Macworld New Complete Mac® Handbook

Macworld New Complete Mac® Handbook

By Jim Heid,
Macworld magazine
"Working Smart" columnist

IDG Books Worldwide, Inc.
An International Data Group Company
Foster City, CA ◆ Chicago, IL ◆ Indianapolis, IN ◆ Braintree, MA ◆ Dallas, TX

Macworld New Complete Mac® Handbook

Published by
IDG Books Worldwide, Inc.
An International Data Group Company
919 E. Hillsdale Blvd.
Suite 400
Foster City, CA 94404

Library of Congress Catalog Card No.: 95-78403

ISBN: 1-56884-484-0

Printed in the United States of America

10 9 8 7 6 5 4 3 2 1

4A/TR/QX/ZV

Distributed in the United States by IDG Books Worldwide, Inc.

Distributed by Macmillan Canada for Canada; by Computer and Technical Books for the Caribbean Basin; by Contemporanea de Ediciones for Venezuela; by Distribuidora Cuspide for Argentina; by CITEC for Brazil; by Ediciones ZETA S.C.R. Ltda. for Peru; by Editorial Limusa SA for Mexico; by Transworld Publishers Limited in the United Kingdom and Europe; by Al-Maiman Publishers & Distributors for Saudi Arabia; by Simron Pty. Ltd. for South Africa; by IDG Communications (HK) Ltd. for Hong Kong; by Toppan Company Ltd. for Japan; by Addison Wesley Publishing Company for Korea; by Longman Singapore Publishers Ltd. for Singapore, Malaysia, Thailand, and Indonesia; by Unalis Corporation for Taiwan; by WS Computer Publishing Company, Inc. for the Philippines; by WoodsLane Pty. Ltd. for Australia; by WoodsLane Enterprises Ltd. for New Zealand.

For general information on IDG Books Worldwide's books in the U.S., please call our Consumer Customer Service department at 800-762-2974. For reseller information, including discounts and premium sales, please call our Reseller Customer Service department at 800-434-3422.

For information on where to purchase IDG Books Worldwide's books outside the U.S., contact IDG Books Worldwide at 415-655-3021 or fax 415-655-3295.

For information on translations, contact Marc Jeffrey Mikulich, Director, Foreign & Subsidiary Rights, at IDG Books Worldwide, 415-655-3018 or fax 415-655-3295.

For sales inquiries and special prices for bulk quantities, write to the address above or call IDG Books Worldwide at 415-655-3200.

For information on using IDG Books Worldwide's books in the classroom, or ordering examination copies, contact Jim Kelly at 800-434-2086.

For authorization to photocopy items for corporate, personal, or educational use, please contact Copyright Clearance Center, 222 Rosewood Drive, Danvers, MA 01923, or fax 508-750-4470.

About the Author

Jim Heid has been writing for *Macworld* since 1984, and has appeared in every issue since March 1985. In the early days, he edited the popular "Open Window" reader tips column. From 1986 through 1993, he wrote the award-winning "Getting Started" column, which focused on a different aspect of Mac fundamentals each month. He currently writes the "Working Smart" column, which provides productivity tips and techniques for people who use the Mac in business. Heid is also a regular contributor to *Macworld*'s features and reviews sections, specializing in Mac technology, printers, typography, multimedia, MIDI, and digital audio — a mix that exploits his background as a typographer, musician, and audio buff. (He grew up in his father's recording studio, which was Pittsburgh's first.)

Prior to writing for *Macworld*, Heid was Senior Technical Editor for *Kilobaud Microcomputing* magazine, where he began writing about the Mac several months prior to its introduction. He has been working with and writing about personal computers since the late seventies, when he computerized his home-built ham radio station with one of the first Radio Shack TRS-80s. He is the author of numerous bestselling books on Macintosh and DOS PC personal computing including *Macworld Word 6 Companion* (IDG Books Worldwide), and frequently speaks at user group meetings, developers conferences, and Macworld Expos. He also taught electronic publishing and typography at the Kodak-founded Center for Creative Imaging in Camden, Maine. He and his wife live on California's scenic Mendocino coast.

Welcome to the world of IDG Books Worldwide.

IDG Books Worldwide, Inc., is a subsidiary of International Data Group, the world's largest publisher of computer-related information and the leading global provider of information services on information technology. IDG was founded more than 25 years ago and now employs more than 7,500 people worldwide. IDG publishes more than 235 computer publications in 67 countries (see listing below). More than 60 million people read one or more IDG publications each month.

Launched in 1990, IDG Books Worldwide is today the #1 publisher of best-selling computer books in the United States. We are proud to have received 8 awards from the Computer Press Association in recognition of editorial excellence, and our best-selling *...For Dummies*™ series has more than 17 million copies in print with translations in 25 languages. IDG Books Worldwide, through a recent joint venture with IDG's Hi-Tech Beijing, became the first U.S. publisher to publish a computer book in the People's Republic of China. In record time, IDG Books Worldwide has become the first choice for millions of readers around the world who want to learn how to better manage their businesses.

Our mission is simple: Every one of our books is designed to bring extra value and skill-building instructions to the reader. Our books are written by experts who understand and care about our readers. The knowledge base of our editorial staff comes from years of experience in publishing, education, and journalism — experience which we use to produce books for the '90s. In short, we care about books, so we attract the best people. We devote special attention to details such as audience, interior design, use of icons, and illustrations. And because we use an efficient process of authoring, editing, and desktop publishing our books electronically, we can spend more time ensuring superior content and spend less time on the technicalities of making books.

You can count on our commitment to deliver high-quality books at competitive prices on topics consumers want to read about. At IDG Books Worldwide, we value quality, and we have been delivering quality for more than 25 years. You'll find no better book on a subject than an IDG book.

John Kilcullen
President and CEO
IDG Books Worldwide, Inc.

IDG Books Worldwide, Inc., is a subsidiary of International Data Group, the world's largest publisher of computer-related information and the leading global provider of information services on information technology. International Data Group publishes over 235 computer publications in 67 countries. More than sixty million people read one or more International Data Group publications each month. The officers are Patrick J. McGovern, Founder and Board Chairman; Kelly Conlin, President; Jim Casella, Chief Operating Officer. International Data Group's publications include: **ARGENTINA'S** Computerworld Argentina, Infoworld Argentina; **AUSTRALIA'S** Computerworld Australia, Computer Living, Australian PC World, Australian Macworld, Network World, Mobile Business Australia, Publish!, Reseller, IDG Sources; **AUSTRIA'S** Computerwelt Oesterreich, PC Test; **BELGIUM'S** Data News (CW); **BOLIVIA'S** Computerworld; **BRAZIL'S** Computerworld, Connections, Game Power, Mundo Unix, PC World, Publish, Super Game; **BULGARIA'S** Computerworld Bulgaria, PC & Mac World Bulgaria, Network World Bulgaria; **CANADA'S** CIO Canada, Computerworld Canada, InfoCanada, Network World Canada, Reseller; **CHILE'S** Computerworld Chile, Informatica; **COLOMBIA'S** Computerworld Colombia, PC World; **COSTA RICA'S** PC World; **CZECH REPUBLIC'S** Computerworld, Elektronika, PC World; **DENMARK'S** Communications World, Computerworld Danmark, Computerworld Focus, Macintosh Produktkatalog, Macworld Danmark, PC World Danmark, PC Produktguide, Tech World, Windows World; **ECUADOR'S** PC World Ecuador; **EGYPT'S** Computerworld (CW) Middle East, PC World Middle East; **FINLAND'S** MikroPC, Tietoviikko, Tietoverkko; **FRANCE'S** Distributique, GOLDEN MAC, InfoPC, Le Guide du Monde Informatique, Le Monde Informatique, Telecoms & Reseaux; **GERMANY'S** Computerwoche, Computerwoche Focus, Computerwoche Extra, Electronic Entertainment, Gamepro, Information Management, Macwelt, Netzwelt, PC Welt, Publish, Publish; **GREECE'S** Publish & Macworld; **HONG KONG'S** Computerworld Hong Kong, PC World Hong Kong; **HUNGARY'S** Computerworld SZT, PC World; **INDIA'S** Computers & Communications; **INDONESIA'S** Info Komputer; **IRELAND'S** ComputerScope; **ISRAEL'S** Beyond Windows, Computerworld Israel, Multimedia, PC World Israel; **ITALY'S** Computerworld Italia, Lotus Magazine, Macworld Italia, Networking Italia, PC Shopping Italy, PC World Italia; **JAPAN'S** Computerworld Today, Information Systems World, Macworld Japan, Nikkei Personal Computing, SunWorld Japan, Windows World; **KENYA'S** East African Computer News; **KOREA'S** Computerworld Korea, Macworld Korea, PC World Korea; **LATIN AMERICA'S** GamePro; **MALAYSIA'S** Computerworld Malaysia, PC World Malaysia; **MEXICO'S** Compu Edicion, Compu Manufactura, Computacion/Punto de Venta, Computerworld Mexico, MacWorld, Mundo Unix, PC World, Windows; **THE NETHERLANDS'** Computer! Totaal, Computable (CW), LAN Magazine, Lotus Magazine, MacWorld; **NEW ZEALAND'S** Computer Buyer, Computerworld New Zealand, Network World, New Zealand PC World; **NIGERIA'S** PC World Africa; **NORWAY'S** Computerworld Norge, Lotusworld Norge, Macworld Norge, Maxi Data, Networld, PC World Ekspress, PC World Nettverk, PC World Norge, PC World's Produktguide, Publish& Multimedia World, Student Data, Unix World, Windowsworld; **PAKISTAN'S** PC World Pakistan; **PANAMA'S** PC World Panama; **PERU'S** Computerworld Peru, PC World; **PEOPLE'S REPUBLIC OF CHINA'S** China Computerworld, China Infoworld, China PC Info Magazine, Computer Fan, PC World China, Electronics International, Electronics Today/Multimedia World, Electronic Product World, China Network World, Software World Magazine, Telecom Product World; **PHILIPPINES'** Computerworld Philippines, PC Digest (PCW); **POLAND'S** Computerworld Poland, Computerworld Special Report, Networld, PC World/Komputer, Sunworld; **PORTUGAL'S** Cerebro/PC World, Correio Informatico/Computerworld, MacIn; **ROMANIA'S** Computerworld, PC World, Telecom Romania; **RUSSIA'S** Computerworld-Moscow, Mir - PK (PCW), Sety (Networks); **SINGAPORE'S** Computerworld Southeast Asia, PC World Singapore; **SLOVENIA'S** Monitor Magazine; **SOUTH AFRICA'S** Computer Mail (CIO),Computing S.A.,Network World S.A., Software World; **SPAIN'S** Advanced Systems, Amiga World, Computerworld Espana, Communicaciones World, Macworld Espana, NeXTWORLD, Super Juegos Magazine (GamePro), PC World Espana, Publish; **SWEDEN'S** Attack, ComputerSweden, Corporate Computing, Macworld, Mikrodatorn, Natverk & Kommunikation, PC World, CAP & Design, Datalngenjoren, Maxi Data,Windows World; **SWITZERLAND'S** Computerworld Schweiz, Macworld Schweiz, PC Tip; **TAIWAN'S** Computerworld Taiwan, PC World Taiwan; **THAILAND'S** Thai Computerworld; **TURKEY'S** Computerworld Monitor, Macworld Turkiye, PC World Turkiye; **UKRAINE'S** Computerworld, Computers+Software Magazine; **UNITED KINGDOM'S** Computing /Computerworld, Connexion/Network World, Lotus Magazine, Macworld, Open Computing/Sunworld; **UNITED STATES'** Advanced Systems, AmigaWorld, Cable in the Classroom, CD Review, CIO, Computerworld, Computerworld Client/Server Journal, Digital Video, DOS World, Electronic Entertainment Magazine (E2), Federal Computer Week, Game Hits, GamePro, IDG Books Worldwide, Infoworld, Laser Event, Macworld, Maximize, Multimedia World, Network World, PC Letter, PC World, Publish, SWATPro, Video Event; **URUGUAY'S** PC World Uruguay; **VENEZUELA'S** Computerworld Venezuela, PC World; **VIETNAM'S** PC World Vietnam.

05/17/95

Dedication

This book is dedicated to Maryellen and to my mother.

The *Macworld Power User Clinic* CD is dedicated to the memory of George Heid, who would have loved this stuff.

Acknowledgments

The columns and articles you read in *Macworld* and the chapters you will read in this book aren't the product of one person; they're the result of a collaborative effort of many, and they all have my sincere thanks and gratitude.

Topping the list is *Macworld* magazine's talented staff, the best group of computer journalists and consumer advocates I've ever had the honor of working with. In the departments section, thanks go to Nancy Dunn, who originally proposed my "Getting Started" column to me and who was instrumental in shaping the column's style and scope; to Cathy Abes, who picked up the torch when Nancy left; and to Dan Littman, who helped me make the transition from Mr. Getting Started to Mr. Working Smart.

My thanks and respect also go to *Macworld*'s Charlie Piller, Galen Gruman, Carol Person, Marjorie Baer, and Elizabeth Dougherty (and to features editors past: Jim Martin, Dan Muse, Cheryl England, and Liza Weiman). Their work has been an inspiration over the years, and their tolerance of the occasional missed deadline — especially as this book came together — is truly appreciated. Thanks also to Wendy Sharp and Michael Fainter of the *Macworld* reviews department; and to *Macworld*'s expert copy editors, whose love of language makes *Macworld*'s writers look good and whose attention to detail never fails to amaze.

On the design and production side, warm gratitude goes to Arne Hurty, who created the gorgeous informational graphics in this book. Arne can make FreeHand sing, and his cheerful personality and dedication to his art make him a pleasure to work with.

Special thanks go to Jerry Borrell for his support of the first edition of this book; and to Adrian Mello, who has been a steadfast supporter and friend since 1984.

I also appreciate the efforts of everyone in Macworld Lab — Mark Hurlow, Danny Lee, Tim Warner, Matthew Clark, and Lauren Black. These are the people who live in the trenches with Macintosh products, running hundreds of tests over thousands of hours so that *Macworld* can guide you to the best products and away from the worst ones. They not only know their stuff, they're fun to work with, too. My thanks also go to Jim Feeley, Tom Moran, Suzanne Courteau, Joanna Pearlstein, Jane Lagas, and Lyn Taylor. And thanks and a squeal of the modem to the people of Macworld Online: Suzanne Stefanac, Steve Costa, Matthew Hawn, Paul Devine, and Kristine Moss.

I also want to thank all the experts of the Macintosh world who have shared their knowledge with me over the years, and the press and marketing representatives who helped supply me with products and product information. There are too many names to list here, but they know who they are, and they have my gratitude.

My warm thanks also go to Dennis Cohen, the technical editor of this book and a good friend. Dennis has forgotten more about the Mac than I'll ever know, and he's been a superb source of technical information and insights over the years. The Macintosh world is lucky to have him in its ranks. If he had stayed at the Jet Propulsion Laboratory, we'd have colonized the solar system by now.

Thanks also go to everyone who agreed to be interviewed for the *Macworld Power User Clinic*, starting with the inspiringly talented Herbie Hancock. Spending time with one of the jazz world's greatest piano players — and one of the music world's most versatile talents — was the highlight of the entire project. And I couldn't have done it without the assistance of Melinda Murphy, who not only scheduled the interviews but also saved my life when I left my tripod at Herbie Hancock's house. Special thanks also go to Darrell Smith, another superbly talented musician, who spent close to an hour setting up a studio full of equipment so that I could get some shots of a mixing board; and also to Chris Chambers of Mercury Records for supplying me with a copy of Herbie Hancock's outstanding new album, "Dis is Da Drum," and for allow me to play excerpts from it on the CD-ROM.

As for the interview victims at Apple, thanks go to Duncan Kennedy, Dave Limp, Rick Rifredi, Michael Hopwood, Eric Gee, Stu Roberson, Vito Salvaggio, and Larry Lightman. Special thanks also go to the hard-working Apple public relations staff, including Maureen O'Connell, Russ Ito, Amy Kavenaugh, Mary Devincenzi, Amy Bonetti, Betty Taylor, Kristen Brownstone, Katy Boos, and especially Jackie Promes, who went above and beyond the call of duty in helping me line up interviews for the CD (and who introduced me to the best restaurant in Cupertino: Apple's own incredible cafeteria).

An extra measure of gratitude goes to Kelly Parnell and everyone at the amazing Berkeley Macintosh Users Group. They worked long hours compiling and testing the Best of BMUG collection on the CD. (Here's the first tip you'll read in this book, and it might be the best: join BMUG! It's an incredible resource. See the BMUG coupon at the end of this book for membership information.) And even more thanks go to the skilled and generous programmers who created the software that makes up the collection.

Another fabulous user group also has my gratitude: the Los Angeles Macintosh Group (LAMG), and Tom Negrino (who's also a friend and *Macworld* colleague), Suzy Prieto, Eliot Kaplan, and Deborah Wagner.

My heartfelt thanks also go to the folks at IDG Books Worldwide, the most innovative book publisher I've ever worked with. Specifically, I want to thank John Kilcullen, for his inspiring enthusiasm and for having the vision to realize what a nifty book this could be (especially if it included a CD-ROM); Mary Corder, for expertly shepherding the book through the production process and for maintaining composure as deadlines loomed and passed and then loomed again; to Jeannie Smith for her expert editing; and to Nate Holdread for assisting the editors. Thanks also go to Nancy Dunn, who I'm delighted to be working with again, and to IDG Books' crack marketing staff. In the production trenches, a tip of the printer's visor goes to Beth Jenkins; Tyler Connor; Valery Bourke; Cameron Booker and everyone in IDG Books' Production department, which handled this book's tricky production demands with aplomb.

And finally, the home front. Roy and Wendy provided encouragement and wonderful astronomical and gastronomical diversions, not to mention close friendship and occasional poodle sitting. Tweed provided much-needed laughs and the best castanet performances north of the border. Rennie Innis of the Mendocino Regional Occupational Program tech center saved my bacon on a few occasions. Trixie was a sweet and constant companion who always seemed to know when it was time for a squeak-squeak break. (You can see Trixie in several screen shots in Chapters 13 and 21, as well as in the "Powering the PowerBook" clinic on the CD-ROM.) And the love of my life, Maryellen Kelly, was there, as always — my general manager, user interface tester, videographer, sound engineer, key grip, and main squeeze. I love you!

(The publisher would like to give special thanks to Patrick J. McGovern, without whom this book would not have been possible.)

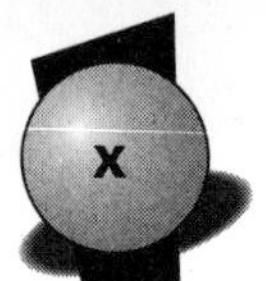

Credits

Group Publisher
Brenda McLaughlin

Acquisitions Editor
Nancy E. Dunn

Brand Manager
Pradeepa Siva

Editorial Director
Mary Bednarek

Editorial Managers
Mary C. Corder
Andy Cummings

Editorial Executive Assistant
Jodi Lynn Semling

Editorial Assistant
Nate Holdread

Production Director
Beth Jenkins

Supervisor of Project Coordination
Cindy L. Phipps

Pre-Press Coordinator
Steve Peake

Associate Pre-Press Coordinator
Tony Augsburger

Media/Archive Coordinator
Paul Belcastro

Project Editor
Mary Corder

Editor
N. Jeannie Smith

Technical Reviewer
Dennis Cohen

Associate Project Coordinator
J. Tyler Connor

Production Staff
Gina Scott
Carla C. Radzikinas
Patricia R. Reynolds
Melissa D. Buddendeck
Dwight Ramsey
Robert Springer
Theresa Sánchez-Baker
Kathie S. Schnorr
Cameron Booker
Maridee Ennis
Angie Hunckler
Drew Moore
Laura Puranen
Anna Rohrer

Proofreader
Charles A. Hutchinson

Indexer
Sherry Massey

Book Design
University Graphics

Contents at a Glance

Table of Contents

CHAPTER 16

The Mac Meets the Telephone 461

Part III: Expanding the Mac 953

CHAPTER 29 Upgrading Strategies 955

CHAPTER 30

CHAPTER

xxxix

Introduction

I am one lucky nerd. For the past eleven years, I've been paid to play with hundreds — maybe thousands — of Mac software and hardware products in the course of writing columns, features, and reviews for *Macworld* magazine. I've been fortunate enough to work with and write about everything from time-billing software to bar-code readers, from mailing-list management packages to high-performance disk arrays, from word-processing programs to video-editing programs.

In this book, I've tried to take this decade-and-then-some of Mac experience and put it between two covers — and on a CD.

Whom This Book is For

Is it stating the obvious to say that this book is for anyone who's into the Mac? I thought so. Specifically, then, this book is intended for:

- Anyone who's thinking about buying a Mac and needs an introduction to Mac terminology, operating concepts, and capabilities.
- Anyone who's mastered the basics and is ready to explore the nooks and crannies, the backwaters, and the dusty attics of the Mac world.
- Mac masters who want a one-stop reference to the Macintosh world, as well as overviews of Mac application categories and hardware concepts to help them choose products and brush up on areas they're unfamiliar with.
- Software hounds who just can't get enough of the stuff — this book's CD contains an incredible collection of top-notch software, all of it compatible with the latest Macs and system software.
- Multimedia buffs who want to explore the worlds of digital video and audio.
- Loyal *Macworld* readers who want an updated and expanded collection of my jibberish for convenient reference.

What's New in this Edition

As the cover indicates, this is the fourth edition of this book. The first edition came out in 1991; the second edition was launched in 1993; and the third appeared in 1994. The third, I'm proud to say, won an award: the Berkeley Macintosh User Group's BMUG Choice award for best general Mac book.

How is this edition different from previous ones? Let me list the ways:

- It's bigger — a hundred or so pages bigger at that. I've added scores of new tips and expanded many chapters to provide more in-depth details on Mac issues and products.
- It's up-to-date. I've revised *every single chapter* to reflect System 7.5 as well as the latest products and latest Mac models — including Mac clones and the second-generation Power Macs, which were announced on the very same day that this edition shipped (August 8, 1995). I've also added more technical illustrations by *Macworld's* award-winning illustrator, Arne Hurty. As with the first three editions, I've aimed for the best of both worlds — magazine-style layout and graphics along with the depth and scope that only a book can provide.
- It's more technical. As the Mac world matures, Macintosh users are becoming more sophisticated. This edition reflects this trend. It contains more technical details on how the Mac works and on how you can customize and fine-tune your system. (If you're a Mac newcomer, don't worry; you'll still find overviews and primers that will get you up to speed in a hurry.)
- It's more authoritative. You can find plenty of books that are filled with little tips and tricks and hidden keyboard shortcuts. (For that matter, *this* book is filled with them.) But this is the *only* mega-page Macintosh book that authoritatively covers the very latest technical issues in the Mac world — the transition to a RISC architecture, the evolution of the Mac's system software, the technicalities behind digital video, and even the world of virtual reality.

What's New on the CD

The second edition of this book was the first general Mac book to include a CD-ROM, which was primarily a vehicle for transporting far more software than a few floppies could contain. The third edition was the first general Mac book to include an interactive CD, which contained not only a ton of software but also a multimedia companion to the book.

This edition continues the tradition of firsts — it's the first general Mac book to include an interactive companion that you can update *every single month*. That's right — every month, I'll post free updates to the book and CD on the America

Online and eWorld services. Download them, stash them in your System Folder, and just like that, you're up to date.

This edition's CD uses QuickTime movies, color graphics, 3-D animation, and digital sound to illustrate the concepts described in many chapters. You can also read and search hundreds of capsule reviews from *Macworld*, and you can watch interviews I conducted with the product managers of many of Apple's latest products — and with one of the most interesting (and certainly the most famous) Macintosh users I've ever met: Grammy- and Oscar-winning musician Herbie Hancock, who uses the Mac in his composing, recording, and performing endeavors.

The new CD also contains new tutorials in which I walk you through the Mac's system software and hardware. You can also read selected sections from the book and search for text. In keeping with this new tutorial perspective, I've called the new CD *Macworld Power User Clinic*. See Appendix A for details on using the CD.

Most CD-ROM titles are developed by a staff of writers, videographers, programmers, and graphic designers. *Macworld Power User Clinic* was entirely my own doing (okay, my wife helped me with the on-location video shoots). I wanted to descend into the trenches of the Mac multimedia world in order to do a better job of writing about it. If you've read previous editions of this book, you'll find that this edition's coverage of multimedia, digital imaging, QuickTime, and CD-ROMs is greatly expanded.

Did the CD's increasingly interactive slant come at the expense of software? Yes and no. This time around, I did not include demonstration software from commercial developers — you won't find trial versions of programs such as Adobe Photoshop or WordPerfect or ClarisWorks. One reason is, frankly, space: I wanted to have more space for tutorials and QuickTime movies. (600MB doesn't go as far as it used to!) Another reason is that you may already have many of the demo programs I used to include; if your Mac came with a CD-ROM drive, chances are you got a demo applications CD. It didn't make much sense for me to include software you might already have.

At the same time, though, I just *had* to make room for a fabulous collection of free software, shareware, and fonts. In fact, there's even more of it this time around: an incredible 100MB worth of great shareware and free software compiled by the Mac world's biggest and best user group, the Berkeley Macintosh Users Group (BMUG). The Best of BMUG collection on the CD was compiled exclusively for this book. You'll also find some terrific utilities and resources that I hand-picked; check out Appendix A and the chapter "On the CD" boxes for more information.

How This Book is Organized

Most computer books begin with chapter after chapter of technical background on bits and bytes and how computers work. But in my experience, the first questions people ask about the Mac aren't "How does it work and what do all those weird words mean?" but "Which machine should I buy and what can I do with it?" That only makes sense: whether you're shopping for a car, a house, or a computer, your first priorities are making an informed purchase and then applying that purchase to your daily life. Learning the technical details usually comes later.

For this reason, this book is organized a bit differently than the rest.

Part I: Using the Mac

In this section, I get right down to business, examining issues you will want to investigate when shopping for a Mac system, and looking at the many ways you can put a Mac to work. I explore the worlds of word processing, desktop publishing, spreadsheets, database management, animation, music, computer-aided design, and more. Each chapter in this section describes the concepts behind an application category and spotlights the leading products in the field. Most chapters have step-by-step boxes that provide detailed instructions for performing various tasks using the most popular programs in that category. You will also find tips for using your programs more effectively, and some shopper's guidelines that will help you choose programs that meet your needs.

As you read this section, check out the "On the CD" boxes that many chapters contain. These boxes list relevant portions of the *Macworld Power User Clinic* CD. When you've finished a given chapter, you might want to explore those parts of the CD to approach the concepts you've read about from a different angle.

Part II: Mastering the Mac

In this section, I take a closer look at what makes the Mac tick and show how to master System 7's most powerful features. This section looks at more advanced topics such as protecting your Mac from computer viruses, customizing your Mac, backing up, exchanging data between programs and computers, troubleshooting, and getting the most out of your printer. (Did you know your laser printer can print iron-on T-shirt transfers?)

The *Macworld Power User Clinic* CD will come in handy as you read this section, too. The CD is packed with free or nearly free software — utility software for customizing and enhancing your Mac and virus protection programs to safeguard it. You'll also find a lot of great games, useful utilities, fun fonts, and more.

Part III: Expanding the Mac

In this section, I look at the kinds of add-ons you might buy to round out your Mac system. Memory, monitors, printers, high-capacity disks, trackballs, and expansion cards are among the hardware vying for your hard-earned money. You will learn what each type of add-on has to offer and what to look for when shopping.

The Rest of the Story

Finally, an appendix describes how to use the *Macworld Power User Clinic* and how to get your free monthly electronic updates. And the quick reference card in the front of the book lists essential System 7 tips and techniques and provides a quick roadmap to the CD.

Conventions Used in This Book

This book contains several types of sidebars, each of which presents a certain type of information.

ON THE CD

If a particular chapter has corresponding software or tutorials on the *Macworld Power User Clinic* CD, this box will tell you so. To quickly locate a program mentioned here, use the Finder's Find command. (See Appendix A for more tips on locating things on the CD.)

The Backgrounder boxes provide additional insights into the subject at hand — the kind of information you might not need if you're just skimming a chapter, but that might be valuable when you need more details on a given topic.

Quick Tips boxes provide, well, quick tips — short, to-the-point time-savers. If you've picked up the book on a rainy day, you might just enjoy browsing the Quick Tips boxes to find shortcuts for your favorite programs or peripherals.

The Step-by-Step boxes provide detailed, stepwise instructions that show how to perform a specific task using a specific program. Even if you don't use all of the programs covered in these boxes, reading the steps will give you a feel for how Mac programs approach various tasks. (Some of the programs covered in Step-by-Step boxes are included on the *Macworld Power User Clinic* CD, so you can try out the steps for yourself.)

These boxes contain tips or background information specific to the PowerBook and PowerBook Duo computers.

Keep those cards and e-mails coming!

In the back of this book, you'll find a pull-out reader response card. Please take a moment to fill it out and mail it. IDG Books really does read these things; even more amazing, they photocopy them and send them on to me. Many of the changes in this edition — more technical meat, more shareware, more product reviews — are my direct response to the feedback on these cards.

If you just can't face communicating the old-fashioned way, send me an electronic mail message (if you don't know what that is, don't worry — it's covered here). I'll respond to any and all comments and questions as time permits. On CompuServe, send messages to 76174,556. On America Online and AppleLink, I'm JimHeid. On eWorld, my address is Heid. And on the Internet, it's jim_heid@macworld.com.

Let's get started!

— Jim Heid

PART I

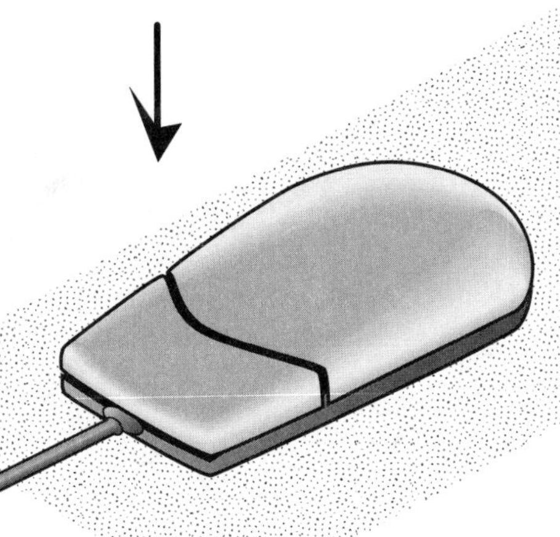

Using the Mac

CHAPTER ONE

1 Buying a Mac and Getting Acquainted

- Buying a Mac — how to determine your needs
- Getting acquainted with the Mac's interface
- An introduction to the Power Macintosh — what's the RISC?
- Understanding and unscrambling Mac acronyms
- Exploring the second-generation Power Macs.

Someday you'll be able to buy a computer without giving much thought to technical specifications, and you'll be able to use it without having to learn a lot of lingo. Whatever you buy will have more power than a Cray supercomputer, and it will adapt itself to your way of working — not the other way around. And if prices keep falling the way they have been, the machine will probably be free with a paid subscription to *Time*.

Wake up — that day is still a dream. This industry is still in its horse-and-buggy days, relatively speaking, and buying and using a computer mean doing some research and learning some terms.

But look on the bright side: at least today's personal computers don't require you to think in binary mode, as did some machines I played with 20 years ago. And a lot of people actually enjoy the thrill of the hunt: the whole process of researching the best models, putting everything together, and conquering the technicalities.

This chapter is dedicated to these silicon thrill-seekers and also to those sane souls who just want to streamline their work. I begin by guiding you through the maze of issues you need to consider when assembling a Mac system, with the goal of helping you decide which combination of hardware is best for you. If you've already bought a Mac and want to start getting acquainted, feel free to skip to "Understanding the Mac's Interface" later in this chapter. If you know these basics, too, you may want to just skim this chapter's sidebars for additional insights into how the Mac works.

First Things First: Buying a Mac

Today's Macintosh shopper faces more decisions than the president on a bad day. Apple offers a full family tree of Mac models, each with different features and performance and each taking a different toll on your bank balance. Hundreds of independent, or *third-party* manufacturers supply thousands of programs and hardware add-ons. You can outfit a system using only Apple hardware or combine components from different firms. You can shop at a local dealer or through the mail. Buy the right system, and you'll wonder how you got along without it. Buy the wrong one, and you'll feel betrayed by technology as you watch your system depreciate and collect dust.

Yes, money is everything. Therefore, take some time to figure out what you need so that you end up with a system that satisfies both you *and* your budget.

Many consultants and Mac gurus suggest that you consider the following questions in determining which Mac to buy:

- ❖ Which tasks do I want to use the Mac for?
- ❖ Which programs can perform them?
- ❖ What kinds of hardware do those programs require?

This approach is valid, but I like to preface it with a more practical question: how much can you spend? The fact is, what you *want* a Mac to do and what the system you can afford *can* do are often two different things. Rule number one: you can't accurately answer the first question until you determine your budget.

Addressing your finances is especially important in the Mac world, where *bargain* often means "cheaper than a car." I'm exaggerating, of course, but Macs do have a reputation for being more expensive than the other major personal computing standard, Windows PCs and clones. That reputation used to be well deserved, but these days, Macs are generally price-competitive with Windows PCs. Better still, the Mac is easier to set up and learn. For more comparisons between the Mac and PC worlds, see the "Mac versus PC" Backgrounder box.

Take a Tour of the Latest Mac Developments

On the *Macworld Power User Clinic,* you can take a tour of Apple's second-generation Power Macs.

In the "Power Mac Update" segment, Power Mac product line manager Dave Limp demonstrates the Power Mac 7000-series' new case design, which lets you gain access to the computer's expansion and memory slots to add upgrades within seconds. You can also see the new Sound & Displays control panel — which is included with the Power Mac 7500 and 8500 — in action.

In the "Performa Update" segment, you can tour the Performa 5200, the slick all-in-one Mac that packs a PowerPC-based multimedia monster into a tilt-and-swivel monitor.

If you're still deciding which Mac to buy — or you want to check the specifications of a particular Mac model — run the GURU utility, which contains a detailed database of the entire Mac family. You can run GURU either by choosing the Guide to RAM Upgrades command from the References menu or by clicking the Guide to RAM Upgrades button in the "Expanding the Mac" segment.

Because the Mac world changes rapidly, be sure to download the free monthly updates from the Macworld Online forums on America Online or eWorld. See Appendix A for details and instructions.

Mac versus PC

If you've browsed some mail-order advertisements in PC-oriented magazines, you've probably noticed that DOS PCs — especially no-name, mail-order brands — are cheaper than many Macs. If your wallet whines when you gaze longingly at a Mac, try using these arguments to shut it up:

❖ *Ease of use* The Mac's *graphical user interface* — the on-screen menus and other devices you use to control your programs — makes the machine easier to learn and use. These days, PCs generally run the Maclike graphical user interface called *Microsoft Windows,* but it isn't as polished or mature as the Mac's interface. The Mac was designed from the ground up to be a graphical computer; PCs weren't and it shows. Macintosh hardware is generally easier to set up, too.

❖ *Superior graphics features* The Mac's sophisticated color features make it the preferred platform for applications such as image scanning and editing, multimedia production, and desktop publishing.

❖ *Superior video display options* It isn't surprising that a computer with superior graphics has superior video features. Fresh from the box, many Macs can display images with photographic realism; those that can't often can with the addition of an inexpensive upgrade. Mac owners can also choose from a large array of sophisticated video cards, including ones that are able to connect to videocassette recorders. Some such boards are available for PCs, but the selection is relatively small. What's more, nothing guarantees that a board works with

(continued on the next page)

(continued from previous page)

all PC programs. The Mac's standardized system software eliminates such compatibility aggravations.

- *More built-in hardware* Macs include hardware that usually costs extra on PCs. This hardware makes it easier and less expensive to connect multiple add-ons, and interconnect Macs to form a network that lets everyone in the office share information and expensive peripherals. Macs containing Apple's audio-visual (AV) technologies can connect to video cameras, video recorders, and television monitors — all you add is the appropriate cable. Many Macs also include or accept an optional CD-ROM drive, which opens the doors to a universe of slick multimedia discs (including the *Macworld Power User Clinic* that's tucked into the back of this book) and much more.
- *Sophisticated sound* Without third-party hardware, most PCs can only beep; by comparison, all Macs can play digitally recorded sounds. Most current Macs — including PowerBooks — can record digital sound, too. You know what the benefit of this capability is: you hear silly beeping sounds when you make a blunder. But seriously, the Mac's built-in sound features also enable you to add sound to documents you create, such as presentations and multimedia productions. You can purchase products that let you send recorded voice messages to other Macs on an office network. And the Power Macintosh family (as well as the Quadra 660AV and Quadra 840AV) can record and play audio with fidelity that approaches that of a compact disc. Other Macs can, too, with third-party hardware.
- *True plug-and-play operation* Adding a new piece of hardware — a CD-ROM drive, a scanner, a network board, whatever — is a breeze: hook up the hardware, copy a file or two to your hard drive, and you're done. PCs don't have anything approaching this — indeed, many PC users joke about having "plug and pray" operation. The long-awaited Microsoft Windows 95 takes a big step forward but still doesn't provide the setup simplicity that Macs have had all along.

Hardware Decisions

You've thought about what you want to do with the Mac and have some ideas about which programs you want to use. Now you're ready to start shopping for hardware. That means addressing the basic features that differentiate each Mac model. Later chapters cover these categories in more detail; for now, here's an overview of what to think about before opening your checkbook.

- *Size* If portability is important — or if you don't have a lot of spare desk space — consider a Macintosh PowerBook or one of the members of Apple's all-in-one Mac line, such as the Performa 5200, which packs a Mac and stereo speakers into an innovative tilt-and-swivel color monitor (see Figure 1-1, "Inside the Performa 5200 Modular Design"). The Performa 630-series and 6200-series machines are relatively compact, too, although they lack the everything-in-one-box convenience of the 5200. And of course, of all these models, only PowerBooks run on batteries.

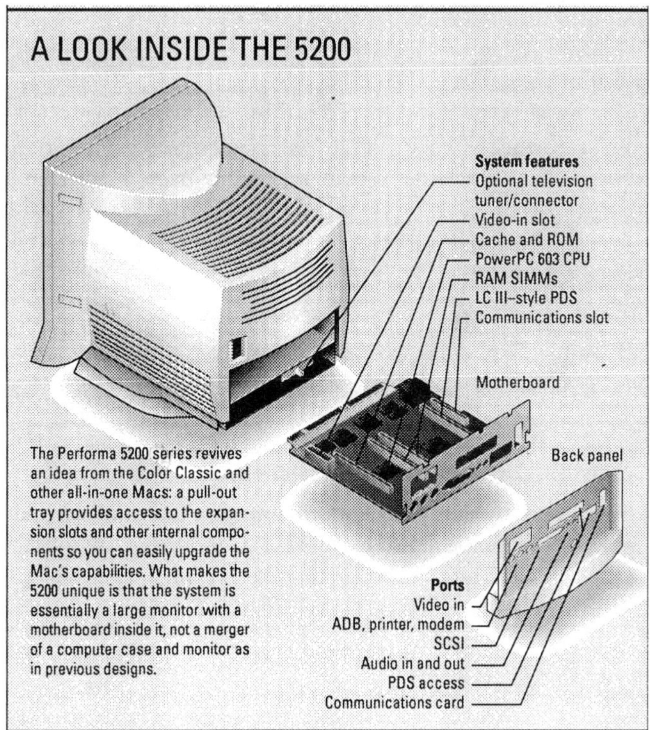
A LOOK INSIDE THE 5200
System features
Optional television tuner/connector
Video-in slot
Cache and ROM
PowerPC 603 CPU
RAM SIMMs
LC III–style PDS
Communications slot
Motherboard
Back panel
The Performa 5200 series revives an idea from the Color Classic and other all-in-one Macs: a pull-out tray provides access to the expansion slots and other internal components so you can easily upgrade the Mac's capabilities. What makes the 5200 unique is that the system is essentially a large monitor with a motherboard inside it, not a merger of a computer case and monitor as in previous designs.
Ports
Video in
ADB, printer, modem
SCSI
Audio in and out
PDS access
Communications card

Figure 1-1: Inside the Performa 5200 Modular Design

- *Speed* Any Mac can handle such tasks as simple word processing and filing, black-and-white drawing, telecommunications, light-duty desktop publishing, and spreadsheet work. But you want a faster Mac for working with large databases or spreadsheets, large word processor documents with indexes and tables of contents, color illustrations or animations, and large desktop publications containing color. That probably means a member of the Power Macintosh family, which uses the much heralded PowerPC microprocessor created jointly by Apple, Motorola, and IBM. More on these models soon.
- *Expandability* Most Macs contain internal *expansion slots* into which you can plug *cards* or *boards* that add to the machine's capabilities, but some machines provide more slots than others (see the "Surveying the Slots" Backgrounder box). *Accelerator boards* boost performance, for example, while *video boards* control monitors. Expansion slots are also an excellent defense against obsolescence. For example, an accelerator board can make a doddering old Mac II-series machine nearly as spry as a young Power Mac. (How do you like that? The Fountain of Youth turns out to be a circuit board.)

- *Networking features* All Macs provide built-in network ports that make it easy to interconnect machines to form a network (see Chapter 32). But built-in networking features vary. Entry-level Macs provide *LocalTalk* network ports, which are adequate for basic networking and printer sharing but transfer data relatively slowly. Costlier Macs (including all Power Macs) provide LocalTalk ports and *Ethernet* ports — the latter transfer data many times faster than LocalTalk does. Ethernet's extra speed is essential for networking tasks that involve large files, such as digital images. (By the way, you can add Ethernet to a Mac that lacks it — see Chapter 32.)
- *Video features* Older Macs and PowerBook models can display only black-and-white screen dots, or *pixels*. All of today's Macs can connect to color and *gray-scale* monitors, which show color or true shades of gray (like those displayed by televisions), respectively. But some Macs have better color capabilities than others. If you're planning to work with a color image-editing program, such as Adobe Photoshop, you want a Mac that supports *24-bit color*, which allows for those photorealistic images I mentioned earlier in this chapter. Many Macs support 24-bit color right out of the box, and many of those that don't accept an inexpensive video-memory upgrade that provides 24-bit capabilities.
- *Memory capacity* If your applications demand speed, chances are they devour memory and disk space, too. In their least expensive configurations, many Macs include 8 megabytes (MB) of memory. If you plan to work extensively with sound, video, and color images — or if you want to be able to run several programs simultaneously — you need more. (I don't recommend anything less than 8MB for a 68040 Mac and 16MB for a Power Mac.) As Chapter 29 explains, you can add extra memory by purchasing memory boards.
- *Disk-storage capacity* Every Mac model includes one floppy disk drive and one built-in, or *internal*, hard disk. Hard disks hold far more information and transfer it much more quickly than do floppy disks — today's complex programs require that speed and capacity. Most of the internal hard disks that Apple currently ships can store at least 500 megabytes (MB), or roughly 200 to 500 million characters. That sounds like a lot and it is, but you will be surprised at how quickly you fill it. If (more likely, when) you fill up your hard drive, you can supplement it with an external hard disk, which attaches to a connector on the back of the Mac. Prices for external hard drives have plummeted in recent years.

Surveying the Slots

To appreciate the benefits of expansion slots, you need to understand the *bus* — an internal freeway that carries data among the Mac's memory, its microprocessor, and a variety of support chips.

All Macs contain two primary buses: the *address bus*, which carries signals from the microprocessor that specify where in memory data is to be stored or retrieved, and the *data bus*, which carries the data itself. With only a few exceptions, all the data that moves within the Mac does so on its data bus. Thus, the speed of the bus is one of many factors that determine a Mac's overall performance.

When you consider the significant role the bus plays, the advantages of tapping into it become clear. With direct access to the microprocessor, memory, and many of the timing and control signals inside the Mac, a device connected to the bus becomes an integral part of the Mac. Accelerator boards, for example, are able to supplant the Mac's microprocessor with their own.

Another advantage is speed. A device connected directly to the bus can transfer data and communicate with memory far faster than it can by using one of the Mac's external connectors. If the bus is a freeway, then a slot is a set of on-ramps and off-ramps, ready to accommodate high-performance add-ons without clips, voided warranties, or fried power supplies.

Comparing slots

Most compact and low-cost Macs — the Classic series, the LC series, and many Performa models — contain one *processor direct slot* (PDS), which allows access to all of the control, address, and data signals that their processors use. (The Quadra 630 and the Performa 5200 and 6200 series also provide a TV Direct slot, which accommodates an optional TV tuner card — see Chapter 20.) Midrange and high-end Macs often contain a PDS, too; an expansion board plugged into a PDS has the potential to deliver faster performance than a NuBus slot. (The old Mac SE also contains one slot; it's much less sophisticated than those of its successors, although it's adequate for accelerator boards and large-screen video cards.)

The primary means of expansion in the Mac II, Centris, and Quadra families is the *NuBus* slot. More NuBus cards are available than PDS cards — one big reason is that Apple has had a habit of changing its PDS design from one Mac model to the next. But NuBus also has some limitations — it generally can't transfer data as quickly as a PDS card can, for example.

As I discuss later in this chapter, Apple's second-generation Power Macs — the 7200, 7500, 8500, and 9500 — use a different type of expansion scheme, called *PCI.* The PCI bus provides faster performance than does NuBus; it also allows for less expensive cards that can often be used in PCI-based Windows PCs as well as in second-generation Macs.

Look for more technical comparisons between slot schemes — as well as a listing of how many slots each Mac model provides — in Chapter 29.

Do you need AV features?

In 1992, Apple introduced its *AV technologies*, which gather together several audio- and video-related features under the AV umbrella. The first AV Macs were the Centris 660AV (later renamed the Quadra 660AV) and the Quadra 840AV. The AV technologies are also available for or built into many of the Power Macintosh models that I discuss shortly.

A Mac with AV features contains additional circuitry and rear-panel connectors that enable you to connect a video recorder or camcorder and capture video scenes that you can edit and play back. Macs with AV features also provide video-out capabilities: connect a video recorder to the Mac's video-out jack, and you can videotape the Mac's screen image — great for taping a presentation that you want to send to the home office or a digital movie that you want to send to your folks (see Chapters 15 and 20).

It used to be that a Mac with AV features had the letters *AV* in its model number. Apple did away with that naming convention in 1995, when it released the second-generation Power Macs. Now it's up to you to know that the Power Mac 8500, for example, provides AV features. Or maybe I should say it's up to me to tell you.

It's also up to me to say that in the pre-Power Mac AV models, *AV* meant more than just video input and output. It also meant speech recognition, high-quality audio, and support for communications features. All Power Macs provide these features as standard equipment; in the Power Mac world, AV technologies refer strictly to video-in and video-out.

So should you buy a Mac with AV features? If you want to work with video, by all means — as Chapter 20 describes, the AV features in the second-generation Power Macs are superb. But note that numerous third-party products are also available for doing digital video and audio work. If you plan to do professional video or audio production — creating video for CD-ROMs, broadcasting, or recording on video-tape — read Chapters 20 and 21 for a look at the issues behind high-end video and audio production.

What kind of monitor should you buy?

All current desktop Macs and most PowerBook models can connect to an external monitor without requiring you to add a video expansion card. What size monitor should you buy? For basic business tasks, the standard 14-inch monitor is a good workhorse, although the trend is toward 15- and 17-inch monitors, which let you see more of a document at once.

If you're thinking of a Mac with AV features, you might also consider Apple's AudioVision 17 monitor. Whether you use an AV Mac for telephony, multimedia, or education applications, the AudioVision 17 monitor is an appealing package.

The AudioVision 17 also includes a built-in microphone and a pair of stereo speakers. It's studded with connectors for audio, video, and the keyboard and mouse, allowing you to make and break connections without groping around the back of the Mac. And its front panel houses convenient controls for adjusting volume, brightness, and contrast.

The monitor's stereo speakers are designed for close-field listening. In other words, they sound best when you're sitting in front of the screen. The monitor contains audio circuitry that automatically adjusts treble and bass to provide the best fidelity at various listening levels. The speakers themselves are magnetically shielded so as not to erase any nearby disks and are housed in a plastic enclosure that adds some oomph to bass. A front-panel mute button lets you turn the sound off instantly.

Of course you want a CD-ROM drive

You need a CD-ROM drive to explore the *Macworld Power User Clinic* CD — as well as the thousands of other CD titles that are available in categories ranging from games to stock photo libraries to encyclopedias to type fonts to ZIP code directories. And you can play your music CDs on one, too.

Chapter 25 details what you should look for in a CD-ROM drive. For now, it's enough to say that a CD-ROM drive is quickly becoming a must-buy peripheral. Most Mac models include built-in CD-ROM drives. Apple's drives are among the best and the least expensive, so if you're buying a new Mac, don't hesitate to get one with an internal CD-ROM drive.

If you already have a Mac, you could consider an external CD-ROM drive; Apple sells its drives in external configurations, and many third-party drives are also available. For more details about connecting Macs and CD-ROM drives to speakers and audio systems, see Chapter 21.

What's All This Stuff on the Back of the Mac?

No matter which Mac you end up buying, you'll find a standard set of connectors for the keyboard, mouse, monitor, external hard drives, and printers. For an introduction to the ports and connectors found on the backs of most Macs, see Figure 1-2, "A Guide to Ports and Connectors." I discuss each port in more detail later.

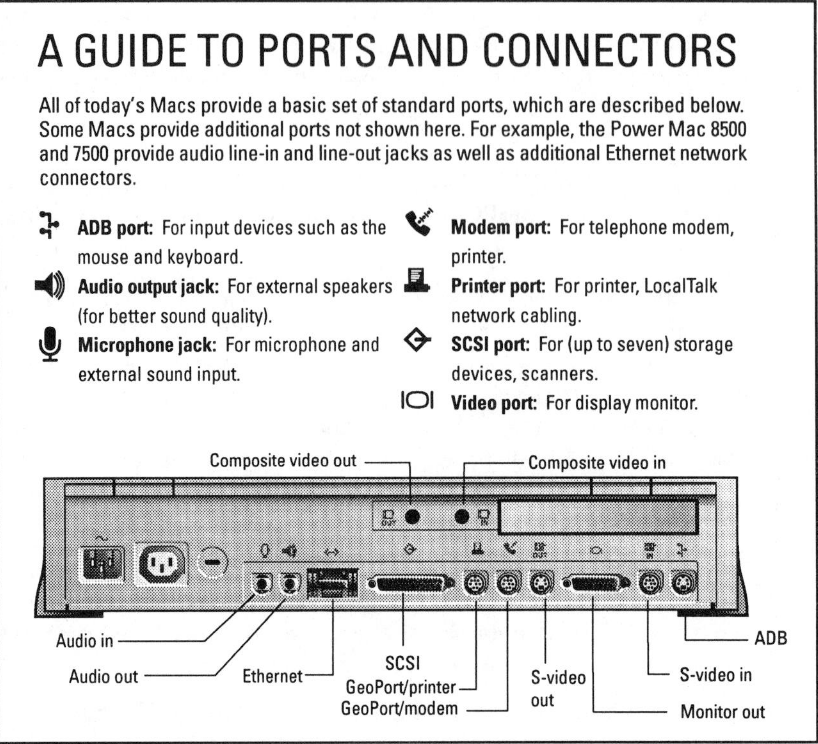

A GUIDE TO PORTS AND CONNECTORS
All of today's Macs provide a basic set of standard ports, which are described below. Some Macs provide additional ports not shown here. For example, the Power Mac 8500 and 7500 provide audio line-in and line-out jacks as well as additional Ethernet network connectors.
ADB port: For input devices such as the mouse and keyboard.
Audio output jack: For external speakers (for better sound quality).
Microphone jack: For microphone and external sound input.
Modem port: For telephone modem, printer.
Printer port: For printer, LocalTalk network cabling.
SCSI port: For (up to seven) storage devices, scanners.
Video port: For display monitor.
Composite video out
Composite video in
Audio in
Audio out
Ethernet
SCSI
GeoPort/printer
GeoPort/modem
S-video out
ADB
S-video in
Monitor out

Figure 1-2: A Guide to Ports and Connectors

PowerPC: What's All the Fuss About?

In 1984, Apple chairman Steve Jobs snorted that IBM's goal was to take over the world and turn it into a version of George Orwell's *1984.* "Apple versus IBM" was one of the main themes of the Mac's early years. (You can hear this story for yourself by listening to the "Mac Intro Highlights" QuickTime movie on the *Macworld Power User Clinic* CD. It's in the Movies and Sounds folder.)

In 1991, Apple and IBM joined forces with Motorola to collaborate on the design of a new microprocessor called *PowerPC.* Why did these companies team up? Three reasons: Microsoft, Microsoft, and Microsoft. Despite the best efforts of Apple's lawyers, Microsoft's Windows software was becoming more and more like the Mac. The Mac remained easier to set up and use (and it still is), but the gap was narrowing.

Actually, there was a fourth reason behind the collaboration: Intel Corporation, which builds the 386, 486, and Pentium processors that drive the vast world of Windows PCs. The fastest Intel processors were delivering better performance than the fastest Motorola processors used in the Mac family. If Apple was going to survive, it would have to do something drastic. By working together with a competitor to design an entirely new microprocessor, it did.

In a nutshell, the PowerPC processors that are built into the Power Macintosh models are faster — a *lot* faster — than the processors used in other Macs. I go into the reasons behind their zip later in this chapter, but for now, suffice it to say that for tasks that demand raw performance, you want a member of the Power Mac family.

Growing pains

The mid-nineties are years of transition for the Mac world, as the entire Mac product line evolves from the older *68000 family* of processors toward the PowerPC chips. To deliver the performance they're capable of, Power Macs require software that has been written to take advantage of their PowerPC chips. The jargon term for this PowerPC-savvy software is *native-mode* software.

When the Power Macs debuted, Apple watchers feared that the relative scarcity of native-mode software cast doubt on the machines' future. Today, however, a vast selection of sizzling native programs are available, and buying a Power Mac has gone from being a forward-looking gamble to being a smart move.

One thing that makes Apple's move to PowerPC so dramatic is that, technically speaking, the new chips are incompatible with the thousands of Mac programs that have already been written. Normally, introducing a computer that doesn't work with existing products is a good way to commit corporate suicide. Apple got away with it when it introduced the original Mac, but it couldn't afford to gamble again.

For the Power Macs, Apple adapted the Mac's system software to allow the new machines to imitate a 68000-family Mac. Programs that came out before the Power Macs *think* that they're running on a 68000-family Mac, a form of computer trickery called *emulation.* It's often another good way to commit corporate suicide — emulation is usually unacceptably slow because the emulation software puts another layer of technical gymnastics between a program and the hardware on which it runs.

But thanks to the speed of the PowerPC chips and the ways Apple took advantage of it, emulation works well on Power Macs. A program running in emulation mode is still much slower than a native-mode version of the same program, but its performance is acceptable — in fact, it is still faster than a lot of low-end 68000-family Macs.

Best of all, Power Macs switch between emulation and native modes without bothering you by telling you about it. Just run the programs you need to run, and the Power Mac's system software handles the details. (For more background on the emulation process, see Chapter 22.)

Common Ground in the Power Mac Family

All Power Macs — whether low-end, high-end, first-generation or second-generation — have numerous features in common:

- ❖ *Speech recognition* AV Macs support Apple's *PlainTalk* speech-recognition software, which lets you use spoken commands to open programs and documents, choose program options, and perform other tasks. I cover PlainTalk in detail in Chapter 33.
- ❖ *Telephony support* As Chapter 16 describes, AV Macs contain additional chips that essentially give them built-in telephone modems *and* voice telephones. Simply put, an AV Mac lets you reach out and touch another computer, a fax machine, or a person. All you have to do is attach the appropriate hardware to the Mac's *GeoPort* connector. (By the way, *telephony* is pronounced *te-LE-phony,* not *tele-PHON-y.* A *telePHONy* is someone who tells lies over the telephone.)
- ❖ *High-quality audio* Power Macs can record and play sound with fidelity approaching that of a compact disc. (Unless you're a recording engineer or a golden-eared audiophile, you may not be able to tell the difference.) As Chapter 21 explains, a Power Mac is a great audio-production workstation.
- ❖ *Two built-in GeoPort connectors* Earlier in this chapter, I mentioned that GeoPort connectors are the gateways to telephony. Power Macs contain not one GeoPort (as do the Quadra AV Macs), but two.
- ❖ *Support for a performance-boosting cache card* Each Power Mac model has a slot that accepts a *Level 2 cache card,* which improves performance by holding recently used instructions and data. Some Power Macs include a cache card, which you can replace with a larger one if you like. See Chapter 29 for more details on caching and cache card options.

First-Generation Similarities

The first-generation Power Macs — the 6100, 7100, and 8100 — also have some common ground.

- ❖ *Multiple monitor support* The Power Mac 7100 and 8100 models can connect to two display monitors with no additional hardware (the AV version of the Power Mac 6100 also has this capability). Macs have had multiple-monitor support since the Mac II was introduced in 1987, but in the past you had to add additional video cards. The Power Mac 7100 and 8100 machines are the first Macs to provide multiple-monitor support right out of the box.
- ❖ *Optional AV technologies* Each first-generation Power Mac model was also available in AV form. As I mentioned earlier in this chapter, in the Power Mac world, AV technologies refer strictly to video input and video output — the capability to display and record video signals from a video recorder or other source and the capability to display the Mac's image on a television monitor or record it on videotape.

The members of the Power Mac family share other similar hardware traits, including their memory-expansion schemes. You'll find all the gory details in Chapter 29.

The first-generation Power Macs

The first three Power Macs — the Power Macintosh 6100, the 7100, and the 8100 — shipped in March 1994. They've since been discontinued, but over a million of them are still out there, so they deserve a look.

These machines form a "good, better, best" hierarchy in all areas: speed, expandability, and video features.

The 6100

The Power Mac 6100 is the smallest, least expensive, and slowest Power Mac. (The word *slowest* does it a disservice, though. When running native applications, the 6100/60 can do some things faster than the Quadra 840AV, the fastest 68000-family Mac Apple ever made.) The Power Mac 6100 uses a pizza-box case design — it's a low, flat package that doesn't take up much room.

The 7100

The Power Mac 7100 is the middle-class Power Mac, offering faster performance and much better expandability than the 6100. The Power Mac 7100 is a taller package; the extra internal real estate provides more room for expansion cards.

In January 1995, Apple speed-bumped the 7100, boosting its clock speed from 66 MHz to 80 MHz and fixing some problems with the computer's NuBus slots.

The 8100

The Power Mac 8100 was the fastest and most expandable of the first-generation Power Macs. In the fall of 1994, an even faster model joined the family: the Power Mac 8100/110, whose processor runs at 110 MHz. In January 1995, Apple bumped the 80 MHz version to 100 MHz.

All three models of the 8100 use a so-called mini-tower case design — the computer is designed to sit alongside your monitor, not underneath it. (You can also stash it on the floor under or alongside your desk.) The 8100 has more room for internal storage devices, such as hard drives and CD-ROM drives, than its juniors.

AV options

All three of the original Power Macs were available with or without AV features. In some ways, however, the AV Power Macs were inferior to the original high-end AV Mac, the Quadra 840AV. They provided only one video-input connector instead of two, for example, and the 7100/66 had particularly slow NuBus slots that hampered its ability to work with third-party digital video cards.

No, it would take another trip to the drawing board for Apple to effectively marry AV technologies and PowerPC chips.

The second-generation Power Macs

In the summer of 1995, Apple unveiled its family of second-generation Power Macs — and what a family it is. At the high end, there's the Power Mac 9500, the fastest and most expandable Mac that Apple has ever made. Then there's the Power Mac 8500, with the best built-in multimedia features you'll find on any personal computer. There's also the 7500, with its upgradable processor and a foolproof expansion design. And at the low end, there's the 7200, which boasts a price/performance ratio that may depress owners of the Power Mac 8100/80.

All of the second-generation Power Macs share a variety of architectural similarities. Some are obvious — the use of PCI slots instead of NuBus slots, for example — while others are more subtle. For an overview, see the Backgrounder box, "Common Ground in the Second-Generation Power Macs."

The 9500

The Power Mac 9500 breaks with the past while also borrowing from it. It's the first Mac to use the PCI expansion bus instead of the NuBus slots that the Mac II introduced back in 1987. It's the first Power Mac to use the second-generation PowerPC 604 chip — and one that you can upgrade, at that.

But like the original Mac II, the 9500 provides a scaled-down set of built-in features. There's no on-board video circuitry; you need to install a PCI-based video card to connect a monitor. (One 9500 configuration includes a video card — more on this shortly.) Even the five-slot Quadra 950, the most expandable 68040 Mac Apple ever made, provided on-board video. The 9500 also lacks AV features — it supports 16-bit, 44 KHz stereo audio recording and playback, but it can't digitize video or route its image to a TV set without third-party hardware.

No, the 9500 is all about speed and expansion — think of it as the most lavish foundation ever built.

The 9500 is initially being offered in two versions: the 120 MHz 9500/120 and the 132 MHz 9500/132. The 132 MHz version includes 16MB of memory, a 2GB hard drive, and a quadruple-speed CD-ROM drive. The 120 MHz version includes 16MB of memory, a 1GB hard drive, a quadruple-speed CD-ROM drive, and an ATI mach64 24-bit video card.

Common Ground in the Second-Generation Power Macs

Here's an overview of the features that the second-generation Power Macs have in common.

From NuBus to PCI With the first-generation Power Macs, Apple often chose compatibility over performance. The first Power Macs' use of NuBus slots was a prime example — faster slots would have yielded faster machines but forced the Mac world to buy new cards. But for a variety of reasons, the first-generation Power Mac NuBus slots (particularly the ones in the 7100) were often significantly slower than those of the Quadra 840AV, whose speedy NuBus implementation makes it popular among digital video producers even today.

The 9500 sheds these constraints by adopting the PCI (Peripheral Component Interconnect) expansion architecture, which is becoming increasingly popular in the PC world, and a de facto standard on Pentium-based PCs. PCI slots provide dramatically faster performance than NuBus slots and make it far easier for hardware developers to create cards that work in PCs as well as Macs. For more details on PCI and its benefits, see Chapter 29.

New memory expansion cards In the first-generation Power Macs, memory expansion was provided through 72-pin single in-line memory modules, or SIMMs. SIMMs transfer 32 bits of data at a time; to accommodate the PowerPC 601's 64-bit memory architecture, upgrading RAM meant installing SIMMs in pairs. The second-generation Power Macs introduce a new memory-expansion board: the 168-pin *dual* in-line memory module, or *DIMM*. DIMMs are described in more detail later in this chapter and in Chapter 29.

Better networking Each of the second-generation Power Macs has not only an AAUI Ethernet port, but also a 10BaseT connector, eliminating the need for an extra-cost adaptor to connect the 9500 to a 10BaseT Ethernet network. See Chapter 32 for more details on networking.

Improved input/output The internal SCSI buses in the 9500 and 8500 provide much faster data transfer than the SCSI buses in first-generation Power Macs. (Chapter 26 gives more details.) Other aspects of the machines' input/output subsystems are also faster, thanks to a new direct-memory access (DMA) scheme that minimizes the processor's involvement in data transfers across the SCSI and PCI buses as well as through the serial and Ethernet ports.

A new emulator Called the Dynamic Recompilation Emulator (DRE), this new OS component runs 680X0 programs faster than did the emulator in the first-generation Power Macs. It's discussed in Chapter 22.

Tweaked system software The second-generation Power Macs include System 7.5.2; this version incorporates numerous tweaks, most of which are to support the new machines' enhanced hardware. Chapter 22 contains more details.

A foundation for graphics acceleration Previously, hardware developers had to devise their own acceleration schemes when designing ultra-fast video cards; for the second-generation Power Macs, Apple defined a structure for graphics acceleration. This should lead to less expensive and more reliable video cards. And in the little-things-that-count department, the Mac's arrow mouse pointer can now be built into and drawn by a video card, a change that eliminates the flickering pointer you see when a QuickTime movie is playing. (In other Macs, the pointer is drawn by the Mac OS.)

Power-saving features The Power Mac 7200, 7500, and 8500 boast energy-saving sleep modes similar to those found on a PowerBook. As Chapter 23 describes, you can specify that one of these Power Macs go to sleep after a period of inactivity. Pressing a key wakes the machine in a flash.

A 604 to go

The Power Mac 9500 delivers on Apple's promise to use new PowerPC-family processors as they become available from IBM and Motorola. The PowerPC 604 sports internal improvements that make it faster than the 601 used in the first-generation Power Macs, and it runs at faster clock rates — at up to 132 MHz now, with faster speeds on the horizon. (By comparison, the fastest 601-based Power Mac, the now-discontinued 8100/110, runs at 110 MHz.)

Macworld Lab's tests confirm the 9500 to be the fastest Mac ever. In overall performance, the 9500/132 was 47 percent faster than the 8100/110, and the 9500/120 was 34 percent faster than the 8100/100. The 9500/132 was a five times faster than the baseline machine, a Centris 650.

Inside Apple's Processor-Upgrade Technology

In the Power Mac 7500, 8500, and 9500, the central processor lives not on the motherboard itself, but on a 4-inch x 7-inch card that you can unplug and replace with a faster one. If you have a 9500/120, for instance, you can quickly turn it into a 9500/132, and you can take advantage of higher-speed 604 processors as they become available. (Apple expects 150 MHz 604 chips to be available relatively soon.) And because the 9500, 8500, and 7500 have identical processor-upgrade slots, trickle-down upgrades are possible: for example, a 9500/120 or 8500/120 owner buys a 132 MHz (or faster) CPU card, and passes the 120 MHz processor card on to someone with a 7500.

Apple is publishing the specifications for its processor-upgrade slot, so expect to see other companies deliver warp-speed processor upgrades, some of which might even combine multiple processors.

Processor upgrades are common options for PC users, where owners of many 486-based systems can buy 486DX2, 486DX4, and even Pentium OverDrive processors that replace a 486DX or 486SX processor. Apple's processor upgrades go a step further. When you install a processor-upgrade card, the 9500's internal buses will run faster, too, boosting video and memory-access performance and SCSI throughput. (That doesn't happen in a PC's OverDrive upgrade.) For example, in the 9500/120 and 9500/132, the processor buses run at 40 MHz and 44 MHz, respectively; when 150 MHz 604 chips become available, however, installing one will bump the buses up to 50 MHz.

At processor clock speeds of between 100 MHz and 150 MHz, the buses run at one third the processor's speed. The buses' upper limit is 50 MHz, however, so don't expect to get 60 MHz buses when you pop in a 180 MHz 604 someday.

Why the 50 MHz upper limit when some PC buses run at 66 MHz? Apple says it's because it puts more on the system bus than do PC manufacturers and because its custom chips are more complex than those used in most PCs.

Expansion galore

The 9500 provides 12 DIMM slots (there's no memory soldered onto the logic board) and can support more memory than any Mac yet: up to 768MB with 64MB DIMMs, and up to 1.5GB with 128MB DIMMs, which can be manufactured using 64MB memory chips. Check your credit card limit before ordering, though — at this writing, 768MB of DIMM-based memory will set you back about $25,000.

The Power Mac 9500 also introduces a new cache memory scheme. (As mentioned earlier in this chapter, Power Mac cache cards boost performance by providing a small amount of very fast memory that the processor can use to hold recently used program code and data.) Where previous Power Macs contained SIMM slots for cache memory, the 9500 contains 512K of cache soldered onto the motherboard. And the cache itself works differently; it provides a 128 bit-wide data path (versus first-generation Power Macs' 64-bit path), and it uses a copy-back rather than write-through scheme. In English: Caching is a lot faster than in first-generation Power Macs.

As for general-purpose expansion, the 9500 provides six PCI slots. Note that you will use up one of them for a video card right off the bat.

Is a 9500 for you?

The Power Mac 9500 is not the second-generation Power Mac for the rest of us — it's too pricey and comes with too little. But the 9500 is an excellent foundation for a high-end production workstation — for color publishing or media production. Its speed and expandability also make it a natural for scientific and technical markets.

What about the rest of us? Read on.

The 8500

The Power Mac 8500 is the connoisseur's second-generation Power Macintosh. It shares the 9500's PowerPC 604 processor, although the 8500's is available only at 120 MHz, not 132 MHz. As in the 9500, the processor resides on a plug-in expansion card. And as in the 9500, the 8500's internal bus speeds notch up when you install a faster processor card, boosting video and SCSI performance.

The 8500 provides eight DIMM memory sockets, which can accommodate up to 512MB of RAM using 64MB DIMMs, and a full 1GB using 128MB DIMMs. There's also 256K of cache memory. Like the Power Mac 9500, the 8500 provides an internal SCSI-2 Fast bus that can transfer up to 10MB per second. The 8500 is available with a 1GB internal hard drive or with a 2GB drive; both configurations include 16MB of memory and a quadruple-speed CD-ROM drive.

The 8500 contains three PCI expansion slots — half the number of expansion slots as its taller sibling. But the 8500 provides built-in video circuitry and a slew of other on-board features, so you have to work pretty hard to fill its PCI slots.

Hot video

Unlike the 9500, the 8500 includes on-board video circuitry — and how. A new, 64-bit video memory (VRAM) scheme makes for fast window redraws and sizzling scrolling. The machine includes 2MB of VRAM, expandable to 4MB using two 1MB VRAM SIMMs. Equipped with 4MB of VRAM, the 8500 can display millions of colors (24-bit video) on monitors with resolutions of up to 1152 x 870 pixels (the standard for a 21-inch monitor), and thousands of colors (16-bit video) at a resolution of 1280 x 1024 pixels — a resolution used for professional image retouching that no previous Mac's on-board video has provided. Chapter 29 contains more details on video-upgrade concepts and strategies.

All this video horsepower terminates in a high-density monitor connector. The same kind of connector found on first-generation Power Macs, it also provides pass-through wires for the Apple Desktop Bus and for audio input and output, eliminating the spaghetti of cables when used with a monitor such as Apple's AudioVision 17.

That high-density connector is the only monitor port you'll find: unlike first-generation Power Macs, none of the second-generation machines comes equipped to drive two monitors. That saves Apple some cost by eliminating a feature that many people don't use. Equipped with 4MB of VRAM, however, the 8500 simultaneously can drive a monitor and a video device such as a TV monitor or camcorder.

The 8500's AV features — video-display, video-input, and video-output — are also dramatic improvements over those of the earlier AV Power Macs and the pioneering Centris/Quadra 660AV and Quadra 840AV. The result is an ideal machine for multimedia production and an excellent foundation for high-end video work. Chapter 20 contains all the details on this remarkable Mac's multimedia features.

The Power Mac 7500

The Power Mac 7500 represents the midrange in the new lineup, providing many of the most innovative features of the second generation at a cheaper price.

As mentioned earlier, the 7500's 100 MHz PowerPC 601 chip resides on the same type of upgradable processor card used by the 8500 and 9500. (Indeed, the 7500 is built to accommodate up to a 150 MHz PowerPC 604.) Eight DIMM slots can house up to 512MB of memory. Another slot can accommodate a cache card, which is not included. Cache cards generally increase performance by 10 to 20 percent; see Chapter 29 for more details.

The 7500 shares the identical on-board video subsystem of the 8500: the motherboard's 2MB of VRAM are expandable to 4MB, and monitor support and resolutions are the same.

Deciphering Power Mac Model Numbers

What's with the long model numbers in the Power Mac family — has someone at Apple taken up numerology? No, it's supposedly Apple's way of clarifying the capabilities of the machine.

The names for Apple's new Macs may seem especially confusing — why, for example, is the 7500 faster than the 8100, when a bigger number usually means a better machine? In Apple's naming scheme, the first digit represents the series:

- A 9xxx series means a tall, tower-style case (like the Quadra 950, Power Mac 9500, or Workgroup Server 9150)
- An 8xxx series means a mini-tower (like the 8100 and 8500)
- A 7xxx means a traditional desktop case (like the Power Mac 7100 or 7200)
- A 6xxx means a flatter, "pizza box" desktop case (like the Power Mac 6100)
- A 5xxx means an all-in-one design (like the Performa 5200)

Within a series, a larger number in the model name means "more features" — the 7500 has more features than the 7200, for example.

Finally, the number after the slash indicates the processor's speed. (The value is in *megahertz,* abbreviated *MHz* — more on what that means later in this chapter.) And effective with the second-generation Power Macs, the *AV* suffix is gone — you'll just have to know which models include AV features.

Is all this number stuff really easier? I'm not convinced. It does make more sense than the old "II, IIx, IIcx, IIci" style of model naming — at least there's some logic behind the new scheme, even if it does take an entire sidebar to explain it.

Easy expansion

Adding memory upgrades to the 7500 is a cinch. Flick two plastic latches to remove the top of the case — no screws. Inside, the storage devices and power supply are mounted on a hinged chassis that swings up to allow complete access to the motherboard beneath. The case also has an additional bay that can accommodate a 3½-inch device, such as a second internal hard drive. Another nice touch is an easily removed baffle that protects any PCI cards while you're upgrading other components.

Apple designed the new case not only to simplify upgrading, but also because the 7100-style case — which originally housed 1992's Mac IIvx and IIvi — was not able to adequately absorb the radio interference generated by the kind of fast processors that the new models can use. The downside is that no upgrade to the 7500 is available for the Power Mac 7100 or earlier Macs using the same case (the IIvi, IIvx, Centris 650, and Quadra 650).

Video conferencing, not video editing

The 7500 lacks the 8500's video-out ports and print-to-video features, but it does provide identical video-input features: S-video and composite video-input jacks, full-screen, full-motion video playthrough, and QuickTime movie captures. It also provides the RCA jacks for audio in and out, and a DAV slot on the motherboard.

Why leave out the video-out? Because Apple is positioning the 7500 as a business-oriented Mac, and its video features as being ideal for video conferencing — the 7500 includes Apple's QuickTime Conferencing software. It's a sensible strategy that reduces the machine's cost without gutting its multimedia capabilities. (CD-ROM producers and QuickTime tinkerers generally don't need video-out features, and if they do, third-party video-out hardware is relatively inexpensive — see Chapter 20.) And if video conferencing ever does take off, the 7500 is ready for it — once you buy a video camera.

The 7200

Redefining the low end of the Power Mac line is the Power Mac 7200, available in 75 MHz and 90 MHz speeds. Yes, the new *low-end* Power Mac has processor speeds that approach or exceed that of the original *high-end* Power Mac, the 8100/80. And with three PCI slots, the 7200 provides a degree of expandability that the now-discontinued previous entry-level business Macs — the Power Mac 6100 and Quadra 630 — never could.

What's the catch?

But to arrive at the 7200's low price, Apple had to omit some of what the 7500 and costlier Macs provide. First to go was the processor upgrade slot: in the 7200, the PowerPC 601 chip is soldered to the motherboard. Other omissions in the 7200 compared to its higher-priced cousins: the low-end machines have a standard DB-15 monitor connector rather than the high-density AV connector. And the low-end machines lack RCA audio ins and outs (they still have miniplugs). Apple also dropped the microphone that comes with the 8500 and 7500.

The 7200 also accepts less memory than the 7500 or 8500: its four DIMM slots allow for up to 256MB of RAM with 64MB DIMMs. The cache and RAM buses are 64 bits wide, as opposed to the faster 128-bit buses in the 7500, 8500, and 9500. As with the 7500, no cache is included, although you can add one.

Both 7200 models share similar on-board video features, although the 7200/90 goes a bit further than the 7200/75. Both include 1MB of video memory; the 7200/75 can be upgraded to 2MB (allowing for 24-bit color on 16-inch monitors), while the 7200/90 supports up to 4MB. In their stock configurations, the machines use a 32-bit-wide graphics bus; when upgraded, the VRAM DIMMs interleave to 64 bits wide.

Which Power Mac is for you?

These mainstream second-generation Power Macs take the basic architectural advances developed for the 9500 and combine them with features aimed for typical users' needs. The 8500 is clearly the power-user choice for color publishers, multimedia producers, and engineers — the 9500 may be faster, but it requires you to add several third-party cards to offer what the 8500 has built in. The 7500 is clearly the power user's desktop Mac, with enough audiovisual and telephony technology to let you dabble in video conferencing, voice mail, and motion-video capture. The 7200 is the Mac that most of us will buy, since it provides great performance without all the bells and whistles that jack up the 7500's price.

But keep in mind that with slower memory architecture and no upgradable processor, the 7200 also offers less room to grow than the 7500. If you anticipate needing more speed in the near future (and who doesn't?) or wanting to dabble with digital video, you might consider spending the extra money for the 7500.

With the 7200, 7500, and 8500, the Power Mac line is no longer hamstrung by the circa-1987 limitations such as SIMMs and NuBus slots. Better still, Apple has crafted a product line whose members have not only strong common denominators — three PCI slots and great performance — but also have important differences that address the needs of specific types of users. And best of all, the leading-edge technology they offer is surprisingly affordable.

And Now, Macintosh Clones

For years, computer industry pundits criticized Apple for retaining a stranglehold on the Macintosh market. "Allow other companies to build Mac clones," they urged. "That's the only way to challenge Microsoft Windows in the market."

They were right, and Apple has finally realized it. Actually, to be fair, Apple realized it a long time ago — it just took a while to leap the technical and political hurdles necessary to open up the Macintosh operating system to other companies.

In any case, the first Macintosh-compatible machines shipped in the spring of 1995. The Mac clone market isn't exactly huge — at this writing, only three companies are shipping Mac clones, and two of them are building expensive, high-end systems designed for publishing and video production. But it's a start.

Meet the Mac OS

One small part of Apple's clone strategy was to create a brand identity for the Mac's system software. Just about everyone knows what Microsoft Windows is, but the Mac's system software has traditionally gone by the rather bland *system* followed by a number. (And that's only a fairly recent tradition: in the Mac's early, touchy-feely days, Apple didn't even use the terms *system software* or *operating system* — it felt they were too technical and intimidating.)

The Mac's system software now goes by the name Mac OS — short for, of course, Macintosh Operating System. To go along with the new name, there's a new face — and it appears when you start up a Mac that's running Mac OS version 7.5.1 or later. You can also expect to see the Mac OS logo appearing in advertisements for Mac clones and on Mac software packages.

Harder hardware steps

If all Apple had to do to create an industry for Mac clones was to create a new logo, we would have seen Mac clones years ago. The real job was much harder. Apple had to figure out a way to ensure that Mac clones would have the same plug-and-play compatibility and ease of use as genuine Macs, lest it lose one of the Mac platform's most significant advantages over Microsoft Windows. One way it has accomplished this is by licensing not only the Mac OS to clone developers, but also key chips that Apple uses on its own Macs. Apple also provides engineering assistance and compatibility certification for clone manufacturers.

This means that Apple has a fine line to walk — it must make many of its crown jewels available to the very companies that it will be competing with. It must support companies that want to make Mac clones while also creating computers that it hopes you'll buy instead. It's a tightrope, and it's easy to see why Apple took so long to step out onto it.

Power Computing

The first company to get an Apple license to produce Power Mac clones was Power Computing, which was founded by a veteran of the PC clone industry. Power Computing's machines are the mainstream Mac clones, providing a solid mix of features and performance at prices slightly lower than Apple's. Like many PC clone vendors, Power Computing sells its machines via mail order rather than through dealers.

Comparing the first Power Computing machines

But in some ways, Power Computing's initial offerings lack the sophistication of Apple's second-generation Power Macs — in fact, they compare more closely to Apple's first-generation Power Macs.

The initial Power Computing family comprises three machines: the Power 80, the Power 100, and the Power 110. All three are built into a horizontally oriented case similar to (but taller than) that of the Power Mac 7100. The case contains room for up to three hard drives.

All three use the PowerPC 601 chip, but each runs it at a different speed — the speed corresponding to its model number. Each machine provides three NuBus slots, a 256K Level 2 cache card (a 512K cache is optional), dual SCSI interfaces,

CHRP: Apple and IBM Get Cozy

The world of Mac compatibles is fairly small now, but if Apple and IBM have their way, it will have the potential to become significantly larger. In the fall of 1994, these two companies, along with Motorola, announced an agreement to build computers that would run each other's system software. One ramification of this — if it all pans out — is that IBM will build computers that run the Mac OS.

Specifically, Apple, IBM, and Motorola defined what they call the *common hardware reference platform,* or *CHRP* — a framework of technical concepts and specifications — that can be used by any hardware vendor to build compatible PowerPC-based computers that can run a variety of operating systems. The plan is for the new hardware reference platform to support the Mac OS; IBM's OS/2 for the PowerPC; AIX, a version of the UNIX operating system; Microsoft Windows NT; and Sun's Solaris. The end result will be extremely flexible computers that will essentially be able to run all of today's mainstream operating systems — and, therefore, application programs.

Each company has its work cut out. Apple's assignment is to adapt the Mac OS to run on the new computers. IBM's efforts will involve OS/2 and AIX, while Motorola will concentrate on Windows NT. Each company also has a lot to gain. By creating a new generation of Power Macs that can also run OS/2 and other operating systems — and by allowing other manufacturers to build computers that run the Mac OS — Apple hopes to increase its market share. For its part, IBM gets a chance to license the Mac OS and establish itself as a player in the world of PowerPC-based computers — something it's been struggling to do.

Before you postpone that new Mac purchase, note that these Swiss army knife computers won't be available until sometime in 1996. To learn more about CHRP and the future of Mac clones, check out the "Mac Clones" segment of the *Macworld Power User Clinic.*

built-in Ethernet, and built-in stereo sound recording and playback. A quadruple-speed CD-ROM drive is standard equipment on some configurations and optional for others. And unlike Apple's machines, the Power Computing models include a keyboard (it's an extended keyboard).

All three Power Computing machines provide on-board video circuitry capable of driving monitors as large as 17 inches. An optional second video card provides 24-bit video on monitors as large as 21 inches.

Radius and DayStar clones

The other two early riders on the Macintosh clone bandwagon are longtime veterans of the Mac world: Radius, best known for its video products and color printers; and DayStar, a major player in Mac accelerators.

The Radius System 100 is a high-end clone tuned for image-editing applications. Based on a Power Mac 8100/110, the System 100 ships with an FWB SCSI JackHammer accelerator (see Chapter 25), two hard drives (2GB and 500MB), at least 40MB of memory, a Radius Thunder video card, a CD-ROM drive, Adobe Photoshop, and Radius Color Composer color calibration hardware. Radius will also be shipping a Mac clone optimized for digital video editing.

DayStar Digital's Genesis MP systems take a different approach to meeting the needs of image-editing and publishing pros. These machines are built around the PowerPC 604 processor and provide PCI expansion slots. The dual-604 Genesis MP includes special software that implements a degree of multiprocessing — so that application programs can split up processor-intensive tasks such as 3-D rendering and image processing.

Future directions for Mac clones

Power Computing plans to ship additional machines later in 1995. A tower-style, high-end machine is in the works, as are machines that provide PCI expansion slots. The company may even develop a hybrid machine that provides both NuBus and PCI slots — not a bad idea.

DayStar is also planning enhancements to the Genesis MP line, including models that pack up to four 604 processors. And Radius will ship clones built around its own, rather than Apple's, logic board designs.

For the latest on the rapidly evolving Macintosh clone industry, keep an eye on the pages of *Macworld.* And be sure to download the monthly *Macworld Power User Clinic* updates from America Online and eWorld. See Appendix A for details.

Running DOS/Windows on a Mac

Dedicated Mac zealots cringe at the idea of running Microsoft Windows on their machines, but it's possible to do so. The ability to turn a Mac into a PC clone can be valuable if you use a PC at work, or if your company insists that all computers it purchases be PC-compatible.

If you have a Power Mac, you can run Insignia Solutions' SoftWindows, which is a special version of Windows 3.1. SoftWindows is the most economical route to Windows compatibility because it doesn't require any additional hardware. But it has some shortcomings, including limited compatibility with Windows sound-oriented software.

For faster performance and better compatibility, there's Apple's Power Macintosh 6100 DOS Compatibility Card, an expansion card for the Power Mac 6100 and Performa 6100 series. This card contains an Intel 486 DX2/66 processor and even supports programs that use the Creative Solutions Sound Blaster card, a popular audio card in the Windows world.

Finally, if you don't have a Power Mac, there's Orange Micro's OrangePC, an expansion card that works in any NuBus-equipped Mac except the Mac IIsi. Orange Micro's Series 400 board is a PCI card for second-generation Power Macs; it provides a user-installable 486 processor, which can be upgraded to a Pentium processor. The Series 400 also accepts an optional, SoundBlaster-compatible sound card.

Visiting the Used Mac Lot

Used Macs have been showing up in classified ads and on college dorm bulletin boards for years. Should you consider one? It depends on the model.

The compact Macs

Avoid the Mac Plus like the plague. It's true that the Plus runs many of today's programs, but the Plus's weakling power supply and lack of an expansion slot make obsolescence-shattering upgrades such as accelerator boards impractical and risky. Besides, the Plus was discontinued many years ago, so the machines that are out there aren't exactly spring chickens.

As for the SE, its single expansion slot gives it a brighter future. Indeed, its expansion slot makes the SE less prone to obsolescence than the Mac Classic that replaced both it and the Plus. Unlike the Plus, the SE can reliably accommodate an accelerator board and an internal hard disk. It's also about 25 percent faster than the Plus and about as fast as a Classic. The SE/30 is a great little Mac that's still well worth considering if the price is right. (Indeed, the SE/30 has advantages over the Classic II that replaced *it*.)

The modular Macs

The modular Macs — ones that lack built-in monitors — provide at least one expansion slot that can accommodate an accelerator board. Chapter 29 lists some upgrade strategies for the members of the Mac family.

But with new Mac prices as low as they are, you need to evaluate carefully whether an old, upgraded machine is a better deal than a brand-new one. A first-generation Power Mac — a 6100, 7100, or 8100 — is the least obsolete, of course. I'd think twice about a used 6100; its expansion capabilities are too limited. The 7100 and 8100 provide better expansion features, although the 7100/66 has relatively slow NuBus slots that make it unsuitable for semi-pro or professional digital video work. (The 7100/80 doesn't have this problem.) The 8100 has the brightest future, since it can be upgraded to the amazing, second-generation Power Mac 8500.

And how about the big, all-in-one Macs — machines such as the LC-500 series and Performa 500 series? The newer models in this family are well worth considering, although their expansion capabilities are much more limited, each generally offering just one slot. These Macs are especially well suited to cramped confines, such as college dorms and home offices. However, they don't provide the performance or design elegance of Apple's latest all-in-one machines, such as the PowerPC-based Performa 5200. Unless you have a chance to pick up an older all-in-one Mac at a rock-bottom price, you're probably better off considering a new 5200 instead.

Macs to Go — the PowerBook Family

The PowerBook family falls into three broad categories — the original all-in-one PowerBooks (I'll call them the classic PowerBooks), the PowerBook Duo family, and the new PowerBook 500-series.

Classic PowerBooks include the PowerBook 100, 145 and 145B, 160, 160c, 165, 165c, 170, 180, and 180c. Most classic PowerBooks contain a SCSI connector for attaching to external hard drives and other add-ons; an ADB port for a mouse or other input device; a modem port and printer port; a floppy drive; and a video-output connector for attaching a display monitor. The older PowerBook 100, 140, and 170 models don't have the video-out connector, and the 100 lacks a floppy drive.

The PowerBook Duo models lack the SCSI connector, video-out jack, ADB port, and floppy drive and provide just one serial port, not two. When you need these ports, you attach a PowerBook Duo to one of several available *docking stations* (see Figure 1-3 "How the Duo System Fits Together"). One station — the Duo Dock — even contains expansion slots. The Duo system is designed to provide the best of both worlds — the portability of a PowerBook with the expansion flexibility of a desktop Mac. Whether it delivers on that goal is a question I address shortly.

Family similarities

All PowerBooks share numerous family traits, starting with a *liquid-crystal display* (LCD) screen. The PowerBook 100, 140, 145, 150, 160, and 165 models use a backlit *supertwist* display; so do the PowerBook Duo 210 and 230. High-end PowerBooks, such as the 170, 180, and 180c, use an *active-matrix* display that is considerably brighter and easier to read. The PowerBook 165c provides a *passive-matrix* color display, while the 180c provides a beautiful active-matrix color display.

The PowerBook 500-series family uses a variety of displays, depending on the model. The PowerBook 520 uses a supertwist gray-scale display, while the 520c provides a dual-scan color display. The 540 and 540c provide active-matrix gray-scale and color displays, respectively. All of the 500-series displays are nice and big: 9½ inches diagonally. The displays in the 520, 520c, and 540 can be upgraded to active-matrix displays.

Passive-matrix displays are prone to a problem called *ghosting* or *shadowing*, in which windows and other items moved on the display leave a shadowy trail in their wake. (For a look at the differences between passive- and active-matrix color displays, see Figure 1-4, "How Color LCDs Work.")

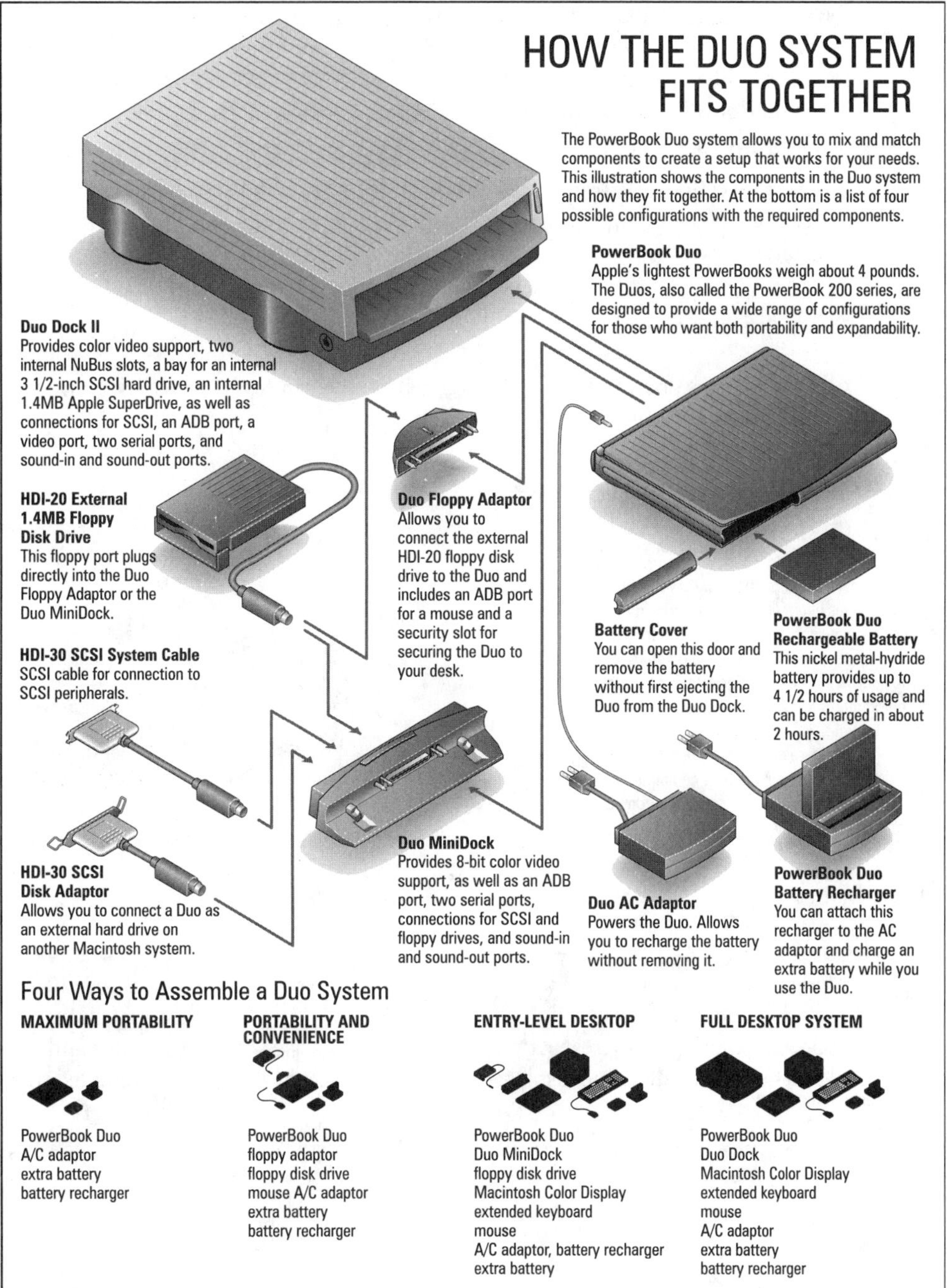
HOW THE DUO SYSTEM FITS TOGETHER
The PowerBook Duo system allows you to mix and match components to create a setup that works for your needs. This illustration shows the components in the Duo system and how they fit together. At the bottom is a list of four possible configurations with the required components.
PowerBook Duo
Apple's lightest PowerBooks weigh about 4 pounds. The Duos, also called the PowerBook 200 series, are designed to provide a wide range of configurations for those who want both portability and expandability.
Duo Dock II
Provides color video support, two internal NuBus slots, a bay for an internal 3 1/2-inch SCSI hard drive, an internal 1.4MB Apple SuperDrive, as well as connections for SCSI, an ADB port, a video port, two serial ports, and sound-in and sound-out ports.
HDI-20 External 1.4MB Floppy Disk Drive
This floppy port plugs directly into the Duo Floppy Adaptor or the Duo MiniDock.
Duo Floppy Adaptor
Allows you to connect the external HDI-20 floppy disk drive to the Duo and includes an ADB port for a mouse and a security slot for securing the Duo to your desk.
Battery Cover
You can open this door and remove the battery without first ejecting the Duo from the Duo Dock.
PowerBook Duo Rechargeable Battery
This nickel metal-hydride battery provides up to 4 1/2 hours of usage and can be charged in about 2 hours.
HDI-30 SCSI System Cable
SCSI cable for connection to SCSI peripherals.
HDI-30 SCSI Disk Adaptor
Allows you to connect a Duo as an external hard drive on another Macintosh system.
Duo MiniDock
Provides 8-bit color video support, as well as an ADB port, two serial ports, connections for SCSI and floppy drives, and sound-in and sound-out ports.
Duo AC Adaptor
Powers the Duo. Allows you to recharge the battery without removing it.
PowerBook Duo Battery Recharger
You can attach this recharger to the AC adaptor and charge an extra battery while you use the Duo.
Four Ways to Assemble a Duo System
MAXIMUM PORTABILITY
PowerBook Duo
A/C adaptor
extra battery
battery recharger
PORTABILITY AND CONVENIENCE
PowerBook Duo
floppy adaptor
floppy disk drive
mouse A/C adaptor
extra battery
battery recharger
ENTRY-LEVEL DESKTOP
PowerBook Duo
Duo MiniDock
floppy disk drive
Macintosh Color Display
extended keyboard
mouse
A/C adaptor, battery recharger
extra battery
FULL DESKTOP SYSTEM
PowerBook Duo
Duo Dock
Macintosh Color Display
extended keyboard
mouse
A/C adaptor
extra battery
battery recharger

Figure 1-3: How the Duo System Fits Together

No mouse in a PowerBook's house

PowerBooks are likely to be used where there may not be roaming room for a mouse. For this reason, they contain a built-in pointing device. Here's the low-down on PowerBook pointing:

- Classic PowerBooks provide a *trackball*, a kind of upside-down mouse (see Chapter 33). Two crescent-shaped buttons surround the top and bottom of the trackball.
- The PowerBook 500 family provides a particularly cool input device called the *trackpad*, which relies on a principle called *coupling capacitance* to sense your finger's location (see Chapter 33 for details). A button is located at the bottom edge of the trackpad.

All PowerBooks provide a large, flat area where you can rest your wrists as you type or use the trackball or trackpad.

HOW COLOR LCDs WORK

Left to their own devices, the liquid crystals in an LCD screen align themselves between the glass plates in a twisted pattern; light can then pass through the panel unobstructed. When an electric current is applied, the liquid crystals untwist **(A)** and light is blocked by the polarizing filter on the glass plate. Different amounts of twist result in different amounts of light passing through.

In color LCDs, there are three subpixels per pixel—one each for the pixel's red, green, and blue components. A film with alternating stripes of blue, red, and green adds color **(B)** to the light emanating from the liquid crystals forming each pixel.

Passive Matrix

The PowerBook 165c uses a grid, or matrix, of electrodes (flat wires). The intersection of current from the horizontal and vertical electrodes — called passive matrix technology — determines the charge at a particular spot in the panel. That charge determines whether that spot is on or off, and its intensity if on. Current moves from electrode to electrode in a cycle. Only one pixel at a time can be activated.

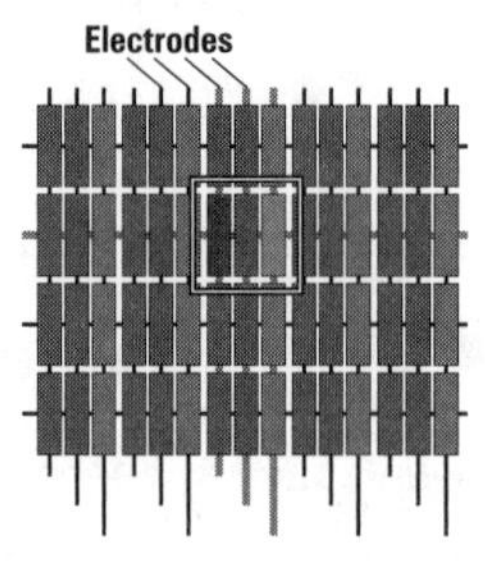

Active Matrix

Active-matrix panels are more complicated and more precise. Rows of horizontal and vertical electrodes, called thin-film transistors, form a grid, or matrix, of pixels. Each pixel can be controlled individually, staying on as long as needed, rather than having to be refreshed periodically the way pixels in a passive matrix display are. Several pixels can be activated simultaneously.

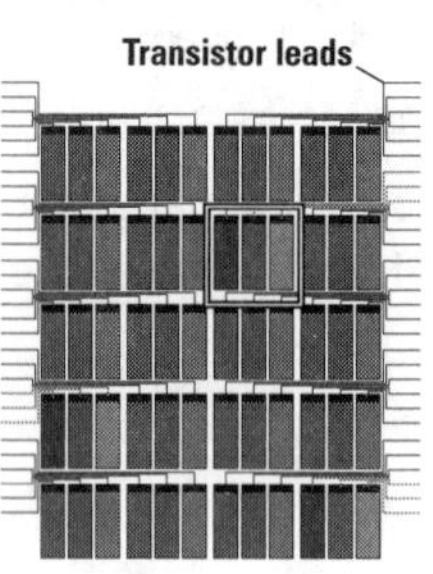

Figure 1-4: How Color LCDs Work

PowerBook sound features

All PowerBooks, except the PowerBook 100 and 150 and the discontinued 140 and 170, contain a built-in microphone. The PowerBook 140 and 170 can attach to the same type of external microphone that desktop Macs use. The PowerBook 100 and 150 do not support a microphone. See Chapter 21 for sound-related PowerBook tips.

The PowerBook 500 series models are the first PowerBooks to include built-in stereo speakers. All previous PowerBooks, except for the PowerBook 100 and 150, provide stereo-sound circuitry, but you have to attach the computer to a sound system or headphones to hear the stereo.

Powering the PowerBook

A PowerBook can run from a slide-in rechargeable battery or from an AC adaptor, both of which are included with the machine. The battery is recharged when the computer is running from AC power. An external battery charger that charges up to two batteries at once is also available. Battery life is determined by many factors — including the screen's brightness setting and the amount of hard and floppy disk activity — but as a general rule, you can expect roughly two to four hours of operating time between charges.

The PowerBook 500-series models use a new, more sophisticated battery design that provides up to three hours of operation on a charge. A 500-series model is unique in that it can house two batteries — just the thing for cross-country flights. The batteries themselves contain a microprocessor and additional circuitry that enables the PowerBook to provide more accurate information about the amount of charge remaining.

PowerBooks provide a variety of power-management features that let you extend the time between recharges. Chapter 23 describes how to take advantage of them.

PowerBook 500-series details

Other noteworthy attributes of the PowerBook 500 series include

- *68040 processors* The PowerBook 500-series machines are the first PowerBooks to use the fast 68040 processor.
- *Expansion slots* The 500-series models provide a processor-direct slot and accept an optional adaptor that lets the PowerBooks use PCMCIA cards, also called PC Cards. (PCMCIA stands for "people can't memorize computer industry acronyms." Actually, it stands for Personal Computer Memory Card International Association, a group that created a standard for compact expansion cards.) PCMCIA support has been available in DOS/Windows portables for some time; now it's finally made its way into the Macintosh world. The PowerBook 500-series PCMCIA adaptor installs in the computer's processor-direct slot and commandeers one of the computer's battery chambers. More details on PCMCIA appear in Chapter 29.

- *Built-in Ethernet networking* All 500-series PowerBooks provide built-in Ethernet ports.
- *PowerPC upgradability* One of the most intriguing things about the 500-series PowerBooks is that they will be upgradable to use PowerPC processors when the low-power version of the PowerPC chip becomes available, probably before September 1995.

Duo details

An all-in-one PowerBook looks downright portly next to a PowerBook Duo. A classic PowerBook weighs about 7 pounds; a PowerBook 500-series machine weighs 6.3 to 7.3 pounds, depending on the model; and a Duo weighs 4.25 pounds. A classic PowerBook is 2.25 inches high, 11.25 inches wide, and 9.3 inches deep; a PowerBook 500-series model is 2.25 inches high, 11.5 inches wide, and 9.65 inches deep; and a PowerBook Duo is 1.42 inches high, 10.87 inches wide, and 8.5 inches deep. A Duo is also less angular, with rounded front edges that should make it more comfortable to carry. Rubber bumpers along the sides of the machine help to cushion it against bumps. Inside the PowerBook Duo, a magnesium subframe adds rigidity and plays an important role in establishing a firm connection between the computer and a docking station.

Honey, I shrunk the input devices

The Duo trackball and keyboard are even smaller than those of a big PowerBook — these computers are not for the ham handed. The Duo's marble-sized trackball measures just 19 mm in diameter, while big PowerBooks have a 31-mm trackball. Pointer movement is surprisingly smooth, though, thanks to three tiny, synthetic ruby bearings that support the trackball. The trackball's tininess keeps it from protruding above the Duo's palm rest, and the two trackball buttons are also recessed. This design makes the whole affair less obtrusive and allows for a thinner lid, but some people may find that it makes pointing and clicking more cumbersome.

The Duo keyboard layout is identical to that of larger PowerBooks, although the keyboard itself is different. The spacing between keys is slightly tighter, making the keyboard a bit more cramped. Also, the *key travel* — the distance a key moves down when pressed — is shorter: about 2.5 mm versus 3 mm. Half a millimeter isn't much, but it makes the keyboard feel a bit more responsive.

Changing batteries

Instead of the nickel-cadmium (NiCad) batteries used in most big PowerBooks, the Duos use a nickel metal-hydride (NiHy) battery that provides more power in a smaller package. NiHy batteries also charge more quickly — in about an hour and a half, versus four to five hours for a classic PowerBook's battery. NiHy batteries are also considered less toxic to the environment. Cadmium has been classified as a toxic material by the EPA, but metal hydride has not been, at least not yet. (The PowerBook 500-series models also use NiHy batteries.)

Unlike all classic PowerBooks except the 100, a PowerBook Duo's battery bay is on the front edge of the machine, not on the side. This location makes it possible to change and recharge batteries while the PowerBook Duo is in the Duo Dock.

Preparing for docking

Before docking a PowerBook Duo, you must choose its Shut Down command; if you insert a sleeping Duo, the dock ejects it and a message appears on-screen (of course, you have to open the lid to read it). After shutting it down, you open the PowerBook Duo's rear door, exposing a 152-pin, palladium-plated expansion connector. The expansion connector is a 32-bit processor-direct slot that allows access to every signal line on the PowerBook's processor.

After opening the expansion door, slide the Duo into the Duo Dock's slot and push gently. As the PowerBook approaches the rear of the slot, two steel alignment pins in the dock meet corresponding holes in the PowerBook's internal magnesium frame, ensuring that the expansion connector mates accurately with its counterpart in the Duo Dock. When the PowerBook Duo is 5 mm from its destination, it trips an optical sensor, activating two motorized hooks that grab the PowerBook's magnesium frame and draw the computer home with a satisfying *thunk*. All this happens in about as much time as it takes to insert a floppy disk in a disk drive.

What a difference a dock makes

Once docked, the 4-pound PowerBook has two serial ports, an Apple Desktop Bus port, a SCSI port, an external monitor port, a larger speaker, and two NuBus slots. The monitor port uses the Duo's video circuitry to display up to 256 colors on monitors as large as 16 inches. The Duo Dock contains a socket for a video expansion card that allows for over 32,000 colors on monitors as large as 16 inches. The dock's case can support a monitor that weighs up to 50 pounds. The Duo Dock also has room for a second hard disk.

The Duo Dock contains a lock-and-key mechanism that lets you lock the Duo and prevent someone from walking away with it. You can also lock a vacant dock to prevent someone else from using it. The Duo Dock includes a standard ADB mouse but does not include a keyboard.

Preparing for departure

When it's time to go, push the Duo Dock's Eject button. If any unsaved documents are open, you're asked whether you want to save them. That accomplished, the PowerBook Duo shuts down and the Duo Dock ejects it. (You can also use the key to manually eject the PowerBook in the event of a power failure.)

The Bad News About Duo Dock Expansion

The biggest compromise in the Duo Dock concerns the NuBus slots. In order to keep the dock's size down, Apple placed the slots underneath the dock's PowerBook bay.

To access the slots, you must remove the upper case lid, disconnect the power supply, remove two screws, and then remove and invert the Duo Dock's insides. Also, because NuBus cards lie parallel to your desktop rather than at right angles to it as they do in most other Macs, you must remove the top NuBus card in order to access the bottom card.

If you swap cards extensively, these gymnastics become bothersome. And there's always the risk that you'll accidentally break something while disassembling and reassembling the Duo Dock. It's a great piece of hardware, but it isn't designed for convenient card shuffling.

Some docking stations are available in the DOS PC world, but they lack the polish of the Duo system. None provides a motorized insert-and-eject mechanism, for example; instead, they rely on strictly mechanical docking schemes that force you to push with some oomph to dock the computer.

But the Duo Dock's motorized mechanism does more than eliminate having to push. Because it's tied to the PowerBook's system software, it can inform the PowerBook that you've pushed the Eject button, giving the PowerBook a chance to ask whether you want to save unsaved documents. Other notebook computers and docking stations lack this intelligence. You can, for example, undock an MS-DOS portable even when unsaved documents are open. When you do, you lose work.

What makes the Duo system so smart?

The underlying glue that ties together the Duo and a docking station is a collection of hardware and software that Apple calls *PowerLatch.* In general, PowerLatch allows for easier transitions between portable and desktop computing. It also keeps you from losing work when you press the Duo Dock's Eject button.

PowerLatch automatically configures the PowerBook for docked operation, activating the math coprocessor chip and video memory expansions installed in the dock and temporarily disabling any power-saving options you activated.

Docking on the road

When your Duo needs ports on the road, there's the 1½-pound Duo MiniDock, which snaps onto the back of the PowerBook Duo and adds a standard complement of ports, including ones for an external floppy drive and color monitor. As with most big PowerBooks, you can specify that an external monitor be treated as an extension of the PowerBook Duo's desktop or that it mirror the contents of the PowerBook display. The latter option is handy for presentations.

If you need only an external floppy drive, consider the Duo Floppy Adaptor, which also provides an ADB port for a mouse and keyboard. The Duo system's PowerLatch technology streamlines connections to the portable docking stations. For example, if you connect either dock to a sleeping PowerBook Duo, you can wake up the computer and immediately use an external floppy drive. You don't have to waste battery power by restarting.

Apple recommends that you disconnect any docking station before transporting the PowerBook Duo to avoid putting undue stress on the expansion connectors and the hooks on the docking station.

Is a Duo for you?

Does the PowerBook Duo system offer you the best of both worlds, or should you combine an all-in-one PowerBook with a desktop Mac?

Start by discounting the notion that purchasing a Duo system saves you a lot of money compared to buying a separate desktop Mac and PowerBook. You save *some* money, but not all that much, especially when you consider that in the end you still have just one computer.

The Duo system becomes particularly expensive if you want NuBus slots at the office *and* a full array of ports when you're on the road. For example, if you frequently need to connect to an external monitor to give presentations when traveling, you need to buy a MiniDock in addition to the Duo Dock you already purchased. Throw in more money if you want a portable floppy drive. You don't have to buy a Duo Dock, but if you buy just the MiniDock, you forgo NuBus slots and all the other expansion opportunities that the Duo Dock provides.

In the end, the Duo system is more about convenience than it is about saving money. The idea of working with just one hard disk whether or not you're traveling is very appealing. (Of course, it also makes a faithfully followed backup routine essential because your sole hard drive is subject to the rigors of the road.)

Macintosh versus Macintosh Performa: What's the Difference?

You're at the local Sears outlet, admiring the shiny new washing machines and the Craftsman air compressors. You round a corner and are greeted by . . . a Macintosh?

No, a Macintosh Performa. The Performa family is a special line within the Macintosh family intended for sales through department stores, electronics superstores, and office-supply outlets — not the usual places you expect to see Macs on display.

As the following table, "A Field Guide to Performas," shows, all the Performa models are based on "regular" Macintoshes.

A Field Guide to Performas

This Performa	*Is Equivalent to*
200	Classic II
400	LC II
405	LC II (with larger hard drive)
410	LC II (with more video memory)
430	LC II (with larger drive and more video memory)
450	LC III
460	LC III (with 33 MHz processor)
466	LC III (with 33 MHz processor and larger hard drive)
467	LC III (with 33 MHz processor and larger hard drive)
475	Quadra 605 (with 160MB hard drive)
476	Quadra 605 (with 230MB hard drive)
550	LC 550
560	LC 550 (included financial software)
575	LC 575 (with 250MB hard drive)
577	LC 575 (with 320MB hard drive)
578	LC 575 (with more memory and 320MB hard drive)
580	LC 575 (with 8MB memory and 500MB hard drive)
600	IIvx (with 68LC040 instead of full 68040)
630	LC 630
635CD	LC 630 (with CD-ROM and 15-inch monitor)
636	LC 630 (does not include fax modem)

This Performa	*Is Equivalent to*
638CD	LC 630 (with 8MB memory, CD-ROM, and 15-inch monitor)
638CDV	LC 630 (as above but with TV tuner card)
5200	5200/75 LC (but with larger hard drives, 4x CD-ROM)

Besides its name, what makes a Performa different?

- *What you get in the box* As mentioned earlier, most Macs don't include a keyboard — you choose the one you want when you buy the machine. Performas don't give you this freedom of choice — they include a keyboard. The Performa 200, 400, and 500 series include the standard Apple Keyboard II (the one without function keys). The Performa 600-, 5000-, and 6000-series machines get the AppleDesign (the big honker with all the function and navigation keys). Many Performa models also include fax/data modems, video displays (either detached or built-in), and TV tuner cards.
- *What you get on the hard disk* A Performa comes with a selection of application software already installed (the specific programs vary). Performas also include Apple's At Ease program-management utility, which provides a simplified method of starting programs (At Ease is discussed in Chapter 22).

Should you buy a Performa or assemble a Mac system yourself? That depends on your needs and your shopping skills. If you prefer the simplicity of the everything-in-one-box approach, get the Performa. If you'd rather assemble a system and software library yourself, consider a "regular" Mac.

Or look at it this way: If you bought an all-in-one stereo system because you dreaded shopping for components and then figuring out how to connect them, you're probably a Performa person. But if you spent weeks reading lab reports, conducting listening tests, and comparing specifications, you would probably be happier assembling your own Mac components. The nice thing about the Performa line is that it gives Mac consumers this choice.

Finding the Best Route

Before you buy a Mac, you need to weigh the differences between each model and determine which features are most important to you. Doing so helps you get the machine best suited to your present and future situation.

Aside from actually writing out the check, figuring out your needs is one of the hardest steps in the purchasing process. At this juncture, you realize just how many ways you can reach your hardware goals. The "Advice for Mac Shoppers" Quick Tips box presents a few buying tips that steer you in the right direction.

One more piece of advice: don't put off a purchase in hopes that some future Mac will offer dramatic new features at half the price. If you really need a machine now, buy one now. Faster machines with new features will supplant it, but if you buy a Mac with expansion slots, chances are you'll be able to buy boards that boost performance or add new features to your existing machine.

More to the point, if you wait to buy a Mac, you miss out on the productivity-boosting benefits that a Mac can provide. It's like waiting to buy a car in hopes that next year's model will be cheaper or get better gas mileage. Maybe it will, and maybe it won't, but one thing is certain: you will do a lot of walking in the meantime.

Advice for Mac Shoppers

In this box, I present some pointers to consider when shopping for a Mac system.

- ❖ Buy the fastest Mac you can afford, even if your present needs are simple. That way, you enjoy top-notch performance and your hardware is better suited to running the latest Mac system software and application programs. At the very least, your system retains its value better should you decide to sell it.
- ❖ Don't be afraid to mix and match components. There may be a certain level of comfort in buying all your components from one company, but that comfort costs you. You can often save money by buying non-Apple hard disks, printers, modems, network connectors, and memory upgrades. And many third-party hard disks and laser printers are faster than Apple's. On the other hand, many third-party products lack the "plug-and-play" setup convenience of Apple's add-ons, which are designed to mesh tightly with the rest of your Mac system. Also, some companies strip away features to arrive at a lower list price; some low-cost laser printers, for example, require you to purchase extra memory if you want to print on legal-size (8½ x 14-inch) paper. The bottom line is that you can save money and often get superior hardware by buying third-party products, but first assess your needs and compare features carefully.
- ❖ To save even more, buy your third-party gear by mail. Items available through most mail-order firms include printers, hard disks, external floppy drives, modems, scanners, video monitors, network cables, software, and memory upgrades. (The latter require careful hands but no special tools to install in a modular Mac; for compact Macs, you're better off having a dealer install extra memory.) The drawbacks: you're likely to suffer delays if a defective component needs to be returned, and you can't turn to one source for technical assistance. Some consumers have also been burned when the manufacturer of their mail-order hard disks filed for bankruptcy after charging their credit cards for goods never delivered. *Caveat emptor:* ask fellow Mac users to recommend prompt, reliable mail-order houses with whom they have done business.
- ❖ Join a user group. Asking other people about products and places to buy them is a good idea no matter how much experience you have. Call 800-538-9696, extension 500, to find the group closest to you. As your experience grows, you may evolve from a question asker to a question answerer, helping newcomers who are treading the same path that you're treading now.

Understanding the Mac's Interface

The Mac is an easy-to-use machine, but it's also powerful and complex. And because it's so easy to learn basic Mac tasks, many people never crawl into the crannies that help make the machine so powerful.

This section is a guide to some of those crannies. It isn't a step-by-step tutorial covering Mac basics: the Mac's manuals contain detailed tutorials, and books that repeat them are only trying to fill pages. Instead, this section gives you a whirlwind tour of the Mac's interface and of basic Mac operating techniques. If you're a Mac

veteran, you probably talk about these things in your sleep. If you're new to the Mac or you use it only occasionally, the information in this chapter forms the foundation that you can build on in the rest of this book.

The Mac's way of doing things

The cornerstones of the Mac's easy operating style are its graphical user interface and its mouse. Many computers require you to memorize and type cryptic commands or choose them from option lists whose workings vary from program to program, but not the Mac. You control the Mac by using the mouse to change the position of an on-screen arrow, called the *pointer*. By rolling the mouse and pointing to the elements you see on-screen and then *clicking* the button on top of the mouse, you can issue commands, work with disks, and much more.

Figure 1-5, "Face to Interface," shows the key elements of the Mac's user interface. Your Mac manual describes them in detail, so I just summarize them here.

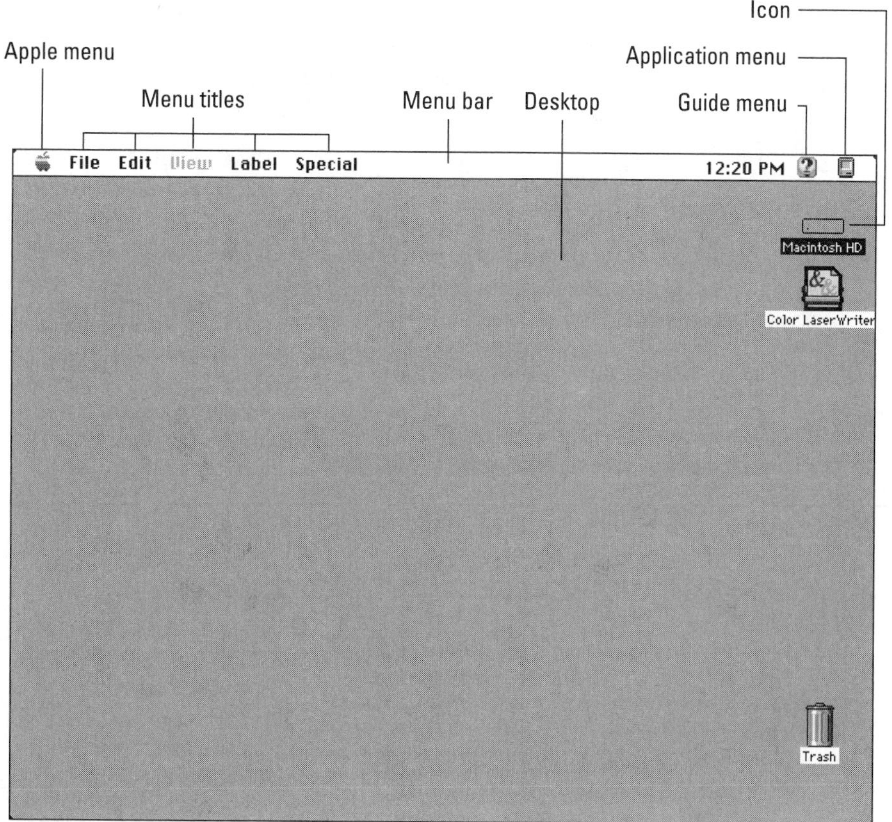

Figure 1-5: Face to Interface The Mac's user interface relies on these standard elements.

- The *desktop* is your electronic work surface, upon which rest *icons*, pictorial representations of objects such as disks, of stored items such as folders and documents, and of functions such as the Trash, into which you toss unwanted icons.
- The *menu bar* contains *menu titles*. When you point to a menu title and then press and hold the mouse button, a list of *commands* called a *menu* appears. To choose a command, move the mouse pointer while pressing the mouse button until the command is *highlighted*, and then release the button. The leftmost menu is the *Apple menu;* it's always available regardless of the program you're using. The remaining menus change depending on the program you're using. When you start a program, it takes over the menu bar, replacing the menus that were there with its own. Nearly all programs provide File and Edit menus, but the menus' commands usually differ from program to program.
- The *Apple menu* lists your available *desk accessories*, which are handy programs you can select while running another program such as a word processor. The Mac comes with numerous desk accessories. Some, such as the Calculator and Alarm Clock, mimic real-world desk accessories. Others, such as the Chooser, let you manage certain aspects of the Mac's operation. Later chapters look at both types of desk accessories and spotlight some third-party desk accessories you may want to add to your collection. You can also add your own often-used files to the Apple menu, as described in Chapter 22.
- *Windows* are viewing portals that let you see the contents of a disk or document. Windows themselves have standard elements that let you move them on the desktop, change their size, *close* them (make them disappear), and *scroll* through them (view information that isn't currently visible within a window's boundaries). Figure 1-6, "Looking at Mac Windows," shows each of these elements. You can have many windows open on-screen at once, but only one is *active*. The active window has thin horizontal stripes in its title bar; an inactive window doesn't.

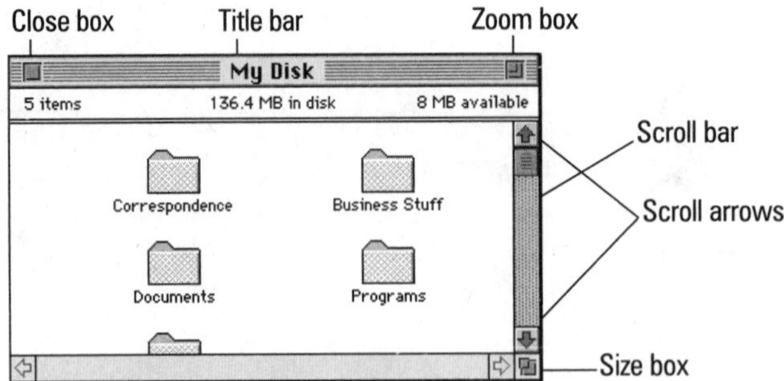

Figure 1-6: Looking at Mac Windows Windows provide standard components, shown here, that let you move, close, scroll through, and resize them. These components operate similarly in all Mac programs, so once you've learned how to work with a window such as this Finder directory window, you can work with windows in any program.

- *Dialog boxes* contain *buttons*, *check boxes*, *text boxes*, and other elements that let you provide more information and select various options after you've chosen a command. For example, when you choose the Print command, you get a dialog box that, among other things, lets you specify which pages you want to print and how many copies you want.

Finder basics

The first piece of software you encounter when you start up your Mac is the *Finder*. The Finder is the link between you and the rest of the Mac's system software, the fundamental software that enables the Mac to run. You use the Finder to start or *launch* programs, delete files, and copy, eject, and erase disks.

The Finder also provides disk-management conveniences — the Get Info command for attaching descriptive text to files, for example — and lets you organize a disk's contents by creating folders and moving documents, programs, or other folders into them. The Finder's Print Window command (in the File menu) also lets you create printouts that show what's on a disk or in a certain folder.

You'll find a collection of tips for the Finder in Chapter 22.

Getting help

It's common for application programs to provide *on-line help* windows that explain program features and eliminate a trip to the manual. Apple has built two help features into the Mac's system software: *balloon help* and *Apple Guide*.

Blowing up balloon help

Peer near the right edge of the menu bar of a Mac that's running System 7 or a later version, and you see a small question mark icon. This icon represents the *help menu* (called the *guide menu* in System 7.5 and later), and it's the gateway to the balloon help feature.

When you turn on balloon help by choosing Show Balloons from the help menu, the Mac displays small, cartoonlike balloons containing descriptive text as you point to different items or menu commands (see Figure 1-7, "Help Is Just a Balloon Away"). The Finder alone contains some 1,300 different help ballons for everything from the Trash to the One Sided and Two Sided buttons in the Erase Disk dialog box.

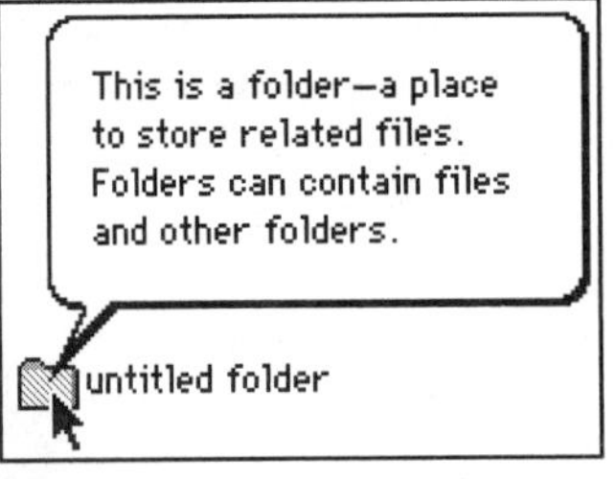

Figure 1-7: Help Is Just a Balloon Away The Mac's balloon help feature, activated by choosing Show Balloons from the Help menu, identifies commands and components. Shown here: a help balloon for the Print dialog box.

Many application programs provide their own help balloons. A publishing program, for instance, might display balloons defining its palette tools when you point to them.

Notice I said that balloon help *defines* things. That's an important point: balloon help generally describes objects or commands, not tasks. Put another way, balloon help answers the question, "What is this?," but not "How do I do that?" So where do you turn when you need instructions about how to accomplish a task? Where do you go when you need guidance?

Getting guidance from Apple Guide

In System 7.5, Apple added another help system to the Mac, one designed to help you accomplish tasks instead of just identifying what you see on-screen. This new help system is called Apple Guide.

By providing what Apple calls *active assistance*, Apple Guide *is* designed to answer the question, "How do I do that?" Apple Guide provides a consistent method for application developers to provide detailed step-by-step help, reference information, shortcuts, and tutorials.

You activate Apple Guide by using the Help menu — the same menu used for turning balloon help on and off. When activated, Apple Guide displays a window that lets you pick a topic from a list of available help topics. Each topic has a number of questions associated with it, such as: "How do I set the time and date?" or "How do I switch to more colors?" or "How to I erase a disk?" When you choose a question, a window appears containing the details you need (see Figure 1-8, "Apple Guide in Action"). Some topics also draw *coach marks* on the screen that point to key areas; for example, the topic on closing windows might draw a coach mark around the window's close box to draw your attention to it. There's even a button named "Huh?" that you can click when you need more hand holding than the instructions provide.

With System 7.5, Apple includes Apple Guide help for general Macintosh topics as well as for some of System 7.5's more advanced features — its built-in electronic mail and network collaboration tools (described in Chapter 32). In the future, as third-party software developers create their own help systems for Apple Guide, you will be able to tap the advantages of active assistance when you're using your application programs, too.

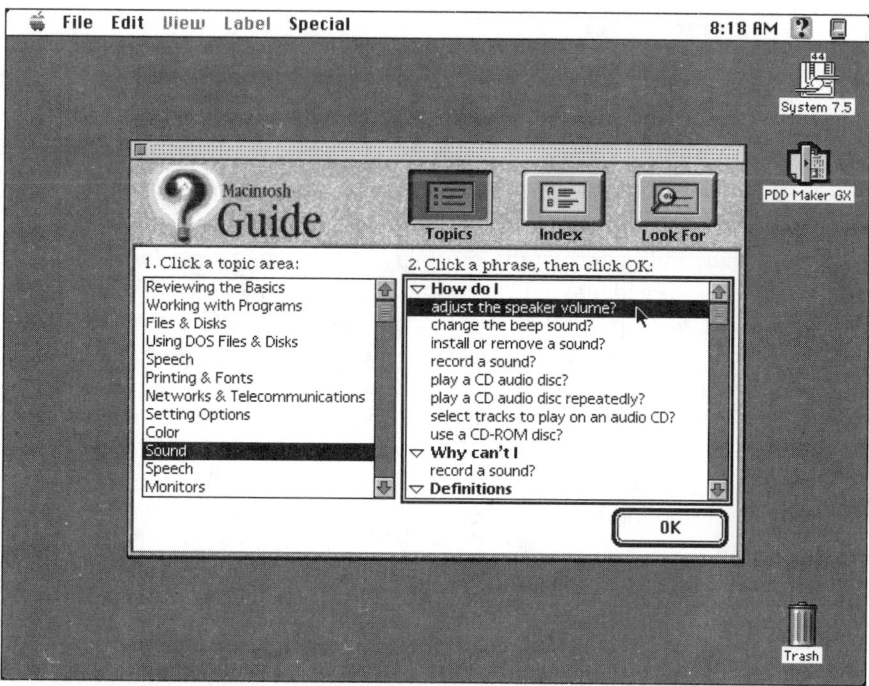

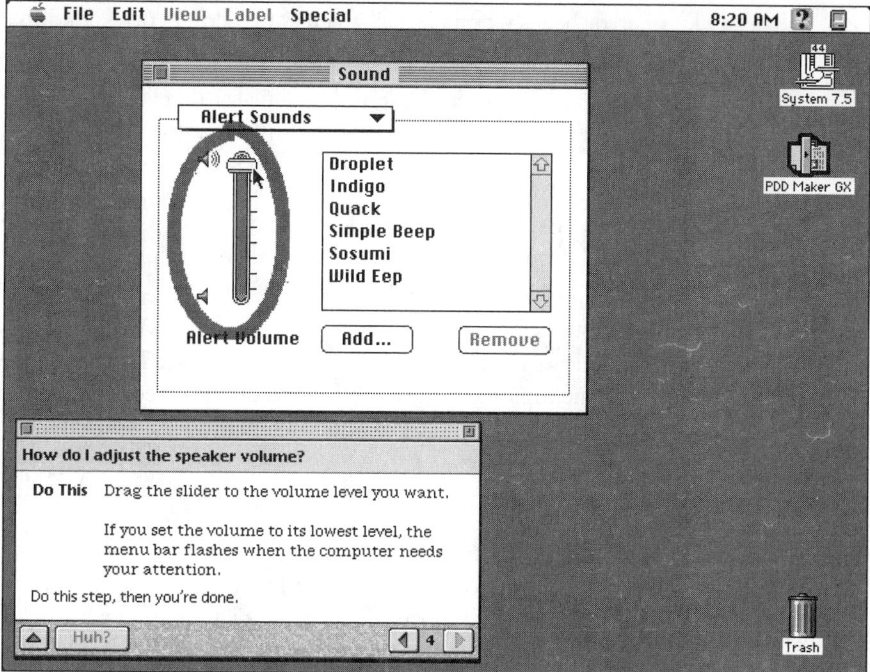

Figure 1-8: Apple Guide in Action Apple Guide's access window (top) displays topics for which detailed help (bottom) is available. Note the coach mark drawn within the Sound dialog box.

Clipboard 101

The Mac's *Clipboard* enables you to move information among programs and has always been one of the Mac's greatest strengths. Thanks to the Cut, Copy, and Paste commands that virtually all Mac programs provide, you can include graphics in a word processor document or paragraphs of text in a drawing.

Copying, pasting, and compound documents

Apple's ads often showcase this capability by depicting a fancy business report with a chart shoehorned into it. Combining text and graphics to create what are often called *compound documents* is certainly one way to put the Clipboard to work. But don't ignore its more mundane uses. Recycle text or part of a graphic by copying it from an older version of a document. If you're always typing a finger-twisting scientific term, copy it to the Clipboard and paste it each time you need it. To remind yourself of what's in a word processor document, copy the first few lines of it and paste them into the Finder's Get Info window for that document — more about Get Info shortly.

Cutting and pasting with the Calculator

If you use the Calculator *desk accessory* (DA), you can copy the result of a calculation and then paste it into a document simply by choosing Copy after performing the calculation. You can also paste numbers or math symbols from the Clipboard to the Calculator. The Calculator's keys even flash to reflect what you've pasted. (You also hear a lot of error beeps if you paste characters that don't correspond to keys on the Calculator.)

You can also paste formulas into the Graphing Calculator that accompanies the Power Macintosh models, and you can copy the graphs that the Calculator creates.

Copying the time and date

Here's a handy way to "stamp" a document with the time you started working on it: choose Alarm Clock from the Apple menu, choose Copy to put the current time and date on the Clipboard, and then paste it at the beginning of your document.

Saving the Clipboard in the Scrapbook

The Clipboard's contents vanish when the Mac is switched off, but you can save them by using the Scrapbook — just open the Scrapbook and choose Paste. Doing so adds a new page containing the Clipboard's contents to the Scrapbook (see Figure 1-9, "Compiling a Scrapbook"). To retrieve an item from the Scrapbook, use the scroll bar to get to the desired page, and then choose Copy from the Edit menu (or Cut to remove the item from the Scrapbook).

The Scrapbook's contents are stored in a file called the Scrapbook File, located in the System Folder. If you want to move your Scrapbook to a different Mac, copy the Scrapbook File to a floppy disk and then copy it to the System Folder on the second Mac. Note that you replace the existing Scrapbook on the second Mac — you may want to stash the existing one in a different folder first or rename it.

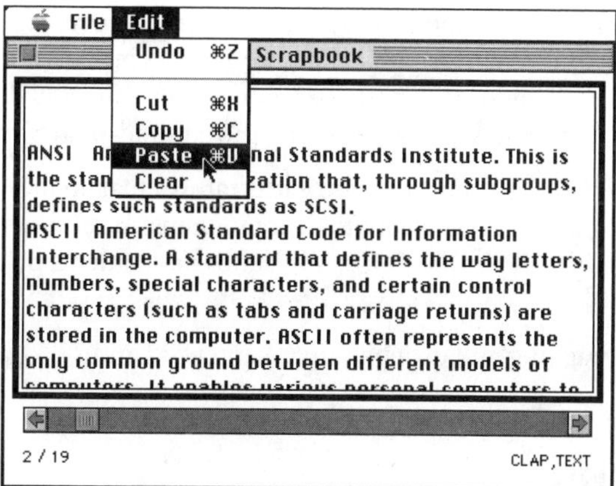

Figure 1-9: Compiling a Scrapbook The Clipboard's contents vanish when the Mac is switched off, but you can save them by opening the Scrapbook (choose its name from the Apple menu) and choosing Paste. To retrieve an item from the Scrapbook, use the scroll bar to get to the desired page and then choose Copy from the Edit menu.

Why cut and paste?

The common denominator behind all this cutting-and-pasting business is saving time. You'll encounter this theme in future chapters — many programs have their own features for storing and recalling often-used text or graphics. Word processors call them glossaries or autotypes; publishing and drawing programs often call them libraries. Whatever the name, the game is the same, because saving time is at least part of the reason most of us bought these machines.

Dragging and dropping

It sounds violent, but dragging and dropping is one of the easiest, most sensible ways to edit and create documents — and it's becoming more and more popular in the Mac world.

It isn't exactly a new concept. Mac owners have been dragging and dropping since January 1984 — you drag and drop when you throw an icon into the Trash or toss a document icon into a folder. System 7 added another aspect to drag-and-drop: you can open a document by dragging its icon onto that of an application program that can open it. For example, you can open a ClarisWorks document by dragging the document's icon over the icon that represents the ClarisWorks program.

More and more application programs support drag-and-drop *within* documents. Microsoft Word, for example, lets you move text within a document by dragging and dropping: select the text and then drag it to its destination.

Some application programs also support drag-and-drop *across* documents. In the Adobe PageMaker and QuarkXPress publishing programs, you can move something from one document window to another simply by dragging and dropping — it's faster, more convenient, and more logical than the cut-and-paste routine.

Apple is enhancing the Mac's system software with features that application developers can use to add drag-and-drop functions to their programs. As more developers take advantage of this feature, you'll be able to assemble entire documents by dragging and dropping.

You'll find details on dragging and dropping in Chapters 22 and 27.

What's Your Version Number?

That line isn't from a Silicon Valley singles bar. Software evolves over time — companies fix bugs, add features, and improve performance. *Version numbers* indicate just how far along the evolutionary timeline a particular program is.

There are a few good reasons to know how to determine version numbers. When you call a dealer or software firm for technical help, you'll probably be asked which version of the Mac's system software you're using. When you buy a program, you want to be sure that you're buying the latest version. And you want to verify its compatibility with the version of the Mac's system software you use.

Determining version numbers

One way to determine a version number is to use the *About* command, which always appears first in the Apple menu. To learn the version number of your Mac's system software, for example, choose the About This Macintosh command. (In System 6, the older version of the Mac's system software that some people still use, the command reads About the Finder.) To learn the version number of an application program, start that program and choose its About command.

Another way to determine a program's version number is to use the Finder's Get Info command. Select the program's icon and choose Get Info from the File menu. The file's version number appears in the Get Info window (see Figure 1-10, "What's Your Version?").

The Get Info command also works for documents you create. A document file doesn't display a version number in the Get Info window, but you can use the text box at the bottom of the window to type descriptive information about the file (or paste a few sentences from it, as mentioned earlier).

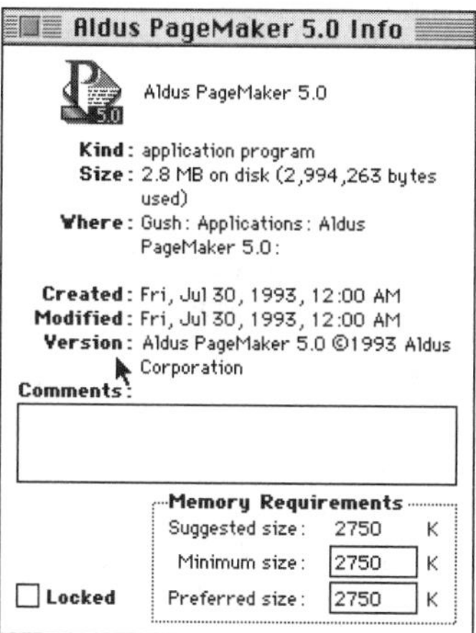

Figure 1-10: What's Your Version? Choosing the Finder's Get Info command displays a window containing statistics about the selected application or document, a check box for locking the file to prevent accidental modification or deletion, and a text box that can contain several paragraphs of descriptive text. The Get Info window for an application program also lists the program's memory requirements.

Decoding version numbering schemes

Manufacturers have no standard for version numbering, although they do follow a general rule. When a product is significantly improved, the number before the decimal point increases. When the revision fixes bugs or has only minor improvements, the number after the decimal goes up. A product label may say, "requires System version 7.x." In this case, you need any version that begins with 7. A manufacturer may also state that its product requires "System version 7.0 or later": In other words, a version with a higher number probably works also.

I threw in that "probably" because system software enhancements sometimes cause a program that worked fine under an earlier system version to choke. Sometimes this happens because developers bend Apple's programming rules (which isn't as big a sin as it sounds: Apple has been know to break its own rules). Other times, it happens because Apple changes the rules or spells them out ambiguously to begin with. At still other times, it's because a new system extension, such as a screen saver, introduced an incompatibility. Whatever the reason, the end result is the same: a program that used to run reliably no longer does. When these software growing pains surface, the program's developer releases a revised version that is compatible with the new system software.

But the new version may not be available immediately, and you don't want to be out of operation in the meantime. For that reason, it's a good idea to verify its compatibility with the programs you use before upgrading your Mac's system software to a new version. Go straight to the source — call the technical support hotlines operated by the companies that publish your programs.

Basic Navigation Techniques

An old bicyclists' maxim says that the easiest way to make your bike five pounds lighter is to lose five pounds. A variation of that truism exists for the Macintosh: the easiest way to boost your productivity with the Mac is to learn how to control it efficiently. Today's fast Macs and high-performance add-ons are great, but you won't get the most out of them until you master all the navigation options provided by the Mac and its programs.

The role of the rodent

You may think that Mac navigation concepts can be summed up in one word — mouse. The mouse doesn't have exclusive domain over Mac manipulation, but there's no denying the rodent's role as the primary link between you and your Mac. That's why navigational expertise is built on three basics — the click, the double-click, and the drag.

Clicking — pressing the mouse's button once — is your way of telling the Mac, "Here's where I want to work." *Here* is where the mouse's on-screen pointer is. In the Finder, pointing to an icon and clicking tells the Mac to *select* the icon — to highlight it for a subsequent action. In a word processor, clicking produces a blinking *insertion point* where you've situated the pointer. In a dialog box, clicking a button performs an action, such as okaying or canceling your choices; clicking a radio button or a check box selects an option. Most Macintosh programs follow these basic rules. Figure 1-11, "Buttons and Bars," shows the differences between check boxes and radio buttons and spotlights some other components of the Mac interface.

Double-clicking — pressing the mouse button twice in rapid succession — creates a kind of super click, a cut above a single click in the mouse-maneuvering hierarchy. Double-clicking an icon in the Finder is the same as clicking it once and then choosing Open from the File menu. When you're editing text, whether in a word processor, a spreadsheet, or the text-entry portions of a dialog box, double-clicking while the pointer is on a word selects that word, which is faster than manually dragging the pointer across the entire word.

Advanced mouse maneuvers

In programs that provide *palettes* — rows of icons that control program functions — double-clicking an icon often performs an action that's an extended version of the icon's normal purpose. In many graphics programs, for example, double-clicking the eraser icon clears the entire drawing window. In Claris's MacDraw series, double-click a tool and you can draw one shape after another without having

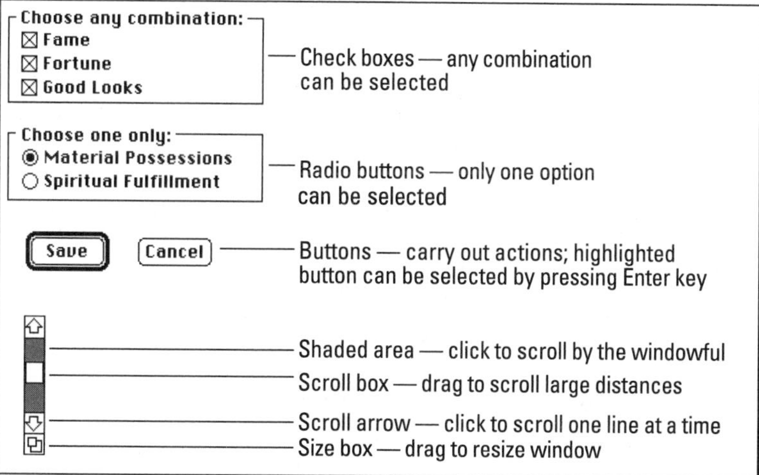

Figure 1-11: Buttons and Bars A guided tour of the interface elements you're likely to encounter in dialog boxes.

to reselect the tool each time. In Claris's FileMaker Pro database manager, double-click a field name to modify it. In QuarkXPress, double-click a text block or graphic to display the Modify dialog box. The list of shortcuts goes on, and you can find the best of them in this book.

By the way, if you find that the Mac isn't treating two clicks as a double-click, you may not be clicking quickly enough. Either speed up your clicking or use the Mouse control panel to tell the Mac to give you more time to double-click. Your Mac manual describes the latter option in detail.

Dragging is the process of moving the mouse while holding down its button. You move windows by dragging their title bars. In the Finder, you move icons by dragging them. In a graphics program, dragging lets you draw with the tool that's selected in the program's palette. You can also reposition items by selecting them and then dragging. And in programs and dialog boxes that let you edit text, you can select text by dragging the pointer across it.

Natural selection

Next to the big three, the most important Mac technique to perfect is *selecting*. In the world according to Macintosh, selection is always the first step in an action: you select something and then tell the Mac what to do with it.

To select an object such as an icon in the Finder or a graphic element in a drawing or publishing program, point to the object and click once. You can always spot Mac owners who are still wet behind the mouse — they habitually click twice when once suffices.

Power techniques for selecting

You can also select multiple objects by enclosing them in a selection rectangle, often called a *marquee* because its dotted lines flow like a movie marquee (see Figure 1-12, "In the Marquee"). You may also hear the marquee referred to as "the marching ants" — for obvious reasons.

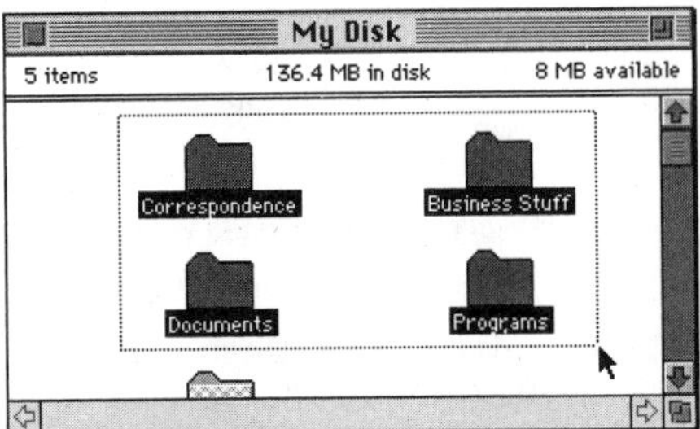

Figure 1-12: In the Marquee In the Finder and in most desktop publishing and drawing programs, you can select multiple objects by enclosing them within a marquee.

To draw a marquee, position the pointer at one corner of the area you want to enclose, hold down the mouse button, and drag to the opposite corner; releasing the button highlights all selected objects. The technique works differently in certain applications. In some, like the Finder, you need only touch an object with the marquee, but with others, the whole object must be enclosed.

You can combine the two main text-selection moves — selecting a word by double-clicking it and selecting a range of text by dragging the pointer across it. Just double-click to select a single word, and then without releasing the button after the second click, drag to select additional text, one word at a time. And if you select text as a prelude to replacing it, don't press Backspace or Delete before typing the new text. Just start typing; the first key you press clears the selected text.

Faster selections with Shift-clicking

When you need to alter a lengthy passage of text, dragging through it all can be a drag in itself. A better solution is to use the *Shift-click* technique. Locate the beginning of the passage you're changing and click to the left of its first character to create a blinking insertion point. Next, locate the end of the section, and then hold down Shift and click to the right of the last character or, to include a Return character, at the beginning of the next line.

Shift-clicking also lets you extend a selection — that is, add additional items to an existing selection. If you realize that you didn't select enough text, just hold down Shift again and click at the appropriate place. To select a slew of icons, you may combine the marquee and Shift-clicking techniques: select icons adjacent to each other by enclosing them in a marquee, and then add ones that are scattered throughout the window by Shift-clicking them. These techniques also apply to most graphics and desktop publishing programs, as well as to database managers that let you create customized forms.

The Shift key takes on an additional function in drawing and publishing programs, letting you *constrain* a drawing action. For example, pressing Shift while drawing with an oval tool produces a perfect circle; with the rectangle tool, you get a perfect square; and with a line tool, you get horizontal, vertical, or diagonal lines.

Scrolling along

As I mentioned earlier, scrolling is the process of moving through a document or disk window so that you can see things that aren't visible within the window's size. If you imagine your document as a scroll and the window as a frame that lets you see part of it, you can understand where the term comes from.

You do so much scrolling in your Mac lifetime that you should be aware of the three ways to do it.

- ❖ To scroll in small increments (such as one line at a time), click the up or down arrow at the ends of the scroll bar. Hold down the mouse button to scroll continuously.
- ❖ Click the shaded area above and below the scroll box to scroll by the windowful, again holding down the mouse button to do so continuously.
- ❖ To scroll large distances in a single bound, drag the scroll box itself (for example, to reach the end of a document, drag the box to the bottom of the scroll bar). With this approach, an outline of the scroll box follows the pointer as you drag; when the outline is where you want it, release the mouse button and the window scrolls.

Navigating with the keyboard

In the navigational realm, the Macintosh keyboard used to be considered a second-class citizen. Apple's philosophy held that keys should be used only for text entry because keyboard commands were considered intimidating and far less intuitive than mouse movements.

That idea was true to an extent, but wordsmiths and data-entry artisans soon began moaning about how constant jumping between keyboard and mouse slowed them down. Fortunately, Apple listened. The Mac Plus keyboard debuted with *direction keys*, which let you move the insertion point, and from then on the Mac's keyboard maneuvering aids have steadily improved.

The power of the ⌘ key

One keyboard control the Mac has always provided is the *⌘-key shortcut* which involves pressing ⌘ along with a letter or number key. ⌘-key sequences let you execute commands from the keyboard so you can bypass the mouse. These shortcuts are especially useful in text-oriented programs such as word processors because they let you issue commands without moving a hand from the keyboard.

A program's designers decide which commands have ⌘-key shortcuts and list them alongside the corresponding menu commands. The most common are ⌘-Q to quit an application, ⌘-O to open a document that you've previously saved, ⌘-S to save your work on disk, and ⌘-P to print. Most programs with Font or Style menus offer ⌘-key shortcuts that let you access other type styles, such as italic or bold. Most word processors also use ⌘-F to summon the Find command. But you shouldn't assume that all applications use the same shortcuts; it's best to explore each application's menus to find out for sure.

Scrolling Tips

When you're searching through a lengthy word processor document, scrolling can be cumbersome and time consuming. If your word processor provides one, use the Go To command to jump to a specific page. If you don't know the general vicinity of the text you're looking for, the Find command is a better option. If possible, select an unusual word or phrase that appears only in the section you're looking for, and the Mac takes you there swiftly with no stops in between.

Most graphics and publishing programs also have a scrolling shortcut that lets you move a document around as though it were a sheet of paper on a desk. In Adobe Photoshop, for example, when you press the spacebar while clicking within the document window, the mouse pointer turns into a hand icon. Now drag the mouse to scroll around without having to futz with the scroll bars.

The best navigation tip you'll ever read

The best navigation habit you can develop is to periodically press ⌘-S to save your document as you work. Do it every few minutes — every time you pause for inspiration or get a phone call — and you won't lose much if a power failure or system error occurs. (Don't panic if a program doesn't have a Save command; many programs, including HyperCard and most database managers, save automatically as you work.)

Keyboard control in dialog boxes

Commands like Open and Find always lead to dialog boxes, which have keyboard-control options of their own. In an Open dialog box, you can locate a specific document or folder by typing the first character of its name. If more than one document or folder starts with the same character, type a few characters. (Unless you type them in fairly rapid succession, though, the Mac assumes that each keystroke is the first character in a different name.)

Many people exploit this trick by preceding the names of often-used folders or documents with a number or punctuation character such as an exclamation mark (!). That way, they can jump to a particular item by typing a single number or character. Any character works except for the colon (:), which is the one character the Mac doesn't let you use in a document or folder name.

If your keyboard has direction keys, you can use them to scroll through the list of document and folder names. To open a document or a folder, select its name and press Return. To close a folder and move up one level in the folder hierarchy, press ⌘-along with the up-arrow key. To cancel the dialog box, press ⌘-. (period). Some people find these key sequences more cumbersome than using the mouse, but keyboard aficionados swear by them. It's another example of how the Mac lets you choose the navigation style that suits you.

The Tab key in dialog boxes

Speaking of dialog boxes, you can use the Tab key to move between their text-entry boxes (see Figure 1-13, "Dialog Box Shortcuts"). For example, to perform a search-and-replace in Microsoft Word, press ⌘-H to summon the Replace dialog box, type the text you want to locate, press Tab to jump to the Replace With box, and type the new text.

When you're finished, there's still no need to reach for the mouse. Because the Find Next button is highlighted with a heavily outlined border, pressing Enter automatically chooses it. This works in any Mac program: in any dialog box with a heavy-bordered button, pressing Enter is the same as clicking that button. Pressing Return usually (although not always) performs the same result.

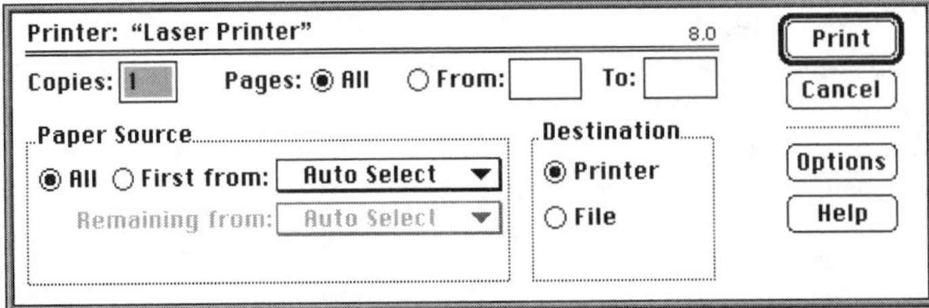

Figure 1-13: Dialog Box Shortcuts In dialog boxes with multiple text-entry boxes, pressing Tab moves the insertion point from one text box to the next. Pressing Return or Enter selects the bold-outlined button. To print a partial range of pages rather than an entire document, you often don't need to type values in both the From and To boxes. For example, to print pages 1 through 5, type **5** in the To box and leave the From box blank. Similarly, to print starting at page 3 and continuing to the end of the document, type **3** in the From box and leave the To box blank.

When you use Tab to jump between text boxes, the Mac selects any text previously entered. That means that you can type new text without having to backspace over an existing entry. Most database managers also let you move from one field to the next by using Tab and to the previous field by using Shift-Tab. Spreadsheets employ Tab and Shift-Tab to move one cell to the right or left and Return and Shift-Return to move up or down one cell.

Assessing your Option key options

In many programs, holding down the Option key while choosing a command or using the mouse produces a different result than that of the original action. Many times, these modified effects aren't discussed in the program's manual; you're left to discover them on your own or hear about them from other sources.

In the Finder, you can close all open windows by holding down Option while clicking a window's close box. In System 6, pressing Option while choosing the Finder's Eject command (or while clicking the Eject button in an Open or Save dialog box) tells the Mac to eject the disk and remove its icon from the desktop — as if you dragged the disk's icon to the Trash. For this trick to work, you need to hold down the Option key until the disk has been ejected from the drive.

In most painting programs, pressing Option while dragging a selection duplicates that selection. Adobe Illustrator uses the Option key to modify the effects of numerous commands. In many Claris products, pressing Option while choosing the About command from the Apple menu displays a window containing technical information about your Mac. Sometimes the Option key even unlocks secret messages created by mischievous programmers. These are often called *Easter eggs*, and many Mac maniacs love to hunt for them.

While Option seems to be the favored modifier key, some programs use Shift, ⌘, or both. In Word, for example, pressing Shift while choosing Open tells the program to display a list of all files, instead of just word processing documents.

Navigation nooks and keyboard crannies

System 7.5's windowshade shortcut is a great solution to the problem of window clutter. The windowshade shortcut lets you shrink a window so that only its title bar is visible. For details, see Chapter 22.

For Mac users who like navigation shortcuts, Microsoft's programs, especially Word and Excel, are what musty secondhand stores are to antique hounds. In dialog boxes, you can double-click a radio button to select it *and* ok the dialog box. Double-click a window's title bar, and the window shrinks to half size; double-click again, and it returns to normal. (Many other Mac developers have adopted this one.) Press ⌘-. (period) to cancel a dialog box. You can also press Esc on keyboards that have one. Faced with a Save Changes? dialog box, press Y, N, or C to answer yes, no, or cancel (this technique works with QuarkXPress and many other programs, too).

Microsoft Word even lets you choose menu commands and dialog box options with the keyboard. Press ⌘-Tab and then the underlined letter of the menu. When the menu appears, press the underlined letter of the desired command (or use the direction keys to highlight the command) and then choose it by pressing Return. In dialog boxes, you can choose a button or pop-up menu option by holding down ⌘ while typing a letter. When you hold ⌘ down for a moment, Word underlines the shortcut letter in each option. (See Chapter 3 for more Word shortcuts.)

Of course, Microsoft doesn't have a monopoly on clever shortcuts. Many other programs let you select dialog box buttons by pressing ⌘ along with the button's first letter. And System 7 and 7.5 provide scads of keyboard shortcuts; see Chapter 22 for a complete list.

Consider a copilot

Any pilot will tell you that navigation is easier when you have a copilot. You can create your own keyboard shortcuts by using a *macro* utility, such as QuicKeys from CE Software or Tempo II Plus from Affinity Microsystems, both of which I cover in Chapter 24.

Other Stops on the Road to Mastery

Familiarizing yourself with the concepts, shortcuts, and commands I present in this chapter takes you a long way toward mastering your Mac. Here are a few more suggestions:

- ❖ *Read* Many advanced Mac users brag that they never crack a manual — even when learning a new program. It's a testament to the Mac's graphical interface and to software designers that this avoidance of the documentation is possible. Nonetheless, every program has its subtle points, and you're unlikely to find them unless you read or at least browse through the manual. If you haven't already, work through the tutorials in the Mac's manual and in your program's manuals. More good places to uncover the hidden treasures of your favorite applications are in *Macworld*'s Quick Tips columns and in user-group newsletters.
- ❖ *Register your software* By sending in the registration cards that accompany new programs, you become eligible for technical support and will be notified when new versions are developed. Many companies offer newsletters containing tips and insights on their wares, and some also operate customer support forums on communications services such as CompuServe, America Online, and eWorld.
- ❖ *Join a user group* As I mentioned earlier in this chapter, user groups are among the best sources of information, assistance, and free or nearly free software.
- ❖ *Take time to play* Set aside time to experiment with your programs and desk accessories and with the Finder's many commands and options. Try selecting text by double-clicking, dragging, and Shift-clicking. Conquer the scroll bars. Use a marquee to select groups of icons in the Finder. Press Option or ⌘ while choosing menu commands or clicking palette icons. Keep exploring. You'll become more adept at using the Mac's interface, you'll develop a better understanding of how the Mac works, and you'll be able to tailor your Mac to your tastes.

Jargon 102 — Mac Acronyms

The computer field abounds with arcane terms, the worst of which are acronyms. Acronyms are those leftovers in language's bowl of alphabet soup — cryptic letter combinations often thrown together without the courtesy of a vowel to make them pronounceable. And pronouncing them is only part of the problem; understanding them is the other.

Behind every acronym are real, sometimes comprehensible words. Understanding those words and their meanings is an important first step in mastering the Macintosh. This section descrambles some acronyms and looks at other jargon you're likely to encounter in the Macintosh world. Don't feel like you have to wade through this material right now. If you're anxious to start learning what the Mac can do, skip to the next chapter; this techie stuff is here when you need it.

ADB — The Apple Desktop Bus

The Mac's *input devices* — its keyboard and mouse — attach to its *ADB* connector. ADB stands for *Apple Desktop Bus*, an expansion system designed for input devices. (In the computer world, a *bus* is a set of wires that forms a common pathway for data.) Some Macs provide one ADB connector; others provide two. (The Plus and earlier Macs use a different, less versatile method to communicate with their mice and keyboards.)

Mac keyboards provide two ADB connectors. That's how Macs with only one ADB connector can accommodate both a keyboard and a mouse — you plug your mouse into one of the keyboard's ADB connectors and then use a cable to connect the keyboard's second ADB connector to your Mac. This technique is called *daisy chaining*.

You can use the daisy-chaining technique to attach up to three ADB input devices to a single ADB connector. Chapter 33 takes a closer look at alternative input devices and ADB.

SCSI — Small Computer Systems Interface

The ADB is a relatively slow bus, transferring only about 4,500 bits — 90 words — per second. That's certainly faster than anyone can type, but it's pretty slow as buses go. It's far too slow for performance-oriented add-ons like hard disks. At about 90 words per second, loading a 10-page document into memory would take over 27 seconds. You'd grow old waiting for a large program to start up.

One way the Mac accommodates high-performance add-ons is with the *SCSI* bus. Short for *Small Computer Systems Interface* and inelegantly pronounced *scuzzy*, the SCSI bus can transfer millions of bits per second. SCSI is most commonly used for hard disks, but it's also used by image scanners, CD-ROM drives, some printers, and tape-backup drives — all add-ons that benefit from fast data transfer.

Like ADB, the SCSI bus lets you daisy-chain peripherals to connect numerous add-ons to a single, rear-panel connector. While the ADB is limited to three devices, SCSI supports up to seven. Nearly all external SCSI devices have two 50-pin connectors, although some use 25-pin connectors like the one on the back of the Mac's case. In either case, you connect the first peripheral to the Mac's SCSI port. Then, if the peripheral has a 50-pin connector, use Apple's *Peripheral Interface Cable* to attach a second peripheral to it. If the device has a 25-pin connector, use another SCSI system cable.

When connecting multiple SCSI devices to the Mac, you need to contend with the black art of SCSI *termination*, which involves using small connectors called *terminators* to tell the Mac where the SCSI bus begins and ends. Chapter 26 provides more details about SCSI addressing and termination.

RAM and ROM — the Mac's memory

Two of the most common acronyms you're likely to encounter are *RAM* and *ROM*. Both refer to types of memory chips used in a Mac.

Prerecorded memory

ROM stands for *read-only memory*. The Mac can read the contents of a ROM chip, but it can't change them. A ROM chip's software is in there for good, prerecorded at the factory like the music on a compact disc. The only real threat to ROM is an electrical mishap such as a power surge or a spark of static electricity.

In most computers, ROM holds only a small amount of system software, the program code that enables the machine to start up. The Mac's ROM plays a much more significant role. It contains software that programmers call on to create pull-down menus, windows, and dialog boxes — all the trappings of the Mac's user interface. (These routines are often collectively described as the *Toolbox*.) This built-in personality is what makes almost all Macintosh programs look alike and operate in the same basic way. ROM also stores diagnostic routines that swing into action when you switch on the Mac, testing its hardware for problems and then displaying the familiar "where's-the-disk?" icon.

Memory that forgets

If a ROM chip is like a compact disc, a RAM chip is like a cassette tape or floppy disk. Initially blank, its contents can be changed over and over again. RAM stands for *random-access memory*. Because it can be written to as well as read from, it's sometimes called *read-write memory*.

RAM performs the vital job of holding the documents you create and the software you use to create them. RAM is the Mac's temporary workspace: when you start a program, one of the Mac's first jobs is to copy the program from disk into RAM. Similarly, the Finder loads into RAM when you start up the Mac.

RAM is versatile but vulnerable. Cassettes and floppy disks store information by using magnetic particles oriented in patterns that remain intact until another magnetic field comes along to change them. A RAM chip, on the other hand, uses millions of microscopic electronic switches that stay in place only as long as the chips have a steady, reliable supply of power. That's why programs have Save commands — and why it's a good idea to use them often.

SIMMs and DIMMs

As mentioned earlier in this chapter, the memory-expansion boards that most Macs use are called SIMMs, short for *single in-line memory module*. (Many laser printers also use SIMMs for memory expansion.) The second-generation Power Macs use DIMMs, short for *dual in-line memory module*.

Chapter 29 contains details on buying and installing memory upgrades; also see the "Installing Upgrades" segments on the *Macworld Power User Clinic* CD that came with this book.

CPU — the Central Processing Unit

RAM, ROM, and the rest would be nothing without the *central processing unit*, or CPU. The CPU is the microprocessor chip that executes the individual instructions that form a program, which shepherds data between disk and memory and between memory and other components. In short, the CPU has a hand in almost every task performed by the computer.

The faster, the better

A microprocessor's activity follows the beat of an extremely stable electronic metronome. Many factors govern a computer's speed, but the number of times per second the machine's metronome ticks is foremost among them. The clock governing the Mac Classic's microprocessor ticks roughly 8 million times per second, giving this Mac a *clock rate* of 8 million hertz (cycles per second), or 8 MHz (pronounced *megahertz*). By contrast, the clock for the Quadra 840AV processor ticks at a sprightly 40 million times per second, or 40 MHz; the clock of a Power Macintosh 8100/80 races at 80 million times per second, or 80 MHz; and the clock of the Power Mac 9500/132 screams at 132 MHz.

The 68000 family

Macs have grown faster and more sophisticated over the years; one key to their evolution has been Apple's use of increasingly powerful CPU chips. The Mac family uses Motorola's 68000 series of microprocessors. The slowest Macs use the Motorola MC68000, usually just called *68000* for short. Examples of 68000-based Macs include the Classic, PowerBook 100, SE, Plus, and the primordial 128K and 512K Macs.

The 68020

The original Macintosh LC used the 68020, often pronounced *sixty-eight-oh-twenty*, or simply *oh-twenty*, for short. The original Macintosh II, introduced in 1987 and discontinued in 1988, also used the 68020. This chip is superior to the 68000 for a few reasons. It's a true *32-bit* microprocessor, which means that it works with information in 32-bit chunks. The less sophisticated 68000 is a hybrid 16- and 32-bit processor: it handles information in 32-bit chunks internally but transfers it to external components such as RAM chips in 16-bit chunks. The 68020, by working with 32 bits of information internally and externally, can shuttle twice the data in the same amount of time. (The Mac LC and LC II don't take full advantage of this feature. These machines use 16-bit external data paths. The Mac LC III doesn't have this shortcoming.)

Another 68020 advantage is its built-in, 256-byte *instruction cache*, high-speed memory that holds the instructions that the CPU used most recently. If those instructions are needed again, the cache supplies them, eliminating the need for the CPU to access RAM, which takes more time.

The 68030

The 68030 is used by the Mac SE/30, Classic II, Color Classic, IIsi, IIci, IIcx, IIx, LC III, IIvx, IIvi, LC520, and Macintosh TV. The PowerBook 140 through 180c models also use the 68030, as do the Duo models.

The 68030 has the same advantages as the 68020 and adds some pluses of its own. One is a built-in *paged memory management unit*, or *PMMU*. The PMMU is used by System 7's virtual memory feature, which tricks the system software into thinking that you have more memory than you actually have. Apple's A/UX, a version of the UNIX operating system popular in many university, engineering, and research settings, also uses the PMMU. As mentioned earlier, Macs that use the 68020 do not support virtual memory unless you buy an optional PMMU chip, the Motorola 68851.

The 68030 also provides a built-in 256-byte data cache, which holds the most recently used data just in case it's needed again. The instruction cache present in the 68020 is here, too. (Note the difference between instructions and data: instructions tell the CPU what to do next, while data is affected by the instructions.)

The 68030 also contains twice the number of internal data pathways as the 68020, and they work in parallel, allowing the CPU to do several things at once — such as access its instruction cache, data cache, and the machine's RAM chips. Adding more data pathways to a chip is like adding lanes to a freeway, letting more traffic move in the same amount of time.

The 68040

The fastest 68000-family Macs use the Motorola 68040, which is faster and more sophisticated still. The 68040 contains 1.2 million transistors — four times the number on the 68030. Like the 030, the 68040 contains a built-in PMMU. The 040 also contains a subset of the 68882 math coprocessor, which enables the 040 to handle most (but not all) of the math calculations that would normally be handled by a math chip.

Other improvements in the 68040 include two built-in 4K caches — one for data and one for instructions. (The 68030 also contains data and instruction caches, but each holds only 256 bytes.) The caches can operate in a faster mode called *copy-back* mode. This mode caused compatibility problems with some application programs when the first Mac Quadra and Centris models were released.

The 68040 also has a six-stage pipeline design. *Pipelining* is the process of decoding and executing several program instructions at the same time. An instruction pipeline works much like an assembly line: each stage works on its own portion of a given program instruction.

The 68060

This new chip is the latest in the 68000 family, and guess what? Apple doesn't use it in any Macs. As this chapter points out, Apple has moved on to the PowerPC family of microprocessors for its high-performance Macs. But you may see accelerator boards and high-performance laser or color printers that use the 68060.

The 68060 is similar to the 68040 but includes some improvements. The 4K on-chip caches are doubled to 8K, and the caches themselves are more efficient. Additional circuits allow the chip to execute two instructions in a single clock cycle. The 68060 contains more than two million transistors.

The PowerPC family: What's the RISC?

One reason Apple didn't use the 68060 is that the chip doesn't provide the necessary performance — it's slower than the PC world's popular Pentium chip. The complex design of the 68000-family processors was becoming a performance bottleneck.

In order to give the Mac family the performance boost it needed to remain competitive, an entirely new chip design was engineered. PowerPC chips use a processor technology called *RISC*, short for *reduced instruction-set computer* and pronounced *risk*. A RISC chip's underlying philosophy is "simpler is better." A RISC chip uses streamlined internal architecture that allows for much faster performance than the other major category of microprocessor — the CISC chip, short for *complex instruction-set computer*. (The 68000 family of chips falls into the CISC category, as do the popular chips in the DOS/Windows world, the 486 and Pentium.)

Compared to a CISC chip, a RISC chip has a more efficient overall design, can do more processing per clock cycle, handles instructions more intelligently, communicates with the computer's memory more efficiently, and has much faster floating-point math performance. (*Floating-point calculations* are those involving numbers with decimal portions, such as 3.1415926. They're used extensively in graphics-intensive programs.)

A RISC chip's simplicity translates into a smaller physical package, lower power requirements, and lower manufacturing costs. And all this translates into less-expensive computers.

Climbing the Power PC family tree

Here's a chip-by-chip look at the first members of the PowerPC family.

The 601

The 601 chip is the processor upon which the first Power Macs are based. At the heart of the chip are three independently pipelined instruction units. (Recall from earlier in this chapter that *pipelining* is the process of decoding and executing several program instructions at the same time.) Together, the pipelines can have up to eight instructions in various stages of execution at any one time.

To accommodate this capacity to do many things at once, the 601 needs to be able to access data and memory quickly. The 601 provides a 32K internal cache (versus the 4K caches in the 68040). The 601 also provides 64-bit pathways to memory, so it can transfer twice as much information in a single clock cycle as a 68040.

One of the real strengths of the 601 chip is its speed at floating-point calculations. The chip's fast, floating-point performance is one of the benefits that IBM brought to the PowerPC collaboration: the portion of the chip that handles floating-point calculations is based on a RISC chip that IBM developed for its workstations.

The 603 and 603e

The 603 family of chips is usually described as the low-power version of the 601 — these chips run software written for the 601 but require only about half the power to do so. The faster 603e also provides a variety of sophisticated power-management features — it can, for instance, turn off portions of itself that aren't being used. As a result, it's a natural for notebook computers. And sure enough, the PowerBook 500-series models are upgradable to 603e chips.

The 603 is also ideal for low-cost desktop Macs; Apple uses it in the Performa 5200 and 6200 series machines. Why? Because low power requirements translate into smaller, less expensive power supplies, smaller fans, smaller cases — and smaller price tags.

Also expect to see the 603 become popular in PowerPC accelerator upgrade boards, especially for low-cost Macs. It won't, however, replace the 601 or 604 chips across the Mac product line; the 601 and 604 provide better performance.

The 604

The 604 chip shipped in 1995 and made its debut in the Power Mac 9500 and 8500. The 604 is the high-performance successor to the 601; it provides a larger pipeline than does the 601, and it provides more advanced instruction-decoding techniques.

You can learn more about the 604 in the "Second Generation Power Macs" segment of the *Macworld Power User Clinic* CD.

The 620

The 620 will be a full 64-bit chip (other PowerPC chips have 64-bit data pathways but use 32-bit address pathways — just as the 68000 was a hybrid 8/16-bit chip, they are hybrid 64/32-bit chips). Combined with other performance enhancements, this design will yield a chip that Motorola hopes will be four to six times faster than a 601.

Coprocessors — CPU sidekicks

Any good business manager knows that being able to delegate work to specialists makes a manager more productive and efficient. Ditto for a computer's CPU, which is able to delegate certain tasks to specialized microprocessors called *coprocessors*. Coprocessors lighten the load on the CPU, freeing it to do what it does best — supervise the overall operation of the computer's components.

Math coprocessors

The most common coprocessor among 68000-family Macs is a *math coprocessor*, a chip with a head for figures. A math coprocessor can perform complex calculations far more quickly than a general-purpose processor like the 68020 or 68030. Specifically, math coprocessors excel at floating-point calculations. Most 68030-based Macs contain or accept an optional Motorola 68882 math coprocessor. The original Mac II used the 68882's predecessor, the 68881.

Specialized coprocessors

The Mac IIfx, Quadra AV, and Power Macs use several specialized coprocessors that assist in transferring data to and from the computer's modem, printer, and SCSI ports. In other Macs, the CPU has to be intimately involved in the transfer of data to or from these ports. In the IIfx, Quadra AV, and Power Macs, specialized processors handle data transfers to and from the modem and printer ports, while another chip shuttles information between RAM and the SCSI port.

Graphics coprocessors

If you plan to do high-end color graphics work on your Mac, you'll probably encounter *graphics coprocessors* like American Micro Devices's *AMD29000* chip. Graphics coprocessors specialize in performing the types of calculations and data transfers involved in drawing complex color graphics on-screen. Many high-speed graphics display cards use the AMD29000.

Digital signal processors

Yet another type of coprocessor is a *digital signal processor (DSP)* chip, such as Motorola's 56001 chip. In the Mac world, DSP chips are most commonly used by digital audio expansion boards such as Digidesign's Audiomedia II card (discussed in Chapter 21). DSP chips are also used in expansion boards that speed the performance of image-editing programs such as Adobe Photoshop (see Chapter 13).

The Quadra AV Macs contain an AT&T 3210 DSP chip. The DSP chip drives these Macs' high-speed GeoPort connector, which is designed for telephony and telecommunications functions. The DSP chip runs its own system software — the Apple Real-Time Architecture (ARTA) — that allows signal processing to occur independently of the Mac's 68040 processor. The Centris/Quadra 660AV's DSP chip runs at 55 MHz; the Quadra 840AV's sizzles at 66 MHz.

The DSP chips in the Quadra AV Macs are key players in their ability to recognize and respond to spoken commands through Apple's PlainTalk technology. Chapter 33 describes PlainTalk and voice recognition in more detail.

Letter Rip

I've covered the most common Mac acronyms and jargon terms in this chapter, but there are many others, as well as a world of abbreviations. You'll find many of them in this chapter's "Concepts and Terms" box. When you run into one that isn't covered in this chapter, consult the index to find where it's discussed.

In the end, most acronyms are just someone's nasty way of turning a few understandable words into a mysterious jumble of letters. You simply have to find out what the letters stand for.

Of course, pronunciation can also be a problem. SCSI may be pronounced as a word, but you'll get strange looks if you ask your friends what kind of *cippu* their Macs contain.

Power Macs: DSPs Need Not Apply

No DSP chip is built into a Power Mac. The PowerPC processors are so fast that they can handle telephony and speech recognition duties in addition to their normal workload.

But if a PowerPC-based Mac is fast without a DSP chip, wouldn't it be even faster *with* one? Probably, and the fact that the first PowerPC Macs did not include DSP chips disappointed some graphics professionals, who need all the processing speed they can get. Some developers were also annoyed that Apple did an about-face, putting a DSP chip in one line of computers and encouraging developers to support the move and then omitting the DSP chip less than a year later.

Why didn't Apple build DSP chips into the Power Macs? The stories range from disputes between the DSP and PowerPC teams to simple economics (omitting a DSP and its support circuits makes the Power Macs cheaper to build). The truth is probably in there somewhere.

What to Read Next?

Where do you go from here? That depends. If you're craving technical details and operating tips for the Mac's system software, jump to Chapter 22. If you'd like to explore hardware concepts in more detail, you might want to move on to Part III.

If you're eager to explore the universe of Mac applications, just continue reading — the tour begins in a few pages.

CHAPTER 1 CONCEPTS AND TERMS

- Finding the right Macintosh involves assessing your requirements in the following areas: speed, portability, expandability, video features, and memory- and disk-storage capacity.
- Of the used or discontinued Macs, those with expansion slots are the least prone to obsolescence.
- If you're interested in a portable Mac, you need to decide between an all-in-one PowerBook (such as a 145B or 180c or the newer PowerBook 500-series) and a PowerBook Duo. The Duo models are smaller but require docking stations to provide most connection ports.
- The Macintosh Performa line, sold in department stores, consumer electronics stores, and office-supply outlets, differs from most other Macs in that the keyboard, video display, and application software are included.
- You can often save money by buying non-Apple products, but be aware that some third-party products may not offer the same features or the plug-and-play convenience of Apple products.
- The Finder is the link between you and the programs and documents on your hard disk. You use the Finder to open programs and documents and manage the contents of disks.
- To use your Mac efficiently, master Mac navigation techniques such as scrolling, selecting, and managing windows.
- Most programs provide keyboard shortcuts that enable you to choose commands and options without having to reach for the mouse.
- Version numbers indicate program revisions. You can determine a program's version number by using the Finder's Get Info command or by choosing the program's About command from the Apple menu.
- Behind every Mac acronym — SCSI, ADB, CPU, and so on — are real words; understanding these words and their meanings is an important first step in mastering the Mac.
- Increasingly powerful CPU chips — the 68000, 68020, 68030, 68040, and the PowerPC 601, 603e, and 604 — have helped the Mac family grow faster and more sophisticated.
- Coprocessors are specialized microprocessors that lighten the load on the CPU, freeing it to do what it does best: supervise the computer's overall operation.

⌘-key shortcut
A keyboard shortcut that involves pressing ⌘ along with a letter or number key. ⌘-key sequences let you execute commands from the keyboard so you can bypass the mouse. These shortcuts are especially useful in text-oriented programs like word processors because they let you issue commands without moving a hand from the keyboard.

32-bit microprocessor
A process that works with information in 32-bit chunks. The 68020, 68030, and 68040 processors are 32-bit processors. The 68000 processor used in earlier Macs is a hybrid 16- and 32-bit processor: it handles information in 32-bit chunks internally but transfers it to external components such as RAM chips in 16-bit chunks.

active window
The frontmost window on-screen, which you can scroll through and manipulate its contents. You can have many windows open on-screen at once, but only one is active. The active window has thin horizontal stripes in its title bar; an inactive window doesn't.

Apple menu
The leftmost menu on the menu bar, represented by the Apple logo (). The Apple menu is always available, regardless of which program you're using. As Chapter 22 describes, you can customize the Apple menu to contain the names of the items you use most.

bus
An internal freeway that carries data among the Mac's memory, its microprocessor, and a variety of support chips. All Macs contain two primary buses: the *address bus*, which carries signals from the microprocessor that specify where in memory data is to be stored or retrieved, and the *data bus*, which carries the data itself. Expansion slots provide electronic on-ramps and off-ramps to this digital freeway.

central processing unit
Abbreviated CPU, the microprocessor chip that executes the individual instructions that form a program and that shepherds data between disk and memory and between memory and other components.

clicking
Pressing and then releasing the mouse button — the cornerstone of Mac operating techniques.

Clipboard
A simple data-exchange system that enables you to move information among documents and programs. The Edit menu's Cut, Copy, and Paste commands are the gateways to the Clipboard.

clock rate
The speed at which the computer's central processing unit (CPU) operates. Many factors influence performance, but generally, the faster the clock rate,

the faster the computer. Clock rates are measured in millions of cycles per second, or megahertz (MHz).

compact Mac
A Mac such as the SE, Classic II, or Color Classic that provides a built-in monitor.

desk accessory
A handy program you can select while running another program, such as a word processor. The Mac comes with numerous desk accessories. Some, such as the Calculator and Alarm Clock, mimic real-world desk accessories. Others, such as the Chooser, let you manage certain aspects of the Mac's operation.

desktop
Your electronic work surface, upon which rest icons for programs, documents, folders, disks, and the Trash.

dialog box
A special kind of window that opens after you choose a command. Dialog boxes contain *buttons, check boxes, text boxes,* and other elements that let you provide more information and select various options after you've chosen a command. For example, when you choose the Print command, you get a dialog box that, among other things, lets you specify which pages you want to print and how many copies you want.

digital signal processor
Abbreviated DSP, a type of coprocessor designed to manipulate massive amounts of data in real time. DSP chips are built into Apple's Quadra AV Macs and are available on expansion boards for many other Mac models.

docking station
A hardware device that attaches to a PowerBook Duo and adds connection ports and, in some cases, expansion slots and other features.

double-clicking
Pressing the mouse button twice in rapid succession. In the Finder, double-clicking is a shortcut for opening an icon.

dragging
The process of moving the mouse while holding down its button. You move windows by dragging their title bars. In the Finder, you move icons by dragging them. In a graphics program, dragging lets you draw with the tool that's selected in the program's palette. You can also reposition items by selecting them and then dragging. And in programs and dialog boxes that let you edit text, you can select text by dragging the pointer across it.

expansion slot
A connector, located on a Mac's main circuit board, into which you can plug *cards* or *boards* that add to the machine's capabilities. *Accelerator boards* boost performance, for example, while *video boards* control monitors. Expansion slots are an excellent defense against obsolescence.

graphical user interface
The on-screen menus and other devices you use to control the Mac and its programs.

icon
A pictorial representation of an object, such as a disk, or of a function, such as the Trash can.

input device
A hardware device that lets you supply information or commands to the Mac. The keyboard and mouse are the primary input devices. On a Mac that supports PlainTalk voice recognition, the microphone is also an input device.

insertion point
The blinking vertical bar that appears in word processors, the text-entry portions of dialog boxes, and any program that works with text. Characters you type always appear at the insertion point.

instruction cache
High-speed memory that holds the instructions the CPU used most recently. If those instructions are needed again, they're supplied by the cache, eliminating the need for the CPU to access RAM, which takes more time.

launch
The meal that New Englanders eat between breakfast and dinner. Also, a term often used to describe the process of starting a program, as in, "I launched Microsoft Word."

liquid-crystal display
Abbreviated LCD, the type of display screen used in PowerBook computers. Some PowerBooks use *passive-matrix* displays; others use *active-matrix* displays, which are brighter and easier to read.

menu bar
The horizontal list of menu names at the top of the Mac's screen. When you start a program, it takes over the menu bar, replacing the menus that were there with its own. Nearly all programs provide File and Edit menus, but the menus' commands usually differ between programs.

modular Mac
A Mac such as a Centris or Quadra model that uses an external monitor.

palette
A row of icons that control a program's functions. Many graphics programs, for example, have palettes containing pencil, eraser, and paintbrush icons (among others). A palette may also be called a *toolbox* or *toolbar.*

pixel
Short for *picture element,* a dot formed on-screen by the electron gun in its video tube. Everything you see on the Mac's screen is formed by an arrangement of pixels.

pointer
The on-screen arrow that moves when you move the Mac's mouse. The pointer is often described (incorrectly) as the *cursor.*

processor-direct slot
An expansion connector that allows access to all the control, address, and data signals of the Mac's microprocessor.

RAM
An acronym for *random-access memory,* the memory that stores the program you run and the documents you create.

reduced instruction-set computer
Abbreviated RISC, a streamlined microprocessor architecture that allows for much faster performance than the other major category of microprocessor — the CISC chip (short for *complex instruction-set computer*).

(continued on the next page)

(continued from previous page)

The Power Macintosh models use a RISC chip — the PowerPC 601.

ROM
An acronym for *read-only memory.* The Mac can read the contents of a ROM chip, but it can't change them. A ROM chip's software is in there for good, prerecorded at the factory like the music on a compact disc.

selecting
The process of marking, or *highlighting,* something as a prelude to a subsequent operation. For example, you select an icon before opening it. You also select text before deleting it or changing its appearance.

Shift-click
A selection technique that involves pressing Shift while clicking in order to *extend* a selection — that is, to add additional items or text to that which is already selected.

Single Inline Memory Module
Abbreviated SIMM, a small circuit board containing memory chips. In most Macs, you add memory by adding SIMMs or by replacing the existing ones with SIMMs of a higher capacity.

system software
The fundamental software that enables the Mac to run. The latest version of the Mac's system software is called System 7.5.

third party
The party you go to after attending the first and second parties. Also, computer industry jargon for a company other than the company that manufactures a given product. For example, Hewlett-Packard is a third-party supplier of Mac-compatible printers, and Microsoft is a third-party software supplier.

window
A viewing portal that lets you see the contents of a disk or document. Windows have standard elements that let you move them on the desktop, change their size, *close* them (make them disappear), and *scroll* through them (view information that isn't currently visible within a window's boundaries). See *active window.*

CHAPTER TWO

Word Processing: The Basics

- Finding the right word processor for you
- Understanding the nuts and bolts of indents
- Organizing tables with tabs and table editors
- Using search-and-replace features to find formatting attributes
- Discovering tricks of the word processing trade

If you're like most Macintosh users, you use a word processor more than any other program. Whether you peck out occasional memos or write reams of technical manuals, a word processor's benefits — convenient text entry, easy revision, and formatting flexibility — are among the best reasons to use a computer.

Regardless of which word whacker you use, chances are your word processing life takes you through similar formatting terrain. This chapter looks at the basics behind word processing and shows you how to conquer common formatting chores with today's most popular word processors. Many of the concepts and instructions explained here also apply to integrated programs such as ClarisWorks and Microsoft Works.

If you're shopping for a word processor, use this chapter to assess how each program handles each task. The Background box "Shopping for a Word Processor" introduces some of the advanced features you'll encounter in the next two chapters.

The Basics

At its simplest level, word processing is using a computer to supplant a typewriter by typing and editing your words on-screen and sending them to paper only when you're satisfied with the results. The cornerstone of a word processor's text-slinging skills is a function called *word wrap*, which brings words that don't fit on a line down to the next line as you type. Word wrap means not having to visit the Return key at the end of every line, and it lets a word processor quickly adjust line breaks when you add or remove text.

Shopping for a Word Processor

Shopping for a word processor has become a lot more complicated than it used to be. Blame it on "featuritis" — software firms' insatiable desire to add more and more features and capabilities to a program. Today's high-end word processors — programs such as Microsoft Word 6 and WordPerfect 3 — have exotic features, such as indexing and automatic cross-referencing, that are powerful, but that many people never use. The problem is, these features take their toll on disk space and free memory, usually causing both to become scarce.

For this reason, one of your first steps in choosing a word processor should be to weigh your word processing needs against your hardware. Don't buy more program than you need — or more than your Mac can run comfortably.

If you have an older Mac — one based on the 68030 or 68020 processors — think twice about a high-end program such as Word or WordPerfect. (In particular, avoid running Word 6 on an older Mac — unless you're very patient.) Consider instead Nisus's Nisus Writer, Claris's MacWrite Pro, or Softkey's WriteNow. Or opt for an integrated package such as ClarisWorks or Microsoft Works; both provide a well-rounded mix of word processing features. (I'm partial to ClarisWorks, which I think is one of the best all-around programs available.)

With this basic advice in mind, here's a look at some helpful word processing features and some more points to consider when shopping.

Shortcuts make editing easier

When the creative juices are flowing, you don't want to have to grope for the mouse to choose common commands. Better word processors provide a selection of keyboard shortcuts for choosing commands and moving text. Microsoft Word, WordPerfect, and Nisus Software's Nisus provide keyboard shortcuts for every command and even let you access dialog box options. Word also has slick shortcuts for copying and moving text without replacing the Clipboard's contents.

WordPerfect, Word, and Nisus let you create macros to automate command sequences. For example, if your last step in creating a document involves selecting all of its text, changing its font, and then choosing the Print command, you can create a macro that performs these tasks for you when you press a single keystroke. Nisus offers the most sophisticated macro and search-and-replace features. It can be a tricky program to learn, but it's fast and powerful and has attracted a loyal, if relatively small, following.

Outliners help you develop the big picture

Many writers develop outlines to determine the structure of a document. Word and WordPerfect contain built-in outliners that let you use the mouse to rearrange your thoughts. Some people also use outliners to create to-do lists and small databases. As explained in Chapter 16, presentation programs such as Aldus Persuasion and Microsoft PowerPoint also provide outlining features.

Glossaries cut keystrokes

A glossary feature lets you store text and/or graphics that you can recall and insert with a couple of keystrokes. Both Word and Nisus include glossary features. (For details on working with Word glossaries and the AutoText feature in Word 6, see Chapter 3.) If you use WordPerfect, ClarisWorks, or Microsoft Works, you can use macros to insert repetitive text.

Style sheets automate repetitive formatting

A *style sheet* is a collection of typographic, line spacing, and margin formats to which you assign a name, such as "body text" or "headline." Style sheets let you switch between formats with a few keystrokes instead of manually choosing formatting commands. Word, WordPerfect, WriteNow, and

MacWrite Pro provide style sheet features, and you can get similar results with macros in other programs.

Spelling checkers help you avoid typos

Many word processors provide built-in spelling checkers. They're useful, but they do have limitations. Spelling checkers don't guarantee accurate spelling or word usage. For example, if you substitute the word *there* for *their,* spelling checkers won't catch the error. But they still can be valuable, especially if your writing contains brand names or industry-specific words. By adding such words to a *user dictionary,* you can tailor your silicon lexicon to your work.

Thesauri help you choose the right word

Several word processors also come with a built-in thesaurus. Because a thesaurus typically offers numerous (and often quite different) synonyms for a given word, it's up to you to choose the one whose meaning fits the context in which you want to use the word. When you find a synonym you like, consult a dictionary as well to ensure that the synonym is appropriate for the meaning you want to convey.

Table editors take the tabs out of tables

As detailed later in this chapter, Word, MacWrite Pro, WordPerfect, and WriteNow offer table-editing features that eliminate the need to set up tabs to create and format multicolumn tables. If you prefer a different word processor, however, you may consider a stand-alone table-editing program such as Macreations's Tycho.

Mail merge makes form letters "personal"

A *mail merge* or *print merge* feature lets you combine your word processor and a database management program to produce personalized form letters. This feature provides the means for those publishing clearinghouses to chum out all those giveaway notices. You find mail merge features in Word, Microsoft Works, ClarisWorks, WriteNow, MacWrite, WordPerfect, and Nisus.

Annotation provides electronic sticky notes

In many businesses, documents must journey from desk to desk for revisions and approval. An *annotation* feature provides an electronic version of those ubiquitous sticky notes, enabling you to attach typed comments to a document. Microsoft Word and MacWrite Pro also support *voice annotations* — recordings you create by using the microphone included with most Macs or with third-party recording hardware, such as Macromedia's MacRecorder. Word 6 has particularly powerful annotation and revision-tracking features.

Indexing features simplify book making

Word, WordPerfect, and Nisus can generate tables of contents and indexes automatically. Nisus's tables of contents and indexes go into a separate file and are fully editable, but they need to be regenerated each time you change the document. Word and WordPerfect update their tables of contents and indexes automatically, but the indexes they generate are usually not fully editable. Beginning with version 1.5, MacWrite Pro can also generate tables of contents.

Equation editors get to the root of things

Word includes a program called Equation Editor that lets you create and edit complex mathematical equations. If you work with equations extensively but don't like Word, consider a third-party equation editor, such as Expressionist from Prescience Corporation, Formulator from Icom Simulations, or Math Writer from Cooke Publications.

All word processors also provide formatting features — the capability to specify margin widths, line spacing, and *justification.* The latter is a leap forward from typewriting; you'll be amazed at how easily word processors let you center lines of text or align them against the left or right margins (or both). And with Mac word processors, you can perform all these formatting tasks by clicking buttons and icons on an on-screen ruler. You can display the rulers in most programs by choosing a Show Ruler command.

Word processors also let you adorn the top and bottom of every page of a document with *headers* and *footers* (text, such as a page number, that repeats at the top or bottom of each page). Most Mac word processors let you create different headers and footers for odd- and even-numbered pages, a useful feature if you plan to bind your final product in book form.

Macintosh word processors also exploit the Mac's text talents, enabling you to format a document by using a variety of fonts, styles, and sizes. And they support the Mac's Clipboard, so you can use the Copy and Paste commands to include text and graphics created in other programs in your documents.

Know Thy Rulers

Before you tackle any word processing job, it helps to understand your program's approach to storing such formatting settings as line spacing, paragraph indents, margins, justification, and tabs. All Mac word processors have on-screen rulers for adjusting these settings. Figure 2-1, "Ruler Reminder," shows the components of the rulers that today's most popular word processors use.

With most programs — including Microsoft's Word and Works, WordPerfect, Softkey's WriteNow, and Claris's ClarisWorks and MacWrite — ruler changes apply only to the paragraph containing the blinking insertion point. If you've selected some text, the changes apply to the highlighted paragraphs. To change an entire document, first select all of it by choosing Select All from the Edit menu. In Word, you can also press the ⌘ key and click in the selection bar along the window's left edge. The bar is invisible, but you know you're there when the pointer changes to a right-pointing arrow.

Secrets of the Lowly Paragraph Indent

Indents are indents, right? Wrong. There's more than one way to bump a paragraph's first line to the right. My favorite method is to press Tab. All programs offer preset tab settings, usually spaced at ½-inch intervals; by pressing Tab at the beginning of a paragraph, you indent its first line ½ inch.

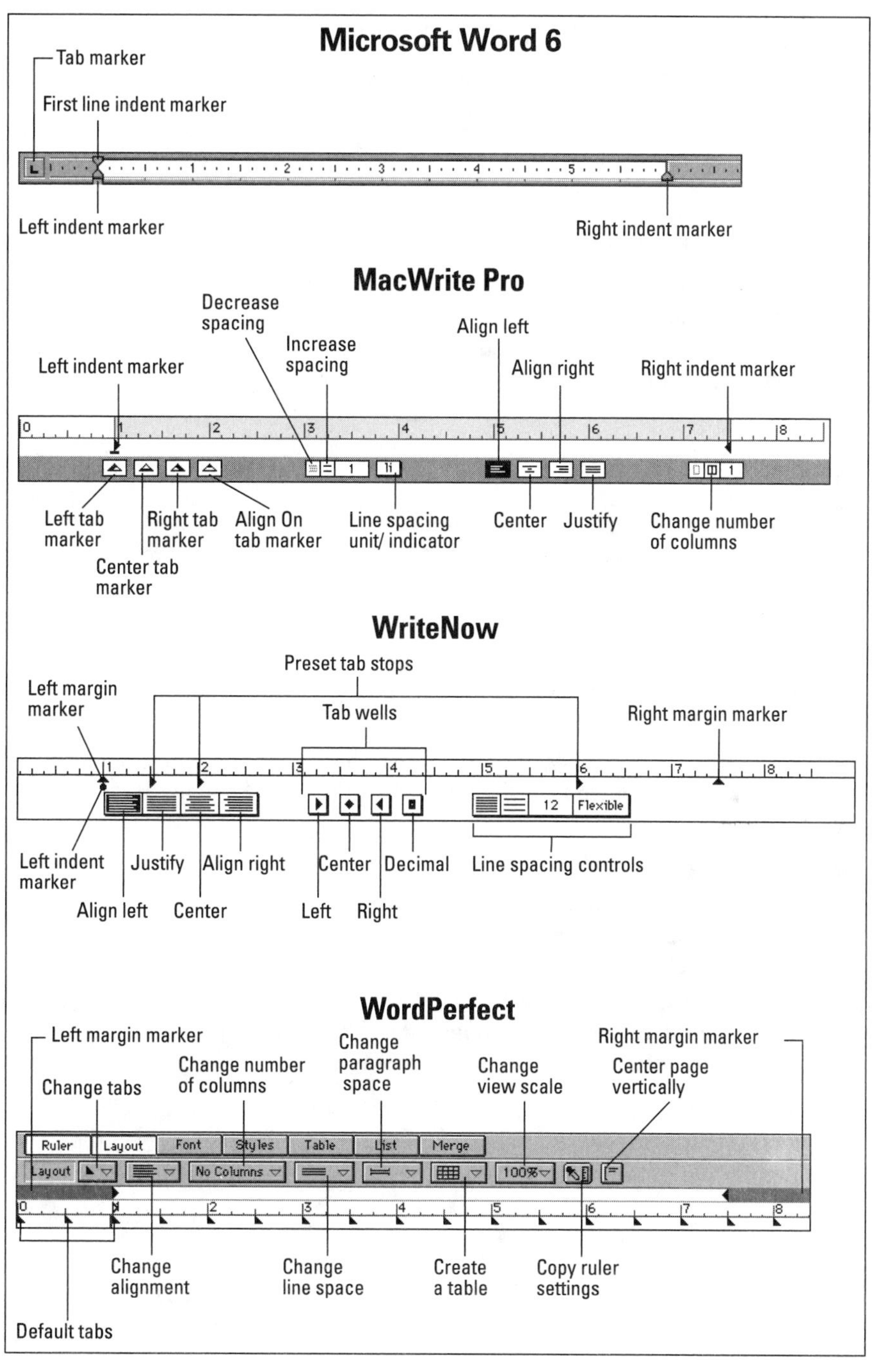

Figure 2-1: Ruler Reminder A ruler is the gateway to a word processor's tab, margin, line spacing, and justification features. Shown here are components you can find on the rulers of today's most popular word processing programs.

First-line indents: the good news

Another method is to use the ruler to create a *first-line indent*, in which the first line of every paragraph — that is, each line following a carriage return — is indented. For instructions for creating a first-line indent, see the "Indenting Paragraphs" Step-by-Step box.

First-line indents: the bad news

There's a drawback to the first-line indenting approach. Because word processors treat any line ending in a carriage return as a paragraph, single-line "paragraphs" (such as headings) are indented, too. To remove the indent, you must reformat each line to appear flush against the left margin. That's one reason I prefer using the Tab key to create first-line indents.

Using the Tab key to indent is essential if you need to save your document in *text-only format* for transmission over the phone lines or to transfer to a program that can't read your word processor's document files. Text-only files discard formatting information such as fonts and indents, but they do retain rudimentary formatting codes such as tabs and carriage returns. Data exchange issues are covered in detail in Part II.

Hanging indents

A variation on the indenting theme is the *hanging indent*, in which the first line of a paragraph begins to the left of subsequent lines. Hanging indents often appear in numbered or bulleted lists of items (see Figure 2-2, "Hanging Indents").

Nested indents

Paragraphs in a legal document or lengthy quotes from another author's work are often indented from both margins. To indent both margins in Word, Works, MacWrite II and MacWrite Pro, or WriteNow, first place the insertion point within the paragraph you want to indent (or select the paragraphs to be indented), and then drag the left and right indent markers toward each other by ½ inch or so. In WordPerfect, choose Left-Right Indent from the Insert menu.

Word 6 provides additional ways to indent paragraphs. You can click the indent tools on the Formatting toolbar, and you can type indent values in the Left and Right boxes of the Paragraph dialog box.

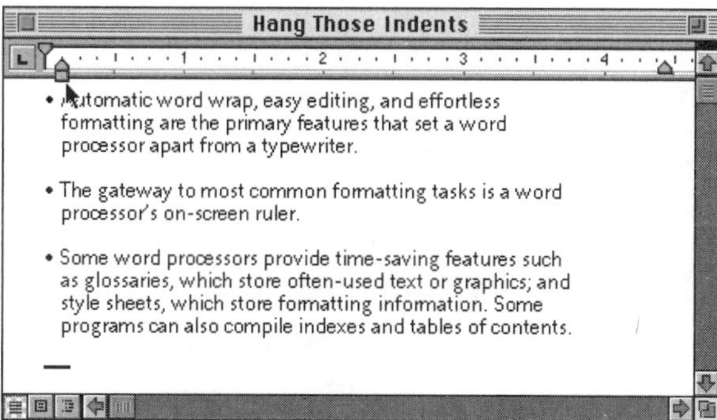

Figure 2-2: Hanging Indents Hanging indents are often used to align the left margins in a list of bulleted or numbered items. Word 6, shown here, lets you create a hanging indent by positioning the indent marker to the right of the left margin marker. Most word processors use a similar technique.

Tables and Tabs

You probably don't spend much time contemplating it, but tables are everywhere. The sports standings in the morning paper, the bus schedule that gets you to work, the spreadsheets you create in the morning, the menu you peruse at lunch, the airport monitor that shows your departure gate, the hotel bill that itemizes your charges, the TV listings you scan at night: tables are the boats that keep you afloat in a sea of facts and figures.

Table basics

A table presents information in a structured, row-and-column format that allows for fast scanning. This structure makes it easy to compare two or more entities: How do the second quarter figures compare to the first quarter's? How are the Giants doing compared to the Braves? How do Apple's laser printers compare to Hewlett-Packard's?

A table can also be a roadmap that helps you find articles in a magazine or chapters in a book (they don't call it a *table of contents* for nothing). Finally, a table allows for the parallel presentation of information. A set of instructions may have English in column A and Spanish in column B. The night's TV listings may put ABC in column 1, NBC in column 2, and CBS in column 3. (For an overview of the components in a table, see Figure 2-3, "Elements of a Table.")

THE ELEMENTS OF A TABLE

Use the techniques shown here to produce tables that are clean, attractive, and easy to read.

Consolidated Global Industries

1993 Sales (in $U.S. millions)

❶ Division	❷ United States ❸ 1993	❹ Change, 1992–1993	Europe 1993	Change, ❻ 1992–1993	Japan 1993	Change, 1992–1993
Construction	$ 4,750	17.9%	$ 883	❼ (24.2%)	$ 14,380	14.6%
Government Services	8,773	73.7	3,211	29.3	0	0
Mining	1,668	(14.5)	❺ 1,844	87.2	0	❽ 0
Transportation	2,795	4.3	5,290	39.9	4,555	5.2* ❾
Total	$17,986	38.1%	$11,228	33.5%	$18,935	12.2%

*July–December only (CGI's Japan Transport opened July 1992).

1) Left-align the heading over the stub (the list of categories in the left-most column).
2) Terminate the rule that divides heads and subheads where the headings end.
3) Center-align heads that straddle more than one column subhead.
4) Indicate ranges with an en dash (Option-hyphen), not an em dash or a hyphen.
5) Use dollar signs, percent signs, and other symbols only on first and last rows. Align symbols in top row with symbols in bottom row.
6) Align single- and multiple-line heads along the bottom line of the multiline heads' type.
7) Put negative numbers in parentheses—don't use a minus sign.
8) Use decimal tabs so that all numbers align at the decimal point.
9) Choose a footnote style to avoid footnotes being read as data—for example, don't use numbers to footnote numbers.

Figure 2-3: Elements of a Table

Creating tables on yesteryear's typesetting systems meant calculating column widths by hand and inserting the cryptic codes and ciphers that separated and positioned each piece of information. Today's word processors make creating and editing tables infinitely easier, but formatting them for legibility is still your job.

Table tools

Microsoft Word, WordPerfect, Claris's MacWrite Pro, and Softkey's WriteNow 4 allow you to create a table in either of two ways: by using typewriter-like tab stops or by using their table editors. You can even combine both techniques to combine their strengths.

What are those strengths? For starters, tabs have the edge when it comes to formatting flexibility. Want to align the decimal points in a column of numbers? Create a *decimal tab*. Want to guide the reader's eye across from one column to another? Create a *leader tab*. (The Step-by-Step box "Creating and Working with Tabs" shows how to apply these concepts to Word and WordPerfect.)

Indenting Paragraphs

Here's how to create first-line indents and hanging indents in several popular programs. These instructions assume that your program's ruler is displayed. If it isn't, display it by choosing the appropriate command (in Word, for example, choose Ruler from the View menu).

Creating a hanging indent is easier when you've typed at least one of the numbered or bulleted items, so do that first. (If you use bullets, put a space between the bullet and the first character of the item. If you want more space, press Tab.)

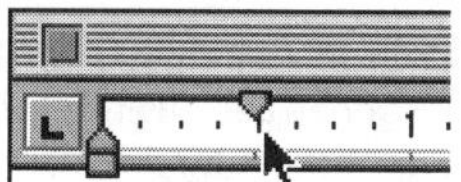

To create a first-line indent in Microsoft Word, WriteNow, or MacWrite:

1. **Place the blinking insertion point in the paragraph to be changed (or before the point at which you want to begin typing).**
2. **Drag the ruler's upper indent marker to the right.**

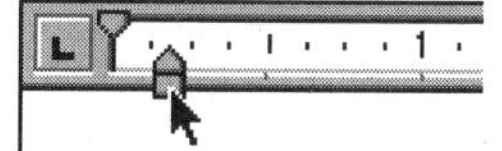

To create a hanging indent in Word:

1. **Place the insertion point within a paragraph, or select multiple paragraphs.**
2. **Press Shift and drag the lower indent marker to the right.**
   All the lines except the first jump to the right.

   You can also use the Format menu's Paragraph command to create a hanging indent. Choose Paragraph and be sure that the Indents and Spacing options are visible (click their tabs if they aren't). Then choose Hanging from the Special pop-up menu.

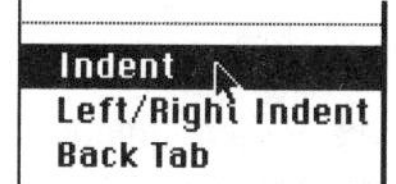

To create a hanging indent in WordPerfect, do the following:

1. **Position the blinking insertion point at the left edge of the paragraph's first line.**
2. **Choose Indent from the Insert menu.**
   The entire paragraph is indented one tab stop to the right.
3. **Press Shift-Tab.**
   The first line moves one tab stop to the left, leaving the rest of the paragraph indented.

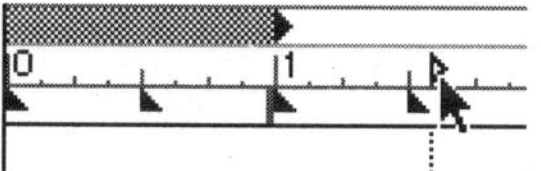

To create a first-line indent in WordPerfect:

1. **Drag the ruler's first-line indent marker (the right-pointing, hollow triangle).**

Creating and Working with Tabs

The instructions in this box tell you how to create and modify tabs in Word and WordPerfect. These basic concepts also apply to other word processors as well as to integrated programs like ClarisWorks. These instructions assume that your program's ruler is displayed. If it isn't, display it by choosing the appropriate command.

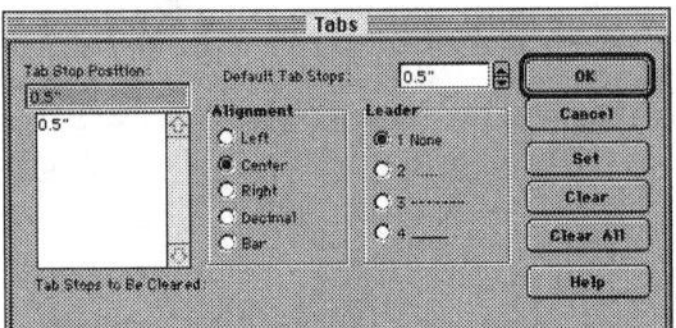

To create a tab in Word:

1. **Be sure that the blinking insertion point is located where the table should begin.**
2. **Optional: Specify the type of tab you want (left-aligned, centered, right-aligned, and so on) by clicking the Tab Alignment button at the left end of the ruler.**
   If you don't perform this step, Word creates a left-aligned tab.
3. **Click the ruler at the location where you want the tab to appear.**
   You can also double-click any tab icon and then specify precise tab locations by using the Tabs dialog box shown here.

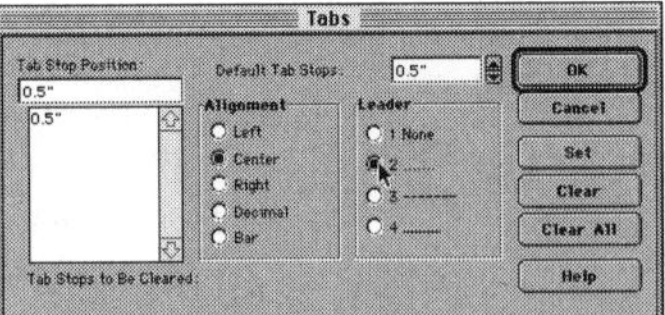

To add leaders to a tab in Word:

1. **If you haven't already, create tabs for each column.**
2. **Double-click the tab to which you want the leaders to point.**
   The Tabs dialog box appears, as shown in this figure.
3. **Choose the kind of leader character you want.**
4. **Click OK to apply the changes and close the dialog box.**

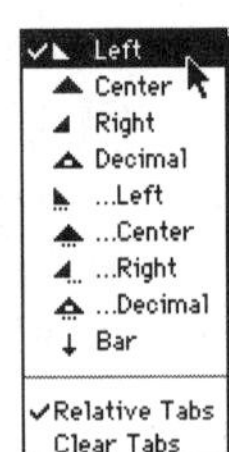

To create a tab in WordPerfect:

1. **Begin by clearing the preset tabs, which appear at ½-inch intervals. Choose Tabs from the Layout menu, click the Clear All button, and then click OK.**
2. **Choose the desired tab type from the layout toolbar's Tabs pop-up menu.**
3. **Create the tabs by clicking at the desired locations on the ruler.**
   You can also use the Tabs dialog box, which you can display by choosing Tabs from the Layout menu or double-clicking any existing tab on the ruler.

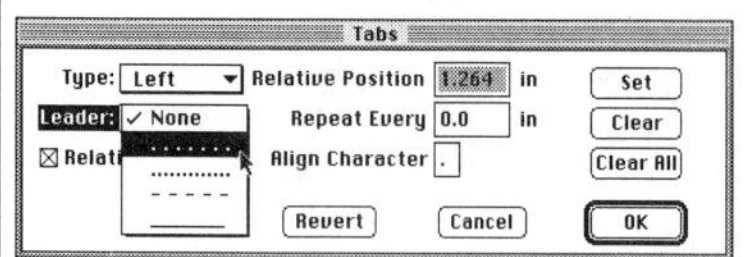

To add leaders to an existing tab in WordPerfect:

1. **In the ruler, double-click the tab to which you want the leaders to point.**
   The Tabs dialog box appears.
2. **Choose the desired leader type from the Leader pop-up menu.**

Tabs are also preferable if you plan to move a finished table into another program, such as Aldus PageMaker. Although all publishing programs can read documents created with these word processors, they can't import tables created in the word processors' table editors. This trade deficit may even occur between two word processors: WordPerfect can open Word documents, for instance, but any tables not created with tabs are ignored. I describe workarounds for these problems later, but the bottom line is that if you plan to move tables between programs, then it's best to use tabs.

The downside of tabs

One big drawback of tabs is that they're harder to set and adjust. Many people have trouble remembering to select a line before adjusting its tabs — they drag their rulers' tab stops left and right and wonder why the column widths don't change accordingly. These hapless souls forget that tabs, like line spacing and indent settings, are paragraph-level formatting attributes — and to a word processor, any text surrounded by carriage returns is a paragraph. Hence the First Commandment of Table Editing: before adjusting a line's tabs, select the line.

The other big tab drawback surfaces with table entries that span more than one line. Instead of being able to type such an entry in one fell swoop, you must divide it across multiple lines in a tedious game of hopscotch between the Tab and Return keys. Editing or reformatting a multiline entry is also cumbersome.

Table editors to the rescue

Table-editing features eliminate these hassles by providing a spreadsheet-like grid of cells that hold the table. Just specify how many columns you want and start typing; the program adds rows as you go. Each cell provides word wraparound, so typing multiline entries is a cinch. When a cell's contents spill onto subsequent lines, the row is made deep enough to accommodate more lines. Besides text, a cell can contain a graphic imported from another program. MacWrite Pro's table editor is especially slick — just click the table tool, drag across the page, and specify the size of the table you want (see Figure 2-4, "Editing the Table"). In MacWrite Pro, a cell can even contain another table.

Virus Table

Virus Name	Nature of Infection	Symptoms	Comments
ANTI, ANTI-B, ANTI-ange	Infects applications only (including the Finder), not oth system files or documents.	Nondestructive but may cause crashes due to its poor programming.	Disinfected applications aren't identical to original, but generally still run. Best approa is to replace infected applicati with an uninfected copy from master disk.
CDEF	Infects DeskTop file only, not system files, programs, or documents.	Slows performance. AppleSha server performance slows significantly.	You can remove this virus fro an infected disk by rebuilding DeskTop file: Press Command and Option while inserting the disk. For hard disks, restart an hold down Command and Option until rebuild dialog bo appears. To avoid infecting an AppleShare server, do not gra "make changes" privilege to th server's root directory (desk to level).
CODE 252	Under System 7, generally infects only the System file. Under System 6 without MultiFinder, it can spread to applications. Spreads only	If an infected system is started up between June 6 and December 31 of any year, the virus displays the following message:	No disks are actually erased, b its sloppy programming can cause crashes and damaged fil

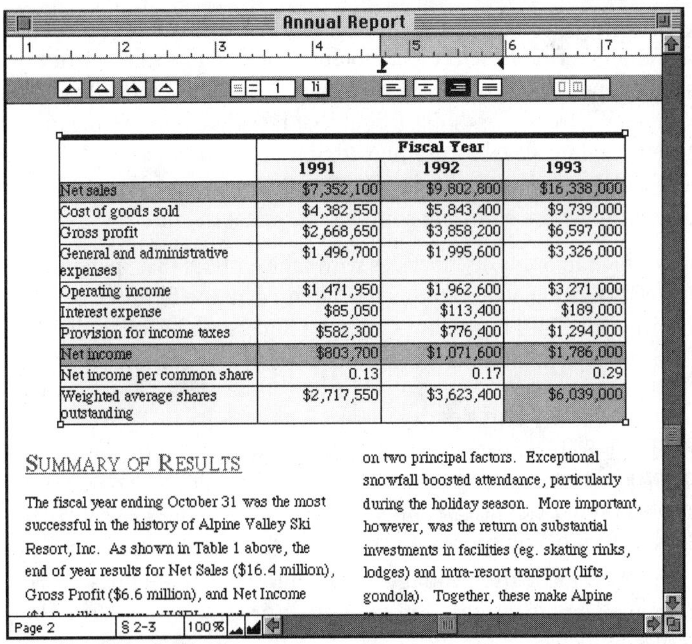

Annual Report

	Fiscal Year		
	1991	1992	1993
Net sales	$7,352,100	$9,802,800	$16,338,000
Cost of goods sold	$4,382,550	$5,843,400	$9,739,000
Gross profit	$2,668,650	$3,858,200	$6,597,000
General and administrative expenses	$1,496,700	$1,995,600	$3,326,000
Operating income	$1,471,950	$1,962,600	$3,271,000
Interest expense	$85,050	$113,400	$189,000
Provision for income taxes	$582,300	$776,400	$1,294,000
Net income	$803,700	$1,071,600	$1,786,000
Net income per common share	0.13	0.17	0.29
Weighted average shares outstanding	$2,717,550	$3,623,400	$6,039,000

SUMMARY OF RESULTS

The fiscal year ending October 31 was the most successful in the history of Alpine Valley Ski Resort, Inc. As shown in Table 1 above, the end of year results for Net Sales ($16.4 million), Gross Profit ($6.6 million), and Net Income

on two principal factors. Exceptional snowfall boosted attendance, particularly during the holiday season. More important, however, was the return on substantial investments in facilities (eg. skating rinks, lodges) and intra-resort transport (lifts, gondola). Together, these make Alpine

Page 2 § 2-3 100%

Figure 2-4: Editing the Table Two table editors in action: Word 6 (top) and MacWrite Pro (bottom).

Three Things to Remember about Tabs

Working with tabs is one of the trickieraspects of word processor formatting — that's why so many word processors now have table editors. Your journeys through the world of tabs will be smoother if you remember the following three points:

- ❖ You can center text within tabs or align it against a tab's left or right edge. Most programs are preset to create left-aligned tabs. To create a different kind of tab, first select the icon on the ruler for the kind of tab you want.
- ❖ With all programs, you adjust a tab's position by dragging it left or right on the ruler. (Word, MacWrite, and WordPerfect also accept measurements in a dialog box for precise positioning.) All programs also let you remove a tab by pointing to it and then dragging it away from the ruler.
- ❖ To refine the tabs in a given line, the blinking insertion point must be in that line, or the line must be selected (highlighted). If you're refining an entire table, select all of it first. You can mutilate a table by dragging tabs left and right without paying attention to the location of the blinking insertion point. You always get the best results by selecting the entire table, adjusting the tabs, and then fine-tuning individual lines (such as headings) as needed.

Adjusting column widths is also easier with a table editor. Instead of dragging tab stops left and right on a ruler, you use the same resizing technique that spreadsheet programs provide: drag the vertical line that separates two columns to the left or the right.

Table editors let you create borders and shade cells to highlight key information or separate each row or column. In WordPerfect and Word 6, you can create simple formulas that calculate the values in a row or column to display a total or an average. In both programs and in MacWrite Pro, you can sort a table according to the contents of given row or column — just the ticket for organizing those sports standings.

A comparison of table editors

Which product has the best table editor? It's a toss-up between WordPerfect and Microsoft Word. Both provide excellent math-calculation features and even let you specify that a set of column headings repeat on each page, a necessity for multipage tables.

MacWrite Pro's table editor has one edge on the rest — you can change a table's location on the page simply by dragging it. Otherwise, MacWrite Pro is relatively lightweight. It can't create multipage tables, for instance, and it doesn't do math.

The ClarisWorks table editor has a unique edge on the table editors that word processors provide. In ClarisWorks, a table *is* a spreadsheet, so it can perform a larger array of math calculation features than a word processor's table editor.

Tips for tables: improving legibility

The aesthetic concerns behind table formatting are the same regardless of the tools you use. The most important aspect of table legibility involves guiding the readers' eyes from left to right along each line. You read horizontally, from left to right — with their strong vertical columns, tables disrupt this flow. In a table, it's easier for readers to inadvertently skip to an adjacent line while scanning across a row, causing them to associate the wrong information with a given subject.

Typographers and designers rely on a bag of visual tricks to keep the eye on the right track. One common device is the *leader tab*, in which a row of periods, or *leader dots*, guides the eye from one column to the next. Leaders are most commonly used between a table's *stub* (its left-most column) and the column to its right — that's usually where the largest gap of white space is (see Figure 2-5, "Fearless Leaders"). In most programs, you assign the leader character to the tab whose column the leaders will point to. For example, to create a leader between columns two and three, assign the leader to column three's tab.

Consolidated Income
in thousands

Western	$30,394
Eastern	43,348
Southern	22,342
Northern	39,678

Figure 2-5: Fearless Leaders Leader characters, usually a row of periods, guide a reader across a line to the next column in a table.

A more contemporary variation (and one used in *Macworld*'s tables) is putting a horizontal line, or *rule*, between each pair of rows of the table. Doing so is particularly easy in a word processor's table editor: use the Cell-Borders command and specify a horizontal border above and below each row. Don't make the rules too heavy — a *hairline* rule usually suffices — and make sure that each row is vertically centered between its surrounding rules. Use a heavier rule between the table headings and the first row. (By the way, if the flow of your table is vertical rather than horizontal — perhaps it contains parallel paragraphs, each in a different language — you may want to put a vertical rule between columns instead of a horizontal rule between rows.)

Yet another variation is shading every other row of a table. The border-and-shading options in word processors make shading easy. Use a very light shade. I suggest 10 percent, lest the shading obscure the text beneath it. If you're printing the final table on a 300-dots-per-inch laser or ink-jet printer, think twice about shading; on a 300-dpi printer, even a 10 percent gray may be too dark.

Lining Things Up

One thing that makes tables so tidy is that the contents of each column are aligned. Or at least they should be. Many table neophytes simply use their programs' left-aligned presets, thus snubbing centuries of typographic tradition. Here's how to do it right (Figure 2-3, "Elements of a Table," found earlier in this chapter, illustrates the following rules):

- ❖ In a column of related numbers, the decimal points must align. Use a decimal tab or, in WordPerfect 3's table editor, the Decimal Align option on the Layout bar. If the column has no decimal values, set the numbers flush right — use a right-aligned tab or table column.
- ❖ If the numbers are monetary values, put a currency sign before the first row's value only — don't repeat the sign in every row. The currency sign must align with the largest value in the column, even if that means putting extra space between the sign and the number following it. (An easy way to do so: type as many zeros as you need to push the currency symbol to the left, and then change the zeros' color to white — they disappear.) By the way, never use a lowercase *l* or capital *I* instead of the numeral *1* or a capital *O* instead of the numeral *0*. Doing so misaligns columns of numbers and causes legions of deceased typographers to spin in their graves.

Some of the formatting gymnastics I just described may require you to combine traditional tabs with a table editor (see Figure 2-6, "Tabs within Tables"). Suppose you want leader dots across the first column of a table that you're creating with a table editor. Using your program's on-screen ruler, put a leader tab near the right edge of the first column (see the figure below). To create the leader dots, type the first column's information and then press Option-Tab (in WordPerfect, press ⌘-Tab).

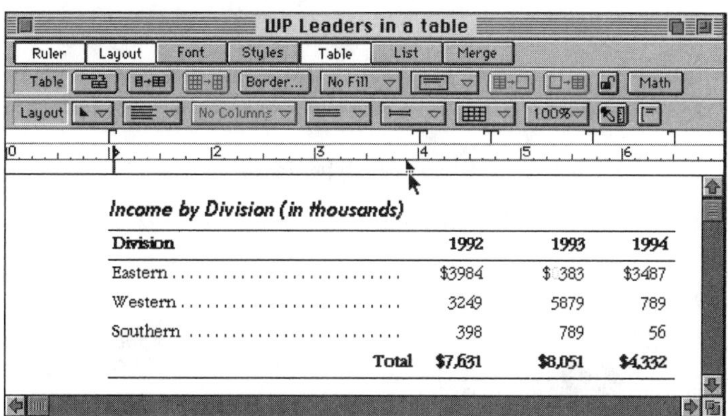

Figure 2-6: Tabs within Tables Most programs let you combine tabs with a table editor; WordPerfect is shown here.

Column headings

Column headings are traditionally centered above their columns. This rule isn't carved in stone, though; many designers prefer to left-align headings, particularly over text-heavy columns, or to right-align headings over numeric columns. If there's a heading over the stub, always left-align it.

Avoid putting long, wordy headings on one line. If headings are considerably longer than the columns below them, there is too much white space between each column, and your readers' eyes need a trapeze to swing from one column to the next. Break long headings into two or more lines to create narrower column widths, and format the headings so that their last lines align vertically. Don't worry about creating a table that fills all the space between the page's left and right margins. There's nothing wrong with a table that goes across only part of a page; on the contrary, a table that's narrower than the margins stands out more and can enliven the page. (Conversely, on a page containing several narrow text columns, try formatting the table so that it spans two or more columns.)

The font and type size you use should also influence your column widths. If you have a lot of information to squeeze into each row, use a space-efficient typeface such as Times or Helvetica Condensed — don't shrink the point size to nearly invisible proportions.

More Table Tips

This box lists some additional tips and techniques for table editing.

- To spice up a table containing yes-and-no values, use symbols to represent the words *yes* and *no*: a check mark for *yes* entries, for example, or a solid (black) bullet for *yes* entries and a hollow bullet for *no* entries. The Zapf Dingbats font has numerous symbols that can replace *yes* and *no.* Consider using an em dash (Shift-Option-hyphen) instead of the text *not applicable* or *n/a.*
- Avoid fouling a table with a flock of footnotes — they undermine the table's structure and may distract the reader. If you must use table footnotes, indicate them with small, superscript numerals or letters, not with symbols such as the asterisk (*).
- If the information in a given cell is the same as that in the cell above it, repeat the information. Never use ditto marks (").
- If your documents contain graphics with captions below them, you can use a table editor to link each caption to its graphic. Simply create a table with one column and two rows. Paste the graphic into the top cell and the caption into the bottom cell. When the graphic moves, the caption moves with it.

❖ All word processors with table editors also have commands that can convert tab-delimited text (whose items are separated by tab codes) into a table. This feature combines nicely with the exporting features that databases and spreadsheets provide: you can import a tab-delimited text file from FileMaker Pro, for example, and turn it into a table with a few mouse clicks. The tabs-to-table feature is also handy when you frequently copy tabular data that you download from an on-line service or mainframe computer. Use the communications programs' Copy As Table command, paste the data into your word processor, and then convert it into a table.

Search-and-Replace Strategies

All programs offer *search-and-replace* features for finding and changing text — changing, for example, all occurrences of *Bush* to *Clinton*. Most programs provide a Find command that lets you search for something and a Replace command that lets you search for something *and* replace it with something else.

But not all programs let you search for one type of formatting attribute (such as tabs and font information) and replace it with another. Want to change all 10-point Helvetica text to 12-point Times Bold? Or get rid of the tabs at the beginning of each paragraph? The capability to search for and replace formatting attributes is a useful feature that lets you quickly change a document's appearance without a lot of manual labor and mistakes.

Finding formatting in Word

Word lets you locate tab characters and carriage returns by typing **^t** or **^p** in the Find What text box (you can also choose these and other codes from the dialog box's Special pop-up menu). Word's Change command also lets you replace one font, size, or style with another (see Figure 2-7, "Changing Formatting in Word").

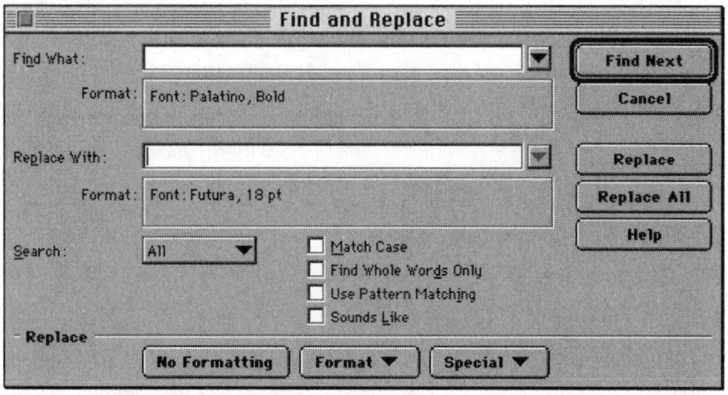

Figure 2-7: Changing Formatting in Word Word's Replace dialog box lets you quickly change formatting. Here, all Palatino Bold text is being changed to 18-point Futura.

Here's a slick trick that lets you use Word's Change command to quickly reformat an entire paragraph. First, copy the carriage return of the paragraph whose format you want to apply elsewhere (choose Show ¶ from the View menu to see carriage return codes). Then select the carriage return of the paragraph to be changed and choose Paste. To automate the process, type **^p** in the Find What box and **^c** in the Replace With box. The latter tells Word to replace the text to be changed with the Clipboard's contents.

Finding formatting in other programs

Like Word, WordPerfect and MacWrite can search for and replace nearly every formatting attribute. To search and replace attributes in MacWrite, choose Find/Change from the Edit menu and check the Use Attributes check box in the Find/Change dialog box that appears. The dialog box changes to include lists of fonts and attributes that you can select. If you're just searching for text attributes (not attributes as well as specific characters), uncheck the Use Text check box.

In WordPerfect, use the Match and Affect menus in the Find window to specify which attributes you're searching for and replacing. To display the Find window, choose Find/Change from the Search menu.

Citizen Mac

One way in which most Mac word processors infiltrate the desktop publishing camp is by enabling you to create multiple columns of text on a page (see Figure 2-8, "Become a Columnist"). Multicolumn pages are common in newsletters, brochures, and menus.

In Word, WriteNow, and MacWrite II, creating multiple columns involves choosing a command and specifying the number of columns you want. In Word, use the Section command from the Format menu. In WriteNow, use Page Setup.

In MacWrite Pro, click one of the ruler's column controls. To create columns of unequal width, double-click the ruler's column number. You can adjust column widths with the mouse by pressing Option and then dragging a column guide. (Choose Show Page Guides from the View menu if you don't see the dotted column guides.)

If you're still using the old MacWrite II, choose the Page command from the Format menu or double-click the column border at the top of MacWrite II's ruler or the page number indicator in the lower-left corner of the document window.

In WordPerfect, you can choose the number of columns by using the ruler's Columns pop-up menu. You can also adjust the columns' widths by dragging the shaded borders in the ruler.

Document6 (Preview)

ARBOR REPORT

Arbor Footwear | Vol. II • No. 12 • Dec. 5, 1991

Foot Facts The children's shoe division walked away with this month's production award, exceeding their production goal by 7 percent!

Production Statistics for the Month

Robot added to work force

Our athletic shoe division took a step toward the twenty-first century this month when it purchased a robot to assist with manufacturing.

The robot threads shoelaces into track shoes at an astounding rate of speed. Human co-workers report that the robot is pleasant to work with and "doesn't complain much." In fact, the robot doesn't talk at all.

scores on arcade computer games. TongueTied rolled away with not only top honors, but the world-record score for all three games.

Although all prizes went to the humans, the company sponsoring the contest created a special plaque for TongueTied to commemorate his win. And what did the kids think of their automated competitor? They had

Employee News

Soccer team wins!

Congratulations to the Arbor Footwear soccer team! They took first place in the recent city competition. Special thanks to team captain **Roy Taylor** (manufacturing), who told a TV reporter, "Great shoes are part of a sound strategy."

Writing contest winner

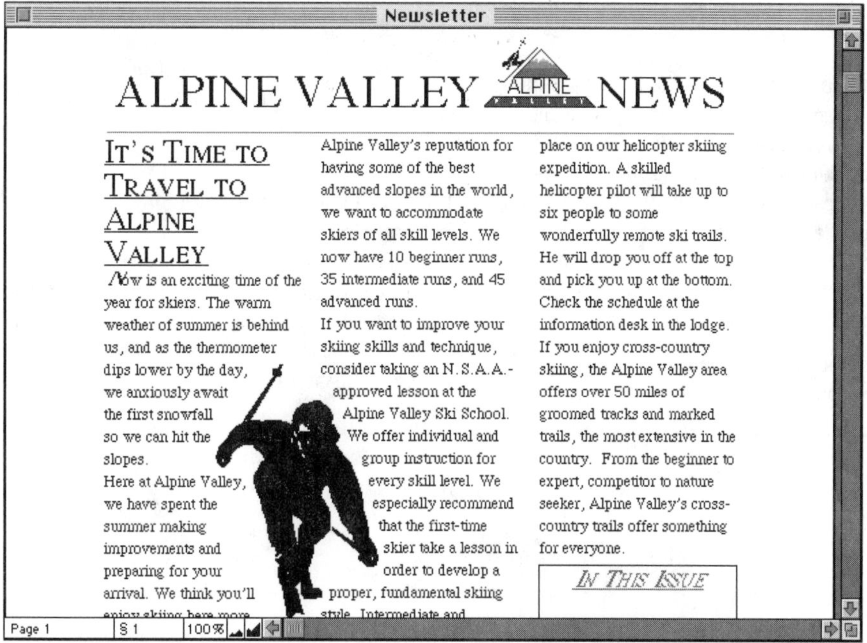
Newsletter

ALPINE VALLEY NEWS

It's Time to Travel to Alpine Valley

Now is an exciting time of the year for skiers. The warm weather of summer is behind us, and as the thermometer dips lower by the day, we anxiously await the first snowfall so we can hit the slopes.

Here at Alpine Valley, we have spent the summer making improvements and preparing for your arrival. We think you'll enjoy skiing here more

Alpine Valley's reputation for having some of the best advanced slopes in the world, we want to accommodate skiers of all skill levels. We now have 10 beginner runs, 35 intermediate runs, and 45 advanced runs.

If you want to improve your skiing skills and technique, consider taking an N.S.A.A.-approved lesson at the Alpine Valley Ski School. We offer individual and group instruction for every skill level. We especially recommend that the first-time skier take a lesson in order to develop a proper, fundamental skiing style. Intermediate and

place on our helicopter skiing expedition. A skilled helicopter pilot will take up to six people to some wonderfully remote ski trails. He will drop you off at the top and pick you up at the bottom. Check the schedule at the information desk in the lodge.

If you enjoy cross-country skiing, the Alpine Valley area offers over 50 miles of groomed tracks and marked trails, the most extensive in the country. From the beginner to expert, competitor to nature seeker, Alpine Valley's cross-country trails offer something for everyone.

In This Issue

Figure 2-8: Become a Columnist You don't need a publishing program to publish. Most word processors, including Word 6 (top) and MacWrite Pro (bottom), let you create complex, multicolumn pages. Note MacWrite Pro's capability to automatically wrap text margins around a graphic.

ClarisWorks and Microsoft Works 4 also let you do multicolumn layout by creating frames that hold text; with both programs, you can even link frames so that text flows from one column to another.

Four Things Everyone Should Know about Word Processing

Don't use the spacebar to align or center

On a typewriter, you may use the spacebar to center text and indent paragraphs. With a word processor, it's better to use the on-screen ruler to control centering, indents, column alignment, and the like. When you use the spacebar for these jobs and then change fonts or sizes, the text is no longer formatted properly — columns don't align, lines and pages don't break in the right places, and you embark on an adventure in manual reformatting.

Don't use extra returns to break a page

If you want a certain paragraph within a document to begin on the top of a page, don't force it there by typing extra carriage returns above it. It's better to insert a page break code. In Word, for instance, choose Page Break from the Insert menu or simply press Shift-Enter. With this approach, you don't have to search through your document for all those extra returns if you reformat the text later.

Note that many programs also provide special paragraph-formatting options that let you specify that a paragraph begin on a new page or that two paragraphs always remain together.

Take advantage of Undo and Redo

If you accidentally delete some text, you can restore it by choosing Undo from the Edit menu before doing anything else. Undo features also make it easy to experiment with your writing. By alternating between Undo and Redo, you can try out different versions of a sentence or a paragraph.

In most programs, Undo also works with formatting commands and ruler alterations. Word 6 has an even more impressive Undo tool that lets you undo multiple actions.

Polish your punctuation for a professional look

If you have a laser or ink-jet printer, following a few simple rules can help make your documents look professionally typeset. See the Quick Reference Card at the front of this book or the "Type Tips" Quick Tips box in Chapter 11.

Some Final Words

If you're just getting started with a word processor, read over the "Four Things Everyone Should Know about Word Processing" Quick Tips box for some reminders. If you're still shopping for a word processor, test drive some programs to find the one whose operating style you like. Doing so is especially important if you plan to spend a great deal of time writing. Every word processor has its own feel — your job is to find one that feels good to you.

When you're shopping, don't be wowed by endless lists of features. Gimmicky formatting and drawing features don't help you put your thoughts into words — indeed, they may tempt you to play with fancy formats instead of making another round of revisions. Word processors exist to make writing easier. That's quite a feat in itself.

Word Processing on the Road

Word processing on a PowerBook portable computer isn't too different from word processing on a desktop Mac, with one big exception: you can process words even when you aren't near a power outlet. Beyond this difference are some less obvious points that you may want to consider.

Keyboard considerations

Older PowerBooks lack the function keys and scrolling keys that Apple's extended keyboards provide. For this reason, you may prefer to use a word processor whose scrolling and editing key sequences can be customized. For example, you can use the Shift and Control keys (not the ⌘ key) in combination with the arrow keys to set up key sequences that move you to the start or end of a document, sentence, or paragraph. If you use a program whose scrolling keystrokes can't be customized, there's still hope: a keyboard-enhancement utility such as CE Software's QuicKeys (see Chapter 24). And, of course, if you've plugged your PowerBook into the wall, you can attach an extended keyboard to its rear-panel ADB port.

Memory and disk space: less leaves more

Many older PowerBooks contain 40MB or 80MB hard drives — not bad, but not large enough to hold dozens of application programs. Unless you want to buy a higher-capacity hard drive, look for a word processor that's as light and lean as the PowerBook itself. The heavy hitters — Microsoft Word and WordPerfect — have big appetites for both disk space and memory. You can reduce Word's disk requirements by not installing optional features, such as the grammar checker. You can also reduce the memory requirements of these and other programs by using the Finder's Get Info command, as described in Chapter 22.

A better choice for portable word processing may be a lean-and-mean program such as Softkey's WriteNow, Nisus Software's Nisus Compact, or WordPerfect's LetterPerfect. Another option: an integrated program such as ClarisWorks or Microsoft Works.

CHAPTER  CONCEPTS AND TERMS

- Automatic word wrap, easy editing, and effortless formatting are the primary features that set a word processor apart from a typewriter.
- The gateway to most common formatting tasks is a word processor's on-screen ruler.
- Some word processors provide timesaving features such as glossaries, which store often-used text or graphics, and style sheets, which store formatting information. Some programs can also compile indexes and tables of contents.
- When you're shopping for a word processor, features to consider include the availability of editing shortcuts, outlining features, glossaries and style sheets, table editors, spelling and grammar checkers, mail merge, and equation editing.
- If you have a PowerBook, you may want to consider a word processor that uses disk space and memory sparingly, such as WriteNow or Nisus Compact.

annotations
Typed (or recorded) comments attached to a document.

columnar tables
Blocks of text that are aligned in columns, such as stock market results or sports standings.

decimal tabs
Tab stops in which the numbers in a column of text are aligned on their decimal points.

first-line indent
A paragraph format in which the first line of every paragraph is indented.

footer
Text and/or graphics that appear at the bottom of every page in a document.

formatting
The capability to specify margin widths, line spacing, justification, fonts, and font size and style.

glossary
What you're reading now. Also, a word processor feature that lets you store and recall often-used text or graphics with a single keystroke.

hanging indent
A paragraph format in which the first line begins to the left of subsequent lines.

header
Text and/or graphics that appear at the top of every page in a document.

justification
Aligning text against the left and right margins.

leader characters
Characters (usually a row of periods) that run across a column and guide the eye along the line to the next column.

search-and-replace
A feature that lets you locate text or a formatting code and either delete it or replace it with something else.

style sheets
Also called *styles,* a named set of character and paragraph formats that you can apply throughout a document.

tabs
Formatting codes that let you indent text or graphics and align columns of numbers in tables.

text-only format
A method of saving a document so that all graphics and most formatting information are discarded, leaving only the text characters and rudimentary formatting such as tab codes and carriage returns.

word wrap
A word processor feature that brings words down to the next line as you type. With word wrap, you don't have to press Return at the end of every line. This feature also quickly adjusts line breaks when you add or remove text.

CHAPTER THREE

Word Processing Power Tips

- Creating glossaries, custom spelling dictionaries, special text effects, and more
- Customizing Word and WordPerfect to match the way you work and write
- Mastering keyboard and selection shortcuts in Word and WordPerfect

A word processing program lets you concentrate on writing instead of mechanics. Go ahead and type — there's no fussing with paper, no pressing Return at the end of every line, and no painting with correction fluid. A variety of fonts, type sizes, and styles are a menu away. And you can do the kind of advanced page formatting that once required a professional typesetter and a room full of equipment.

Whether you write a memo a week or a chapter a day, you can save time by mastering and customizing your word processor. I start off this chapter with a look at common business word processing chores — the little formatting grunts and groans that are a part of word processing life. I show how to tackle each chore by using today's most popular programs (some of which are included on the *Macworld Complete Mac Interactive CD*).

After you master those chores, put on your explorer's boots for a journey into the world of word processor customizing, a place where menus contain only the commands you use, keyboard shortcuts make sense, and all you have to do is concentrate on your writing. The customizer's dream destinations are Microsoft Word 6 and WordPerfect Corporation's WordPerfect 3, so that's where I take you. (For advice on applying these customizing tips to programs such as Softkey's WriteNow, Claris's MacWrite II and MacWrite Pro, ClarisWorks, and Microsoft Works, see the "Customizing Other Programs" Quick Tips box.)

Along the way, I also pass along some tips and techniques that let you create special effects, navigate through documents quickly, and more.

Customizing Other Programs

If you don't use Word or WordPerfect, you can still apply many customizing techniques to other programs.

Custom spelling checkers

All popular word processors and integrated packages have spelling checkers and support custom dictionaries.

Stationery

You can create stationery with ClarisWorks, Softkey's WriteNow 3, and Claris's MacWrite II and MacWrite Pro. It's worth noting that with System 7 you can create stationery from a document created in any program. At the Finder, select the document, choose Get Info from the File menu, and then check the Stationery Pad box. Thereafter, when you open the stationery document, the Finder duplicates the stationery document and then opens the duplicate. Apple built this feature into System 7 to let you create stationery for programs whose Save dialog boxes don't contain a Stationery option.

AutoText and glossaries

Only Word has a glossary feature (called AutoText in Word 6), but ClarisWorks and Microsoft Works have macro recorders that let you record and play back key sequences. You can also save and insert repetitive text in any program by using CE Software's QuicKeys keyboard-enhancement utility.

Styles

WriteNow has excellent style features. MacWrite II and ClarisWorks provide a custom styles feature that lets you store and recall character formatting but not paragraph-level formatting such as line spacing, margins, and indents. (MacWrite Pro does provide paragraph-level styles.) ClarisWorks and Microsoft Works lack style features, but you can simulate them by recording macros that choose formatting commands.

Menu and keyboard customizing

You can use ClarisWorks or Microsoft Works macros to create your own keyboard shortcuts. Better yet, use QuicKeys to create shortcuts for all your programs.

Macros

You can add macro features to any program with CE Software's QuicKeys. It doesn't offer all the power and flexibility of a built-in macro feature, but it does let you record and play back repetitive tasks. And it lets you customize other aspects of your Mac.

Finding Your Center

How many times have you printed a one-page memo or letter only to find that your salutation prints on top of your letterhead? Adding half a dozen blank lines at the beginning of the document fixes the problem but creates another: when you edit or reformat the document, the letter isn't vertically centered anymore. They can send a man to the moon — can't they make a word processor that vertically centers a one-page letter? Yes, they can.

Vertical centering in Word

Word 6 makes vertical centering a cinch. Choose Document Layout from the File menu and then click the Document Layout dialog box's Layout tab. Then from the Vertical Alignment pop-up menu, choose Center.

If you're still using Word 5, you need to use frames. Word's Frame command is designed for fancy tasks like creating sidebars and positioning graphics, but you can also use it for this simple but common chore. After typing the letter, choose Select All from the Edit menu. Next, choose Frame from the Format menu. In the Vertical area of the Frame dialog box, choose Center from the left-hand pop-up menu and Page from the Relative To pop-up menu. Click OK or press Return, and you're done. The text remains vertically centered even if you edit or reformat it. When you work in Page Layout view (the view that shows all your headers, footers, and frames in position), you may notice delays during editing as Word works to keep the text centered. After centering text by using this technique, you may want to work in Normal view only. Or you may want to upgrade to Word 6.

Vertical centering in WordPerfect

WordPerfect's Center Page command does the job in one step. With the blinking insertion point located anywhere on the page, open the Page submenu (in the Layout menu) and then choose Center Page. To check your work, choose Print Preview from the File menu.

Making and Tracking Revisions

In many businesses, documents must run the approval loop gauntlet, which involves everyone adding his or her two cents' worth. *Revision-tracking* features make it easy to spot the text that has changed since the last go-around.

The most useful revision-tracking feature is the capability to display vertical *change bars* in the margin next to altered text. Sometimes called *redlining*, this feature enables readers to quickly scan for new or edited text.

Revision tracking in Word 6

Word 6 provides terrific revision-tracking features. To activate them, choose Revisions from the Tools menu. When you do, the Revisions dialog box appears. Check the box named Mark Revisions While Editing, and then click OK or press Return. From this point on, Word keeps track of the revisions you make and indicates them in the following ways (see Figure 3-1 "Making Revisions in Word"):

- ❖ A vertical change bar appears in the left margin adjacent to revised lines. This bar makes it easy to spot text that you change.
- ❖ An underline appears under any text that you add after turning on revision tracking.
- ❖ Any text that you delete after turning on revision tracking has a line through it.

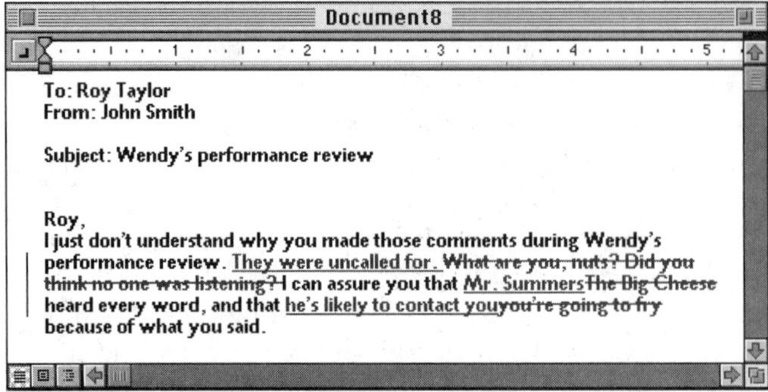

Figure 3-1: Making Revisions in Word When Word 6's revision-tracking features are active, the program indicates changed text with change bars, underlining, and strikethrough text.

You can change the ways Word indicates revisions by clicking the Options button in the Revisions dialog box or by choosing Options from the Tools menu and then clicking the Revisions tab.

Reviewing and incorporating revisions

Word's revision-tracking features don't just mark changed text — they let you (or someone else) work through the document and either accept or reject the revisions. You read that right; you can reject a specific revision, and Word actually restores the text to the state it was in prior to the edit.

To review revisions, choose Revisions from the Tools menu and click the Review button. The Review Revisions window appears (see Figure 3-2 "Reviewing Revisions"). In this window, you can examine each change in the document and decide to accept or reject it. When you reject a change, Word deletes the change and restores the text to the state it was in before you turned on revision tracking. When you accept a change, Word incorporates the edit.

The Review Revisions window is powerful, but sometimes you may not need to double-check every revision. In these cases, you can simply use the Revisions dialog box's Accept All or Reject All buttons to keep or discard all revisions.

Revision tracking in WordPerfect

Compared to Word 6, WordPerfect's revision-tracking features are wimpy. For starters, WordPerfect can't automatically create change bars as you work. You need to indicate new or changed text manually by choosing a command — an easy step to overlook when you're frantically making the boss's changes.

To create a change bar in WordPerfect, choose Redline from the Style menu. This command places a (red) change bar adjacent to the line containing the blinking insertion point.

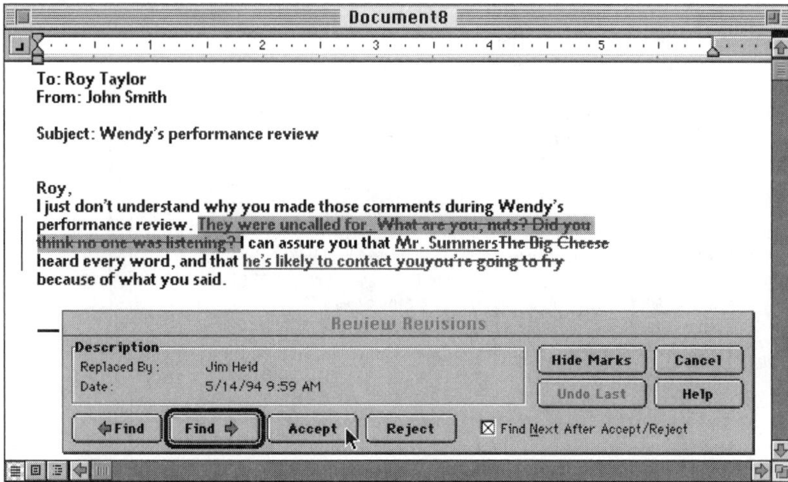

Figure 3-2: Reviewing Revisions Word's Review Revisions dialog box lets you step through each change in the document and decide to accept or reject it.

DocuComp II: advanced revision tracking

If you're willing to introduce another program and another step to your revision tracking, consider Advanced Software's DocuComp II utility. This program compares two files and describes the differences between the two (see Figure 3-3 "Comparing Documents"). DocuComp II can also create a third document that details the differences between the two versions. DocuComp II directly supports Microsoft Word and WordPerfect documents and can also read text-only files. (With the latter capability, you can even compare two spreadsheets by saving each as a text-only file. Be sure to save them in their native formats first so you don't lose any formatting.)

Word 6, by the way, has built-in document-comparison features. Just click the Compare Versions button in the Revisions dialog box. Nisus Software's Nisus word processor also has built-in document-comparison features, including the capability to synchronize two windows so that when you scroll one, the other tags along.

Electronic Annotations

Word and MacWrite Pro offer on-line annotation features — electronic sticky notes that you attach to documents. These features are handy for adding comments without fouling the document's text itself, but readers may not notice the small icons these programs use to indicate annotations. Another problem: annotations don't print when you print the document. The beauty of real sticky notes is that they stick out like flags — electronic annotations are a bit too unobtrusive for my taste.

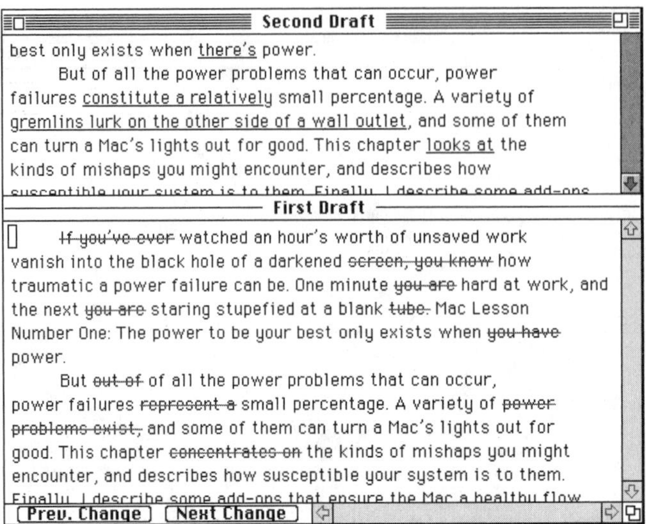

Figure 3-3: Comparing Documents Advanced Software's DocuComp II can compare two documents and show the differences between them. You can also save a report (not shown here) that summarizes the differences.

On-line annotation features are common in electronic document-interchange programs — packages such as Adobe Acrobat, Farallon's Replica, and No-Hands Software's Common Ground. (You'll find more details on these programs in Chapter 28.) There's also Mainstay's MarkUp, which lets you electronically scrawl comments and note insertions and deletions — complete with standard proofreader's marks (see Figure 3-4 "Marking It Up"). MarkUp lets you set up a separate layer for each person who reviews the document. You can then choose which layers you want to view.

I'm not a big believer in electronic document annotation — the risk of missing a comment (or with MarkUp's layer feature, an entire set of comments) is too great. If your documents travel around a single physical location, I say mark them up with pencils and sticky notes. But if you send them to other locations via e-mail or remote-access network software, electronic annotations are worth considering as long as they are used with care.

As for the voice annotation features Word and MacWrite provide, don't waste your disk space or time. One five-second voice annotation uses as much disk space as hundreds of typed comments. Documents with voice annotations also take far longer to transfer over networks.

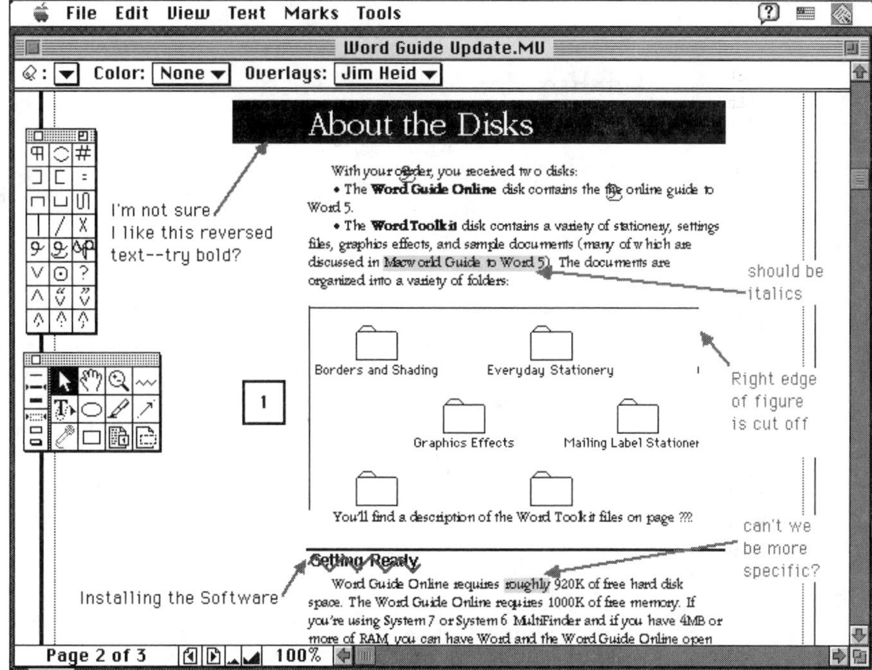

Figure 3-4: Marking It Up With Mainstay's MarkUp, you and your colleagues can electronically annotate documents. The Marks palette in the upper-left corner contains standard proofreader's marks, while the Tools palette below it lets you attach typed or recorded annotations, draw arrows and other shapes, and highlight text. The boxed numeral 1 indicates a note — double-clicking the numeral opens a window containing the note's text.

How to Make Watermarks

If you hold a sheet of letterhead or other high-quality paper up to a window, you can probably see the paper manufacturer's logo. This is called a *watermark*. In the word processing world, a watermark is text or graphics that appear beneath the copy on a page. Watermarks are often used to emblazon a document with a message that you don't want readers to miss, such as Confidential, Draft Version, or Final Notice.

This section describes how to create watermarks within Word and WordPerfect. If you use QuickDraw GX or any of several Apple printer drivers, you can also create watermarks using any program. See Chapter 31 for more details.

Ten Hot Tips for Using Microsoft Word

- **Know when to disable fast saves** Word's fast save feature is true to its name — when the feature is active, Word's Save command operates in a flash. That's good because it encourages you to save more often. But there are times when it's better to disable fast saves. Here's why: When the fast save feature is active, Word tacks on changes to the end of the document file, which causes file sizes to grow and wastes disk space. (If you're transferring files over networks or phone lines, it also increases transfer times.) By disabling fast saves, you can keep file sizes as small as possible. Another important time to disable fast saves is when you plan to import your files into a publishing program such as PageMaker or QuarkXPress — these and other publishing programs often have trouble reading files saved in fast-save format. To disable fast saves, choose Options from the Tools menu, click the Save tab, and uncheck the Allow Fast Saves box.

- **Know your double-click shortcuts** You can make a lot happen in Word by double-clicking — if you know where to double-click. You can split a document window by double-clicking the split bar — the heavy black bar just above the document window's vertical scroll bar. (You can also use this shortcut to close annotation and footnote windows.) You can display the Document Layout dialog box by double-clicking the ruler, the Columns dialog box by double-clicking the ruler's column separator, and the Go To dialog box by clicking the page number area of the status bar. You can turn an anchored toolbar into a floating toolbar (and vice versa) by double-clicking it. You can enlarge a window to fill the screen by double-clicking its title bar. When in Page Layout view, you can edit a header or footer by double-clicking it. And in dialog boxes, you can choose an option *and* okay the dialog box by double-clicking the desired option.

- **Use shortcut menus to cut down on trips to the menu bar** Shortcut menus appear when you press the Control key (not the ⌘ key) while pressing the mouse button. Word is smart about which shortcut menus it displays: if the mouse pointer is in the document window when you Control-click, you get menus for formatting, cutting, copying, and pasting. If the pointer is in a toolbar when you Control-click, you get a menu of available toolbars. If the pointer is in a table, a menu of table-editing commands appears. Shortcut menus save time especially when you have a large-screen monitor — they can save you from making the long journey up to the menu bar.

- **Create AutoText entries for often-used text or graphics** Look for step-by-step instructions later in this chapter.

- **Create templates that store often-used formatting, macros, AutoText entries, and custom menu, toolbar, and keyboard settings** As you'll see later in this chapter, Word 6 templates are incredibly powerful: they store not only boilerplate text and formatting, but also AutoText entries, customized menu, toolbar, and keyboard settings, and macros. You essentially can change Word's user interface by opening a specific template. Take advantage of this power by creating templates that streamline the types of documents you create.

- **Set bookmarks in lengthy documents** Word lets you create electronic bookmarks that make it easy to navigate large documents. To insert a bookmark, choose Bookmark from the Edit menu, type a name for the bookmark (the name can't include any spaces), and then click Add. To jump to a specific bookmark, choose Go To from the Edit menu, select the Bookmarks option, and then choose the desired bookmark from the pop-up menu.

- **Keep often-used dialog box windows open** You can leave many of Word's dialog box windows — Find and Replace, Go To, Spelling, Mark Index Entry — open as you edit text; you don't have to close them to return to the document window. Leaving these windows open can save a lot of time when you're in the editing phase of a project. If you have a second monitor, you may want to stash these windows there so they don't get in the way of your text.
- **Use drag-and-drop editing and the spike** These editing features are more versatile and often faster than the Clipboard's Cut and Paste commands. I describe both later in this chapter.
- **Use the Go Back key sequence for fast edit navigation** Word remembers the last three locations where you edited or typed text. The Go Back key sequence — Shift-F5 — returns the blinking insertion point to each of these locations. I used Word's Customize command to reassign the key sequence to the numeral 0 on the numeric keypad, a more convenient location.
- **Use Word's cross-referencing features** In manuscripts and books, "to" references to other sections and to figures and tables (for example, "See the section 'All About Poodles' on page 198") are common. Keeping track of and updating these cross-references as page numbers change is a real chore. Word provides automatic cross-referencing features that eliminate the manual labor. To continue the aforementioned example, suppose that you change the "All About Poodles" section name to "Poodles for Industry" and that other edits cause the section to move to page 203. Word's automatic cross-referencing features change the reference appropriately, automatically updating both the section name and the page number.

And of course, you should master Word's keyboard shortcuts. You'll find a list of the most useful ones later in this chapter. Use them when you're in the writing phase of a project and don't want to take your hands from the keyboard.

Making watermarks in Word

Word 6's watermark feature relies on Word's built-in drawing features and on headers and footers. In a nutshell, you use the Drawing toolbar to create the text and/or graphics for the watermark, and you place that text and/or graphics in a header to make it appear on each page.

First, click the Standard toolbar's drawing button to display the Drawing toolbar. Next, choose Header and Footer from the View menu. On the Header and Footer toolbar, click the Show/Hide Document button to hide the text and graphics in your document. Now use the Drawing toolbar's text tool to create the watermark's text.

After you've typed and formatted the watermark's text, drag the text to the desired location on the page. (You don't have to confine the text to the dotted header and footer areas; you can put the text anywhere.) Finally, click the Send Behind Text button in the Drawing toolbar.

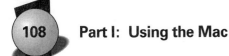

Microsoft Word 6: The Good, Bad, and Ugly

Word 6 is the latest version of the Mac world's most popular word processor. It's been lynched on-line and at user groups; it's been tossed in the Trash and returned to dealers; and it's lost market share to Novell's WordPerfect, which had for years been a relatively minor player among high-end Mac word processors.

What happened? Three things: First, Microsoft updated Word's interface to make it identical to that of Word for Windows 6.0, and the differences annoyed many Word 5.1 loyalists. Second, Microsoft included such a huge array of add-on utilities, document templates, and gimmicky auto-formatting "Wizards" that a full installation of Word 6 swallows 25MB of hard disk space. Third, Microsoft shipped a program that is often dramatically slower than its predecessor — so much so that it doesn't run acceptably on 68030-based Macs, or even on slower 68040 Macs such as the Quadra 610.

Several months after Word 6 shipped, Microsoft shipped version 6.0.1, which fixes some of the program's worst problems. Specifically, version 6.0.1 sports a much faster Word Count command (now it's faster than Word 5.1's); it starts up much faster (version 6.0 was particularly sluggish on systems containing a large number of fonts); it fixes numerous incompatibilities between Word and third-party extensions (Microsoft, in its questionable wisdom, failed to test Word 6 with older versions of many extensions — versions very likely to be installed on users' systems); and it fixes a variety of bugs, one of the most notable being Word 6.0's frequent inability to print envelopes.

Is Word 6 a perfect word processor? Hardly. Its setup program is still finicky, and certain aspects of Word don't work the way a standard Macintosh application's should. Still, there are flashes of brilliance in Word 6, and the new cross-platform compatibility is a boon to businesses that mix Macs and Windows machines.

But before you upgrade, you need to weigh Word's innovations against its greed for hard disk space and horsepower. If you can benefit from Word's laundry list of automation features — cross-referencing, AutoText, automatic numbering and renumbering, macros — you stand a good chance of saving more time over the course of a day than you'll lose waiting for some of Word 6's slower operations. I say if you can put Word 6's features to work and if you have a Quadra 650 or faster Mac, take the plunge — but use the custom installation option to pare down the program's disk space requirements.

If you need advanced word processing features but you don't have the fastest Mac in the world, Novell's WordPerfect is a much better choice. And if your needs are more basic — if you just want to use a word processor to, say, *write* — forget both Word 6 and WordPerfect and get ClarisWorks or MacWrite Pro.

Making watermarks in WordPerfect

WordPerfect's watermark feature also relies on the program's built-in drawing window. When you choose New from the Watermark submenu (in the Tools menu), the drawing window appears. Create the watermark's text and/or graphics, and then choose Close Graphic from the File menu. Choose Print Preview to see the watermark. WordPerfect lets you create two watermarks. You can put a different watermark on odd- and even-numbered pages or use one for graphics and the other for text. You can also use the Suppress command (in the Page submenu of the Layout menu) to prevent a watermark from printing on a given page.

See You in Court

Legal documents often have numbers running along the left margin to allow for quick reference. Microsoft Word, WordPerfect, and Nisus can automatically add these numbers.

Numbering lines in Word

To create line numbers in Word, choose Document Layout from the File menu and be sure that the Layout tab is selected in the Document Layout dialog box. Next, click the Line Numbers button. The dialog box that appears lets you number lines by page, by section, or continuously throughout the document. You can also choose the numbering interval to number, for example, every other line or every fifth line. The From Text box lets you specify the distance between line numbers and the lines they number.

To turn off line numbering for certain lines, select them, choose Paragraph from the Format menu, and then select the Text Flow tab. Next, select the Suppress Line Numbers option.

Line numbers don't appear in Word's Normal view. To see them, switch into Page Layout or Print Preview mode. To change the font and size in which line numbers appear, edit the style named Line Number.

Numbering lines in WordPerfect

In WordPerfect, place the insertion point where you want numbering to begin or select the text you want to number. Open the Line submenu (in the Layout menu) and then choose Format. In the Line Format dialog box, choose Continuous or Restart Each Page as desired and specify other options, such as the numbering interval. If you want a vertical line between the numbers and the text, draw it by using WordPerfect's drawing window.

Other features for legal eagles

Barristers can benefit from several other word processor features. A print merge feature, normally used to create personalized form letters, can be handy for combining boilerplate contract text with the names of each party (see Chapter 4). And as you'll see later in this chapter, AutoText and macro features let you insert boilerplate text with a few keystrokes.

Word's Bullet and Numbering commands (in the Format menu) provide paragraph-numbering and renumbering features. These features make it easy to create numbered lists, such as for instructions in a manual. You can also use Word's Bullet and Numbering commands to automatically number an outline in standard outlining style.

WordPerfect and Word 6 provide features that streamline the creation of a table of authorities — a kind of bibliography that lists the cases cited in a legal brief. The process is too complicated to describe here (hey, sue me), but in a nutshell, it involves marking each citation, choosing a location and formatting style, and then generating the table of authorities.

Creating a Personal Dictionary

Although a word processor's spelling checker can't guarantee perfect spelling, it can help. But what if you use words that aren't in the program's dictionary? Names, scientific jargon, abbreviations, and slang can confound a spelling checker. And when you're in a hurry to complete a document, it's tempting to click the spelling checker's Ignore or Skip button to bypass terms you know are spelled correctly.

But wait — instead of telling your program to ignore those terms, add the terms to your user dictionary. Sometimes called a *custom dictionary*, this separate file supplements the program's built-in dictionary. Adding terms to a user dictionary essentially expands your word processor's vocabulary. The spelling checker runs faster, you don't have to click Ignore all the time, and your documents are that much more accurate.

For instructions for adding words to a custom dictionary in Word and WordPerfect, see the "Customizing a Dictionary" Step-by-Step box.

Word can work with numerous custom dictionaries at once; consider creating separate dictionaries for different types of terms — legal terms, names, and so on. Use the Spelling portion of the Options dialog box to switch between custom dictionaries. While the Options dialog box is open, explore its other options — as you'll see later in this chapter, they let you tailor nearly every aspect of Word's operation.

Other ways to fine-tune spelling

Word and WordPerfect also let you customize other aspects of their spelling checkers. You can use the Spelling portion of the Options dialog box to tell Word to ignore words in all capitals as well as words containing numbers (such as 100K).

You can use Word's AutoCorrect command (in the Tools menu) to fine-tune the workings of Word's AutoCorrect feature, which proofreads your work as you type to correct common errors such as transposed letters and misspelled words. If you always type *nieghbor* instead of *neighbor*, for example, you can add these words to the AutoCorrect list, and Word makes sure that your mistake never appears in print again.

The AutoCorrect feature is also great for creating em dashes — those long dashes that set off a portion of a sentence for emphasis (there's one in this sentence). In the AutoCorrect dialog box, type two hyphens in the Replace box and an em dash (Shift-Option-hyphen) in the With box.

As for WordPerfect, you can use the Check menu in WordPerfect's Speller dialog box to tell the program to watch for duplicate words (such as "and and") and ignore words containing numbers. WordPerfect's Preferences submenu, located in the Edit menu, is also rich with customizing opportunities.

Shopping for customized dictionaries

Can your word processor spell *thrombocytopenia*? Or *habeas corpus ad subjiciendum*? Or *nondiversifiable*? Or *3-ethoxy-1,3-pentadiene*? Every profession has its own jargon and abbreviations, but word processor spelling checker dictionaries don't know them. One solution is to manually teach your program new words as it encounters them. But besides taking forever, this approach has a risk — you might add an incorrect spelling to your dictionary, ensuring that all occurrences of a word are misspelled.

Customizing a Dictionary

Adding terms to a user dictionary essentially expands your word processor's vocabulary to include specialized terms you may use. This section shows you how to add a highlighted word to a Word or WordPerfect user dictionary.

To add a word in Word:

1. **Optional: To add a word to a specific custom dictionary, select the dictionary's name from the Add Words To pop-up menu.**
   If you don't perform this step, the word is added to the dictionary named Custom Dictionary.
2. **Click the Add button in the Spelling dialog box.**

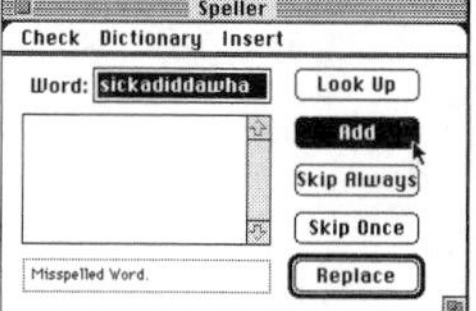

To add a word in WordPerfect:

1. **Click the Add button in the Speller dialog box.**
   To edit the user dictionary, use the ST Utility program that comes with WordPerfect.

A better way to expand a word processor's vocabulary is to add specialized dictionaries. WordPerfect and Nisus Software (619-481-1477) sell medical and legal dictionaries for their programs. For Microsoft Word, the best source for custom dictionaries is Alki Software (206-286-2600), which distributes expanded dictionary and thesaurus packages licensed from Microsoft. Alki's Comprehensive Spelling package adds 74,100 medical, legal, business, financial, and insurance terms. Alki's Word Proofing Tools includes expanded dictionaries, thesauri, and hyphenation files and is available in 14 languages.

Medina Software sells a Word dictionary of biblical proportions: the $16.95 Medina Spelling Dictionary contains proper names, geographical names, abbreviations, and topics of the Bible, along with a variety of computer industry, medical, and electronics terms. Medina's ¡Correctamente! is a Spanish spelling dictionary for Word.

Working with Stationery and Templates

Chances are you always create similar types of documents. If so, you should take advantage of the labor-saving stationery and template features most word processors provide.

Creating your own stationery

If you always create similar types of documents, such as memos, letters, fax cover sheets, or contracts, consider creating stationery for them. A stationery document is electronically preprinted with whatever text, graphics, and formatting information you use in a certain kind of document, just as a piece of company stationery is preprinted with a name and address. Stationery for a letter might contain your return address. Stationery for a newsletter might contain the publication name, placeholder text for the headlines and table of contents, and formatting settings for multicolumn pages.

Using a stationery document is easy: simply open it and start writing. Couldn't you simply open an old newsletter or memo and replace its contents? Yes, but you might accidentally choose Save instead of Save As, thereby losing the old document. By contrast, your word processor opens the stationery document as a new, untitled document, so you can't accidentally save over it.

To create a stationery document, look for the Stationery option in the Save As dialog box. In Word and WordPerfect, you'll find this option in a pop-up menu. In other programs, you may have to click a File Format button to choose the Stationery format.

Word templates: stationery on steroids

Microsoft Word 6 provides a much more powerful variation of stationery documents, called *templates*. Indeed, the single biggest difference between Word 6 and earlier versions is Word 6's concept of document templates.

If you're a Word 5 veteran, you know that you can create stationery documents that hold boilerplate text and formatting. You also know that you can create glossary files that store often-used text and graphics for quick recall. And you know that you can create and switch between settings files, which store customized Word menus and keyboard shortcuts.

A Word 6 template combines the functions of stationery, glossary, and settings files into one file and throws in some additional capabilities for good measure. A template can hold boilerplate text, glossary entries (which, as mentioned earlier, are called AutoText entries in Word 6), and your customized keyboard shortcuts, menus, and toolbars.

Using templates

Templates provide some powerful possibilities. Using Word 6's macro language, you (or a consultant or software developer) can create customized menus that supplement or even replace Word's menus. A template for a weekly status report might have a menu called Assemble containing commands that retrieve report contributions from several coworkers and then put them together into one formatted document.

A writer can create a template called Manuscripts that customizes Word's menus to remove advanced formatting commands that the writer never uses. A corporate publications director can create a template called Documentation that puts customized versions of Word's automatic indexing and cross-referencing commands close at hand. Templates are like stationery on steroids.

Accessing and applying templates

When you choose Word 6's New command, instead of getting a blank, untitled window, you get a dialog box asking you to choose a template upon which to base the new document. (Word 6 ships with a dozen or so canned templates for documents ranging from newsletters and resumes to fax cover sheets and employee time sheets.) You can bypass this dialog box by using the ⌘-N keyboard shortcut or the Standard toolbar's New button instead of choosing New with the mouse. Doing so tells Word to create a new, untitled document window based on the Normal template. AutoText entries and custom menus and keyboard shortcuts are always stored in this template unless you specify otherwise.

One potential drawback to Word's templates can surface when you have multiple documents open and some are based on templates containing different custom menu, toolbar, and keyboard settings. In this scenario, Word's user interface actually changes as you switch from one document window to another — commands disappear and reappear and keyboard shortcuts and toolbars change. It's a recipe for potential confusion.

Cut Down on Typing with AutoText

Chances are you frequently use certain terms or sections of text — a return address, a closing for a letter, tendon-tangling scientific terms, or contract clauses. Instead of typing them over and over again, store them as AutoText entries in Word 6.

An AutoText entry can contain any amount of text, from a single character to an entire document, including graphics such as a company logo or a scanned version of your signature. You can insert an AutoText entry into a document with a few keystrokes.

QUICK TIPS

How to Speed Up Word 6

Word 6 packs far more power than its predecessor, but it's often dramatically slower — so much so that it doesn't run acceptably on 68030-based Macs, or even on slower 68040 Macs such as the Quadra 610.

Here are five ways to boost Word 6's performance.

- **Hide all toolbars, the status bar, and the ruler.** This dramatically decreases the time required to start Word.
- **Don't let a floating toolbar overlap the document window.** This slows scrolling significantly.
- **When in page-view mode, hide the rulers when you aren't using them.** This speeds up scrolling.
- **Give Word more memory.** If you have 8MB or more of memory, use the Finder's Get Info command to boost Word's allocation to at least 3000K.
- **Fine-tune Word's advanced settings.** You can make a big difference in Word 6's performance by tweaking the way it uses memory. For example, if your documents rarely contain graphics, you can tell Word to allocate less memory to graphics and more to the program's code itself. You do so by modifying an advanced Word setting called BitMapMemory.

Here's how. First, you need to add the Advanced Settings command to Word's Tools menu: choose Customize from the Tools menu, click the Menu tab, and under Categories, select Tools. In the Commands list box, select ToolsAdvancedSettings, and then click the Add button. Finally, click the Close button.

To modify the BitMapMemory value, choose Advanced Settings from the Tools menu. In the Categories box, choose Microsoft Word. In the Option box, type **BitMapMemory**, and then move to the Setting box and type **512**. Click Set and then OK.

Now quit and restart Word. If Word doesn't run faster — or worse, if it runs slower — remove the BitMapMemory setting. To remove it, choose Advanced Settings from the Tools menu, and choose Microsoft Word in the Categories box. In the Options box, click the BitMapMemory setting and then click Delete.

For more details on advanced Word 6 modifications you can make, you'll need a copy of a Microsoft technical note called *Mac Word 6.0 FastTip: Setup & Performance Optimization*. You'll find it in the Macworld Online forums on America Online and eWorld.

Working with AutoText in Word

Word's AutoText feature cuts down on repetitive typing by allowing you to store and recall often-used text. Here's how to work with AutoText entries in Word.

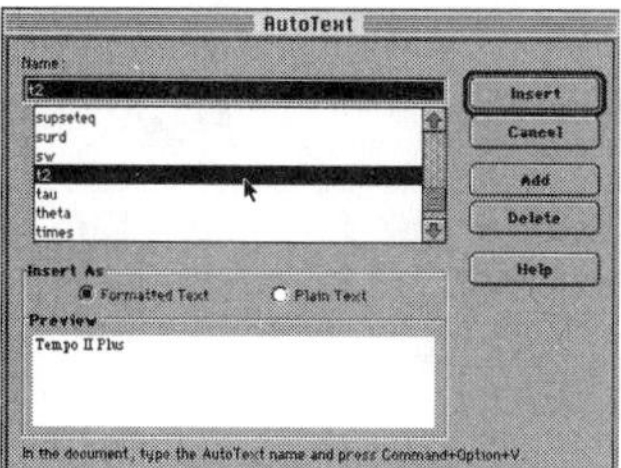

To create an AutoText entry:

1. **Select the text and/or graphics that you want to store.**
2. **Choose AutoText from the Edit menu or click the AutoText button on the Standard toolbar.**
   The AutoText dialog box appears.
3. **In the Name box, type a short name for the entry.**
   If you're creating an entry for your name, for example, you might type your initials.
4. **Optional: Choose the template in which you want to store the AutoText entry.**
   If you omit this step, Word stores the entry in the Normal template.
5. **Click Add or press Return.**

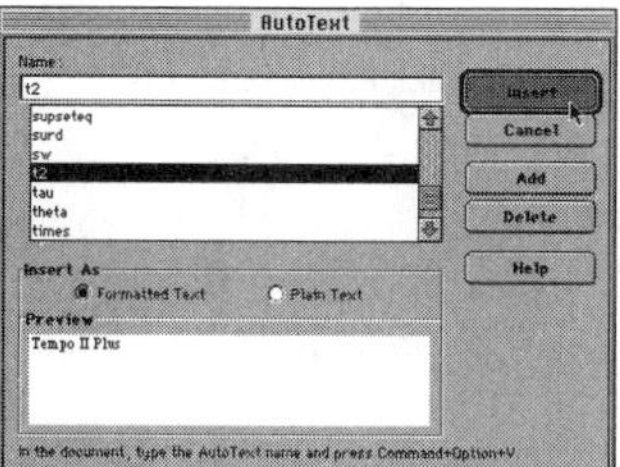

To insert an AutoText entry in a document:

1. **Position the blinking insertion point in the location you want the entry to appear.**
2. **Type the entry's name, and then press ⌘-Option-V.**
   Alternatively, you can choose the AutoText command and double-click the entry's name in the AutoText dialog box. Use this method when you've forgotten the name you gave the entry.

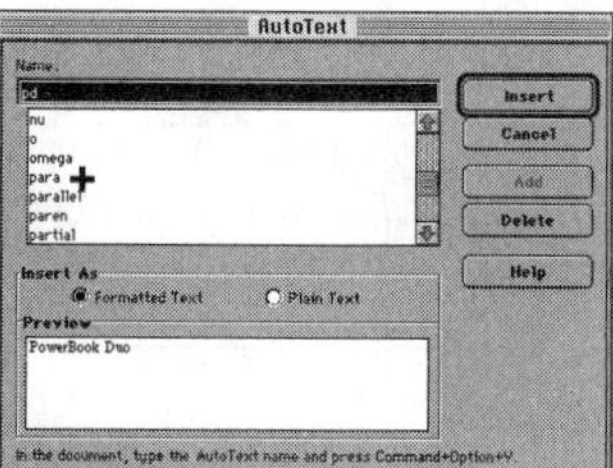

To add an AutoText entry to Word's Edit menu:

1. **Choose AutoText from the Edit menu.**
2. **Press ⌘-Option-equals (=).**
   The mouse pointer turns into a plus sign (+), as shown at left.
3. **Click the entry's name.**
   The menu bar flashes and the entry is added to the Edit menu.

A Microsoft Word Cheat Sheet

No word processor offers more slick keyboard and mouse shortcuts than Microsoft Word. The following tables show just a few of the shortcuts Word provides. (For a complete list, I humbly suggest that you check out another of my IDG books, *Macworld Word 6 Companion, Special Edition.)*

Selection Shortcuts

To Select This	*Do This*
A word	Double-click on the word
A sentence	⌘-click within the sentence
A paragraph	Triple-click within the paragraph or double-click the selection bar adjacent to the paragraph
A single line	Click once in the selection bar adjacent to the line
A carriage return character	Double-click to the right of the last line of the paragraph
The entire document	⌘-click in the selection bar, triple-click in the selection bar, or choose Select All from the Edit menu
A table column	Press Option and then click anywhere within the column
An entire table	Press Option and then double-click anywhere within the table
A table cell	Click within the cell selection bar on the cell's left edge

Table-Editing Shortcuts

To Do This	*Do This*
Delete a selected row or series of rows	Press ⌘-Control-X
Insert a row or series of rows	Press ⌘-Control-V
Move a row	Switch to Outline view and then drag the row
Insert a blank paragraph above a table	Move the insertion point to the beginning of the first cell in the table and then press Enter
Move to the first cell in a row	Press Option-Home
Move to the last cell in a row	Press Option-End
Move to the first cell in a column	Press Option-Page Up
Move to the last cell in a column	Press Option-Page Down

Outlining Shortcuts

To Do This	*Press This*
Promote the heading containing the insertion point	Shift-Option-left arrow
Demote the heading containing the insertion point	Shift-Option-right arrow
Move the paragraph containing the insertion point up	Shift-Option-up arrow
Move the paragraph containing the insertion point down	Shift-Option-down arrow
Expand or collapse an entire outline to a specific level	Control-Shift along with numeral 1–8
Expand the heading containing the insertion point	Plus key (+) on the numeric keypad
Collapse the heading containing the insertion point	Minus key (–) on the numeric keypad
Expand an entire outline	Multiply key (*) on the numeric keypad or Control-Shift-A
Show or hide formatting	Slash key (/) on the numeric keypad
Show all body text or just the first line	Control-Shift-L

Character Formatting Shortcuts

For This Style	*Press ⌘-Shift and*
Bold	B
Italic	I
Underline	U
Word underline	W
Double underline	D
SMALL CAPS	K
ALL CAPS	A
Hidden (appears as dotted underline)	H

Unless you say otherwise, the AutoText entries that you create are stored in the Normal template. Word uses this template for all documents you create (again, unless you specify otherwise). When you want an AutoText entry to be available in all new documents, be sure to store it in the Normal template. On the other hand, if you want certain AutoText entries to be available only when you choose a particular template in the New dialog box, store those entries in the appropriate template. For example, if you create an AutoText entry that types your name, you may want to store it in the Normal template, because you'll probably use it often. On the other hand, if you create an AutoText entry that types a complex technical term that you use in reports, you should store the entry in the template that you use for reports.

The "Working with AutoText in Word" Step-by-Step box shows you how to use Word's AutoText features. WordPerfect lacks these features, but you can obtain the same keystroke-saving benefits by creating a macro — a series of keystrokes and menu choices that you record and save for later playback. See the section about macros later in this chapter.

Automate Formatting with Styles

If you frequently switch between text formats within a document, you should be using styles. A *style* is a set of text formats — font, size, type style, line spacing, and so on — that you can apply in one fell swoop. For example, suppose you always format reports to have double-spaced 14-point Helvetica Bold headings and single-spaced 10-point Times body text. If you define a style for headings and body text, you can format these elements with a single mouse click or keystroke — no traveling from menu to menu and threading through dialog boxes.

Besides saving time, styles help ensure consistent formatting. They can be especially valuable for projects involving numerous writers. You can create a stationery document containing the styles used in a project and then give each writer a copy.

Fast formatting — and reformatting

Styles have additional advantages. If you change a style's description — perhaps to switch from 10-point Times body text to 12-point Palatino — the program reformats all text formatted under that style. This capability lets you experiment with different formatting options without doing a lot of manual reformatting. Word and WordPerfect styles are also supported by publishing programs such as Adobe PageMaker and QuarkXPress. You can import a Word or WordPerfect document into either of these programs and retain the original style definitions and formatting.

Linking styles

Both Word and WordPerfect let you link one style to another so that the program automatically switches from one style to the next when you press Return (or Enter in WordPerfect). For example, if you link your heading style to the body text style, the program automatically switches to body text style after you type a heading. Both programs also let you base one style on another. If, for example, you create two styles that use the same line-spacing settings but different fonts, you can base the second style on the first. If you want to change line-spacing settings later on, you need alter only the first style.

The next chapter is devoted to the wonderful world of styles and contains step-by-step instructions for creating and working with styles in Word, WordPerfect, and WriteNow.

Tailoring Keyboard Shortcuts and Menus

You can customize your word processor with keyboard shortcuts and menus. Word lets you change its keyboard shortcuts and even reorganize commands within its menus. If you never use the commands related to footnoting and indexing, for example, you can remove them to tidy up your menus.

Better still, you can add commands that correspond to options within Word's dialog boxes. For example, Word's Font dialog box is the gateway to most character-formatting operations. But when you're doing serious formatting, choosing Character over and over again gets old quickly. The solution: add the desired fonts to Word's menus, where you can choose them directly.

More Word customizing tips

You can also use the Customize dialog box to add or remove commands to or from Word's other menus and save your customization settings (see Figure 3-5 "Command Performance").

It's important to know that your custom menus and keyboard shortcuts are stored in a template document — specifically, in the Normal template, unless you choose a different template by using the Customize dialog box's Save Changes In pop-up menu. This differs from previous Word versions, where customized settings were stored in a special settings file.

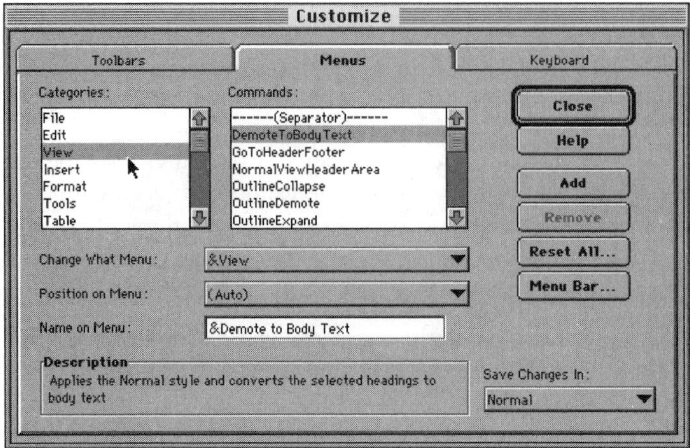

Figure 3-5: Command Performance Word's Customize dialog box is the gateway to modifying the program's menus to your own specifications.

The fact that menu and keyboard shortcuts are stored in templates has some important ramifications. For one thing, you can completely change Word's user interface — from its keyboard shortcuts to the contents of its menus — simply by applying a different template after choosing the New command. Indeed, if you have two documents open and each is based on a different template, Word's interface changes as you switch between the two documents — menu commands may disappear and reappear, and keyboard shortcuts may change. This can be confusing to newcomers, but it allows power users to create a fast, responsive, custom-tailored word processor.

If you do a lot of customizing, your templates represent a lot of work. Back them up to avoid having to reconfigure Word if the worst happens.

Customizing WordPerfect

Like Word, WordPerfect lets you change and create keyboard shortcuts for menus and the style sheets and macros you create. Unlike Word, WordPerfect lets you reorganize the positions of keyboard characters themselves. For example, if you use the trademark symbol (™) frequently, you may want to assign it to the Option-T key sequence instead of its usual (and more forgettable) Option-2 sequence.

Power Editing in Microsoft Word

Microsoft Word packs several shortcuts that let you move or copy text and graphics without replacing the contents of the Clipboard. As this Quick Tips box describes, one shortcut relies on the mouse and the other depends on the keyboard.

Drag-and-drop editing

Word's drag-and-drop editing feature lets you move text or graphics by simply dragging them to the desired location. To activate drag-and-drop editing, choose Options from the Tools menu, click the Edit tab, and then check the Drag-and-Drop Text Editing box.

To drag text elsewhere within a document, simply select the text and then point to it. The mouse pointer turns into a left-pointing arrow. Press and hold down the mouse button and then drag. As you drag, you see a dotted vertical bar that follows the mouse pointer. Drag the bar until it's located where you want the text to appear, release the mouse button, and Word moves the text to that location. That's all there is to it. To make a copy of the text instead of moving the original, press the Option key before beginning the drag-and-drop.

By the way, it's worth noting that Word 6 — unlike Word 5 — even lets you drag and drop text from one document window to another. When the drag-and-drop mouse pointer moves into the other document window, that window becomes active.

This degree of drag-and-drop editing is becoming more and more common — PageMaker and QuarkXPress also let you drag and drop between documents. Unfortunately, none of these programs lets you drag and drop between *programs*: for example, you can drag text from one Word 6 document to another Word 6 document, but you can't drag text from a Word 6 document to a PageMaker document. This kind of drag-and-drop editing is coming to the Macintosh, but it isn't here yet (see Chapter 27).

Moving text and graphics with the spike

One drawback of the Mac's Clipboard is that it can hold only one item at a time — when you copy or cut an item to the Clipboard, the Clipboard's previous contents vanish. This flaw usually hits home when you copy something and realize that the Clipboard contained some important text that you hadn't yet pasted. (When this unfortunate event occurs, choose Undo before doing anything else.)

Word 6 provides a special editing feature that doesn't have the Clipboard's one-item-at-a-time limitation. The feature is called the *spike.* If that seems like a bizarre name for an editing feature, think about those tall, stiff needles that office workers use to impale phone messages and other scraps of paper (you also see them alongside cash registers in some restaurants). The spike — whether in an office or in Word 6 — *accumulates* items. In Word 6, when you add an item to the spike, the item joins whatever text and graphics were already on it. You can then insert the contents of the spike elsewhere in the document or in a different document.

To move text or graphics to the spike, select it and press ⌘-F3 (that's the F3 function key on an extended keyboard). Next, move the insertion point to the location at which you want the spike's contents to appear (or select a range of text to be replaced). Finally, press ⌘-Shift-F3.

The ⌘-Shift-F3 sequence inserts the spike's contents *and* empties the spike. If you want to retain the spike's contents — perhaps to insert them in yet another document — press ⌘-Option-V instead.

You can also insert the contents of the spike by using the AutoText tool on the Standard toolbar: in your document, type **spike** and then click the AutoText tool. And you can view the contents of the spike by choosing AutoText from the Edit menu and selecting Spike from the list of AutoText names.

Customizing Word and WordPerfect

File...
Frame
Picture...
Object...
Database...

To remove a command from Word's menus:

1. **Press ⌘-Option-hyphen (the key to the right of the zero key).**
   The mouse pointer turns into a bold minus sign (–).
2. **Choose the command you want to remove.**
   The menu bar flashes and the command is removed. You can restore the command by using the Customize dialog box.

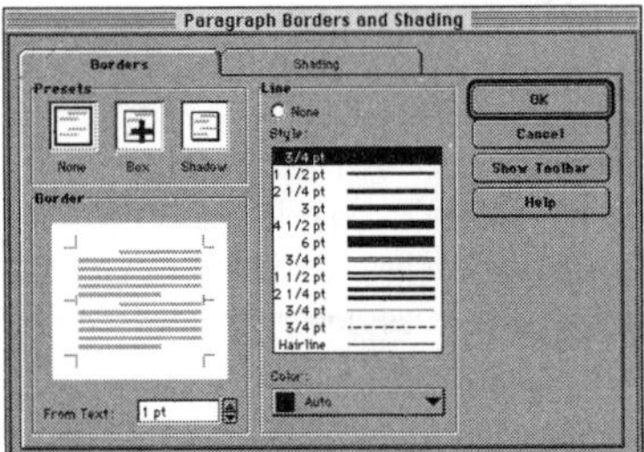

To add a Word dialog box option to a menu:

1. **Open the dialog box containing the option you want to add and then press ⌘-Option-equals (=, to the left of the Delete key).**
   The pointer turns into a bold plus sign (+).
2. **Click the desired dialog box option.**
   If the pointer remains a bold plus sign, the option you clicked lacks a corresponding command. To restore the normal pointer, press ⌘-period (.) or the Esc key.

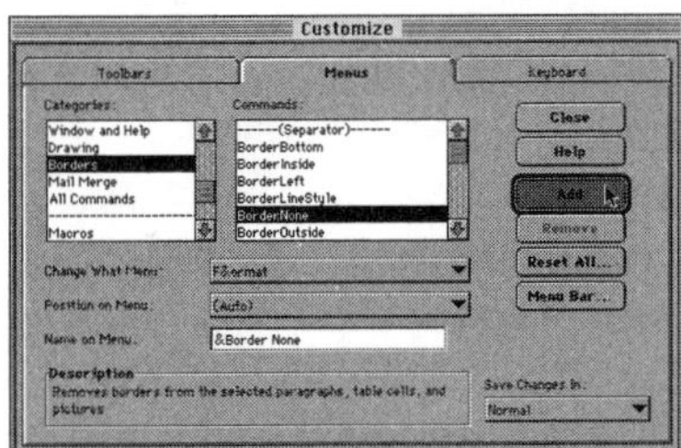

To add commands to Word's menus:

1. **Choose Customize from the Tools menu.**
   The Customize dialog box appears.
2. **Select the Menus tab.**
   The Menus options appear (shown at left).
3. **In the Categories box, select the category containing the name of the command or item you want to add to a menu.**
   For example, if you want to add border-related commands to a menu, select the Borders item in the Categories box.
4. **In the Commands box, select the item that you want to add to a menu.**
   For example, if you want to add a command to remove borders, choose the BorderNone item in the Commands box.
5. **Optional: Using the Change What Menu pop-up menu, specify the menu to which you want to add the new command.**
   If you omit this step, the new command is added to the menu Word deems most appropriate.

6. **Optional: Using the Position pop-up menu, specify the location within the menu for the new command.**
   If you omit this step, Word uses the (Auto) option, which groups similar menu items together.
7. **Click the Add button.**

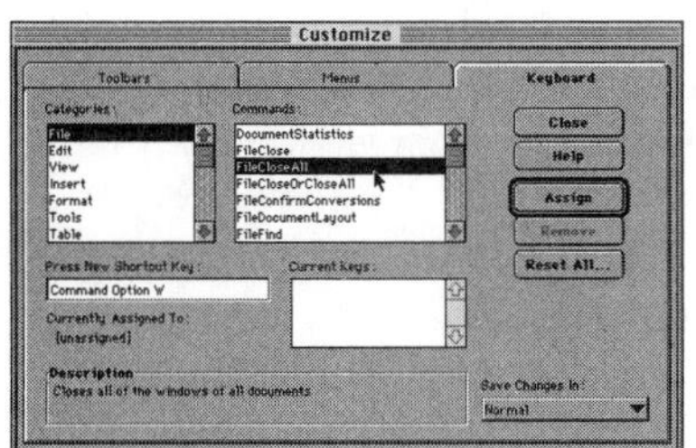

To create or change a command's keyboard shortcut in Word:

1. **Choose Customize from the Tools menu.**
   The Customize dialog box appears.
2. **Select the Keyboard tab.**
   The Keyboard options appear (shown at left).
3. **Use the Categories and Commands boxes to locate the command for which you want to change or create a keyboard shortcut.**
   For example, if you want to add a shortcut to the Close All command, click File in the Categories box and then locate the Close All command in the Commands box.
4. **Type the key sequence you want to use.**
   If the sequence is already assigned to a different command, that command's name appears in the dialog box.
5. **Click the Assign button.**

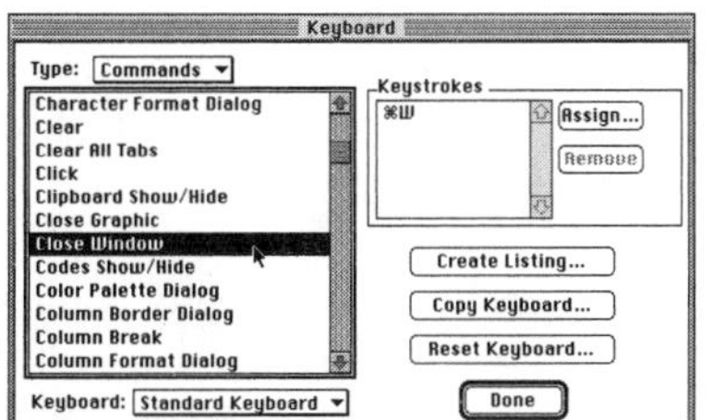

To customize WordPerfect's keyboard:

1. **Choose Preferences from the Edit menu.**
   The Preferences dialog box appears.
2. **Click the Keyboard option.**
   The Keyboard dialog box (left) appears.
3. **From the Type pop-up menu, choose the type of modification you want to make.**
   For example, choose Characters to change a keyboard character, Commands to assign or remove a keyboard shortcut, or Styles to assign a shortcut to a style.
4. **Select a character, menu command, style, or macro name, and use the Assign or Remove buttons to add or remove a keyboard shortcut.**
   WordPerfect keyboard settings are stored in a *keyboard template.* You can create as many keyboard templates as you like and switch between them by using the Librarian.

Macros: Word Processing on Autopilot

If you use Word 6 or WordPerfect and frequently perform the same sequence of steps, consider recording those steps in a macro for later playback. Macros can perform simple jobs, such as inserting often-used text or automatically changing all double hyphens (- -) to typesetters' em dashes (—). But a macro can also perform a sequence of events — opening a document, searching for some text and replacing it with something else, saving the document, and then printing it. You can even create macros that display dialog boxes and then make decisions based on your response. For example, you can create a form letter whose contents vary depending on whether a client's account is paid up or past due.

Two paths to macro mania

You can create macros by pecking out statement after statement of macro-language code — much like programmers do when they're writing programs. But that's the hard way. The easy way is to use your program's macro recorder to create macros automatically.

A macro recorder essentially watches over your shoulder and records what you're doing: the command you're choosing, the dialog box options you're selecting, and even the text you're typing. You create a macro by simply switching into record mode, performing the tasks you want to automate, and then turning off record mode. You can then play back the steps you recorded by playing back the macro.

It's common to combine the manual and automatic macro-creation techniques: start by recording a series of tasks, and then use your word processor's macro editor to fine-tune the result.

Recording a macro in Microsoft Word 6

Word 6 provides a powerful macro language called WordBASIC. If you're familiar with the BASIC programming language, many aspects of WordBASIC should feel familiar. If you don't know BASIC, don't worry: thanks to Word's macro recorder, you can go a long way with Word macros without having to understand how they work.

To record a macro in Word, double-click the REC indicator in Word's status bar (you can also choose Macro from the Tools menu and then click Record in the Macro dialog box). In the Record Macro dialog box that appears, type a name for the macro and click OK. The Macro Record toolbar appears.

Now perform the tasks you want to automate. If you want to perform some actions without recording them, click the Pause button in the Macro Record toolbar. When you're done recording, double-click REC again or click the Stop button in the Macro Record toolbar.

You can assign a recorded macro to a menu, toolbar, or keyboard shortcut. To do so, use the appropriate buttons in the Record Macro dialog box. You can also assign a macro to a toolbar, keyboard shortcut, or menu after the fact in the Customize dialog box.

Macros are stored in the Normal document template unless you specify otherwise. (To store a macro in a different template, use the Make Macro Available To pop-up menu in the Record Macro dialog box.) You can also use the Organizer dialog box to copy a macro to another template.

Macros created in Word 6 are also compatible with Microsoft Word for Windows and vice versa. You can move macros between Macs and Windows PCs.

Recording a macro in WordPerfect

To record a macro in WordPerfect, choose Record from the Macro menu. Type a name for the macro and then click New. Next, perform the steps you want to record. If you need to scroll while recording, use the keyboard's scrolling keys, not the mouse. When you finish recording, choose Stop Recording from the Macro menu. (You can also pause recording to perform an activity that you don't want to record by choosing Pause from the Macro menu's Options submenu; choose Resume to continue recording.) When asked to save changes, click Yes.

Unless you say otherwise, WordPerfect stores macros in your private library; this file, located in your System Folder, can hold macros, styles, keyboard templates, and more. Items in the private library are available in any open document. If you want a macro (or a style, keyboard template, or other item) to be available only when a certain document is open, save it in that document.

Spend Time Now to Save Time Later

Customizing a word processor takes some time at first but pays off in the long run. As you create dictionaries, styles, and stationery, tweak menus and keyboard shortcuts, and write macros, you tailor your program to your writing habits. You can create a word processor that feels just right.

Fine-Tuning Memory and Disk Space

Free memory and disk space are often in short supply on a PowerBook. If you're willing to forgo some performance and features, you can dramatically reduce your program's appetite for kilobytes.

To reduce any program's memory requirements, select its icon at the Finder and choose Get Info from the File menu. In the Get Info window, specify how much memory you want to give the program by typing the value in the Current Size box. (In system versions prior to 7.0, this box reads Application Memory Size. In System 7.1 and later versions, it reads Preferred Size.) I'll provide some memory-size guidelines shortly. For more details about tweaking program memory sizes, see Chapter 22.

Word 6 runs on as little as 3MB of memory, although performance suffers. You may also encounter low memory messages during a lengthy search-and-replace operation or when compiling an index or table of contents. As for saving disk space, Word 6's modular design makes pruning the program easy. Use Word's Setup program to remove modules and converters you don't want. The grammar checker is one candidate for the Trash; it and its accompanying file use nearly a megabyte of disk space.

WordPerfect 3 runs on as little as 800K of memory, but like Word, it slows down. To save disk space, delete file converters you don't need by dragging them out of the Conversions folder. To access the Conversions folder, open the System Folder, the Preferences folder, and then the WordPerfect folder.

Reducing disk space requirements means doing without. Remove files corresponding to features you don't use, such as sample documents, tutorials, and unneeded converters that enable your program to swap documents with other programs.

CHAPTER 3 CONCEPTS AND TERMS

- You can save time and cut down on repetitive typing and formatting by mastering the customizing options your word processor provides.
- Adding words to a custom dictionary tailors your word processor's spelling checker to the type of writing you do.
- If you create a certain type of document often, consider creating a stationery document that reflects its formatting and boilerplate text.
- Style sheets let you automate and easily change complex formatting.
- One way to fine-tune a word processor for efficiency is to customize its keyboard shortcuts — adding shortcuts to the commands you use most and changing any shortcuts you have trouble remembering.

converters
Special files that enable a program to swap documents with other programs.

glossary
A word processor feature that lets you store and recall often-used text and/or graphics with a single keystroke. In Word 5, glossary entries are saved in a special document called a glossary file. In Word 6, the glossary feature is renamed AutoText.

keyboard template
A WordPerfect settings document that describes which key sequences summon which characters and commands.

private library
A special WordPerfect document, located in your System Folder, that stores macros, styles, keyboard templates, and more. Items in the private library are available in any open document.

revision tracking
A word processor feature that highlights or otherwise marks text that has changed since the preceding revision of a document. Most revision tracking features place vertical change bars in the margin adjacent to changed text.

settings file
In Microsoft Word 5, a special document that stores your Word preferences, including customized menus and key sequences. In Word 6, settings files are replaced with templates (see *template*).

spike
In Microsoft Word 6, an editing feature that lets you accumulate text and graphics and then insert them in one fell swoop in the same or a different document.

stationery
A special type of document that holds boilerplate text, graphics, and formatting. If you routinely create a certain type of document, save it as stationery to cut down repetitive formatting.

template
In Microsoft Word 6, a type of document that holds boilerplate text and formatting information, keyboard shortcuts, custom menu settings, AutoText entries, and macros.

user dictionary
Sometimes called a *custom dictionary,* a file that supplements a program's built-in spelling checker dictionary.

watermark
Text or graphics that appear beneath the copy on a page. Watermarks are often used to emblazon a document with a message such as Confidential or Final notice.

CHAPTER FOUR

Fast Formatting with Style Sheets

- Using style sheets to automate formatting tasks
- Understanding the consistency, speed, and formatting ease that style sheets provide
- How to create and work with styles in Word, WordPerfect, and WriteNow

Writing is only part of what you do with a word processor. The other part is formatting — choosing fonts, adjusting margins, changing line spacing, and setting tabs. It's the manual labor that can make you feel more like a typesetter than a writer.

What's frustrating about formatting is that so much of it is repetitive: 12-point Helvetica headings, 10-point Times body text, and back again. Maybe you also put an extra line space above the headings, or you center the headings over justified body text. Switching between these formats as you create a document means trip after trip to the menu bar and through the same old dialog boxes.

Or does it? Four of today's most popular word processors — Microsoft Word, WordPerfect, Claris's MacWrite Pro, and Softkey International's WriteNow — provide features that let you automate repetitive formatting chores by creating *style sheets*, or *styles* for short.

If you read the preceding chapter, you know that a style is a collection of formatting settings — font, point size, line spacing, tabs, margins, borders, and more — stored under a single name, such as "Heading" or "Body text." If you create a style for centered 12-point bold Helvetica headings, you can turn any text into a heading with one mouse click or keystroke. Styles let you leap tall formatting tasks in a single bound.

Besides enabling you to quickly apply complex formats, styles make reformatting easier. If you decide that your headings look better in 14-point Bookman italic, just change the description of the heading style, and all headings are instantly changed — no need to scroll through the document and manually change each one. You can even tell your word processor to switch from one style to another when you end a paragraph.

All this automation has another benefit. Styles help ensure that a long document has a consistent appearance, even if you redesign it midstream.

As with any word processor customizing task, defining styles for a document is one of those jobs in which some up-front work simplifies life in the long run. So why do so many people ignore their program's style features? One reason may be the initial setup time — even a minute of advance planning is too much for some folks. But another reason may be that styles can seem complicated. They aren't, especially when you start with the basics.

The Elements of Styles

One key to understanding how styles work is to remember the two basic kinds of formatting you can perform in any word processor — character-level formatting and paragraph-level formatting. When you change an individual word from bold to italic, for example, you're formatting at the character level. When you change indents, tabs, or line spacing, you're formatting at the paragraph level. And remember, to a word processor, a paragraph is any piece of text — even a single letter — that is surrounded by carriage returns (see Figure 4-1 "Paragraphs Illustrated").

Try Getting Stylish

If you'd like to get some hands-on experience with style sheets in several popular programs, you can. The Software and Demos folder of the *Macworld Complete Mac Interactive CD* contains demonstration versions of the following programs:

- ❖ WordPerfect 3.0a: This powerhouse program runs in native mode on Power Macs.
- ❖ Claris MacWrite Pro: This approachable program provides character-level and paragraph-level styles.
- ❖ ClarisWorks: As mentioned in this chapter, ClarisWorks lacks a style sheet feature, but you can use macros to simulate style sheets. Compare this approach with real style sheets.
- ❖ Aldus PageMaker: This leading publishing package provides its own style sheet features, and it can import styles created in word processors.

```
start·with·the·basics.¶
¶
The·Elements·of·Styles¶
♦    One·key·to·understanding·how·styles·work·is·to·remember·
the·two·basic·kinds·of·formatting·you·can·perform·in·any·word·
processor.¶
```

Figure 4-1: Paragraphs Illustrated To a word processor, any text surrounded by carriage returns (generated by pressing Return) is a paragraph. There are four paragraphs here.

The basic style features in Microsoft Word, WordPerfect, MacWrite Pro, and WriteNow operate on the paragraph level. When you define a style in these programs, the style stores not only the desired font and type size, but also the line spacing, indents, tabs, and other formatting attributes that can apply to paragraphs. WriteNow, Claris MacWrite Pro, and Microsoft Word 6 also provide character-level styles that store only font, size, and type-style information. I'll spotlight some advantages of character-level styles later.

The easiest way to create a style in these three programs is to format a paragraph as desired — including any special margin indents, tabs, or line spacing settings — and then define a style that holds the formatting (see Figure 4-2 "Creating a Style"). Be sure to select the text whose formatting you want to store. Then consult the appropriate Step-by-Step box in this chapter for further information about your specific program.

After you define a style, you can apply it to existing text or to new text that you type. In these four programs, applying a style is no different than choosing a font or other formatting command. If you're reformatting existing text, select the text first; if you're typing new text, place the insertion point where you want the text to appear and then apply the style.

For faster formatting, create a keyboard shortcut for a style or add it to a menu. The Step-by-Step boxes that cover working with styles show you how.

Simulating Styles in Other Programs

If you use a program that doesn't provide style-sheet features — Microsoft Works, ClarisWorks, or MacWrite II, for example — you can simulate styles by using a keyboard customizing program such as CE Software's QuicKeys. With Microsoft Works and ClarisWorks, you can create macros to automate formatting. As Chapter 6 shows, the Microsoft Excel spreadsheet program has some slick style features of its own that let you automate the formatting and alignment of spreadsheet cells.

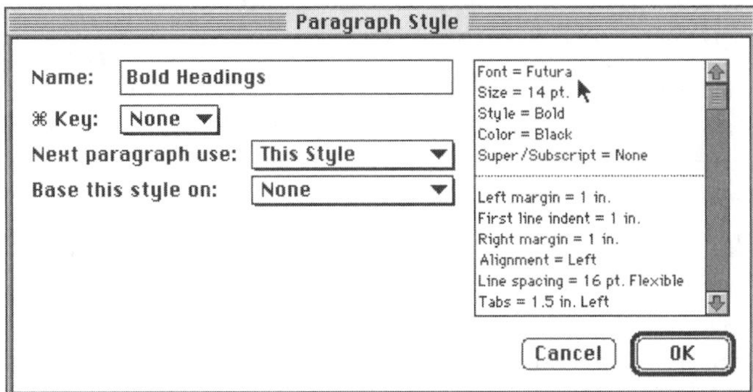

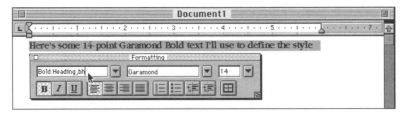

Figure 4-2: Creating a Style Click in the Word ruler's Style box (top), and then type a name for the style. WordPerfect's New Style dialog box (middle) lets you add an optional description to remind you of the style's purpose or revision history. WriteNow's Paragraph Style dialog box (bottom) lists the formatting attributes that make up the new style.

Advanced Style Techniques

Normally, when you press Return to begin a new paragraph, your word processor applies the current style to the new paragraph. But what if you frequently switch formatting from one paragraph to the next? In an instruction manual, you may alternate between bold step-by-step instructions to plain-text explanations of each step (see Figure 4-3 "Next Style"). In a newsletter or book, you may switch from headings in one font to body text in another.

Next styles: linking one style to another

You can automatically switch to a different style when you end a paragraph by defining a *next style* (called a *linked style* in WordPerfect). This chapter's Step-by-Step boxes show you how to define a next style for a style that you've already created, although all four programs let you specify a next style as you create a new style.

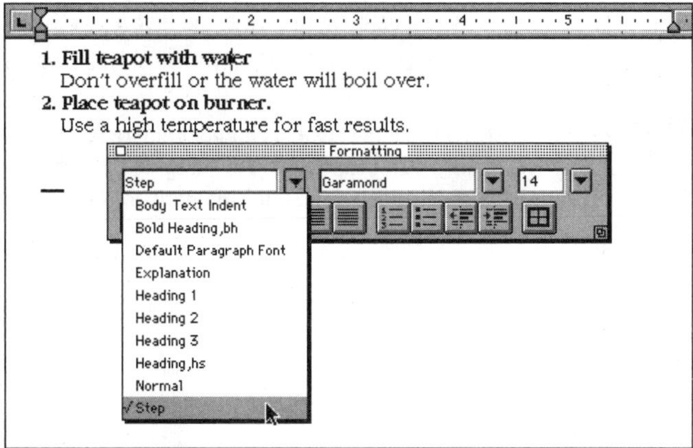

Figure 4-3: Next Style These instructions use two styles: Step and Explanation. Each step is linked to the other with the next style option; pressing Return after typing a step automatically switches to the Explanation style.

In either case, before defining a next style, first create the style that you want to switch to. You can't specify a next style if the first style doesn't yet exist.

Working with Styles in Word

Microsoft Word 6 introduces some potent new style-related features, including an AutoFormat command that applies styles automatically based on your document's content. Word 6 also provides a style gallery that lets you browse the predefined styles in the templates that accompany the program you create.

Word 6's AutoFormat features are easy to use: simply choose the AutoFormat command and stand back. But Word's classic style features can still cause some head-scratching. Spare your scalp and read the instructions in this box to learn how to create and work with styles in Word 6.

(continued on the next page)

(continued from previous page)

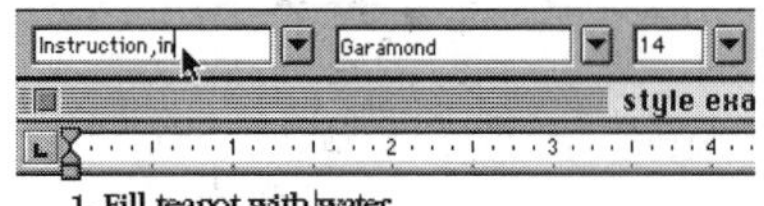

To define a style:

1. **Format some text as desired.**
2. **Display the Formatting toolbar.**
3. **With the blinking insertion point in the text, click once within the Formatting toolbar's Style pop-up menu.**
4. **Type a name for the style and then press Return.**

   To create an alias for the style name, type a comma.

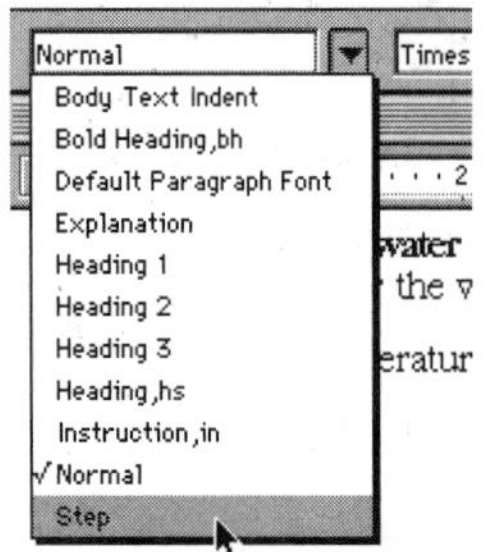

1. **To apply the style to another paragraph, place the insertion point within the paragraph and then choose the style's name from the Formatting toolbar's Style pop-up menu.**

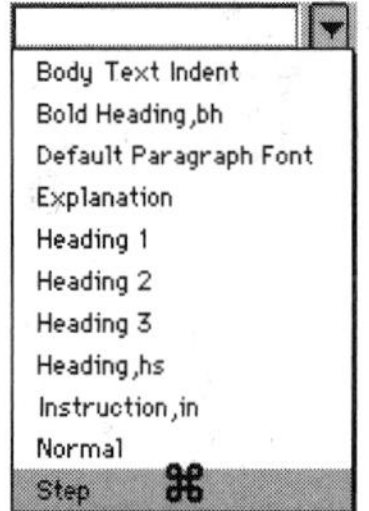

To create a keyboard shortcut for a style:

1. **Be sure that the Formatting toolbar is visible.**
2. **Press ⌘-Option-plus (+). (That's the plus on the number keypad, not the one next to the Delete key.)**

   The mouse pointer turns into a ⌘ symbol.
3. **Choose the desired style from the Formatting toolbar's Style pop-up menu.**

   The Keyboard portion of the Customize dialog box appears.
4. **Type the keystroke by using the ⌘ key or any other desired modifier keys (Control, Option, Shift).**

   If the keystroke you typed is already assigned to a different command, Word displays that command's name in the Currently Assigned To area. Think of a different keystroke if you don't want to reassign the keystroke sequence.
5. **Click the Assign button.**

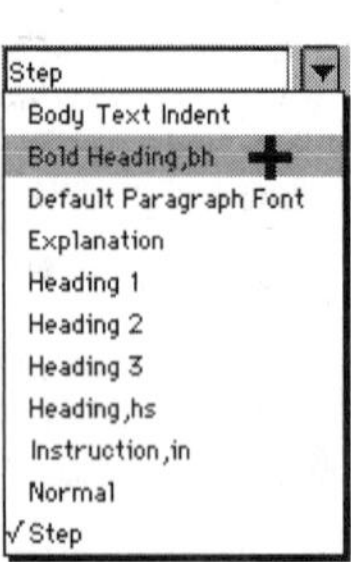

To add a style to Word's menus:

1. **Press ⌘-Option-plus (+) (use the plus key next to the Delete key).**
2. **Choose the desired style from the Formatting toolbar's Style pop-up menu.**

   Word adds the style's name to the Format menu. You can use the Menus portion of the Customize dialog box to move the style to a different menu if you like.

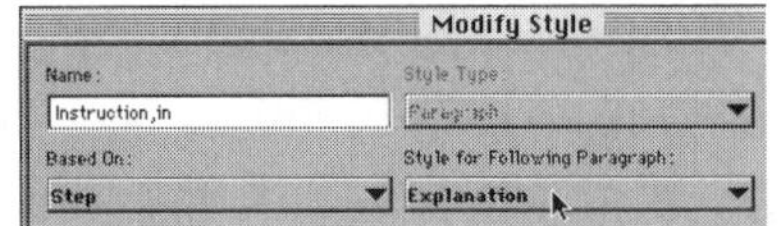

To define a next style:

1. **Choose Style from the Format menu.**
2. **Select the style for which you want to define a next style.**
3. **Click the Modify button.**
4. **Use the Style for Following Paragraph pop-up menu to choose the style to which you want to switch.**
5. **Click OK or press Return.**

   If you want to override the next style, press ⌘-Return to start a new paragraph. When you press ⌘-Return, Word applies the current style to the new paragraph instead of switching to the next style.

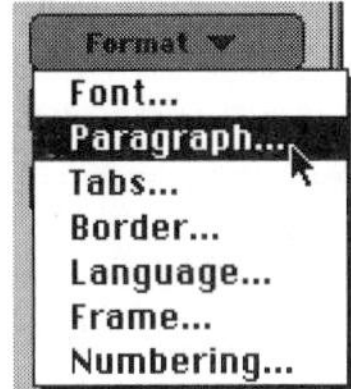

To redefine the Normal style:

1. **Choose Style from the Format menu.**
2. **Select the Normal style from the Styles list box.**

   If you don't see the Normal style, be sure that the All Styles option is chosen in the List pop-up menu.
3. **Click Modify.**
4. **Use the options in the Format button to specify the desired formatting for the Normal style.**
5. **Optional: If you want Normal style to be used in all new, untitled documents you create by using the active template, check the Add to Template box.**

   If you don't perform this step, the changes you make to the Normal style apply to the currently active document only.

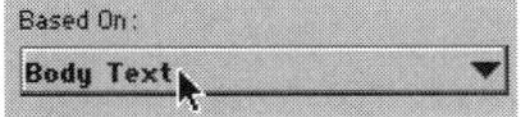

To change the style upon which another style is based:

1. **Choose Style and then select the style you want to change.**
2. **Click the Modify button.**
3. **Choose the desired base style from the Based On pop-up menu, and then click OK.**

   In Word, all styles are based on the Normal style unless you specify otherwise.

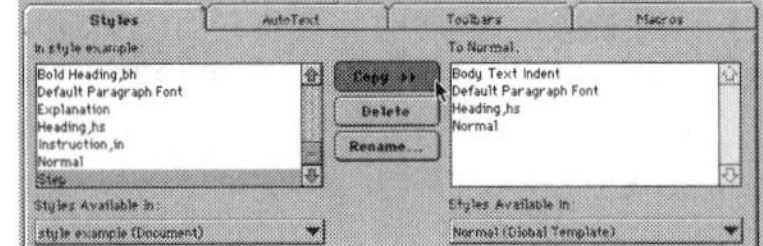

To make a style available to all new, untitled documents created with the Normal template:

1. **Choose Style from the Format menu.**
2. **Click the Organizer button.**
3. **In the left-hand list box, select the style you want to copy to the Normal template.**
4. **Make sure that the heading above the right-hand list box reads `To Normal`, and then click the Copy button.**
5. **Click the Close button.**

Basing one style on another

When defining styles, you can base numerous styles on one base style that reflects the bulk of the formatting information. A well-designed document may have many different elements — headings, body text, sidebars, tables — but most elements share some common formatting. You may, for example, use Palatino Bold for headings and plain Palatino for body text, headers, and footers. If you need to do a major redesign — maybe the boss wants the Futura font family instead of Palatino — you can simply change the base style.

All four programs — Word, WordPerfect, WriteNow, and MacWrite Pro — provide a base style that they apply to text unless you specify a different style. In Word and WordPerfect, this base style is called *Normal.* In WriteNow, it's called *Body Style.* In MacWrite Pro, it's called *Default.* All four programs also provide predefined styles for headers, footers, footnotes, and other parts of a document. In Word, MacWrite Pro, and WriteNow, these predefined styles are based on the Normal, Default, or Body Style styles, respectively. By modifying these base styles, you can change the appearance of headers, footers, and other elements, too.

You don't have to base a style on the Normal or Body Style style — you can base a style on a custom style that you create. You can create a base style named *Newsletter* and then create your own header, footer, and caption styles that are based on the Newsletter style.

The Step-by-Step boxes in this chapter show you how to work with base styles and next styles.

Working with Styles in WordPerfect

In this Step-by-Step box, you'll find instructions for creating and managing styles in WordPerfect.

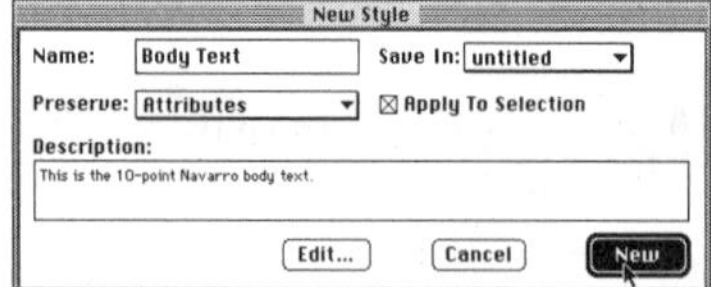

To create a style:

1. **Format some text as desired.**
2. **Click the control bar's Styles button to display the Styles bar.**
3. **With the insertion point within the text, click the Styles bar's New button.**
   The New Style dialog box appears. The Preserve pop-up menu lets you choose to store only character formatting (the preset Attributes option), only ruler settings (the Formatting option), or both.

4. **Type a name for the style and then click New.**
   You can also type an optional description to remind you of the style's purpose.

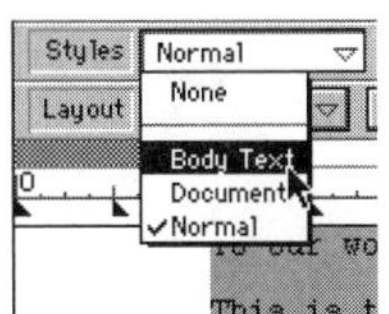

To apply the style to another paragraph:

1. **Place the insertion point within the paragraph whose formatting you want to change.**
2. **Choose the style's name from the Styles bar's Styles pop-up menu.**

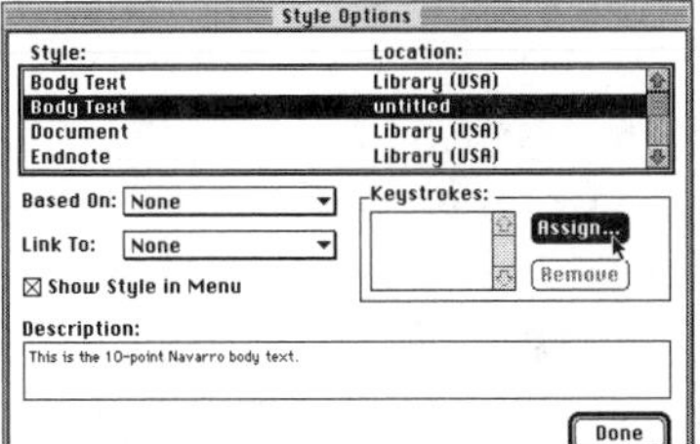

To create a keyboard shortcut for a style:

1. **Click the Options button in the Styles bar.**
2. **Select the desired style.**
3. **In the Keystrokes area, click the Assign button and then type the keystroke.**
   If you don't want the style to appear in the Styles submenu, uncheck the Show Style in Menu box.
4. **When you've finished defining shortcuts, click Done.**

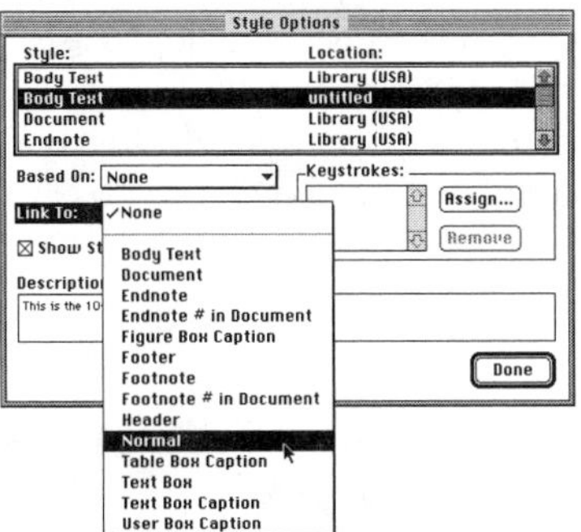

To define a next style (a linked style):

1. **Click the Options button in the Styles bar.**
2. **Select the style for which you want to define a next style.**
3. **Choose the next style from the Link To pop-up menu, and then click Done.**
   Unlike Word and WriteNow, WordPerfect doesn't switch to the next style when you press Return. To call up the next style, end a paragraph by pressing Enter instead.

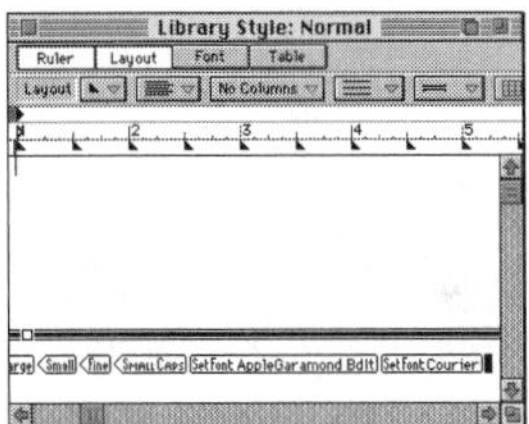

To redefine the Normal style:

1. **Click the Edit button in the Styles bar.**
2. **Double-click the Normal style.**
3. **Specify the desired formatting and then close the Normal style window.**
   If you want to base the header, footer, footnote, and other element styles on the Normal style, edit each style and choose Normal from the Based On pop-up menu.

(continued on the next page)

(continued from previous page)

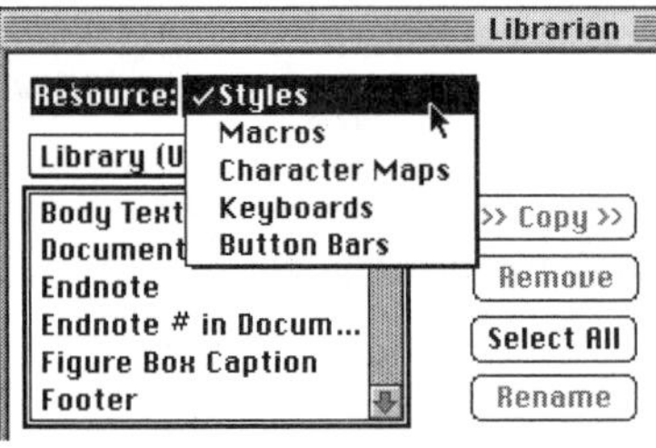

To make a style available to all documents:

1. **Choose Preferences from the Edit menu and then click the Librarian icon.**
2. **Choose Styles from the Resource pop-up menu.**
3. **Select the style you want to copy, and then click Copy.**
4. **Click Done or press Return.**

Redefining a Style

One advantage of styles is that you can use them to redesign a document in one fell swoop. This chapter's Step-by-Step boxes show you how to redefine the Normal or Body Text styles. You can use these same steps to redefine a style that you've created.

You can also use these steps to redefine a program's built-in styles, such as its header, footer, or footnote style. In WriteNow and WordPerfect, these styles automatically appear in the style-editing dialog box. In Word, however, they don't automatically appear. To display Word's *standard styles,* choose the All Styles option from the List pop-up menu in the Style dialog box. When you do, you see a list of over 50 predefined styles. Some control the appearance of headings created in Word's outline view; others govern the formatting of index and table of contents entries. All of these standard styles are based on the Normal style.

Working with Styles in WriteNow

The instructions in this box show how to create and work with styles in WriteNow.

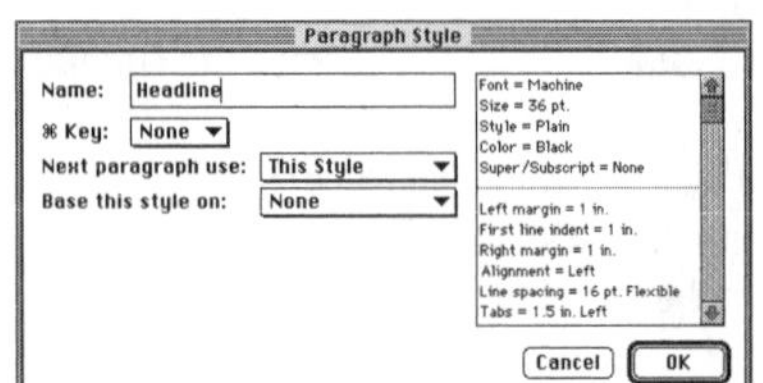

To create a style:

1. **Format some text as desired and then select it.**
2. **Choose New from the Custom menu's Paragraph Style submenu.**

   You can also choose New Paragraph Style from the Paragraph Style pop-up menu at the bottom of WriteNow's document window. This pop-up menu doesn't appear unless you've already defined at least one style for the document.
3. **Type a name for the new style and click OK.**

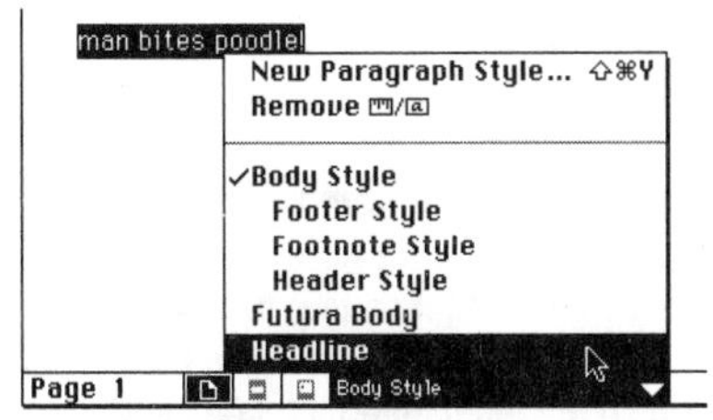

To apply a style:

1. **If you're reformatting existing text, select the text to which you want to apply the style.**
2. **Choose the desired style from the Paragraph Style pop-up menu.**

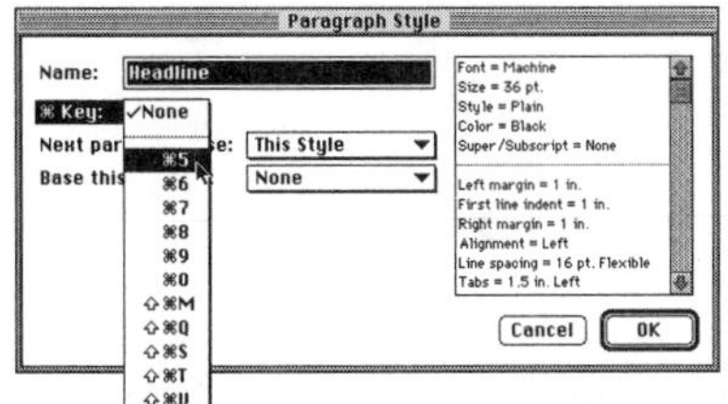

To define a keyboard shortcut for a style:

1. **Choose Edit/Delete Style from the Custom menu, and then double-click the desired style.**
2. **Choose the desired keystroke from the ⌘-key pop-up menu.**
   WriteNow doesn't let you make up your own keystroke sequence as a style shortcut, but instead provides 11 predefined ⌘-key sequences from which to choose.
3. **Click OK.**

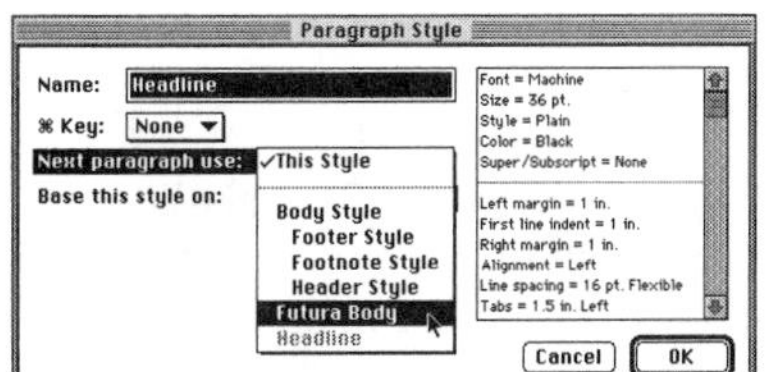

To define a next style:

1. **Choose Edit/Delete Style from the Custom menu.**
2. **Double-click the style for which you want to define a next style.**
3. **Choose the desired next style from the Next Paragraph Use pop-up menu, and then click OK.**
   To override the next style when ending a paragraph, press Option-Return instead of Return.

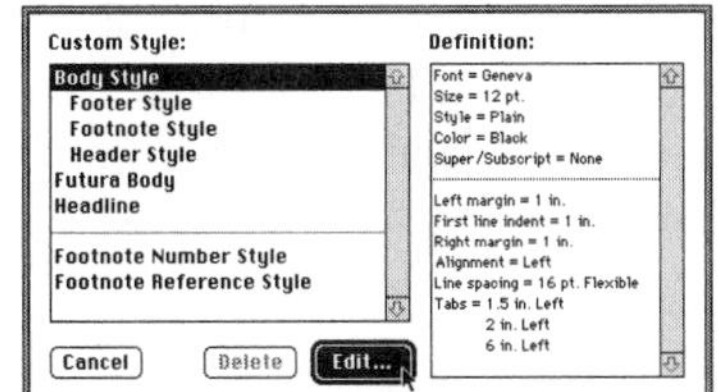

To redefine the Body Style style:

1. **Choose Edit/Delete Style from the Custom menu.**
2. **Double-click the style named Body Style.**
   You can also select the style and then click Edit.
3. **Use the ruler or the Font, Size, and Style menus to change formatting, and then click OK.**
   To base a new style on the body text style, choose Body Style from the Base this style on pop-up menu when creating the new style.

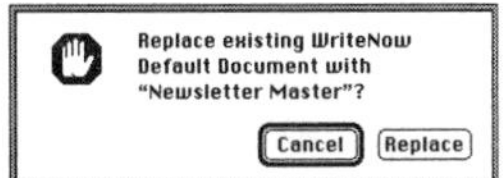

To make custom styles available in all new, untitled documents:

1. **Save the document to make sure that your latest changes are committed to disk.**

(continued on the next page)

(continued from previous page)

2. Delete all the text in the document, including that of headers and footers (unless you want that text to appear in all new, untitled documents).

3. Choose Save As Default Document from the File menu and then click Replace.

4. If you want to restore the document's text to continue working on it, choose Revert to Saved from the File menu. Otherwise, close the document and then click Don't Save.

Making a Style Available in All Documents

When you define a new style, it's available only in the document that is active when you create the style. But as this chapter's Step-by-Step boxes show, it's easy to make one or more of your custom styles available in the new, untitled documents you create.

Other ways to sling styles around

Word and WriteNow provide other ways to move styles from one document to another. In Word, you can access the styles in a different document by using the Organizer. After opening the document whose styles you want to access, choose Style from the Format menu and then click the Organizer button in the Style dialog box. In the Organizer dialog box, select the style or styles you want to copy, and then click the Copy button.

You can also copy a style simply by copying a paragraph formatted with that style and then pasting it into another document. Or you can do it by copying the last paragraph mark (the ¶ symbol visible when you click the ¶ button on the Standard toolbar) in a document and pasting it into the new document.

Moving styles in WriteNow

In WriteNow, you can use the Custom menu's Import Styles command to access another document's styles. All four programs also let you create stationery documents that store styles and other often-used elements.

Styles and Publishing Programs

Publishing programs such as Aldus PageMaker and QuarkXPress can interpret the styles you've defined in your word processor. This means that you can do text formatting with your word processor and then bring that text and its styles into the publishing program. If you need to reformat text after importing it into the publishing program, you can redefine the appropriate styles right there in the publishing program.

This function works the other way, too: if you use the publishing program's Export command to create a word processor file containing the text in a publication, the publishing program exports the styles as well as the text. Indeed, IDG Books' production department used this technique for this book. They exported the text from the third edition of the book, specifying PageMaker's Microsoft Word export filter. They then sent me the resulting files, which I used as the foundation for this edition. Because all the styles remained intact, IDG Books had a lot less manual formatting to do when they began producing the fourth edition.

Overriding a Style

You can override a style you've applied by using your program's formatting features in the conventional way. Each program has its own way of indicating that you've overridden a style with manual formatting (see Figure 4-4 "Overriding Styles").

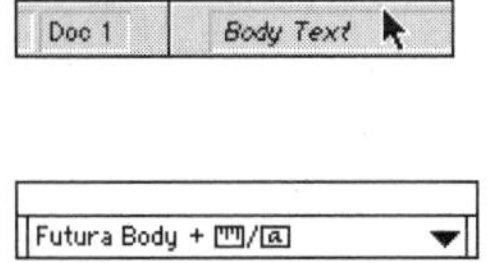

Figure 4-4: Overriding Styles WordPerfect and WriteNow tell you when you've overridden a style with manual formatting: WordPerfect's italicized style name (top), and WriteNow's plus sign plus ruler- and character-formatting icons (bottom).

When would you override a style? One common reason is to apply additional character formatting — to italicize a word in a sentence, for example. Another reason is to change paragraph formatting, such as centering a paragraph instead of justifying it.

Try to avoid extensive overriding, which defeats the purpose of styles. If you find yourself frequently overriding a style in the same way, consider creating another style that's based on the style you've been overriding.

The benefits of character-level styles

The character-level styles that WriteNow, Word 6, and MacWrite Pro provide can also eliminate the need to override a style in order to apply additional character formatting. For example, if you always italicize the first occurrence of a technical term, you can create a character style that reflects this formatting. (Another word processor, Nisus Software's Nisus, also provides character-level styles.)

Easy Ways to Become Style Conscious

Okay, styles can seem complicated, especially when you start wading through next style and based-on options. But you don't have to start out in these backwaters. Start by creating some simple styles for the types of documents you create:

- ❖ For your correspondence, define a return-address style that automatically indents your address and closing.
- ❖ For a newsletter or manual, define styles that automatically format your headings and body text.
- ❖ Try redefining the Normal or Body Text style so that you don't have to change fonts, tabs, or margins every time you create a new document.

Trying any of these techniques cuts down on repetitive formatting and gives you more time to refine your writing. Isn't that why you use a word processor?

CHAPTER 4 CONCEPTS AND TERMS

- Style sheets, or styles, let you automate complex formatting.
- Most programs provide a base style named Normal or Body Text upon which it bases new styles, unless you specify a different base style.
- Most word processors provide standard styles for common document components — headers, footers, tables of contents, footnotes, and more. By redefining the standard styles, you can control the appearance of these components.
- If you routinely switch from one style to another, use your word processor's next style or linked style feature to automate the process.
- Publishing programs such as Aldus PageMaker and QuarkXPress can interpret the styles you create in a word processor.

base style
A style upon which other styles are based. In Word and WordPerfect, the base style is called *Normal.* In WriteNow, it's called *Body Style.* In MacWrite Pro, it's called *Default.*

next style
A style to which a word processor automatically switches when you end a paragraph. This is called a *linked style* in WordPerfect.

standard styles
Built-in styles that control the formatting of common document components, such as headers, footers, page numbers, and footnotes.

style
A named set of text formats — font, size, type style, line spacing, and so on — that you can apply with a single keystroke or menu choice.

CHAPTER FIVE

Spreadsheet Basics

- How spreadsheets enable you to explore different approaches to a problem
- Tips on formatting and designing spreadsheets
- How to manage and navigate large spreadsheets
- Including spreadsheet data in other programs

The spreadsheet has been around in one form or another for centuries. In the 1800s, spreadsheets were big, leather-bound books — the kind in which Cratchet scratched his quill. In this century, leather gave way to leatherette, and Cratchet evolved into a paunchy guy in baggy pants who plays a mechanical adding machine like a Stradivarius.

For years, the spreadsheet remained essentially the same: a large ledger with pages divided into rows and columns for convenient organization of text and numbers. Then in the late '70s, a Harvard MBA candidate named Dan Bricklin got the idea that a computer program could mimic a ledger and also calculate numbers. His finance professor dismissed the idea as having no commercial value, but Bricklin was undaunted, teaming up with programmer Bob Frankston to create a wildly successful program called VisiCalc. The electronic spreadsheet was born, and the skeptical professor joined the ranks of history's great antivisionaries.

Since then, the spreadsheet program has become as much a mainstay of business as the expense account (and deservedly so). A spreadsheet lets you record numbers more neatly and efficiently than a ledger does, and it lets you calculate and analyze them. You can plug in new values and watch the spreadsheet recalculate accordingly. You can ask "What if?" questions: What if interest rates rose to 12 percent? What if we got a 20-year mortgage instead of a 30-year mortgage?

A spreadsheet does for you what a flight simulator does for a pilot: it lets you explore different approaches to a problem without the risk. And because life is full of problems and risks, spreadsheets have 1,001 uses. You can use them to create business plans and profit-and-loss statements, forecast sales figures, track stock market data, and print loan-amortization tables — in short, any endeavor that involves playing with numbers. And their orderly approach to storing information makes them ideal for other tasks, from managing address files to creating columnar tables (see the Quick Tips box "Other Ways to Use a Spreadsheet").

Other Ways to Use a Spreadsheet

A spreadsheet's capability to neatly pigeonhole text and numbers makes it a good basic database manager. When using a spreadsheet for data management, label columns with your field names (such as Name, Address, and Phone) and build downward from there, making each row a record. There's no need to fuss with field definitions and maximum character lengths. Every cell accepts any combination of text or numbers, and most spreadsheets hold up to 255 characters per cell. You can also use the spreadsheet's library of functions and math features to analyze data and create reports.

Many spreadsheets provide additional commands for managing data and for creating data-entry forms that show one record at a time. But remember, spreadsheets generally don't offer the sophisticated form-layout features or the extensive entry-checking features of true databases.

Finally, a spreadsheet's columnar bent can make it a wonderful table processor. (Indeed, most of the large product-feature tables you see in *Macworld* articles began life as spreadsheets.) You can add new columns or rows with a mouse click and resize columns in a flash instead of struggling with rulers and tab settings. If you need fancy formatting, move the completed table into a word processor by copying its cells to the Clipboard or by saving it as a text-only file.

Everything in Its Cell

The secret to a spreadsheet's organizational virtues is its grid-like approach to storing information. A blank spreadsheet is divided into horizontal and vertical lines that create a grid of boxes called *cells* (see Figure 5-1 "Spreadsheet Basics"). The horizontal lines form *rows*, and the vertical lines form *columns*. Rows are labeled by number and columns by letter to give every cell its own address: A1 is the cell in the upper-left corner of the spreadsheet. B4 is the cell in the second column, four rows down. (Some spreadsheets number both rows and columns: A1 becomes R1C1, and B4 is R4C2. Many programs let you choose the numbering scheme you prefer.)

Each cell can hold a number, some text, or a *formula* — a combination of cell addresses and math symbols that tell the program what to do with those numbers. A simple spreadsheet contains text *labels*, which describe the numbers in adjacent cells, and a formula (see Figure 5-2 "Weekly Pay").

The real power of a spreadsheet surfaces when you create formulas that manipulate the results of other formulas. In Figure 5-3 "Monthly and Yearly Pay," I've tied two new formulas to the result of "Weekly Pay." Doing so causes any changes in the *Hours Worked* or *Hourly Wage* cells to show up in the *Weekly Pay*, *Monthly Pay*, and *Yearly Pay* cells. To answer the question, "What if I earned $15 an hour instead of $10?" simply type **15** in cell B2 and press Return.

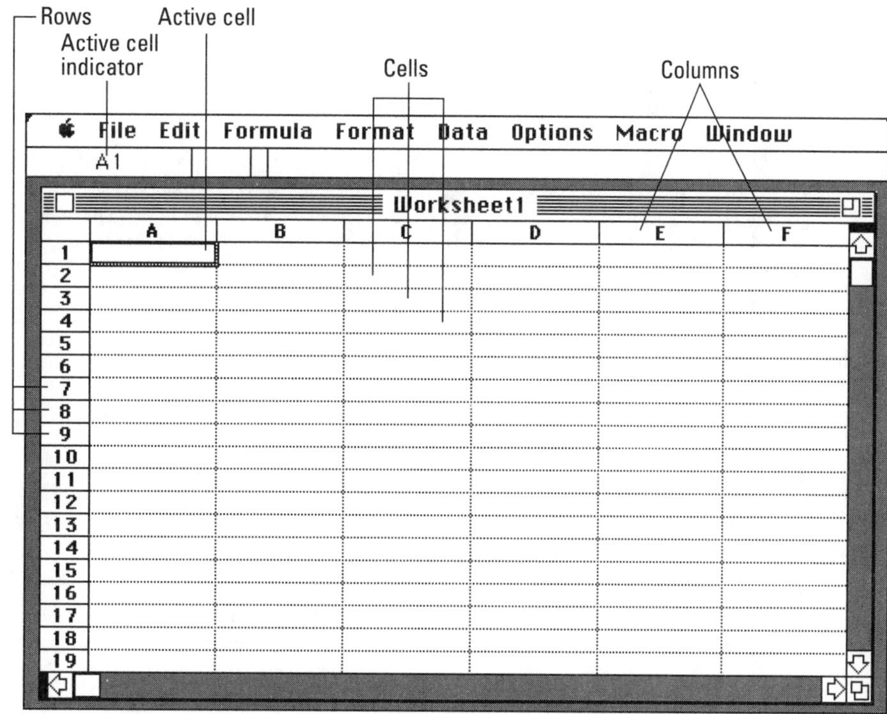

Figure 5-1: Spreadsheet Basics Horizontal and vertical lines divide a spreadsheet's window into a grid of boxes called cells, each with its own address (A1 is the cell in the upper-left corner). A bold rectangle indicates the active cell.

File Edit Formula Format Data

B4 =B1*B2

Worksheet-1

	A	B
1	Hours Worked	40
2	Hourly Wage	10
3		
4	Weekly Pay	400
5		

Figure 5-2: Weekly Pay This spreadsheet uses a formula to calculate weekly income based on number of hours worked and hourly wage. The formula itself appears in cell B4 and tells the spreadsheet program, "Multiply the contents of cell B1 by the contents of cell B2, and display the result here."

B5	=B4*4	
	A	B
1	Hours Worked	40
2	Hourly Wage	$10
3		
4	Weekly Pay	$400
5	Monthly Pay	$1,600
6	Yearly Pay	$19,200
7		
8		

Figure 5-3: Monthly and Yearly Pay Building on the formula in Figure 5-2 "Weekly Pay," the monthly pay formula multiplies weekly pay by 4, while the Yearly Pay formula multiplies monthly pay by 12. As you enter different wage and hour values, the spreadsheet instantly recalculates the weekly, monthly, and yearly pay.

Cell Selection Strategies

Selecting (highlighting) cells is one of the most common tasks you perform in a spreadsheet. Creating graphs, formatting cells, reorganizing a worksheet, and transferring information into another program are only some of the tasks that begin with selecting.

All spreadsheet programs provide similar mouse and keyboard sequences, which are summarized in the following table.

Selecting cells

To Select	*With the Mouse*	*With the Keyboard*
One cell	Click the cell	Move the cell pointer by using the arrow keys
Several adjacent cells	Drag across them, or click the first cell and then Shift-click the last cell	Hold the Shift key and then use the arrow keys
An entire row	Click the row heading	Press ⌘-Shift-right arrow or ⌘-Shift-left arrow
An entire column	Click the column heading	Press ⌘-Shift-up arrow or ⌘-Shift-down arrow
The entire worksheet	Click the box above and to the left of the first row and column	Press ⌘-A
Cells not adjacent to each other	Select the first cell or group of cells and then press ⌘ to select the others	

Navigating in a Spreadsheet

In all Mac spreadsheet programs, you select a cell by pointing to it with the mouse and then clicking or by using your keyboard's directional keys to move the *cell pointer*, a dark rectangle that encloses the active cell. Once you've honed in on a cell, simply begin typing. The characters you type appear within the *formula bar*, a text-entry box just below the spreadsheet's menu bar. (In 1-2-3 and Excel 5, they also appear in the cell as you type — these programs provide what's sometimes called *live editing* within cells.) You can edit text in the formula bar just as you do in other Mac applications. Pressing the Return key stores the text in the cell.

How does the spreadsheet know whether you've typed a label, a numeric value, or a formula? Most programs follow this approach: If you type only numbers, the entry is treated as a value. If it contains any letters or spaces, it's treated as a label. If the first character is an equals sign (=), the spreadsheet considers it a formula. If the first character is a double quote ("), the spreadsheet considers the text a label.

Basic Spreadsheet Formatting in Microsoft Excel

This box shows how to perform common spreadsheet formatting tasks in the Mac world's most popular spreadsheet program, Microsoft Excel. These basic concepts also apply to Lotus 1-2-3, although the specific commands and tool palettes vary.

To format a cell or range of cells:

1. **Select the cell or range of cells you want to format.**
2. **Click the desired formatting button in the toolbar, or choose Cells from the Format menu and then click the appropriate tab, as shown in the following table.**

Formatting Cells

To Do This	*Choose this Cells dialog box tab*
Change the way numbers are displayed	Number
Specify the alignment of values within cells	Alignment
Change the typeface, size, style, or color of a cell's contents	Font
Add a border to a cell or change a cell's border style or border color	Border
Add shading to a cell or change the pattern, color, or shading	Patterns

(continued on the next page)

(continued from previous page)

To change the width of a column:

1. **In the column heading area, point to the vertical bar that separates the column from the one to its right.**
   The mouse pointer turns into an arrow pointing left and right, as shown here.
2. **Drag left or right to change the width of the column.**
   If you select multiple columns before performing step 2, each column's width is changed to match the one you resized.

— or —

1. **Select any cell in the column.**
   You can also select the entire column or a series of columns.
2. **Choose Column from the Format menu.**
   The Column Width dialog box appears.
3. **Type a value of between 0 and 255.**
   Pressing 0 (zero) is the same as choosing the Hide button.
4. **Click OK or press Return.**
   Or you can double-click the vertical bar that separates the column from the one to its right in the column heading area. Excel changes the column's width to accommodate the longest cell entry in the column. This is the same as choosing the AutoFit Selection option in the Column Width dialog box. Excel bases the width on the screen font you're using. To get an accurate preview of how your hard copy will look, use the Print Preview command. You can also adjust the width of columns in the Print Preview window.

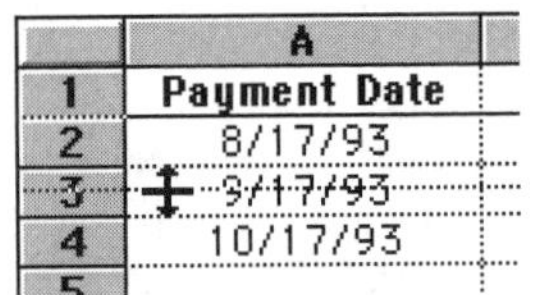

A
1
Payment Date
2
8/17/93
3
9/17/93
4
10/17/93

To change the height of a row:

1. **In the row heading area, point to the horizontal bar that separates the row from the one below it.**
   The mouse pointer turns into an arrow pointing up and down, as shown here.
2. **Drag up or down to change the row's height.**
   If you select multiple rows before performing step 2, each row's height is changed to match the one you resized.

— or —

1. **Select any cell in the row.**
   You can also select the entire row or a series of rows.
2. **Choose Row from the Format menu.**
   The Row dialog box appears.

3. **Type a value of between 0 and 409.**
   Pressing 0 (zero) is the same as choosing the Hide button.
4. **Click OK or press Return.**
   Or you can double-click the horizontal bar that separates the column from the one below it in the row heading area. Excel changes the row's height to accommodate the largest font size in the row. This is the same as choosing the AutoFit Selection option in the Row dialog box.

Manipulating Data with Functions

Spreadsheet programs also contain a number of preprogrammed formulas called *functions*, which provide advanced math skills. You needn't remember complex math symbols to use a function; simply type its name (or choose it from a dialog box or menu) and enclose the required values, called *arguments*, within parentheses. The function performs its preprogrammed calculation on the arguments and returns a result.

One statistical function that all spreadsheets provide is SUM, which adds its arguments. In a spreadsheet function, a colon (:) or space between two cell addresses indicates a *range* of cells, while a comma between cell addresses denotes individual cells. For example, the Excel formula =SUM(B1:B3) adds the contents of cells Bl through B3 (the short form of =B1+B2+B3), and the formula =SUM(B1,B5,B7) adds the contents of cells B1, B5, and B7. (Unless otherwise noted, I use Excel in all the examples in this chapter because it's the Mac world's most popular spreadsheet program. All of the concepts here apply to other spreadsheets, too, but the exact spelling — the *syntax* — of formulas or functions may differ.)

Other statistical functions include AVERAGE, which calculates the average value of given arguments, and MAX and MIN, which return the largest and smallest values, respectively, within the list of arguments. Spreadsheets also provide mathematical functions such as ABS, which returns the absolute value of an argument; and ROUND, which rounds off the value to a specified number of digits. Then there are trigonometric functions like COS, which gives the cosine, and TAN, which calculates the tangent. Text functions search and manipulate text. Financial functions calculate present and future values, rates of return, and more. Date functions return the current date and time and calculate differences between dates or times. A spreadsheet's seemingly endless library of functions is its ultimate weapon for manipulating text and numbers.

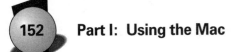

Resizing Column Widths Instead of Using Blank Columns

When a spreadsheet's column headings are wider than the data below them, the headings intrude into adjacent columns and obscure each other. To fix this problem, many people put a blank column between each column. Although this solution works, a better solution is to resize the columns themselves by using the techniques described in this chapter. Resizing columns uses memory more efficiently and makes it easier to scroll through the spreadsheet.

Functions become even more powerful when you nest them within other functions so that one function uses the value returned by another function as an argument. For example, the Excel formula =MID(A1,1,SEARCH(",",A1,1)-1) uses two text functions, MID and SEARCH, to extract the last name from a cell (A1) containing names in last name, first name format. Excel first executes the SEARCH function to locate the comma. SEARCH reports its findings to MID, which takes over to extract all the characters up to the comma.

Sprucing Up Data with Formats

Spreadsheets calculate numbers with a high degree of precision, using many decimal places (14, in Excel's case) to represent fractional values as accurately as possible. But that kind of precision is overkill for some data. A dollars-and-cents value doesn't look like one when 14 digits follow the decimal point.

Cell formats enable you to specify how you want numbers and text to be displayed. You can have dollars-and-cents figures appear with a dollar sign and only two digits after the decimal point. You can have percent signs appear after values that represent a percentage of other values. For date values, you can specify display formats such as 8/17/94 or 17-Aug-94. Appropriate display formats can make spreadsheet values more meaningful.

Another aspect of spreadsheet formatting involves specifying the alignment of data within cells. Numbers, for example, are usually lined up against the right edge of their cells with their decimal points aligned. Text is usually aligned against the left edge. You can also choose to center text within a cell — handy for a title that appears above a column of numbers.

Mac spreadsheets provide other formatting options as well, including the capability to format cells in different fonts and styles. Excel and Lotus 1-2-3 support color graphs and cell formats. These programs also let you create borders and lines and add shading to cells to highlight key figures or underscore totals. You can use these border features to create worksheets that look like paper forms. The next chapter contains more details about borders and shading.

Making Things Manageable

A single spreadsheet document provides thousands of blank cells ready for facts and formulas. But as you scroll from one area of the spreadsheet to another, you'll probably run out of memory and patience long before filling all of them.

Linking documents together

One solution to both problems is a program that enables you to link separate documents, causing changes you make in one to appear in the other. Linking separate spreadsheets lets you work around memory limitations and simplifies creating and using a complex spreadsheet application.

While the specific steps vary between products, you usually link spreadsheets by creating a formula in one spreadsheet that refers to one or more cells in the second spreadsheet. For example, assume you're working with two spreadsheets named Income and Expenses, and you want to link them so that the contents of the Income spreadsheet's Net Income cell are copied into the Net Income cell of the Expenses worksheet. To do so in Excel, create a formula in the Net Income cell of the Expenses worksheet reading =Income!$E2.

Saving time with macros

Another way to tame a spreadsheet is through *macros*, a series of formulas and commands that carry out actions at your command. A macro is like an electronic autopilot you can program to perform repetitive tasks — anything from choosing commands to entering formulas to performing complex calculations. You can find basic macro features in Microsoft Works and ClarisWorks and far more advanced ones in Excel and Lotus 1-2-3.

You can create macros from scratch by typing their commands one at time, but an easier way is to use the program's *macro recorder*. Activate the macro recorder, and the program records your work, translating your actions into macro statements. When you replay the resulting macro, it repeats the steps you performed. You can also edit macros to add additional functions.

Creating customized dialog boxes

The macro languages in Excel and 1-2-3 go even further in enabling you to create customized dialog boxes, menus, on-screen buttons, and other user interface elements. You can use these features to create customized spreadsheets that work like standard Mac applications. For example, a business may create an accounting system with menu commands such as Display Outstanding Invoices or Print Inventory Report. Behind these commands are macro statements that perform the appropriate tasks. An administrative assistant or temporary employee who may not otherwise know how to generate graphs or display outstanding invoices can use such spreadsheets to perform these functions.

These customized applications are often called *turnkey applications*, because, metaphorically speaking, all you have to do to be off and running is turn the key. You may also hear a turnkey spreadsheet application described as a template. A large library of spreadsheet templates is available from Heizer Software.

Using on-screen tool palettes

Today's spreadsheet programs offer additional time-savers — on-screen tool palettes for choosing often-used commands and formatting options. Microsoft Excel has a particularly extensive collection of these palettes, which Microsoft calls toolbars. The next chapter describes these and other spreadsheet streamliners.

Including Spreadsheet Results in Other Programs

When you're preparing a report, you may need to transfer numbers or graphs from a spreadsheet program to a document you're creating with a word processor or desktop publishing program. In this Step-by-Step box, you'll find instructions for copying information from a spreadsheet and pasting it into another program. Chapter 27 has all the details on the Mac's data-exchange features, including System 7's slick publish-and-subscribe features. The Step-by-Step box "From Excel to Word: How to Publish and Subscribe" in the next chapter shows you how to use publish and subscribe to include spreadsheet data in another program.

To move the contents of some cells into another program:

1. **Select the cells whose contents you want to appear in the other program.**
   For a look at the ways you can select spreadsheet cells, see the Quick Tips box "Cell Selection Strategies" earlier in this chapter.
2. **Choose Copy from the Edit menu.**
   The contents of the cells are placed on the Mac's Clipboard.
3. **Start or switch to the program into which you want to paste the cells.**
   If you want to paste them into a document you've already started working on, open that document.

4. **Choose Paste from the Edit menu.**
   The data is pasted into the active document. If you paste from Excel to Microsoft Word, the data appears with formatting intact as a Word table. If you paste into another word processor or into a publishing program, each cell is separated by a tab character. You may need to use the formatting ruler in the word processor or publishing program to adjust the tabs for better spacing between columns.

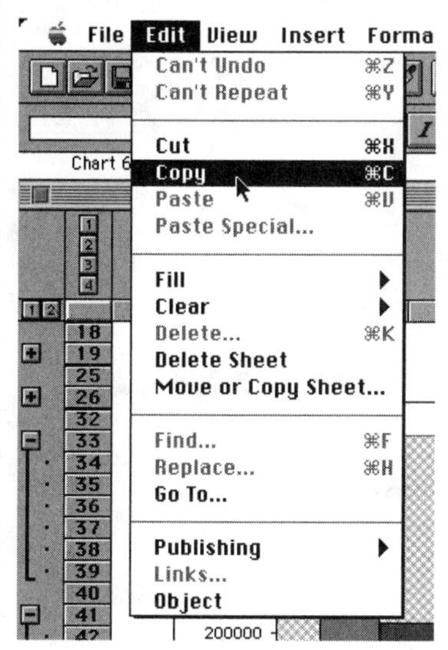

To copy a graph into another program:

1. **If the graph is part of a worksheet, select the graph by clicking it once.**
   If the graph is in an Excel chart window, you don't have to perform this step.
2. **Choose Copy from the Edit menu.**
   The graph is placed on the Mac's Clipboard.
3. **Start or switch to the program into which you want to paste the graph.**
   If you want to paste the graph into a document you've already started working on, open that document.
4. **Choose Paste from the Edit menu.**
   If you paste a graph into a drawing program (or into the drawing module of an integrated program), you can modify the individual components of the graph — its bars, text labels, and so on. See Chapter 12 for some graph customizing ideas.

Creating Charts and Graphs

Besides number-analyzing prowess, Mac spreadsheet programs often include a variety of features that can transform monotonous rows and columns of numbers into graphs and charts, interesting-looking reports, or powerful forecasting tools.

Many spreadsheet programs have built-in graphing features that create spiffy bar, line, or pie charts. You can even place your spreadsheets and graphs on the same page (see Figure 5-4 "Tables and Charts"). In Excel, you can resize a bar or line in a graph and change its corresponding spreadsheet data. This feature is useful for *goal-seeking tasks* — for example, if you want sales to increase by 10 percent next year, you can drag the appropriate line in a chart, and Excel changes the underlying spreadsheet to show what you need to meet your goal.

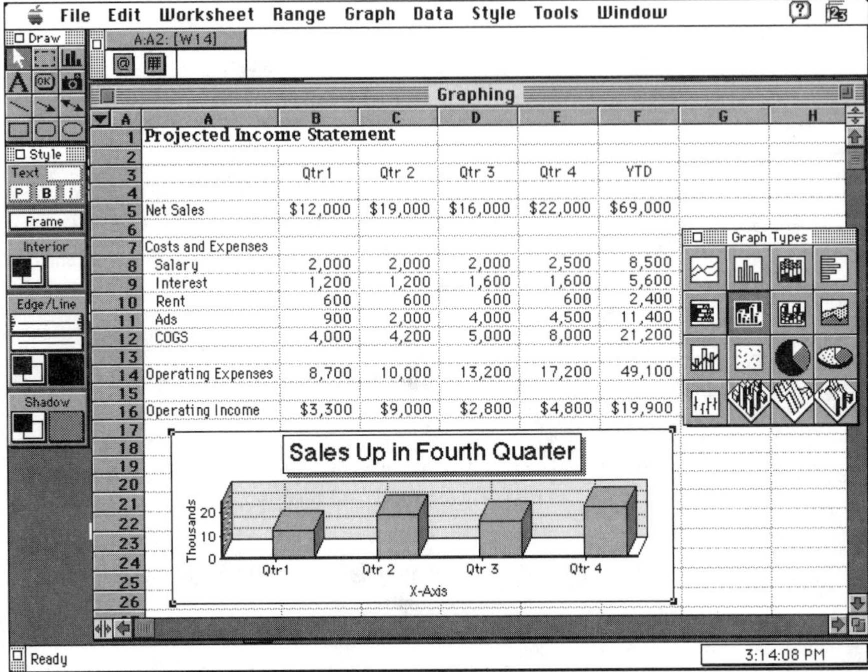

	A	B	C	D	E	F
1	Projected Income Statement					
2						
3		Qtr 1	Qtr 2	Qtr 3	Qtr 4	YTD
4						
5	Net Sales	$12,000	$19,000	$16,000	$22,000	$69,000
6						
7	Costs and Expenses					
8	Salary	2,000	2,000	2,000	2,500	8,500
9	Interest	1,200	1,200	1,600	1,600	5,600
10	Rent	600	600	600	600	2,400
11	Ads	900	2,000	4,000	4,500	11,400
12	COGS	4,000	4,200	5,000	8,000	21,200
13						
14	Operating Expenses	8,700	10,000	13,200	17,200	49,100
15						
16	Operating Income	$3,300	$9,000	$2,800	$4,800	$19,900

Figure 5-4: Tables and Charts Excel and Lotus 1-2-3 (shown here) let you mix graphs and spreadsheet cells in the same document. Both programs also support 3-D graphs and color.

Spreadsheet programs can also create graphs that look three-dimensional, and they even enable you to rotate the graph and change its perspective. Graphs and spreadsheets team up well for analyzing numbers and spotting trends; a rising or falling line tells a more compelling story than a nondescript table of numbers.

Because graphs and tables often end up in reports, all spreadsheet programs let you copy graphs and spreadsheet cells to the Clipboard for subsequent pasting into a word processor or desktop publishing program. Most programs also support System 7's publish-and-subscribe features, which, as the next chapter explains, enable you to create a link between a spreadsheet document and another program. The next chapter also contains tips for creating and formatting graphs.

How to Keep Headings Visible When You Scroll

A common annoyance with large spreadsheets is that their row and column headings disappear when you scroll — the headings go out the window, you might say. To remember what kind of data a given row or column holds, you need to scroll all the way back to the top or left edge of the worksheet.

Or do you? Most spreadsheet programs have window-management features that enable you to keep row and column headings visible while the rest of the spreadsheet scrolls around them. One technique is to split the spreadsheet window by using the split bars that all spreadsheet programs provide.

To split a spreadsheet window, first scroll the window so you can see the row or column headings you want to keep in view. Drag the window's horizontal or vertical split bar until it's below the column headings or to the right of the row headings. (The split bars are located above and to the left of the vertical and horizontal scroll bars, respectively.)

If you use Excel, you can neaten up the window — removing the extra scroll bars and borders created when you split a window — by choosing Freeze Panes from the Window menu. If you need to adjust the panes later — maybe you changed the headings' font or size, and now they don't fit the original size — choose Unfreeze Panes and then drag the split bar as needed.

You can apply this window-splitting technique to Lotus 1-2-3, but using 1-2-3's Titles command, located in the Worksheet menu, is better. To freeze a row of horizontal titles, simply select any cell directly below the titles and then choose Titles from the Worksheet menu. In the Worksheet Titles dialog box, choose the Horizontal option and then click OK or press Return. To freeze a column of vertical titles, select a cell to the right of the titles, choose the Titles command, and then choose the Vertical option. To freeze both the row and column titles, choose the Both option.

Unlike Excel, 1-2-3 doesn't let you change the contents of frozen cells. If you need to edit a heading, choose Titles and click the None option. (You don't have to select a specific cell first.)

Tips for Spreadsheet Shoppers

For basic spreadsheet needs, it's hard to beat an integrated program such as Microsoft Works or ClarisWorks, which take a Swiss army knife approach by consolidating spreadsheet, word processing, graphing, database management, and telecommunications features.

Integrated programs are convenient, but remember that the Mac's Clipboard and Scrapbook let you create your own integrated workplace by cutting and pasting information between programs. System 7 (or the System 6 MultiFinder) lets you do so without quitting and restarting each application — provided your Mac has enough memory, of course.

If you need a spreadsheet only occasionally, an integrated program may be the most convenient way to include spreadsheet data in your documents. But if you plan to spend a great deal of time asking "What if?" you'll be better served by a powerhouse spreadsheet like Excel, relying on the Clipboard or System 7's publish-and-subscribe features to exchange and combine data within other applications as needed. (You can find instructions for using publish-and-subscribe with spreadsheets in the next chapter.)

If you create complex formulas containing flocks of functions and parentheses, look for a program that lets you attach notes to cells. Cell notes, electronic versions of sticky notes, effectively describe how large formulas work or how the spreadsheet is structured — details that are easy to forget and difficult to decipher.

If memory is at a premium, consider Bravo Technologies' MacCalc. It's fast, easy to use, and compares favorably to its more corpulent competitors. There's also Zedcor's Desk, a collection of desk accessories, one of which, DeskCalc, is a mini-spreadsheet. In the shareware arena, BiPlane comes in both application and desk accessory versions (see Chapter 17 for details about shareware). BiPlane is included on the CD-ROM that came with this book.

If you're shopping for a heavy-duty spreadsheet, make things easy for yourself and buy Microsoft Excel. Lotus 1-2-3 is a powerful program, but Excel is more powerful and far more popular. (Indeed, in early 1994, Lotus announced that it was discontinuing work on future versions of 1-2-3 for the Macintosh.)

Spreadsheet Design Basics

Creating an effective, easily understood spreadsheet requires an organized approach and plenty of advance planning. According to John M. Nevison's excellent *Elements of Spreadsheet Style* (Brady, 1987), a spreadsheet "should be straightforward to build, easy to read, receptive to change, and, above all, free of error." Here are a few of Nevison's 22 spreadsheet rules:

Make a formal introduction

Explain the spreadsheet's purpose and design as well as how to use it. Describe cells holding key information and provide a table of contents listing key data sections.

Label every assumption

So that your readers can better understand your spreadsheet's structure, state up front all its assumptions (for example, a 5 percent annual growth rate with a 7 percent annual depreciation rate).

Explain tricky formulas

If your spreadsheet offers cell-notation features, use them. Later, when you have to modify your formulas, you'll be glad you did. If a formula is particularly complex, consider dividing it across several cells.

Use cell naming

If your spreadsheet program lets you, assign names to a cell or range of cells to explain key formulas. The formula =HoursWorked*HourlyWage says a great deal more than =B7*B6.

Graph to illuminate

Be sure that graphs summarize their data well. Proofread them for style and content. And put each graph's conclusion in its title. For example, the title "Sales Up 20 Percent This Year" says more than "Year-to-Date Sales Results."

The Power of Numbers

As you master the workings of your spreadsheet program, don't forget the importance of good spreadsheet design. Creating a spreadsheet that's easy to understand and maintain requires forethought and an understanding of the problem you're analyzing. You can find advice for creating effective spreadsheets in the Quick Tips box "Spreadsheet Design Basics."

Finally, don't underestimate the potential for spreadsheet abuse. These days, business plans and sales forecasts come with an entourage of facts and figures depicting profits and prosperity. Often, those statistics are supplied by the project's proponents, and therein lies the potential problem. Anyone can doctor a spreadsheet to give the desired results simply by beginning with preselected figures and then designing a spreadsheet to produce them. In such cases, the spreadsheet changes from a tool for evaluating options to a tool that supports decisions that have already been made.

The moral? Don't take someone else's spreadsheet figures at face value. Question the spreadsheet's underlying assumptions: Did its creator assume that profits will increase 20 percent each year, that interest rates will fall, that no competition exists, or that costs will remain the same?

George Canning, a prime minister of Britain in the nineteenth century, said it best: "I can prove anything by statistics — except the truth."

CHAPTER 5 CONCEPTS AND TERMS

- A spreadsheet is divided into horizontal and vertical lines that create a grid of boxes called cells, which hold numbers, text, or formulas.
- Spreadsheet programs contain preprogrammed formulas called functions, which perform calculations on values you specify.
- You can format a spreadsheet by specifying how you want numbers and text to appear and how you want the data aligned within cells.
- Ways to manage spreadsheets include linking separate worksheets together and using *macros,* which are a series of formulas and commands that automate repetitive tasks.
- If you use a spreadsheet only occasionally, consider an integrated program such as ClarisWorks.

cell
A box that can hold a numeric value, text, or a formula. Cells are arranged in horizontal *rows* and vertical *columns.* Each cell has its own address; cell A1, for example, is in the upper-left corner.

cell pointer
A dark rectangle that encloses the current cell.

formula
A combination of math symbols and cell addresses that tell the spreadsheet program what to do with the values in those cells.

formula bar
A text-entry box that usually appears just below the spreadsheet's menu bar and displays a formula, value, or text label as you type it. You edit text in the formula bar just as you do in other Mac applications.

functions
Preprogrammed formulas that accept required values, called *arguments,* and return a result. All spreadsheet programs provide a large library of functions for statistical and financial calculations as well as for text.

goal-seeking
A method of spreadsheet analysis that involves supplying the desired result and allowing the spreadsheet to calculate the values required to obtain that result.

label
Descriptive text that appears in a cell adjacent to a value.

link
The process of tying two spreadsheet documents together via a formula in one spreadsheet that references one or more cells in the other. It's often easier to manage large spreadsheet projects if you divide them into separate documents and then link them.

macro
An automated series of formulas and commands that carry out specific actions.

range
A series of adjacent spreadsheet cells.

template
A "canned" spreadsheet that you purchase from a software developer and use as is or modify to suit your needs.

CHAPTER SIX

Excel Power Tips

- Working efficiently with cell pointing and range naming
- Adding borders and shading to spreadsheet cells
- Structuring spreadsheets for fast performance and easy navigation
- Creating cross-platform worksheets and macros

Business without spreadsheets? It's easier to imagine soup without sandwiches or Abbott without Costello. The spreadsheet program has been around for only a little more than a decade, yet it's hard to imagine doing business without it. Creating budgets and business plans, estimating profit and loss, forecasting sales, experimenting with mortgage options, analyzing statistics — spreadsheets have tamed these and myriad other calculation-intensive chores.

The basic concepts are simple. As you saw in the preceding chapter, a spreadsheet is divided by horizontal and vertical lines into a grid of boxes called *cells*. You type numbers in the cells and then create formulas that describe the relationship between the numbers. You can then ask "What if?" questions — that is, you can plug different numbers into the formula to see how they impact the end result. Each time you change a number on which a calculation is based, the spreadsheet program recalculates the spreadsheet accordingly. In doing so, the spreadsheet enables you to learn the best approach for a specific problem and set of conditions.

Today's spreadsheet programs do much more than crunch numbers. You can turn rows of numbers into graphs that illustrate trends and relationships. The Mac's fonts and graphics features can make your spreadsheets easier to read and can enable you to create forms that look like they came from a publishing program. And data-exchange features let you include numbers and graphs in memos and reports. You can even use the publish and subscribe features in System 7 to automatically update the graphs and numbers in a report when the spreadsheet changes.

In this chapter, I show you how to take advantage of these and other spreadsheet features with Microsoft Excel. Much of the information here also applies to Lotus 1-2-3 as well as the spreadsheet modules in integrated packages such as Microsoft Works and ClarisWorks.

Spreadsheet Techniques for Microsoft Excel

This box shows you how to apply the techniques described in this chapter to Microsoft Excel.

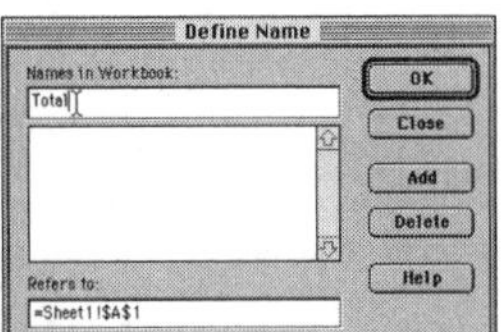

To name a cell or range of cells:

1. **Select the cell or cells to be named.**
   The preceding chapter summarizes the techniques you can use to select cells.
2. **Choose Name from the Insert menu, and then choose Create.**
   You can also use the ⌘-L keyboard sequence.
3. **Type a name and then click OK or press Return.**
   If the cell to the left of the active cell contains text, Excel proposes that text as the cell's name. If that's what you want, simply click OK.

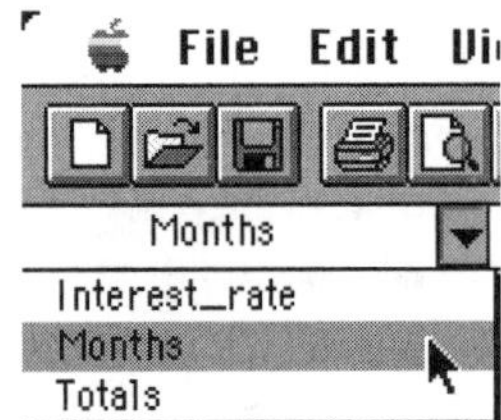

To use a name in a formula:

1. **Choose the desired name from the Name box in the formula bar.**

To change a number or date format:

1. **Select the cell or range of cells containing the numbers or dates you want to reformat.**
2. **Click the desired format on the formatting toolbar.**
   If the format you want isn't on the toolbar, choose Cells from the Format menu and then click the Number tab. Double-click the desired format.

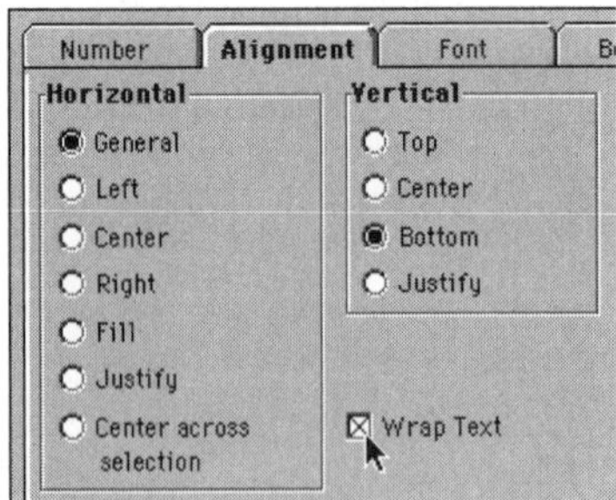

To format lengthy text labels so that they wrap around to the next line within each cell:

1. **Select the cell or cells containing the labels.**
2. **Choose Cells from the Format menu, and then click Alignment.**
3. **Check the Wrap Text box.**

To reuse a set of number and text-formatting options:

1. **Format a cell as desired.**
2. **Type a brief, descriptive name in the style portion of the toolbar, and then press Enter.**
   To apply that style to another cell, select that cell (or select a range of cells) and then choose the style's name from the toolbar's pop-up menu.

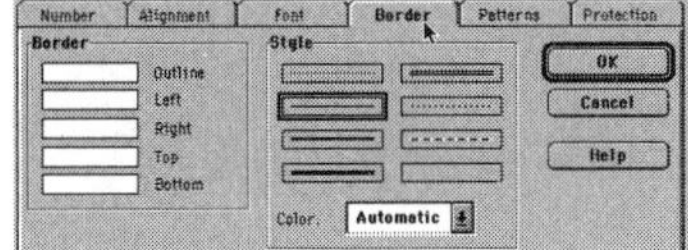

To add a border or borders to one or more cells:

1. **Choose Cells from the Format menu and then click the Border tab.**
   The Border dialog box appears.
2. **Select the desired option, as described in the following table.**

To	*Choose This Option*
Border all four edges of each cell within a range	Left, Right, Top, and Bottom
Border only certain edges, such as the top and bottom	Only those edges
Border the outer edges of a range	Outline
Shade the selected cells	Shade
Add color to the selected cells	Desired color from the Color pop-up menu

Keep the following tips in mind when formatting cells with borders or shading:

❖ You can use the Style area of the Border dialog box to choose from eight line widths and patterns.

❖ You can reuse a border and shading arrangement elsewhere by selecting a bordered or shaded cell and then creating a style as described in the previous set of instructions.

❖ You can change the pattern Excel applies to shaded cells by using the Format menu's Patterns command.

❖ Excel's AutoFormat tool lets you apply a variety of preset border and shading schemes to a range of cells. Check out the options described in Excel's manual; they may save you a lot of formatting time.

❖ The Format Painter tool is another handy way to copy formats. First, select the cell containing the formats you want to copy. Then click the Format Painter button and drag through the cells you want to reformat.

(continued on the next page)

(continued from previous page)

To include a graphic in a spreadsheet:

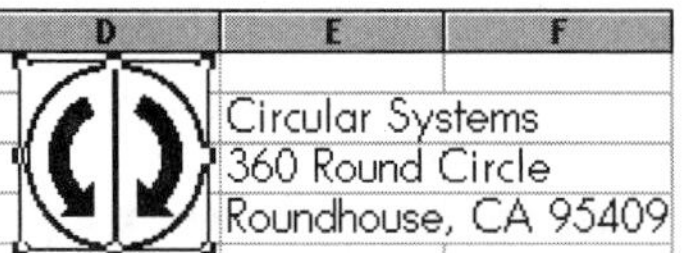

1. **Open the graphic in the appropriate program, and then select it and choose Copy.**
   The graphic is placed on the Mac's Clipboard.
2. **Switch to or start Excel and open the desired worksheet.**
3. **Select the cell in which you want the graphic to appear.**
4. **Choose Paste from the Edit menu.**
   You can resize the graphic by dragging its handles. Press Shift while dragging a corner handle to resize the graphic and maintain its original proportions.

Spreadsheet Techniques for Lotus 1-2-3

Lotus 1-2-3 was a hot Mac spreadsheet that appeared too late to weaken Excel's hold on the Mac spreadsheet market. Lotus has halted development on future versions of 1-2-3, but thousands of copies (or at least hundreds) are still out there in daily use. This box shows you how to apply the techniques described in this chapter to Lotus 1-2-3.

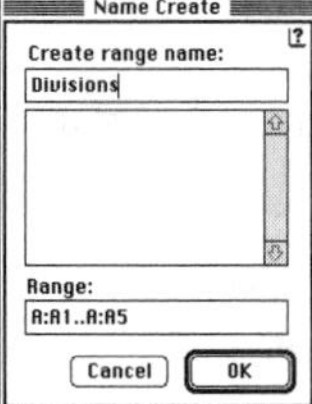

To name a cell or range of cells:

1. **Select the cell or cells you want to name.**
2. **Choose Create from the Range pop-up menu located in the console.**
   You can also choose Create from the Name submenu in the Range menu, or press the ⌘-R keyboard shortcut.
3. **Type a name for the cell or range of cells.**
   If you like, you can use spaces in the name.
4. **Click OK.**
   When naming cells, you can also tell 1-2-3 to use the text in adjacent cells by using the Name submenu's Label Create command.

To add a cell or range name to a formula:

1. **Begin by creating the formula as you usually do.**
2. **Select the name from the Range pop-up menu.**
   1-2-3 inserts the name at the location of the blinking insertion point.

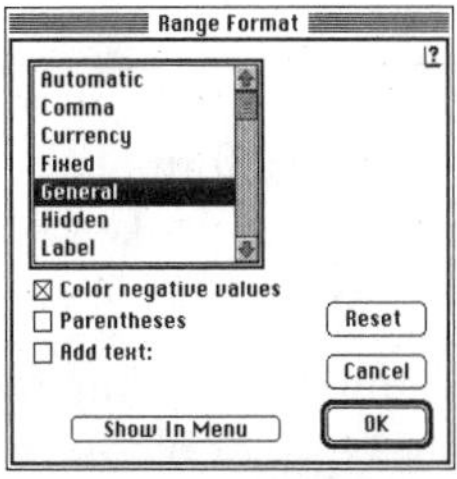

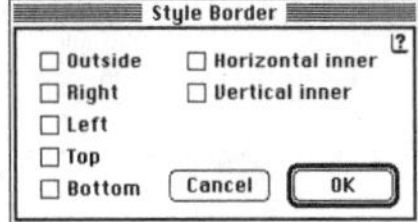

To change a cell's number or date format:

1. **Choose Format from the Range menu.**

   The Range Format dialog box appears.

2. **Select the format you want, and then click OK or press Return.**

   You can also use the Range Format dialog box to add often-used formats to the Range menu.

To add a border or borders to one or more cells:

1. **Choose Border from the Style menu.**
2. **Select the desired option, as described in the following table.**

To Border	*Choose This Option*
The edges of a single selected cell	Outside
The top and bottom edges of a single selected cell	Top, Bottom
All four edges of each cell within a range	Outside, Horizontal inner, and Vertical inner
The outer edges of a range	Outside

Keep the following tips in mind when formatting cells with borders and shading:

- ❖ You can also choose border options from the Style floating palette.
- ❖ You can shade a cell by choosing one of the light shaded patterns from the Style palette's pattern pop-up menu.
- ❖ You can apply an existing border or shading arrangement to other cells by selecting the bordered or shaded cells and choosing Copy. Next, select the cells you want to reformat and choose Paste Special. In the dialog box that appears, select the Styles and Formats option.

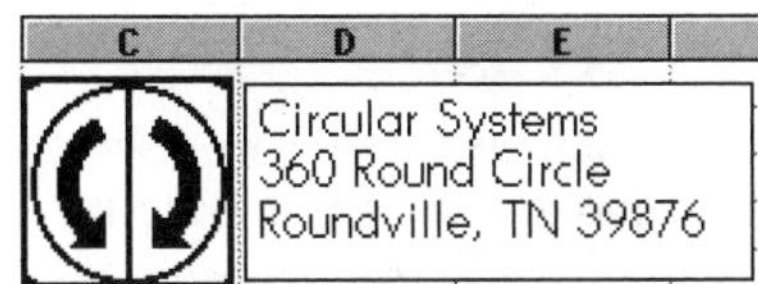

To add a graphic created in another program to a worksheet:

1. **Open the graphic in the appropriate program, and then select it and choose Copy.**

   The graphic is placed on the Mac's Clipboard.

2. **Switch to or start 1-2-3 and open the worksheet to which you want to add the graphic.**
3. **Select the Draw palette's Picture tool (the camera).**
4. **Click the worksheet in which you want the picture to appear.**

   You can resize the picture by dragging its corner handles; press Shift to avoid altering its proportions. To import the picture at a specific size, select the Picture tool and then drag across the worksheet to create a box of the desired size. To restore a picture's original size, double-click it.

Tips for Creating Formulas

Because formulas form the backbone of a spreadsheet, I begin this section with a few formulaic tips. One of the most tedious parts of creating a formula is specifying cell addresses. Add B4 to B2 and divide by G6 — it's enough to make you feel like yelling "Bingo!"

The *cell pointing* feature that all spreadsheets provide simplifies creating formulas by eliminating the need to type addresses. After typing the equal or plus sign that denotes the beginning of a formula, simply point to the first cell to be included in the formula and then click. The program enters that cell's address in the formula. If you drag across a range of cells, the program creates the range reference for you.

There are two kinds of references: *absolute* and *relative*. An absolute reference refers to a specific cell address or range, such as D4. A relative reference refers to a cell by providing "directions" from the cell containing the formula. An absolute reference is like giving someone directions by spelling out each street: "Turn left at Lookout Hill, then right on Salem Drive." A relative reference is like saying, "Go up two blocks, turn left, then go west three blocks." Use a relative reference when you want to refer to the same cell, regardless of where the formula is located on the spreadsheet.

Name That Cell

A blank Excel worksheet looks like an aerial map of a midwestern city. A grid of 16,384 horizontal rows and 256 vertical columns creates a total of 4,194,304 cells, each of which can hold a number, a text label, a note, or a formula. But with this kind of wide-open space come some navigational challenges. Like a business, a spreadsheet gets hard to manage as it grows, and even a seemingly simple task like scrolling to a specific location can become a challenge.

Commuter lanes for spreadsheet cells

Several Excel features let you create express lanes from one part of a worksheet to another. One technique is to assign descriptive names to cells or range of cells. For example, if your worksheet contains a summary section, give that range of cells a name such as *Summary_Info*. (Excel won't let you put a space in the name — to simulate one, use the underscore character — Shift-hyphen — as I did here.)

Once you've named a cell or range, you can use the Go To command to jump to that spot. Choose Go To from the Edit menu and double-click the name. Excel instantly beams you there and selects the cell or range. When you use the Go To command, Excel remembers your previous four locations and automatically displays them in the Go To dialog box the next time you choose Go To. This command streamlines jumping back and forth between various sections of the worksheet.

Other benefits to cell naming

Faster scrolling is only one reason to assign names to cells or ranges. A bigger payoff is self-documenting formulas. For example, if you've named the cells that hold deposit and withdrawal figures, your formula for the Balance cell can read =Deposit-Withdrawal. That says more about what the formula does than =F12-F13. And the biggest payoff is increased accuracy. It's easy to make a mistake when entering a cell reference — typing *F12* instead of *F13*, for example. But you're unlikely to type *Deposit* when you want to refer to a cell named *Withdrawal.*

After selecting worksheet and using
Create and Apply from the Names submenu ...

Range B2:B4 is named "Jan" | Range C2:C4 is named "Feb" | Range D2:D4 is named "Mar"

	A	B	C	D
1		Jan	Feb	Mar
2	Deposits	342	535	234
3	Withdrawals	232	235	119
4	Balance	110	300	115

The Go To dialog box lists the new names —
double-clicking one selects the corresponding cell or range

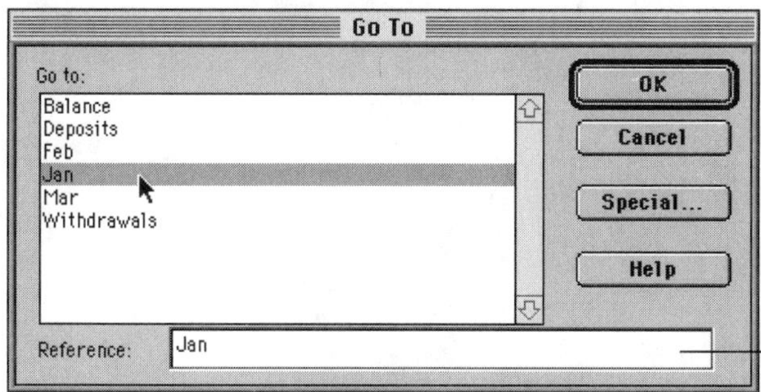

You can also type a name along with a reference operator (colon, space, or comma) to select combinations of cells within each range. For example...

Typing... | Yields this selection...

feb balance

	A	B	C	D
1		Jan	Feb	Mar
2	Deposits	342	535	234
3	Withdrawals	232	235	119
4	Balance	110	300	115

jan,mar

	A	B	C	D
1		Jan	Feb	Mar
2	Deposits	342	535	234
3	Withdrawals	232	235	119
4	Balance	110	300	115

deposits,feb:mar

	A	B	C	D
1		Jan	Feb	Mar
2	Deposits	342	535	234
3	Withdrawals	232	235	119
4	Balance	110	300	115

Figure 6-1: Range Intersections Illustrated

Excel's range-naming features go well beyond the example I just outlined. With the Insert menu's Name command, you can turn row and column headings into range names and then locate and select rows or columns by specifying those names in various combinations. Better still, you can tell Excel to automatically replace cell references within that range with the appropriate names, yielding clearer formulas. See Figure 6-1 "Range Intersections Illustrated" for details.

Formatting Cells Appropriately

Spreadsheet programs calculate numeric values very accurately, using over a dozen decimal places. That's comforting, but it's often more precision than you really need. Dollars-and-cents values, for example, require two decimal places. The answer is cell formatting. Telling your spreadsheet to format currency values appropriately gives you not only an appropriate number of decimal points, but also a dollar sign (or the currency symbol of your choice). You can specify other types of numeric formats for noncurrency values (see Figure 6-2 "Numbering Your Options").

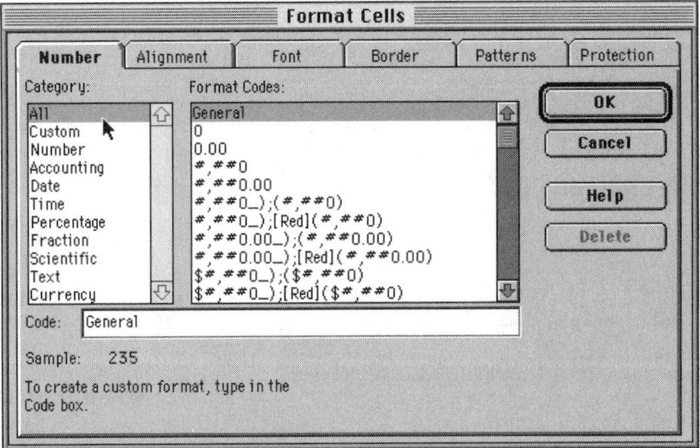

Figure 6-2: Numbering Your Options Excel gives you complete control over how numbers and date values appear in cells.

Cell-formatting features go beyond numbers to include text and date values. You can specify whether text appears aligned against the left or right edge of a cell or centered within it. You can choose a variety of date formats that include the day of the week and various date and month abbreviation schemes. Most programs also let you specify that negative numbers appear in color, bringing new meaning to the phrase "in the red."

Tips for font formatting

All spreadsheets enable you to apply the Mac's variety of fonts, sizes, and type styles to cells. For example, you can format headings or key cells in bold. Want to fit more data on a page? Decrease the type size of every cell or use a narrower font, such as Helvetica Condensed. (If you use a laser or ink-jet printer, you can accomplish the same result by specifying a reduction percentage in the Page Setup dialog box. This approach yields more cells per printed page without forcing you to squint at tiny cells on-screen.)

If you've changed a cell to appear in bold or in a larger type size, the cell's contents may not fit within the column's width. Excel and 1-2-3 provide a quick fix — double-click the cell's right column boundary, and the program resizes the column to accommodate its widest cell.

Most programs also provide a variety of keyboard shortcuts for changing cell alignment and type style. I summarize Excel's shortcuts in the Quick Tips box "Microsoft Excel Keyboard Shortcuts."

Quick Fills with Excel's Autofill Feature

Many spreadsheets require lists of incrementing or decrementing data called *data series.* One example is the sequence of numbers from 1 to 10. Other examples include the days of the week and the 12 months or four quarters of a year. Instead of manually typing each item in a data series — January, February, March, and so on — use Excel's Autofill feature.

Begin by typing the first item in the series: for example, January. Then point to the *fill handle* — the small black box — at the lower-left corner of the cell containing the entry you just typed. Next, click and drag down or to the right (depending on where you want the rest of the data series to appear). As you drag, the current value in the series appears at the left edge of the formula bar. When you release the mouse button, Excel creates the series.

You can use the Autofill feature to create almost any kind of repeating data series. If you want to create a series that increases or decreases by more than one unit in each cell, type the first two data items in the series. For example, to create a series of odd numbers, type **1** in one cell and **3** in the next cell. Then select both cells and drag the fill handle. Excel figures out the difference between the two entries and bases the rest of the series on this difference.

You can also use the fill handle to delete the contents of a cell or range of cells. Simply drag the fill handle up until a gray pattern fills the cell or cells, and then release the mouse button.

Microsoft Excel Keyboard Shortcuts

This box lists some handy keyboard shortcuts for commonly used commands and options in Microsoft Excel.

Toolbar Shortcuts

To Do This	*Do This*
Quickly display any toolbar	Point to any visible toolbar, press Control (⌘-Option in Excel 4), and then choose the desired toolbar from the shortcut menu.
Access cell-format commands	With the mouse pointer in the worksheet area, press Control (⌘-Option in Excel 4), and then choose the desired command.
Move a toolbar	Double-click within the toolbar (but not within any buttons) or drag the toolbar until the dotted outline changes shape.
Turn a floating toolbar into a fixed toolbar	Double-click within the toolbar (but not on any buttons) or drag the toolbar until the dotted outline changes shape.

Editing Shortcuts

To Do This	*Press This*
Enter the current date	⌘-hyphen (-)
Enter the current time	⌘-semicolon (;)
Create an outline border	⌘-Option-O (Excel 4 only)
Copy a value from the cell above the active cell into the formula bar	⌘-Shift-double quote mark (")
Insert a tab character in the formula bar	Option-Tab (Excel 4 only)
Insert a line break in the formula bar	⌘-Option-Enter
Fill a selected range of cells with a formula	Option-Enter

Formatting Shortcuts

For This Format	*Press This*
General	Control-Shift-L (Excel 4 only)
Currency	Control-Shift-$

Percentage	Control-Shift-%
Exponential	Control-Shift-^
Date (day, month, year)	Control-Shift-#
Time (hour, minute, AM/PM)	Control-Shift-@
Two decimals, with commas	Control-Shift-!
Left border	⌘-Option-left arrow
Right border	⌘-Option-right arrow
Top border	⌘-Option-up arrow
Bottom border	⌘-Option-down arrow
Outline border	⌘-Option-0 (zero)
No borders	⌘-Option-hyphen (-)
Plain text	⌘-Shift-P
Bold	⌘-Shift-B
Italic	⌘-Shift-I
Underline	⌘-Shift-U

Note: To select the style box, press ⌘-Shift-L.

Outlining Your Spreadsheet

When a spreadsheet reaches gargantuan proportions, it becomes difficult to see the forest for the cells. Key figures such as totals and summaries get lost in the details, and you end up doing more scrolling and squinting than analyzing.

Excel is the only spreadsheet program with an outlining feature that lets you collapse a spreadsheet to show only the bottom-line results, expand it to show every ugly detail, or expand only those sections you want to concentrate on at the moment.

Automatic outlining

What's especially slick about Excel's outlining is that the program can automatically create the outline structure for you. Simply structure the range (or the entire worksheet, if that's what you're outlining) so that the rows and columns that contain summary values such as totals appear below and to the right of the details, respectively. Most people lay out their spreadsheets this way, anyway.

If you've used this common structure, simply select the area you want to outline, choose Group and Outline from the Data menu, and then choose the Auto Outline command. You can even tell Excel to automatically format the totals in bold: in the Outline dialog box (which appears when you choose Settings from the Data menu's Group and Outline submenu), check the Automatic Styles box and then click Apply Styles. (Tip: If you want to change the way the totals or any other level of the outline appears, redefine the style for that outline level.)

Manual outlining

You can also specify the outline levels manually. Use this technique when you've structured a range or worksheet in a way that prohibits Excel from deciphering its structure — or if you want to set up various outline levels before entering formulas and values.

Experimenting with outlining

The best way to appreciate the benefits of Excel outlining is to play with the sample file named Annual Budget, included with Excel. This model depicts a typical annual budget for a firm with five sites. Click two outlining buttons, and you can completely collapse the spreadsheet to show only the total budget expenditures for each site along with a grand total — a total of 12 cells from a model that uses nearly 1,000. But by clicking other outlining buttons in the worksheet, you can zoom in to view, for example, each monthly expenditure for each site in each fiscal quarter.

Strength in Numbers: Linking Worksheets

If you actually fill each of the four million cells that an Excel worksheet can contain, you're a candidate for a different kind of cell — a padded one. When you're creating very large models, take advantage of Excel's capability to link separate worksheet documents. As the preceding chapter introduces, linking worksheets involves creating a formula in one worksheet that refers to one or more cells in other worksheets.

The benefits of linking

Linking has several benefits. When you divide a large model across numerous worksheet documents, Excel runs more efficiently — the model recalculates, opens, and saves faster than if everything was stored in one worksheet. You can also create different views in the model to examine it from different angles — create one worksheet containing all the data and formulas, and then link it to separate worksheets that act as reports. You can also use linking to integrate the efforts of a workgroup — each team member contributes his or her worksheet, and you link to them a summary worksheet that presents the key figures from each one.

How to make a link in Excel

Linking one worksheet to another is easy. If you're creating a formula and you want to refer to a cell or range in a different worksheet, simply activate that worksheet, select the cell or range, and then switch back to the first worksheet. The resulting formula contains an *external reference* to the other worksheet. Another way to link two worksheets is with the Copy and Paste Special commands: in the source worksheet, select the cell(s) to which you want to refer and then choose Copy. Next, switch to the worksheet into which you want to paste the linked data and choose Paste Special from the Edit menu. In the Paste Special dialog box, click the Paste Link button.

One final tip on working with multiple worksheets: to quickly clean up a cluttered screen, use the Window menu's Arrange command, which lets you rearrange open windows in a variety of ways.

Workbooks: Digital Binders

In Excel 4, you can bind linked worksheets (as well as unlinked worksheets and often-used charts and macro sheets) into a *workbook*. A workbook document is a digital three-ring binder, a way to transport and easily open a collection of related documents.

To create a workbook in Excel 4, choose New from the File menu and double-click the Workbook option. In the workbook window that appears, click the Add button and then specify the documents you want to bind. Finally, save the workbook. From now on, you can open the files as a group in one fell swoop — simply open the workbook.

Copying Excel Cells as a Picture to Retain Formatting

Word and Excel mesh beautifully, but if you paste some cells you copied from Excel into a different program, you lose any text or border formatting that you did in Excel.

If you want to retain borders, shading, and other formats, copy the spreadsheet cells as a picture: In Excel, select the cells and then press Shift while opening the Edit menu. Notice that the Copy command now reads Copy Picture. Choose Copy Picture and then select the As Shown When Printed option. Now switch into the second program and paste. (Note that you can't edit the data you've pasted — if you need to change it, you have to return to Excel.) You can also use this technique to move a chart into another program.

Workbooks in Excel 5

In Excel 5, all worksheets are workbooks — that is, you don't have to go through the process I just described to create a digital binder. Workbooks contain individual sheets, which you can switch between by clicking tabs at the bottom of the workbook window. A default workbook opens with 16 sheets; you can insert or delete sheets as needed.

From Fonts to Forms: Formatting Tips

Before the Mac, spreadsheets were dull tables of numbers that only a bean-counter could find attractive. But not only do Mac spreadsheets provide access to the Mac's typographic talents, they also sport features that encroach on desktop publishing territory. In fact, when you need to create fill-in-the-blank forms such as invoices and insurance applications, a spreadsheet may be a better tool than a publishing program. The spreadsheet's row-and-column grid ensures that a form's elements visually align with each other. You can configure cell borders to act as lines and boxes, and you can add shading to cells, rows, or columns to set them apart. Best of all, you can use the spreadsheet program itself to fill out and calculate values on the form.

Accessing Often-Used Formats and Styles

Chances are you use similar number, text, and border formats throughout a spreadsheet. Instead of making trip after trip to the menu bar or tool palette to change formats, take advantage of the labor-saving features that your program provides.

If you use Excel and you frequently use a specific font, size, and style combination, create a cell style for that combination as described in this chapter. It's the best way to cut down on repetitive formatting.

If you use Lotus 1-2-3 and you frequently use specific formats, click the Show In Menu button before closing the Style Font dialog box. (You can also use the Style floating palette to summon the plain, italic, or bold styles.) Remember that you can also use the Range Format dialog box to add often-used formats to the Range menu.

1-2-3 also lets you apply an existing border or shading arrangement to other cells: select the bordered or shaded cells and choose Copy. Next, select the cells you want to reformat and choose Paste Special. In the dialog box that appears, select the Styles and Formats option.

Adding borders and shading

Even if you don't have publishing aspirations, you can use borders and shading to create more readable spreadsheets. If a spreadsheet contains long rows, add a top and bottom border to the cells in each row. This creates a line (in graphic arts parlance, a *rule*) that visually separates each row, lessening the chance that a reader's eyes will stray to adjacent rows as they scan across the spreadsheet. If your spreadsheet contains dozens of rows, consider adding a blank row after every five or ten rows to make the spreadsheet less dense on-screen. If you plan to print the spreadsheet, consider applying a light shading to every other row. Figure 6-3 "Borders and Shading" illustrates these techniques.

Spreadsheets created with Excel, 1-2-3, and Resolve can even contain images created in other programs. As the Step-by-Step boxes in this chapter show, you can take advantage of this feature to add a company logo or scanned image to forms or spreadsheets.

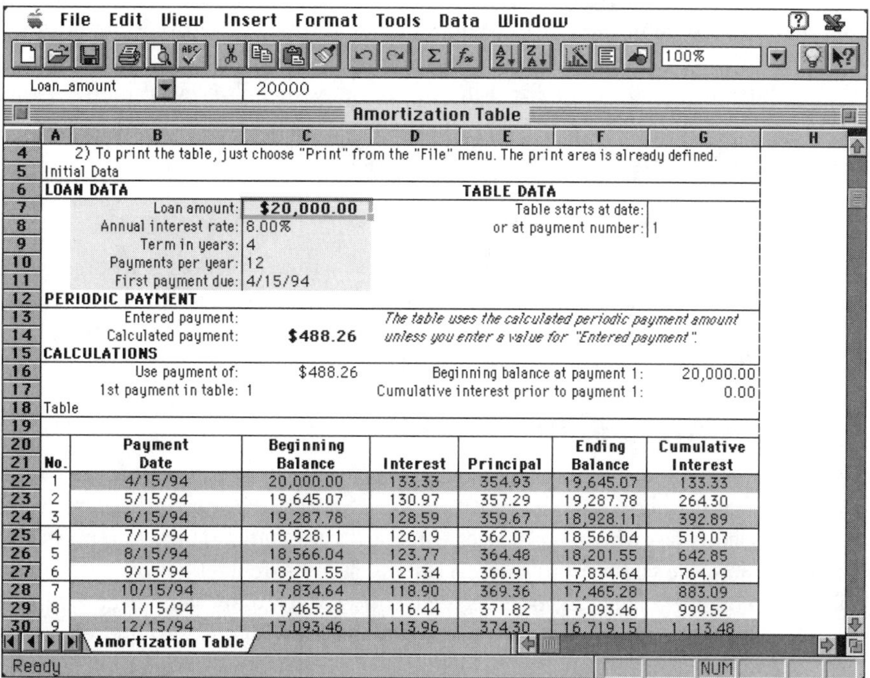

Figure 6-3: Borders and Shading Appropriate use of cell borders and shading can make a spreadsheet easier to read and use. In this spreadsheet, top and bottom cell borders separate each line of the loan-amortization table, lessening the chance that readers' eyes will skip to an adjacent row as they scan from left to right. Colored shading helps highlight key areas of the spreadsheet.

Accuracy is Everything

A spreadsheet that yields inaccurate results is not only worthless, it's dangerous. Modeling gurus refer to the process of proofreading a worksheet and verifying its accuracy as *auditing*. Auditing involves understanding the flow of a model's logic — in essence, understanding its goals and how it attempts to reach them — as well as verifying that its calculations are accurate.

The best way to clarify what a model's goals are is to state them explicitly. Every model should include built-in documentation that describes the model's purpose, states its assumptions, and documents key formulas. You'll find some guidelines in the preceding chapter.

Zoom out for the big picture

As for verifying accuracy, Excel provides several features that can help you in your journey along the audit trail. One is the View menu's Zoom command, which lets you zoom out to show more cells in the window. (The Zoom Control box also lets you zoom in and out.) By zooming out to show the entire worksheet, you can get the big picture of how the worksheet is organized — it's like viewing the worksheet from 50,000 feet up. By using the Window menu's New Window command along with the Zoom command, you can even create multiple views of a worksheet, with each showing it from a different electronic altitude.

Finding the cells referenced in a formula

When you're double-checking to see whether a formula is accurate, you often need to refer back to the cells referenced in the formula. Excel makes this easy: double-click a cell containing a formula, and Excel selects the cells referenced in the formula. If those cells are in a linked worksheet, Excel even activates that worksheet for you.

Power auditing with the Select Special command

One of Excel's most powerful auditing tools is the Edit menu's Go To Special feature (choose Go To and then click Special). Choosing this command displays a dialog box whose options let you select cells that meet the criteria you specify. Suppose you want to delete a cell but aren't sure whether other formulas need its contents. Select the doomed cell, choose Go To Special, select the Dependents option, and click OK. If a different cell's formula refers to the cell, Excel selects the dependent cell. (In the spreadsheet world, a *dependent* cell refers to the active cell; a *precedent* cell is referred to by the active cell.)

The Go To Special command can also locate inconsistencies in rows or columns (the Row Differences and Column Differences options), errors in formulas (the Formula Errors check box), and much more.

Customizing Excel's Toolbars

If you use Excel, customize the program's toolbars to reflect the commands and options you use most. It's easy: simply choose Toolbars from the View menu, click the Customize button, select a tool category, and then drag the tools to the appropriate toolbars.

If you're into macros, check out the Custom category of tools (click the Customize button, and then select the Custom option in the Categories box). You can assign your own macros to this collection of miscellaneous tools — click a tool, and its macro runs.

To reset the toolbars to their default (original) settings, choose Toolbars. Select the toolbar you want to reset and then click the Reset button.

Optimizing Performance and Memory

As a model grows, Excel slows. You can optimize Excel's performance and use memory more efficiently by observing a few basic guidelines.

Don't format gratuitously

Formatting can use up to half the amount of memory and disk space that a model requires. If you're working with a large model, reformat cells only when necessary. If your model requires a large look-up table (such as a table of sales tax percentages for each state), put the table in a separate, unformatted worksheet. Then link other worksheets to the table.

Strip formatting from macros

Similarly, when creating macros, you may be tempted to format them to enhance their legibility. That approach is sound, but it gobbles memory. When you're sure the macro sheet is debugged, choose Select All and then Clear (both from the Edit menu). In the Clear dialog box, double-click the Formats option. This option wipes out formatting while retaining everything else. (You may want to save a copy of the formatted macro in a different macro sheet, too.)

It's better to format an entire row or column rather than a large range of cells within the row or column. When you format an entire column or row, Excel makes an internal notation saying, for example, "Column A is bold." That requires less memory than saying "Cells A1 through A120 are bold." And don't forget Excel's cell style feature. If you want to change the font of all cells in a worksheet, redefine the style named Normal instead of selecting the entire worksheet and then choosing a different font.

Another Way to Create Links Between Word and Excel

The Step-by-Step box "From Excel to Word: How to Publish and Subscribe," later in this chapter, shows one technique for creating a link between Excel and Word. You can also use Word's Paste Special command. In the Paste Special dialog box, select the Excel option and then click the Paste button. Thereafter, you can edit the spreadsheet by double-clicking the cells you pasted. (You need at least 8MB of memory to run both Word and Excel at the same time.) When you return to Word, you see that it has automatically updated the document to reflect your edits.

This technique relies on a data-exchange system called *object linking and embedding,* or OLE for short. For details about OLE, see Chapter 27.

Work down rather than across

As you build a large worksheet, try to work down rather than across — Excel allocates memory by rows. If you want to add extra space between rows or columns, do so by adjusting the height or width of the rows or columns, not by using blank rows and columns. But don't be afraid to put large blank areas between sections of a worksheet. Excel uses a *sparse-matrix* memory-management scheme that lets it all but ignore large blank areas. (But remember that a cell is not considered blank if it contains formatting such as borders or shading.)

Get faster recalc speeds

As for boosting performance, Excel recalculates in an upper-left to lower-right direction, so you get faster recalcs by placing summary information in the lower-right corner of the worksheet. If you put summary info in the upper-left corner, Excel has to make multiple passes through the model when recalculating.

Automatic Updating with Publish and Subscribe

In the preceding chapter, I show how to move some spreadsheet cells or a graph into another program by using the Mac's Clipboard. The Clipboard's a cinch, but it has a big limitation. If the data changes in the originating program — in this case, if your spreadsheet figures change — you need to repeat the copy-and-paste routine in order to bring the latest version into your word processor or desktop publishing program.

System 7's publish-and-subscribe features enable you to quickly update the word-processed or desktop-published document when the original spreadsheet changes. All major-league spreadsheets support publish and subscribe, as does the ClarisWorks integrated program. If you use a word processor or publishing program that also supports publish and subscribe, you can use its Subscribe To command to include published cells or graphs in your documents, as shown in the Step-by-Step box "From Excel to Word: How to Publish and Subscribe."

The graphs that spreadsheet programs create are actually object-oriented graphics; you can modify these graphics by using the drawing features in an integrated package such as ClarisWorks, or in a graphics program such as ClarisDraw, Adobe Illustrator, or Macromedia FreeHand. (For more details on graphing, see Chapter 12.)

From Excel to Word: How to Publish and Subscribe

With System 7, you can create links between a spreadsheet or graph and a document created in a word processor — or any other program that supports System 7's publish-and-subscribe features. The instructions in this box show you how to include a graph from Microsoft Excel in a Microsoft Word document. You can apply these general steps to most Mac programs — they all support publish-and-subscribe in similar ways.

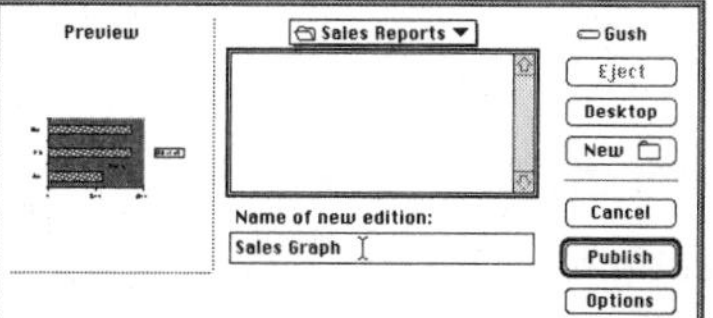

To publish the graph:

1. **Select the graph you want to publish.**
2. **Choose Create Publisher from the Edit menu's Publishing submenu.**
3. **Type a name for the edition file (the graph) and then click Publish or press Return.**
   The graph is published.

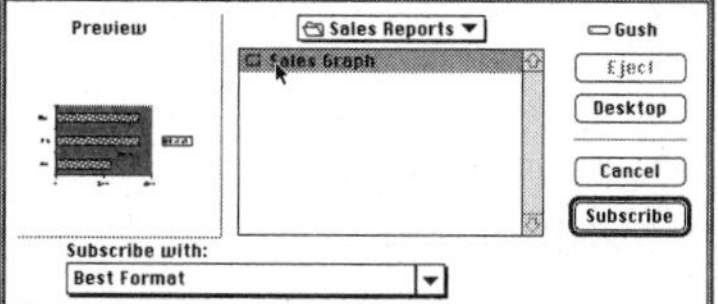

To bring the published graph into Microsoft Word:

1. **Choose Subscribe To from the Edit menu's Publishing submenu.**
   The Mac automatically selects the edition file you just created and shows a preview of it.
2. **Click Subscribe or press Return.**
   The graph appears in the Word document. To change the way the graph is updated when it or its underlying data changes, use Word's Subscriber Options dialog box or the Publisher Options dialog box in 1-2-3 or Excel. These dialog boxes let you specify when and how Word should receive an updated version of the graph.

Bridging the Mac-PC Gap

Microsoft says that most large firms use Excel on both Macs and DOS PCs running Microsoft Windows. It's no wonder — the program's interface and file format are the same on both platforms, so exchanging documents and switching between environments are relatively easy. Excel can even convert a worksheet's custom graphics (such as a company logo) when you move it from one platform to the other.

There are some potential hurdles, but you can work around them by establishing a few standard practices.

Use TrueType fonts

Both the Mac and Windows support TrueType fonts directly. You avoid having to reformat worksheets because one system's fonts aren't available in the other.

Use DOS filenames — even on the Mac

A DOS filename can have up to eight characters and is followed by a period and a three-character *extension* that identifies the file's type. An Excel for Windows worksheet has the extension .XLW. It's a shame to trade the Mac's 31-character filenames for names like BUDGET95.XLW, but you can simulate longer names by binding the file into a workbook and then using the workbook window's Options button to specify longer, more descriptive names.

Have your macros find out where they are

In macros, use the =GET WORKSPACE function to enable the macro to determine which platform it's running on. Then use IF . . . THEN statements throughout your code to adjust the macro's workings accordingly.

Use OLE instead of publish and subscribe

For worksheets containing hot links to other worksheets, use object linking and embedding (the Paste Link command) instead of the Mac's publish-and-subscribe commands. Microsoft Windows supports OLE, and as far as it's concerned, pub-and-sub is a bar and sandwich joint.

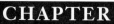

CHAPTER 6 CONCEPTS AND TERMS

- Instead of typing cell addresses by hand when creating formulas, use the cell-pointing feature that all spreadsheet programs provide.
- Excel lets you assign descriptive names to cells and cell ranges. You can take advantage of this feature to create more descriptive formulas and quickly go to different sections of a spreadsheet.
- Choosing the appropriate number format (a currency format that uses two decimal places, for example) and adding cell borders can make a spreadsheet easier to read and more meaningful.
- With System 7's publish-and-subscribe feature, you can establish links between spreadsheet documents and documents you're working on in other programs that automatically update tables or graphs when the underlying spreadsheet data changes.

auditing
The process of proofreading a worksheet and verifying its accuracy. Auditing involves understanding the flow of a model's logic — understanding its goals and how it attempts to reach them — as well as verifying that the model's calculations are accurate.

border
A line on one or more edges of a spreadsheet cell. In graphic arts parlance, a rule.

cell pointing
Adding cell addresses to formulas by pointing with the mouse pointer or the arrow keys instead of typing the cell addresses manually.

data series
A list of incrementing or decrementing data, such as the sequence of numbers from 1 to 10 or the months of the year.

dependent
In the spreadsheet world, a cell that refers to the active cell; see *precedent.*

external reference
A formula that refers to a cell or range of cells in a different worksheet. When you link Worksheet A to Worksheet B, Worksheet A contains an external reference.

fill handle
In Microsoft Excel, the small black box at the lower-left corner of a selected cell. By pointing to the fill handle and then dragging into adjacent cells, you can repeat the values in the selected cell or create a data series.

naming
Assigning a descriptive name, such as QuarterlySales, to a cell or range of cells. If you name a cell or range of cells, you can refer to the name in formulas, thereby making the formulas easier to understand.

object linking and embedding
Abbreviated OLE, a method of establishing links between two documents (or between parts of one document) in certain Microsoft products and in Aldus PageMaker 5.

toolbar
In Microsoft Excel, a window containing buttons that perform various tasks when clicked.

precedent
A cell referred to by the active cell.

sparse-matrix memory management
An efficient method of spreadsheet storage that doesn't waste memory on empty cells, letting you squeeze more into the machine's memory.

workbook
In Microsoft Excel, a digital three-ring binder: a file that can hold multiple worksheet, chart, and macro sheet documents. In Excel 5, all worksheets are workbooks.

CHAPTER SEVEN

The Delights of Databases

- From fields to records — database basics
- Tips for choosing database programs
- Customizing fields and layouts in FileMaker Pro
- Tracking time with time-billing software

Life is filled with facts to file. In any office, near the "You don't have to be crazy to work here, but it helps" sign, file cabinets entomb paper that has run the course from in-box to out-box. Rolodex files swell with cards, and sticky notes spread like moss on the surfaces of overcrowded folder holders. "While you were out" messages stack up in corners, each one a clear reminder of *why* you were out.

If this description fits your workplace, the notion that a computer can get you organized and keep your head above paper can be enticing enough to inspire a purchase. But this inspiration is often built on the vague idea that computers have miraculous powers of organization, that putting one on your desk somehow gives you one-key access to those tedious tidbits you have to root for now.

Speed, disk storage, and eraserless revisions do give a computer powerful filing capabilities — when they're tapped by a *database manager*. These electronic file clerks let you store, sort, retrieve, revise, and print information. You can store an entire file drawer of facts and figures on a floppy disk and locate any one of them in the time it would take you to open the drawer.

But a database manager isn't a panacea for organizational ills. For one thing, a computer database can't create itself. You have to decide how to organize your information and then set up the database manager accordingly. And information doesn't file itself in a database; you (or someone else, if you're lucky) have to set aside time for that tedious task called *data entry*. A database may enable you to effortlessly retrieve information, but it requires endless maintenance.

Variations on the Database Theme

Every database manager handles the details of field formatting and range checking in its own way, but most database managers work within the standard framework of fields and records. One interesting exception is Apple's HyperCard. As Chapter 19 describes, HyperCard is much more than a database manager; you can use it to create interactive multimedia productions, for example. But its capabilities to sort, search, and store make it a useful data filer.

If you want to replace your Rolodex with something electronic, check out electronic address book programs such as Prairie Group's In Touch, Now Software's Now Contact, Claris's ClarisOrganizer, Attain's In Control, or Adobe's TouchBase Pro. These programs, often called *personal information managers,* can track names, addresses, and phone numbers and can even dial the phone for you (see Chapter 16). Many address book programs include small binders that you can use to create hard-copy versions of your address book. Several free or shareware address book programs are also available (see the "Best of BMUG" collection on the CD that accompanies this book).

Many personal information managers can also help you manage your time as well as your data. Now Software's Now Up-to-Date, Claris's ClarisOrganizer, Attain's In Control, and Adobe's DateBook Pro are among the programs that enable you to set up schedules and print daily to-do lists in a variety of formats. (Also see the section on time-billing packages later in this chapter.)

For publishers and multimedia producers, managing a hard drive containing images, QuickTime movies, and digital sounds can be more of a challenge than managing client databases or schedules. If you're in this group, you may want to consider one of the new breed of so-called *mixed-media* databases such as Imspace's Kudo Image Browser, Adobe Fetch, or Canto's Cumulus series. These programs enable you to catalog, browse, and retrieve illustrations, sounds, clip art, and QuickTime movies. You can create media categories — outdoor scenes, background music, sound effects, and politicians — and then organize your graphics and multimedia files according to those categories. You can find more details about these multimedia databases in Chapter 14. A demo version of Kudo Image Browser is included on the CD that accompanies this book.

Data Basics

Unlike a file folder, database managers don't let you stuff information anywhere just to get it out of sight. They hold data within a rigid structure, and planning that structure is the most important step in setting up your database. You can reorganize an electronic database after you've entered data, but it's not much easier than reorganizing a paper filing system.

Phase 1: Set up the structure

A database structure is formed by two building blocks — *fields* and *records.* A field is a single piece of information for an entry; together, the fields for an entry make up the record (see Figure 7-1 "A Matter of Record"). In a database version of a Rolodex, for example, all of the information on a single card is a record and each element — first name, last name, company, zip code, and so on — is a field. When you define a database's structure, you create fields and give each one a name that reflects its contents, such as First Name or Street Address.

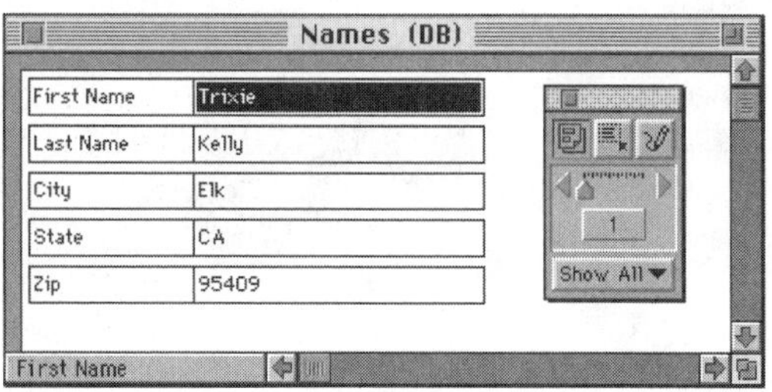

Names (DB)

First Name	Last Name	City	State
Trixie	Kelly	Elk	CA
Roy	Taylor	Albion	CA
Anita	Taylor	Albion	CA
Fred	Fargoyle	Fredville	CA
Joe	Smith	Fort Bragg	CA

Figure 7-1: A Matter of Record In a database, a field is a single piece of information for an entry; together, the fields for an entry make up a record. The window (top) shows a single record from a Microsoft Works database. The window (bottom) shows five records displayed in a spreadsheet-like, row-and-column format.

Phase 2: Create forms and reports

In addition to defining the structure, creating a database involves specifying how information will be presented on-screen. The screen layout of fields and their names is called a *form*. Most programs provide a preset, quick-and-dirty form layout to use when you just can't wait to start entering data. Many programs also let you design your own forms — you can even create on-screen versions of the paper forms that probably clutter your desk. Macintosh database managers tend to offer more design options than a decorator supply house, enabling you to choose fonts and styles, draw lines and boxes, and add graphics, such as company logos (see Figure 7-2, "In Fine Form").

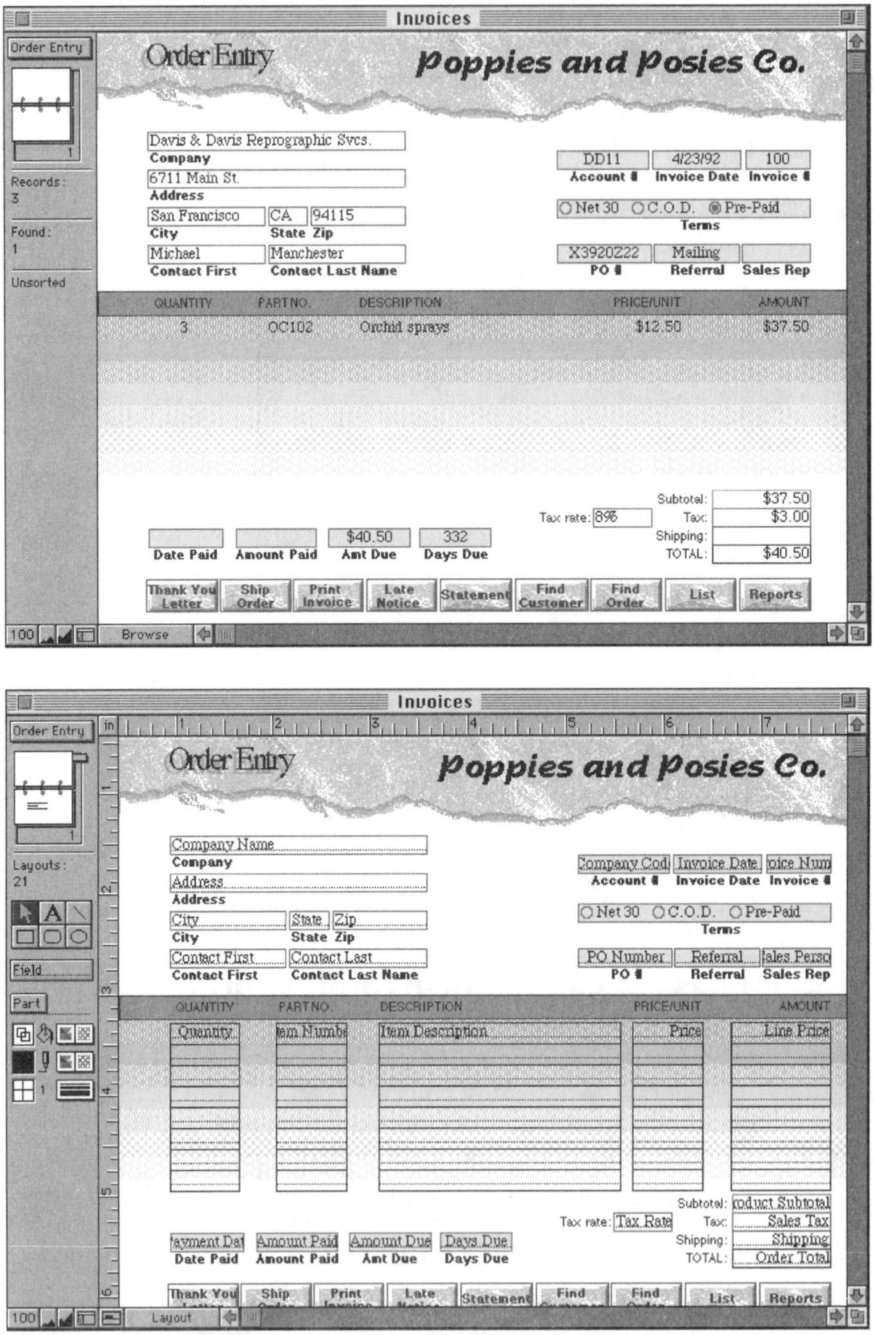

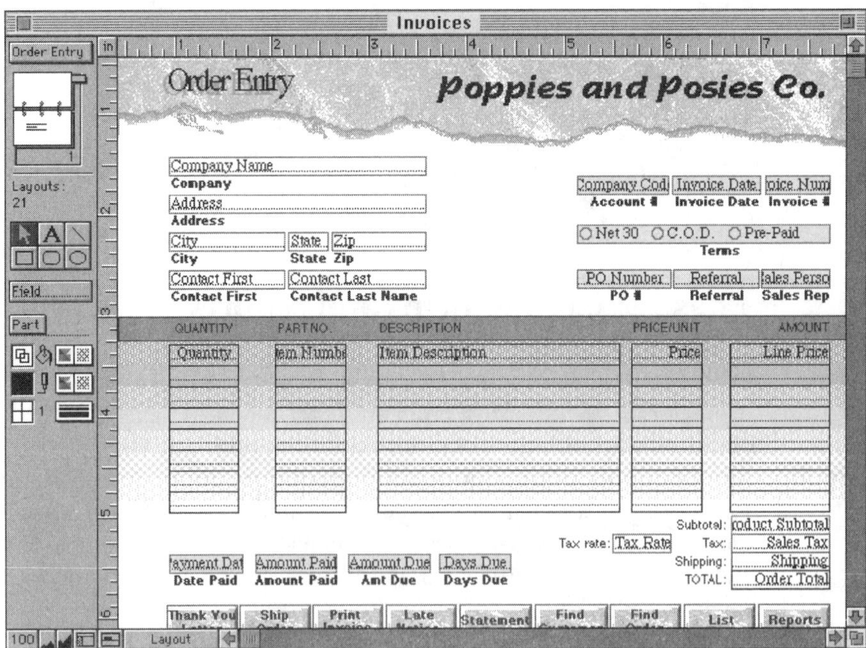

Figure 7-2: In Fine Form Many Mac database managers provide layout features that let you create sophisticated forms for data entry and reporting. The invoice form (top) was created using the powerful form-design features in FileMaker Pro. The window (bottom) shows the form in FileMaker Pro's Layout mode and the tools on the left for drawing shapes and creating text items.

Many database managers also let you view and enter data in a spreadsheet-like, row-and-column format. This *table view* can be a good way to step back for the big picture — it's like looking at a baseball card team photograph instead of having to paw through each player's card separately. Programs that provide a table view (also called a *columnar view*) include Claris FileMaker Pro, ClarisWorks, and Microsoft Works.

Different Fields for Different Yields

Database managers provide different types of fields for different kinds of information. All data managers offer two basic field types. *Text fields* hold letters, numbers, and any other keyboard character. Number, or *numeric*, fields hold numeric values — an employee's hourly wage in a personnel database or a balance-due value in an accounting database, for example.

Most data managers provide additional field types. *Date fields* hold only date values. *Picture fields* hold graphics that you paste in from the Clipboard. *Logical fields* hold only one of two values — yes or no. For example, you may create a logical field called Past Due that indicates whether a client's account is paid up. *Formula fields* obtain their values not from the keyboard but by processing values in other fields according to a formula you specify. An example of a formula field is a Gross Pay field that multiplies the value in an Hours Worked field by that in an Hourly Wage field.

Tips for improving accuracy

One way to improve your accuracy in data entry is to use a program that lets you assign *range checking* values to fields. You may specify, for example, that an error message be displayed if someone enters only five digits in a Social Security Number field. If your company opened in 1993, you can tell the data manager to reject employee hire dates earlier than January 1, 1993.

If text fields can hold any character, why are there special fields for numbers, dates, and yes or no values? One reason is to guard against inaccuracy. Most database managers don't let you store a text value in a number field, and therefore, thwart someone typing a lowercase letter *l* for the number 1 or an uppercase letter *O* for a zero. Having numeric fields also simplifies generating totals and subtotals in reports.

Choosing and changing field types

Choosing the correct field type is especially important for fields that hold numbers or date values. Although you can store numbers or dates in a text field, it isn't a good idea. Most data managers can apply calculations to the values in a number field — adding a sales tax percentage to a subtotal to arrive at a grand total, for example — but they can't calculate numbers stored in a text field.

Can you change a field's type if you realize that, for example, a text field really should be a date field? Generally, yes, but depending on the program you use — and the change you're proposing — you may lose some or all of the data in that field. The best way to eliminate field-conversion worries is to think about each field's type before you start entering data.

Basic Data Management in FileMaker Pro

Its straightforward operating style, excellent form-layout features, and speed have made Claris's FileMaker Pro the top-selling Macintosh data manager for some time. In 1992, Claris shipped a PC version of FileMaker Pro that runs under the Microsoft Windows environment and can share databases with its Mac cousin. This box shows how to specify field types, add error-checking options, and create buttons and scripts in FileMaker Pro.

To specify a field type:

1. **Choose Define Fields from the Select menu.**
   When creating a new database, you don't have to perform this step — the Define Fields dialog box appears automatically.
2. **To change an existing field's type, select it.**
3. **In the Type section of the Define Fields dialog box, click the desired field type.**
   You can also press ⌘ along with a letter, as shown at left.

Type
- (•) Text ⌘T
- ( ) Number ⌘N
- ( ) Date ⌘D
- ( ) Time ⌘I
- ( ) Picture or Sound ⌘P
- ( ) Calculation ⌘C
- ( ) Summary ⌘S

4. **If you change an existing field, the Change button is highlighted. Click it or press Return.**
   Depending on the field type you specify, a message may appear warning you that some or all data in that field will be lost.
5. **When you've finished defining, creating, or customizing fields, click Done.**

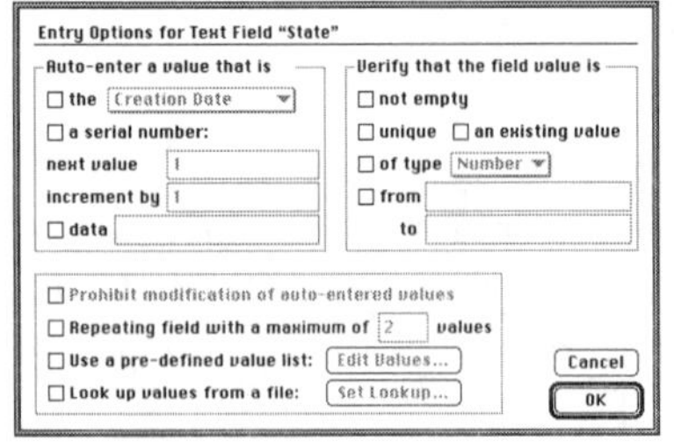

To specify a range, a list of choices, or other data-entry options for a field:

1. **When defining the field, click the Options button. If you've already defined the field, select it and then click Options.**
   The Entry Options dialog box (left) appears.
2. **Select the appropriate options as described in the following table.**

To...	*Select...*	*And Then...*
Have FileMaker Pro automatically enter data	One or more auto-enter options	Specify the type of information to enter
Have FileMaker Pro "proofread" entries	One or more verify options	Specify additional options, such as Type (number, date, time) or a range (From and To)
Restrict data entry to a fixed number of choices	The box labeled "Use a pre-defined value list"	Type each value, pressing Return after each one
Have FileMaker Pro enter values from another file when certain conditions are met	The box labeled "Look up values from a file"	Select the file, and then specify the conditions in the Lookup dialog box

To create radio buttons or check boxes for a field based on a list of values:

1. **If you haven't already, use the Define Fields dialog box to specify the list of values for the field.**
2. **Switch to layout mode by choosing Layout from the Select menu.**
3. **Select the field you want to modify by clicking it once.**
   If you double-click the field, the Text Format dialog box appears. Click Cancel and repeat step 3.
4. **Choose Field Format from the Format menu.**
   You can also press ⌘-Option-F. The Field Format dialog box appears.
5. **Choose the desired element (buttons, check boxes, and so on) from the Display Type pop-up menu.**
6. **Click OK or press Return.**

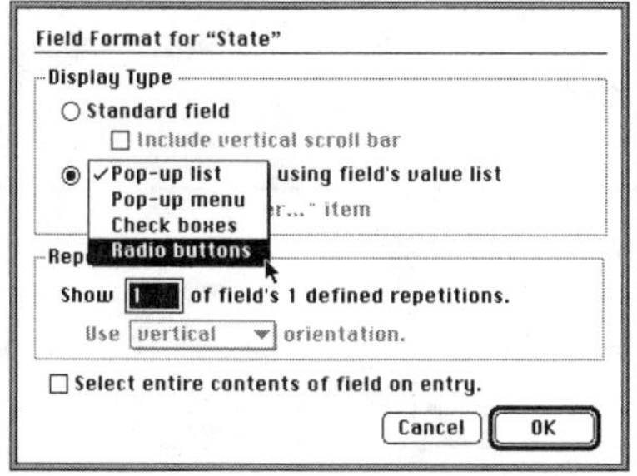

To create a script:

1. **Choose ScriptMaker from the Scripts menu.**
2. **Type a name for the script.**
   Use a descriptive name that reflects the script's purpose, such as *Print Outstanding Invoices.* If you don't want the script to appear in the Scripts menu, uncheck the Include in Menu box.

(continued on the next page)

(continued from previous page)

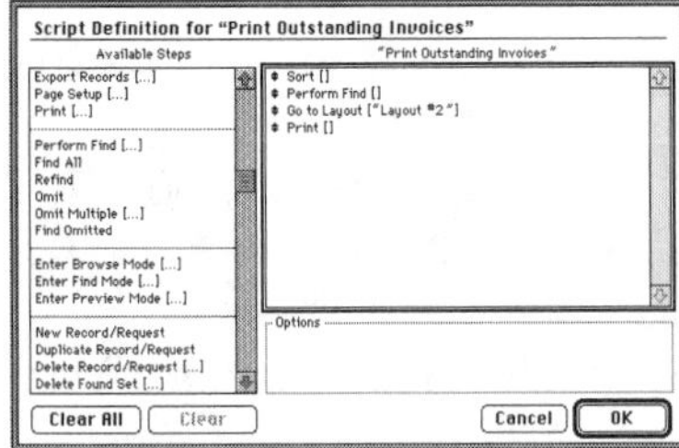

3. **Click the Create button or press Return.**

   The Script Definition dialog box appears.

4. **Specify the steps you want the script to perform by double-clicking them in the Available Steps box.**

   You can change the order in which a step appears by pointing to the up-and-down pointing arrows next to the step and then dragging.

5. **Click OK or press Return.**

   The Define Scripts dialog box reappears.

6. **To define another script, return to Step 2. Otherwise, click Done.**

To assign a script to a button:

1. **Choose Layout from the Select menu.**
2. **Create the new button by drawing a square and then typing the button's name within it.**
3. **Select the button and choose Define Button from the Scripts menu.**

   The Define Button dialog box appears.

4. **Click the Perform Script option, and then select the desired script's name from the pop-up menu.**
5. **Click OK or press Return.**

   At this point, you may want to switch back to Browse mode and try the new button.

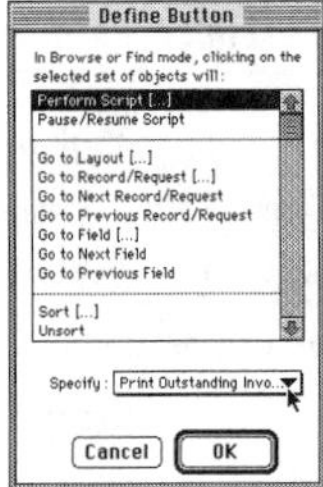

When Is a Zip Code Not a Number?

When creating a database for addresses, many people make the mistake of using a number field to hold zip codes. The problem is that eight states (as well as Puerto Rico) have zip codes that begin with 0, and a number field generally lops off a leading zero, leaving you with just the last four digits. Many non-U. S. postal codes also contain a mishmash of letters and numbers. The moral: use a text field for zip codes. Doing so enables you to enter a hyphen if you're one of the few people in the world who actually uses nine-digit zip codes.

Sorting Out Your Data

Using appropriate fields is also important when it comes to sorting data. Suppose you want to sort an employee database according to each employee's date of birth. If you store the birth date values in a text field, your database manager places values beginning with December ahead of those beginning with September, because *D* precedes *S*. A date field knows better. When you use a date field, the program recognizes that September precedes December and sorts your records accurately.

A database manager's capability to sort information in alphabetic or numeric order makes your data more useful by letting you look at it from different perspectives. In a personnel database, you can view a list of employees sorted according to salary, date of hire, or number of sick days taken. You can view a database of videotapes according to title, star, running time, or genre (see Figure 7-3, "Filing Movies").

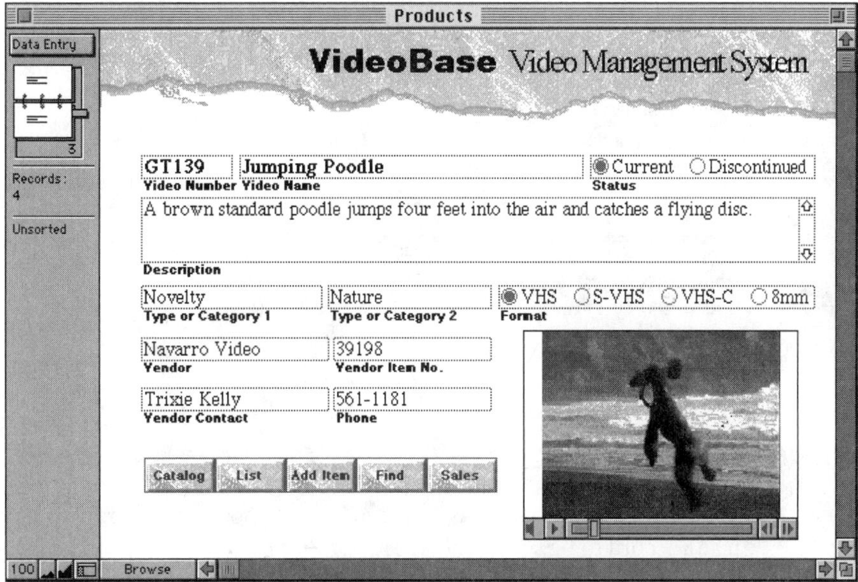

Figure 7-3: Filing Movies This FileMaker Pro database stores information about videos, with a picture field holding QuickTime movie clips. To import a movie into a database, choose Import Movie from the File menu's Import/Export submenu.

Sorting on multiple levels

But what if you want to view an employee list organized by salary within each department or an alphabetized list of horror movies presented in the order they were made? That's where sorting levels come in. Most database managers let you sort data according to multiple levels: last name, then first name; last name, first name, hire date, and department; or last name, first name, age group, income, and city. Multiple sorting levels multiply the angles from which you can view your data (see Figure 7-4, "New Levels of Sorting").

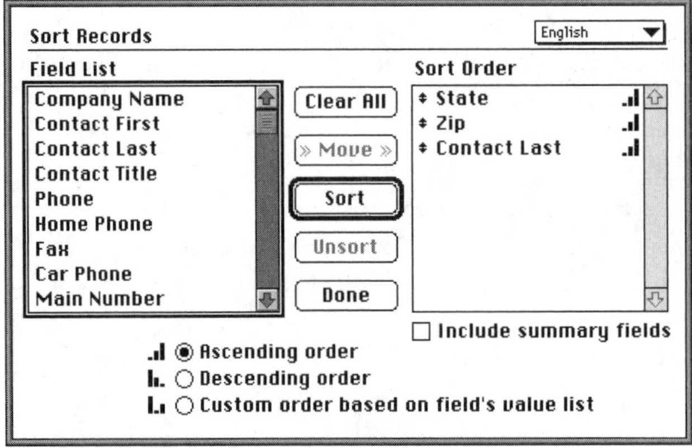

Figure 7-4: New Levels of Sorting This FileMaker Pro database is sorted on three levels — first by state, then by zip code, and then by last name. The rising bars next to each field name denote an ascending (A–Z) sort.

More Tips for Improving Accuracy

A database is only as useful as it is accurate. A typographical error in a field can cause a record to be sorted incorrectly or not found during a search. And if the field contains numbers — an employee's hourly wage, an item's price, or the number of widgets in stock — the inaccuracy can cost you money. No database manager can ensure 100-percent accuracy, but most programs have features that guard against certain kinds of mistakes, making it easier to enter frequently used information.

Use entry checking to avoid typos

Entry-checking features are data-entry proofreaders that compare what you enter to a list or range of acceptable values. Suppose you're creating a personnel file containing a Department field. If your company has four departments, you can specify that the program reject anything other than their names (see Figure 7-5, "Labor Savers").

Power Tips for FileMaker Pro

Finding — and preventing — completely empty records

Choose Find from the Select menu and then type an equal sign (=) in each field. Click Find, and FileMaker Pro selects only those records that are completely empty. Now you can delete them. To prevent a field from being left blank, choose Define Fields from the Select menu and then double-click the field's name. Now check the Not Empty box in the Verify area of the dialog box.

Creating sorted value lists

FileMaker Pro's ability to enter data based on choices you make from a pop-up menu is a real keystroke saver. A nice, tidy value list — whether it's a list of departments or countries — is in sorted order. Problem is, FileMaker Pro can't sort the values within a value list. The solution: Paste the value entries into a word processor that has a Sort command, such as Microsoft Word. Sort the entries, and then paste them into the value list box that appears in the Define Fields dialog box's Options box.

Hide the control panel to gain extra screen space

This trick is especially handy on small-screen Macs. Squint at the lower-left corner of the database window, and click the little icon located to the right of the zoom controls. Click the icon again to make the control panel area reappear.

Ignore the snap-to grid with the ⌘ key

You can override the Layout window's snap-to grid by pressing the ⌘ key while dragging a field or text label.

Bypassing the warning when deleting records

Just press the Option key while choosing Delete. Note, however, that you can't undo a record deletion, so be sure that you really want to delete the record before Option-deleting.

Speeding up field formatting, part 1

When you're creating a form or report, it's tedious to use the Font, Size, and Style commands to fine-tune each field's formatting. An easier way is to format one field as desired, and then ⌘-click it. Any new fields you add to the layout now have the same formatting as the first.

Here's a variation: Format one field and then press Option while dragging it. This action makes a copy of the formatted field. When you let up on the mouse button, however, a dialog box appears from which you can assign a new field for the copy you just made.

Speeding up field formatting, part 2

Another way to format fields quickly is to specify a default font, size, and style before you create the fields. This one is a little weird, but it works. When the Define Fields dialog box appears, click the Done button — that's right, click Done before defining any fields. Next, choose Layout from the Select menu and use the Format menu's commands to specify the default formatting you want. *Now* choose Define Fields from the Select menu and create your fields.

Dragging one part over another

Normally, FileMaker Pro doesn't let you drag one form part (such as a header) over another (such as the body portion of a form). To override this restriction, hold down the Option key while dragging.

Shrinking those database files

You can save disk space by resaving database files in compressed form. Choose Save a Copy As from the File menu, and then choose the Compressed (Smaller) option from the pop-up menu in the Save dialog box. Type a new name for the database and then click Save or press Return.

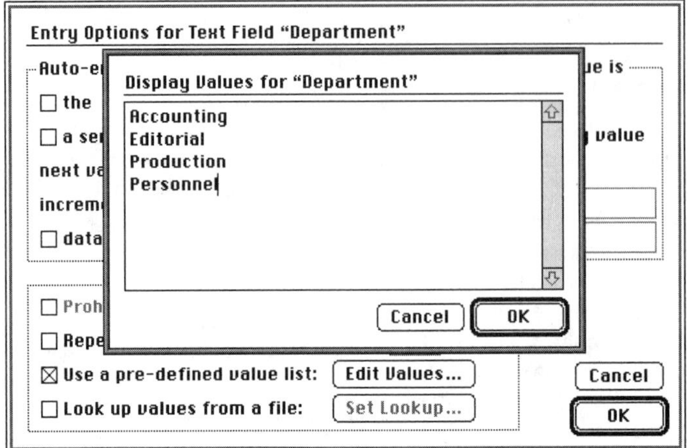

Figure 7-5: Labor Savers FileMaker Pro is among the database managers that let you specify a list or range of acceptable field values. Here, four departments are being specified for a file named Department.

Use input patterns to simplify data entry

Many programs also let you specify *input patterns*, series of characters that affect the text you type. For example, an input pattern for a telephone number field may read *(nnn) nnn-nnnn*. When you enter data into a field with this pattern, you can simply type ten numbers and the data manager inserts the parentheses and hyphen for you. And if you type more or fewer than ten numbers — or throw in some letters — the program lets you know.

Use range checking to keep entries in the ballpark

A cousin to entry checking is *range checking* — ensuring that numbers or dates are within a specified range. If you know the price of a Type A Widget is always between $10.95 and $12.95, you can assign that range to the Price field. Attempting to enter a price outside that range earns you an error message.

Use auto-entry to cut down typing

In many databases, the contents of certain fields stay the same from one record to the next (most of a company's employees live in the same state, for example). To streamline data entry, most programs can enter data into certain fields for you when you create a new record. Most programs can also carry over information from corresponding fields in the previous record.

For those times when the data differs, you can replace automatically entered data by simply backspacing over it. ProVUE Development's Panorama II boasts a love-it-or-hate-it feature called *clairvoyance* — if you type San F and a previous record contains San Francisco, the program inserts the rest of the text for you. You can override the guess by simply continuing to type. You can also turn the feature off when you don't feel like having fields finished for you.

Certain types of fields — ones that list marital status, sex, or whether an account is past due, for example — contain one of only two possible values. Other types of fields are based on a rigid list of values — such as the list of colors available for Type A Widgets or the expense categories in a budget database. Most database programs enable you to specify these kinds of restrictions and select a value from a list of options by clicking on-screen buttons or check boxes. Use these multiple-choice features to improve accuracy and eliminate the drudgery of repeatedly typing the same values.

Golden Retrievers

Unlike the file cabinets I have known, a database manager doesn't teleport information it receives into the Twilight Zone. When you want to find something, you can do so in a few simple ways.

Just browsing

The simplest way to move around in a database is by browsing — moving from one record to the next, either to view the records you just sorted or to admire how much better they look on-screen than in a box of index cards. When you locate the record you want, you can alter it or just move on to the next.

Specifying your search criteria

When you're looking for something specific instead of just browsing, you use what are called *search specifications* or *search criteria* — phrases that tell your database manager what to look for. A search can be simple ("Find Dave Byrd's record"), complex ("Find all married male employees in accounting earning more than $35,000 but less than $50,000"), or downright impossible ("Find all Tonya Harding fans in Nancy Kerrigan's house").

When you perform a complex search, you use *search operators* — characters like the greater-than and less-than signs (> and <) — to find entries above or below a certain value. You also use the *logical operators* AND, OR, and NOT to combine search criteria. In the complex search example, the logical AND appears twice: "Find all employees whose Sex field is male AND whose Department field is accounting AND whose Salary field is greater than 35,000." With the logical AND, all criteria must be true for a given record to be considered found. With a logical OR, only one need be true: "Find all clients in Minneapolis OR St. Paul."

Simplifying complex searches

Fortunately, complex searches aren't complex to conduct. Most Mac database managers provide dialog boxes that make performing complex searches a matter of clicking the desired options, typing the data you're looking for, and then clicking OK (see Figure 7-6, "Search for Data").

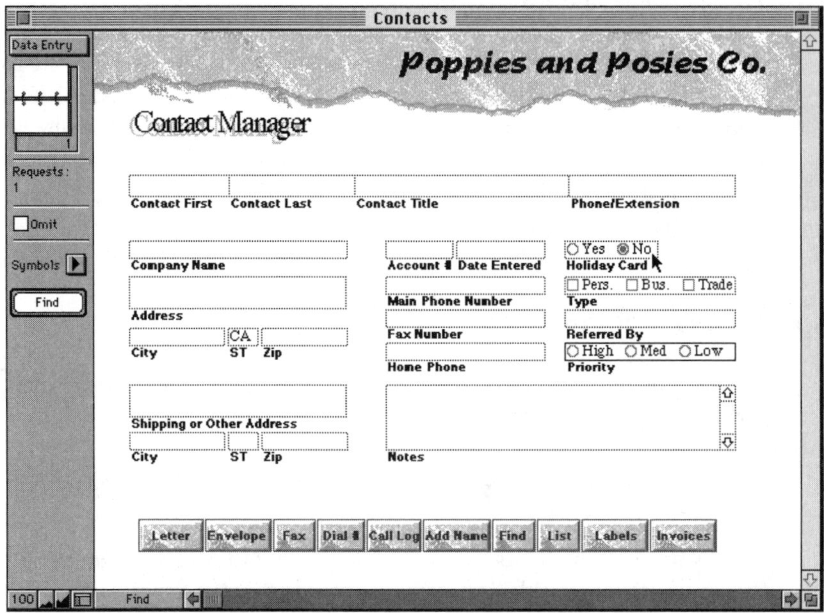

Figure 7-6: Search for Data Most Mac data managers let you search for data by typing the values you're looking for in the appropriate fields. Here, a FileMaker Pro search is being specified for all contacts in California that did not receive a holiday greeting card.

Creating Your Own FileMaker Help Screens

A polished program provides its own on-line help screens, and so can your FileMaker Pro database. Simply create a new layout, and instead of putting fields on it, put several paragraphs (or more) of help — advice for using your reports or scripts, tips for searching or sorting, or reminders for data entry. Name your layout *Help,* and users can view your on-line help by choosing its name from the layout pop-up menu. Many sample databases included with FileMaker Pro use this technique.

Tips for Designing Database Forms

Mac database managers have layout features that encroach on desktop publishing territory. You can find on-screen measuring rulers and T-squares and tools for drawing lines, circles, and boxes. You can also add text and graphics such as a company name and logo. And you can change the font, style, and size in which fields and labels appear.

All these layout tools also make it easy to create visually busy database forms. Graphically tasteless forms don't present your data in its best light, and they make data entry — never a picnic anyway — more arduous.

If you're working in FileMaker Pro on a large-screen Mac and want to design a form that fits on the screen of a small Mac such an SE or Classic, open the FileMaker Help database and use its size as a template — it's designed for 9-inch monitors.

Because most data managers let you create numerous forms and switch between them, I recommend creating separate forms for data entry and for printing. Make the data-entry forms simple, without a lot of extraneous text and graphics. If several people are entering data, consider including some brief help text to guide less-experienced users through the process.

If possible, position fields so that you can review data and move between fields without having to scroll; besides showing an entire record at once, doing so helps prevent people from skipping over fields they can't see. And use fonts that are designed for the Mac's limited screen resolution, such as New York and Geneva. Laser printer fonts such as Times and Helvetica aren't as legible on the Mac's screen (although the TrueType versions of these fonts don't look bad).

For forms that you print on a laser printer, the opposite applies — avoid city-named fonts such as New York, Chicago, and Geneva. They don't laser-print well. Many graphic designers recommend sturdy, sanserif fonts such as Helvetica and Franklin Gothic for forms (see Chapter 1 for more advice about choosing fonts for forms).

Position fields to take advantage of the paper size you're using; because scrolling isn't an issue for printing, don't let yourself be hemmed in by the size of the Mac's screen. If you're printing on preprinted forms such as invoices or label stock, use your program's rulers to position items so they appear in the proper place. Throw in some graphic embellishments if you like. Let your creative juices flow — but not gush.

Reporting the results of a search

The result of all this searching is usually a *report*, a printed copy of the records meeting your search criteria, sorted in a specific order. Although a report can be a form that shows just one record, it's more typically a *columnar report* showing many records, with each field in its own column and each record in its own row, like baseball team standings or stock exchange tables.

The Mail Merge Angle

How does Ed McMahon find time to personally address those publisher's giveaway mailings? He's discovered *mail merge*, a variation on the reporting theme that involves merging a stock form letter with a database to produce "personal" form letters. Mail merge is often performed with powerful word processors like Microsoft Word, but a database manager that lets you create lengthy text items on a form can also do the job.

With mail merge, you first type the stock portion of a letter, inserting field names where you want the custom text to appear. Using *conditional statements* such as IF . . . THEN, you can create different letters based on information in the database — congratulating clients with paid-up accounts or telling clients whose accounts are overdue to reach for their checkbooks, for example.

If you're interested in putting mail merge to work, I reveal all the gory details (except for Ed McMahon) in the next chapter.

Understanding Relational Databases

When searching for a database manager, you run head-on into the brick wall known as *relational database management.* Though the term causes great confusion, the difference between the two types of databases is actually simple. The type I've discussed so far is the *single file*, or *flat file*, database, where one file contains all the fields and records in the database. A *relational database*, however, comprises two or more files linked by the database manager to enable one file to access data in the others. Relational databases also provide the most headaches for newcomers to computer databases.

Comparing single-file and relational databases

Unlike a single-file database, a relational database isn't easily compared to a real object like an index-card file. If you squint and pretend, however, you can compare it to a cross-referenced filing system. In such a system, an employee's personnel entry may say "See the payroll file for this employee's salary history." In the payroll file, each employee salary history can be accompanied by a note saying "See the personnel files for this employee's address and Social Security number." By cross-referencing the two files, you eliminate the need to store each employee's address and Social Security number in the payroll file and the need to store payroll information along with personnel history (see Figure 7-7, "When Files Relate"). Elimination of redundancy is a relational database's strong suit.

Another relational-database plus is that cross-referencing is automatic. An employee's address and Social Security number can appear on-screen next to his or her payroll information. When employees leave, you can expunge all references to them by deleting their records in just one file.

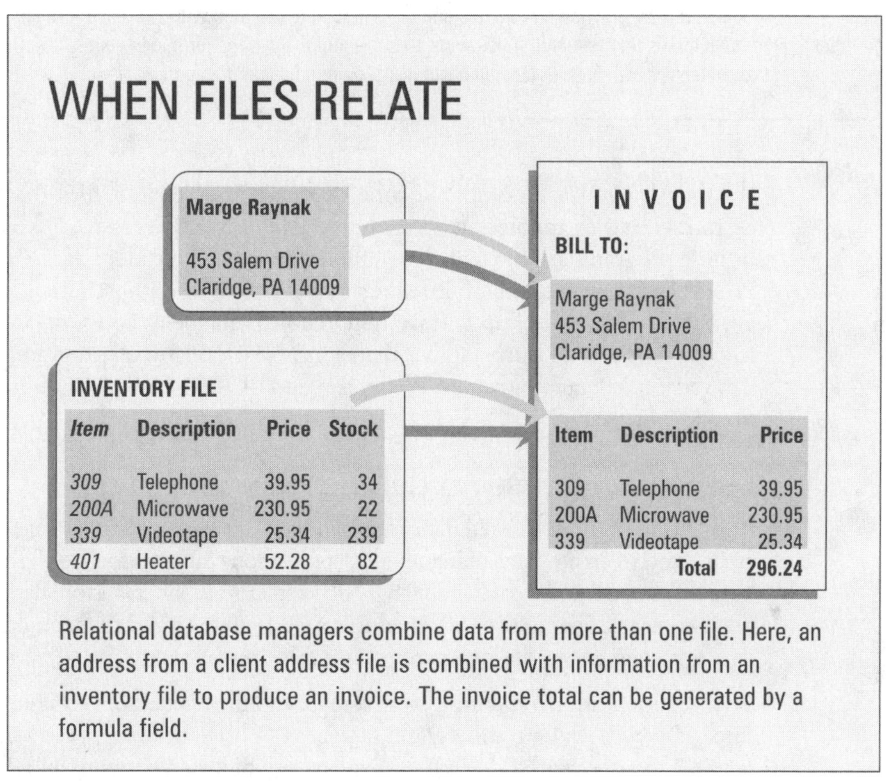

Relational database managers combine data from more than one file. Here, an address from a client address file is combined with information from an inventory file to produce an invoice. The invoice total can be generated by a formula field.

Figure 7-7: When Files Relate

Choosing the right database for the job

These strengths don't mean that every data-management task demands a relational program. Unfortunately, no sharp boundary separates single-file applications from multifile applications, so deciding when to make that leap can be difficult. As a rule, consider a relational data manager such as ACI's 4th Dimension or Microsoft's FoxPro when the data you're storing can be used in more than one way or when

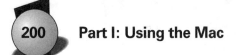

Flashier Buttons in FileMaker Pro

This chapter's Step-by-Step box shows you how to create a simple button by drawing a rectangle and then typing the button's text within it. If you want to dress up your database with flashier-looking buttons, copy one of the button designs from the Buttons template included with FileMaker Pro and then paste it into the desired form in Layout mode. Or draw your own graphic and import it.

you find that you're entering the same information in separate files. (Alas, FoxPro's performance is disappointing compared to that of its predecessor, FoxBase+/Mac.) If those programs are too daunting (and they can be), consider Claris's FileMaker Pro. Technically speaking, FileMaker Pro is a flat-file database manager; however, it provides a lookup feature that enables one file to access data in another. And it's far easier to learn and use than a full-blown relational program. FileMaker Pro version 3.0, due to be available by the end of 1995, will provide fully relational features.

Generating custom database applications

At the head of the relational data-management class are *application generators*, which enable you to create data-management applications tailored for specific tasks such as inventory management or client billing. Such applications, often custom designed for a single company, enable people who don't need to understand the technicalities of data management or file structures to use the information in the database.

With an application generator, someone sets up the needed file structures, relationships, range-checking routines, and search-and-sort specifications and then ties them all together with (ideally) self-explanatory pull-down menus and dialog boxes. The advantage: anyone can use the application immediately without having to master the data manager. The drawback: a change in reporting needs or business practices requires that you modify the application, which can bring work to a halt while you're making the changes.

Database Shopping Tips

Before shopping for a database manager, first assess the way you work with information now and then try to find the program that makes the transition to electronic filing as smooth as possible. If you need to create data-entry forms that resemble their paper counterparts, you need a program with complete form-layout features, such as FileMaker Pro.

For complex accounting or inventory applications, a relational program such as 4th Dimension or Microsoft's FoxPro is in order. For maintaining a mailing list, a simple filer such as Software Discoveries' RecordHolder Plus may be all you need. For simple mail merge tasks, consider an integrated program such as ClarisWorks or Microsoft Works.

Spreadsheets as databases

As I mention in Chapter 5, spreadsheet programs make serviceable database managers, thanks to their sorting and searching features and their libraries of functions for manipulating data. But where most true database managers enable you to store as much data as fits on disk, most spreadsheets enable you to store only as much as fits in memory. Try to maintain a huge database using a spreadsheet program, and you risk running out of memory or, at the very least, slowing the spreadsheet program to a crawl.

Most spreadsheets also lack the built-in error-checking features that data managers provide. You can construct error-checking routines yourself by creating formulas, but if you have to resort to that, you're probably better off with a database manager.

A Database Variation: Time-Billing Software

Time is not money — not when you aren't keeping track of it. Many professionals, from attorneys and architects to consultants and freelancers, bill by the hour. But too many folks rely on time-billing systems that are, shall I say, informal: notebooks with entries scrawled in margins, slips of paper tossed in an envelope, or guestimates jotted down on the bus ride home. And every time these casual timekeepers forget to log a phone call or record a consultation, they lose money.

If you're in this group, you should know about an entire category of software that exists to help you track — and charge for — your time. Time-billing software combines a database manager's filing skills with the calculating capabilities of a spreadsheet program. Also in the recipe is a dash of accounting software: time-billing packages can generate invoices based on your entries, and many programs can link into an accounting program's accounts-receivable file. Some programs even add some project-management spice, offering features that create charts and reports showing how you've allocated personnel to projects.

You don't hear much about time-billing programs — they don't exactly have the glitz of multimedia or digital imaging software — but a surprisingly large selection is available. Probably the best known are Timeslips Corporation's Timeslips and its nomadic cohort, LapTrack, which is designed for PowerBooks. Satori Software offers Legal Billing II and Project Billing, as well as the more comprehensive Components Job Cost/Time Billing. Brainchild Corporation sells Shortlist, a contact management and scheduling application that also has rudimentary time-billing features. Timeslips Corporation also sells a version of Timeslips that runs on the Apple Newton. In-the-field time tracking — what a great use for a personal digital assistant. And there's even a shareware time-billing program, and it's first-rate: Maui Software's TimeTracker. You'll find a copy on the CD-ROM disk that accompanies this book.

How Time-Billing Software Works

At the core of a time-billing package is a database manager that stores each variable in the time-billing equation: the names of your clients, the tasks you perform for them, the personnel who perform the tasks, and the rates you charge for each task.

The inevitable setup chores

Setting up a time-billing program generally begins with specifying a list of the kinds of services you render along with the hourly rate you charge. During this phase, you specify details such as whether the activity is taxable, billable, or nonbillable. You can also make entries into an expenses category for keeping track of costs such as couriers and mileage. And you can specify a markup or discount on labor and expenses for certain clients.

Another phase of the setup process involves pecking in the names and addresses of existing clients. This information appears in the windows you use when tracking your time as well as in the invoices and reports you print. If you've already entered this information somewhere — for example, in a database or a contact-management program — there's a good chance that you'll be able to import it into the time-billing package instead of having to retype everything. Most programs can import tab- or comma-delimited text files (I provide some details about database importing and exporting shortly).

I've described the setup process as two distinct phases, but you don't necessarily have to perform them in this order. All time-billing programs let you enter new clients and define new activities at any time. But it's a good idea to define a set of activities at the outset to ensure that you're naming them consistently. This step is especially important if several employees use the program on a network (more about network issues in a moment).

If yours is a one-person shop, your initial setup chores are done. In an office setting, though, you also need to specify a list of the employees for whose time you charge. In most companies, rates vary depending on three criteria: the employee (consulting with a senior partner may command a higher rate than that with a junior partner), the task (an architect may charge more for design work than for drafting), and the client (a high-volume customer may get a discount). Overall, Timeslips III, Satori's Project Job Cost/Time Billing, and DesignSoft Time &

Billing can accommodate this three-dimensional billing grid better than the competition. Brainchild's Shortlist doesn't even let you specify a different rate for each employee — not surprising, given this program's personal information manager orientation.

Timing Is Everything

The real fun begins after you've survived the initial setup data entry and actually begin tracking your time. You can do so by manually entering data in batches — at lunchtime, at the end of the day, or whenever you get a moment. But unless you have an elephant's memory, the batch-entry method requires you to write down that information somewhere else until your data-entry session — and that's not much better than the notebook or shoebox method you may be using now.

A stopwatch in your Mac

If you're next to your computer, it's easier to use the built-in timers that Timeslips III, LapTrack, Job Cost/Time Billing, and Project Billing provide. These timer features work with the Mac's built-in clock to let you begin and end time-recording sessions.

In keeping with the traditions of manual time billing, most programs call their time-tracking windows *time slips*. Creating a time slip generally involves selecting a client, specifying the activity you're performing (and in an office, who's performing it), and noting whether it's a billable activity (see Figure 7-8, "Making a Time Slip"). You can then either manually enter the time data or activate the program's timer. All programs also let you annotate time slips with comments that can optionally appear in the invoices or reports you create, such as *Discussed upcoming skating competition; recommended a whack on the kneecap.*

Customer relations tip: hide the stopwatch

If your client can see your screen as you work, you may not want to use your program's timer. A time-billing program displays a running tally of how much a given activity is costing, and a client may not appreciate seeing the charges mount in real time. Only taxi drivers can get away with that sort of thing.

The search-and-sort angle

Like database managers, time-billing programs provide search features that let you locate existing time slips according to various criteria — the person who performed the work, the type of work, the client, and more. You can use a search feature to determine who worked on a particular project on a given day — perhaps to follow up on a customer's question or complaint. Or you might use it to determine how much nonbillable work was performed on a given job — perhaps to monitor an employee's performance or to locate the weak links in the production process.

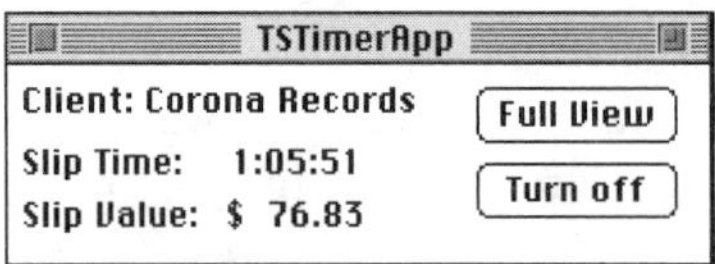

Figure 7-8: Making a Time Slip The time slip windows in Timeslips III and LapTrack share this same basic design (top); note the incrementing dollar value, indicated by the mouse pointer. Clicking the Mini View button shrinks the slip window to show only the client, time, and current charges (bottom).

Reporting Results

One thing that makes database managers valuable is the way they let you create reports to examine and analyze the information you've stored from different angles. The same plus applies to time-billing software.

Bill me

Chances are that the reports you create most often are invoices that summarize the work performed for clients and show the amounts due (see Figure 7-9, "Time for Billing"). If you already use accounting software, you can export the data to that program's accounts receivable module. Better still for Timeslips III users is Timeslips Corporation's Timeslips III Accounting Link, which ties Timeslips III into many popular accounting packages. Satori's Job Cost/Time Billing meshes with Satori's own Components series of accounting modules.

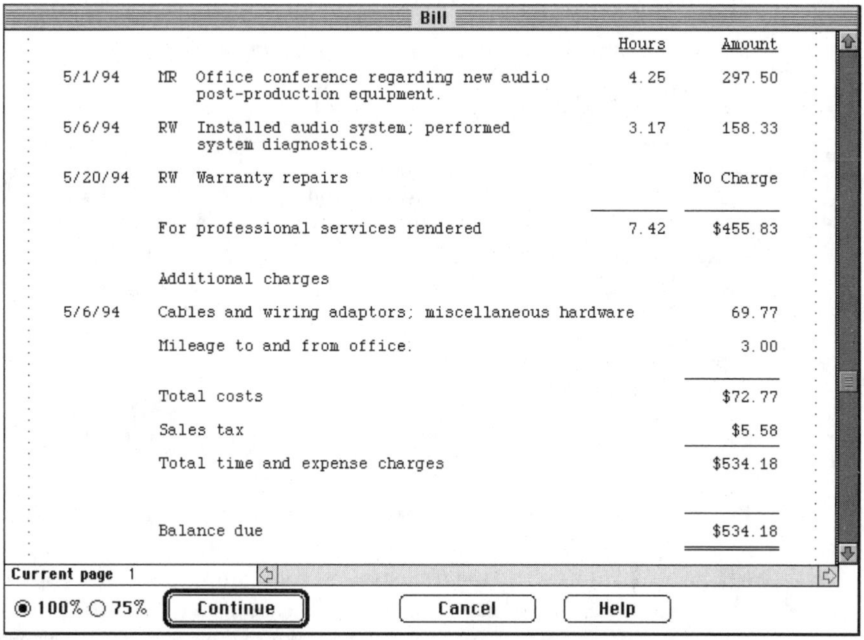

Bill

			Hours	Amount
5/1/94	MR	Office conference regarding new audio post-production equipment.	4.25	297.50
5/6/94	RW	Installed audio system; performed system diagnostics.	3.17	158.33
5/20/94	RW	Warranty repairs		No Charge
		For professional services rendered	7.42	$455.83
		Additional charges		
5/6/94		Cables and wiring adaptors; miscellaneous hardware		69.77
		Mileage to and from office.		3.00
		Total costs		$72.77
		Sales tax		$5.58
		Total time and expense charges		$534.18
		Balance due		$534.18

Current page 1

100% 75% Continue Cancel Help

Figure 7-9: Time for Billing A time-billing program can generate invoices based on the information in its time slips, incorporating markups for materials and sales tax. This invoice was created by using the reporting features in Timeslips III.

Check up on me

What other types of reports should you create? That depends on what you want to know. Employee-oriented reports let you see who does what for which clients. They're good for monitoring employee performance and for determining who's available to take on a new project. You can apply multiple sorting levels when creating the report to look at each employee's activities from different angles: time spent on specific tasks, on specific projects, and so on.

Client-oriented reports can tally up the year-to-date or monthly billings for specific clients, show past-due amounts, or list the activities performed for a given client. Work-in-progress reports can give you the up-to-the-minute status of an account to help you make informed decisions about billing.

In the time-billing world, Satori's Job Cost/Time Billing has the best report-design features (it should given its $1,495 price tag), providing on-screen rulers and other layout tools for creating the report's design and straightforward dialog boxes for specifying the report's contents. (Reports can even contain charts that graphically depict billings by employee by month, for example.) Saved report designs appear in a menu for quick recall; the program comes with over 25 canned report designs.

The reporting features in Satori's Legal Billing II and Project Billing are less comprehensive. Overall, these programs lack the depth of Timeslips III and Job Cost/Time Billing. But they're good basic programs, and they need only about 300K of memory to run (Job Cost/Time Billing, by comparison, needs 1.4MB) — something to keep in mind if you're using a PowerBook or entry-level Mac.

Timeslips III also has strong reporting features, although its layout tools aren't as polished. LapTrack's reporting features are less complete but are adequate for a program intended to be used on the road. LapTrack provides other features useful to road warriors, such as a telephone dialing command that lets you use a PowerBook's internal modem to call customers. LapTrack can even automatically begin logging time when you finish dialing.

Time Billing through Window Watching

I've mentioned that time-billing packages let you make entries manually and also provide a stopwatch-like timer that you can start and stop. But if the work you charge for takes place on the Mac itself — for example, freelance copywriting in Word or page layout in PageMaker — there are even easier ways to track your time. Coral Research's TimeLog and ASD Software's WindoWatch are utilities that watch over your shoulder and automatically record the amount of time you spend in various applications and documents.

TimeLog and WindoWatch can even take into account when you've paused to answer the telephone or grab a bite — you can tell either program to stop logging after a specified period of inactivity. Both programs include a control panel that does the actual monitoring and an application program that lets you create reports showing usage times and omit certain windows from the logging process (do you really need to know how much time you spend in the Clipboard window?).

Timeslips III and LapTrack take advantage of System 7's Apple events mechanism, which enables programs to send data and commands to each other. Their Apple events support allows you to create your own links between them and any other application or utility program that also supports Apple events, such as FileMaker Pro. You can use CE Software's QuicKeys to create a keyboard shortcut that automatically begins or ends a timing session. Developers creating telephone-dialing applications may include Apple event features that automatically create a new time slip when you dial a number. Consultants creating customized FileMaker Pro or Microsoft Excel templates may use Apple events to automatically retrieve a client's time slip data when you type the client name into a field or cell. And because the Apple events mechanism works over networks, each of these scenarios does, too.

Time-billing for QuarkXPress

Finally, if you're a QuarkXPress user and want to track only your page-layout time, consider Trias Development's Time Logger, a $49 Quark Xtension that records the total amount of time you spend working with a QuarkXPress document. It's available through the Xtensions clearinghouse XChange (800-788-7557 or 303-229-0620).

How Not to Use Time-Billing Software

There are additional benefits to using a time-billing package besides getting paid for your time (they're outlined in the Backgrounder box "Other Benefits of Time Tracking"). These side benefits share a common thread: a time-billing program helps you gauge your business's efficiency. Just as some dieters do better when they write down everything they eat, some business people are more successful when they keep track of how they spend their work time.

At the same time, though, don't let yourself become enslaved to a time-billing program's data. Anyone who has worked in a service business that charges by the hour knows that time slips can be fudged and finessed to cover an extra-long lunch break or an error that required work to be redone, for example. Basing major staffing decisions solely on time-billing data ignores the way people actually work.

What's more, monitoring an employee's minute-by-minute activities has an Orwellian feel to it. Nonetheless, it's happening more and more in fields that rely on computers — for example, each call taken by a directory assistance operator is timed, and operators who don't meet their quotas can expect to hear from their supervisors. I'd hate to see this kind of digital dogging make its way into the personal computer world. Time may be money, but employees are people.

Data Processing: Massaging Your Data

If you've read this far, you know that database managers are powerful tools for storing and retrieving information. But the field of data management can be choked with brush that slows you down. Does your mailing list contain duplicate entries that cost you in paper and postage? Did a temporary employee enter 948 records with the CAPS LOCK KEY DOWN? Is the data you need stored in some oddball format on the company mainframe? Do you need to combine the data from two files into a third file containing only those entries found in both files? And how can you get those product descriptions from a FileMaker Pro database into a catalog you're laying out with a publishing program?

Other Benefits of Time Tracking

Making it easier to track and charge for your time is reason enough to consider a time-billing package. But there are additional side benefits, too.

- ❖ By allowing you to track chargeable as well as nonchargeable time, a time-billing program can help you find weak links in a process. For example, if you're a graphic artist and you often spend an hour of nonchargeable time driving into town to print jobs on a service bureau's color printer, tallying up all those nonbillable hours may show that it makes more sense to buy your own printer.
- ❖ If you charge flat rates for your work, you can use a time-billing program to find out just how much you're making on each aspect of each job — by regularly comparing reality against your estimates, you can adjust future estimates so that they're more realistic.
- ❖ If you're a department manager, a time-billing package can help you keep track of how many jobs and how much work goes through your department. That information can help you determine staffing requirements. Large institutions can also use time-billing software for interdepartmental billing — for example, an in-house publishing department can track the time it spends on jobs for the marketing, training, and personnel departments.

You don't hear much about problems like these — except in bars and on therapists' couches. Before you get that desperate, read on. This section concentrates on tools and techniques for converting, combining, and otherwise massaging and manipulating databases. The stars of the show are several inexpensive utilities that provide the kind of data-manipulation and conversion features most database programs leave out. I'm not talking glamourware here — the utilities I describe are no-frills affairs from the unsung heroes ward. But when you need their data-massaging skills, they're priceless.

How Data Processing Utilities Work

The utilities I'll concentrate on are WorksWare's DataMate, Seawell Microsystems' DataMerge, and Main Street Software's Rosanne. Rosanne actually comprises numerous separate utilities, each of which performs a specific job.

These packages are, to resurrect a term from the sixties, *data processing* utilities. Unlike database managers such as FileMaker Pro and ACI's 4th Dimension, data-processing utilities don't have features for creating fancy data-entry screens, typing new records, or browsing. Data-processing utilities work with existing databases — either ones you've created by using Mac data managers or ones you've transferred to the Mac from other computers.

Just the text, ma'am

Data-processing utilities operate on text-only files — files containing only unformatted text characters. If you need to modify a database created with a data manager such as Claris's FileMaker Pro, you must export it to create a text-only file. You can also use a data-processing utility to process spreadsheet data — just export the spreadsheet as a text-only file first.

The data-processing process

A data-processing utility accepts one or more of these text-only *input files*, modifies the data according to your specifications, and then creates a text-only *output file* containing the modified database. After manipulating the file, you'll probably import it back into your database program in order to sort records, create and print reports, format text, and do all the other things you do to data. Or you may want to run it through the utility again to perform still more modifications; indeed, data processing is often a multistep process in which each step modifies the database in its own way. This kind of data processing benefits from some advance planning, but when it works, it is, to resurrect another term from the sixties, groovy.

Case Workers: Converting All-Caps Entries

A database whose entries are in all-capital letters is fine for printing mailing labels and the like, but it's unsuitable for tasks such as creating customized form letters with a word processor's mail merge feature — nothing gives away a form letter more than a salutation such as "Dear MR. DAVE BYRD."

Low-end databases, such as those built into ClarisWorks and Microsoft Works, lack case-conversion features. Using the scripting and programming features in databases like FileMaker Pro, ACI's 4th Dimension, or Microsoft's FoxPro, you can write a program that examines each entry and capitalizes only its first character. But an easier way is to use WorksWare's DataMate.

Converting case in DataMate

After specifying the input file, indicate which fields you want DataMate to include in the output file. Select all the fields unless you also want to strip some fields out of the database — a job I describe later. Next, select the field (or fields) whose case you want to convert and choose Text Conversion from the Options menu. Select the desired conversion option, click OK, specify a name for the output file, and then click Process.

Converting Fixed-Record Files

A thornier data-processing chore involves modifying a database that was created on a different type of computer, such as a minicomputer or mainframe. Perhaps you downloaded a large database from an on-line service or the company mainframe. Or maybe you purchased a large mailing list as a prelude to doing a mass mailing. Whatever the circumstances, your first step is the same: in order to bring the data into a Mac data manager, you must ensure that the database is properly delimited — that each field and record is separated so that your database program can tell where one ends and the next begins.

Most Mac database managers (and spreadsheets, for that matter) can import two formats of delimited text files. In a *tab-delimited* file, each field is separated by a tab code, while each record is separated by a carriage return. In a *comma-delimited* file, fields are separated by commas instead of tabs.

If your database came from a minicomputer or mainframe, it may not have these delimiters. Mini- and mainframe databases often have *fixed-length records* — instead of each record's length varying to accommodate the data within it, all records are the same length, and the database manager gives each field a specific number of characters — 15 characters for a last name, for example, or two characters for a state abbreviation. If a given field isn't full, the database manager simply tacks on a bunch of spaces to the end of its contents.

DataMate can convert a fixed record-length database, and so can Seawell Microsystems' DataMerge and Main Street Software's Rosanne. The specific steps vary between packages, but the process generally involves identifying each field in the input file and then specifying which kind of delimiters you want to include in the output file (see Figure 7-10, "Data Processing on the Mac").

Removing Duplicates

As a database grows, so do its chances of containing duplicate records. This problem is especially common in mailing list databases, where differences in last names or addresses can cause a household to receive multiple copies of a catalog or other mass mailing. DataMate and Rosanne have features that let you locate and delete duplicates. Purging duplicates from a mailing list not only results in a more accurate, more efficient database, but it also lowers your mailing costs and reduces waste.

To purge duplicates by using DataMate, specify the input and output files and then choose Duplicate Records from the Options menu. The Duplicate Record Eliminator dialog box lets you fine-tune what DataMate considers a duplicate. You can, for instance, tell DataMate to check the capitalization of field entries when comparing them. Activating this option lets you snare subtle duplications, such as

Jack McDuff and *Jack Mcduff*. You can tell DataMate to save the duplicates in a separate file as it deletes them from the main database, which lets you inspect the duplicates to make sure that you really want to delete them. If you want to be informed each time DataMate finds a duplicate, check the Alert On Duplicate Fields box. When this option is active, you can choose to keep or discard each duplicate as the program encounters it.

Oftentimes, you want to check only certain fields for duplicates. If you're processing a mailing list, for instance, you probably don't want to check the City, State, or Zip Code fields for duplicates — a mailing list database is filled with them. In such cases, DataMate lets you specify that only certain fields be checked for duplicates.

DATA PROCESSING ON THE MAC

A typical data processing task involves preparing mainframe data for use in a Mac database or mail merge. In this example, the data is in fixed-length format; each field is the same length in every record and must be converted with a data processing utility to a delimited format, in which a delimiter (such as a comma) separates each field.

Fixed-Length Format

In this mainframe data file, the LASTNAME field contains 10 characters—if the name is shorter, as is SMITH, the field is filled up with blank spaces (a longer name would be truncated).

```
LASTNAME..FIRSTNAME.STREET..........CITY........ST.ZPCOD
SMITH.....JOSEPH....15 MAIN ST......SMALLTOWN...NH.03458
CAMPBELL..AMY.......328 GEORGE ST...NEWVILLAGE..WI.52044
TAYLOR....ROY.......43900 RIDGE RD..WAZOOA......CA.99328
```

Delimited Format

A data processing utility strips out extra spaces and inserts commas so that the Mac can recognize where each field ends and the next field begins.

```
LASTNAME,FIRSTNAME,STREET,CITY,ST,ZPCOD
SMITH,JOSEPH,15 MAIN ST,SMALLTOWN,NH,03458
CAMPBELL,AMY,328 GEORGE ST,NEWVILLAGE,WI,52044
TAYLOR,ROY,43900 RIDGE RD,WAZOOA,CA,99328
```

Figure 7-10: Data Processing on the Mac

Stripping and Changing Fields

Suppose your company has a client database containing names and addresses along with buying histories and credit information. You want to use those names and addresses in a new database, but you don't need the other information. The exporting features in some Mac data managers let you select which fields you want to export, but if the database in question originated on a mainframe or other machine, turn to a data-processing utility.

Stripping out certain fields involves first specifying the input file and then specifying which fields you want the output file to contain. DataMate, DataMerge, and Rosanne let you do just that.

Rosanne has a unique feature that lets you change the values within fields. The *recode* option is Rosanne's answer to the search-and-replace features that word processors provide. With it, you can tell Rosanne to look for a certain value in the input file and replace it with a different value in the output file. Suppose your input file contains a State field, but you want the output file to simply reflect whether a given client is in a given sales territory — Northwest, Western, Midwest, and so on. Supply Rosanne with a list of the states that comprise each territory, and Rosanne examines each record's State field and generates the appropriate territory value in the output file.

Merging Ahead

Another data-processing scenario involves combining two or more databases to create a new database containing data from the old ones. For example, if you have several databases, each containing sales information about a specific county, you can merge them to produce a statewide sales database.

DataMerge and Rosanne have merging features. In DataMerge, merging databases involves specifying the input files and then selecting the fields that you want it to write to the output file (see Figure 7-11, "Merging Databases").

Rosanne's merging features are more sophisticated. You can, for example, perform a relational merge, in which a record is written to the output file only if one of its fields contains a value present in all input files. You can use this feature to combine a database of customer names and addresses with a database of recent purchases. A relational merge of these files yields a database of names and addresses *and* those customers' recent purchasing histories. You can also tell Rosanne to save reject records — ones that aren't present in both files — to a separate file. You can choose this option to locate customers who haven't purchased recently.

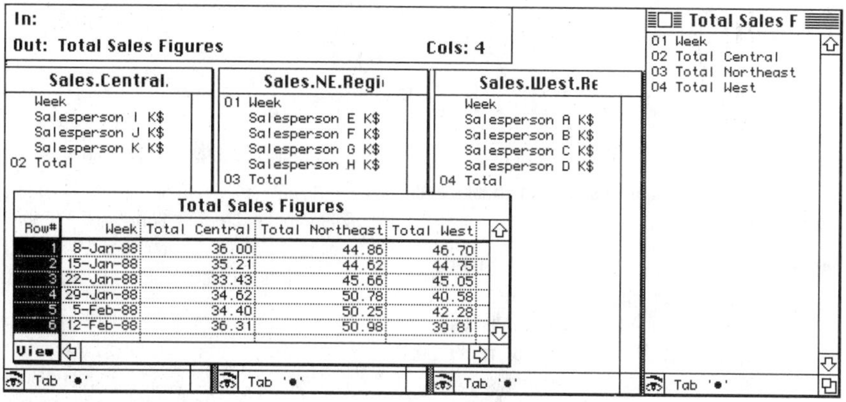

Figure 7-11: Merging Databases In this DataMerge session, sales data from three tab-delimited files are being merged into a tab-delimited summary file (the window named Total Sales Figures).

Plan Ahead for Best Results

That's sound advice for any database management endeavor because databases tend to be resistant to change. But it's especially important for data-processing jobs, given these programs' capability to alter and delete your data. Be sure to keep a backup copy of your input files handy in case you accidentally damage one. If you're performing a multistep data-processing job, sketch out the steps on paper ahead of time, noting what kinds of modifications each one should perform.

Parting Thoughts about Data Management

A database manager can streamline your filing, provided that you realize it isn't a surefire cure for disorganization. If you learned filing from Oscar Madison, that slob's slob of a sportswriter from *The Odd Couple*, your records are probably as disorganized electronically as they are on paper.

Some tasks are better handled on paper. Flipping through Rolodex cards is often still faster than typing search criteria. And until the Mac has a sauce-proof keyboard, recipes belong in card files and cookbooks. Don't try to shoehorn the computer into areas of your filing life that work efficiently now. Even Oscar Madison always knew which dirty sock held the witty, poignant conclusion he planned to use the next time he got the chance.

Pardon me while I check my laundry basket.

Other Data Processing Jobs

I've covered the primary uses for data-processing utilities; here's a brief look at some other tasks that you can perform:

- Zip code processing. As the next chapter describes, the U. S. Postal Service offers discounted rates on mass mailings that use the ever-popular nine-digit zip code. For no charge, the Postal Service adds the extra four digits to mailing list files that you submit — if those files are in a specific format. DataMate can create those files for you.
- Sampling. Sometimes, you may want to extract only a certain number of records from a huge database. Perhaps you want 10,000 records out of a 100,000-record database in order to do a test mailing of a new promotional piece. Or perhaps you have thousands of records generated by a piece of laboratory equipment and you want to extract a representative sampling of them for statistical analysis or graphing. You can tell DataMerge and Rosanne to write only every *nth* record to the output file — every third, every tenth, and so on.
- Scripting. If you frequently work with and modify the same type of database, specifying field and conversion options over and over again gets old quickly. Rosanne is the only data-processing package that lets you automate processing tasks by writing scripts in Apple's scripting language, AppleScript (for an introduction to AppleScript, see Chapter 24). If you grew up with the mainframe world's Job Control Language (JCL), you can think of the Rosanne-AppleScript combination as a kinder, gentler, and more powerful JCL. Rosanne's AppleScript support lets you combine its data-massaging features with the application programs you use to view and analyze your data. You can, for instance, create a script that not only processes a database but also opens Microsoft Excel, imports the data, selects it, and creates a chart.
- Report generation. If you ultimately import your databases into a Mac data manager, you're likely to use its report layout and printing features. But if you're working with minicomputer or mainframe databases — or even dBASE or Lotus 1-2-3 files stored on DOS PCs — check out Snow International's Snow Report Writer. Snow Report Writer enables you to create reports that include data from multiple external database files. The program provides on-screen rulers and other form-layout features that are similar to (but not as complete as) those of a Mac database manager. Reports can calculate values in fields to produce totals and summary information. You can also specify that fields or records appear in a report only if certain conditions are true — for example, you can create an accounts receivable report that prints only the records for clients whose accounts aren't paid.

You can print a completed report or tell Snow Report Writer to save its contents in a variety of file formats. The latter option turns Snow Report Writer into a data-processing and file-conversion utility. If you frequently create the same type of report, you can save it in *run-time* form. This option creates a small application program that generates the report when run. You can distribute this small application throughout a department or company, and each recipient can run the report without needing a copy of Snow Report Writer.

CHAPTER 7 CONCEPTS AND TERMS

- A database allows easy storing, sorting, retrieving, revising, and printing of information, but it requires careful advance planning and frequent maintenance.
- Databases provide a variety of field types. Text fields hold text or numbers, number fields hold only numeric values, date fields hold date and time values, logical fields hold yes and no values, and picture fields hold graphic images.
- Choosing the appropriate field types when setting up a new database helps ensure accuracy when entering data and sorting.
- You can locate data in a database by browsing (moving from one record to another) or by typing specific search criteria.
- In a flat-file database, one file holds all the fields and records in the database. In a relational database, two or more files are linked by the database manager to allow one file to access data in others.

application generators
Programs such as Acius's 4th Dimension that enable you to create data-management applications tailored for specific tasks such as inventory management or client billing, complete with their own dialog boxes and pull-down menus.

delimiters
Characters, such as commas or tabs, that serve as boundaries that tell an importing program where one field or cell ends and the next begins. The most common field or cell delimiter is a tab character (ASCII code 9); the most common row or record delimiter is a carriage return (ASCII code 13).

entry checking
A data-entry feature in which the database program restricts what you enter to a list or range of acceptable values.

field
A single piece of information for an entry, such as a person's last name or street address.

flat-file database
The most common type of Macintosh database, in which one file contains all the fields and records in the database.

form
The on-screen or printed layout of fields and their names with optional fixed text, graphics, lines, and other embellishments.

formula field
A field that obtains its values not from the keyboard but by processing values in other fields according to a formula you specify.

input file
The file that you supply to a data processing utility for modification. The utility massages the file according to your specifications and then creates an output file containing the results.

input pattern
A series of characters that you specify in order to restrict the format of data in a particular field. For example, a State field may have an input pattern that enables only two capital letters to be entered.

mail merge
The process of combining or merging a stock form letter with a database to produce "personal" form letters.

range checking
A data-entry feature in which the database program ensures that data you enter is within a specific range.

record
A collection of fields for a single entry, such as a person's name and address.

relational database
A database consisting of two or more files linked by the database manager in a way that enables one file to access data in the others.

report
A printed copy of the records that meet your search criteria, often sorted in a specific order and enhanced with totals, subtotals, and other summary information.

search criteria
Information you specify to tell the database manager what you're looking for. You can combine criteria by using logical operators such as AND, OR, and NOT.

search operators
Characters, such as the greater-than and less-than signs (> and <), that tell the database to look for values or dates greater than, less than, equal to, or not equal to the search criteria you specify.

tab-delimited text file
An ASCII file whose data items (cells or fields) are delimited by tabs.

table view
A spreadsheet-like, row-and-column display format that shows numerous records at once.

CHAPTER EIGHT

Managing Mail Merge

- How to create personalized form letters
- Preparing a FileMaker Pro database for mail merge
- Using mail merge in Microsoft Word, WordPerfect, and WriteNow
- After the merge: how to do a bulk mailing

Dear <name:> If you're like many <job title,> you've compiled a database of customers who use your <product.> Now and then, you want to notify them of a <sale/special offer.> Or perhaps you want to inform them that their accounts are <paid up/past due.> In any case, if you want your letters to be personally addressed — none of that *Dear valued customer* stuff — you're a candidate for *mail merge.*

Mail merge is the science behind all those publisher's sweepstakes mailings, magazine subscription offers, and check-up reminders from your dentist. Mail merge, also called *print merge,* is the process of combining or merging information from a database program with a text document. The text document, usually created in a word processor, contains the letter's *boilerplate text* — the stuff that doesn't change from one recipient to the next. The database contains the information (names, addresses, account information, and so on) that merges with the boilerplate text to create that oxymoronic marvel of the computer age — the personalized form letter.

In this chapter, I walk you through the step-by-step process of performing a mail merge with today's most popular Mac word processors. But a successful mailing campaign doesn't end when the form letters come out of the printer — you also need to know how to take advantage of the discounted mailing rates that the Postal Service provides. For this reason, I also provide some background on the fine art of bulk mailing.

Merging and Mac Word Processors

The Mac world's most popular word processors have mail merge features that go beyond simple form letters. Microsoft Word, MacWrite Pro, and Softkey's WriteNow allow conditional merges — if *x* is true, insert text *y;* otherwise insert *z.* If an account is paid up, thank the recipient; otherwise, remind the deadbeat to mail that check. Word, WordPerfect, and WriteNow enable you to type information from the keyboard during the merge. This capability allows you to add personal comments to some letters. You can also use it to prepare other types of documents (such as legal contracts) — store all the boilerplate contract text in one document, and then type specific information during the merge.

Mail merge is one of those word processor features that gets dusty from disuse. True, many people don't need to send personalized form letters. But another reason may be that the merging process isn't as easy as point-and-click. Merging data with canned text means walking the dark alleys of data export and import — transferring information out of a database program and into a word processor. Mail merge also requires some advance setup time and troubleshooting, lest you get weird results such as *Dear Mr. 123 Main Street.*

This chapter shows you how to use the mail merge features in Word, WordPerfect, and WriteNow. For a database program, I use Claris's popular FileMaker Pro. See the Quick Tips box "Merging with an Integrated Program" for an introduction to the mail merge features in two popular integrated programs, ClarisWorks and Microsoft Works. Their mail merge features aren't as sophisticated as those of the word processors, but they're easier to use because you don't have to move data from one program to another.

Merging with an Integrated Program

If you don't need conditional merges or the capability to supply information from the keyboard during a merge, consider using an integrated program for mail merge. ClarisWorks and Microsoft Works both have straightforward, approachable mail merge features that don't force you to grapple with text-only files, export and import, delimiters, and arcane field codes.

With either program, create the database document as you normally would. Next, create a word processor document containing the template text — the text that you want to merge with the database. Before continuing, make sure that the database document is open.

Using Microsoft Works 4

To insert a field at a given spot in a template, choose Database Field from the Insert menu and select the desired database and field. Use the Print Preview command to preview the form letters. To print the letters, choose Print and be sure that the Print Merged Fields option is checked.

Using ClarisWorks

To insert a field in the template, choose Mail Merge from the File menu. Select the database, click OK, and then select the desired field. To print the letters, click the Print Merge button in the Mail Merge dialog box.

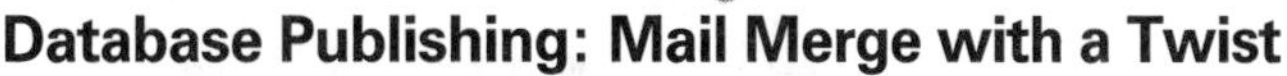

Database Publishing: Mail Merge with a Twist

In this chapter, I concentrate on word processors and FileMaker Pro, but these programs don't have a monopoly on the mails. If you need fancier page-layout and typographic features than a word processor provides, consider *database publishing* — combining data with a desktop publishing program. The basic concepts are similar, except you use a publishing program and a third-party utility to create the template documents.

For Adobe PageMaker, the best database publishing tool is Digital Composition Systems' DataShaper. For QuarkXPress, try Em Software's xdata.

Both programs also include a special zip code font for printing the bar codes that enable you to obtain discounted postal rates.

Preparing to Merge

A mail merge project generally requires the following three components (see Figure 8-1 "Mail Merge Illustrated"):

- A database containing the information you want to insert arranged in typical database fashion — a collection of fields (name, address, city, state, zip code, and so on) and records (all the fields for one entry — for example, one person's name and address information).
- A word processor document containing the data from the database. Word and WriteNow call this document the *data document*, and WordPerfect calls it the *data file*.
- A word processor document containing the boilerplate text. Word calls this document the *main* document; WriteNow, the *template* document; and WordPerfect, the *form* file. This document includes field-name codes that show where the information from the data document goes.

After you assemble these three pieces, you tell your word processor to begin merging. The word processor then creates a new, untitled document — the *merge document* — containing the boilerplate text as well as the data from each record of the data document, with page breaks separating each form letter.

There are variations to these basic steps. You can instruct your program to discard the merge document after it prints it, or you can choose to save it. You can work without a data document, typing all your information from the keyboard as each new letter appears. You can also create the data document within your word processor, for which Word's table feature comes in handy. In Word and WordPerfect, you can run a *macro* (an autopilot-like series of commands) during the merge. I'll show you some of these merge variations shortly.

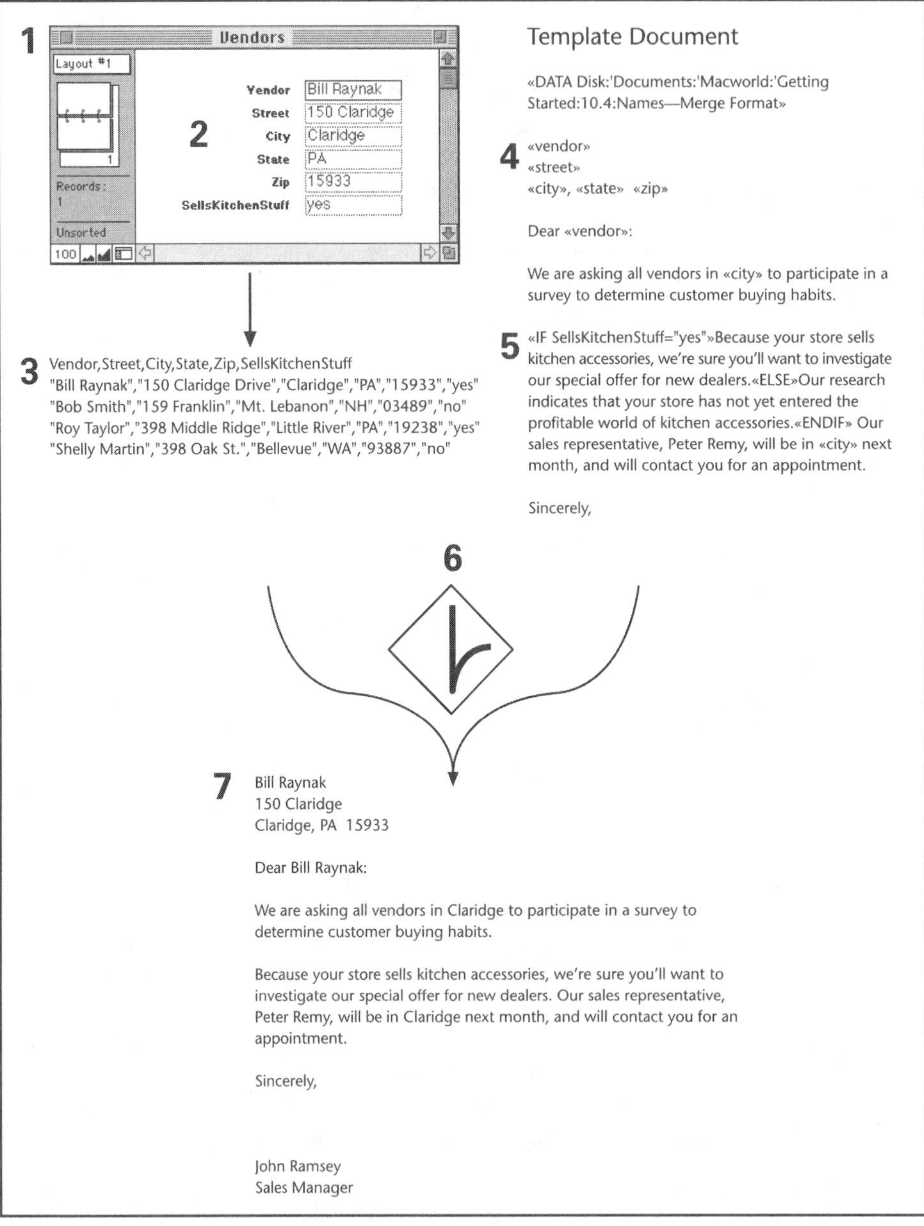

1
Vendors
Layout #1
Records:
1
Unsorted
100
2
Vendor Bill Raynak
Street 150 Claridge
City Claridge
State PA
Zip 15933
SellsKitchenStuff yes
3
Vendor,Street,City,State,Zip,SellsKitchenStuff
"Bill Raynak","150 Claridge Drive","Claridge","PA","15933","yes"
"Bob Smith","159 Franklin","Mt. Lebanon","NH","03489","no"
"Roy Taylor","398 Middle Ridge","Little River","PA","19238","yes"
"Shelly Martin","398 Oak St.","Bellevue","WA","93887","no"
Template Document
«DATA Disk:'Documents:'Macworld:'Getting Started:10.4:Names—Merge Format»
4
«vendor»
«street»
«city», «state» «zip»
Dear «vendor»:
We are asking all vendors in «city» to participate in a survey to determine customer buying habits.
5
«IF SellsKitchenStuff="yes"»Because your store sells kitchen accessories, we're sure you'll want to investigate our special offer for new dealers.«ELSE»Our research indicates that your store has not yet entered the profitable world of kitchen accessories.«ENDIF» Our sales representative, Peter Remy, will be in «city» next month, and will contact you for an appointment.
Sincerely,
6
7
Bill Raynak
150 Claridge
Claridge, PA 15933
Dear Bill Raynak:
We are asking all vendors in Claridge to participate in a survey to determine customer buying habits.
Because your store sells kitchen accessories, we're sure you'll want to investigate our special offer for new dealers. Our sales representative, Peter Remy, will be in Claridge next month, and will contact you for an appointment.
Sincerely,
John Ramsey
Sales Manager

Figure 8-1: Mail Merge Illustrated Mail merge begins with a database (1), with its fields and records (2). You prepare a data document by exporting the database as a text-only file (3). This example is a comma-delimited file — each field is separated by commas, and each field item is enclosed within quotes. The first line of the data document is a header record that identifies the field names. The form letter's contents are determined by the template document, which uses field codes (4) to tell the word processor where to insert information from the data document. Word and WriteNow allow conditional merges (5) that insert text only if a certain field contains a specified value. The data and template documents meet during the merge itself (6). The result is a personalized form letter (7).

Exporting the Database

Before you start up a word processor, you need to export your database, creating a text-only file that you then import into the word processor to create the data document. This export-import routine is one of mail merge's tallest hurdles — it's the reason that many people resort to the *Dear valued customer* approach.

Exporting and importing is necessary because a word processor can't directly read a database program's files — they're different types of tools. You can't use a word processor to open a FileMaker Pro database any more than you can use a can opener to open a bottle of wine.

Getting your delimiters right

For your word processor to distinguish one field from another and one record from the next, you must separate fields and records with special characters called *delimiters.* The most common delimiting scheme involves separating each field by a tab character and each record by a carriage return (see Figure 8-2 "Separating Fields and Records"). A file organized this way is often called a *tab-delimited* text file.

Another scheme involves separating fields with commas instead of tabs, with each field item enclosed within quotes — the *comma-delimited* format. Microsoft Word and WriteNow can work with either format. WordPerfect requires data documents to be in a special format. See the section "Merging with WordPerfect" later in this chapter.

Preparing the header record

A word processor needs another important piece of information before it can accomplish a successful merge — a line at the top of the data file, often called a *header record,* that contains the name of each data field being used (refer to Figure 8-2 "Separating Fields and Records").

If you're using FileMaker Pro to create a data file, simply save the data file in FileMaker Pro's *merge format.* Specifically designed for mail-merge applications, the merge format is identical to the comma-delimited format, with one exception — it automatically inserts a header record into the data file. If you use a database or spreadsheet program that can create only standard comma- or tab-delimited text files, you need to type the header record yourself after you import the data file into your word processor.

```
Vendor,Street,City,State,Zip,SellsKitchenStuff
"Bill Raynak","150 Claridge
Drive","Claridge","PA","15933","yes"
"Bob Smith","159 Franklin","Mt. Lebanon","NH","03489","no"
"Roy Taylor","398 Middle Ridge","Little
River","PA","19238","yes"
"Shelly Martin","398 Oak St.","Bellevue","WA","93887","no"
```

```
Vendor→    Street→    City→State→     Zip→ SellsKitchenStuff¶
Bill Raynak→    150 Claridge Drive→ Claridge→ PA→  15933
→    yes"¶
Bob Smith→159 Franklin→   Mt. Lebanon→    NH→  03489→     no¶
Roy Taylor→     398 Middle Ridge→    Little River→  PA
→    19238→     yes¶
Shelly Martin→ 398 Oak St.→    Bellevue→ WA→  93887→     no¶
```

Figure 8-2: Separating Fields and Records A comma-delimited text file (top) separates each field with a comma and each record with a carriage return. The quotes enclosing each field item allow fields themselves to contain commas (for example, "Smith, John"). A tab-delimited text file (bottom) separates fields with tab codes, visible here as right-pointing arrows. The first line of each file is a header record that defines names for each field.

Creating a FileMaker Pro Merge File

Before using a FileMaker Pro database in a mail merge project, you need to export the database as a merge file. The instructions in this box show you how.

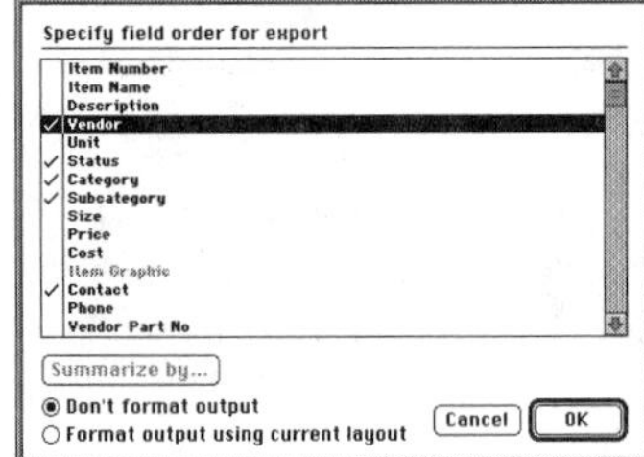

To create a merge file:

1. **Be sure that the records you want to export are selected.** If you previously used the Find command to select only certain records, only those records are exported. To export the entire database, choose Find All from the Select menu.
2. **Pull down the File menu and choose Export Records from the Import/Export submenu.** A Save dialog box appears.
3. **Choose Merge from the File Type pop-up menu.**
4. **Type a name for the merge file and click New or press Return.** A dialog box appears that lets you choose which fields to export.
5. **If you don't want to export certain fields, click the check mark next to their names. If you want to change the order in which fields are exported, rearrange the fields by dragging them.**
6. **Click OK after you've finished.** FileMaker Pro exports the database.

Merging with Microsoft Word

The merge file is your data document — it contains the information that is inserted in each form letter. Your next job is to prepare the template document — the one that tells your word processor where and how to insert information from the data document. You don't need to use the database program from this point on, so you can quit it and start your word processor.

Word 6 provides a *print merge helper* that walks you through the process of choosing a data document and creating the template document. Details about using the print merge helper appear in the following Step-by-Step box "Word Mail Merge Techniques."

Word Mail Merge Techniques

The instructions in this box tell you how to perform a mail merge in Word.

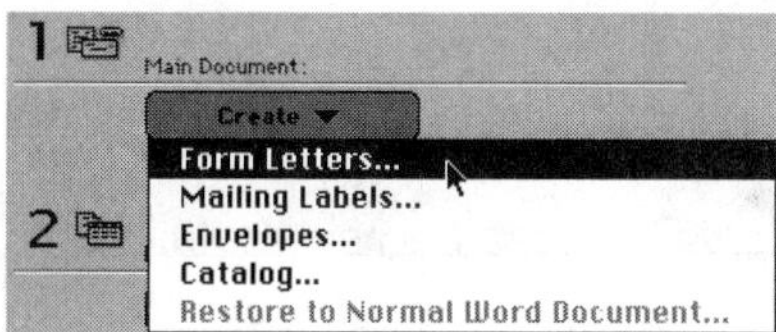

To begin a new template document:

1. **Choose Mail Merge from the Tools menu.**
   The Print Merge Helper dialog box appears.
2. **From the Create pop-up button, choose the Form Letters command.**
   A dialog box appears asking whether you want to use the active document window for the form letter or create a new main document. If you've already started typing the document's text in the active document window, click Active Window. Otherwise, click New Main Document. In either case, a new pop-up button, named Edit, appears alongside the Create button. You can choose the main document's name from this button to edit the document's text, or you can proceed to the next step and do your editing later.
3. **From the Get Data button, choose Create Data Source or Open Data Source, depending on whether you want to create a data document from scratch or open an existing one.**
   If you choose Create Data Source, a dialog box appears asking you to specify the fields that you plan to use.

(continued on the next page)

(continued from previous page)

4. **Use the adjacent Edit buttons to create the main document and edit the data source document as desired. You can also use the Mail Merge Helper dialog box's Query Options button to specify that only certain records be selected — such as those for everyone living in a certain state.**
   The following steps show you how to insert fields in the main document.

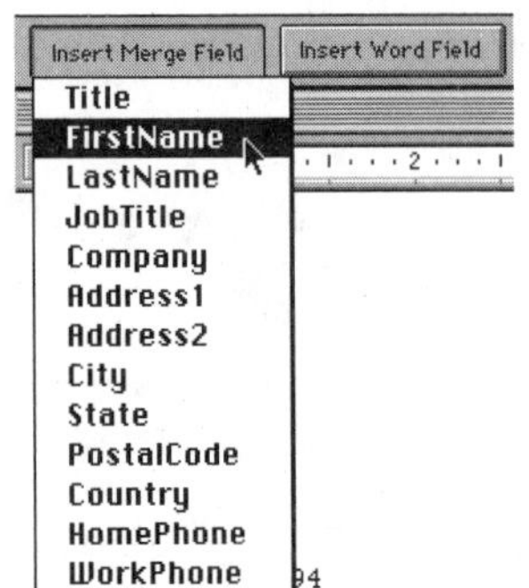

To prepare the main document:

1. **Type and format the boilerplate text as you normally would.**
   Add fields and keywords as described in the following steps.
2. **To insert a field name, position the blinking insertion point where you want the field's contents to appear, and then choose the field's name from the Insert Merge Field menu on the Mail Merge toolbar.**
3. **To insert a keyword in a template, choose the keyword from the Insert Word Field pop-up menu.**
   A dialog box appears asking for additional information. For example, when you're inserting an IF . . . ENDIF series of keywords, the dialog box lets you specify which field you want to test, the type of test you want to perform, and the value you want to compare against.
4. **After you finish the main document, save it.**

To perform the merge and create a new document containing the form letters:

1. **Choose Mail Merge from the Tools menu.**
   The Mail Merge dialog box reappears.
2. **Click the Merge button.**
   The Merge dialog box appears (left).

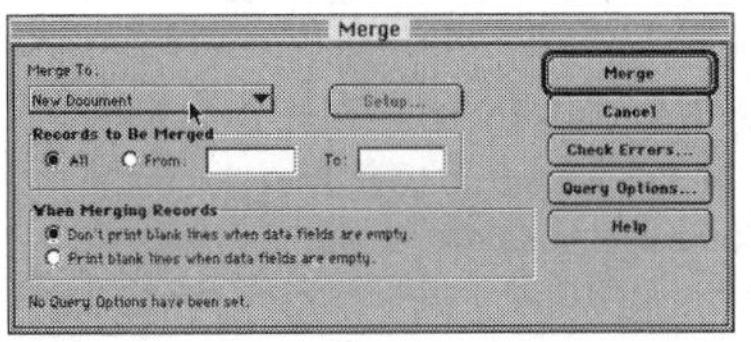

3. **From the Merge To pop-up menu, choose New Document. Also specify any other desired options, such as the number of records to merge.**
4. **Click the Merge button.**
   Word performs the merge, creating the new letters in a document named Form Letters1.
5. **Proofread the resulting document, making sure that each piece of data has the right number of word spaces around it.**
   It's easy to wind up with incorrect spacing, especially when you're inserting one field immediately after another or using the IF . . . ELSE keywords.

Tips for creating the template document

As mentioned in the previous Step-by-Step box, when you want to insert the contents of a certain field, choose its name from the Insert Merge Field Name pop-up menu. Some lines — such as the recipient's address in a business letter — may contain only field names. If you want a field's contents to appear in a different font, size, or style, select (highlight) the field name and then specify the format.

Next to the Insert Merge Field Name pop-up menu on the Print Merge toolbar is the Insert Word Field pop-up menu. This menu lets you insert keywords that tap Word's specialized print-merge features. For example, the IF keyword lets you create those conditional merges I mentioned earlier. The ASK keyword displays a dialog box that lets you type some information during the merge.

Deciphering the main document's window

The way a main document appears on-screen depends on several things. One is how you've configured Word's View options (in the Options dialog box). If the Field Codes box is checked, you see the actual codes that Word inserts for each data field and keyword. If the Field Codes box is not checked, you see the results of each field — that is, the data or field names themselves (see Figure 8-3 "Merging with Word").

Preview your merge as you edit the main document

You can toggle between viewing the actual merged data or the field names by clicking the View Merged Data button on the Mail Merge toolbar. Get in the habit of clicking this button now and then as you prepare a main document and its data document — it's a great way to preview your form letters. You can advance from one data record to the next by using the tape recorder-like buttons on the Mail Merge toolbar.

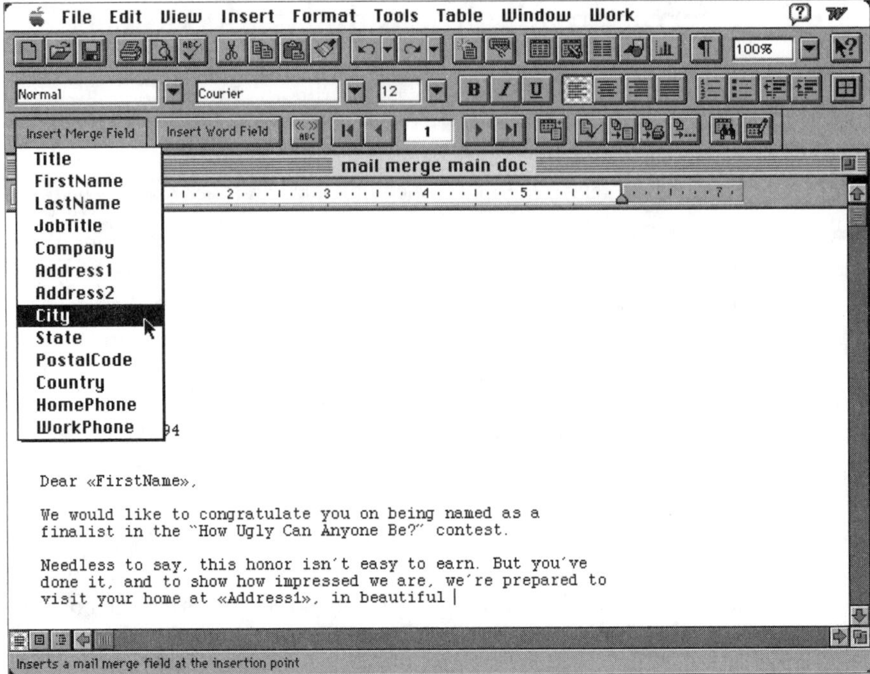

Figure 8-3: Merging with Word The pop-up menus in Word's Print Merge toolbar simplify adding field names and keywords to a template document. The first line of this template document is the DATA statement, which tells Word where to find the data document for this merge project.

You can't type field codes manually anymore

In Word 5, you can manually type the international quotation mark characters — « and » — that surround the names of merge fields. (Word 5's Print Merge Helper bar inserts these characters automatically as you choose field names and other merge statements.) This feature doesn't work in Word 6 — you must insert fields by choosing them from the Insert Merge Field menu on the Mail Merge toolbar.

Reviewing the results

After you generate the form letters, notice that each one is separated by a section break, which appears as a double-dotted line when you're viewing the document in Normal view. These breaks cause each letter to begin on a new page. You can see this by switching to Page Layout view.

If the form letters look correct, you can print them. You can save the merge document if you anticipate having to print the letters again. Or you can always generate the merge document again if you save the data and template documents.

Merging with WriteNow

The basic concepts behind merging with WriteNow are similar. WriteNow 4 also provides a print merge helper that streamlines the process of cooking up field names and keywords.

Preparing the template document

To display WriteNow's merge helper, choose Merge Helper from the File menu. The window that appears makes it easy to insert commands and field names. All merge instructions are enclosed in international quote symbols « and ».

When you choose Merge Helper, WriteNow scans the active document in search of a DATA statement, which tells the program which file contains the data that you want to insert in each form letter. If no DATA statement is present, WriteNow displays a dialog box asking you to locate a data document.

Performing the merge

To perform a merge in WriteNow, choose Merge from the File menu. In the dialog box that appears, click the New Document button. (You can click the Printer button, but it's better to merge to a new document that you can proofread for errors.)

After you click New Document (or Printer, if you're feeling confident), a dialog box appears asking whether the data document has line breaks inserted. Click No, and the merge takes place. Like Word, WriteNow formats the merge document so that each form letter begins on a new page.

QUICK TIPS

Print Merge + Fax Modem = Fax Merge

If your Mac has a fax modem (described in Chapter 16), you can use mail merge to churn out personalized faxes. All the information in this chapter applies; simply use the Chooser desk accessory to select your fax modem driver before using the Print command.

To avoid errors and wasted phone calls, it's a good idea to proofread each personalized fax before you send it.

Merging with WordPerfect

A WordPerfect template document, called a *form file*, looks much like a Word or WriteNow template document, with field codes indicating where information from the database is inserted. The field codes themselves are a bit different; field names, for example, are enclosed in greater-than and less-than signs, not the « and » characters (see Figure 8-4 "WordPerfect Merging"). Also, WordPerfect lets you simply number fields instead of requiring you to give them descriptive names.

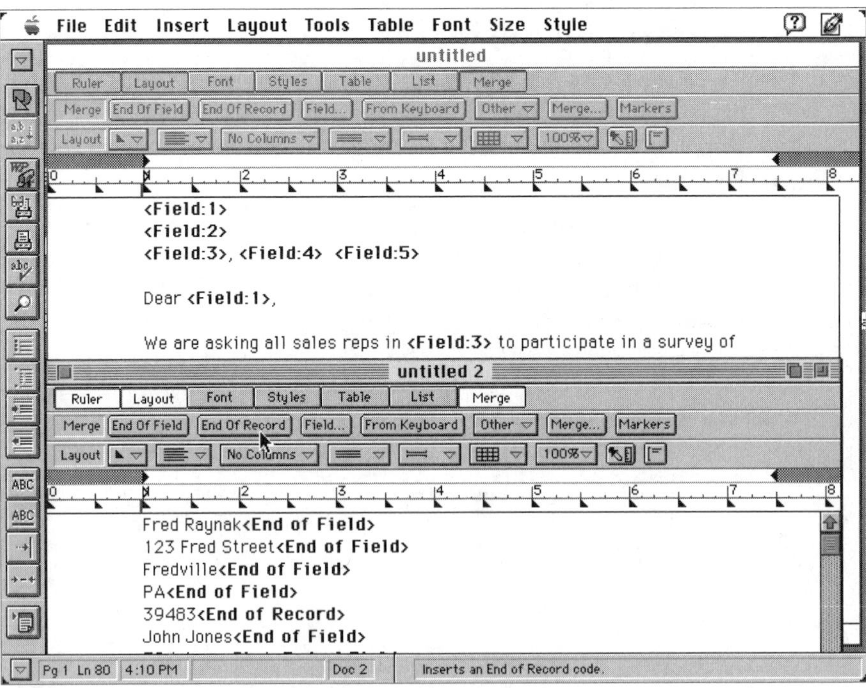

Figure 8-4: WordPerfect Merging WordPerfect's Merge dialog box lets you insert field numbers and the end-of-field and end-of-record codes shown in the lower window.

Making a WordPerfect data document

Where the data document is concerned, WordPerfect breaks from the pack. WordPerfect can't use any of the standard text-only formats I described earlier — tab-delimited, comma-delimited, or merge. Instead, you need to manually indicate where fields and records end by inserting *end of field* and *end of record* codes. Doing so adds extra work to the merging process.

WordPerfect Mail Merge Techniques

The instructions in this box explain how to perform a mail merge in WordPerfect.

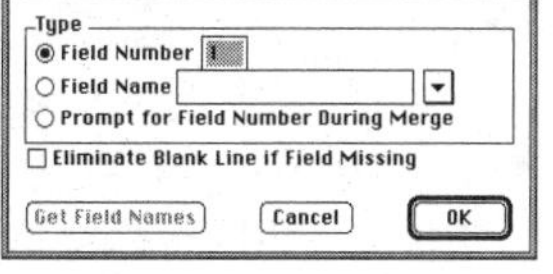

To begin a new form file (the template document), follow these steps:

1. **Choose New from the File menu.**
2. **Click the Merge button on the control bar.**
3. **To insert a field code, click the Field button in the Merge control bar, and then specify a name or number for the field in the Merge Field Number dialog box.**
   If you want to be prompted for a field name or number during the merge, choose the Prompt for Field Number During Merge option.
4. **Save and close the primary file after you finish.**

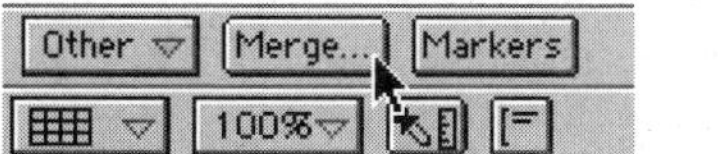

To perform the merge, do this:

1. **Choose New from the File menu.**
2. **Click the Merge button on the control bar.**
3. **Click the Merge button on the merge control bar.**
   A dialog box appears asking you to select the form file.
4. **Select the form file.**
   A dialog box appears asking you to select the data file.
5. **Select the data file.**
   WordPerfect performs the merge, inserting a page break between each form letter.

Use Find/Change to create the codes

Fortunately, you can use the Find/Change command to automate some of the work. Here's how: When exporting your database, create a tab-delimited text file. Open this file in WordPerfect and use Find/Change to change each carriage return code to a carriage return followed by an end-of-record code and a carriage return. (The carriage return is called a *hard return* in the Find/Change dialog box's Insert menu.) Next, use Find/Change to change each tab code to an end of field code followed by a carriage return. If you like, you can give descriptive names to each field; see the Merge section of the WordPerfect user guide for details. Save the resulting file as a WordPerfect document, and then close it.

For details about creating a template document and performing a merge, see the Step-by-Step box "WordPerfect Mail Merge Techniques."

After the Merge: A Primer on Bulk Mailing

The United States Postal Service doesn't get a lot of respect. Sometimes it deserves the criticism: a year or two ago, while wallowing in an eight-figure deficit, the Service spent $7 million to replace its eagle logo with . . . an eagle logo.

To be fair, the Service's bad press overshadows the advancements it has made in delivering the billions of pieces of mail it handles every day. Postal distribution centers now use automated sorting equipment that scans addresses. The Service has also developed several schemes to manage what comprises the largest percentage of its volume: direct-mail pieces. Special offers, pleas for donations, Victoria's Secret catalogs — examine the labels on these and other pieces of junk mail, and you can see that they all bear similar codes. The sorting techniques behind these ciphers make it easier for the Postal Service to deliver the pieces.

The Postal Service offers discount rates to organizations that use these delivery-streamlining schemes. It used to be that only big commercial mailing houses knew about and exploited these cut-rate mailing options. Now, thanks to a variety of software and hardware, small businesses and nonprofit organizations can take advantage of them, too.

Taking the direct-mail plunge isn't easy — you have to contend with forms that are often arcane and regulations that can seem inane. There is, for example, only one officially sanctioned way to put rubber bands around letter bundles. Mailing software can help (although not with the rubber bands). Even if you aren't about to tackle a thousand-piece mailing, read on. Some of the products I cover in this section simplify small-scale label and envelope printing and may even get your letters there a day or two sooner. And if you decide to let a commercial mailing house do your mailing after all, the background I provide helps you understand what you're paying for.

Know Your Mailing Options

The Postal Service offers a variety of mailing options, each with its own delivery, parcel weight, and pricing considerations. To summarize them:

- First-class mail gets there in two to five days but is the costliest of the big four mailing options. (I won't be foolish enough to print the prices here, as I did in the previous edition of this book. We all know that postal rates go up faster than taxes do. The basic concept behind each of the four delivery classes doesn't change, however: the faster the delivery, the more it costs.)
- Second-class mail is used for periodicals. To qualify, a publication must publish at least four times per year — and meet innumerable other criteria relating to such matters as the ratio of advertising to editorial and whether the publication is a general, paid-circulation magazine (such as *Macworld*) or a free-to-qualified-subscribers trade rag. As part of a very complex application process, a Postal Service representative scrutinizes your circulation records as well as several issues of the publication to determine whether you qualify. Delivery time varies; second-class mail is generally faster than third class but slower than first class.
- Third-class mail represents the bulk of direct mail, encompassing everything from subscription offers to catalogs. Delivery time: 3 – 10 days.
- Fourth-class mail is the so-called *book rate*, reserved for bound, printed material weighing one to ten pounds. Delivery time: 4 – 10 days.

What determines your rate?

Many factors influence what you pay to mail each piece, including

- Whether you're a commercial or a nonprofit mailer (nonprofits pay less).
- Whether you use bulk mailing or not. Bulk mailing earns you a better discount, but to qualify for bulk rates, your mailing must comprise at least 200 pieces or weigh at least 50 pounds. You also need to deliver the mailing pieces to the Postal Service — no dumping them in the corner mailbox. You generally deliver the mailing pieces to a Bulk Mail Center, a Postal Service facility that handles third- and fourth-class bulk mail. In some cases, you can save more money by delivering the mailing to a facility closer to the pieces' destinations.

More bulk-mailing requirements

For bulk mailing, you also must *presort* the mailing pieces. Presorting involves bundling together those pieces that are going to the same general location — or, more accurately, to the same zip code groups. For example, the zip codes on a stack of catalogs going to the San Francisco metropolitan area all have the same zip code prefix: 941. This stack qualifies for 3-digit presort discount. A stack of catalogs going to *Macworld*'s neighborhood all have the 94107 zip code; they qualify for a 5-digit presort discount.

Large-scale bulk mailings are often sorted by carrier routes, which are the streets or areas to which mail is delivered. (The text CAR-RT on a piece of junk mail indicates that it has been carrier-route sorted.) Sorting by carrier route can earn you steep discounts, but to qualify, your mailing must meet stringent sorting requirements.

There's more to presorting than this section reveals, but you get the idea: the more you do, the less the Postal Service has to do, and the more you save. But you have to do it right — and that's one area where mailing software can earn its keep.

How the Mac Can Help

Programs such as Satori's Bulk Mailer Plus, Synex's MacEnvelope Professional, or Software Publishers' AccuZip6 combine database-management features that let you enter and edit mailing lists with printing features that produce envelopes or mailing labels in the appropriate formats (see Figure 8-5 "Bulk Mail Masters"). All mailing programs can also import existing databases from general-purpose database managers such as FileMaker Pro.

A closer look at mailing software

At first glance, a mailing program seems similar to a general-purpose data manager. There are big differences. FileMaker Pro and its ilk are generalists, able to manage anything from a client list to a videotape database. Mailing programs are specialists designed for the rigors of bulk mailing.

Less initial work

For starters, there's less initial setup — when you create a new mailing list or import data from another program, fields for names, addresses, and the like are created automatically. Similarly, the programs have a variety of preset printing formats for common label sizes and configurations.

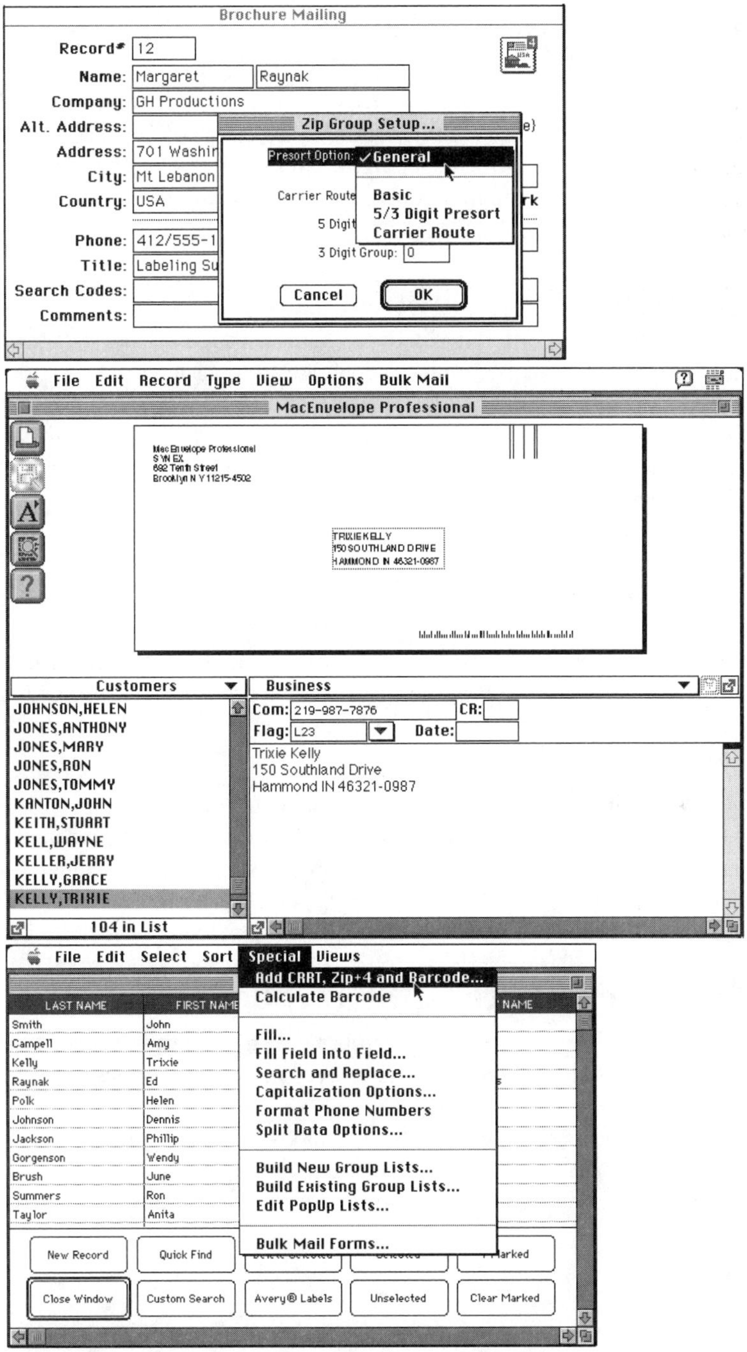

Figure 8-5: Bulk Mail Masters Satori Software's Bulk Mailer Plus (top) sorts records to meet postal requirements. Synex's Mac Envelope Professional (middle) has preset templates for common label and envelope sizes. Software Publishers' AccuZip6 (bottom) can automatically clean up addresses, correct zip codes, and fine-tune mailing lists.

Better features for eliminating duplicates

To cut paper and postage waste, mailing programs sport slick features for snaring duplicate entries. Satori's Bulk Mailer Plus is particularly clever about duplicates; its Close Calls options can snag phonetically similar names (such as *Cathy* and *Kathy*) as well as names with similar spellings (as in *Barr* and *Barre*). And you can tell the program to display suspected duplicates before deleting them so that you can verify that they really are duplicates.

Better printing features

Another significant difference between mailing programs and data managers surfaces at printing time. Not only do mailing programs have preset printing formats for envelopes and mailing labels, they can also print *POSTNET* bar codes that the Postal Service's automatic sorters can scan. (POSTNET stands for Postal Numeric Encoding Technique.) Including the correct POSTNET bar codes on bulk mailing pieces earns you a lower rate.

CASS: Postal Proofreading

Here's where the gap between mailing software and database managers turns into a canyon. Several mailing programs can actually proofread and alter a mailing list's entries, adding accurate zip+4 codes and more. They do so by supporting the Postal Service's *Coding Accuracy Support System*, or *CASS*.

Here's how it works: When you've finished entering and editing a mailing list, you run it through a CASS-certified utility, which adds the extra four digits to each entry's zip code. The utility gets those zip+4 codes from an included CD-ROM that contains the entire Postal Service zip code directory — that fat book you browse at the post office when you don't know someone's zip code.

Other benefits to CASS certification

Using a CASS-certified utility has other benefits. The utility corrects a zip code if it's wrong or has changed since you entered it, and it massages addresses so that the Postal Service's automated sorters can scan them more accurately. This massaging process also helps root out duplicates. Suppose a given address was entered twice — once as *Post Office Box 743* and once as *Box 743*. The CASS utility changes both to PO BOX 743, making it possible for the mailing list program to spot the entries as duplicates.

A Field Guide to Postal Bar Codes

POSTNET bar codes come in several flavors (see the following figure). The most basic is a bar code version of the addressee's five-digit zip code. A step up from there is the zip+4 bar code, which reflects the addressee's nine-digit zip code; the extra four digits include more specifics about the delivery location.

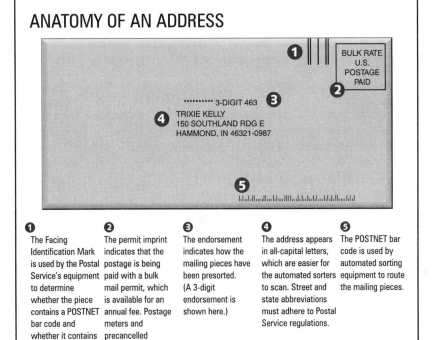

ANATOMY OF AN ADDRESS

BULK RATE U.S. POSTAGE PAID

********** 3-DIGIT 463

TRIXIE KELLY
150 SOUTHLAND RDG E
HAMMOND, IN 46321-0987

1. The Facing Identification Mark is used by the Postal Service's equipment to determine whether the piece contains a POSTNET bar code and whether it contains a stamp that requires cancellation.
2. The permit imprint indicates that the postage is being paid with a bulk mail permit, which is available for an annual fee. Postage meters and precancelled stamps can also be used to pay for bulk mailing.
3. The endorsement indicates how the mailing pieces have been presorted. (A 3-digit endorsement is shown here.)
4. The address appears in all-capital letters, which are easier for the automated sorters to scan. Street and state abbreviations must adhere to Postal Service regulations.
5. The POSTNET bar code is used by automated sorting equipment to route the mailing pieces.

The most complex POSTNET bar code is the *Delivery Point Bar Code*. Also called the *Advanced Bar Code,* this code includes not only the zip+4 bar code, but also the *walk sequence number,* which is usually the last two digits in the street address or post office box. In postal parlance, the *walk sequence* is the actual order in which letter carriers physically deliver the mail — criss-crossing streets, for example, or working their way across a bank of mailboxes.

Organizing mail into the correct walk sequence is the final stage in the manual sorting process that takes place in your local post office; when bulk mail is presorted and encoded with delivery point bar codes, this stage is eliminated — and you save money. As of March 21 of 1993, the Postal Service requires Delivery Point Bar Codes on all bulk mail for which you want the bar code discount rates.

(continued on the next page)

(continued from previous page)

Yet another type of bar code, the *facing identification mark,* or *FIM,* is most often used on business-reply cards and envelopes. Among other things, the FIM tells the post office's equipment whether the piece contains a POSTNET bar code and whether it bears a stamp that requires cancellation.

By the way, some vendors I've talked to claim that including POSTNET bar codes on individual (not bulk) mailing pieces can speed delivery; others say that they haven't seen any hard evidence of it. It can't hurt, but don't buy a bulk mailing package just to try. Azalea Software's $59 POSTools includes a POSTNET bar code font and a simple utility that prints bar codes.

Small-time mailers need not apply

A CASS-certified utility isn't for the occasional, small-scale mailer. For starters, you pay more for the software: Software Publisher's CASS-certified AccuZip6 retails for $899, while Satori's Bulk Mailer Plus lists for $395. The software isn't a one-time expense, either. Zip+4 codes are always changing, and the Postal Service requires CASS software vendors to update their CD-ROMs quarterly. (The utilities won't run after their expiration dates.) A one-year subscription to AccuZip6's CD-ROM updates costs $200.

Another CASS-certified package is Semaphore Corporation's ZP4. Unlike AccuZip6, Bulk Mailer Plus, and MacEnvelope Professional, ZP4 doesn't have data-entry features; it's primarily designed to batch-process mailing lists created in other programs (one reason that it's only $125). With its support of System 7's Apple events mechanism, ZP4 can talk to other programs to exchange data and commands. MacEnvelope Professional takes advantage of this feature — choose its Clean Address command, and MacEnvelope Professional collaborates with ZP4 to massage the currently displayed address. ZP4 also includes utilities that enable it to clean up FileMaker Pro mailing lists via Apple events. Utilities for controlling ZP4 via AppleScript and UserLand's Frontier are also included.

CASS alternatives

Satori sells a program similar to ZP4 called Bulk Mailer CASS. Bulk Mailer CASS can communicate via Apple events with Bulk Mailer Plus and also batch-process existing Bulk Mailer Plus mailing lists and text-only files. Both Bulk Mailer CASS and ZP4 can print the Postal Service form you're required to submit to show that your mailing list has been CASSified.

If you want the low mailing rates that CASS certification allows but you can't justify the cost of CASS software, there's another option: send disks containing your mailing list to the Postal Service's National Customer Support Center in Memphis, Tennessee, which offers a free, one-time CASSification service. The disks must be in MS-DOS format, but fortunately, the Mac's ability to read and write DOS disks makes this obstacle surmountable — if you can structure your database according to the Service's requirements. These requirements are described in a free Postal Service brochure, *Address File Standardization on Diskette* (PS Form 5603). For a copy, call 800-238-3150 and ask for Diskette Processing Services.

Better yet, use Satori's Bulk Mailer Plus, which can export mailing lists in the required format. Synex offers a utility called Mac to Memphis and Back, which also structures mailing list files appropriately. To get either program's efforts onto DOS disks, use a utility that lets DOS disks appear on the Mac's desktop; for example, Apple's PC Exchange, which is included with System 7.5. (See Chapter 28 for details on PC Exchange.)

Printing Time

Most of those predefined label formats that mailing programs provide are for Avery labels — the most common peel-and-stick labels for computer printers. Avery labels are available for laser and dot-matrix printers, so you can use your existing printer to address your mailing pieces.

If you don't want to tie up the office printer with this grunt work, consider CoStar's AddressWriter, a compact dot-matrix printer designed for envelope printing. The AddressWriter's envelope feeder holds up to 100 envelopes and 200 post cards; an optional label feeder allows the printer to accept one-across labels. For higher-volume addressing, CoStar sells Address Express, a faster ink-jet printer that handles both envelopes and labels. Both printers attach to the modem or printer port; CoStar also sells an AppleTalk adaptor that lets you share them on a network. Both printers include a version of Synex's MacEnvelope.

Mailing software can help with other aspects of hard copy, too. The Postal Service wouldn't be a government agency if it didn't require plenty of paperwork — when you deliver your mailing, you need to supply forms that describe it and the mailing methods you're using. (AccuZip6 supports the largest variety of Postal Service forms.) Mailing programs can also print the tags and labels that you must attach to each sorted bundle of mail.

For More Mailing Information

If you're contemplating the bulk mail plunge, you need more background than I've had room to provide here. The best source of information is the Postal Service itself: its *Domestic Mail Manual* is *the* comprehensive guide to mailing in the United States. It's available for $36 from the Superintendent of Documents, US Government Printing Office, 941 N. Capitol St. NE, Washington, DC, 20402. To order by phone, call 202-783-3238. A smaller, more digestible publication, *Third-Class Mail Preparation,* is free and available at your local post office. While you're there, ask the postmaster about bulk mailing discounts as they relate to your specific needs.

Which bulk mailing program should you buy? I find Satori's Bulk Mailer Plus the easiest to learn and use. AccuZip6 has a steeper learning curve and a less approachable interface (the program is built around ACI's 4th Dimension database program, although you don't need 4D to run it). But AccuZip6 is more powerful; besides including the CASS-certified CD-ROM, it supports a larger array of mailing options and even includes a built-in word processor that lets you create customized form letters by using the entries in your mailing list.

Bulk Mailing for the Rest of Us

Bulk mailing programs are having the same impact on the direct-mail world as page-layout programs have had on the publishing world: they've taken what was once a costly, specialized service and put it on the desktop (and in the service bureau: a growing number of bureaus and print-shop chains use these programs to provide mailing services).

And as with publishing, this migration gives businesses more control over their efforts. Given the value of a mailing list, the costs of dealing with a mailing house, and the savings possible with bulk mail discounts, that's a significant advantage.

CHAPTER 8 CONCEPTS AND TERMS

- A word processor's mail merge features enable you to combine a database with boilerplate text to produce personalized form letters and other documents.
- A mail merge project generally requires two files — a merge file (created with your database program's export features) and a template document (created with your word processor).
- In addition to field names that show where to insert each piece of information, template documents may contain keywords such as IF . . . ENDIF, which enable the word processor to insert information only when certain conditions are met.
- If your mail merge needs are simple, you may want to use an integrated program such as ClarisWorks or Microsoft Works to avoid the time and trouble of exporting and importing a database.
- The Postal Service offers a variety of discounted mailing rates, but to qualify for them, you must prepare your mailing according to strict guidelines.
- Mailing list programs can help you meet Postal Service requirements for bulk mailing and also make it easier to manage a large mailing list.

Coding Accuracy Support System
Abbreviated *CASS,* a method of certifying and formatting addresses to ensure that their zip codes are correct and that they're formatted in a way that best supports the Postal Service's scanning equipment.

comma-delimited text file
A file in which fields are separated by commas, with each field's data enclosed within quotes.

conditional merge
A merging option in which the text inserted by the word processor depends on the presence of certain values in the database.

data document
In Word and WriteNow, a word processor document into which you import the information from the database. Called the *secondary file* or the *address file* in WordPerfect.

delimiter
In an exported database file, a special character (usually a tab code, sometimes a comma) that separates one field from the next.

delivery-point bar code
Also called the *Advanced Bar Code,* this bar code includes not only the zip+4 bar code but also the *walk sequence number,* which is usually the last two digits in the street address or post office box. This bar code must be present in order to earn the lowest possible mailing rates.

end-of-field code
In WordPerfect, a code that indicates where fields end.

end-of-record code
In WordPerfect, a code that indicates where records end.

facing-identification mark
Abbreviated *FIM,* a bar code most often used on business-reply cards and envelopes. Among other things, the FIM tells the post office's equipment whether the piece contains a POSTNET bar code and whether it bears a stamp that requires cancellation.

header record
A line at the top of an exported database file that contains the name of each data field being used.

keywords
Special command words such as IF . . . THEN that you insert in a template document to control the merging process.

merge format
A FileMaker Pro export file format specifically designed for mail merge applications. A merge-format file is comma-delimited and begins with a header record.

POSTNET
Short for Postal Numeric Encoding Technique, a variety of bar codes that, when printed on bulk mailing pieces, earn you lower postal rates.

presorting
Bundling together those mailing pieces that should go to the same general location — or, more accurately, to the same zip code groups. You must presort mailing pieces in order to obtain low postal rates.

print merge helper
In Word and WriteNow, a feature that walks you through the process of choosing a data document and creating the template document.

tab-delimited text file
A file in which each field is separated by a tab character and each record by a carriage return.

template document
A word processor document containing the boilerplate text, including field-name codes that show where the information from the data document goes. Word calls it the *main document,* and WordPerfect calls it the *form file.*

CHAPTER NINE

Desktop Publishing Basics

- Why electronic publishing is replacing traditional layout techniques
- What to look for in publishing software
- Comparing PageMaker and QuarkXPress

In the last thirty years, the graphic arts industry has seen more revolutions than any third-world country. In the sixties, the turn-of-the-century Linotype and Monotype hot-metal typesetters based on medieval printing technologies rapidly began to be displaced by phototypesetting machines whose speed and output improved in quantum leaps — each machine becoming obsolete within a few years of its introduction. The seventies saw large publishing houses, printers, and newspapers begin to use on-screen page-makeup systems that enabled graphic artists to lay out pages electronically — without T squares, Exacto knives, and the other tools of mechanical pasteup.

Although electronics played a prominent role in the evolution of phototypesetting and electronic page-makeup equipment, personal computers didn't. They lacked the processing power to calculate precise character widths and line endings and the graphics to display various fonts and sizes. Then the Macintosh appeared. Armed with electronic publishing programs, the Mac has picked off the expensive page-layout systems, sniped at typesetters, and forced established type houses either to join the revolution or retreat.

As a computer user, I'm excited to see that technology has advanced enough to enable nonprofessionals to set type and paste up pages with a $1,000 Macintosh. But as a former typographer, I cringe when that technology is misused. Properly producing a printed piece takes time, patience, and at least a rudimentary knowledge of design and typographic concepts. In this chapter, I discuss the basics behind electronic publishing and the responsibilities you assume when you start producing your own publications. In the next chapter, I show you how to accomplish common publishing tasks by using PageMaker and QuarkXPress, the two most popular Mac publishing programs.

The Desktop Difference

In the world of electronic page makeup, a video screen and a mouse replace the traditional layout table and its tools (see the Background box "Layout and Pasteup the Old-Fashioned Way"). You add rules, halftone windows, and crop marks with electronic drawing tools, and then send the whole shebang to a phototypesetting machine — an *imagesetter* — that delivers a camera-ready page.

If you're willing to invest some time and effort in learning a sophisticated word processor or an electronic publishing program and some fundamentals of publishing design, you can do what used to require several specialists and expensive typesetting equipment. Using the Mac, you can write and proofread copy, design a layout, and create camera-ready pages on a laser printer or an imagesetter. If you don't own a laser printer (or an imagesetter), you can use one at any of the growing number of copy shops and computer stores that rent time on electronic publishing systems.

With commercial typesetting and graphic arts firms charging $20 an hour and up (way up), it doesn't take long for an electronic publishing system to pay for itself. And there's the convenience factor. You can experiment with different designs or make last-minute type corrections in the time it takes to call a typesetting service and place an order. Best of all, the Mac can serve you in other areas when you aren't wearing your printer's apron.

Outfitting a Publishing System

You have to spend before you can save. The road to electronic publishing has a number of alternate routes, and each takes a progressively higher toll on your bank account.

The cheap route: Mac and rubber cement

The least expensive involves combining the Mac's typographic prowess with conventional pasteup methods. By preparing text with a word processor, printing it on a laser printer, and then pasting it up by hand, you can dramatically reduce your typesetting and production costs, which are often the most expensive part of a job.

If you're willing to rent time on a laser printer, the only vehicle you need to travel this path is a Mac with a word processor. A rusty 128K Mac and the original version of MacWrite will do, but I'd suggest at least a Mac Classic and an integrated program such as ClarisWorks, which combines a powerful word processor with graphics features that let you lay out pages (I have more to say about software shopping shortly).

Layout and Pasteup the Old-Fashioned Way

Before you can fully appreciate how the Mac streamlines the publishing process, it helps to know how printed materials are produced without it (see the figure below). Initially, a graphic designer develops a concept by drawing rough, or thumbnail, sketches. Later, comprehensive drawings, called *comps,* are produced, which show how the final piece will look.

Next, the designer chooses the typefaces and type sizes for the text, using a tedious process called *copyfitting* to make sure it fits the available space. From there, the text is marked up with specifications for line lengths, fonts (a typeface in a particular size), and spacing. The typesetter may key in the text from the marked-up copy or convert the author's disk files, adding the necessary typesetting codes.

The layout artist then creates a *dummy,* a preliminary layout that shows how and where the text and graphics go on each page. The artist refers to the dummy when pasting up the finished type on cardboard sheets, using T squares, triangles, and sharp eyes to make sure that everything's straight. If the design calls for them, the artist draws lines (called *rules*) with a drafting pen or adds stick-on rule tape (clear adhesive tape on which rules have been machine drawn).

If the page includes photographs, a screened negative called a *halftone* must be made from each photo to convert its various shades into dots that can be printed. The artist cuts a matching window from opaque film (such as Parapaque or Zipatone) and pastes it on the board to show the printer where to position the halftone. Line art — graphs or line drawings — does not require halftones.

The artist then draws crop marks to denote the page's boundaries and may attach a protective sheet of tissue paper on which to mark ink colors or paper stock. Finally, when the cardboard sheet (called a *mechanical*) is camera ready, the printer shoots an actual-size negative from which the printing plate is made.

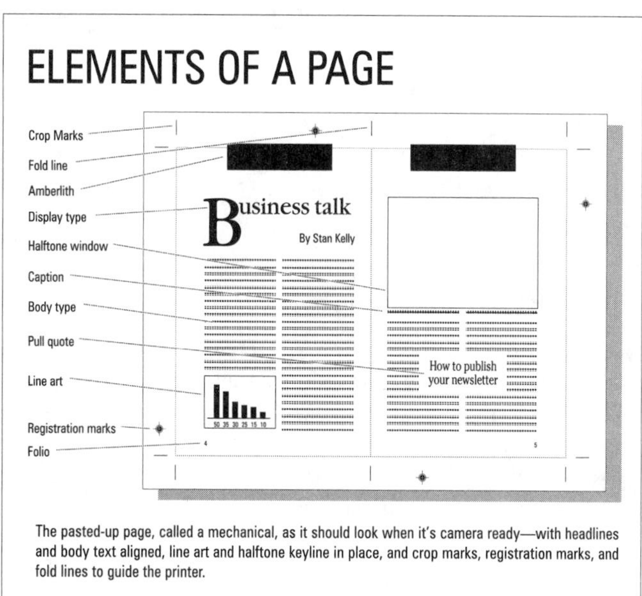

The pasted-up page, called a mechanical, as it should look when it's camera ready—with headlines and body text aligned, line art and halftone keyline in place, and crop marks, registration marks, and fold lines to guide the printer.

The more direct route: a publishing program

The more direct route that most people take involves using a publishing program to paste up pages electronically. Most publishing programs mimic conventional pasteup methods. After you specify basic information about your publication — its page size, number of pages, and whether the final product should be printed on both sides — the program presents you with a blank page into which you can import word processing documents and graphics created with drawing or business graphics programs. The toll for the latest layout programs: A Mac with a fairly large (preferably 500MB or larger) hard drive and at least 16MB of memory (preferably more). And for satisfying performance, the Mac itself should be at least a 68040 machine such as a Quadra 650, with a Power Mac preferred.

The upscale route: all the trimmings

The third route to electronic publishing traverses the same terrain as the second but includes some high-priced stopovers to pick up a large-screen display and a scanner. Large-screen displays are just that — big screens that let you view an entire 8 ½ x 11-inch page — or even two pages, side-by-side, without having to scroll (see Chapter 31).

Scanners are add-ons that use optical sensors to convert photographs or other artwork into graphic documents where the original image is represented by a series of dots (see Chapter 14). Scanners range in price from a few hundred dollars for handheld models such as Thunderware's LightningScan series to around $1,000 for scanners such as Apple's Color OneScanner and Hewlett-Packard's ScanJet series, which can produce images that look at least as good as a high-quality newspaper photo.

Scanners earn their keep in another way: When driven by the appropriate software, they become optical character recognition (OCR) devices, able to "read" typed or typeset pages of text and create disk files you can edit and reformat with a word processor (see Chapter 18).

The Software Side

Most Mac publishing programs create on-screen versions of an artist's layout table. You can zoom in on the page to position something precisely or zoom out to get the big picture of a single page or a two-page spread. You can position text and graphic elements by dragging them with the mouse. In keeping with the Mac's what-you-see-is-what-you-get (WYSIWYG, pronounced *wizzy-wig*) philosophy, the screen accurately reflects the appearance of the final page.

PageMaker versus QuarkXPress

If you plan on buying a mainstream publishing program, your decision probably boils down to two programs: Quark's QuarkXPress or Adobe PageMaker. QuarkXPress has become extremely popular among graphics professionals in the past few years. It's a great program, but so is my favorite — PageMaker.

Why do I prefer PageMaker? For one thing, I like its way of operating. QuarkXPress's draw-a-frame-and-then-import routine gets in my way. But more importantly, I believe — as do some of the industry's top electronic publishing experts — that PageMaker's typographic features are superior to QuarkXPress's. That's important because a publishing program is, first and foremost, a typesetting program.

Here are some more comparisons between the two programs:

- PageMaker provides five tracking levels versus QuarkXPress's one, giving you better command of intercharacter spacing. But QuarkXPress 4.0, due to ship late in 1995, will provide character-level style sheets (see Chapter 4); PageMaker 6 provides only paragraph-level style sheets.
- QuarkXPress doesn't let you disable automatic kerning for individual paragraphs; PageMaker does and lets you control it through style sheets. That's ideal when you want to automatically kern text in some fonts or elements but not others.
- PageMaker's ranked hyphenation scheme allows for better, more accurate automatic hyphenation.
- Although QuarkXPress's frame approach lends itself to structured documents, PageMaker remains the better program for producing books and manuals, thanks in part to its ability to link separate documents and generate a table of contents and index that spans all linked documents. (Indeed, PageMaker's indexing features are among the best anywhere.) Quark is addressing long-document production with version 4.0 of QuarkXPress, which will provide indexing and table-of-contents generation features.
- PageMaker's unique word processor – like story editor lets you edit without having to weave through a publication's pages.
- PageMaker also provides a better system of managing the links between the publication file and the text and graphics files you import into it. That system simplifies updating publications when their source files change and makes it easier to send publications to imagesetting service bureaus.
- PageMaker 6 is tightly integrated with Adobe's other publishing products, particularly Photoshop. For example, if you double-click a Photoshop image that you've placed in a PageMaker publication, PageMaker switches to Photoshop, where the image is opened. (For more on PageMaker 6's new features, see the Backgrounder box, "What's New in PageMaker 6?" later in this chapter.)
- PageMaker's printing features, manual, and on-line help are better. And PageMaker has historically been more reliable than QuarkXPress, thanks in part to its mini-save feature, which automatically saves the page you're working on when you switch to another page. Adobe's technical support is also better.
- PageMaker 6's Control palette provides even more slick positioning aids than QuarkXPress's Measurements palette. In fact, beginning with version 5, PageMaker has most of the layout goodies — text and graphics rotation, built-in color separation, and editable kerning and

(continued on the next page)

(continued from previous page)

tracking data — that have helped make QuarkXPress so popular. PageMaker 6 adds numerous additional enhancements, including multiple master pages (a feature QuarkXPress has provided for some time), support for Kodak's Precision Color color-management system, and the ability to create documents for use on the Internet. (For details on the last enhancement, see the Backgrounder box, "From Desktop Publishing to Internet Publishing," later in this chapter.)

QuarkXPress does have the edge over PageMaker in several areas. As I describe in the next chapter, far more software add-ons have been developed for QuarkXPress. Also, its frame-oriented approach has made it very popular for periodical publishing.

In the end, both programs are among the best you'll find, and it's possible to produce top-notch publications in either one. Many publishing professionals buy both programs and apply each one's strengths to the appropriate jobs — a smart approach. But if you can buy only one program, my pick is PageMaker.

What publishing programs do

Most publishing programs offer similar features: on-screen rulers for measuring and aligning elements; the capability to import word processing documents with formatting attributes and style sheets intact; rudimentary text editing for making corrections or typing short passages; master pages for holding page numbers and other elements that repeat on each page; and formatting commands that let you change the appearance of text and create tables.

Most programs also let you type position values in a dialog box — handy for precise positioning. (For more comparisons between PageMaker and QuarkXPress, see the Background box "PageMaker versus QuarkXPress.")

Two different layout philosophies

It's important to assess how the programs you're considering approach the challenges of electronic publishing. The most basic point of comparison concerns the way you position text and graphics on the page. Two schemes predominate — the on-the-fly, import-and-place scheme exemplified by Adobe PageMaker, and the draw-a-frame-and-then-import approach of QuarkXPress and most other programs.

To bring a text or graphics document into PageMaker, you simply choose the Place command and choose the document. The mouse pointer changes shape to indicate that it's "loaded" with text or a graphic. Click within the layout, and PageMaker places the item on the page (see Figure 9-1 "Making Pages with PageMaker").

With QuarkXPress and most other programs, before you can bring in a text or graphic, you must draw a box on the layout to indicate where you want the item to appear. Then you select the box and choose a Get Text or Get Picture command (see Figure 9-2 "Layout Librarian").

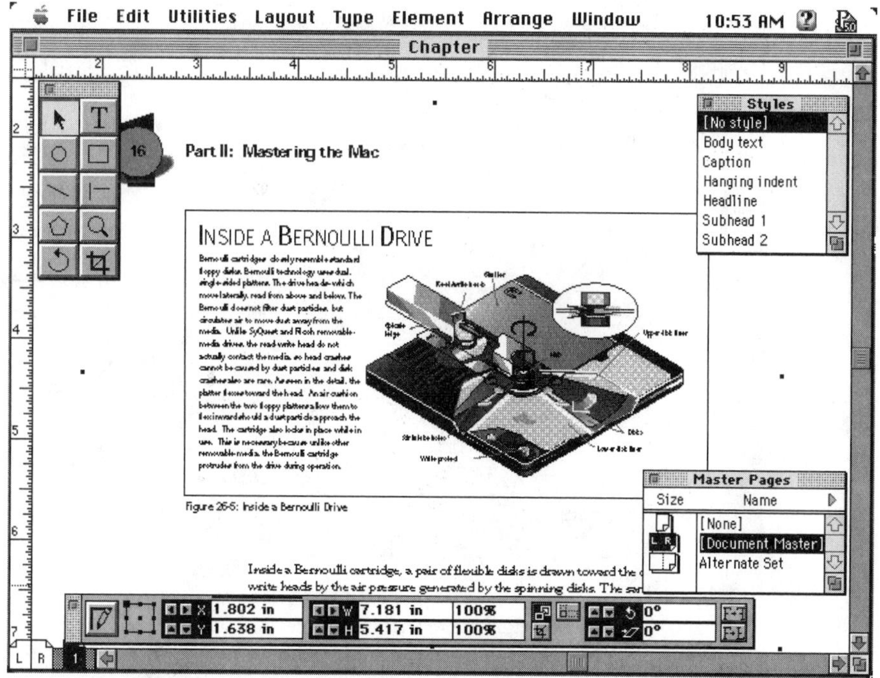

Figure 9-1: Making Pages with PageMaker Publishing programs such as Adobe PageMaker provide on-screen layout tables upon which you electronically attach text and graphics. You can also use these tables to temporarily hold text or graphics much like a pasteup artist might tack a strip of text to the edge of a layout table. The dotted ruler guides aid in positioning and aligning elements, while the Styles palette lets you assign style sheets to text. The icons in the lower-left corner enable you to access other pages in the publication. The icons labeled L and R correspond to left and right master pages, which hold page numbers and other elements that appear on each page. Also note the drawing tools for creating boxes, lines (also called rules), and other shapes.

Which approach is best? Many people prefer the PageMaker approach for experimenting with layouts — it's also more akin to the way a layout artist works. The frame-oriented scheme lends itself to periodicals, books, and manuals, where consistency and advance planning are paramount.

Color on the leading edge

Besides being able to import images from graphics programs, publishing programs provide tools for drawing rules, boxes, and circles. They also let you create *spot color* — a single color dropped into certain page elements (such as a headline or a horizontal bar) used to grab readers' attention. When you print a publication containing spot color, the program prints a separate sheet of paper for each color. Each sheet contains registration marks that a printing company uses to align colors.

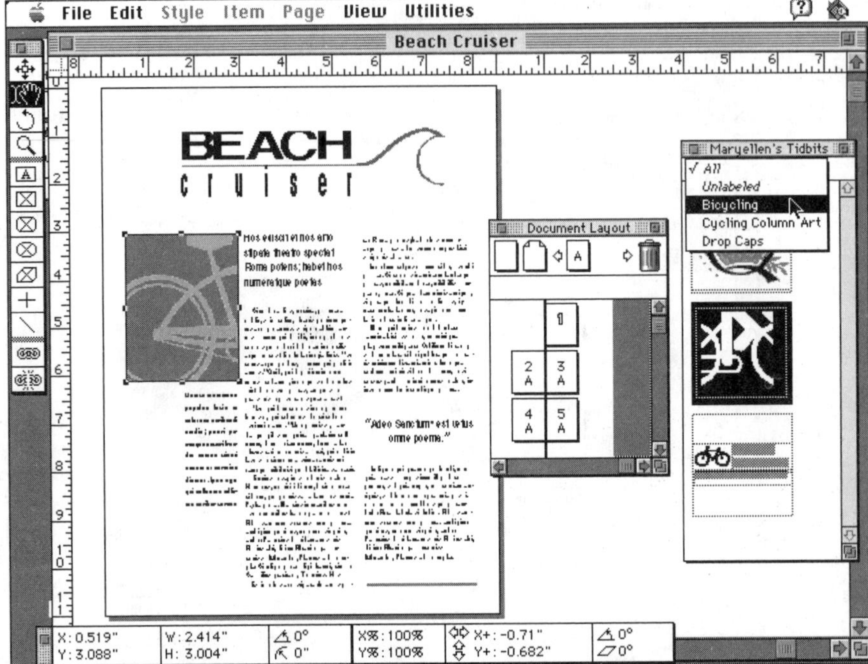

Figure 9-2: Layout Librarian QuarkXPress's innovative library feature lets you store and recall often-used text or graphics. Retrieving an element from the library is a simple matter of dragging it from the library window (here, called "Maryellen's Tidbits") onto the page. (PageMaker 5 has a similar library feature that also works with the Aldus Fetch image database software.) Also visible here is QuarkXPress' Document Layout palette, which lets you rearrange and quickly access a publication's pages. The measurements palette at bottom displays information about the selected element and lets you conveniently modify its position, text, and other attributes.

Adobe PageMaker, QuarkXPress, and Manhattan Graphics' ReadySetGo can also import color images and print *color separations* that a professional printer uses to create the four printing plates (cyan, yellow, magenta, and black) used to print color images on offset printing presses. This technique is the leading edge of electronic publishing, and you need a sense of adventure and some pioneer spirit to reach it.

Many publishing pros have learned the hard way that it's often easier and more economical to stick with traditional color-separation techniques, which usually involve sending color images to separation houses that use ultra-expensive computer systems from firms such as Crossfield and Scitex. The printer then strips the resulting separations into place by hand.

Some publishers strike a middle ground, using a publishing program's color features for proofing and then using conventional separation techniques for the final product. Technology is improving rapidly, however, and companies like Crossfield and Scitex are building their next-generation separation systems around the Macintosh. Each year brings more affordable and less experimental desktop color separation products.

For an overview of some popular publishing programs, see the Quick Tips box "Publishing Software at a Glance."

What's New in PageMaker 6?

When PageMaker 5 shipped several years ago, it incorporated some significant enhancements: the ability to have multiple publications open simultaneously, the Control palette, enhanced color separation features, text and graphics rotation, and more.

In the summer of 1995, Adobe shipped PageMaker 6 — the first new version of PageMaker since the merger of Adobe and Aldus took place. PageMaker 6 sports more than 50 new features. Here's a summary of the best of them.

- **A tweaked Tools palette.** The palette now looks more like its counterparts in Adobe Photoshop and Illustrator. And as in those programs, you can adjust the settings of many of its tools by double-clicking their palette icons. The palette also provides a new polygon-drawing tool (great for drawing the starbursts that you often see in advertisements) and a new zoom tool that lets you enlarge and reduce the layout view.
- **Multiple master pages.** You can now create up to 256 different master pages for a single publication and switch between them by using a new Master Pages palette or by clicking the L and R master page icons in the publication window.
- **Enhanced color support.** High-end publishers will appreciate PageMaker 6's support for the Kodak Precision Color Management System, which works behind the scenes to improve color accuracy as a publication makes the long and complex journey from monitor to paper. (If you have complex color publications that you created in PageMaker 5, you can also specify that PageMaker 6 use the old PageMaker 5 color management system.) PageMaker 6 also has new features for converting RGB images to CMYK format; for importing and enhancing Kodak PhotoCD images; and for creating ultra high-quality color separations that use high-end printing technologies such as HiFi Color and Pantone Hexachrome.
- **Tighter integration with other Adobe products.** This is a big side benefit of the Adobe/Aldus merger, and great news for the thousands of publishers who live in programs such as Photoshop and Illustrator. In PageMaker 6, you can open a Photoshop image that you've placed in PageMaker by double-clicking it. PageMaker 6 also supports Adobe Photoshop filters, so you can apply special effects to images without having to go through the export/import routine. And a new plug-in module, named Create Adobe PDF, lets you create Portable Document

(continued on the next page)

(continued from previous page)

Format files for use with Adobe Acrobat (described in Chapter 28).

- **A new Arrange menu.** This menu, similar to its counterparts in other Adobe programs, lets you move page elements in front of or behind other page elements; lock elements to prevent them from being moved or deleted; and group multiple elements so that you can move or resize them as a unit.
- **New plug-in modules.** In PageMaker 5, these software add-ins were called *Additions.* In PageMaker 6, they're *plug-ins,* which is what they're called in most other programs, including Photoshop and Illustrator. Some of PageMaker 6's new plug-ins include Guide Manager, for creating on-screen layout grids and guides; Scripts, for managing automation scripts (discussed in the next chapter); Alignment, for aligning objects; and Photoshop Effects Filters, for accessing Photoshop plug-ins.
- **Object-masking features.** With the new Mask command, you can superimpose a shape (such as an oval or starburst) over an image and then turn the shape into a mask so that the image shows through the shape. You can also create masks for text.
- **Printing enhancements galore.** From automatic built-in trapping features to a sophisticated two-way communication scheme with PostScript printers to a Non-Printing command that lets you specify that an object appear on-screen but not be printed, PageMaker 6 offers numerous printing-related enhancements.
- **Support for QuarkXPress keyboard shortcuts.** If, as Adobe hopes, you like PageMaker 6 so much that you decide to switch from QuarkXpress, you can configure PageMaker 6 to respond to the same keyboard shortcuts you memorized for QuarkXPress.

Power Publishing with FrameMaker

A notch or two above PageMaker, QuarkXPress, and ReadySetGo, you find Frame Technology's FrameMaker, a so-called workstation publishing program (see Figure 9-3 "High-End Publishing"). FrameMaker provides interactive layout features, too, but it supplements them with features aimed at producing lengthy documents such as books and technical manuals. FrameMaker lets you create and manage footnotes, tables of contents, and indexes. It can automatically revise page numbers in cross-references (such as "see 'mouse' on page 150") as you add text to or remove it from a publication.

FrameMaker also provides template features that automate the production of documents in which each page has a similar layout. (Ventura Publisher has many of these features, too; indeed, the program's prowess at handling lengthy, structured documents has helped make it one of the PC world's most popular publishing programs. The Macintosh version appeared in late 1990 but never really developed much of a following.)

Publishing Software at a Glance

In this box are the nuts and bolts of the popular publishing programs you have to choose from.

Entry-Level Programs

- **Adobe Home Publisher:** Formerly called Aldus Personal Press, this simple program does what a low-end publishing program should: it streamlines publishing for nonpublishers. You can use its AutoCreate feature to automate production of documents that don't demand finely finessed type. It's also extensible with file import/export modules and scanner drivers. And its $49.99 price tag is hard to argue with. (A $69.99 version includes the SuperPaint graphics program.)
- **Integrated programs:** Programs such as ClarisWorks and Microsoft Works may not be called desktop publishing packages, but they can certainly handle basic publishing tasks such as simple newsletters and brochures. Their ability to manage data also makes them useful for simple database publishing tasks such as phone directories and price lists. And unlike mainstream publishing programs, integrated packages run well on slower Macs.

Mainstream Programs

- **Adobe PageMaker:** The best typography in its class, solid printing and bookmaking features, extensibility, and an elegant interface combine to make PageMaker the best all-around mainstream package. As described elsewhere in this chapter, version 6, the first new release to appear since the Adobe/Aldus merger, builds on the program's strength with an enhanced tool palette, tighter integration with Adobe imaging programs, and support for up to 256 master pages per publication.
- **Quark QuarkXPress:** Another professional-level tool, QuarkXPress has earned praise for its speed, responsiveness, and control over type and graphics. Its frame-oriented approach is ideal for structured publications, and sophisticated software add-ons are available for high-volume production. QuarkXPress's learning curve is steep, but pros find plenty of power at the summit. Version 4.0, due for release by the end of 1995, will provide index- and table of contents–generation features, character-level style sheets, and an enhanced interface. QuarkXPress 4 will also be tightly integrated with Quark's Photoshop-like image-editing program, Xposure.
- **Manhattan Graphics ReadySetGo:** Mainstream Publishing's also-ran, ReadySetGo is strong on typography and color support, but previous versions' limitations have slowed its acceptance. The program has the hooks to allow for powerful software add-ons, but few have been developed.

Long-Document Programs

- **Frame Technology FrameMaker:** Powerful and well designed, FrameMaker is the best choice for scientific and technical publishing, and an excellent choice for preparing documents destined for the Internet. It has a fine table editor, allows manual kerning, and can import and print color, but its power demands commitment and a fast machine.

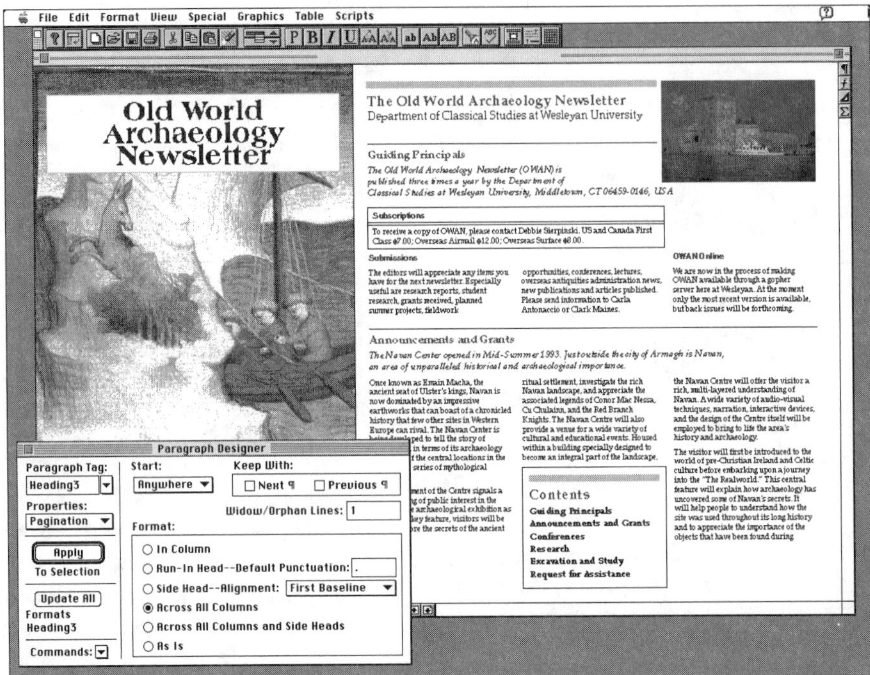

Figure 9-3: High-End Publishing Frame Technology's FrameMaker is a workstation publishing program designed for the production of lengthy documents. FrameMaker provides built-in word processing and drawing features that go far beyond those of general-purpose publishing programs like PageMaker. Note the extensive object-manipulation features in FrameMaker's tool palette (which can be collapsed to show only the most often used tools).

All-in-one publishing

Besides handling lengthy documents, FrameMaker enables you to produce complex publications without having to use separate word processing and graphics programs. FrameMaker provides powerful drawing features you can use to create technical illustrations and schematics. The program also sports a built-in word processor with advanced features such as revision tracking and equation editing.

Workstation publishing programs get their name because they were originally developed for minicomputer-based workstations such as those made by Sun Microsystems and Digital Equipment Corporation. Indeed, FrameMaker is still available for such workstations (as well as for Microsoft Windows), and you can transfer publications between the Mac version and its counterparts on other platforms.

From Desktop Publishing to Internet Publishing

The phrase "electronic publishing" used to refer to the process of laying out pages with computers. These days, "electronic publishing" means delivering publications in electronic form — on CD-ROMs, through on-line services, or over the Internet.

As Chapter 16 describes, the World Wide Web (WWW) is one of the hottest aspects of the Internet, thanks in part to its support for hypertext — the ability to jump from one document or area on the Web to another by clicking on words or images. Many businesses and other organizations are establishing sites on the Web — to promote products, to distribute information, or just to convey the impression that they're on the cutting edge.

If you're creating a Web site, you need to prepare documents with the proper codes that describe the document's appearance and hypertext links. On the Web, this formatting is described by a language called *Hypertext Markup Language,* or *HTML*. HTML relies on *tags* — text codes such as </HEAD>— that describe a document's structure and also refer to external files such as graphics.

One way to create these tags is by using a program that can translate an existing document into HTML format, and that's where publishing programs come in. PageMaker 6 and FrameMaker 5 can both create HTML-format documents from existing publication files. With these programs, you can create your publication using the program's page-layout features, and then use its HTML converter to generate the HTML file that you post on your Web site.

PageMaker 6 provides HTML support via a plug-in module named HTML Author. FrameMaker 5 provides an export option that creates HTML documents. FrameMaker's HTML export feature even lets you assign specific FrameMaker paragraph style sheets to HTML tags and also support hypertext links within documents and to external documents. The HTML exporter can also create hypertext links between table-of-contents and index entries and the text they refer to.

Adobe Acrobat provides its own Internet publishing angle. As Chapter 28 describes, Adobe has teamed up with Netscape Communications (whose Netscape software is one of the most popular Web browser programs) to provide Internet support for Portable Document Format files created using Adobe Acrobat. With the Acrobat Weblink, a utility included with Acrobat, you can create glitzy Web screens (called *pages*) containing sophisticated text formatting as well as graphics. By comparison, Web pages created using HTML tools are graphically rather bland. The goals of the Adobe/Netscape collaboration are to allow Web publishers to create visually attractive Web pages and also to enable them to easily adapt their existing paper documents for distribution on the Web.

The face of Internet publishing is changing quickly, with new products and new concepts appearing almost as fast as new Web sites. Where all this will lead is anyone's guess, but one thing is certain: publishing is making the leap from the printed page to the screen, and publishers who don't want to be left behind may want to make the same leap themselves.

FrameMaker 5, released in the summer of 1995, provides several significant new features, including support for text runarounds and for headings that straddle multiple text columns. FrameMaker 5 also provides enhanced text- and graphics-importing features.

FrameMaker 5 is also a powerful electronic publishing tool: with the included FrameViewer utility, you can create electronic versions of publications, with hypertext features that enable you to, say, jump to a certain section by clicking its table-of-contents entry. And as described elsewhere in this chapter, FrameMaker 5 lets you prepare electronic publications that will be distributed on the Internet's World Wide Web.

On the negative side, FrameMaker can be difficult to learn. Also, its all-in-one approach makes sense for high-end workstations, where there isn't a huge selection of third-party software, but it's less of an advantage in the Mac world, where you can choose from and combine dozens of powerful word processors and graphics programs.

Essential Reference Books

If you're after professional results, you should take time to proofread your publication's text carefully to ensure that words are spelled correctly, lines are hyphenated accurately, and punctuation characters are correctly positioned.

For checking spelling and hyphenation, you want a standard dictionary (such as *Merriam-Webster's Collegiate Dictionary, Tenth Edition,* Merriam-Webster, 1993. Webster's is available on CD-ROM from Highlighted Data, Inc.) To learn about the ins and outs of punctuation, grammar, and style, buy a style manual such as the *Chicago Manual of Style* (University of Chicago Press, 1993) or *Words into Type* (Prentice-Hall, 1974).

In the meantime, I provide some guidelines for punctuation and other typographic details in Chapter 11.

Scaling the command-driven mountain

On the fringes of the electronic publishing world are *code-oriented* (also known as *command-driven* or *batch-processing*) programs that require typed formatting codes in the text. With code-oriented programs, typed codes such as \hsize = 155mm replace the mouse and menus for positioning and formatting text. This substitution makes them more difficult to use; indeed, you need mountain-climbing gear to scale the learning curve of programs like Textures from Blue Sky Research. Textures is based on the TeX (pronounced *tek*) typesetting language, which was developed in part to streamline the production of lengthy publications containing complex mathematical equations. Another TeX package, OzTeX, is available free through user group libraries and on-line services.

Display Type Made Easy

If you are creating advertisements, large headlines, or package designs, you probably want a display type program such as Broderbund's TypeStyler (top) or Letraset's LetraStudio (bottom). These programs let you stretch, condense, squeeze, and otherwise alter the appearance of text. Finally, if you plan to include graphics in your publications, see Chapter 12 for a look at painting and drawing programs.

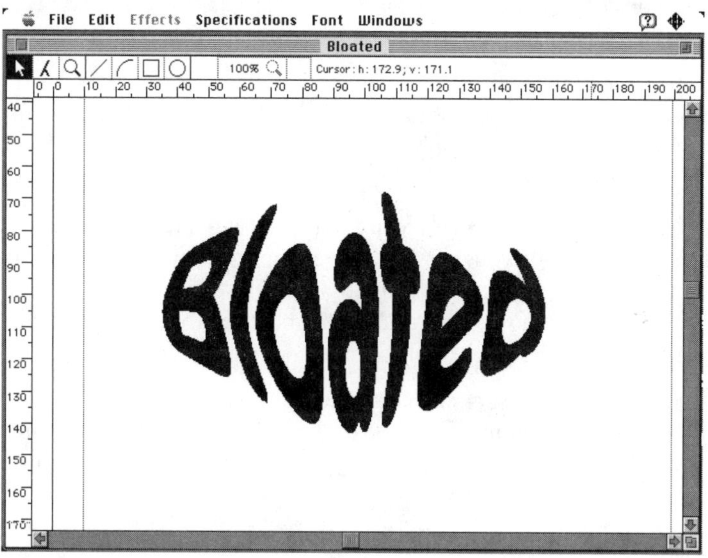

But there are rewards at the summit. Not only can Textures create documents of virtually unlimited size, but it can also create footnotes, tables of contents, and indexes automatically. Textures also provides preview windows that show how the final product will appear. The program is best for producing large publications that require a consistent appearance throughout, such as books and training manuals. And because formatting codes are embedded in the original text, a code-oriented program is ideal for publications that need frequent revision.

Publishing Alternatives

With the boundaries between text processing and publishing becoming increasingly blurred, the best electronic publishing program for your needs may actually be a word processor. A word processor is an ideal tool for documents that have relatively simple layouts and whose text undergoes frequent revision.

The Mac world's word processing powerhouses have features formerly associated with publishing programs. Microsoft Word, Nisus Software's Nisus, and WordPerfect Corporation's WordPerfect can create footnotes, tables of contents, and indexes. Word also lets you create mathematical equations. WordPerfect, Nisus, and Claris's MacWrite Pro can even wrap text around an irregularly shaped graphic. Word 6 encroaches on FrameMaker's territory in many ways — it provides automatic cross-referencing features, automatic kerning, and a plenty of page-layout options.

If you're new to publishing or don't need exotic color-separation and text-spacing features, consider Adobe's HomePublisher entry-level publishing package. You may also consider an integrated program such as ClarisWorks or Microsoft Works. Both enable you to mix text, graphics, and even spreadsheet data on a page.

Illustration programs such as Macromedia FreeHand and Adobe Illustrator are ideal for creating small, graphically oriented publications, especially ones requiring special typographic effects. Adobe Illustrator handles text particularly well, even enabling you to link frames so that text flows from one to another.

Then there's Multi-Ad Service's Multi-Ad Creator, which lets you create documents containing numerous versions of a single page. With its PageMaker-like place-and-go layout scheme, built-in library of PostScript special text effects, and superb style sheet features, it's an excellent choice for producing display advertisements and other single-page publications.

If you're determined to stick with a mainstream publishing program, look for shopping advice in the Quick Tips box, "A Publishing Program Shopping List."

A Publishing Program Shopping List

The best way to choose a publishing program is to assess your needs and then find the program that best meets them. Be sure to select a program whose operating style you can live with. Here are some features and factors to consider.

What is its maximum document length?
Early publishing programs were limited to short documents of about 16 pages. Today's programs support much longer documents, 999 pages in PageMaker's case, and as many pages as fit on disk with QuarkXPress and ReadySetGo. FrameMaker is particularly well suited for the production of lengthy, structured documents such as books and manuals.

What sizing and positioning features does it offer?
PageMaker used to rely exclusively on the mouse for sizing and positioning items on a page, but it, like QuarkXPress and ReadySetGo, now lets you type values that describe an element's size and position. Some people prefer typing these values to dragging with the mouse.

What kind of text-editing features do you need?
Unless you're using a workstation publishing program, you want to use a word processor to write your publication's text, saving your publishing program's text-editing features for simple tasks such as last-minute corrections and revisions. QuarkXPress and ReadySetGo provide search-and-replace features and other rudimentary text-editing functions. PageMaker provides these same goodies, but also adds an extremely useful *story editor,* a mini-word processor that makes it easy to revise text and even write small passages within PageMaker.

PageMaker also provides linking options that let you easily update your original word processor files to reflect last-minute editing changes. Updating your original files to match the publication's text is important if you plan to use the originals again in other publications. PageMaker, QuarkXPress, and ReadySetGo also support System 7's publish-and-subscribe features for moving data between programs. PageMaker also supports Microsoft's OLE data-exchange system, described in Chapter 27.

Can you control spacing adequately?
The spacing between characters and between words plays an important part in determining a publication's overall legibility. Most publishing programs offer a variety of features that improve intercharacter and interword spacing. *Kerning* features let you move characters closer together to improve the spacing of certain letter combinations, such as To and AT (see the figure "Kerning Characters"). An automatic kerning feature enables the publishing program to kern characters based on kerning tables that developers build into most of their fonts. A manual kerning function lets you fine-tune spacing by hand to improve the spacing of large text such as headlines. Word-spacing features let you increase or decrease interword spacing.

A track kerning feature lets the program uniformly decrease intercharacter spacing as the type size increases. Most publishing programs provide automatic and manual kerning, but only Adobe PageMaker, QuarkXPress, and ReadySetGo provide track kerning. Ventura Publisher claims to provide tracking, but its tracking feature simply tightens intercharacter spacing and isn't dependent on type size.

You often hear QuarkXPress zealots praise their program for being more precise than PageMaker because QuarkXPress allows smaller kerning and positioning increments (1/20,000 em compared to PageMaker 6's 1/1000 em). But the fact is, at most type sizes, 1/20,000 em is finer than almost any output device can render. For example, at 3,386 dots per inch, 1/20,000 em has no effect on type sizes below 400 point. Mechanical output devices — with their belts, rubber rollers, and film that expands and contracts with the weather — aren't precise enough to render such minute measurements. In short, you may feel

(continued on the next page)

(continued from previous page)

better specifying a teeny kerning or positioning value in QuarkXPress, but you're unlikely to see the difference in your hard copy.

Can the program import your documents?
All publishing programs can import word processing and graphics files created by popular Mac programs, and some programs, such as WordPerfect, also support popular IBM PC file formats. But it's always a good idea to verify in advance that a publishing program can import the types of documents you create.

Is third-party support available?
PageMaker and QuarkXPress users can choose from a large variety of training materials and software add-ons that enhance their programs. Add-ons range from utilities that arrange pages for booklet printing to database publishing software such as Digital Composition Systems' DataShaper (for PageMaker) and Em Software's xdata (for QuarkXPress). DataShaper and xdata let you use the data stored by a database management program to create a variety of publications. For example, a video rental store might use its videotape database to produce catalogs for customers, inventory reports showing which tapes are checked out, and labels for the videotapes themselves. Database publishing simplifies the production of publications whose text is sorted and organized into categories. Typical database publishing applications include catalogs, classified advertisements, telephone directories, and television listings.

I give more details on software add-ons for PageMaker and QuarkXPress in the next chapter.

What are your needs and limitations?
To pick the right program, first determine which types of publications you want to create. Brochures, menus, newsletters, books, scientific papers, advertisements — every piece has its demands, and some programs meet them better than others. Next, consider your hardware. Low-end packages run on Mac Classics and the like, but mainstream programs demand a Quadra-class machine or better still, a Power Mac. Finally, consider yourself — your design and layout skills and the extent to which you want to immerse yourself in publishing minutiae.

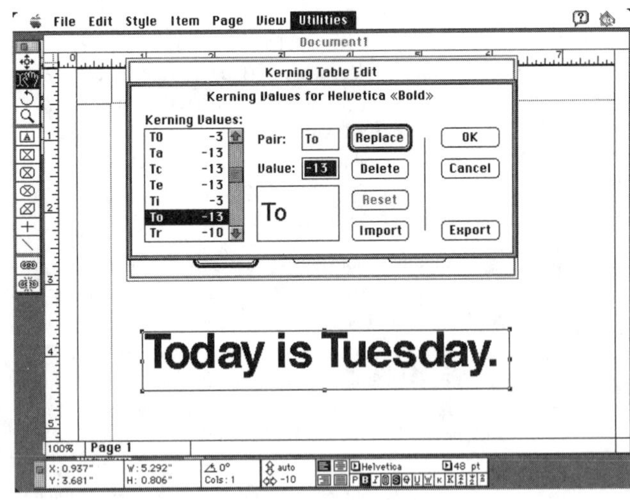

Kerning Characters The legibility of text, especially that of large headlines such as the one visible here, improves when key letter pairs are kerned. Automatic kerning features rely on kerning tables built into a font by its designer. QuarkXPress, ReadySetGo, and PageMaker 5 let you edit kerning tables to suit your typographic tastes. (QuarkXPress's kerning table editor is shown here.) You can also use third-party kerning table utilities such as The Software Shop's Kern-Rite and Pairs Software's KernEdit.

Putting the Issue to Bed

Before you take the publishing plunge, prepare yourself. It's hard work. The Mac makes producing an attractive, readable page easier than it used to be, but it's still not a breeze. To get results that do justice to your message, you need to develop an awareness of design and typography.

One way to get off to a good start is to hire a graphic designer to create a conceptual framework — a foundation on which you can build each issue. Many companies also sell canned template documents for common publishing jobs like newsletters and reports. Most programs also come with a library of templates that you can use as is or modify to suit your tastes. Even with one of these approaches, however, the quality of your publication's typography is still up to you. The tips and advice in Chapter 11 should help.

When you start up that page-layout program, you assume a responsibility for conveying ideas in an aesthetically pleasing way, both visually and verbally. Ignore that responsibility and you ignore centuries of printing tradition. And it isn't just the designers and typographers of the world who notice. They may not be aware of it, but your readers are excellent judges of good design and typography. Don't let them find you guilty of crimes against legibility.

CHAPTER 9 CONCEPTS AND TERMS

- Investing some time and effort in learning a sophisticated publishing program can allow you to do what used to require several specialists and expensive equipment — but you have to know what you're doing.
- The two most popular publishing programs are Adobe PageMaker and QuarkXPress, but for lengthy documents and technical manuals, workstation programs such as FrameMaker can be more appropriate.
- When you're shopping for a publishing program, features and factors to consider include maximum document length, positioning and sizing features, text-editing features, text-spacing controls, and third-party support.
- Although electronic publishing makes it easier to produce printed materials, you need to develop an awareness of design and typography in order to get the best results.

camera ready
A page that's ready to be sent to a printer for printing.

code-oriented programs
Also known as *command-driven* or *batch-processing* programs, a category of publishing programs that don't rely on the mouse for layout but instead require typed formatting codes in the text.

color separation
An essential step in producing color publications, the process of dividing a color page into cyan, yellow, magenta, and black components and printing a separate page for each ink color.

comp
Short for *comprehensive,* a detailed drawing that shows how a final printed piece will look.

copy
Publishing jargon for text.

copyfitting
A tedious process in which a designer or typesetter uses formulas to calculate how much space a given amount of text requires when printed in a particular font and size.

crop marks
Those weird round circles in British farmers' fields, supposedly created by aliens. Also, horizontal and vertical lines that indicate a page's boundaries.

dummy
Anyone who thinks that a publishing program automatically makes him or her a graphic artist. Also, a preliminary layout that shows how and where the text and graphics should go on each page.

halftone
A technique of converting a photograph into a series of dots.

Hypertext Markup Language
Abbreviated HTML, a text-coding language used to prepare documents that will be published on the Internet's World Wide Web. PageMaker 6 and FrameMaker 5 both provide HTML support.

imagesetter
A kind of printer that produces its hard copy on photographic film or paper.

kerning
The process of adjusting the space between certain character pairs, such as *To.*

line art
Black-and-white drawings or graphs.

mark up
The process of annotating a page of copy to indicate the desired fonts, line lengths, spacing, and other specifications.

master pages
In a publishing program, special pages for holding page numbers and other elements that repeat on each page or on odd- and even-numbered pages.

mechanical
A piece of heavy cardboard upon which the text and graphics for a page are pasted.

optical character recognition
A software technology that enables a computer to "read" typed or typeset pages of text and create disk files you can edit and reformat with a word processor.

registration marks
Special symbols printed outside the margins that a printing shop uses to align the plates that print each color.

rules
Lines that appear on a page.

scanner
A photocopier-like device that creates electronic image files from photographs or other artwork.

spot color
A single color dropped into certain page elements (such as a headline or a horizontal bar) used to grab readers' attention.

spread
A low-fat alternative to butter. Also, two facing pages.

strip
A printing industry process in which page negatives are cut into place and prepared for printing.

tracking
A publishing program feature that automatically adjusts the space between every character. With small sizes, spacing is increased to open up the text and make it less dense. In large sizes, spacing is decreased to tighten up the text.

CHAPTER TEN

10 Publishing Techniques and Power Tips

- Performing common publishing tasks in Adobe PageMaker and QuarkXPress
- Creating oversized publications with your program's tiling features
- Ensuring your publications are TC — typographically correct
- Expanding a page-layout program with software add-ons

Today's publishing programs are capable of turning out top-quality publications. But are you? If you were a publishing professional before the Mac appeared, chances are you've made the transition to the desktop without too much pain (assuming that you didn't lose your job in the process — according to the International Typeface Corporation, there are half as many typesetting houses today as there were before the Macintosh was introduced).

But if you're new to publishing — if you used to produce that newsletter with an IBM Selectric and a couple of type balls — you may be overwhelmed by the array of options that programs such as Adobe PageMaker or QuarkXPress provide. Smart quotes, kerning, tracking, letter spacing, spot color — it's almost enough to make you long for the old Selectric.

Some publishing neophytes address this feature onslaught by ignoring it, relying on their program's default settings for page size, spacing, and the rest. As a result, many desktop publications *look* like desktop publications — the efforts of someone with a powerful program but without the knowledge to fully apply it.

Fortunately, it's not too difficult to take the desktop out of desktop publishing. In this chapter, I spotlight several techniques for adding polish to publications. Although the instructions here apply to QuarkXPress and PageMaker, similar concepts apply to all publishing programs and even to some word processors.

If you're already a publishing veteran, you may just want to browse this chapter's Quick Tips boxes for tips and insights into PageMaker and QuarkXPress.

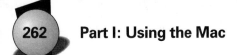

Making Banners at the Local Copy Shop

Many copy shops have blueprint photocopiers that can accept originals up to a few feet wide, with no length limit. You can produce some mighty impressive banners by using your publishing program's tiling feature and then photocopying the assembled page.

Page Size Decisions

One of the most basic decisions behind any publication is the choice of page size, or *trim size*. Chances are you frequently opt for the 8½ x 11-inch page size offered by QuarkXPress and PageMaker. After all, that's probably the largest paper size your laser printer can handle, and it's the most common size used by print shops.

But before okaying that New dialog box, consider the options. For starters, consider a *landscape*, or wide, orientation — 11 by 8½ inches. It may work well for a small poster, a publication with wide graphics, or a calendar. (By the way, the more common orientation is called *portrait*, or tall.)

Two sides are better than one

If you're a bit more ambitious, consider turning that letter-sized sheet into a two-sided job. By folding the sheet one or two times, you can create an attractive booklet, menu, or brochure (see Figure 10-1 "One Fold and Two Folds"). A two-sided job costs more to print, but exactly how much more depends on many factors, including the quantity you print, the paper you use, the number of printers in your area, and the type of equipment each printer has. It's a good idea to get several estimates.

Print on offbeat paper for a hot look

If you're printing a small run on your laser printer, investigate the wide selection of specialty papers available from mail-order houses such as Paper Direct (800-272-7377). Besides stiff card stocks, Paper Direct also sells paper preprinted with splashes of color and interesting patterns around which you can structure your design. (See Chapter 31 for more details about alternative paper stocks.)

ONE FOLD AND TWO FOLDS

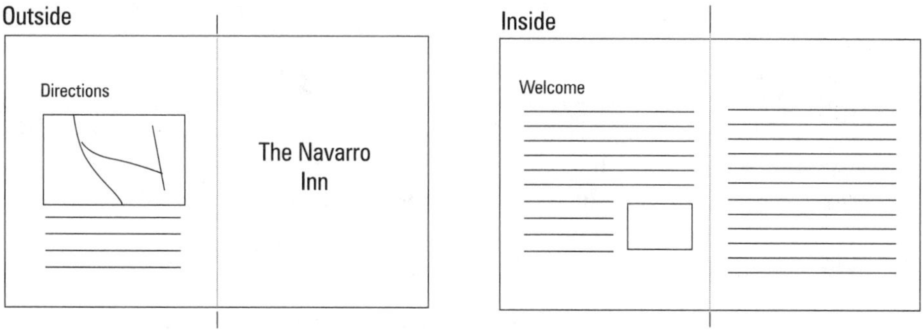

A single fold yields a four-page booklet. A horizontal orientation is usually preferable, since it allows for wider text margins. How to: Specify a wide page orientation, and then create a ruler guide at the 5½- inch mark. You may also want to draw vertical rules above and below the fold point; these crop marks will indicate where the printer should fold the page.

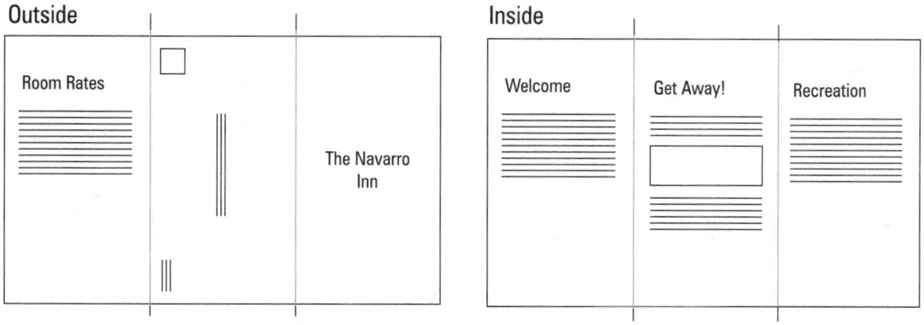

Two fold points yield a six-page booklet that folds nicely for mailing or for insertion in a standard business envelope. How to: Specify a wide page orientation, and then create ruler guides and crop marks at the 3⅞- and 8-inch marks. To create a mailing address on the back page, rotate the text 90 degrees.

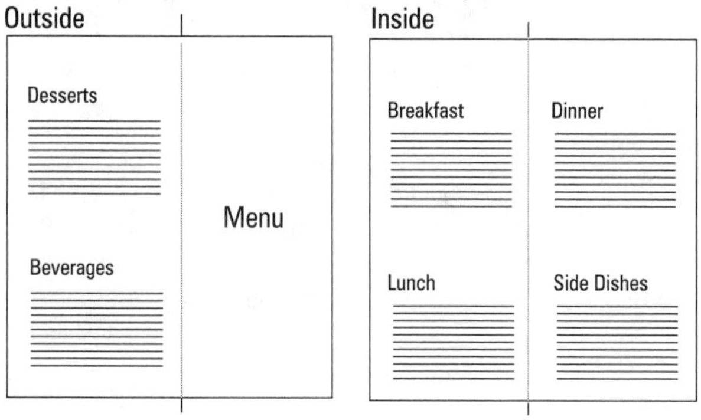

A vertical orientation may be appropriate for a phone directory or menu, where narrow lines are common. How to: Create a ruler guide at the 4¼-inch mark and draw crop marks to indicate the fold point.

Figure 10-1: One Fold and Two Folds

Use tiling for oversized publications

If you're producing a poster or newsletter, don't be caged in by your laser printer's maximum paper size. You can produce tabloid- or even billboard-size publications by using your program's *tiling* feature. Simply specify the desired final page size when setting up the document, and then activate the tiling option when you print. You get a raft of letter-sized pages that you can tape together or paste up on layout board. A large-size tabloid (11 x 17 inches) costs more to print than a letter-size publication but gives you more flexibility in designing your layout. Try to adjust the tiles to avoid cutting lines of type in half; pasting the tiles together will be all the harder. It's better to divide tiles between lines or columns.

Working Faster in PageMaker and QuarkXPress

Complex documents with lots of graphics and a variety of type styles and sizes can slow down a publishing program. Here are a few tips for speeding up PageMaker and QuarkXPress. Unless otherwise noted, the following tips apply to both programs.

Other ways to speed up these and all other programs include increasing their memory allocation by using the Finder's Get Info command (see Chapter 22) and, of course, speeding up your Mac with a faster hard disk or accelerator board (see Part III).

Additional tips that are specific to PageMaker or QuarkXPress appear elsewhere in this chapter.

Use picture placeholders

If your pages have a lot of graphics on them, you can speed up the screen display by choosing to view picture placeholders instead of the graphics themselves. Scrolling is faster, as is switching between pages and magnification views.

In QuarkXPress, choose General from the Preferences submenu (in the Edit menu) and check the Greek Pictures option. When this option is active, QuarkXPress displays a graphic as a gray box; click the gray box to see its actual graphic. In PageMaker, choose Preferences from the File menu. In the Graphics section, choose the Gray Out option.

In PageMaker, you can dramatically speed up printing by choosing to print picture placeholders instead of the actual graphics. This technique is a real time-saver when you're proofing a project. In the Print dialog box, check the Proof box. Each graphic prints as a rectangle with an *X* in it. If you want faster printing but you need to see the graphics, click the Print dialog box's Options button and then choose Low TIFF Resolution from the Graphics pop-up menu. This option prints TIFF images at a relatively coarse 72 dots per inch. (For more details about TIFF images and other graphics file formats, see Chapter 12.)

Greek that text

Displaying a page of text — especially one that uses multiple fonts, sizes, and styles — can slow the Mac at least as much as displaying lots of graphics. To speed up page displays, use the *text greeking* option that PageMaker and QuarkXPress provide. When active, text greeking displays each line of text as a gray bar.

Both programs let you specify a greeking threshold — a type size below which all text is greeked. In PageMaker, choose Preferences and click the Options button. In the Text area, type a size in the Greek Text Below box. In QuarkXPress, choose General from the Preferences submenu and type a value in the Greek Below box.

Use PageMaker's story editor to edit text

Publishing programs aren't word processors. Performing extensive text editing in a publication can be cumbersome as you jump from page to page and column to column. PageMaker's unique word processor-like story editor lets you edit without having to weave through a publication's pages. Just triple-click on a block of text to open the story editor window. (Or select the text block and choose Edit Story from the Edit menu.)

The story editor shows text in a single font and size — normally, 12-point Geneva. This option can be handy when you're working with tiny type or with a fancy script font that's difficult to read on-screen. You can change the font and size by clicking the Options button in the Preferences dialog box.

Use the quick-drag technique when moving items

If you begin dragging immediately after clicking an object, PageMaker and QuarkXPress display an outline indicating the item's size as you drag. However, if you hold down the mouse button for a moment without moving the mouse, both programs display the actual item as you drag. The latter approach lets you see the actual text or graphic as you move it, but it takes longer. (The mouse pointer turns into a wristwatch as the program prepares the display.) When you just want to sling something across a page, use the quick-drag technique: begin dragging immediately after clicking an object.

Use the on-screen palette for formatting and sizing

Both programs provide floating palettes that, among other things, let you format text, resize text blocks and graphics, and change the position of items on a page. In QuarkXPress, the palette is called the Measurements palette; in PageMaker, it's the Control palette. Using this palette is often faster than traveling up to the menu bar, especially when you have a large screen.

Both programs' palettes provide a slick shortcut for changing the size or position of an item: you can change size or position mathematically. For example, suppose an item is positioned 2½ inches from the left margin and you want to move it 3¾ inches to the right. Instead of having to calculate the desired position and then type it into the palette, you can simply type **+3.75** in the appropriate box.

PageMaker's Control palette takes this feature one step further by enabling you to multiply and divide. If you want to double the width of a text block, just type ***2** in the Control palette. PageMaker's Control palette also has numerous keyboard shortcuts for choosing fonts and other options, which the PageMaker manual describes.

Store often-used items in a library

Both programs provide library features that let you store and recall often-used items — graphics, logos, text blocks, and so on. Take advantage of this feature to store page elements that you use often.

Are You Typographically Correct?

The easiest way to spot a desktop-published job is to look at the punctuation. Are the quotes and apostrophes “curly” (like the ones I just used), or are they those tacky "typewriter" quotes (like those)? Are there two spaces after periods (the style taught in Typing 101) or just one (the typographically correct style)? Also look for double hyphens -- how gauche -- which should be true em dashes — that's better.

PageMaker and QuarkXPress help with punctuation by translating typewriter quotes and double hyphens found in word processor files into their typographically correct counterparts. This translation occurs automatically when you import the word processor file.

But automatic punctuation conversion doesn't address text that you type directly into the publishing program, such as headlines and last-minute corrections. You can use the smart quotes option in PageMaker or QuarkXPress to automatically convert quotes as you type, but that option doesn't guard against double word spaces or double hyphens. That's your job.

You can give your tendons a break and use one of the keyboard-modifying system extensions available through user groups and on-line services (see the Quick Tips box "Smart Punctuation Made Easy").

Use search-and-replace to convert dashes

If you've imported word-processed text that's laden with double hyphens, use your publishing program's search-and-replace feature to look for each occurrence of two hyphens and replace it with an em dash (press Shift-Option-hyphen to get an em dash). While you're on your search-and-destroy mission, look for occurrences of two consecutive spaces and replace them with a single space.

Needless to say, this technique works in word processors, too.

Smart Punctuation Made Easy

You can add a smart quotes feature to any program by using a free system extension called SmartKeys, written by Maurice Volaski and available through user groups and on-line services. SmartKeys not only converts quotes as you type, but it also optionally converts double hyphens into em dashes, uses ligatures when available, and prevents you from typing more than one consecutive space.

If you can't find SmartKeys, look for Quote Init, a $15 shareware extension that performs the same basic functions, but not as elegantly.

Note that most on-line services can't recognize smart quotes and em dashes, so when you're creating electronic mail, you may need to disable your keyboard's smarts. SmartKeys makes it easy by enabling you to specify a list of programs in which its conversion features should be disabled.

Using auto ligatures in QuarkXPress

QuarkXPress has an interesting option that automatically generates *ligatures* — connected character pairs such as fi and fl — as you type or import text. You can activate this feature by using the Typographic Preferences dialog box, as described in the Step-by-Step box "Basic Publishing Tasks in QuarkXPress."

Basic Publishing Tasks in QuarkXPress

This box shows you how to use QuarkXPress to perform the tasks described in this chapter.

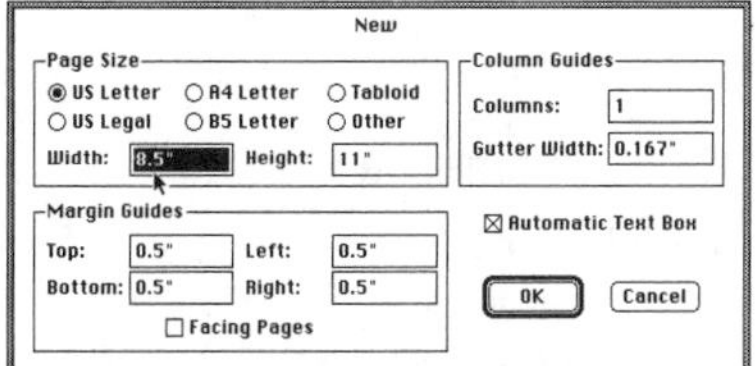

To specify a wide rather than tall page orientation:

1. **Type the appropriate dimensions in the New dialog box's Width and Height boxes.**
   If you've already started a publication and need to change its orientation, choose Document Setup from the File menu and type the appropriate dimensions.

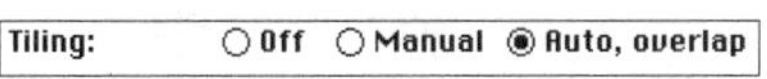

To create an oversized publication:

1. **Specify the final page size in the New dialog box.**
2. **When you're ready to print, choose Print and then click the Manual or Auto, Overlap tiling button, depending on the desired tiling scheme.**

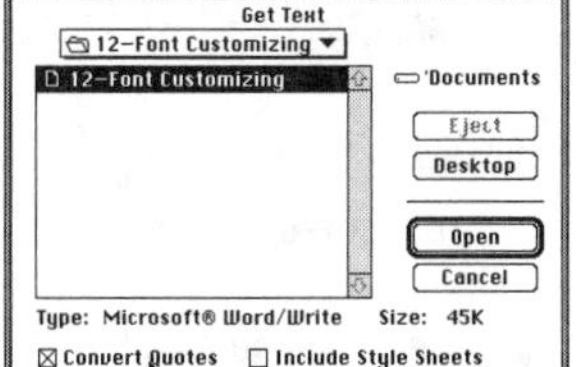

To convert quotes and double hyphens when importing text:

1. **Check Convert Quotes in the Get Text dialog box.**

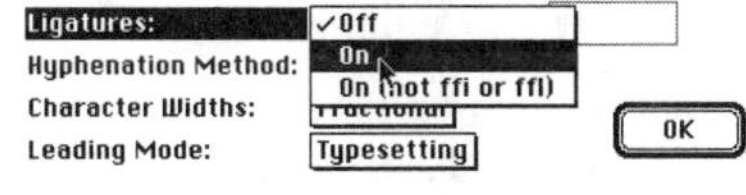

To automatically generate ligatures:

1. **Choose Typographic from the Preferences submenu (in the Edit menu).**
   The Typographic Preferences dialog box appears.
2. **Choose the On option from the Ligatures pop-up menu.**
3. **Click OK or press Return.**

(continued on the next page)

(continued from previous page)

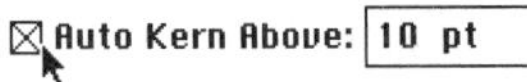

To activate tracking and automatic kerning:

1. **Choose Typographic from the Preferences submenu.**
2. **Check the Auto Kern Above box.**

   If you like, you also can specify a type-size threshold for automatic kerning.

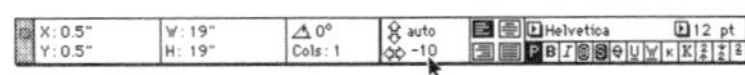

To manually kern two characters:

1. **Place the blinking insertion point between the two characters you want to kern.**
2. **Press ⌘-Shift-{ or, for finer kerning, ⌘-Option-Shift-{.**

   For more kerning shortcuts, see Table 10-1. You can also click the kerning arrows in QuarkXPress's measurements palette or type a kerning value in the area to the right of the kerning arrows. Type a negative value (for example, **–2**) to reduce the spacing. You can also kern a range of characters by using these techniques.

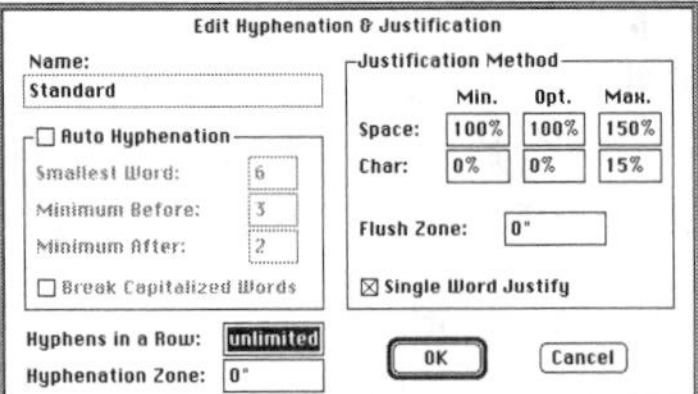

To edit the standard H&J or create a new one:

1. **Choose H&Js from the Edit menu.**
2. **To edit the standard H&J, double-click the H&J named Standard. To create a new H&J, click the New button and then name the new H&J.**
3. **Specify the desired spacing and hyphenation settings in the Edit H&J dialog box.**
4. **Click OK or press Return.**
5. **Click Save.**

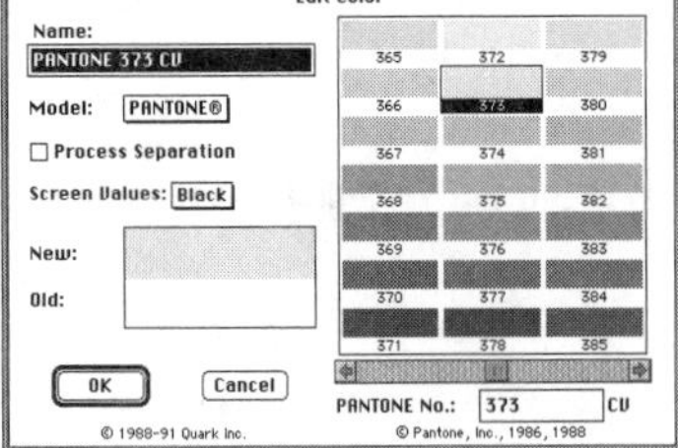

To add a Pantone color to QuarkXPress's color palette:

1. **Choose Colors from the Edit menu.**
2. **Click New.**

   The Edit Color dialog box appears.

3. **Choose Pantone from the Model pop-up menu.**
4. **Select the desired Pantone color and then click OK.**
5. **Click the Save button in the Colors dialog box.**

To assign a color to text or a graphic element:

1. **Select the text or element.**
2. **Click the color name in the Colors palette.**

   If the Colors palette isn't visible, choose Show Colors from the View menu.

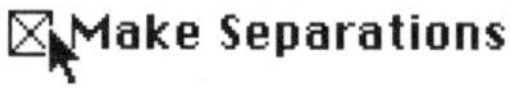

☒ Make Separations

To print the separations for each spot color:

1. **Choose Print from the File menu.**
2. **Check the Make Separations box.**
   To help the print shop align the plates correctly, you may also want to check the Registration Marks button. See the *Using QuarkXPress* manual for more color details.

Improving Character Spacing

To determine how much space to put between words and characters, a publishing program relies on information built into a font. This spacing data is designed to (and usually does) produce attractive results within the range of body text sizes — roughly 8 to 12 points. But with larger sizes, the spacing between characters and words can appear exaggerated. By tightening the spacing with your program's *tracking* and *kerning* features, you can improve the legibility of headlines (see Figure 10-2 "Tracking and Kerning").

Away Today
Away Today
Away Today

Figure 10-2: Tracking and Kerning
To improve headline spacing, start by tightening overall spacing, and then selectively kern where necessary. Begin with a 24-point Helvetica Bold headline (top) with no kerning, apply PageMaker's Normal track option (middle) to tighten overall spacing, and then use selective manual kerning (bottom) to finish the job.

The truth about tracking

Tracking is probably the most misunderstood character-spacing feature in the publishing world. Every Mac book I've seen defines it as the process of removing space between letters. Wrong. As it's defined in the traditional typesetting world, tracking adjusts the space — it removes *or adds* space — between characters, depending on the type size.

With small sizes, you increase spacing to open up the text and make it less dense. In large sizes, you decrease spacing to tighten up the text. This latter aspect of tracking is useful for headlines.

PageMaker sports the best tracking features of any publishing program, offering five tracking commands ranging from Very Loose to Very Tight. For tightening up headlines and other large sizes, try the Normal track for starters.

Improving spacing through kerning

Kerning involves adjusting the space between only certain character pairs. Kerning features come in two flavors: manual lets you specify how much space is to be removed and from where, and automatic lets the program remove space from certain letter pairs, such as *To*, based on information built into the font you're using. Automatic kerning adds polish to body text, but for large headlines, you should use manual kerning to achieve the best look (see Tables 10-1 and 10-2 for kerning specifics).

Don't kern too tightly; characters should not touch. You may need to zoom in on the characters you're kerning to see the results. Or better yet, print some test pages as you work.

Table 10-1
Kerning from the Keyboard in PageMaker

Kern Option	***Key Sequence***
Tighten coarse	⌘-left arrow or ⌘-Delete
Tighten fine	⌘-Shift-left arrow or Option-Delete
Loosen coarse	⌘-right arrow or ⌘-Shift-Delete
Loosen fine	⌘-Shift-right arrow or Option-Shift-Delete
Remove all manual kerning	⌘-Option-K or Option-Shift-keypad Clear or ⌘-Option-Shift-Delete

Table 10-2
Kerning from the Keyboard in QuarkXPress

Kern Option	***Key Sequence***
Tighten coarse	⌘-Shift-{
Tighten fine	⌘-Option-Shift-{
Loosen coarse	⌘-Shift-}
Loosen fine	⌘-Option-Shift-}

PageMaker is preset to automatically kern sizes above 12 point. You can change that size value by using the Spacing Attributes dialog box — choose Paragraph from the Type menu and then click the Spacing option. (Specifying a smaller value slows PageMaker's performance in formatting body text.)

PageMaker provides a plug-in module called Expert Kerning that lets the program automatically do fine kerning by relying on the spacing data that's built into a font. It isn't a substitute for hand kerning, but it does a remarkably good job. PageMaker also lets you edit tracking and kerning data to fine-tune spacing for your particular jobs and tastes.

In PageMaker, automatic kerning is a paragraph-level attribute — you can turn it off or on for a given paragraph. To use (or disable) automatic kerning for only certain paragraphs, select those paragraphs before choosing the Paragraph command.

Better Spacing with Justified Type

The type in newsletters and magazines is often *justified* — aligned against the left and right margins. To justify text, a program adds space between characters and words. Therein lies the potential for poor spacing. With narrow columns, a program often has to insert too much space between words or characters, resulting in distracting rivers of white space (see Figure 10-3 "Clear the Rivers").

With a word processor, there's little you can do to avoid rivers aside from hyphenating the text so that more fits on each line. (You can also reduce the point size or increase the column width, but these measures may compromise your original design.) But publishing programs give you far more control over interword and intercharacter spacing. By tweaking your H&J (hyphenation and justification) settings, you can keep those rivers within their banks.

Adjusting justified spacing

Both QuarkXPress and PageMaker enable you to specify three characteristics for spacing — minimum, the least amount of space that can be put between characters or words; optimum, the spacing specified by the font's designer; and maximum, the largest allowable amount of intercharacter or interword spacing. By adjusting any or all three of these settings for both word and character spacing, you can finely control how text is justified.

Because every publication is different, no specific settings guarantee good justification. Experiment with these two general rules to find the ideal spacing settings for a specific job:

- ❖ Increasing the maximum amount of letter spacing results in fewer large spaces between words, but too much letter spacing can cause words to appear to run together.
- ❖ Decreasing the amount of space between characters allows more text to fit on a line, but the text can appear too dense.

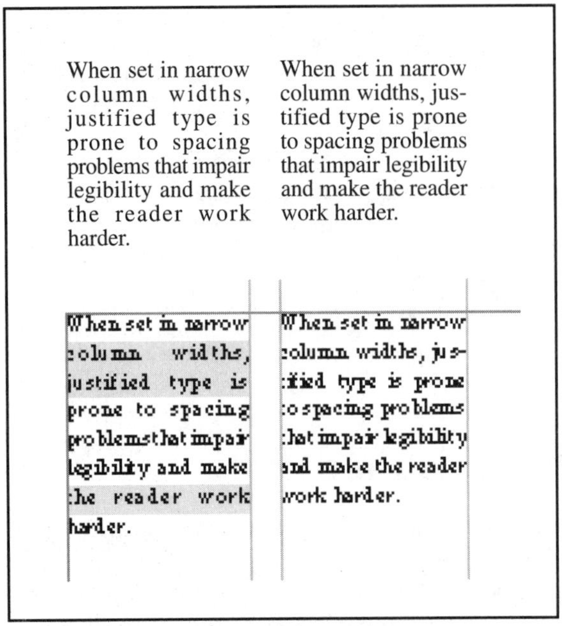

When set in narrow column widths, justified type is prone to spacing problems that impair legibility and make the reader work harder.

When set in narrow column widths, jus-tified type is prone to spacing problems that impair legibility and make the reader work harder.

When set in narrow column widths, justified type is prone to spacing problems that impair legibility and make the reader work harder.

When set in narrow column widths, jus-tified type is prone to spacing problems that impair legibility and make the reader work harder.

Figure 10-3: Clear the Rivers Note the river of white space (top) that runs through the second, third, and fourth lines of the left example. At right, the problem is fixed by hyphenating a word. When PageMaker's Show Layout Problems option is active (bottom), the program highlights poorly spaced lines.

Hyphenating with discretion

Sometimes the easiest way to fix a spaced-out line is by hyphenating. QuarkXPress and PageMaker have automatic hyphenation features and also enable you to manually insert *discretionary hyphens.* A discretionary hyphen tells the program, "If the letters to the left fit on the previous line, divide the word here and insert a hyphen. If they don't fit, don't divide the word." If reformatting or editing changes the line breaks later, the hyphen disappears, but the discretionary hyphen code remains. Discretionary hyphens are sometimes called *soft hyphens* to distinguish them from hard (permanent) ones.

To create a discretionary hyphen in either program, position the insertion point at the possible word break and then press ⌘-hyphen. (By the way, Microsoft Word, WordPerfect, ClarisWorks, and MacWrite Pro also support discretionary hyphens.)

QuarkXPress calls a set of spacing and hyphenation specifications an H&J and lets you create as many H&Js as you like. If you modify or create an H&J when no documents are open, your changes will be available in all future documents you create.

PageMaker has a unique feature that highlights lines with bad spacing, making it easier to spot them. To activate the feature, choose Preferences from the Edit menu and then check the Loose/Tight Lines box.

A Spot of Color

A good way to enliven a publication is by using color. I'm not talking about full-color photographs or illustrations, which can be technically complex to work with and expensive to print, but *spot color* — color added to elements that would otherwise be black, such as headings, lines, and boxes. Using spot color is an easy way to add emphasis and pizzazz to a page, and it doesn't require any exotic hardware. You can even work with spot color on a monochrome Mac such as a Classic, although you obviously can't see the colors on-screen.

When you print a publication containing spot color, you tell the program to print a separate page, or *overlay*, for each spot color you use. You then supply these pages to the print shop, which creates a printing plate for each color.

Because you must run a multicolor job through a press more than once (or through a press capable of printing more than one color at once), it costs more than when you use just one color. Costs for multicolor jobs can vary dramatically from one printer to the next. You'll get a better price at a printing company that has a press designed to print two-color jobs than at a printer that runs the publication through a one-color press two times.

Just as paint stores use standardized swatch books, the printing industry uses standardized color-matching systems that let you choose hues. One of the most popular systems is called Pantone. Both PageMaker and QuarkXPress let you assign Pantone colors and see them on a color monitor. When you take your artwork to the printer, you specify by number which Pantone colors you want — as in Pantone 350.

Both PageMaker and QuarkXPress let you assign color to elements by clicking an on-screen color palette. Normally, the palette lists only a few basic colors such as red, green, and blue. You need to use a command to add other colors to the palette (see the Step-by-Step boxes that discuss basic publishing tasks in QuarkXPress and PageMaker).

Basic Publishing Tasks in Adobe PageMaker

This box shows you how to perform the tasks described in this chapter by using Adobe PageMaker.

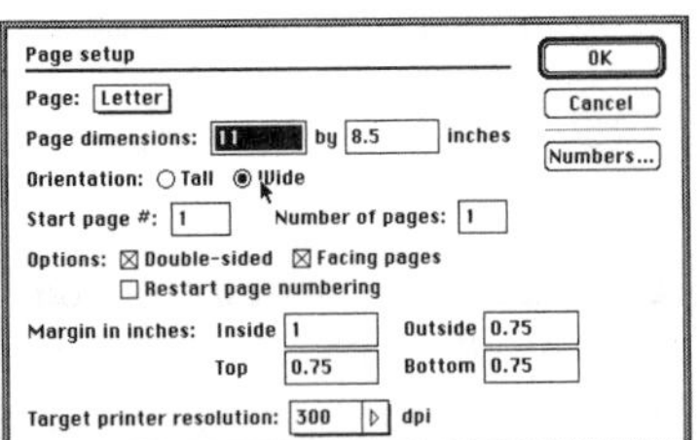

To specify wide rather than tall page orientation, click the Wide button in the Page setup dialog box:

1. If you've already started a publication and need to change its orientation, choose Page Setup from the File menu and choose or specify the desired dimensions.

To create an oversized publication:

1. Choose Page Setup from the File menu.
2. Specify the final page size.
3. When you're ready to print, choose Print and then click the Paper button.
4. Check the Tile box in the Paper Options dialog box.

To specify that PageMaker convert quotes and double hyphens when importing a file:

1. Check the Convert quotes box that appears in the Place document dialog box.

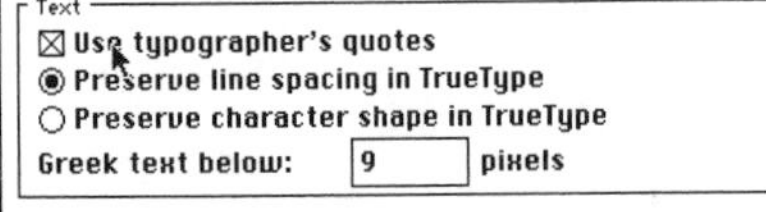

To specify that PageMaker convert quotes as you type or edit text:

1. Choose Preferences from the File menu.
2. Click the Other button.

   The Other Preferences dialog box appears.
3. Click the Use typographer's quotes box.
4. Click OK or press Return.

   The Preferences dialog box reappears.
5. Click OK or press Return.

To manually kern two characters:

1. **Place the blinking insertion point between the characters you want to kern.**
2. **Press ⌘-Delete or, for finer kerning, Option-Delete.**
   For more kerning shortcuts, see Tables 10-1 and 10-2. You can also kern a range of characters by using the same key sequences; simply select the characters first. You can also use the Control palette to kern manually (shown at left).

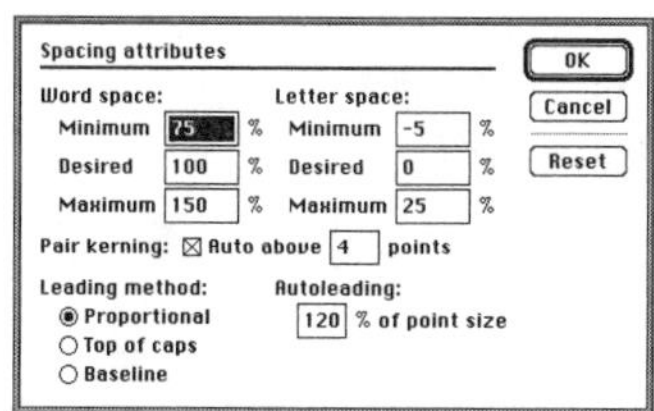

To change the spacing settings for a given paragraph:

1. **Select the paragraph you want to change and then choose Paragraph from the Type menu.**
   Pressing ⌘-M also displays the Paragraph Specifications dialog box.
2. **In the Paragraph Specifications dialog box, click the Spacing button.**
   The Spacing attributes dialog box appears.
3. **Type the desired spacing values in the appropriate boxes.**
4. **Click OK or press Return.**
   Other tips to keep in mind when changing spacing settings include the following:

   ❖ To change the default spacing settings for an entire document, use the Paragraph command when no text is selected.

   ❖ To change the defaults for all new documents, use the Paragraph command when no document is open.

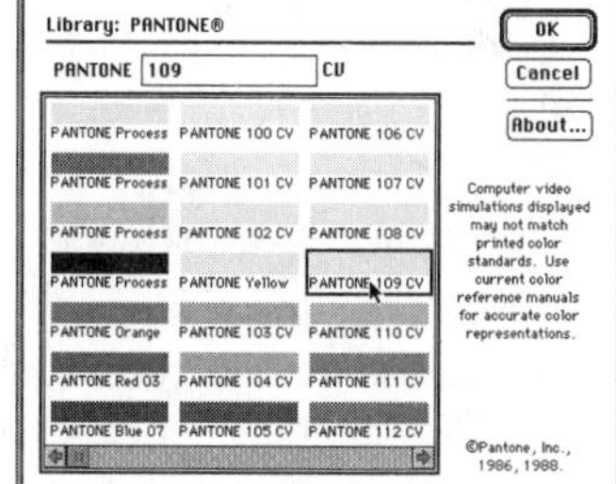

To add a Pantone color to PageMaker's Color palette:

1. **Choose Define Colors from the Element window.**
2. **Click New.**
3. **In the Edit Color dialog box, choose Pantone from the Libraries pop-up menu.**
4. **Select the desired color and click OK.**

(continued on the next page)

(continued from previous page)

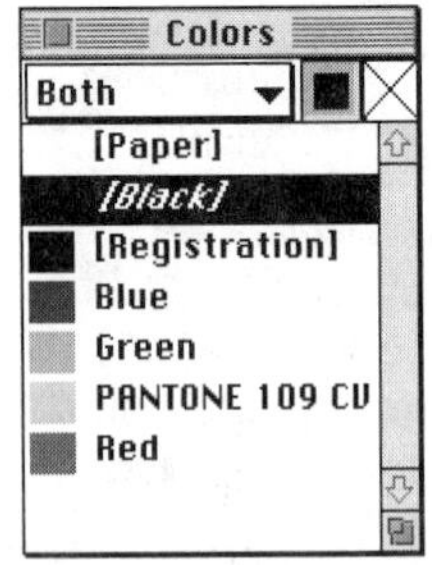

To assign a color to text or a graphic element such as a rule:

1. **Select the text or element.**
2. **Click the color name in the Colors palette.**
   If the Colors palette isn't visible, choose Color Palette from the Windows menu or use the ⌘-K keyboard shortcut.

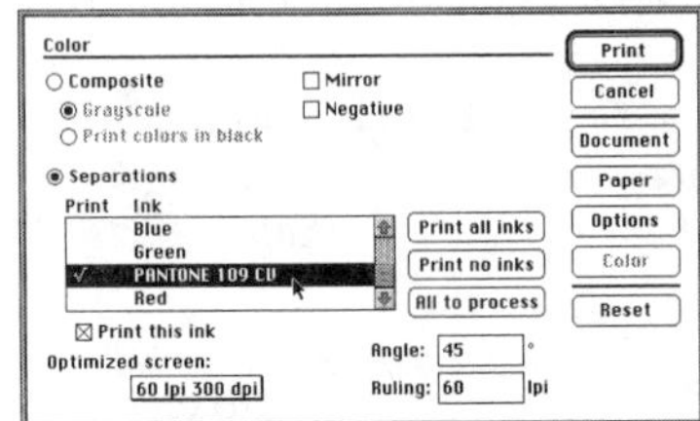

To print overlays for each spot color:

1. **Choose Print from the File menu.**
2. **Click the Color button.**
   The dialog box displays color-printing options.
3. **Click the Separations button.**
4. **Select the name of each spot-color ink you want to print, and check the Print this ink box.**
   To print all colors, click Print all inks.
5. **Click Print or press Return.**
   For more details on working with color, see the PageMaker reference manual.

Expanding Your Page-Layout Program

No program can be all things to all people. That truism is the driving force behind one of the latest trends in desktop publishing software — extensibility. Just as you can buy plug-in boards and external add-ons that enhance your Mac, you can buy software that plugs into QuarkXPress or Adobe PageMaker and adds new features.

Why extensibility?

To understand why extensibility is desirable in publishing software, walk through any large publishing department. Of course, you find typesetters and pasteup artists, but you also find the specialists on which every publishing niche relies. Darkroom technicians prepare the publication's images. Proofreaders and editors check spelling and compile indexes. Strippers organize the elements on a page and then organize a publication's pages so that they're in the correct order after being printed, cut, folded, and bound. Research assistants cull through databases and wire service reports. Managing editors monitor the big picture and shepherd stories through the production process. Advertising coordinators sell, track, and manage ad space.

An equivalent publishing add-on exists for every one of these job specialties. Over 100 QuarkXPress extensions and stand-alone utilities are available from Quark and

third-party developers. Far fewer are available for PageMaker, which is a relative latecomer to the extensibility party.

When choosing between PageMaker and QuarkXPress, you're also buying into an extensibility technology. Understanding how those technologies differ may help you choose the program that can grow to meet your specific needs.

Understanding software add-ons

Unlike expanding a Mac, expanding a publishing program involves no expansion slots or static-sensitive circuit boards. To install a utility, simply copy it to the appropriate folder on your hard disk. Depending on the complexity and quantity of the add-ons you're using, you may also need to use the Finder's Get Info command to increase the amount of memory allocated to the publishing program (see Chapter 22). When you start the publishing program, it examines that folder and loads the add-ons it finds. The names of the add-ons appear in one or more of the program's menus.

Quark's XTension technology

Beyond these basics, however, the programs' underlying approaches to extensibility diverge. Quark's XTensions technology enables extensions to tap into QuarkXPress's software code. Quark provides dozens of software routines that extensions developers use to create dialog boxes and manipulate style sheets, ruler guides, text and picture boxes and their contents, and menus — every aspect of QuarkXPress. XTensions can add commands to any QuarkXPress menu, and it can dim (make unavailable) those commands when it doesn't make sense to choose them. XTensions can display floating tool palettes that are always available and operate like QuarkXPress's own palettes. They also can weave themselves into QuarkXPress and become part of it.

Because extensions are intimately tied to QuarkXPress, however, compatibility problems often arise when Quark releases a new version of the program. Before buying an extension, verify that it works with your version of QuarkXPress.

Adobe PageMaker plug-ins

Adobe aims to avoid the extension compatibility problem by putting some distance between PageMaker and its add-ons, which are called *plug-in modules,* or *plug-ins,* for short. Instead of granting developers access to PageMaker's code, Aldus created what it calls the *interface manager,* a middleman that enables plug-ins to interact with PageMaker through two text-based languages. One language comprises commands: put a ruler guide at the 3-inch vertical mark, create a new tabloid-size document, import a file, and so on. The other language handles queries: which font does the selected text use, where is the ruler's current zero point, and what are the current tracking settings? Both languages are fairly easy to understand because they're derived from PageMaker's menu commands and mouse actions. (See Chapter 24 for more details about scripting languages.)

QuarkXPress Power Tips

QuarkXPress is a fast, responsive program, which has always been one of its major strengths. This box contains some tips that will make *you* faster as you work in the program.

Keep a tool selected for reuse

Normally, when you activate one of QuarkXPress's palette tools, the tool becomes inactive as soon as you use it, and the Content tool (with the little hand and I-beam) is reactivated. That's a real pain when you want to draw several text boxes in rapid succession, for example. The solution: press the Option key while activating a tool. When you do, the tool remains active after you use it.

Here's a related tip: when you've activated a tool by Option-clicking but want to use the Item tool to, for example, move a text box, press the ⌘ key. The Item tool is active as long as you keep the ⌘ key pressed.

Use the Apply button to check dialog box settings

Many QuarkXPress dialog boxes contain an Apply button. Click it (or use the ⌘-A shortcut) and QuarkXPress applies the changes you've made without closing the dialog box. If you decide that your changes need altering, you can do so without having to reopen the dialog box.

And by the way, if you can't see your changes because the dialog box obscures them, you can move the dialog box out of the way by dragging its title bar.

Navigate publications faster

To scroll through a publication one page at a time, press Shift while pressing the Page Up and Page Down keys on an extended keyboard.

Select something that's behind something else

In a complex layout, some objects may overlap. To select an object (such as a text block) that's behind another object (such as a rule or box), press ⌘-Option-Shift while clicking the layout. Each such click sequence selects the object another layer down.

Undo changes in a dialog box

You've made a slew of changes in a dialog box and now you wish you hadn't. Just press ⌘-Z, and QuarkXPress reverts to the dialog box's previous settings. (Microsoft Word and Excel dialog boxes had a similar "local undo" feature, but alas, Microsoft has taken it out of the latest versions of these programs.)

Type symbols and dingbats with a quick keystroke

Need to type a single a character from the Symbol or Zapf Dingbats font? Don't touch that Font menu — press ⌘-Shift-Q (for Symbol) or ⌘-Shift-Z (for Zapf Dingbats) instead. The next character you type appears in that font.

Recognize the power of three (and four and five) clicks

Sure, all Mac programs let you select a word by double-clicking. QuarkXpress also lets you select a line by triple-clicking, an entire paragraph by quadruple-clicking, and an entire story chain by quintuple-clicking.

Use precise zooming

Want to zoom in on a specific spot in your layout? Activate the Zoom tool (the magnifying glass) and then drag across the layout to draw a rectangle around the area you want to zoom. There it is, up close and personal.

You can also type a specific zoom percentage in the zoom readout at the lower-left corner of the document window.

Know the priceless "Indent to Here" shortcut

When you're creating hanging indents for bulleted and numbered lists, don't struggle with the rulers to align your runover lines — use QuarkXPress's Indent to Here shortcut. With the blinking insertion point located where you want runover lines to indent, press ⌘-\ (that's the backslash character just above the Return key). Your runover lines indent to this point.

How to Speed Printing in PageMaker 5

To print to PostScript printers, PageMaker 5 relies on LaserWriter 8, an enhanced version of the printer driver software that enables the Mac to communicate with PostScript printers. (See Chapters 30 and 31 for details about PostScript and the LaserWriter 8 driver.)

LaserWriter 8, in turn, relies on special files called *PostScript printer description* (PPD) files. PPDs tell the driver about a specific printer's capabilities: its output resolution, how much memory it contains, the number of fonts and paper trays it has, and so on. Before a print job, PageMaker consults the PPD for your printer and uses the information it finds in the PPD to control the job.

If you've added a memory upgrade or additional fonts to your printer as described in Chapter 30, PageMaker can print faster — but only if it knows that the extra memory and fonts are present. The stock PPD that came with your printer (or with the LaserWriter 8 driver) doesn't have this information. One undesirable side effect of this digital ignorance is that PageMaker may download fonts that are already stored on the hard drive connected to the printer.

To fix this problem, you have to modify the PPD to reflect your printer's capabilities. To create a custom PPD file, you can use the Update PPD addition that accompanies PageMaker. Before launching PageMaker, use the Chooser to select the LaserWriter 8 driver and your printer. Then start PageMaker and open the Update PPD addition. Select the PPD for your printer and then click Update. Save the customized PPD, and you're done. If you've upgraded to PageMaker 6, you don't need to perform any of these steps. PageMaker 6 provides a two-way printer-communication scheme that enables it to find out how much memory your printer has as well as which fonts it currently contains.

Drawbacks to the PageMaker approach

The problem with languages — especially computer languages — is that they have finite vocabularies. A PageMaker script can't make PageMaker do anything that PageMaker doesn't already know how to do. Imagine the plug-in mechanism as a set of wires leading to a puppet's limbs. Now imagine Quark's XTension technology as not only providing those wires but also enabling developers to add entirely new limbs.

This isn't to say that plug-ins can't make PageMaker do new things. They can, but they must ultimately rely on the command and query languages to put their efforts on PageMaker's pasteboard.

A more direct limitation of the PageMaker plug-in technology is that a plug-in must complete its work before you can return to the publication window. As a result, plug-ins generally can't provide floating tool palettes that are always available (many such extensions are available for QuarkXPress). Nor does the plug-in mechanism enable a plug-in to appear in any PageMaker menu — all plug-ins appear in the Options menu. (In PageMaker 6, plug-ins created by Adobe can appear in other menus, but third-party plug-ins can't.)

But the PageMaker plug-in mechanism also has some advantages over the XTension technology. For example, you can write scripts in PageMaker's command language. Want to automate a repetitive task? Type a script on PageMaker's pasteboard or in its story editor, and then select the script and choose the Run Script command (see Figure 10-4, "PageMaker on Autopilot"). PageMaker 6 provides a Script palette that makes working with scripts even easier; PageMaker 6 also includes a large selection of canned scripts that you can use as is or modify for specific jobs. PageMaker hackers often litter their pasteboards with timesaving scripts that make fractions, apply kerning, shift baselines, reflow text, import files, and much more. (Quark gurus can now do the same, thanks to the AppleScript support in QuarkXPress 3.2 and later versions.)

```
new                             --create a new publication
pagesize 8.5, 11                --make it an 8.5 by 11 incher, tall
pageoptions off,off             --turn off double-sided, facing pages
pagemargins 1, 1.5, 1, 1        --set page margins
page RM                         --go to right master page
columnguides 2 0.5              --two-column format, half-inch gutter
guidehoriz 1.5                  --make ruler guide 1.5 in from page top
linestyle thickthin             --use double-rule, thick/thin line style
line (1,1),(7.5,1)              --draw a line across top of page
line (1,10),(7.5,10)            --draw a line across bottom of page
page 1                          --go to first page
autoflow on                     --turn Autoflow on
import "report"                 --import file named "report"
place (column 1 left, 1.5)      --place it starting at col. 1
page 1                          --return to page one when done
view fit                        --switch to fit-in-window view
```

Figure 10-4: PageMaker on Autopilot This PageMaker script shows how you can use scripts to automate the production of a weekly status report. The text comments following each set of double hyphens describe each statement's purpose.

Where to get add-ons

Many extensions are developed by small software shops that aren't equipped to take orders and ship products. The best source for purchasing extensions is an XTensions distributor called XChange (800-788-7557). The firm also helps put publishing companies that want customized extensions in touch with freelance extensions programmers. Quark also publishes a detailed extensions directory that's free upon request. A large collection of XTensions is available on on-line services such as CompuServe and America Online.

Who's more expandable?

So who wins the extensibility contest? For sheer numbers, Quark does. Whether you want to create complex impositions, track ad placement, customize style sheets, create crossword puzzles, or have QuarkXPress play sounds as you work, you can find an extension to do the job. The large selection of top-quality extensions makes QuarkXPress the most versatile publishing program available. Many extensions are geared toward high-end pagination and publication management, giving QuarkXPress additional appeal for newspaper and periodical publishing.

Taking the Next Step

If you're committed to making publications look professionally typeset, you may want to investigate the expert sets sold by Adobe and other font vendors. Expert sets include special characters not found in most fonts, including true small capitals, old-style numerals, and fractions (see Figure 10-5 "Expert Characters").

But NASA's greatest triumph came 2-1/2 years later, with the 1969 launch of Apollo 11.	But NASA's greatest triumph came 2½ years later, with the 1969 launch of Apollo 11.

Figure 10-5: Expert Characters Many font vendors offer expert edition fonts that contain additional characters such as small capitals, fractions, and old-style numerals, which have ascenders and descenders. Adobe's Caslon is shown here. The large capitals (left) overwhelm the surrounding lowercase characters, the phony fraction looks tacky, and the numerals break up the rhythm of the line. Small capitals (right) make acronyms less acrimonious, and the true fraction and old-style numerals add a touch of class.

The next chapter contains more advice for using type. An excellent guide to typographic style is *The Desktop Style Guide* by James Felici (Bantam, 1991). For general advice about publication design, I recommend *Graphic Design for the Electronic Age* by Jan V. White (Watson-Guptill Publications, 1988).

When you're starting a new project, don't forget that most publishing programs include a library of predesigned templates for common types of publications, including newsletters, brochures, invoices, and books. PageMaker includes an especially attractive template library; the program's manual has tips for modifying the templates to suit your needs.

Perhaps a future generation of publishing programs will have the smarts to handle many design and typographic chores for you. Until then, you must make the same decisions that designers and typesetters have been making for centuries, decisions aimed at one goal — conveying your message in an appropriate, aesthetically pleasing way.

PageMaker Power Tips

Here are some PageMaker-specific tips for navigating through publications, keeping file sizes down, zooming, saving, and more.

Switch all page views at once

Want to use the same magnification scale for every page in the publication? Just press Option while choosing the desired magnification scale. Now every page appears at the same magnification.

View your pub in slide-show mode

Want to spot-check each page in your publication? Press the Shift key while choosing Go To Page from the Layout menu. Press ⌘-period or just click the mouse to end the show. This tip teams up nicely with the previous one: switch each page's zoom scale to Fit in Window before you start the slide show.

You can also leaf through your document one page at a time by pressing ⌘-Tab.

Select something that's behind something else

In a complex layout, some objects may overlap. To select an object (such as a text block) that's behind another object (such as a rule or box), just press ⌘ while clicking the object you want to select.

See the world

Pressing ⌘-0 switches the viewing scale to what Aldus calls *Fit in world* view. In this view, PageMaker's entire pasteboard is visible, and you can see elements that you may have stashed there and forgotten about.

Selecting toolbox tools from the keyboard

You can select any PageMaker toolbox tool from the keyboard by using the shortcuts listed in the following table. Note that these sequences use the Control key, not the ⌘ key (the first shortcut is an exception).

To Select This Tool	*Press*
Pointer tool	Control-Shift-F1 or ⌘-spacebar
Line tool	Control-Shift-F2
Horizontal/vertical line tool	Control-Shift-F3

(continued on the next page)

To Select This Tool	*Press*
Text tool	Control-Shift-F4
Rectangle tool	Control-Shift-F5
Round rectangle tool	Control-Shift-F6
Ellipse tool	Control-Shift-F7
Cropping tool	Control-Shift-F8

Set defaults

You can specify defaults for nearly everything in PageMaker, from fonts and sizes to Page Setup options to the measuring system that PageMaker's rulers use to the type of round corners drawn by the Round rectangle tool. Moreover, you can set these defaults on a global level (your settings apply to all new documents) or a local level (your settings apply to the open document only).

To specify global defaults, choose the appropriate commands when no publication window is open. To specify defaults for one publication only, make your choices when its window is open.

Create styles by example

Remember the Chapter 4 sections about creating style sheets by example? You can do the same thing in PageMaker. Format your text as desired, open the Style palette (⌘-Y), and then ⌘-click the No Style entry. The Edit Style dialog box appears, where you can name the new style.

Nudge with the arrow keys

You can move selected items in one-pixel increments by pressing the keyboard's arrow keys. To move items in five-pixel increments, press ⌘ along with the arrow keys.

Use Save As to reduce file bloat

Every now and then, use the Save As command to save your publication under a new name. You can cut down the file size dramatically.

Use the mini-save safety net

PageMaker provides a priceless *mini-save* feature that can save your bacon — or at least your hard work. The mini-save intermediate saves everything you did since the last time you chose the Save command. PageMaker does a mini-save when you perform any of the following: move to another page, insert or delete a page, print, switch between layout view and story editor, use the Clipboard, click the active page's icon, or change the publication's page setup. If your Mac crashes while you're working, you can recover your document up to the last mini-save by reopening the publication file. If you hadn't saved the file yet but did something that caused a mini-save, you can probably recover your work. Restart the Mac and then double-click the Trash — it should contain a folder named "Rescued items from *your hard disk name.*" Drag this folder out of the Trash (it doesn't matter where you drag it — the desktop is fine) and then open it; you should see a file with a cryptic name, such as ALDTMP01. Double-click this file, and PageMaker starts and opens your untitled publication.

By the way, you can revert to the last mini-saved version of your publication by pressing the Shift key while choosing Revert from the File menu.

Force a mini-save to commit your work to disk

The preceding tip mentioned that PageMaker does a mini-save every time you click the active page icon. Get in the habit of clicking the icon to force a mini-save.

(continued on the next page)

(continued from previous page)

Save everything!

Have a bunch of open documents that you want to save? Press Option while opening the File menu, and you notice that the Save command reads Save All. Choose Save All, and PageMaker saves all open documents.

Applying master pages

PageMaker 6's support for multiple master pages is long overdue. One way to apply master pages is using the new Master Pages palette. But there's another way, and it can be faster, especially if the Master Pages palette isn't open: just point to the L and R master page icons in the lower-left corner of the publication window, and then click and hold down the mouse button. A pop-up menu appears listing available master pages — choose the one you want.

CHAPTER 10 CONCEPTS AND TERMS

- The techniques you can use to enliven a publication include using wide instead of tall orientation and adding spot color.
- You can produce pages that are larger than the maximum size your printer accepts by using a publishing program's tiling feature, which splits oversized pages into separate pages that you tape or glue together.
- Using true typographers' quotes as well as em and en dashes adds a professionally typeset look to your document's text.
- You can improve the appearance of justified text by fine-tuning paragraph spacing and by hyphenating.
- PageMaker and QuarkXPress are extensible — you can add new features to either program through the use of small software modules.
- Quark's XTension technology allows for more sophisticated software add-ons than does PageMaker's plug-in mechanism, but compatibility problems can arise when Quark releases a new version of QuarkXPress.

discretionary hyphen
Also called a *soft hyphen,* a code you can insert between syllables to tell a publishing program where to divide a word if possible. If reformatting or editing changes the line breaks later, the hyphen disappears, but the discretionary hyphen code remains.

em dash
A dash that typographers use instead of double hyphens to set off part of a sentence (— instead of --).

expert set
A font that includes special characters not found in most fonts, such as true small capitals, old-style numerals, and fractions.

H&J
Short for *hyphenation and justification,* a generic term that refers to a program's hyphenation and text-spacing features. In QuarkXPress, a set of hyphenation and justification settings.

landscape orientation
Also called *wide orientation,* a page that is wider than it is tall — for example, 11 x 8½ inches.

ligature
Connected character pairs such as fi and fl.

overlay
A separate page containing only the items that print in a specific color.

Pantone
A popular printing industry system for specifying colors.

portrait orientation
Also called *tall orientation,* a page that is taller than it is wide — for example, 8½ x 11 inches.

smart quotes
A software feature that automatically generates typographers' quotes (for example, "these") as you type or import text.

tiling
A publishing program feature that lets you create publications larger than your printer can print by splitting oversized pages into separate pages that you tape or glue together.

trim size
The final size of a printed publication.

CHAPTER ELEVEN

Fonts and Typography

- From bitmaps to outlines — how fonts work
- Tips for choosing fonts and formatting text
- Surveying font customizing tools
- How to determine the appropriate type size and line length

The Mac's capability to set type in a variety of fonts, sizes, and styles has always been the cornerstone of its personality. This chapter tours the Mac's type talents and guides you through using them tastefully. I wrap up with technical details about Mac font formats and include a cookbook of font-customizing tips. For the latter, you need to know how to install fonts in your system; instructions are included in Chapter 22. For help with troubleshooting font-related problems, see Chapter 28.

Fonts 101: The Basics

Like any specialized field, the typesetting world has its own language. This section describes the terminology you encounter as you work with fonts.

Typefaces versus fonts

First, I need to clarify the difference between the terms *typeface* and *font.* A typeface is a unique design of uppercase and lowercase characters, numerals, punctuation marks, and symbols. A font is the implementation of a typeface in one size.

In the not-so-good-old-days of hot metal type, when different molds were required to cast different sizes of type, the distinction between *typeface* and *font* was important. (The word *font* is derived from the verb *found* — to pour into a mold in a foundry.) If you had 12-point Times, 14-point Times, and 18-point Times, you had three fonts.

Today, the terms *typeface* and *font* are often used interchangeably. In fact, the only people who still count each size or style separately are those who sell fonts.

Typefaces are often grouped together into *families*. In the Macintosh world, a type family usually contains four *styles:*

- Roman, the upright version of the typeface. On the Mac, the roman style is called *normal* or *plain.*
- *Italic*, a calligraphic variant often used for emphasis. This book uses italic to emphasize new terms.
- **Bold,** a heavier version of the roman style, often used for headings.
- ***Bold Italic*,** a bold version of the italic style.

A field guide to character components

Figure 11-1 "Character Components" shows the primary components that form characters. The shape and combination of these and other components give each typestyle its unique appearance and personality — more about that later in this chapter.

These components and characteristics include the following aspects:

- **Ascender.** The portion of a character that extends above the top of lowercase characters.
- **Bowl.** The round portion of characters such as *b*, *p*, and *d*.
- **Counter.** The white space within a character that helps to define the character's shape.
- **Descender.** The portion of a character that extends below the *baseline*, the imaginary line upon which characters rest.
- **Serif.** Ornamental flourishes attached to the edges of characters. Serifs help lead the eye across a line of type. A typeface whose characters have serifs (such as Times) is called a *serif typeface;* a typeface that lacks serifs (such as Helvetica) is described as *sanserif* (without serifs).

Figure 11-1: Character Components

Oblique: Faux Italics

You may also encounter a style called *oblique,* a slanted version of the roman style. That may sound identical to italic, but it isn't. An italic style is a completely different rendering of a typeface, while an oblique style is simply a slanted version of the roman or bold style. If you don't have the true italic version of a font installed in the Mac, the Mac uses the oblique technique to simulate italic on the screen.

- **Stem.** The vertical portion of a character.
- **X-height.** The height of the lowercase characters (specifically, of the lowercase *x*) in a given typeface.

Units of measurement in the type world

Old-fashioned inches weren't good enough for pioneering typographers, who needed finer units of measurement. Their units and measuring systems have survived to this day, and include

- **Point.** A unit equal to 1/72 inch. (Technically, a typographer's point is equal to .351 millimeters, so there are actually 72.27 points per inch. In the Macintosh, however, a point is exactly 1/72 inch.)
- **Pica.** A unit equal to 12 points. Picas are often used to specify the width of columns.
- **Em.** A unit of horizontal space equal to the square of the type size. For example, in 10-point type, an em is 10 points wide and 10 points high. In the typesetting world, em spaces are often used to specify the width of paragraph indents.
- **En.** A unit of horizontal space equal to half of an em space. Also called a *nut* space.
- **Thin.** A unit of horizontal space equal to half an en space.

The point is the most important common measuring unit. Points are used to measure and specify the vertical size of type. In a 72-point typeface, for example, there are 72 points of space between the lowest descender and the highest ascender.

Points are also used to specify *leading* — the amount of vertical space between lines. Leading (pronounced *led-ing*) is measured from baseline to baseline. The term comes from the hot metal type era, when strips of lead were used to add space between lines.

When specifying type size and leading, typesetters and designers write a fraction in which the type size is the numerator and the leading is the denominator. For example, text that uses 12-point type and 14 points of leading is described as 12/14 and pronounced *twelve on fourteen* or *twelve over fourteen.*

Monospaced versus proportional fonts

On most typewriters, every character has the same width: A lowercase *i* uses as much horizontal space as an uppercase *M.* Fonts whose characters have the same width are called *monospaced* or *fixed-width* fonts.

Fixed-width fonts are fine for mechanical typewriter mechanisms, but they aren't as legible as *proportional* fonts — fonts whose character widths vary. Proportional fonts are easier to read and are preferred for publishing applications. Examples of proportional fonts include Times and Helvetica; monospaced fonts include Courier and Monaco.

Even in proportional fonts, all the numerals and math symbols have the same width so that the decimal points align in tables. This is called *tabular spacing.*

Pi fonts: what a bunch of characters

In the old days of conventional typesetting, most fonts lacked special characters such as math and copyright symbols. To get these characters, typesetters had to switch to special fonts called *pi fonts*. Pi fonts contained nothing but special characters — in essence, they are forerunners to today's Symbol font.

Most Mac fonts *do* provide a wide range of special characters — in computer jargon, the Mac provides a large *character set.* You can access most special characters through finger-breaking Option-Shift keyboard sequences. (For some help in finding these crazy characters, see the Step-by-Step box "Finding Special Characters.")

Another useful tool for finding special characters is PopChar, a free system extension by Günther Blascheck.

Improving Your Desktop Typography

When you use the Mac, you're setting type. When you choose different fonts, sizes, or styles — be it in a publishing program, word processor, spreadsheet, or database — you're making the same decisions typographers have made for centuries. You're specifying the type characteristics that convey your message clearly and attractively.

Finding Special Characters

To help them remember the keystrokes that summon accents, fractions, and other special characters, typesetters often refer to printed charts called keyboard layouts. For desktop typographers, the Mac provides an electronic keyboard layout chart called the Key Caps desk accessory, which displays an on-screen keyboard with a text-entry box above it.

You can access the Mac's special characters through combinations of the Option and Shift keys. When you press these keys, Key Caps updates its graphical keyboard to reflect the characters they summon.

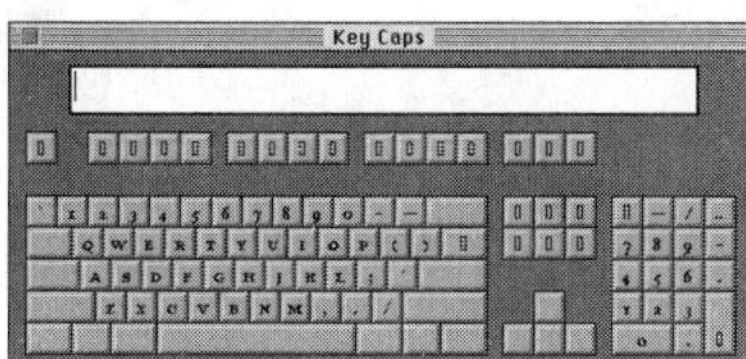

To locate a certain character in a given font:

1. **Choose the font's name from the Key Caps menu.**
   This step is important because not all fonts provide the same characters in the same keyboard locations. (Adobe's Caslon expert set is shown at left.)
2. **Press Option with and without Shift until you locate the character on the Key Caps keyboard.**
3. **When you find the character, continue holding down the Option and/or Shift key, and then click on the character's key with the mouse.**
   The character appears in the text entry window above the keyboard. Repeat this step for any additional characters you need (such as the slash and denominator to complete a fraction).
4. **Select the character(s) in the text-entry window and choose Copy or Cut from the Edit menu.**
5. **Return to your document, position the blinking insertion point where you want the character to appear, and then choose Paste. If necessary, change the font to the desired typeface.**

   Other tips to consider when using Key Caps include the following:

   - As an alternative to copying the character to the Clipboard, you can type the character directly by pressing its appropriate key, as displayed by Key Caps.
   - Close the Key Caps window when you're done with it; leaving it open while you type in other programs slows the Mac as the Key Caps keys flash merrily in the background.
   - Creating an accented character such as *é* or *ñ* requires a two-step key sequence. First, press Option along with the accent's character. Next, type the character that should appear under the accent. For example, to create an *n* with a tilde over it (ñ), press Option-N and then press N.

Or are you? Do you choose fonts that are appropriate to your message, or do you flit from font to font because the Mac makes it easy to do so? Do you choose type size, line spacing, and line length with readability in mind, or do you use whichever combination strikes your fancy?

The fact is, fine typography requires training and experience. Because type and fonts play such a large role in the Macintosh world, it's important to understand the basics of typography. In this section, I present some techniques for making your documents more readable.

Tips for Choosing Fonts

The most basic typographic choice is usually that of a typeface. Each typeface has a personality; some are sophisticated, some are casual, and others are forceful and bold (see Figure 11-2 "Font Personalities"). Your goal is to choose typefaces whose personality complements your message.

ITC Franklin Gothic is legible and honest.

ITC Franklin Gothic Heavy carries weight.

Futura is geometric and "moderne," no?

ITC New Baskerville is delicate and graceful.

Helvetica Condensed is space-efficient, yet legible.

ITC New Century Schoolbook is easy to read.

Helvetica Condensed Bold Oblique is progressive.

ITC Lubalin Graph is sturdy and distinctive.

Figure 11-2: Font Personalities A sampling of eight Adobe Systems PostScript typefaces shows how the shape and thickness, or weight, of each character contributes to a typeface's overall appearance. Special flourishes such as Futura's flashy question mark and the square serifs in ITC Lubalin Graph also add interesting personality traits.

Better serif than sorry

Although some studies show little difference in legibility between serif and sanserif fonts, it's generally believed that serif typefaces are more legible and therefore better suited to lengthy text passages. I recommend that typographic newcomers follow this rule of thumb.

Mix and match within families

Another issue concerns whether to use the same font for all the elements of a document or to use a different font for headings and subheadings. One way to get good results is to use different fonts within the same family. For example, you may use Garamond for body type (or body text), Garamond Bold for headlines, and Garamond Italic for captions. Or you can mix typefaces by using, for example, New Baskerville for body text and Helvetica Black for headlines. Just be consistent throughout a document, and don't mix with abandon.

Condensing copy when space is tight

The amount of copy you have may also influence your choice of typeface. To squeeze a lot of text into a small space, consider a space-efficient *condensed* typeface. The downloadable font libraries from Adobe Systems, Bitstream, Compugraphic, and other font vendors include attractive condensed versions of typefaces such as Helvetica, Univers, and Futura. A large selection of free or inexpensive, high-quality downloadable fonts is also available through user group libraries and on-line services and from software clearinghouses such as Educorp.

Line Length and Type Size Decisions

After choosing a font, you need to settle on the width of text columns and the type size. Both decisions are related and have one goal — putting a manageable number of words on each line.

Tips for determining the ideal line length

Two rules of thumb exist for determining line length. One states that each line should have roughly 8 to 11 words. Another says that a column should be just wide enough to accommodate 2½ lowercase alphabets in the typeface and size you plan to use (see Figure 11-3 "How Long a Line?"). Experimentation with both rules reveals that they often provide the same results. The bottom line: Strive for lines containing between 50 and 70 characters.

abcdefghijklmnopqrstuvwxyzabcdefghijklmnopqrstuvwxyzabcdefghijklm

One rule of thumb for determining line length states that a line should be wide enough to accommodate 2.5 lowercase alphabets in the typeface and size you plan to use. This works out to roughly 8 to 11 words per line—not so many that the eye gets lost, but enough to retain the smooth flow of the text.

Figure 11-3: How Long a Line? One way to determine the ideal line length for a given font and size is to type 2½ lowercase alphabets, as demonstrated here in 10-point Optima.

Most people read groups of three or four words at a time rather than individual words. If there are too many words on each line, the eyes tire as they journey from left to right. If there are too few words on each line, then line breaks and excessive hyphenation disrupt the flow of the text.

Deciding on a type size

The amount of text you have and the space into which it must fit should influence your choice of type size. For documents duplicated on a laser printer or photocopier, you probably won't have a preconceived number of pages, or *page count,* in mind. If that's the case, simply choose a type size that works with your column width to provide 8 to 11 words per line.

For a document that is to be commercially printed, however, you must determine the page count in advance to make sure that your text fits within it. Before WYSIWYG (what-you-see-is-what-you-get) screen displays, designers and typographers endured a complex copyfitting routine that involved crunching through formulas to calculate character widths. Today's WYSIWYG programs and displays let you adjust the type size as you work. Of course, on-the-fly tweaking is effective only to a point. In a newsletter, for example, you wouldn't adjust each article's type size to accommodate its text. That would destroy the publication's uniformity, and uniformity is a cornerstone of good typography and design. When an article is a tad long, try hyphenating more lines (this tactic works best with text that's set ragged right). If it's still too long, consider cutting some text.

When an article is too short, try removing hyphens, breaking long paragraphs into shorter ones, or narrowing the width of the columns. If these techniques fail, consider filling the leftover space with a graphic element such as a straight line (or rule) or an ornamental dingbat. Other possibilities include lengthening the article by using subheads or pull quotes. Or you can leave the space blank. Just as silence is an integral part of music, white space is an integral part of graphic design.

Leading Guidelines

Another way to do your readers a favor is to use appropriate use of line spacing, or leading. For body text, the general rule is to lead at 20 percent of the type size. For 10-point type, for example, use 2 points of lead for a total of 12 points from one baseline to the next. The Mac's fonts contain built-in autoleading specifications that use this 20-percent rule. When you specify *auto* in your word processor or desktop publishing program, the program uses the font's autoleading value.

Use more leading for long line lengths

The 20 percent rule is a good starting place, but many other factors should influence your choice of leading. Line length is one. With long lines, too little leading causes readers to occasionally read the same line twice, a phenomenon known as *doubling*. Longer lines benefit from more leading.

Type size should also influence how much leading you use. Large type (14 point or larger) generally needs more leading than body type (8 to 12 point). Type that's smaller than 8 point sometimes needs more than 20 percent leading to make the tiny type appear less dense.

Use less leading for headlines

The rule "Large type requires more leading" doesn't always apply to headlines. Headlines often look better when set solid — with no extra space. (For example, a 24-point headline set solid has 24 points of space between baselines.) With some fonts, you may even consider *minus line spacing*, such as 22-point leading with 24-point type. Just watch that the line's descenders don't touch the next line's ascenders.

Understanding Alignment Issues

Another major aspect of type formatting concerns the alignment of the left and right margins. You're probably familiar with the three most common forms of alignment: flush left, ragged right; justified; and flush right, ragged left. But which to use, and when?

Traditionally, large passages of text are set justified. Many designers believe that neatly aligned left and right margins are best suited to sustained reading because they give pages a quiet look that lets readers concentrate on content.

To justify text, word processors add space between each word. Some desktop publishing programs, including Adobe PageMaker and QuarkXPress, can also add space between characters in a process called *letterspacing*. Letterspacing helps eliminate the large word spaces and the rivers of white space that can occur (see Figure 11-4: "Justifying Your Actions"). Hyphenation also helps, although you should never hyphenate more than two or three consecutive lines.

Justified text, long preferred for its smooth appearance, is less readable when there's too much space between words. Distracting "rivers" of white space can appear. This problem is especially common with narrow column measures. Letterspacing and hyphenation can help eliminate the problem.	Justified text, long preferred for its smooth appearance, is less readable when there's too much space between words. Distracting "rivers" of white space can appear. This problem is especially common with narrow column measures. Letterspacing and hyphenation can help eliminate the problem. Don't letterspace excessively, and never hyphenate more than two or three consecutive lines.

Figure 11-4: Justifying Your Actions Appropriate use of letterspacing and hyphenation can dramatically improve the appearance of justified type. Also note that because more text can fit on each line, the same amount of copy takes up less space. Adobe's Melior typeface is used here.

Ragged-right margins

These days, ragged-right margins have become more popular, even in such bastions of justification as textbooks and magazines. Ragged-right text requires fewer hyphenations, and its consistent word and letterspacing give it a clean, even texture (see Figure 11-5 "Running Ragged"). And because the eyes stop at a different point in each line, reading it can actually be less fatiguing than reading justified text.

Ragged left and centered

As for the other alignment options — centered or flush right and ragged left — both can be effective in small doses. Centering, for example, is ideal for short passages such as headlines. But because centered and ragged-left text force you to hunt for the start of each line, they can be hard to read over the long run.

Display Type: Details Count

Headlines and other large, attention-getting blocks of type are called *display type*. Showing attention to detail in display type is an important step in making documents look professionally typeset.

Whether a ragged-right margin is more readable depends in part on the contour, or *rag*, of the right margin. A good rag has a rhythm, with text alternating between longer lines and shorter ones. The best typographers ensure that each line ending contributes to the margin's profile, even if they have to break certain lines by hand.

Whether a ragged-right margin is more readable depends in part on the contour, or *rag*, of the right margin. A good rag has a rhythm, with text alternating between longer lines and shorter ones. The best typographers ensure that each line ending contributes to the margin's profile, even if they have to break certain lines by hand.

Figure 11-5: Running Ragged In the top paragraph, notice that most lines hover around the same width, making the right margin look poorly justified, not ragged. When the word "with" is brought down to the next line in the bottom paragraph, the right margin assumes a more ragged contour. This example uses ITC New Baskerville.

With display type intended to grab the reader's interest, you may be tempted to use all capital letters for added oomph. Resist the urge. A mix of uppercase and lowercase characters gives words an overall shape that aids in recognition; text set in all caps lacks these patterns. It's generally better to capitalize only the first letter of important words, leaving conjunctions and articles such as *and*, *in*, and *the* lowercase. That way you avoid putting undue emphasis on less important words.

Kerning for better spacing

After you settle on case, concentrate on the space between characters and words. As I mention in the last chapter, most fonts produce too much space between certain character pairs, especially in large type sizes. You can improve the look by tightening those spaced-out pairs with a process called *kerning*.

In smaller type sizes, kerning usually involves tightening only certain letter pairs, such as *To* and *Av*. But in large sizes, almost every combination of characters is a candidate (see Figure 11-6 "Kerned versus Unkerned"). Use the manual-kerning features in your desktop publishing program or word processor to remove space between characters until they are tight but not touching. Also, decrease the spaces between words. Just be sure to apply the same degree of kerning and word spacing throughout a document. Inconsistent spacing is worse than none at all.

You'll say, "wow."

You'll say, "wow."

Figure 11-6: Kerned versus Unkerned In display type, nearly every character is a candidate for kerning. Here, space was removed between the Y and the o, around the apostrophe, between the y and the comma, between each w, and between the period and the closing quotes. A little less space was removed between the a and the y. Notice how the kerned headline uses less space. This headline was created with Letraset's LetraStudio display-type program, which simplifies manual kerning tasks by enabling you to position individual characters by dragging them.

Letterspacing for that elegant look

A variation on the letterspacing theme in headlines involves adding space between each character to obtain an airy, elegant effect. This letterspacing technique can be effective when used sparingly.

Be sure to also add more space between words so that they don't run together, and avoid letterspacing heavy, condensed typefaces such as ITC Machine. Type set in Machine actually looks better when certain characters touch slightly, or *kiss* (see Figure 11-7 "Headline Spacing").

For best results, use the Return key

With body text, you usually let your word processor or publishing program end each line for you. With display type, however, you should take a more active role in determining line breaks and use the Return key to *force* line endings. Good typographers end lines at logical stopping points, such as after a comma or a key phrase (see Figure 11-8 "Breaking for Sense"). The best advertising typographers also apply this technique to body text.

For body text, you get a more attractive rag if the text tends to alternate between long lines and shorter ones. This gentle zigzagging of line endings reinforces the notion of a ragged-right margin, and some people say that it reduces reader fatigue.

Shrink those symbols

In headlines containing trademark or copyright symbols, the symbols are usually much too large and obtrusive. Use a smaller type size for the symbol itself, and then move the symbol so that its top aligns with the top of the text (see Figure 11-8).

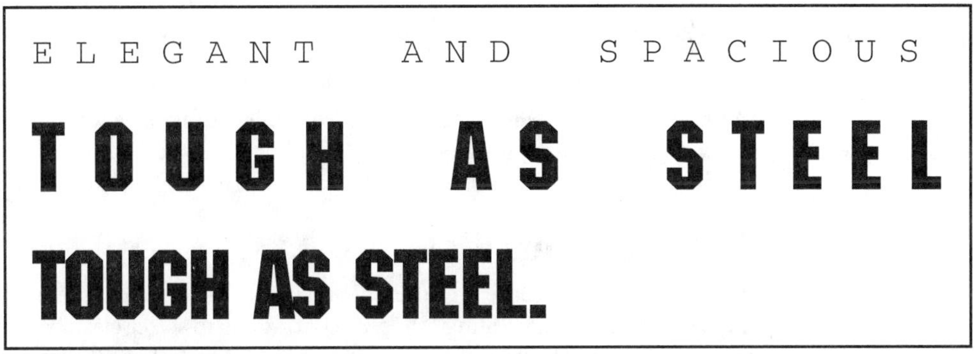

E L E G A N T   A N D   S P A C I O U S

TOUGH AS STEEL

TOUGH AS STEEL.

Figure 11-7: Headline Spacing Letterspaced headlines like the one at the top can create an airy, dignified effect, especially when you use a typeface with such elegant capitals as Italia's. Extra space between words keeps them from running together. Heavy, condensed faces such as ITC Machine don't letterspace well and are best set tight. Note the kissing T and O, A and S, and S and T. In the bottom headline, the word spaces were tightened slightly, too. A period gives the slogan added authority.

Today and tomorrow, the Southcom 300® will be there. We guarantee it.

Today and tomorrow,
the Southcom 300®
will be there.

We guarantee it.

Figure 11-8: Breaking for Sense Readability of display type (here, 18-point Futura Extra Bold) is improved by breaking each line at a logical stopping point. Extra leading before the final sentence adds emphasis. This example also shows you how to deal with a large, distracting register mark: select it, choose a smaller type size (in this case, 8 point), and then move it until its top aligns with the top of the text.

Designing Forms and Faxes

One document that imposes unique typographic requirements is the form. Forms range in size and style from reply cards, with their blank lines for names and addresses, to tax forms, with their dozens of cubbyholes and instructions. If you use a database manager, you probably use on-screen forms to enter and view data.

Choosing fonts for forms

A form's primary purpose is to present and obtain information in a structured format. The first step in creating that sense of order is to select clean, readable typefaces. Sanserif fonts such as Helvetica and News Gothic are particularly well suited to forms (just ask the IRS). Univers is another sanserif font that works well in forms.

When designing forms, group related information together. If the form will be filled out by hand, leave enough space for people to write comfortably. Put 18 to 24 points of space between each line, and make lines long enough to accommodate long names and addresses.

Choosing fonts for the screen

Creating on-screen forms for data entry requires similar considerations, with an added twist: Most laser printer fonts don't have particularly readable screen fonts. The Mac's screen resolution is roughly one-fourth that of a laser printer's, which is insufficient to render the subtleties of most fonts accurately.

One solution is to use fonts designed for the Mac's screen, such as New York and Geneva. On laser printers, however, these fonts print poorly. The best method is to use separate forms for data entry and report printing. Use readable screen fonts such as New York and Geneva for on-screen data-entry forms and laser-printer fonts for report-printing forms.

Choosing fonts for faxes

Faxes present their own challenges. The resolution of most fax machines is only about 200 dots per inch, so avoid delicate serif fonts such as Baskerville. Sturdy, sanserif faces such as News Gothic and Univers work well. For serif faces, try Lucida or ITC Stone Informal. Avoid type sizes smaller than 9 point. Also, avoid placing page numbers and the like at the very bottom of the page — your faxes will take longer to send. For more tips on faxing, see Chapter 16.

Sweating the Details

One of the easiest ways to make documents look typeset is to replace the Mac's typewriter-like punctuation characters with characters that typesetters use (see the Quick Tips box "Type Tips" as well as the quick reference card in the front of this book).

Styles to avoid

Avoid gimmicky font styles such as shadow and outline. And avoid superimposing type over a gray-shaded background. Type is most legible when it's easily distinguished from the background; black-on-gray isn't exactly a high-contrast combination.

Also, think twice about using the small-caps option that many programs provide. To create small caps, typesetting systems provide special fonts in which the small capitals are drawn to match the texture and line thickness of the large capitals. On the Mac, programs with small-caps options simply use a smaller type size for the small capitals. The resulting small caps have lighter *stem weights* than the large ones, giving the text an uneven appearance. Similarly, in *derived fractions* — ones made up of small inferior and superior characters with a slash sandwiched between them — the tiny numerals have such light stem weights that they often don't print well.

The answer? True-cut small caps and fractions. More and more font developers are offering fonts containing small caps and fractions whose stem weights are designed to match the rest of the typeface. Several of Adobe's fonts, for example, have optional expert sets that include true small caps, a variety of ready-made fractions, and separate numerals that were born to be numerators or denominators.

These collections often include other mainstays of fine typography, such as old-style numerals (ones with descenders and ascenders) and ligatures (connected character pairs, such as fi and fl). They aren't cheap (Adobe's expert sets retail for $275), but they're an essential part of a desktop typographer's toolbox. Fraction fonts are also available on many on-line services; later in this chapter, I show you how to use a font-editing program to create fonts containing fractions.

Where to use small caps

If you commit to buying true small caps, don't relegate them to headlines or special applications. Use them in body text where appropriate — for acronyms (such as NASA or CIA), for the chronological designations A.M., P.M., B.C., and A.D., and in other instances where large capitals overwhelm surrounding lowercase text. (For an example illustrating the use of small caps, see Figure 10-5 in the preceding chapter.)

Type Tips

I acquired an appreciation for fine typography while working as a typesetter for Davis & Warde, a 100-year-old printing company in Pittsburgh. I learned the trade from old-school masters who wore visors and referred to text as *matter*: headline matter, body matter, it didn't matter — no job was too complex. There, an apprentice typographer started out melting down old type into lead bars and loading and unloading 75-pound font "magazines" into Linotype machines. (You think installing fonts on the Mac is a pain.) After a six-year apprenticeship, he — rarely she, in those days — became a journeyman.

"You learned your trade through association with experienced people," said Bill Darney, who started as an apprentice in 1959 and graduated to shop foreman and, later, vice president. "There were shop standards for aesthetics and consistency you had to learn and live by — or die. Those standards are exactly what's lacking today. When you have so many people creating type in so many ways, [standards and consistency] fall by the wayside."

The death of hot-metal type forced Davis & Warde to make the painful transition to "cold" type — big phototypesetting machines, later to be supplemented by Macs. They succeeded, partly because they knew the basics of quality typography that transcend technology. Here are some ways to keep up that tradition on the Mac:

Use em and en dashes

Use these instead of double hyphens. To get an *em dash* (—) on the Mac, press Option-Shift-hyphen; for an *en dash* (–), press Option-hyphen. You use an en dash to express a range, standing for *to* between numbers or words.

Use true quotes

Press Option-] and Shift-Option-] for open and closed single quotes; for double quotes, press Option-[and Shift-Option-[. (Also, put commas and periods inside quotation marks; colons and semicolons go outside quotes.) Most word processors offer a smart quotes option that inserts the proper quotes as you type. As the preceding chapter describes, desktop publishing programs also offer a quote-conversion option that causes the program to automatically convert quotes when you import word processing files.

Don't put two spaces after punctuation

I know, your high school typing teacher taught you otherwise. Things are different now. Put only one space after periods, colons, and semicolons.

Don't use a lowercase l for the numeral 1

Though similar on a typewriter, they look different in typographic fonts. And because the l is narrower than the 1 in most fonts, using the l misaligns number columns in tables. The same rules apply to the letter O and the numeral 0.

Hyphenate judiciously

Make sure that words break correctly — between syllables. Try not to end more than two or three consecutive lines with hyphens, and avoid two-letter divisions (on-ly, un-til). Double-check the results of your program's automatic hyphenation against a dictionary — some words are spelled the same but hyphenated differently (for example, *pro-ject* the verb and *proj-ect* the noun). Also, see the tips about discretionary hyphens in the preceding chapter.

Shrink those symbols

The register mark (®) and trademark symbol (™) in Macintosh fonts are far too big (maybe Apple's legal department created them). Shrink them down by several sizes and then shift them vertically so that their tops align with the top of the text. Ditto for bullets — if the artillery-sized ones the Mac gives you overwhelm the text they're supposed to accent, shrink them. But remember to move them up so that they're vertically centered within the line.

Hang that punctuation

When a line begins with an opening quote symbol ("), typesetters often adjust the left margin so that the quote "hangs" outside of it, thus avoiding little pockets of white space that disrupt the margin's perfect edge. Some typographers also hang hyphens outside the right margin in justified text. A typographer named Johann Gutenberg started that tradition in 1455. And when closing quotes (") follow a comma or period, many typographers hang them directly over the comma or period — if the client wants it. At a type house where I once worked, we had to reset an entire university course catalog because the hanging closing quotes weren't stylistically correct.

Align runover lines in bulleted or numbered lists

When you're formatting a series of paragraphs that begin with a bullet character or number, you're likely to have runover text — text that continues on to subsequent lines. Generally, it's a good idea to indent these runover lines so that they align with the first character that follows the bullet or number. This practice sets the list apart from the rest of the body text. And never type multiple spaces to align runover lines (or anything else). Use tabs or adjust the margin to create a hanging indent. If you use QuarkXPress, use the fantastic indent-to-here keyboard shortcut (⌘-\), described in the preceding chapter.

Proofread early and often

Don't wait until you've poured text into a layout to proofread it for the first time. Use your word processor to print it out in double-spaced Courier, and look for misspellings. Then switch to a proportionally spaced font such as Times and tweak dashes, quotes, and other special characters. (Dashes are difficult to discern in Courier.) If you make edits after you lay out the text, be sure to type true quotes and dashes. And as the page comes together, manually kern the type, break for sense, hang punctuation, and sweat all the other little details.

One more thing about fractions

If you can't justify buying a fraction font, create derived fractions instead of using full-sized figures (as in 1/2). A derived fraction is better than no fraction at all.

Italics versus Obliques

Another subtle point to be aware of is the difference between true italic text and derived italics, or *oblique*, text. In most typefaces, especially serif faces, italics are specially drawn to have their own script-like characteristics and to complement the stroke width of the roman version of the face.

How to see oblique text for yourself

The Mac can electronically slant the upright, or *roman*, version of a font to create a kind of pseudo italic. To see an example, type some text in a font such as Geneva, Chicago, or New York, and then choose the italic style.

Illustration programs such as Macromedia FreeHand and Adobe Illustrator also let you create oblique text by slanting a block of roman text to the angle you specify.

Choosing between oblique and italics

Oblique text can be a useful design element for headlines and other special purposes, but for body text, you generally want to use the font designer's true italics. In most cases, it's easy — simply install the italic versions of the font's screen and printer fonts. But some font packages don't include true italics. Adobe's ITC Benguiat package, for example, includes only roman and bold versions, even though Benguiat has beautiful italics. In this case, the solution is to buy from Bitstream, which sells a complete version of the Benguiat family.

The true-versus-derived issue applies to bold text, too, although generally you encounter derived bolds on the Mac's screen more often than in hard copy, and then only when you fail to install the actual bold screen or TrueType font that accompanies a typeface package.

Closing Thoughts on Typography

As you create and format documents, choose fonts, guesstimate line lengths, and make fractions, remember that the best typography is always appropriate to the message it conveys. Every formatting command you issue should be aimed at improving your document's readability.

Aaron Burns, chairman of the International Typeface Corporation, sums it up best: "In typography, function is of major importance; form is secondary; and fashion, almost meaningless."

Recommended Reading

If you're interested in learning more about typography, you may want to investigate the following books: *Designing with Type* by James Craig (Watson-Guptill Publications, 1971); *Graphic Design for the Electronic Age* by Jan White (Watson-Guptill Publications, 1988); *Basic Typography* by John R. Biggs (Watson-Guptill Publications, 1968); *The Mac Is Not a Typewriter* by Robin Williams (Peachpit Press, 1990); and *The Elements of Typographic Style* (Hartley & Marks, 1992).

Two more excellent sources of type tips are Adobe's "Font & Function" catalog ($6 from Adobe Systems, 1585 Charleston Road, P.O. Box 7900, Mountain View, CA 94039), and the International Typeface Corporation's free quarterly, *U&lc* (write to U&lc Subscription Department, International Typeface Corporation, 2 Hammarskjold Plaza, New York, NY 10017).

Under the Hood: How Fonts Work

The Mac's fonts are a type of *resource* — a collection of data that programs can use when they're running. The font resources themselves can be structured in either of two very different ways — one is much more versatile than the other.

Bitmap versus outline fonts

Think of a font resource as a description — a kind of recipe — that tells the Mac how to draw a given typeface in a given size and style. These font descriptions can take the form of *bitmaps* or *outlines*. You're likely to encounter both types of fonts as you use the Mac, so it helps to understand both approaches in order to use and choose fonts effectively.

Bitmaps: one recipe for each size

In a bitmapped font, the font description specifies the exact arrangement of pixels that forms a given character *in a given size*. Bitmapped fonts require a separate description to accurately render each size. If a program needs a size for which no description exists, the Mac must create that size by altering, or *scaling*, an existing size. The results of that scaling process are usually chunky, awkward-looking characters.

Outlines: one recipe fits all

With outline fonts, the font description is a mathematic recipe that describes the characters' properties: their proportions, the size of their bowls, stems, ascenders, descenders, and other components. Unlike a bitmap font, an outline font doesn't require a separate font description for each type size. Instead, the Mac (or a printer) can use one outline font description to create characters of any size.

To appreciate this difference, imagine that you have the job of describing the letter O by using toy wooden blocks — bits. First, you arrange the blocks in the shape of an O, and then you note the arrangement and number of blocks required to form the letter. If you need an O of a different size, you must assemble a completely different arrangement of blocks. This is the bitmapped approach.

Now assume that you have to describe an O by using the outline approach. This time, your tool isn't a set of blocks, but a fat rubber band. Because the rubber band describes the properties of the O — it's round — you don't need to create a separate arrangement of blocks for each size. To create a larger O, you simply stretch the rubber band proportionally. To create a stretched or compressed O (in type terms, an *expanded* or *condensed* O), you stretch the rubber band more in one direction than the other.

The downside of outlines

Like a rubber band, the outline approach is flexible — but there's a catch. The Macintosh uses a bitmapped screen, so ultimately it must describe a character as a bitmap. So rendering a character from an outline description requires two basic steps:

1. The Mac consults the outline description to learn the character's properties.
2. It constructs a bitmap from that description to create a character of the required size and proportions.

This process of building a bitmap from an outline description is called *rasterizing*, and it requires the Mac (or a printer) to perform numerous calculations that slow the display or printing of text. You can see this for yourself by typing a sentence such as *The quick brown fox jumped over the lazy dog's back* and then reformatting it in a variety of fonts, sizes, and styles using both bitmap and outline fonts. When you're formatting with outline fonts, you'll probably notice that the text takes longer to appear.

Outline font advantages

If outline fonts take longer to display or print, why use them? Two reasons:

- Unlike bitmapped descriptions, outline font descriptions are *resolution independent* — they aren't tied to a specific number of dots per inch. The character isn't described as a bitmap until moments before it's displayed (or printed). This flexibility allows one font description to work on any device, regardless of its resolution, and take maximum advantage of that resolution. Thanks to resolution independence, you can use the same font on a 72-dots-per-inch Macintosh video screen, a 300-dpi laser printer, and a 2540-dpi Linotronic imagesetter.
- Outline fonts can create sharp characters in a virtually unlimited range of type sizes. A computer or printer that uses outline fonts can generate text in virtually any size as well as expand or condense a font to create an entirely different look.

Another benefit of outline fonts surfaces in programs that let you view documents in varying degrees of magnification. (Different magnification views are most common in desktop publishing, presentation graphics, and drawing programs. Such programs allow you to view documents at actual size, half size, and double size, for example.) Because outline fonts allow the Mac to create any size it needs, programs that offer different magnification scales can display sharp, distortion-free text in all their viewing scales.

My wood block-versus-rubber band example oversimplifies the technicalities behind bitmapped and outline fonts. But it does show the basic differences between the two approaches, which are summarized in Table 11-1.

Table 11-1
Summary of Differences between Bitmap and Outline Fonts

Bitmap Fonts	***Outline Fonts***
Often require more storage space because each size needs a separate description	Efficient to store because one description can be used to generate any size
Resolution dependent — a given font can't be resized without distortion	Resolution independent — one font description can be used on any output device, whether screen, printer, or imagesetter
Fast to display and print; no extra processing required, provided that a description of the required size is available	Can be slower to display and print because the outline must be converted, or rasterized, into bitmaps of the required sizes

Understanding Outline Font Formats

Within the outline font category are two more categories, or *formats:* TrueType fonts and PostScript fonts. Within the PostScript font category are three subcategories: Type 1 fonts, Type 3 fonts, and Multiple Master fonts.

The underlying mathematics behind each of these outline font formats is different; that is, each format takes its own approach to describing the characteristics of characters. Unless you plan to design your own fonts, you don't have to worry about understanding the gory details of these font formats. But knowing the basics behind each format helps you choose fonts that work best with your Mac and printer.

TrueType fonts

On the surface, TrueType and Adobe Type Manager (ATM) are the same — both provide rasterizing software that enables the Mac to translate font outlines into bitmaps for the screen and for non-PostScript printers. But unlike ATM, TrueType does not rely on PostScript fonts — in fact, TrueType doesn't rely on PostScript for anything. You can print TrueType fonts on a PostScript printer, but TrueType is designed for non-PostScript devices: the Mac's screen as well as Apple's non-PostScript printers. Apple has also licensed TrueType to Microsoft, which has built TrueType into Microsoft Windows 3.1 and later.

You can also use TrueType with System 6.0.7 or 6.0.8 by adding the TrueType system extension to your System Folder.

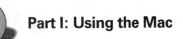

The Essential Font Utility: Adobe Type Manager

For the first several years of its life, the Macintosh relied exclusively on bitmap fonts for its screen display. That changed when Adobe Systems introduced its Adobe Type Manager (ATM) system extension. ATM essentially teaches the Mac how to rasterize Type 1 PostScript fonts — the most popular type of outline font used with PostScript printers such as Apple's LaserWriter Pro series. ATM was the first program to bring all the benefits of outline fonts to the Mac's screen and to non-PostScript printers such as Apple's ImageWriter II and StyleWriter and Hewlett-Packard DeskWriter. ATM was an instant success and has become one of the most popular extensions in the Macintosh world. ATM also enlarged the market for Type 1 PostScript fonts by allowing these fonts to be used on non-PostScript printers.

Valuable as ATM is, bitmap fonts still have their place. Because bitmap fonts are faster to display, you can boost your Mac's performance by installing bitmap versions of common font sizes in your System Folder. If you have a Power Mac, use ATM version 3.8 or later.

Comparing TrueType and PostScript fonts

TrueType fonts have some advantages over PostScript fonts. Because TrueType is part of the Mac's system software, it's easier to install and remove TrueType fonts than it is to install and remove PostScript fonts, especially if you use System 7 instead of System 7.1. When you add a TrueType font, it's immediately available; when you add a PostScript font, you must restart the Mac in order for ATM to recognize the new font. Also, for some technical reasons described in Chapter 30, TrueType fonts have the capability to look better than Type 1 fonts at small sizes (below 12 point).

But if you use a PostScript printer, TrueType fonts have some drawbacks. Because TrueType knows nothing of PostScript, the Mac's LaserWriter printer driver must perform some technical gymnastics in order to print a TrueType font on a PostScript printer. This process usually translates into longer printing times and can result in memory shortages on some PostScript printers. Again, Chapter 30 contains all the details.

PostScript Font Details

PostScript fonts are the most widely used fonts in the Mac world, thanks to the popularity of ATM and PostScript printers. But not all PostScript fonts are identical; there are several types of PostScript fonts — and each comes with its own set of technicalities.

Type 1 Fonts

Type 1 fonts are the most popular kind of PostScript font. These fonts are built into PostScript printers. Type 1 fonts are also the most popular format for *downloadable* fonts — fonts stored on your Mac's hard disk and transferred to a PostScript printer's memory during a print job. Adobe Systems and most other font developers sell fonts in Type 1 format.

In a Type 1 font, the mathematical outlines are structured in an efficient way that allows the font to use disk space and printer memory sparingly. Type 1 fonts are also compatible with Adobe Type Manager; ATM can read the Type 1 outline and create a bitmap for the screen or for a non-PostScript printer.

Type 3 Fonts

Type 3 fonts, sometimes called *user-defined* fonts, are much less popular than Type 1 fonts. Some font developers sell Type 3-format fonts, and you may find some free Type 3 fonts floating around in user groups and on on-line information services, but generally, Type 3 fonts play second fiddle to Type 1 fonts. (By the way, there is no such thing as a Type 2 font. That name was reserved for a font technology that never panned out.)

Because Type 3 fonts don't use the special encoding techniques present in Type 1 fonts, they're generally larger than equivalent Type 1 fonts. Therefore, they use more printer memory and take longer to print than Type 1 fonts.

But the Type 3 format allows for certain effects that aren't available in Type 1 fonts. A Type 3 font can contain a gray fill — characters outlined in black but filled in a gray shade. A Type 3 font can also contain complex characters that are, in fact, PostScript illustrations. Using font-editing software discussed later in this chapter, you can create a Type 3 font whose characters are pictures — your company logo, for example.

Serving Multiple Masters

Adobe's Multiple Master font technology enables you to slant, skew, and horizontally scale fonts without compromising the original type design. Multiple Master fonts are a font customizer's dream. Besides being able to expand or condense a font, you can also create any weight from extra light to extra bold. As the next section of this chapter describes, many capabilities provided by Multiple Master fonts are also available in QuickDraw GX.

With Multiple Master fonts, you can create a limitless number of font variations from a single typeface. For example, instead of having only three type weights — light, medium, and bold — to choose from, you can generate any weight ranging from ultra-light to extra-bold. Similarly, instead of having only condensed, normal, and expanded styles, you can generate any width — from ultra-skinny to bloated, including any width in between.

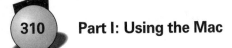

Font Files and Their Icons

When you get a new font, its file has one of a number of different icons. As the illustrations in this box show, each icon indicates a different type of font file:

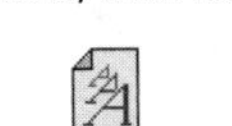

TrueType outline font
This file's icon shows several different-sized capital As, indicating that a TrueType font can generate any size.

Bitmap font file
This file has a single capital A to indicate that the font file contains a bitmapped description for only one size. A bitmap font file usually has the size in its name — for example, New York 24 or Venice 14.

Suitcase file
A *suitcase file* has an icon that looks like — that's right — a suitcase. These files can contain more than one font, size, and style.

PostScript font file
A PostScript font outline may have any of a few different icons, depending on the font vendor or the program used to create the font. The icon shown here is used by Adobe Systems. To use a PostScript font file, you also need a corresponding bitmap font for the System file (or the Fonts folder in System 7.1 and later versions).

When you double-click a TrueType or bitmapped font file, the Finder displays a window showing a sample of the font. A TrueType font sample shows several sizes, while a bitmapped font sample shows only the size represented in that file. (If you want to change the text of the sample that appears, see Chapter 24 for instructions.)

If you double-click a suitcase file, a window opens listing the fonts contained in the file. This window is very similar to the standard directory windows that the Finder uses to show what's on a disk or in a folder.

See Chapter 22 for details about installing and removing fonts.

How Multiple Master fonts work

Each of these style variations is called a *design axis*. Most Multiple Master fonts offer at least two axes. The weight axis governs lightness or boldness, while the width axis controls condensation or expansion.

Each end of each design axis in a Multiple Master font has a *master design*. For example, the weight axis has light and bold masters. All other weights in between are generated — in tech talk, *interpolated* — from these masters. This explains the Multiple Master name: A given typeface's appearance is actually determined by multiple masters instead of just one master.

The Multiple Master format allows for two additional axes. The *optical scaling* axis provides masters designed for small type sizes as well as large ones. (Multiple Master's support for an optical scaling axis represents a major milestone in digital typography; the Backgrounder box "Optical Scaling Advantages" explains why.) The *style axis* controls the actual design of the typeface. A Multiple Master font with a style axis can enable you to generate sanserif, small serif, medium serif, or large serif fonts — or anything in between.

More memory required

Using Multiple Master fonts has one potential drawback: They devour printer memory. Because of the complexity of the Multiple Master format, Adobe recommends that you have at least 3MB of memory in your PostScript printer. If you have a low-end or midrange PostScript printer, you may need to add memory to it in order to print a Multiple Master font. (See Chapter 31 for details about adding memory to PostScript printers.)

Ares Software's Chameleon Technology

Ares Software's Chameleon technology provides features similar to those of Adobe Multiple Master fonts, but it adds some additional capabilities.

Optical Scaling Advantages

In the days of hot metal type, casting different sizes of type required different molds. As a result, type designers cut a separate mold for each point size and made small adjustments to letter spacing, character proportions, and weight so that each size would be as legible as possible.

When phototype and digital type became popular, this practice of creating separate masters for each size went out the window. Instead, most typesetting equipment used one master font and scaled the type to the size required — originally by moving lenses closer to or further away from the font negative, later by mathematically scaling a font outline. In both cases, small type became less legible because it was simply a scaled-down version of a larger size.

The optical scaling axis brings the legibility advantages of separate masters to the digital typographer. In Adobe's Minion Multiple Master typeface, as the type size increases, the space between characters, the *letterfit,* decreases; the spaces within characters, the *counterforms,* close up; the serifs become finer; the overall weight of the type becomes lighter; and the x-height becomes smaller. These are the same basic techniques — updated for the digital age — that a hot-metal type designer used to optimize legibility at various sizes.

Like Multiple Master technology, Chameleon relies on master descriptors from which a limitless variety of fonts can be interpolated. But one key difference is that every Chameleon descriptor provides multiple design axes — you can control weight, width, height, serif shape, and slant by moving sliders in Ares's Font-Chameleon application (see Figure 11-9 "FontChameleon in Action").

Another key difference between Chameleon and Multiple Master technology is that Chameleon can make TrueType fonts as well as PostScript Type 1 fonts. Multiple Master fonts are intimately tied to PostScript — not surprising, given that Adobe invented them.

The Chameleon technology relies on a single master font outline that's about 350K in size and contains width, weight, serif, oblique, and x-height design axes.

This master descriptor is manipulated by font descriptors, which are small (about 5K) files whose information tells Chameleon's built-in rasterizer how to modify the master font outline. The FontChameleon product includes 220 descriptor files.

Confused about the differences between Chameleon and FontChameleon? Here's the scoop: Chameleon is the underlying technology — the master font outlines, the descriptors, and the rasterizer. FontChameleon is a font-generating utility that includes the Chameleon technology.

Figure 11-9: FontChameleon in Action Ares Software's FontChameleon lets you create an unlimited number of fonts by adjusting the sliders in the application.

QuickDraw GX: Fine Type for the Rest of Us

If you use System 7.5, you have still more typographic options open to you — and still more technicalities and compatibility issues to contend with. System 7.5 includes Apple's QuickDraw GX, an enhanced version of the Mac's QuickDraw graphics routines, which are responsible for creating everything you see on the Mac's screen.

An important component of QuickDraw GX is TrueType GX — an enhanced version of the TrueType font format. The QuickDraw GX/TrueType GX combination yields some significant benefits where fonts, typography, and printing are concerned. In this section, I describe the typographic benefits; for details about how QuickDraw GX makes printing easier and more convenient, and for an overview of the other enhancements in System 7.5, see Chapters 22 and 31.

An overview of QuickDraw GX benefits

What's so great about the QuickDraw GX/System 7.5 combination?

- **All font formats are equal.** In System 7.5, PostScript Type 1 fonts are no longer considered second-class citizens to TrueType fonts. In fact, System 7.5 *includes* a version of Adobe Type Manager, called ATM GX, that provides rasterizing for Type 1 fonts.
- **Smart fonts.** QuickDraw GX extends the TrueType and Type 1 font formats to enable font developers to create what Apple calls *smart fonts* — fonts that automatically perform a variety of typographic operations.
- **Sophisticated line-layout features.** QuickDraw GX includes a new set of routines that application programs can tap in order to perform the kinds of typographic finessing that you'd otherwise have to do by hand. As the term *line layout* implies, these features have to do with positioning text on a line — adjusting its horizontal positioning (for kerning and tracking, for example) or even its vertical positioning (to create superscripts, subscripts, or just bouncy-looking type).

The down side: You need new fonts and programs

It's important to note that most of these benefits require updated fonts as well as updated application programs that are written to take advantage of QuickDraw GX's capabilities. So at first, many of the typographic enhancements of QuickDraw GX aren't accessible.

Over time, developers will add QuickDraw GX support to their programs, but it may take awhile. These days, most developers create versions of their programs for the Mac and for Microsoft Windows, and many developers have expressed concerns about adding features to their Mac applications that they won't be able to add to their Windows versions. One of the first programs to support GX fonts is Pixar's Typistry 2.1, the 3-D text effects program discussed in Chapter 14. Another is Manhattan Graphics' ReadySetGo, which actually *requires* QuickDraw GX.

More on Smart Fonts

Here is a closer look at the benefits that QuickDraw GX smart fonts can provide.

Lots of characters

One key benefit of smart fonts is that they can contain a whole lotta characters. Most non-GX TrueType and PostScript fonts provide only 255 characters. That isn't enough to hold the range of characters that used to be mainstays of traditional fine typography: true-cut small capitals, old-style numerals, real fractions, ornamental swashes, and ligatures. (This is why these characters have been relegated to expert-set fonts — and why they've fallen into disuse.)

A QuickDraw GX font can contain a whopping 65,536 characters. This greatly expanded character set not only means that a single font can hold a huge array of special characters. It's also extremely useful for typesetting in languages other than English — complex, non-Roman text systems such as Japanese and Chinese can rely on thousands of different characters.

Contextual substitution tables

That's a mouthful, but it simply means that a smart font can automatically substitute one or more characters you type with another character. Examples include automatically substituting curly quotes when you type the tacky kind, inserting a real fraction when you type **1/2**, using an ornamental swash instead of the plain version of a character, or using a ligature when you type **fl**. With a smart font, you don't have to remember the Option-Shift-sneeze key sequence required to obtain special characters; the font spews them out automatically.

Contextual substitution is also valuable for non-Roman writing systems. For example, in text systems such as Arabic and Hindi, the appearance of some characters changes in relation to their position within a word or relative to vowels. If the proper smarts are built into the QuickDraw GX font, the font can automatically make these substitutions, thereby maintaining grammatical accuracy — not to mention making life easier for the person doing the typing.

Built-in bitmaps

Earlier in this chapter, I mentioned that you can boost font-display performance by including bitmaps of commonly used font sizes. In recognition, QuickDraw GX outline fonts can contain built-in bitmaps — no need to fuss with separate font files or packing custom font suitcases.

Unlimited style variations

Smart fonts can contain the same types of design axis and stylistic variants as Adobe Multiple Master fonts, including support for optical scaling. Indeed, an application program that has QuickDraw GX-savvy can provide a slider that lets you create stylistic variants on the fly, as shown in Figure 11-10 "Changing Styles."

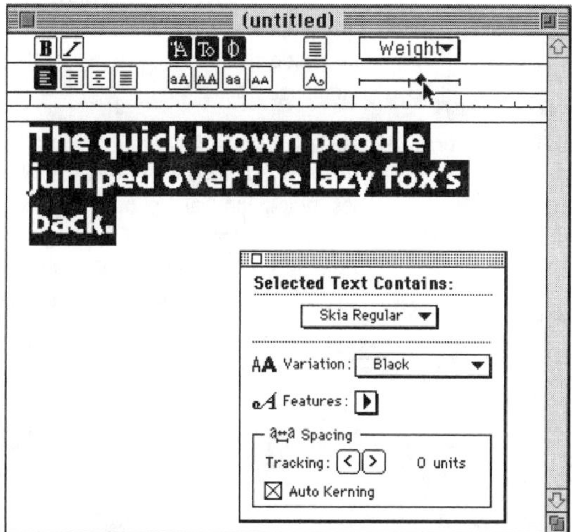

Figure 11-10: Changing Styles In a QuickDraw GX-savvy application program, you can alter character widths by dragging a slider, as shown here in an Apple prototype application.

It's worth mentioning that Ares's Chameleon technology, discussed earlier in this chapter, operates as a system extension under QuickDraw GX. With a GX-savvy application program, you can create unlimited style variations without having to use the FontChameleon utility.

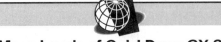

The Many Levels of QuickDraw GX Support

I've mentioned that developers must adapt their application programs in order to take advantage of QuickDraw GX's enhanced typographic features. There are actually several levels of QuickDraw GX support, and you're likely to encounter each level as QuickDraw GX momentum builds.

The levels of QuickDraw GX support include

- **QuickDraw GX unaware.** Programs in this category don't implement any QuickDraw GX features; when such a program is running on a Mac containing QuickDraw GX, QuickDraw GX translates all QuickDraw printing and drawing commands into QuickDraw GX equivalents. Many of QuickDraw GX's unique printing features are still accessible with these programs—see Chapter 31. All applications developed prior to QuickDraw GX's release fall into this category.
- **QuickDraw GX aware.** Programs in this group provide a core set of QuickDraw GX printing features but retain compatibility with documents created using earlier versions. Generally, QuickDraw GX-aware programs support QuickDraw GX's enhanced Print dialog box and all the slick things it makes possible, such as printing each page of a document on a different paper size or routing a document from one printer to another.
- **QuickDraw GX savvy.** The application implements full support for QuickDraw GX graphics, typography, and printing features. It also retains compatibility with documents created in earlier versions.
- **QuickDraw GX dependent.** The application *requires* the presence of QuickDraw GX graphics, typography, and printing routines to function. You aren't likely to see GX-dependent programs for some time, at least not until the vast majority of Macs are running QuickDraw GX.

More on GX Line-Layout Features

This section details the benefits of QuickDraw GX's line-layout capabilities.

Automatic kerning and tracking

Prior to the release of QuickDraw GX, only high-end publishing programs supported features like automatic kerning and tracking. QuickDraw GX's line-layout routines enable any GX-savvy application — from a word processor to an integrated package to a personal information manager — to provide these features. As a result, QuickDraw GX makes it easier to get professional-quality type from a wide variety of applications.

And by the way, QuickDraw GX does tracking correctly — that is, it increases spacing of small sizes and decreases spacing of large ones.

Automatic optical alignment

The eye has a weird quirk: When a round character such as an O is directly above a vertical character such as an L, the two characters do not appear to be aligned — the O looks like it's slightly to the left of the L.

Typographers have known about this phenomenon for centuries and have developed a technique called *optical alignment* to compensate for it. Optical alignment simply means adjusting the line containing the round character until the two lines *appear* to be aligned. The process involves fiddling with margins and indents and doing a lot of test printouts. QuickDraw GX enables application programs to do optical alignment automatically.

Automatic hanging punctuation

In the Quick Tips box "Type Tips" earlier in this chapter, I mentioned that when a line begins with an opening quote symbol ("), typesetters often adjust the left margin so that the quote "hangs" outside of it, thus avoiding little pockets of white space that disrupt the margin's perfect edge. Doing this "by hand" requires a lot of manual labor — adjustments of the left margin and indent markers. QuickDraw GX's line-layout features can hang punctuation automatically.

International advantages

As with smart fonts, QuickDraw GX's line-layout features make it easier for developers to write application programs that handle non-Roman writing systems. One aspect of laying out lines involves positioning characters in the right order: from left to right in English, from right to left in Hebrew, and from top to bottom in Japanese.

Font Customizing and Special Effects

Because outline fonts are as flexible as rubber bands, they're naturals for special typographic effects. By stretching a font vertically, you can create a skinnier, *condensed* version of the original typeface. Stretching the font horizontally gives you a wider, *expanded* font. You can attach an outline font to a curved line to create wavy-looking text or stretch it to fit an irregular shape. You can even alter the characters themselves to create logos, special symbols, and fractions.

Numerous font-editing utilities let you perform these and many other font-customizing jobs. Macromedia's Fontographer lets you alter fonts and create new ones from scratch. Ares's FontMonger, Type Solutions's Incubator Pro, and Macromedia's Metamorphosis Professional are best suited to modifying existing fonts — converting them from one outline format to another, expanding or condensing them, or creating fractions.

Type effects programs such as Letraset's LetraStudio, Brøderbund's TypeStyler, and Adobe TypeTwister let you twist, stretch, squeeze, mold, mirror, and otherwise modify type. These programs excel at display type — fancy headlines, product labels, and logos. They let you do with a mouse what used to require hours of labor over a layout table or in a darkroom.

Expand and Condense

Expanding or condensing, or *horizontally scaling*, a typeface can give it a new, distinctive personality. This point isn't lost on Apple — its corporate font is a condensed version of Garamond. A condensed font looks more delicate and allows more text to fit on a page; an expanded font has a weightier look (see Figure 11-11 "Expanding and Condensing").

Times Roman.
Thin and elegant.
Stretch out.

Figure 11-11: Expanding and Condensing
Expanding or condensing a font can give it a new personality. The original Times Roman (top), condensed 20 percent (middle), and expanded 30 percent (bottom) present three different faces.

Expanding and condensing within a program

Adobe PageMaker and QuarkXPress let you expand or condense text formatted in existing fonts. In PageMaker, use the Type menu's Set Width submenu. In QuarkXPress, use the Style menu's Horizontal Scale command.

Drawing programs such as Macromedia FreeHand and Adobe Illustrator can also expand and condense. In FreeHand, use the Horizontal Scale portion of the Text Inspector window. In Illustrator, use the Horizontal Scale portion of the Character palette.

Font Customizing: The Legal Angle

Font customizing brings up some legal issues. Specifically, you can't legally modify an existing commercial font (or use it to create fractions) and then distribute the resulting font or post it on an on-line information service — even if you change the font's name. Doing so is as much a form of software piracy as copying a word processor for a friend.

Expanding and condensing with a font utility

Using a program's horizontal scaling command works, but wouldn't it be more convenient to have fonts that are expanded or condensed to begin with? That way, you can use them in programs that don't have horizontal scaling commands, such as word processors. You can scale fonts in advanced programs like Fontographer, but it's often easier in the basic (and more economical) font-customizing programs. To learn how to scale fonts in Incubator Pro, see the Step-by-Step box "Scaling Fonts."

Don't scale too much

Because horizontal scaling distorts the proportions of a typeface, it compromises the original type design. To remain as faithful as possible to the original design, avoid scaling by more than 25 percent or so in either direction unless you're after a particularly dramatic or gaudy effect.

As you explore the world of font customizing, keep your sense of good taste close at hand. Don't go crazy with glitzy effects. Good font customizers work like jazz musicians — they improvise and customize, but they also preserve the essence of the original.

Some effects lengthen printing times

Note that some font-customizing tasks — for example, fitting text to a shape, stretching and condensing a font, and applying special PostScript effects and gradients — lengthen printing times, especially for a PostScript-based imagesetter. If you're creating a document laden with effects, prepare to wait — and to pay more if you use a service bureau that charges by the hour.

Scaling Fonts

Expanding or condensing a typeface can give it a new, distinctive personality. These instructions show you how to scale a font by using Incubator Pro.

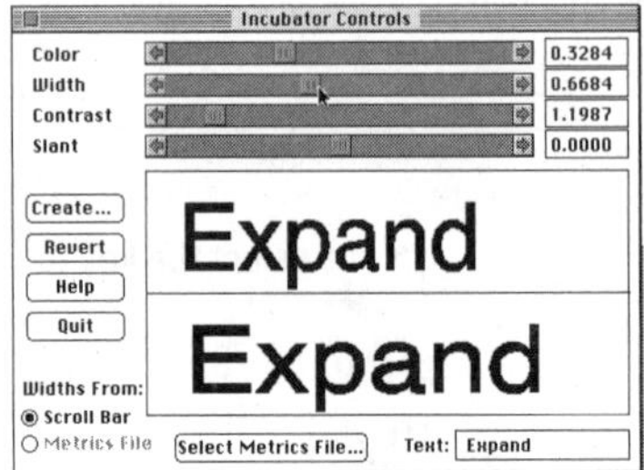

To scale a font with Incubator Pro:

1. **Choose the font you want to modify from the Font menu.**
2. **Use the Width scroll bar to condense or expand the font.** Use Incubator Pro's sample text display and preview window to see the results.
3. **Click the Create button.**
4. **Type a name for the font, click OK, and then click Save.**
5. **Install the resulting font file in your system.**

Let's Get Fractional

If I had a dime for each time I saw a phony fraction such as 1/2 in an otherwise good-looking publication, I'd be rich. Besides taking up more space, phony fractions are unattractive and dead giveaways of desktop publishing. You can create your own fractions the hard way by reducing the type size of the numbers and then, if your word processor or publishing program allows, shifting the numerator up by a few points. As I describe in the preceding chapter, you can also buy fonts that contain ready-made fractions; best of all are the expert sets some font vendors sell, which have true-cut fractions designed to match a specific typeface, with the design of the small numerals tweaked for better legibility. (Some fraction-only fonts are included on this book's CD-ROM.)

You can also customize an existing font to create your own fractions — even oddball ones like $^{15}/_{128}$. It's easiest in FontMonger. You can find instructions for creating fractions in FontMonger in the Step-by-Step box "Makin' Fractions."

Makin' Fractions

Using actual fractions instead of full-size numerals can add a professional touch to your documents. The following instructions show you how to make fractions in FontMonger.

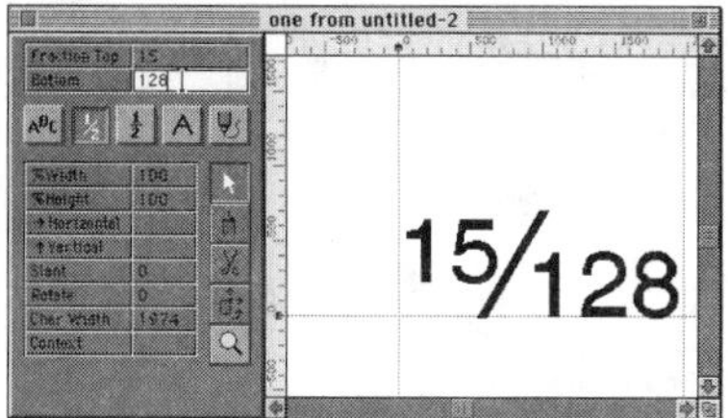

To make a fraction in FontMonger:

1. **Use the Open command to open the font for which you want to create a fraction.**
2. **When the keyboard display appears, select the key to which you want to assign the fraction.**
   To use an Option-key or Shift-Option-key sequence, click the appropriate modifier key in the keyboard display.
3. **After selecting a spot for the fraction, choose Alter Character(s) from the Alterations menu.**
   The Alter Character window opens.
4. **Select the type of fraction you want and then type the numerator and denominator in the appropriate text boxes.**
5. **Click the window's Close box.**
6. **Save the font under a different name to avoid replacing the original.**
7. **Install the resulting fonts in your system.**

Turning Text into Pictures

Many company logos consist of text that has been stylized, reshaped, shaded, or otherwise modified. Using Macromedia's Metamorphosis Professional (Meta Pro, for short), you can convert a passage of text into an object-oriented PICT graphic that you can paste into a graphics program and polish as you please. (See Chapter 12 if you're unfamiliar with graphics formats such as PICT, TIFF, and EPS.)

In Meta Pro's main window, click the Convert Text button, choose the PICT to Clipboard option from the Format pop-up menu, and choose the Type Your Own option from the Text pop-up menu. Select the desired font, style, and size from their respective menus (a large size such as 100 point gives the best results — you can scale it down later). Type the text you want to convert in the text box and then click Convert (see Figure 11-12 "Prose to Picture").

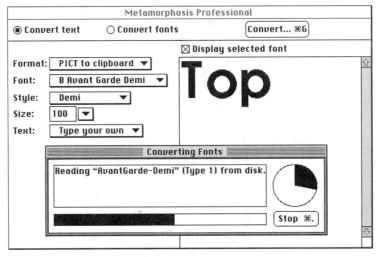

Figure 11-12: Prose to Picture Metamorphosis Pro can convert text you type into a PICT graphic that you can modify by converting the text (top) and then pasting it into MacDraw Pro, where you can reshape the T and apply a gradient fill (bottom).

After the conversion is complete, switch to a graphics program and paste. When you paste into Claris MacDraw Pro or ClarisDraw, you can reshape an individual character by selecting it and then choosing Reshape from the Edit menu. Keep in mind that you can't edit or reformat the text after you make it a graphic. If changes are required, you have to return to Meta Pro and start over.

Meta Pro can also save converted text in a PICT or Encapsulated PostScript (EPS) file that you can open by using an object-oriented drawing program or import into a publishing program. Meta Pro can also convert fonts themselves from one format to another. If you have Type 3 PostScript fonts, for example, you can convert them to Type 1 format for use with Adobe Type Manager. Meta Pro can even convert fonts for or from a DOS PC. If you have a Mac and a PC, you can convert Mac fonts into ones that the Mac-like Microsoft Windows software can use.

Turning Pictures into Text

Another customizing task involves adding a graphic such as a scanned image or an image from a clip art collection to an existing font. You can start by scanning an original — your signature or company logo, perhaps — and then saving the resulting image. Scan a large original if possible (if you're scanning your signature, for example, write big); you get more detail in the resulting font. After scanning the original, import the scan into Fontographer and use the program's *autotrace* feature to trace the image. If you have a PostScript illustration program such as FreeHand or Illustrator, you may prefer to trace the image by using that program. In either case, the result is an outline character of the art you scanned.

Font developers work by using this scan-and-trace process: A designer hand-draws large masters for each character, scans them, and then traces them. You can apply these techniques yourself to create an entirely new font. Create a font of your handwriting or printing (great for architects, but not recommended for physicians).

A relatively painless way to try your hand at font-making is to make a font from a sample in an old type specimen book — many books containing old display type and a variety of ornamental dingbats are available from Dover Books. To get good results, you need to do a great deal of fine-tuning and print a ream or two of test output to check spacing in all sizes and character combinations. When done, you'll have a new appreciation for the skill and patience of a professional type designer.

Creating Stylish Display Type

The font-customizing programs I've covered so far let you create and modify fonts that you then install in your system to use with other programs. Letraset's LetraStudio and Brøderbund's TypeStyler are designed to let you create special typographic effects by using fonts already in your system. (Both programs also provide their own proprietary outline fonts.) The result of a LetraStudio or TypeStyler session is typically a PICT or EPS file that you import into a publishing or illustration program. (Adobe sells a similar program called TypeTwister.)

How type-effects programs work

With either LetraStudio or TypeStyler, start by typing text and then formatting it in the desired font. Next, you can fine-tune the character spacing; instead of requiring you to use awkward ⌘-key sequences to adjust spacing (as do publishing programs), both programs let you simply drag characters left or right — a more efficient and direct technique. After you tweak the spacing, you can draw a shape and resize the type to fit within it (see Figure 11-13 "Styling Type"). Nothing illustrates the flexibility of outline fonts like watching characters recast themselves to fit a shape you draw.

Both TypeStyler and LetraStudio can work with PostScript and TrueType fonts and also include a few display typefaces. If you work with display type frequently, investigate Letraset's Fontek library of over 100 display typefaces. Each Fontek package includes both TrueType and Type 1 PostScript versions of the first-rate display type that Letraset has been selling for years.

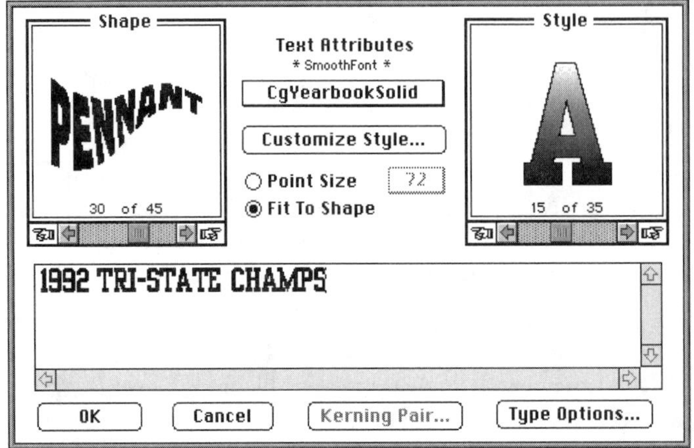

Figure 11-13: Styling Type When you create display type with TypeStyler, you can specify the text, the desired font, the effect, and the shape the text should fit into (top), and then display the resulting effect (bottom).

PostCraft's Effects Specialist

A simpler effects program is PostCraft International's Effects Specialist, which lets you apply 120 special effects to text you type. Effects Specialist isn't in the TypeStyler or LetraStudio league — it doesn't, for example, let you fit type to irregular shapes and manually kern by clicking and dragging characters. But it does provide more special effects than TypeStyler and LetraStudio, and you can modify those effects in a dizzying number of ways.

Bigger, better banners

For those who think big, there's Brøderbund's BannerMania. This fun program lets you create, yes, banners — choose one of the 50 built-in designs, type your text in any of 19 built-in fonts (or use any Type 1 PostScript font), apply one of the 34 built-in special type effects and 134 built-in color schemes, print, and then assemble the resulting pages. You can also customize designs, type effects, and color schemes. It's a sign-maker's playground.

Font Things to Try

The *Macworld Power User Clinic* CD contains numerous items for your Mac's type foundry.

- **theTypeBook.** This terrific (and free) program by Jim Lewis prints font-specimen pages that show samples of your fonts. It also prints extremely handy charts that indicate where each font's special characters are hiding.
- **BitFont.** This handy utility generates bitmaps of the size you specify from any PostScript or TrueType font. If you frequently use a large type size of a particular font, use BitFont to create a bitmap of that size. Install that bitmap, and text in that size will display much faster.
- **Fonts galore.** The CD contains roughly 100 PostScript and TrueType fonts — everything from company logos to fractions to exotic headline fonts.

You'll find all of the items in the Fonts folder, within the Best of BMUG folder.

CHAPTER 11 CONCEPTS AND TERMS

- Outline fonts such as PostScript and TrueType fonts are more versatile than bitmapped fonts because one outline can be used to generate any type size.
- Another plus for outline fonts is their ability to expand or condense.
- Fonts and type play large roles in the Mac world, making an awareness of typographic basics important.
- The first step in choosing a font involves deciding between sanserif and serif designs.
- To arrive at the ideal line length, strive for an average of 8 to 11 words per line.
- Body text generally looks best when you choose a program's autoleading option. Consider setting headlines with no extra leading.
- Justified body text is prone to rivers of white space, which you can eliminate with judicious hyphenation and letterspacing.
- In display type, almost every character combination can benefit from kerning.
- For professional looking fractions, small capitals, and old-style numerals, use an expert set version of a font.
- Font utilities such as Fontographer, FontMonger, Incubator Pro, FontChameleon, FontStudio, and Metamorphosis Professional enable you to customize and create fonts.
- Adobe's Multiple Master fonts can be expanded and condensed without compromising the original design; they have other sophisticated advantages over conventional outline fonts as well.
- With display type programs such as LetraStudio and TypeStyler, you can create special text effects and meticulously spaced headlines.

ascender
The part of a character such as *f* or *d* that rises above the body of the letter.

autotrace
A feature in font-editing (and some illustration) programs that generates an outline from a bitmap image.

baseline
The imaginary line on which the body of a character sits. Leading is measured from baseline to baseline.

bitmap font
Also called a *fixed-size font,* a font in which an arrangement of bits describes characters. Each type size requires a separate arrangement, making bitmap fonts less flexible than outline fonts.

body type
Also known as body text, the typeface used for the main text of a job.

condensed
A skinnier version of a given typeface.

descender
The portion of a character such as *j* or *g* that drops below the baseline.

dingbat
Also called an *ornament,* a decorative graphic element.

downloadable font
A font that is stored on a floppy or hard disk and downloaded into a laser printer's memory before use.

drop cap
A decorative capital at the beginning of a paragraph set in a larger size than the surrounding body text and lowered to occupy more than one line.

em space
A fixed amount of space equal to the point size of the typeface you're using. In 12-point type, an em space is 12 points wide.

en space
Also called a *nut space,* a fixed amount of space equal to half an em space.

expanded
A fatter, stretched version of a given typeface.

family
A group of related typefaces. For example, Times Roman, Times Italic, Times Bold, and Times Bold Italic are all members of the Times family.

font
All the characters for one typeface and, historically, in one size. Today, *font* and *typeface* are often used interchangeably.

hanging punctuation
Positioning punctuation outside the even left or right margin of text for better visual alignment. Also, the technique of hanging quote symbols over a period or comma to tighten up the text.

leading
The amount of space between two baselines (pronounced *led-ing*).

letterspacing
Adding space between letters to create an airy effect in a headline or to justify body text.

old-style numerals
Numerals with ascenders and descenders, often used in body type for better legibility.

optical scaling
The process of adjusting character shapes and spacing for maximum legibility at a given point size.

outline font
A font in which mathematical equations describe characters; by processing these equations, the Mac can create characters of virtually any size.

pica
A unit of measurement that is equal to 12 points.

point
A unit of measurement equal to .01384, or approximately 1⁄72, inch. The point size of a given typeface is the distance between the top of the highest ascender and the bottom of the lowest descender.

pull quote
A phrase extracted from the body text and set in large type to attract the reader's attention.

rag
An uneven left or, more often, right margin.

resident font
A font that is built into a printer.

sanserif
A typeface without serifs. Sanserif typefaces include Helvetica, Futura, and the Mac's Geneva screen font.

scale
The process of deriving a required type size from a bitmap of a different size.

serif
A line crossing the main strokes of a character. Serifs lead the eye across a line of type. Serif typefaces include Times, Palatino, Century Schoolbook, and the Mac's New York screen font.

small caps
Capital letters with the same height as the lowercase characters.

subhead
A heading within the text that's used to split up lengthy passages and draw the reader's attention.

thin space
A fixed amount of space equal to half an en space.

tracking
Also called *track kerning,* uniformly adjusting letter and word spacing over a range of text. Track kerning generally adds space between characters in very small sizes and decreases space between text in large sizes.

Type 1 font
The most common and preferable format for PostScript downloadable fonts.

Type 2 font
There is no such beast — Type 2 was reserved for a font technology that never panned out.

Type 3 font
A less-common PostScript outline font format that generally delivers inferior results on laser printers.

x-height
The height of a typeface's lowercase letters, excluding ascenders and descenders.

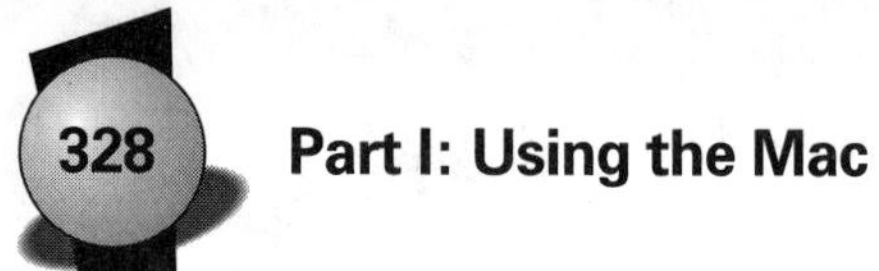

CHAPTER TWELVE

Painting, Drawing, and Graphing

- Object-oriented versus bitmapped: how graphics programs work
- How to put a graphics program to work — even if you aren't a Mac Monet
- Creating special effects with Macromedia FreeHand and Adobe Illustrator
- A survival guide to graphics file formats
- How to create great graphs

Word processors may be the Macintosh world's most popular applications, but graphics programs are the most appealing. Start up a word processor for a few friends and they'll probably show lukewarm interest. But fire up a graphics program and watch them line up for their turn at the mouse. People who would never dream of standing in front of an easel and canvas suddenly become artists-in-training, spilling paint all over the screen.

Perhaps graphics programs are enticing because people traditionally view a computer as a tool for calculating, not as an artistic medium. Or maybe it's the sense of experimentation that draws you in. Move the mouse, get a circle. Oops, erase that mistake. Hey, the little spray can works just like a real one.

Ever since MacPaint blazed the trail in 1984, graphics programs have been instrumental in the success. You can create images with the Mac in more ways than you can process words — proof of the machine's graphical bent. In this chapter, I explore some of the technicalities behind Macintosh graphics and spotlight the features you find in the most popular graphics programs. And because not everyone has artistic aspirations, I include tips throughout the chapter that describe other ways to put graphics software to work.

Putting a Graphics Program to Work #1: Spruce Up a Business Graphic

The graphs and charts that programs such as Microsoft Excel and Lotus 1-2-3 create are actually object-oriented drawings. You can use the Clipboard to move them into a draw program for further polishing.

To copy a graph, select it and choose Copy from the Edit menu. Start or switch to your graphics program and choose Paste. If you're working in an integrated program, simply create a new graphics document and then choose Paste.

When you paste a graph, the drawing program treats it as a single object. To modify an individual element such as a bar or axis line, you need to ungroup the object by selecting the graph and then choosing your program's Ungroup command. (In most drawing and integrated programs, the Ungroup and Group commands are in the Arrange menu.)

After you ungroup the graph, what changes should you make? Try adding gradient fills to bars or pie wedges. Change the font, size, or style of the graph's labels and legends (you can do so in your spreadsheet or graphing program, too). Add icons, logos, or scanned images. Replace the bars in a bar chart with icons that represent the data (for example, use automobile icons in a car-sales chart); use a clip art collection or characters from pictorial fonts such as Zapf Dingbats or Zeal.

Different Strokes

All graphics programs share the same basic operating style. Start one up, and you get a new, untitled document window surrounded by one or more tool palettes for creating various shapes — circles, rectangles, lines, arcs, and so on — and for adding text to an image. To create a shape, you click the tool for that shape, move the mouse pointer into the window's drawing area, and drag (see Figure 12-1 "Electronic Easels").

Graphics programs come in two basic flavors — *bitmapped* and *object oriented.* Their different approaches to storing and printing images suit each type of program to specific purposes. For this reason, some programs combine both approaches. In any case, understanding the differences between bitmapped and object-oriented graphics is an important first step in choosing graphics software and using it effectively.

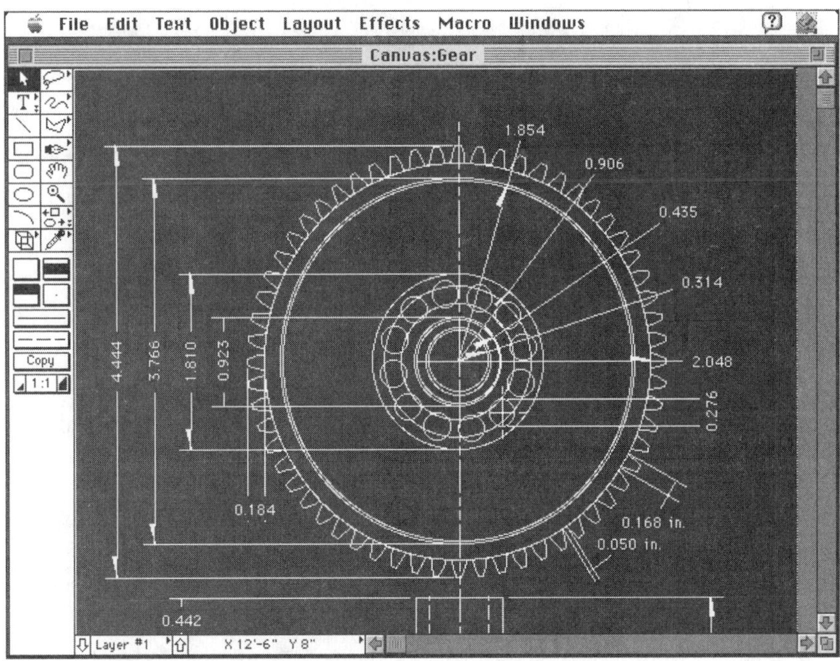

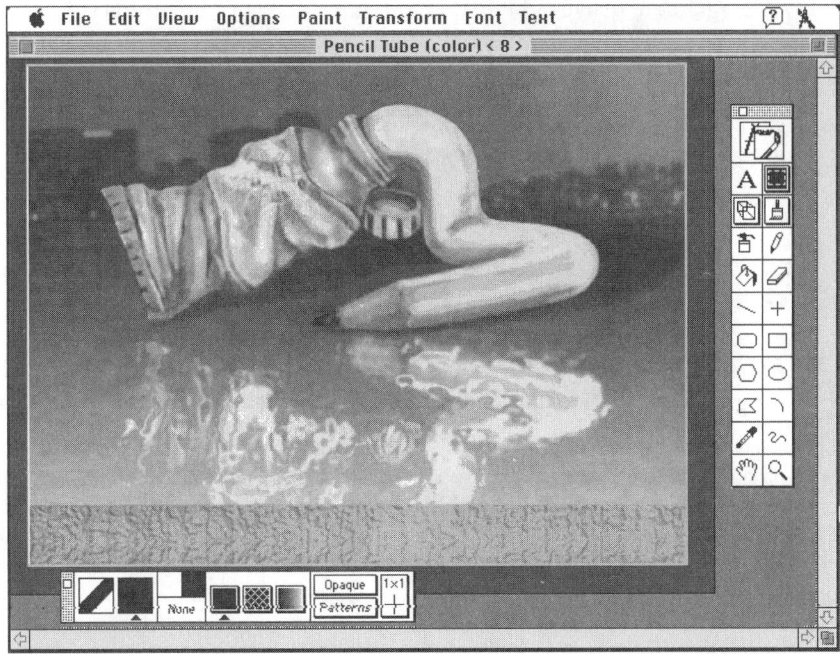

Figure 12-1: Electronic Easels Two popular graphics applications: Deneba Software's Canvas (top) and Adobe SuperPaint (bottom). Note the similar tools that each provides for drawing, selecting, and modifying images.

Try Your Hand at Digital Drawing

The Best of BMUG collection on the *Macworld Power User Clinic* CD contains some great free and shareware painting and drawing programs. They're in the Graphics folder.

Also on the CD is a copy of NIH Image, an amazing freeware image processing program. See the "On the CD" box in the next chapter for more details on this program.Bitmapped, or paint, programs

Bitmapped, or paint programs

Bitmapped graphics, or *paint*, programs store images as a series of bits — ones and zeros — in the Mac's memory. With monochrome (black-and-white) paint programs such as the original MacPaint, each screen dot, or *pixel*, in an image corresponds to one bit in the Mac's memory. If a dot is black, its bit is a one; if a dot is white, it's a zero. Think of a sheet of graph paper. Each square is a bit, and you create images by darkening some squares and leaving others white. To change part of the drawing, get out your pencil and eraser and change black squares to white ones and vice versa.

Color paint programs such Fractal Design's Painter work similarly, except that they assign more than one bit to each pixel. It's as if you laid several sheets of graph paper on top of each other and selectively blackened squares on each layer. The on-off combinations of a pixel's bits tell the Mac what color that pixel is (see Figure 12-2 "Bitmaps versus Objects").

Putting a Graphics Program to Work #2: Make Quick-Reference Cards

Can't remember which dialog box contains that certain option or which menu holds the command you need? Use the Mac's snapshot feature (press ⌘-Shift-3) to create a PICT image of the screen; then annotate the image with text. Print the result, and you have a custom quick-reference card. The Mac names snapshot files *Picture 1, Picture 2, Picture 3,* and so on.

The snapshot feature can capture color screens, although it can't capture pulled-down menus or any event that involves pressing the mouse button. To capture pulled-down menus, you need a utility such as Mainstay's Capture. See Chapter 24 for more details about utilities.

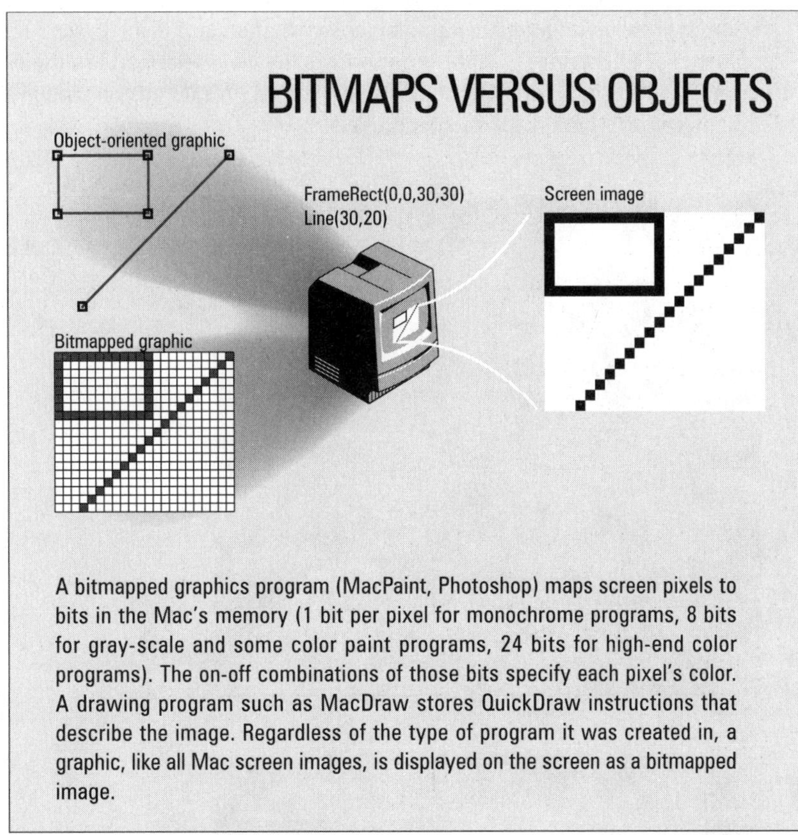

A bitmapped graphics program (MacPaint, Photoshop) maps screen pixels to bits in the Mac's memory (1 bit per pixel for monochrome programs, 8 bits for gray-scale and some color paint programs, 24 bits for high-end color programs). The on-off combinations of those bits specify each pixel's color. A drawing program such as MacDraw stores QuickDraw instructions that describe the image. Regardless of the type of program it was created in, a graphic, like all Mac screen images, is displayed on the screen as a bitmapped image.

Figure 12-2: Bitmaps versus Objects

Image-processing programs

Close cousins to paint programs are *image-processing* programs such as Adobe Photoshop and Quark XPosure. Like color paint programs, they work with bitmapped images containing multiple bits per pixel. But image-processing programs are designed primarily for retouching and modifying images created by a scanner or video camera. Chapter 13 contains details about image-processing programs and the up-and-coming field of filmless photography.

To use an image-processing program effectively, it's best to have a Mac capable of displaying millions of colors — or, technically speaking, a Mac that supports 24-bit color. If you use an image-processing program on a Mac that supports only 16-bit video (thousands of colors) or 8-bit video (a paltry 256 colors), the Mac must use a technique called *dithering* to simulate colors that it can't display (see Figure 12-3 "Darn that Dithering"). To find out how many colors your Mac supports, check your Monitors control panel. And see Chapter 29 for details on video upgrades that enhance your Mac's display capabilities.

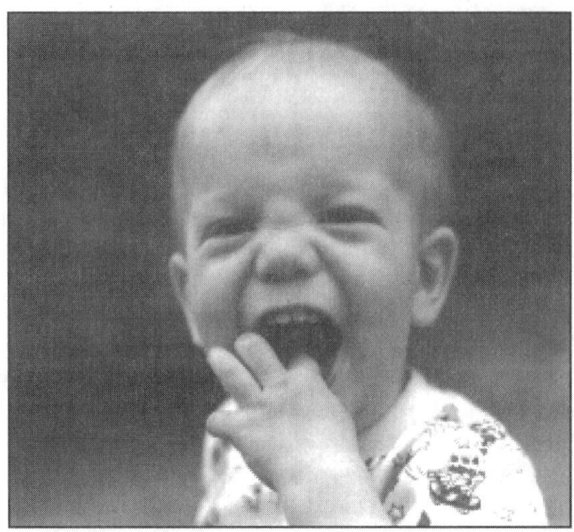

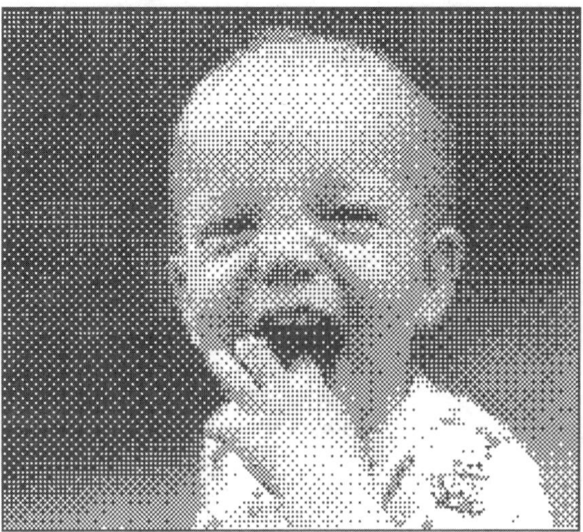

Figure 12-3: Darn that Dithering
Dithering is the process of simulating colors or gray shades through the use of dot patterns. This extreme example shows the difference between a true gray-scale display (top) and a dithered black-and-white display (bottom).

Creating a Zoom-Text Effect with FreeHand

Want to spice up a poster or advertisement? Try creating a zoom-text effect, in which a line of text appears to be zooming toward you. Macromedia FreeHand provides a zoom-text feature. The steps in this box show you how to use it. (Note that using a zoom-text effect lengthens printing time.)

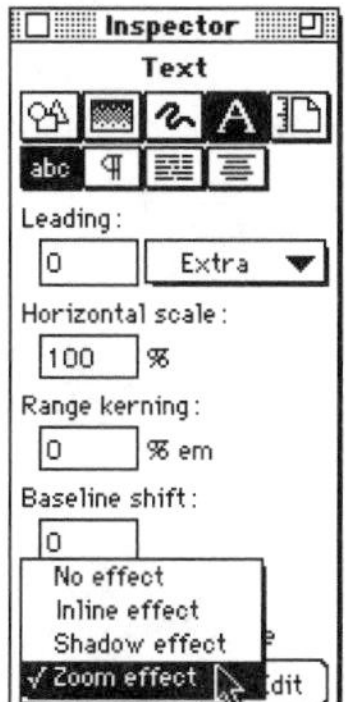

To create a zoom-text effect:

1. **Type the text you want to zoom by using FreeHand's Text tool and format it in the desired font, size, and style.**
2. **Open the Text Inspector window and then click the character icon.**
3. **In the Text Inspector window, choose Zoom Effect from the Effects pop-up menu.**
   FreeHand adds a zoom effect to the text.
4. **To fine-tune the zoom effect, click the Edit button at the bottom of the Text Inspector window.**
   The Zoom Effect dialog box lets you specify the beginning and ending colors for the effect as well as the horizontal and vertical offsets for the text — that is, the location of the zoom text in relation to the original text.

Drawing Distinctions

When you create an image, such as a circle, with a paint or image-processing program, the circle loses its identity as a circle and becomes simply a series of pixels as soon as you deselect it. You can't change the circle's size, line thickness, or any other characteristics; instead, you must erase its pixels and create a new circle.

Not so with images created by an object-oriented, or *draw*, program. Programs such as Claris's MacDraw series and ClarisDraw treat images not as a series of bits but as a series of drawing instructions for QuickDraw, the fundamental graphics routines that are responsible for everything you see on the Mac's screen. When you draw a circle, the program stores a set of QuickDraw instructions that describe the circle's characteristics — its radius, line thickness, pattern fill, and so on. To change the circle's size, you simply select and resize it. The program then updates the circle's QuickDraw instructions. It's as if you're creating images not by blackening squares on graph paper but by creating a list of instructions that tell your pen — the electron beam in a monitor, the print wires in an ImageWriter, the ink nozzles in a StyleWriter, or the laser in a LaserWriter or imagesetter — how and where to move.

The same pixels-versus-objects issue also applies to text. With paint programs, editing or reformatting text means retyping it. Draw programs let you use the same editing and formatting techniques as a word processor.

Grouping objects

A finished drawing consists of numerous separate objects — sometimes thousands of them. But what if you want to move or modify several objects as a group? For example, after drawing a floor plan for a bathroom, you may want to duplicate the layout for another bathroom elsewhere in the house. One solution is to select all the objects and then copy and paste, but a better technique is to use the Group command that all drawing programs provide.

A Group command tells a drawing program: "From now on, treat the objects I've selected as a single object." When you group objects, you can select, move, and modify them as if they were one object (see Figure 12-4 "Before and After Grouping").

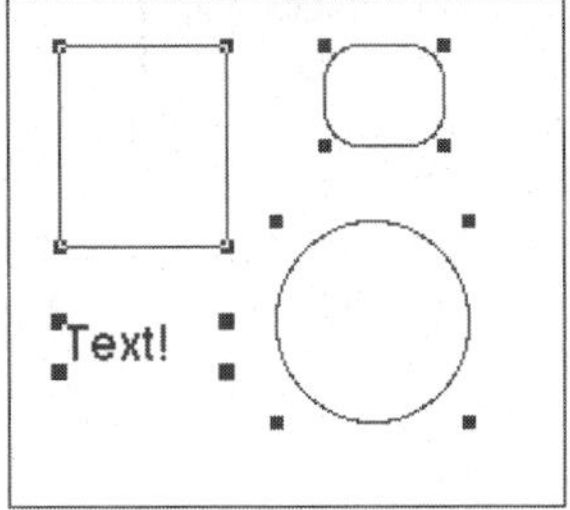

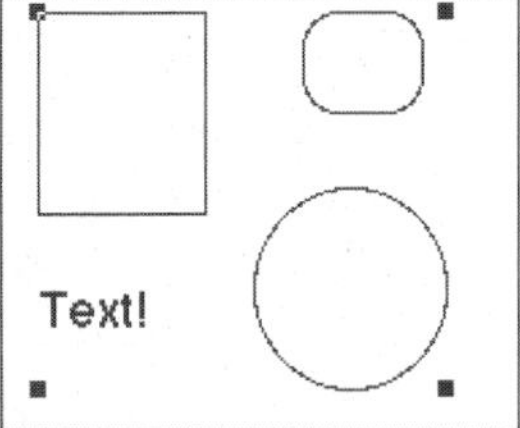

Figure 12-4: Before and After Grouping The Group command tells a drawing program to treat a series of selected objects (top) as one object (bottom). After grouping objects, you can select, resize, and reposition them as if they were one object.

When you group objects into one object, you can't modify an individual item within the group. For example, if you decide to make the bathroom sink larger after you've grouped all the bathroom objects, you can't simply select the sink and resize it. In order to modify an object within a group, select the group and choose your program's Ungroup command.

Selecting elements

Speaking of selecting, drawing and painting programs each provide their own types of tools and techniques for selecting parts of an image. The Backgrounder box "Graphics Selection Tools" describes the most common tools you encounter and provides some tips for using them.

Putting a Graphics Program to Work #3: Make a Start-Up Screen

You can replace the Mac OS's start-up screen with any image you like. Many monochrome paint programs, including MacPaint and SuperPaint, can create start-up screens. The image must be named *StartupScreen* and reside in the top level of the System Folder — not within any folders such as the Extensions folder.

You can also create color start-up screens. For the Mac to display a color start-up screen, the image file must be saved in a special format (technically, it must be a PICT file that contains a PICT resource with an ID number of 0 — that's the number zero). Several popular programs, including Canvas, SuperPaint, and PixelPaint, can create start-up screen PICT files. You can also create start-up screen PICT files with a shareware program called The Giffer, by Steve Blackstock.

If you have more than one monitor, you can specify which monitor you want to use for the start-up screen. You may want to do so if you have one color monitor and one full-page monochrome monitor and you want the start-up screen to appear on the color monitor.

To control where the start-up screen appears, open the Monitors control panel and press the Option key. When you press Option, a Mac with a smiling face appears on the monitor displaying the start-up screen. If you want the start-up screen to appear on a different monitor, continue pressing Option while you drag the smiling face to that monitor.

Graphics Selection Tools

Painting and drawing programs provide several tools for selecting parts of a drawing. The illustrations in this box show the most common graphics selection tools and techniques.

Selection Techniques in Paint Programs

Tool	What it Does	Example	Tips
(Lasso)	Selects irregularly shaped areas		You don't have to completely enclose the area you're selecting; when you release the mouse button, the program completes the selection for you.
(Marquee)	Selects rectangular areas		Double-click to select an entire image.

Selection Techniques in Draw Programs

Tool	What it Does	Ways to Use	Example
(Arrow)	Activates selection mode, deactivating previously active tool	Click an object to select it	Object 1
		To select multiple objects, draw a selection marquee around them	Object 1 Object 2 Object 3
		– or –	
		Click the first object, and then Shift-click subsequent objects	Object 1 Object 2

Hard Copy Differences

Another big difference between paint and draw programs becomes evident when you print images, especially on a laser printer or imagesetter. With paint programs, images are tied to a specific resolution, a fixed number of dots per inch (dpi). For example, a MacPaint image's resolution matches that of the Mac's screen — 72 dpi. Print a 72-dpi image on a 300-dpi laser printer, and you notice jagged-edged text and shapes. (You can even out the jaggies somewhat by using the Page Setup dialog box's Graphics Smoothing option, but the results still aren't great. Another option is to print the image at 92 percent of the original size.)

Some paint programs let you create bitmaps with higher resolutions (such as 300 dpi), but that solution isn't perfect either. For one thing, a 300-dpi image is still locked into a specific resolution. For another, high-resolution bitmap images devour memory and disk space — a 300-dpi 8½ x 11-inch monochrome image uses about a megabyte of disk space. Multiply that by eight and more for gray-scale and color images.

ImageWriter Printing Problems: When to Use Tall Adjusted

ImageWriters are prone to a subtler problem when printing bitmapped images. When you choose the ImageWriter's Faster or Best print-quality options, the ImageWriter prints roughly 80 horizontal dots per inch. When you print a 72-dpi bitmapped image on an ImageWriter, the slight difference in resolution can cause bitmapped images to appear distorted, compressed by about 13 percent — not a lot, but enough to turn a circle into an oval.

The solution: select the Tall Adjusted option in the Page Setup dialog box. Tall Adjusted compensates for the difference in resolution, but at a price: Text is widened along with the adjusted picture. A 5-inch column of text expands to over 5½ inches.

Putting a Graphics Program to Work #4: Create Organizational Charts

Many businesses rely on organizational charts to visually spell out the pecking order. You can create an organizational chart by using the box and text tools in any drawing program, but if you have to revise organizational charts frequently (Apple, take note), consider a program that's built for the job, such as Kaetron's OrgChart Express. Adobe IntelliDraw and ClarisImpact also have smart linking features that streamline the creation of organizational charts.

An organizational chart is a type of *tree chart.* You can also use tree charts for family trees, block diagrams, and time lines. Many presentation programs can also create tree charts. Use the program's built-in outliner to specify the reporting structure, with subordinates indented from their supervisors. Then tell the program to create a tree chart.

Images created with draw programs, on the other hand, tend to use far less disk space and memory and are not tied to a specific resolution. You can print the same image on an ImageWriter, StyleWriter, LaserWriter, or 2540-dpi imagesetter and get progressively better results. You play back the same drawing instructions each time you print, but with a progressively sharper electronic pen.

Object-oriented graphics can also be resized without the distortion and undesirable patterns to which bitmapped graphics are prone. And because draw programs know that text is text, they can take advantage of the tack-sharp outline fonts used by PostScript printers, Adobe Type Manager, and Apple's TrueType. (See Chapters 11 and 30 for more details about printer font outlines.)

Putting a Graphics Program to Work #5: Add Graphics to a Database

Most database managers let you create custom forms and paste images from the Clipboard into your form designs. Use this technique to add a logo to a form. Create the logo in a graphics program, and then copy and paste it into the form.

And as explained in Chapter 7, Claris's FileMaker Pro lets you create on-screen buttons that execute scripts when clicked. You can create basic buttons in FileMaker Pro, but if you want a flashier look, create them in a drawing program and then use the Clipboard to paste them into a FileMaker Pro layout. Buttons with graduated fills or 3-D shading can give a fashionable look to your database.

Choosing Between Paint and Pen

So how do you decide whether you need a paint or a draw program?

When to use a paint program

A paint program is the tool of choice when you need to create images with photographic details, fine shading, or brush-like effects. Paint and image-processing programs are also required for working with scanned images because these images are always bitmapped.

All paint programs provide tools for drawing simple shapes, selecting a portion of an image to move or copy to the Mac's Clipboard, and zooming in on an image to work with individual pixels. Paint programs provide a variety of brush shapes, a pencil tool, and a spray can for creating on-screen graffiti. Advanced programs such as Fractal Design's Painter provide these tools as well as tools for obtaining charcoal, airbrush, and watercolor effects (see Figure 12-5 "Painting with Painter").

But calling Painter an "advanced paint program" is like calling Michaelangelo an "advanced painter." Over the years, Fractal Design has expanded Painter's features to provide an amazing array of capabilities. Painter's innovative *image hose* lets you

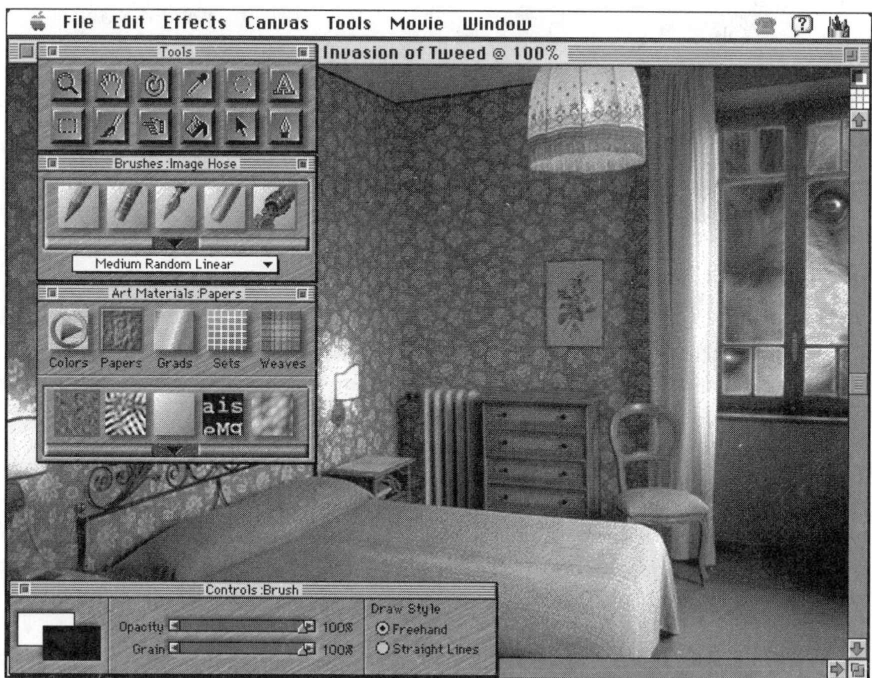

Figure 12-5: Painting with Painter Fractal Design designed Painter to electronically re-create the tools and techniques of traditional painting. With the brush palette shown here, you can customize the operation of Painter's tools. Fractal's Sketcher provides similar natural-media tools for gray-scale work.

apply not dabs of digital paint, but actual images, such as clouds or flowers. Painter also addresses the multimedia world, with features that let you do frame-by-frame painting on QuickTime movies. (The image hose also supports QuickTime movies, enabling you to "paint" with a movie.) And Painter can also handle the kinds of image-editing tasks Adobe Photoshop is used for. (Indeed, beginning with version 3.1, Painter is compatible with Photoshop 3 documents and layers.)

When to use a draw program

Draw programs are better suited to creating line drawings such as architectural floor plans, newspaper graphics, and technical drawings. Programs like Deneba Software's Canvas, and Claris's MacDraw II and ClarisDraw provide features that help you create drawings to scale. In most draw programs, you also find *dimensioning* features that automatically display an object's dimensions in your choice of measuring systems.

Layering features let you divide a drawing into layers, each of which is like a sheet of clear plastic. If you're creating a house floor plan, you may use one layer to show the location of furniture, another to show carpets and rugs, and another to show lamps. You can selectively show and hide layers to examine one detail or show the big picture. And because many drawings involve reusing the same shapes or symbols — chairs, bathroom fixtures, doors, windows — most drawing programs provide *symbol library* features that let you store and retrieve often-used shapes.

Putting a Graphics Program to Work #6: Create Special Text Effects

It's easy to stretch or condense text by using a draw program in conjunction with a desktop publishing program or word processor. First, type the text in the draw program. Next, select the entire block of text (not its individual characters) with your draw program's arrow-shaped selection tool and then copy the selection to the Clipboard. Switch to a word processor or publishing program and choose Paste, and you have a picture of the text that can be resized.

If you don't have Adobe Type Manager and you aren't using TrueType fonts, the resized text will probably look ragged on-screen, but it should print with sharp edges. Note that this technique may not work with every combination of word processor and drawing program. For example, when you paste text from MacDraw II or MacDraw Pro into Microsoft Word, it appears as conventional text, not as a graphic.

Illustration programs

Adobe Illustrator and Macromedia FreeHand approach drawing from the standpoint of a graphic designer or technical illustrator, not a draftsperson. The technical illustrations you see in *Macworld* and in this book (such as Figure 12-2 "Bitmaps versus Objects") are produced by using FreeHand and Illustrator. You don't find automatic dimensioning features in these programs, but you find features geared toward the production of technical illustrations, package designs, and advertising art.

You also find extensive text-manipulation features and options for taking advantage of PostScript's printing prowess. For example, FreeHand, Illustrator, and MacDraw Pro can all create *graduated fills* — patterns in which one shade smoothly blends into another. (The shading that appears in many of the illustrations in this book is a graduated fill.)

Illustrator introduced the Macintosh world to Bezier curves — a method of describing the path that a digital pen travels as it inscribes lines, curves, and shapes (see Figure 12-6 "How Bezier Curves Work"). When Illustrator debuted back in 1987, critics claimed that its method of drawing curves was too complex. History and the marketplace have proven them wrong, as almost all current illustration programs use the Bezier technique.

Putting a Graphics Program to Work #7: Make a Poster

Most draw programs can print poster-size drawings by tiling — printing sections of the drawing on individual pages that you attach to each other. You can use this feature to create large posters — up to 81 square feet in Canvas.

If you print a huge poster on a typical laser printer, be prepared for an hour or so of taping or gluing to assemble the tiles. A better alternative for frequent poster-makers is a large-format ink-jet printer, such as Hewlett-Packard's DesignJet, which can print on pages as large as 2 x 9 feet — in color, no less. (A larger-format model is also available that handles 3 x 9 feet output.) LaserMaster Corporation's DisplayMaker is a similar device.

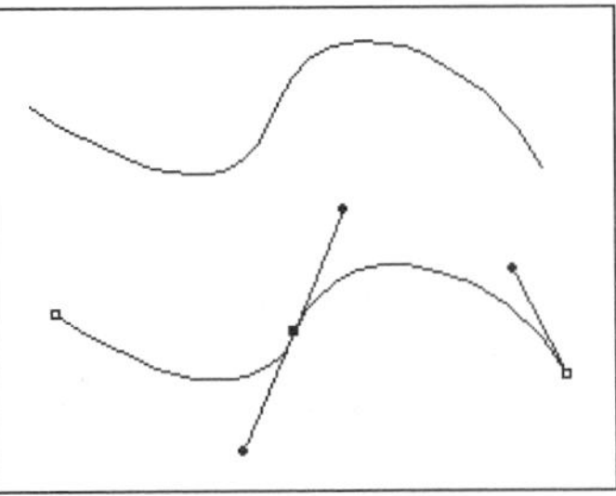

Figure 12-6: How Bezier Curves Work
The shape of a Bezier curve (top) is determined by its control points (bottom). By dragging the control points, you can reshape the curve. Imagine the curve as a piece of soft wire and each control point as a nail around which the wire is wound.

Text as a design element

For many illustration jobs — product packaging, advertisements, company logos — type is just another form of graphic. Illustrator, FreeHand, and Deneba's Canvas also let you dissect Type 1 and TrueType printer font outlines to break characters down into their individual curves and lines. After converting a font into outlines, you can reshape characters — perhaps to create a company logo or package design. Illustrator and FreeHand let you create linked text blocks and flow text across multiple columns as if you were using a publishing program. Both programs even provide automatic hyphenation features.

All three programs can also bind text to an arbitrarily shaped path — handy for printing text in a circle on the label of a compact disc, for example. Some of the Step-by-Step boxes in this chapter show you how to create these and other popular special text effects.

Putting a Graphics Program to Work #8: Create a Publication

With their rulers, line-drawing tools, and alignment features, draw programs make serviceable publishing programs, especially for small jobs such as brochures or one-page fact sheets. Many programs even have spelling checkers. Integrated programs such as ClarisWorks and Microsoft Works are particularly well suited to basic publishing, especially if your publications require graphs or data from a spreadsheet or database. Both programs (as well as Adobe Illustrator and Macromedia FreeHand) let you link text blocks and flow text across multiple columns.

Mixed Media

Fortunately, choosing between paint and draw graphics isn't an either/or proposition. Programs such as Deneba's Canvas and Adobe SuperPaint provide both painting and drawing features, as do integrated packages such as ClarisWorks and Microsoft Works. You can also move images between separate paint and draw programs by using the Clipboard. You can paste a bitmapped image into a drawing program to annotate it with text. You can also paste an object-oriented drawing into a bitmapped program, but it becomes just another bitmap floating in a sea of pixels.

Several drawing and illustration programs also provide *autotrace* features that enable you to create an object-oriented version of a bitmapped image. For example, you can scan your corporate logo and then autotrace the resulting bitmapped image.

Remember, you can combine paint or draw programs with other types of software. You can use the Clipboard to paste images into a word processor, page-layout program, data manager, and any other program that supports graphics. Because images can be large, however, you should probably rely on disk files instead of the Clipboard to import and export images. If you take this route, familiarize yourself with Macintosh graphics-file formats to choose the one that represents your image accurately and takes up the least amount of storage space (see Table 12-1).

Putting a Graphics Program to Work #9: Create a Presentation

Claris's MacDraw series, ClarisDraw, ClarisImpact, and ClarisWorks provide features for creating overhead transparencies and slides. MacDraw Pro, ClarisDraw, ClarisImpact, and ClarisWorks also provide features for giving a presentation. You can, for example, specify special visual effects for slide transitions, such as a wipe, in which one image is pushed off-screen by another. In some of these programs, a presentation can even contain QuickTime movies. If you give presentations on a regular basis, you'll probably be better served by a program such as Adobe Persuasion or Microsoft PowerPoint (both are covered in Chapter 15). But if you're an occasional presenter, a drawing program may be all you need.

Table 12-1
Storing Pictures

Format	*Best for*	*Comments*
EPS	Text and bitmapped or object-oriented graphics to be printed on a PostScript printer	Widely supported in both Mac and PC worlds. Generally used to export images from PostScript printer drawing programs or scanning applications to desktop publications.
GIF	Bitmapped images	Developed by CompuServe for exchanging graphics between different systems. Allows up to 8 bits per pixel. GIF translators are available for most computers.
JPEG	Bitmapped images	Uses compression to reduce storage requirements.
MacPaint	72-dpi bitmapped images	Widely supported, even by some DOS PC graphics and publishing programs.
PICT	Bitmapped or object-oriented graphics	Usually used to transfer object-oriented graphics between programs.
PICT2	Bitmapped or object-oriented graphics	A newer version of the PICT format that supports color.
RIFF	Bitmapped images, especially scanned	Developed by Fractal Design and used by Painter and Sketcher. Supported by QuarkXPress, but not by Adobe PageMaker. Files are usually smaller than TIFF counterparts.
TIFF	Bitmapped images, especially scanned	Widely supported in both Mac and PC worlds. Able to represent color and gray-scale images at virtually any resolution. Files can be large.

Putting a Graphics Program to Work #10: Modify Clip Art

Many companies sell libraries of canned illustrations that you can use in desktop publications. Instead of just using a clip art drawing as is, copy it to a graphics program and personalize it — add some shading, slant it by using a shear tool, or flip it horizontally. You can also autotrace a bitmapped clip art image to improve its appearance.

Focus on Charts and Graphs

Future archaeologists may be unable to decipher our written languages, but at least they'll have pie charts to learn where our tax dollars went. Charts and graphs from spreadsheet and graphics programs like Microsoft Excel and Lotus 1-2-3 have become the hieroglyphics of our time. Printed as is or spruced up with a drawing program, they provide at-a-glance insights into tables of yawn-worthy numbers.

A good graph is worth a thousand numbers and can illustrate trends and relationships far more effectively. Why? Over the millennia, people have become adept at locating the edges of shapes and discerning the size and color differences between them. Skills that helped our ancestors hunt and gather now help us track previous quarters' sales results. Now that's evolution.

All major spreadsheet and integrated programs have built-in graphing features. You also find graphing features in presentation programs such as Microsoft PowerPoint and Gold Disk's Astound as well as in Adobe Illustrator and even Microsoft Word. And there are stand-alone graphing packages such as Computer Associates' CA-Cricket Graph and DeltaPoint's DeltaGraph Professional.

Each of these programs can create several types of graph: bar, column, line, scatter, radar, and pie. Which to use, and when? In this section, I provide pointers to help you match the data to the graph along with tips for creating graphs that get your message across.

Graph basics

The first step involves choosing a graph format that illustrates what your numbers represent. Are you trying to show where each research-and-development dollar went? Do you want to illustrate trends in population growth or market share? Do you need to show the correlation between population growth and freeway congestion? Do want to compare the sales figures for each of several regional offices? Each scenario calls for a different type of graph. Figure 12-7 "A Field Guide to Graphs" shows the most popular graph formats and describes what each is best for.

Field Guide to Graphs	
Graph type	Description
	Area — shows the relative change of values over time. Similar to line, but emphasizes the amount of change.
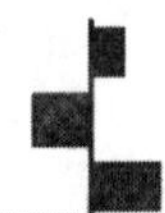	Bar — compares items or shows individual values at a given time.
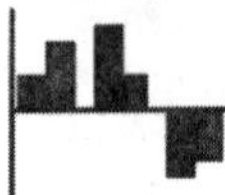	Column — compares items or shows variation in values over time. Similar to bar, but positions categories horizontally and values vertically.
	Line — shows trends or changes in values over time. Similar to area, but emphasizes the passage of time rather than the amount of change.
	High, low, close — a type of line graph, used for stock quotes, that shows the highest, lowest, and closing value of a stock.
	Pie — shows the relationship of parts to a whole. Always contains just one data series.
	Radar — shows data changes relative to a center point; useful for making relative comparisons between items. Each category has a value axis that radiates from the center point; lines connect a given series' data markers.
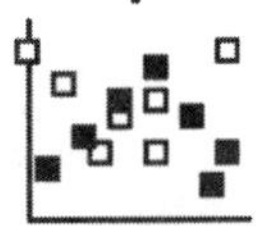	Scatter — shows the relationship between the values in several data series; useful for finding trends or determining if one set of values depends on or affects another.
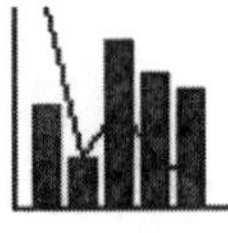	Combination — combines a main chart and an overlay chart to compare two data series — for example, actual sales versus projections.

Figure 12-7: A Field Guide to Graphs

Graphing Features Everywhere

Although you usually find graphing features in spreadsheet and integrated programs, they do pop up elsewhere. Adobe Illustrator can create graphs, and one word processor, Microsoft Word, includes a graphing program. It's called — can you guess? — Microsoft Graph, and it can generate a graph based on data contained in a Microsoft Word table (there's that close relationship between tables and graphs again).

Microsoft Graph also supports the Microsoft OLE data-exchange system. Double-click a graph that you've inserted in a Word document, and Word automatically starts Graph, which opens the graph. Make your changes and close the graph, and the new version appears in your document. (See Chapter 27 for more details about OLE.) Microsoft Graph doesn't have all the graphing features of Microsoft Excel, but it uses far less memory, making it more practical to run Graph and Word simultaneously.

For industrial-strength graphing features, check out Computer Associates' CA-Cricket Graph III. The latest version of this veteran graphing package is laden with drawing and text-annotation features — ideal for creating presentation materials. Cricket Graph III provides a built-in data sheet into which you can paste row-and-column data that you want to graph. Another powerhouse graphing program is DeltaPoint's DeltaGraph Professional.

What does a stand-alone graphing program bring to the table? A wider selection of graph formats, for one thing. Excel provides a dozen or so graph types, while DeltaPoint Professional, for example, provides 57 varieties. DeltaPoint Professional can also create pictographs (graphs whose data series are represented by icons) and provides more formatting options to give you more control over a graph's appearance. And if you frequently create a particular type of graph, you can create templates or macros that automate repetitive formatting chores.

Stand-alone graphing packages typically provide a better selection of formats and features for scientific and statistical graphing. For hard-core scientific and statistical work, however, you might turn to a program such as Systat's Systat, which can even create animated QuickTime movies that show how, for example, a data set changes over time. Other technical and scientific programs with graphing features include WaveMetric's Igor, Synergy Software's KaleidaGraph, Jandel Scientific's SigmaPlot, Abacus Concepts' MacSpin, and Wolfram Research's Mathematica.

By the way, graduating to a stand-alone graphing program doesn't mean throwing away the data that's already locked up in spreadsheet cells. All graphing programs can import data from Excel and other spreadsheets.

The elements of a graph

No matter which program you use to create graphs, you generally begin by specifying the *data series* — the lists of numbers that the graph represents. A line chart showing a month's worth of closing stock prices contains one data series. So does a pie chart depicting where each tax dollar went. On the other hand, a bar chart comparing the quarterly profits of General Motors, Ford, and Chrysler contains three data series.

Most types of graphs have two axes — a horizontal *X* and a vertical *Y* axis. (Have trouble remembering which is which? Remember that the letter *Y* has stems that point up and down — it's *vertical.*) The categories of data — for example, the sales quarters you're comparing — are usually plotted along the horizontal axis. The data values themselves — the sales figures — are usually plotted on the vertical axis. Indeed, the X axis is often called the *category axis,* while the Y axis is often called the *value axis.* (Note that these two axes are reversed in bar graphs: The categories are stacked vertically, while the bars extend horizontally to indicate values.)

Each data item in a graph — the first quarter's sales figures, the percentage of a tax dollar that goes to space shuttle toilet design — is a *data point.* In most programs with graphing features, the category names and their data point values are stored in a grid of rows and columns — either in a spreadsheet document or in a data window that looks a lot like a spreadsheet (see Figure 12-8 "From Grid to Graph").

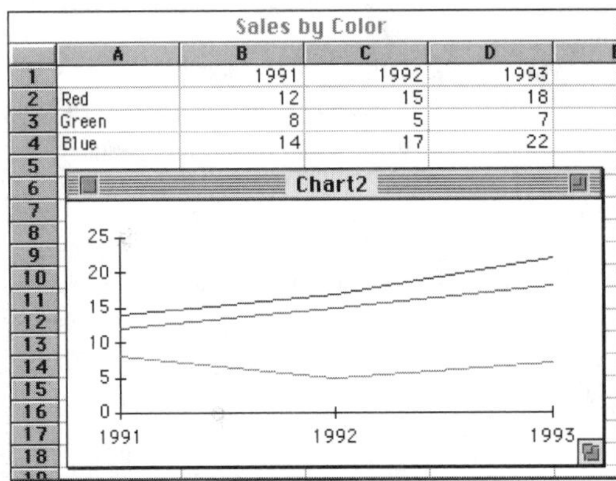

Figure 12-8: From Grid to Graph A spreadsheet's row-and-column orientation makes it a natural place to store data in a graph.

Tips for titling graphs

Every graph has the basic components I just described, but most graphs can also benefit from additional furnishings. A *title* is one of the most important — it should not only tell the reader what the graph is about, but it should also summarize the graph's key message.

Most people miss that second point and create bland titles like *1995 Sales Summary by Territory* and *Home Sales by County.* Better versions of these titles are *1995 Sales Up 10% in East* and *Lake County Leads in Home Sales.* If you're creating a graph that's intended to persuade, you may even want to make the title a bit assertive: *Western Territory Needs More Sales Reps.*

When titling a graph, ask yourself what the graph's primary message is and then name accordingly. If you can't think of a primary message, you may not need a graph. If the graph has multiple messages of equal importance, you may want to split your data into multiple graphs. Doing so creates opportunities for creative titles that tie the graphs together. You've probably seen this approach in newspapers: One graph may be titled *Inventories Grew Last Quarter...*, while an adjacent one is titled *...While Exports Fell.* The ellipsis (...) after and before the titles reinforce the notion that the two graphs present related data. (Don't put any space between the periods in the ellipses, and use only three periods.)

Choosing colors and patterns

When a graph has multiple data series, you want to set each series apart by using different colors, patterns, or gray shades for its bars, wedges, or lines. Whether you opt for colors, patterns, or gray shades depends on the graph's final resting place. Patterns or gray shades are preferable for monochrome-printed output, while colors are better for slides and electronic presentations.

If you're using patterns, be sure to choose ones that differ significantly. Studies indicate that the brain has trouble differentiating between patterns whose frequency is less than 2 to 1: At a quick glance, a diagonal line pattern with 8 lines per inch looks a lot like a pattern with 11 lines per inch, but it's clearly different from a pattern with 16 lines per inch. Rather than fuss over pattern frequency, consider using gray shades instead. Patterns can appear to shimmer on the page and distract the eye from the data.

For color graphs, consider choosing hues that complement the data: red for a bar graph of a summer heat wave, for example, or green for a profitable quarter and red for a bad one. Or you can color one significant element in an otherwise monochrome chart: your company's performance in a color that matches your logo, the competition's in black and white. If you use multiple colors, choose sharply contrasting ones — many people have trouble distinguishing between similar hues.

Legendary advice

Any graph with more than one data series is a candidate for a *legend* — a key that tells readers which bars, wedges, or columns relate to which data series names. I confess to a bias against legends — graphs that require jumping between the graph elements and a legend seem less forceful and require more effort to interpret. When the graph contains only a few data series, consider labeling bars, wedges, or whatnots with callouts within the graph itself (see Figure 12-9 "Living Legends"). This approach may not be practical in graphs with many data series.

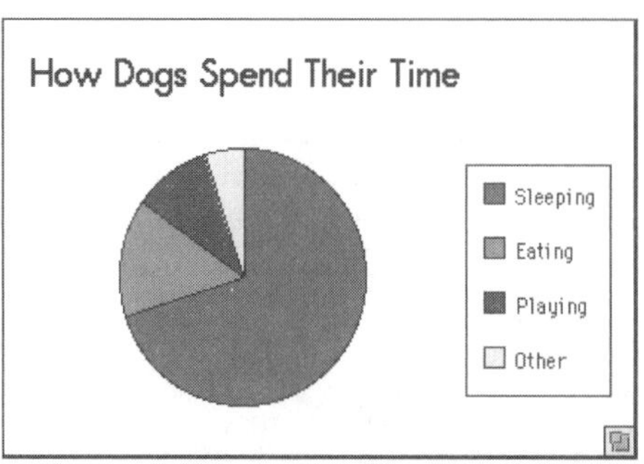

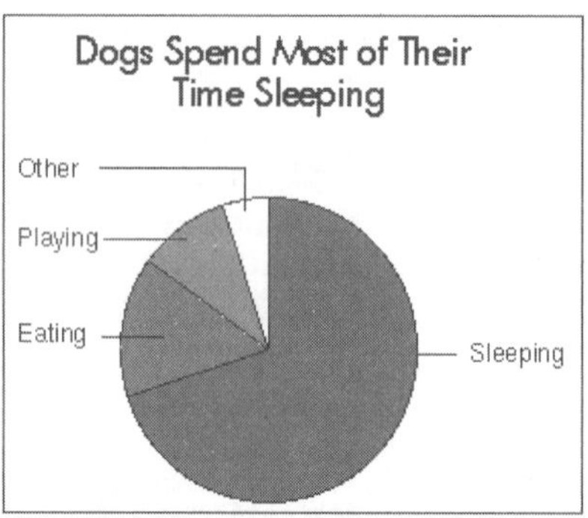

Figure 12-9: Living Legends The pie chart on the right reflects two principles of good graph design that are lacking in the left pie chart. The right chart's title summarizes the chart's message instead of merely summarizing its topic, and it employs callouts that enable you to do away with the legend.

Programs with graphing features usually let you specify where you want a legend to appear: to the right of the graph or below it, for example. The location you choose affects the size of the rest of the graph. For instance, putting the legend below a column chart allows your program to create wider columns, but the chart's vertical axis is compressed. In a column chart, this compression may cause similarly sized columns to look identical. Choose the legend location that intrudes least on the graph's data points.

Adding precision and legibility

A graph's first job may be to provide an at-a-glance look at trends or data, but there's no reason why a graph can't also convey hard facts. By adding data series values to the graph, you can provide an extra level of detail for readers who want to give the graph more than just a passing glance. This technique works especially well for bar, pie, and column graphs.

If a graph contains many data series, you may need to use a space-efficient font in order to fit the values between each column, wedge, or bar. Helvetica Condensed and Helvetica Narrow are good candidates. Don't over-condense a font in an effort to shoehorn the values in, however — if you have that many data series (or your graph is that small), it may not be practical to include data values.

More type tips for graphs

Speaking of graph typography, avoid using all-capital letters for value or category names or graph titles. If this text is coming from spreadsheet cells, you need to address this aspect of graph design when creating the original spreadsheet. When you are deciding which fonts to use, consider the final medium. For titles on slides and overheads, stick with sturdy, sanserif faces: Helvetica Bold or ITC Franklin Gothic Bold, which is available as a downloadable font from Adobe Systems and other font vendors. (See Chapter 15 for more advice on choosing typefaces for presentations.)

Improving legibility with gridlines

Another way to enhance legibility in bar, column, and line charts is to add gridlines. These horizontal or vertical lines run at right angles to the value axis, serving to guide the eye from a particular data point to its closest value on the value axis. Don't add gridlines just because your program supports them, but only when they genuinely help readers interpret the data. If your program allows, consider making the gridlines a light gray or other unobtrusive color that doesn't draw attention away from the data points.

Dealing with problem data

For all the effort you can expend in improving legibility, sometimes your data works against you. For example, if two or more pie graph wedges are similar in size, it's difficult to discern the difference between them. One solution to this problem is to *explode* the wedge you want to accentuate — drag it a short distance away from the rest of the pie. Another solution is to use a bar or column graph — the eye can see small differences in edges more easily than it can discern differences in area.

Another problem can surface if you have one data series whose values are dramatically different from the others. (Maybe sales in one quarter skyrocketed after an unexpected endorsement by Oprah.) In such a case, you may want to change the scale of the graph's value axis to reflect the largest of the similar values and then extend the oddball bar beyond the graph's boundaries.

You may need to move a graph into a drawing program such as ClarisDraw or Adobe Illustrator to perform this kind of modification. See the Quick Tips box "Transporting Graphs" for some advice on moving graphs between programs.

Transporting Graphs

A graph you create in a spreadsheet or graphing program often needs to end up in a different program, such as a word processor or publishing program. You can generally move graphs into other programs in either of two ways:

- **Through the Clipboard.** Select the chart or open the chart window, choose Copy, start or switch to another program, and then paste.
- **Using Publish and Subscribe.** If you anticipate having to revise the chart's underlying data, you can use this System 7 feature to automate the process. Use the Edit menu's Create Publisher command to create an edition file to which you can then subscribe within another program.

Remember that a graph is actually an object-oriented graphic — the same kind drawing programs such as ClarisDraw create. If you paste a chart into a drawing program, you can then modify its elements — change the columns in a graph of downtown office occupancy into skyscrapers, for example.

The role of decoration in graphs

These days, it's fashionable to decorate graphs with cartoons, icons, symbols, and other gimmicks that supposedly make the graph more approachable and attractive. *USA Today* is often guilty of creating garish graphs, and many newspapers and magazines are jumping on the bandwagon. Some programs even provide features that make creating these kinds of graphs easier. In Adobe Illustrator, for example, you can specify that a symbol or shape be used instead of a plain bar, column, or other data point marker.

Many graphing gurus despise this kind of decoration. To me, a little bit of decoration — pencils instead of bars in a graph about scholastic test results, for example — isn't a cardinal sin. A bigger offense is the use of a three-dimensional graph to represent two-dimensional data. Most graphing programs let you create 3-D bar, column, and line charts, in which each column looks like a little skyscraper or each line looks like a ribbon. This kind of graph not only makes it harder to decipher the original data, its 3-D perspective can distort or deemphasize some of the data. Don't enter the third dimension unless your data really is three-dimensional.

For more background on the elements of graph design, read *The Visual Display of Quantitative Information* by Yale University's Edward R. Tufte (Graphics Press, 1983). This beautiful book is the definitive guide to creating data graphics. One of Tufte's principles of graphical excellence should be emblazoned on the wall of everyone who uses a graphing program:

> Graphical excellence is that which gives to the viewer the greatest number of ideas in the shortest time with the least ink in the smallest space.

Text on a Curved Path in FreeHand and Illustrator

A common text effect involves attaching a line of text to a wavy baseline. The instructions in this box show you how to bind text to a curved path by using Macromedia FreeHand and Adobe Illustrator.

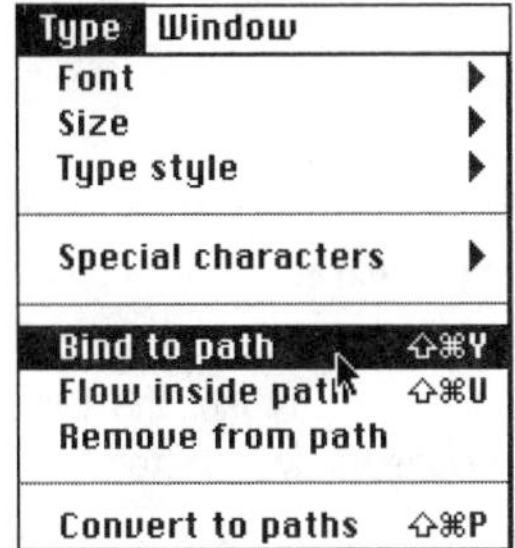

To bind text to a curved path in FreeHand:

1. **Press and hold the Shift key, select a text box, and then select the path to which you want to bind the text.**
2. **Choose Bind to Path from the Type menu or press Shift-⌘-Y.**
   FreeHand joins the text.

   Other tips for binding text to a curved path include

   ❖ You can fine-tune the way the text is joined by using the Text Inspector. For example, you can specify that the text be rotated along the path or that characters appear skewed to the path's shape.

   ❖ Selecting text that you've bound to a curved path can be tricky. The easiest way to do so is to draw a selection marquee around part or all of the text.

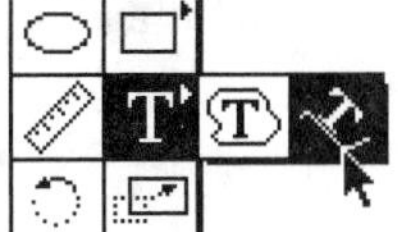

To bind text to a curved path in Illustrator:

1. **Create the path.**
2. **Select the Path-type tool (highlighted at left).**
3. **Position the pointer on the path and then click the mouse button.**
   A blinking insertion point appears on the path.
4. **Type the text.**
   Illustrator automatically positions the text along the path as you type. You can move the text along the path by selecting the text, pointing to the large I-beam at the beginning of the line of text, and then dragging.

Using Mirror and Shadow Effects in FreeHand and Illustrator

Both FreeHand and Illustrator provide tools that let you skew or distort part or all of an image. In FreeHand, it's called the Skewing tool; in Illustrator, it's the Shear tool. You can use these tools to create mirror-image or shadow effects. The instructions in this box show you how to create mirror and shadow effects by using FreeHand and Illustrator. I used a text block for these examples, but you can substitute any type of object — a shape you've drawn, a piece of clip art, or even a scanned image that you've imported.

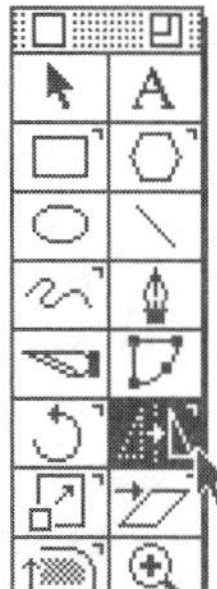

To create a mirror effect in FreeHand:

1. **Select the item you want to mirror.**
2. **Choose Clone from the Edit menu.**
   FreeHand duplicates the item and positions the duplicate on top of the original. The clone is now selected.
3. **Activate the Mirror tool (highlighted at left).**
4. **Press and hold the Option key while clicking the object.**
   The Transform window appears.
5. **In the Transform window, type 180 in the Reflect Axis box and click Apply.**
   The clone now appears upside down.
6. **Activate the Selection tool (the arrow) and drag the clone down so that its top just touches the original object.**

   Notes to keep in mind when creating mirror effects in FreeHand include

   ❖ To change the angle of the reflection, use the Skewing tool.

   ❖ To make the reflection look more realistic, you may want to change its fill pattern to a lighter shade than the original object. If you're working with text, use the Fill and Stroke command in the Type menu's Effect submenu. If you're working with an object, use the Fill and Line commands in the Attributes menu.

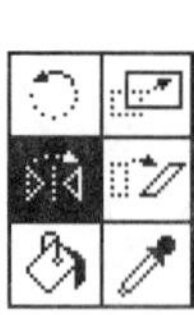

To create a mirror effect in Illustrator:

1. **Select the item you want to mirror.**
2. **Duplicate the item by pressing the Option key while dragging the item.**
   As an alternative, you can choose Copy and then Paste. This method, however, replaces the Clipboard's preceding contents.

3. **Double-click the Reflect tool (highlighted at left).**

   The Reflect dialog box appears.

4. **Select the Horizontal Axis button, and then click OK.**

   Illustrator reflects the selected item.

5. **Fine-tune the duplicate's position if necessary.**

   Keep the following in mind when creating mirroring effects in Illustrator:

   - To change the angle of the reflection, use the Shear tool.
   - To make the reflection look more realistic, you may want to change its fill pattern to a lighter shade than the original object. Use the Object menu's Paint Style command.

Computer-Aided Design — Drafting on the Mac

This is not a good time to be in the T-square manufacturing business. Computers are replacing traditional drafting tools in the same way that word processors are supplanting typewriters. A detail-minded category of drawing program, computer-aided design (CAD) software can turn computers into electronic drafting tables that make creating and revising complex drawings easier than ever.

A brief history of CAD

CAD was born in the sixties, when some automobile and aircraft manufacturers began augmenting their pencil-and-paper drafting methods with floor-sagging mainframe computers tied to large graphics terminals. These systems — which had a fraction of the Mac's speed, memory, and graphics resolution — cost millions of dollars to buy and hundreds of dollars an hour to run. Because of their cost, CAD systems' benefits were reserved for the designers of such complex beasts as cars, planes, and missiles. Everyone else used T squares, triangles, mechanical pencils, compasses, and protractors.

As the cost of computers shrank and their capabilities grew, CAD became feasible for smaller firms. Shortly after personal computers debuted, CAD appeared on desktops, thanks largely to two DOS PC programs — Autodesk's AutoCAD and VersaCAD Corporation's VersaCAD. The Mac, despite its superior graphics, wasn't part of the picture. Using the original Mac's 9-inch screen to view blueprint-size CAD drawings would be like viewing the ceiling of the Sistine Chapel through a keyhole.

Today, thanks to large-screen monitors and fast Macs, the Macintosh is becoming a force in personal computer CAD. What follows is a beginner's guide to the jargon and concepts behind Mac CAD — a starting point for your own investigation.

Categories of CAD

CAD programs are object-oriented drawing programs on steroids. Like general-purpose drawing programs such as ClarisDraw, CAD programs provide tools for drawing shapes and provide commands for altering those shapes and displaying their dimensions. You can also create boilerplate designs and adapt them as needed. Fast-food chains, for example, use CAD programs to adapt their basic building designs to specific sites, allowing their buildings to maintain that "Anytown, USA" look while still adapting to the characteristics of a specific site.

Three basics categories of CAD exist — mechanical, architectural, and electrical engineering.

Mechanical CAD

Mechanical CAD is the broadest category. It involves the design of objects — cars, planes, trains, machine parts, lamp shades, thumbtacks, you name it. Most mechanical CAD programs create two-dimensional drawings that, like soap opera characters, have height and width, but no depth.

Architectural CAD

Architectural CAD, as you can guess, involves the design of buildings. Architects create many kinds of drawings — elevations depicting a building's profile; floor-plans showing room dimensions, door locations, and furnishings; and maps of the building's plumbing, heating, and electrical systems. Many CAD programs provide drawing tools for creating parallel lines, making it easy to draw walls. Some architectural CAD programs let you create a 3-D view that you can rotate and examine from different angles.

Electrical engineering CAD

Electrical engineers use CAD programs to design circuits and schematics — those symbols and lines that show how electronic components are interconnected. CAD programs designed specifically for circuit design are often called *schematic capture programs.* In addition to letting you easily draw a schematic diagram, these programs work behind the scenes to keep track of what's connected to what. When you're finished, you have not only a schematic drawing, but also a parts list and a list of connections. That list of connections can go to a circuit board layout program such as Douglas CAD/CAM Professional System, which can map out the copper highways and byways that traverse a multilayer printed-circuit board.

At this advanced level, CAD programs play a direct role in executing a design. Many programs can shuttle their data directly into computer-aided manufacturing (CAM) equipment, which uses the measurements and specifications in the CAD drawing to control industrial robots or machining tools to create the parts in the drawing. Such Buck Rodgers CAD/CAM is primarily the province of six-figure workstations.

Life with a CAD program

If you suspect that software with this kind of power is complex, you're right. Forget diving into a CAD program without opening the manual. You need weeks (or months) of practice to master the hundreds of drawing, measuring, and annotating features that a powerhouse CAD program provides.

Similarities to drawing programs

If you use any version of Claris MacDraw, you have a head start. From the features standpoint, MacDraw is to a CAD program what a tricycle is to a Harley-Davidson. But they have similarities in their basic approaches to electronic drafting. You begin with a blank, untitled document window and create a drawing by choosing tools from on-screen palettes and using the mouse to draw shapes.

To help you draw straight lines and position objects accurately, most drawing programs provide a snap-to feature that draws the mouse pointer to an invisible grid as it moves. But CAD programs offer more ways to snap. For example, most programs let you specify that an object snap to a particular point on another object or to the point at which two objects intersect.

A powerful array of specialized tools

Basic drawing programs such as ClarisDraw provide tools for drawing several different shapes, but a CAD program's palettes bristle with specialized tools that make creating complex drawings easier. A CAD program's *geometric facilities* replace compasses and protractors and enable you to quickly draw objects requiring calculations or measurements. Need to measure an angle or calculate the midpoint of a line? Want to draw a line perpendicular to a slanted line, parallel to it, or tangent to an arc (such as a belt connecting two pulleys)? Such chores are a common part of an engineer's or architect's life. A CAD program reduces these tasks to a mouse click.

CAD programs also simplify altering the objects you draw. As in any drawing program, you can move or resize an object by selecting it and dragging the mouse. Many CAD programs also let you enter measurement or position values from the keyboard for greater precision. Most programs also provide on-screen rulers and *coordinate windows* that display the mouse pointer's position as it moves within the drawing window.

Chamfers and fillets

A more advanced level of object altering involves creating chamfers and fillets. A *chamfer* is a beveled corner formed by a diagonal line that connects two lines. If you chamfer all four corners of a box, you get an octagonal shape similar to that of a stop sign. A *fillet* (pronounced *fill-it*) is similar, except that the object connecting the two lines is an arc, not a diagonal line. If you fillet all four corners of a box, you get a box with round corners or, if the arcs are large enough, a circle. Geometrically speaking, a fillet is an arc tangent to two objects.

Other labor-saving features

CAD programs also give you more ways to tame complex drawing jobs. One such life simplifier that nearly all CAD programs provide is a layering feature similar to that of many draw programs. Engineers and architects often build drawings by using layers of transparent acetate, each showing a particular component or system. An architect can show a plumbing system on one layer, walls on another, electrical systems on a third, and room dimensions on a fourth.

CAD layering features

CAD layering features work similarly. You can move objects between layers and selectively show and hide layers, depending on how much detail you want to see. You can assign a color to each layer to color code the systems in a drawing. Many CAD programs also let you open bitmapped graphics, place them on one layer, and then trace over them by using the CAD program's tools. You can use this technique to transfer old blueprints or schematics into a CAD program. First digitize the images by using a scanner, and then import them and trace over their bitmaps.

Dimensioning features

Mechanical drawings and architectural blueprints always show the dimensions of their components. CAD programs provide dimensioning features that create those dimension values for you. Simply choose a command or click a palette icon and select the item you're measuring, and the CAD program adds the dimension to the drawing, complete with arrows and lines. All programs that provide dimensioning features let you choose the measuring system in which dimensions appear, and many also let you choose from several styles of arrows and extension lines. Most programs that provide dimensioning also provide *auto-dimensioning*. When an auto-dimensioning feature is active, the program changes dimension values for you when you change an object's size.

The kinds of objects you can measure vary from program to program. Some programs provide only *linear dimensioning* — measuring the distance between two points. Others also support *angular dimensioning* — measuring the size of angles. Still others go a step further, offering *radial dimensioning* — the capability to measure the radii of circles.

CAD symbol libraries

Drawings and schematics often contain multiple copies of the same object, be it a bolt, a sink, or a transistor. Most CAD programs offer symbol libraries that make it easy to create, store, and reuse often-used symbols of your trade. Some programs come with libraries of common architectural or electronic symbols.

Libraries can also be extra-cost options available from the program's developer or third parties. With many programs, you can assign a name to each symbol, such as "3-inch carriage bolt" or "conference chair." Some programs can use those names to print a parts list showing how many times a given component appears in a drawing, enabling you to easily generate a parts list and bill of materials. This feature is often called *attribute tracking* or *associativity*. High-end CAD programs can often export these lists to database managers.

Zoom and redraw halting

And because even a large-screen monitor can't show an entire blueprint-size drawing at actual size, all CAD programs offer zoom commands that let you move in for a close-up look or zoom out to get the big picture. Redrawing an image containing thousands of objects can also take time, even on the higher-end Macs. To eliminate the wait, most programs offer a *redraw halting* feature that lets you stop the redrawing process. You can use redraw halting to stop further redrawing after the object you've zoomed in to see appears.

CAD and Power Macs: A Perfect Match

For a microprocessor, CAD is hard work. Keeping track of the thousands of objects that a CAD drawing might contain, rotating them, resizing them, and displaying them as you zoom in and out — these are complex jobs that demand as much processing horsepower as they can get.

Given this, it isn't surprising that Power Macs are the computers of choice for Mac-based CAD. When we tested native Power Mac CAD programs against their 680X0-family counterparts at Macworld Lab, we found that the native Power Mac programs were several times faster.

Of the five CAD programs tested, the native program that most outperformed its 680X0 twin was Graphsoft's Blueprint, which was, on average, a whopping 11 times as fast. (If you're using Blueprint on a 680X0 Mac, drop this book now and upgrade to a Power Mac and the native version.) In a test involving a 90-degree rotation of a complex image, Blueprint's native version was 26 times faster than its 680X0 version, completing the task in 45 seconds instead of 20 minutes. This obviously helped the program's overall score, but Blueprint did well in other tests, too, with the native version performing two to five times as fast as the 680X0 version. Graphsoft's MiniCAD was similarly impressive, with the native version averaging nearly four times as fast as the 680X0 version.

Ashlar's Vellum is another native CAD program that humbled its 680X0 cousin. The native version of Vellum was, on average, twice as fast as the 680X0 version. The native version was especially quick when switching views and redrawing an image, performing about six times as fast as the 680X0 version.

Exchanging and printing CAD images

If you work in an organization that already uses a CAD system — whether a large workstation or a DOS PC — you may want to investigate the data-exchange options that Mac CAD programs provide. There is no single standard for moving CAD drawings between systems, but some established formats exist. Perhaps the most popular is IGES, short for Initial Graphics Exchange Standard, developed by the American National Standards Institute (ANSI). You find support for IGES files in CAD systems running on microcomputers, minicomputers, and mainframes. Another popular format is the DXF file, popularized by Autodesk's AutoCAD package for DOS PCs (and also available for Macs).

Some Mac CAD programs can import and export IGES and DXF files. With others, file-translation modules are extra-cost options. Most advanced CAD users rely on translation programs such as Kandu Software's CADMover, which can translate among IGES, MacDraw, MiniCAD, HPGL, PICT, DXF, and many other formats.

Plotter output

A CAD drawing's final destination is a piece of paper, and some CAD programs can get it there in more ways than others. In the CAD world, the dominant output device isn't a LaserWriter or an ImageWriter but a pen plotter, which prints by zipping special felt-tipped pens across a sheet of paper or mylar film. Most plotters can hold between 4 and 12 different colored pens in a turret mechanism, switching between them as the CAD program instructs.

Plotters are often described according to their maximum paper size, with each size labeled by a letter. An A-size plotter can create 8½ x 11-inch drawings; B-size drawings measure 11 x 17; C-size, 17 x 22; D-size, 22 x 34; and E-size, 34 x 44. Nearly all Mac CAD programs can print to a plotter and support plotters from such industry leaders as CalComp, Hewlett-Packard, Houston Instruments, and Roland.

Plotters take too long to accurately render the subtle serifs and fine details of Mac fonts, so most CAD programs with plotter support include *stroke fonts* for their output. Stroke fonts enable the plotter to quickly draw text by using — you guessed it — single strokes of its pens. Stroke fonts, sometimes called *vector fonts*, resemble the letters created with a Leroy lettering set, a stencil lettering kit popular in the drafting world.

CAD output options

Mac CAD programs also support ImageWriters and LaserWriters to varying degrees. Some can print in only low-resolution draft modes, but most offer both low- and high-resolution ImageWriter and LaserWriter output. Low-resolution output is useful for producing quick proofs of a drawing. High resolution takes longer, but it takes advantage of your printer's maximum resolution.

Another output option is a large-format ink-jet printer such as Hewlett-Packard's DesignJet series or LaserMaster's DisplayMaker, all discussed earlier in this chapter (see the Quick Tips box "Putting a Graphics Program to Work #7: Make a Poster"). If you don't need colossal output, you might consider a tabloid-size laser printer, which can handle 11 x 17 sheets. See Chapter 30 for more printer buying advice.

The cost of CAD

If you're drooling at the prospects of working CAD into your life, dry up — at least until you check your bank balance. Software with the capabilities that I've described doesn't come cheap.

To get satisfying performance from a CAD program, you need at least a Quadra or accelerated Mac — better still, a Power Mac. If you prefer to spend your time drawing rather than scrolling, you need a large-screen monitor, too.

Then there's the cost of the programs themselves. Their complexity and a relatively small market combine to place CAD programs among the Mac's most expensive software. High-end CAD programs such as Gimeor's Architrion II, Autodesk's AutoCAD, and InterGraph Corporation's MicroStation Mac each cost over $3,000. Between $1,000 and $3,000, you can find programs such as Ashlar Vellum.

You can also get extremely capable programs for less than $1,000. Examples include Engineered Software's PowerDraw and Graphsoft's MiniCad. But be aware that some programs in this under $1,000 ballpark don't include the plotter support and file-exchange features included with their higher-priced brethren. If you need those features, be sure to tally the total cost before buying.

Mac CAD at affordable prices

The most reasonable CAD programs are Graphsoft's BluePrint, and Abracadata's Design Your Own Home Architecture, both of which retail for less than $300. These programs can't match the capabilities of AutoCAD or Architrion II, but they're ideal tools for exploring the CAD world. And if you outgrow them, chances are you'll be able to import their drawings into a more powerful program.

Choosing the program that suits your needs

Besides the features I've described here, other factors may influence your choice of a CAD program. For example, if you need to exchange drawings with DOS PCs, you can get more consistent results with a program that has a PC counterpart, such as AutoCAD. If you're buying CAD software that people with varying levels of CAD experience need to use, a midrange product such as PowerDraw or Forthought's Snap may be in order. And don't forget to match the program's appetite for hardware to the systems you have. Try to run a high-end CAD program on a midrange Mac, and you'll be disappointed with the results.

Serious about Graphics? Get a Tablet

If you're serious about CAD or any form of computer graphics, consider supplementing your mouse with a *graphics tablet* such as those made by Wacom and CalComp. Graphics tablets have a flat surface (usually 12 x 12 inches or larger) upon which you draw by using a pencil-like stylus, which is generally wireless.

Many of today's tablets are pressure-sensitive: You can press harder and get darker or wider lines. (Programs that support pressure-sensitive tablets include Adobe Photoshop and Illustrator, Macromedia FreeHand, and Fractal Design's Painter and Sketcher.) Many artists and CAD devotees find graphics tablets more natural than the mouse for drawing and tracing.

For complete details on graphics tablets and other alternative input devices, see Chapter 33. But beware — if you think that graphics programs are appealing when used with a mouse, wait until your friends start scribbling with a stylus. They may never go home.

CHAPTER 12 CONCEPTS AND TERMS

- Bitmapped, or paint, programs store images as a series of bits, one (or more) for each pixel in the image. Paint programs are best for creating subtle shading effects and manipulating scanned images.
- Object-oriented, or draw, programs store images as a series of instructions for QuickDraw or PostScript. An object-oriented image can take full advantage of your printer's resolution. Draw programs are best for creating technical illustrations, blueprints, electronic schematics, organizational charts, and other forms of line art.
- Computer-aided design, or CAD, programs are sophisticated draw programs that provide features for measuring objects, creating multilayer drawings, and tracking the materials required for a project.
- Some programs, including Adobe SuperPaint and Deneba's Canvas, combine drawing and painting features.

attribute tracking
Also called associativity, a CAD program feature that enables you to generate a parts list and bill of materials based on the objects you've drawn.

autotrace
A drawing program feature that automatically traces a bitmapped image and generates an object-oriented version of it.

Bezier curve
A method of describing the path that a digital pen travels as it inscribes shapes. You can reshape the path by dragging one or more control points.

bitmapped image
An image in which each dot, or pixel, corresponds to a bit in the Mac's memory. With a monochrome (black-and-white) bitmapped program, a bit with a value of 1 creates a black dot, while a bit with a value of 0 creates a white dot. Gray-scale or color bitmapped programs assign multiple bits to each pixel — the bits' on-off combinations indicate the pixel's gray shade or color.

chamfer
A beveled corner formed by a diagonal line that connects two lines. If you chamfer all four corners of a box, you get an octagonal shape similar to that of a stop sign.

coordinate window
A window that displays the mouse's position as you move it.

data point
A single value — such as the sales results for one quarter — in a graph such as a bar chart.

data series
A set of related values — such as the sales results for an entire year — in a graph.

dimensioning
A feature provided by many draw programs for adding measurements to a drawing by clicking the objects you want to measure. Most draw programs provide linear dimensioning — measuring the distance between two points. CAD programs often add angular dimensioning (measuring the size of angles) and radial dimensioning (measuring the radii of circles).

dithering
A technique of simulating gray shades or colors through the use of patterns.

draw program
A term often used to describe an object-oriented graphics program.

fillet
Pronounced *fill-it,* an arc tangent to two objects. If you fillet all four corners of a box, you get a box with round corners or, if the arcs are large enough, a circle.

geometric facilities
The features in a CAD program that enable you to draw objects requiring calculations or measurements.

graduated fill
A pattern in which one shade smoothly blends in to another.

graphics tablet
A mouse alternative that provides a flat surface on which you scrawl with a pen-like stylus.

image-processing program
A program that works with bitmapped images and is primarily designed for retouching and otherwise modifying scanned or video-captured images.

layering
A feature that enables you to divide an image into multiple layers, each of which acts like a see-through plastic overlay. You can selectively show and hide layers to examine one detail or show the big picture. Layering features are most commonly found in draw programs.

legend
In a graph (such as a bar chart), a box adjacent to the chart that shows category names alongside the patterns in which their data points appear.

object-oriented image
An image comprised of discrete objects, such as lines, circles, arcs, rectangles, and free-form paths. An object-oriented image requires less memory to store than a bitmapped image and is resolution independent — that is, not tied to a specific number of dots per inch.

paint program
A term often used to describe a bitmapped graphics program.

pen plotter
A type printer, popular in the CAD world, that produces output by zipping special felt-tipped pens across a sheet of paper or mylar film.

(continued on the next page)

(continued from previous page)

pixel
Short for picture element, a single dot on the Mac's screen.

redraw halting
A timesaving feature that enables you to interrupt a program while it's drawing a complex image.

schematic capture program
Another term for a computer-aided design program designed specifically for circuit design.

snap-to grid
A drawing program feature that helps you draw straight lines and position objects accurately by drawing the mouse pointer to an invisible grid as it moves.

stroke font
Also called a vector font, a type of simple font that many CAD programs provide.

symbol library
A drawing program feature that enables you to store and recall often-used shapes, such as chairs, bathroom fixtures, doors, and windows.

CHAPTER THIRTEEN

13 Digital Imaging

- Combining photography with computers in the electronic imaging revolution
- Gray maps, histograms, gamma correction, filters: image-processing jargon defined
- Tips for outfitting an electronic darkroom
- Shortcuts and tips for Adobe Photoshop
- Surveying the field of filmless cameras

Photography is going electronic, and the Mac is helping to take it there. Conventional film and processing techniques haven't yet gone the way of the daguerreotype, but more and more publishers, photographers, designers, and scientists are relying on computers to help them publish, retouch, and analyze images. Electronic imaging can be faster and more flexible than conventional photography, and it's environmentally sound, requiring no chemicals, silver halides, or other toxins.

The techniques behind electronic image manipulation are called *image processing*, and they're the subject of many technical and even ethical and legal discussions. Image-processing hardware and software can be complex and costly, especially where color images are concerned. Ethical questions arise when someone alters a photo's content. The common view of photography as a realistic medium is shattered when you learn that people can change news, police, or spy satellite photos with a few mouse clicks. And legal issues surface when designers and artists use portions of copyrighted images in their works.

This chapter covers the concepts behind image processing as well as the hardware and software it requires. I also examine some advanced image-processing and printing concepts and provide some tips for the Mac world's most popular image-processing program, Adobe Photoshop.

Experience Digital Imaging for Yourself

The best way to appreciate the power of digital imaging is to try it for yourself. Here are some things you might want to try as you read this chapter.

- **NIH Image.** This amazing program, from Wayne Rasband at the National Institutes of Health, is the freeware world's answer to Photoshop. Image editing, macros, plug-ins, filters, video frame grabbing — it does it all. And it's free — the NIH has put the program in the public domain.
- **Graphics shareware.** You can find some great graphics programs and file-conversion utilities in the Best of BMUG collection.
- **A tour of the Apple QuickTake 150.** In the Digital Imaging segment of *Macworld Power User Clinic,* you can see Apple's latest digital camera in action and compare the images from three filmless cameras.

Turning Pictures into Pixels

Before you can bring an image-processing program's powers to bear, you need images. While some people use image-processing programs to create original artwork, most people work with images generated by a variety of hardware add-ons. The most popular are scanners, those cousins to copiers that take photographic prints or slides and translate them into series of gray or colored dots (see Figure 13-1 "Anatomy of a Scan").

Gray-scale scanners

For scanning black-and-white photographs, you need a gray-scale scanner such as Apple's OneScanner, Hewlett-Packard's ScanJet 3p, or Microtek's ScanMaker IIG. These 8-bit scanners are capable of discerning roughly 256 levels of gray. Many older scanners (including Apple's original Apple Scanner) were of the 4-bit variety, capable of detecting only 16 levels of gray. These older scanners deliver inferior results when used with continuous tone images such as photographs.

As for sharpness, most gray-scale scanners can produce images with resolution of up to 300 dots per inch (dpi) — more than adequate for creating and printing gray-scale scans.

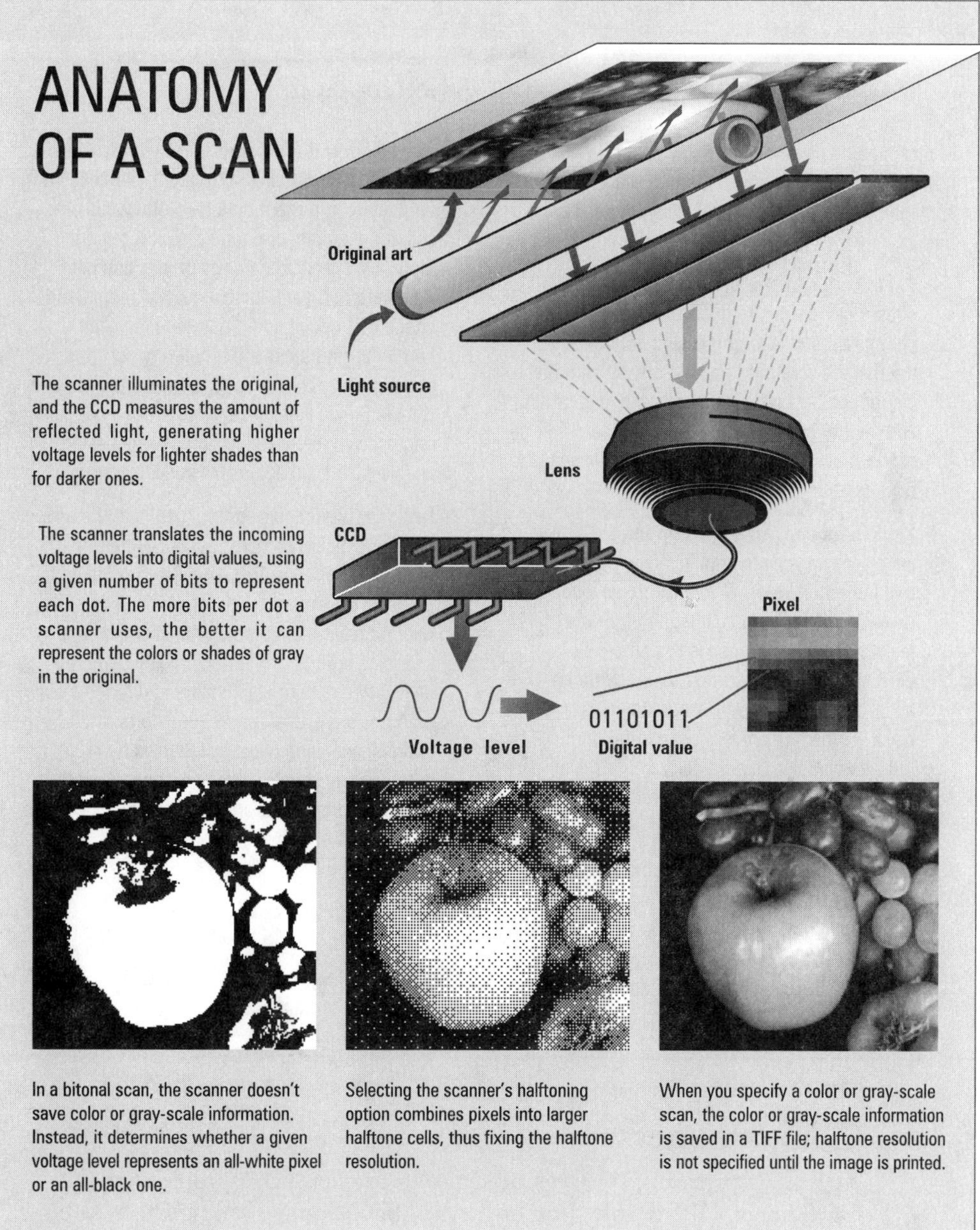

ANATOMY
OF A SCAN
Original art
Light source
The scanner illuminates the original, and the CCD measures the amount of reflected light, generating higher voltage levels for lighter shades than for darker ones.
Lens
The scanner translates the incoming voltage levels into digital values, using a given number of bits to represent each dot. The more bits per dot a scanner uses, the better it can represent the colors or shades of gray in the original.
CCD
Pixel
01101011
Voltage level
Digital value
In a bitonal scan, the scanner doesn't save color or gray-scale information. Instead, it determines whether a given voltage level represents an all-white pixel or an all-black one.
Selecting the scanner's halftoning option combines pixels into larger halftone cells, thus fixing the halftone resolution.
When you specify a color or gray-scale scan, the color or gray-scale information is saved in a TIFF file; halftone resolution is not specified until the image is printed.

Figure 13-1: Anatomy of a Scan

Digital Imaging: Who Needs It?

Digital imaging used to be a highly specialized field; now it's accessible to anyone with a Mac. This box spotlights the types of professionals who can benefit from it.

- **Publishers and photographers:** These folks often need to crop, retouch, and otherwise alter photographs. Image-processing software lets them erase scratches and blemishes, remove distracting backgrounds, and improve contrast and brightness. It also offers a safety net that no airbrush or retouching pencil affords — an Undo command.
- **Publishers and printing companies:** Getting full-color images into print involves performing two important steps. *Color correction* involves tweaking the hues in an image for greater realism. *Color separation* is the process of dividing a color image into four separate images, one each for cyan, magenta, yellow, and black — the four *process colors* that printing presses combine to print color images. Until recently, the Mac wasn't involved in this upper stratum of imaging; now it's a major player.
- **Illustrators, designers, and artists:** Image-processing software helps them create special effects that otherwise require hours of darkroom work or can't be done any other way. Some programs can even make an image look like it was painted in a pointillist style.
- **Scientists and educators:** These professionals use image-processing software to enhance and emphasize important details — the walls of a cell, for example, or a tumor in an X-ray. In factories, specialized image-processing hardware and software guide industrial robots and check that circuit board parts are installed correctly. And those interplanetary portraits phoned home by the Voyager space probes and Hubble Space Telescope wouldn't be nearly as impressive were it not for image-processing specialists at the Jet Propulsion Laboratory.
- **Ordinary business people:** Thanks to the new, low-cost, digital cameras such as Apple's QuickTake 100 and 150, anyone who wants to illustrate documents with images can do so without having to grapple with scanners and scanning software. High-end digital cameras deliver film-quality results; low-end models such as Apple's are ideal for creating corporate ID badges, snapping photos of houses for real-estate listing sheets, documenting insurance claims, and other tasks for which film-like image quality isn't essential.

Color scanners

To scan color photographs, you need a color scanner such as Apple's Color OneScanner, HP's ScanJet IIcx, or La Cie's SilverScanner series. These 24-bit scanners can discern millions of colors. In experienced hands, they can deliver quality that approaches that of five- and six-figure color scanners from firms such as Dainippon Screen and Scitex. Most color scanners offer scanning resolutions of between 300 and 600 dpi; some use software *interpolation* to simulate resolutions as high as 1200 dpi. Resolutions this high are often overkill for desktop publishing work.

Slide scanners

Slide scanners such as Nikon's Coolscan and Leaf Systems' Leafscan 35 and Leafscan 45 work with color slides. They generate considerably sharper images: 2700 dpi for the Coolscan and up to 4800 dpi for the Leafscans. The Coolscan is unique in that it actually fits inside a Mac — you can install one in the bay that's usually used for a second internal hard drive or for a removable-media drive.

Slide scanners often have a wider dynamic range than flatbed scanners — that is, they're able to detect a wider range of color and brightness values. A wide dynamic range is important: If it's narrow, all dark areas of an image go black, and subtle shadow details disappear.

Drum scanners

Service bureaus and professional publishing houses use high-end scanners that use a photomultiplier tube instead of CCD. Drum scanners from firms such as Crosfield and Optronics provide the widest dynamic range and yield the sharpest scans. They also cost $10,000 and up, which is why you generally find them only in service bureaus and printing houses. Expect to pay $25 to $100 for a scanning job at a service bureau — relatively steep, but a bargain considering the quality you get.

Hand scanners

Hand scanners look like huge mice and roll across an original document, scanning in swaths about 4 inches wide. They have serious limitations and deliver mediocre results. See Chapter 18 for more details.

The software side

Most scanners include rudimentary image-processing software as well as software modules that enable you to scan from within an image-processing program such as Adobe Photoshop. Many products include a limited-edition version of Photoshop — some even include the full version. When you're shopping, be sure to consider software bundles. If you haven't bought Photoshop yet, you can save a lot of money by buying a scanner that includes it.

For some tips on getting high-quality scans, see the Quick Tips box "Tips for Better Scans."

Tips for Better Scans

Following the rules outlined in this box will help you get the most from your scanner — and your disk space.

Save disk space by scanning at a lower resolution

A laser printer's low halftone frequency creates an opportunity to save disk space and memory and decrease the time required to print images. Many scanners can create 300- or even 600-dpi images, but scanning photographs at that maximum resolution often wastes disk space. Generally, you can get excellent results by scanning photographs at a resolution twice the final halftone frequency — a 106-dpi scan for a 53-lpi halftone, for example, and a 240-dpi scan for a 120-lpi halftone. This is just a rule of thumb, however. For images lacking fine details, you can often get away with even lower scan-to-halftone ratios — as low as one-to-one. (Always scan line art at your scanner's maximum resolution, provided that resolution isn't higher than that of the printer you plan to use to print the art. For example, scanning line art at 1200 dpi wastes disk space if you'll be printing it on a 600-dpi printer.)

Scan in gray or color and save as TIFF

Always scan continuous-tone originals by using your scanner software's gray-scale setting or color and save the result as a TIFF or RIFF file. Doing so lets you alter the image's grays or color balance, change its halftone resolution and angle, and resize the image without distorting its halftone screen. If you use the scanning software's halftoning options instead, the settings of these key components are carved in stone during the scan.

Crop the image before you save it

If you only plan to use a portion of an image, crop the image appropriately before you save it — that way, you don't waste a lot of disk space storing portions of the image that won't ever appear. You also save time when you import the image into a publishing program because the program has a smaller file to read.

An easy way to crop before saving is to use your scanner's prescan feature, which does a quick-and-dirty scan so you can draw a selection marquee around the area you want to include in the final scan.

Perform tonal correction to lighten up the scan

Most desktop scanners yield images that print too dark — partly because of the scanner's optics and partly because of a phenomenon called *dot gain.* When you prepare an image for printing — shoot negatives, make plates, and then run the presses — halftone dots tend to merge together, yielding muddy images. This problem is especially apparent with poor-quality paper stocks (such as newsprint) and high halftone-screen frequencies.

The solution to dark images is to perform nonlinear gamma correction to brighten the image and bring out the details in the dark areas (but without washing out the highlights). See the section about gamma correction later in this chapter for more details.

Sharpen the image

The optics in most desktop scanners aren't the best in the world, and the images they deliver often have a fuzzy appearance. Fortunately, image-processing programs provide software-sharpening routines that work beautifully. Most experienced scansters run their images through Photoshop's Sharpen or Unsharp Masking filters to sharpen up details.

Digitizing hardware

If your subject is at hand or on videotape, you can bypass the time and expense of photography with a video camera or an electronic photography system. Most camcorders and videocassette recorders have video-output jacks that you can connect to digitizing hardware. At the low end of the digitizer spectrum are products such as Digital Vision's Computer Eyes, which connects to the Mac's SCSI port (and therefore works with low-end machines such as Classics and Pluses).

For faster, higher-quality video digitizing, you can use a Mac equipped with video-input hardware: an AV Mac, a Power Mac 7500 or 8500, a Quadra 630 or Performa equipped with the video-input card, or any Mac that can accept a third-party digitizing board such as Radius's VideoSpigot series.

With these options, you simply connect a camcorder or VCR to the video-input jack. Accompanying software captures an image in as little as 1/60 second. Sometimes called *frame grabbers*, these boards are designed for multimedia applications (see Chapter 20).

Filmless cameras

Photojournalists and others are embracing still video cameras that save images not on film but in the camera's memory or on tiny floppy disks. Electronic photos currently lack the quality of conventional ones (they're gaining fast), but they don't require processing. They're ideal for newspapers and low-budget catalogs, service manuals, and newsletters. Now that Apple has entered the camera market with the QuickTake 100 and its successor, the QuickTake 150, filmless photography is getting more attention than ever. (The *Macworld Power User Clinic* contains a segment on the QuickTake 150 and on electronic photography in general.)

For a look at the other add-ons that you can find in a well-equipped digital-imaging setup, see the Backgrounder box, "Outfitting an Electronic Darkroom."

Kodak's PhotoCD System

One of the most exciting developments in the electronic imaging field comes from a company that has a bit of experience in conventional photography — Kodak. I'm referring to the Kodak PhotoCD system, which puts high-quality scans of conventional photographs on CD-ROM.

PhotoCD supplements conventional film and processing instead of replacing it. (Kodak knows on which side its bread is buttered.) When you take a roll of 35mm film to a photo lab that provides PhotoCD services, you get not only your slides or prints and negatives, but you also get a CD-ROM that contains scanned, color-corrected versions of the images.

Outfitting an Electronic Darkroom

If you're fired up about digital imaging, a look at its cost may hose you down. You can perform simple image editing on a low-end Mac system, but day-in, day-out image processing requires a significant investment.

A color Mac

To get realistic grays or any color, you need a Mac capable of displaying them. Some low-end image-processing programs run on the monochrome Classic, SE, and Plus models, but these Macs must simulate shades of gray by dithering (combining patterns of dots), making detailed retouching and gray-map adjustments difficult. Low-end Macs aren't fast enough for complex filtering and resizing tasks, either.

For realistic color, you need at least 16-bit color video circuitry. Most current color Macs support 16-bit color (some require a video memory upgrade to do so). Better still is the 24-bit video built into many members of the Quadra and Power Mac families and available through add-on cards for many other Macs. Throw in a large-screen monitor to avoid constant scrolling. (See Chapter 29 for details about video upgrade options.)

Color calibration hardware

Working with colors on-screen introduces a problem: A color monitor does not render the colors in the same way as a color printer or printing press. Color monitors create colors by adding red, green, and blue light in various ratios; printed output, on the other hand, creates colors by subtracting some colors and reflecting others. (In color jargon, monitors use an *additive* color model, while printed materials use a *subtractive* model.)

The answer? More hardware — specifically, color calibration hardware such as Radius's PrecisionColor Calibrator or SuperMatch Display Calibrator, Kodak's ColorSense, or Light Source's Colortron.

Most calibration devices use a small sensor cup that attaches to the surface of your monitor and provides feedback to the video board, which adjusts its signals to provide accurate on-screen colors. See Chapter 30 for details about color matching.

A CD-ROM drive

Besides wanting a CD-ROM to access Kodak PhotoCD discs (described later in this chapter), you may want one to tap the growing number of CD–ROM-based stock photo libraries. Stock photo libraries are the image-processing world's version of clip art, offering scenes such as business, nature, sports, science, medicine, and more. Copyright and usage restrictions vary from product to product: with most libraries, you have to pay additional fees to use an image commercially. Sources for stock photo libraries include PhotoDisc, Inc. (Seattle, WA), Gazelle Technologies (San Diego, CA), and Comstock (New York, NY). Comstock also offers an on-line retrieval service for stock and news photography.

More incentive for purchasing a CD-ROM drive: Adobe offers a CD-ROM version of the Photoshop program that adds a stock photo sampler, additional filters and plug-in modules, technical notes, utilities, and a variety of Adobe typefaces (the Type on Call library, from which you can "unlock" typefaces by calling a toll-free number with credit card in hand).

Memory and disk space

Finally, you need to find room for all those bits that represent your images. A 5MB Mac is adequate for gray-scale work, but 8MB or more are essential for color work. It isn't unusual to find dozens of megabytes of memory in an imaging professional's Mac.

As for hard disk space, you need it, too. A gray-scale image can scarf half a megabyte in one sitting, and a large color file can consume ten times that. A 240MB drive is a bare minimum for gray-scale work; you want at least twice that for color. Look for a fast hard drive, too: You spend less time waiting for files to open, save, and even appear on-screen. Serious image processors often supplement their hard drives with SyQuest, Iomega, or magneto-optical removable-media drives. (See Chapter 25 for storage shopping advice.)

Compression software

Another weapon against "disk full" messages is compression software such as Storm Technology's PicturePress. PicturePress uses compression routines built around a standard called JPEG, short for an industry organization called Joint Photographic Experts Group. Some image quality is lost in the compression process — JPEG uses what is called a *lossy* compression scheme — although you can control the degree of compression to minimize that loss. Some DSP boards, including DayStar Digital's Charger, also include PicturePress, as discussed later in this chapter.

You can also reduce storage requirements by using a general-purpose compression program such as Aladdin Systems' StuffIt Deluxe.

Remember, too, that you can reduce disk requirements simply by learning how to fine-tune your scanner settings to obtain the best quality at the lowest possible scanning resolution.

How PhotoCD works

PhotoCD scans come in a variety of resolutions — some for viewing images on-screen, others for high-quality publishing applications. The PhotoCD is enclosed in a standard plastic CD case (a so-called *jewel box*); the front cover of the case contains a contact sheet that shows a thumbnail version of each image. (If you've been shoehorning your photos into shoe boxes, you're probably starting to get excited about the efficiency and convenience of electronic photo storage.)

A PhotoCD can hold approximately 100 photos. Thanks to a special multisession CD recording technique, you don't have to fill the CD at one time. Simply take the CD back to the photo finisher when you drop off your next roll of film, and the lab adds the new images to the existing ones. You can also take the CD to a photo lab to have prints made from the digitized images — no holding negatives up to a window to determine which one you want to have reprinted.

Kodak also offers several PhotoCD options for professional photographers, such as PhotoCDs that store images from large-format, such as 70mm and 4 x 5-inch, cameras. *Pro PhotoCDs*, as they're called, can also incorporate three security features — a special identifier bearing copyright information, an encryption scheme that prevents unauthorized access to images, and an option that prints a watermark (such as the word *PROOF*) over an image.

PhotoCD players

Kodak sells a variety of PhotoCD players that can also play audio CDs. They're fine machines with some slick options, such as the ability to zoom in on part of an image and to play images in a specific order. But Kodak's players attach to a television set, not a Macintosh. To work with PhotoCD images on a Mac, you need a CD-ROM drive that supports XA Mode 2, the special recording mode used to create multisession PhotoCDs. Most of today's CD-ROM drives support XA Mode 2. Apple's AppleCD 300 and 600 families (and their internally mounted cousins, the AppleCD 300i and 600i) are among them, and they include software that lets you view PhotoCD images on the desktop (see Figure 13-2, "Accessing PhotoCD Images").

PhotoCD and older CD-ROM drives

Some older CD-ROM drives that use Sony mechanisms can read the first session on a PhotoCD — that is, the first set of images that were recorded to the CD — but are unable to access subsequent sessions. Apple's now-discontinued AppleCD 150 is one such drive.

Figure 13-2: Accessing PhotoCD Images Apple's CD-ROM drives include software that makes working with PhotoCD images more convenient. The Slide Show Viewer utility lets you browse through the images on a CD by using the QuickTime movie controller (upper left). Note the various folders on the CD itself — each holds images at various resolutions. Open a folder and you see a thumbnail version of each image.

If you have an older CD-ROM drive that lacks PhotoCD support, get FWB's CD-ROM Toolkit. It includes PhotoCD driver software as well as caching capabilities that boost CD-ROM performance.

Imaging software

The software that comes with a scanner or frame grabber is sometimes called *image-acquisition* software. It works with the hardware to acquire the ones and zeros that represent the original image and enables you to save it on disk. Most image-acquisition programs also have rudimentary editing features — for cropping out unwanted borders, for example.

Image-acquisition programs

One of the better image-acquisition programs is LightSource's Ofoto, which comes with Apple's scanners and is also available separately for use with other popular scanners. Ofoto includes numerous features that streamline the scanning process: The program automatically straightens out crooked scans, for example. Ofoto also provides sophisticated calibration features that make it easier to get high-quality results with a good balance of gray tones or colors (see Figure 13-3 "Inside Ofoto").

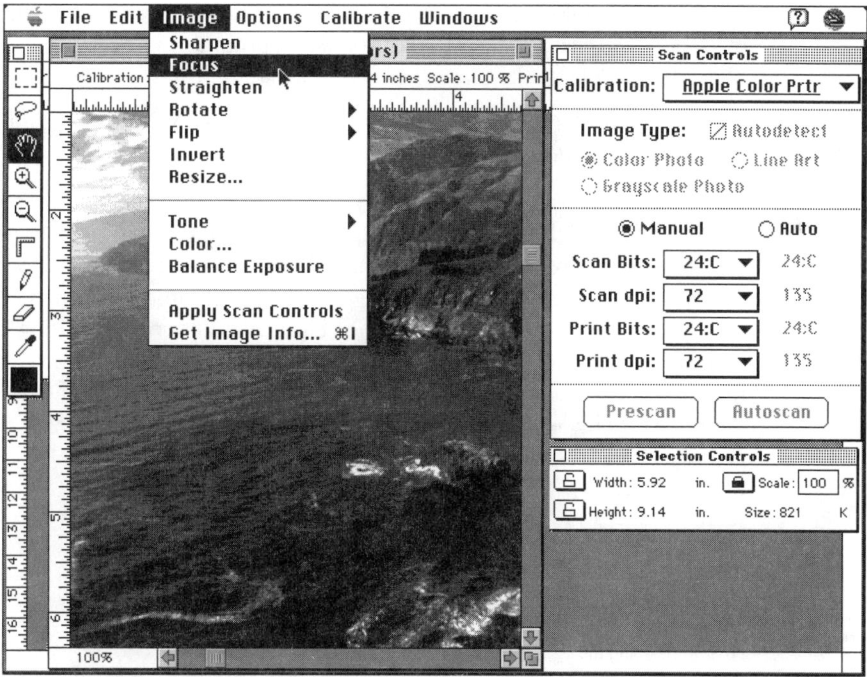

Figure 13-3: Inside Ofoto Light Source's Ofoto, included with Apple's scanners and available separately for third-party scanners, is a sophisticated scanning application that automates much of the grunt work behind scanning — cropping, straightening, and adjusting brightness and contrast.

Image-processing programs

As powerful as Ofoto is, for serious electronic retouching you want an image-processing program. Like the lowly MacPaint and SuperPaint, image-processing programs work with bitmapped graphics, which, as you saw in the preceding chapter, are images whose individual dots, or pixels, correspond to a series of ones and zeros, or bits. And like paint programs, image-processing programs let you alter an image's underlying ones and zeros and thus alter the image itself.

Image-processing and painting programs have much in common. Both provide on-screen tool palettes containing electronic erasers, pencils, and paintbrushes as well as tools for typing text and drawing lines, circles, and squares. You can zoom in on individual pixels for detail work or zoom out to fit an entire image on-screen. And you have two basic ways to select part of an image to move or modify it: A Marquee tool lets you select rectangular areas, and a Lasso tool lets you select irregularly shaped areas.

Gray-scale or color?

Just as some paint programs are color blind, some image-processing programs work only with gray-scale images. Gray-scale programs include Fractal Design's Sketcher and a first-rate but little-known program, MicroFrontier's Enhance.

In the color field, the market leader is Adobe's amazing Photoshop, followed by Fractal Design's Painter.

Quark, best known for its QuarkXPress publishing program, is also entering the field with QuarkXPosure. QuarkXPosure takes a unique approach to image editing: it keeps track of the modifications you make on an image but does not apply the modifications to the original image until you save it in a non-native file format, such as TIFF. Quark says this approach eliminates a lot of the waiting associated with complex image-editing tasks. Another benefit of QuarkXPosure's approach is that you can save a list of the tasks you performed and apply them to other images. This can be a big time-saver for repetitive operations such as opening an image, resizing it, adjusting its color balance, and then saving it.

Another Photoshop competitor is HSC Corporation's LivePicture, which uses a unique method of file management that enables you to work with huge files (for example, 500MB images) in real time. Like QuarkXPosure, LivePicture saves the changes you make to an image, but doesn't actually apply them until you save the image. LivePicture has been relatively slow to catch on in the marketplace, in part because early versions had stiff memory requirements and stiff price tags. The program has improved in both areas, however, and is gradually establishing a loyal following.

How Image-Processing Programs Work

Image-processing programs differ from most of their painting partners in that they provide more tools for drawing and modifying. Most programs provide an electronic airbrush whose flow rate and nozzle size you can adjust for painting anything from fine details to digital graffiti. A Smudge tool lets you smear part of an image as though it were a charcoal drawing and the mouse pointer was your fingertip. A Blur tool softens part of an image; a Sharpen tool does the opposite. A Rubber stamp tool duplicates one part of an image as you drag the mouse over a different part.

More tool options, too

The tools in an image-processing program are also laden with options for tailoring how they work. How fat should the pencil point be? Should paint flow continuously from the Paintbrush tool or fade as you paint? Or should it fade, then strengthen, and then fade again as though you're repeatedly applying short brush strokes? Should the paint or pencil lead be opaque, obscuring whatever it touches, or should it be transparent like watercolor?

Photoshop versions 2.5 and later provide two tools that anyone who has worked in a darkroom should find familiar — the Dodge and Burn tools. The Dodge tool lets you lighten an area as if you blocked part of the light coming from a photographic enlarger (see Figure 13-4 "Dodging Photoshop"). The Burn tool lets you darken an area as if you allowed light to reach an area for a longer length of time.

Figure 13-4: Dodging Photoshop Photoshop's Dodge tool simulates a common darkroom technique — blocking part of the light coming from a photographic enlarger in order to lighten an area. In the right image, the hull of the sailboat has been lightened by using the Dodge tool.

A plethora of palettes

Image-processing programs also provide palettes that let you choose from a variety of gray shades and, in some programs, colors. If you're retouching a scratch out of a photo, you can use the palette to select the gray shade or color you need before applying it with the Paintbrush tool. Better still, use the program's Eyedropper or Pickup tool. Point to a spot adjacent to the scratch and click, and the program automatically selects the gray shade or color you need (see Figure 13-5 "Pick Me Up").

Figure 13-5: Pick Me Up Retouching scratches in an old photograph is simplified by the Eyedropper tool, which lets you pick up a color or gray shade to use elsewhere. The Eyedropper tool picks up a gray shade (top) for retouching the scratch on the face to create the final retouched image (bottom). The Blur, Rubber stamp, and Smudge tools are also useful for retouching.

Antialiasing: text without jaggies

One classic drawback of bitmapped graphics programs is that the edges of shapes you draw appear jagged, especially when laser-printed. Image-processing programs eliminate this drawback through *antialiasing*, which smooths jaggies by adding shaded pixels. Most programs can apply their antialiasing talents to text when you use TrueType or Adobe Type Manager (Photoshop includes the latter).

Text is still a second-class citizen in image-processing programs. You can't edit or reformat it as you can in a drawing program such as ClarisDraw, Adobe Illustrator, Macromedia FreeHand, or Deneba's Canvas. If you need to add a lot of text to an image, import the image into a drawing or page-layout program.

Selecting and Masking

You often need to select part of an image as a prelude to moving or modifying it, but for selecting fine details, the basic Marquee and Lasso tools aren't enough. Most image-processing programs provide an advanced selection tool that is a magic wand; point to a spot and click, and the program selects all contiguous pixels of the same or similar color or gray shade. You can adjust the wand's tolerance to select a wide range of similar colors or grays or only ones identical to the spot you clicked.

One especially powerful selection tool is the Adobe Photoshop pen. It lets you select portions of an image by drawing Bezier curves, those geometric constructions that form the foundation of PostScript illustration programs and type fonts. Like the lasso, the Pen tool is best suited to selecting irregularly shaped portions of an image. But the pen allows for far greater precision, and it lets you fine-tune the selection area by clicking and dragging the curves' control points. You can even save the selection paths you draw to reapply them elsewhere in that image or in other images.

Figure 13-6: Feathering Illustrated By specifying a feathered selection, you can create a vignette effect such as this one. Feathered selections help minimize jarring transitions when you're pasting one image into another.

In most image-processing programs, even the lowly Lasso and Marquee tools have powerful options that simple paint programs lack. You can specify a feathered selection, for example; instead of selecting only the pixels within the selection boundary, the program throws in extra pixels on either side of the boundary and fades them (see Figure 13-6 "Feathering Illustrated").

Photoshop Power Tips

This box includes a collection of my favorite Photoshop tips. For tips on boosting Photoshop's filtering performance, see the Quick Tips box "Speeding Up Photoshop Filters" in this chapter.

Zooming shortcuts

Photoshop provides several shortcuts that let you zoom in and out on an image without having to first activate the Zoom tool. The first two shortcuts even work when a dialog box is open on-screen.

Palette tips

Photoshop's palettes are the gateways to many of the program's features. Beginning with version 3.0, Photoshop lets you customize palettes in several ways. You can rearrange a palette by dragging its tabs. For example, if you never use the Scratch portion of the Picker palette, drag the Scratch tab away from the palette, and it becomes a smaller palette unto itself. You can also create your own mega-palette by dragging the tabs you use most often to a particular palette.

Photoshop saves the positions and grouping of palettes when you quit the program. When you start it up again, the palettes are where you left them. If you'd rather Photoshop restore the palettes to their default positions, uncheck the Restore Dialog Positions box in the More Preferences dialog box.

Finally, you can hide Photoshop's many tool palettes by pressing the Tab key. Press Tab again to redisplay the palettes. Also remember that you can display and hide individual palettes by pressing the function keys on an extended keyboard.

Two ways to kern text

As I mention several times in this chapter and the preceding one, bitmapped programs such as Photoshop don't know text from any other bitmap. As a result, Photoshop doesn't have the kinds of fine text-spacing controls you find in publishing and illustration programs.

Still, you can adjust the spacing of text in two ways. One is to type a negative or positive value in the Spacing box of the text dialog box. (Type a negative value to decrease character spacing.) The other method is to use the little-known text-selection lasso. After you've created some text, leave it and the Text tool selected. Then press the ⌘ key to turn the mouse pointer into a lasso. You can use the lasso to deselect any of the characters and then use the arrow keys or the mouse to adjust the position of the remaining text.

View file information

The lower-left corner of Photoshop's document window normally displays the file size. If you press Option while clicking the file-size display, a little window pops up that displays statistics about the file: its size, number of channels, and resolution. If you press ⌘ while clicking the display, a different set of stats appears, this one listing the document's tiling information (which is useful when you're creating an oversized image that you'll print as a number of separate tiles). If you click the file size display without pressing any keys, a page preview window pops up that shows where the image appears in relation to the currently active Page Setup settings.

Zoom Shortcuts

To...	*Do This...*
Zoom in	Press ⌘-spacebar and click
Zoom out	Press Option-spacebar or ⌘-Option-spacebar and click
Switch to actual-size view	Double-click the Zoom tool
Zoom to fill the screen	Double-click the Hand tool

(continued on the next page)

(continued from previous page)

Gain quick access to the Eyedropper tool

You often use the Eyedropper tool (which picks up a color or gray shade) while working with other tools, such as the Text tool. Instead of traveling to the palette to activate the eyedropper, just press Option. As long as Option is pressed, the mouse pointer becomes an eyedropper. This shortcut works when the Text, Line, Paint can, Pencil, Gradient, and Airbrush tools are selected.

Press Option to pick up a background color

Normally, the Eyedropper tool changes the foreground color. To make it change the background color instead, press Option while clicking the color you want to pick up. This trick works only when the Eyedropper tool is explicitly selected in the palette — it doesn't work in combination with the Option-key shortcut in the preceding tip.

Open a second (or third or fourth) window

If you have a large-screen monitor or multiple monitors, consider opening multiple windows into a document by using the Window menu's New Window command. Each window can have a different zoom scale, allowing you to see your image from several vantage points at once.

Use crosshair pointers for precision

When the Caps Lock is down, many of Photoshop's tool pointers — the Paintbrush, Pencil, Eyedropper, and so on — look like crosshairs. Use this crosshair pointer when you need to zero in on a particular spot.

Keys to selection shortcuts

Photoshop's image-selection tools are incredibly powerful, but some of their power is hidden behind the Option key or similar sequences. The table below summarizes Photoshop's hidden selection shortcuts.

Selection Shortcuts

To	*Do This*
Create polygonal selections with the lasso	Press Option as you click at the corners of the area you want to select
Have the lasso enclose what's inside it	Select the area, select the magic wand, and then ⌘-click within the selection
Create a copy of the selection	Press Option and then drag or use the arrow keys
Move the marquee without moving the selection	Press ⌘-Option while dragging or using the arrow keys
Deselect an area within the selection	Press ⌘ and drag within the selection
Add an area to the selection	Press Shift and drag across the area you want to add
Connect separate selections	Press Shift-Control (not ⌘) and drag
Select a circular or rectangular area	Press Shift while selecting

Make your own function key shortcuts

With the Commands palette, you can create your own keyboard shortcuts for the function keys on an extended keyboard. Choose Show Commands from the Palettes submenu (Windows menu), and then use the Commands palette's menu to change commands. You can even save and load different sets of function key shortcuts — consider creating one for each of the types of projects you work on.

Access the last filter's dialog box

Every Photoshop fanatic knows that you can press ⌘-F to reexecute the last filter you used. But did you know that when you press ⌘-Option-F, you get the dialog box corresponding to the last-used filter? This sequence is handy when you want to apply the same filter but with different settings.

These selection variations help in two ways — in modifying parts of an image and in creating masks. Just as masking tape prevents stray paint from staining woodwork, a *mask* prevents stray pixels from fouling part of an image. You can use a mask to protect an area adjacent to the spot you're retouching or to add a new background by combining images (see Figure 13-7 "Moon Over Chicago").

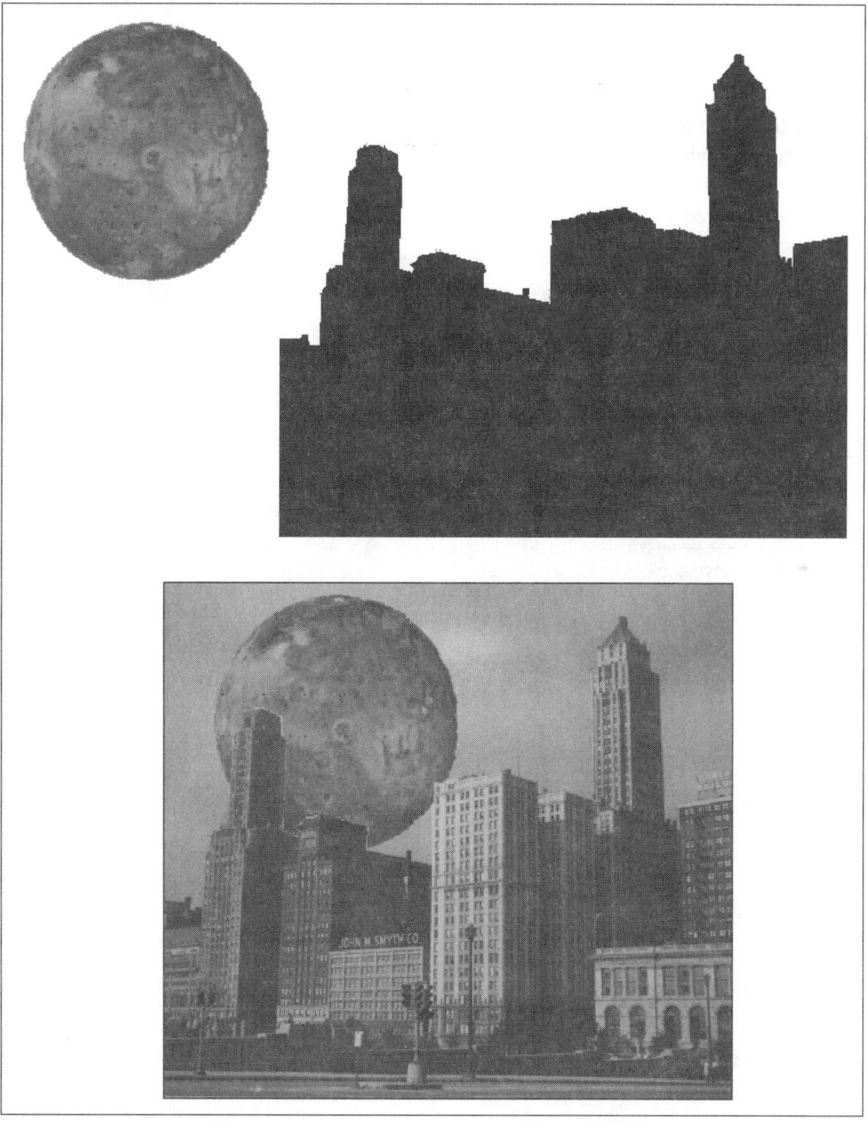

Figure 13-7: Moon Over Chicago Io, one of the moons of Jupiter, rises over Chicago. This composite was created by giving the moon (top left) a slightly feathered edge, creating a mask for the skyline (top right), and then pasting the moon into position (bottom). The mask protects the buildings, enabling the moon to appear behind them.

Layering and floating selections

If you worked with bitmapped imaging programs in their earlier days, you've experienced the following frustration: You paste one image into another, deselect what you've pasted, and then realize that you want to move the pasted image slightly. With most paint programs, you can't; as soon as you deselect part of an image, it becomes part of the sea of pixels that makes up the entire image. It's the classic drawback of bitmapped graphics programs — and, you might recall from the previous chapter, it's a drawback that object-oriented drawing programs don't share.

Today's higher-end imaging programs address this drawback by supporting multiple image *layers*. Think of an image layer as a sheet of clear plastic upon which you can paint or paste an image. You can create multiple layers and place a different image on each one. The final image is made up of the images contained on each layer.

Placing different portions of an image on different layers makes it easy to rearrange the final image. Suppose you're working on a promotional poster for a new Godzilla movie, and you've just pasted Godzilla's image into a picture of the Pittsburgh skyline. (Godzilla's heading west in this sequel.) You've positioned the big ape atop the old Gulf Building but decide later that he'd look better mauling the Westinghouse Building. Simply activate the layer containing Godzilla, and you can move the monkey by dragging him. If you save a bunch of little airplanes in their own layer, you can move them, too. And if you create a layer for the sky, you can create one version of the poster that contains blue skies and another version that contains thunder and lightning.

When you add a layer to an image, you can specify how it affects the underlying layers. You can specify that a layer completely obscure the image it covers, appear transparent, invert the underlying image, and much more.

Painter also lets you save floating selections in a Portfolio, which is Painter's equivalent to the library features found in publishing programs such as Adobe PageMaker and QuarkXPress. A Portfolio window lets you save and recall image selections for quick reuse.

Gamma and Color Correction

Anyone who has struggled to print a poorly exposed photo in a darkroom will want an image-processing program just for its *gamma-correction* features. By assigning different colors or gray shades to the underlying ones and zeros that describe each dot, an image-processing program can change the brightness, contrast, and color balance of an image.

Techniques for adjusting brightness and contrast

For adjusting brightness and contrast, most programs provide on-screen sliders and a window containing a *gray-map* graph, which graphically shows the relationship between the ones and zeros in the image file and the shades of gray on-screen. You can tailor the gray map by drawing with a Pencil tool. Most programs let you save gray maps on disk, enabling you to apply them to similarly exposed images in the future. Most also let you apply corrections to only part of the image — useful for bringing out details in a washed-out face.

One common pitfall of gray-scale scanning (and of black-and-white photography, for that matter) is the failure to get a complete range of gray tones. An image should have a wide distribution of gray shades — from white, for bright areas such as highlights; to black, for dark areas such as shadows. In between those extremes are *midtones* — the light, medium, and dark grays that represent most of the image's details. An image whose range of grays is too narrow lacks contrast and is often described as *flat.* An image that has bright whites and dark blacks but few midtones has too much contrast and doesn't show details well.

I just mentioned that most programs have brightness and contrast controls — on-screen sliders that let you adjust the overall brightness and contrast of the entire image or a part of it. Many publishing programs have similar controls. But brightness and contrast controls, while enhancing one aspect of the image, often cause degradation elsewhere. If you boost brightness to bring out shadow details, light areas of the image become washed out and their details disappear. Similarly, if you increase contrast, you lose details in both light and dark areas.

Linear versus nonlinear correction

A better way to improve brightness and contrast involves using another of the contrast-adjustment features I mentioned earlier — a gray-map display. This graph's horizontal axis shows the original brightness values in the file — the *input values* — and its vertical axis shows the new brightness values, or *output values.* By altering the shape of the graph, you tell the image-processing program to assign new values to the image's underlying data, thus changing its brightness and contrast (see Figure 13-8 "Working with Grays").

When you draw a custom gray-map curve, you're performing *nonlinear* correction; you're altering the original image's data in varying degrees to improve the image's appearance. By comparison, when you use a brightness or contrast control, you're performing *linear* correction — remapping all the values to the same degree, which can lead to the loss of details in bright or dark areas.

You can also use a gray-map graph to create special effects. Draw a line shaped like a *V*, for example, and you get a solarized effect similar to that produced in a darkroom when a developing print is briefly exposed to light.

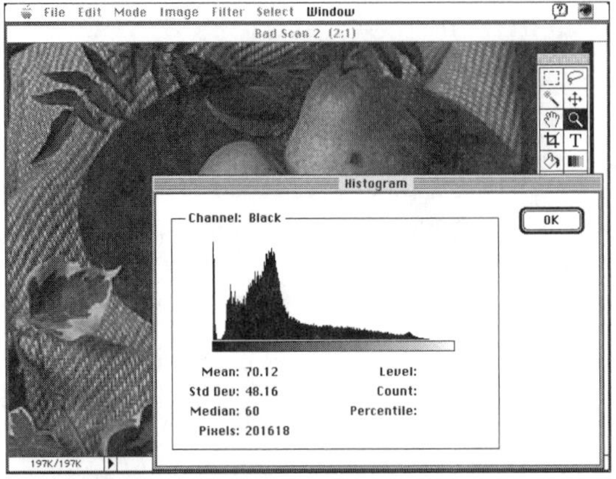

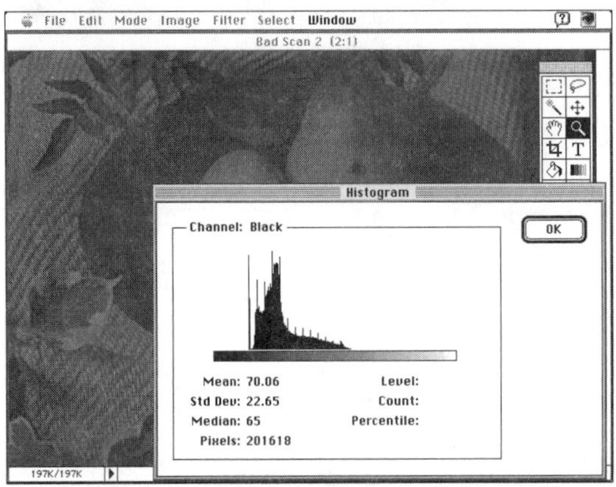

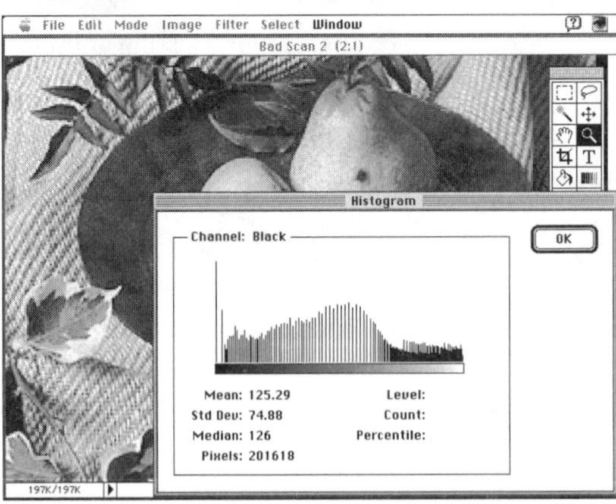

Figure 13-8: Working with Grays
Brightness and contrast controls and gray-map displays let you finely tailor brightness and contrast, and histograms let you view the distribution of gray levels. The original image (top) has its brightness, contrast, and gray map unchanged. The image is too dark: note that the histogram shows more dark shades than light ones. An image lacking contrast (middle) appears flat, and its histogram lacks values at the light and dark ends of the spectrum. Brightness and contrast have been tweaked (bottom) to produce a more appealing image and a wider distribution of grays in the histogram. I used Adobe Photoshop for these examples.

Reading a histogram display

One particularly powerful correction aid is a *histogram*, a bar chart that shows which gray shades appear in an image and to what degree. You can use a histogram to determine the kind of correction an image needs and to judge the effectiveness of your correction techniques.

For example, if most of a histogram's bars are at the left or right end of the chart, the image is probably too dark or too light. As a general rule, an image's histogram bars should form a fairly smooth curve (refer to Figure 13-8 "Working with Grays").

If an image's histogram looks like a mountain range alternating with plains, the image probably has too much contrast. A flat image's histogram is narrow, with most of the bars appearing in the midtone area and few or no bars at the black and white ends of the graph.

Adjusting images with the Equalize command

In many cases, improving a mediocre image doesn't require fiddling with contrast controls, gray maps, or histograms. Most programs provide an Equalize command, which mathematically adjusts the image's data to produce a more even range of light and dark shades. Examine a histogram after equalizing, and you see that the graph reflects a broader range of grays.

Color-Correction Features

Color image correction relies on similar concepts, except that the concepts extend beyond grays to include red, green, and blue — the three additive primary colors the Mac mixes to create color images.

Adjusting color with the Variations display

If you've ever done color darkroom work, Photoshop's color-correction features should feel familiar. The Variations window (available in Photoshop 2.5 and later) provides an on-screen *color ring-around* that displays numerous versions of an image, each with its own color balance, contrast, and saturation (color purity) settings. You can choose the one that looks most pleasing and use it as is or as a basis for further refinements (see Figure 13-9 "Color Variations").

You can find this multiple-choice approach in other image-editing applications, including Cachet from Electronic for Imaging (EFI). Cachet doesn't provide the wide array of retouching tools that Photoshop does. It's a color-correction specialist designed to supplement programs such as Photoshop. (Indeed, EFI calls Cachet a *color editor*, not an image-processing program.)

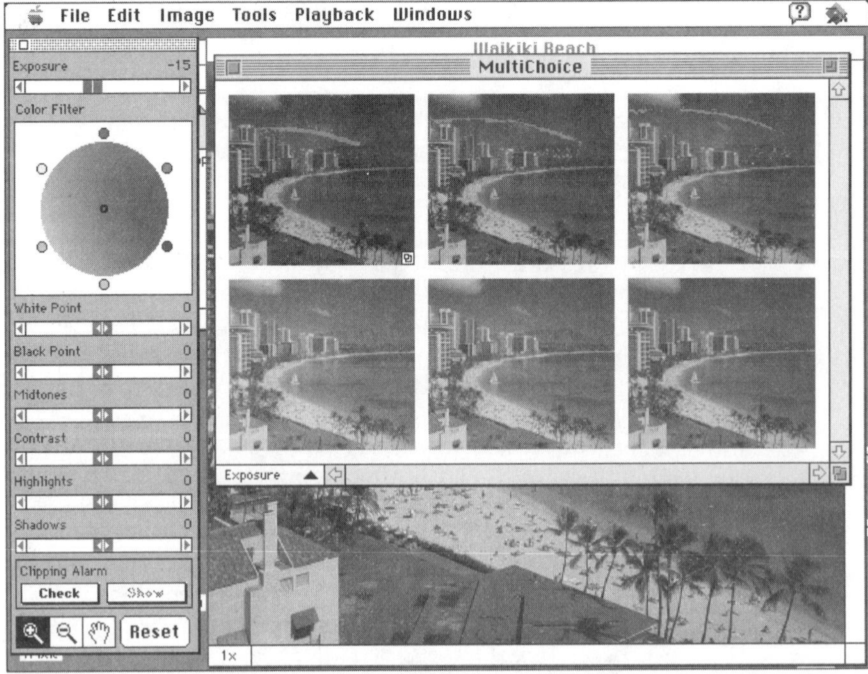

Figure 13-9: Color Variations The Variations window in Photoshop (top) provides an on-screen color ring-around that displays numerous versions of an image, each with its own color balance, contrast, and saturation settings. EFI's Cachet is shown at the bottom.

For Best Results, Use a High-Quality Original

The best way to get an ideal range of grays or pleasing color balance in a scanned image is, of course, to scan a photograph that has it to begin with. Similarly, if you're capturing an image with a video camera, the key is to light the subject properly. For example, diffused light produces less contrast than direct sunlight.

Often, however, you must make do with substandard photographs or lighting. In photography, a darkroom technician can compensate for contrast problems when printing an image. With scanned images, you can improve contrast by using an image-processing program.

Cachet's clever approach to color correction eliminates the hassle of calibrating a monitor and printer. You adjust the on-screen colors of an image to match the colors of a reference image that has already been corrected in Cachet. When your image's colors match the reference, the image is color-corrected. EFI calls this approach *edit by reference.* Cachet includes a large library of reference images, which you can supplement with your own corrected images.

Filtering

Histogram and gray-mapping features alter an image's grays; *filters* alter the image itself. By examining an image's underlying data and then applying calculations to it, an image program can modify the image (see Figure 13-10 "A Filter Sampler"). Some filters enhance the quality of an image; a sharpening filter, for example, can bring out details lost during scanning.

Producing special effects

Other filters produce special effects, with Photoshop's filters leading the pack. Its Motion Blur filter simulates motion by blurring the image in a single direction, and the Zigzag filter creates rippling effects — as if viewing an image through water. The Pointillize filter makes an image look like it was painted in a pointillist style. The Swirl filter simulates an image's journey down a drain, and the Spherize filter simulates a fish-eye lens or a Christmas tree bulb. You can spend hours exploring Photoshop's filters — and waiting for the results. It can take a Quadra-class machine half an hour to filter a large color image.

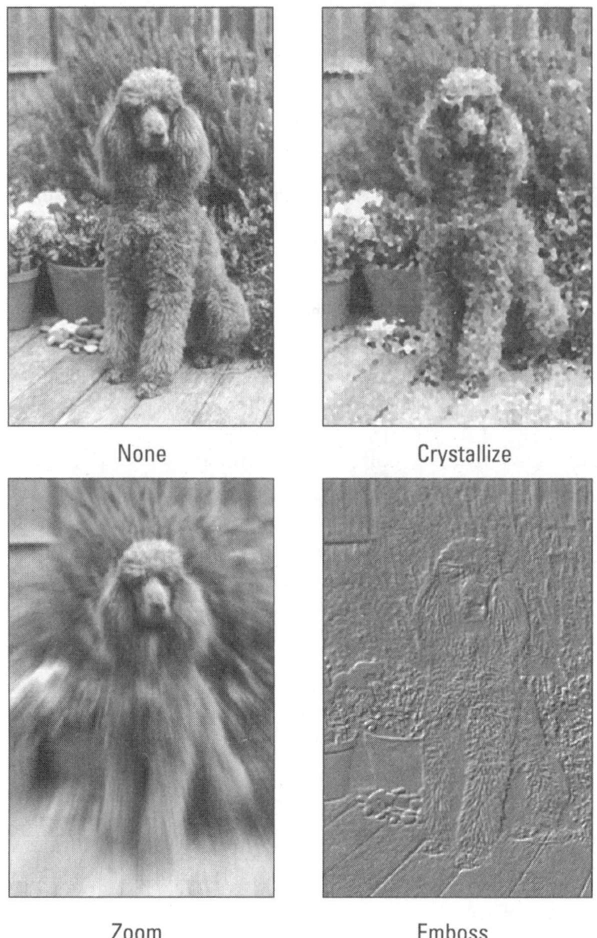

Figure 13-10: A Filter Sampler A sampling of Adobe Photoshop's special effects filters.

Some filters hint at image processing's scientific applications — edge-detection filters alter an image so that only its edges appear and can be useful for creating unusual embossed effects. Photoshop also enables you to create new filters by editing a table of data (technically, a *convolution matrix*) that tells the program how to alter pixels based on their neighbors.

Plug-in filter modules

Most programs come with several filters and enable you to add new ones by using *plug-in modules*, separate miniprograms that add new features to the program. This is the concept of software extensibility that I discussed in Chapter 10 — applied to the imaging world.

Choosing Your Image-Enhancement Weapon

Brightness and contrast controls, gray-map displays, histograms, Equalize commands: How do you decide which correction scheme to use? Try the Equalize command first. It's the easiest of the four techniques, and it's often all you need. If it isn't, the Undo command puts you back to square one, where you can try the other techniques, relying on the histogram and your eyes to get the results you want.

Fix brightness and contrast before retouching

If you retouch an image by using the Paintbrush, Smudge, Rubber stamp, or other tool discussed earlier, fix the image's brightness and contrast problems before retouching. Otherwise, the image may have odd splotches of gray and other undesirable artifacts. Also, remember that some image-processing programs let you save gray-map curves and apply them to other images. This option can be a big time-saver when you're working with numerous images that share the same brightness and contrast characteristics.

This software expandability has created a market for filters. Adobe's Gallery Effects series, for example, includes filters for texture, watercolor, pen-and-ink, and other effects. Three volumes of Gallery Effects are available; each provides 17 different filters.

The Photoshop plug-in format has become so popular that other programs now support it. You can, for instance, use Photoshop plug-in filters with Fractal Design's Painter and even with video-editing programs such as Adobe's Premiere and After Effects. (For tips on using the same filters with more than one program, see the Quick Tips box "Using Plug-in Modules with More than One Program.")

Other popular filter and plug-in libraries include HSC Software's Kai's Power Tools, Xoas Tools' Paint Alchemy, and Andromeda Software's Photography Filters and Three-D Filters.

Variations on the plug-in theme

It's worth noting that some plug-ins aren't filters, but instead add new features to Photoshop, such as the capability to control a scanner — a timesaving feature that enables you to scan, enhance, and retouch within a single program. Most scanners now include these Photoshop *import modules.* Similarly, some color printers include a Photoshop *export module* that enables you to bypass the Mac's standard printer driver when printing images, a scheme that results in better image quality and faster print times.

Using Plug-in Modules with More than One Program

If you're a serious digital imager, chances are you have more than one program that supports Photoshop plug-in filters. You could install your favorite filter libraries into each application's Plug-ins folder, but you'd waste a tremendous amount of disk space.

Here's a better way: First, install the filters just once — for example, in the Photoshop Plug-ins folder. Next, open the Plug-ins folder, select the filters that you also want to use in a different program, and choose Make Alias from the Finder's File menu. Finally, copy the aliases to the other program's Plug-ins folder. When you start the program, it will use the aliases to locate the original filters.

If you want the filters to be available to a third application program, make aliases of the original filters and copy the aliases into the third program's Plug-ins folder.

See Chapter 22 for more tips on using aliases.

Batch-processing images in Photoshop

If you use Photoshop in a production setting, chances are a lot of your work is repetitive: open an image, resize it, resample it, apply the Sharpen filter, tweak the brightness and contrast, save the image, and then repeat. It gets old quickly.

Daystar Digital's PhotoMatic allows you to set up scripts that batch-process images. With PhotoMatic, you record Photoshop functions by using low-resolution files and then tell PhotoMatic to apply them to your high-resolution originals. PhotoMatic is essentially a "watch me" macro recorder — invoke the record mode, perform some tasks, and then turn off the record, and you get a script that reflects what you did. PhotoMatic scripts are saved in AppleScript-compatible format (see Chapter 24), so you can edit them to add, remove, or fine-tune a particular step.

Storing it Away: Choosing an Image File Format

All image-processing programs support several file formats (indeed, Photoshop supports nearly all of them). Your goal is to settle on one that uses disk space efficiently, is supported by your desktop publishing program, and is compatible with all other software you plan to use on the images.

Fractal Design's RIFF format is efficient and supported by the QuarkXPress and Manhattan Graphics ReadySetGo publishing programs, not to mention Fractal's Painter and Sketcher programs (both covered in the preceding chapter). PageMaker and Photoshop do not support RIFF.

Adobe PageMaker supports several varieties of TIFF format, including those saved with LZW and RLE encoding. These acronyms refer to compression schemes that save space by replacing groups of identical values with a code. You use a similar technique when you say "a dozen eggs" instead of saying "egg" 12 times.

For a quick reference to these and other graphics file formats, see Table 12-1 in the preceding chapter.

Speeding Up Photoshop Filters

Complex filtering operations can take a long time, even for a fast Mac. Here are some tips for speeding up Photoshop filtering operations.

A DSP Board or Quadra 660AV or 840AV

A DSP board — as well as the Quadra 660AV and 840AV — contains a specialized processor designed for the number-crunching demands of image processing. Unlike a general-purpose accelerator, a DSP board doesn't speed your Mac's overall operation. It's specifically designed to speed up filtering, selecting, and other common Photoshop operations.

Some DSP boards designed for Photoshop include DayStar Digital's Charger and Radius's Thunder series. All are available for NuBus-equipped Macs.

Radius's PhotoBooster for the Mac Quadra family is a processor-direct slot (PDS) board. PhotoBooster uses an AT&T DSP3210 — the same 32-bit DSP chip used in Apple's AV Macs. The PhotoBooster is compatible with the Apple RealTime Architecture (ARTA) that the Quadra 840AV and 660AV use (see Chapter 33). DayStar Digital's Image 040 accelerator contains twin DSP chips *and* a fast 68040, thus providing overall acceleration as well as Photoshop acceleration.

Beginning with version 3.0, Photoshop takes direct advantage of DSP hardware. If you're using Photoshop 2.5, use Adobe's AV DSP Power plug-in to boost Photoshop's performance. This plug-in speeds 18 Photoshop operations, including Blur, Blur More, Gaussian Blur, Sharpen, Sharpen More,

(continued on the next page)

(continued from previous page)

Unsharp Mask, Sharpen Edges, Find Edges, High Pass, Custom, Despeckle, Emboss, Fragment, Resize, Rotate, Skew, Perspective, and RGB-to-CMYK mode changes.

The PowerPC Alternative

Filtering is one area where the PowerPC family of RISC chips can really earn their keep. Their sizzling performance at floating-point math (of which there is plenty in filtering operations) enables Power Macs and other PowerPC-equipped Macs to perform filtering jobs several times faster than a 68040-based Mac.

As with DSP support, Photoshop provides direct Power Mac support beginning with version 3. If you're using version 2.5 of Photoshop, you need Adobe's PowerPC Accelerator plug-in. This plug-in replaces Photoshop's image-processing engine with one that runs in PowerPC native mode.

If you're using a PowerPC-equipped Mac, be sure to use filters that are written in native PowerPC code (look for the "Accelerated for Power Macintosh" sticker on the box). HSC's Kai's Power Tools run in native mode. Beginning with version 1.5.1, Adobe's Gallery Effects also run in native mode.

PowerPC upgrade cards

If you currently have a 68040 Mac but you want to apply PowerPC performance to your Photoshop work, consider a PowerPC accelerator such as Daystar Digital's PowerPro. Designed to install in the processor-direct slot of a Mac IIci, Quadra 700, 800, 900, 950, or Centris 650, the PowerPro card uses a PowerPC 601 chip running at 66 MHz or 80 MHz. The card has a 64-bit data bus and accepts an optional 128MB of on-board memory for even higher performance.

If you have a Power Mac 9500, 8500, or 7500, you might consider upgrading to a faster processor — for example, upgrading from the 100 MHz PowerPC 601 that's in the Power Mac 8500 to a 132 MHz PowerPC 604 chip. See Chapter 29 for more details on Power Mac upgrades.

Filter a small area to save time

Whether or not you use a DSP chip or a Power Mac to speed up Photoshop, remember that you can preview a filter's effects by selecting a small portion of an image before applying the filter. When you're experimenting with filter settings, this approach is much faster than filtering an entire image. If you're happy with the preview results, use the Undo command to restore the image and then apply the filter to the entire area you want to modify. If you aren't happy with the preview results, choose Undo and try, try again.

Shore up your Mac's storage system

You probably don't need me to tell you this, but Photoshop is a disk-intensive program. The faster your storage system, the better Photoshop's performance. Serious Photoshop users often rely on high-speed SCSI adapters and disk arrays to improve performance. You can find full details about these add-ons in Chapter 25.

The Problems with Printing

You've tweaked grays, retouched scratches, and filtered an image into a digital masterpiece. The next step — paper. This stage is often the most disappointing part of desktop image processing. Because of the way most printers handle gray-scale or color images, your printed results can't match the quality you see on-screen.

The heartbreak of halftoning

Several factors contribute to the disappointing look of printed images, but foremost among them is halftoning. Unlike monitors, monochrome printers can't produce shades of gray, but must simulate grays by using black dots of varying size. Similarly, most color printers must combine cyan, yellow, magenta, and black dots in various patterns to create their hues.

To create these dots, a printer combines the smallest dots it can create into clusters called *cells* and then turns on varying numbers of dots within each cell. The number of cells per inch corresponds to the screen frequency and is usually measured in lines per inch (lpi). (The term *screen frequency* derives from conventional photographic halftoning, in which an image is photographed through a special mask containing thousands of minute, regularly spaced holes.)

When printer dots are combined into larger cells, the printer's resolution effectively plummets. A 300-dpi laser printer's ideal halftone screen frequency is only about 53 lpi — short of the 85-lpi screens often used in newspapers and of the 133- to 150-line screens used in magazines.

Using high-resolution printers

The key to better digital halftones is printing on a device with higher resolution. Laser printers with resolutions of 600 dpi and higher are common: examples include Apple's LaserWriter Pro series, Hewlett-Packard's LaserJet 4M and 5M, and Lexmark's Optra series (which prints at up to 1200 dpi). A 600-dpi printer can produce attractive 85-lpi halftones.

Better still is Apple's PhotoGrade technology, which is built into most of today's LaserWriters as well as into the older LaserWriter Pro 600 and 630 and LaserWriter IIf and IIg printers. PhotoGrade finely controls these printers' lasers to yield 106-lpi halftones (see Chapter 30 for output samples and more details on resolution-enhancement techniques). Best of all, of course, is an imagesetter, which can produce magazine-quality halftones.

Many other variables influence the appearance of printed images. The printer itself is one; printers and imagesetters vary in their ability to accurately translate grays in an image to halftone cells on a page. Paper is another; every stock has unique texture and light-reflection properties. And when you photocopy a printed image or print it on an offset printing press, you introduce still more variables.

Advice to Budding Digital Imagers: Look Before You Leap

Matching file formats is one of the easier aspects of electronic imaging. Although programs like LightSource's Ofoto streamline the scanning process, getting top-notch results is not a point-and-click proposition. Before taking the image-processing plunge, step back and assess your goals. If you want high-quality halftones in desktop publications, you may be better off using conventional photographic halftones, which are inexpensive and can be superior to digital halftones.

Many publishers are committed to pushing the technology and adopting all-electronic publishing techniques, but with that commitment come myriad technical and logistic hurdles. If conventional techniques are working for you now, take a slow and steady approach to going electronic. The problem with pushing technology is that technology often pushes back — usually when you're on a deadline.

Printer calibration curves

To compensate for these variables, use your image-processing or scanning software to create a *printer calibration curve.* This document's data describes the relationship between the grays in an image and the grays that your printing process reproduces. It's a kind of gray map for printing. For an overview of the process, see the Step-by-Step box "Calibrating a Printer."

Calibrating a Printer

A calibration curve tells an image-processing program how a given printer or printing process handles grays, enabling you to get more accurate and more consistent output. The specific steps for creating a calibration curve vary from program to program, but the general routine is outlined in the steps below.

To create a calibration curve:

1. Print the gray-scale test chart built into the image-processing or scanning program, using the paper you normally use.

2. If you'll be offset printing or photocopying your final images, run the printed test chart through your printing process, using the same ink, imagesetter, printing press or copier, and paper stock that you will use for the final product.

(continued on the next page)

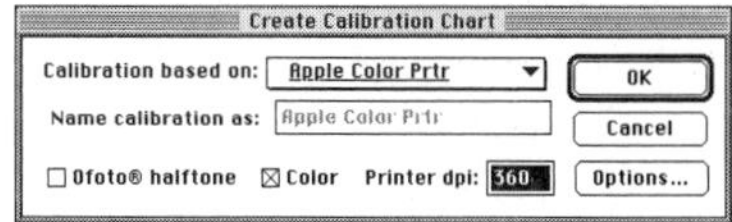

3. Scan the chart (or its photocopied or offset-printed version).

4. Depending on the software you use, you may at this point have to use the program to measure the scanned gray shades and manually enter values for the calibration curve.

   Programs such as Ofoto, the software that accompanies Apple's OneScanner, perform this chore automatically.

5. **Save the calibration curve.**

   Apply the curve to an image just before printing it (or just before saving it, if you plan to import it into a publishing program). Because the curve alters the image's brightness and contrast, don't apply it until you've performed other retouching and correction steps.

Focus on Filmless Photography

Electronic cameras combine photographic optics with the wizardry of computer imaging — and do away with film expenses, caustic chemistry, and processing delays. Professional photographers can transmit images from remote locations without having to first process and then scan them. Business people can quickly include images in newsletters and reports. For economy-minded amateurs and deadline-driven professionals — and for anyone who wants to include images in computer-generated documents — a filmless camera seems like a dream come true.

I wrote a *Macworld* feature on electronic cameras a while back and spent quite a bit of time working with numerous electronic cameras, including Apple's original QuickTake 100, Canon's RC-570, and Kodak's high-end DCS-200, which has since been replaced by the DCS-460.

The verdict? There's still room for improvement in both cost and image quality. For example, Apple's QuickTake 150 costs more than a 35mm single-lens reflex camera that accepts interchangeable lenses, yet it's a snapshot-grade camera — a disposable camera from the corner drugstore provides better image quality. There are some good reasons to take the electronic photography plunge, but low equipment costs and film-like image quality are not among them.

The best arguments for today's electronic cameras revolve around deadlines, convenience, and computers themselves. With a filmless camera, you can see an image an instant after you take it — with some cameras, in even less time than it takes to peel a Polaroid. What's more, it's becoming increasingly common for an image's final resting place to be a computer — in a page-layout program, database, or multimedia package. A filmless camera eliminates the multistep process of taking a photo, having it processed, and then scanning and tweaking it to obtain a high-quality digital version.

Behind the Lens

Shopping for an electronic camera means addressing conventional camera issues — lens quality and characteristics, exposure controls, and size and weight — as well as those factors unique to the electronic field: the camera's imaging method, the way images are stored, and the way you transfer them to the Mac.

Electronic cameras share a common characteristic with video cameras and scanners: They contain a *charge-coupled device*, or *CCD*, a chip containing photosensitive cells that generate voltage when struck by light. The design of the CCD and the way the information it generates is processed within the camera play key roles in determining image sharpness, color quality, and light sensitivity.

How still-video cameras work

The field of filmless cameras is divided into two main camps: still-video cameras and digital cameras. Think of a still-video camera as a camcorder without a tape drive; it generates an analog video signal that you can display on a TV monitor, record with a video recorder, or capture with an AV Mac or video frame grabber board. The still-video cameras I tested include Sony's Pro Mavica MVC-7000 and Canon's RC-570. Both cameras provide a composite video-out jack, and the Sony also accepts an optional S-video output adapter. (S-video generally provides a sharper image because the signal's color and brightness information travel on separate wires; a composite video signal merges this information.)

All of the first electronic cameras were of the still-video variety: being able to use existing CCDs and support circuitry was convenient for their manufacturers. But still-video technology has some inherent limitations. Still-video cameras use CCDs designed to capture a full frame in two passes, grabbing first the even-numbered scan lines and then the odd-numbered ones. To accommodate this *interlacing*, a still-video camera's CCD has smaller light-sensitive cells than the *full-frame* CCDs used by most digital cameras. To compensate, a still-video camera has to apply more image processing to the CCD's data, making images more prone to aliasing and other artifacts.

The still-video approach has other drawbacks. Image quality often suffers because of the extra signal processing required to convert the CCD's information into an interlaced analog video signal and then into digital form when you capture the image. When used for still photography, CCDs designed for video applications are prone to undesirable artifacts: fuzzy fringes surrounding the objects in a high-contrast scene or vibrant colors that bleed slightly into surrounding areas (see Figure 13-11 "Comparing Image Quality").

How digital cameras work

A digital camera's CCD and its support circuitry are designed from the ground up to deliver a digital result. Because the CCD doesn't require the additional elements needed for interlacing, its light-sensitive cells can be larger and closer together. And because the CCD's signal starts out digital and remains that way, you avoid the distortion that can take place in the conversion between the analog and digital worlds.

How filmless cameras store images

A lowly roll of film can store more images than almost any filmless camera. Digital images devour storage space, and to hold them, filmless cameras use either battery-powered memory chips or small floppy or even hard disk drives.

Most digital cameras, including Apple's QuickTake 100 and 150 and Kodak's Digital Camera 40, store images in internal memory. One drawback to storing images in memory is that you have to transfer them to the Mac when you reach the camera's capacity — otherwise, you're done shooting.

The QuickTake 100 holds either eight 640 x 480 – pixel images or 32 photos at 320 x 240 pixels. Its replacement, the QuickTake 150, holds either 16 high-quality images or 32 standard-quality images. In either case, the image resolution is 640 x 480 pixels. (The QuickTake 150's other improvements over the 100 include a close-up lens, improved color reproduction, a better viewfinder, and improved image-transfer software. You can learn more about the QuickTake 150 by watching the *Macworld Power User Clinic*'s Digital Imaging segment.) You have to delete all the images to free up memory.

The Kodak DC 40 provides an image resolution of 756 x 504 pixels — somewhat higher than that of the QuickTake 150. The DC 40 provides 4MB of internal memory that enable it to store 48 high-quality images and 99 images at a lower-quality resolution of 378 x 256 pixels.

Figure 13-11: Comparing Image Quality These images were taken with filmless cameras by San Francisco photographer Stan Muselik. Top: Apple's QuickTake 100; middle: Kodak's DCS-200; bottom: Canon's RC-570. Note the blurry edges in the RC-570 image, an artifact of its still-video technology. The QuickTake 100 has since been replaced by the improved QuickTake 150, and the DCS-200 has been replaced by the DCS-460, but these images are still useful for comparison purposes. (You can see color versions of these images in the *Macworld Power User Clinic*'s Digital Imaging segment.)

Other Factors That Influence Image Quality

Many subtle factors influence the quality of a filmless camera's image.

The size of the CCD

Each of the CCD's photosensitive cells corresponds to a single pixel in the final image. The more cells the CCD provides, the higher the potential resolution of its image — and the larger the image can be scaled without distortion. For example, Logitech's FotoMan Plus, a low-end, black-and-white digital camera, uses a 178,560-pixel CCD, while the CCD in Kodak's high-end DCS-200 and DCS-420 have over 1.5 million pixels. Impressive as that sounds, consider that a fine-grain 35mm slide film has an estimated resolution equivalent to 20 million pixels.

The way the CCD records color data

Some high-end cameras — including Sony's MVC-7000 — provide three separate CCDs, one each for red, green, and blue. Within the camera, a beam splitter sends light to each CCD. The separate CCDs pay off: the Sony MVC-7000 delivers much better image quality than the single-CCD Canon RC-570.

But three separate CCDs increase complexity, size, and cost. Most cameras use a single CCD whose cells are covered with a filter pattern that makes some cells sensitive to red, some to blue, and some to green. The camera then averages, or *interpolates,* the data from these cells to create the final image.

The CCD's filter pattern

Even the quality of the CCD's filter pattern affects image quality. The design of the interline sensors used by still-video cameras, for example, prohibits the CCD from having an evenly spaced array of green cells. As a result, the camera has to do more interpolation, which can lead to color fringing and other distortions.

Apple's QuickTake 100 and 150 and the Kodak Digital Camera 40 use a Kodak-patented filter pattern called a Bayer pattern. Kodak originally developed this pattern for its $10,000 DCS-200. For the QuickTake 100 and 150, Apple and Kodak collaborated on a CCD design that provides the image-quality benefits of the Bayer pattern for less money.

To reduce storage requirements, most digital cameras store images in compressed form. But compression takes time, which means that you can't shoot multiple images in rapid-fire succession. The QuickTake 150 generally takes a few seconds to compress an image (the exact time depends on the image). By comparison, the Canon RC-570 still-video camera offers a continuous-photo mode that takes two images per second.

Floppies instead of film

The Sony and Canon cameras store images on tiny floppy disks. The 2-inch disks hold up to either 25 or 50 images, depending on whether you shoot in *frame* or *field* mode. Frame mode provides better image quality by combining two interlaced fields from the CCD, but it uses twice the disk space in the camera. You can mix image modes on a single floppy, and you can delete individual images to free up space. Best of all, when a floppy fills, you can eject it and insert a new one.

The Kodak DCS-200 accepts an optional internal hard drive and connects to an external drive through a built-in SCSI interface. The model I tested contains an 80MB hard drive capable of storing up to 50 images. To prolong battery life, the hard drive spins only after you take an image, spinning down again several seconds later. It takes about four seconds for the drive to spin up and another four seconds for the camera to copy the image from its internal memory, which can hold only one image. The Kodak DCS-420 also has a SCSI interface, and it accepts removable PC cards (also called PCMCIA cards) that can contain memory or hard drives.

The primary drawback to storing images on floppy or hard drives is that the drives themselves can go south under physical abuse. Disk drives also require more power than memory chips, which means less time between battery charges when you frequently insert and eject disks or review the pictures you've shot.

From camera to Mac: transferring images

So how do you get images from the camera into the Mac — and how long does the transfer take? The answers depend on the camera. Most cameras include or accept optional cables and image-transfer utilities that make it easy to transfer some or all images to the Mac. The Sony MVC-7000 camera relies on a video-output jack; this approach has some limitations and advantages that I'll discuss shortly.

All image-transfer utilities work similarly. A window displays thumbnail versions of the images in the camera; double-clicking a thumbnail downloads the image, which appears in a new window (see Figure 13-12 "Comparing Transfer Utilities"). Some utilities have rudimentary image-enhancement features such as sharpening commands, brightness and contrast adjustments, and cropping tools, but you still need a program such as Adobe Photoshop for serious image editing.

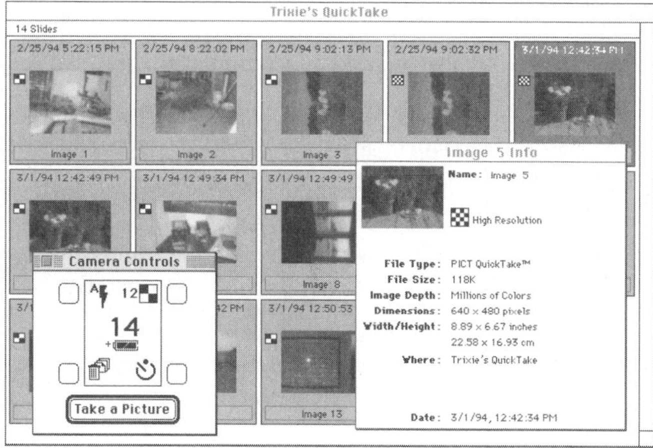

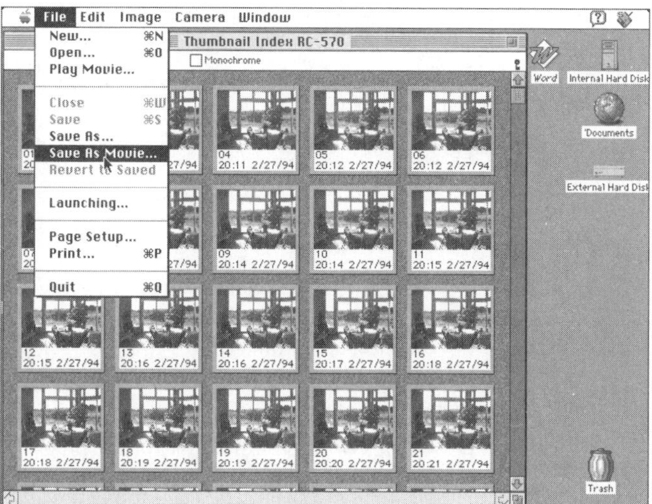

Figure 13-12: Comparing Transfer Utilities Image-transfer utilities display thumbnail versions of the images in the camera's memory or on its disk. Top: Apple's PhotoFlash provides useful Get Info windows that display details about a selected image. The Camera Controls window mimics the QuickTake's buttons and LCD panel. Middle: The QuickTake Setup control panel puts the QuickTake's contents on the Mac's desktop — as if the camera were just another disk. With System 7's file sharing features, you can even make the camera available to other Macs on the network. Bottom: The Save As Movie command in Canon's SV Mac utility lets you make time-lapse QuickTime movies from a series of images.

The Canon RC-570 can work with an optional NuBus board whose cable connects to a multipin interface tucked within the camera's battery chamber. Because the board requires a NuBus-equipped Mac, you can't transfer images to a PowerBook when you're in the field. On the plus side, Canon's transfer utility is the best of the bunch, offering features that let you add antialiased text to images, resize images, and even save a sequence of images as a QuickTime movie — a capability that lets you use the camera to make time-lapse movies.

Kodak's DCS-200 and DCS-420 include a Photoshop Acquire plug-in that lets you import images by using Photoshop's Acquire command. Canon's SV-Mac interface board also includes a Photoshop Acquire module.

If your images will wind up in a multimedia production or an on-screen presentation instead of being printed, you can use a video-out port instead of an image-transfer utility to move images to the Mac; just capture the image with the software that came with your frame-grabber. This approach is faster than using a transfer utility, but the resolution of the grabbed image is only 72 dots per inch — too low to yield sharp printed results.

Sony doesn't offer a transfer utility or Mac interface for the otherwise excellent MVC-7000 — its video-out jack is the only way to move images to the Mac. This limitation makes the MVC-7000 less than ideal for applications that involve transferring images to the Mac before printing them. The camera is superb, however, for images that you will view on a monitor, and it also has the unique capability to work as a video camera. Connect the MVC-7000 to a videocassette recorder, and you record moving video. Connect it to a TV monitor, and you have a closed-circuit TV system. Attach it to an AV Mac or a frame-grabber, and you can digitize live video. Its live-video capabilities make the MVC-7000 appealing for multimedia, QuickTime, and video work.

The camera angle

Enough of CCDs, transfer utilities, and video jacks — how do these things stack up as *cameras?* Low-end units such as Apple's QuickTake 150 and Kodak's Digital Camera 40 compare to typical auto-everything 35mm cameras, providing built-in flash units and using noninterchangeable lenses. They also provide additional controls for disabling the automatic flash, activating the self-timer mode, and choosing an image-quality mode. The settings of these functions appear on a small display screen, which also displays low-battery warnings and other messages.

The QuickTake 150 includes a snap-on close-up lens that lets you take pictures at distances of between 10 and 14 inches. The lens also diffuses the flash so that it doesn't wash out the subject. The Kodak DC 40 accepts screw-on lens attachments; available attachments include wide-angle, telephoto, and close-up lenses.

The Apple QuickTake 100 and 150 use standard AA batteries. The camera includes three rechargeable NiCad batteries, but if you lose them or you can't wait for them to recharge, you can use standard AA alkaline cells. Kodak's DC 40 uses four AA batteries. Canon's RC-570 uses proprietary rechargeable batteries, so be sure to take some extras along for extended photo shoots. All of these cameras can also operate from AC power when used with their battery chargers or adapters. (The QuickTake 100 and 150 use the same AC adapter as a classic PowerBook.)

The Canon RC-570 loses points for its poor battery chamber design. It's easy to insert the battery upside down — a mistake you won't catch until you replace the removable door and try unsuccessfully to turn the camera on. The fact that the door is removable — and therefore easy to lose — is another drawback, especially because you have to remove the door and set it aside when using the SV Mac digitizing board.

The Sony MVC-7000 and Kodak DCS-200 have the same amenities found on a 35mm single-lens reflex camera. Both accept interchangeable lenses designed for Nikon or Canon bayonet mounts. (The Kodak DCS-200 actually uses a Nikon 8008 body.) Both provide through-the-lens viewing, hot shoes for attaching a flash unit, and center-weighted or spot-metering options. Unlike most cameras, both also allow you to select a specific ISO rating in order to control depth of field (the distance range within which objects are in focus).

The Sony MVC-7000 is a sumo-sized camera that weighs nearly six pounds including the 8 – 48mm zoom lens that's standard equipment. You don't want to use this camera without a tripod for very long. The DCS-200 and DCS-420 are a bit more manageable, weighing four pounds and sporting rounded contours that make them more comfortable to hold.

Should you consider a filmless camera?

Filmless cameras are far more expensive than conventional ones and they deliver inferior image quality. It doesn't sound like a formula for success, but the no-film, no-processing convenience of an electronic camera goes a long way toward offsetting the image-quality drawbacks.

Who should consider the current crop of cameras? Low-end and mid-range models are best for business and industrial applications: real estate agents snapping houses for listing sheets and databases, insurance claims adjusters recording dents and accident scenes, personnel departments snapping photos for ID badges, and professionals wanting a fast way to include images in documents such as reports, newsletters, and brochures.

In this league, the Apple QuickTake 150 and Kodak Digital Camera 40 are the best. The Canon RC-570's image quality is inferior, but the camera's zoom lens, floppy drive, video-out jack, and the superb SV Mac board and transfer utility make it a much more versatile system. Indeed, the ideal filmless camera would combine the RC-570's goodies with the image quality and superior industrial design of the Apple and Kodak cameras.

In the consumer photography market — the weekend and vacation snapshooters — don't expect digital cameras to supplant film any time soon. Consider the components required: a computer with good graphics capabilities and lots of storage, color calibration software, image-enhancement software, image-database software, and a continuous-tone printer. Throw in the expertise required to use it all, and you're likely to have a new appreciation for the simple slogan that helped George Eastman build his photographic empire: "You push the button, we do the rest."

High-End Filmless Photography

High-end filmless cameras such as Kodak's DCS-200 and Sony's Pro Mavica are well suited to newspaper photojournalism, law enforcement and military documentation applications, and scientific and medical imaging. High-end cameras are also becoming popular for low-budget catalog and newspaper advertising photography, neither of which demand film's crystal clarity or capability to be enlarged significantly and both of which can benefit from filmless photography's instant gratification. The Kodak DCS-200 is the best and most popular camera in this class, although the Sony MVC-7000's video features give it a multimedia appeal that the DCS-200 lacks.

At the summit of the electronic photography world are some specialized high-end devices. The $36,000 Leaf Digital Camera Back from Leaf Systems works with several popular medium- and large-format cameras: the Hasselblad 500 EL and 553 ELX series, the Mamiya RZ67, and certain Sinar and Cambo view cameras. The Digital Camera Back uses a sophisticated CCD with more than 4 million pixels to produce images that really do look photographic — even when enlarged to poster size. The Leaf Digital Camera Back has become the major digital player in commercial studio photography.

To better serve the needs of fast-shooting photojournalists, Kodak collaborated with The Associated Press to create the NewsCamera 2000, which can take up to two images per second and provides better light sensitivity than the DCS-200. Built around a Nikon N90 body, the camera can store 75 images on a removable 105MB hard drive. The camera can also transfer images to memory cards that work with AP's PhotoLynx hardware, which can transmit images back to the home base via cellular phone connections. The NewsCamera 2000 even provides a voice-annotation feature for recording notes or captions. It sells for $16,995 to AP members and $17,995 to non-AP members.

Nikon and Fuji have collaborated on a family of high-end digital cameras, which includes the Fujix DS-505 and DS-515 and the Nikon Digital Camera. These cameras provide 1.3 million pixel CCDs as well as video-out connectors, and they accept plug-in PC cards for storing images. Kodak and Canon have also combined efforts to develop the Kodak EOS-DCS 5, which has a 1.5-million pixel CCD and voice-annotation features.

These cameras illustrate a trend toward specialization — studio photographers and photojournalists have unique needs, and no single digital camera can meet all of them. Expect to see more niches being filled as filmless photography matures.

CHAPTER 13 CONCEPTS AND TERMS

- The trend toward electronic photography is fueled by its speed, convenience, flexibility, and environmental friendliness.
- To generate electronic images, you need a scanner (gray-scale, color, or slide), a still-video camera, video-capture hardware, or a CD-ROM drive capable of reading Kodak PhotoCD discs. A large selection of stock photographs is also available on CD-ROM.
- Most scanners include image-acquisition software that controls the scanner and provides basic editing features. Some machines also include Adobe Photoshop.
- Image-processing programs are bitmapped (paint) programs that provide sophisticated tools for controlling brightness, contrast, and color balance and for editing and retouching images.
- Most image-processing programs provide filters that can sharpen, blur, and otherwise modify all or part of an image. Adobe Photoshop provides the largest array of filters and can accept additional ones through software plug-in modules.
- An image-processing program's histogram and gray-map graphs can be useful tools for analyzing and fine-tuning the range of grays or colors in an image.
- Laser printers and other relatively low-resolution output devices often yield disappointing results due to the halftoning process. The higher a device's resolution, the better the quality of its halftones.
- Helpful hardware for advanced image processing includes a CD-ROM drive, a large-screen color or gray-scale monitor, a color-calibration device, an accelerator board, and a memory upgrade.

8-bit scanner
A scanner that assigns eight bits to each pixel and is capable of discerning roughly 256 levels of gray.

24-bit scanner
A scanner that assigns 24 bits to each scanned pixel and can discern millions of colors.

antialiasing
A technique that smooths the jagged edges of characters or shapes by adding shaded pixels.

color correction
Tweaking the hues in an image for greater realism.

color ring-around
A multiple-choice color-correction feature that displays numerous versions of an image, each with its own color balance, contrast, and saturation (color purity) settings. You can choose the one that looks most pleasing and use it as is or as a basis for further refinements.

color separation
Dividing a color image into four separate images, one each for cyan, magenta, yellow, and black — the four *process colors* that printing presses combine to print color images.

continuous tone image
An image, such as a photograph, that has subtle variations in gray levels or colors.

digital signal processing (DSP) board
A hardware add-on containing a specialized processor designed to speed up filtering, selecting, and other common image-manipulation operations.

feathered selection
A selected area whose edges are faded slightly instead of being sharp, providing a less jarring transition.

filter
A software routine that alters an image by examining its underlying data and then applying calculations to it.

flat
An adjective applied to images whose range of grays is too narrow, resulting in insufficient contrast.

gamma correction
Assigning different colors or gray shades to the underlying ones and zeros that describe each dot, thereby changing the brightness, contrast, and color balance of an image. *Nonlinear correction* involves altering the original image's data in varying degrees to improve the image's appearance. *Linear correction* involves remapping all the values to the same degree, which can lead to the loss of details in bright or dark areas.

gray map
A graph that depicts the relationship between the ones and zeros in the image file and the shades of gray on-screen. The horizontal axis shows the original brightness values in the file — the input values — and the vertical axis shows the new brightness values, or output values.

halftoning
Simulating shades of gray or colors by using black or colored dots of varying size. To create these dots, a printer combines the smallest dots it can create into clusters called cells and then turns on varying numbers of dots within each cell. The number of cells per inch corresponds to the screen frequency and is usually measured in lines per inch (lpi).

(continued on the next page)

(continued from previous page)

image acquisition software
Software included with a scanner that works with the hardware to acquire the ones and zeros that represent the original image and enables you to save it on disk. Most image-acquisition programs also have rudimentary editing features.

Kodak PhotoCD
A Kodak-developed technology that provides high-quality, CD-ROM-based electronic images along with conventional prints or slides.

mask
An electronic version of masking tape that you can use to prevent stray pixels from fouling part of an image. You can use a mask to protect an area adjacent to a spot you're retouching or to add a new background by combining images.

midtones
The light, medium, and dark grays that represent most of an image's details.

multisession CD
A special CD-recording technique that enables you to add images to an existing Kodak PhotoCD disc. To work with multisession PhotoCD discs, you need a CD-ROM drive that supports XA Mode 2.

plug-in modules
Separate miniprograms that add new features to a program. A plug-in module may be a filter that modifies an image, an import module that lets you control a scanner from within a program, or an export module that lets you save an image in a special format or print it on a color printer.

printer calibration curve
A document whose data describes the relationship between the grays in an image and the grays that your printing process reproduces.

slide scanner
A scanner designed specifically for scanning color transparencies, usually 35mm slides.

still-video camera
An all-electronic camera that saves images not on film but in memory or on tiny floppy disks. Still-video cameras generally deliver inferior results compared to digital cameras, whose CCDs are designed from the ground up with still imaging in mind.

video digitizer
Also called a *frame grabber,* a hardware add-on that creates editable images from a video source such as a camcorder or VCR.

Glossary of common image-editing tools

airbrush
A tool that simulates an airbrush. You can adjust the tool's flow rate and nozzle size.

blur
A tool that softens part of an image.

burn
A tool that lets you darken an area of an image as if you were allowing extra light from a photographic enlarger to reach a piece of photographic paper.

dodge
A division of Chrysler Corporation. Also, a tool that lets you lighten an area of an image as if you were blocking part of the light coming from a photographic enlarger.

Eyedropper
A tool that lets you select a gray shade or color by clicking an existing portion of an image. Called a Pickup tool in some programs.

lasso
A tool for selecting irregularly shaped areas.

magic wand
An advanced selection tool that lets you select all contiguous pixels of the same or similar color or gray shade by pointing to a spot and clicking.

marquee
A tool for selecting rectangular areas.

multiple floating selections
A powerful image-editing feature provided by Fractal Design's PainterX2 that lets you save selections and move them around freely.

pen
A tool that lets you select portions of an image by drawing Bezier curves, geometric constructions that form the foundation of PostScript illustration programs and type fonts.

rubber stamp
A tool that duplicates one part of an image as you drag the mouse over a different part. Called a Clone tool in some programs.

sharpen
A tool that sharpens part of an image.

smudge
A tool that lets you smear part of an image as though it were a charcoal drawing and the mouse pointer were your fingertip.

CHAPTER FOURTEEN

Graphics in the Third Dimension

- Creating photorealistic 3-D images
- Modeling, extruding, rendering, ray tracing, and other 3-D jargon defined
- Equipping your Mac to run 3-D programs
- Using Pixar Typistry and StrataType 3d to create text with depth
- How Apple's Quick-Draw 3D will change the third dimension
- Getting good results in less time

Mac graphics programs are taking on a new dimension — the third dimension. Painting and drawing programs mimic canvases or drafting tables, but a growing number of programs mimic the real world, where objects have height, width, depth, shadows, textures, and perspective — and where those characteristics appear to change as you move around. Many programs also provide animation features that let you put those objects in motion.

Architects can use 3-D programs to create animated walk-throughs that enable clients to tour a building before it exists. Programs such as Virtus's WalkThrough hint at the brave new world of virtual reality, where you can create and explore places that exist only in the digital domain.

Engineers and industrial designers use 3-D programs to create realistic renditions of space stations, cars, lampshades — you name it. Package designers create 3-D mock-ups of packaging and wrap text and images around their labels. Graphic designers create special text effects, such as glittering logos that appear to be cast in chrome. Film and television studios can experiment with different set designs and camera angles without having to construct the real thing. Artists can create images that would be difficult or impossible to produce with programs such as Adobe Illustrator or Macromedia FreeHand. And graphics buffs can experiment with creating the photorealistic images that make 3-D programs so enticing.

You're About to Enter the Third Dimension

The Multimedia Theater segment of the *Macworld Power User Clinic* contains two animations created with Specular Infini-D and with Pixar's Typistry. Notice the great image quality in these movies — anyone who says that the Mac can't do professional-level 3-D animations hasn't seen the latest programs. (My thanks to Specular and Pixar for providing these animations.)

Three-dimensional graphics programs are among the most complex programs you can find on a personal computer; to use them, you need to come to terms with a bevy of brain-bending technical and geometric concepts. Forget trying to learn a 3-D program without opening the manual, even if you've already mastered a 2-D program. You need every tutorial a program's manual provides along with hours of practice just to master the basics.

You may need hours of patience, too. It isn't unusual to wait an hour or more for a 3-D program to create a complex photorealistic scene. You can almost raise a family in the time required to create a 3-D animation containing hundreds of separate images. Most programs require a high-end machine or an accelerator board and benefit greatly from a Power Mac's processing punch. For best results, throw in a memory upgrade to bring your Mac up to at least 16MB, a high-capacity hard disk, 24-bit video hardware, and a large-screen monitor.

But cost is relative. Many 3-D programs have features that not long ago were found only on six-figure workstations. For businesses that can't afford such hardware — or that don't want to waste their workstations on small jobs — waiting while a Mac 3-D program generates a complex image is a small price to pay. The third dimension can be a fascinating and rewarding place — if you approach it with the proper perspective (pun intended). As this chapter describes, that involves understanding the concepts behind 3-D graphics and then choosing a program that can handle the types of images you want to create.

Three Steps to 3-D

The best way to understand the process of creating a 3-D image is to imagine that you're an architect building a house model that you will then photograph for publication. Your first step is to cut pieces of balsa wood into the appropriate shapes to represent the roof, windows, chimney, doors, and other components of the house. You glue them together and then paint the model to make it look more realistic — shingles on the roof, a brick-like pattern on the chimney, and woodgrain on the siding. Finally, you supply the completed model to a photographer who illuminates it and then photographs it using a variety of camera angles and lenses.

Phase 1: modeling

The steps are similar in a 3-D graphics program; they just take place within the Mac. First, you use the mouse to draw shapes corresponding to the house's components. Next, you "glue" them together by dragging the shapes until they're positioned appropriately. This draw-and-glue phase is called *modeling*.

In the modeling phase, you can also specify textures and perhaps colors for the surfaces in the model, assigning a shingle pattern to the roof, a brick pattern to the chimney, and a woodgrain pattern to the siding. In doing so, you electronically paint your model.

Phase 2: scene description

Setting up the final image — the equivalent of preparing a photographic set — is called *scene description*. In this phase, you specify the number and position of the lights illuminating your model, along with their characteristics — for example, whether they're bright or dim and whether they're spotlights or floodlights. You can also specify the color of the light itself, choosing, for example, a yellowish hue to simulate late-afternoon sun.

In the scene-description phase, you also play the role of photographer, choosing the camera angles and lenses that best capture your model. It helps to know a bit about photography at this stage because a 3-D program's electronic lens acts much like a real camera's. A wide-angle lens distorts somewhat and provides better depth of field, for example, while a telephoto lens reduces the degree of perspective visible in the final image.

Phase 3: rendering

The final phase of a 3-D imaging project is *rendering*. This stage of the process puts your Mac through its paces, as the 3-D program grinds through the calculations required to simulate a 3-D scene. More about this step later.

I've described the modeling, scene-description, and rendering phases separately, but they don't necessarily have to occur in this order. You can, for example, adjust lighting and camera angles before assigning textures and performing other rendering tasks. What's more, not all 3-D products can handle all three phases. Some programs are modeling specialists and have minimal rendering and scene-description features. Other products handle rendering and scene description based on models you create by using a different company's modeler. Still other products handle all three tasks, using either one program or separate modeling and rendering programs that you switch between as you work.

Model Shops

Modeling out of balsa wood means using a knife to cut out shapes that you attach to each other. Modeling with a 3-D program isn't as straightforward. You create basic shapes not by cutting them out, but by drawing them with the mouse. Trickier still, you assemble those shapes not in the three-dimensional space in front of you, but in the simulated 3-D world that your program projects on the Mac's screen.

Drawing some primitives

Different modelers provide different drawing features, but in general, creating a model's basic shapes often begins with drawing *primitives* — circles, rectangles, polygons, or curves. Like drawing and painting programs, modeling programs provide on-screen palettes for their various drawing tools. But drawing a primitive is only a starting point. To create a 3-D object, you need to use either your program's lathe or extrusion features (see Figure 14-1 "Extrusion versus Lathing").

Lathing and extruding

A modeler's lathe features let you create objects with radial symmetry — goblets, bowls, baseball bats, doughnuts, doorknobs, or the letter O. When you're using a lathe, or *sweep*, feature, you generally draw half of the object — a profile — and the program rotates what you draw around an axis to create the 3-D object.

Extrusion creates a 3-D object by copying the primitive, moving the copy, and then adding edges to create a surface that connects the copy to the original. The result is a shape with a complex cross section and plain sides — as if the shape were cut out with a jigsaw or cookie cutter.

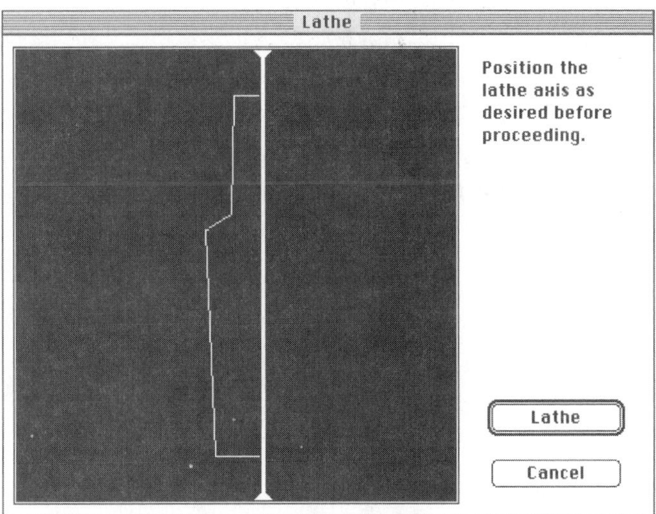

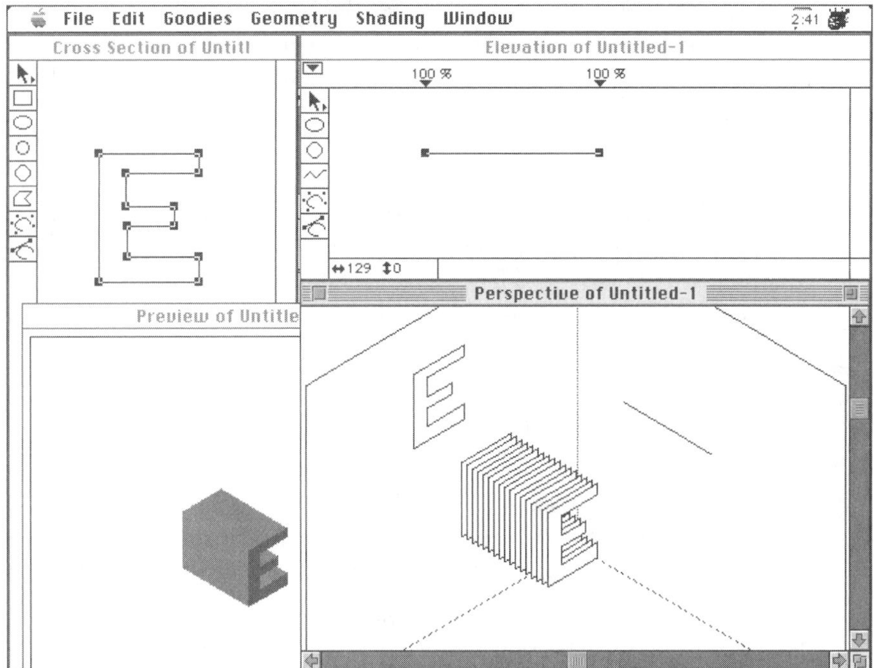

Figure 14-1: Extrusion versus Lathing The lathing feature in Macromedia's Swivel 3-D Professional (top) is used to create a wine bottle. Ray Dream Designer's extrusion feature (bottom) is used to create a 3-D letter.

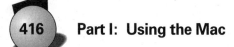

Industrial-Strength Modeling Features

High-end programs such as Alias Research's Sketch and Strata's Vision 4 and Studio build on the basic modeling features I describe in this section and also add some sophisticated ones.

Vertex editing lets you manipulate the individual points that define an object's shape or surface mesh.

Lofting applies a skin over a series of modeled elements, such as applying wall panels over a building's frame.

Boolean operations modify objects that intersect by describing the way the objects interact.

Spline-based modeling uses curves to form objects that have smooth flowing lines — jetliners, for example. Spline-based modelers provide greater precision than programs that simulate curves by using straight line segments.

The positioning challenge

Creating shapes is easy compared to assembling them into complex objects and images. The fact that your link to the program's 3-D space is a 2-D screen makes it more difficult to accurately position shapes in relation to each other — just as it's harder to assemble a balsa model with one eye closed.

Most 3-D programs tackle this problem by providing multiple views of your scene (see Figure 14-2 "From Many Angles"). Modifications you make in one view are reflected in the others, thus giving you the feedback you need to position objects accurately. With programs that show just one view at a time, you may need to do a bit more work in moving around your model to verify that objects are positioned correctly.

Assembling the Pieces

When you're creating a complex object out of separate shapes, you need to tell the program that the shapes are related. After all, when you rotate a car body to view it from other angles, you want its tires to go along for the ride. Some programs provide a Group command that combines the objects you select into one.

Other programs use a more complex but more powerful hierarchical scheme. When creating a hierarchical model, you lock one or more *child objects* to a *parent object.* If you model a human figure, for example, you can use the torso as the applying constraints to those objects; you can create a model that more accurately represents the real thing.

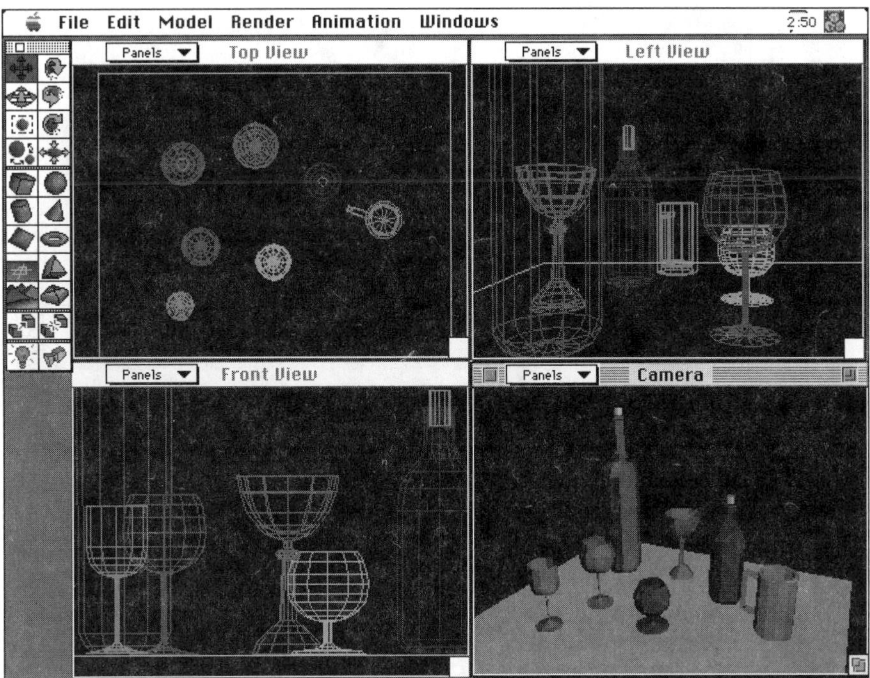

Figure 14-2: From Many Angles Most 3-D programs, including Infini-D, shown here, enable you to view a scene from several angles simultaneously, simplifying the process of positioning objects. Most also let you resize individual views to fill the screen and close views that you aren't using.

Some programs provide a library feature that lets you store and recall objects for reuse. Many programs also include libraries of commonly used shapes and objects. DynaPerspective, for example, includes architecture and interior design-oriented shapes such as doors, plumbing fixtures, and office equipment.

3-D text features

As for text, you can't simply click a text tool and start typing 3-D text in your favorite font. Some modelers can generate an outline from text stored in a PICT or Adobe Illustrator file. Other programs provide a text tool that generates outlines from text you type. With either approach, you can add depth to the text by extruding the resulting outline.

If you plan to work with 3-D text extensively, investigate one of the 3-D programs that specializes in text, such as Pixar's Typistry or Strata's StrataType 3d (see Figure 14-3 "Text on a 3-D Stage"). You can find details about these programs in the Background box "Text with Depth."

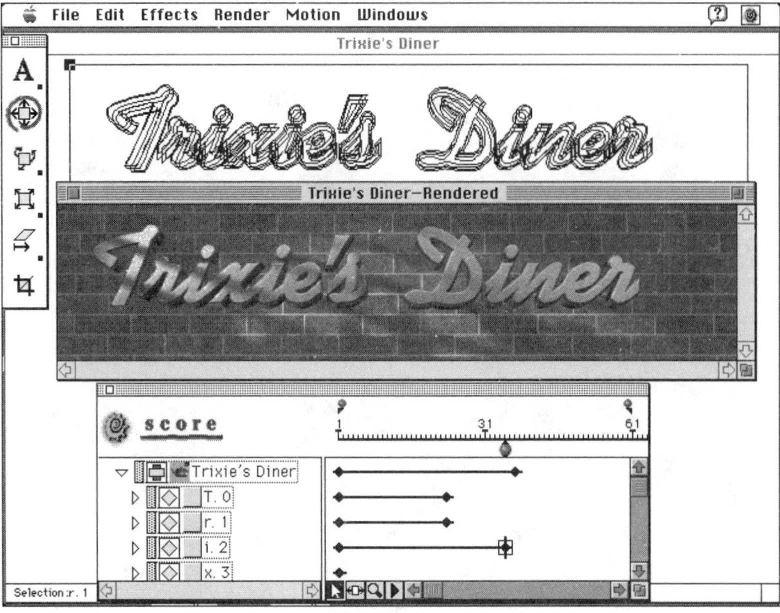

Figure 14-3: Text on a 3-D Stage Pixar's Typistry (top) and Strata's StrataType 3d enable you to create 3-D renderings from any TrueType or PostScript Type 1 font. The Typistry screen shows an image rendered in the program's highest-quality setting. The Score window at the bottom of the Typistry screen lets you create 3-D animations.

Text with Depth

Until recently, if you needed photorealistic 3-D text for a publication, presentation, or multimedia production, you had to use a 3-D modeling-and-rendering package. Buying such a package to generate a 3-D text effect is overkill. What's more, general-purpose 3-D packages often have limited text features — if they have them at all.

Pixar Corporation's Typistry and Strata's StrataType 3d can generate photorealistic 3-D text from nearly any TrueType or Type 1 PostScript outline font. Typistry can simulate motion as well as depth. By using its straightforward animation controls, you can create the kind of animated text that pervades TV station breaks and movie-of-the-week openings. You can save completed animations in a variety of formats, including QuickTime movies.

Both programs have straightforward operating styles that invite experimentation. Start either program, and you get an untitled document window along with a tool palette for creating new text objects as well as for moving, rotating, resizing, and extruding text. (You can also use dialog boxes to specify precise rotation, extrusion, and resizing values.)

When you're typing new text, you can also choose from a variety of bevel styles to give letters a rounded, routered, or sharp-edged appearance. You can also specify the size of the bevel. When you're done, a wire-frame version of the object appears in the document window (see Figure 14-3 "Text on a 3-D Stage").

After you build an object, you can position it and assign textures to its surfaces and adjust lighting. As in Pixar's Showplace, surfaces in Typistry are called *looks.* Typistry includes a selection of looks for common surfaces — shiny metal, stucco, bricks, wood, and plastic. You can also add looks that are sold separately by Pixar and third-party firms such as The Valis Group. StrataType 3d includes a wide variety of textures as well as a utility that lets you create new textures.

In the 3-D world, you view objects from the vantage point of an electronic camera. Typistry lets you use one of several lenses — normal, fisheye (exaggerates perspective), and zoom (flattens perspective). In this regard, Typistry is a bit less flexible than StrataType 3d, which provides one lens whose focal length is continuously variable.

Typistry provides 18 light sources — nine front lights and nine back lights. You can customize each light's intensity, color, and position, as well as assign electronic gels that cast shadows to simulate windowpanes, a spotlight, venetian blinds, and more. You can also specify that a light pointed at an object move along with the object. Combine this feature with Typistry's animation features, and you can create a spotlight that follows a moving object. StrataType 3d lets you create an unlimited number of light sources, each of which can have gels. StrataType 3d even lets you create your own custom gels.

For creating animations (a capability StrataType 3d lacks), Typistry uses a simple keyframe scheme. Move an object or a light, choose Next Keyframe, and then repeat the process. Typistry calculates the intermediate frames for you.

As for StrataType 3d, versions 2.0 and later fix most of the shortcomings of the first version — although animation isn't provided. StrataType 3d now supports an unlimited number of light sources, which can have gels. The program also provides a kerning feature, an optional alpha channel, more control over textures, and improved rendering quality.

Another hot program for creating 3-D text and animations is Specular International's LogoMotion. This program is unique in that it includes a large selection of canned backgrounds and animation effects — everything from 3-D checkerboards to animated sparkles that travel across your text. Unlike Typistry and StrataType 3d, LogoMotion also contains some modeling features — you can draw shapes with its built-in tools and then sweep or extrude them.

Changing your view

I've already mentioned one benefit of a 3-D program — its capability to show a completed model from different angles. Most programs provide a variety of clever navigation tools that let you rotate a model or move your vantage point, which is usually called the *camera.*

To enable you to move objects and your vantage point without having to wait for the program to redraw the image, most 3-D programs use a wire-frame rendering technique, in which they draw only the edges of objects. Many programs can also display higher-quality versions with shading — but at the price of performance.

Need to Model People? Use Poser

Using a modeling program to create a shape as complex as the human body is a formidable job. If you work with human forms in 3-D renderings, you need Fractal Design's Poser.

Poser is a modeling and rendering program that lets you create 3-D human figures that can be posed, rendered with surface textures and multiple lights, and incorporated into 2-D and 3-D imaging programs. Poser provides male, female, and stylized models that can be moved and shaped into any pose and viewed from any angle. You can specify body sizes in any range, from infant to adult to, as Fractal Design says, "super hero." Body parts are scaleable — you can size them independently to create, for example, long arms, big heads, or fat stomachs.

Poser also lets you adjust the size and dimension of individual body parts such as arms, legs, and torsos. To adjust body position, simply drag the appropriate part of the figure, and Poser adjusts related limbs accordingly. For example, if you grab the hand and move it, the arm and shoulder follow along appropriately.

Once you've fine-tuned your digital model's position, you can add bump and texture maps and up to three light sources and then render a final version of the image. You can export the final composition as a RIB, DXF, or PICT file.

One Step Closer to Realism

So when do you see those stunning, photorealistic results? In time; first, you need to apply textures and other details to the surfaces of your model.

How texture mapping works

Texture-mapping features, found in most midrange and high-end programs, enable you to apply an image to a surface — like applying a decal to a balsa model. The image may represent woodgrain or bricks, or text created in a different program and saved in a PICT file. A package designer may use the latter technique to wrap a label around a 3-D bottle.

Because a texture map is an electronic decal that rests on an object's surface, it doesn't allow for realistic rendering of materials such as wood or marble, whose texture patterns change throughout the material's thickness. The answer — *procedural textures*, also called *shaders*, supported by Ray Dream Designer, Strata's StrataVision 3d, Specular International's Infini-D, and Byte-by-Byte's Sculpt 3-D, to name a few.

A shader for wood, for example, isn't a 2-D picture of woodgrain; it's a set of mathematical routines that describe the characteristics of wood — the undulations and spacing of its veins as well as the colors of winter and summer growth. When you cut a solid-textured object in half, you can see the grain pattern inside.

Adding roughness with bump mapping

Another characteristic that affects an object's appearance is its roughness: Bowling balls and oranges are spheres, but their vastly different surfaces cause them to reflect light differently. *Bump-mapping* features give surfaces a 3-D roughness that would be grueling to model by hand. Most programs let you adjust the degree of bumpiness, allowing you to render everything from the nubs of an orange peel to the craters of the moon.

Specifying surface properties

Creating a photorealistic scene also requires you to specify an object's *surface properties* — the object's degree of transparency and the way its surface reflects light and objects around it (see Figure 14-4 "Light Show"). You can also create and position additional light sources to better illuminate the scene or simulate a certain time of day.

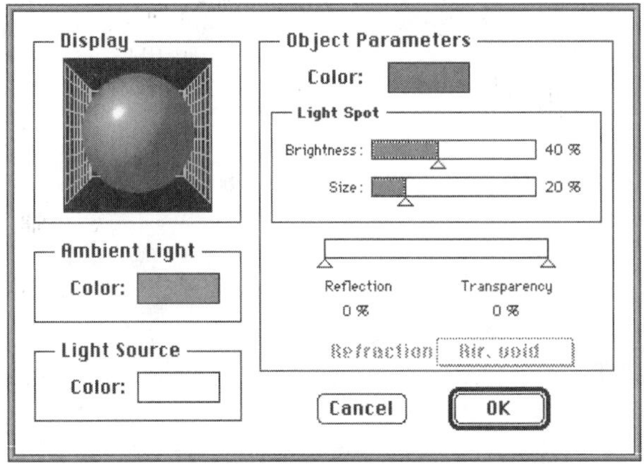

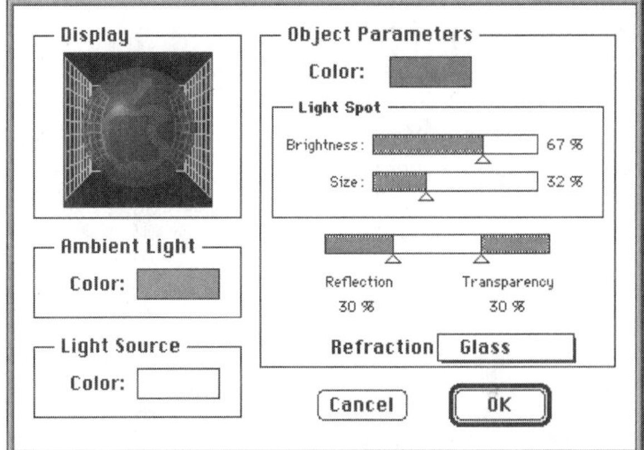

Figure 14-4: Light Show Like most 3-D programs, Ray Dream Designer lets you modify an object's surface properties to simulate various materials. The preview (top) shows the program's preset values of no transparency or reflection. Reflection and transparency (bottom) have been modified. Note that the grid is reflected in the sphere, and an object (the Apple logo) is visible through the sphere.

How Rendering Works

Now it's time to let your rendering program earn its keep by slogging through the myriad calculations required to create the final image.

Rendering techniques compared

The most calculation-intensive rendering technique is *ray tracing.* Most 3-D programs, including Ray Dream Designer, StrataVision 3d, Infini-D, Sculpt3-D, and Alias Sketch, provide ray tracers.

A ray tracer projects an imaginary ray of light from the center of the camera into the scene and then back again, calculating the effects of the scene's light sources as they illuminate each object's surfaces, capturing highlights, shadows, and reflections. This process occurs for every screen dot (pixel) that appears in the final image, so the larger the image, the longer you wait.

Faster but less realistic rendering techniques involve shading routines (not to be confused with the shaders described earlier, which simulate solid textures). Figure 14-5 "Three Ways to Shade" illustrates the three most common shading techniques — *flat*, *Gouraud*, and *Phong*.

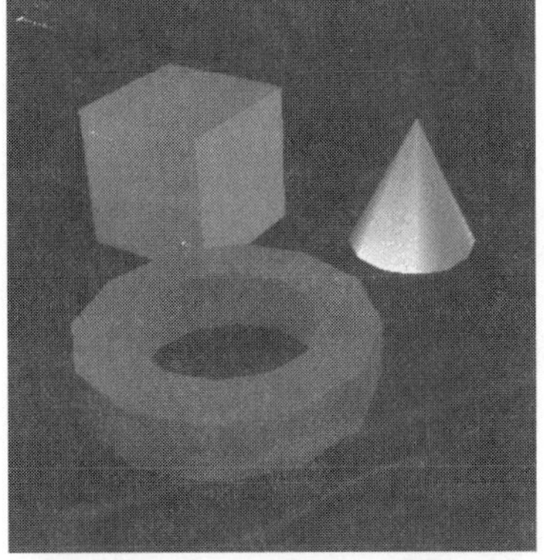

Figure 14-5: Three Ways to Shade
Three common shading techniques exist — flat (top left), Gouraud (top right), and Phong (bottom). Each provides progressively more realistic results but requires more processing time.

After you choose your program's Render command or its equivalent, sit back and wait for the final results. If you're running System 7 (or System 6 MultiFinder) and if the program can render in the background (most can), you can switch to a different program. But increasing your Mac's workload only slows down the renderer, so you may just want to go out for lunch — or out for a long weekend, if you're ray-tracing a huge, complex scene.

After the rendering: saving and printing

When the renderer completes its chores, you can save the results on disk, generally in PICT, TIFF, or EPS formats. You can also print images, although you need a high-end color printer or a film recorder to do justice to a full-color, ray-traced image.

Most rendering programs have antialiasing features that help eliminate the jagged edges that are common in computer-generated images. You can also fine-tune an image after it's rendered by putting it through Ray Dream's JAG II utility. Its name is short for *jaggies are gone*, and it lives up to the moniker (see Figure 14-6 "Jaggies Are Gone").

Figure 14-6: Jaggies Are Gone Ray Dream's JAG is an antialiasing utility that smooths the edges of 3-D art as shown before JAG (left) and after JAG (right).

The Adobe Dimension

Capable as most 3-D programs are, their final results are bitmapped images, which you can't resize without introducing distortion. As Chapter 12 describes, bitmapped images are also tied to a specific number of dots per inch, so they aren't able to take full advantage of high-resolution output devices such as imagesetters and film recorders.

The object-oriented approach

Adobe Dimensions takes a different approach to 3-D — the vector, or object-oriented, approach. The end result of a Dimensions session isn't a PICT or TIFF file, but an Illustrator or Macromedia FreeHand file. You can open this file in a variety of drawing programs and modify it — change its stroke and fill attributes, resize it, rotate it, disassemble it, and reshape it by using the Bezier controls that are the foundation of PostScript-oriented drawing programs. Dimensions bridges the gap between the third dimension and PostScript drawing programs.

If you use Adobe Illustrator, you'll feel at home in Dimensions (see Figure 14-7 "The Adobe Dimension"). Dimensions provides a floating tool palette and bottom-of-the-window information bar that work similarly to their Illustrator counterparts, as do Dimensions' tools for scaling and rotating.

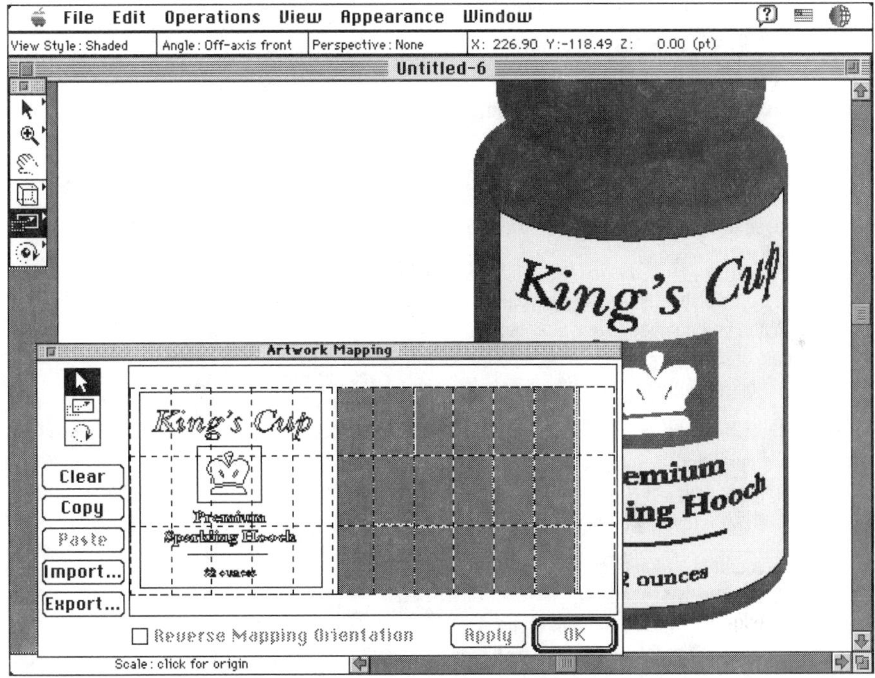

Figure 14-7: The Adobe Dimension Dimensions' artwork-mapping window lets you apply an Illustrator or FreeHand file to a 3-D object. Here, a label created in Illustrator is applied to a bottle.

Dimensions is designed to be used with Illustrator or FreeHand or by itself. To create 3-D objects, you can draw them in Dimensions or draw 2-D versions of them in Illustrator or FreeHand and then import the file into Dimensions. You can then extrude the shapes or revolve them. Extrusion adds depth to an object's boundaries, while revolving spins an object around one axis — as though you're turning a block of wood on a lathe. You can rotate 3-D objects by using Dimensions' Trackball tool or by typing specific rotation values.

Making Rendering Faster

They say that time is the fourth dimension, and 3-D programs eat up plenty of it. Of all the tasks you can perform with a Mac, none take longer than rendering a complex 3-D scene. In this box, you can find some tips for speeding up your 3-D program.

Illuminate judiciously

Use only enough lights to get the effect you want. The more lights you create for a scene, the longer it takes to render, because your program has to calculate shadows for each light. Too many lights can also make a scene look washed out.

Create proofs to check your work

Calculating shadows and reflections are among the most time-consuming aspects of rendering. Most programs let you specify that an image be rendered without shadows and reflections. When you're in the initial stages of a project, use these options to create proof versions of a scene.

Most programs also let you render only a portion of a scene. When you do need to see shadows and reflections, consider rendering just the portion of the scene that contains them.

Upgrade your Mac

I may be stating the obvious, but the faster your Mac, the faster your 3-D program. Several types of upgrades can improve rendering performance:

- *More memory* You can speed up most rendering programs by allocating more memory to them with the Finder's Get Info command, as described in Chapter 22. Unless you have a Power Mac, avoid using System 7's virtual memory feature: it slows the program instead of speeding it up.
- *A faster hard disk* Most rendering programs swap information between memory and a hard disk as they work. A faster hard disk allows those swaps to occur more quickly.
- *An accelerator board* As Chapter 29 explains, an accelerator board boosts performance by replacing your Mac's processor with a faster one. A board that uses a PowerPC chip yields the fastest results — rendering relies extensively on floating-point calculations, and floating-point math is one of the PowerPC family's strengths.
- *A rendering accelerator* A general-purpose accelerator boosts your Mac's overall performance. But for top rendering performance, consider a RISC-based rendering accelerator such as Yarc Systems' NuSprint or Hydra. Both are built around RISC processors; the NuSprint uses a single AMD 29050, while the Hydra packs four PowerPC 601 chips. The Hydra is available as a NuBus board or as a PCI card for the second-generation Power Macs. Most major 3-D programs are available in versions that support these cards. You can boost performance even more by using multiple cards.

Consider network rendering

Network rendering involves dividing a rendering job across a network of Macs, with each Mac handling a portion of the image. This rendering team effort is sometimes called *distributed rendering.* Several rendering packages, including Ray Dream Designer and MacRenderMan, are available in versions that support network rendering. You can also use one or more Radius Rocket accelerators in combination with Radius's RocketShare to set up a distributed rendering system on a single Mac. Before taking the network rendering approach, however, investigate a RISC card such as Yarc's NuSprint or Hydra, which have the potential to provide better performance and reliability.

One fun aspect of working with a conventional 3-D program is giving objects surface textures such as marble, stucco, or red bricks. Dimensions doesn't support these kinds of textures, which is understandable, considering that textures are essentially bitmaps and Dimensions is an object-oriented program. Dimensions is limited to creating smooth surfaces with finishes ranging from matte to glossy. When you use Dimensions' rendering commands to generate the 3-D image, the program creates PostScript blends that simulate shading and depth.

As for lighting your 3-D world, Dimensions lets you create any number of light sources and specify their position and intensity. Dimensions 1.0 was color blind, but version 2 lets you create colored lights.

Mapping 2-D to 3-D

One of Dimensions' slickest features is its capability to map an Illustrator or FreeHand drawing onto a 3-D surface. If you're designing a package, you can create its label in Illustrator or FreeHand and then use Dimensions to electronically apply the label to a shape such as a bottle or box. Dimensions accurately retains the characteristics of the art while also giving it the appropriate perspective. Besides being a boon to package designers, the artwork-mapping feature also makes it easy to add accurate perspective to 2-D art.

The end result of a Dimensions session is an Illustrator or FreeHand file, but you can also tell Dimensions to render an image and place it on the Clipboard for subsequent pasting into a publishing or word processing program.

It's no Walt Disney

Dimensions has a limited animation capability: specify the beginning and ending attributes for a shape, and Dimensions generates the in-between frames and saves each as an Illustrator file. Unlike Pixar's Typistry and many conventional 3-D programs, Dimensions can't create QuickTime movies. You can, however, create a movie by importing the Illustrator frames into Adobe Premiere (discussed in Chapter 21).

If you're used to working with conventional 3-D programs, you may think that Dimensions is very limited, what with its white-only light and no surface texturing. Only when you realize that Dimensions performs its 3-D illusions within the object-oriented, resolution-independent world of PostScript does it hit home that this program is groundbreaking. Dimensions is an excellent 3-D tool for anyone who works extensively in Illustrator or FreeHand.

Choosing a 3-D Program

Should you use an all-in-one program such as Infini-D or StrataVision, or should you combine a modeler with a stand-alone renderer such as MacRenderMan?

One advantage to combining separate programs is that you can tailor your 3-D toolbox to your tastes. But there are drawbacks, too, not the least of which is that you'll probably spend more. A more serious problem is that one firm's renderer may not accurately import another's models.

Apple's QuickDraw 3D

When Apple released its QuickTime technology in 1991, it made it easier for developers to create programs that could work with time-based data such as video and sound. And that inspired an explosion of multimedia products that took digital video out of the research labs and put it into the hands of anyone with an inexpensive video digitizer or even just a CD-ROM drive.

Apple's QuickDraw 3D is designed to have the same effect on the 3-D world. Like QuickTime, QuickDraw 3D isn't a program that you open and run — it's a system software foundation that developers can use to build application programs that can create and work with 3-D images. Designed for Power Macs (no version will be available for 680X0-family Macs), QuickDraw 3D will make it easier for developers to add 3-D features into programs, and it will provide a standardized user interface; — just as all QuickTime-savvy programs provide the standard QuickTime movie controller bar for working with movies, all QuickDraw 3D programs will provide the same standard tools for rotating and scaling images.

QuickDraw 3D has several noteworthy, um, dimensions.

- **A standard 3-D file format** For representing models, QuickDraw 3D introduces a standard file format, called 3DMF (short for *3-D metafile)*. Applications that support this format can swap files easily — just as applications that support the PICT format can easily exchange two-dimensional graphics.
- **3-D cut-and-paste** With application programs designed to work with QuickDraw 3-D, you can cut and paste models using the Edit menu. You can also paste models into the Mac's Scrapbook, and even rotate them in the Scrapbook window (see Figure 14-8 "A 3-D Scrapbook")
- **An extensible architecture** QuickDraw 3D accepts plug-in software modules for rendering acceleration. This should simplify life for companies that want to develop accelerator boards for 3-D rendering.

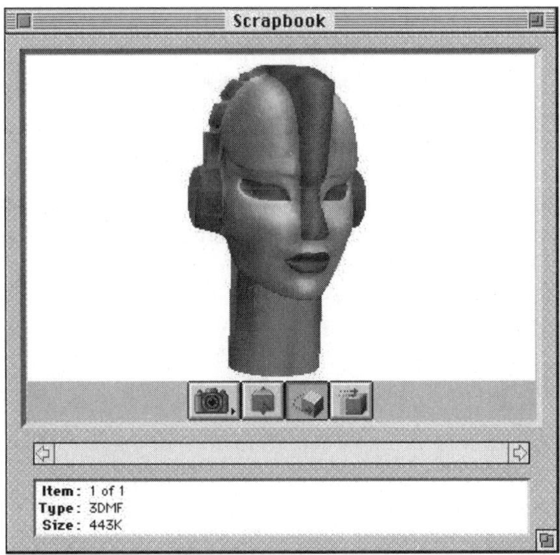

Figure 14-8: A 3-D Scrapbook Apple's QuickDraw 3D enables you to exchange 3-D models using the Edit menu's Cut and Paste commands. The new Scrapbook also supports the QuickDraw 3-D 3DMF data format and allows you to rotate, translate, and zoom any 3DMF model or scene. The camera button allows you to take advantage of any special camera views that may have been saved with the file as well as restore standard views.

- **Windows support** Apple is making QuickDraw 3D available to the Windows platform. The Windows version should be available by early 1996.
- **Toward a growing third dimension** Initially, expect to see QuickDraw 3D support primarily in 3-D modeling and CAD applications. (All major 3-D and CAD vendors plan to support QuickDraw 3-D.) But QuickDraw 3D's sphere of influence is likely to grow beyond the modeling and CAD worlds. You may see it surfacing in games and educational software, and even on on-line services. And Apple has hinted that future versions of the MacOS might have some built-in 3-D features.

File exchange formats

A common file format for exchanging models is called DXF. Another is Pixar's RenderMan Interface Bytestream, or RIB, format. Pixar designed the RIB format to be a standard format that lets you use any RIB-compatible modeler to create models that are then rendered with the MacRenderMan rendering software. A third popular format for importing and exporting model geometry is IGES, which many CAD programs support (discussed in Chapter 12).

Most 3-D programs support DXF, IGES, and RIB files, but there's no guarantee that each adheres exactly to DXF or RIB standards. If you're considering combining separate 3-D modeling and rendering programs, ask their developers if they know of any file compatibility problems.

Remember, too, that switching among programs isn't as fast or convenient as using an all-in-one program. But just as professional publishers often combine numerous programs to tackle a tough job, you may need to combine different programs for professional-level 3-D work. For example, for broadcast-quality animation, it's hard to beat the combination of Macromedia's MacroModel for modeling, Macromedia Three-D for animation control, and MacRenderMan for rendering.

Try before you buy

Because 3-D programs are so complex, I recommend trying a few before buying one. Most developers offer demo packages that include scaled-down versions of their programs, videotape demonstrations, or both. They're an inexpensive way to sample 3-D. (Demo versions of several 3-D packages are included on the *Macworld Complete Mac Interactive CD* that accompanies this book; see the "On the CD" box near the beginning of this chapter.)

That 3-D graphics programs are difficult to learn is no reflection on their designers. Simulating the real world is not an easy job. But if you can make a 3-D program earn its keep and invest the time required to master it, you can find new ways of looking at your design jobs. Working with a good 3-D program can also give you a new appreciation for light, shadows, textures, perspective, and all the other phenomena that contribute to that mental miracle called sight.

CHAPTER 14 CONCEPTS AND TERMS

- Architects, artists, industrial designers, and graphics buffs are only some of the groups that can benefit from a 3-D graphics program.
- Many 3-D programs provide animation features that let you create walk-throughs and special effects.
- Creating a 3-D scene involves three basic steps: modeling (creating the scene's basic shapes and describing their surfaces); scene description (creating and adjusting light sources and choosing an angle and focal length for the program's electronic camera); and rendering (the time-consuming process in which the 3-D program calculates and creates the image's shapes, shadows, surface textures, and other characteristics).
- You can speed up image rendering by accelerating your Mac, adding a memory upgrade, or by buying a specialized rendering accelerator board.
- A 3-D program requires more time to learn than a conventional drawing program. Besides learning about lighting, textures, and rendering options, you need to adjust to the challenge of describing 3-D scenes within a 2-D space — the Mac's screen.
- Pixar Typistry and StrataType 3d are specialized 3-D programs that let you create 3-D text from TrueType or Type 1 PostScript fonts. Typistry can also create animations.

3DMF
Short for *3-D metafile,* the standard file format that Apple's QuickDraw 3D technology provides for 3-D models. (See *QuickDraw 3D.*)

bump mapping
A feature that automates giving surfaces a 3-D roughness that would be grueling to model by hand.

camera
The vantage point from which a 3-D scene is viewed.

distributed rendering
Dividing a rendering job across multiple networked Macs. Each Mac handles a portion of the job, enabling the final image to be rendered faster.

extrusion
The process of creating a 3-D object by copying the primitive, moving the copy, and then adding edges to create a surface that connects the copy to the original.

hierarchical model
A model in which you lock one or more child objects to a parent object. If you are modeling a human figure, for example, you may use the torso as the parent object and make the limbs and head child objects.

lathe
Also called sweep, a modeling feature in which you generally draw half of the object — a profile — that the program rotates around an axis to create the 3-D object. You generally use a lathe feature to create objects with *radial symmetry*: goblets, bowls, baseball bats, doughnuts, doorknobs, and the letter *O*.

modeling
The process of drawing shapes, positioning them, attaching them to each other, and describing their surfaces and textures.

primitives
The basic shapes — circles, rectangles, polygons, and curves — used in a scene.

procedural textures
Also called shaders, mathematical routines that describe the characteristics of a material, such as wood.

QuickDraw 3D
An Apple software technology that enables developers to create 3-D applications and provides 3-D cut-and-paste, consistent 3-D user interface controls, and a standard file format for exchanging 3-D information.

ray tracing
A rendering technique in which 3-D software projects an imaginary ray of light from the center of the camera into the scene and then back again, calculating the effects of the scene's light sources as they illuminate each object's surfaces, capturing highlights, shadows, and reflections.

rendering
The phase of a 3-D project in which the 3-D program grinds through myriad calculations to produce a final image based on the work you did during the modeling and scene-description phases.

RenderMan Interface Bytestream
Abbreviated RIB, a file format for storing models that are rendered with Pixar's MacRenderMan software.

scene description
The process of creating and adjusting light sources and choosing camera angles and focal lengths.

surface properties
Everything about an object's surface — for example, its degree of transparency and the way its surface reflects light and objects around it.

texture mapping
Applying an image to a surface as if you're applying a decal to a balsa model.

walk-through
A 3-D animation that simulates a trip through a space, usually a building.

wire frame
A fast rendering technique in which only the edges of objects are drawn.

CHAPTER FIFTEEN

Presentation Tools and Tips

- Comparing presentation and publishing software
- Choosing a medium: slides, overheads, or the Mac itself?
- Projecting the Mac's image onto a large screen or TV
- The interactive angle — adding branching to presentations

Now and then, everyone dons a Willie Loman outfit and becomes a salesperson. Some people sell products, and others sell ideas and concepts. Whatever your wares, the steps are the same: you gather your facts, shine your shoes, and present your argument.

The Mac can't shine your shoes, but it can help with the rest of the process. Presentation software can help you refine your ideas and create presentation aids such as slides, overhead transparencies, and audience handouts. The whole process smacks of desktop publishing, and indeed, there are plenty of parallels between publishing and presenting. There are also significant differences.

In this chapter, I show you the world of presentation graphics software and hardware. I wrap up the chapter with some tips for preparing presentations.

Present or Perish

Desktop publishing implies that there's permanence to your work: you're preparing documents that can be printed and kept — at least for a while. With presentation graphics, however, your efforts are often more transitory: your audience sees each visual just briefly. Because of their fleeting nature, it's important to create visuals with impact and plan your presentation so that your message sinks in.

Another key difference between desktop publishing and presentation graphics lies in the output media. With desktop publishing, your efforts rest on paper. With presentation graphics, your results are usually projected onto a screen, the most common types of output media being 35mm slides and overhead transparencies. The Mac itself is another medium. Using hardware I discuss later, you can project Mac screen images onto a large screen or route them to a television set.

Combining text and graphics is something most Mac programs do with ease. So do you really need a presentation program? The truth is, if you make only one or two presentations a year, you can probably get by with a drawing program such as ClarisDraw or Deneba's Canvas, a spreadsheet program such as Microsoft Excel or Lotus 1-2-3, or a word processor or desktop publishing program. The ClarisWorks integrated package contains impressive presentation features, too. But if presentations are a regular part of your job, you need the specialized features of a presentation program.

How Presentation Software Works

Word processors and publishing programs are generalists. Presentation programs are specialists; their text-editing and graphics-manipulation features are geared specifically toward producing presentation materials. Toward that end, most presentation programs play three primary roles: they help you develop and refine your ideas, create visuals, and structure and deliver your pitch.

When you're first developing a presentation, you need to organize and reorganize your ideas on the fly. Built-in outlining features, found in Adobe Persuasion, ClarisImpact, and Microsoft PowerPoint, help you do just that (see Figure 15-1 "Outlining a Presentation"). If you use a program that lacks built-in outlining, team it with Symmetry's Acta Advantage outliner desk accessory, or do your brainstorming with a word processor that has outlining features.

Presentation programs encroach on word processing territory in other ways. Many provide search-and-replace commands for making wholesale changes to your text. And because typographical errors can turn a presentation into an embarrassment, you can find spelling checkers in Microsoft PowerPoint, Adobe Persuasion, and ClarisImpact and ClarisWorks. But remember, spelling checkers aren't usage checkers. They don't know *capital* from *capitol* or *its* from *it's*, so keep your dictionary handy.

The Components of a Presentation

After you've refined your ideas, you're ready to produce visuals, which can contain three basic elements: text, graphics, and backgrounds.

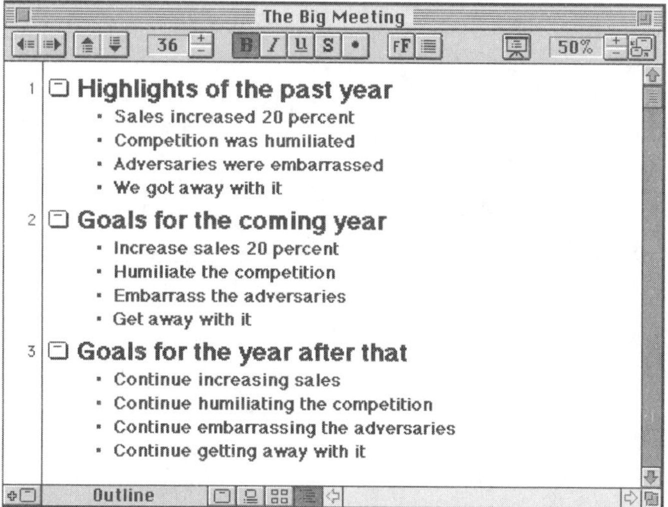

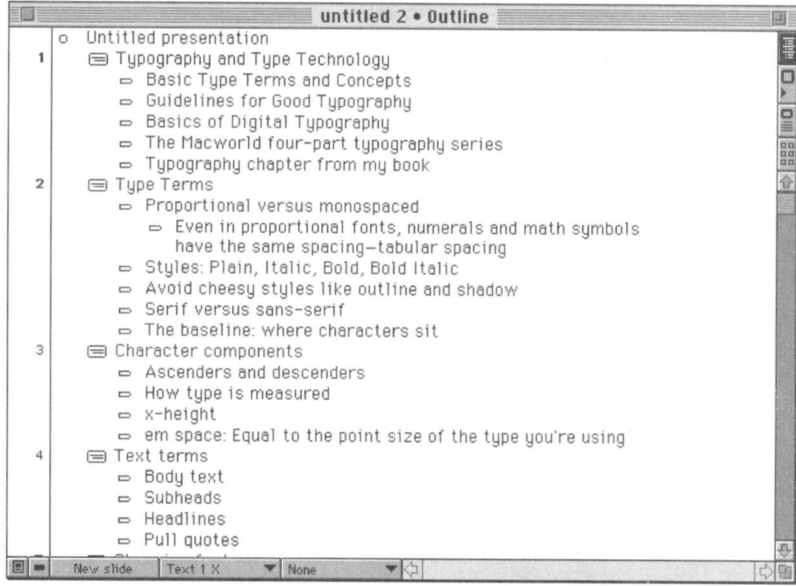

Figure 15-1: Outlining a Presentation Microsoft PowerPoint (top) and Adobe Persuasion (bottom) offer built-in outlining features that let you organize your thoughts before creating visuals. Both can turn outlines into bullet charts with one command or mouse click.

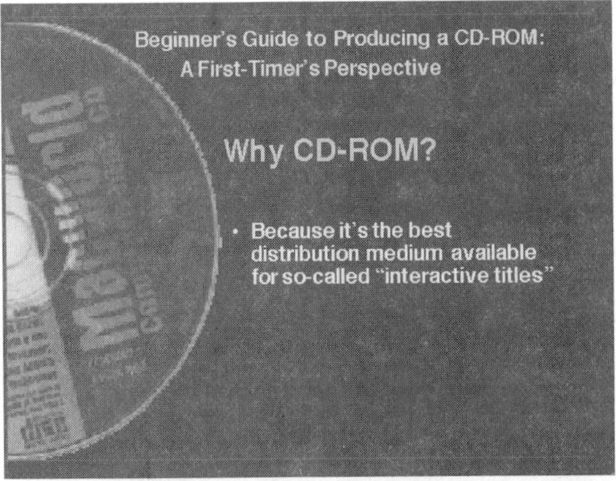

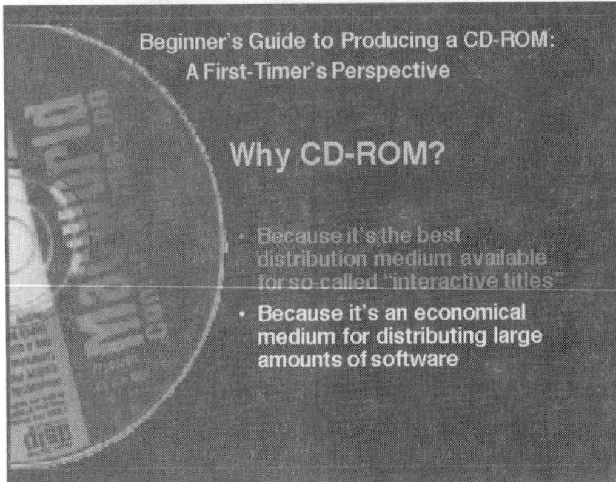

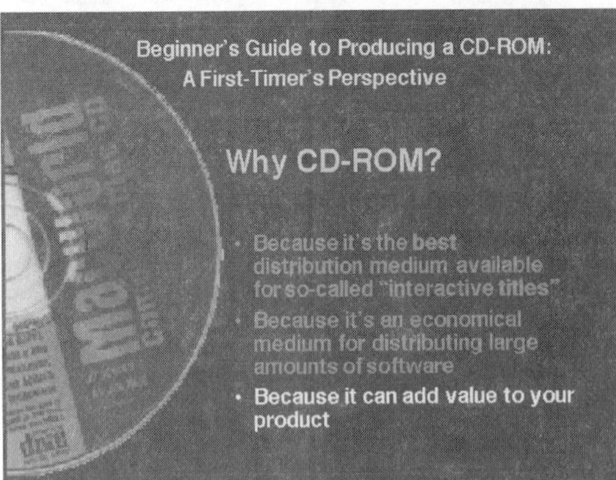

Figure 15-2: Bullet Charts Bullet charts present their information in short phrases, organized in bulleted list form. Many presentation programs let you specify that the bulleted items in a list appear one at a time on consecutive visuals, as shown here. This technique is called a build.

Text elements

Text usually consists of short passages, often organized as bullet charts for fast reading (see Figure 15-2 "Bullet Charts"). Persuasion, ClarisImpact, and PowerPoint let you turn outlines into bullet charts with one command or mouse click. Many programs also let you specify that the bulleted items in a list should appear one at a time on consecutive visuals, a technique called a *build.* By using builds, you can make your case and discuss it point by point. PowerPoint also lets you include Microsoft Excel worksheets in slides. PowerPoint uses Microsoft's OLE linking technology (discussed in Chapter 27) to let you link a slide to a worksheet. Double-click a worksheet that you've imported into PowerPoint, and PowerPoint starts Excel and opens the worksheet for editing.

Graphic elements

A picture is often worth a thousand bullets. Graphs can visually depict trends or market shares, organization charts can spell out the corporate pecking order, and diagrams and drawings can illustrate complex concepts. Persuasion, PowerPoint, and ClarisImpact provide built-in graphing features that let you create graphs from numerical data that you type or import from a spreadsheet (see Figure 15-3 "Built-in Graphing").

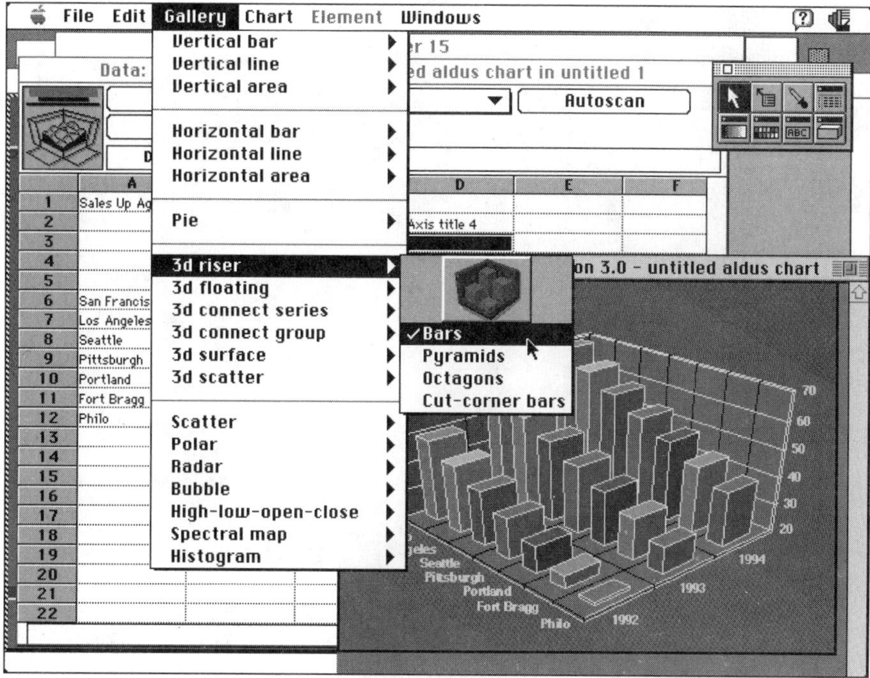

Figure 15-3: Built-in Graphing Persuasion provides built-in graphing features that let you create graphs from numeric data that you type or import from a spreadsheet. A 3-D bar chart is shown here.

PowerPoint includes a separate graphing program, Microsoft Graph, which I discuss in Chapter 12. Other programs let you import graphs created in other programs such as Excel, but importing graphs isn't as convenient as creating them within the presentation program.

As for other types of graphics, Persuasion and ClarisImpact can automatically generate organizational charts based on the indent levels in an outline. All presentation programs have drawing tools for making diagrams, and most can also import images created with a scanner or a drawing program. Persuasion, PowerPoint, and ClarisImpact presentations can also incorporate QuickTime movies.

Background elements

On printed documents, text and graphics generally appear against the white background of paper. But presentation visuals are usually projected onto a white screen in a darkened room, and in that setting, dark text against a white background is hard on the eyes. It's better to use white or brightly colored text against a dark background. All presentation programs let you specify such schemes. Many also provide special background effects that give visuals an elegant, professional look (see Figure 15-4 "The Right Background").

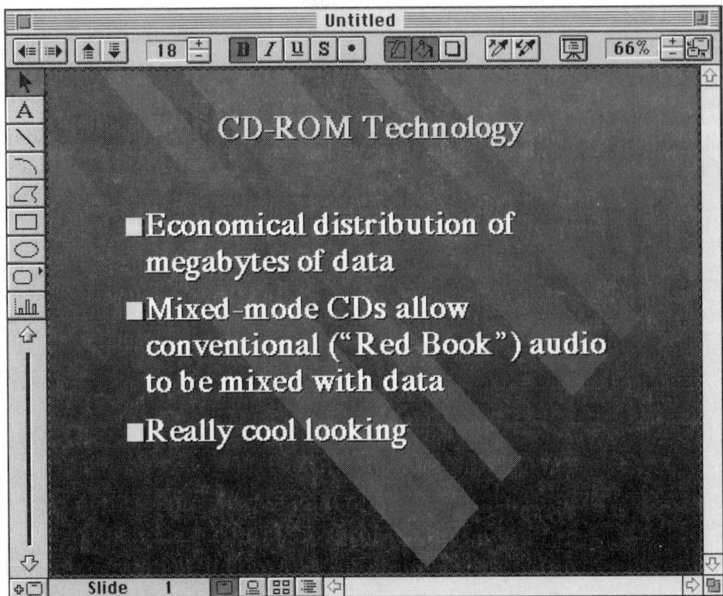

Figure 15-4: The Right Background Most presentation programs provide canned templates that you can use to create your visuals. This one is from Microsoft PowerPoint.

Drawing and Layout Features

For assembling these components, presentation programs provide drawing and layout features that let you position text, create boxes and borders, paste graphics created in other programs, and draw various shapes. Most also provide on-screen rulers and alignment guides for precise positioning.

True, you can find all these features in publishing and drawing programs. But presentation programs put a different spin on many of them. For example, publishing programs don't know overheads from slides, but presentation programs provide page-setup options for both. Thus, instead of having to calculate the proper dimensions for a slide or overhead and then type them into a Page Setup dialog box, you simply choose your output medium from a dialog box.

Consistency is everything

A presentation is more effective if its visuals are designed with care. Well-designed visuals use a consistent background and color scheme and have a uniform layout to give the viewer's eye familiar points of reference. One way to achieve this continuity is to repeat a company logo or graphic on each visual. Most presentation programs let you store such repetitive elements on a *master slide* (see Figure 15-5 "Master Slides").

Figure 15-5: Master Slides Presentation programs use master slides to hold elements that repeat on each slide, such as a company logo, a set of lines, or a background. The contents of a master slide are combined with each individual slide to create a composite containing both the text and graphics.

For typographic consistency, many programs also provide word processor-like style features that let you store and recall text formats. Persuasion, PowerPoint, and ClarisImpact let you create templates to store your formatting preferences for future use. These programs also include an assortment of predesigned templates, some of which look great.

Descriptive titles

Most presentation programs let you assign descriptive titles to each visual in a presentation, so you can tell at a glance what the slide or transparency contains. You can also use these names to sort and organize the visuals by using your program's sorting features.

Keyboard Shortcuts for Microsoft PowerPoint

The tables in this box list some handy keyboard shortcuts for Microsoft PowerPoint.

Slide Show Shortcuts

To Do This	*Press*
Display the next slide	Page Down, N, space, down arrow
Display the previous slide	Page Up, P, up arrow
Blank/restore the screen	B, period
Go to a specific slide	<*number of slide*> and Return

(continued on the next page)

(continued from previous page)

Selection Shortcuts

To Do This	*Press*
Select the next object	Tab
Select the previous object	Shift-Tab
Select text	Shift and an arrow key
Add to or subtract from the selection	Shift-click

Dragging and Resizing Shortcuts

To Do This	*Do This*
Constrain movement vertically or horizontally	Press Shift while dragging
Ignore grids and guides	Press ⌘ while dragging or resizing
Duplicate	Press Option while dragging
Constrain resizing	Press Shift while resizing
Resize from the center of an object	Press Option while clicking a resizing handle
Restore shape	Double-click a resizing handle

Text-Editing Shortcuts

To Do This	*Press*
Create a new paragraph	Return
Create a new line in a paragraph	Shift-Return
Move the insertion point one word at a time	⌘-left arrow or ⌘-right arrow
Move the insertion point one paragraph at a time	⌘-up arrow or ⌘-down arrow
Increase font size	⌘-Shift-period
Decrease font size	⌘-Shift-comma
Raise baseline	⌘-Shift-Option-period
Lower baseline	⌘-Shift-Option-comma

Outlining Shortcuts

To Do This	*Press*
Promote paragraph	Shift-Option-left arrow
Demote paragraph	Shift-Option-right arrow
Move paragraph up or down	Shift-Option-up arrow or Shift-Option-down arrow

Sorting and Showing

What ultimately separates presentation programs from most of their publishing and drawing kinfolk are features that let you sort and arrange visuals and present them on the Mac's screen.

People who work with slides often use an illuminated stand called a *slide sorter* to view and organize their images. On-screen slide sorters — provided by PowerPoint and Persuasion — perform the same role by displaying numerous slides reduced to fit within a window (see Figure 15-6 "Sorting Slides").

Within the slide sorter window, you can change the sequence of slides in your presentation simply by dragging them to different positions. The slide sorter windows in PowerPoint and Persuasion also let you cut or copy slides to the Clipboard for pasting elsewhere in the same presentation or into a different one altogether. Most programs also provide title sorters that display only the titles of the slides. ClarisImpact lacks a slide sorter window, but it does provide a slide manager dialog box that lets you rearrange slides by dragging their names.

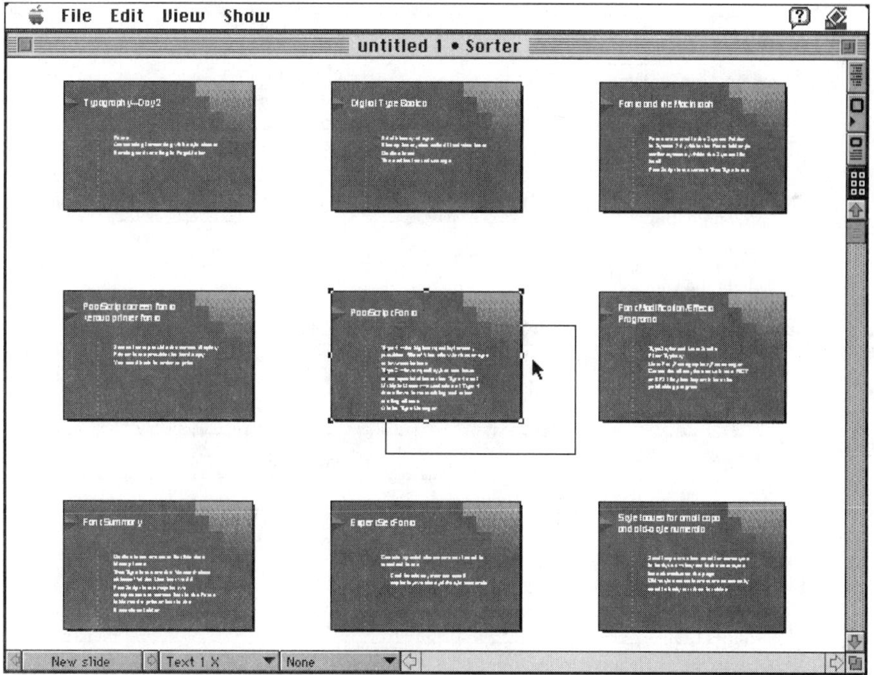

Figure 15-6: Sorting Slides PowerPoint and Persuasion (shown here) provide on-screen slide sorters, which display numerous slides reduced to fit within a window. You can reorganize the sequence of the presentation by dragging the visuals within the sorter window.

Slide show features

Finally, presentation programs provide slide show features to help you exhibit your visuals. Choose your program's Slide Show command, and the Mac becomes a projector, displaying each visual on-screen without the menu bar and tool palettes. In slide-show mode, the mouse becomes a remote control: click it to advance to the next visual. PowerPoint and Persuasion also let you use visual effects such as a *wipe*, which causes one visual to push the preceding one off-screen.

Power Shortcuts for Persuasion

The tables in this box list some keyboard shortcuts for Adobe Persuasion.

General Shortcuts

To Do This	*Press This*
Design an AutoTemplate	Shift-⌘-N
Show/hide the tool palette	Option-⌘-1
Show/hide the color palette	Option-⌘-2
Show/hide the text palette	Option-⌘-3
Show/hide the line palette	Option-⌘-4
Show/hide the nudge palette	Option-⌘-5
Cancel a dialog box	⌘-period (.)

Outline View Shortcuts

To Do This	*Press This*
Create a new heading at the next higher level	Shift-⌘-L
Create a new heading at the next lower level	Shift-⌘-R
Move an empty heading right	Tab
Move an empty heading left	Shift-Tab
Move a non-empty heading right	⌘-]
Move a non-empty heading left	⌘-[
Start a new line within the same heading	Shift-Return

To Do This	Press This
Turn a heading into a title	Option-⌘-T
Turn a heading into a subtitle	Option-⌘-S
Turn a heading into body text	Option-⌘-B
Add notes	Option-⌘-N
Collapse selection	⌘-K
Expand selection	⌘-E
Collapse entire outline	Shift-⌘-K
Expand entire outline	Shift-⌘-E

Slide Show Shortcuts

To Do This	Press This
Show or hide the menu bar	⌘-M
Show or hide the control bar	Shift-⌘-C
Display next slide or layer	Right arrow or N (or click)
Display the preceding slide	Left arrow or P (or double-click)
Go to the first slide	Home or H
Go to the last slide	End or E
Go to the first layer of the first slide	Shift-H or Shift-Home
Go to the first layer of the last slide	Shift-E or Shift-End
Go to the first layer of a specific slide	A slide number and then Return
Stop or resume a slide show that's on auto-advance	Spacebar
Show or hide the mouse pointer	A
Show or hide the blank screen	B or comma (,)
Turn the screen black	Shift-B or period (.)
Exit the slide show	⌘-period (.)
Exit the slide show and quit	⌘-Q

Swapping Mac and Windows presentations

If you use PowerPoint or Persuasion, you can use a Windows PC to show presentations created on a Mac or vice versa. Both PowerPoint and Persuasion have equivalent versions that run under Microsoft Windows.

You can transfer PowerPoint or Persuasion documents to the Windows PC by using a floppy disk, network file server, or cable-transfer utility. (Chapter 27 shows you how to swap files with DOS PCs.) Both programs also come with player applications that you can use to play presentations created under the same or a different platform.

Because of the differences between the two systems, you may have to fine-tune some formatting and visual transitions, so don't transfer your presentation moments before the big meeting begins. To avoid too many formatting hassles, use fonts available on both systems — generally TrueType fonts. Also, if you use movies, sounds, or native-platform graphics formats (such as PICT on the Mac or BMP and PCX on Windows), you have to transfer them separately and re-import them into the presentation program after transferring the presentation to the destination platform.

Output Alternatives

And now for the output: after you create your visuals, how do you bring them to your audience? I just mentioned the Mac-as-slide-projector technique. With this route, however, you may need some additional hardware — unless you can convince a roomful of people to crowd around your Mac.

Large-screen monitors

One option for owners of color Macs is a 19-inch color monitor. If you can spare about $8,000, consider one of Mitsubishi's gargantuan 37-inch color monitors, which are guaranteed to get noticed.

But giant monitors weigh and cost a great deal. And in a large room, even a 37-inch screen can seem small. A more practical solution may be an LCD-projection panel such as those offered by nView Corporation, Sayett Technology, In Focus Systems, Sharp Electronics, and others.

A Mac with video-out and a TV set or VCR

The AV-series Macs as well as the Power Mac 8500 have video-out connectors that let you attach a TV monitor or video recorder. A variety of third-party firms also sell video-out adaptors that connect to desktop Macs and PowerBooks alike. With any of these products, you can show a presentation on any television set that provides a composite or S-video input. (A TV set that provides these connectors is often described as a *TV/monitor*.) You can also record your presentation by connecting the Mac's video-out jack to a VCR or camcorder.

For details on connecting a Mac with video-out features to a TV or VCR, see the Step-by-Step box "How to Put the Mac on TV" in Chapter 20. In a nutshell, you connect the Mac's video-out connector to the video-in connector on the TV set, VCR, or camcorder. (If both the Mac and video device have S-video connectors, use them for a sharper picture.)

Next, use the Monitors control panel to route the Mac's video signal to the television set as described in the Step-by-Step box that I just mentioned. (If you have a Power Mac 8500, use the Video and Sound control panel instead of Monitors.) Note that the outer edges of your visuals will be cut off unless you use the Monitors or Video and Sound control panels to specify a screen resolution of 512 x 384 pixels.

If you want to record the presentation on videotape, connect the VCR's video-in connector to the video-out jack of your television set. Or connect the Mac's video-out jack to the VCR's video-in connector and then connect the VCR's video-out jack to the TV set.

LCD projection panels

LCD projection panels work with an overhead projector. You plug the panel into your Mac and then lay the panel on the projector as though it were a transparency. The Mac creates a video image on the panel's liquid crystal display (LCD) screen, and the projector shows the image on the room screen. Some LCD panels create monochrome (black-and-white) images only, while others support color. Some panels even contain memory into which you can load your visuals, eliminating the need to carry your Mac along.

Video projection

A better way to project color images is to use a video projector such as Sayett's Mediashow. Video projectors can create wall-size images with the same vivid color and fast screen updating you see on-screen. Many LCD projection pads include built-in projectors.

For some tips on getting the best results from an LCD projection pad or video projector, see the Quick Tips box "Projecting the Best Image."

Overheads and Slides

The biggest drawback to most video-oriented presentation hardware is that you need to lug your Mac along. When portability, color, and economy are important, overhead transparencies and slides are better alternatives.

If you're like me, you probably slept through a few overheads in high school. Ah, but our teachers didn't have the output options that we enjoy today. By printing your visuals on transparency film, you can produce impressive overheads that do your teachers proud.

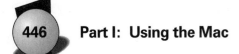

Projecting the Best Image

Here are some tips for getting the best results from an LCD projection pad or video projector.

Use a high-quality screen
Don't project an image onto a wall; you get more vivid colors and a brighter image when you use a screen. Matte-finish screens provide a wide viewing angle — good when your audience is spread out to the far sides of a room. Glass-beaded screens are brighter and have a fairly wide viewing angle, but they can be fragile. Lenticular screens have a relatively narrow viewing angle, but within that angle, the image is bright and sharp.

Let your hardware warm up
Give a projection pad or video projector at least 20 minutes to warm up before you try to adjust its colors. And if you've just taken your hardware out of a cold car, let it adjust to room temperature so condensation doesn't form on its optics.

Ship the hardware carefully
Video projectors and projection pads are delicate. If your unit didn't include a hard carrying case, buy one. And avoid storing a unit in a hot car.

Printing overheads

For laser printers, use 3M Type 154 Transparency Film or its equivalent. (Generally, you can use any transparency film designed to withstand temperatures of 392° F or 200° C — the temperature present in a laser printer's fusing rollers.) For ink-jet printers such as Apple's StyleWriter series or Hewlett-Packard's DeskWriter series, use 3M CG3480 Transparency Film.

Need color? Use one of the new breed of affordable color ink-jet printers, such as the Apple StyleWriter 2400 or Hewlett-Packard's DeskWriter C series. Bigger budgets may spring for a printer such as Tektronix's Phaser 340 or the Apple Color LaserWriter. (See Chapter 30 for more details about color printers.)

Overhead drawbacks

Overhead transparencies are eminently portable: dozens of them can fit in a binder, and overhead projectors are almost as ubiquitous as photocopiers. But overheads have drawbacks, too. You must manually flip from one transparency to the next, which can make an otherwise sophisticated presentation seem amateurish — especially if the projector's fan blows half your visuals off the table. (Don't laugh; it happens.)

What's more, overheads can scratch and smudge, and the hues produced by inexpensive color printers can't approach the vividness of the ultimate presentation output medium — the color slide.

Professional Slide Presentations

Two slide projectors and a dissolve unit (available from photographic and audiovisual suppliers) help you create professional-looking presentations with special visual effects. When used with a dissolve unit, one projector's tray holds even-numbered slides; the other holds odd-numbered ones. By alternating between projectors and fading the lamps in and out, a dissolve unit creates smooth transitions between slides, eliminating the jarring on-and-off flash between slide changes. By varying the speed of the lamps' fade-ins and fade-outs, the dissolve unit can create slow, graceful dissolves or instant cuts.

The most sophisticated multimedia audiovisual applications combine dissolve units, multiple slide projectors, one or more motion picture projectors, and a multitrack audio tape recorder. One track of the audio recording holds inaudible pulses that control the dissolve units and projectors, while the remaining tracks hold narration, sound effects, and music.

Slide advantages

Slides are portable, too, and you can carry them in a tray, where they're always properly sequenced and ready to show. In addition, slides are inexpensive to duplicate, so it's easy to prepare extra sets as backups or for colleagues. And slides give you the vivid colors that only film can provide. Slides also have the greatest dazzle potential. By combining two or more slide projectors under the control of a dissolve unit, you can create impressive presentations containing fancy visual effects (see the Backgrounder box "Professional Slide Presentations").

Making slides with film recorders

To create slides with a presentation program, you need a film recorder such as Lasergraphics' Personal LFR or Polaroid's Digital Palette HR-6000 (also sold by GCC Technologies as the ColorFast II). I recently tested several film recorders for my *Macworld* column and found these models to be the best. Think of a film recorder as a printer that creates images on film instead of paper. Most film recorders contain a camera aimed at a video tube. Sandwiched between those components is a wheel containing red, green, and blue filters. The film recorder paints an image on the video tube, making separate passes for red, green, and blue light — three primary colors for video with which it can create a palette of over 16 million hues. A complete exposure usually takes a few minutes.

Not only do film recorders provide spectacular color, but they also offer tack-sharp resolution — usually in the ballpark of 4000 horizontal lines per slide. By comparison, a 14-inch color monitor displays 480 horizontal lines, and commercial television has 525-line resolution.

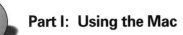

Photo Opportunities

Although film recorders are generally associated with making 35mm slides, they can produce other types of photographic output, too. Because a film recorder accepts standard 35mm film, you can load any type of film — to create black-and-white or color prints, for example.

One type of film that you might consider using is Polaroid's PolaChrome, an instant slide film that produces high-contrast images; it's ideal for title slides. PolaBlue is an instant slide film that produces white-on-blue images; it's designed for simple title slides and for line art, such as diagrams and architectural drawings. PolaPan is an instant black-and-white slide film.

To process an instant slide film, you need a Polariod AutoProcessor; this gizmo is about the size of a small telephone and contains rollers and gears that apply a developing jelly located in a cartridge that accompanies each roll of instant slide film. Load the developing cartridge and your exposed roll of film into the AutoProcessor, turn a crank, wait the specified amount of time, and then admire (or reshoot) your images — no darkroom needed. You can then mount the slides in standard slide mounts; Polaroid's Illuminated Slide Mounter makes the job fairly straightforward.

Another noteworthy option involves replacing the film recorder's 35mm camera back with a sheet-film adaptor. This enables you to use professional 4 x 5-inch sheet films as well as Polaroid's 669 Instant Pack film for making instant prints — handy for proofing your visuals before exposing film. Polaroid also offers a 4 x 5 instant transparency film called 691 Overhead Projection Instant Pack film (for transparencies). With Polaroid's Overhead Adaptor, you can project these transparencies using a standard overhead projector.

The service bureau alternative

Hardware this sharp isn't cheap; film recorder prices generally start at about $6,000. A less expensive alternative is to use a slide-service bureau. Most cities have service bureaus and large copy shops that can create slides for you from documents that you supply on a floppy disk or transmit via modem. Your slides arrive from one to several days later, depending on the turnaround time you're willing to pay for. Service bureaus also provide other types of output, such as high-resolution overhead transparencies and color prints.

Most publishers of presentation software have cooperative arrangements with nationwide slide-service bureaus such as Genigraphics. Included with the software is a driver for the type of film recorder the bureau uses; you copy the driver to your System Folder and use the Chooser desk accessory to select it prior to creating your visuals. The driver provides straightforward dialog boxes that automate communications with the service bureau (see Figure 15-7 "Dialing for Dazzle").

For tips on choosing between and designing slides and overheads, see the Quick Tips box "Presentation Pointers."

Presentation Pointers

You're scheduled to give a presentation. Which medium should you use — slides or overheads? And what typefaces would be best? Use the table below to help you decide.

	Overhead Transparencies	Slides
Best applications	Informal presentations to small groups	Formal presentations to large groups; repeating presentations at trade shows or public places
Advantages	Inexpensive; can be shown in lit room, allowing interaction; can be written on	Vivid colors; impressive looking; special effects possible with multiple projectors; easy to duplicate; remain sorted in trays
Disadvantages	Can scratch and smudge; bland colors; can become disordered	Relatively expensive; turnaround time required for service bureaus; less personal — requires darkened room, which discourages interaction
Design tips	One concept per transparency; use about seven words per line, and no more than seven lines per overhead	One idea per slide; use bulleted lists and *builds* for complex topics; avoid more than four lines of type per slide, use the same orientation for all slides — don't switch between horizontal and vertical slides
Typographic tips	Avoid type sizes smaller than 18 point; text should be readable from 10 feet away before projection	Set type tight but not touching; use reverse type (light type on dark background); avoid centering; avoid varying type size from one slide to the next
Presentation tips	Be sure visuals are in order before beginning	Be sure slides are properly sequenced and oriented in their trays; use a large number of slides — don't force the audience to stare at one image
Graphics tips	Use bar graphs to show relationships between data; use line graphs to show trends; use pie charts to show percentage relationships	
Typeface tips	Use bold, sanserif fonts such as Helvetica Bold and Franklin Gothic Heavy; also consider the square-serif Lubalin Graph; don't use more than two typefaces per visual, and use the same typefaces throughout the presentation; for slides, use reverse type (light type on a dark background)	

Genigraphics Driver Job Instructions

Copies: 1 sets, 35mm Slides (plastic mounts)
0 sets, 35mm Slides (glass mounts)
0 sets, 8"x 10" Overheads
0 sets, 8"x 10" Prints

Send via: ◉ Modem ○ Diskette
Return via: ◉ Courier ○ Mail ○ Hold for Pickup

Save As: Geni-Genigraphics Disk

OK
Cancel
Custom

Figure 15-7: Dialing for Dazzle Most presentation programs include a driver that lets you transmit visuals to a nationwide slide-service bureau such as Genigraphics. Note the options for delivery method.

Tips for Planning Your Presentation

Your teeth chatter, your heart pounds, your palms sweat. You hear your name — time for the big presentation. Standing up, you hear chuckles and feel terror as you realize: you're in your underwear!

Presentation Pointers for PowerBooks

A PowerBook is ideal for presentations. All PowerBooks except the 100, 140, 145, 145B, 150, 170, and the PowerBook Duo models provide a connector to which you can attach an external monitor. You can then use the Portable Display control panel to put the PowerBook's video circuitry into video-mirroring mode.

Mirroring causes the PowerBook to display the same image on the external monitor as appears on the PowerBook's display, enabling you to see your presentation without having to look behind you at the large screen. When the PowerBook isn't in mirroring mode, the external monitor extends the Mac's desktop.

If you have a PowerBook that lacks a built-in monitor port, you can add external video support by using a third-party upgrade, such as Power R's PB-10. (See Chapter 29 for more video options.)

For PowerBook Duo models, consider buying a docking unit that provides an external video port. Apple's Duo Minidock provides one, as do several third-party docks. Radius's Presentor even lets you use a TV set as a monitor.

Whew — just a bad dream. The presentation isn't until next week, and it's been months since you forgot to dress for work. Besides, this time you'll be prepared. You've read the background information in this chapter and chosen a presentation package; now all you need is the guidance to take advantage of it. In this section, I present some pointers for presenters.

Choosing a medium

Before you start creating presentation visuals, you need to choose an output medium. Are you creating overhead transparencies? 35mm slides? Do you plan to use the Mac as a projector? You can change Page Setup options after you've created visuals, but you may have to reposition some elements to make them fit.

Several factors influence your choice of an output medium:

- *Whether you want to encourage or discourage audience participation.* Generally, a darkened room suggests a more formal presentation and discourages audience participation. Slides all but require a darkened room; overhead transparencies can be shown in lighted rooms and suggest a less formal presentation. You can also write on overheads to highlight or annotate a point. For Mac-based presentations, the lighting conditions depend on how you project the Mac's screen. A 35-inch video monitor yields a vivid image that looks fine in a lighted room; a video projector and movie screen usually benefit from dimmed lights.
- *The equipment at the presentation location.* If you know that there is a Mac and a large-screen monitor (or you plan to lug along your own hardware), you may be more inclined to use the Mac as your medium. Otherwise, slides or overheads are in order.
- *Your willingness to live on the edge.* Electronic presentations (ones shown with the Mac) can include fancy visual effects, soundtracks, and QuickTime movies. But I've seen many glitzy presentations go awry because of system crashes, power glitches, kicked cords, or Murphy's Law. It's better to keep a presentation simple than to risk embarrassing delays or total failure. This rule is especially true if you plan to show the presentation by using a Mac other than your own; differences in configuration — fonts, system extensions, available memory — are common causes of presentation pickles.

Creating visuals

If you want your audience to swallow your ideas, you have to make your visuals digestible. That means putting a manageable number of words and lines on each visual — a job you tackle during the outlining phase.

Generally, use a separate visual for each main idea or concept. Then use bullet points to elaborate on each idea (see Figure 15-8 "Building a Visual").

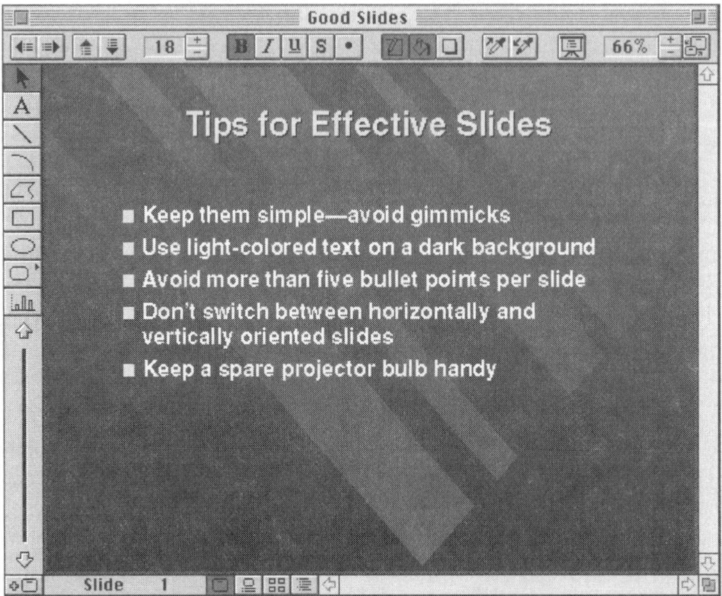

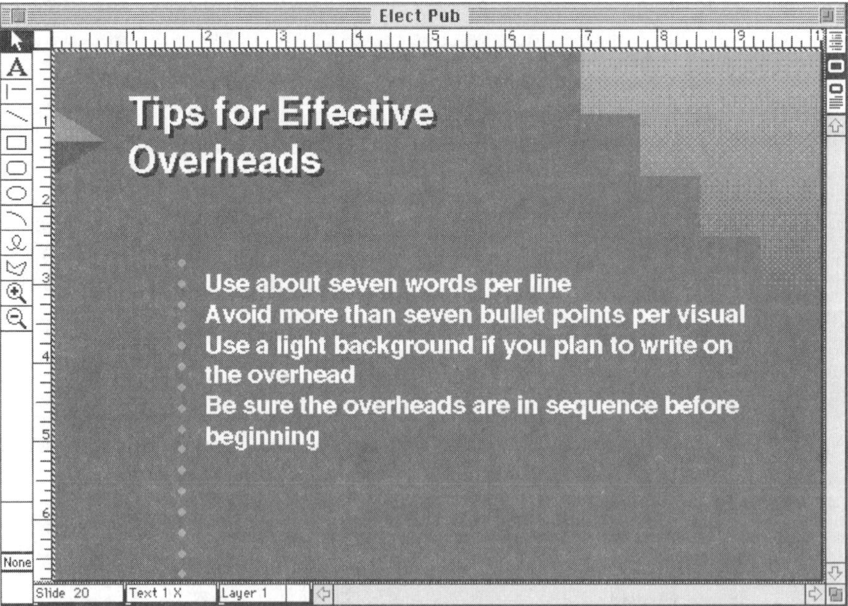

Figure 15-8: Building a Visual Both Microsoft PowerPoint (top) and Adobe Persuasion (bottom) include templates that provide attractive backgrounds and color schemes. Two of my favorites are shown in these slides, which also illustrate capitalization guidelines for slide titles and bullet points.

Don't be wordy — your visuals should be signposts, not eye charts. For overhead transparencies, use about seven words per line and no more than about seven lines of text per overhead. Put no more than four or five lines on a slide or electronic visual. If a heading takes more than one line, you're probably trying to cram too much information onto a single visual. If a bullet point takes two or more lines, break it into two or more separate points. Use initial capitals for slide titles ("Goals for Next Quarter") and sentence capitals for each bullet item ("Torch the competition's factory").

For slides or electronic visuals, consider using builds to present and discuss each bullet point separately. Don't use builds for overheads.

Creating builds in PowerPoint and Persuasion

To create a build in PowerPoint, display the appropriate slide and choose Build from the Tools menu. (In PowerPoint 3, choose Build from the Slide menu.) Check the Build Body Text box. If you want to gray the preceding bullet point when you advance to the next point, check the Dim Previous Points box. For electronic presentations, you can use the Effect pop-up menu to choose an effect for the build. Choosing Fly From Right, for instance, causes each bullet point to slide into place from the right edge of the screen. Choose effects judiciously — and use them sparingly.

To specify that Persuasion use builds for all visuals, switch to the Master slide and then select the placeholder for the bullet items. Choose Build Layers from the Master menu and specify the number of layers you want to build.

Designing visuals

All presentation programs come with a large library of ready-to-use design templates, each with its own combination of color schemes, type attributes, and graphic flourishes. If you aren't an experienced designer, a template is the safest way to get good results.

Still, there may be times when you want to create a design from scratch (or times when you may *have* to — perhaps you didn't install the space-consuming templates on your PowerBook, and now you're on the road). You can find some advice in the Quick Tips box "Tips for Designing Presentation Visuals."

Getting Glitzy with Graphics and Movies

PowerPoint, Persuasion, and ClarisImpact let you import graphics and even QuickTime movies into a presentation. In Persuasion, use the File menu's Import command. In PowerPoint, use the Insert menu. (In PowerPoint 3, use the Edit menu's Insert submenu.) In ClarisImpact, use the Place File command in the File menu to bring in graphics. To import QuickTime movies, use Import to open the movie and Place File to place the movie in the current document.

Tips for Designing Presentation Visuals

For most jobs, you'll probably be happy with one of the canned design templates that accompany your presentation program. But if you aren't — or if you didn't install the templates before hitting the road — here are some tips for designing visuals.

Slides

Use a dark background color and light-colored text. (White or yellow text on a blue background is popular and looks classy.) A bright background in a darkened room creates too much contrast and may give your audience headaches. PowerPoint and Persuasion also let you create a gradient fill, an effect in which one color gradually blends into another — an elegant look if you choose colors carefully. A fill that graduates from blue to black looks great on a big screen. (PowerPoint's built-in array of color schemes makes choosing colors a breeze.)

Laser-printed overheads

Use black text on a white background. If you have a color printer, consider using light-colored text on a dark background, but choose colors carefully. You get the best results from pure colors that don't require dithering (patterns of dots), such as yellow and blue. This restriction doesn't apply to dye-sublimation printers, which don't dither. (See Chapter 30's sections about color printers for more details on printing transparencies.)

Backgrounds

While you're creating a background, consider adding an element to the master slide, whose contents appear on each visual. (To display the master slide in PowerPoint, choose Master Slide from the View menu; in Persuasion, choose Current from the View menu's Slide Master submenu.) A company logo or the title of a conference is a typical candidate for a master slide. Be sure to position the repeating element so that the contents of each visual don't obscure it. And if you need to resize a logo or other graphic, remember to hold the Shift key while resizing to avoid changing the image's proportions.

Font choices

I'm fond of Helvetica Bold — it's sturdy and stands up well under projection. Serif typefaces such as Baskerville, Caslon, and Century Schoolbook often look fuzzy. Avoid type sizes smaller than 18 point for transparencies.

Importing

What should you import? A photo showing the new product or the new CEO (a digital camera such as Apple's QuickTake 150 is handy for taking such images — ones that you view on the monitor). A scan of the annual report or the new package design. Or a graph showing the latest market shares.

Be careful with QuickTime movies, though. I once attended an Apple presentation that included a QuickTime snippet in which a focus group talked about the features they longed for. Good idea, bad execution: although such a clip could have added objective support for the presenter's claims, the video was fuzzy and the audio unintelligible. Don't use a QuickTime movie or a digitized sound unless it says — and says clearly — something that words and still images can't.

Animate sparingly

Besides supporting movies and digitized sounds, Gold Disk's Astound invades animation territory — you can create graphs that tumble into view or assemble themselves bar by bar. Astound has more glitz than an Oscar awards ceremony. A Timeline window lets you orchestrate a cast of sounds, movies, and visuals to play back automatically — ideal for self-running presentations.

These features can be effective when used tastefully and sparingly — and therein lies the rub (or at least one of the rubs: Astound's astounding appetite for disk space and memory is another). Too many flashy effects are distracting and tacky. And of course, inviting sound and motion to the party increases the amount of disk space and memory your presentation requires — as well as the odds that something will go wrong.

Adding interactivity to presentations

In the past, only programs such as Macromedia Director and Passport Producer could produce interactive presentations that incorporate sound effects and music. Now, even mainstream presentation packages provide a path to the interactive world.

By *interactivity*, I don't mean audience interaction with you, but audience interaction with your presentation. Astound and Persuasion let you create on-screen buttons that display other slides when clicked. With this feature, you can create interactive presentations that viewers can navigate on their own — it's interactive multimedia without the expense and learning curve of a program such as Macromedia Director.

Of course, you don't want audiences branching around within your presentation while you're on-stage. But if you know that your audience members have Macs (or Windows machines), you can create an interactive version of a presentation and pass it out on floppy disks. Astound and Persuasion include Mac and Windows player applications that you can copy freely to enable others to view your efforts.

Don't forget HyperCard

Then there's HyperCard. As a presentation program, Apple's software toolkit has serious limitations, most notably, limited color support and weak screen-layout tools. But it does provide a selection of visual effects and can play back sounds and movies. And by combining its built-in programming language with on-screen buttons, you can create dynamic presentations that people can use and navigate through on their own. Beginning with HyperCard 2.2, you can save your work as a stand-alone application program that you can give to anyone who has a Mac (see Chapter 19).

Everyone's Looking for a Handout

Flashy visuals are great, but audiences also like hard copy. A hard copy of your presentation enables them to take notes during your pitch and refresh their memories later. Hard copy also shows that you care enough about your ideas to commit them to paper and enough about your audience to go to the trouble of doing so.

Creating handouts

PowerPoint and Persuasion can automatically generate handouts based on the visuals you create. You can also print and pass out the presentation in outline form, but an outline doesn't look as good and leaves little room for notes.

Both programs can create two types of handouts: *note* pages, each containing a single visual, with blank space below for doodles; and *handout* pages, which print several visuals on each page.

If you're using handout pages, avoid printing too many visuals on each page. You may save paper by printing six slides on each page, but you leave little room for notes, and readers have to squint to read each slide. I prefer one to three visuals per page. Also, don't neglect the opportunity to spiff up the handouts — add a company logo and your presentation title, for example, and create some lines on each page for audience notes (see Figure 15-9 "Better Handouts"). To create lines, switch to the handout master and draw one line. Then select the line and use the program's Duplicate command to create more. Be sure to leave enough space to write — to allow for fast scribbling, put three quarters of an inch to one inch of space before each line.

Printing and binding handouts

If your visuals use a graduated background fill and you're using a monochrome printer, you can cut printing time dramatically by telling your program not to print the fills. In PowerPoint's Print dialog box, check the Black and White Only box. In Persuasion's Print dialog box, check the Proof Print box.

After you've printed the handouts, staple or otherwise bind them to keep them in order. (Paper Direct, at 800-A-PAPERS, has a great selection of presentation binders and other specialty papers.) And distribute handouts before your presentation begins. Nothing dilutes a presentation's impact more than audience members passing wads of paper to each other while you talk. If you anticipate note-taking, distribute pencils or pens so audience members don't spend the first few minutes of your show looking for something to write with.

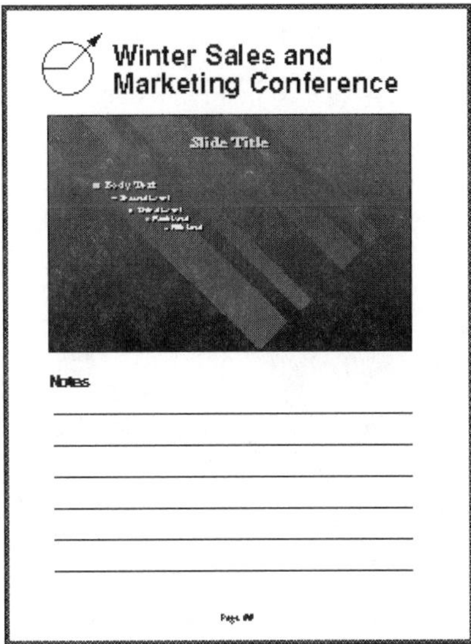

Figure 15-9: Better Handouts You can enhance a handout by adding repeating elements such as a company logo and text describing the presentation and by adding lines for handwritten notes. Be sure to leave plenty of room to write between the lines — people tend to write larger when they're taking hurried notes.

Showtime!

Before the big day arrives, visit the Room of Doom and case the joint. What should you look for? Signs of sabotage? No, just the basics.

Here's a checklist of things to do before the crowd starts filing in. For more tips on presentation giving, see the Quick Tips box "Don't Let 'Em See You Sweat."

- If there's a public-address system, adjust it so you don't deafen attendees with microphone feedback or spend the first few minutes asking, "Can you folks in the back hear me?"
- Make sure that the screen is visible from each seat.
- Don't put yourself between the screen and the audience. Position the screen to your right or left and at a 45-degree angle.
- If you're using a slide or overhead projector, keep a spare bulb close by — or to be extra safe, replace the bulb with a new one before you begin.
- Get everything up and running and do a dry run. Making frantic, last-minute preparations while your audience waits makes you look like an amateur.

In the end, the keys to a successful presentation are preparation and practice. The more often you speak before a group, the more natural it becomes. Organize your thoughts, create simple, tasteful visuals, and make sure that the room and everything in it are ready. And don't forget to dress.

Don't Let 'Em See You Sweat

About to give a big presentation? Don't panic. Or at least don't let them *see* you panic. And read the tips in this box before you step on-stage.

Picture yourself a success

I'm wading into hot-tub psychology here, but I really believe that it helps to visualize yourself giving the presentation. Imagine being introduced and making your remarks and fielding questions with confidence.

Set the tone for the audience

Speaking of questions, if you don't want to take any until the end, be sure to say so either at the outset or when the first hand goes up. If you want an informal, give-and-take exchange, let your audience know — although you risk the event going in its own direction.

Cover your props

If your presentation relies on props — maybe you're unveiling the new widget — keep the props covered or hidden until you need them and put them away when you're finished with them. This way, they don't distract the audience.

Make eye contact

During the presentation, look at and talk to the audience, not the screen. Make eye contact with your audience — a second or two per victim. Don't keep your hands in your pockets or folded on a lectern, but use natural hand gestures for emphasis.

Do an honest Q&A

If you're taking questions at the end, make sure that the entire audience hears each question — repeat it if necessary or, for large rooms, station a microphone in an aisle and ask that anyone with questions use it. If someone asks a question you can't answer, be honest: say that you don't know but will find out. Don't try to fudge an answer — someone in the audience may know that you're doing so.

CHAPTER 15 CONCEPTS AND TERMS

- If you give presentations only occasionally, consider using Claris MacDraw Pro or ClarisWorks, both of which combine drawing and graphics with basic presentation features. Frequent presenters should use a presentation program such as Adobe Persuasion or Microsoft PowerPoint.
- Visuals contain three basic elements — text, often organized into bullet charts; graphics, including graphs, organizational charts, diagrams, and drawings; and backgrounds, which spice up the visual and help make text more readable on-screen.
- A presentation program's features for sorting, arranging, and presenting visuals set it apart from a drawing or publishing package.
- Overhead transparencies, slides, and handouts are the most common forms of presentation hard copy. You can also use the Mac to display your visuals by using an LCD projection pad, video projector, or large-screen monitor.

build
A display technique in which the bulleted items in a list appear one at a time on consecutive visuals. By using builds, you can discuss each bullet point individually.

bullet chart
A series of text points, each of which is preceded by a bullet (•) or similar character.

dissolve unit
A device that connects two slide projectors and alternates between them to avoid jarring flashes of light between each slide.

film recorder
A hardware add-on that lets you create 35mm slides.

LCD projection panel
A hardware add-on that uses a liquid-crystal display (LCD) enclosed in a frame that sits on an overhead projector, enabling the LCD's screen image to be projected.

master slide
A slide that holds the background and other elements that repeat on each slide.

slide-show mode
An operating mode in which a presentation program hides the Mac's menu bar and windows, leaving only the visuals themselves. You can advance to the next visual by pressing the mouse button.

transparency film
A clear film that you can run through a laser or ink-jet printer to produce visuals that you can project by using an overhead projector.

video projector
A hardware add-on that lets you project the Mac's screen image onto a large screen.

wipe
A visual effect in which one slide appears to push the preceding one off-screen.

CHAPTER SIXTEEN

The Mac Meets the Telephone

- All about modems — and why your Mac needs one
- Tips for choosing and using on-line services
- Fax modem survival tips
- An overview of the Internet
- Telephony: the Mac as an answering machine and telephone

With some inexpensive hardware and software, your Mac can use a phone line to reach out and touch other computers. You can exchange files with a colleague at the office or a friend in another city. You can dial up *bulletin boards*, electronic meeting places for hobbyists and user group members. You can send *electronic mail* to friends and coworkers, even if they don't have computers. You can transmit documents to desktop publishing service bureaus for output on their typesetting equipment. You can subscribe to any number of *on-line services* from which you can access current news and vast libraries of free and nearly free software. You can send and receive faxes. And as Chapter 32 shows, with Apple's Apple Remote Access software, you can even dial into a Mac located somewhere else in order to copy files or print documents.

These days, Macs can reach out and touch more than just computers and fax machines. With the right products, a Mac can dial the customers in your contact database and let you talk to them. The Quadra AV models started the built-in-telephone trend, and the Power Macs have picked up the torch.

Macs can also be the hub of a voice-mail system (press 1 if you're intrigued, press 2 if you hate voice mail). They can run automated fax-back systems, which let customers phone in to order product brochures, technical updates, horoscopes, you name it. Callers punch in numbers and the documents arrive via fax shortly thereafter. A Mac-based voice-mail and fax-back system can make a small business look bigger.

Naturally, there's a buzzword behind all this phone fun: *telephony*. Pronounced *te-LE-phony*, it's one of the hot trends in computing. Apple is actively involved in this area; besides building telephony capabilities into the AV and Power Macs, Apple has enhanced the Mac's system software to add telephony features that any application program can take advantage of. Indeed, telephony gurus talk of a rosy future in which our computers are also videophones that let us beam our smiles across the miles. We shall see. In the meantime, here's a look at some of the genuinely useful ways in which a Mac can tie up a telephone line.

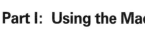

See You in Cyberspace

The Best of BMUG collection on the *Macworld Power User Clinic* CD contains some shareware and free software you can use to get on-line.

- **Zterm** David Alverson's shareware telecommunications program is legendary — and pretty powerful, too. It supports macros, scripting, and all the popular file-transfer protocols. It also includes great documentation.
- **First Class Client** First Class is a graphical BBS system that's true to its name.
- **BBS directories** The CD contains several lists of bulletin board systems — everything from user group bulletin boards to computer company support boards to boards with, shall I say, offbeat themes. If you want to explore the eddies and backwaters of cyberspace, use this list as your roadmap.
- **AT command reference** Need a handy on-screen reference to the world of AT commands, which modems use to dial numbers, connect, and more? You can find some in the Telecom Tools folder, within the Shareware and Freeware folder.

Private Lines and Party Lines

You can telecommunicate on two basic levels — directly with another computer (which may be anything from another personal computer to a Cray supercomputer), or through an intermediary such as an information service or bulletin board (see Figure 16-1 "Two Ways to Connect"). With the direct route, you arrange the communications session ahead of time by determining who will call whom and then setting up your communications gear accordingly. A business traveler can use this technique to transfer a file to a colleague at the home office.

Communicating directly

Communicating directly costs only the phone call, but it forces you to contend with several communications technicalities. For example, the choice of a *file-transfer protocol* causes data to be electronically proofread to eliminate garbled files as it's received. Plan on making a troubleshooting call to iron out the wrinkles. Also, plan for some scheduling predicaments. You and your fellow communicator should be at your machines to ensure that things go smoothly, which can be awfully inconvenient if you're in different time zones.

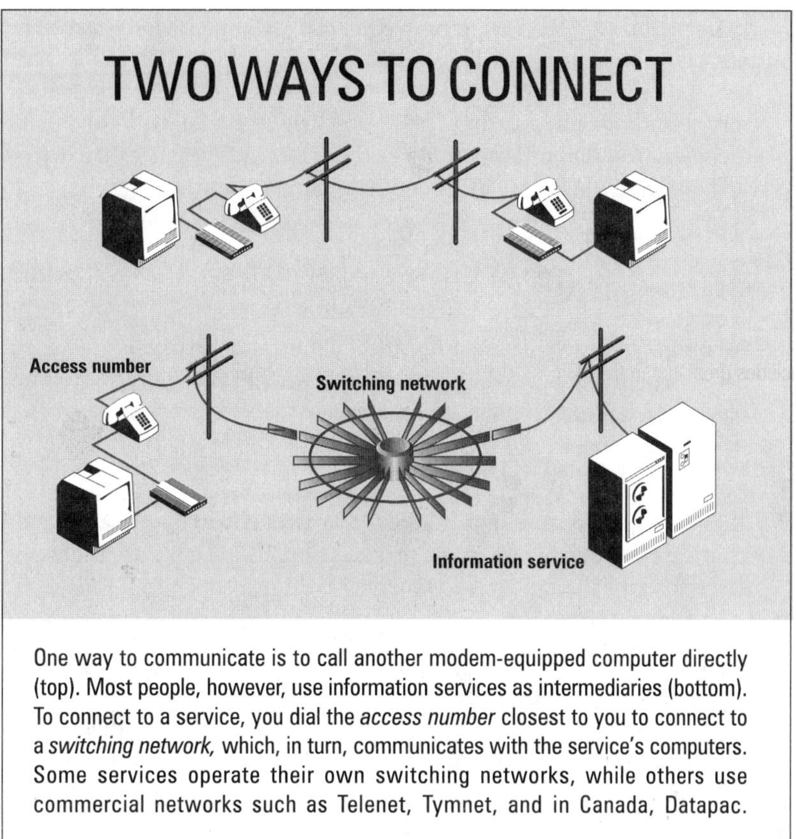

One way to communicate is to call another modem-equipped computer directly (top). Most people, however, use information services as intermediaries (bottom). To connect to a service, you dial the *access number* closest to you to connect to a *switching network,* which, in turn, communicates with the service's computers. Some services operate their own switching networks, while others use commercial networks such as Telenet, Tymnet, and in Canada, Datapac.

Figure 16-1: Two Ways to Connect

Communicating via an on-line service

Using an information service is a more convenient and more flexible way to communicate. When connected to one, your Mac talks to a roomful of refrigerator-size mainframe computers. Those mainframes may, in turn, be talking to thousands of your fellow subscribers simultaneously, divvying up their time between each one. It's called *timesharing,* and it's one of the oldest ways of getting computer power to individuals and small companies. (Indeed, some on-line services, including CompuServe, began life years ago by selling mainframe computer time to businesses for payroll management and similar tasks.)

Information services used to have ugly, text-only interfaces — artifacts from the early days of computing. These days, all major information services provide graphical *front ends* — Mac programs that you use to access and navigate through the service and that provide some insulation from the cold world of communications technicalities. And information? It's there in quantities that may overwhelm you at first and cost you a fair sum in connect charges after that.

What's On-Line?

An information service is a post office, library, stockbroker, travel agent, meeting hall, computer club, and software flea market all rolled into one phone call. This section describes what you can find on most services.

Electronic mail

You can exchange messages and disk files with other subscribers in a flash and cut your express courier bills in the process. Simply *upload* files and messages to the service; recipients can *download* them at their convenience.

With many services, you can exchange *e-mail* with other subscribers only. Some services, however, provide *gateways* to other services. CompuServe and America Online users, for example, can exchange mail with MCI Mail subscribers. Other services, including MCI Mail and GEnie, can combine e-mail with paper mail. Transmit your message to the service, and it's laser printed and then mailed or delivered by courier. Most services can also send your e-mail to any fax machine.

News

Most services offer up-to-the-minute news from wire services such as The Associated Press, United Press International, and Reuters, and from newspapers such as the *Wall Street Journal* and the *Washington Post.* The NewsNet information service specializes in government and industry news, offering the full text of hundreds of specialized newsletters.

Most services let you locate items of interest by typing sets of keywords. For example, the keyword phrase *offshore and regulation* would snag stories on offshore drilling laws. Some services also let you set up electronic clipping folders: specify your keywords, and the service constantly scans the wires for you and saves stories containing them. When you go back on-line, you find the relevant stories waiting.

Research

Of all the major consumer information services, CompuServe has the largest electronic research room. You can summon detailed information about nearly 10,000 publicly traded companies and demographic reports for thousands of towns and cities. Also available are data from the Bureau of the Census, transcripts of television news programs, thousands of articles from *Consumer Reports* and numerous computer publications (including *Macworld*), and on-line versions of *Books in Print* and *Who's Who*. On several services, you can find all ten million words of *Grolier's Academic American Encyclopedia*. There are also specialized research-oriented services, such as NewsNet and Dialog.

Travel information

Most services have on-line travel agents that can help you plan trips. On CompuServe, you can search for fellow subscribers willing to swap houses for vacations. Frequent flyers can access the Official Airline Guide (OAG) database, the same flight-information service that travel agents use.

Shopping

Yes, you can say "charge it" on-line. CompuServe and GEnie both have on-line malls containing music and video stores, florists, pharmacies, and cookie shops — everything except acres of asphalt and socializing teenagers. GEnie and America Online offer gateway access to Comp-U-Store, which offers member discounts on 250,000 products.

Special-interest forums and chats

With special-interest forums, you can communicate with other subscribers about a wide range of issues, including technical questions about using Mac hardware and software. You can also download megabytes of software, including fonts, scanned images, sounds, utilities, movies, and more. Many programs are free, while others are *shareware*. You're expected to pay a modest registration fee, usually less than $25, if you decide to keep a shareware program. (You can find instructions for downloading software in the next chapter.) Most major software and hardware firms also operate forums, offering technical tips and program updates.

Many information services also operate *chat* events, in which you and your fellow subscribers meet in an electronic auditorium, where you can talk to each other via the keyboard and interact with the host and, usually, a special guest. Most chat events are question-and-answer sessions between audience members and the guest. Yours truly appears as a regular guest in *Macworld's* Macworld Online forum on America Online. (eWorld 1.1 extends the chat metaphor by supporting the Mac OS's text-to-speech capabilities — eWorld 1.1 can actually read aloud the text of chats as they occur.)

Tips for Choosing a Service

Choosing an information service involves assessing your budget as well as your information needs and then deciding how important a Mac-like interface is to you. Initial membership costs and connect charges vary depending on the service and when you use it.

Most services used to bill like the phone company: they charged you according to how much time you spent on-line, and evening and weekend rates were lower than daytime weekday rates. Most services have since borrowed from the cable TV industry by offering a basic package of services for a fixed monthly rate, with extra premium services available for additional costs.

Your on-line intentions should be a major factor in your choice. Business people may lean toward MCI Mail, Dow Jones/News Retrieval, and NewsNet, while Mac hobbyists who want access to shareware may find America Online, eWorld, CompuServe, or GEnie more appealing. People who work in the Mac field as consultants, dealers, writers, and developers may use AppleLink, Apple's worldwide communications network.

Comparing on-line service interfaces

Then there's the interface issue: some services take better advantage of the Mac's operating style than others. America Online and eWorld take the prize with attractive and easy interfaces that make excellent use of the Mac's personality traits (see Figure 16-2 "The Face of Communications"). America Online is also available for Windows machines; the service looks and works the same on both Macs and PCs, making it a good choice for businesses that mix machines. (A Windows version of eWorld is in the works, too.)

On-Line Services and Cable TV Companies: Strange Bedfellows or Tomorrow's Communications Giants?

Many services are not only borrowing from the cable TV industry, they are uniting with it. Several services are working on pilot programs in which customers can access the service by using their cable TV systems.

The benefit for customers is much faster response times — cable TV lines can carry data far more quickly than can plain old telephone systems, commonly abbreviated POTS. This faster bandwidth makes it possible for on-line services to provide new types of offerings, such as digital video.

What's in it for the cable companies? They're in a better position to take advantage of the embryonic market for interactive television and all that information superhighway hype that you've undoubtedly been reading about.

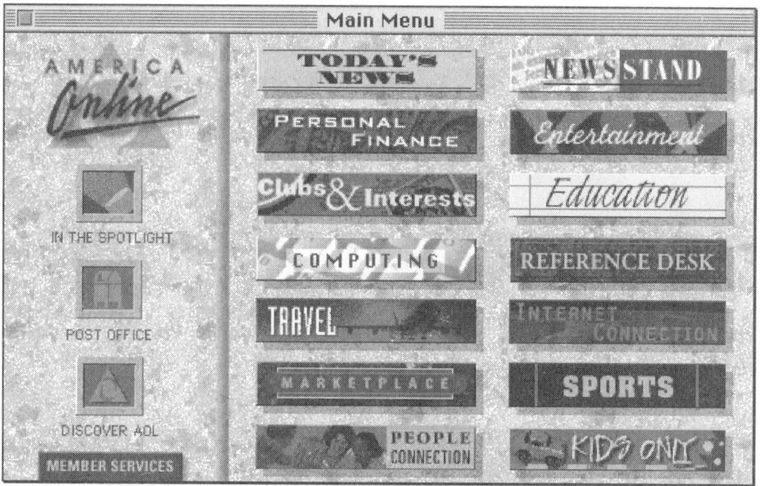

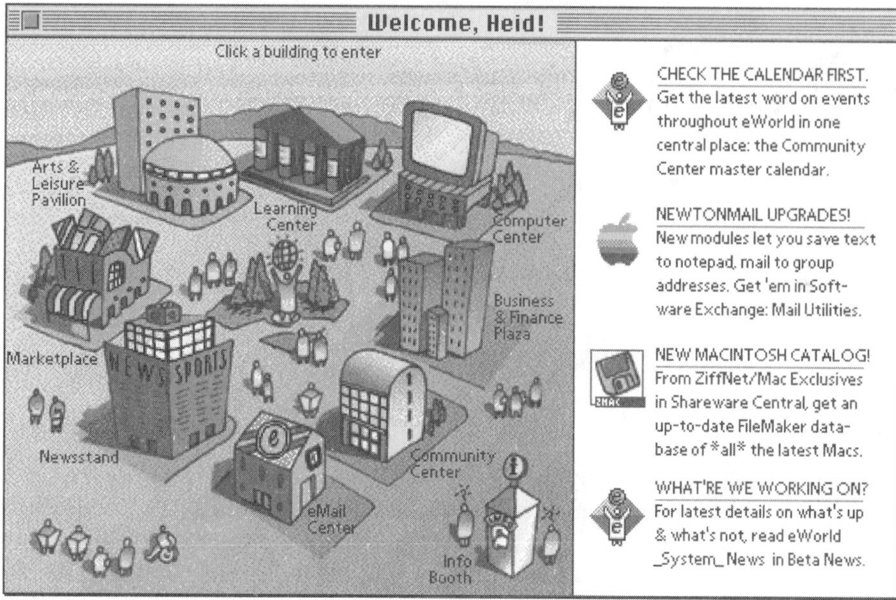

Figure 16-2: The Face of Communications Two information services — America Online (top) and Apple's eWorld (bottom).

For its part, eWorlds uses a community metaphor, with a digital town hall, bank, library, bookstore, and more. You navigate the electronic world by clicking icons that look like buildings. In eWorld 1.1, you can even customize the town square, adding snow to the rooftops, for example.

As for CompuServe, MCI Mail, Dow Jones, and GEnie, their interfaces are, well, not so pretty. All of these text-oriented services require typed commands in response to text menus. However, you can find Mac front-end programs that graft a Macintosh interface onto these services. CompuServe's CompuServe Information Manager provides point-and-click access to some (but not all) of CompuServe's nooks and crannies (see Figure 16-3 "CompuServe Makeover").

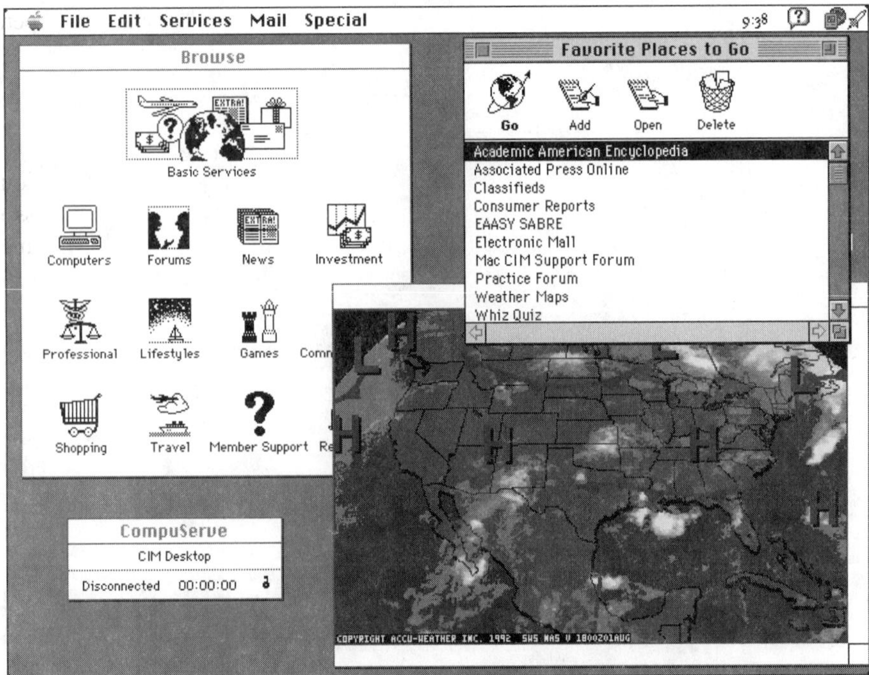

Figure 16-3: CompuServe Makeover The CompuServe Information Manager is a friendly facade for CompuServe. You choose menu commands and double-click forum names, and CompuServe Information Manager sends the commands that CompuServe expects to see. The program also offers a terminal mode that lets experienced users control CompuServe conventionally.

Matching services to your needs

My personal picks? For sheer quantity of information, it's hard to beat CompuServe. For ease of use and economy, however, America Online and eWorld win. Both AOL and eWorld are good choices for *Macworld* readers, too: *Macworld* has forums on both services in which you can search through and read reviews and news stories from past issues of *Macworld* and exchange ideas with *Macworld* editors, contributors, and fellow readers. Apple now bundles the eWorld software with most Macs, making it easy to test the eWaters.

But limiting yourself to just one service is like reading only one newspaper or watching only one television station. Because you use the same hardware (and in some cases the same software) to communicate with each service, subscribing to additional services may not greatly increase your communications expenses.

Doing Business and Research On-Line

You've subscribed to an information service and you've toured its various offerings. Now it's time to get down to business. There's a gold mine of business and research information on-line, and not just current stock quotes and timely news from major wire services — two things often cited as good reasons to use (and tax-deduct) a modem. I mean *real* business information:

- Demographic data that can help you decide whether to open a branch office or a new business. Type a ZIP code, and you get screens full of lifestyle and demographic information for a specific community.
- Abstracts and full-text articles from major newspapers and hundreds of business, industry, scientific, and medical newsletters to keep you abreast of developments in your field. You'll find everything from major publications such as the *Wall Street Journal* and *Business Week* to esoterica such as *Blood Weekly* and my personal favorite, *Money Laundering Alert*. Many on-line services provide *clipping file* features that automatically snare articles containing information of interest.
- Corporate data, such as disclosure statements filed with the Securities and Exchange Commision and company evaluations prepared by Standard and Poor's, that can help you plan investments and keep an eye on the competition.
- Data from Uncle Sam: census results, Commerce Department reports and forecasts, details on federal projects and contracts, and technical summaries of government-sponsored research projects.

You don't have to be a corporate raider or work in a walnut-paneled office to benefit from cyberinfo. There's a lot for small business owners, researchers, and students, too: directories of all kinds, from telephone books to *Who's Who* to *Books in Print*; newspapers and publications galore, from *Consumer Reports* to transcripts of "60 Minutes" episodes; and on-line encyclopedias from Grolier and Compton.

How to Use Shortcuts for Faster On-Line Navigating

You can point and click your way through an on-line service, but you might wind up with a wrist injury. There's a faster, more efficient way to get from one area of a service to another: shortcuts. These are one-word abbreviations or keywords that take you directly to a particular forum or section.

- ❖ On America Online, shortcuts are called keywords. To enter one, press **⌘-K.** The keyword dialog box appears. Type the keyword, press Return, and you're there. For example, to get to Macworld Online, press **⌘-K**, *macworld,* press Return.
- ❖ On eWorld, shortcuts are called, well, shortcuts. Press **⌘-G**, type the shortcut, and press Return.
- ❖ With CompuServe Information Manager, choose the Go command and type the shortcut word. If you're using CompuServe with a terminal-emulation program, type **go** followed by the shortcut word and then press Return.

To find out what the shortcut words are for your favorite area, check the "About" message for a particular forum. You can also get lists of shortcuts in America Online and eWorld by clicking the Help button in the keyword or shortcut dialog box.

Many of these information gold mines are available on eWorld, America Online, and CompuServe. (Throughout this section, I list the shortcut keywords for each forum mentioned. If you don't know how to use shortcut keywords, see the Quick Tips box "How to Use Shortcuts for Faster On-line Navigating".) Some of the best libraries and databases, however, are on the outskirts of cyberspace, in specialized business and research services such as NewsNet and Dialog. These services can cost far more than mainstream services and they're considerably harder to use, but their depth and scope are unmatched.

eWorld's Offerings

Given that eWorld is a relative newcomer with far fewer subscribers than the competition, I didn't expect to find much in the way of eBusiness eInfo. I was eSurprised: the Business and Finance Plaza has a solid foundation of basic business offerings — and access to all of them is included in the basic eWorld subscription rate.

Much of eWorld's business information is geared toward small businesses and home office workers. For example, there's Working Solo (shortcut: solo), a forum for entrepreneurs and home business operators looking for guidance and connections. The forum's software libraries contain business-oriented templates for popular application programs. For on-line networking, there's an Introductions area where you can post a brief resumé and list of services you offer. *Inc* magazine also operates a forum (shortcut: inc online) containing entrepreneurial tips and magazine excerpts.

Another useful forum for small business types is the Nolo Press Self-Help Law Center (shortcut: nolo), where you can read interesting (and understandable) articles on topics such as incorporation and contract law, and ask Nolo Press staff legal questions. And although the Annoying Neighbors folder sports the largest number of queries, you'll also find questions and answers on business-related topics such as filing copyright and patent applications and collecting past-due accounts.

Of broader interest is the Business Sector Profiles forum (shortcut: bsp), operated by The Reference Press (800-486-8666), an Austin, Texas-based business publisher. Business Sector Profiles contains expanded and annotated versions of reports and forecasts issued by the U.S. Department of Commerce for over 200 industries. Profiles typically contain tables of industry revenues, employment, and market-share data; industry projections to 1998; and descriptions of key companies and products in a given field.

(The Commerce Department also operates its own bulletin board. You can join by having your modem call 202-482-3870. Access to the board costs $45 per year plus per-minute connect-time charges, which vary depending on the time of day you connect. You can also obtain reports through a fax-back service by calling 900-786-2329; the service costs 65 cents per minute. For more information on these services, call 202-482-1986.)

Similar, though less comprehensive, reports are also available in the Vital Statistics section of the Real-Time Marketing forum (shortcut: rtm), operated by Regis-McKenna, a marketing and public relations firm that counts Apple among its major clients. If you're in the advertising biz, you might also want to visit the Ad Age/Creativity Online forum (shortcut: ad age), run by Crain Communications, which publishes *Advertising Age* and *Creativity* magazines.

If you're looking for company information, check out the Hoover's Company Profiles forum (shortcut: hoovers). This forum, also operated by The Reference Press, contains nicely done profiles of nearly 1,000 public and privately held corporations — overviews, founder's names and company histories, headquarter addresses, lists of divisions, and more. The profiles are from The Reference Press's *Hoover's Handbook* series.

An American Online

Most of the business information offerings on America Online (AOL) are in the News & Finance area (click the Departments button on AOL's main screen and then click News & Finance).

The Hoover's Company Profiles are available on AOL, (keyword: hoovers), as are the business profiles (keyword: company). If you're a fan of public television's "Nightly Business Report," you might enjoy NBR Online (keyword: nbr), which contains transcripts of selected NBR interviews and commentaries, business news summaries, and reports on market trends.

If your company is a federal contractor, check out *Commerce Business Daily* (keyword: cbd), which lists notices of proposed government contract awards for amounts in excess of $25,000 as well as sales of government property and other procurement-related tidbits. The Government Printing Office produces the *Commerce Business Daily*; Federal Information & News Dispatch, Inc. provides the publication in electronic form. Each edition contains approximately 500–1,000 notices — proof that your tax dollars are at work.

Anyone who works in the publishing or communications industries should visit the Cowles/SIMBA Media Information Network (keyword: cowles). The Cowles/SIMBA Media Daily contains stories on everything from book and magazine publishing to cable-and-telephone company wars to satellite broadcasting. The forum also contains an active bulletin board where you'll find debates on media-related technologies, companies, and issues.

Investors will be interested in the Morningstar forum (keyword: morningstar), which ranks mutual funds in a wide variety of categories. From this forum, you can also get stock quotes and set up an electronic portfolio to track your favorite companies' stocks. (eWorld has a similar feature.) There's also the Wall Street SOS Forum (keyword: sos), which, among other things, offers a daily stock market and mutual fund report.

Business news junkies will be in heaven on AOL. The Business News window (keyword: business) lets you read current news by industry or search for articles containing keywords you specify. And forums are operated by *Worth* magazine (keyword: worth), *The New York Times* (keyword: nyt), the *San Jose Mercury News* (keyword: mc news), and the *Chicago Tribune* (keyword: chicago). Generally, these free forums offer only a subset of their respective publications; as I'll describe later, the full text of many publications is available, but it'll cost you.

Sleepless in CompuServe

eWorld and America Online look like small-town libraries compared to CompuServe. You can spend days — and hundreds of dollars — exploring CompuServe's business information offerings.

CompuServe's Business menu (shortcut: go business) is the gateway to dozens of profession-specific forums. Among them: a work-at-home forum (go work), a public relations and marketing forum (go prsig), an inventors' forum (go innovations), a legal forum (go lawsig), an office automation forum (go oaforum), an international trade forum (go trade), and a court reporter's forum (go crforum). As with the forums on eWorld and AOL, these forums are available to all subscribers at no additional charge.

News hounds will howl over CompuServe's on-line newspaper and magazine offerings. The Associated Press wire service is available (go aponline); news stories are updated hourly. The Business Wire (go tbw-1) carries company information and press releases. And researchers will want to explore the newspaper archives (go newsarchive), which let you search for and download full-text articles from over 50 American and British newspapers dating back to the late '80s. The News Source USA area (go newsusa) provides a similar service, and adds a dozen or so major magazines — from *People* and *Sports Illustrated* to *Fortune* and *Forbes.* The Magazine Database Plus area (go magdb) lets you search for and retrieve articles from 140 magazines, from the *New Republic* to *Cosmopolitan.*

Equally impressive is CompuServe's range of reference materials. You can get TRW credit reports and business information on more than 13 million organizations (go trwreport). You can get astonishingly detailed demographic data on cities, towns, neighborhoods, census tracts, specific Nielsen TV ratings areas, and more (go demographics). You can search every phone book in the country (go edu-8). The full text of the *Commerce Business Daily* is also available (go combus). Also available are searchable versions of *Books in Print* (go bip) and Marquis *Who's Who* (go biography). And the IQuest service (go iqu-1) is a collection of nearly 1,000 databases in every imaginable category. Type search keywords that describe your area of interest, and IQuest will return either a list of article citations (publication name, date, author, and title) or the full text. If you need help crafting a query, type **SOS** and an IQuest representative will help you. There's no additional charge for on-line help, although you do pay for the searches themselves (generally, $1 to $5 per search, depending on the type of search and the databases that you're searching).

Note that many of the best reference resources on CompuServe carry additional surcharges. Some services carry an additional hourly charge of up to $24, others charge for each article you retrieve or each search you conduct, and still others combine both approaches. All premium-priced services provide menu options that describe pricing details and provide tips on searching; it's a good idea to read this information before embarking on what could be a costly trip to the digital library.

The Big Guns: Dialog and NewsNet

One of the ways CompuServe can provide such a staggering array of information is through *gateways* — connections to external information services. When you order a TRW credit report or search a magazine database, for example, CompuServe's computers actually connect to yet another information service. This is one reason why many areas carry a surcharge.

Two of the information services that many CompuServe gateways rely on are Dialog and NewsNet. Each of these services is also available directly. Dialog (800-334-2564 or 415-858-7026) is the world's largest on-line bibliographic company, with over 200 million searchable items spread across 370 databases. Databases include the full text of 33 major newspapers as well as scientific journals; government, business, and corporate publications; and law and reference books. You can retrieve the full text of articles or even have hard copies mailed or faxed to you.

Dialog can be daunting. Besides the vast array of searchable materials, the service's interface is archaic, relying on cryptic, typed commands. Conducting searches is an art in itself; choose keywords carelessly, and you wind up with hundreds of irrelevant citations.

Dialog's Knowledge Index is a subset of the full service specializing in science and education. Knowledge Index is available only through CompuServe (go KI); there's a $24 an hour surcharge for access.

NewsNet (800-345-1301 or 610-527-8030) specializes in business information, providing full-text access to 700 business and industry publications and 20 international newswires that together post 17,000 new items every day, according to the company. Here you'll find not only mainstream newspapers, but ultra-specialized newsletters: *Blood Weekly*, *Drug Detection Report*, *Indoor Air Quality Update*, *Pharmaceutical Litigation Reporter*, *Toxic Materials News*, *Wine Business Insider*, and *Asbestos and Lead Abatement Report.* Costs depend on the publication you're reading, and vary from 40 cents to several dollars per minute of connect time.

Clipping Services: Creating Personalized Papers

With all this information out there, how can you possibly snare the stuff that's of interest to you? One way is to take advantage of the clipping services many on-line services provide. Specify keywords describing your areas of interest, and the information automatically scans specified publications, scarfing up items that meet your criteria. When you sign on, you'll find a kind of personalized newspaper containing items that meet your criteria.

NewsNet's clipping service is called NewsFlash, and lets you specify keywords, publications you want to search (and explicitly exclude from the search), and the maximum number of *hits,* or articles that meet your criteria. CompuServe's clipping service is available through its Executive News Service, and can snare items of interest from a variety of wire services and newspapers. eWorld offers a similar service called HeadsUp.

Each of these clipping services has its own surcharges, which vary widely depending on the service, on whether you elect to retrieve full text or article abstracts, and on the number of news items found by your search criteria.

And speaking of search criteria, you may find your personal paper contains articles that aren't all that personal — that is, items that technically meet your criteria but aren't really of interest to you. Say you're interested in snagging stories on Mexico, but you aren't interested in news about Mexican sports. You specify the search criteria *Mexico not sports,* but find a listing littered with articles on New Mexico high school football. It's at times like these that you realize just how sophisticated the human search engine is — and how primitive an on-line service's is. And the killer is that you're still charged for these items — as far as the on-line service is concerned, you asked for them.

The key, then, is to be extremely specific about what you ask for by spelling things out in detail. In the preceding example, instead of specifying *Mexico not sports,* you might specify *Mexico not football or baseball or basketball or soccer or tennis.* You might also specify *not "New Mexico,"* (you often have to enclose a multiword phrase within quotes) although doing so would cause you to miss an article titled *President-Elect Zedillo Promises a New Mexico*.

Some services, including Dialog and NewsNet, let you specify the list of databases to which your criteria are applied. Doing so is another good way to avoid snaring irrelevent items.

When a service displays a list of hits, you often get the opportunity to start your search over or to retrieve the full text of each hit. If you'll need the full text, retrieve it at this point. Otherwise, you'll have to repeat the search later — and that'll cost you.

What About the Internet?

I was afraid you'd ask. The Internet is a vast, worldwide computer network that arose from scientific and academic computing but has since become the fashionable place for businesses and cyberspace explorers to meet. The amount of information and software available on the Internet can make commercial on-line services such as CompuServe look like small town bookmobiles.

Like any gem, the Internet has numerous facets.

- **Electronic mail.** You can swap e-mail with anyone on the Internet — or anyone on a commercial on-line service.
- **Software libraries.** Called *ftp sites* (ftp stands for *file-transfer protocol*), these are software libraries where you can download files of all kinds, from programs to images to audio clips to text files.
- **Mailing lists.** Everyone knows what a mailing list is — the Internet takes the concept into cyberspace. You can subscribe to a mailing list by simply sending e-mail to the address of the *list server*, which is a program that manages a particular list. After you subscribe, the list server automatically e-mails whatever you subscribed to you. (See the Quick Tips box "How to Join a Mailing List.")
- **Usenet newsgroups.** These are the Internet's equivalent to bulletin boards — places where people post public messages about particular topics. The range of discussion topics on the Internet, however, goes well beyond anything you find on a commercial on-line service. (Indeed, some people — including some legislators — say it goes too far, and have stirred up a heated debate concerning on-line censorship.)
- **The World Wide Web.** The Web was originally developed in 1989 at the European Center for Particle Physics (known by its French acronym, CERN) as a way for scientists to share documents over the Internet. Today, for many netsurfers, the Web is where the action is. Why? Because the Web makes it possible for anyone to publish electronic books, promotional materials, and other documents for a *global* audience.

The Web is organized by hypertext-linked screens, or *pages*, containing text and graphics. One organization's collection of pages is called a *Web site*. (When you overhear people at a hip coffee bar saying, "We've just got to get our Web site up," it means they, like so many other organizations and companies, are clamoring to establish a presence on the Web. Many companies are doing so in the hopes that they will be able to sell products and services. Presently, however, commerce and the Internet don't dovetail smoothly, and many companies are spending far more on Internet sites than they're earning from them. They're hoping the investment will pay off as the Internet grows and its commercial side evolves.)

What makes the Web particularly exciting is that sites can be linked to each other — clicking a button or word in one site can take you to another, where you might branch off to still others. They don't call it a web for nothing.

The Web is becoming increasingly graphical, with many organizations and companies creating sites that look and feel a lot like a CD-ROM title — attractive navigation buttons for you to click, and even sounds and movies you can download. Note that you need a fast modem for satisfying performance — a 14.4Kbps modem is an absolute bare minimum, with 28.8Kbps being more reasonable. (More about modem speeds shortly.) Serious netsurfers often have special *ISDN* — Integrated Services Digital Network — phone lines installed, which provides speeds of roughly four to eight times faster than a 14.4Kbps modem.

Accessing the Internet

So how do you get a piece of all this action? The good news is that as interest in the Internet grows, a growing number of commercial on-line services, including CompuServe, eWorld, Delphi, and America Online, are providing access. America Online has done the best job of making the Internet accessible. AOL's Internet Connection (keyword: internet) lets you search for mailing lists, join newsgroups, and access ftp sites (see Figure 16-4 "Internet via AOL"). 1995 will be remembered as the year all the major information services added World Wide Web access to their array of Internet services. By the end of the year, AOL, eWorld, and CompuServe will provide Web access.

How to Join a Mailing List

Internet mailing lists are a great way to get useful (and useless) information automatically. And you don't have to have direct Internet access — you can subscribe to a mailing list using any on-line service that provides gateway e-mail access to the Internet.

Subscribing

To subscribe to a mailing list, you send an e-mail message to the list's manager. The message itself contains a specific series of commands — usually, the word *subscribe* followed by the list's name followed by your name.

For example, say you want to subscribe to David Letterman's Top 10 List (yes, you can do this — see below). In the instructions for subscribing (which you can find on America Online's Internet Connection), you are instructed to "send e-mail to listserv@listserv.clark.net; in the body of the message type **SUBSCRIBE TOPTEN** followed by your real name." In this example, you would create a new America Online e-mail message (choose Compose Mail from the Mail menu or press ⌘-M) and then fill it out as shown in the accompanying figure (of course, you will probably want to substitute your own name for Trixie Kelly's).

Leaving a list

To leave a mailing list — to "drop" your subscription — the process is usually similar, except your request e-mail should contain the appropriate command — usually **unsub**, **unsubscribe**, or **signoff**.

Some lists to consider

Here are just a few useful (and useless) mailing lists you might want to subscribe to.

- ❖ Apple's Information Alley. This is a terrific electronic newsletter published by Apple's Austin, Texas-based technical support group. It contains tips, troubleshooting suggestions, product information, and much more. To subscribe, send e-mail to listproc@spock.austin.apple.com, and type **subscribe infoalley *yourname*** as the message text. (Remember, replace ***yourname*** with your real name. For example, **subscribe infoalley Jim Heid**).
- ❖ Inclass. This list is a newsletter on using the Internet in classrooms. To subscribe, send e-mail to listproc@schoolnet.carleton.ca, and type **subscribe SUBSCRIBE INCLASS *yourname*** as the message text.
- ❖ David Letterman's Top 10 List. Yes, it's available in mail list form, direct from the home office in...oh, you know. Send e-mail to listserv@clark.net with the text **subscribe topten yourname.**

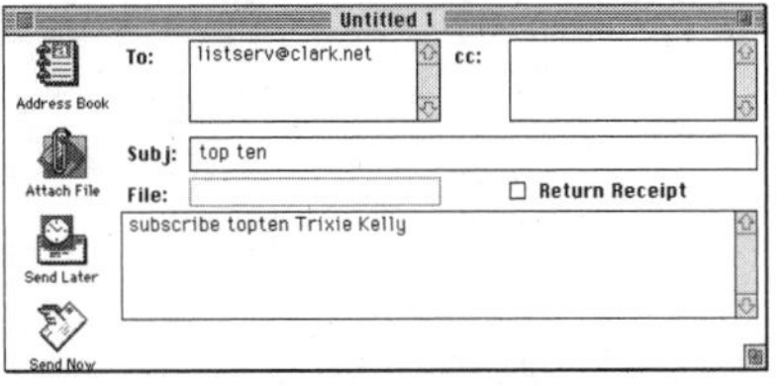

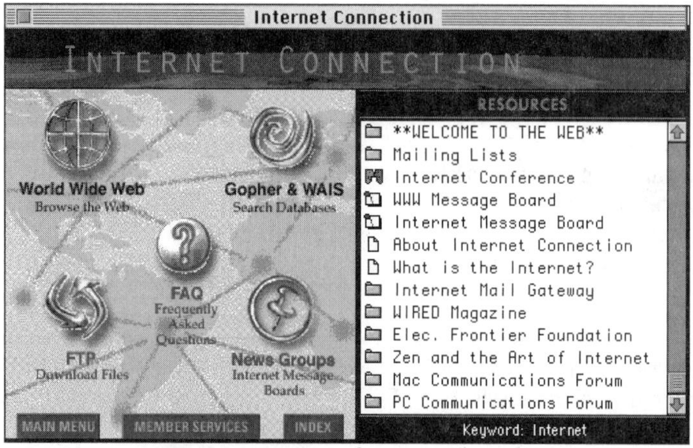

Figure 16-4: Internet via AOL Top: America Online's Internet Connection (keyword: internet) lets you access many aspects of the Internet. Bottom: Apple's home page on the Web, as seen through the AOL browser

It's possible to access the Internet without using a commercial on-line service, of course, but it can be a complex process. You need to sign up with an Internet service provider and install some special software that implements the Internet's data-transmission protocols. When you overhear those coffee-slurping hipsters say, "I just got MacTCP and a SLIP account, and am I jazzed," they're referring to an Apple control panel (MacTCP) and the *serial-line interface protocol*, a method of transmitting data.

The advantage of connecting to the Internet through an Internet service provider is that you can take advantage of a growing number of sophisticated programs for browsing newsgroups and the Web. One of the best-known Web browsers is a program called Mosaic, created by the National Center for Supercomputing Applications at the University of Illinois. Mosaic has inspired an industry of Web browsers, such as Netscape Communications's Netscape Navigator. For browsing ftp sites, there's a $10 shareware program called Anarchie; it lets you download files by dragging them directly to your hard drive — as if the Internet's ftp sites were just a bunch of huge hard drives connected directly to your Mac.

So You Want to Be an Internet Publisher

So how do you move from being an Internet surfer to making some waves of your own by establishing your own Web site? This, too, is a subject for a book. What follows is an overview of your options.

One easy way to start might be to contact one of the growing numbers of Internet service providers that offer Web site services — for an initial setup charge and monthly fees in the $30 ballpark, they will set up and maintain a Web site for you on their computers. All you supply is the content — the graphics, HTML-format text files, sounds, and the like, that you want to make available on your site. (See Chapter 9's Backgrounder box "From Desktop Publishing to Internet Publishing" for an introduction to HTML files.)

As your needs grow, you might prefer to operate your own Internet server. In this case, one option is Apple's Internet Server Solution, which comprises one of Apple's PowerPC-based Workgroup Servers and a large software bundle that, among other things, includes an editor for creating HTML files; AppleSearch software, for indexing documents on your server and making them available to the Web; MacHTTP software, which allows the Workgroup Server to serve HTML documents to the Web; and Web page templates that you modify to suit your needs.

If you want to establish an on-line presence but aren't ready to take the Internet plunge, just get yourself a company account on an on-line service such as America Online. Publish the account number in your promotional materials, your manuals, and wherever else it's appropriate. This will at least give your net-savvy customers a way to reach you electronically.

Evolution ahead

The entire Mac-to-Internet interface is in constant flux, with on-line services adding new access features and new Internet service providers appearing all the time. That's one reason why I haven't provided detailed instructions for getting wired into the Internet in this chapter.

Another reason is that details about accessing the Internet with a Mac would fill a book. In fact, they have filled many books. My friend and *Macworld* colleague, Charles Seiter, wrote one of the best. *The Internet For Macs For Dummies* (IDG Books Worldwide). Read it — and in the meantime, check out America Online's Internet Connection.

Tips for Modem Shoppers

A computer's link to the on-line world is a *modem* (pronounced *mow-dem*). A modem converts, or modulates, the data coming from the Mac into audio tones that phone lines can carry and demodulates the incoming tones into data the Mac can comprehend. Indeed, the word modem is a short form of the words *MOdulate* and *DEModulate.*

Modem options

Every Mac has a modem port that enables you to connect an external modem. An external modem also has an extra jack into which you can plug a telephone. These days, many external modems are also *fax modems* — they enable you to send and receive faxes to and from fax machines (or other fax modems).

When shopping for an external modem, look for one that provides status lights. They aren't essential, but they can help you troubleshoot a sticky file-transfer session by showing when a connection exists and when it's sending and receiving data. Like a car without gauges, a modem without status lights doesn't tell you much when problems arise.

If you have an AV Mac or a Power Mac, you have another communications option: Apple's GeoPort Telecom Adaptor. I discuss this option later in this chapter.

Modems to go

The Mac PowerBook family can accommodate internal modems, which live inside the case, providing greater portability and a less cluttered desk. With its battery-powered operation, a PowerBook is an ideal Mac for keeping in touch. All Mac communication software runs on the PowerBook family. Things differ in the hardware: Apple has offered a variety of modems for the PowerBook family.

Macintosh PowerBook Internal Fax/Data Modem

This cleverly named modem works in most classic PowerBook models. (The modem was included with the PowerBook 170.) A 2400-bps data modem, it can also send (but not receive) faxes. The modem includes somewhat limited but easy-to-use fax software. Select the Fax Sender icon in the Chooser desk accessory, and your programs' Page Setup and Print commands change to read Fax Setup and Fax. (Tip: You can eliminate a trip to the Chooser by pressing the Shift and Control keys while opening a program's File menu. Doing so temporarily changes the printing commands into faxing commands.) The Fax Setup command lets you specify paper size and orientation, enlargement or reduction, and fax quality; the Fax command lets you add and remove telephone numbers from a built-in directory and specify whether a cover page should be printed (see Figure 16-5 "PowerBook Faxing"). I have a lot more to say about fax modems later in this chapter.

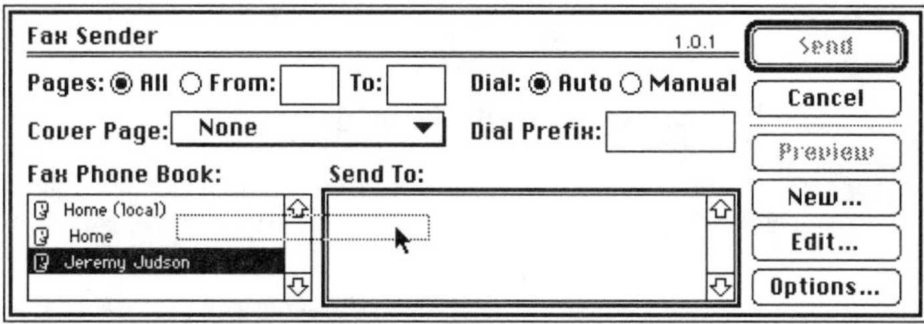

Figure 16-5: PowerBook Faxing Sending a fax with the software that accompanies Apple's PowerBook Internal Fax/Data Modem.

Macintosh PowerBook Express Modem Kit

This modem works in later PowerBook models, such as the 160, 165c, 180, and 180c as well as in PowerBook Duos. It costs a bit more than the preceding modem, but it's faster, supporting up to 14.4Kbps connections, and it can receive faxes as well as send them. The Express Modem is partially implemented in software; as a result, when the modem is active, it reduces the amount of free memory in your Mac by about 300K.

Macintosh PowerBook Express Modem II

This improved version of the Express Modem is included in the PowerBook 500-series models that are sold in the Pacific and European markets. In the United States and Canada, PowerBook 500-series machines are available with a 19.2Kbps Global Village fax/data modem.

Third-party PowerBook modems

Several firms offer internal fax/data modems that include better software than is included with the Apple's PowerBook modems. Global Village Communications' PowerPort series gets good marks for its high-quality software. The Platinum 288 PowerPort supports speeds of up to 28.8Kbps.

Using an external modem with a PowerBook

If you anticipate using your PowerBook for communications only occasionally and you have other computers, consider buying a compact external modem. You have one more piece of equipment to carry with you, but you can also use the modem with your other computers. (After connecting the modem, open the PowerBook control panel and select the External Modem option.)

Tips for Mobile Modems

On the road with a PowerBook? Here are some survival tips to help you make and keep your connections:

Ask in advance about phone services

When making hotel reservations, ask whether the hotel's phones provide connectors for portable computers. A growing number of hotel telephones contain so-called datalink ports — standard RJ-11 telephone jacks into which you can plug your PowerBook's modem cable. You may also want to seek out hotels that offer free local calls.

Don't forget your phone numbers

Another aspect of planning ahead involves making sure that you have the local phone access numbers for the area to which you're traveling and the on-line services you'll be using. All on-line services have commands that list these numbers for you: consider saving the list on your PowerBook's hard disk so you won't misplace it.

Connecting to hotel phones

If you're patronizing an as-yet unenlightened innkeeper whose phones can't accommodate your PowerBook, check to see whether the phone is hard-wired into the wall. If it isn't, unplug it and plug your PowerBook modem into the wall jack.

If the phone is hard-wired, you may be able to make a connection by disassembling the phone's handset or wall outlet and connecting directly to the red and green wires within. (Don't try this technique unless you're comfortable working around wires: you can get an electrical shock, although phone line voltages aren't as dangerous as those inside a power outlet.) Radio Shack sells a cable with a male RJ-11 jack on one end and spade lugs on the other (catalog number 279-391). You can also make your own: cut a standard RJ-11 cable in half and then strip the insulation off the red and green wires and connect an alligator clip to each one.

Dialing through a hotel system

Remember that most hotels require you to dial 8 or 9 to make an outside call. If you're using your modem's autodial capability, be sure to add the required prefix. Put a comma (,) between the prefix and the phone number you're dialing to tell your modem to wait a moment after dialing the prefix.

Carry an extension cord

Hotels have a tradition of putting power outlets in illogical or inaccessible places. If you plan to use your AC adaptor with your PowerBook (and you probably need to, because using a modem drains the battery faster), bring along an extension cord, too.

After the call, save battery power

An internal modem uses battery power whenever a communications program is running. After you make your call, quit the communications program. Also, keep in mind that a PowerBook won't go to sleep if its modem is in auto-answer mode.

How fast a modem do you need?

Place of residence aside, the primary difference between modems is the speed at which they transfer data. It used to be that most modems transmitted data at 1200 or 2400 bits per second, or bps. (Historical note: my first modem ran — or crawled — at 300 bps.) A few years ago, 9600 bps was the speed record; today, 14.4Kbps and 28.8Kbps modems are commonplace.

But whether you should consider one of these warp-speed modems depends on your communications tasks. Many on-line services support high-speed connections, but generally, only access numbers in urban areas support this fast rate. Connect charges are generally higher for high-speed operation, too, although the faster data rate often more than makes up for the extra cost. (America Online is one exception to this rule; it does not tack on a surcharge for high-speed access.) If you're thinking of a high-speed modem and your communications plans center around on-line services, make sure that you'll be able to get high-speed access to your favorite services from your location.

Similarly, if you plan to communicate directly with another computer user (that is, without using an on-line service), make sure that the other user also has a fast modem before you buy. Otherwise, you might consider a slower, less-expensive modem.

If you plan to use Apple's Apple Remote Access software or other remote network access software, buy the fastest modem you can afford. (For some background on how modems transfer data and how their speed is measured, see the Backgrounder box "Bits and Bauds: Understanding Modem Speeds" later in this chapter.)

Features and price

Modems vary in the features they provide and in how deeply they invade your wallet. Feature-laden modems such as Supra's SupraFaxModem add faxing capabilities and even voice-mail features, but cost considerably more than simple data modems. Let your need for features be your guide. Just make sure that any modem you're considering is fully Hayes compatible — which means it understands the Hayes command set of dialing and connection commands, often called the *AT command set.*

If you have several Macs interconnected on a network, consider Shiva's NetModem, which all the machines on your network can share (see Chapter 32).

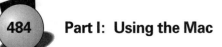

What AT Commands Do

Communications programs transmit AT commands in order to dial the phone, establish a connection, hang up, and manage everything in between. Even the volume of the modem's squeaks and squawks is controllable by an AT command. The list of commands a communications program sends prior to the dialing process is often called a *modem string.*

You can control your modem "by hand" by typing AT commands and modem strings yourself with a communications package such as Smartcom II, MicroPhone, or SITcomm. For example, to make your modem dial a number, you can type **ATDT555-1212**. You can also examine and change the modem's internal settings.

You can find a complete listing of AT commands on the CD-ROM that accompanies this book.

Using an AV or Power Mac for communications

The GeoPort connectors in Apple's AV and Power Macs give these machines a head start in telecommunicating. An AV or Power Mac essentially contains a built-in 14.4Kbps modem that can also send and receive faxes.

Going on-line via GeoPort

To connect an AV or Power Mac to a standard phone line, you need a GeoPort Telecom Adaptor, which attaches between the Mac's GeoPort connector and the telephone line. The GeoPort Telecom Adaptor includes Apple's Express Modem software, which works with any communications program that supports the Apple Communications Toolbox (all of today's popular communications programs do). The adaptor includes a second RJ-11 phone jack into which you can plug a telephone.

Note that the standard GeoPort Telecom Adaptor works only with analog phone lines, not with the PBX systems that many large businesses have.

Early versions of the GeoPort and Express Modem software had a reputation for being quirky; some commercial communications programs balked when you used them with the GeoPort/Express Modem system. These days, the software works well — I use a GeoPort Telecom Adaptor daily. (Be sure to use the latest version — at this writing, it's 2.0.1, and it includes the terrific MegaPhone telephony software described later in this chapter. You can download the software from eWorld or from Apple's Internet ftp sites, or get it from a friendly dealer.)

By the way, you can connect a conventional external modem to a GeoPort-equipped Mac, so if you upgrade to a Power Mac, don't think that you have to buy a GeoPort in order to go on-line. Your old modem should work just fine.

Reclaiming memory by turning off the Express Modem software

One final tip for Express Modem software: you can reclaim roughly 500K of system software memory by using the Express Modem control panel to turn off the Express Modem software when you aren't using a telecom program. The modem software is automatically turned on when you use a telecom program for the first time after starting up, but it isn't automatically turned off when you're done. To see your savings, open the About This Macintosh window before you turn off the Express Modem — you see the memory-usage bar graph shrink and the amount of memory used by the system software drop by nearly 500K.

Bits and Bauds: Understanding Modem Speeds

The speed at which modems exchange data is measured in terms of *baud rate,* also called *bit rate.* A combination of eight bits, or a *byte,* can represent any character on the Mac's keyboard. Internally, the Mac shuttles these bits among memory and microprocessor and disk drives in *parallel:* the eight bits travel alongside each other, each in its own wire, like marchers in a parade striding eight abreast. When conversing with a modem or printer, however, the Mac sends bits in *serial form* — one bit after another, in single file, like commuters threading through a subway turnstyle.

To show the computer at the other end of the line where one byte ends and the next begins, a communications program adds extra bits, a *start bit* and a *stop bit,* to the eight bits in the byte itself. This means that it takes roughly ten bits to send one character. One baud equals one bit per second, so you can calculate how many characters a modem sends per second by dividing the bit rate by ten. Many people prefer the acronym bps because baud is old-fashioned and less precise.

There are numerous standards regarding the format of data communications, and all of them have the kind of boring names that you'd expect to come from a standards committee. Here are quick definitions of the jargon you're likely to encounter. You don't have to understand what these standards mean or do in order to go on-line; if reading about the activities of standards committees isn't your idea of a good time, feel free to skip this gibberish.

V.22bis: The standard for 2400-bps communications.

V.32: The standard for 9600-bps communications.

V.32bis: The standard for communications at speeds of up to 14.4Kbps.

V.42: This standard is actually for error correction — a method of digital proofreading that enables two communicating computers to ensure that data hasn't been garbled. For the proofreading process, the V.42 standard uses what's called the Microcom Networking Protocol, or MNP. (To be precise, V.42 uses Levels 2 through 4 of MNP.) In a nutshell, MNP checks for transmission errors and automatically requests that data be resent if any errors occur.

V.42bis: This standard specifies data-compression methods that enable more data to be sent in a given amount of time. Many high-speed modems also support another compression standard, MNP Class 5.

Modem and Communications Technicalities

This section defines the serial-communications terms you're most likely to encounter as you work with communications software and telephone modems. If you'd rather not ingest more jargon at the moment, feel free to skip to the section "Choosing Communications Software" later in this chapter.

Start and stop bits

Earlier in this chapter, I said that in serial data transmission, the bits that form each byte travel in single file, with one bit behind another. In many cases, some additional bits travel along with each byte. Two such specialized bits — *start bits* and *stop bits* — mark the beginning and end of each byte.

Start and stop bits frame each byte. If you imagine each byte as a presidential motorcade, the start and stop bits compare to the police escorts at the beginning and end of the motorcade.

Parity bits

Another specialized bit in serial communications is the *parity bit.* A parity bit serves as a data proofreading device: it allows the receiving device to verify that it has accurately received a given byte. With parity checking, the transmitting device processes the bits in a given byte according to a formula and then sets the parity bit accordingly. When the receiving device receives a given byte, it processes its bits according to the same formula and then verifies that it comes up with the same result. If it doesn't, it can tell the transmitting device to send the byte again.

In working with communications software, you encounter three possible parity settings:

- **Odd:** With odd parity, the transmitting computer always sends an odd number of 1 bits (bits with a value of 1). When a given byte contains an even number of 1 bits, the sending device adds an additional bit. The receiving device then verifies that it received an odd number of bits.
- **Even:** With even parity, the transmitting computer always sends an even number of 1 bits. When a given byte contains an odd number of 1 bits, the sending device adds an additional bit. The receiving device then verifies that it received an even number of bits.
- **None:** With this setting, no parity bit is transmitted or expected on the receiving end. This setting is the most common in microcomputer communications.

When a parity bit is used, it's positioned before the stop bit that marks the end of a given byte.

Asynchronous versus synchronous

Start and stop bits make possible a form of communications called *asynchronous* communications. The word *asynchronous* means *without synchronization.* In the computer world, it means that two devices are not communicating under the control of rigid timing signals. Instead, they use start and stop bits to denote the beginning and end of each byte. Asynchronous communication is a very flexible method of data transmission; the transmitting device can send data as it's ready. As long as the two devices are set up to send and recognize the right combination of start and stop bits, the message should get through.

Asynchronous communication has a drawback, too: it's inefficient. Start and stop bits don't carry actual data; they simply go along for the ride, telling the receiving device when to expect the data. This excess baggage effectively reduces the overall transmission speed — time that could be used exchanging data is wasted sending and receiving start and stop bits. Think about how much roadway those presidential motorcades require.

Synchronous communication reduces this inefficiency by using a timing clock to regulate data transmission. With synchronous communications, data is transmitted in chunks (typically containing 256 bytes) called *frames* or *packets.* Each frame is preceded by timing information that tells the receiving device how many characters to expect in a given amount of time. The receiving device then uses this timing information to count incoming characters. Start and stop bits aren't required, and as a result, the two communicating devices can exchange more data in the same amount of time.

In the personal computer world, asynchronous communication is far more common than its synchronized counterpart. Synchronous communication is generally used in mainframe computers and in local-area networks (including LocalTalk).

Most low- to medium-speed modems (those providing speeds up to and including 2400 bits per second) use asynchronous communication. Many of today's high-speed modems also support synchronous communication.

Full duplex versus half duplex

Another aspect of serial communication involves whether both devices can transmit and receive simultaneously, or whether only one device can transmit at a time. The former is called *full-duplex* operation; the latter is *half-duplex.*

Both types of communication have parallels in the noncomputer world. Full-duplex operation compares to telephone calls: both people on the line can speak and listen at the same time. Half-duplex operation is similar to two-way radio: only one person can talk at a time and that person must signal the other person when it's his or her turn to speak.

Personal computer communication almost always uses full-duplex mode.

Handshaking

When two serial devices are communicating, the receiving device may occasionally need to tell the transmitting device to pause momentarily. For example, when you're printing to an ImageWriter, the printer's internal memory may fill periodically, and the printer must tell the Mac to stop sending more data, lest some characters get lost. When the printer is ready to resume receiving data, it needs a way to tell the Mac to continue. Similarly, if you're connected to an information service and you're saving incoming data on disk, the Mac must periodically tell the transmitting computer to pause while it accesses the disk.

This wait-and-resume is called *handshaking*, or *flow control.* Two forms of handshaking exist:

- In *software handshaking*, the receiving device transmits a software code to the sender. The most common form of software handshaking is called *X-on/X-off.* When the receiving device requires a pause in data transmission, it sends an X-off code. When it's ready to resume receiving, it sends an X-on code. When using a communications program, you can often send an X-off code by pressing Control-S and an X-on code by pressing Control-Q. Some programs may use the ⌘ key instead of the Control key.
- In *hardware handshaking*, the receiving device changes a voltage on a signal line in order to pause transmission.

Software handshaking is generally used in remote communications applications, such as when you're connected via modem to an information or electronic mail service. Hardware handshaking is common in links between a computer and a serial add-on, such as a printer (although software handshaking can be used here, too). High-speed V.42bis modems also use hardware handshaking.

Choosing Communications Software

Communications software falls into two basic categories — customized front-end programs such as those used by AppleLink, eWorld, and America Online (as well as CompuServe Information Manager); and *terminal emulation* programs such as Hayes' Smartcom II, Software Venture's MicroPhone II, The FreeSoft Company's White Knight, and Aladdin Systems' SITcomm. Many integrated programs, such as ClarisWorks and Microsoft Works, have basic communications features, too.

Front-end or terminal emulation software

Front-end programs are tailored to a specific service; you can't use America Online's software to access AppleLink any more than you can use your front door to enter your neighbor's house. Terminal-emulation programs, however, are general-purpose communicators: they can talk to just about any computer that answers. You can use terminal-emulation programs to access CompuServe,

MCI Mail, Dow Jones, and GEnie in their native text modes and to tap into hobbyist bulletin boards. You can't use a terminal-emulation program to access a strictly graphical service such as America Online, eWorld, or AppleLink.

Both types of communications software are intermediaries between the Mac and the modem. When you start a communications session, the program transmits dialing commands to the modem; then it waits for the modem to report when a connection is made and at what speed. After the connection is made, however, each type of program works differently. A front-end program performs much of its work behind the scenes, receiving instructions from the service telling it which icons and windows to display and sending commands to the service as you click icons and choose menu commands. A terminal-emulation program, in contrast, simply displays incoming text on-screen and transmits your typing to the other computer to which you're connected.

Using script languages

Most terminal-emulation programs also provide features that streamline your on-line sessions. *Script languages* let you automate communications sessions by transmitting commands for you. A script can dial a service in the middle of the night (when phone rates and service activity are low), sign on, retrieve waiting mail, and then sign off. Less ambitious scripts may simply take you to a specific forum when you choose a menu command or type a keyboard shortcut. With careful scripting, you can create your own front end for text-oriented services.

Deciding which program is for you

Hayes's Smartcom II is my favorite terminal-emulation program. It's elegantly designed and easy to use, although it lacks some of the features found in MicroPhone II and White Knight. (The latter was formerly called Red Ryder and is the Mac world's shareware success story. Its fervent followers have inspired programmer Scott Watson to release updates at frequent intervals. Some people joke that you don't buy White Knight, you subscribe to it.)

If you plan to explore text-only services and bulletin boards extensively, you may be better served by MicroPhone II or White Knight. MicroPhone II has a particularly powerful scripting language.

Aladdin's SITcomm is unique in that it provides excellent support for Apple's AppleScript scripting technology (described in Chapter 24). With SITcomm's AppleScript support, you can not only automate communications sessions, but you also can do so from other programs that support AppleScript. And it's from the same company that brings you the wonderful StuffIt series of file-compression utilities (also described in Chapter 24 as well as in the next chapter). SITcomm automatically compresses and decompresses files for you, thereby saving you time and connect charges.

When the Mac Meets the Fax

Can you imagine business life without fax machines? The folks at Federal Express probably fantasize about it, but the rest of us wouldn't dream of doing away with those warbling wonders and the cheesy thermal paper that most of them use.

Most of the world relies on desktop fax machines to beam documents about, but the fax modem is another alternative. Combine a fax modem with your favorite application programs, and you essentially attach your Mac to millions of printers around the world. Combine a fax modem with a laser or ink-jet printer, and you have a plain-paper alternative to that flimsy parchment. If the quality of an incoming fax is good enough, you can even run it through an optical-character recognition (OCR) program to generate an editable text file.

This section provides tips for getting higher-quality faxes, reducing fax transmission times, and taking advantage of the timesaving features that most fax modem software provide. I also describe some additional ways to put your fax modem to work and spotlight PostScript fax, a hot faxing technology that's finally catching on.

The best use for a fax modem is sending documents that you've created on the Mac. The superior quality, efficiency of not having to print documents first, and convenience features offered by fax software combine to make fax modems far superior to desktop fax machines.

Choosing fax software

If you have an AV or Power Mac and Apple GeoPort Telecom Adaptor, you already have all the faxing software you need: the adaptor comes with Apple's Express Fax software, which is easy to use and reliable, although not as fully featured as some third-party programs. (Note that versions prior to 2.0 can cause slowdowns on Power Macs; see Chapter 28 for details.)

As for third-party programs, Global Village's GlobalFax software is outstanding, but it works only with Global Village's modems. STF Technologies' FaxSTF and Delrina's FaxPro, on the other hand, work with most any modem, including Apple's GeoPort Telecom Adaptor. FaxSTF's and FaxPro's interfaces aren't as polished as GlobalFax's, but the programs are powerful.

What kinds of features do third-party programs provide that Apple's Express Fax software lacks? Support for gray-scale faxing is one — with FaxPro and GlobalFax, you can fax scanned images to other gray-scale-capable fax machines and modems, and they won't come out looking like ink blots on the other end. (GlobalFax supports up to 64 levels of gray, while FaxPro supports 16.) FaxPro and GlobalFax also provide more sophisticated address book functions. For example, while the Express Fax software supports only one address book, these programs let you create and switch between as many as you like.

When to Use a Desktop Fax Machine Instead

A big part of working smart involves knowing when to turn away from the Mac and toward a different tool. There are times when a conventional desktop fax machine is preferable to a fax modem, including the following:

- *When you're sending faxes of hard copy originals.* To fax a newspaper clipping with a fax modem, you need to scan it first. That's a lot of work compared to simply using a desktop fax. (You may get better results, however — Mac scanners have much better optics than fax machines.)
- *When you're not expecting a fax but want to be able to receive any that may come in.* That a fax modem lets you organize and print incoming faxes is appealing, but leaving a Mac on 24 hours a day wastes energy and shortens a hard drive's life. Some workarounds: If you have a PowerBook or other Mac that supports a "wake-on-ring" function (such as a Power Mac 7200, 7500, or 8500), you could set it to wake up when the phone rings. You can do the same with Sophisticated Circuits' PowerKey Remote, described later in this chapter. (See the Backgrounder box "More Ways to Put Modems and Telephony to Work.") Or just use a compact desktop fax machine, which uses a mere ten watts in standby mode — about a nightlight's worth. And it's completely silent, at least until an incoming fax makes it sing.

One more reason I sometimes prefer a fax machine for receiving: when a fax modem detects an incoming call, its software activates, temporarily slowing down the Mac. That's distracting — and annoying or worse if you're watching or creating a QuickTime movie. Also, as someone who religiously chooses the Save command before switching to a different program, I'm not always comfortable with the idea of my Mac suddenly starting up another task on its own.

Shutting off auto-answering

Most products let you disable automatic answering, usually by unchecking a box or menu command. For example, with the fax software that accompanies Apple's Express Modems, run the Fax Terminal application, choose Preferences from the Fax menu, and uncheck the box that reads Answer Calls to Receive Faxes After *X* Rings.

Getting the best of both worlds

What's my approach to the fax modem/fax machine dilemma? I use both. When I'm expecting a lengthy fax, I turn on my fax modem's auto-answer feature and use it to receive the missive. Otherwise, I leave the auto-answer feature off and rely on a desktop fax machine that's always on guard. I get better performance from the Mac (which also gets to sleep at night), I get the fax modem's benefits for long faxes, and I don't lose touch with that slimy fax paper.

Choosing the fax without using the Chooser

You can access fax drivers — the software that translates a document into a form that a fax modem can understand — by using the same tool you use to choose other output devices: the Mac's Chooser desk accessory. Select the fax driver's Chooser icon, and your programs' printing commands turn into faxing commands: Fax Setup replaces Page Setup, and Fax replaces Print.

That's all well and good — unless, like most people, you alternate between printing and faxing. If that's the case, do you need to travel to the Chooser each time you want to switch output devices? Fortunately, no. Most fax software provides shortcut keys that temporarily change your printing commands to faxing commands. With the software that accompanies Apple's Express Modem software, press Shift-Control while pulling down the File menu. With most third-party fax software, press Option while pulling down the File menu. Most programs also let you define your own shortcut keys.

Another benefit to using shortcut keys is that you don't have to worry about your document's margins changing when you switch output devices. But with this plus comes a potential minus: because your application program still thinks it's preparing the document for a printer, the document may not fax properly if it contains effects that depend on that printer. For example, when I used shortcut keys to fax a Microsoft Word document containing gray shades created with Word's Border command, the fax contained PostScript shading commands instead of the gray shades. Word had prepared the document for a PostScript printer — the last Chooser device I had selected. If a fax you send by using shortcut keys doesn't look right, select the fax driver with the Chooser and then try again. Better yet, use the Preview button that most fax software provides. It lets you see what will be sent before you dial.

Beginning with version 2.5, Global Village's GlobalFax software supports Apple's QuickDraw GX printing architecture. This means you can create a desktop printer icon (or, more accurately, a desktop faxer icon) and send faxes by simply dragging documents to it. (Versions 2.0 and later of Apple's Express Fax software also support GX.) For more details on QuickDraw GX's desktop printers, see Chapter 31.

Print = Fax — The Squirrelly Excel 4 Filename Bug

If you use Excel 4, you probably know about the most recently used files option; the program's File menu lists the four files you opened most recently for convenient access. If any of those filenames contain the word *print,* you notice a funny bug when your fax modem software is active: Excel changes the word to *fax.* I first encountered this phenomenon when working on one of my mega printer overviews for *Macworld* and saw that a worksheet named *Printer Table* showed up as *Faxer Table.*

You don't have to have a computer science degree to figure out this one. When you select fax modem software in the Chooser, any occurrence of the word *print* in the File menu is changed to *fax.* There's no need to worry, though — the right file opens when you choose its name. More to the point, Microsoft fixed the problem in Excel 5.

Tips for better fax quality

The phrase "fax quality" is as much a contradiction in terms as "military intelligence." But you can take some steps to get the best possible results from a fax modem.

Use TrueType fonts or Type 1 PostScript fonts and Adobe Type Manager

These font formats are so popular that you're probably using them already, so I won't belabor this point. Suffice it to say that these outline font technologies result in smooth text at any size — an important plus for printed and faxed documents alike.

Use sturdy fonts

Keep in mind that relatively low faxing resolution distorts type. The subtleties of delicate typefaces such as Caslon and Garamond disappear in a shower of pixel shrapnel. Use sturdy fonts that have been designed to withstand the rigors of low-resolution imaging — Adobe's ITC Stone Informal is a good choice, as is Lucida.

Use the right resolution

Standard fax resolution is 200 horizontal dots per inch x 100 vertical dots per inch. If you're faxing documents formatted for wide orientation (for example, 11 x 8½ inches instead of 8½ x 11), those figures reverse — horizontal resolution is only 100 dpi. For this reason, you get better quality when you fax horizontally oriented documents in fine mode, which provides 200 x 200-dpi resolution (this tip applies to conventional fax machines, too). Keep in mind, though, that doubling horizontal resolution slows faxing times.

Think twice about using EPS art

If you want to include artwork in a fax — for example, an illustration or electronic letterhead with a company logo — don't use encapsulated PostScript (EPS) artwork. Unless installed in a PostScript printer, a fax modem is a QuickDraw-based device — it relies on the Mac's built-in graphics routines for imaging text and graphics. If you fax an EPS image, it's transmitted at a chunky 72 dpi versus a fax's 200 dpi. The solution: Import EPS art into a QuickDraw-oriented drawing program such as MacDraw, and then save the art as a PICT file. Finally, import the PICT image into the document you're faxing.

If you must fax EPS art, here's a workaround that yields better resolution: create the art three to four times larger than its intended size and then import the art into any program that lets you reduce it by the same amount.

Create a scanned version of your signature

If you're faxing correspondence, you may want to create an electronic version of your signature so that your faxed correspondence looks signed. (Source: *Etiquette in the Fax Age*.) If you have a scanner, scan your John Hancock and then save the image as a TIFF or PICT file. If you don't have a scanner, use a drawing program.

First, use the Mouse control panel to select the Tablet speed (you have finer control over the rodent), and then draw your signature at roughly twice its normal size. Save the result as a TIFF or PICT file.

When it's time to "sign" a document, import the image and scale it down to 50 percent. If you're signing documents created with Microsoft Word or another word processor that has a glossary or autotext feature, you can store the signature as a glossary entry and retrieve it with a keystroke or two. Or paste the image into the Mac's Scrapbook, where you can copy it for pasting into any program (or with System 7.5, drag it into a drag-aware application — see Chapter 22).

Save time — don't go gray

Speaking of slow faxing, avoid using extensive areas of gray shading in a document. When you send a fax, the fax software compresses the page image by replacing groups of identical white or black pixels with a code (this *run-length encoding* is the foundation of most image-compression techniques). Gray shades made up of alternating black and white dots can't be efficiently compressed.

In one test I performed, a page containing several large 50-percent gray shades took over five minutes to transmit. The same page without the gray areas took only a minute and a half. When I replaced the 50-percent gray shades with a lighter, 10-percent gray (which can be compressed to some extent), transmission time improved to just under two minutes — not much slower than the grayless version. The lesson: If you want to use gray shading to dress up a page or highlight a row of spreadsheet figures, use a light pattern such as 10 percent. (Shades darker than 50 percent or so usually end up printing as black, by the way.)

Scan hard copy at 200 dots per inch

If you are scanning some hard copy as a prelude to faxing, set up your scanner software to scan at 200 dpi. If you scan at 300 dpi or more, the fax software slows down as it works to downsample the page image to 200 dpi.

Tips for setting up a fax address book

The phone book feature that all fax software provides is a big time-saver. It allows you to enter and save address and phone information for the people you fax.

Importing addresses from another program

If you already store names and numbers by using a contact database or other address book software, you can import your existing database into your fax phone book — if your fax software supports it. The software that accompanies Apple's PowerBook fax modems doesn't. Most third-party fax programs can import a standard tab-delimited text file — a data-exchange format most databases and spreadsheets can create (see Chapter 7). Global Village's Global Fax software can directly read databases from many popular address book programs, including Address Book Plus, Dynodex, and TouchBase.

More Ways to Save Time with a Fax Modem

An obvious way to save time when faxing is to nix the cover page — does every fax have to be announced with a full-page fanfare? Put the to-and-from information at the top of the first page or in a header or footer. If you don't want to foul your pages with address information, consider using a short cover page. FaxSTF provides a half-page cover sheet as well as one called QuickFax that measures just six inches long. If you use a different fax program, create a short cover page of your own by using the cover-page customizing software that all programs include. Even if the receiving fax is a sheet-fed machine (which uses the same-sized sheet of paper no matter how short the original is), the shorter cover page takes less time to transmit.

If you just want to send a quick note ("The express package arrived safely — thanks"), consider using the quick-faxing desk accessory that many fax programs include. Desk accessories such as FaxSTF's QuickFax let you peck a quick note and beam it on its way. But they don't let you save your miniature missives. If you need a record of what you sent ("I faxed a counteroffer at noon — didn't you get it?!"), use a word processor and fax it conventionally.

Exploring advanced fax-addressing options

Most fax programs provide advanced addressing options, such as support for *groups* — collections of multiple addresses. If you frequently send the same fax to a number of locations, automate the process by creating a group (see Figure 16-6 "Grouping Faxes"). Many programs also let you defer faxing until a specific time — such as after 11p.m., when phone rates drop. Combine deferred faxing with group faxing, and your Mac can send a flock of faxes while you sleep.

If your fax software supports multiple phone books and your fax recipients fall into general categories — clients, suppliers, family members — consider creating a separate phone book for each category. Then switch between phone books by using the Fax dialog box. With this approach you do less scrolling when you try to locate a name. And back up your phone book file often.

Dealing with long-distance access codes

Most third-party fax programs let you enter long-distance access numbers and credit card codes. With many programs, when you dial a number that isn't in your area code, the software automatically dials the access and credit card codes for you.

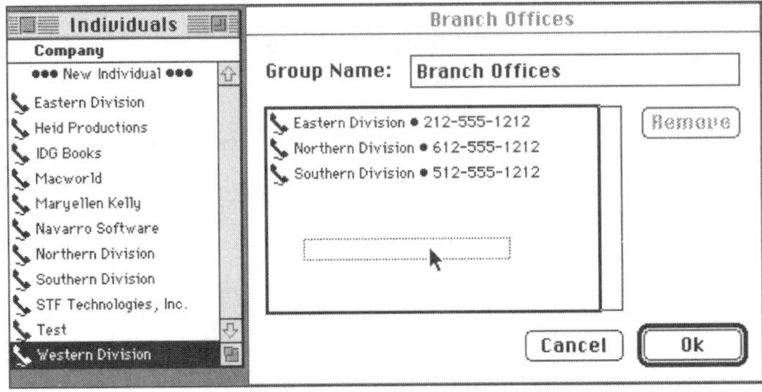

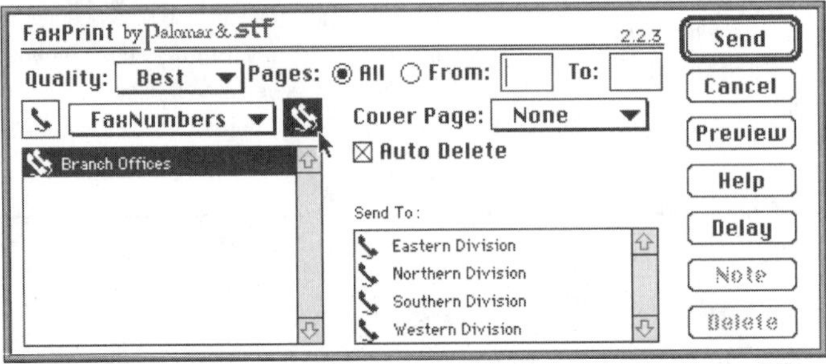

Figure 16-6: Grouping Faxes By creating a group — a collection of fax addresses — you can automate the process of sending the same fax to several locations. With FaxSTF's Fax Manager (top), you can create a group by dragging individual addresses to the group's window. At faxing time, click the group icon in the Fax dialog box (bottom) and then drag the group name to the Send To box. Note that the box then lists the group's members.

Dealing with incoming faxes

I've already confessed my bias toward desktop fax machines for receiving faxes. If you disagree with my preference — or you don't have a conventional fax — here are some tips for dealing with incoming faxes.

Save your eyes: view at 200 percent

If you've received a small fax that you don't want to print out, use your fax software's viewing feature to zoom the page image to 200 percent. The text is much more readable on-screen.

Print on a QuickDraw printer for faster results

If you want to print a received fax, you see your output more quickly if you print it to a QuickDraw-based printer such as an HP DeskWriter or an Apple LaserWriter Select 300 or Personal LaserWriter 300. A PostScript printer connected via LocalTalk is likely to take longer to print the fax, given LocalTalk's relatively slow speed and the need to convert the page image from QuickDraw to PostScript. A

Level 2 PostScript printer combined with Apple's LaserWriter 8 driver (also known as Adobe's PSPrinter driver) provides better performance, as the driver can compress the page image before sending it to the printer. See Chapter 31 for LaserWriter 8 details and tips.

Converting a fax to text with OCR

Some fax programs offer OCR options that can turn faxed text into editable text. You get the most accurate results with fine-mode faxes containing 12-point or larger text. Simple fonts such as Courier help, too. Even then, don't expect anything near 100-percent accuracy. (See Chapter 18 for details on OCR.)

Dealing with fax files

If you receive a lot of faxes, you need a fair amount of disk space to store them. If you're sure that you're finished with a received fax, delete it. Or do an occasional purge of the fax folder, printing faxes you want to keep or copying them to floppies or other backup medium.

The lowdown on PostScript faxing

When you look at an office laser printer sitting idle while a fax machine or fax modem works overtime alongside it, you probably wonder why some company doesn't come out with a laser printer that doubles as a fax. Actually, some have. Apple, NEC Technologies, Compaq Computer, and others offer optional fax modems for their printers. The fax modem board turns the printer into a plain-paper fax that can receive faxes even as it handles incoming print jobs. The included software also lets you send faxes from a Macintosh or Windows PC.

Faxing on the Road

If you're on the road with a PowerBook, fine-tune your phone book ahead of time to remove prefix characters (such as 9 followed by a comma — the sequence often used to access an outside phone line from an office) or add long-distance access codes.

If you use the fax software on your desktop Mac as you do on your PowerBook, you might want to copy the desktop Mac's address book to the PowerBook. With Apple's Express Modem software, the address book is stored in a file named Fax Addresses, located in the System Folder's Preferences folder. Most third-party faxing programs let you store address books anywhere.

Finally, don't forget about one of the most useful ways to put a PowerBook's fax modem to work: sending faxes to yourself. If you need hard copy of a document you've created and you don't have (or forgot to pack) a portable printer, just fax the document to your hotel's fax number, with your name in the "To" portion of the cover sheet.

The marriage of a PostScript printer and a fax modem is a happy one. For one thing, you can send PostScript artwork and get recognizable results — none of that 72-dpi QuickDraw business. You get even better results if you have a PostScript fax at both ends of the line. In this case, the receiving printer prints the document at the printer's maximum resolution — 800 dpi for Dataproducts printers, and 600 for the Apple machines. The received fax looks as gorgeous as if you printed it from a Mac on your own network. It's remote printing without the snail-like performance provided by modems and software such as Apple Remote Access.

Industrial-strength faxing options

If you work in a fax-happy office, consider setting up a network fax server instead of equipping each Mac with a fax modem. Network fax systems such as Cypress Research's FaxPro II and CommForce's 4-Sight let you set aside a modem-equipped Macintosh for your network's faxing needs. With a fax server, the Macs on your network are free from the grunt work of receiving faxes and converting documents for faxing.

Cypress's FaxPro II also lets you create a database of documents that you fax frequently — brochures, price lists, technical notes, and so on. A document in a fax database has already been converted into faxable form; when you need to fax it, the server simply dials and faxes the converted document. Claris uses FaxPro II for its automated fax-back system, which lets you order technical notes and other information by pressing a few keys on your telephone. Within a few minutes, a fax of the requested information is on its way. (Many other software and hardware firms offer similar services — they're a great way to put your fax modem to work.)

4-Sight offers a similar feature, but its real strength is its tight link to the Microsoft Mail and CE Software QuickMail electronic mail systems. (CommForce is jointly owned by CE Software and 4-Sight Systems, a British company.) With 4-Sight, you can send faxes by using the desk accessory that you use to send e-mail. Fax numbers are stored in the e-mail system's address book.

Telephony: Making and Taking Calls

So much for talking to other computers and fax machines — what about using the Mac to talk to other *people?* This section spotlights Mac telephony applications and tools.

Number, please

The simplest form of telephony is wrapped around the commendable concept that you shouldn't have to dial a phone number manually that you or someone else has already typed. Automatic phone dialing saves your fingers from unnecessary walking — or hikes, if you use long-distance services that need a dozen digits' worth of access codes. At its best, autodialing means having the Mac dial a number regardless of where it's stored — in a contact database, e-mail message, text document, or CD-ROM phone book.

There are a few routes to autodialing. Many personal information managers (programs such as Adobe TouchBase Pro) can dial by using your Mac's modem — you simply pick up the phone after the dialing has finished. This scheme has several flaws, the first of which is that it assumes that your modem and telephone are connected to the same phone line. That may be the case in a small home office, but most businesses dedicate separate lines to voice and data.

The Mac itself can produce the standard tones used for tone dialing. Many programs also provide an option for through-the-speaker dialing: you simply hold the telephone handset up to the Mac's speaker before choosing a dialing command. In my experience, though, this method works poorly — too many wrong numbers and incomplete calls caused by the phone not picking up the tones accurately. And of course, through-the-speaker dialing doesn't work at all with phone systems that require pulse dialing.

Reliable dialing with an autodialing box

One solution to these problems is an autodialing box, which connects the Mac and a telephone. I've played with Sophisticated Circuits' Desktop Dialer and Micromachines' TurboDialer and found that each has good and bad points.

TurboDialer connects to the Mac's sound-output jack; that's bad news if you're into CD-ROMs and multimedia, in which case a pair of external speakers probably occupies your sound-output jack. Desktop Dialer, by comparison, connects to the Apple Desktop Bus (ADB) — a much more flexible scheme.

Have QuicKeys, Will Autodial

If you have CE Software's QuicKeys, you have all you need to test the waters of modem- or speaker-based autodialing. QuicKeys includes an extension called Phone Dialer that dials a number that you've copied to the Clipboard.

Here's how to find it. In QuicKeys' Define menu, open the Extensions submenu, and then open the Network and Device Tools submenu. You should find Phone Dialer there.

TurboDialer lets you dial any number simply by selecting it and then pressing a ⌘-key sequence. To dial a number with Desktop Dialer, you must first copy it to the Clipboard — that adds a step to the dialing routine and, more significantly, replaces the Clipboard's previous contents. But to its credit, Desktop Dialer supports dialing via System 7's Apple events mechanism. You can set up any program that can send Apple events, such as Claris FileMaker Pro or Apple's HyperCard 2.2 or later, to communicate with the dialer. Desktop Dialer also includes a bare-bones address book program that stores up to 20 names and addresses. In all, it's the better of the two dialers. It's also directly supported by most contact managers and other dialing-aware programs.

Another dialing detail concerns area codes and long-distance access codes. You want an autodialing program to dial them for long-distance numbers, but not for local ones. How does the program know which is which? Both dialers use a simple scheme, which begins with you entering your local area code in a setup dialog box. Thereafter, when you dial a number, the dialer checks to see whether its area code matches the local one. If it does, the program doesn't dial the area code.

Both dialers also let you specify prefixes for accessing outside lines or long-distance services; you can insert a pause between prefix and the number by typing a comma after the prefix. Many long-distance companies also require a suffix, which is your calling-card number.

Dialing and calling

One way in which Apple is pushing telephony is by building GeoPort connectors into the AV Macs and Power Macs. GeoPort promises to do for telephony what LocalTalk did for networking: make hardware connections easy and economical.

The AV and Power Macs have enough processing horsepower to generate and decode the squeaks and squawks that are normally the exclusive vocabulary of data or fax modems. All an AV or Power Mac needs is a hardware interface that connects it to telephone lines. That's where Apple's GeoPort Telecom Adaptor comes in — it's a simple interface box that connects the Mac to analog phone lines (the kind you have in your house). As I mentioned earlier in this chapter, if you plug a GeoPort Telecom Adaptor into an AV or Power Mac, you have a high-speed data and fax modem.

Using an AV or Power Mac as a telephone

GeoPort isn't just for data — it's also capable of carrying voice conversations. Unfortunately, for the first year or two of the GeoPort architecture's life, this aspect of Mac telephony was more of a promise than a reality. The problem was that Apple had delivered the hardware — the GeoPort connectors and GeoPort Telecom Adaptor — but had not delivered the software that would enable programmers to write telephone applications.

That has finally changed, thanks to versions 2.0 and later of the GeoPort software. GeoPort 2 incorporates a new set of system routines called the Telephone Manager, which provides standard telephony features that any program can access (see the Backgrounder box "Inside the Macintosh Telephony Architecture"). The Telephone Manager talks to software drivers, called *telephone tools*, that tell the Telephone Manager how to access a specific piece of hardware. Unlike previous versions of the GeoPort software, GeoPort 2 includes a telephone tool for the GeoPort Telecom Adaptor.

Cypress Research Corporation has taken advantage of this to create a terrific screen-based telephony program called MegaPhone (see Figure 16-7 "Talking into MegaPhone"). MegaPhone turns an AV or Power Mac into a speakerphone — you talk into the microphone that came with the Mac and listen through the Mac's speaker (or through headphones connected to its sound-output jack). MegaPhone performs some sophisticated audio processing to eliminate the coffee-can audio quality that conventional speaker phones suffer from.

MegaPhone also lets you set up address books and provides a speed-dialing feature. The program provides automatic links to databases and contact managers such as FileMaker Pro and TouchBase Pro, so you can swap names and phone numbers between MegaPhone and your existing name-and-address files.

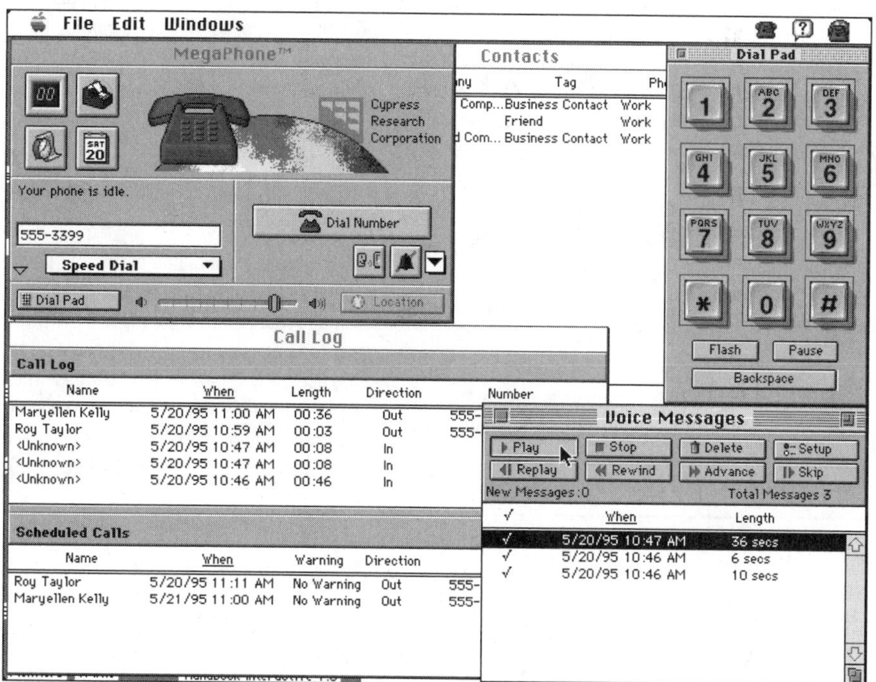

Figure 16-7 Talking into MegaPhone Cypress Research's MegaPhone is a full-feature telephony program that turns the Mac into speaker phone, auto dialer, and answering machine.

Better Telephony with the Jabra Ear Phone

History has recorded for all time the first words that Alexander Graham Bell said to his assistant through the telephone: "Come here, Watson, I need you." But few people know that the great inventor also designed the first speaker phone. Upon hearing Bell through the contraption for the first time, Watson reportedly replied, "Hey boss, why are you talking into a coffee can?"

I have yet to hear a speaker phone that doesn't sound like an empty can of Folger's, and that includes the speaker phone that's essentially built into AVs and Power Macs. A smarter way to put AV telephony to work is with Jabra Corporation's Ear Phone.

The Ear Phone looks like, well, an earphone — the kind that lets you listen to the TV without waking your spouse — but it also contains a microphone sensitive enough to pick up your voice. A six-foot cable terminates in a tiny black box, from which extend two short cables: one plugs into the Mac's microphone jack and the other into its external audio jack. You can connect an Ear Phone in less time than it takes to read this paragraph. (You can also connect an Ear Phone to an Apple AudioVision 14 monitor, but configuring the monitor's control panel for the proper sound levels is a bit cumbersome. It's easier to use the Mac's rear-panel jacks.)

What's it like to wear this thing? It's reasonably comfortable, although it began to bother me after prolonged use. A small foam cover makes the earpiece — the ear bud, as Jabra calls it — more comfortable than a typical earphone. For the fashion conscious, Jabra also sells replacement foam covers in several colors. I have a white one for formal occasions, a blue one for everyday use, and red and green ones I use alternately during the Christmas season.

The Ear Phone also includes plastic loops in several sizes; the loop snaps on to the ear bud and then hooks over the top of your ear to hold the ear bud in place. The Ear Phone box also contains a coupon advertising a custom cup — sorry, an *ear mold* — available in several sizes for $35 each.

Perhaps the biggest drawback of the Ear Phone is that because it disables the Mac's speaker, you can't hear all the other sounds a Mac makes — like the modem making a call and connecting or an audio CD playing in play-through mode — unless you unplug or wear the Ear Phone. This shortcoming isn't so much the Ear Phone as it is a side effect of having a computer that also acts as a telephone, modem, and CD player. The fact remains, though, that the unplug-and-plug routine can become tiresome, not to mention hard on the Mac's jacks.

If you have a Power Mac 7500 or 8500, this drawback doesn't apply because these Macs have two sets of audio-output jacks: the headphone jack and the RCA line-output jacks.

By the way, if you're one of the four people who actually use the AV and Power Macs' PlainTalk voice-recognition features, you'll be glad to know that the Ear Phone works with them. In fact, recognition accuracy improves a bit because the microphone is always a consistent distance from your mouth and because Jabra's engineers fine-tuned the audio levels for better results.

Using MegaPhone to take calls

MegaPhone can also serve as an answering machine — it lets you digitally record an outgoing message and digitizes incoming messages and saves them on your hard disk. The program provides a slick array of message-management features: you can set up a password to check your messages from the road, for example, and you can specify that MegaPhone inform you with a tone when a new message comes in. If you've installed Apple's PowerTalk software (discussed in Chapter 32), you can even tell MegaPhone to put new messages in your In Tray.

How to get MegaPhone

MegaPhone is included with second-generation Power Macs such as the 7500 and 7200. If you have an earlier Power Mac or AV machine, you can download the GeoPort 2.0 software and MegaPhone from Apple's customer-support forum on eWorld or from Apple's Internet ftp sites. (A knowledgeable dealer can also provide or let you copy the disks.)

Oh, one more thing — the version of MegaPhone Apple includes (and that you can download) is fully functional for only 30 days. After that trial period, it turns into Basic MegaPhone, a simple speakerphone and answering machine that lacks most of MegaPhone's best features. Fortunately, if you become hooked during the 30-day trial period, you can upgrade to the full version — over the phone, of course.

Desktop voice mail

Like them or not, voice-mail systems are coming on strong — and they're doing more than just routing calls and taking messages. You can program them to place calls — to conduct surveys, for example, or remind patients of upcoming dental appointments. They can act as order-entry systems that allow callers to order products or services by pressing keys on their phones. And they can drive those fax-back systems I mentioned earlier.

Dedicated voice-mail systems, whose prices start at about $4,000 and skyrocket into the six-figure range, are beyond the budgets of most small businesses. That's where the Mac can help. Products such as Cypress Research's PhonePro and Magnum Software's TFLX (pronounced *tee-flex*) let you turn a Mac into a voice-mail system. Neither system is limited to voice mail — other applications include calling numbers in a database and playing a recorded message (a doctor's office can use this feature to set up an automatic appointment-reminder system), automatic order entry (callers enter item numbers from a catalog and the system records the orders), or telephone surveys (the system plays multiple-choice recordings and the survey victim presses keys to respond).

Tips for MegaPhone

Making the transition to screen-based telephony? Here are some tips for Cypress Research's MegaPhone.

- **Use the Return key to dial and hang up.** You don't have to click the Dial button after typing a number — just press Return. Press Return again to hang up.
- **Use commas for dialing pauses.** If you're dialing using a credit card and you need a pause between, say, the phone number and your credit card number, type a comma (,) between those numbers.
- **Set up a MegaPhone hot key.** If you use CE Software's QuicKeys utility, set up a hot key that opens MegaPhone when you press a keyboard shortcut.
- **Watch your disk space.** MegaPhone uses 17K of disk space for each second of recorded sound, so long incoming messages can fill a hard drive quickly. If you're going away for a while, consider freeing up some disk space first, or specify that MegaPhone store messages on the highest-capacity hard drive you have. (To change the drive, click the Setup button in the Voice Messages window and then click the Change button in the Messages Folder area of the Setup window.)
- **Limit message length.** Another way to avoid filling the hard drive is to limit message length. MegaPhone is preset to limit messages to two minutes, but you can change that using the Setup window.
- **How MegaPhone stores messages.** MegaPhone records each message as a standard System 7 sound file. This means you can play back a message by simply double-clicking its icon in the Finder. (Check the Setup window to determine where your messages are being stored.) And if you want to save a message to a different disk, just copy its file.
- **A MegaPhone practical joke.** Want to play a mean joke on a coworker? Record a System 7 sound (or download one from an on-line service) and copy its file into his or her MegaPhone messages folder — it will show up in the Messages window as if it were left over the phone. (See Chapter 21 for details on System 7 sound files.)

Some of MegaPhone's additional goodies include

- **Letter-to-number translation.** If you type numbers such as (800) BIG-DEAL, MegaPhone translates the letters into the appropriate numbers.
- **Call logging.** When you hang up, MegaPhone displays a dialog box that lets you record information about the call — great for attorneys, consultants, and other professionals who charge for their telephone time. You can also call back any number in the log by simply double-clicking it.
- **Automatic call navigation.** Don't you hate call-routing systems that make you press five different keys to get to the proper option or department? MegaPhone can record those keystrokes and then play them back for you.

Inside the Macintosh Telephony Architecture

Apple's Macintosh Telephony Architecture relies on several layers, each of which deals with a certain aspect of the Mac-to-telephone interface. This layered approach makes it easier for developers to implement telephony features that run across a wide variety of hardware.

At the top layer are telephony-aware applications — programs that can make use of telephony services. Examples include a database manager that dials stored numbers; a client-tracking system that uses caller ID to display clients' data when they call; or a personal-information manager that reminds users of scheduled calls and then places the calls automatically.

Telephony-aware applications can rely on Apple event messages to communicate with either of two types of applications: screen-based telephony applications (which may include an answering machine program, a program that displays caller ID information, or a graphical switchboard) and programmed telephony applications (which may include voice-mail systems or automated paging and call-routing systems).

Screen-based and programmable telephony applications in turn communicate with the Telephone Manager, a system software extension. The Telephone Manager talks to telephone tools, which are drivers that tell the Telephone Manager how to access a specific piece of hardware, such as a GeoPort Telecom Adaptor.

Programming a voice-mail system

Behind every voice-mail system is a program that does different things — plays a message, records a message, transfers a call, and so on — depending on the keys pressed at the other end of the line. In order to create a voice-mail system that's tailored to your business, you need to create a program that tells the system how to respond to the caller's keystrokes. It's the biggest part of setting up a voice-mail system, and PhonePro and TFLX take remarkably similar approaches to the task.

Instead of providing text windows into which you type programming statements, both provide graphical programming environments: you program the system by dragging and linking icons representing tasks and functions, such as answering the phone and responding to key presses. A completed voice-mail program looks more like a flowchart than a computer program (see Figure 16-8 "Visual Voice Mail").

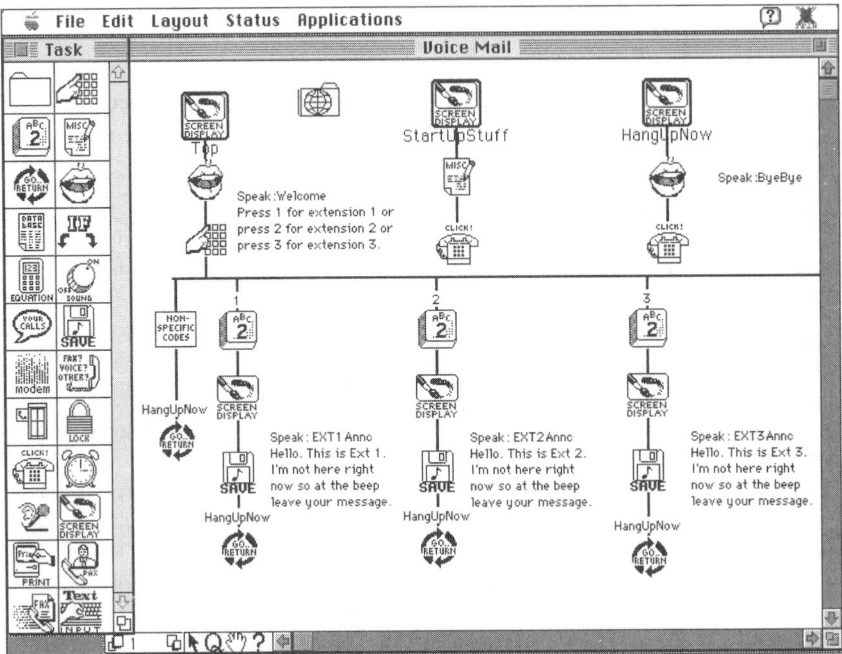

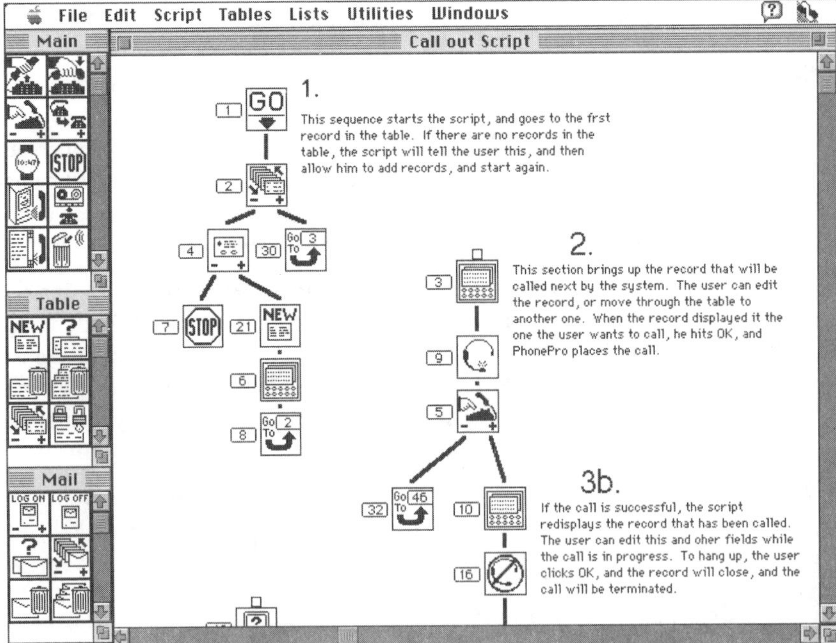

Figure 16-8: Visual Voice Mail Cypress Research's PhonePro and Magnum Software's TFLX turn a Mac into a voice-mail system that you program by dragging and connecting icons. The PhonePro script (top) dials numbers that are stored in a database. The TFLX script (bottom) is the basis of a simple voice-mail system that lets callers enter an extension number and leave a message.

PhonePro is often sold along with a high-speed SupraFAX modem that has been upgraded with a chip that enables the system to play back outgoing messages (such as "If you know your party's extension number, press it now"). In order to shoehorn voice recordings through the modem port, the recordings must be compressed in a way that compromises fidelity. A version of PhonePro that doesn't require separate hardware is also available. This version uses the Apple Telephone Manager software described earlier. And because it doesn't have to shoehorn a voice recording through the modem port, it sounds better, too.

In the summer of 1995, Cypress Research shipped PhonePro for GeoPort, a version of PhonePro that runs on GeoPort-equipped Macs (AV and Power Macs) and requires no specialized modem hardware except for a GeoPort pod. PhonePro for GeoPort works together with the Apple Telephony Architecture and GeoPort 2.0 software discussed earlier in this chapter. But its most exciting new feature is support for Apple's text-to-speech software: PhonePro for GeoPort can read aloud *over the phone.* That makes possible a whole new set of telephony applications: one that reads account balances to callers, for example, or one that reads your e-mail to you.

As for TFLX, it uses custom hardware that connects between the phone line and the Mac's sound-output jack. Outgoing sounds are uncompressed and played at the Mac's standard 11KHz or 22KHz sampling rate, which yields very good fidelity (at least by telephone line standards).

Magnum has created an impressive demonstration of TFLX that's only a phone call away. Call 818-701-5051 and ask for the TFLX demo. If you call after hours (Pacific time), you connect to it automatically.

Several entry-level voice-mail products are also available. Prometheus Products' Home Office includes a 2400-bit per second modem and answering-machine software that supports up to 999 password-protected mailboxes; Ultima Home Office includes a 14.4Kbps modem.

The trouble with telephony

For all their promises, some aspects of computer telephony still have some rough edges. For example, most people have their modems and voice phones connected to separate phone lines. The Mac doesn't support this basic requirement — a GeoPort-based modem and Mac phone are connected to the same line.

Another problem is that Apple's GeoPort Telecom Adaptor works only with analog phone lines — the kind your house has — but many big businesses have private-branch exchange (PBX) or other digital systems through which the adaptor can't dial. Apple has been saying that PBX-compatible GeoPort adaptors will be available since it released the AV Macs a few years ago, but none have appeared as of mid-1995.

More Ways to Put Modems and Telephony to Work

The worlds of telecommunications and telephony aren't limited to the applications and products described in this chapter. Additional applications include

- **Remote access:** With Apple's Apple Remote Access software, you can dial a remote network to access its printers, file servers, and e-mail systems (see Chapter 32). You can use remote access to keep in touch with the main office or simply to retrieve a forgotten file from the Mac at home. A remote network node can do anything a local node can do, albeit in slow motion — even with a 14.4Kbps modem, accessing a remote network feels a lot like trying to sprint in a swimming pool.
- **Remote control:** For a variation on the remote-access theme, combine ARA with Farallon Computing's Timbuktu Pro, which, as Chapter 32 describes, lets you actually control a remote Mac or even a Windows PC. You can run programs, choose their commands, and print documents — but again, in slow-motion. Note the subtle but important difference between Apple Remote Access and Timbuktu/Remote: ARA allows you to dial a remote network to access its services, while Timbuktu Pro allows you to see what's on a remote Macs screen and control the Mac as if you were sitting at it. You can't control or view the screen of a remote Mac by using ARA alone. (If you're on a budget, you can buy Timbuktu/Remote, which doesn't require ARA but also has fewer features.)
- **Remote power-on/power-off:** The problem with remote-access products — and, for that matter, fax modems and Mac-based voice-mail systems — is that you have to leave your computer on all the time to take advantage of them. Or do you? System 7.5 includes a control panel called Auto Power On/Off that lets the Mac turn itself on and off at intervals you specify. If you're going on the road but anticipate having to call in (to retrieve a file, for example), you can set up the control panel so that the Mac is on during business hours. See Chapter 23's section on environmentally friendly computing for a list of the Macs that are compatible with Auto Power On/Off.

For the Mac that doesn't support the Auto Power On/Off control panel, check out Sophisticated Circuits' PowerKey and PowerKey Remote. PowerKey is a small box that connects to the Macs ADB port and provides three power outlets. An included control panel lets the box turn the Mac and up to three peripherals on or off at specified times. PowerKey also lets you press the keyboard's power-on key to turn on Macs that don't normally support this key, such as the Quadra 605 or Power Mac 6100/60. (Macs that do support the key are often described as supporting *soft power* — the capability to be turned on and off under software control.)

The PowerKey Remote add-on lets you turn the Mac on with a phone call. PowerKey Remote includes a control panel that turns the Mac off after a specified period of inactivity. If your Mac supports keyboard power-on and you just want to be able to turn it on remotely, all you need is PowerKey Remote. Macs that don't support soft power require both PowerKey and PowerKey Remote.

Finally, it's impractical for a home-office or small-business user to leave a Mac on all the time to act simply as an answering machine or telephone. Conventional phones, answering machines, and fax machines aren't about to go the way of the telegraph key. Computer-based telephony tools supplement, rather than supplant, the phone equipment to which we've become addicted. That's as it should be.

Paving the Information Highway

When the first information service appeared, industry gurus began forecasting a day when people would do all their banking, learning, and shopping on-line. That day hasn't arrived — partly because the refinement and widespread acceptance of a technology always takes longer than its initial birth, but mostly because you can't endorse a check, go on a field trip, or try on clothes over the phone.

Still, communications is becoming a consumer commodity. Many banks offer bank-by-modem services, and the Internal Revenue Service even lets taxpayers file their returns by modem and get their refunds faster.

To some people, the real consumer communications age won't arrive until telecommunications meets television. Imagine looking up the latest on-line news and seeing a television news report instead of a window full of text, or browsing an on-line encyclopedia and not only reading about Martin Luther King, Jr. but also seeing and hearing him give his most famous speeches. This kind of interactive news and video exists today, thanks to CD-ROMs and QuickTime, but it's unlikely to meet the on-line world for a while.

But it won't be long. When I wrote the preceding paragraph for the first edition of this book several years ago, the marriage of telecommunications and television seemed a million years away. Today, with telephone and cable TV companies investing millions in interactive television tests, it's closer than ever.

In the meantime, today's world of communications has a great deal to offer, and I encourage you to sample it. If you do, drop me an e-mail note and let me know how you use it. On CompuServe, I'm 76174,556; on America Online and AppleLink, I'm JIMHEID.

CHAPTER 16 CONCEPTS AND TERMS

- You can telecommunicate on two basic levels — directly with another computer or through an intermediary such as an information service or bulletin board.
- Most on-line services provide electronic mail (exchanging messages and disk files with other subscribers); research (consumer articles and demographic reports, for example); travel (travel news and information and on-line flight-reservation systems); shopping (on-line malls); and special-interest forums (communicating with other subscribers about a wide range of issues).
- Choosing an information service involves assessing your budget and information needs and then deciding how important a Mac-like interface is to you.
- A modem is the computer's link to the on-line world. It converts, or modulates, the data coming from the Mac into audio tones that phone lines can carry and demodulates the incoming tones into data that the Mac can understand.

bulletin board
A small-scale on-line service operated by computer hobbyists that acts as an electronic meeting place for user-group members.

download
To receive a file from an on-line service or bulletin board.

electronic mail
Correspondence exchanged via on-line services.

file-transfer protocol
A method of transferring a disk file that causes data to be "proofread" to eliminate garbled data.

front end
A program that presents a Mac-like interface for a text-oriented on-line service such as CompuServe.

gateway
A link provided by one on-line service that lets you access or exchange mail with users of another on-line service. For example, CompuServe provides a gateway that lets you exchange mail with MCI Mail subscribers.

modem
The hardware that connects a Mac to the telephone line. The word modem is a short form of the words *modulate* and *demodulate.* Direct-connect modems attach between a phone jack and the Mac's modem or printer port and have a jack into which you can plug a telephone. Acoustic modems contain cups into which you snug a telephone handset. Fax modems let you send, and often receive, faxes.

on-line service
A commercial communications service that charges hourly or monthly rates for access to news, shopping services, special-interest forums, and vast libraries of free and nearly free software.

script language
A command language that lets you automate communications sessions by transmitting commands for you in response to prompts from an on-line service. Most terminal-emulation programs provide script languages.

shareware
A program that you can try at no cost but are expected to pay a modest fee for if you decide to keep it.

terminal-emulation software
A program, such as Hayes's Smartcom II or Software Ventures' MicroPhone II, that turns a modem-equipped Mac into a terminal that can access an on-line service.

upload
To transfer a file to an on-line service or bulletin board.

(continued on the next page)

(continued from previous page)

Glossary of Internet Terms

browser
A program that lets you explore Internet World Wide Web sites. One of the most popular browsers is the freeware program Mosaic.

FTP
Short for *file-transfer protocol,* a method of moving files across the Internet. *FTP sites* are Internet locations from which you can download software and other files.

HTTP
Short for *hypertext transfer protocol,* the method of transmitting hypertext documents across the Internet. HTTP is used on the World Wide Web.

Internet
A network of networks — a collection of interconnected networks that spans the globe.

MacTCP
An Apple control panel that implements TCP/IP, the communications protocols used by the Internet.

mail list
A list you can join by sending an e-mail message to the list's manager. Thereafter, you receive regular electronic mailings, such as newsletters.

Mosaic
See *browser.*

newsgroups
Internet public discussion groups, each dealing with a specific topic. You can read newgroup messages and contribute your own.

home page
The first screen you see when you connect to a specific site on the World Wide Web.

HTML
Short for *hypertext mark-up language,* a method of formatting documents for the World Wide Web. When creating a Web site, you create a series of HTML documents that contain text as well as references to graphics and other types of data (such as sounds and movies), and to other Web sites.

PPP
Short for *point-to-point protocol,* a method of encoding data for transmission over serial lines. Often used in high-speed Internet connections. (Also see *SLIP.*)

SLIP
Short for *serial-line Internet protocol,* a method of encoding data for transmission over serial lines. Often used in high-speed Internet connections. (Also see *PPP.*)

URL
Short for *universal resource locator,* a standard electronic address for computers connected to the World Wide Web. A typical URL might read http://www.mac.com/homepage.html.

Web server
A computer that contains the screens and related files that comprise a Web site. If you're setting up your own Web site, you need a Web server.

World Wide Web
The fashionable place to be on the Internet, the Web is a matrix of computers running HTTP. One Web site can provide hypertext links to other Web sites. Web sites can support graphics and multimedia elements such as sounds and movies.

CHAPTER SEVENTEEN

How to Download Software

- Getting on-line
- Choosing a file-transfer protocol
- Downloading from CompuServe, America Online, and eWorld
- Decompressing files after downloading

Your Mac is but a phone call away from a library of free and inexpensive software. All you need to tap into the world of *freeware* and *shareware* are a modem and a communications software package. Then you can dial hobbyist bulletin board systems or, better still, subscribe to an on-line service such as CompuServe, eWorld, or America Online.

What's Available?

You name it. There are utilities that check your system for viruses and others that compress files to save disk space. There are fonts, programs that modify fonts, and programs that print font samples. If you're obsessed with time, there are programs that display a digital clock in your menu bar, synchronize your Mac's clock with the government's atomic clock, and let your Mac speak the time when you press a key.

Do you have a PowerBook? You can find utilities that make it easier to locate the pointer on a dim screen, automatically dim the display after a few minutes to save battery power, and let you put the hard disk to sleep with a single keystroke.

Want fun stuff? How about a program that lets the Mac play different sounds when you insert or eject disks, empty the Trash, and perform other activities? And there are sounds themselves, more sounds than you have disk space for: clips from *Star Trek*, *Terminator II*, *Twin Peaks*, *Ren and Stimpy*, *The Simpsons*, and more. That goes double for QuickTime movies.

There's also plenty for the serious-minded; for example, a full-featured spreadsheet program as well as spreadsheet templates for loan amortization, investment analysis, and more. HyperCard buffs can find stacks galore, from one that tracks your videotape collection to a mixology stack containing (hic!) 137 drink recipes (see Chapter 19 for more details about HyperCard).

How Shareware Works

The shareware system illustrates the generosity and sense of community you find on-line. You can download a shareware program from a bulletin board or on-line service and try it out for a week or two. If you find the program a useful addition to your software library, send a check to the author. In return, you often get a printed manual (most shareware programs come with on-screen documentation) and a disk containing the latest version of the program.

How much does a shareware program cost? Payment usually ranges from $5 to $50, although some programmers prefer more creative forms of remuneration. One programmer asks for a postcard from your home town, another requests a donation to UNICEF, a third wants $25 or a case of beer, and another requests Grateful Dead concert tapes.

Freeware doesn't cost a cent (aside from the cost of the phone call and the on-line service's connect-time charge — two tariffs that almost always apply when you're on-line). But don't get the idea that a free program isn't worth anything. The best virus-detection utility is free (and is included on the CD-ROM that accompanies this book), as is a popular utility for managing system extensions and control panels. Freeware programmers are often inspired by fellow subscribers. On Friday, someone may ask whether a certain kind of program is available; by Monday, it often is.

Downloading software from a bulletin board or information service is fairly easy, although few technical hurdles can trip up communications newcomers. In this chapter, I describe the key technicalities behind downloading and show you how to download from three services — CompuServe, eWorld, and America Online. If you don't have a modem, see the preceding chapter to learn about what to look for.

Other Downloading Opportunities

I concentrate on freeware and shareware forums in this chapter, but there are other on-line sources for software, too. Many top software developers have customer-support forums on CompuServe, eWorld, and America Online. These company-run forums have their own software libraries containing demonstration versions of their programs, sample documents, answers to commonly asked questions, software updates, and more. Hardware companies often post the latest versions of the system extensions that their products require. Apple also posts its Mac OS system updates on its eWorld and AppleLink services (and on its Internet ftp site). Downloading updates is faster and more convenient than sending away for a disk — or a set of disks. The downloads are free except for connect-time charges.

Bulletin boards

Then there are bulletin board systems (BBSs), small-scale on-line services often run by user groups or communications fiends. Many bulletin boards used to be difficult to use, with ugly, text-based interfaces. Today, however, many bulletin boards provide attractive graphical interfaces, thanks to BBS software such as FirstClass. The legendary Berkeley Macintosh User Group (BMUG) operates outstanding bulletin boards called Planet BMUG (see Figure 17-1, "Visiting Planet BMUG"). Access to these bulletin boards is available to any BMUG member. (See the BMUG membership page at the back of this book for details.)

A HyperCard stack called The Mac BBS Stack (available on-line) contains a partial list of bulletin board systems. A list of bulletin boards also accompanies White Knight and the *Macworld Power User Clinic* CD-ROM that accompanies this book (in the "Best of BMUG" collection).

Where to begin?

How do you find all these software treasures? You could just browse various forums until you find something of interest, wandering like a library patron among the stacks. But the local library doesn't charge for access — and on-line services do. A more efficient and economical alternative is to use the searching features that on-line services provide to locate items based on dates or subject keywords. I describe how to use these features later in this chapter.

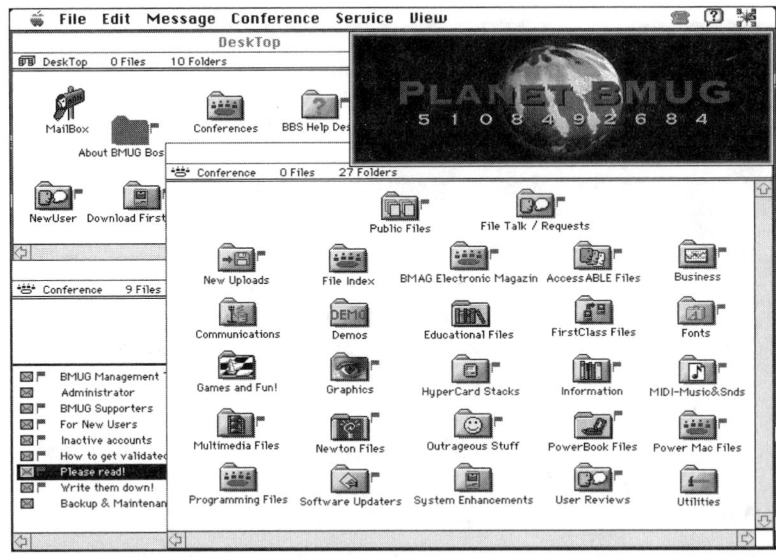

Figure 17-1: Visiting Planet BMUG Bulletin board systems driven by SoftArc's FirstClass software provide a graphical user interface, complete with a Finder-like desktop. One of the best FirstClass bulletin boards is the Berkeley Macintosh User Group's Planet BMUG, on which you swap messages with BMUG members, download software, read reviews contributed by BMUG members, and much more.

Choosing a Transfer Protocol

Accuracy is paramount when downloading software, because even one missing or garbled bit can render a downloaded program useless. If you're using a general-purpose communications program to access CompuServe or a bulletin board, you need to perform another step before you can begin downloading — choose a *file-transfer protocol.* This three-dollar phrase refers to a set of rules that both computers use to ensure that they transfer files accurately. If you're using eWorld, CompuServe Information Manager, or America Online, you can skip this section — these services' software choose file-transfer protocols automatically.

With a file-transfer protocol, the sending computer (for example, the on-line service's) sends the file in chunks called *blocks.* When your Mac receives a block, it compares notes with the on-line service to make sure that it received the block accurately. If it didn't, it requests the block again. If it did, it gives the go-ahead to send the next block. "This Did-you-get-it? Yes-I-did" banter continues until the entire file has been transferred. (For details about transfer protocols, see the Backgrounder box "More about Transfer Protocols" and Table 17-1 "File Transfer Protocols at a Glance.")

Table 17-1
File Transfer Protocols at a Glance

Protocol	***Description***
XMODEM	The original file-transfer protocol. Uses block sizes of 128K. Widely supported, but slower than its successors.
XMODEM-CRC	Uses a more accurate error-checking method called a *cyclic redundancy check.*
YMODEM	Similar to XMODEM, but lets you send a batch of files with a single command. Also uses CRC error checking.
YMODEM-G	Faster than YMODEM, but performs no error correction. If an error occurs during transmission, it cancels the entire transfer. Useful with modems containing error-correction hardware such as MNP.
ZMODEM	Another fast protocol with better reliability than YMODEM-G. The protocol to use if both computers support it.
Kermit	Very flexible but slow. Often useful in swapping files with mainframes that don't support other protocols.
CIS B Plus	A CompuServe protocol used by CIM and supported by some communications programs.
MacBinary	Actually not a protocol, but a format for protocol transfers that ensures the transfer of the file's unique Mac attributes: its data and resource forks (see Chapter 24's discussion of resources), icons, creation and modification dates, and so on. You generally want to use MacBinary protocol transfers when exchanging Mac files.

In the end, the underlying details behind these protocols aren't important. What is important is that you set up your program to use a transfer protocol that the sending computer also supports. I recommend starting out with YMODEM or ZMODEM if your service supports it. (CompuServe, for instance, does not support ZMODEM.) To choose a protocol, look for a command called File Transfer Protocol or Protocol Transfer.

As you become an experienced downloader, you may want to experiment with other protocols to see whether they reduce downloading times, and if so, by how much.

Tips for CompuServe Downloading

One way to locate files available for downloading is to enter a specific forum (games, utilities, sounds, fonts, and so on) and then look around. Suppose you want to see what's been added to the arcade and action games section of the games forum within the last week.

More about Transfer Protocols

Several file-transfer protocols exist — XMODEM, YMODEM, ZMODEM, Kermit, CompuServe A, CompuServe B, and MacTerminal. Each type of protocol even has variants within it — XMODEM-CRC, XMODEM-1K, and CompuServe B Plus, for example. All text-oriented services, such as CompuServe, support XMODEM. Microphone II, Smartcom II, SITcomm, and White Knight support XMODEM, YMODEM, ZMODEM, and their variants as well as Kermit. MicroPhone II and Smartcom II also support the CompuServe B Plus protocol. (The shareware ZTerm, included with this book, supports XMODEM, YMODEM, and ZMODEM.)

Each file-transfer protocol and variation thereof uses different block sizes, different error-checking techniques, or both. For example, the original XMODEM uses a 128-byte block size, while XMODEM-1K uses 1024-byte blocks. This larger block size means that the on-line service spends less time asking your Mac if things are okay and more time transmitting the file. The down side: if the phone lines are noisy, the transmitting computer has to spend more time resending blocks. Small block sizes are best for noisy connections, while large block sizes are best for clean connections. (ZMODEM shines in this area — block sizes are adjusted for conditions, and if you lose the connection, you can pick up where you left off.) If you choose a protocol that uses a large block size (such as XMODEM-1K) and find that you're getting a lot of *retries* — retransmitted blocks — during a download, chances are you have a noisy connection and may benefit from choosing a protocol that uses a smaller block size (such as plain XMODEM).

If you use CIM, America Online, or eWorld, you don't have to fuss with choosing a transfer protocol. CIM automatically uses the CompuServe B Plus protocol, and America Online and eWorld use their own transfer protocols.

From any CompuServe menu, type **go macfun** and press Return. (If you use CIM, choose Go from the Services menu and then type **macfun**.) When the forum menu appears, press 3 and then press Return to enter the file libraries. When the menu of libraries appears, press 2 and then press Return to enter the Arcade/Action Games library. Finally, type **cat/des/age:7** and press Return. This sequence displays a catalog (*cat*) and description (*des*) of files added within the past seven days (*age:*7).

Searching with keywords

You can also add a keyword to narrow your search; for example, **cat/des/age:7/key:poker** narrows the search to up-to-week-old poker games. Keywords let you search according to descriptive words assigned to the file when it was originally uploaded. Omit the *age* portion of the command to search all files regardless of when they were uploaded.

Searching with the file finder

CompuServe also provides a file-finder feature that lets you automatically search all Mac forums at once instead of having to enter a specific forum and then look around. This feature is handy when you're not sure where to find a certain type of file.

To access CompuServe's file finder, type **go macff** at any CompuServe menu and then press Return. The file finder lets you search by numerous criteria — submission date, forum name, and so on — but you'll probably find the keyword option the most useful.

The main drawback of CompuServe's file finder is that you can't directly download a file when it's found; instead, you need to jot down its name and location and then move to that forum to download it by using the techniques just described. This drawback doesn't apply if you're using CompuServe Information Manager.

Deciphering file descriptions

CompuServe's file descriptions include a variety of information (see Figure 17-2 "Deciphering Descriptions"), but the most important information is the filename as it's stored on CompuServe's computers. When you find a file that you want to download, type that name.

Doing the download

Suppose you want to download the file profiled in Figure 17-2. At CompuServe's Enter choice! prompt, type **dow ataxx.cpt** and press Return. CompuServe responds with a menu of available file-transfer protocols. Choose the desired protocol. Depending on the protocol you chose, you may have to tell your program to begin receiving the file — generally by choosing a Receive File command or clicking a corresponding button or icon.

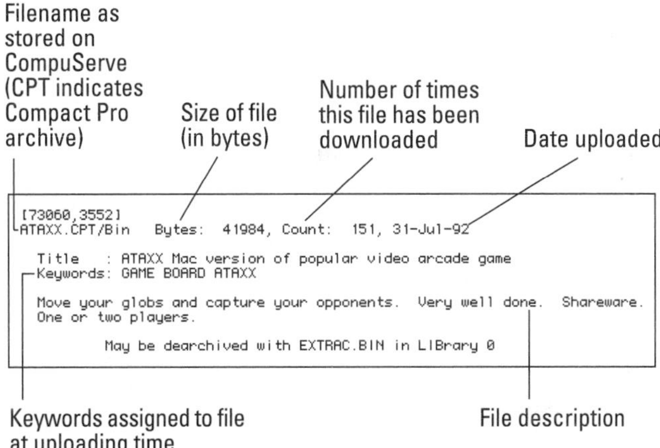

Figure 17-2: Deciphering Descriptions A typical CompuServe file description.

Tips for America Online Downloading

Accessing CompuServe by using a general-purpose communications program means typing your way through a maze of text menus. CIM streamlines the process, but it's still clunky compared to America Online.

Browsing AOL's software libraries

As with CompuServe, you can locate files on America Online by visiting each forum or by using a file-search feature. To jump directly to the software libraries, choose Keyword from the Go To menu (or press **⌘-K)**, type **quickfind**, and then click OK. The file-finder window appears (see Figure 17-3 "Finding on America Online").

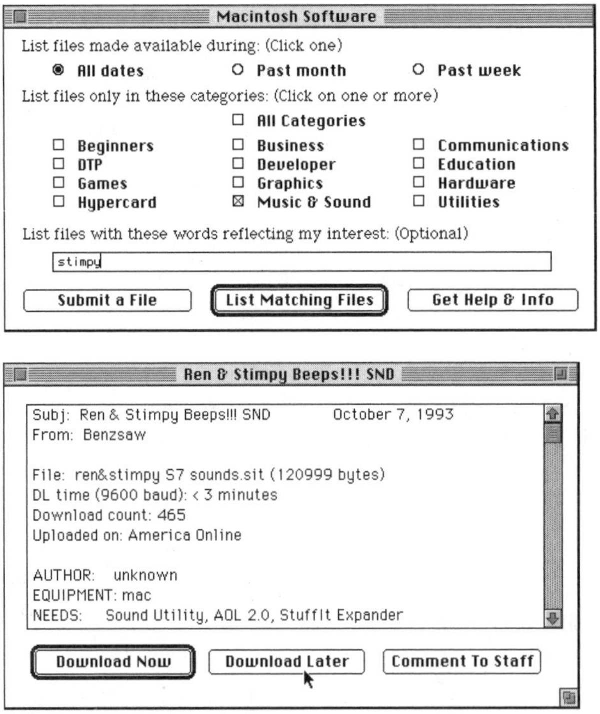

Figure 17-3: Finding on America Online America Online's file finder makes locating files easy. If you're on the prowl (top) for digitized Ren & Stimpy sounds, note the keyword. The File List window in the background (bottom) lists files located by the file finder. Double-clicking an entry opens another window that contains a description of the file and a button for downloading it.

Finding the most popular downloads

America Online also offers fast access to the most popular downloads. In the Macintosh Software Center window, click the Macintosh Top Downloads icon to display a window of the current month's most popular downloads.

If a given file sounds interesting, double-click its entry to display a description window (again see Figure 17-3 "Finding on America Online"). The description window tells you how long the file will take to download at the connection speed you're using.

To download the file, click the description window's Download File button and then specify a location for the file. America Online lets you know how much time downloading should take, and when it's done, a digitized voice announces, "File's done."

Deferring downloads: the Download Manager

America Online also lets you mark a group of files for deferred downloading. Instead of having to download files one at a time, simply select all the files you want, and America Online downloads them in one fell swoop.

To use the download manager, click the Download Later button in a file description dialog box. To begin the batch download, choose Download Manager from the File menu and use its options to specify where you want to store the files and to begin the actual downloading.

Tips for eWorld Downloading

Downloading from eWorld is very similar to downloading from America Online. eWorld even provides a deferred downloading feature, too. To mark a file for later downloading, click the Get File Later button that appears in a file description dialog box (see Figure 17-4 "Deferred Downloading in eWorld").

To begin a batch download, choose Files to Get from the File menu and use its options to specify where you want to store the files and to begin the actual downloading.

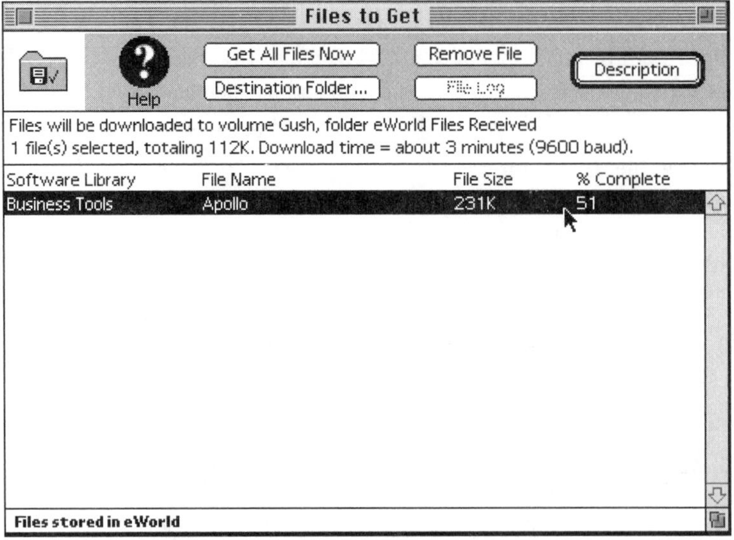

Figure 17-4: Deferred Downloading in eWorld eWorld's Files to Get window lets you download a batch of marked files in one step.

Pausing and Resuming Downloads in AOL and eWorld

eWorld and America Online let you pause or cancel a download and resume it later.

To pause a download on either service, click the Finish Later button that appears in the download progress dialog box.

To resume a paused or interrupted download, choose Files To Get from the eWorld's File menu or Download Manager from AOL's File menu. Next, double-click the file whose download you want to resume. (Notice that the window indicates the percentage of the file that was already received.)

When the file's description window appears on eWorld, click the Get File Now button or press Return. On AOL, click the Download Now button or press Return.

Decompressing Files after Downloading

After you download a program, you're probably dying to try it out. Hang on — you have to perform one more task.

Files that you download from an on-line service are stored in a compressed form that takes up less disk space and, more importantly, requires less time to upload and download. The person who uploaded the file used a file-compression utility such as Aladdin Systems' StuffIt series or Bill Goodman's Compact Pro to create what's often called an *archive* — a single disk file that contains one or more compressed files. Before you can try out the programs you've downloaded, you must decompress them to their original form.

Self-extracting archives

The compression utilities I just mentioned have the capability to create *self-extracting archives* — archive files that you can decompress without having to own a copy of the compression utility. These days, many programs and files available on information services arrive as self-extracting archives.

You can recognize a self-extracting archive by looking at its name; self-extracting archives usually have the characters *sea* tacked onto their names, as in "Great New Game.sea." Decompressing a self-extracting archive is easy: double-click its icon and then specify where you want to store the decompressed file or files.

Decompressing by hand

If the file's name ends with other characters, it probably isn't a self-extracting archive, and you need a copy of the compression utility (or a compatible one) to open and decompress the archive. Archives whose names end in *sit* were created with StuffIt: most files available on-line are either self-extracting archives or StuffIt archives.

You can decompress StuffIt files by using the shareware StuffIt Lite, which is available on-line as a self-extracting archive (it's also included on the CD-ROM that accompanies this book, as is Compact Pro.). If you don't want to pay the shareware fee, you can download StuffIt Expander, a free, stripped-down StuffIt that can decompress files but not compress them. A free, decompress-only version of Compact Pro is also available on-line. StuffIt Expander can also decompress Compact Pro and AppleLink archives.

AOL and eWorld can unstuff for you

America Online and eWorld also streamline the decompression process. They contain software that can automatically decompress StuffIt-format archives as soon as you sign off.

Final Tips for Downloading

The technicalities behind downloading can seem complicated at first, especially if you use text-oriented services like CompuServe. Just remember these tips:

- ❖ Make sure that your communication settings and transfer protocols match those of the service.
- ❖ Use the service's file-finding feature if it provides one — searching for a file based on keywords is a lot faster (and therefore cheaper) than rooting around for it by hand.
- ❖ Decompress your files after downloading them.

CHAPTER 17 CONCEPTS AND TERMS

Don't forget to pay shareware fees, even if you aren't a Grateful Dead fan.

- On-line services and bulletin board systems are bursting with megabytes of free or nearly free software as well as digitized sounds, scanned images, QuickTime movies, and technical support advice.
- Shareware is software that you can use at no cost for a limited amount of time. If you like a program, you send the author a small fee, which often entitles you to a printed manual and an update to the latest version.
- To ensure that software is transferred with no garbled bits, you use a file-transfer protocol when downloading files.
- Numerous file-transfer protocols exist. XMODEM MacBinary is the most common, but faster, more-capable protocols such as YMODEM and ZMODEM are rapidly supplanting it.

- CompuServe, eWorld, America Online, and other on-line services provide search features that let you locate downloadable files based on keywords, dates, categories, and other criteria.
- On-line services usually store files in a compressed form that requires less time to download. After you download a file, you have to decompress it by using a program such as StuffIt or Compact Pro.

blocks
The chunks in which a file is transferred under a file-transfer protocol such as XMODEM. The transmitting computer sends a block, compares notes with the receiving computer, and then either transmits the next block or resends the block until it's received accurately.

freeware
A program that's distributed free of charge. Freeware programs are often called *public-domain programs,* but the latter term is usually inaccurate; the freeware programmer still retains copyrights to the program, but he or she permits the program to be copied freely.

MacBinary
A format for protocol transfers that ensures the transfer of a file's unique Mac attributes: its data and resource forks (see Chapter 24's discussion of resources), icons, creation and modification dates, and so on. You generally want to use MacBinary protocol transfers when exchanging Mac files.

shareware
A program that's distributed on a try-before-you-buy basis. Try the program for a week or two, and if you decide to keep it, pay the author the requested fee.

CHAPTER EIGHTEEN

Optical Character Recognition

- Choosing a scanner and OCR software
- The six steps of scanning
- Improving OCR accuracy
- Scanning by hand

Every so often, you're reminded that the Mac is incompatible with the most widely used data-storage medium in the world — paper. This revelation may dawn when you have to laboriously retype a financial table from last year's annual report or spend hours pawing through magazines to locate something you read a few months ago. Wouldn't it be wonderful if you could apply the Mac's sorting, searching, and storing skills to the printed material that touches your life every day?

I have some good news and some bad news. The good news is that you can bridge the gap between the Mac and the printed page, thanks to *optical character recognition*, or OCR, software. When teamed with a scanner, OCR software lets a Mac read, or *recognize*, printed pages and create files containing their text. You can edit the resulting text, reformat it, run it through spelling checkers, save it, or paste it into databases or HyperCard stacks for quick searching. Pop a page into your scanner, click a button, and voilà — instant text, ready to be sliced and diced as you see fit.

The bad news is that it isn't as rosy as all that. Some OCR programs read certain kinds of text better than others, and to get the fastest, most accurate results, you need to match the program to the OCR task at hand. What's more, OCR software craves memory and processing power. Some low-end OCR programs run (albeit slowly) on Mac Pluses, Classics, and SEs, but extensive OCR work demands a fast Mac with plenty of memory.

Finally, OCR isn't a magic potion that automatically saves time and keystrokes. The best results come from practice and experience and still require careful proofreading. If you're compiling a digital library of text scanned from publications, you must develop an electronic filing system that lets you find what you've scanned. You also need a hard disk that can hold it all and a backup regimen to keep it safe. In this chapter, I describe how OCR programs work and include some tips for improving OCR accuracy.

Who Needs to Read?

OCR isn't a panacea, but it is useful. The following sections provide a sampling of OCR applications.

Printers and typesetters

A printing service bureau or typesetting company uses OCR for clients who submit copy on paper rather than on disk. Of course, proofreading is still essential — no matter how you use OCR — but not having to retype all that text can save you a lot of time and cut typesetting costs.

Lawyers

A law firm scans legal briefings and contracts that were produced before the office became computerized. Having those old documents on disk enables the firm to reuse sections of them as needed and allows for fast searching of client histories.

Brokers

A stock brokerage scans company prospectuses and pastes the numeric data into Microsoft Excel to generate graphs that show companies' financial statuses. The text from prospectuses and annual reports is pasted into a FileMaker Pro database that brokers can use to advise their clients.

Office librarians

An office that once distributed weekly photocopies of newspaper and trade-magazine clippings now scans them and stores the resulting text files on a network file server, where they are available to everyone. Employees can quickly search the electronic clippings and copy key sections for inclusion in reports or for distribution to others. The information is more accessible, and the office saves filing space as well as paper and photocopying costs. And cutting paper use benefits the environment as much as it does the bottom line.

Personnel specialists

A corporation's human resources department receives hundreds of resumes each day. They're scanned, and the resulting text is imported into a database manager, which sorts them into job categories and then creates a text file for each category. The resulting files are forwarded via electronic mail to appropriate personnel managers in offices across the country. No photocopying, no express courier charges, just increased efficiency.

Common denominators

These scenarios share a common thread — OCR used department-wide or company-wide, not at individual desks. That isn't to say that individuals can't benefit from OCR; they can if they have enough text to scan or their typing is bad enough. But given its cost and the time required to use it, OCR makes the most sense when a group of people can share its benefits — as they do with the office photocopier.

These scenarios also involve a variety of hard-copy originals, from manuscripts and contracts to resumes and magazine pages. Manuscripts and contracts aren't too tricky; they are often produced in a simple typewriter font such as Courier.

Magazine and newspaper pages are another matter. They can use just about any font and format, from justified left and right margins to irregularly shaped columns that wrap around a photograph or illustration. And resumes may be the ultimate formatting wild card. You never know what fonts you'll find, and you may receive a photocopy rather than an original. This variety of hard copy makes it important to match the OCR program to the scanning task at hand.

Six Steps to OCR

A typical OCR job has six phases. Each phase impacts the accuracy of the final product and also imposes its own demands on a scanner, an OCR program, and your skill as an OCR operator. What follows is an overview of the process along with comments on how some of today's top OCR packages — Xerox's Accu Text, Caere's OmniPage Professional and OmniPage Direct, and ExperVision's TypeReader — handles each phase. The Backgrounder box "Choosing OCR Software" summarizes the key issues to consider when shopping.

Setting up for the scan

At this stage, you specify details such as the scanning resolution (generally 300 dpi) and brightness. The OmniPage series and TypeReader also let you choose to retain or discard formatting such as italic or bold type. Some programs can also scan and separately save the graphics from an original document — handy when you're updating an old technical manual containing schematics and diagrams.

Scanning the original

An OCR program can't deliver accurate results without a high-quality image. Accuracy plummets if the scan is crooked or poor brightness adjustments create a muddy or washed-out image. An overly dark image causes problems because characters tend to touch and the hollow portions of round characters (such as *e*) tend to fill in. A washed-out image complicates recognition because fine character details are lost. For example, if the top and bottom of an *O* are lost, a program may misread the character as two parentheses ().

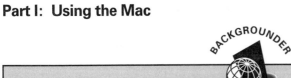

Choosing OCR Software

Here's a checklist of features to look for when shopping for OCR software:

- *Direct support* for your scanner lets you scan pages and recognize text by using just one program. If an OCR program cannot directly control your scanner, you need to scan pages by using the software that accompanies the scanner and then save them in a format that the OCR program can read — a time-consuming approach.
- A *built-in editor* lets you review and alter the resulting text without switching to a word processor. Search-and-replace commands are useful for correcting problems that occur throughout, such as when a *w* is read as two *v*s.
- *Format recognition* retains formatting attributes such as boldface, underlining, italics, centering, and justification. Some programs can also distinguish between multiple columns, enabling you to read them as a single table or as snaking (magazine-style) columns.
- *Support for multiple file formats* increases the odds that you'll be able to move recognized text into another application while retaining its formatting. Some programs can save documents in text-only format; others support popular word processing and spreadsheet formats.
- A *spelling checker* helps with (but doesn't eliminate) proofreading. Some OCR programs provide spelling checkers that are tuned to look for substitution and other typical OCR-oriented errors.
- *Graphics recognition* lets you save the graphics that appear in an original document. This feature can be useful when, for example, you're producing a new version of a printed manual containing illustrations.
- *Background operation* lets the OCR program decipher a page while you work in another application. Some programs also offer a *batch mode* that lets you scan a stack of pages but defer the actual recognition process until a later time.
- *Landscape support* lets you scan documents printed in landscape orientation (for example, 11 x 8½ instead of 8½ x 11).

A relatively recent development addresses the need for a high-quality image. Hewlett-Packard's AccuPage technology, supported by scanners from HP and other firms, automatically adjusts brightness during the scan for optimum results (see Figure 18-1 "Bringing Type Out of the Background").

Most programs support the *automatic document feeder* (ADF) attachments that are available for many flatbed scanners (but not for Apple's). TextBridge, OmniPage Pro, and TypeReader even enable you to scan double-sided originals: First run the odd-numbered pages through the ADF and then scan the even-numbered ones, and these programs automatically put the pages in the correct order.

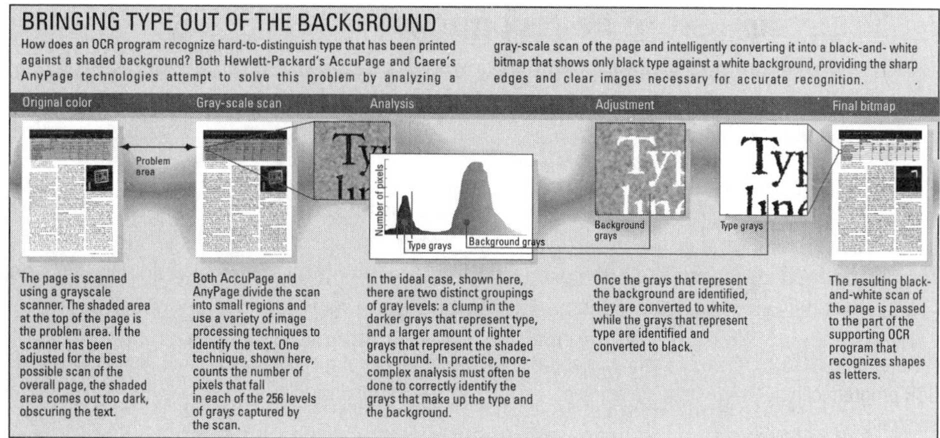

How does an OCR program recognize hard-to-distinguish type that has been printed against a shaded background? Both Hewlett-Packard's AccuPage and Caere's AnyPage technologies attempt to solve this problem by analyzing a gray-scale scan of the page and intelligently converting it into a black-and- white bitmap that shows only black type against a white background, providing the sharp edges and clear images necessary for accurate recognition.

| Original color | Gray-scale scan | Analysis | Adjustment | Final bitmap |

The page is scanned using a grayscale scanner. The shaded area at the top of the page is the problem area. If the scanner has been adjusted for the best possible scan of the overall page, the shaded area comes out too dark, obscuring the text.

Both AccuPage and AnyPage divide the scan into small regions and use a variety of image processing techniques to identify the text. One technique, shown here, counts the number of pixels that fall in each of the 256 levels of grays captured by the scan.

In the ideal case, shown here, there are two distinct groupings of gray levels: a clump in the darker grays that represent type, and a larger amount of lighter grays that represent the shaded background. In practice, more-complex analysis must often be done to correctly identify the grays that make up the type and the background.

Once the grays that represent the background are identified, they are converted to white, while the grays that represent type are identified and converted to black.

The resulting black-and-white scan of the page is passed to the part of the supporting OCR program that recognizes shapes as letters.

Figure 18-1: Bringing Type Out of the Background

The Twain Shall Meet After All

Perhaps the best news for OCR (and for scanning in general) is that software developers and scanner manufacturers are edging toward a standard set of commands for controlling scanners, video frame grabbers, and other graphic input devices. A specification called Twain enables software developers to create programs that let you scan from directly within a program such as Adobe PageMaker.

Instead of having to run a separate OCR program and then save the recognized text as a word processor file, you can choose a command such as Scan or Acquire directly within any program that supports Twain. The resulting text then appears directly in your application. Twain also supports image scanning, of course. (The specification's name derives from the phrase "never the twain shall meet" — a phrase that seems all too true when you're struggling to get a given software package to work with one of today's primitive scanner drivers.)

Twain makes it possible for software developers to support a variety of scanners without having to create and test a driver for each one, and for customers to use their scanners with a wide variety of applications without struggling with incompatible drivers. In theory, if both a scanner and an application program support Twain, they can work together. Some Mac software developers who are riding the Twain bandwagon include Adobe, Caere, LightSource (which develops Ofoto, the scanning software included with Apple's OneScanner), and Kodak. Participating hardware developers include Hewlett-Packard, Agfa, Logitech, Ricoh, and Howtek. The specification also works under the Microsoft Windows environment.

Selecting text to be recognized

If you're scanning a complex multicolumn page, you need to tell the OCR program which columns you want to recognize and in what order. All programs provide a marquee tool that enables you to select the areas, or *zones*, that you want to recognize (see Figure 18-2 "Zoning in Progress").

Instead of manually selecting zones, you may prefer to rely on a program's automatic zoning or *page decomposition* feature, where the program looks for areas of horizontal and vertical white space to differentiate columns and text blocks. But problems can arise. The sidebars and captions in a magazine or newspaper page can wind up interspersed with the main text. A program may try to recognize the text in a letterhead when you want only the letter's contents. Or it may try to treat the columns in a table as newspaper-style snaking columns, recognizing each column separately from top to bottom instead of reading across each row.

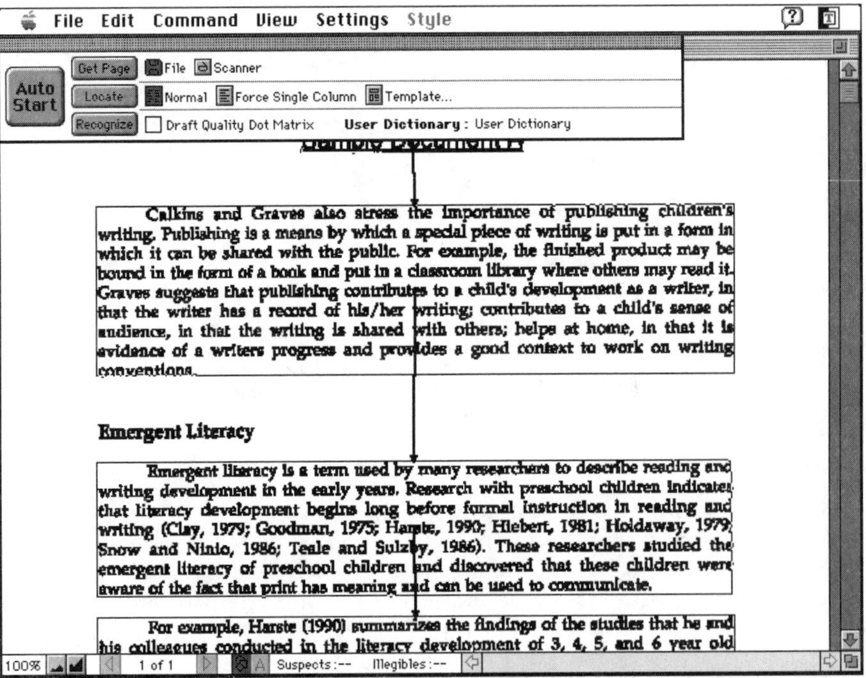

Figure 18-2: Zoning in Progress Most programs let you specify which zones you want to recognize and in what order. Here, three zones have been defined and linked in TextBridge. If you used automatic zoning for this page, the figure captions in the middle column would end up in the middle of the text.

To work around these problems, most programs let you indicate which zones you want to recognize and in what order. Most programs also let you save templates that describe the zone boundaries for a specific page layout. This feature can be a big time-saver if you frequently scan the same page design.

Recognizing

Recognizing is the main event. When deciphering the bitmapped image from the scanner, an OCR program employs complex shape-analysis techniques to differentiate the components that make a character unique.

TextBridge and the OmniPage series also provide *training* features that you can use to teach the program to recognize unusual typefaces, special symbols, or defective or poorly scanned characters (see Figure 18-3 "Literacy Lesson"). A separate class of programs used to require training to read anything other than a small range of sizes and fonts. Today's programs are of the *omnifont* variety, able to recognize a wide range of sizes and fonts.

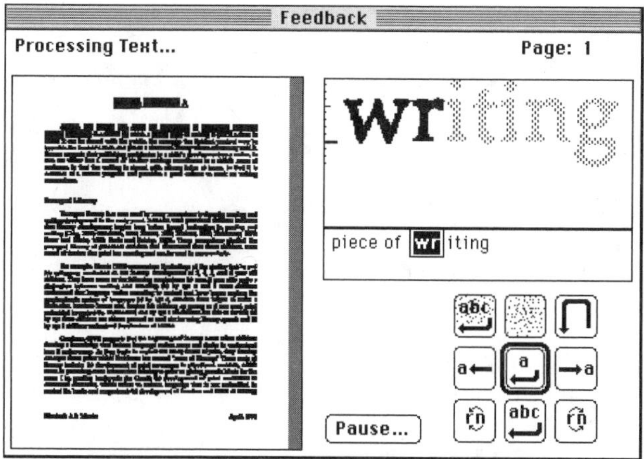

Figure 18-3: Literacy Lesson Using TextBridge's verifier window to improve accuracy.

Some programs offer special recognition options. *Deferred recognition* lets you scan a stack of pages but postpone the recognition process until a convenient time — such as after you've gone home. *Background recognition* relies on the MacOS's multitasking features to let you switch to a different program while recognition occurs behind the scenes. That option sounds appealing, but it's practical only if you have a fast Mac and at least 8MB of memory, preferably more. Even then, your Mac may slow unacceptably as it juggles tasks.

Proofreading and polishing

Most programs display recognized text in a window where you can make corrections. Characters such as an at sign (@), bullet (•), or tilde (~) indicate misread characters. (You can specify a different character in case your original happens to contain a raft of at signs or tildes.) By searching for these symbols, you can quickly locate obvious errors.

OCR errors can confound a word processor's spelling checker because they differ from conventional typographical errors. To address this problem, most programs provide spelling checkers geared toward OCR-oriented blunders. Xerox and Caere also sell foreign-language dictionaries, and Caere sells medical and legal dictionaries.

OmniPage Professional has the best editing features. Besides enabling you to change fonts, sizes, and styles, its editing window has a ruler for specifying alignment and creating and adjusting tabs, margins, and first-line and hanging indents. You can also display a portion of the scanned page's bitmap to correct an error manually (see Figure 18-4 "Check the Original"). Many programs provide a similar feature.

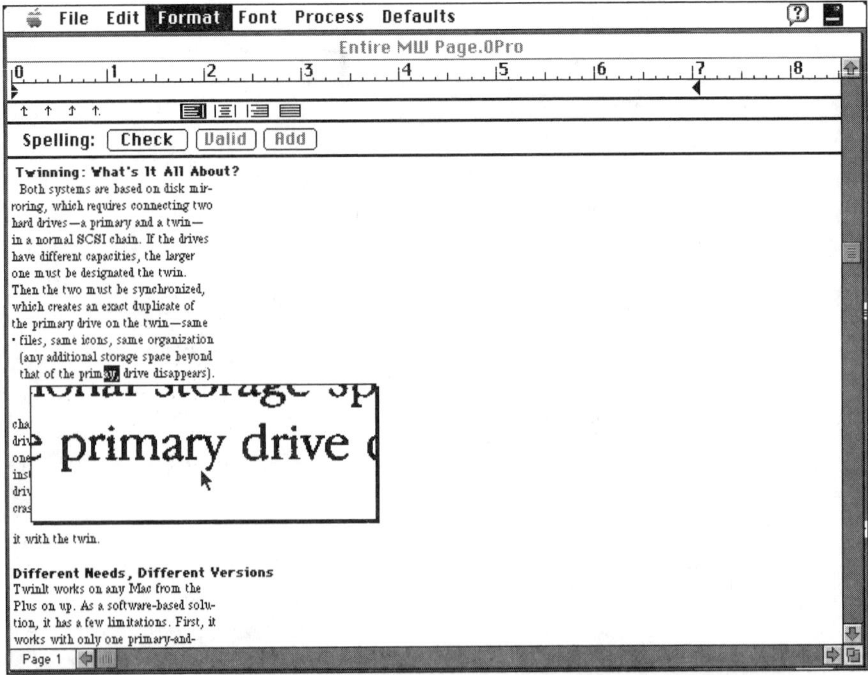

Figure 18-4: Check the Original OmniPage Professional is among the programs that let you display the original bitmap for a section of a document. By doing so, you can see where the program has stumbled and determine how to manually correct the error. (Here, you can see that the touching r and y caused OmniPage Professional to misread the y as a y followed by a comma.) Also, note the wide range of formatting features provided by OmniPage Professional's text-editing window.

Saving the file

Programs that can retain formatting information let you save recognized text in a variety of popular word processor formats. Many programs also support database- and spreadsheet-oriented formats such as SYLK.

How OCR Programs Work

To turn pixels into pages, OCR programs employ a battery of complex analysis techniques (see Figure 18-5 "OCR Approaches Compared"). With the simplest recognition technique, *matrix matching*, the program compares each character to a library of templates, also called *type tables* or *matrices*, for specific fonts and type sizes. Think of those tests where kids insert different-shaped pegs into matching holes in a pegboard. Now imagine the OCR program trying to insert each character it has scanned into a hole shaped like a letter, number, or other symbol. When a character seems to fit a particular hole, the OCR program calls it a match.

Teaching your OCR program to read

Programs that offer training modes let you create your own digital pegboards for new fonts as you encounter them. But *trainable* means that you train it, and that means work. It may take only a few minutes to train a program to read a document with one or two fonts, but it can take an hour or two to teach it to read a typical magazine page. The program can apply its newfound knowledge to future documents, but that's no consolation if you never scan those fonts and sizes again.

Still, a training mode is ideal for some applications. Consider a manuscript produced on a typewriter that types a defective character — for example, an *e* whose crossbar always prints too lightly. An automatic program will probably always misidentify the character as a *c*, but a you can teach a trainable program to recognize it. Trainable programs are also well suited to large projects that involve a lot of scanning, such as books or catalogs. The program is finely tuned to the fonts at hand, which can boost performance and accuracy.

The omnifont advantage

Automatic, or *omnifont*, programs such as OmniPage Professional and TypeReader use a whole bag of recognition tricks to read just about any font and type size. With one such technique, *feature extraction*, the program studies the shape of a character's components — its stems, loops, bowls, and so on — and compares them to the program's internal knowledge of letterforms. For example, if an automatic program sees a character with a vertical stem that descends below the baseline and has a loop attached to its upper-right side, the program knows that it's found a *p*. There are significant variations between fonts — some have ornamental serifs, and some have heavier stems than others — but generalized descriptions like this one apply to all characters.

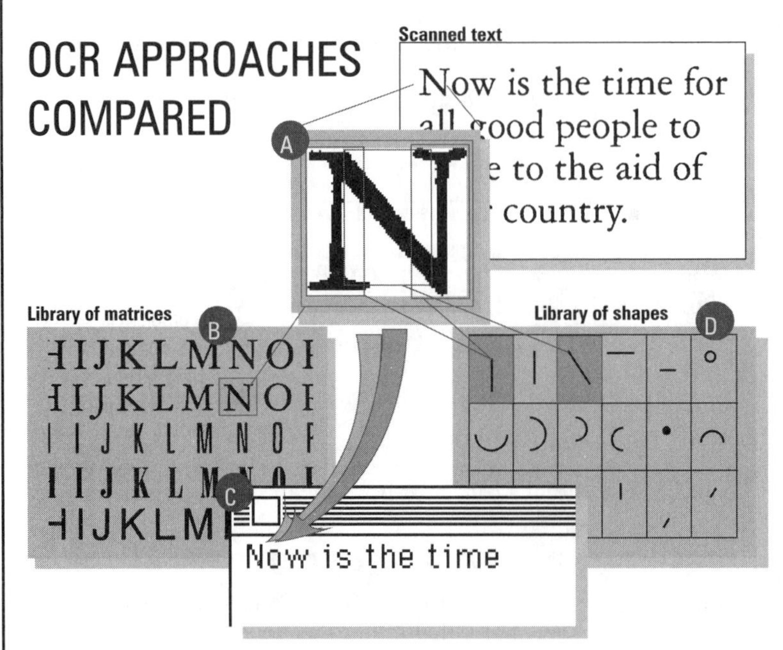

Matrix-matching and automatic, or omnifont, programs use different techniques for recognizing text. Matrix-matching compares a given character (A)—here, a capital N—to a library of matrices (B), each for a different font and type size. When a match is found, the character is added to the new document (C).

Feature extraction, one of the text-recognition techniques used by automatic programs, compares the components of the character (A) for the *N*, two vertical lines and a diagonal line, to a library of shapes (D). The program then determines the character based on its features and their relative positions.

Figure 18-5: OCR Approaches Compared

Some typefaces bend these rules, and poor-quality documents make them difficult to enforce. In such cases, an automatic program may resort to additional techniques such as *topographical analysis*, which examines the character's shape for recognizable characteristics, and *context recognition* (also called *context intelligence)*, which uses built-in rules and dictionaries that know, for example, that when the program recognizes *q*, the next character is likely to be *u*.

QUICK TIPS

Improving OCR Accuracy

You can improve your OCR accuracy by following the guidelines outlined here. Some of these tips are based on the advice from the first-rate manual that accompanies ExperVision's TypeReader.

Keep the scanner clean

Spots and streaks on the scanner's glass can translate into recognition errors. Check your scanner's manual for recommendations of cleaning solutions and techniques.

Position the original carefully

If the original document is crooked, accuracy can suffer along with recognition speed. Your OCR program is also likely to have trouble decomposing the page into columns and paragraphs. If the text is straight on the page, use the scanner's guides to ensure that the page is positioned properly. If the text itself is crooked, adjust the paper so that the text is scanned in straight. After scanning, use the OCR program's preview window to determine whether the text lines are straight. If they aren't, tweak the paper's position and try again.

Remove markings on pages

Handwritten notes on pages can slow down recognition. If the notes overlap the text, they can cause recognition errors. Use correction fluid to paint over markings. But avoid using correction fluid near the text itself: you may make the problem even worse. If you don't want to paint correction fluid on the original document, make a photocopy, touch it up, and then scan the copy.

Coping with thin paper

Thin paper, such as newsprint, is translucent. The scanner's bright light may cause the type on the back side of the page to show through and become part of the page image, which can impair performance and accuracy.

One way to fix this problem is to use the OCR program's brightness control to turn down brightness. Another technique is to put a couple of sheets of white paper on top of the page you're scanning.

Dealing with dot-matrix output

Some OCR programs provide an option for reading dot-matrix printer output, where the dots that form each letter often don't touch. If your program doesn't provide a dot-matrix option, try photocopying the original and scanning it. The photocopying process can cause the dots to blend together, thereby improving accuracy.

Adjust brightness carefully

Use your OCR program's brightness settings to adjust the scanner so that the resulting page image is as crisp and clear as possible. If the scan is too dark, characters such as *o* and *e* fill in. If the scan is too light, thin portions of characters become lost, and an *O* becomes ().

Create a user dictionary

If your program lets you add words to its spelling dictionary, do so. You spend less time cleaning up the resulting document.

Scanning the Field

I've said little about the hardware half of the OCR equation — the scanner, which uses a mechanism similar to a photocopier or fax machine to examine a page and create a digital image of its contents. I examine scanner technology in detail in Chapter 13, but from an image-scanning, not an OCR, perspective. For now, here's a quick look at the field:

❖ *Flatbed scanners* such as the Apple OneScanner series look like small copiers, with a lid covering a piece of glass upon which you lay the original document. Flatbed scanners can accommodate books and other originals too thick to fit through a sheetfed scanner's rollers. For accuracy, it's important to keep the glass spotless. As mentioned elsewhere in this chapter, many scanners accept automatic document feeders, which hold a stack of pages and feed them to the scanner as needed — useful for high-volume OCR work.

❖ *Handheld,* or *hand, scanners* are small boxes that you can roll across an original page. Costing only a few hundred dollars, hand scanners are inexpensive but have limitations. You need to move the scanner at a slow and steady pace — about an inch per second — to get good results, and you can scan only a few inches of a document at a time (see the Backgrounder box "Reading by Hand").

Adjusting Your Expectations

When shopping for an OCR system, take along several test documents, preferably ones similar to the documents you plan to scan. Don't take only war-torn, barely legible documents in an attempt to stump the OCR software — you'll succeed. If you have trouble reading a page, an OCR program will, too. That's especially true if the document contains fine print: OCR programs have more trouble with it than I do.

Advice for accuracy

After you scan a test page, proofread it carefully. Some errors are easy to spot: A capital *D*, for example, can be misread as a vertical bar followed by a parenthesis |). And the OCR program itself flags characters it doesn't recognize, usually by substituting an at sign (@), bullet (•), or tilde (~).

Substitution errors are the hardest to find. A *w* can become *vv*, an *m* can become *rn*, *S* can become *5*, and an italic *h* can become a *b* — to name only several ways OCR programs can suffer from mistaken identity. In one document I scanned, OmniPage turned PS/2 (a model of IBM personal computer) into P512. Catching that kind of blunder requires a watchful and experienced eye. Anyone who is unfamiliar with IBM computers may not know that P512 isn't a valid model number. And every field — from law to medicine to plumbing — has these kinds of specialized terms and ciphers.

Reading by Hand

If you can't justify or afford a flatbed scanner, consider a handheld scanner such as Caere's OmniScan, Logitech's ScanMan Model 32, or Thunderware's LightningScan Pro. Hand scanners look like huge mice and roll across an original document, scanning in swaths about four inches wide. And therein lies one rub: to scan text columns (or images) wider than the scanner, you must make multiple passes and then use the scanner's *stitching* feature to attach the swaths.

Getting a high-quality scan from a hand scanner can be a challenge. You must be careful to move the scanner steadily — about an inch per second — and not skew the image by tilting the scanner to the left or right (see "Getting the Best Scan by Hand", below). Scanning a page from a book or magazine is complicated by the binding (the manual for the OmniScan actually suggests that you tear pages out to scan them). And although the scanners themselves are small, they require external SCSI interfaces and power adapters, so they aren't practical PowerBook companions.

A hand scanner can be a workable alternative if you usually scan narrow columns or images anyway. Thunderware's LightningScan Pro comes with Olduvai's ReadIt as well as a gray-scale image-editing program. Logitech bundles CatchWord Pro with the ScanMan, while Caere's OmniScan includes Caere's OmniPage Direct and Image Assistant GS for gray-scale image editing.

For OCR work, Caere's OmniScan is the best of the bunch. If you scan carefully, you can get OmniPage-caliber accuracy. OmniScan is also the only package that can insert recognized text directly into an application.

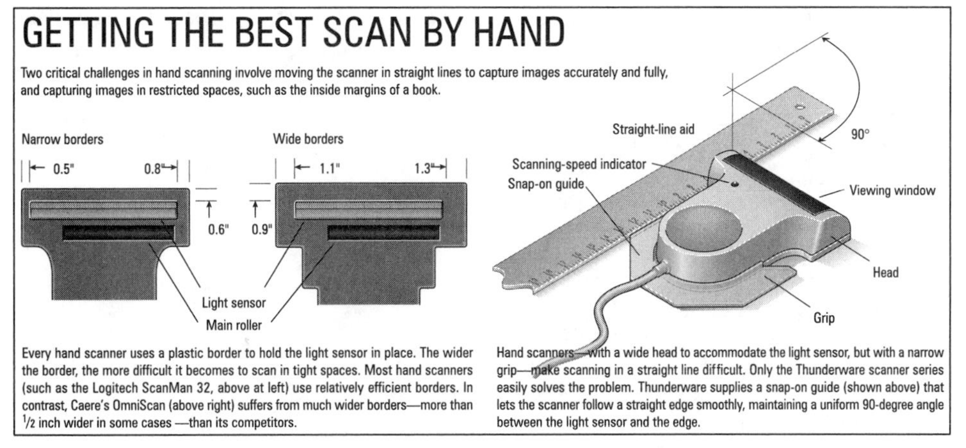

Every hand scanner uses a plastic border to hold the light sensor in place. The wider the border, the more difficult it becomes to scan in tight spaces. Most hand scanners (such as the Logitech ScanMan 32, above at left) use relatively efficient borders. In contrast, Caere's OmniScan (above right) suffers from much wider borders—more than 1/2 inch wider in some cases —than its competitors.

Hand scanners—with a wide head to accommodate the light sensor, but with a narrow grip—make scanning in a straight line difficult. Only the Thunderware scanner series easily solves the problem. Thunderware supplies a snap-on guide (shown above) that lets the scanner follow a straight edge smoothly, maintaining a uniform 90-degree angle between the light sensor and the edge.

The moral? No OCR program is 100-percent accurate, regardless of its developer's claims. But no typist is 100 percent accurate, either. If you approach OCR with the knowledge that the results will not be perfect and require careful proofreading, you won't be disappointed.

I'm still swimming in paper

I'm sold on the keystroke-saving benefits of OCR, but I haven't made it a part of my day-to-day business life. I once fantasized about scanning all the press releases that litter my office, but I soon realized that it would take far too long to be practical. A handheld scanner may streamline the process by enabling me to scan just the portions of a press release that interest me, but as I mentioned before, hand scanners are usually second-best OCR devices.

As mentioned in the Background box "Reading by Hand," Caere Corporation's OmniScan is a hand scanner designed for OCR. OmniScan isn't as finicky about speed as other hand scanners and, better still, OmniScan inserts the text it reads directly into whatever application you're using — no grappling with a separate OCR program, and no cutting and pasting or fussing with file formats to move text into the program where it will ultimately be used. (OmniPage Direct has this advantage, too.)

It sounds appealing, but don't believe it until you see it in action with the types of documents you plan to scan. Indeed, that's a good way to approach OCR in general — believe it when you see it. And when you proofread it.

CHAPTER 18 CONCEPTS AND TERMS

- OCR software and a scanner enable the Mac to read, or recognize, printed pages and create files containing their text.
- Most OCR programs can retain formatting such as bold and italic as well as type-size information. You need a fast Mac with at least 5MB of memory for good performance, however.
- A typical OCR job has six phases — scanner setup (adjust brightness and resolution settings, specify format retention and page-decomposition modes); scanning (generate a bitmapped image of a page); text selection (specify which portion of a page you want to recognize); recognition (sit back while the OCR program deciphers the text); clean-up (proofread and polish the resulting text file); and saving (store the recognized text in the desired file format).
- The scanner is the hardware half of the OCR equation. It uses a mechanism not too different from that of a photocopier or fax machine to examine a page and create a bitmapped image of its contents. Flatbed scanners can scan pages from books, magazines, and other bulky originals. Most scanners accept automatic document feeders that streamline multipage jobs. Handheld scanners roll across a page and scan in narrow swaths; they're economical but finicky.

background recognition
An OCR program feature that relies on System 7 or System 6 MultiFinder to let you switch to a different program while recognition occurs behind the scenes.

context recognition
Also called *context intelligence,* a recognition technique that uses built-in rules and dictionaries that know, for example, that if the program recognizes a *q,* the next character is likely to be a *u.*

deferred recognition
An OCR program feature that lets you scan a stack of pages but postpone the recognition process until a convenient time.

feature extraction
A recognition technique in which the program studies the shape of a character's components — its stems, loops, bowls, and so forth — and compares them to the program's internal knowledge of letterforms.

matrix matching
A recognition technique that compares each scanned character to a library of templates.

omnifont
A term sometimes applied to OCR programs that can recognize a wide range of sizes and fonts.

page decomposition
An OCR program feature in which the program looks for areas of horizontal and vertical white space to differentiate columns and text blocks.

recognition
The phase of an OCR job in which the program examines the scanned version of a page and deciphers its contents.

substitution error
A hard-to-find type of OCR error in which the program substitutes one or more characters for another: for example, *w* can become *vv, m* can become *rn, S* can become *5,* and an italic *h* can become a *b.*

training
Teaching an OCR program to recognize unusual typefaces, special symbols, or defective or poorly scanned characters.

Twain
A standard that enables you to scan directly into a program. Instead of having to run a separate OCR program and then save the recognized text as a word processor file, you can choose a command such as Scan or Acquire directly within any program that supports Twain. The resulting text then appears directly in your application. Twain also supports image scanning.

zoning
The process of telling the OCR program which columns you want to recognize and in what order.

CHAPTER NINETEEN

HyperCard

- Looking at HyperCard's versatility and possibilities
- Designing effective HyperCard stacks
- Customizing HyperCard
- Creating stacks that run without HyperCard

HyperCard defies simple definition. Call it a database manager, and you short-shrift its MacPaint-like painting features. Call it a paint program, and you ignore its capability to store and retrieve information. HyperCard isn't educational software or a game, but it can educate and entertain. It isn't part of the Mac's System Folder, but like the Finder, it can start applications and open documents. It isn't a programming language, but it has introduced thousands of people to the fun and frustration of programming.

Appreciating HyperCard's versatility is easier if you consider the code name it bore during its gestation — WildCard. In poker, a wildcard can represent any card and can make a winning hand. Similarly, HyperCard can be sculpted into nearly any kind of application, thus rounding out your computing toolbox.

In this chapter, I examine this software wildcard and spotlight some of the stellar ways in which you can use HyperCard. For those who haven't gone beyond browsing around in HyperCard, I include a short exercise that introduces customizing basics.

The Three Keys to HyperCard

Three factors combine to give HyperCard its wildcard versatility — its card-and-stack metaphor, its painting features, and its built-in programming language, *HyperTalk*.

Cards and stacks

HyperCard presents and stores information on cards. In an electronic address book, for example, each person's name and address is stored on its own card. Cards that accept information from you contain *fields*, each of which stores a piece of information, such as a name or phone number. A card can also contain *buttons* — hot spots you click to perform an action, such as moving to a different card for more information. A collection of related cards — such as all the cards in the address book — forms a *stack* (see Figure 19-1 "Fields, Cards, and Stacks"). You can have numerous stacks open simultaneously; each appears in its own window.

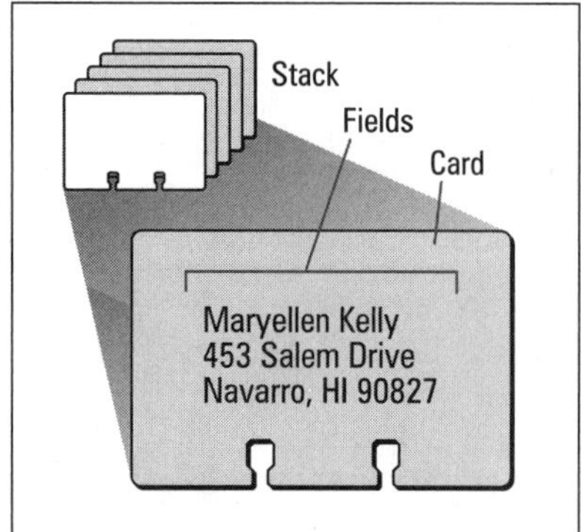

Figure 19-1: Fields, Cards, and Stacks
HyperCard presents and stores information on cards. Cards that accept information from you contain fields. A collection of related cards forms a stack.

A card can be up to 18 inches tall or wide. (In HyperCard 1.*x*, card sizes were fixed to match the size of a 9-inch Macintosh screen.) You specify card dimensions in the dialog box that appears when you choose New Stack from the File menu.

Painting and graphics tools

HyperCard's painting tools are similar to the ones provided by all painting (bitmapped) programs — besides the electronic eraser, pencil, and spray can, there are tools for creating rectangles, ovals, lines, and text. You can create text and graphics on individual cards or on backgrounds, which appear beneath cards in a stack (see Figure 19-2 "In the Background").

You can also paste graphics from the Clipboard to create a scrapbook of drawings — or to store a scanned photo of each person listed in your address book. HyperCard 2.0 and later versions also enable you to display color PICT images in separate windows.

HyperCard's color and multimedia features

HyperCard started life in a black-and-white world, but its color and multimedia features have been improving steadily (if slowly). HyperCard 2.3 provides the best color and multimedia support of any HyperCard version to date. For starters, HyperCard 2.3 provides 24-bit painting features; in previous HyperCard versions, you had to create 24-bit images in a separate painting program and then import them — a process HyperCard 2.3 still allows.

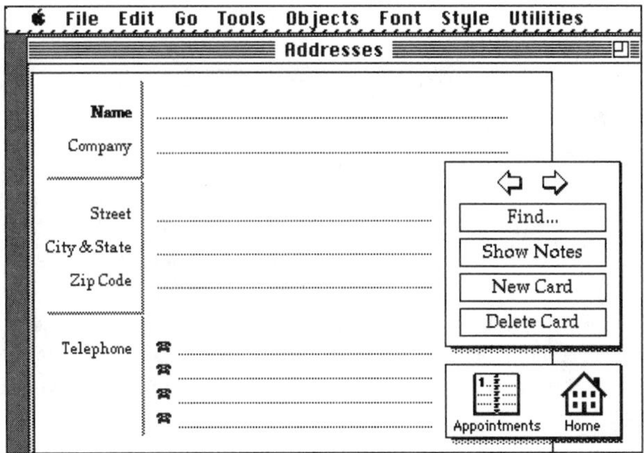

Figure 19-2: In the Background A stack's background holds fields, graphics, and buttons that appear on every card (in this case, HyperCard's Addresses stack). To view a stack's background, choose Background from the Edit menu. HyperCard displays stripes in the menu bar to indicate that you're working with the background.

As for multimedia, HyperCard's QuickTime Tools stack lets you add QuickTime movies to stacks. (I used HyperCard to create the *Macworld Power User Clinic* CD-ROM bundled with this book.) HyperCard can also play digital sounds, and version 2.3 can even read text aloud using Apple's PlainTalk software (see the Backgrounder box "What's New in HyperCard 2.3?").

What's New in HyperCard 2.3?

For years, people have been predicting HyperCard's demise, but Apple has been proving them wrong. (Creative third-party developers have helped — the best-selling CD-ROM title of all time, Myst, was developed in HyperCard.)

HyperCard 2.3, released in the spring of 1995, provides a welcome array of improvements.

- ❖ **Color painting tools** Finally, you can create 24-bit color images without having to use a separate paint program.
- ❖ **Power Mac support** HyperCard 2.2 introduced a significant new feature: the ability to save stacks as stand-alone application programs that anyone could run without having to own HyperCard. HyperCard 2.3 builds on this strength by enabling you to create stand-alones that run in native mode on Power Macs. The section "Turning Stacks into Applications," later in this chapter, contains more details on creating stand-alone applications.

(continued on the next page)

(continued from previous page)

- **Button tasks** Think of these as templates that enable you to create buttons without having to do any programming. With button tasks, you can create buttons that, when clicked, go to other cards, play QuickTime movies or sounds, launch another program, apply visual effects, or read text aloud using PlainTalk.
- **PlainTalk support** HyperCard 2.3 supports Apple's PlainTalk text-to-speech technology, enabling you to create stacks that read aloud. This makes possible some slick educational applications, such as stacks that teach a foreign language.
- **Bundled multimedia utilities** HyperCard 2.3 includes several multimedia utilities from Motion Works. The bundle includes AddMotion II, an animation program, and Multimedia Utilities, a collection of programs for QuickTime movie editing, sound recording and editing, and morphing. (See Chapter 20 for the good news and bad news about Multimedia Utilities.)

Tying it together with HyperTalk

HyperTalk ties HyperCard's features together. By creating HyperTalk *scripts* — short command sequences that control HyperCard's actions — you determine how a stack responds to its users. A script for a button named Next may tell HyperCard to advance to the next card when you click the button. A script for a field named Date may tell HyperCard to display an error message if someone enters an invalid date, such as February 31. You can also design HyperCard scripts to control videodisc players, CD-ROM drives, and music synthesizers, or to play digitally recorded sound (see Figure 19-3 "Hearing HyperCard"). I spotlight some of these advanced applications of HyperCard when I examine multimedia in the next chapter.

A complete HyperCard stack — be it a business-management application, a children's story, or an introduction to bird anatomy — makes extensive use of the three elements I just described. The stack's cards use text and graphics to convey information. The cards may also use fields to display information or accept new information and buttons for moving to other cards, playing QuickTime movies, or otherwise controlling the stack. Behind the scenes, HyperTalk scripts define each button's action, calculate numbers, display messages, produce sound, play movies, and do whatever else the stack requires.

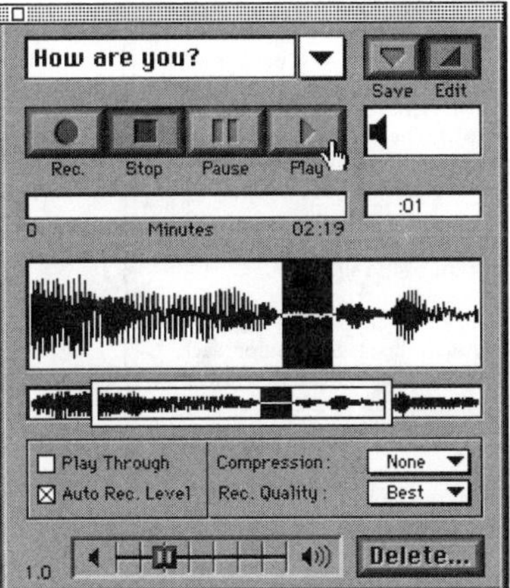

Figure 19-3: Hearing HyperCard The easiest way to record sounds for playback in HyperCard is to use a Mac that includes sound-recording circuitry and a microphone. These Macs include the HyperCard Audio Palette (shown here), which lets you add sounds to HyperCard stacks. For other Macs, you can use Macromedia's MacRecorder Sound System Pro — its SoundEdit application lets you record sounds and modify them by using numerous digital effects. For more ambitious applications of digital audio, The Voyager Company's Voyager CD AudioStack enables HyperCard to play audio from a compact disc in a CD-ROM drive. With the tools in the AudioStack, you can create HyperCard stacks that incorporate the audio from a CD. See Chapter 21 for more details about Mac audio products.

From the Obvious to the Subtle

If HyperCard provided only fields, stored graphics, and contained a programming language, it would be no different than many Mac database managers. What makes HyperCard different is the myriad ways in which its components can work together. Everything in HyperCard seems to have obvious applications and subtle ones.

Making hot spots with transparent buttons

Take buttons, for example. Their obvious use is to provide icons for moving to the next or the preceding card and for returning to the *Home stack.* (The Home stack serves as your base of operations in HyperCard — just as the Finder does for the Mac.) Navigation buttons often appear as icons and always have HyperTalk scripts that run when you click the buttons (see Figure 19-4 "Navigation Buttons").

You can specify that a button have no icon or text but be *transparent.* By placing transparent buttons over key portions of a graphic, you can define a relationship between each area of the graphic and other cards, fields, or stacks. Thereafter, when you click a portion of the graphic, HyperCard takes you to a different card or stack.

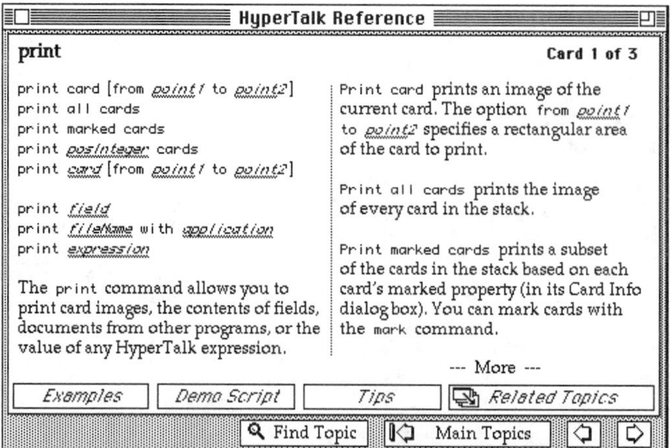

Figure 19-4: Navigation Buttons In this HyperTalk Reference stack, you use navigation buttons to access information about the HyperTalk language. The buttons at the bottom of the window let you display examples and related topics, search for topics, and move to the next and preceding cards.

Many educational stacks use this technique. One superb example is Bird Anatomy, a stack created by Yale University's Patrick Lynch and published by The Voyager Company (an earlier version of Bird Anatomy is available through user groups and on-line services). This stack combines beautifully drawn images with transparent buttons that, when clicked, display additional details about avian anatomy (see Figure 19-5 "See-Through Buttons").

I used see-through buttons throughout the *Macworld Power User Clinic* that accompanies this book. For example, in the "Meet the Mac" segment, there's a transparent button behind each component — monitor, keyboard, mouse, and so on — in the illustration.

Realizing the hidden power of fields

Fields also have their obvious and subtle uses. As in any database manager, they accept and store information. But they can also serve a read-only role — displaying text you can't edit. You can also display or hide them by using HyperTalk scripts. Combine both traits with buttons, and you have another way to convey information — *pop-up fields* that appear when you click a button (see Figure 19-6 "Pop-Up Fields").

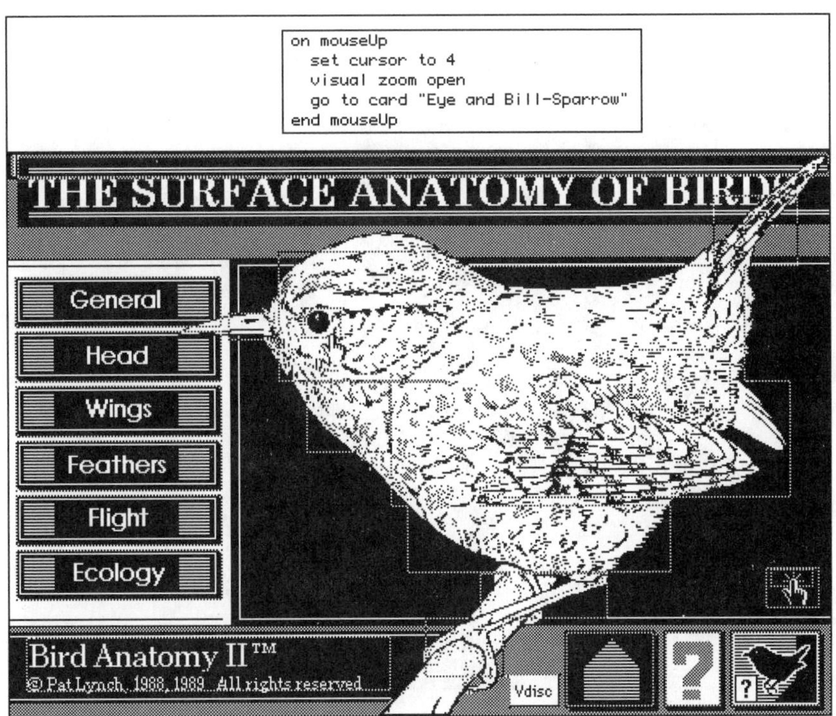

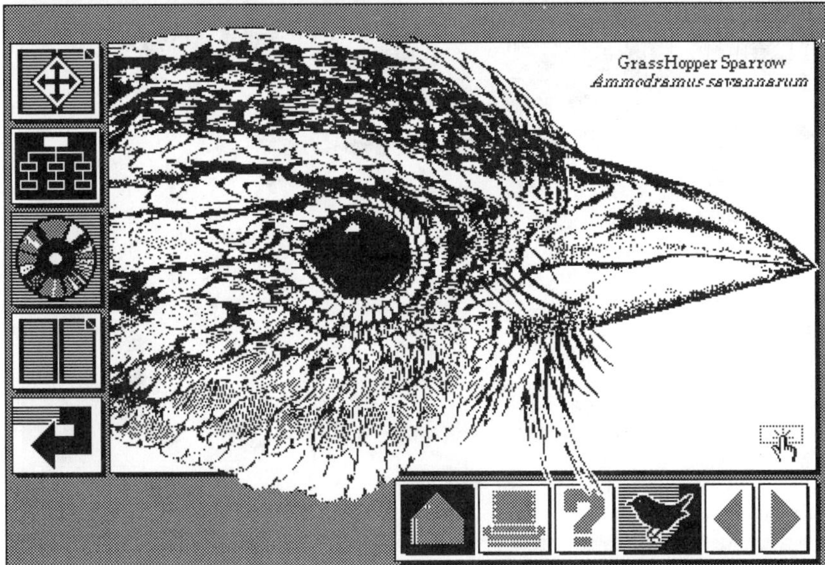

Figure 19-5: See-Through Buttons In Patrick Lynch's Bird Anatomy II stack, transparent buttons are placed over key anatomical areas and become temporarily visible when you press ⌘-Option. Here, the Browse tool is pointing at the button whose HyperTalk script appears above the screen (top). Clicking this button tells HyperCard to go to the card shown at bottom, which also contains transparent buttons that reveal additional details when clicked.

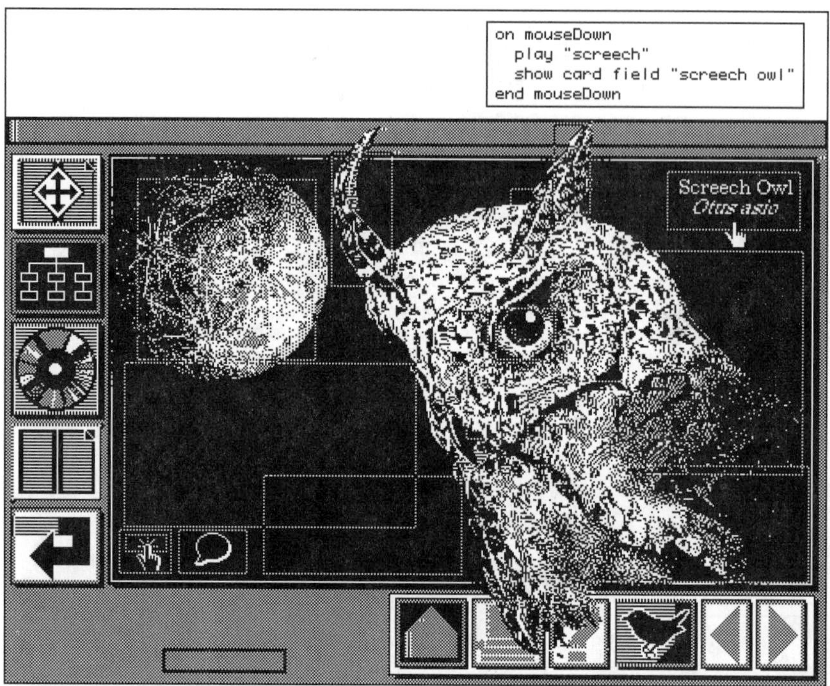

Figure 19-6: Pop-Up Fields Pop-up fields are ideal for conveying small tidbits of information. Shown here is another card from Bird Anatomy II. Clicking the Screech Owl button executes the HyperTalk scripts shown above the card (top), which plays back a digitized recording of a screech owl and then displays the card field shown at bottom. That card contains another HyperTalk script (not shown) that causes HyperCard to hide the field when you click it.

You can mix fonts, sizes, and styles within a single field. You can also specify that a word (or sentence or paragraph) act as a hot spot that users can click to go to a different card, display a definition for a term, play a QuickTime movie, or display a color PICT image, for example.

Buttons and fields can appear on individual cards or in the background. Stack-navigation buttons are often in the background, so they appear on each card and provide a consistent way for you to navigate. Transparent buttons that lead to other cards or display pop-up fields generally appear on individual cards and correspond to a graphic.

Keyboard Shortcuts for Browsing Stacks

This box lists some keyboard shortcuts for browsing HyperCard stacks.

HyperCard Browsing Shortcuts

To Do This	*Press*
Go to the HyperCard Help stack	⌘-?
Go Home	⌘-H
Go to the stack's first card	⌘-1 or ⌘-left arrow
Go to the stack's last card	⌘-4 or ⌘-right arrow
Go to the preceding card	⌘-2 or left arrow
Go to the next card	⌘-3 or right arrow
Go back through cards viewed	Tilde (~), Esc, or down arrow
Go forward through retraced cards	Up arrow
View miniature versions of recently viewed cards	⌘-R
Select the Browse tool	⌘-Tab
Store the current card's location for quick return	⌘-down arrow
Return to stored location	⌘-up arrow
Go to the next field	Tab
Go to the preceding field	Shift-Tab

So You Want to Be an Author

Because the best way to learn about HyperCard is to play with it, I put together an exercise that exposes you to HyperCard customizing. For a hands-on introduction to *authoring* — the fashionable term for HyperCard customizing — see the Step-by-Step box "A HyperCard Tutorial" and Figure 19-7 "HyperCard's Tools."

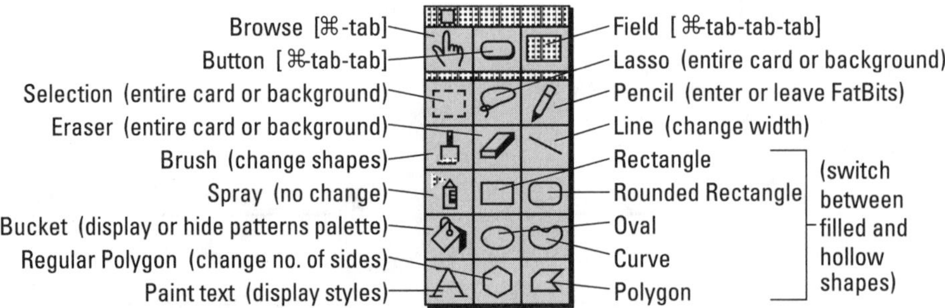

Figure 19-7: HyperCard's Tools HyperCard's Tools menu is the gateway to many of its painting and stack-design features. To access the secondary functions shown in parentheses, double-click the appropriate tool. In HyperCard 1.2 and later versions, you can select the Browse, Button, and Field tools by using the key commands shown in brackets.

You may think that the exercise in "A HyperCard Tutorial" is too simple and that HyperTalk scripts are usually longer. Not so; HyperTalk is an efficient language. Scripts rarely exceed 10 or 20 lines and often have just a few. To see for yourself, explore the scripts in HyperCard's stacks (see Figure 19-8 "HyperCard User Levels"). To quickly open any button's script, press ⌘-Option while clicking the button. (Note that your user level must be set to 5, the Authoring level, for this technique to work.)

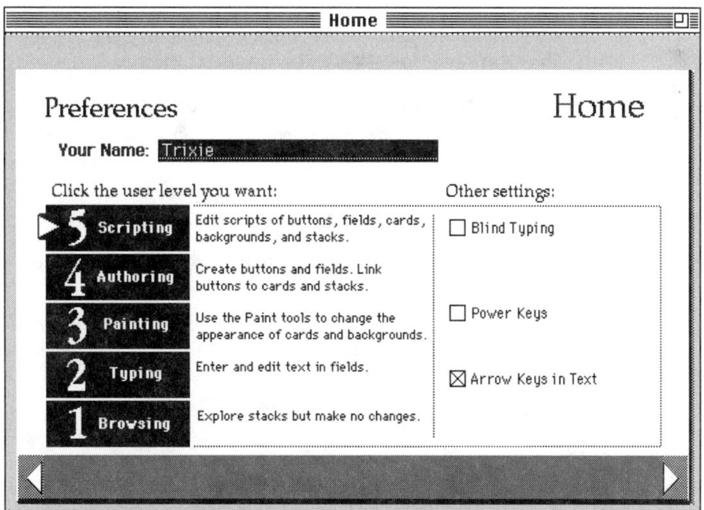

Figure 19-8: HyperCard User Levels HyperCard offers five user levels, each providing more access to HyperCard's programming and customizing features than the level beneath it. The Blind Typing option lets you type messages without having to open the message box. Checking the Power Keys option enables HyperCard's power keys, a number of keys on the keyboard that you can press to choose a command when a paint tool is active.

A HyperCard Tutorial

In this exercise, you exploit HyperCard's capability to start other programs by adding a button to HyperCard's Home card that, when clicked, uses a HyperTalk script to take you to the word processor of your choice. You must know the exact name of your word processor as it's stored on your hard disk. If you aren't sure, return to the Finder and find out. Finally, for insurance, you may want to use the Save a Copy command in HyperCard's File menu to make a backup copy of your Home stack.

Changing your user level

You can use HyperCard on any of five levels, each of which provides more access to HyperCard's customizing features than the one before it. To work with HyperTalk, go straight to the most powerful level — the Scripting level. (See Figure 19-8 "HyperCard User Levels," which precedes this sidebar.)

To change the user level:

1. With the Home stack open, choose Preferences from the Home menu to display the User Preferences card.

(continued on the next page)

(continued from previous page)

2. **Click the Scripting button in the User Preferences card.**
   Two new menus, Tools and Objects, appear. HyperCard's Tools menu contains its painting, button, and field tools (see Figure 19-7 "HyperCard's Tools"). The Objects menu lets you create, examine, and change information and scripts for buttons, fields, cards, backgrounds, and stacks.
3. **Return to the first card of the Home stack by choosing Home Cards from the Home menu.**
   HyperCard remembers which user level you chose, so you need to perform these steps only once.

Create a new button

Now that you have the authority to author, you can create the new button on the first card of the Home stack.

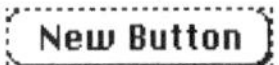

To create a new button:

1. **Choose New Button from the Objects menu.**
   A button named New Button appears in the center of the screen.
2. **Drag the button to a free area of the Home card.**
   Don't worry about its exact position; you can fine-tune it shortly.

Refine the button

Your next step is to make the button look like the other buttons in HyperCard's Home stack — icons with text below them.

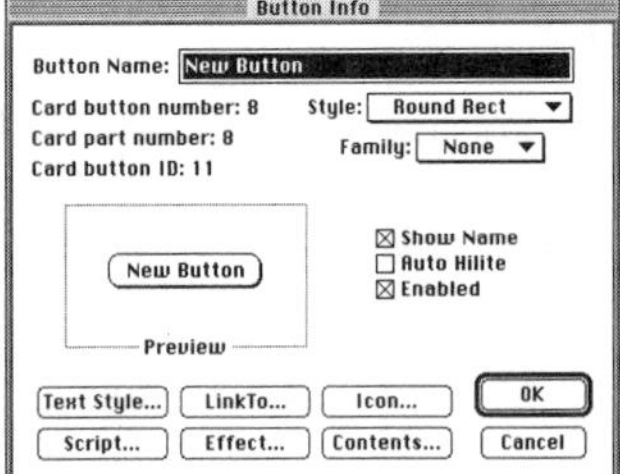

To edit the button:

1. **Choose Button Info from the Objects menu, or simply double-click the new button.**
   HyperCard's Button Info dialog box appears.
2. **In the Button Name text box, type your word processor's name exactly as it's stored on the hard disk.**
   Because the dialog box's Show Name option is checked, the button name appears on the card.
3. **Click the Auto Hilite check box.**
   This step tells HyperCard to invert the button (turn white areas black and vice versa) when you click it. This way, the button provides visual feedback and operates like a standard Macintosh button.
4. **In the Style area of the dialog box, choose the Transparent option. Don't click OK yet.**
   When using this option to create an invisible button over a graphic, uncheck the Show Name option.

Add an icon

Next, you can add an icon to the button from one of the dozens built into HyperCard.

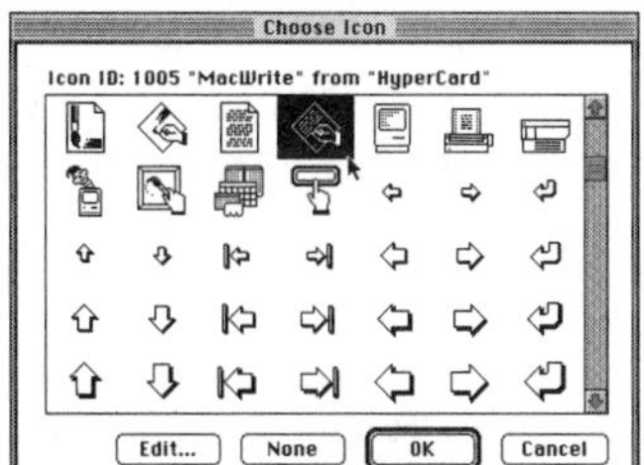

To add an icon to a button:

1. **In the Button Info dialog box, click the Icon button.**
   A dialog box showing HyperCard's built-in icons appears. For your word processor, use the icon located in the upper-right corner of the dialog box.
2. **Select the icon you want by clicking it, and then click the OK button.**
   The button changes to reflect its new icon. But because the button is rectangular, it obscures part of the icon. In the next steps, you can resize the button to see the entire icon, and you can fine-tune the button's position.

To resize a button:

1. **Make sure that the Button tool is active and that the button is selected.**
2. **Point to any of the button's four corners, and then click and drag until the button is the desired size.**
   In this example, resize the button until the entire icon and the text below it appear.
3. **Drag the button as needed to align it with any adjacent buttons.**

Create the script

If you click the new button now, HyperCard highlights it, but nothing else happens. In this final phase, you create the HyperTalk script that tells HyperCard what to do when you click the button.

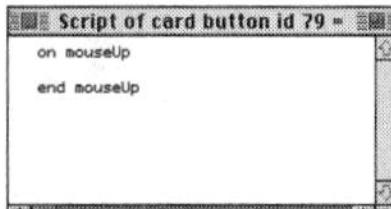

To create the script:

1. **Choose the Button tool from the Tools menu.**
2. **Double-click your new button to reopen the Button Info dialog box.**
3. **Click the Script button.**
   HyperCard's script editor window appears.

   Before you type a script, here is some background on scripts:

   - A script consists of one or more *handlers.* A handler is a collection of HyperTalk statements that HyperCard executes when it receives a message that an event has occurred — in this case, when you press the new button.

(continued on the next page)

(continued from previous page)

- A message handler for a button always begins with *on mouseUp* and ends with *end mouseUp.* The commands between these two lines tell HyperCard what to do when you press and release the mouse button while the browsing pointer is within the button's boundaries. Note that a blinking insertion point exists between the two lines. You type the script there.

To type the script:

1. **Type (include the quotes) open "Microsoft Word" (or the name of the word processor of your choice as it's stored on your hard drive).**
   Be sure to type the name exactly as it appears in the Finder.
2. **Check your work, and then click the script window's close box.**
   Click Yes when asked to save changes.
3. **Choose the Browse tool — the pointing finger — from the Tools menu, or access it from the keyboard by pressing ⌘-Tab.**
   Test the button now. Depending on the organization of your disk folders, one of two things happens: HyperCard dutifully starts the word processor, or a dialog box appears asking where the application is stored. If the latter occurs, use the dialog box to aim HyperCard in the right direction. From now on, HyperCard looks for applications in that folder. (By editing the Search Paths cards in the Home stack, you can also add path names to the list of folders that HyperCard automatically searches.)

Extending HyperTalk's Vocabulary

HyperTalk contains a large vocabulary, but no programming language meets every need. Knowing that, HyperTalk's designers devised a way for HyperTalk to access routines written in conventional programming languages. These *external commands* (XCMDs) and *external functions* (XFCNs) can perform specialized jobs that exceed HyperTalk's capabilities, such as controlling a videodisc player or CD-ROM drive.

HyperCard itself includes several XCMDs. For example, the QuickTime Tools stack includes XCMDs that enable stacks to open and play QuickTime movies.

Using Other Scripting Systems

Beginning with version 2.2, HyperCard supports Apple's Open Scripting Architecture (OSA), which provides a mechanism for controlling multiple applications with scripts. The OSA is a framework into which you can plug scripting languages such as Apple's AppleScript (covered in Chapters 22 and 24). HyperCard's OSA support allows you to augment HyperTalk with additional scripting languages to combine the strengths of each.

Using AppleScript with HyperCard

To use AppleScript in your stacks, your Mac must be running System 7.0 or later and both the Apple Events Manager and the AppleScript extensions must be installed. (If you use AppleScript in stacks that you distribute to others, make sure that the system software on their Macs meet these requirements.)

Where to Get XCMDs and XFCNs

User groups and on-line services such as America Online and CompuServe offer hundreds of free or inexpensive XCMDs and XFCNs. Libraries of XCMDs and XFCNs are also available from a variety of sources, including Heizer Software (800-888-7667), Clear Lake Research (713-242-3494), and APDA, Apple's source for developer tools (800-282-2732).

As Chapter 22 describes, AppleScript sends messages, called *Apple events*, to applications. When a HyperCard script containing AppleScript statements runs, HyperCard sends the statements to the AppleScript extension. The AppleScript extension interprets the statements and sends Apple events to the appropriate applications, which respond by performing the actions specified in the script — opening a document, performing a calculation, or changing some formatting in a document.

Applications can also send Apple events back to the AppleScript extension to report results. The AppleScript extension returns these results to HyperCard, where your script can display them or respond to them.

Why bother with AppleScript?

With HyperTalk built into HyperCard, why should you bother with AppleScript? Because AppleScript opens HyperCard to the outside world — other applications. With AppleScript and HyperCard, you can combine multiple applications into a single unified system, taking advantage of the unique features that each provides.

For example, an AppleScript script can collect information from a database program and then copy it to HyperCard. The script in Figure 19-9 "HyperCard to FileMaker Pro" does just that: it returns all the names of the fields in an open FileMaker Pro database.

```
checkFileMakerOpen() -- subroutine below
if the result is false then return
tell application "FileMaker Pro"
    copy name of every field to fldList
    repeat with i from 1 to length of fldList
      copy "\"" & item i of fldList & "\"" to item i of fldList
    end repeat
end tell
fldList  -- this is the result

on checkFileMakerOpen()
  do script ("there is a program \"FileMaker Pro\"")  -- "do script" is HyperCard's
  if the result is true then
    tell application "FileMaker Pro"
      exists document 1
      if the result is true then return true
    end tell
  end if
  answer ("You must have a FileMaker Pro database open to run this script.")
  -- "answer" is HyperCard's
  return false
end checkFileMakerOpen
```

Figure 19-9: HyperCard to FileMaker Pro This script uses AppleScript and Apple events to enable HyperCard to communicate with the Claris FileMaker Pro database application.

An AppleScript script can also work in the opposite direction: it can send information from HyperCard (for example, a selection you made from a field or button) to another application, which may, in turn, perform some action and then return the result to HyperCard. All you need to know is how to use the AppleScript language to request the actions or results that you want from the programs with which you're communicating.

HyperCard's AppleScript support teams up well with System 7.5, whose Finder is scriptable. With System 7.5 and HyperCard, you can create stacks that control the Finder — to copy files and folders, for example.

HyperCard 2.2 includes numerous examples of how you can put AppleScript to work. They're on the AppleScript Stacks disk, along with stack-based documentation for HyperCard's AppleScript-related features.

Turning Stacks into Applications

Beginning with version 2.2, HyperCard makes it easy to turn a stack into a stand-alone application — a program that you can run directly from the Finder without having to use HyperCard. HyperCard's built-in application builder lets you use HyperCard as an application development system to create programs that you can sell, give away, or use in your own business. (Note that you must be running System 7.0 or a later version in order to use HyperCard's application builder.)

Creating an application

Creating a stand-alone application is a cinch. From the File menu, choose Save a Copy. In the Save dialog box that appears, choose Application from the File Type pop-up menu. (If the pop-up menu isn't available, it's probably because you don't have the StackToApp translator installed in the Stack Translators folder, which is located in the same folder as the HyperCard program itself.)

After you type a name for the application-to-be and then press Return, another dialog box appears that lets you specify additional information about your program — I describe this information in a moment. If you're in a hurry to see your new program, you can just click OK without specifying any additional info.

Testing an application-to-be

A stand-alone application is its own Home stack. A stand-alone doesn't have to be named "Home," but if you're creating other stacks (or applications) that access the stand-alone, the scripts in those stacks should use the HyperTalk statement **domenu "Home"** or **go home** to go to the application. They should not use **go stack "Home"** — this statement causes HyperTalk to go to a stack named "Home."

Here's how to test how a stack will behave as a stand-alone application. If HyperCard is running, quit it. Next, rename your current Home stack (the new name doesn't matter — *Old Home* is fine). Now start up HyperCard; when you're asked to locate Home, select the stack that you plan to turn into a stand-alone.

Don't delete your original stack

Keep it handy — if you find a bug in your stand-alone or you want to add a feature, you need to make the change to the original stack and then create a new stand-alone.

Specifying Finder information

When you save a stack as a stand-alone, a dialog box that lets you specify copyright and version number information appears . This information appears in the Finder's Get Info window for your program (see Figure 19-10 "Specifying Version Information").

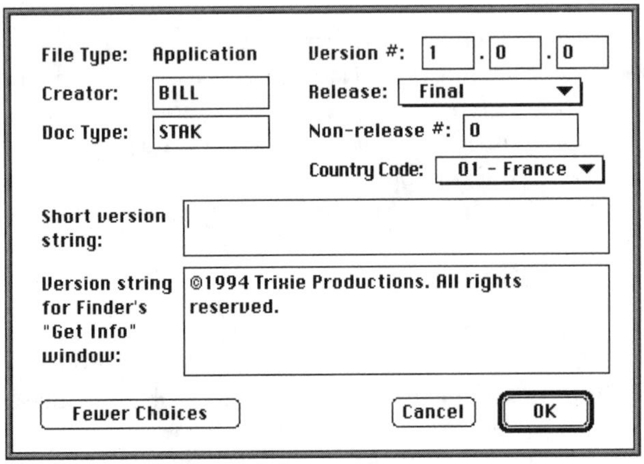

File Type: Application
Version #: 1 . 0 . 0
Creator: BILL
Release: Final
Doc Type: STAK
Non-release #: 0
Country Code: 01 - France
Short version string:
Version string for Finder's "Get Info" window: ©1994 Trixie Productions. All rights reserved.
Fewer Choices
Cancel
OK

Figure 19-10: Specifying Version Information When you save a HyperCard stack as a stand-alone application, a dialog box (top) asks you to specify copyright and version number information, which appears in the Finder's Get Info window (bottom).

If you're familiar with the Mac concept of resources, this dialog box adds a VERS resource to your application. (I describe resources in Chapter 24.)

Stack Design Tips

Knowing your way around HyperCard and HyperTalk doesn't guarantee stunning stacks. The best guide to stack design I've seen is Apple's *Stack Design Guidelines* (Addison-Wesley, 1990). Its nine basic guidelines, summarized here, provide sound advice for budding stackware authors.

Determine your audience
Do they have experience with computers and HyperCard? Imagine designing stacks about dinosaurs for kids and for paleontologists. How would the stacks differ?

Focus the subject matter
Decide how detailed the stack should be. From this standpoint, you get ideas about how to present it. Disk space and scheduling considerations may influence your decisions.

Decide how to present the subject
Doodle on paper and on-screen. Solicit opinions. Consider a metaphor. A book metaphor may use a table of contents as a gateway to various cards. A videotape metaphor may use on-screen rewind, stop, play, and fast-forward buttons.

Teach people how your stack works
Provide help screens that explain the stack's workings, but make them unobtrusive so experts won't be slowed down.

Make the stack easy to navigate
Consider how users access other cards. Put key navigation buttons on backgrounds so they appear in the same place on each card. Consider using visual effects such as dissolves and wipes to convey a sense of movement within a stack, but don't overdo the effects or you'll induce motion sickness.

Integrate text, graphics, and audio design
Avoid amateurish graphics and sound effects. Use text sparingly. Put navigation buttons near the edge of the screen.

Refine the stack as you work
As Apple says: "Your goal should be to produce the best possible stack, not to defend your first beloved idea." Make changes as you think of new presentation styles and navigation methods.

Test early and often
Don't wait until the stack is done before soliciting feedback from users to find out where they stumble.

When you've finished, check the stack again
Make sure that there are no typographical or grammatical errors and that all your buttons, dialog boxes, and scripts work.

Where Does HyperCard Fit In?

Is HyperCard a revolution, or has it survived simply because Apple has kept it alive? I'm less impressed by HyperCard's data-management applications than I am by its educational and entertainment possibilities. Database managers, personal information managers, and even spreadsheet packages are better filing programs.

But for presenting information — as a medium for electronic publishing — HyperCard excels. It's a boon to people who want to tinker with buttons and other aspects of the Mac interface without grappling with conventional programming.

With the color and QuickTime support in the latest versions, HyperCard is a great way to test the multimedia waters without having to shell out big money for programs such as Macromedia Director. The capability to create stand-alone applications that you can sell or give away without having to pay licensing fees is another big plus. And HyperCard's AppleScript support makes the program an excellent front-end for tapping into scriptable applications.

A different way to assess HyperCard's significance may be to ask someone who has learned to read thanks to a stack called Alphabet for Adults by Michael Giamo. Developed for Drexel University's adult literacy program, this stack combines graphics and digitized sound to familiarize users with letters and words.

A software wildcard that teaches adults to read: who can say that isn't revolutionary?

CHAPTER 19 CONCEPTS AND TERMS

- Three factors combine to give HyperCard its versatility — its card-and-stack metaphor, its painting features, and its built-in programming language, called HyperTalk.
- By attaching HyperTalk scripts to buttons, fields, and text within fields, you can create on-screen hot spots that users can click to navigate within a stack and otherwise control its operation.
- Specialized jobs that exceed HyperTalk's capabilities can be performed by external commands (XCMDs) and external functions (XFCNs). These software routines, created with conventional programming languages, extend HyperCard's capabilities.

authoring
The fashionable term for HyperCard customizing.

background
A special painting layer that appears beneath cards in a stack. Backgrounds contain images as well as buttons and fields.

button
An on-screen hot spot that you click to perform an action, such as moving to a different card for more information. Generally, when you click a button, HyperCard executes the script that's attached to that button.

card
HyperCard presents and stores information on cards.

external command (XCMD)
Pronounced *ex-command,* an XCMD is a software routine created in a conventional programming language and installed in a HyperCard stack that extends HyperTalk's capabilities — to control a CD-ROM player, for example.

external function (XFCN)
Pronounced *ex-function,* an XFCN is a software routine created in a conventional programming language and installed in a HyperCard stack that extends HyperTalk's capabilities.

field
A named container that stores a piece of information, such as a name or a phone number.

handler
A collection of HyperTalk statements that HyperCard executes when it receives a message that an event has occurred.

Home
A stack that serves as your base of operations in HyperCard — just as the Finder does for the Mac.

HyperTalk
HyperCard's built-in programming language. Using HyperTalk, you can create scripts and attach them to buttons, fields, cards, and stacks.

script
A sequence of HyperTalk statements that controls HyperCard's actions. For example, a script for a button named Next may tell HyperCard to advance to the next card when you click the button.

script editor
The HyperCard window in which you type, edit, and debug scripts. You can open the script editor window for a button by pressing the ⌘ and Option keys while clicking the button.

Scripting level
Level 5 in HyperCard's Preferences cards — the HyperCard operating level that lets you create HyperTalk scripts.

stack
A collection of related cards — such as all the cards in an address book.

transparent
A property that you can give a button so that the image beneath it remains visible. By placing transparent buttons over key portions of a graphic, you can define a relationship between each area of the graphic and other cards, fields, or stacks. Thereafter, when you click a portion of the graphic, HyperCard takes you to a different card or stack.

CHAPTER TWENTY

Making Multimedia with QuickTime

- Exploring the applications and implications of interactive multimedia
- Outfitting a multimedia system
- Surveying multimedia production and effects software
- Examining the technical concepts behind QuickTime and QuickTime VR
- Understanding video compression

Multimedia is many things — literally and figuratively. Literally, multimedia is the integration of more than one communications medium. It's the use of words, sounds, and still and animated pictures to convey ideas, sell products, educate, and entertain. It's built around the premise that anything words can do, words, sounds, and pictures can do better. The more, the media.

Figuratively, what multimedia is depends on who you talk to. Some say that it's the future of computing, a harbinger of an era when computers will convey information by using sound and motion as well as text and static images, and when television will become more interactive and less passive. Some say that multimedia is the future of communication itself, the ideal way of conveying the complex ideas and concepts of the twenty-first century.

But others say that multimedia represents the victory of television over literature, the triumph of sound bites and flashy visuals over the slow-moving but more thought-provoking printed word. Multimedia, they say, is just one more technological diversion for a society addicted to entertainment and distracted by trivia.

Multimedia can be all these things. It brims with potential and the potential for misuse. Multimedia can also be technically complex and, in its most advanced forms, quite expensive. In this chapter, I explore the world of multimedia, particularly as it relates to QuickTime, the Apple system software that enables programs to work with digital video. Along the way, I pass along some tips and techniques for QuickTime movie making, gleaned from my experience in putting together the movies on the *Macworld Power User Clinic.*

The Multi Levels of Multimedia

At its most basic level, multimedia may involve jazzing up a slide presentation with background music or narration. This kind of multimedia doesn't require a great deal of equipment or technical expertise. You can create title slides and other visuals by using a presentation program such as Adobe Persuasion or Microsoft PowerPoint and then use a stereo cassette deck to record and play the soundtrack. Not long ago, the combination of soundtrack and visuals was about all there was to multimedia.

The latest versions of PowerPoint and Persuasion provide multimedia features that enable a presentation to have animation, such as bullet chart items that slide onto the screen, and flashy transitions, such as dissolves and fade-outs between visuals. Creating a presentation that uses these basic visual tricks isn't difficult, but the results can be livelier and more engaging than a simple slide show (see Chapter 15). In the past, you had to use an *authoring* program such as HyperCard or Macromedia Director to get those kinds of results.

QuickTime animation

A more advanced level of multimedia may involve using QuickTime animation sequences that illustrate complex concepts, such as how a steam engine works or how heart valves operate. At this level, your role as producer becomes more demanding. Designing and executing a complex animated sequence requires artistic skills and knowledge of animation techniques. It may also require software with more advanced animation features than HyperCard's — more about that later.

ON THE CD

Take a Tour of the Mac's Multimedia Talents

The *Macworld Power User Clinic* itself is a demonstration of the Mac's multimedia capabilities, illustrating how multimedia titles rely on on-screen hot spots on which you click to display images or text and also play QuickTime movies.

Speaking of QuickTime movies, I used all the tools and techniques described in this chapter to create the movies in the *Macworld Power User Clinic*. I digitized the movies using Adobe Premiere running on a Quadra 840AV equipped with a Radius SpigotPower AV card. I edited the movies using Adobe Premiere and Adobe After Effects. I prepared the movies' soundtracks using Digidesign's Audiomedia II card and SoundDesigner II software, both of which are described in the next chapter.

On the *Macworld Power User Clinic*, you can watch an interview with QuickTime product manager Duncan Kennedy and learn about the latest QuickTime developments, including the amazing QuickTime VR. In the Multimedia Theater segment, you can watch several types of QuickTime special effects and see a demonstration of a digital video camera that costs less than $100 — Connectix's QuickCam.

Also on the CD is a trio of QuickTime shareware utilities: Paul C.H. Ho's Movie Trilogy, which lets you edit QuickTime movies, add soundtracks to them, and do cool things with the video digitizing hardware in an AV Mac. You can find Movie Trilogy in the Movies and Sounds folder. Also in this folder is a copy of PetersPlayer, a great freeware movie-playing utility.

Capturing video

A multimedia production may also incorporate moving or still images captured from a video camera or videocassette recorder. A corporate presentation may include shots of the new factory; a medical tutorial may show images captured from a videotape of a surgical operation. For this type of operation, you need additional hardware and software, not to mention some knowledge of video and lighting techniques.

Videodiscs

Most multimedia producers rely on Apple's QuickTime to display video on-screen, but interactive multimedia can also make use of yet another piece of hardware: a videodisc player, whose discs look like a cross between a phonograph album and a compact disc.

Videodiscs and interactive multimedia complement each other beautifully, primarily because, unlike a videocassette, a videodisc is a random-access medium. One side of a videodisc contains 54,000 numbered *frames*, and a player under the Mac's control can skip to any one of them almost instantly. The player can play frames continuously to show up to 30 minutes of moving footage or freeze any one frame to show a still.

Thus, a multimedia production can include moving and still pictures stored on the same videodisc — along with up to 30 minutes of two-channel audio per side. You can use those two audio channels for stereo or use them separately to hold, for example, narration in two languages.

Sound recording

Then there's sound, which authoring programs support in a few ways. They can play back short sound passages you record directly into the Mac by using the recording circuitry built into most Mac models or by using an add-on such as Macromedia's MacRecorder Sound System Pro. So your animated heart can beat to the sound of a recorded heart, and the animated steam engine can chug as a locomotive sound plays. You can also create audio-only QuickTime movies in order to play back audio clips that are too large to fit into memory.

With QuickTime 2, you can convert standard music MIDI files (described in the next chapter) into movies that take up so little disk space that an entire symphony can fit on a floppy disk. These music movies can play on any Mac containing the QuickTime 2 extension. If that Mac happens to be connected to a MIDI musical instrument, the movies automatically take advantage of that instrument's superior sound-generating capabilities. (The next chapter contains full details on QuickTime 2's music architecture.)

Authoring programs can also control electronic synthesizers and CD-ROM players. Thus, a corporate presentation can play to the sound of CD-quality background music, or a music tutorial can display text on-screen while a piece plays.

Passive Versus Interactive

Multimedia productions can be linear affairs — watched from start to finish, like a slide show or a TV program. But the most significant aspect of Mac multimedia — and the thing that gets its evangelists and doomsayers so excited — is *interactivity.* The most advanced multimedia productions are nonlinear and interactive. Instead of passively sitting through them from beginning to end, you use the Mac to interact with them, setting your own pace and branching to different topics and areas as they interest you.

Tools for interacting

With interactive multimedia, the Mac and authoring programs such as Apple's HyperCard and Macromedia's Director become more than devices that present various media — they become tools for navigating through the media themselves. The primary tools of multimedia navigation are on-screen buttons and other on-screen hot spots that, when clicked, take you to other screens, display windows containing additional information, or play sounds or video sequences.

A Closer Look at the Pieces

I mentioned in passing many of the software and hardware components involved in multimedia. Figure 20-1 "Multimedia to the Macs" illustrates how they interrelate. Here's a closer look at the pieces and a partial list of products from each category.

Focus on authoring software

The key player in multimedia is authoring software — it's the stage that lets you direct your production's cast of audio and visual characters. An authoring program is to multimedia what a publishing program is to printing — it lets you integrate the output of various programs into a finished product.

HyperCard

The jack-of-all-trades HyperCard is Apple's most popular authoring program; its relatively easy-to-learn programming language, HyperTalk, lets you create simple animations and establish links between on-screen hot spots and other cards. As the preceding chapter describes, HyperCard 2.3 provides better support for QuickTime and color than did previous versions, and it can create stand-alone applications.

Allegiant's SuperCard

Allegiant's SuperCard is more sophisticated, with better color and animation support and more features geared toward professional development. When SuperCard was abandoned by Aldus (which inherited the program when it purchased Silicon

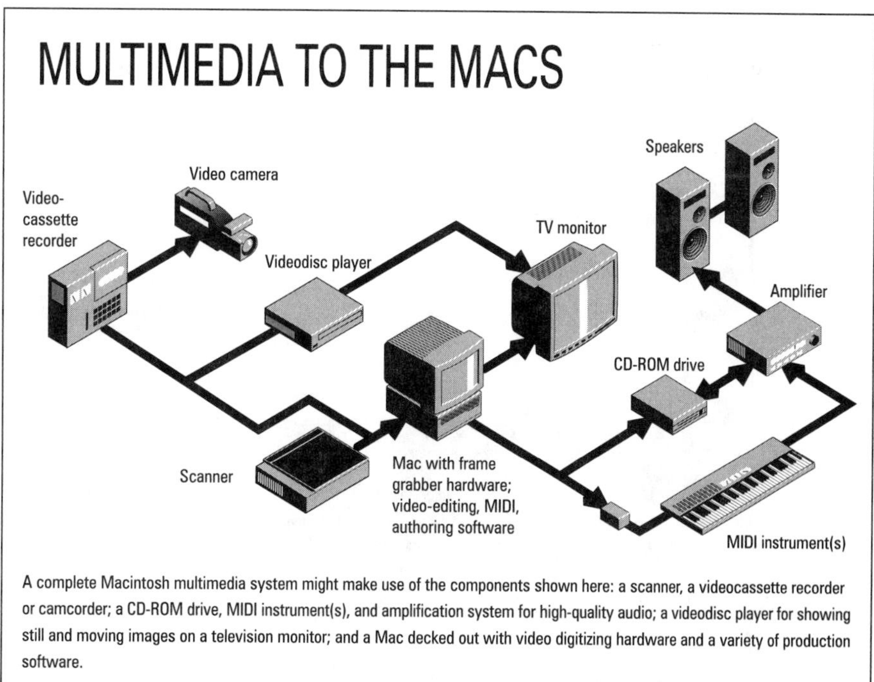

A complete Macintosh multimedia system might make use of the components shown here: a scanner, a videocassette recorder or camcorder; a CD-ROM drive, MIDI instrument(s), and amplification system for high-quality audio; a videodisc player for showing still and moving images on a television monitor; and a Mac decked out with video digitizing hardware and a variety of production software.

Figure 20-1: Multimedia to the Macs

Beach Software), the program's future was unclear. But its creators formed Allegiant and have resurrected the program, breathing new life into it and establishing it as a multimedia authoring contender.

Indeed, for multimedia productions that involve extensive calculations and database processing, SuperCard can be preferable to more fashionable programs such as Macromedia Director. An example of such a production is a promotional piece put together by a major auto manufacturer — as you select various options, the screen displays the total purchase price. Putting together a production like this with a program such as Director, which is geared toward animation rather than calculation and data processing, would be infinitely harder than it is in SuperCard.

Electronic book toolkits

The Voyager Company's Expanded Book Toolkit is designed to support electronic book publishing; Voyager uses it to create its own electronic book titles and also makes it available to other developers. The Expanded Book Toolkit enables authors to produce interactive books with automated word-search and annotation options. It's geared more toward text-oriented electronic publishing than to QuickTime and digital video.

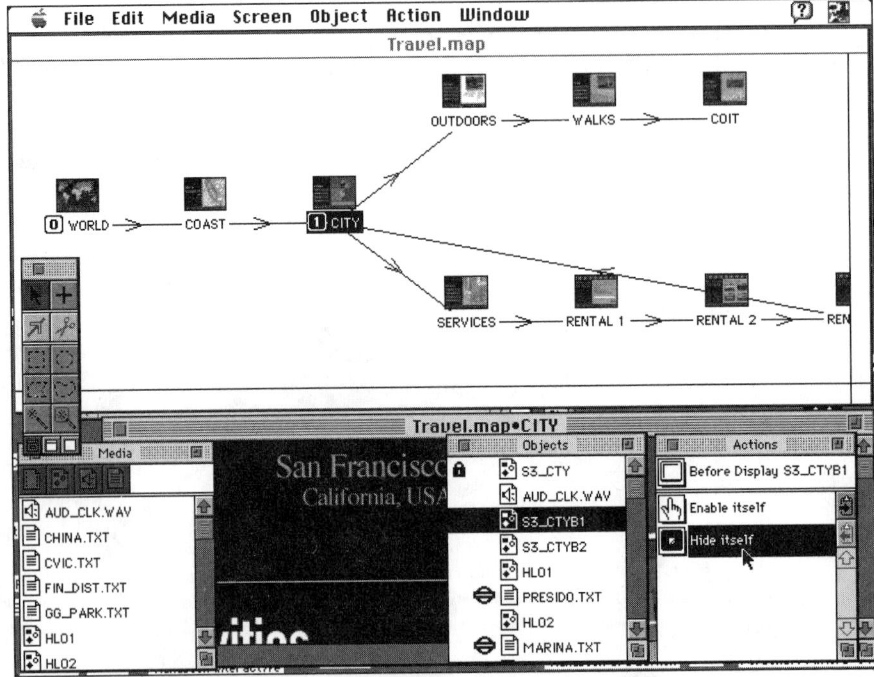

Figure 20-2: The Apple Media Tool AMT's Map window (top) graphically depicts the relationship between each screen in a production. The windows at bottom specify the objects on each screen and the events that occur when you click the objects.

The Apple Media Tool

Apple's most impressive authoring package is the Apple Media Tool, a program that lets you create interactive productions with absolutely no programming (see Figure 20-2 "The Apple Media Tool"). With the Apple Media Tool, or AMT, as it's affectionately known by its fans, you import artwork, movies, text, and sounds created in other programs, and then you specify on-screen hot spots and buttons and the actions that occur when users click them. AMT also accepts a software add-on, the AMT Programming Environment, that allows programmers to add additional capabilities to AMT productions.

Besides its easy operating style, AMT's real strength is that it lets you create a final, stand-alone application that runs on the Mac or on PCs running Microsoft Windows. This versatility makes AMT an ideal environment for creating dual-platform multimedia projects.

The Apple Multimedia Program

The Apple Multimedia Program (AMP) isn't a program that you run — it's a program that you join. AMP is an organization for developers of multimedia products and projects. AMP provides members with quarterly mailings, including technical guidebooks, market research reports, discounts on Apple and third-party gear, videos on interface design, and current information about Apple's directions in multimedia. It costs a few hundred bucks a year — about a dollar a day. For more information, contact Apple at 408-974-4897.

Macromedia's authoring offerings

More sophisticated authoring programs include Macromedia Director and Authorware Professional. Director began life as an animation program, but it now has a HyperTalk-like language called Lingo that lets you create interactive animations containing navigation buttons. In Director, the components in production are stored in the Cast window. The Cast window is a kind of multimedia database, an electronic casting office that holds the audio and visual cast of characters in your production. You add a cast member to the screen by dragging it from the Cast window to the stage or by using the Score window, which graphically depicts the events in the animation (see Figure 20-3 "In the Director's Chair"). Director includes a player application that lets others use your productions without having to own Director.

Figure 20-3: In the Director's Chair Macromedia Director stores the components of a production — QuickTime movies, screen backgrounds, images, text, and so on — in the Cast window, visible at the bottom of this screen. The Score window above it graphically depicts the events in the production. Other windows let you test a production, view QuickTime movies, and paint 24-bit color images.

Authorware Professional is a high-end authoring package that provides sophisticated animation features and lets you create interactive productions without programming by drawing links between the production's components (see Figure 20-4 "Professional Authoring").

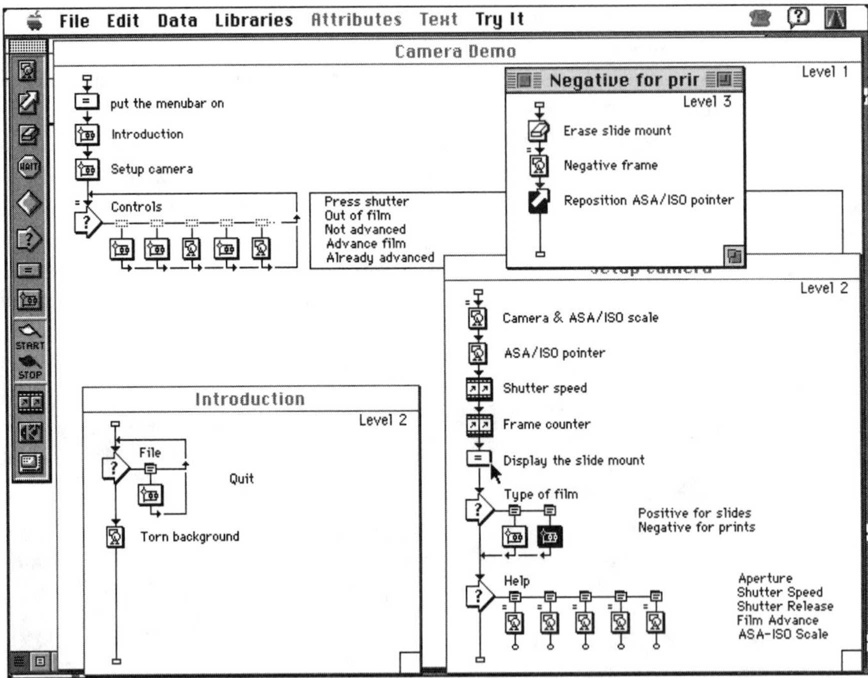

Figure 20-4: Professional Authoring Authorware Professional from Macromedia lets you create productions by drawing links between components.

Adobe ScreenReady: Software for Making Screens

The components of an interactive multimedia production — the movies, the text boxes, the graphics, and so on — don't just appear on a blank screen. Instead, they appear superimposed over screen layouts containing static text, an attractive background pattern or color, and images that represent navigation buttons.

A big part of creating an interactive production is creating these screens. The process is much like page layout, except that you're designing not for the printed page, but for the screen.

To create multimedia screens, many producers combine Adobe Illustrator with Adobe Photoshop, using Illustrator to create and position the text of each screen, and then importing the text into Photoshop, which can create anti-aliased (smooth-edged) text. The layering features in Photoshop make it well-suited to creating screen designs — you can, for example, put a background pattern on one layer, the text on another, and the button images on a third. (Fractal Design's Painter has the same advantages.)

Layering features streamline the screen-layout process, but only to an extent. If you have to revise text, for example, you must return to Illustrator, make the changes, and then re-import it into Photoshop. For a multimedia production containing dozens or hundreds of screens, this is not an efficient way to work.

A new utility, Adobe ScreenReady, eliminates these multistep hassles by allowing you to use a page-layout program such as Adobe PageMaker to do your screen design. You can apply the layout program's text-management and graphics-importing prowess as if you were creating a design for a printed piece. When you've finished, simply process the document through ScreenReady; the end result is a PICT file containing gorgeous anti-aliased text.

I used ScreenReady to prepare all of the screens in the *Macworld Power User Clinic*, and can say that it saved me countless hours. I'd never want to make screens in Photoshop again.

Video hardware

Multimedia can make use of every category of video hardware. For capturing video images from camcorders, videodiscs, or VCRs, you can use any Mac with video-input features, such as a Power Mac 7500 or 8500; an AV Mac; a Performa with the optional Video System card installed; or a Mac equipped with third-party digitizing hardware such as Radius's VideoVision.

If you want to videotape the Mac's screen — perhaps to transfer a completed QuickTime movie to videotape — you need an AV Mac, a Power Mac 8500, or a Mac equipped with third-party video-output hardware. I describe such hardware later in this chapter.

As for videodisc players, Pioneer and Sony make the largest assortment of players with interfaces that can connect to the Mac.

Audio equipment

I've already discussed CD-ROM players and entry-level recording hardware such as Macromedia's MacRecorder. To record and play back CD-quality audio, you need an AV or Power Mac or a board such as Digidesign's Audiomedia II. Throw in a big, fast, hard disk, too, because CD-quality stereo requires 10MB of disk space per minute.

The speaker in most Macs wasn't designed to reproduce anything except error beeps. (The exceptions include all-in-one multimedia Macs such as the Performa 5200, which includes built-in stereo speakers.) For better fidelity, you should connect the Mac to a pair of high-quality speakers such as Bose's VideoRoommates. Several so-called multimedia monitors containing stereo speakers are also available; examples include Apple's AudioVision 17 and discontinued AudioVision 14. The next chapter contains details on attaching the Mac to an external audio system.

For composing and playing music, use a MIDI interface to connect your Mac to one or more MIDI synthesizers. This enables you to record and play back MIDI sequence files, which use far less disk space than digitized sounds. The next chapter explores digital sound concepts as well as MIDI and MIDI gear.

QuickTime Close-Up

The Mac was the first affordable computer that made it easy to combine text and graphics in the same document. Apple's QuickTime software extends this innovation to include dynamic, time-based data — animation, video clips, and sound. (Still images and text are static data — you can't play a scanned image or a paragraph of text.)

QuickTime isn't an application program that you double-click and run; it's an extension to the Mac's system software that application programs can tap into in order to enable you to cut, copy, paste, record, and play dynamic data, which in QuickTime's world are called *movies.* QuickTime teaches the Mac how to move.

In Apple's words, QuickTime provides people with "powerful new tools for communication more closely approximating the richness of the world in which we live." I may not be that effusive about QuickTime, but there's no denying that it is a genuine innovation and a preview of the way we'll use computers and television in the future. At the very least, it's a fun way to make the Mac's screen come to life.

Using QuickTime

As with any medium, QuickTime's effectiveness depends on how you use it. Before looking at the technicalities behind QuickTime, I'll spotlight some application scenarios.

Dynamic documents

Today's most popular word processors, database programs, and integrated packages enable you to incorporate QuickTime movies in your documents (see Figure 20-5 "Moving Documents"). Because QuickTime movies use so much disk space and because most business documents are ultimately printed, however, I'm a bit skeptical of this aspect of QuickTime. Perhaps the era of dynamic documents will dawn along with the arrival of the "Paperless Office" — next year, or the year after, or maybe the year after that.

Electronic publishing

Imagine an electronic version of your favorite magazine: you not only read its text, but you also double-click illustrations and watch them come to life. Double-click a photo in a movie review to see a preview, a music-note icon to hear a snippet of a new hit song, a photo in an interview to see the actual interview, or a stock market graph to see the trends animated.

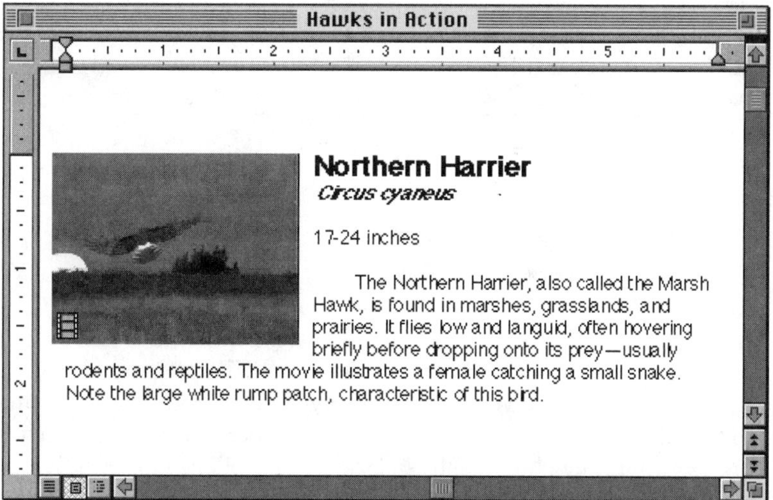

Figure 20-5: Moving Documents You can add QuickTime movies to documents created in most word processors, including Microsoft Word, shown here. The small movie icon in the movie's lower-left corner is called a badge and distinguishes the movie from a still graphic. The badge disappears when a movie is playing.

This brave new world is here now. Numerous encyclopedias are available in CD-ROM form; Microsoft's Encarta is highly regarded. A multimedia, CD-ROM-based magazine called *Nautilus* delivers interactive articles and interviews as well as software (freeware, shareware, and commercial demonstrations) in each issue. And of course, the *Macworld Power User Clinic* CD that comes with this book uses QuickTime movies and searchable text to enable you to explore Macintosh components and concepts, and meet interesting people in the Mac community.

Tips for the QuickTime Controller

QuickTime provides a standard controller — a kind of special horizontal scroll bar — that you can use to play movies, pause them, and adjust their volume.

You can also perform some special tricks with the controller by using the shortcuts in the following table.

QuickTime Controller Shortcuts

To Do This	*Do This*
Make a movie play backward	Press Shift while double-clicking in the movie window
Mute the sound	Press Option while clicking the speaker icon (Option-click the speaker to restore the sound)
Play the movie backward or forward at various speeds with sound	Press Control while clicking the step-forward or step-backward buttons
Adjust the movie's sound volume	Press the up- and down-arrow keys

Many book and magazine publishers are testing the waters of interactivity, creating CD-ROM versions of encyclopedias, magazines, memoirs, and more. One example: the Voyager Company's The Complete Maus, a fascinating CD-ROM version of cartoonist Art Speigelman's Pulitzer Prize-winning *Maus*, a moving story of his family's tribulations during World War II. To research *Maus*, Speigelman recorded hours of interviews with his aging father, a concentration camp survivor. In the CD-ROM version, you can hear these interviews as well as view digitized Speigelman family photographs and watch QuickTime movies.

Education

Educational software such as Knowledge Revolution's Interactive Physics uses animated sequences to illustrate scientific concepts. History software can show clips of historic events and speeches.

Some such products were available long before QuickTime's debut. Indeed, one of the best examples of the educational applications of multimedia is a series of videodisc packages produced by ABC News Interactive and Optical Data Corporation. In the Martin Luther King, Jr. package, you use HyperCard to explore a videodisc brimming with footage of civil rights protests, vintage news reports, and King's speeches, as well as still photographs, maps, and charts. You can watch the entire "I

Have a Dream" speech while reading King's prepared text on-screen — and you can see where, halfway through, he diverged from the prepared text to capture the attention of millions.

Other ABC News Interactive presentations include *In the Holy Land, The Great Quake of '89*, and *AIDS*. The state of Florida has distributed the latter package along with videodisc players to all its schools.

Each package in the ABC News Interactive series also includes a "documentary maker" that lets students assemble their own documentaries based on the videodisc's images and news footage. It's this feature that raises red flags among interactive multimedia critics, who wonder whether students are learning about Martin Luther King, Jr. or learning how to produce TV documentaries and splice sound bites. Are they learning about AIDS? Or are they learning that "learning can take the form of an entertainment and ought to," in the words of professor and media critic Neil Postman, author of *Amusing Ourselves to Death: Public Discourse in the Age of Show Business* (Penguin, 1985).

TV and film production

Broadcasting and film professionals can use QuickTime to create animated storyboards that show camera angles and scene progressions, and to create mock-ups of animations that they will produce by using high-end broadcasting equipment such as Quantel's Paintbox. And with high-end Macintosh video products such as Radius's Telecast and Fast Multimedia's Fast Video Machine, they can produce broadcast-quality video on the Mac itself.

Some broadcasters are also using QuickTime to create electronic catalogs of their vast film and videotape libraries. Apple is positioning QuickTime as a platform for the world of interactive television by encouraging developers of interactive TV boxes — the so-called set-top boxes — to adopt QuickTime as their digital video technology.

Entertainment

QuickTime is nothing if not fun. It's easy to digitize snippets of home videos, and it's fun to play director and piece them together into your own productions. (I guarantee that you won't bore friends and neighbors, either: QuickTime movies use so much disk space that most of your productions will be over within minutes if not seconds.)

And, of course, there's the entire universe of entertainment CD-ROMs that rely on QuickTime — products such as Broderbund's legendary Myst. One of my favorites is the Voyager Company's Baseball's Greatest Hits, in which you can explore hours of sound and video clips of baseball's greats and read columns by legendary sportswriter Red Smith.

Macintosh training

Products such as Strata's InstantReplay and MotionWorks's CameraMan let you record on-screen action and then save it as a movie. A Mac consultant or trainer can exploit this capability to create customized training software for specific tasks or programs. Or the movie can be part of a program's on-screen help system. Instead of reading how to resize an object in a drawing program, you can play back a movie that shows you. Indeed, Apple Guide, the help system built into System 7.5, supports the playback of tutorial QuickTime movies.

Presentations

Programs such as Adobe Persuasion enable you to create on-screen slide shows. By supporting QuickTime, presentations can also incorporate sound and motion. A medical presentation can contain an animated sequence that illustrates a new discovery. An architect's presentation can include an animated walk-through that takes clients on a tour of an unbuilt building. An attorney's presentation can include video clips of the scene of a crime. A trade show information kiosk can incorporate movies promoting products or exhibitors.

Science and engineering

Time-based data doesn't have to be video clips or sounds. The data transmitted by seismic equipment is dynamic; a QuickTime movie can record this data so that seismologists can play it back at various speeds to study a quake and its aftershocks. Similarly, meteorologists can record data from weather instruments or photos from weather satellites for later analysis or animation. Scientific programs such as Mathematica can create animated sequences from the data you supply.

Two ways to approach QuickTime

As all of these examples show, you can approach QuickTime from two perspectives — as a viewer who primarily works with commercially produced education or entertainment software or as a producer who creates his or her own QuickTime movies. The path you choose (and you may tread both) should influence your shopping list.

Required Equipment

To use QuickTime, you need a color Mac with a hard disk running System 6.0.7 or later. The 8-bit (256-color) video hardware built into most color Macs will do, but for the best image quality, you want video circuitry that can display thousands or millions of colors — 16- or 24-bit video (see Chapter 29). QuickTime also runs on the PowerBook 140 and 170, but color movies are little more than recognizable on their monochrome screens.

Memory a must

As for RAM, 8MB is a bare minimum, but 16MB or more delivers better performance when recording and saving movies. And don't expect any help from virtual memory, that System 7 feature that lets the Mac treat part of a hard disk as RAM. QuickTime movies may play back poorly when virtual memory is on, and you can encounter disconcerting delays when recording.

The QuickTime extension

You also need the QuickTime extension itself, which is included with System 7.5. It's also generally included with QuickTime-oriented software, including the CD-ROM that accompanies this book.

A CD-ROM drive

Speaking of CD-ROM drives, they aren't required for multimedia or QuickTime work, but you probably want one — the vast majority of commercial QuickTime-based multimedia is distributed on CD-ROM.

With street and mail-order prices falling below $200, CD-ROM drives have become mainstream add-ons. Most current Mac models include an internal CD-ROM drive. The second-generation Power Macs — the 7200, 7500, and 8500 — as well as the Performa 5200 and 6200 series include quadruple-speed CD-ROM drives. (See Chapter 25 for CD-ROM drive details and tips.)

Several companies, including Macromedia, Alpha Technologies, and CD Technology, also offer CD-ROM libraries of canned video clips, sound effects, and animations. (Beware: some clip CD-ROMs are candidates for "America's Hokiest Home Videos." Try a few before buying — or make sure that the company has a money-back guarantee.) Some QuickTime-oriented programs also come with clip discs.

Making Your Own Movies

To many people, making QuickTime movies involves digitizing video from a camcorder or videocassette recorder. As I mentioned earlier, this means either buying a Mac with built-in video-capture hardware or buying a third-party video-capture board. Either option gets you the circuitry that accepts an analog video signal and translates it into digital data, as well as the software that you use to record clips and save them to disk.

In this section, I examine the techniques and technicalities behind making movies with a Mac containing built-in video-digitizing features. Let's begin our tour with the AV Macs, and then we'll check out the enhanced video features of the second-generation Power Macs, particularly the Power Mac 8500 — the best multimedia Mac yet.

Digitizing with an AV Mac

With their built-in connectors for video input and output, Apple's AV-series Macs are ready-made for video production — almost. Although Apple went to the trouble to build video-digitizing circuitry into the AV models, it chose digitizing chips that were woefully inadequate for anyone except the QuickTime tinkerer. Forget making full-screen movies at the standard 30 frame per second (fps) rate — a quarter-screen, 15-fps movie is about the best a stock AV machine can do.

But what the rest of us call a shortcoming Apple calls a third-party opportunity. The AV machines contain a special connector, called the *digital audio-video*, or *DAV*, slot. The DAV slot provides direct access to the stream of video data generated by the AV's digitizer. Apple included the DAV slot so that third-party firms could build boards that enhanced the AV's movie-making capabilities (see the Quick Tips box, "Enhance Your AV Video with the SpigotPower AV").

Enhance Your AV Video with the SpigotPower AV

Radius's SpigotPower AV is not a digitizing card such as Radius's Spigot II Tape or VideoVision-series products. Rather, SpigotPower AV is a compression/decompression card that works with the AV's on-board digitizer to enable you to make full-screen, 30-fps flicks.

The SpigotPower AV works with the Quadra 660AV and 840AV as well as with the Power Mac 7100AV and 8100AV models. You can't use it with the Power Mac 6100AV, whose sole expansion slot is occupied by Apple's AV Technologies card. And although the SpigotPower AV is compatible with the original Power Mac 7100/66, that machine's relatively slow NuBus transfer rates may require the use of lower-quality recording settings when making 30-fps movies. The Power Mac 7100/80 doesn't have this limitation.

Installing the SpigotPower AV is particularly easy in the Quadra 660AV or 840AV models because the DAV connector in these Macs is positioned directly adjacent to the NuBus slot in which the SpigotPower AV card installs. In the Power Mac 7100AV and 8100AV models, you must first install the SpigotPower AV and then connect an included ribbon cable between it and the DAV connector located on the Apple AV Technologies card.

For software, the SpigotPower AV includes an extension that adds its compressor/decompressor (codec) to QuickTime; a simple utility that plays back SpigotPower AV movies; and a plug-in module, Print to SpigotPower AV, that lets you output final movies from within Adobe Premiere. SpigotPower AV does not include software for recording movies; you'll need to use the Fusion Recorder application that's included with the AV Macs or the movie-capture feature of a program such as Adobe Premiere.

With many digital video products, you need a disk array or at least an extremely fast drive mechanism to capture video without losing frames. (Disk arrays are discussed in Chapter 25.) SpigotPower AV does such a good job of compression that its hard drive requirements are relatively modest — any drive with sustained throughput of at least 2.5MB per second works fine. (I use a 1.2GB Quantum Empire drive.) In any case, be sure to use a hard disk whose driver software supports the AV Macs' SCSI Manager 4.3 software (see Chapter 25). And think big — expect to burn roughly 100–150MB per minute for full-screen, 30-fps movies.

Because SpigotPower AV taps into the existing AV architecture, it's a breeze to use — you connect your video and audio gear to the jacks on the Mac and use the standard QuickTime dialog boxes to choose the SpigotPower AV codecs and quality settings. (SpigotPower AV provides two codecs, both variants of JPEG. One captures movies at 640 by 240-pixel resolution and uses hardware interpolation to fill the screen; the other captures at 640 by 480 and also captures movies in interlaced — 60 fields per second — form.)

SpigotPower AV complements an AV Mac's audio capabilities nicely — you can record in 44kHz, 16-bit stereo while capturing full-screen video. (If you use Adobe Premiere for capturing, be sure to use version 4.0.1 — earlier versions contain a bug that results in loss of audio sync when using a 44kHz sampling rate.)

Although the board isn't designed for it, you can also use SpigotPower AV to create full-screen, 30-fps computer animations using programs such as Strata's StudioPro or Pixar's Typistry. When making the final animation, just select one of the SpigotPower AV's codecs in your animation application. This makes SpigotPower AV a great tool for animators looking to create demo tapes or rough animations for client approval.

SpigotPower AV captures movies in full 24-bit color, but because of the way Apple designed its AV architecture, the number of colors you can display at playback time depends on the amount of video RAM (VRAM) you have. On a Quadra 660AV, you're limited to a rather unsatisfying 256 colors — movies look grainy and dithered. An 840AV has the same limitation unless you upgrade its VRAM to 2MB, in which case movies play back in 16-bit color. The Power Macs' AV card includes 2MB of VRAM, and thus also plays back SpigotPower AV movies in 16-bit color. Because an AV Mac can't play back full-screen movies in 24-bit color, you may notice some color banding, although the relative fuzziness of television obscures much of this when you print to videotape.

Another Radius board, SpigotPro AV, addresses the 16-bit limitation by providing its own, 24-bit video-output circuitry. It does cost several hundred dollars more than SpigotPower AV, however.

The SpigotPower AV was designed for CD-ROM movie production and for off-line editing — creating rough versions of videos whose final versions will be produced on high-end equipment. It excels at these tasks, but is also suitable for creating in-house training or presentation videos, demonstration tapes, and other projects that require full-screen, full-motion video but don't demand broadcast-quality results. In short, SpigotPower AV is a tremendously versatile board that puts the "V" in an AV Mac.

Making connections

Whether you're using a stock AV Mac or one equipped with a SpigotPower AV card, your first step is to connect your video equipment's video-out connector to the Mac's video-in connector (see Figure 20-6 "Digitizing Video"). The Quadra 660AV and 840AV each provide two video-in ports — one for a composite video signal and one for an S-video signal. You can switch between the ports using QuickTime's standard Video Settings dialog box. Power Mac AV models, by comparison, have only a single S-video video input, and include an adaptor cable that lets you connect a composite cable. In this regard, the 660AV and 840AV are more flexible than the first-generation Power Macs that replaced them. I use both composite and S-video equipment with a Quadra 840AV and a Power Mac 7100/80AV, and far prefer switching between video sources with a dialog box to disconnecting and reconnecting cables. In any case, use S-video if your video equipment has an S-video output — composite video is less sharp.

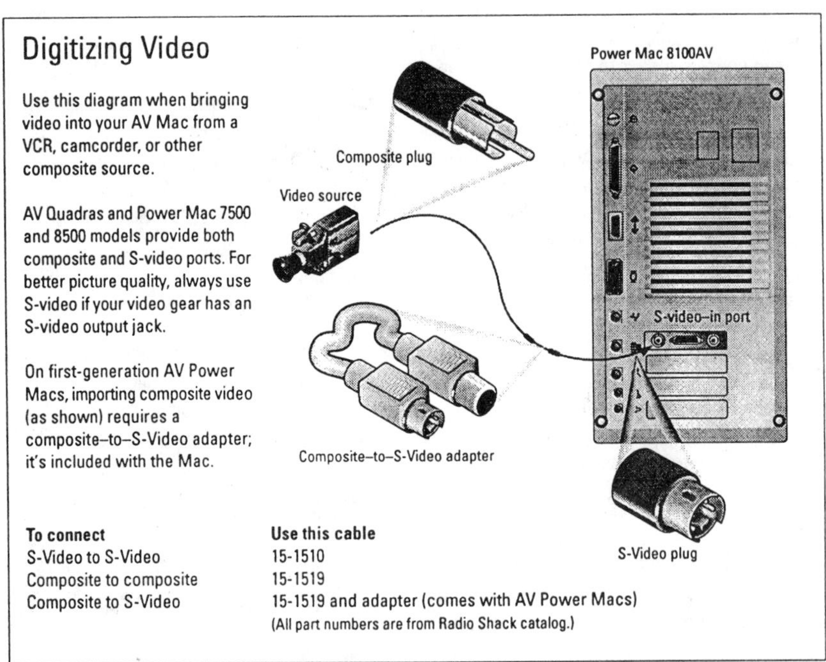

Digitizing Video
Use this diagram when bringing video into your AV Mac from a VCR, camcorder, or other composite source.
AV Quadras and Power Mac 7500 and 8500 models provide both composite and S-video ports. For better picture quality, always use S-video if your video gear has an S-video output jack.
On first-generation AV Power Macs, importing composite video (as shown) requires a composite–to–S-Video adapter; it's included with the Mac.
Power Mac 8100AV
Composite plug
Video source
S-video–in port
Composite–to–S-Video adapter
S-Video plug
To connect
S-Video to S-Video
Composite to composite
Composite to S-Video
Use this cable
15-1510
15-1519
15-1519 and adapter (comes with AV Power Macs)
(All part numbers are from Radio Shack catalog.)

Figure 20-6: Digitizing Video

And...action!

After you've made your connections and tweaked your image settings as described in "Tips for Adjusting Capture Settings," you're ready to digitize your video. For some additional tips, see the Quick Tips box "Tips for Making Better Movies," later in this chapter.

Tips for Adjusting Capture Settings

Regardless of the Mac model you use, you should use your video capture program's Video Settings dialog box to adjust image brightness, hue, and other settings before digitizing.

I sometimes find QuickTime's default brightness setting to be too high, and usually turn it down to avoid washing out bright areas of the image. In any case, you want to adjust brightness and contrast so that black areas of the video are truly black and white areas are pure white. Doing so makes it easier for QuickTime to compress the movie, and that means better movie quality.

While you have the Video Settings dialog box open, specify the video compressor you want to use. If you have a SpigotPower AV or other third-party board, choose its compressor. If you have a stock AV Mac, use the Video compressor. If you'll be recompressing the movie later — perhaps after editing in Adobe Premiere — consider this trick: choose the Photo-JPEG compressor and specify post-compression (more on the latter in a moment). You'll get stuttering movie playback in your video-editing program — the Photo-JPEG compressor is too slow for smooth movie playback — but you will get excellent image quality. When you make your final movie, specify the Video or Cinepak compressor.

In post-compression mode, the capture program defers compression until after you stop recording. This enables the Mac to devote its full attention to keeping up with the incoming video. To use post-compression in Fusion Recorder, choose Record Preferences from the Record menu and then check the Post Compress box. In Adobe Premiere, choose Recording Settings from the Movie Capture menu and check the Post-Compress Video box.

If you're using a board such as SpigotPower AV, consider recording the audio at 44kHz/16-bits for best quality. (With a stock AV Mac, you may have to settle for a lower sampling rate and 8-bit sound in order to get a reasonably fast frame rate.) If you do opt for 44kHz audio and you're using Adobe Premiere, be sure to use version 4.0.1, the latest at this writing. Versions 4.0 and earlier have a bug that results in loss of audio sync when using a 44kHz sampling rate.

Digitizing with a Power Mac 8500 and 7500

The Power Mac 8500's video input features are dramatically improved over those of the AV Power Macs and the pioneering Centris/Quadra 660AV and Quadra 840AV. The 8500, in particular, is an ideal machine for multimedia production and an excellent foundation for a high-end video work. (And note that there is no non-AV 7500 or 8500; the following features are standard equipment.)

For getting video into the 7500 or 8500, there are both S-video and composite video input jacks. (AV Power Macs, by comparison, lack composite inputs and rely on an easy-to-lose adaptor cable to connect composite gear.) You can digitize video using the Apple Video Player application, an enhanced version of the video utility that originally debuted with the Quadra 630 (it's discussed later in this chapter). If you have an 8500, you can also digitize using Avid VideoShop — the full version of VideoShop is bundled with the 8500 (more about VideoShop shortly).

A stock 8500 can capture 30 frames per second at a quarter-screen movie size (320 by 240 pixels, a standard size for CD-ROM-based QuickTime movies). Previous AV Macs could muster only between about 8 and 15.

The 7500 and 8500 motherboards each have a digital audio-video (DAV) connector that lets third-party cards directly tap into the machine's digitizer. Existing DAV cards such as Radius's SpigotPower AV won't work — the new DAV slot isn't compatible with those of earlier AV Macs.

The audio angle

Apple didn't neglect the "A" half of the AV equation, either. The 7500 and 8500 sport audio line-input and -output jacks — the same kind of RCA phono jacks used in stereo equipment and on VCRs. Finally, audiophiles need not use those cheesy 1/8-inch stereo miniplugs (which are also provided). There's a genuine audio-quality benefit, too: the miniplugs are prone to crosstalk (one channel's signal leaking into the other channel) and noise.

Editing Your Video

After capturing video, you enter the post-production phase of your project: editing the video, adding soundtracks, and creating titles and special effects.

You can do basic video editing — cutting and pasting scenes, for example — using a program such as Apple's Movie Player or using the capture programs that come with most video-digitizing products.

Premiere or VideoShop?

For serious editing, though, you need a program such as Adobe Premiere or Avid VideoShop. These programs let you assemble movies, edit them, add sound tracks, and specify transitions such as dissolves and fades (see Figure 20-7 "Now Premiering").

Both VideoShop and Premiere also provide filters that alter the appearance of clips — for example, you can distort a scene to look like it is reflected in a glass globe. If you've used Adobe Photoshop, the concept of filters should be familiar; indeed, Premiere and VideoShop can use Photoshop-compatible filters. (Tip: As described in Chapter 13, if you want to use Photoshop filters with a video-editing program, make an alias of the filters and copy them to the editing program's plug-ins folder.)

Adobe Premiere is my favorite video editor, and it's certainly the industry's most popular one. But VideoShop is a terrific program, too. Apple apparently agrees — it bundles VideoShop with the Power Mac 8500. One reason VideoShop has been slower to establish a following is that early versions used an often-confusing, HyperCard-based interface. But VideoShop has shed that awkward baggage, and today's versions are fast and straightforward.

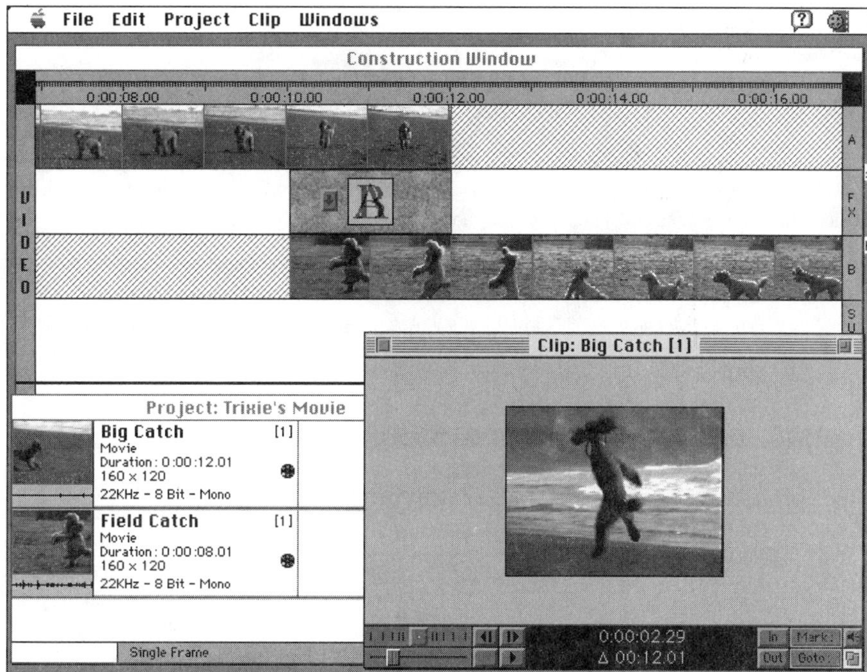

Figure 20-7: Now Premiering Adobe Premiere lets you assemble QuickTime movies into larger movies, called projects, complete with special visual effects. At the lower left, the project window lists available movies along with their characteristics. You include a movie in a project by dragging it from the project window to the construction window (top). The construction window has an adjustable time ruler that shows the project's length. This construction window shows a two-second dissolve between two movies — one movie fades out as the second fades in. Creating such an effect involves simply dragging two movies into position and then dragging the desired effect from Premiere's effects window (not shown). The clip window (lower right) lets you view and modify individual movies. After you finish a project, you can create a movie of its contents by choosing the Make Movie command.

Other editing alternatives

Premiere and VideoShop don't have a lock on video editing. Radius Edit is a powerful editor that ships with Radius's Telecast, a high-end ($15,000) video production system. And a low-end program, Nuts Technologies's MediaFactory, provides basic editing features at a more reasonable price. Radius QuickFlix, another entry-level editing program, is often bundled with video cards.

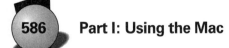

Understanding QuickTime's Concept of Tracks

The editing windows in Premiere and other video-editing packages graphically illustrate how a QuickTime movie consists of *tracks,* usually a video track and a soundtrack.

QuickTime isn't limited to these types of tracks, however. A movie can also contain a text track that displays, for example, closed-caption text or subtitles. Here's another subtle point: A QuickTime movie can also have *multiple* sound or video tracks, which you can selectively enable or disable under software control. A movie may, for example, have a second sound track for a foreign language, and an application program (such as a multimedia production) could offer an option for activating this second track.

QuickTime 2's music architecture adds support for music tracks — tracks containing MIDI note data that you can send to a music synthesizer or to QuickTime 2's built-in sound-playback software.

QuickTime's variety of tracks can be combined in some interesting ways. Consider a movie containing only a text track and a MIDI track — the text track may contain text from a slide presentation while the MIDI track contains background music. Such a movie can be ten or twenty minutes long — and still fit on a floppy disk.

Future enhancements to QuickTime may provide additional types of tracks. If such enhancements become available, you'll install them simply by dragging files into your System Folder. The new features will immediately be available to QuickTime-savvy programs: You won't need to upgrade your application software — another benefit of QuickTime's expandability.

Creating special effects

Needless to say, you can create a huge variety of special effects with QuickTime-savvy programs. Some examples include

- *Morphing* Programs such as Elastic Reality Inc.'s Elastic Reality and Gryphon Software's Morph let you jump on this crowded effects bandwagon. With morphing, one object or character appears to change form and melt into another (see Figure 20-8 "Morphing in Movies"). Elastic Reality is the better program for morphing professionals, but it has a fairly steep learning curve. (You can see some sample Elastic Reality morphs in the Multimedia Theater segment of the *Macworld Power User Clinic.)*
- *Rotoscoping* By combining a video-editing program with an image-processing program, you can paint individual video frames to add special effects. With Premiere, for instance, you can save a video clip as a *filmstrip* — a large file containing each frame in the clip. You can then open this filmstrip in Photoshop and modify it to your heart's content — add animated laser bolts coming out of a toy ray gun, use the Photoshop rubber-stamp tool to create multiple copies of your kid, and so on. You can then bring the filmstrip back into Premiere and play it as a video clip. Strata's MediaPaint and Fractal Design's Painter 3 also let you paint on movie frames.

- *Filtering and compositing* Numerous filter sets perform all manner of special-effects magic. Adobe After Effects is an amazingly powerful program that lets you combine movies and images, warp them, animate them, and do everything else that you see on flashy TV commercials. Its image quality is stunning — generally better than that of Adobe Premiere. And its filters can do everything from removing video noise to simulating the scratches and dust fuzzies that your old family home movies have.
- *Transitions* With transition libraries such as Elastic Reality's TransJammer, you can spice up movies with broadcast-quality transitions (see the Backgrounder box "Transjammer: A Transitions Toolbox").

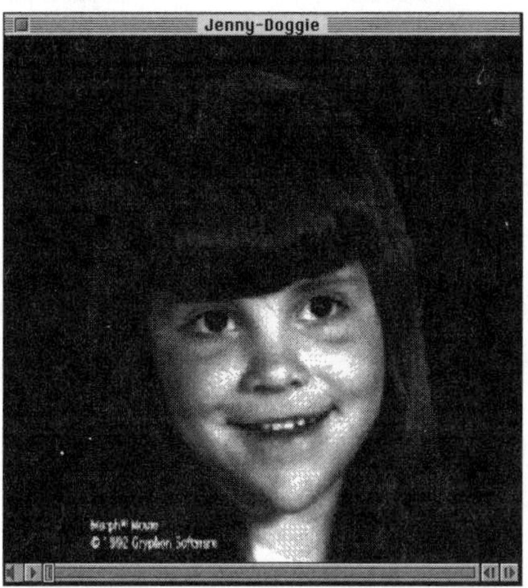

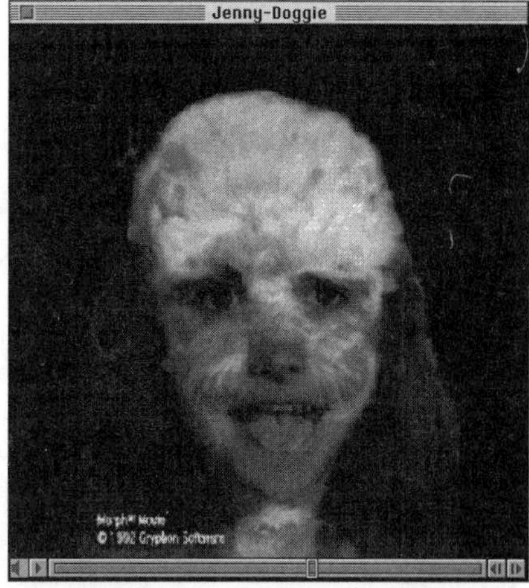

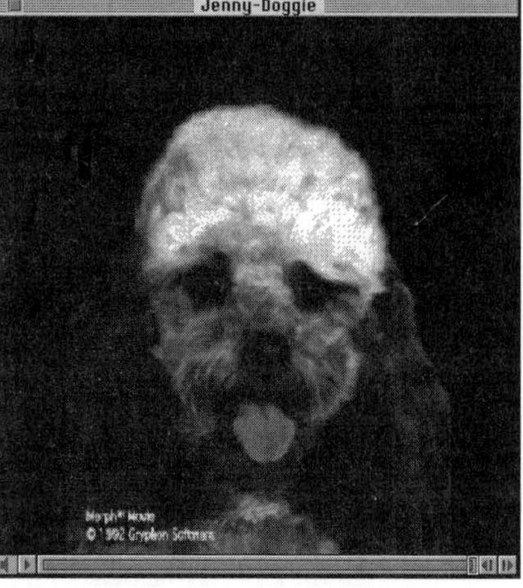

Figure 20-8: Morphing in Movies It's a bird! It's turning into a plane! No — it's turning into . . . Morph! This slick program lets you play with one of Hollywood's most fashionable special effects — morphing, in which one object (or character, if you saw *Terminator II*) appears to change form and melt into another. Creating movies with Morph is easy: you specify key points to identify common areas of each image (such as the eyes, noses, and mouths on two faces), and Morph generates the intermediate frames necessary to create the illusion, as these three frames show.

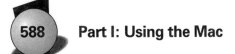

Transjammer: A Transitions Toolbox

Transitions are the spice of video life. Scene A dissolving into Scene B, a title peeling away to reveal a different scene beneath — transitions like these are mainstay seasonings in a video producer's kitchen. Like any spice, they can be overused, but in appropriate doses, they enliven and enhance a video.

Elastic Reality's TransJammer is a spice rack of 100 transition effects for Adobe Premiere and Avid VideoShop. TransJammer operates as a plug-in for these programs, so it's easy to learn — simply install it in your program's plug-ins folder.

So what's included? You name it. There are classic as-seen-on-TV transitions: a rotating cube explodes to reveal a new scene, for example. There are variations on common effects: one scene wipes another off the screen, but in a herky-jerky way. There are all-business effects: Scene B appears in a chart whose animated bars grow until Scene A is no longer visible. And there are effects you're not likely to see on *World News Tonight* any time soon: scene A is replaced by profiles of cows — yes, cows — falling from the top of the screen to the bottom, with scene B appearing within each cow's shape. This effect alone makes TransJammer a must-buy for every video producer in the dairy industry.

How do they look? Great — the quality of TransJammer's effects is as good as anything you'll see on television. But if you have a 680X0 Mac, give yourself time, because TransJammer all but demands a Power Mac. In my tests, a one-second transition that took 9 seconds to render on a Power Mac 7100/80 took over a minute on a Quadra 840AV.

Many of TransJammer's effects are corny, but there are as many gems as there are cows in this collection. If you're tired of the same old transitions — and you have an appropriate sense of restraint — you'll find plenty of uses for TransJammer.

QuickTime Technicalities

Because QuickTime performs its playback magic with no additional hardware, your Mac's processor must do all the work. As a result, your machine's speed determines how well it can play back QuickTime movies.

Two key factors combine to determine just how hard your Mac has to work in order to play back a movie.

The frame rate

The frame rate is the number of frames per second the movie displays. The faster the frame rate, the more fluid the motion — and the more data your Mac must read from disk (or a CD-ROM) every second. An old color Mac such as an LC or original II can show about 10 frames per second (fps) — a rather slow frame rate that gives movies a jittery, Keystone Cops flavor. A midrange 68040 Mac can play about 15 fps, just shy of the frame rate used by Super 8 movies (remember them?). A Power Mac can play 30 fps — the television industry standard in the United States.

The size of the movie window

When QuickTime 1.0 came out in 1991, QuickTime movies measured 160 by 120 pixels — about the size of an Elvis postage stamp. Improvements in the QuickTime software and in the overall performance of the Mac family have boosted frame sizes significantly. These days, a common movie size is 320 by 240 pixels — one fourth of the standard Mac's screen size of 640 by 480 pixels. This size, sometimes called a *quarter-screen* movie, is what I used for the *Macworld Power User Clinic.*

Frame rate x movie size = hard work

If you do some multiplication, you realize that a single frame of a 160 by 120 QuickTime movie contains 19,200 pixels. A single frame of a 320 by 240 movie contains 76,800 pixels.

QuickTime 2: What's the Difference?

For digital video buffs, QuickTime 2 is the most important thing to happen since, well, QuickTime 1.0. You'll find coverage of the new features in QuickTime 2 throughout this chapter; here's a summary of the most significant enhancements in the new version.

- *Bigger, faster, smoother video* By making refinements to QuickTime's "data pipe" — the software mechanisms used to shuttle movie data through QuickTime — Apple was able to improve QuickTime's performance dramatically. Even a relatively low-end Mac such as Quadra 605 or 610 can play back 320 x 240, 15-frame per second movies. And a Power Mac can play 30-fps movies at full-screen (640 x 480) resolution. (For full-screen playback, QuickTime 2 uses a technique called *pixel doubling,* which results in some chunkiness.)
- *The QuickTime Music Architecture* QuickTime 2 essentially turns your Mac into a General MIDI sample-playback instrument — that is, it enables your Mac to play digital reproductions of musical instruments. See the next chapter for full details on QuickTime 2's music architecture.
- *MPEG support* MPEG is an emerging standard for professional digital video distribution. QuickTime 2.0's MPEG support makes QuickTime an ideal format for the distribution of multimedia data. In trendy terms, QuickTime 2 is equipped to haul cargo on the Information Superhighway.

QuickTime 2 offers a host of other enhancements, including improved timecode support for professional video editing applications and better support for movies containing text tracks. But you can see and hear the key improvements for yourself.

Now multiply that pixel count by the number of frames per second to get an idea of how much data has to be slogged around each second. To play a 320 by 240 movie at 15 fps, a Mac has to display 1,152,000 pixels *every second.* And that's for frame rates and movie sizes that are slower and smaller than what you're used to seeing on television. (QuickTime provides numerous features that reduce the actual number of pixels that must be displayed each second; I have more to say about this topic later.)

Factors that influence playback performance

QuickTime has to do a lot of work in order to play back a movie, but it can't do the work unless your Mac is up to the task. Several factors influence your Mac's capability to play back movies.

The speed of the CPU

When QuickTime plays a movie, it must decompress the data that comprises each frame. (I describe QuickTime's compression/decompression concepts in more detail shortly.) The speed of your Mac's central processor determines how quickly the computer can compress and decompress video. Power Macs are best at this processor-intensive task.

For Best Results, Use Multimedia Tuner

QuickTime 2 has many wonderful attributes, but complete stability isn't one of them — the software has some bugs and some architectural changes that cause problems with many video-editing programs and video-digitizing cards as well as with some commercial CD-ROM titles.

Apple has released a patch called Multimedia Tuner that, by and large, fixes these problems. Multimedia Tuner improves the performance and reliability of some programs and multimedia titles that use QuickTime under System versions 6.0.7, 7.0, 7.0.1, 7.1, 7.1.1 (System 7 Pro), 7.1.2 (for Power Macintosh), or 7.5. Multimedia Tuner is also included with System 7.5 Update 1.0 and with System 7.5.2, both discussed in Chapter 22. Multimedia Tuner also improves the reliability of Quadra 660AV and Quadra 840AV systems when these machines are running under low-memory conditions.

But Multimedia Tuner wasn't exactly perfect in *its* first release, either. At this writing, the current version is 2.0.1. If you're using QuickTime 2, be sure to use Multimedia Tuner 2.0.1, too. How do you get it? You already have it — it's included on the *Macworld Power User Clinic* CD-ROM.

The speed of your storage devices

All the data that comprises a QuickTime movie has to be stored somewhere; that "somewhere" is usually a hard drive or CD-ROM. A storage device must be fast enough to supply the data that QuickTime needs, when it needs it.

CD-ROM drives are notoriously slow — Apple's CD-300 series drives, for example, can transfer a maximum of about 300,000 bytes per second. (By contrast, a fast hard drive can blast anywhere from 3 to 10 million bytes per second across the SCSI bus.) Although Apple's latest quadruple-speed drives have transfer rates of roughly 600,000 bytes per second, the vast majority of CD-ROM producers still prepare their movies with double-speed drives in mind — otherwise, their products wouldn't work on the majority of today's Macs. And that means going through some technical gyrations to create movies that play back smoothly from a CD (more about this subject later).

The speed of your video circuitry

This is a subtle one. It's easy to see why CPU and hard drive performance influence movie playback; video speed isn't as straightforward.

Video performance affects playback because of the sheer number of pixels that must be displayed every second. The data that represents those pixels must travel from the Mac's video memory and through the digital-to-analog converters and all the other circuitry responsible for painting pixels on-screen.

If that circuitry is located on a NuBus video card — that is, if you're using a video card instead of the on-board video circuitry that most Macs have — you face an additional bottleneck: the NuBus slot, whose rules about data transfers limit speed with which data can move between NuBus cards and the rest of the Mac's circuitry.

Yet another video-related performance issue is the number of colors your video hardware can display. If your Mac has only 8-bit video circuitry (the maximum setting in the Monitors control panel is 256 colors), QuickTime must translate the colors in the movie into ones that your Mac can display. This *dithering* process takes time — time that the Mac could spend reading data from the disk and decompressing it.

What happens when your Mac isn't fast enough?

In a word, dropped frames (okay, in *two* words). If you run a QuickTime movie that, for any reason, exceeds your Mac's capabilities — its frame rate is too fast, its window is too large — QuickTime drops frames as necessary in a near-futile struggle to keep the video synchronized with the audio. The results are jerky video that is poorly synchronized. (If you try to play back the movies on the *Macworld Power User Clinic* using a slow Mac, you see this outcome for yourself.)

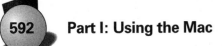

Understanding QuickTime's Modular Architecture

QuickTime doesn't necessarily have to rely on the Mac's processor for everything. Its modular design enables it to take advantage of specialized coprocessor hardware designed for the demands of digital video and audio.

With NuBus boards such as Radius's VideoVision Studio and SpigotPower AV, you can record and play back full-screen — 640 by 480 pixels — movies at 30 frames per second. Some boards also handle CD-quality stereo recording and playback. Each board comes with its own codecs that you add to your System Folder (they generally use variants of JPEG, such as *Motion-JPEG*). Because the codecs plug into QuickTime, the boards become compatible with any application program that supports QuickTime — from Microsoft Word or WordPerfect to Adobe Premiere or Avid VideoShop.

QuickTime's modular design is one of its best attributes. QuickTime owes its modular personality to the Component Manager, a portion of the QuickTime software that enables software to plug into QuickTime to enhance its capabilities — by adding compressors, for example. The Component Manager also isolates application programs from the nitty-gritty details of the hardware they're running on. This feature enables you to create movies on one machine and play them back on others — even ones with different performance and video capabilities.

What do you need for smooth playback?

By now, you should be getting an idea of the kinds of features a Mac needs to be able to handle the demands of dynamic data. In a nutshell, they are

- *A fast processor* A 68040 or PowerPC chip is best.
- *A fast storage device* A speedy hard drive is ideal; for CD-ROM work, a double-speed drive is essential.
- *Fast, built-in, 16-bit video* The ideal video circuitry for QuickTime movie playback is located on the Mac's logic board (not in a NuBus slot) and provides support for 16-bit color (the Thousands setting in the Monitors control panel). Although 24-bit color is acceptable, too, 16-bit color is the standard for QuickTime work.

Squeeze Play: QuickTime Compression

Whether your QuickTime movies come from an animation program or a camcorder, one of the biggest problems you face as a QuickTime movie producer is that movies can use astronomical amounts of disk space. A *five-second* movie recorded with sound uses almost 10MB of disk space — that's 2MB per second. When you run out of hard disk space while making your first movie, you realize just how ill-equipped many Macs really are for the digital video revolution.

Fortunately, QuickTime's compression features dramatically reduce disk space requirements — and in the process, they make movie playback easier for the Mac.

How QuickTime compression works

If you've used programs such as Aladdin's StuffIt, you know that you can compress a file to use less disk space and then decompress it when you want to use it. QuickTime's compression and decompression features are similar, but much more sophisticated. For example, QuickTime decompresses movie frames on the fly as a movie plays. That QuickTime can decompress and display 10 to 30 color images every second with no additional hardware is remarkable, and a testament to the talent of QuickTime's programmers.

QuickTime includes several compressors, each of which provides a different degree of space savings and image quality (see the Quick Tips box "Choosing a Compressor").

Compression almost always means trading image quality for disk space, but it's a worthwhile trade-off, especially because the results are still more than adequate for most applications. By using the Video compressor at its lowest-quality setting, QuickTime can squeeze that same five-second, 10MB movie down to 722K — almost a fifteen-fold savings.

Compression can also allow for faster playback frame rates on slower Macs — or from slower storage devices. Indeed, the incredible compression capabilities of QuickTime's Cinepak compressor enable smooth movie playback from CD-ROM drives.

Choosing a Compressor

Which QuickTime codec should you choose for your movies? Use the following table as a guide.

Compressor Name	***Best Used For***	***Comments***
Photo - JPEG	Still images or archiving video clips that you plan to recompress	Decompression is too slow for smooth movie playback unless you have a JPEG board
Animation	Animated sequences, including recorded Mac screen activity	Yields poor results with digitized color video
Video	Digitized video	Very fast decompression, reasonably fast compression
Graphics	8-bit (256-color) still images and movies	Provides better compression but slower playback speeds than the animation compressor
Cinepak	Digitized video	Very slow compression but fast decompression — the best compressor to use for smooth video playback
None	Clips requiring high quality	Devours disk space — generally only suitable for short clips that you plan to recompress

In a word, use Cinepak. This compressor delivers the smoothest, cleanest results with digitized video. The Cinepak compressor also lets you specify a data rate for the finished movie. If you know that the final movie will be played back from a slow storage device — an older hard drive or, more typically, a CD-ROM drive — you can specify the maximum data-transfer requirements that the movie can impose on the storage hardware. For movies that will be played back on a double-speed CD-ROM drive using QuickTime 2, specify a data rate of 250K to 300K per second. Don't specify a lower data rate than you have to: the lower the data rate, the poorer the image quality.

The drawback of the Cinepak compressor is that compression takes forever — on my Quadra 840AV, about an hour for each minute of video. In techie terms, the Cinepak compressor is *highly asymmetric* — compression takes far longer than decompression. Cinepak compression is, however, considerably faster on a Power Mac than it is on a 68000-family Mac, thanks to the fact that QuickTime runs in native mode on Power Mac systems.

Temporal and spatial compression

Many of QuickTime's compressors incorporate two kinds of compression — *temporal* and *spatial.* Spatial compression saves space by removing information within a single image or video frame. Consider an image that's half blue sky: instead of QuickTime describing the image by saying, "Row one is blue, row two is blue, row three is blue," and so on through row 60, it can simply say: "The first 60 rows are blue."

Temporal compression saves space by describing only the changes between frames. For example, if an airplane is flying across that blue sky, instead of describing each frame in its entirety, QuickTime records only the differences between each frame. Temporal compression is also called *frame differencing.*

Understanding key frames

When you use temporal compression, you generally have a *key frame* — a frame that contains every pixel in the image — at regular intervals. Key frames are especially important if you want fast random access to different parts of the movie; if you plan to drag the movie controller back and forth a lot to skip around within the movie, you want enough key frames.

How many are enough? It's common practice to have one key frame for every second — for example, one key frame every 15 frames in a 15-fps movie. The more key frames you have, however, the higher the movie's data-transfer requirements — and the greater the chance that the movie won't play smoothly on slower Macs.

QuickTime's approach to compression is modular, too. By adding new *codecs* (compression/decompression extensions) to your System Folder, you can enhance QuickTime's compression capabilities. Some video-capture boards include codecs that provide better compression than Apple's.

Peg your hopes on MPEG?

An up-and-coming standard for digital video compression is MPEG, short for *Motion Picture Experts Group.* MPEG appears to be the standard that will be used by the first interactive television systems and the brave new world of 500-channel cable systems.

There are two variants to MPEG. MPEG 1 is designed to allow movie playback from CD-ROM drives at 320 by 240 pixels and 30 frames per second. MPEG 2 provides a 704 by 480 pixel movie size at 30 fps. This variant is being adopted by the satellite broadcast and cable industries. Both variants require hardware assistance — coprocessors to do decompression — for playback.

Apple's MPEG card — finally

In the summer of 1995, Apple finally introduced the MPEG playback card, which had been rumored for at least a year. The MPEG Media Card works in any Mac or Power Mac with an LC processor-direct slot. (It doesn't work in LC630 DOS Compatible or the Performa 640 DOS Compatible because the DOS compatibility card in those Macs uses the processor-direct slots.) The card supports full-screen video playback at 30 frames per second. It includes an enhanced version of the Apple Video Player utility that provides VCR-like buttons playing and navigating through MPEG movies.

A Field Guide to QuickTime Trade-Offs

Making QuickTime movies is all about making trade-offs — between disk space, data-transfer rates, and movie quality. This section details the factors that you must weigh against one another when making your own movies.

Frame size

As mentioned earlier, the size of the movie window not only impacts the movie's storage requirements but also how well the movie plays back on Macs with slower video hardware. A larger movie window — 320 by 240 pixels, for example — generally imposes more performance demands than does a smaller window, such as 240 by 180.

Frame rate

The number of frames displayed per second also impacts storage requirements and playback quality. A movie with 10 fps uses less disk space than a 15-fps movie, but it looks jerky. Thirty fps yields the smoothest results but uses three times the disk space as 10 fps.

For "talking head"-style movies — like the interviews on the *Macworld Power User Clinic CD* — 15 fps usually delivers very good results.

The color depth

The higher the bit depth of a movie — the more bits that are assigned to each pixel — the larger the movie and higher its data rate. Fortunately, 16-bit color (the Thousands setting in the QuickTime compression dialog box) delivers image quality that's virtually indistinguishable from 24-bit color (the Millions setting).

Tips for Making Better Movies

In the course of producing the video segments on the *Macworld Power User Clinic*, I learned more than I wanted to learn about QuickTime movie production. What follow are some tips gleaned from my experiences using the built-in digitizer on a Quadra 840AV. These basic concepts apply to any video digitizing endeavor.

Use a high-quality original

The higher the quality of your original videotape material, the better the finished movie. A Hi-8 or S-VHS camcorder delivers far better video than a VHS machine. The VHS signal is much noisier, which actually impairs QuickTime's capability to compress the video efficiently. That contributes to poorer overall movie quality.

Also, if you can, digitize from the original copy of a tape rather than from a dub, which is noisier than the original.

Use a fast, defragmented hard drive

The faster, the better. I used a 1GB Quantum Empire drive with my 840AV; when initialized with FWB's Hard Disk Toolkit software (which supports the 840AV's faster SCSI Manager 4.3), I got sustained transfer rates of over 3MB per second — more than adequate for 15-fps, quarter-screen movies. To ensure that I was getting the best possible performance from the drive, I also defragmented it regularly by using the Norton Utilities' Speed Disk program. For more details about boosting SCSI performance and using SCSI Manager 4.3, see Chapter 26.

Use postcompression

Most digitizing programs can do their work in either of two ways: by compressing each video frame as it's being captured or by *postcompressing*. In the latter mode, the program saves the video in an uncompressed (and space-devouring) form during the capture itself. Only when you stop capturing does the program go back and compress what you've captured.

Because of the time required to compress a frame of video — especially with the Cinepak compressor — it's best to use postcompression if your Mac doesn't have compression coprocessing hardware such as a Radius VideoVision board. The only drawback of this approach is that you need a lot of free disk space to do the initial capture; indeed, you may have to digitize a lengthy scene in multiple passes.

Run lean

So that your Mac can devote its full processing power to recording your movie, disable all but the most essential extensions and use the Chooser to turn off AppleTalk. When digitizing to my Quadra 840AV, I turn off every extension except for QuickTime itself. As soon as I'm done digitizing, I restore my usual extension collection. (See Chapter 24 for details about extension-management utilities.)

Disable counters and read-outs

Many video digitizing programs can display elapsed-time counters during the recording process. If your program allows you to turn off these counters, do so. By not having to calculate and display the counter's data, the program can concentrate fully on digitizing your movie.

The audio track

I haven't said much about the audio half of the QuickTime equation — the next chapter covers music and sound in detail. As with video, however, the higher the quality, the more demanding the movie. A 44kHz, 16-bit soundtrack (CD quality) in stereo imposes far more processing, storage, and data-transfer demands than a 22kHz, 8-bit soundtrack in mono. You need to balance your audio requirements against the capabilities of the Mac that will be playing your movies.

A 22kHz, 8-bit soundtrack generally yields good results with voice or music. (I used these specs for the movies on the CD.) For voice-only sound-tracks that don't require excellent sound quality, consider dropping down to 11kHz.

If you *must* have a high-quality stereo soundtrack in a particular movie, you can still ensure that the movie will play smoothly on slower Macs by using the Cinepak compressor and specifying a desired data rate. The Cinepak compressor reduces the movie's image quality significantly, but the movie should meet the data-rate requirement you specified. And you have the great soundtrack to make up for the pixelated appearance of the movie.

Recording Your Efforts on Videotape

It's fun to show QuickTime movies on-screen, but if you want to distribute your productions to people who don't have computers, you probably want to record them on videotape. Creating professional-quality video is a subject for an entire book. An introduction to the challenges of recording to video, as well as some product information to get you started, follows.

Technical differences between the Mac and TV

At the simplest level, uniting a Mac and video recorder means routing the Mac's video output signal to the video recorder's video-input connector. But you also need to be sure that the Mac is sending a signal that the video recorder can understand. And that's when the differences between Macintosh video and broadcast video become critical.

The first of these differences concerns those horizontal scan lines that form video images. On all video tubes, these lines are formed by an electron gun (or with most color monitors, three electron guns) within the video tube. The gun fires a stream of electrons at the tube's inner surface, causing its phosphor coating to glow briefly.

A 14-inch color monitor contains 480 horizontal scan lines, and they're painted one at a time, from left to right, from the top of the screen to the bottom. One complete set of scan lines forms a frame. Most Mac video boards repaint the entire frame roughly 60 to 70 times per second, which translates into a refresh rate of 60 to 70Hz.

Interlaced versus noninterlaced video

By contrast, American television uses 512 horizontal scan lines painted in a very different manner. Instead of painting one frame's worth of scan lines from top to bottom, a TV set paints them in two separate passes, or *fields.* First, all the odd-numbered lines are scanned, and then all the even-numbered lines are scanned. Each field is painted 30 times per second, giving broadcast video a frame rate of 30Hz. Thanks to the persistence of vision — the same phenomenon that makes movies appear to move — we see the two fields as one image. This two-fields-per-frame approach is called *interlaced video.* The Mac's approach of painting all the scan lines in one pass is called *noninterlaced* video.

Color differences

Mac video and TV also handle color differently. In the Mac, the signals for red, green, and blue — the primary additive colors from which all colors are created — travel on separate wires. Other wires carry synchronization, or *sync,* signals. This approach is called *RGB video.*

In the TV world, the red, green, and blue signals merge with the sync signals into a *composite* signal that's technically simpler but lacks the sharpness and clarity of RGB video.

Size differences

The technicalities don't stop there. Because of a television industry practice called *overscan,* in which the image projected onto a television's video tube is too large to fit, the outer edges of the Mac's screen don't appear on the television or videotape.

Overscan was born in television's early days, when the image on a picture tube would gradually shrink as the tube aged. Today's picture tubes don't suffer from this flaw, but overscan remains, partly to accommodate the elderly televisions still out there and partly because television manufacturers would rather fill an entire screen than have a black border around its image. On the other hand, computer monitors *underscan* — they project an image smaller than the tube's surface in order to show every precious pixel.

Because of overscan, it's best to design titles and other graphics to occupy the center of the Mac's display — although you still may need to adjust the position of the text after you connect the Mac to your video gear.

In many ways, an NTSC signal is technically inferior to a color Mac's video signal. That's to be expected, given the less-demanding nature of television. A TV image doesn't have to be sharp enough to display small text that's legible at arm's length. In short, to record to video from the Mac, you need to tell the Mac to lower its standards.

Designing for Television

Television graphic design has its own unique requirements. Because of television's limited resolution, images and text tend to appear soft and diffused. This and the fact that a TV image is interlaced require some special approaches to graphic design.

Avoid thin lines

Lines that are one scan line wide flicker badly, and even lines that are two scan lines wide tend to break up. Use horizontal lines that are an even number of pixels (2, 4, 6, and 8) high.

Avoid tight spacing

Tightly spaced parallel lines, small boxes, and tight concentric circles are prone to flicker because they conflict with the TV's scan lines. Make them heavier and space them farther apart than you would for a printed graphic. Think of the stock market graphs you see on the news: they're often superimposed over a grid, but the grid boxes are large. Use a minimum box size of one square inch, as seen on a 19-inch television.

Avoid lightweight fonts

Fonts such as Helvetica Light or Univers 45 and serif typefaces in small sizes are risky because they tend to become blurred and hard to see. Bodoni, for example, doesn't work well in small sizes because the serifs and thin portions of characters are too thin. Times and Caslon don't always work well, either. Century Schoolbook is better because its thins aren't very thin.

Don't space characters too tightly

Avoid excessively close kerning. The edges of characters bloom when televised, so the characters appear closer together than they really are. To compensate, space characters so that they look a bit too loose on the Mac's monitor.

Choose colors carefully

As a general rule, combine colors that are very different, like a light blue and a dark red, not a medium red and a medium blue. Use a full range of pastel colors, and they all may end up looking the same. Also, avoid colors that are too hot, like hot pink or lemon yellow. If you want yellow, use a more golden yellow. If a color is too hot, it can bleed past its borders or appear to vibrate.

For titles not superimposed over an image, use a black background and white or colored text. Black or colored text on a white background is rarely used in television for the same reason that it's rarely used in presentation graphics: an all-white background tends to be too glaring and harsh.

Superimposed titles

For titles that are superimposed over an image, keep the text simple. Use a font such as Univers 65 or Helvetica Medium and choose a color that enables the text to be visible over the background. Don't use white text, for example, if the background is a snow-covered ski slope.

Video Output Hardware

With hardware add-ons such as Radius's VideoVision and SpigotPower AV, you can capture full-screen QuickTime movies and record full-frame video on videocassette recorders. These high-end products not only support the 30-fps playback rate that's essential for high-quality video, they also support the 60 *fields* per second that interlaced television's approach to video requires.

Recording video from an AV Mac

If you have an AV Mac, you don't need additional hardware to record full-frame video — except for a video recorder, of course.

If your video recorder supports S-video, connect the AV's output to the recorder's input (see Figure 20-9 "Making Video Connections"). If the recorder supports only composite video, connect the AV's output to the recorder's composite input. (On Power Macs, use the output adaptor cable.) To also record the Mac's audio signal, connect the speaker jack to the recorder's audio input jack or jacks. Connect a TV set to the video recorder's video-out jack — this will enable you to see the Mac's screen. If you're using a camcorder, you can omit this step and just squint into the viewfinder, although connecting an external monitor to the camcorder will make videotaping a lot easier. (Many companies sell 4-inch color LCD monitors with composite video inputs; they make ideal monitors for camcorders or VCRs.)

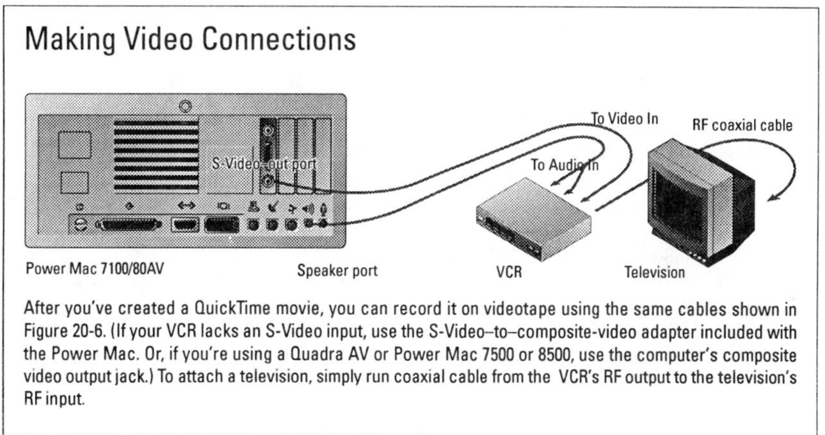

After you've created a QuickTime movie, you can record it on videotape using the same cables shown in Figure 20-6. (If your VCR lacks an S-Video input, use the S-Video–to–composite-video adapter included with the Power Mac. Or, if you're using a Quadra AV or Power Mac 7500 or 8500, use the computer's composite video output jack.) To attach a television, simply run coaxial cable from the VCR's RF output to the television's RF input.

Figure 20-9: Making Video Connections

Because navigating and choosing commands can be difficult when the screen is displayed on a fuzzy TV set or in a tiny viewfinder, consider making an alias of the Monitors control panel and stashing the alias on the Finder's desktop. If you use a macro utility such as CE Software's QuicKeys, make a keyboard shortcut for Monitors. This will make it easier to reactivate the Mac's monitor when you've finished recording.

The key to rerouting the Mac's screen image is the Monitors control panel. Open it, specify the desired number of colors, and then click the Options button (see Figure 20-10 "Switching to TV"). Click the button labeled Display Video on Television. Next, in the Select Monitor Type list, choose the appropriate resolution:

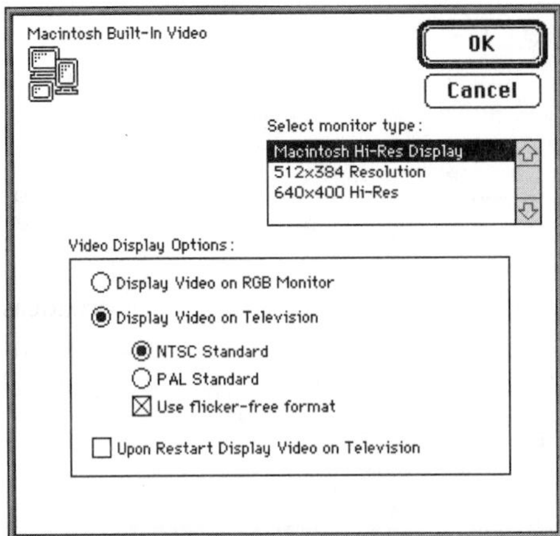

Figure 20-10: Switching to TV The Monitors control panel on an AV Mac provides additional options that let you route the video signal to a television or videorecorder. To switch to TV, click the Monitors control panel's Options button (not shown here) and then select the NTSC or PAL option as needed. If you want the entire Mac screen to fit in the video image, select the 512 x 384 option in the Select monitor type box. You may also want to check the Use flicker-free format box to avoid jittery horizontal lines.

- For recording Mac screen activity — the menu bar, windows, and the like — choose 512 by 384; this will prevent the outer edges of the screen image from being cut off. Also check the Use Flicker-Free Format box; this prevents thin horizontal lines, such as those in window title bars, from flickering. (Note that for flicker-free format to be available, the Monitors control panel must be set to 256 or fewer colors.)
- For recording QuickTime movies, choose 640 by 480, and do not check the Flicker-Free box. Note that because TV sets overscan — they project an image slightly larger than will fit on the picture tube's surface — the outer edges of the movie will not be visible on TV sets. TV producers take overscan into account during production by ensuring that titles and essential parts of a scene fit within a *safe zone*. QuickTime producers should, too.

When you click OK, a dialog box appears asking if you really want to switch the screen image. Verify that your video recorder is properly connected — if it isn't, you won't be able to see the Mac's screen image — and then click the Switch button.

If you have a SpigotPower AV card, use its SpigotPower AV Player application to play movies created with the card. Otherwise, you can use a video-editing program or Apple's Movie Player utility to play movies that you want to videotape. With QuickTime 2 and the Movie Player 2.0 application, you can use the Print to Video command's zooming options to play a quarter-screen movie in full-screen mode. The relative fuzziness of television (compared to a sharp computer monitor) will smooth out most of the jagginess that you would otherwise see on the Mac's screen.

The NTSC video that the AV Macs produce isn't 100-percent broadcast quality, but it looks great. AV machines also support the PAL video standard that's used in Western Europe, Africa, and Asia. For France, which uses a standard called SECAM, you need to use a PAL-to-SECAM converter, which is a common video accessory in that country.

Recording video from a Power Mac 8500

The Power Mac 8500's video-output capabilities are dramatically improved over those of the AV Macs. The same basics apply: you can connect a video device — camcorder, VCR, TV monitor — and tape or display QuickTime movies, screen activity, or presentations.

Beyond these basics, however, everything is new and improved. The 8500 can display 24-bit video on a video device; previous AV models were limited to 16-bit video, which caused color banding. At least as important, when you upgrade the 8500's VRAM to a full 4MB, you don't have to shut down the computer's monitor to send the screen image to a video device: You can set up the 8500 to mirror its screen on both the monitor and the video device, or to treat the video device as a second monitor. With the stock 2MB of VRAM, the 8500 works similarly to previous AV Macs — when video-out is active, the monitor goes dark.

The 8500 also supports a hardware zoom feature that lets you fill the screen with a QuickTime movie whose actual dimensions are 320 by 240 pixels (quarter-screen resolution). QuickTime 2 supports a software-only full-screen playback mode, but it uses pixel doubling — it simply duplicates each horizontal and vertical pixel. The 8500's hardware zooming, by comparison, actually creates new pixels that are blends of the movie's actual pixels, a process called *interpolation*.

For controlling this AV studio-in-a-box, there's a new control panel, named Video and Sound (see Figure 20-11 "Central Switching"). Sound & Displays provides a visual view of the machine's sound and video capabilities and simplifies the process of configuring monitors. (It also provides some enhancements over the Monitors control panel; for example, you don't have to restart after dragging the menu bar from one monitor to another, and you can activate display mirroring by simply dragging one display's icon to another's.)

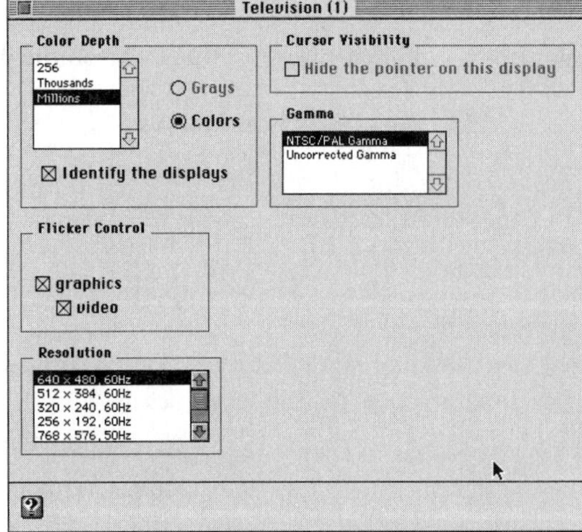

Figure 20-11: Central Switching The Sound & Displays control panel lets you manage the video and sound features of the Power Mac 7500 and 8500. Top: The control panel with both its Map (the icons) and List (the text boxes) view displayed. Checked items are activated. In this example, a television monitor is connected to an 8500's video-out connector. Bottom: Configuring the television's resolution and anti-flicker options. Configuration dialog such as this one appear when you click a component's icon or text label and then choose commands from the Configure menu.

Recording video from a converter box

Numerous companies, Apple included, make converter boxes that attach to the Mac's monitor connector and convert the Mac's video signal to NTSC or PAL format.

Apple's inexpensive Apple Presentation System connects to any Mac with a 15-pin monitor connector — including many PowerBooks — and lets you display the Mac's screen image on any NTSC or PAL television. Connect the box to a video recorder, and you can record QuickTime movies.

The Apple Presentation System provides both composite and S-video outputs. Software bundled with the box lets you activate a flicker filter and choose from several display resolutions. In short, the product provides the same video-out capabilities as AV Macs.

Actually, the Apple Presentation System does the AVs one better by supporting mirroring — the capability to display an image on a Mac monitor *and* a TV set simultaneously. With AV Macs, when you switch to TV output, the Mac's monitor goes dark — which complicates life if you haven't connected your cables properly.

Numerous video-out boxes are available from third-party firms, but the Apple Presentation System's aggressive price is likely to narrow the field — or bring down prices. This appealing little box should find a home in schools or businesses that want to use large-screen monitors for training, the briefcases of PowerBook owners who want to connect to TV sets for presentations, and on the desks of people who want to record Mac screen images and QuickTime movies.

Performas and Multimedia: QuickTime Made Easier

Apple's entry-level Macs — the Quadra 630 and Performa 630 series machines as well as the Performa 5200 and 6200 series — sport logic board and case designs geared toward multimedia: from their optional TV tuner boards to their front-panel remote-control sensors, these computers are designed for the television age.

These computers' TV talents fall into two broad categories: support for video digitizing and support for broadcast and cable television.

The Apple Video System card

Apple's Apple Video System, which installs in one of the computer's specialized expansion slots, provides video digitizing features similar to those of AV Macs. (Indeed, the card uses the same Phillips digitizing chips.) Connect a videocassette recorder, camcorder, or other video source to the card's input jacks, and you can create QuickTime movies, grab individual video frames, and display video in a window on-screen. The price: only $199.

Like an AV Mac, the Apple Video System card provides both composite and S-video connectors. (S-video generally provides a sharper image because the signal's color and brightness information travel on separate wires; in a composite video signal, this information is merged.) Unlike an AV Mac, the card also provides a standard RCA-style audio-input jack — no struggling to find a miniplug-to-RCA adaptor when you need to connect the card to an audio source.

Using the Apple Video Player application

For QuickTime digitizing, the Apple Video System card includes a simple program called Apple Video Player. This program lets you grab individual frames, digitize movies, and switch between video sources (see Figure 20-12, "Apple Video Player"). It's preinstalled in the Apple menu for convenient access.

As this chapter has discussed, a critical phase of any QuickTime project involves compressing the movie so that it uses less disk space and plays back smoothly. This process can be one of the most confusing aspects of QuickTime; the compression world is laced with technical jargon and concepts. The Apple Video Player software simplifies things by providing three compression settings: none, normal, and most.

These settings correspond to the following:

- ❖ The Most setting corresponds to the highest-quality Video codec setting (Apple Video Player uses QuickTime's Video compressor).
- ❖ The Normal option corresponds to the normal Video codec setting.
- ❖ None, of course, means no compression.

You make these adjustments in the Apple Video Player's Preferences dialog box. The Apple Video Player's Controls window is where you do your actual digitizing (see Figure 20-12 "Apple Video Player").

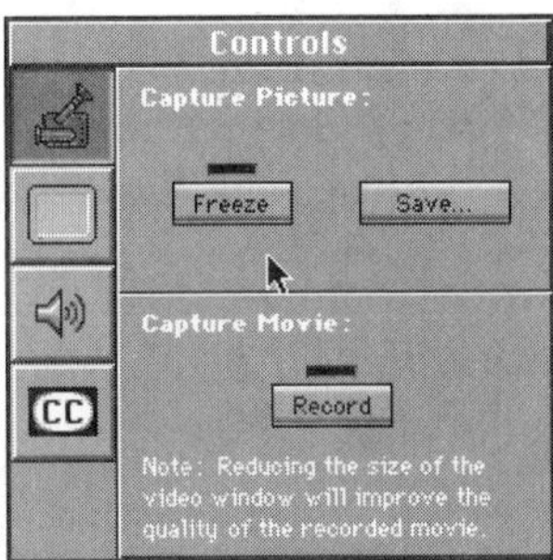

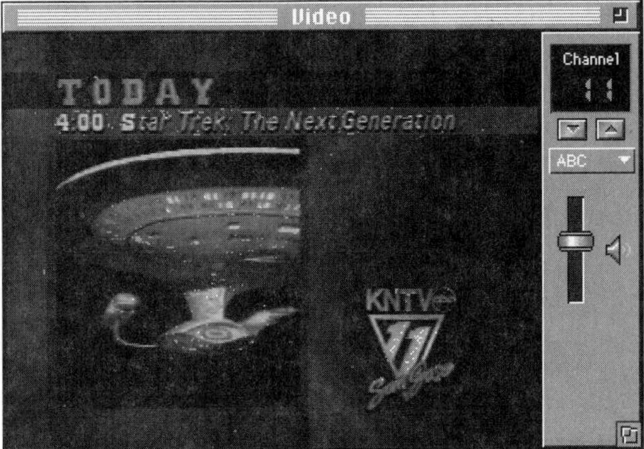

Figure 20-12: Apple Video Player The Apple Video Player utility (top) provides a simple, one-window interface for choosing the video source, capturing a single video frame, and recording a QuickTime movie. TV from the Video/TV System cards (bottom), displayed in a resizable window.

They don't sound as good

Sound is one area where entry-level Macs fall short of AV and Power Mac standards. Their sound-digitizing and playback circuitry uses 8-bit sampling resolution rather than the cleaner-sounding 16-bit sound of the AVs and Power Macs. Also, the Quadra 630 and Performa 630 series can't record stereo sound (although it can play back stereo QuickTime movies and compact discs). In general, the audio features in entry-level Macs are adequate for viewing multimedia CDs and creating amateur-level content, but they aren't intended to meet the needs of professional producers.

Watching TV

In 1993, Apple built one production run of a computer called Macintosh TV, which combined a slick but flawed TV tuner with a relatively slow 33MHz 68030 Mac. Now there's a better way to put *The Simpsons* alongside your spreadsheets: an entry-level Mac equipped with the Apple Video/TV System, which also includes the Apple Video System digitizing card.

The Mac TV's biggest flaw was that it forced you to choose between full-screen TV or a full-screen Mac desktop. The Apple Video/TV System lets you view television in a resizable window. You can digitize QuickTime movies of TV programs and also do still captures of single video frames.

Using the Apple Video/TV System software

The Apple Video/TV System's software is similar to that of the old Macintosh TV (see Figure 20-13 "TV Tuning"). A control panel lets you activate an automatic scan mode in which the card scans each of the 181 channels it's capable of receiving and locks out inactive ones, so you can channel surf without static.

Other options let you activate closed-captioning and assign text labels, such as call letters or network names, to channels. You can specify a keyboard shortcut for displaying the TV window and specify a password that must be typed before the window appears. (The security system is as easy to defeat as the Mac TV's: just yank the TV Preferences file out of the System Folder and restart, and the passwords are gone.) And a handy new Reminder option lets you program the Apple Video/TV System to automatically display given channels at specified times — no missing *Home Improvement* because you were mired in homework.

The Apple Video/TV System includes a compact remote control that lets you not only control the TV functions, but also turn the computer on and off and play audio compact discs with the computer's built-in CD-ROM drive. (You can also train a programmable universal remote control to control the computer's tuner and CD-ROM.)

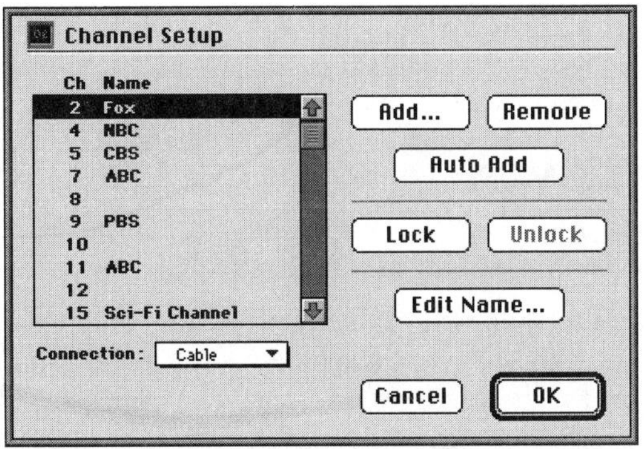

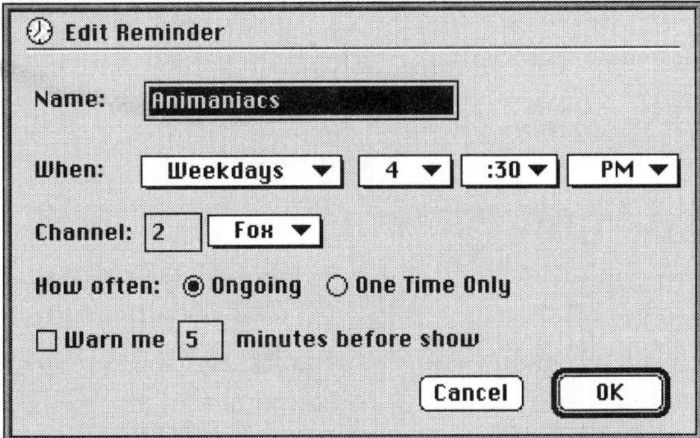

Figure 20-13: TV Tuning The software that accompanies the Apple Video/TV System lets you configure the tuner to lock out inactive channels, specify TV station call letters and network affiliations, and password-protect access to specific stations (top). You can also specify that the TV window appear automatically so you don't miss a favorite program (bottom).

Tips for Choosing a Video Recorder

You can use a consumer VCR to record QuickTime movies, but for more advanced applications (or bigger budgets), you may want to use a machine that your video editing program can control. Sony, Canon, Panasonic, NEC, and other big-name video manufacturers offer such machines.

The Sony Vbox system

The Sony Vbox controller, for example, is a video/computer interface that lets you control a wide range of Sony consumer video gear, including VCRs and 8mm camcorders, from within presentation and multimedia applications. With the Sony Vbox interface, the Mac can accurately control multiple video devices and lets you search for and identify specific video segments to incorporate into a production.

The Sony Vbox uses Sony's Video System Control Architecture (VISCA) protocol, designed by Sony as a standard set of command codes for synchronized computer control of multiple video peripherals. With the Vbox interface and a video production program that supports VISCA, your Mac can control a VISCA-supported video recorder such as Sony's Vdeck.

Camcorders with consumer timecodes

Most camcorder manufacturers sell mid- to high-priced camcorders that support one of several consumer timecodes. These machines record a code on the videotape that the camcorder uses to locate scenes precisely. The camcorder also provides an interface jack designed to connect to video editing gear — or to a computer.

One of the most popular consumer timecodes is Sony's Recordable Consumer Time Code (RCTC), which has also been licensed by Canon. I used a Canon L2 camcorder, Canon's high-end consumer Hi-8 machine that supports RCTC, to shoot the video on the *Macworld Power User Clinic*.

The controlled capture alternative

Another plus to using a computer-controllable video deck is that you can get higher-quality results when digitizing movies by doing your digitizing on a slower, frame-by-frame basis — a technique sometimes called *controlled capture*. (The opposite of controlled capture is live capture — digitizing movies in real time, as a videotape plays back or as you simply point a camcorder at the subject.)

Controlled captures also enable you to digitize at a faster frame rate or larger movie size than your Mac can handle in real time. Your Quadra 650, example, is too slow to handle 30 fps in real time, but it's certainly able to single-step a video recorder and grab frames at its own pace.

One drawback of a controlled capture, as you might guess, is that it's *slow*, far slower than a live capture. That's especially true when you use a slow compressor such as Cinepak. Another drawback to controlled captures is that they tend to impose more wear and tear on your videotapes and your video recorder or camcorder, because the machine is always alternating between pausing and advancing a frame.

Abbate's VideoToolkit

An inexpensive program that lets you do controlled captures is Abbate Video's Video Toolkit. Video Toolkit includes a Mac-to-videorecorder control cable and supports most popular consumer video timecodes and controllable camcorders. (I've used it with good results with my Canon L2.) The program has extensive logging features that let you make notes about scenes, specify in-points and out-points, and then do the final digitizing. VideoToolkit's amazing interface cable can also connect to a second video recorder to enable you to dub your scenes directly to a second tape.

VideoToolkit can be quirky and its HyperCard-based interface is a bit confusing at times, but it is an inexpensive way to do controlled captures and videotape logging.

The service bureau option

You probably won't be shocked to hear that professional and semiprofessional video gear is costly. But just as graphics service bureaus enable you to output text and graphics to a high-resolution imagesetter, video service bureaus are appearing that enable you to rent time on high-end video production equipment.

You create your rough edit by using a program such as Premiere or VideoShop, and then you export an *edit-decision list* (EDL) — a list of all the clips, transitions, and special effects in the production. You can then supply your original videotapes and the EDL to the service bureau, which returns them along with a master of your final, edited production. And a bill.

QuickTime VR: Virtual Reality for the Rest of Us

Virtual reality — that goggles-and-gloves technology that immerses you in photorealistic 3-D worlds where you can explore — requires more computing horsepower and hardware than a personal computer provides. Apple's QuickTime VR technology brings the best parts of virtual reality — user-controlled exploration and examination — to Macs and Windows computers. QuickTime VR doesn't demand goggles or gloves; you view a virtual world on the computer's screen and move around with your mouse or keyboard. As such, QuickTime VR doesn't provide the total immersion of true virtual reality, but neither does it impose its hardware requirements. Think of it as virtual VR.

The QuickTime VR experience

Initially, QuickTime VR will find its way into multimedia CD-ROM titles, where it will join images, sounds, text, and conventional QuickTime movies. QuickTime VR adds a unique benefit: the ability to explore scenes and objects for yourself. A developer who uses QuickTime VR creates a virtual world that you can control instead of simply observe.

A conventional, or *linear*, QuickTime movie is like a videotape: you can watch it from start to finish or skip around within it, but your view of the subject — say it's of an orchestra on a stage — was cast in stone when the original video was shot.

With a VR movie, you can change your view by clicking and dragging within the movie or by using the keyboard's left-and-right arrow keys. For example, dragging to the left causes the view to change as if you were turning your head to the left, while dragging up is the equivalent of looking up (see Figure 20-14 "Moving Within Movies"). You can not only see the orchestra, you can turn around to see who's sitting in the row behind you. You can zoom in on the orchestra for a closer look, or zoom out to see the big picture. A VR movie that provides this freedom of navigation is called a *panoramic* movie.

Figure 20-14: Moving Within Movies
QuickTime VR lets you explore locations using the mouse or keyboard's arrow keys. The scenes shown here are from the first CD-ROM to use QuickTime VR, Simon & Schuster Interactive's Star Trek: The Next Generation Interactive Technical Manual. Top: We're on the bridge of the U.S.S. Enterprise. We can look left and right or zoom in and out if we want, but in this screen, we're about to jump to a different bridge location — the helm station. (The arrow pointer means the mouse is over a hot spot that leads to a different location.) Middle: We've arrived at the helm station and we're in the process of turning to the right, as indicated by the right-pointing arrow. Bottom: We've turned around almost 180 degrees to look at where we came from. Here, the mouse is over the hot spot that, if clicked, will return us to that location.

Creating VR movies

When creating a panoramic movie, a developer uses Apple's QuickTime VR authoring software to create a 360-degree image; it's this image that you navigate. Because the panoramic movie is actually a single still image, it can't contain motion — you can see the orchestra and audience, but you can't see the conductor's blurring baton or the latecomers scurrying to their seats. This is QuickTime VR's biggest trade-off compared to goggles-and-gloves virtual reality.

QuickTime VR movies can also contain hot spots — areas upon which you can click to perform an action, such as displaying some text, playing a sound, or most commonly, switching to a different VR movie. Our VR movie of the concert hall might have a hot spot below the exit sign — click it, and you're suddenly transported to the lobby.

There's a key difference between QuickTime VR hot spots and the hot spots you've probably encountered in CD-ROM titles: a QuickTime VR hot spot is within the movie itself, and moves along with its object as you move around within the panoramic. In non-VR CD-ROM titles, hot spots are just static points on the screen; they aren't part of linear QuickTime movies.

Clicking a hot spot might also allow you to examine a specific object from different angles by clicking and dragging — it's the QuickTime VR equivalent to picking up an object and turning it around. This kind of exploration is provided by a different type of QuickTime VR movie: the *object* movie.

QuickTime VR movies differ from their linear counterparts in another way: they're expensive and complex to create. The first release of Apple's QuickTime VR authoring tools, the only software available for making VR movies, cost $2,000, require a fast Mac with 40MB of memory, and are difficult to use. ("You've got to be a wirehead to get this stuff to work," one QuickTime VR developer once told me.) The authoring landscape may change over time, but initially, most of us will be QuickTime VR consumers, not producers.

Fortunately, QuickTime VR's consumer hardware requirements are modest. Apple recommends a 25MHz 68030 or faster Mac with 5MB of memory, or a 33MHz 386 Windows machine with 8MB of memory. QuickTime VR movies themselves are remarkably compact — one panoramic movie uses only about 800K of disk space.

Photographing for QuickTime VR

If you're a shutterbug, you've probably experimented with panoramic pictures: snap a picture, turn, snap another, and so on until you've photographed a vista too grand for a single picture. When your photos arrive, you arrange them on a tabletop, aligning them where they overlap.

The first steps in creating a QuickTime VR panoramic movie are similar. Mount a camera on a tripod, orienting it vertically to capture as much of the subject's height as possible. To avoid distortion, the camera must be level and aligned so that it rotates around its optical center. Because a camera's tripod mount is on the camera body and not on the lens, a tripod-mounted camera will not rotate around its optical center unless it's offset slightly. Creating this offset means using a heavy-duty tripod and an array of brackets and tripod heads containing levels. (Peace River Studios, a developer in Cambridge, MA, has developed a low-cost bracket that simplifies camera mounting and enables the use of lightweight tripods.)

The number of pictures required for a full panorama depends on the camera and lens. Apple recommends using a 35mm camera with a 15mm lens. (A fisheye lens won't work.) Apple also recommends that each image have 25 to 40 percent overlap with the adjacent images. That's more overlap than you'd use for tabletop panoramics, but it leads to a better panoramic movie — I'll describe why shortly.

It's worth noting that you can also take a 360-degree image using panoramic cameras. These contain motorized mechanisms and special shutters that can capture a 360-degree image in one fell swoop. One drawback, however, is that panoramic cameras are expensive, ranging in price from $1,000 to more than $15,000. Another drawback is that the resulting image is likely to have areas that are poorly exposed — for example, in a panoramic of a sunrise scene, the area opposite the sun will be too dark. By comparison, if you take individual photos and adjust the exposure for each, the QuickTime VR software can blend each image to provide a smooth dynamic range across the panorama.

You'll snap a dozen or so photos to capture a 360-degree scene. Your next job is to get them into digital form by scanning them or having them transferred to Kodak PhotoCDs. The QuickTime VR developers I talked to prefer the PhotoCD approach — PhotoCD scanners yield better images than most desktop scanners, the PhotoCD supplier does the grunt work behind scanning the images, and the discs themselves are an ideal archiving medium.

The previous descriptions assume you're working with photographs, but you can also create a VR movie from a series of images generated by a 3-D rendering program — a prospect likely to lead to a new generation of Myst-like adventure titles.

Stitching Time

The job of combining individual images into a 360-degree panorama is performed by a program called the *stitcher*, part of the QuickTime VR authoring kit. Of all the components comprising QuickTime VR, the stitcher may be the most magical. And the most important — without it, creating a photographic QuickTime VR movie would *require* one of those expensive and inflexible panoramic cameras.

How the Stitcher works

The stitcher combines multiple images into a single file. That's the simple description. Under the hood, the stitcher performs what computer graphics gurus call *enviromapping* — it maps, or projects, an environment (such as a concert hall) onto the inside of a shape, such as a cube or a sphere — or, in QuickTime VR's case, a cylinder. When you navigate a QuickTime VR movie, you are in essence moving within a vertically oriented tube whose inner walls contain the panoramic image. The stitcher's job is to distort the original images — which were intended to appear on a flat surface — and then combine them into a seamless panoramic. In technical terms, the stitcher mathematically converts an image from a planar projection to a cylindrical projection.

The stitcher can usually perform its magic automatically by comparing the pixels in each image to locate the points where they overlap. If the images don't overlap neatly — perhaps one was scanned crookedly or the tripod moved during the photo session — you can use a manual stitching mode, which lets you use the keyboard's arrow keys and number pad to move and resize images. But manual intervention is the exception rather than the rule: according to Apple, 80 to 90 percent of properly photographed panoramics can be stitched automatically. On a Power Mac 8100, automatic stitching takes about five minutes; on a Quadra 900, it takes about 40. Exact stitching times depend on the resolution and quantity of the images.

As it combines images, the stitcher also blends the intensity levels of each one to compensate for differences in lighting or exposure. The more you overlapped the images, the smoother the blends.

Painting Hot Spots

The stitcher's end product is a PICT file containing the complete panoramic. Opened in an imaging program such as Adobe Photoshop, the PICT file appears warped and distorted. But the scene is clearly recognizable, and you won't find a single seam that gives away its past as a dozen separate images.

At this phase, you can use any imaging program to modify the panoramic — correct its color balance, retouch a flaw, remove an unwanted object. You can also create hot spots that will cause things to happen — such as a text description to appear or an object movie to be displayed.

A different approach to hot spots

If you've created hot spot buttons in an authoring package such as HyperCard, Apple Media Tool, or Macromedia Director, you're probably used to using a click-and-drag tool to select the area to be made hot. QuickTime VR approaches hot spots differently: you actually paint them using an imaging program. For example, to create a hot spot for a sculpture, you paint over the sculpture with a solid color. To create another hot spot for another sculpture, choose a different color and then paint it. Giving each hot spot a unique color enables QuickTime VR to distinguish between hot spots.

When you've finished painting hot spots, erase the rest of the image and then use the Save As command to create a new image file containing only the hot spots. During a later phase of the development process, a QuickTime VR authoring tool combines this hot spot image with the original panoramic. The painted hot spots don't appear on the screen when the VR movie is playing, but QuickTime VR knows where they are. (Under the hood, QuickTime VR stores the hot spots in a disabled video track.) When the mouse pointer is over a hot spot, its shape changes to tell the viewer that he or she can click the spot to make something happen.

The painting approach to creating hot spots is more laborious than an authoring program's draw-a-selection approach, but it has unique advantages. It allows you to create extremely precise hot spots — right down to the single pixel level. And this makes possible dramatic on-screen effects, such as everything except the hot-spot object disappearing when the object is clicked.

From One Place to Another: Controlling User Navigation in QuickTime VR

An important part of the QuickTime VR experience involves moving between locations. Making this experience possible requires creating a separate panoramic for each location, or node, and then using QuickTime VR's HyperCard-based scene editor to link the locations.

Making a conventional QuickTime movie means thinking like a movie director; making a multinode QuickTime VR movie means thinking like a tour planner. You must address questions such as, Where is a user looking now? Where can the user go from this location? Multimedia developers have always had to think about navigation, but QuickTime VR puts a new spin on the challenge: because a VR movie can display any portion of a 360-degree panoramic, developers must decide which portion of a panoramic should be visible when a user jumps to it. That view is likely to be different depending on where the user is coming from. For instance, in my concert hall example, when you click the exit sign hot spot to jump to the lobby, you'd expect to be looking out at the lobby when you arrive there. It wouldn't make sense to click the exit sign and then find yourself looking at the lobby door that leads back into the concert hall.

The scene editor helps you plan a virtual tour by enabling you to draw a top view of the entire scene and then add nodes corresponding to each of the panoramics you've created. You can draw hot spots on a given panoramic that, when clicked, will display other panoramics. You can specify what part of a panoramic will be displayed when a user jumps to it.

The scene editor generates a series of PICT files containing the hot spots along with a file containing information that tells QuickTime VR what part of a panoramic to display when it's activated. Another utility in the QuickTime VR authoring kit combines these files into a finished QuickTime VR movie — a single file containing as many locations as you defined.

The bigger picture

Most QuickTime VR movies are built into multimedia productions that also contain text, sound, still graphics, and linear QuickTime movies. Apple has created a series of external commands (XCMDs) that enable developers to access QuickTime VR movies within either Director or Apple's HyperCard. The XCMDs extend Director's and HyperCard's capabilities, enabling them to open QuickTime VR movies, scale them to a specific size (most CD-ROM titles display QuickTime VR movies at quarter-screen resolution: 320 by 240 pixels), and display a specific portion of a movie at a specific zoom setting. From a developer's perspective, integrating finished QuickTime VR movies into a production is similar to working with linear movies.

The QuickTime VR XCMDs also enable QuickTime VR to communicate with the authoring program by sending messages when various events take place. It's these messaging features that enable a production to display text or pictures when a VR movie's hot spot is clicked.

Sound and QuickTime VR

Developers can also use the messages to play sounds — indeed, this is the only way the first release of QuickTime VR can work with sound. Future versions of QuickTime VR are likely to have more sophisticated sound features that will enhance the virtual reality experience. Imagine navigating through a virtual forest and hearing a babbling brook become louder as you approach it, or navigating through a hotel room and hearing traffic noise increase as you approach the window. For now, you will have to imagine these things because the current incarnation of QuickTime VR is geared toward the eyes, not the ears.

CHAPTER 20 CONCEPTS AND TERMS

- Multimedia is the use of words, sounds, and still and moving pictures to convey ideas, sell products, educate, and entertain.
- At its most basic level, multimedia may involve jazzing up a slide presentation with music and narration. More advanced levels of multimedia use an authoring program to provide interactivity.
- QuickTime is a system extension that enables Mac programs to work with dynamic data such as sound, video, and animation. A piece of dynamic data is called a movie. You can create QuickTime movies by using a video recorder or with a wide variety of programs, such as animation and 3-D drawing packages.
- Multimedia and QuickTime can make use of every category of video hardware. For capturing video from a camcorder, videodisc player, or VCR, you need a frame-grabber board. For recording your productions on videotape, you need a board (or a Mac) that can output NTSC video.
- The rules that describe the format of a composite video signal were developed about 30 years ago by the National Television System Committee (NTSC). In many ways, the Mac's standard video signal is technically superior to NTSC video.
- To create final QuickTime movies from digitized clips, you need a video editing program such as Adobe Premiere or Avid's VideoShop.
- To design titles and other graphics to look their best within the limited resolution and 30Hz frame rate of NTSC video, avoid thin parallel lines and choose fonts and colors carefully.

authoring program
A program, such as HyperCard, Apple Media Tool, Macromedia Director, or Authorware Professional, that lets you integrate text and visuals and add on-screen buttons and other hot spots that enable users to interact with the production by branching to different areas of interest.

broadcast video
Another term for NTSC video — the standard format for commercial television in the United States and Japan.

codecs
Compression/decompression extensions that add specific compression capabilities to QuickTime.

composite video
A video-display technique in which the red, green, and blue signals merge with the sync signals into a technically simple composite signal that lacks the sharpness and clarity of RGB video (see *RGB video*).

compression
Reducing the storage requirements of an image or video sequence. Spatial compression saves space by removing information within a single image or video frame. Temporal compression, also called *frame differencing,* saves space by describing only the changes between frames.

controlled capture
Digitizing a movie one frame at a time by using a videodisc player, VCR, or other video device that is attached to and controlled by the Mac (see *live capture*).

edit-decision list
Abbreviated EDL, a list of all the clips, transitions, and special effects in a production. EDLs are used by professional video production equipment to assemble a final production from the source tapes.

field
In NTSC video, a set of odd- or even-numbered scan lines. Each field is painted 30 times per second, giving NTSC video a frame rate of 30Hz and a field rate of 60. Generating 60 fields per second requires professional video hardware.

frame
In video, one complete set of odd- and even-numbered scan lines. In animation, one of many still pictures that, when played rapidly, provide the illusion of motion.

frame grabber
An add-on board that enables the Mac to digitize video frames and create a QuickTime movie of the results.

frame rate
The number of frames displayed per second.

interlaced video
A video technique in which each frame is painted in two passes: the odd-numbered scan lines are drawn first, followed by the even-numbered scan lines.

live capture
Digitizing movies in real time, as a videotape plays back or as you simply point a camcorder at the subject (see *controlled capture*).

movie
A recorded sound and/or series of video frames stored in QuickTime's MooV format.

overscan
A television industry practice in which the image projected onto a television's video tube is too large to fit (see *underscan*).

RGB video
Short for red-green-blue, the video-display technique used by the Mac. With RGB video, the signals for red, green, and blue travel on separate wires. Other wires carry synchronization signals (see *composite video*).

underscan
A video-display technique in which the image projected on the video screen is smaller than the tube's surface. Computers underscan in order to show every pixel.

CHAPTER TWENTY-ONE

Music, MIDI, and Sound

- Looking at the Mac's many musical roles
- Applying digital audio — from error beeps to presentations to compact discs
- Attaching your Mac to a stereo system for better sound quality
- How to turn an AV or Power Mac into a digital audio recorder
- Tips for recording sound and editing QuickTime soundtracks

For Mac owners with a musical ear, this is a wonderful time to be alive. The Mac may be best known for changing the way people publish, but it has become a prominent force in the way people make and record music, too. Whether you're a beginner who has trouble pecking out "Chopsticks," a film score composer, or lead guitarist for the Bleeding Eardrums, there's a place for the Mac in your musical life.

And you don't have to break the bank to find it. You can sample the world of computer music applications for nothing more than the price of a program and a cable to hook your Macintosh into a stereo system. When you're ready to move up to a synthesizer, you'll be pleasantly surprised. The same electronics advances that have spawned $9.95 digital watches have made possible synthesizers that cost less than a color television.

What Can You Do with Sounds?

The Mac's capability to record, manipulate, and play back sound is also opening doors to new applications in education, entertainment, music, business, and science. And of course, on a more basic level, it lets you change the way your Mac sounds when you make a mistake: when you explored the Sound control panel, you noticed that you can choose from several digitally recorded beep sounds — a simple beep, a clanking sound, a springy "boing" (reminds me of the suspension on my first car), or a monkey's squawk, which, for you Mac trivia buffs, was actually created by a woman named Sandi Dobrowolsky, now a Claris employee.

In this chapter, I show you the ways in which you and a Mac can make beautiful music together, and I examine the roles that digital audio plays in the Mac world. Along the way, I spotlight some sound-oriented products available for the Mac. The Quick Tips box "The Mac Sounds Off" explains how to modify your System file to add your own digitally recorded system beeps, and it reveals some sources for prerecorded sounds.

The Mac Sounds Off

You can add to the Mac's repertoire of digital beep sounds by adding sound resources to your System file. Thousands of prerecorded sounds are available through on-line services such as America Online and CompuServe, user groups, and public domain and shareware clearing houses. And the *Macworld Power User Clinic* CD that accompanies this book includes a small collection of sounds to get you started (see the "Now Hear This" box in this chapter).

So how do you get sounds into the System file? If the sounds are stored as standard System 7 sound files, you can simply drag them to the icon of the System Folder. When the Finder asks if you want to install them in the System file, click OK. (Here's an easy way to tell if a sound is a standard System 7 sound file: in the Finder, double-click its icon. If it's a System 7 sound file, the sound plays.)

As for sounds stored in other formats, most of the sound-editing programs I discuss in this chapter — including Macromedia's SoundEdit 16, Digidesign's Sound Designer II, and Passport Design's Alchemy — can save sound resources directly in the System file (or in any other file, for that matter). You can also use SoundMover, a shareware utility by Riccardo Ettore, or Apple's ResEdit. And as an alternative to installing sounds directly in the System file, you can use a system-resource management utility such as Suitcase II or MasterJuggler, both described in Chapter 24.

Regardless of the program you use, you should make a backup copy of your System file in case something goes awry during the modification process.

After you add a sound to the System file, use the Sound control panel to select it as the current system beep.

If you use System 7.5, you can have your Mac play four separate sounds on the hour and at 15, 30, and 45 minutes past — turn your Mac into Big Ben or a grandfather's clock or, perhaps more appropriate, a cuckoo clock. Just open the Date & Time control panel and click the Clock Options button. In the Chime portion of the Options dialog box, check the Chime on the Hour box and then choose sounds and options as desired (see the accompanying figure).

(By the way, if you're using a system version prior to 7.5, you can have the same chime options using a free extension called SuperClock!, by Steve Christiansen. Indeed, the chime features in System 7.5 are based on SuperClock!.)

Using a variety of shareware system extensions, you can make your Mac sound off at other times, too. The best such sound extension is the shareware SoundMaster, by Bruce Tomlin. SoundMaster lets the Mac play sounds when you perform any of over a dozen tasks (such as inserting or ejecting a disk). MasterJuggler and Suitcase II have similar features.

Clock Options

To have System 7.5 play sounds at regular intervals, click the Clock Options button in the Date & Time control panel and use the options in the Chime portion of the subsequent dialog box.

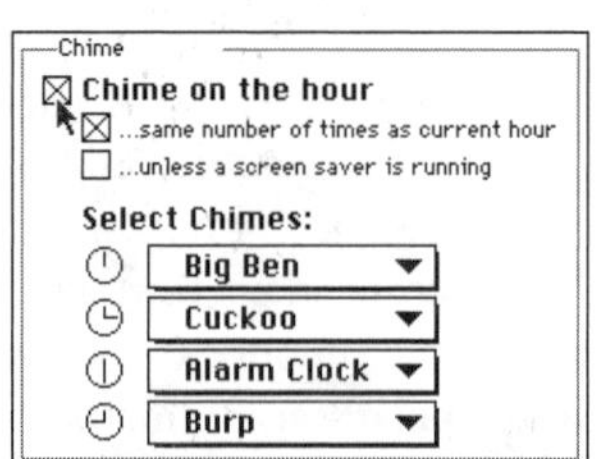

The Macintosh is a multitalented performer. In fact, a Mac can play so many musical roles that it may help to briefly audition each role before taking a closer look.

Sequencing

Several programs turn the Mac into an electronic multitrack recorder that records, edits, and plays back performances by using one or more synthesizers attached to the Mac. The magic that makes this possible goes by the name *Musical Instrument Digital Interface (MIDI)*, a synthesizer-communications standard built into virtually every synthesizer and electronic instrument made today. With QuickTime 2.0, included on the CD that accompanies this book, your Mac itself can become a MIDI synthesizer; more about this subject later.

Scoring

The process of putting notes on paper is traditionally a grueling task for composers, who must wrestle with staff paper and correction fluid, and for music publishing houses, which often use a mutated typewriter called a Musicwriter. Scoring programs do for composers what word processors have done for writers.

Composition

A fascinating genre of programs lets the Mac collaborate with you, storing groups of phrases you enter, analyzing their structure, and rearranging the notes into new rhythms and patterns based on the originals.

Sound editing

With many electronic instruments, adjusting the knobs and buttons required to produce a desired sound is so difficult that many players stick with the instruments' built-in sounds, often called *patches* (named in honor of the pioneering synthesizers of the sixties, whose many sound-generating modules were linked by patch cables like those for a telephone switchboard). Patch-editor programs let you draw and manipulate the waveforms that describe a sound's qualities and then transfer them to a synthesizer's memory.

Patch management

Most synthesizers can store dozens of patches, but that isn't enough for real sound hounds. *Patch librarians* are database managers for patches; these programs transfer the settings that make up each patch to or from a Macintosh disk. Patch librarians also let you cut and paste patches from one file to another, so you can organize sounds according to your performance needs. Most patch editors also provide librarian features.

Soundtrack production

For years, film and recording studios have used a timing standard called the *SMPTE* edit time code (SMPTE, pronounced *simpty*, stands for Society of Motion Picture and Television Engineers). The SMPTE code enables engineers to synchronize a soundtrack with an action. Many sequencers, as well as a variety of *cue* programs, work with the SMPTE code to simplify the chore of calculating how long a musical passage must be in order to fit a given scene.

Surveying Entry-Level Music Options

You're neither a synthesizer owner nor a soundtrack composer? You can still choose from a combination of programs designed to let you sound off with a minimal musical background and no additional equipment.

ConcertWare Pro

Foremost among such packages is ConcertWare Pro from Jump Software (formerly marketed by Great Wave Software). With ConcertWare Pro, you enter music on conventional staves by using the mouse and on-screen palettes, which provide one-click access to note and rest values. ConcertWare Pro also lets you cut, copy, and paste passages and print your compositions, which can have up to 32 parts. The program isn't intended to be a full-fledged scoring tool: you probably wouldn't use it for music publishing applications that I discuss later. But the program is ideal for composers and students.

ConcertWare Pro is also an ideal tool for learning about sound. Using the package's Instrument Maker program, you draw and edit waveforms and define a sound *envelope*, which governs a sound's percussiveness (see Figure 21-1 "Designing Instruments"). For example, a piano has a sharp attack (as the hammers hit the strings) and a gradual decay (as the strings stop vibrating and the sound fades out). Wind instruments have a gradual attack and little decay until the musician runs out of breath.

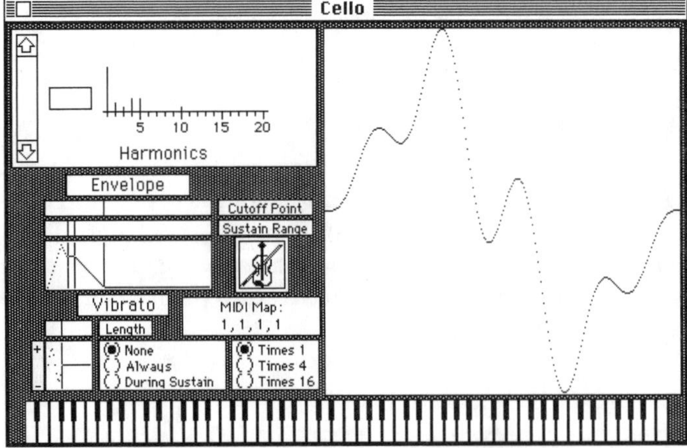

Figure 21-1: Designing Instruments ConcertWare Pro's Instrument Maker lets you design instruments by specifying the characteristics of their waveform, harmonics, and envelope. You can hear your efforts by clicking the on-screen piano keyboard, and you can save instruments for use with ConcertWare Pro.

Considering the Mac's limited sound-synthesizing capabilities, the end product of ConcertWare Pro's Instrument Maker program is surprisingly good. But if it's not good enough for you, ConcertWare Pro can send songs to a synthesizer or let you enter songs from a synthesizer.

If the notion of playing a song and then printing out its score sounds too good to be true, it is. Any performer's rendition of a piece varies from the precise timing specified by music notation. ConcertWare Pro, as well as professional sequencer and scoring packages, must attempt to round off variances in timing through a process called *quantization.* Generally, the process works well, but you still must fine-tune the final score.

Jamming with the Mac

A fun way to turn your Mac into an easy-to-play musical instrument is with Bogas Productions' Super Studio Session or Jam Session, both of which use *sampled* sound.

As I describe later in this chapter, sampled sound is a digitized version of the real thing, produced by feeding an audio signal into a hardware device called an *analog-to-digital converter*, which turns a continuously varying (analog) sound wave, the kind our ears recognize, into a series of numbers stored by sampling software. If you've ever marveled at a compact disc's startling clarity, you've experienced the most common application of sampled sound.

The instrument sounds included with Super Studio Session and Jam Session can't approach a compact disc's realism. Still, both programs are remarkable. Jam Session includes numerous songs in a variety of styles, from reggae to rock to classical to country. Each key on the Mac's keyboard is assigned to a prerecorded *riff* (a series of notes) or a sound effect such as a cheering or applauding crowd. You can improvise solos (and cheer yourself on) by pressing keys as a song plays, and Jam Session works to ensure that everything you play is in the right key and tempo. And on-screen, an animated band boogies to your beat.

Super Studio Session includes additional features, including a music editor that lets you create new songs. CompuServe, America Online, and user-group libraries are brimming with songs and additional instrument sounds. You can also create your own sounds by using a Mac with sound-recording hardware.

Bogas Productions also sells the Studio Session MIDI Utility, which lets you save your songs as standard MIDI files, and also lets you use Super Studio Session to play existing MIDI files.

The Scoop on MIDI

In 1982, the largest companies in the electronic music industry overcame their normally secretive and competitive urges and agreed to cooperate. The result of their collaboration was not a hot new musical instrument, but a 13-page document that has literally changed the way the world makes music.

That document describes the MIDI specification. MIDI was developed to enable musicians to connect electronic instruments to each other and to computers. The MIDI specification spells out the types of wires and connectors that unite musical instruments, as well as the commands and codes that MIDI-equipped instruments transmit and respond to. Generally, any piece of equipment with MIDI — whether a musical instrument or a computer — can talk with any other piece of MIDI gear.

On a basic level, MIDI lets you create a network of two or more instruments that you can play from just one instrument. Musicians often use this technique, called *layering*, to play multiple instruments simultaneously to obtain richer sound.

On a somewhat more advanced level, MIDI lets you connect one or more instruments to a computer to record and play back music and add accompaniments. This aspect of MIDI has helped create a new phenomenon — the home recording studio. And at its most advanced level, MIDI lets you combine a computer-controlled network of instruments with audio equipment and even stage lighting to automate an entire performance environment.

MIDI Basics

MIDI data can travel in two directions at the same time — from an instrument to a computer and from a computer to an instrument. To accommodate this two-way traffic, every MIDI device has two connectors — MIDI In and MIDI Out. Some devices have another connector called MIDI Thru, which can be used to chain MIDI devices together.

How MIDI interfaces work

Peer behind the Mac and you notice there are no such connectors. Unlike some personal computers, Macs don't come equipped for MIDI. They need a separate piece of hardware called a *MIDI interface*, which connects to the Mac's modem or printer port and provides MIDI In and MIDI Out connectors.

Several MIDI interfaces are available for the Mac, ranging from Opcode's $59 MIDI Translator II to Mark of the Unicorn's $595 MIDI Time Piece II Interface and Opcode's $1195 Studio 5LX. High-end MIDI interfaces provide more MIDI In and MIDI Out connectors, enabling you to create a larger MIDI network. They also provide sync features that allow the Mac's MIDI playback to be synchronized with an external device such as an audiotape recorder. More about syncing later.

Understanding MIDI data

Figure 21-2 "The Ins and Outs of MIDI Connections" shows three different ways to connect MIDI instruments with an interface to relay MIDI data (also called *messages* or *events*) between instruments and a Mac.

What kind of data travels via MIDI? First and foremost, *note data.* When you play a MIDI instrument's keyboard, it tells the Mac which keys were pressed and for how long. Velocity-sensitive keyboards also note how hard you pressed each key, letting the Mac capture the varied dynamics of your performance.

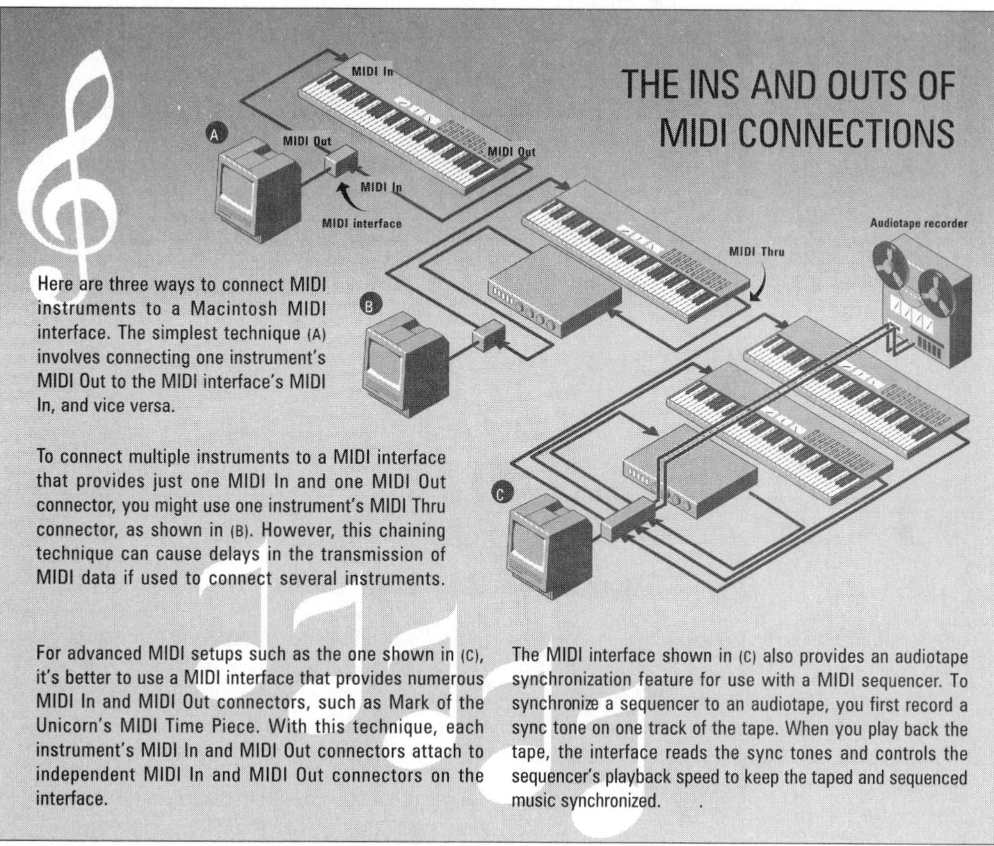

THE INS AND OUTS OF MIDI CONNECTIONS
A
B
C
MIDI In
MIDI Out
MIDI Out
MIDI In
MIDI interface
MIDI Thru
Audiotape recorder
Here are three ways to connect MIDI instruments to a Macintosh MIDI interface. The simplest technique (A) involves connecting one instrument's MIDI Out to the MIDI interface's MIDI In, and vice versa.
To connect multiple instruments to a MIDI interface that provides just one MIDI In and one MIDI Out connector, you might use one instrument's MIDI Thru connector, as shown in (B). However, this chaining technique can cause delays in the transmission of MIDI data if used to connect several instruments.
For advanced MIDI setups such as the one shown in (C), it's better to use a MIDI interface that provides numerous MIDI In and MIDI Out connectors, such as Mark of the Unicorn's MIDI Time Piece. With this technique, each instrument's MIDI In and MIDI Out connectors attach to independent MIDI In and MIDI Out connectors on the interface.
The MIDI interface shown in (C) also provides an audiotape synchronization feature for use with a MIDI sequencer. To synchronize a sequencer to an audiotape, you first record a sync tone on one track of the tape. When you play back the tape, the interface reads the sync tones and controls the sequencer's playback speed to keep the taped and sequenced music synchronized.

Figure 21-2: The Ins and Outs of MIDI Connections

Note that data is by no means the only kind of information that can travel on MIDI cables. Instead of playing notes, the following MIDI messages play other roles in the performance:

❖ *Program changes* instruct an instrument to switch sounds — from piano to strings, for example.

❖ *Continuous data* generally modifies the way a sound is played. For example, many instruments have *pitch bend* wheels or levers that let you slide between pitches the way guitar players do when they bend a string. Another kind of continuous data is *aftertouch*, which describes how hard you hold down a note key. By pressing harder on a key after you press it, you may add vibrato or cause a string sound to get progressively louder. Not all keyboards send aftertouch, but those that do allow for a greater range of expression.

❖ *Clock* or *sync data* carries information about the timing of a MIDI performance. It's often used to synchronize a network of MIDI instruments to an audiotape recording.

❖ *System-exclusive data* includes information pertinent to a specific model of MIDI instrument, such as the contents of its internal memory or the MIDI-channel assignments of its sounds. By transferring system-exclusive data to the Mac, you can store and alter an instrument's sounds and then transfer the data back to the MIDI instrument.

Alternative MIDI controllers

MIDI instruments don't necessarily have to have piano-like keyboards. They can take other forms, ranging from the self-explanatory MIDI guitar and drum pad to the not-so-self-explanatory saxophone-like wind controller. MIDI-equipped accordions are available, as are retrofits that add MIDI to organs and acoustic pianos.

Instruments that generate MIDI data are often called *controllers.* Many musicians combine one controller with several *sound modules* — boxes containing sound-generating circuitry and MIDI connectors, but no keyboards. E-mu Systems' remarkable Proteus series is among the most popular, but Yamaha, Roland, Korg, and others also have offerings.

If you think that the Mac world changes fast, you wouldn't believe how often music hardware developers rework their product lines. Check out a local music store or a copy of *Electronic Musician* or *Keyboard* magazine for the scoop on the latest gear.

Understanding MIDI channels

MIDI instruments can receive or transmit data on any of 16 independent *channels* — electronic mailing addresses that accompany MIDI data and specify its destination. Not only can you specify the channel MIDI instruments use to transmit data, you can also configure them to respond to data sent on all MIDI channels (omni mode) or only to certain ones (poly mode).

This capability to channel MIDI data is important because many MIDI setups comprise more than one instrument, some of which may be *multitimbral* — capable of simultaneously producing different types of sounds, such as those of a drum set and a horn section. If you couldn't assign certain MIDI data to certain channels, nothing would stop one instrument from playing another's part.

Surveying MIDI Software

Without a computer, MIDI data plays a valuable but limited role: it lets you play numerous instruments using just one controller. MIDI was originally created for this humble role.

How MIDI sequencers work

But MIDI data becomes much more useful when you combine it with a computer and software that can store and manipulate it. The most popular kind of MIDI software is the *sequencer*, a kind of tapeless tape deck that lets you build your own arrangements by recording parts one track at a time. You can start with a drum or bass track to establish a rhythm, and perhaps specify that it *loop*, or repeat, continuously. Next, you can add a guitar melody and then add some strings to sweeten things up. During playback, you route the tracks to the appropriate instruments or to the appropriate sounds within a multitimbral instrument by specifying a different playback channel for each one (see Figure 21-3 "Laying Down Tracks").

Sequencers versus audio recording software

On the surface, a sequencer seems similar to a multitrack tape recorder or to digital audio-recording software such as Digidesign's Sound Tools or OSC's Deck II. But a sequencer doesn't store sound; instead, it stores the sequence of MIDI data that describes what you played.

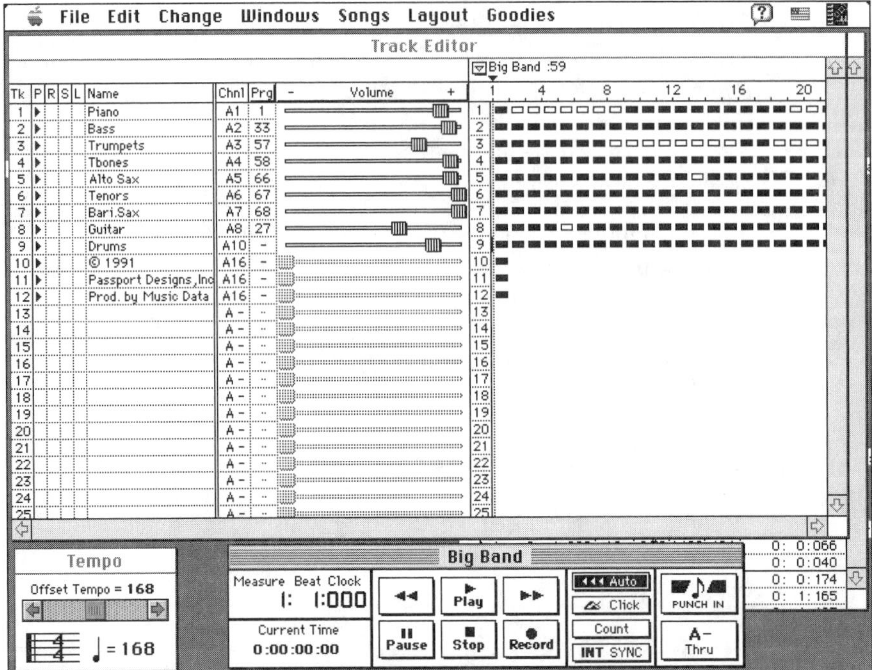

Figure 21-3: Laying Down Tracks Sequencers (such as Passport Designs' Pro 5, shown here) let you record and play back MIDI data. The dark bars on the right indicate the presence of MIDI data in those measures. At the top of the window is a marker (here named Big Band), which you can create to quickly access a specific point. Most sequencers provide these basic features.

MIDI's storage technique has a few significant pluses. First, MIDI data requires far less disk space than digital audio data does. A ten-minute, CD-quality stereo audio recording requires 100MB of disk space; a ten-minute MIDI sequence may use 30K or so. MIDI's bird-like appetite for disk space is what makes MIDI movies so efficient in QuickTime 2.0; more about this topic later.

Also, because the MIDI data in a sequence isn't tied to a particular sound, you can change an instrument's settings before or during playback to hear how that electric guitar part sounds when played by an acoustic guitar or an oboe, for example. You can also work up an arrangement by using an economical home system and then take your disk into a recording studio and play the sequence with state-of-the-art gear.

And because you're working with MIDI data, you can continue adding tracks without compromising sound quality. With analog audio recording, each time you bounce two or more tracks to a single track to free up a track for recording, the sound quality of the older tracks suffers. With a sequencer, the tracks exist in the Mac's memory, not on audiotape. So you can add as many tracks as you have memory for, and every playback is an original performance.

MIDI Vanilli?

Perhaps best of all (at least for those of us who can't practice eight hours a day), you can use a sequencer's extensive editing features to correct misplayed notes or add more dynamic expression. You can cut and paste sections of a recording, for example, to remove extra verses or repeat a part. And with a sequencer's step-recording mode, you can manually enter difficult parts one note at a time or slow down the tempo and record them at a more leisurely pace. Is it cheating? Some say yes, but it lets you make better music, and the results go a long way toward soothing your guilt.

Sequencer Editing Features

Here's a closer look at the kinds of features you can find in Macintosh sequencers.

Editing features

For correcting or inserting notes in existing tracks, three basic schemes exist. Graphic editing displays a track's contents on a music staff-like grid, except that notes are shown as horizontal bars, with longer bars representing longer notes. Graphic editing lets you select and drag notes from one position to another by using the mouse. Because a graphic editing display resembles a player piano roll, it's often called a *piano roll display*. Some programs, including Mark of the Unicorn's Performer and Opcode's Studio Vision Pro, can also display a sequence in standard music notation.

Event-list editing displays a track's contents as a table of MIDI data. It doesn't give you the click-and-drag convenience of graphic editing, but it allows for greater precision because you can type and edit the exact values that describe individual notes or other MIDI data. Better sequencers provide both types of editing windows (see Figure 21-4 "Editing Tracks").

Quantizing: keeping time

For tweaking the timing of notes, sequencers provide quantizing features, which cause the program to move notes to the nearest note value you specify. If used excessively, however, quantizing can give sequenced music an overly mechanized feel; after all, no one plays every note exactly on time. To eliminate this undesirable side effect, most sequencers let you specify a margin within which notes aren't quantized, thus you can neaten up your playing without making it sound robotic.

Some sequencers also provide a humanize option, which does the opposite of quantizing: it nudges notes off their exact beat values to improve the feel of a passage that was overly quantized or entered by using a step-recording mode.

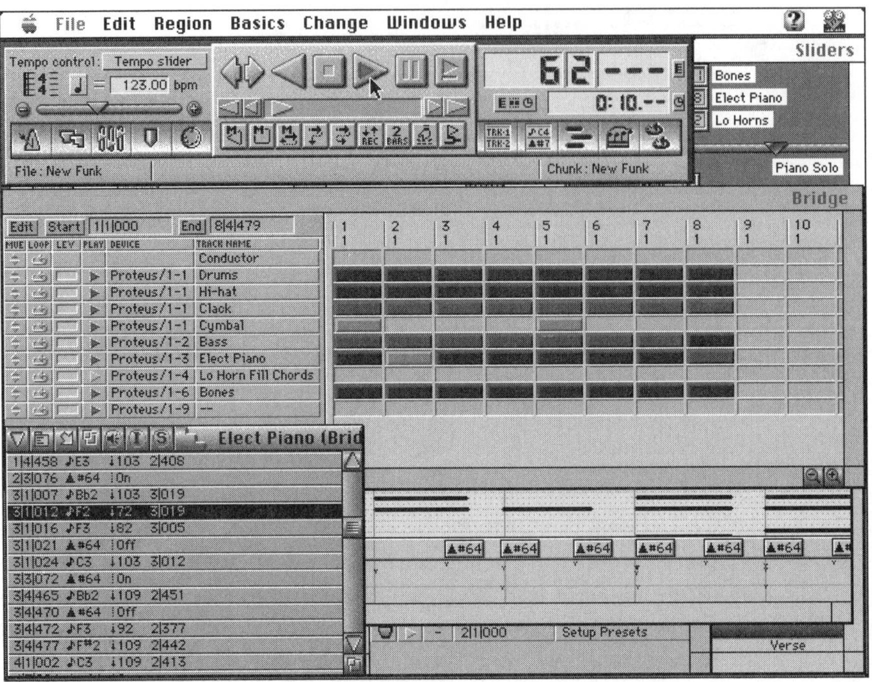

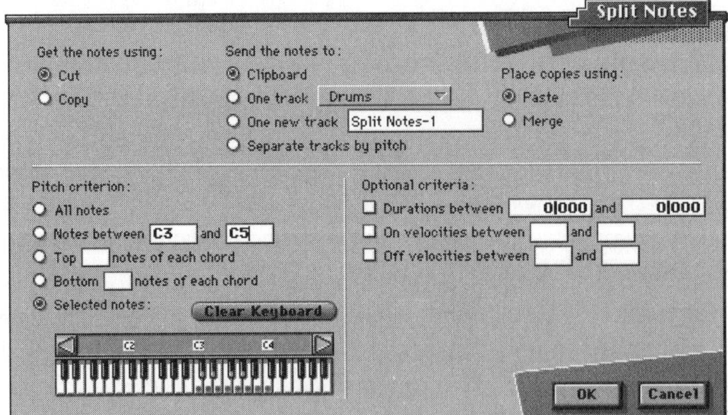

Figure 21-4: Editing Tracks The graphic and event list-editing windows in Mark of the Unicorn's Performer (top). The entries reading #64 indicate the press and release of a MIDI keyboard's sustain pedal. Performer's Split Notes dialog box (bottom) lets you extract certain notes from a track. One use for Split Notes is to separate the left- and right-hand parts of a track.

Conductor tracks and tempo maps

Many pieces of music don't have the same tempo throughout. To accommodate such pieces, sequencers provide a special track, often called a *conductor track*, that stores tempo information. Using the conductor track, you can create a tempo map that describes the tempo changes in the piece.

With some sequencers — including Mark of the Unicorn's Performer, Opcode Systems' Vision, and Steinberg-Jones's Cubase — you can specify the tempo by tapping a key on a MIDI keyboard.

Synchronizing with external equipment

If you combine a sequencer with external equipment, such as a multitrack audiotape recorder or a high-end video recorder, you need a sequencer that you can lock to synchronization codes sent by that external source. By recording a sync track on a tape recorder and feeding that track into a sync-supporting MIDI interface such as Opcode's Studio 5LX or Mark of the Unicorn's MIDI Time Piece II, you keep the sequencer and recorder in exact synchronization.

You can use sync to add sequenced electronic music to an acoustic recording or to create a multitrack audio recording by using a single MIDI instrument to record one track at a time, synchronizing the sequencer's playback with the tracks you've already recorded on tape. Sync features are commonly used in TV and movie soundtrack production, in which MIDI sequences of music or even sound effects are synchronized to visual action. In these cases, a sequencer is synchronized to a film editor or videotape recorder with the industry standard SMPTE time code.

Combining MIDI with digital audio

At the leading edge of the sequencer world, you can find sequencers that can combine MIDI data and digitally recorded audio in the same file, enabling you to add vocals or acoustic instrument recordings to a sequence. It's the best of both worlds.

Sequencers that support hard disk digital audio recording include Mark of the Unicorn's Digital Performer, Opcode's Studio Vision Pro and Studio Vision AV, and Steinberg's Cubase Audio. The Studio Vision programs and Steinberg's Cubase Audio require no additional audio-recording hardware when used with an AV or Power Mac. Digital Performer requires third-party audio hardware, such as Digidesign's Audiomedia II (discussed later in this chapter). The Studio Vision programs and Cubase Audio also work with Digidesign hardware.

The leading program in this category is Opcode's Studio Vision Pro 3.0, which provides an astonishing audio-to-MIDI conversion feature that actually translates recorded audio into MIDI data that you can edit and then convert back into audio data. Here's just one way to use this amazing feature: Say you've recorded a vocal track containing an off-key note. With Studio Vision Pro, you can convert the track into MIDI data, correct the note, and then convert it back into audio!

Freestyle sequencing with FreeStyle

If you like to compose using a sequencer, check out Mark of the Unicorn's FreeStyle. As its name implies, FreeStyle is less structured than a conventional sequencer; its approach to sequencing makes it easy to experiment with different tracks and arrangements. It's a great program for someone who wants to spend more time composing and playing than setting up track and MIDI channel assignments.

Introducing standard MIDI files

If you're a pro, you may end up using more than one sequencer. Fortunately, virtually all sequencers support a standard file format for exchanging sequences. This format is called, amazingly enough, the *standard MIDI file* format, and it enables sequencers — even ones running on different computers — to exchange recordings.

If you're familiar with Mac graphics concepts, think of standard MIDI files as the PICT files of the MIDI world — a file format that all programs can understand. When you want to move a MIDI sequence from one program to another — or if you want to convert a sequence into a QuickTime music movie — you save the sequence as a standard MIDI file, usually by using a Save As or Export command.

Often, you also use MIDI files along with scoring programs — the next stop on your MIDI tour.

Music Processors

Scoring programs let you print music by using conventional notation. They do for composers what word processors do for writers — enable you to easily correct and revise a piece without a lot of erasing (see Figure 21-5 "Scoring Software").

Even more exciting, scoring programs can transcribe music as you play it on a MIDI keyboard. Real-time music transcription has been a fantasy of musicians for years, and the dream still hasn't been completely fulfilled. The primary problem is one I mentioned before: nobody plays every note exactly on time. A real-time transcription is likely to have a large number of awkward rests and unusual note values you need to clean up by using the scoring program's editing features.

Scoring programs help you get better results by quantizing data as you play it (or load it from a MIDI file), but don't expect perfect notation the first time around. These real-time entry features are most effective when used as a starting point.

Numerous scoring programs are available for the Mac, including Mark of the Unicorn's Mosaic, Passport Designs' Encore, Coda's Finale, Opcode's MusicShop, and Jump Software's ConcertWare Pro.

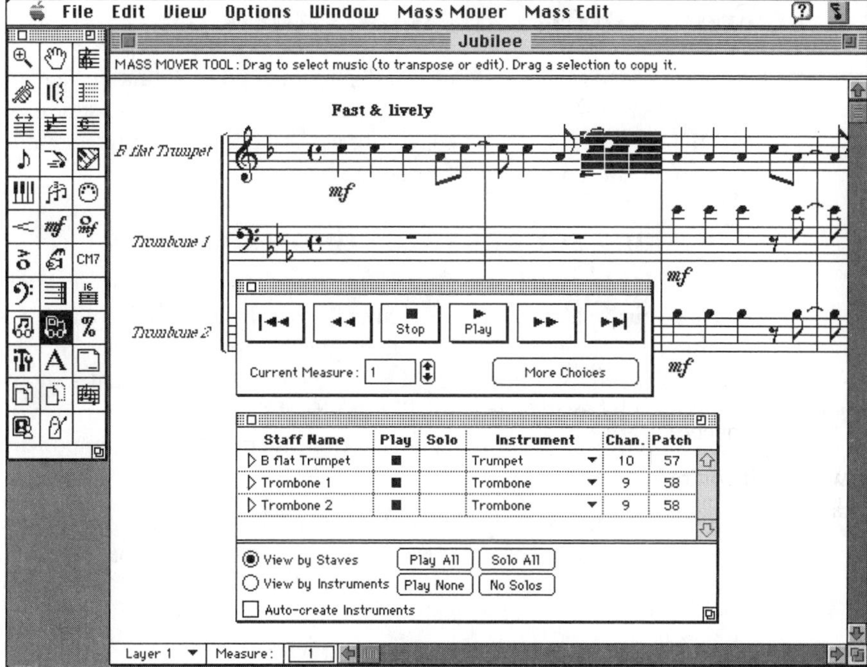

Figure 21-5: Scoring Software Notation programs such as Finale (shown here) let you commit music to paper by entering notes individually from a tool palette, playing a MIDI instrument, or importing a MIDI file created by a sequencer. The latter two approaches sound especially appealing, but music entered directly from a performance often requires extensive quantizing to compensate for minor timing inaccuracies.

Fonts for music scoring

All of these programs take advantage of Adobe Systems' Sonata music font to produce sharp copy on LaserWriters and other PostScript printers. (Many programs, including Coda's, include additional PostScript fonts for producing specialized notation symbols such as guitar chord patterns.) Beyond that, each program provides its own notation strengths; if you're a serious composer, you should evaluate them all to find the one that best handles the notation requirements of the style of music and the instruments for which you're writing.

You may also want to investigate free or shareware scoring programs such as Lime, from the CERL Music Group at the University of Illinois and the Department of Computer and Information Science at Queen's University. Lime and a large selection of music notation fonts are available through most user groups and on-line services.

Surveying Editor/Librarian Software

As I mentioned at the beginning of this chapter, editor/librarians let you manage, alter, and save a MIDI instrument's sounds by manipulating system-exclusive MIDI data. You may use an editor/librarian to tweak an existing sound to your liking or create a new sound from scratch.

Tweaking sounds with editor/librarians

You can alter a MIDI instrument's sounds by using its front-panel knobs and switches, but an editor/librarian makes it easier by taking advantage of the Mac's graphical operating style. For example, giving a sound a sharper, more percussive quality may require 15 minutes of twiddling with an instrument's knobs while squinting at its small, calculator-like display. With an editor/librarian, you can edit an on-screen version of the sound, clicking and dragging its components until you get the sound you want.

Editor/librarians are available for all popular MIDI instruments. Some, such as Opcode's Galaxy and Mark of the Unicorn's Unisyn, can work with numerous instruments and are often called *universal editor/librarians.*

Summoning patches by name

One recent trend has seen MIDI software vendors integrating their universal editor/librarians with their sequencers. Doing so provides a more convenient sequencing environment in which you can summon patches by name instead of by number. Opcode's Galaxy editor/librarian works with Vision and Studio Vision Pro, while Mark of the Unicorn's Unisyn works with Performer and Digital Performer.

Software for Samplers

Just as digital sound has made its mark in the Mac world, it has also significantly influenced the music industry. Musicians are embracing a new generation of keyboards called *samplers.* Like a Mac with a microphone or a MacRecorder, a sampler digitally records and plays back sound.

But with a sampler, you can play the sound at different pitches simply by pressing different keys on a musical keyboard. Record just one pitch of a given instrument, and you can instantly play that instrument from the sampler's keyboard.

Actually, most samples sound artificial when transposed too high or too low. Therefore, most sampling keyboards divide the range of notes into multiple samples, each of which plays a range of only an octave or so. This technique, called *multisampling,* avoids having to transpose a sample too high or low.

Passport Design's Alchemy lets you simultaneously view and alter a sampler's sounds. This capability is especially useful for setting a *loop point*, a portion of a sample that repeats as long as a key is pressed. Because few samplers display waveforms graphically, it's difficult to find the perfect loop point by using a sampler's editing commands. When you can see the waveform, however, setting loop points is far easier.

One of Alchemy's primary strengths is its capability to change the sampling rate of a recorded sound. This resampling capability enables you to transfer sounds between samplers that use different rates. Musicians can store all their sound samples on the Mac and use Alchemy to shuttle them between samplers as needed for more versatility.

If you have a sampler, you may also want to investigate Digidesign's Turbosynth software, which lets you design synthesized sounds on the Mac and then transfer them to a sampler for playback. Turbosynth gives a sampler, whose normal purpose is to play back digital recordings of real instruments, the sound-generating versatility of a synthesizer.

A Salute to General MIDI

A classic problem with MIDI is that one MIDI instrument's patches may be assigned to different patch numbers on a different MIDI instrument. Try to play a song created for one synthesizer on a different model, and you may find that a trumpet section is playing the drum part and a choir is singing the lead guitar solo.

The General MIDI solution

A version of the MIDI specification called *General MIDI* is designed to fix this problem by establishing a standard set of 128 patches, organized into 16 families — piano, percussion, organ, guitar, bass, strings, ensemble, brass, reed, pipe, synth lead, synth pad, synth effect, ethnic, percussive, and sound effects. Within each family are eight sounds. The patch numbers assigned to these sounds are standardized, so you can be sure, for example, that Patch #7 is always a harpsichord and Patch #74 is always a flute — regardless of which company made the instruments. Table 21-1 "General MIDI Patch Listing" lists the instruments assigned to General MIDI's 128 patches.

Table 21-1
General MIDI Patch Listing

1. Piano 1	33. Acoustic Bass	65. Soprano Sax	97. Ice Rain
2. Piano 2	34. Fingered Bass	66. Alto Sax	98. Soundtrack
3. Piano 3	35. Picked Bass	67. Tenor Sax	99. Crystal
4. Honky-tonk Piano	36. Fretless Bass	68. Baritone Sax	100. Atmosphere
5. E. Piano 1	37. Slap Bass 1	69. Oboe	101. Brightness
6. E. Piano 2	38. Slap Bass 2	70. English Horn	102. Goblin
7. Harpsichord	39. Synth Bass 1	71. Bassoon	103. Echo Drops
8. Clavichord	40. Synth Bass 2	72. Clarinet	104. Star Theme
9. Celesta	41. Violin	73. Piccolo	105. Sitar
10. Glockenspiel	42. Viola	74. Flute	106. Banjo
11. Music Box	43. Cello	75. Recorder	107. Shamisen
12. Vibraphone	44. Contrabass	76. Pan Flute	108. Koto
13. Marimba	45. Tremolo Strings	77. Bottle Blow	109. Kalimba
14. Xylophone	46. Pizzacato Strings	78. Shakuhachi	110. Bag Pipe
15. Tubular-Bell	47. Harp	79. Whistle	111. Fiddle
16. Santur	48. Timpani	80. Ocarina	112. Shannai
17. Organ 1	49. Strings	81. Square wave Bell	113. Tinkle
18. Organ 2	50. Slow Strings	82. Saw Wave	114. Agogo
19. Organ 3	51. Synth Strings 1	83. Syn. Calliope	115. Steel Drums
20. Church Organ	52. Synth Strings 2	84. Chiffer Lead	116. Wood Block
21. Reed Organ	53. Choir Aahs	85. Charang	117. Taiko
22. Accordion	54. Voice Oohs	86. Solo Vox32	118. Melo Tom
23. Harmonica	55. Synth Vox	87. 5th Saw Wave	119. Synth Drum
24. Bandeon	56. Orchestra Hit	88. Bass & Lead	120. Reverse Cymbal
25. Nylon Guitar	57. Trumpet	89. Fantasia	121. Guitar Fret
26. Steel Guitar	58. Trombone	90. Warm Pad	122. Breath Noise
27. Jazz Guitar	59. Tuba	91. PolySynth	123. Seashore
28. Clean Guitar	60. Muted Trumpet	92. Space Voice	124. Birds
29. Muted Guitar	61. French Horn	93. Bowed Glass	125. Telephone
30. Overdrive Guitar	62. Brass 1	94. Metal Pad	126. Helicopter
31. Distortion Guitar	63. Synth Brass 1	95. Halo Pad	127. Applause
32. Guitar Harmonics	64. Synth Brass 2	96. Sweep Pad	128. Gun Shot

ON THE CD

Now Hear This!

The best way to appreciate the Mac's sound capabilities is to hear them. Here's how to do just that using the *Macworld Power User Clinic*.

- You can hear examples of various sound sampling rates — and see how much disk space each uses — in the Multimedia Theater segment of the *Macworld Power User Clinic*. You can also listen to a QuickTime music movie. This movie is over four minutes long, but thanks to the efficiency of MIDI data, it's tiny — only about 15K.
- Digitized sounds: The Movies and Sounds folder contains a small collection of digitized sounds, which you can also access through the *Macworld Power User Clinic*'s Multimedia Theater segment. You'll also find some sounds and sound utilities in the Best of BMUG's Sound folder.
- MIDI file converters: The DesktopMovie utility, part of the Movie Trilogy collection, can convert standard MIDI files into QuickTime music movies. The All MIDI utility can also convert MIDI files into music movies. (The Step-by-Step box "Where to Find MIDI Files and How to Convert Them into Music Movies" describes how to covert MIDI files.) These utilities are located within the Movies and Sounds folder.

All major synthesizer vendors sell General MIDI sound modules. General MIDI is ideal for entry-level MIDI work, home entertainment applications (including games), multimedia, and any application that involves moving sequences among different brands or models of gear.

General MIDI doesn't guarantee that a sequence will *sound* identical regardless of the module used to play it — every module has its own audio qualities and peculiarities. But General MIDI does eliminate twiddling with knobs and flipping through manuals to make sure that your MIDI orchestrations are at least played by the right instruments.

General MIDI and QuickTime 2.0

QuickTime 2.0's music architecture provides a library of digital sounds licensed from Roland Corporation and mapped to the General MIDI channel assignments. In simpler terms, QuickTime 2.0 can play General MIDI files.

QuickTime 2.0's music architecture is scalable — if you have a MIDI instrument connected to your Mac, QuickTime uses it to play back the music. (You do have to configure QuickTime to do so by using the PatchBay application, described shortly.) If you don't have a MIDI instrument, QuickTime 2.0 uses its own musical instrument sounds, which don't exactly sound like a high-end sampler (they're not bad, though, as you can find out by playing the MIDI movie on the CD that comes with this book).

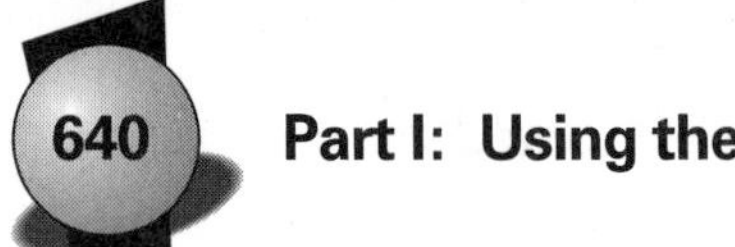

Problems in MIDI Land

A PowerBook is a perfect musician's computer — or is it? The PowerBook family's power-management features, which are designed to extend the life of each battery charge, can cause data-transmission errors between the PowerBook and MIDI instruments. These errors most often occur when the PowerBook is receiving a large amount of system-exclusive MIDI data such as a sound sample. The problem occurs because the PowerBook's power-management software periodically interrupts the computer's central processor. When these interruptions occur, MIDI errors can occur, too.

The PowerBook family does work well for most MIDI applications, including sequencing. But if you need to transfer large amounts of system-exclusive data, you may encounter problems. One solution is to use the Open Music System (OMS) driver (see the "Every Band Needs a Manager" section later in this chapter). OMS Versions 1.2 and later fix the PowerBook communications problem. OMS-supporting music software includes the OMS driver.

Where to Find MIDI Files and How to Convert Them into Music Movies

QuickTime 2.0's music architecture lets you experiment with the flexibility of MIDI without having to buy a MIDI instrument and interface. But where to find MIDI files? There are hundreds — no, make that thousands — available from on-line services and in user-group libraries.

Once you find some MIDI files, you can convert them into QuickTime music movies using any program that supports the QuickTime music architecture. Apple's Movie Player 2.0 program does, as does Strata's Instant Replay screen recorder utility. A variety of free and shareware programs also do, including Paul Cho's MovieTrilogy and AllMIDI (included on the CD) as well as Roland Corporation's MIDI2Music.

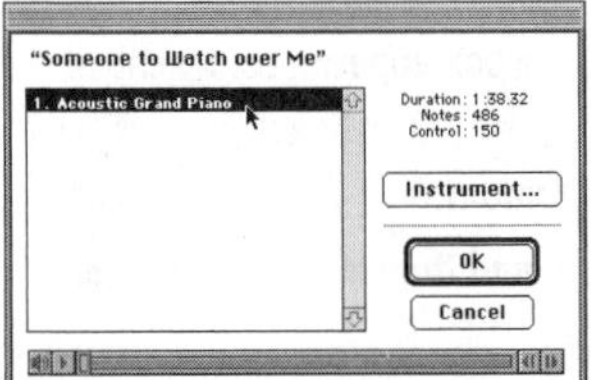

To open the MIDI file:

1. **Choose Open (or Import) from the File menu, and double-click the MIDI file to be converted.**
   A Save dialog box appears. (Some programs don't display the Save dialog box, but instead immediately display the Options button at left. If your program is one of these, you can skip step 2.)

2. **To examine the track and instrument assignments, click the Options button.**
   When you do, a dialog box (left) appears that displays the tracks in the file and the instruments to which each is assigned. Instructions for reassigning a track to a different instrument appear later in this box.
3. **Type a name for the movie and click Save.**

To reassign a track:

1. **In the Convert Options dialog box, select the track you want to reassign.**

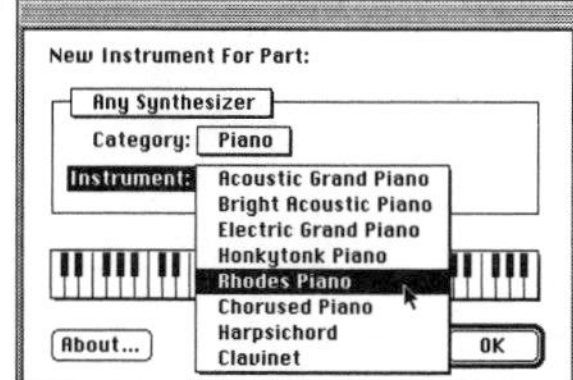

2. **Click the Instruments button.**
   The Instrument picker appears (left). This standard dialog box appears in any application that supports the QuickTime 2.0 music architecture.
3. **Choose the desired instrument.**
   You can switch between instrument families by using the Category pop-up menu. To view only instruments installed in your Mac, choose Macintosh Built In from the pop-up menu at the top of the dialog box. After you choose Macintosh Built In, instruments not installed in your Mac appear in *italics*. You can audition any instrument by clicking the keys in the dialog box's piano keyboard.
4. **Click OK or press Return.**

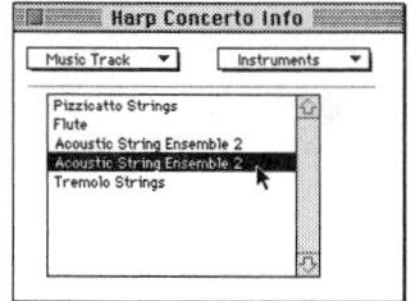

To examine or change a music movie's instrument assignments:

1. **Choose Get Info from the Movie window.**
   The Info window appears.
2. **From the Movie pop-up, choose Music Track.**
3. **From the right-hand pop-up, choose Instruments.**
   The window displays the movie's track and instrument assignments.
4. **Double-click the track whose assignment you want to change.**
   The Instrument picker dialog box appears, as described above.
5. **Choose the desired instrument.**
6. **Click OK or press Return, and then save the movie.**

Every Band Needs a Manager

If you try to run several MIDI programs simultaneously under System 7 (or System 6 MultiFinder), you may experience compatibility problems. That's because some MIDI programs monopolize the Mac's communications chips, preventing other programs from using them.

But chances are all your MIDI programs can peacefully coexist if you use Apple's MIDI Manager, an enhancement to the Mac's system software that lets multiple MIDI programs run simultaneously and even share the same MIDI data. Instead of accessing the hardware directly, programs access the MIDI Manager, which in turn deals with the hardware. You can establish connections between the various MIDI programs and hardware you use by using Apple's PatchBay application (see Figure 21-6 "MIDI Patching").

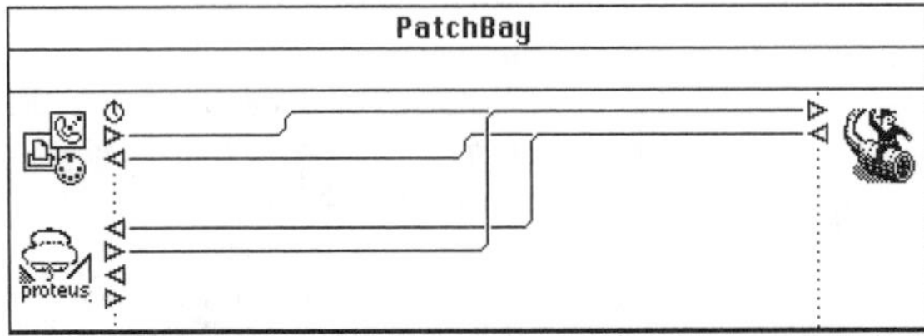

Figure 21-6: MIDI Patching Apple's PatchBay application graphically depicts the connections between the MIDI Manager (upper-right icon) and your MIDI hardware and software. Here, connections have been established between the MIDI Manager and Digidesign's MacProteus (far left) and the MacProteus' Front Panel application, which lets you adjust instrument settings and MIDI parameters. MacProteus is a version of E-mu's Proteus that plugs into a NuBus slot.

Most current MIDI products are compatible with MIDI Manager. Nonetheless, if your setup requires that you use MIDI Manager, it's a good idea to verify that a given piece of MIDI software is compatible with it before you buy it. If you don't have to use MIDI Manager, however, don't. It slows your Mac's overall performance.

An alternative to MIDI Manager is the Open Music System (OMS). Developed by Opcode (and originally known as the Opcode MIDI System), the OMS system extension acts as a central MIDI driver for OMS-compatible software to communicate with MIDI hardware. OMS also gives you a place to define and store information, such as patch names, about each of your MIDI devices. OMS can then supply this information to other OMS-compatible programs. It can work with or without MIDI Manager. As mentioned elsewhere in this chapter, the OMS driver also fixes the MIDI data errors that can occur with the Mac PowerBook family (see the PowerBook Angle box "Problems in MIDI Land").

Mark of the Unicorn has developed its own alternative to OMS. Called FreeMIDI, it's used by the company's sequencers (Performer, Digital Performer, FreeStyle), editor/librarian (Unisyn), and composing software (Mosaic).

Opcode and Mark of the Unicorn each claim their MIDI-management software is superior to the other's. I won't try to settle the debate here, although it does seem that OMS is gaining more widespread industry acceptance than FreeMIDI. And in 1995, Apple and Opcode announced that OMS would be incorporated into a future version of QuickTime.

Performance Software

One of the most fascinating categories of MIDI software almost defies categorization. I'm referring to *performance software,* programs with which you interact to improvise compositions, and in some cases, store and analyze phrases and then improvise music with some characteristics of the originals.

Jam Factory

Musical Luddites who aim their noses skyward at the notion of computer-composed music haven't played with Jam Factory, one of several intelligent instrument programs from Dr. T's Music Software. In Jam Factory, four players store notes played at a MIDI keyboard, and then the program analyzes the music. From there, the program generates new passages that contain the notes you played, but in a more random order. The order isn't completely random, however, because the probability of a given note occurring depends on how often it occurred in the original phrase. That's what enables Jam Factory's improvisations to resemble the original phrases.

The basic concepts behind Jam Factory aren't new. In 1961, computer music scientists developed what they called an analog composing machine. In one experiment, they used it to analyze Stephen Foster songs and compose new songs that had that Dixie flavor. And even Mozart once experimented with random composition, using dice to choose notes and then building a melody and supporting harmony based on those selections.

He would have loved Jam Factory. The screen is jam-packed with performance controls, buttons, and graphs for altering the phrases Jam Factory plays — their tempo, rhythm, randomness, key signature, and more. Jam Factory turns the Mac into a musical instrument, letting you change the program's renditions of your phrases by playing the on-screen controls. You can store the results of a performance to commit that flash of brilliance to disk and replay it later.

Where to Learn More About MIDI

If you want to learn more about computer music applications and synthesizers, consider subscribing to *Keyboard* magazine (Cupertino, CA) or *Electronic Musician* (Emeryville, CA).

Both magazines review the latest in synthesizers and computer software, but not at the expense of the creative aspects of music making. *Keyboard,* in particular, provides more coverage of musical theory and the professional music scene.

Music Miscellany

Sequencers, editor/librarians, and scoring programs are the primary players in the MIDI software world. On the fringes, you find programs such as Ars Nova Software's Practica Musica, which is designed to help you train your musical ear and learn music theory. For creating slick drum and rhythm patterns, check out Dr. T's UpBeat. If you're into jazz, look into MiBAC's Jazz Improvisation Software, which lets you quickly create and play along with a MIDI jazz trio accompaniment consisting of piano, bass, and drums. Choose the form, key, and tempo and then type the chords: MiBAC Jazz does the rest.

Several companies sell prerecorded MIDI sequence libraries that include elaborately produced sequences of hundreds of Top-40, rhythm-and-blues, country, and classical music pieces. You may use a canned sequence to fine-tune your arranging or improvisation skills or as an accompaniment to a live performance. Metatec, the publishers of the Nautilus CD-ROM magazine, sell a library called The Best of MIDI Connection. Educorp offers a product called Loops: Music For Multimedia, which also includes music clips recorded in a variety of digital audio formats.

You can also find MIDI support in authoring and production programs such as Macromedia Director and Passport Producer Pro. Their MIDI support lets you trigger a sequenced piece of music or sound effect at a particular time during a production. HyperCard users can also choose from a variety of XCMDs and XFCNs to add MIDI-control features to stacks.

Surveying Digital Sound Applications

The Mac is not only transforming the way you create and perform music, but it's also changing the way you record and listen to sound in general. As with music and MIDI, digital audio can play so many roles that it may help if I summarize each one before taking a closer look at how digital sound is produced.

Education

Digital sound is used to teach concepts that are difficult to grasp through written words or pictures. What does a red-tailed hawk sound like? How are numbers pronounced in Spanish? What's the difference between legato and staccato? For explaining these types of concepts, a sound is worth a thousand words.

Entertainment

Digital sound enlivens games with realism that phony beeps and squawks can't match. In some arcade games, for example, you hear the screaming of fighter jets or the wash of helicopter blades or invading alien spacecraft. Some games use stereo sound to add additional realism — if an alien ship is on the left side of the screen, you hear its sound coming from the left speaker. And CD-ROMs, with their large storage capacity, can hold background music that sets the mood for scenes in adventure titles such as Myst.

Music

In music, digital sound plays three roles. On one level, it makes possible Bogas Productions' remarkable Jam Session, whose digitally recorded instruments turn the Mac into a six-piece band that can make even novice musicians sound good. On another level, the Mac's sound features enable musicians to alter sounds played by digital sampling keyboards such as those made by Ensoniq, E-mu Systems, Roland, Kurzweil, and others. On still another level, the Mac can become a professional audio workstation that can record and play back sound with the fidelity of a compact disc.

Business

Digital sound can enliven business presentations and training software. But you must don yet another hat to add the dimension of sound. You may already be playing photographer, videographer, graphic artist, writer, and producer. Recording your own soundtracks means becoming a recording engineer, too. You can bypass much of the work by using prerecorded music clips, but it still helps to understand technicalities such as volume levels, sampling rates, and MIDI.

Science

Scientists and medical researchers use Mac sound products to analyze brain waves and study heart rhythms. And at Scotland Yard, some cutting-edge criminologists are using Macs to view and analyze voiceprints, which depict the characteristics of an individual's voice. Like fingerprints, no two are alike.

How Sound Sampling Works

To understand how the Mac records and plays back sound, think of a movie. By taking 24 photographs per second, a movie camera captures a reasonably accurate sampling of the action in front of it. When those samples are played back, the illusion of smooth motion is created.

Digital audio also samples motion, like the moving air molecules that make up sounds. Vibrating objects — whether strings, saxophone reeds, vocal chords, or slamming car doors — produce *sound waves*, variations in air pressure that travel outward from the sound source like the ripples from a stone dropped into a pond.

A digital audio recorder samples these sound waves thousands of times per second. Each sample is a digital image of the sound at a given instant (see Figure 21-7 "Snapshots of Sound"). The samples, each recorded as a series of bits, are stored in memory and can be manipulated. Bits can be added or removed, their order can be altered, or their very values changed. Each modification alters the overall image of the sound wave, so when the samples are played back, you hear a different sound.

Being Seen, Not Heard

If you use a PowerBook in meetings, you may want to turn the speaker volume down all the way to avoid annoying colleagues with occasional error beeps — especially if you've customized your beep to sound like The Three Stooges' Curly Howard.

But the original PowerBooks have a quirk: if you start up or restart with the speaker volume all the way down, you get a full-volume start-up chord. If you have to restart or start up your PowerBook during a meeting and you don't want to disrupt the proceedings with a start-up chord, insert a miniplug in the PowerBook's audio output jack (on the rear panel) to disable the speaker entirely.

Apple fixed this problem with the PowerBook Duo line as well as the PowerBook 160, 180, and later models. When you choose the Simple Beep sound and turn the volume down all the way, the PowerBook starts up without a peep.

Sampling rates and resolution

With movies, taking too few pictures per second results in jittery, unrealistic motion. With sound, taking too few samples per second results in a distorted recording that doesn't faithfully convey all the frequencies present in the original sound. The faster the *sampling rate*, the more accurate the recording, and the better the recorder is able to capture the highest frequencies.

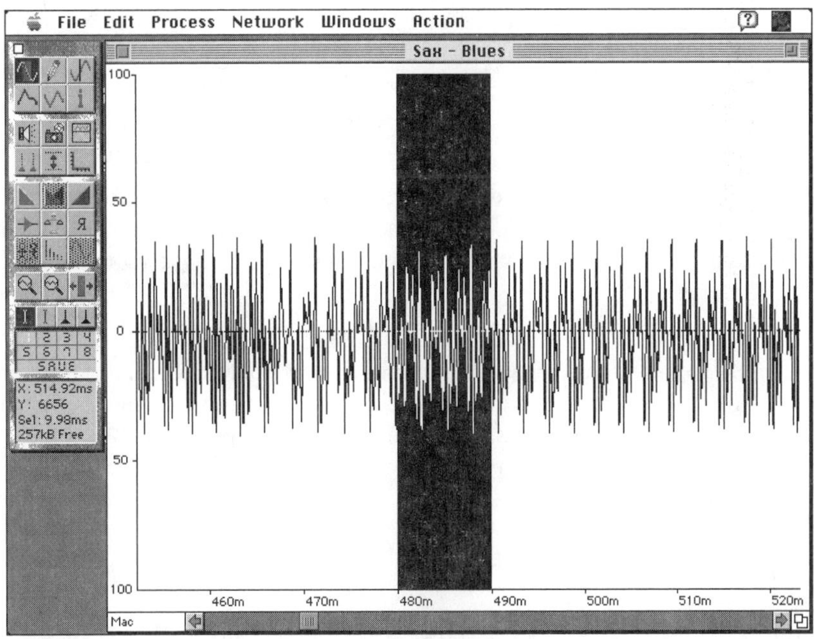

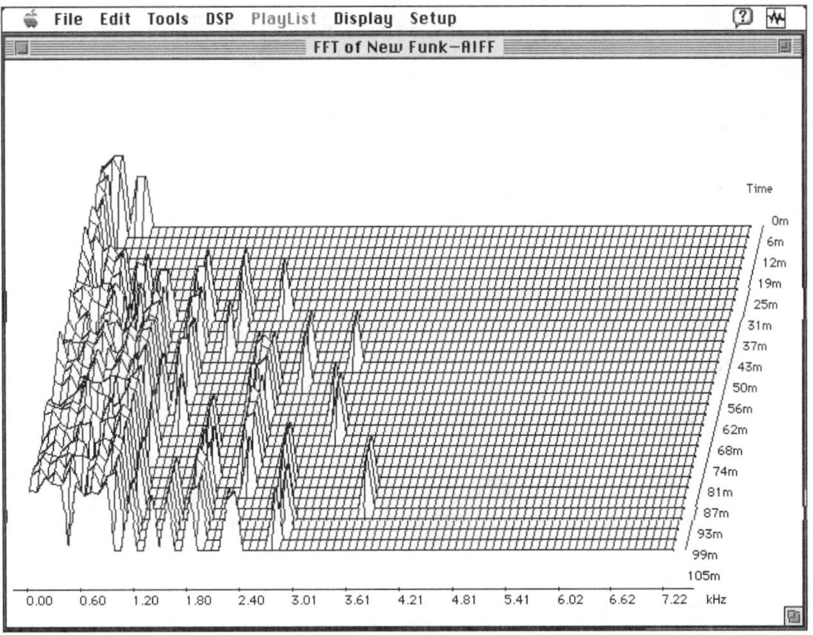

Figure 21-7: Snapshots of Sound Sound-editing programs graphically display sampled sounds and let you edit them. At top, 10 milliseconds of a sampled sound have been selected in Passport Design's Alchemy. At bottom, Digidesign's Sound Designer II depicts how a sound changes over time by using a sound-analyzing technique called a fast Fourier transformation, or FFT.

Compact discs are recorded at a rate of 44,100 samples per second, or 44.1kHz. Without specialized sampling hardware, a non-AV or non-Power Mac's maximum sampling rate is 22kHz — too slow for recording-studio quality, but fast enough to enable the Mac to sound at least as good as an ordinary table radio.

Another factor that influences digital sound quality is the *sampling resolution* — the number of bits assigned to each sample. These bits store information about the sample's *amplitude*, or loudness. The more bits assigned to each sample, the more accurately the recorder can store and re-create the original sound's variations in loudness.

A compact disc player (and an AV or Power Mac) has a 16-bit sampling resolution, enabling it to reproduce thousands of distinct volume levels. Non-AV and non-Power Macs have 8-bit sampling resolution; they re-create only 256 volume levels. (Entry-level Power Macs such as the Performa 5200 and 6200 series also have 8-bit sound resolution.) When a given sample's amplitude lies between two levels, it's rounded to the nearest one. This rounding of amplitude information, called *quantization*, causes distortion.

What You Need to Play and Record Audio

Before digitally recorded sound can be played back, the discrete bits of digital data generated during sampling must be translated back into continuously varying volume levels. A hardware component called a *digital-to-analog converter* performs this job. Because all Macs contain one, they can play digital sound without additional hardware.

Connecting the Mac to an audio system

For better sound quality, however, you can attach the Mac to a stereo system or external amplifier, as shown in Figure 21-8 "Wired for Sound." You might also consider Apple's AudioVision monitor, which contains a pair of great-sounding speakers and provides convenient front-panel controls for adjusting volume. The AudioVision monitor also contains a built-in microphone similar to the one that accompanies an AV Mac. Apple's Multiple Scan 15 monitor also provides built-in stereo speakers (but no microphone).

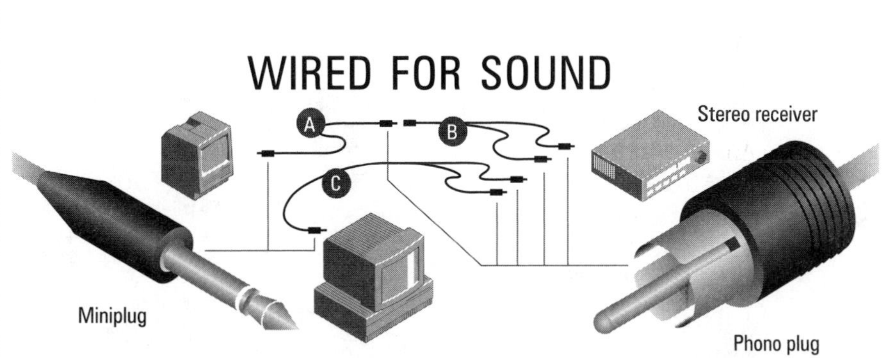

For better sound quality, connect a Mac to a stereo system. For monophonic Macs, one cable has a 1/8-inch miniplug on the Mac end, and a phono plug (Radio Shack catalog number 42-2444) on the other end (A). The other cable is a "Y" adapter with a phono plug on one end and two phono plugs (Radio Shack number 42-2435) on the other (B). For stereo Macs, all you need is a cable with a 1/8-inch stereo miniplug on the Mac end and two phono plugs (Radio Shack number 42-2475) on the other (C). Important: Before turning your stereo on, turn its volume control all the way down and use the Mac's Sound control panel to turn the Mac's speaker volume all the way down. Then turn the stereo on and adjust its volume and the Mac's to a comfortable listening level.

Figure 21-8: Wired for Sound

Recording your own audio

Unlike older machines, all current Mac models can record digital sound. To do so, they use a circuit called an analog-to-digital converter, which measures the voltage levels coming from a microphone or other sound source and translates them into digital data.

Power Macs and AV Macs can record stereo sound; most older Macs are limited to mono recording unless you add additional hardware, such as Macromedia's MacRecorder Sound System Pro.

Recording your own beep sounds

The Sound control panel lets you record your own beep sounds. When you click its Add button, a recording dialog box appears that lets you choose the desired recording settings and adjust the record volume (see Figure 21-9 "Now Recording").

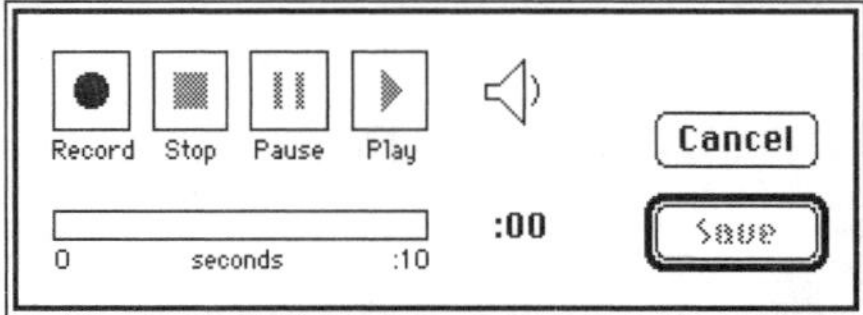

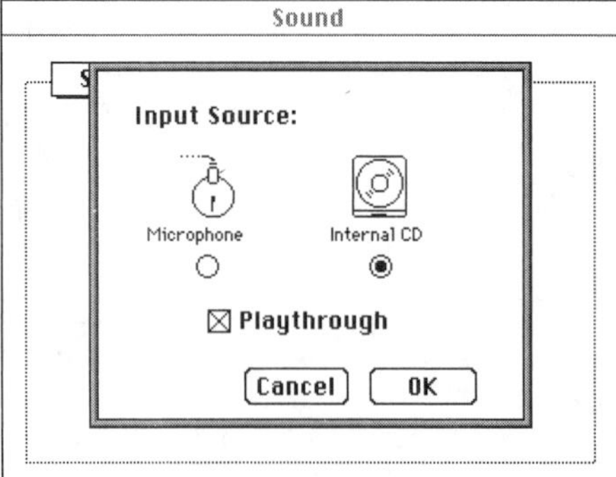

Figure 21-9: Now Recording The Sound control panel lets you record your own error beeps. Recording begins when you click the Record button, and the graph and seconds display below the speaker icon indicates its progress (top). After you finish recording, you can click the Save button to name and save the sound. The Sound control panel that accompanies an AV or first-generation Power Mac also lets you specify whether you want to record from the microphone or CD (bottom). The Power Mac 7500 and 8500 models use the Display & Sound control panel for these settings (see text).

The Mac's Clipboard also supports sound, so you can cut and paste sounds between applications that support it. And if you paste a sound into the Mac's Scrapbook, you can play the sound by clicking the Play button.

The Mac's Sound Manager (the portion of the Mac OS that handles audio recording and playback) also offers a compression feature that decreases storage requirements (and fidelity) by assigning fewer bits to each sample. Called Macintosh Audio Compression and Expansion (MACE) scheme, it compresses sound by 3:1 or 6:1 ratios. In most sound-recording programs — and in the audio-settings dialog box that QuickTime digitizing and editing programs provide — you can specify whether you want to use either of these compression settings. Generally, you should avoid audio compression unless disk space is very tight and your quality needs (or standards) are very low.

Recording with an AV or Power Mac

An AV Mac can record and play 48kHz, 16-bit stereo sound; for that matter, so can all Power Macs (AV and non-AV) except for the Performa 5200 and 6200 series. Although these specifications exceed those of audio compact discs and match those of digital audiotape (DAT) recorders, the audio circuitry in an AV or Power Mac isn't of the caliber found in professional audio gear, which contains higher-quality amplification and sound-generating circuitry than a general-purpose personal computer. As a result, sound pros will probably need to add additional hardware, which I describe later in this chapter.

Still, a stock AV or Power Mac can be adequate for producing CD-ROM soundtracks, which typically use 22kHz, 8-bit sound. Musicians making demo or rehearsal recordings will also be content with a stock machine, as would corporate producers making audio training or sales tapes. Many small radio stations also use stock machines.

Several AV- and Power Mac-compatible audio programs are available; I describe them later in this chapter. For now, here's a look at the connection and recording concepts you need to know before you hit the Record button.

Making connections

Your first step is to connect the audio outputs of your sound source (for example, a music keyboard or a camcorder) to the Mac's microphone jack (see Figure 21-10 "Digitizing Audio"). If you have a Power Mac 7500 or 8500, connect the audio output to the Mac's line-input jacks instead of to its microphone jack.

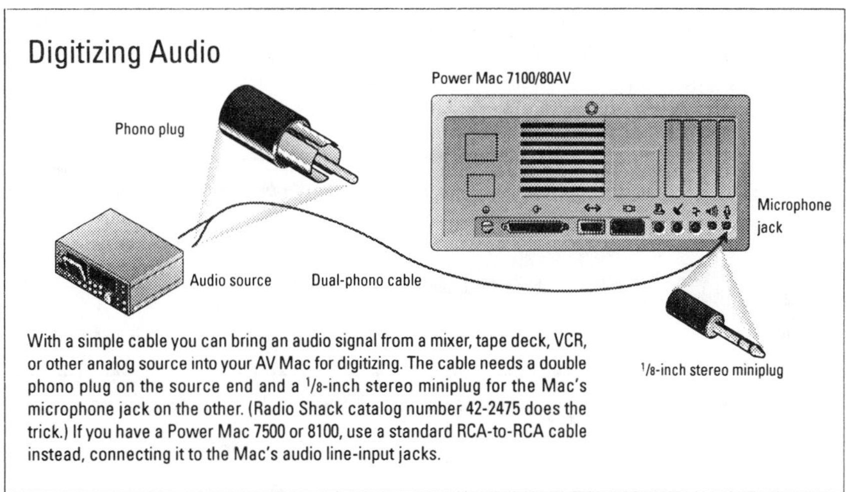

With a simple cable you can bring an audio signal from a mixer, tape deck, VCR, or other analog source into your AV Mac for digitizing. The cable needs a double phono plug on the source end and a 1/8-inch stereo miniplug for the Mac's microphone jack on the other. (Radio Shack catalog number 42-2475 does the trick.) If you have a Power Mac 7500 or 8100, use a standard RCA-to-RCA cable instead, connecting it to the Mac's audio line-input jacks.

Figure 21-10: Digitizing Audio

If you have a sound mixer connected to an amplifier and a set of speakers, consider connecting the Mac's sound-output jack to the mixer's stereo return inputs. (For the Power Mac 7500 and 8500, connect the line-output jacks to the mixer's stereo return inputs.) This enables you to use the mixer to monitor not only your original sound sources, but also the recordings you make. (If you need a mixer, consider the Mackie

Designs Microseries 1202 or the larger 1604. Both are popular among multimedia producers; I use a 1202 and am impressed with its versatility and sound quality.)

Depending on your hardware setup and needs, you may want the sound you're recording to play through your Mac's sound-output jack, so you can listen to the audio through headphones or external speakers. To activate this *playthrough* mode, open the Sound control panel, select the Sound In item from the pop-up menu, click Options, and then check the Playthrough box. (On the Power Mac 7500 and 8500, use the Sound & Displays control panel.)

Tips for better recordings

Setting record levels properly is a vital step. To avoid a noisy recording, adjust your program's levels so that the sound signal registers as high as possible on the program's volume meters without illuminating the very top meter segment. If the top segment illuminates, the recording will be distorted, or, in digital audio parlance, *clipped.* (see Figure 21-11 "Setting Levels"). If the level is too low, the sound isn't loud enough and background noise and any digital distortion is proportionally louder.

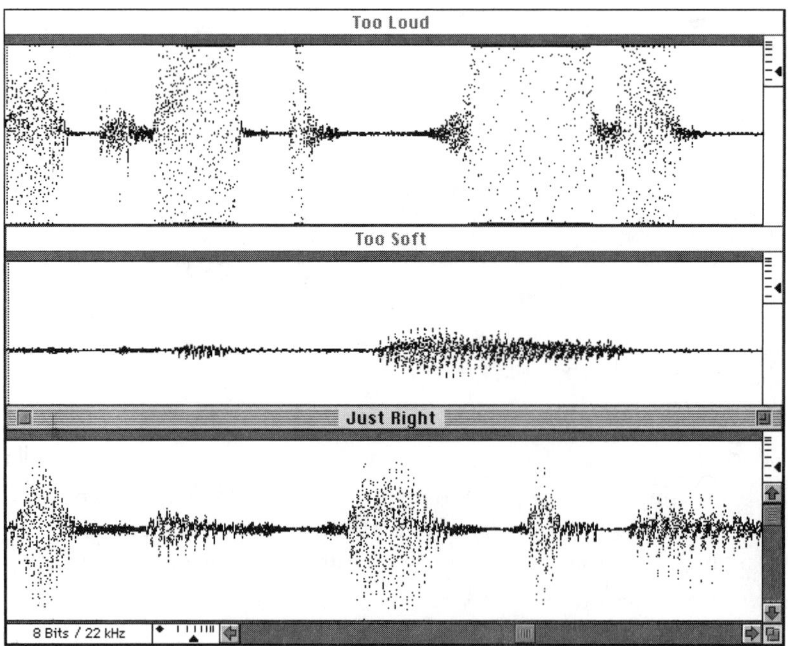

Figure 21-11: Setting Levels The sound in the top window was recorded at too high a volume setting: note how the waveform seems to crash into the upper and lower edges of the display. The sound in the middle window is too quiet: notice that the loudest portions of the waveform aren't that much louder than the background noise. The sound in the bottom window was properly recorded: the waveform peaks almost reach the top and bottom of the display.

Adjusting levels in SoundEdit 16

Macromedia's SoundEdit 16 doesn't provide a record-level adjustment. If you're using SoundEdit 16, you must adjust levels at the source. For example, if you're recording a narration, your narrator needs to speak more loudly or more quietly, or you need to adjust the position of the microphone. Or plug the microphone into a mixer that has volume-adjustment controls and then attach the mixer to the Mac's sound-input jack.

Adjusting levels in multitrack programs

If you're using a multitrack recording program such as OSC's Deck II, Opcode's DigiTrax, or Digidesign's Session, adjust the levels using the program's on-screen mixer, as described later in this chapter.

If you're using a Power Mac and Deck II, you should also use the Audio Input Level menu (in the Options menu) to specify a level of 0. Power Macs contain a low-quality audio preamplifier that can introduce noise; setting this level to 0 turns off the preamplifier. (This step isn't necessary with 680X0 AV Macs, which, incidentally, some people regard as having slightly better-sounding audio than the first-generation Power Macs — the 6100, 7100, and 8100. Also, some audio gurus maintain that first-generation Power Mac audio quality improves as you climb the family tree — that costlier models sound better than cheaper ones — due to the location of the audio circuitry on the logic boards.)

Tips for Positioning a Microphone

If you're recording a narration, locate the microphone at least a few inches from the narrator's mouth to avoid breathy results. As a test, record the phrase "pretty poppies." If the result sounds like a hurricane, back off.

You might want to consider using a tie-clip microphone, which tends to be less susceptible to breath-induced pops. Radio Shack tie-clip microphones are inexpensive but deliver surprisingly good results — I used them for the recordings on the *Macworld Power User Clinic* CD. (I have to admit I was embarrassed handing a Radio Shack mike to music legend Herbie Hancock — until I heard his coproducer Darrell Smith say, "Yeah, I've used them before — they're not bad!")

Also, move as far away from the Mac as possible to avoid recording hard disk and fan noise. If you're still picking up Mac noise, consider turning the Mac off and using a high-quality audiotape recorder or camcorder to make the recording. Then connect the recorder's line-output jacks to your Mac and digitize the results.

Adjusting levels in QuickTime recording programs

If you're doing your audio recording with Adobe Premiere's Audio Capture command, adjust volume levels with the Sound Settings command. And if you're recording audio while also recording video — using Premiere's Movie Capture command, for example, or the Fusion Recorder application that comes with AV Macs — use Gain slider in the standard QuickTime Sound Settings dialog box.

Choosing a sampling rate

If you can spare the hard disk space, always record sound using 44kHz, 16-bit settings. Even if you're recording sound destined for a CD-ROM, you'll get better sound quality by recording at 44/16 and then *downsampling* the audio to 22kHz/8-bit. Alas, downsampling adversly impacts sound quality. Quiet portions of a recording — the pauses between sentences, for example — develop static-like artifacts. This is one reason it's important to record at as high a level as you can. You can also make these artifacts less apparent by combining narration with a music soundtrack.

Deck II, SoundEdit 16, and Opcode's DigiTrax can downsample. Deck II 2.2 does the best job of it; its Mix to Disk command lets you choose from a variety of downsampling options. (For best results, use either the Rounding or Dithering options — each massages the audio in ways that minimize the distortion inherent in 8-bit audio.) Adobe Premiere 4.0.1 also has an effective downsampling filter. To apply it, select an audio track in the Construction window, choose Filters from the Clip window, and double-click the Downsample filter.

Hardware Enhancements for Power Mac/AV Mac Audio

The primary audio shortcoming of an AV or Power Mac is its lack of digital inputs and outputs (I/O). If you want to record from or to an audio DAT machine, you must connect the DAT machine's analog ins or outs to the Mac's 1/8 stereo miniplugs (or to the line-inputs or line-outputs on a Power Mac 7500 or 8500). Audio pros would rather keep digital signal in the digital domain — especially onsidering the Mac's analog circuits aren't up to pro-audio par.

The answer, at least for NuBus-equipped Macs, is a Digidesign Audiomedia II, a NuBus card that provides digital I/O as well as digital-signal processing (DSP) circuitry. Audiomedia II includes Digidesign's first-rate recording and editing program, SoundDesigner II. Deck II also supports Audiomedia II. I take a closer look at Audiomedia II shortly.

An Audiomedia II card has an additional benefit for CD-ROM producers: it enables you to use a SoundDesigner II plug-in, the L1 Ultramaximizer from Waves Ltd. This amazing utility makes soundtracks sparkle. Technically, it provides peak-limiting features that boost a recording's level while minimizing digital distortion, and it can downsample 16-bit audio to 8-bit. Practically, if you're serious about sound, you need L1.

The Formats of Sound

Every program category has its standard file formats, and sound-editing software is no exception. Here's an overview of the sound formats that are most common in the multimedia world.

SND resources

If there's a sound you want to use as a system-error beep in a HyperCard stack, you must save it as an SND resource. Technically, two types of SND resources exist. Format 1 resources are generally system beeps, and Format 2 resources are used by HyperCard and other sound-playing applications.

(Historical note: In the early days of digital Mac sound, the distinction was more important; you couldn't use Format 2 SND resources as system beeps. Beginning with System 6.0.2, however, Apple made the Mac's Sound Manager a bit less picky. With System 6.0.2 and later versions, you can use either format for system beeps.)

AIFF files

The Audio Interchange File Format (commonly referred to as either AIFF or Audio IFF) lets one program open a digital recording created by another program — it's the PICT format of the digital audio world.

You can find support for AIFF files in professionally oriented sound software such as Passport Designs' Alchemy and Digidesign's Sound Designer, as well as in sound-editing programs such as SoundEdit 16 and OSC's Deck II, and in video-editing packages such as Adobe Premiere. AIFF is the preferred format for swapping files between such programs.

System 7 sound files

Sometimes called the sfil format, this is the format that allows you to play sounds by double-clicking them at the Finder. An example of when you might want to use this format is while creating a special error beep sound.

WAV files

This is a common file format in the DOS/Windows world. WAV files generally end with the characters .WAV. SoundEdit 16 can open and save WAV files, as can S/Link, a sound-conversion utility from New England Digital.

MOD files

The MOD format is a special format that stores sound samples. Originally developed for the Commodore Amiga computer, MOD files are used by music programs such as Sound-Trecker, which is included on the *Macworld Power User Clinic* CD. (If you haven't tried it yet, do it! It's quite cool.)

Sound at the High End

If you don't have an AV or Power Mac but do want to reach the upper strata of Mac digital audio, you need hardware such as Digidesign's Audiomedia II board, which is compatible with most NuBus-equipped Macs. Audiomedia II contains a Motorola digital signal processing chip, a microprocessor designed for the data-shuffling demands of digital audio. (Audiomedia LC, a version of the board for the Mac LC family of machines, is also available.)

A closer look at Audiomedia II

The Audiomedia II board enables the Mac to record and play back stereo CD-quality audio directly to and from a Mac's hard disk. Thus, sound length is limited only by available disk space. You still may feel rather limited, however: a one-minute monophonic recording uses 5MB of disk space; double that for stereo.

On the back of the Audiomedia II board are a microphone jack and six RCA jacks. Two are inputs that accept audio from a tape deck, compact disc player, or other sound source. Audiomedia II can record from the RCA and microphone jacks simultaneously, enabling you to record a voice narration and background music in one step. Two RCA jacks are outputs that send an analog signal to a stereo amplifier or mixer, and the remaining two are digital outputs (S/PDIF-type) that can connect to a digital audiotape recorder.

Audiomedia and hard drives

Audiomedia II includes Digidesign's Sound Designer II, which you use to record, alter, and play back recordings. The Audiomedia hardware is also compatible with OSC's Deck II as well as the Digital Performer and Studio Vision Pro sequencers, so you can use these programs to record.

Each recording, or sound file, appears in its own window (see Figure 21-12 "In the Studio"). While recording, Sound Designer II expertly shuttles incoming data from the Mac's memory to your hard disk — provided the hard disk has a 28ms or faster average access time. If the disk isn't fast enough, parts of the recording will be lost, and you'll need to try again with a slower sampling rate.

If you want to use the Audiomedia II board with a sequencer such as Digital Performer or Studio Vision Pro or Studio Vision AV, you need an 18ms or faster drive. Most of today's high-capacity hard drives meet this requirement.

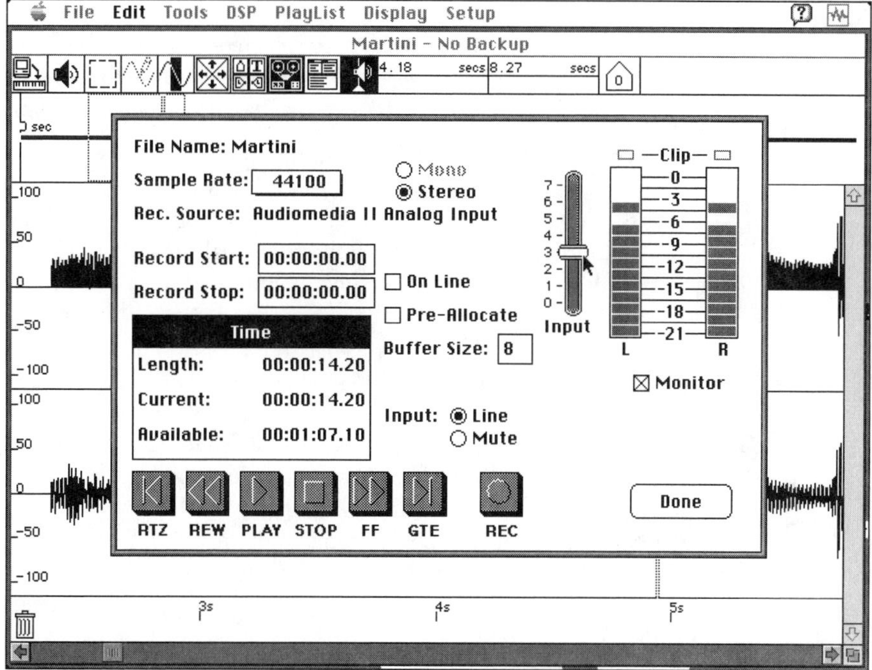

Figure 21-12: In the Studio Audiomedia's record window has a volume slider and dancing volume meters that let you adjust the input volume before recording. Familiar-looking tape-transport controls let you record, rewind, fast-forward, and play back the recording.

Editing with Sound Designer II

Sound Designer II's editing features enable you to cut and paste portions of a recording. You can also alter individual sound samples by using a MacPaint-like pencil icon. To locate exact spots on the recording, a scrub tool lets you slowly play the recording forward and backward — like rocking the reels of a reel-to-reel tape recorder back and forth.

The remarkable Playlist editing feature lets you rearrange a recording — remove or rearrange words, cut or add verses to a song, or repeat a section — without changing the original sound file. You do so by selecting specific areas of the recording (such as a single verse), naming them, and then arranging those names in the playlist window. Just as a baseball manager can change the batting order by simply rearranging names on the lineup card, you can change how a recording plays back by rearranging names in its playlist window. You can create and save as many playlists as you like.

You can also mix two recordings or fade from one to the other. You can change a recording's tonal qualities by using an on-screen graphic equalizer and hear each change as you make it. You can even change a recording's length without altering its pitch — handy if you have a 35-second music passage that has to fit a 30-second animation.

As mentioned earlier in this chapter, SoundDesigner II accepts optional plug-in modules that add additional features, such as peak limiting and equalization. Waves Ltd. offers the largest selection of plug-ins for this program; examples include the L1 mentioned earlier, and the Q10 parametric equalizer. All of Waves' plug-ins are top-quality audio enhancements — highly recommended.

Tape Decks on a Disk

Two remarkable digital audio programs are OSC's Deck II and Opcode's DigiTrax. DigiTrax turns an AV or Power Mac into a six-track, CD-quality, digital audio recorder. Deck II works with an AV or Power Mac and also supports third-party audio hardware, such as Digidesign's Audiomedia II. Deck II also works with RasterOps' MediaTime card and with Spectral Innovations' NuMedia card, both of which use the same AT&T 3210 digital signal processor (DSP) chip as the Quadra 660AV and 840AV.

They even look like tape recorders

The main screens in DigiTrax and Deck II are faithful to the multitrack recording metaphor, with volume meters that show sound levels, sliding faders that adjust recording and playback volumes, and transport controls that let you record, play back, fast forward, and rewind (see Figure 21-13 "Digital Decks on the Desktop"). If you've used conventional multitrack decks, you'll feel at home with most of what you see. And you'll be delighted with some of the differences, such as instantaneous rewinding.

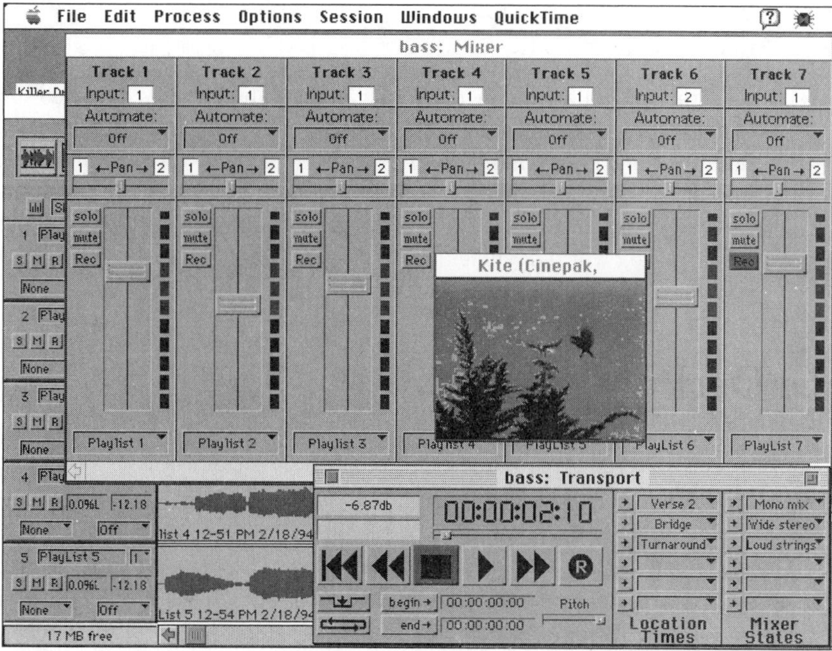

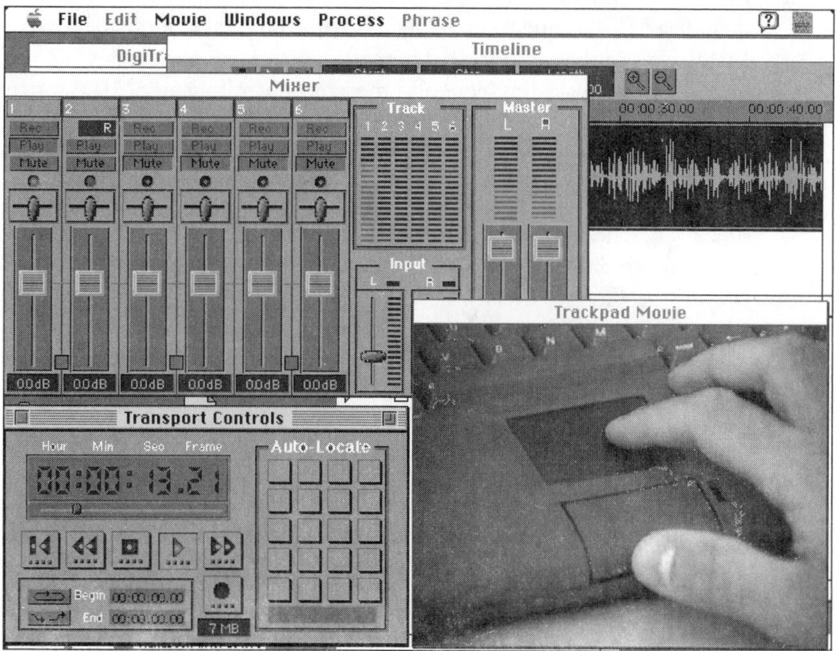

Figure 21-13: Digital Decks on the Desktop OSC's Deck II (top) and Opcode's DigiTrax (bottom) turn the Mac into multitrack digital audio recorders.

Recording a track

Recording a track with Deck II or DigiTrax involves selecting the desired track, adjusting the input volume to avoid clipping (which causes distorted sound), and then clicking the Record button. After you record one track, you can record additional tracks. If you fill all six or eight tracks and still need more, you can merge two or more tracks into one, freeing the others for reuse. This technique, called *bouncing*, is often used with conventional multitrack decks, too. But bouncing tracks in the analog world degrades a recording's quality — not so with Deck II or DigiTrax.

Adding digital EQ

DigiTrax also enables you to alter the sound of a track during playback. It supports several digital effects, ranging from a digital equalizer, which lets you accentuate or attenuate certain frequencies, to a stereoizer, which processes a monophonic recording to simulate stereo. Beginning with version 2.5, Deck II supports plug-in EQ modules that are written to conform to the Adobe Premiere plug-in standard.

Adding MIDI sequences to Deck II recordings

Another big difference between Deck II and conventional recorders is that Deck II can import and play back a MIDI composition created with sequencer software. To include a MIDI sequence in a Deck II recording, save the sequence as a standard MIDI file and then import it. Thereafter, when you play back your audio recording, Deck also plays the sequence, thereby controlling any MIDI instruments attached to your Mac. A musician may use this feature to combine sequenced instrumentals with vocals or acoustic instrumentals. A multimedia producer may use it to add voice narration to an instrumental soundtrack.

Deck II reaches out to the MIDI world in another way: it lets you assign, or *map*, one or more of Deck's on-screen faders to the physical sliders on a MIDI fader box such as J.L. Cooper Electronics' FaderMaster. (A *fader box* contains slider knobs that transmit MIDI data when you move them.) With this feature, you can control the playback volume of one or more tracks by moving the sliders on the fader box instead of using Deck's on-screen sliders.

Automating the final mix

The final step in any recording session is the *mix-down*, which involves adjusting the playback volume of each track while recording in standard two-track stereo on a second deck. As the multitrack recording plays back, a recording engineer often adjusts the volume of certain tracks, changes their apparent location in the left-right stereo spread, and makes other fine adjustments to arrive at the best-sounding final product. Twiddling all those knobs as a piece plays requires some dexterity, and twiddling them in the exact same way each time is all but impossible. For these reasons, professional recording equipment often provides automated mix-down features that remember the adjustments the engineer makes so the final mix can be re-created if needed.

Deck II brings automated mix-down to the desktop. You can save and restore hundreds of different combinations of fader and effects settings. During playback, Deck II's faders and other on-screen knobs move to the appropriate positions by themselves. Automation files are stored separately from the recording itself, enabling you to apply different automation files to a single recording to see which you prefer. (DigiTrax has some automation features, too, but they aren't as sophisticated or complete as those of Deck II.)

(By the way, I'd be remiss if I didn't mention that Deck II uses a form of copy protection, albeit a relatively unobtrusive one. You can install the program on up to two hard drives by "authorizing" the drives using the installation program. If you simply copy the program's icon to your hard drive, you're asked to insert the master floppy each time you start Deck II. Unlike some early authorizing schemes, Deck II's is not affected by disk defragmenting programs.)

Sound at the Summit: High-End Audio Tools

At the summit of the Macintosh digital audio world, you can find products such as Digidesign's Pro Tools system, which you can use to record and edit CD-quality digital audio, synchronize to motion picture and videotape soundtracks, and use digital audiotape (DAT) to create masters that you send to a compact disc manufacturer for pressing. This professional-quality digital audio recording and mastering system runs on a computer that smiles when you switch it on.

Pro Tools comprises a NuBus board containing the DSP chip and its support circuitry, an external box that contains the analog-to-digital converter, circuitry for synchronizing audio to video, and Apogee antialias filters to improve sound quality. (Apogee filters are popular in the professional digital audio world.)

Other high-end digital recording products from Digidesign include the Session 8 family. The Session 8 provides 8-track digital recording and is designed for home studios. The Session 8 XL is designed for professional applications and includes the same audio interfaces that ship with Digidesign's Pro Tools and Sound Tools II systems. Both Session 8 models are available for Macs as well as DOS PCs running Microsoft Windows.

Digidesign and Prosonus (a leading developer of sampled sounds for music samplers) have collaborated on a CD-ROM packed full of production music and sound effects designed for audio and multimedia productions. Called Clip Tunes, it contains 350MB of music in a variety of styles and 250MB of sound effects, all in Sound Designer II format. Prosonus also offers Mr. Sound FX, a collection of sounds in SoundEdit Pro format.

Digidesign's Session Software

Feeling the heat from Deck II and DigiTrax, Digidesign has introduced its own software-only recording package, called Session Software. The program can record two tracks simultaneously and plays back up to 16. Like Deck II and DigiTrax, Session Software also lets you work with QuickTime movie soundtracks.

Unlike its competitors, however, Session Software also supports plug-in software modules developed for Digidesign's high-end recording tools — so you can use those modules from Waves Ltd. that I've raved about earlier in this chapter. Session Software does not run on the Quadra 660AV or 840AV, but you can use it on the Quadra 840AV if you have Digidesign's Audiomedia II card.

Tips for Sound in Multimedia Productions

Sound helps put the *multi* in multimedia. You can add the dimension of sound to multimedia productions in several ways (see Table 21-2). The least expensive technique involves using the Mac's built-in sound circuitry for recording and playback. If you use a Power Mac or AV Mac, this option might be all you need — as I've described earlier in this chapter, these Macs have excellent built-in audio features.

The sections that follow show how several popular multimedia presentation and production programs handle sound.

Table 21-2
Ways to Sound Off

Technique	***Pros***	***Cons***	***Tools***
Digitized music clips played through the Mac's sound circuitry	Inexpensive; you can move productions to another Mac without adding sound hardware to the machine	Sound isn't CD quality on many Macs; digitized clips use up destination disk space	For older Macs, a MacRecorder; for newer Macs, appropriate cables; optional: a CD-ROM drive and clip music collection (Macromedia MediaClips recommended)
Music clips played through Digidesign's Audiomedia II board	CD-quality sound; board can be used to record and mix voice-overs, too; board includes Sound Designer II sound-editing program	Costly; CD-quality stereo sound requires lots of disk space; sound plays only on Audio-media II-equipped Macs	Audiomedia II; a CD-ROM drive and Digidesign Clip Tunes (SoundDesigner-format production music)

Technique	*Pros*	*Cons*	*Tools*
MIDI music sequences played through sound modules	High-quality sound; MIDI sequences use very little disk space	More hardware to buy and transport; must use Apple MIDI Manager in most production programs	MIDI sound module (see text); MIDI interface; amplification system; clip music collection (Opcode MIDIClips; Passport Music Data Company; also on-line services and user groups)
Music movies played through QuickTime 2.0's music architecture	MIDI sequences use very little disk space; efficient; reasonably good sound, depending on instruments used	Sound isn't as good as that provided by a MIDI playback module	MIDI files; QuickTime 2.0; QuickTime-savvy application software
Conventional CD audio played through a CD-ROM drive under control of Passport Producer Pro	You can play tracks from any audio CD, in any order. CD audio uses no disk space.	Potential copyright problems; limited control over audio	Passport Producer Pro; CD-ROM drive; any audio CD
Conventional CD audio played through a CD-ROM drive under control of a HyperCard stack and The Voyager Company's CD AudioStack software	You can play tracks from any CD, in any order; you can create interactive stacks that play passages when buttons are clicked or that display running comments during playback; CD audio uses no disk space	You must work in HyperCard — not always the ideal multimedia production tool	Voyager CD AudioStack software; CD-ROM drive; HyperCard; any audio CD

Sound in Persuasion and PowerPoint

The voice-over is a common device: a graph or other image appears while a voice elaborates on it. You can apply this technique to simple presentations created with Adobe Persuasion.

Persuasion 2.1 and later versions support sound via QuickTime. If your original sounds are stored as AIFF files, you must convert them into sound-only QuickTime movies. Persuasion 3.0 performs this conversion process automatically when you use the Sounds command in the Import submenu (File menu). Persuasion can also convert System 7 sound files.

If you place a sound-only QuickTime movie on a slide's first layer, the movie plays as soon as the slide is displayed. If you place the movie on a different layer, it will play only when that layer is displayed.

As for Microsoft PowerPoint, it too handles audio via QuickTime movies. You can import movies by using the Edit menu's Insert submenu.

Sound and Macromedia Director

Director provides two sound channels, so you can put background music in one channel and a voice-over in the other.

Director provides a few ways to import sound. You can use Director's Import command to add a sound to the Cast window and then drag the sound from the Cast window to the desired sound channel in the Score window. If you use a sound in several Director productions, you can save memory and disk space by adding the sound to a shared cast movie as described in Director's documentation. You can also install sound resources in Director's Sound file; this option is best for sound effects and other short sounds.

When you start playing sounds in one channel and then introduce a sound from the second channel, the volume of the first channel drops by about half. If you want the volume of both sound channels to be the same throughout the movie, put Director's *null sound* in all the consecutive empty sound channel cells that precede the second channel's sound. You can also control the volume of each channel by using Director's Lingo scripting language.

Tips for Working with Sound in QuickTime

For many of today's multimedia producers, QuickTime is where the action is. Unfortunately, synchronization of sound and video tracks can be poor on slow Macs — QuickTime talkies often look like English-dubbed foreign films. This problem occurs because QuickTime concentrates first on playing sound without distracting interruptions, and it discards video frames when necessary in an attempt to maintain synchronization. Another problem: if a QuickTime movie starts with a sharp, percussive note, part of the note is often cut off during playback.

Working with sound in Adobe Premiere

Here's a look at the issues and options behind working with soundtracks in the most popular video-editing program.

Premiere can record audio and video simultaneously if you have a Mac equipped with sound-input hardware. You can also record voice-overs and music within Premiere, using the Sound Settings dialog box to adjust levels and choose sampling rates.

You can also use an audio-recording program such as Deck II, DigiTrax, SoundDesigner II, or SoundEdit 16. If you use these programs, save the finished recording in AIFF format and use Premiere's Import command to bring it into the Project window. Then drag the sound to the Construction window.

Premiere has multiple sound channels and excellent mixing features (see Figure 21-14 "Sound and Premiere"). Each audio clip has a fade control; to adjust the level of an audio track, drag its fade control up or down. You can start a movie with a music score playing at full volume and then fade the music to 50 percent volume as a voice-over or talking head begins speaking. (Tip: For faster Premiere performance, use the Preferences command to turn on the audio-approximation feature.)

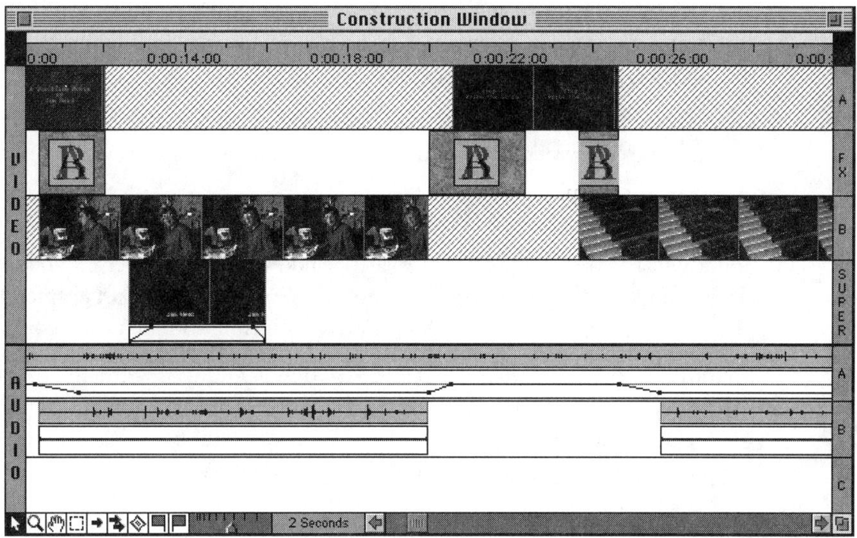

Figure 21-14: Sound and Premiere Adobe Premiere lets you adjust the level of audio tracks. Here, a music score in Track A is faded to 40 percent of its normal volume as a narration begins in Track B. When the narration ends, the music resumes its normal volume and then fades again as the next voice-over begins.

Beginning with version 3.0, Premiere lets you zoom in to view soundtracks at a resolution of 1/600 second. Premiere 3.0 and later versions also support Apple's Sound Manager 3.0, which enables programs to record and play CD-quality audio on an AV or Power Mac or other Mac equipped with appropriate third-party hardware.

Premiere also lets you export soundtracks as AIFF files. Why would you bother? One reason is if you want to tweak a movie's soundtrack using a program such as SoundDesigner II or Deck II. You can export a completed movie's soundtrack as an AIFF file, import the AIFF file into your audio program, make your changes, save the changed version as an AIFF file, and then import it *back* into Premiere and sync it up with the movie's video track. It's a chore, but it's often a necessary evil.

Tools for editing QuickTime soundtracks

As mentioned earlier in this chapter, three terrific tools for working with QuickTime movie soundtracks are Deck II, DigiTrax, and SoundEdit 16. All three programs can import soundtracks from QuickTime movies and export their own recordings as QuickTime soundtracks.

You can use these features to import an interview of a QuickTime movie, add a musical background, and then replace the movie's original soundtrack with the interview and the music. Or you can import a movie's soundtrack in order to "sweeten" it — that is, to enhance its sound quality, perhaps by processing it through the equalizer in DigiTrax or SoundEdit 16.

Deck II and DigiTrax can also display live video from a camcorder or VCR connected to the video-input jack on an AV Mac or a Power Mac 7500 or 8500.

SoundEdit 16's advantages

SoundEdit 16 doesn't support a live-video window, but unlike Deck II and DigiTrax, it lets you add *multiple* soundtracks to a movie. (Recall from the last chapter's discussion of QuickTime tracks that a movie can have multiple sound and video tracks.)

SoundEdit 16 also can also open and save digital audio files created for the Microsoft Windows environment. Such files are called *wave* files; their filenames generally end with the characters .WAV. This capability makes SoundEdit 16 a good tool for cross-platform sound work.

CHAPTER  CONCEPTS AND TERMS

- The Mac can perform many musical roles, including sequencing (recording, editing, and playing back performances); scoring (putting notes on paper); composing (analyzing phrases and generating new ones); sound and patch editing (manipulating an instrument's sounds); and producing soundtracks.
- Programs such as Concertware Pro, Jam Session, and Super Studio Session let you experiment with music and sound with little additional equipment.
- The Musical Instrument Digital Interface (MIDI) was developed to let musicians connect electronic instruments to each other and to computers. MIDI lets you create a network of two or more instruments that you can play from one instrument. MIDI also lets you combine a computer-controlled network of instruments with audio equipment and even stage lighting to automate an entire performance.
- MIDI sequencer programs let you build arrangements by recording parts one track at a time. Scoring programs let you print music by using conventional music notation; many programs can transcribe music as you play it on a MIDI keyboard. Patch librarians let you manage, alter, and save a MIDI instrument's sounds by manipulating system-exclusive MIDI data.
- The Mac's capability to record, manipulate, and play back sounds has opened doors to new applications in education, entertainment, music, business, and science.
- To digitally record audio, you must take thousands of samples per second. Compact discs use a 44.1kHz sampling rate; Macs can sample at this rate when equipped with hardware such as a Digidesign Audiomedia II board. The AV and Power Macs can also sample at 44.1kHz. Other Macs are limited to a 22kHz sampling rate.
- Macromedia's SoundEdit series are popular programs for working with sound. Professional-level sound-editing programs include Digidesign's Sound Designer II and Passport Design's Alchemy.
- Most multimedia authoring and production programs support digital sound resources as well as MIDI and compact disc audio.
- QuickTime 2.0's music architecture makes it easy to include MIDI data in movies. Because it stores only note data and not actual digitized audio, a music movie uses far less disk space than digital audio does.

analog-to-digital converter
A circuit, essential for digital audio recording, that turns a continuously varying (analog) sound wave into a series of numbers that the Mac can store, manipulate, and play back.

Audio Interchange File Format
Abbreviated *AIFF,* a standard file format for storing digital recordings.

channels
Electronic mailing addresses that accompany MIDI data and specify its destination. The MIDI standard provides 16 channels.

clipping
The undesirable outcome of recording at too high a volume level. A digital recording in which some samples have been clipped often sounds distorted.

conductor track
A special sequencer track that stores tempo information and lets you vary the tempo within a piece.

continuous data
MIDI data that generally modifies the way a sound is played. For example, many instruments have *pitch bend* wheels or levers that let you slide between pitches the way guitar players do when they bend a string. Another kind of continuous data is *aftertouch,* which describes how hard a note key is being held down.

controller
A device that generates MIDI data. Controllers are usually piano-like keyboards, but MIDI guitars and wind controllers are also available.

digital signal processor
Abbreviated *DSP,* a microprocessor designed to manipulate real-time streams of digital data. An AV Mac contains an AT&T 3210 DSP chip; third-party DSP boards such as Digidesign's Audiomedia II often use a Motorola DSP chip.

digital-to-analog converter
A hardware circuit that translates digital data such as samples into analog signals such as sound waves.

envelope
A graphical depiction of a sound's percussiveness.

event-list editing
A sequencer editing mode that displays a track's contents as a table of MIDI data. It doesn't give you the click-and-drag convenience of graphic editing, but it allows for greater precision. Also see *graphic editing.*

General MIDI
A version of the MIDI standard that establishes a fixed set of 128 patches, organized into 16 families. General MIDI is designed to prevent problems that can occur when you play a sequence created for one model of synthesizer on a different model.

(continued on the next page)

(continued from previous page)

graphic editing
Often called a *piano roll* display, a sequencer editing mode that displays a track's contents on a music staff-like grid, except that notes are shown as horizontal bars, with longer bars representing longer notes. Graphic editing lets you select and drag notes from one position to another by using the mouse. Also see *event-list editing.*

layering
Playing multiple instruments simultaneously to obtain a richer sound. MIDI is often used for layering.

MIDI file
A standard file format that lets you move sequences between different sequencers, even ones running on different computers.

MIDI interface
A piece of hardware that connects to the Mac's modem or printer port and provides MIDI In and MIDI Out connectors.

multisampling
A technique employed by most samplers that improves realism by dividing the range of notes the instrument can play into multiple samples, each of which plays a range of only an octave or so. This technique avoids having to transpose a sample too high or low.

multitimbral
Capable of simultaneously producing different types of sounds, such as those of a drum set, piano, and horn section.

omni mode
A MIDI configuration mode in which an instrument responds to data sent on all MIDI channels. Compare with *poly mode.*

patch
One of a synthesizer's sounds, such as a piano or guitar. Patches are named in honor of the pioneering synthesizers of the sixties, whose many sound-generating modules were linked by patch cables like those for a telephone switchboard.

patch editor
A program that lets you draw and manipulate the waveforms that describe a sound's qualities and then transfer them to a synthesizer's memory.

patch librarian
A program that serves as a database manager for patches, transferring the settings that make up each patch to or from a Macintosh disk and enabling you to name, sort, and organize patches.

poly mode
A MIDI configuration mode in which an instrument responds to data from only certain MIDI channels. Compare with *omni mode.*

program change
A type of MIDI command that instructs an instrument to switch sound — from piano to strings, for example.

quantizing
A sequencer and scoring program feature that moves notes to the nearest note value you specify, essentially correcting timing errors.

sampled sound
A digitized version of a sound, produced by feeding an audio signal into a hardware circuit called an analog-to-digital converter.

sampling rate
The number of sound samples taken per second. The higher the rate, the better the fidelity of the resulting sound.

sampling resolution
The number of bits assigned to each sample. These bits store information about the sample's *amplitude,* or loudness. The more bits assigned to each sample, the more accurately the recorder can store and re-create the original sound's variations in loudness.

sequencer
A program that turns the Mac into a tapeless tape deck that lets you build your own arrangements by recording parts one track at a time and then plays them by using one or more synthesizers attached to the Mac.

SMPTE edit time code
A synchronization system used in the motion picture, television, and recording industries. SMPTE, pronounced *simpty,* stands for Society of Motion Picture and Television Engineers. The SMPTE code is often used to synchronize a musical soundtrack or sound effects to film or videotape and to synchronize the playback of audio from a tape recorder with a MIDI sequence.

SND resources
A standard resource format for digital sounds. The sounds in your System file are SND resources.

sound module
A box containing sound-generating circuitry and MIDI connectors, but no keyboard.

sound waves
Variations in air pressure that travel outward from the sound source like the ripples from a stone dropped into a pond.

step recording
A sequencer recording mode that lets you manually enter music one note at a time.

system-exclusive data
MIDI data that is pertinent to a specific model of MIDI instrument, such as the contents of its internal memory or the MIDI-channel assignments of its sounds. By transferring system-exclusive data to the Mac, you can store and alter an instrument's sounds and then transfer the data back to the MIDI instrument.

universal editor/librarian
A patch editor and librarian that is compatible with numerous instruments. Two popular universal editor/librarians are Opcode's Galaxy and Mark of the Unicorn's Unisyn.

velocity-sensitive keyboard
A synthesizer or sampler keyboard that measures how hard you press each key, allowing you to play loudly or softly and enabling the Mac to capture the varied dynamics of a performance.

PART II

Mastering the Mac

CHAPTER TWENTY-TWO

Everything You Need to Know About System 7, 7.5, and Beyond

- Understanding how the Mac and your software use memory
- Adjusting program memory sizes to make best use of your Mac's memory
- Adding fonts in System 7
- Making the most of System 7's multitasking features
- Exploring the enhancements in System 7.5

The System Folder, that folder with the small Mac icon on it, is really what transforms a box of chips into a Macintosh. Knowing what goes on inside the System Folder can help you diagnose problems, customize and fine-tune your system for better performance, use disk space more efficiently, and remain up to date with the latest system software.

This chapter describes the workings of the System Folder and provides tips for customizing yours. After that, you can look under the hood to learn how System 7 operates on Power Macs and how System 7's multitasking features work. I also provide some strategies to help you take better advantage of System 7 multitasking.

Unless otherwise noted, the information in this chapter applies to System 7.0, System 7.1, and System 7.5. When I say System 7, I'm referring to all of these versions. When I refer to a specific version, I include its decimal portion — for example, System 7.1.

For advice on troubleshooting system problems — and on avoiding them to begin with — see Chapter 28.

Oh, and one more thing — the *Macworld Power User Clinic* CD contains interactive tutorials that elaborate on many of the tips and techniques described in this chapter. Check them out!

What's in the System Folder?

When you open the System Folder for the first time, you may feel like you've stepped into a maze. But once you understand how the System Folder is organized, you'll find that it's actually pretty straightforward. Here's the big picture.

When you open the System Folder, you see a directory window that resembles the one in Figure 22-1 "Inside the System Folder." As this figure shows, the System Folder contains several folders of its own as well as several files that are loose within the System Folder. Of these loose files, two — System and Finder — form the backbone of the Mac's system software.

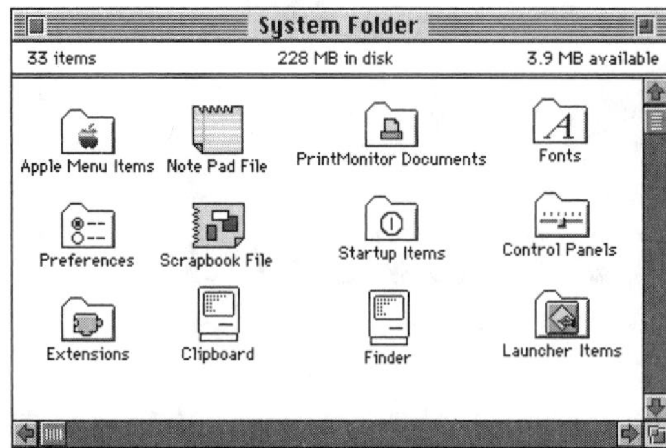

Figure 22-1: Inside the System Folder When you open your System Folder, you see an arrangement similar to this one. (The specific files and folders as well as their icon locations may vary.)

Each of those folders holds related files. The following is an overview of each folder; you can find tips for each one later in this chapter.

❖ *Apple Menu Items* holds items whose names appear in the Apple menu.

❖ *Startup Items* holds items that you want the Mac to open automatically when it starts up.

❖ *Fonts* holds the type fonts whose names appear in your programs' Font menus. The Fonts folder is present in System 7.1 and later versions.

❖ *Preferences* holds the preferences files that many programs create as they run. If you change certain settings in a program — such as the font it uses for new, untitled documents — the program probably saves your settings in a preferences file within this folder.

❖ *Control Panels* contains control panels, those small programs that allow you to adjust and customize the Mac's operation.

❖ *Extensions* contains extensions, those files that often load into memory during startup and add features or capabilities to the Mac.

❖ *PrintMonitor Documents* is a temporary storage place for files that are waiting to be printed by the Mac's background printing software, called PrintMonitor.

- *Launcher Items* holds icons that you want to appear in the Launcher. If you have the Launcher control panel (it's included with Performas as well as with System 7.5), you have this folder.
- *Shutdown Items* holds items you want the Mac to open automatically before shutting down.

The Finder and System Files

As I mentioned, the files named Finder and System are the key players in the disk-based portion of the Mac's operating system. The file named Finder, as you can probably guess, holds the software for the Mac's Finder.

The System file performs a dual role. It contains portions of the system software that aren't in ROM, and it contains *system resources* such as sounds and, in system versions preceding 7.1, fonts. These resources are generally available to all application programs.

Introducing FKEYs

The System file can also accommodate a cousin to the desk accessory, the *function key*, or *FKEY*. FKEYs, like desk accessories, are small programs that are generally available in any application. To run an FKEY, you type a ⌘-Shift keyboard sequence. The Mac includes three FKEYs:

- ⌘-Shift-1 and ⌘-Shift-2 eject the disk in the internal or external floppy disk, respectively. (On a two-floppy Mac SE or SE/30, ⌘-Shift-1 ejects the disk in the lower drive and ⌘-Shift-2 jettisons the disk in the upper one; on a two-floppy Mac LC, II, IIx, or IIfx, ⌘-Shift-1 ejects the disk from the left-hand drive and ⌘-Shift-2 ejects the disk from the right-hand one. Of course, no current Mac supports two floppy drives — internal or external — so pressing ⌘-Shift-2 gets you nothing but an error beep.)
- ⌘-Shift-3 creates a screen *snapshot*, a PICT file containing whatever is displayed on-screen when you press the key sequence.

A Closer Look at Extensions

Just as expansion slots make a Mac more versatile by allowing you to add new hardware, system extensions allow you to add new features to the Mac's system software. You can pick and choose the extensions that your work requires and thus tailor your system software to match your needs and your Mac's capabilities.

This section describes the key extensions that accompany System 7 and also some of the optional extensions that Apple has developed.

Chooser extensions

Chooser extensions are those files whose icons appear in the window of the Chooser desk accessory. The most common Chooser extension is the *printer driver*, which enables the Mac to communicate with a specific type of printer.

How printer drivers work

Printer drivers act as intermediaries between a program that has something to print and the printer itself. The driver translates the commands that describe a document's appearance into the specific commands required by a given printer. See Chapter 31 for tips on specific printer drivers.

The complete guide to Mac OS extensions

Here's a file-by-file roundup of the extensions you're likely to encounter in your System Folder. Note that you may not have every single one of these puppies — some are present in System 7.5 only (not in System 7.0 or 7.1), while others may not be installed on your particular machine.

One more thing — if you're running low on disk space (and everyone does now and then), you can safely delete extensions you don't use. The best candidates for the Trash are drivers for printers you don't have — they're worthless to you and they use more disk space than just about any other type of extension. If you never use System 7.5's Apple Guide help system, you can also expunge the Apple Guide help files to gain a couple of megabytes of disk space. Here we go....

- *A/ROSE* is used by NuBus cards, such as Apple Token Ring 4/16 NB card or the Apple Serial NB card, that run the Apple Real-Time Operating System.
- *About Apple Guide* provides information about Apple Guide. When you choose About Apple Guide from the Finder's Guide menu (the question mark), it's this file's text that appears.
- *Apple CD-ROM* loads the driver software needed to access an Apple CD-ROM drive. If your Mac came with a CD-ROM drive, you have this extension.
- *Apple Guide* implements the active-assistance help system built into System 7.5. (Weird note: If you don't have this file and you choose Apple Guide from the Guide menu, a message appears saying "Apple Help extension was not found." Not only is the extension name wrong, but the message isn't exactly helpful, is it?)
- *Apple Photo Access* is that part of Apple's CD-ROM software that lets you view Kodak PhotoCDs, described in Chapter 13.
- *AppleScriptLib* implements the AppleScript Open Scripting Architecture (OSA) component.
- *AppleScript* lets you automate repetitive tasks within scriptable programs; it's discussed later in this chapter and in Chapter 24.

- *AppleShare* enables you to connect to a shared hard disk by using System 7's file-sharing features, described later in this chapter.
- *AppleTalk ImageWriter* is the printer driver for a networked ImageWriter printer.
- *Audio CD Access* is that part of Apple's CD-ROM software that lets you play audio CDs through a CD-ROM drive. You also need the AppleCD Audio Player or equivalent; see Chapter 25 for details on playing audio CDs and on CD-ROMs in general.
- *Assistant Toolbox* is for PowerBooks; it works along with the Auto Remounter control panel and provides support for the persistent RAM disk and for deferred printing. Note that this extension conflicts with the LaserWriter Select 310 printer driver and can prevent printing. The workaround is to turn off background printing.
- *Caps Lock* works only on PowerBooks; it displays an arrow symbol at the right end of the menu bar when the PowerBook's Caps Lock key is active. This extension is helpful because the Caps Lock key on an older PowerBook doesn't remain down when the caps lock feature is active. You don't need this extension with a PowerBook Duo or 500-series model; the Caps Lock key on the Duo keyboard lights when active.
- *Clipping Extension* implements the desktop clippings feature — the ability to drag a text or graphics selection to the desktop and create a clippings file, as described in Chapter 27.
- *Color Picker* implements the standard color-choosing dialog box that many graphics-oriented programs support — the color wheel with the scroll bar alongside it and the text boxes that let you enter precise color values.
- *Desktop PrintMonitor* implements the desktop printing conveniences of Apple's latest printer drivers — LaserWriter version 8.3 as well as the printer drivers that accompany the Color LaserWriter, the StyleWriter 1200, and the Color StyleWriter 2200 and 2400. See Chapter 31 for more details on how these drivers make printing easier.
- *EtherTalk Phase 2* is the driver software that lets a Mac connect to an Ethernet network.
- *File Sharing Extension* loads some of System 7's file-sharing software into memory during startup.
- *Find File Extension* lets you bring up the System 7.5 Find File window by pressing ⌘-F. If you trash this extension, you can still open Find File — but only by choosing its name from the Apple menu. If you press ⌘-F when this extension is not loaded, the old, pre-System 7.5 Find dialog box appears.
- *Finder Help* contains the text that appears in the Finder's help balloons.
- *Finder Scripting Extension* adds AppleScript support to the Finder.

- *Foreign File Access* is that part of Apple's CD-ROM software that lets you access non-Macintosh CDs such as ISO 9660 or High Sierra formats.
- *High Sierra File Access* is that part of Apple's CD-ROM software that lets you view non-Macintosh file system CDs created in the High Sierra format.
- *IIci/IIsi Monitors* describes the capabilities of the built-in video circuitry in the Mac IIci and IIsi; it's used by the Monitors control panel.
- *ImageWriter* is the printer driver for Apple ImageWriter dot-matrix printers.
- *ISO 9660 File Access* is that part of Apple's CD-ROM software that lets you view non-Macintosh file system CDs created in the ISO 9660 format.
- *LaserWriter 8* is the printer driver for LaserWriter and other PostScript printers. It's covered in detail in Chapter 31.
- *MacinTalk Pro* implements the PlainTalk text-to-speech features that let the Mac read text documents aloud.
- *Macintosh Guide* is the main Apple Guide database file.
- *MacTCP Token Ring Extension* implements the TCP/IP communications protocol on Token Ring networks.
- *Mailbox Extension* provides Mailbox support under PowerTalk.
- *My Speech Macros* is used by the PlainTalk speech-recognition solftware.
- *Network Extension* is used by System 7's file-sharing features to select network options.
- *ObjectSupportLib* works along with the AppleScript software to implement the Apple Open Scripting Architecture's object model, which is what developers use to add AppleScript support to their programs.
- *Personal LaserWriter SC* is the printer driver for the long-discontinued Apple Personal LaserWriter SC.
- *PowerBook Guide Additions* is an Apple Guide database describing PowerBook-related topics.
- *PowerBook Monitors Extension* describes the capabilities of the PowerBooks' video circuitry; it's used by the Monitors control panel.
- *PowerPC Finder Update* expands the width of the Finder's About This Macintosh window to prevent longer Power Mac names from being cut off. (Power Mac names tend to be longer than the non-Power Mac names, and without this extension, part of the name may not be displayed in the About This Macintosh window.)
- *PowerPC Monitors Extension* provides support for the Apple AudioVision 14 multimedia monitor.

- *PowerTalk Extension* implements the PowerTalk communications features (discussed in Chapter 32). This extension also contains information used by the PowerTalk keychain.
- *PowerTalk Guide* is an Apple Guide database containing PowerTalk-related help.
- *PowerTalk Manager* provides management of the PowerTalk Mailbox and other services.
- *Printer Descriptions* is not an extension, but a folder containing PostScript printer-description files; it's used by the LaserWriter 8 driver and is discussed in Chapter 31.
- *PrinterShare* works together with non-PostScript printer drivers (such as the StyleWriter drivers) to enable you to share a non-PostScript printer on a network (see Chapter 31).
- *PrintMonitor* manages the printing process when you have Background Printing enabled; it's discussed later in this chapter and in Chapter 31.
- *Quadra AV Monitors Extension* describes the capabilities of the built-in video circuitry of the Centris/Quadra 660AV and the Quadra 840AV; it's used by the Monitors control panel.
- *Quadra Monitors Extension* describes the capabilities of the built-in video circuitry of the non-AV Centris and Quadra models; it, too, is used by the Monitors control panel.
- *QuickTime* enables the Mac to work with dynamic data such as movies; it's covered in detail in Chapter 20.
- *QuickTime PowerPlug* provides native PowerPC code for QuickTime 2.0. You can install this extension on non-Power Macs, but it has no effect.
- *QuickTime Musical Instruments* contains the Roland Corporation sound samples used by the QuickTime 2 music architecture, described in Chapter 21.
- *Scripting Additions* extend the AppleScript language with special features, such as finding the date or time of day.
- *SCSI Manager 4.3* is an update to the portion of the Mac OS responsible for accessing hard drives. It improves hard drive performance on 68040 Macs; SCSI Manager 4.3 is built into the ROMs of Power Macs, so you don't need this extension if you have one. See Chapter 26 for details on SCSI Manager 4.3.
- *Shortcuts* is the Apple Guide database that describes Finder shortcuts.
- *Speech Guide Additions* is the Apple Guide database containing speech-recognition help.
- *Speech Recognition* implements the PlainTalk speech-recognition software described in Chapter 33.

- *SR Monitor* is used by PlainTalk to monitor and interpret speech.
- *StyleWriter II (or 2400)* is the printer driver for the Apple StyleWriter ink-jet printer.
- *System 7 Tuner* fixes some bugs in System 7, speeds certain tasks such as disk and file copying, and improves System 7's performance during those times when free memory is low. The System 7 Tuner extension is part of Apple's System 7 Tune-Up package, which was released in early 1992. It's not used in System 7.1 or later versions.
- *System Speech Rules* is used by the PlainTalk speech-recognition software.
- *TokenTalk Phase 2* is a driver for Apple's Token Ring networking card.
- *TokenTalk Prep* implements Apple's TokenTalk Phase II networking software.
- *Video Guide Additions* contains Apple Guide help for video-related topics.
- *WorldScript Power Adaptor* provides support for Language Kits on Power Macs.

Easier Interface: Apple's At Ease

Apple's At Ease software is included with Macintosh Performa models. At Ease creates a simplified desktop for starting programs and opening documents, and it provides some basic security features.

For starters, At Ease replaces the standard Finder desktop with two on-screen cards: one labeled Applications and one labeled Documents. Each card contains program or document icons. You can open an item by clicking its icon once — no double-clicking needed.

When At Ease is active, you can neither rename or delete icons nor open the System Folder or any control panels. A menu command lets you access the full Finder, but you must first supply a password. You can also configure At Ease so that new documents must be saved to a floppy disk instead of to the Mac's hard disk. This feature may appeal to schools that don't want students cluttering computer lab hard drives with their own files.

At Ease is designed primarily for home and educational use, but one attribute makes it appealing to almost anyone: when you run under At Ease instead of the full System 7 Finder, you have roughly 200K more RAM available for running programs. It's also easy to switch between the Finder and At Ease. At Ease adds a Go To At Ease menu command to the Finder's File menu; simply choose it and the traditional desktop surrenders to At Ease. Balloon help is still available when At Ease is active.

Apple also sells a business version of At Ease, called At Ease for Workgroups. This version provides the same basic features as its home-bound cousin, but adds additional security and network-oriented features. For example, you can set up At Ease for Workgroups so that a user must save documents on a file server instead of on the local hard drive. At Ease for Workgroups also has activity logging features that track who uses which applications, for how long, and how often.

For some troubleshooting tips regarding At Ease, see Chapter 28.

Control Panels

As I mentioned earlier in this chapter, control panels are small programs that let you adjust system-related settings such as the time and date of the Mac's built-in clock. Control panels live in the Control Panels folder (within the System Folder). When you choose Control Panels from the Apple menu, the Mac switches to the Finder if necessary and then opens the Control Panels folder for you.

(Another name for a control panel is *cdev*, which is short for *control panel device* and generally pronounced *SEE-dev*. You may encounter this technical term in programming books or in older Mac books.)

Keeping track of the Mac's control panels is a bit easier when you group them into the categories, as shown in Table 22-1.

Table 22-1
Control Panel Categories at a Glance

Control Panel Category	*What It Does*	*Examples*
System settings	Adjusts various technical aspects of the Mac's operation	General Controls, Monitors, Keyboard, Mouse, Memory, Startup Disk, Map, PowerBook, Date & Time
Interface customizing	Fine-tunes the workings and appearance of the Mac's interface	Color, Sound, Easy Access, Sound & Displays
Finder customizing	Tweaks the way the Finder displays icons and determines the contents of disks and folders	Views, Labels, WindowShade
File sharing	Activates and adjusts System 7's file-sharing features and monitors how others are using your Mac's hard disk	Sharing Setup, Users & Groups, File Sharing Monitor, Auto Remounter

A complete guide to Mac OS control panels

Here's a file-by-file roundup of the control panels you're likely to encounter in the System 7.5 Control Panels folder. As with extensions, you may not have every single one of these — many are not present in system versions prior to 7.5, while others may not be installed on your particular Mac model.

You can find tips for many of the control panels elsewhere in this chapter. You can also use the index in System 7.5's Apple Guide feature to get more details.

- *Apple Menu Options* lets you enable or disable hierarchical menus, and specify how many recent documents, applications, and servers will be listed.
- *ATM GX* is Adobe Type Manager (ATM), the Adobe font utility for Type 1 PostScript fonts.
- *Auto Power On/Off* lets you set your computer to turn on and/or off at a specified time on a daily basis or on a specified date. See Chapter 23.
- *AutoRemounter* lets you put a PowerBook to sleep without having to see the warning dialog box about losing network services. When the PowerBook wakes up, it also remounts any file servers that were connected when you put the machine to sleep.
- *Brightness* adjusts screen brightness on Macs with soft brightness control, such as the Classic and Classic II.
- *Button Disabler* lets you disable the buttons on the front of the Mac or Performa 500 series so that users (read: students) cannot adjust the volume or brightness.
- *Cache Switch* is installed only on 68040-based Macs. It enables or disables the 68040 processor caching. It's just about obsolete these days, although you may need to use it to disable the cache if you're running an old version of a program on an 040 Mac.
- *Color* sets the color of highlighted (selected) text as well as the border color of windows.
- *CloseView* magnifies the display for easier viewing; it works on all Macs *except* for Power Mac models.
- *ColorSync System Profile* is part of Apple's ColorSync color-matching system, described in Chapter 31.
- *Date & Time* lets you set the Mac's built-in clock, specify the date format, and choose clock options such as playing a sound at regular intervals.
- *Desktop Patterns* lets you change the pattern or color of the desktop background in System 7.5.
- *Easy Access* lets you, among other things, control the Mac's pointer by using the keyboard — handy when your mouse breaks. See the Quick Reference card at the front of this book for details.
- *Extensions Manager* lets you choose which extensions load at startup time. This powerful weapon against extension conflicts and system errors is covered later in this chapter and in the Chapter 28 Quick Tips box "Extension Troubleshooting Strategies."
- *File Sharing Monitor* lets you see who is accessing drives you've made available through System 7 file sharing.

- *General Controls* lets you tweak a variety of System 7.5 settings, including whether the desktop remains visible when you start a program; whether the Launcher appears at startup; and whether the System and Application folders are protected; as well as the rate at which the insertion point blinks; how many times a menu command blinks when chosen; and more.
- *Keyboard* sets the repeat rate and delay before repeat for your keyboard and, in System 7.5, lets you choose a keyboard layout. (Keyboard layouts are described in Chapter 24.)
- *Labels* lets you customize the color and text of Finder document labels.
- *Launcher* provides fast access to often-used items, as described later in this chapter.
- *MacTCP* lets the Mac connect to network services via the TCP/IP protocol.
- *Macintosh Easy Open* helps put an end to "application not found" messages by searching for programs that can open a document that you double-click (see Chapter 27).
- *Map* displays a world map and lets you set the Mac's time zone as well as determine the time difference between your location and another location.
- *Memory* lets you tweak memory-related settings, including the disk cache, virtual memory, and RAM disk. See the section "Memory Maximizing Tips," later in this chapter.
- *Monitors* adjusts monitor settings, including the number of colors or shades of gray that are displayed.
- *Mouse* sets the tracking speed and double-click speed of your mouse.
- *Network* lets you choose between network ports and options installed in your computer. For example, most of today's Macs provide both LocalTalk and Ethernet connectors; to choose the active connector, you use the Network control panel.
- *Numbers* lets you specify the format of currency values (for example, what kind of currency symbol is used) as well as the position of the decimal point in numeric data.
- *PC Exchange* lets you access DOS-format disks as if they were Mac disks; it's described in detail in Chapter 27.
- *Power Macintosh Card* is included with Apple's Power Macintosh Upgrade Card (see Chapter 29). This control panel lets you choose whether you want to start up with the 68040 processor or the PowerPC processor.
- *PowerBook* provides control over PowerBook-related settings: hard drive sleep, system sleep, display dimming, and the like. The next chapter contains tips for this control panel.

- *PowerBook Display* controls the video-mirroring feature on PowerBooks that support video mirroring.
- *PowerBook Setup* lets you specify the PowerBook's SCSI address for SCSI Disk Mode (discussed in Chapter 26) and also lets you choose between the so-called "normal" and "compatible" modes for the serial port, as described in the next chapter's Quick Tips box "When Is It Normal to Not Be Compatible?"
- *Screen* controls the brightness and contrast of the built-in monitor on certain Mac models.
- *Serial Switch* is for the Mac IIfx and Quadra 950. Some programs that use the printer or modem port have problems on these Macs; with these programs, choose the More Compatible option.
- *Sharing Setup* lets you configure file sharing and supply a network name for your Mac; it's discussed in detail later in this chapter.
- *Sound* lets you choose an alert sound, adjust the speaker volume, and record new sounds. The second-generation Power Macs use the Sound & Displays control panel.
- *Sound & Displays* is included with System 7.5.2 and works on second-generation Power Macs; it provides a one-stop source for tweaking sound and video settings.
- *Speech Setup* enables speech recognition and lets you fine-tune recognition settings (see Chapter 33).
- *Startup Disk* lets you specify the hard drive or volume that the Mac starts up from. If you have more than one hard drive connected (or you've partitioned a hard drive into multiple volumes), you can store a different System Folder on each drive or volume and then use this control panel to specify which one the Mac should start from.
- *Text* is part of Apple's WorldScript software; it affects "text behavior" such as sorting and case conversion.
- *Trackpad* lets you fine-tune the trackpad settings on PowerBooks that provide trackpads.
- *Users & Groups* lets you specify lists of network users who can access your hard drive when file sharing is on. It's discussed later in this chapter.
- *Views* lets you tweak the way the Finder displays disk and folder windows; it's also discussed later in this chapter.
- *WindowShade* lets you hide a window by double-clicking its title bar.

When does a control panel act like an extension?

If you think about it, extensions and certain control panels have one big similarity. Consider Easy Access, the control panel that, among other things, lets you move the mouse pointer by using the keyboard's numeric keypad. Part of the Easy Access control panel loads into the Mac's memory at startup time and always watches your typing, on the alert for the key sequences that activate the sticky keys or mouse keys features.

But how can a *control panel* load software into memory during startup? Isn't that what extensions do?

Yes, and there's the similarity: like an extension, a control panel can load software into memory during startup. That's because a control panel can have a snippet of software called an *INIT resource* attached to it. When the Mac starts up, it scans the Control Panels folder as well as the System Folder. If any control panels contain INIT resources, the Mac loads their software into memory.

As it turns out, INIT resources are the key to loading software into memory during startup. System extensions, Chooser extensions, and control panels — all can have INIT resources and thus can load software into memory during startup.

Adding Control Panels and Extensions

The control panels discussed here aren't the only ones a System Folder can contain — not by a long shot. Many software developers and Mac programming hobbyists have created control panels and extensions that perform some very useful jobs.

I describe some of these control panels and extensions in Chapter 24. For now, here's a look at the process of installing them in your System Folder. It's actually very simple: Simply drag the file to the *closed* System Folder icon. The Mac displays a message telling you that the control panel or extension needs to be stored in the Control Panels or Extensions folder, as shown in Figure 22-2 "Installing Control Panels and Extensions." (Curious about how the Mac knows where to put what? See the Backgrounder box "File Signatures: How the Mac Identifies Files.")

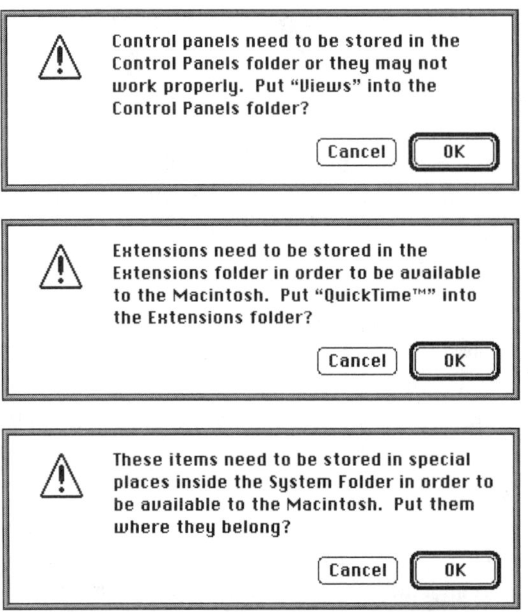

Figure 22-2: Installing Control Panels and Extensions The Finder displays one of these three dialog boxes when you drag control panels and extensions to the System Folder icon. Top: Installing a control panel. Middle: Installing an extension. Bottom: Installing a control panel and an extension.

If you need to install a control panel or extension in a folder other than the one in which System 7 thinks it belongs, drag it to the open System Folder directory window. Suppose you're having a system problem that you suspect is related to the loading order of a particular control panel. You want to change the order in which the control panel loads, so you put it in the top level of the System Folder by dragging it there.

Tips for System Software Customizing

The System 7 Finder provides many more built-in customizing options than did previous Finders. A good first step in conquering the Mac's system software involves tweaking the Finder to fit your tastes and work habits. You can find additional tips for extra customizing opportunities in System 7.5 later in this chapter.

File Signatures: How the Mac Identifies Files

Have you ever wondered how the Finder knows that control panels belong in the Control Panels folder, while extensions belong in the Extensions folder? Or how the Mac knows which program to start when you double-click a document? Or why your PageMaker documents don't show up in Microsoft Word's Open dialog box?

The answer is the *file signature*, which identifies a file as well as the program that created it. A file signature has two components:

- The *type* is a four-character code that identifies the file. A control panel's type is *cdev,* a system extension is an *INIT,* and a Chooser extension is an *RDEV.* (Note the capitalization — *cdev* is lowercase, but the others are all capitals.) When you drag a file to the System Folder's icon, the Finder examines the file's type code. If the type is cdev, the Finder knows that it's working with a control panel and asks you if you want to store the file in the Control Panels folder.
- The *creator* is a four-character code that identifies the program that created the file. For example, a Microsoft Word document has a creator code of *MSWD.* When you double-click a document, the Finder consults the creator code to determine which program to start in order to open that document.

Most of the time, you don't have to concern yourself with file signatures — the Mac keeps track of them for you behind the scenes. But there can be times — such as when you're swapping files with Windows PCs — that knowing how to change signatures can be useful. Chapter 24 describes the process.

Customize directory windows with Views

Using the Views control panel, you can change the type font and size of the text in directory windows and choose to see as much or as little information as you like about the items on your disks. Note that unchecking items such as size, date, and kind also eliminates those commands in the View menu. If you uncheck Kind, for example, you can't sort the contents of a window according to icon type (folder, application, or document).

Other tips: Think twice about checking the Calculate Folder Sizes box; it can slow the Finder significantly under some circumstances. If you're a neatnik, check the Always Snap to Grid box. This command puts the Finder in what I call *mom mode* — it always cleans up after you.

You can switch between views by using the Finder's View menu, but there's a faster way — click the view heading in the active directory window. If you have a large screen, doing so can be faster than moving the mouse pointer all the way up to the menu bar.

The Finder stores your Views settings in the file named Finder Preferences, stored in the Preferences folder within the System Folder.

Power Tips for the Launcher

System 7.5 and Mac Performa models include a handy control panel called Launcher that gives you one-click access to the programs and documents you use most. If there's a program, document, or alias you want fast access to, just add it to the Launcher.

To display the Launcher, choose Launcher from the Apple menu's Control Panels submenu. To have the Mac display the Launcher automatically when you start up, open the General Controls control panel and check the box named Show Launcher at system startup. (When you check this box, the Mac creates an alias for the Launcher in the System Folder's Startup Items folder.)

Adding Items to the Launcher

If you're using System 7.5.1 (that is, System 7.5 with the System 7.5 Update 1.0 described later in this chapter) or System 7.5.2, you can add an item to the Launcher by simply dragging its icon to the Launcher window. To remove an item's button, press Option and drag the button out of the Launcher window and into the Trash. Note that this just deletes the item's Launcher button — it doesn't actually delete the file or item the button points to.

If you're using System 7.5 or an earlier system version, adding items to the Launcher window takes a little more work. First, make an alias of the item (if you don't know how, see the section on aliases later in this chapter). Next, move the alias into the Launcher Items folder, which is located within the System Folder. (You can, by the way, store original application and document files in the Launcher Items folder, but it's more efficient to create aliases of them.)

Making Launcher Topic Buttons

Normally, the top of the Launcher window contains two buttons — Applications and Documents. When you click Applications, the Launcher displays the buttons you've created for applications. When you click Documents, you see the buttons that you've created for your often-used documents.

You can also create additional topic buttons to further subdivide your Launcher items. For instance, instead of just having an Applications button, you may want to create one button for graphics programs, one for text programs, and one for communications programs. Ditto for documents — create a button for memos, one for pictures, and one for QuickTime movies.

To create a topic button, first open the Launcher Items folder (remember, it's in the System Folder). Next, create a folder and give it the desired button name. But preceed the button name with a bullet character (that's •, the Option-8 key sequence). For example, to create a button named Jim's Stuff, name the folder •Jim's Stuff, as shown in the adjacent figure. Finally, copy the aliases or files that you want to appear in each topic button into its appropriate folder.

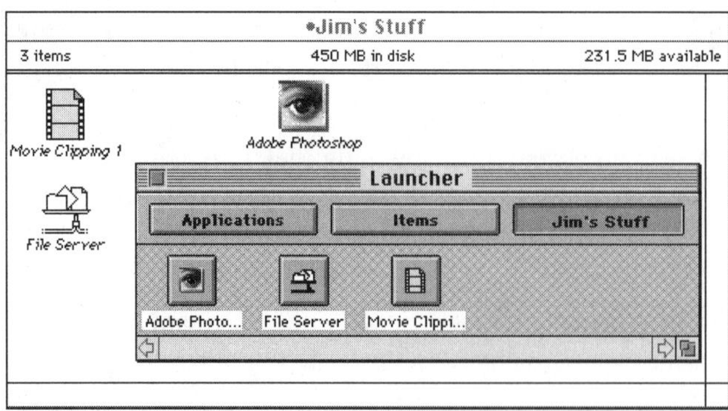

Need to perform some maintenance on a folder with the Launcher Items folder? Don't double-click your way through folder after folder. Press Option while clicking on the topic button, and the Finder opens the topic's folder for you.

Moving Buttons from One Category to Another

With the Launcher in System 7.5.1 and later versions, it's easy to move an item's button from one category to another: press Option and drag the button to the desired category button. Release the mouse button, and the item is beamed to its destination.

Changing the Size of Launcher Buttons

In the Launcher in System 7.5.1 and later versions, you can have small, medium, and large buttons. Press ⌘ while clicking within the Launcher window, and then choose the desired button size from the pop-up menu that appears. Your choice applies to the current topic only — repeat this procedure for your other topic buttons. Or use different button sizes for different topics, as you see fit.

Who wrote the Launcher?

Press ⌘-Option while clicking the shaded area that surrounds the Launcher's topic buttons to find out.

Getting rid of the Empty Trash warning dialog box

Normally, the Finder warns you when you choose the Empty Trash command. If you don't want the warning, you can temporarily bypass it by pressing the Option key while choosing Empty Trash.

You can also get rid of the warning permanently: Select the Trash icon and choose Get Info from the File menu. In the Info window, uncheck the Warn Before Emptying box. You'll never see the warning again. (You'll never be rescued by it, either.)

Assigning text labels and colors to icons

Using the Labels control panel, you can create descriptive labels (Personal, Work in Progress, Urgent, To Be Trashed, and so on) and then assign them to files or folders with the Finder's Label menu. You can then use the View menu to sort directory windows according to labels or colors. To be honest, I don't know anyone who uses this feature — maybe you'll be the first.

Customizing the Apple menu

Would you like fast access to a particular program, control panel, or document? Make an alias of the item (as described later in this chapter) and then move the alias into the Apple Menu Items folder, located within the System Folder.

And if you haven't upgraded to System 7.5, which provides a hierarchical Apple menu, use a utility such as Microseed's HAM, Now Software's Now Utilities, or Alsoft's Menu Extend (part of the Alsoft Power Utilities package). Chapter 24 covers these and other utilities.

Selecting Icons with the Keyboard

When using the Finder, you can select an icon on the desktop or in the active directory window by quickly typing the first few characters of its name — just as you can select items within an Open or Save dialog box.

If the item you want isn't in the active window, you can still locate and select it from the keyboard — just use the Find command as described in the section "Fast Finding" in this chapter.

You can also select icons by using the keyboard's arrow keys as well as the Tab key and Shift-Tab key sequence. See the Quick Reference card at the front of this book for a list of System 7 Finder shortcuts.

Creating stationery documents

The Get Info window for a document contains a new check box called Stationery Pad. When you check this box, you turn the document into a *stationery pad.* The stationery feature lets you create masters for the types of documents you create — letterheads, business letters, fax cover sheets, newsletter designs, and so on. By creating a document and then turning it into a stationery pad, you can reuse its contents without worrying about accidentally saving over them. When you open a stationery pad, the Finder makes a copy of the document and asks you to name the new copy (see Figure 22-3 "Personal Stationery").

As Chapter 3 describes, many programs can also save documents as stationery. For details about creating stationery within two popular word processors — Microsoft Word and WordPerfect — see the Chapter 3 Step-by-Step box "Creating Stationery."

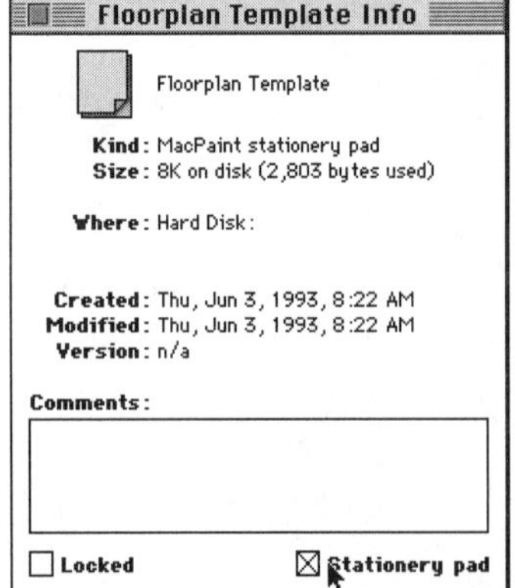

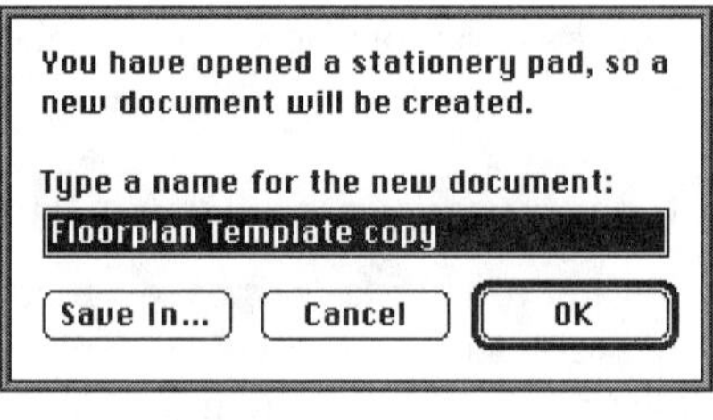

Figure 22-3: Personal Stationery To turn a document into a stationery pad, click the Stationery Pad check box in the document's Get Info window (left). When you open a stationery pad, the Finder asks you to provide a name for the new document (right), which is a copy of the original. To save the docu-ment in a different folder or on a different disk, click the Save In button.

Customizing disk, file, and folder icons

When I was a kid, creating custom icons meant a fantastic voyage into Apple's ResEdit resource-editing utility (also discussed in Chapter 24). System 7 makes it easier. Select an icon and choose Get Info. In the Info window, click the icon (a border appears around it) and then choose Copy (see Figure 22-4 "Picture an Icon").

Now start up a paint program such as Adobe Photoshop. Paste the icon, and then use the paint program's tools to tweak it as desired. (Designing a good-looking icon is the hard part.) After you're done, select the modified icon and copy it to the Clipboard. Return to the Info window from which you copied the icon, make sure that the icon is still selected, and then paste.

You can also use scanned images as icons: when you paste a large image into the Info window, the Finder shrinks it to fit a standard icon size. With this technique, you can turn a disk or folder window into a thumbnail catalog of scanned images.

I used custom icons to dress up the folders on the *Macworld Power User Clinic* CD. And speaking of the CD, you can find dozens of great-looking custom icons for Apple and third-party equipment in the Utilities folder of "The Best of BMUG" collection. Using them is a great way to dress up your desktop and also to distinguish between the types of Macs and storage media you use (for example, you can use the SyQuest icon for your SyQuest cartridges or one of the PowerBook icons for your PowerBook's hard disk).

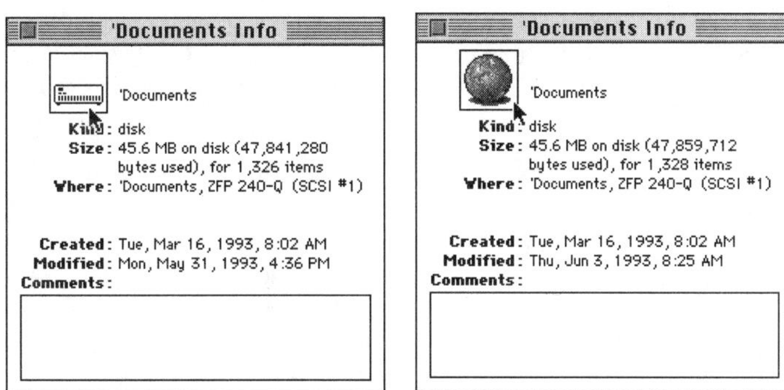

Figure 22-4: Picture an Icon System 7 lets you customize the icons of most items by using the Get Info window. First, select the image in a graphics program and choose Copy. Next, select the icon in the Get Info window; if the icon can be modified, it appears within a rectangle (left). Finally, choose Paste, and the Mac scales the graphic to fit and turns it into an icon (right).

Standard Shortcuts for the Open and Save Dialog Boxes

All System 7 versions provide several standard shortcuts for directory dialog boxes. Mastering these shortcuts, which work with any program, can save time when opening or saving files.

Locating a file or folder

To locate a file or folder in an Open dialog box, use the up- or down-arrow key or quickly type the first few characters of the item's name.

Using Return or Enter to confirm the dialog box

After you locate the file or folder you want, you don't need to reach for the mouse to click the Open button: you can open it by pressing Return or Enter. If you have selected a file, pressing Return opens it. If you have selected a folder, the Mac opens the folder and displays its contents in the dialog box.

Opening and closing folders

To close a folder and move up one level in the storage hierarchy, press ⌘-up arrow. To open a folder, either select it and press Return or select it and press ⌘-down arrow.

Moving up one level in the hierarchy

To use the mouse to quickly move up one level in the storage hierarchy, click the disk name that appears in the directory dialog box. Each click moves you one level closer to the desktop level.

Using Tab to switch between the file list and the text-entry box

In the Save or Save As dialog box, you can press the Tab key to switch the keyboard focus between the file list and the text-entry box. When the keyboard focus is on the file list, you can select folders by typing the first few characters of their names; when the keyboard focus is on the text-entry box, you can type a name for the file. By using the Tab key to switch the keyboard focus, you can open a particular folder and then type a document name — without reaching for the mouse. When the keyboard focus is on the file list, a bold border appears around it; when the focus is on the text-entry box, a bold border appears around it.

Accessing the desktop

To quickly jump to the desktop level, simply press ⌘-D or ⌘-Shift-up arrow.

Creating a new folder

You can create a new folder within a currently open folder by pressing ⌘-N.

Canceling the dialog box

If you decide not to open or save a document after all, you can cancel the directory dialog box by pressing ⌘-period (.) or the Esc key instead of clicking the Cancel button.

Moving to a folder automatically

You can tell System 7.5 to automatically take you to the folder containing your application programs or to the folder you last used in a program when you choose Open or Save. To do so, open the General Controls control panel and, in the Documents area, choose the appropriate option.

Installing and Removing Fonts

System 7 makes adding fonts or removing fonts from your system a breeze. This section shows you how to add and remove fonts in System 7.0 and 7.1/7.5.

Adding a font to System 7.0

Before adding a font, quit any programs you've already started. (You can't modify the system when programs or desk accessories are running.) Then drag the font file to the System Folder icon. A dialog box appears asking whether you want to install the fonts, as shown in Figure 22-5 "Font Moving Made Easy." Click OK or press Return, and the Mac installs the fonts in the System file.

You can also add more than one font at a time by selecting each font file and then dragging it to the System Folder icon.

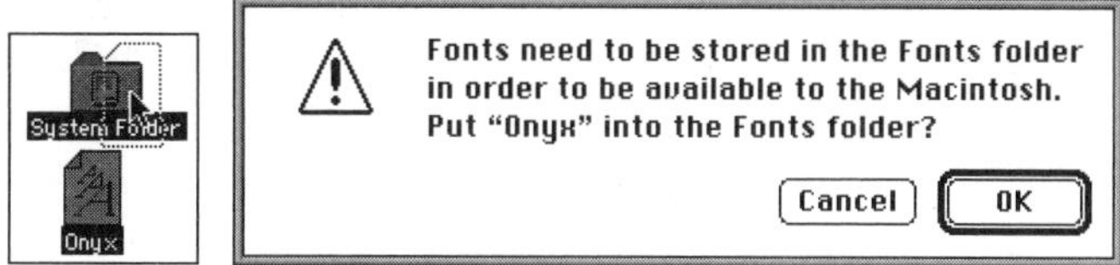

Figure 22-5: Font Moving Made Easy To install a font in System 7.0, drag its icon to that of the System Folder (left). When the Mac asks whether you want to put the fonts in the System file (right), click OK. One catch: You must quit any open programs and close any desk accessories in order to install or remove a font.

Better Balloons

Most people either love or hate System 7's balloon help feature, which explains menu commands, dialog box options, and tool palette icons when you point to them. The Finder alone contains some 1,300 different help balloons for everything from the Trash to the One Sided and Two Sided buttons in the Erase Disk dialog box.

One of the less-likable aspects of balloon help is that you must travel up to the menu bar to turn it on — a long journey when you have a big screen. Using a shareware extension called Helium (by Robert Mathews), you can activate balloon help by using the keyboard. If the help balloons are a little small for your tastes, you can use Helium to change the font and size in which help text appears.

CE Software's QuicKeys keyboard-enhancement utility also lets you turn balloon help on or off from the keyboard. Open the QuicKeys control panel, pull down the Define menu, open the Extensions submenu, and then choose the System 7 Specials command. In the subsequent dialog box, choose the Toggle Balloon Help option and then type the key sequence you want to use. (I use Control-Help on my extended keyboard and Control-? on my PowerBook. Note that it's Control, not ⌘. You can use ⌘-Help, but some programs may use that sequence themselves. Besides, the Control key is closer to the Help key, making it easier to turn help on or off with one hand.)

In most cases, the text for balloon help is stored in a separate disk file, so you can free up disk space by removing the help file if you like. The Finder's help balloons are stored in a file called Finder Help, located within the System Folder's Extensions folder.

As an alternative to dragging a font to the System Folder icon, you can also drag it to the System file icon or to the opened System file window. But you can't install a font by dragging it to the open System Folder window. When you try, the Mac simply moves the font into the top level of the System Folder — it doesn't install the font in the System file.

Removing fonts in System 7.0

To remove one or more fonts, first quit any open application programs or desk accessories, open the System Folder, and then open the System file. The directory window that appears lists the installed fonts. Select the font or fonts you want to remove, and then drag them to the Trash. Better still, drag the fonts to the desktop or to a disk or folder window or icon: you may want to reinstall the fonts later. After you finish removing fonts, close the System file window and the System Folder window.

Adding a PostScript outline font in System 7.0

Adding a PostScript font involves two steps. After installing the screen font by using the techniques I just described, install the printer outline font. (The screen fonts have suitcase icons. Printer font icons vary depending on the font vendor; Adobe's icons have a large *A* on them.) Printer outline font files can go in the top level of the System Folder or in the Extensions folder within the System Folder. (The Finder recognizes PostScript outline files. When you drag the outline files to the System Folder icon, the Finder asks whether you want to store the files in the Extensions folder.)

Removing a PostScript font from System 7.0

To remove a PostScript font, first remove the bitmap font from the System file by using the techniques described earlier and then remove the PostScript outline font from the Extensions folder.

Adding and Removing Fonts in System 7.1 and 7.5

System 7.1 and 7.5 store all fonts — TrueType, PostScript, or bitmap — within the Fonts folder (located within the System Folder). This location makes adding and removing fonts easier and faster than with System 7.0.

Adding a font in System 7.1 or 7.5

To add a font, drag the font file to the System Folder icon. A dialog box appears asking whether you want to install the fonts in the Fonts folder. If any programs or desk accessories are open, a second dialog box appears telling you that the font will not appear in the currently running programs: you need to quit the programs and start them again (you don't have to restart the Mac). Click OK or press Return. The Mac installs the fonts in the Fonts folder.

Removing a font in System 7.1 or 7.5

To remove a font, first quit any programs or desk accessories that you previously started. Then open the Fonts folder and drag the font out of the folder. Or simply use the Finder's Find command to locate the font for you.

Font-Management Strategies

As this chapter has shown, the Mac's System Folder holds a variety of resources. But only one category helps you express yourself: fonts. Professional publishers have huge font libraries, but the rest of us aren't far behind. Many printers and programs come with font collections. Free and shareware fonts abound. Fonts are fun — after all, you can never have too many ways to express yourself.

Until, that is, you start falling victim to the many side effects of fontmania. The time required to start programs increases as the programs work harder to create their Font menus. The Font menus themselves sag to the bottom of the screen, making it hard to locate the font you want. And your System Folder bloats and becomes a ball and chain at backup time.

This section details a font-management strategy designed to avoid these problems. If you're unfamiliar with font formats such as *TrueType* and *Type 1*, or with font-related terms such as *suitcase file* and *screen font*, you'll find some essential background in Chapter 11.

Font management: The big picture

If you have a moderate-sized font library, you probably don't need to worry about font-management issues. Simply stash the fonts in your System Folder and go about your business. (A moderate-sized library might be ten or so font families, with a family encompassing the standard four styles: plain, italic, bold, and bold italic.)

But when a font collection grows to a dozen or more font families, it isn't efficient to just chuck every font into the System Folder. A better approach is to keep only a base set of your everyday fonts in the System Folder, and then organize the rest of your fonts according the way you use them. A set of fonts for the company newsletter. Another set for the quarterly technical manuals. A set of flashy fonts for invitations and certificates. You get the idea: when you organize your fonts the way you organize your documents — into logical, related categories — it's easier to manage them.

Third parties to the rescue

The Mac's operating system doesn't provide these kinds of font-management luxuries, but you can get them by combining the features it does provide with one of two third-party utilities: Symantec's Suitcase and Alsoft's MasterJuggler. Both utilities allow you to open and close suitcase files, those special document files that can hold TrueType and fixed-size (bitmapped) fonts. I recommend MasterJuggler; it's easier to use and has a much more up-to-date manual.

Creating a streamlined font filing system involves three phases: grouping fonts into suitcase files; organizing those suitcase files, along with their related printer font files, into folders; and then using Suitcase or MasterJuggler to open and close suitcase files and create font sets as needed. Opening a suitcase file is the equivalent of installing its fonts in the System Folder — it makes the fonts available to your programs. Similarly, closing a suitcase file is like removing the fonts from the System Folder. (There are some important caveats behind both steps, though — more on them shortly.)

Phase 1: Packing suitcases

The Mac used to include a utility, Font/DA Mover, that allowed you to create suitcase files and move fonts in and out of them. Font/DA Mover is still around, but it's no longer included with the Mac's system software. (It is included with Suitcase and some other font-related products, and it's available for downloading from America Online. To locate it, press ⌘-K, type **quickfind** and press Return; then type **Font/DA Mover** and press Return.)

Packing suitcases with the Finder

By doing some futzing in System 7's Finder, you can create and pack suitcase files without using Font/DA Mover. The secret is to set up an empty suitcase file and then use it as the starting point for your font-organizing efforts. To create an empty suitcase file, first copy any existing suitcase file — perhaps one from your Mac's system disks or from a font package you bought — to your hard drive. Now double-click it, and a window opens listing the fonts in the suitcase file. Choose Select All and then drag the fonts to the Trash. Empty the Trash and close the suitcase file's window. Finally, change the suitcase file's name to *Empty Suitcase* or something similar. From now on, each time you want to create a new suitcase file, use the Finder's Duplicate command to make a copy of the empty suitcase and then modify the duplicate. To prevent accidental modification of your "master" empty suitcase, lock it using the Finder's Get Info command.

Suitcase-packing strategies

Everyone has his or her own suitcase-packing techniques — whether you're talking Samsonites or fonts. For the latter, what I do is pack all four styles of a given font family into a suitcase that I've named after the family. For example, for a family of

PostScript Type 1 fonts named Tweed, I'd pack the Tweed, Tweed Italic, Tweed Bold, and Tweed Bold Italic fonts into a suitcase file named *Tweed Screen Fonts*. For a TrueType font, I'd pack all the fonts into a suitcase named *Tweed TT*.

When you're packing the fixed-sized fonts that the Mac uses for its screen displays, you have another decision to make: how many fixed sizes to include in the suitcase. The Mac needs only one fixed size in order to be able to use a PostScript font; it doesn't need any fixed sizes in order to use a TrueType font. Thus, you can save some disk space by not storing a lot of fixed-sized fonts.

But there's a catch: When you choose a font size for which no fixed size exists, the Mac must generate, or *rasterize*, the size on the fly. (For PostScript fonts, this is done by the Adobe Type Manager utility; for TrueType fonts, it's done by the Mac's system software.) This rasterizing process takes a moment or two; the delay can be especially apparent on slower Macs. For this reason, you'll get the best scrolling and text-display performance if you retain the fixed-size fonts for the type sizes you use most often.

So how do you do the actual packing? Use the Finder. First, quit any open programs or desk accessories, and then open up the System Folder's Fonts folder (or the System file itself in System 7.0). Finally, drag each font into the empty font suitcase you created earlier. If the fonts you want to move are already stored within a suitcase file (as they can be in Systems 7.1 and 7.5), you can either drag the entire suitcase file into the new suitcase, or you can open up the suitcase file and drag the actual fonts within it. You might take the latter approach if you want to install only certain font sizes in the new suitcase.

Phase 2: Filing the fonts

At this point, you've created one suitcase file for each of your font families, and you've copied to each suitcase file that family's fixed-sized fonts along with any TrueType fonts. But organizing font styles is one thing; organizing the font *suitcases* is another. This phase involves deciding where you're going to store all the suitcase files, and then moving them there along with the printer font files that PostScript fonts require.

Setting Up a Font File Server

One of the beauties of using Suitcase or MasterJuggler is that you aren't restricted to storing fonts in your System Folder. You can stash them in separate folders on your hard drive, on a removable cartridge drive, or even on a network file server. The file server approach has important advantages for a large office: It makes it easy to standardize on a consistent set of fonts, and it eliminates the need to store PostScript outline fonts on each user's hard drive. If you store a given typeface's outline fonts in the same folder as its suitcase file, the Mac's PostScript printer driver as well as Adobe Type Manager will still be able to find the outlines. Note, though, that accessing fonts over a LocalTalk network isn't exactly speedy; the file server approach is most practical for Ethernet networks.

The font server approach can even be handy for PowerBooks. For example, I keep only a bare minimum set of fonts in my PowerBook's System Folder — the fonts I use when I'm on the road. Back at the home base, I connect the PowerBook to my main machine and use System 7 file sharing and MasterJuggler to tap into my desktop font library, which I store in a folder named Fonts Folder on my Mac's hard drive. This scheme gives me the best of both worlds: a lean font collection that doesn't take up precious PowerBook disk space, and hundreds of additional fonts just a network cable away.

Note that if you want more than one person to be able to open a given suitcase file, you need to tell MasterJuggler or Suitcase to open that file as shared — otherwise, the second person who tries to open a suitcase will get an error message saying the file is in use. In MasterJuggler, press Option while opening the suitcase file. In Suitcase, check the Shared box before opening the file. (Tip: You can also force either utility to open a suitcase as shared by locking the suitcase file using the Finder's Get Info window.)

Phase 3: Using the utility

Using MasterJuggler or Suitcase to access fonts is easy: just use either utility's Open button to open the suitcase files you need. Both utilities let you specify that certain suitcases be automatically opened when you start up.

But there are some flies in the font-management ointment, and they deal with the way Mac programs access fonts. A program builds its Font menu when you start it up — if you open a suitcase after starting a program, the fonts you open won't show up in the program's Font menu. To access them, you'll have to quit the program and then relaunch it.

A related though potentially more serious problem surfaces when you close a font suitcase while a program is running. Mac programs aren't smart enough to know that a given font is no longer available — the font still shows up in their Font menus. If you choose the closed font's name, the program could crash.

You don't encounter these pitfalls with System 7's standard font-handling features because System 7 won't let you install or remove fonts when programs or desk accessories are open. But MasterJuggler and Suitcase let you open and close suitcases at any time (they do display appropriate warning messages). Fortunately, it's easy to avoid both problems: Just remember to open the fonts you need before starting the program in which you'll use them, and to quit that program before closing those fonts' suitcases.

Creating font sets

I've mentioned that a good font-management technique is to create font sets for the types of documents you work with. One way to do this is to create a suitcase file containing those fonts — for example, the Baskerville you use for the text of your monthly reports, and the Futura Bold you use for its headings.

The problem with this approach is that you can end up with a lot of suitcase files that contain some of the same fonts. Both MasterJuggler and Suitcase let you define named sets of suitcase files — you can, for instance, create a font set named *Report Fonts* that automatically opens the Baskerville and Futura suitcase files (see Figure 22-6 "Font Streamlining"). It's usually more efficient to use this feature rather than creating a multitude of suitcase files. This avoids the disk waste that occurs when some fonts are stored in more than one suitcase. And it keeps your font library organized the way it should be: according to the fonts themselves.

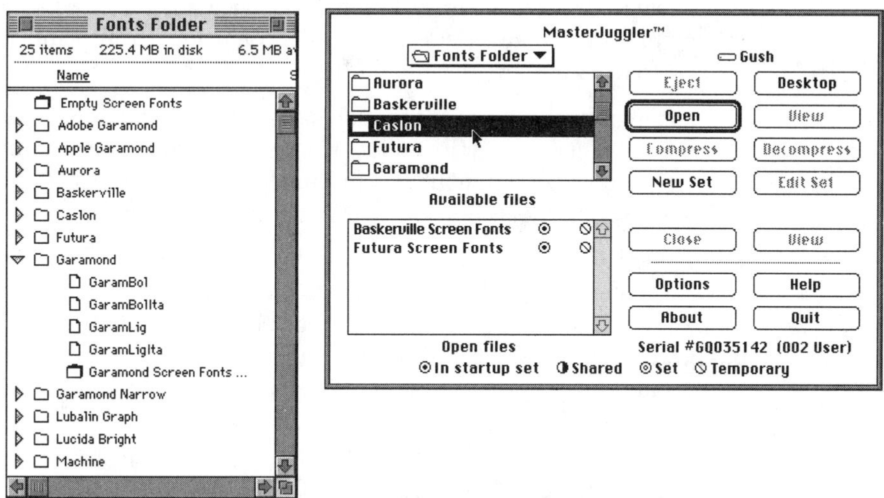

Figure 22-6: Font Streamlining After organizing printer and screen fonts into folders (left), use MasterJuggler (right) or Suitcase to open fonts and create font sets.

The Amazing Alias

One of System 7's biggest conveniences is the *alias*. An alias is a small file that acts as a remote control for another item, usually another file or a folder. When you double-click an alias, the Mac opens the item to which the alias points. You can keep programs and files within their folders but still have fast access to them from other places, such as the desktop or the Apple menu.

Instructions for creating aliases by using the Finder appear in the Step-by-Step box "Making an Alias."

Other ways to make aliases

After you've mastered aliases, you may want to experiment with an alias utility. One is an extension called FinderHack, by Donald Brown, the creator of CE Software's QuicKeys.

FinderHack adds a menu to the Finder called Futz (I said it was easy, not poetic). Select an icon and choose the FinderHack command called Make Alias in Apple Menu. FinderHack creates an alias of the icon and puts the alias in the Apple Menu Items folder for you. Its Make Alias As command gives you a dialog box that lets you name the new alias and specify where you want to store it. FinderHack also provides commands that instantly delete selected icons or move them to the Trash.

If you want the Finder to append something other than *alias* to an alias name, use Adam Stein's shareware utility, Adam Stein's System 7 Pack, which can perform several other useful System 7 modifications. (It's included in the Best of BMUG Collection on the CD that came with this book.)

Another handy alias maker is AliasThis!, by Bruce Oberg and Gordon Sheridan. Drag an item to the AliasThis icon, and AliasThis creates an alias of that item in the Apple menu. Better still is Lawrence Harris's shareware called Alias Director, which even lets you create aliases that don't have icons — a nice way to avoid clutter if, like me, you like to keep aliases on the desktop. It's also included on CD.

Styling and trashing aliases

To show that an item is an alias, the Finder puts its name in italics. Bill Monk's Alias Stylist utility lets you specify a different type style for alias names.

One problem with aliases is that they remain on your hard disk even if you delete the items you aliased. To fix that problem, try Maurice Volaski's free TrashAlias, a control panel that automatically deletes an alias when you delete the item to which it points. Cliff McCollum's shareware utility, the AliasZoo, helps you keep track of aliases and can also delete orphaned ones.

The Quick Tips box "Alias Ideas" describes some ways to use aliases.

The Power to Find Your Best

It's a good idea to organize documents and programs within folders. But as your filing system gets complex — with folders within folders within folders — locating and opening a particular file can become cumbersome.

In System 7, the File menu contains a Find command that lets you locate files. In System 7.0 and 7.1, choosing Find displays a dialog box whose options I'm about to describe. In System 7.5, choosing Find opens the Find File desk accessory, which I cover at the end of this section.

Exploring the System 7.0/7.1 Find dialog box

The Find dialog box contains a button called More Choices. When you click More Choices, the Find dialog box is replaced by a larger dialog box containing pop-up menus that enable you to search by using a variety of different criteria (see Figure 22-7 "Detailed Searching"). To specify that the Finder locate and select all the items that meet the criteria, click the All at Once check box. When this option is unchecked, the Finder stops each time it locates and selects an item.

Making an Alias

The instructions in this box show you how to create an alias by using the Finder.

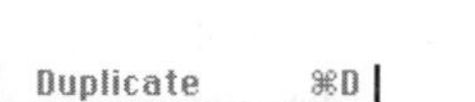

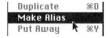

To create an alias:

1. **Select the original file or folder by clicking it once.**
2. **Choose Make Alias from the Finder's File menu.**
   The Finder creates the alias. The alias's icon appears adjacent to the original and has the word *alias* tacked onto its name; you can rename the alias if you like. An alias by another name . . .
3. **Drag the alias to its final destination.**
   You may want to keep it on the desktop or in the Apple Menu Items folder.

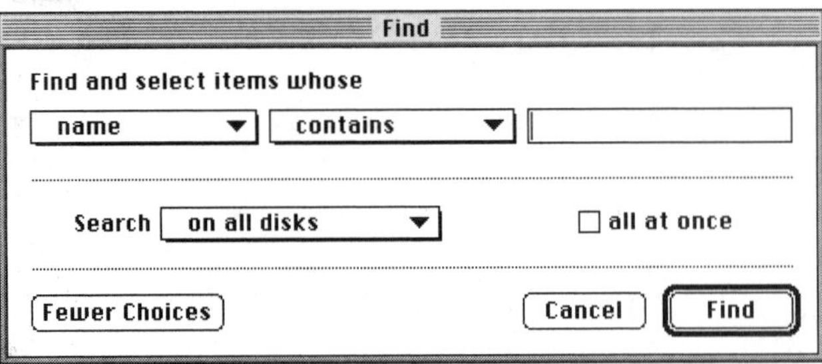

Figure 22-7: Detailed Searching When you click More Choices in the Finder's Find dialog box, a new dialog box appears whose pop-up menus give you more ways to search. Clicking the All at Once button tells the Finder to find and select all the files rather than stopping after the first one it finds. The All at Once button isn't available in System 7.5, whose Find File desk accessory displays found items in a window.

Alias Ideas

There are almost as many ways to use aliases as there are ways to use the Mac. Here's a collection of ideas to get you started.

Put items in your Apple menu

Don't move an original program, document, or folder to the Apple Menu Items folder. Create an alias of it and put the alias in the Apple Menu Items folder. Remember that you can rename the alias if you like.

By the way, if you use aliases in your Startup Items folder, you should know that they open after any "real" programs located in the Startup Items folder.

Access a frequently used folder

Perhaps you always use a certain folder that you keep buried within other folders. For fast access to that folder, make an alias of it and move the alias to your desktop. You can then open or modify the contents of the folder by opening its alias — not by opening folder after folder to get to the one you want. You can even copy items to the folder by dragging them to its alias.

Access a file-server volume

An alias provides an easy way to mount an AppleShare file-server volume or a disk or folder made available through System 7's file-sharing features. (See Chapter 32 for an introduction to AppleShare and file servers; System 7's file-sharing features are discussed in this chapter's section "File Sharing 101.")

First, mount the volume as you normally would, and then select it and choose Make Alias. Rename or move the alias as desired. Thereafter, to connect to the server, simply open its alias, and you receive the standard AppleShare log-on dialog box. (You don't even see the log-on dialog box if you access the server as a guest when making the alias.) You can even use this technique to copy a file to a server volume that you haven't yet mounted: Just drag the file to the alias icon and respond to the log-on dialog box as necessary. The Finder connects to the server and then copies the file.

Access your hard disk from any Mac on your network

First, use the Finder's Sharing command to make your hard disk available. Next, make an alias of your hard disk, and then copy that alias to a floppy disk. To connect to your hard disk from a different Mac in your network, simply insert the floppy disk and double-click the alias.

Access an extension or control panel from somewhere else

Normally, system extensions reside in the Extensions folder, which is in the System Folder. If you want to access an extension from the Control Panels window, make an alias of the extension and move the alias to the Control Panels folder (also within the System Folder). Similarly, if you want to access a certain Control Panel directly from the Apple menu, make an alias of it and move the alias to the Apple Menu Items folder.

Start programs and open documents

If you make an alias of a program, you can start the program and open a document by dragging the document icon to the alias icon. When you do, you see the alias icon become highlighted — just as a folder or disk icon is highlighted when you copy an item to it. Release the mouse button, and the Mac starts the program and opens the document. If the application icon doesn't highlight when you drag the document icon to it, the application may not be able to open that type of document. See Chapter 27 for more details about drag-launching and data exchange in general.

Quickly access all the programs on your hard disk

First, create a folder to hold the aliases. Next, use the Finder's Find command to search for all applications at once. (See the section "The Power to Find Your Best.") After the Mac has found and selected all the applications, choose Make Alias. The Mac makes an alias of every application it finds. You can then move those aliases into a single folder to have quick access to every program on your hard disk.

Automate access to archived files

Many people use file-compression utilities such as StuffIt to compress and archive older files that they copy to floppy disks and then delete from their hard disks to free up space. If you're in this group, you can use aliases to easily locate your archives — no more rooting through floppies trying to locate the disk that contains a certain archive.

First, make your archive file as you normally do and then copy it to a floppy disk. Next, make an alias of the archive on the floppy and then copy the alias from the floppy to your hard disk — perhaps to a folder called Archive Aliases. Finally, delete the archive from your hard disk. When you need to access the archive, just double-click its alias. The Mac then asks you to insert the appropriate floppy.

The Find dialog box's expanded searching options enable you to perform some surprisingly powerful tasks. (Table 22-2 describes each search option and its criteria.)

Table 22-2
Find Options

When Searching By...	*Your Options Are...*	*You Specify...*
Name	Contains, starts with, ends with, is, is not, doesn't contain	Part or all of the item's name
Size	Is less than, is greater than	A size value (in K)
Kind	Contains, doesn't contain	Alias, application, document, folder, or stationery
Label	Is, is not	A label name or None
Date Created	Is, is before, is after, is not	The current date or use arrows to change to the desired date
Date Modified	Is, is before, is after, is not	The current date or use arrows to change to the desired date
Version	Is, is before, is after, is not	A version number
Comments	Contains, does not contain	Text that appears in the Get Info command
Lock	Is, is not	Locked or unlocked

Using Find to open a program with the keyboard

If you know part of a file or folder name, you can use the Find command to open the item with a few keystrokes — no matter how many folders it's buried in. Choose Find from the Finder's File menu (or press ⌘-F), type part of the item's name, and then press Return. When the Finder locates the icon, it displays and selects it. Press ⌘-O to open it.

Using Find to create a program launching pad (not for System 7.5)

Here's how to quickly create an alias for every program on your hard disk. First, create a new folder named *Programs* and move it to the desktop. Choose Find, click More Choices, and then set up the pop-up menus to read *Kind Contains Application.* (Choose Kind from the leftmost pop-up menu, Contains from the middle one, and Application from the rightmost pop-up menu.) Next, check the All at Once button and then click Find.

The Finder locates and selects every application program on your hard disk (except those located on the desktop). Choose Make Alias from the File menu, and the Finder creates aliases and selects them. Drag one of the aliases to the Programs folder you created; the other aliases are still selected, so they tag along. Now you can use the Programs folder as the gateway to any program on your hard disk.

Using Find to do a quick backup

Here's how to use the Find command to perform a quick backup of all the files that you change on a given day. Click the Find dialog box's More Choices button and then configure the pop-up menus to read *Date modified is* followed by the current date. (In System 7.0 and 7.1, also check the All At Once box.) Click Find. After the Finder has located and selected all the modified files, drag one of them to the icon of a backup disk (the others follow because they're still selected). Of course, you need sufficient free space on the backup disk to hold all the files.

More Find Options in System 7.5

It's baa-aack — the Find File desk accessory, that is. Apple included a desk accessory by that name in the old System 6 days, but replaced it with the just-described Find command in System 7.0 and 7.1. In System 7.5, Find File is back — and like they say at the movies, it's meaner than ever.

How Find File works

Find File is actually very similar to the System 7.0/7.1 Find dialog box (although Find File sports a flashy 3-D window style). The pop-menus work in the same way, although their specific options have changed. You can't search by Get Info comments anymore (don't everyone start crying at once), but you can search by several new criteria, listed in Table 22-3 "System 7.5 Find Additions." (For background on the file type and file creator search options, see the Backgrounder box "File Signatures: How the Mac Identifies Files" earlier in this chapter.)

Table 22-3
System 7.5 Find Additions

When Searching By...	*Your Options Are...*	*You Specify...*
Folder attribute	Is, is not	Empty, shared, mounted
File type	Is, is not	A four-character file type
File creator	Is, is not	A four-character creator code

Searching for multiple criteria at once

The bad thing about the Find command in System 7.0/7.1 is that it doesn't let you search according to multiple criteria — you can't, for instance, find all files modified on a certain day *and* in Adobe Photoshop *and* larger than 1MB.

That sort of thing is easy in Find File. Click More Choices, and another set of pop-up menus appears. Configure them to specify your second set of criteria. You can click More Choices again and again — until you have eight sets of pop-up menus to work with. You can get pretty specific with Find File.

Using drag-and-drop with Find File

You can fill in the text boxes in Find File by dragging icons to them. For example, to find all Excel files, set up the first two pop-up menus to read File Type Is and then drag an Excel icon to the text box. Find File will extract the icon's file type and enter it into the box. Similarly, if you drag a 500K file to the Size text-entry box, the Finder enters *500* for you. And if you have several hard drives or other storage devices mounted, you can restrict the search to one drive by dragging its icon to the Find Items pop-up menu.

What Apple didn't tell you about Find File

Find File has a terrific undocumented feature — press Option before clicking on the criteria pop-up menu, and additional search options appear. The two most useful are

- **Searching for text within files.** Choose Contents, and you can type text that you want to locate *within* files. It's great for those times when you've forgotten a filename but can remember a phrase that's within a file. Searching file contents isn't speedy, but it can be faster than manually opening file after file after file.
- **Searching for files with custom icons.** Choose Custom Icon, and you can locate files that do or do not contain custom icons. You might not use this one every day, but it's there if you need it.

Unleashing the power of the Results window

Another big improvement is Find File's Results window, which lists the files your specifications turn up (see Figure 22-8 "The Files I've Found").

Here's the best part: the Results window isn't just a listing — you can actually work with the items that Find File has found. You can

- Open items by double-clicking them
- Drag found items to folders or disks
- Throw away items by dragging them to the Trash
- Set file-sharing information for disks or folders by choosing the Sharing command from the File menu
- Get information about items by choosing Get Info from the File menu
- Make an alias of an item by pressing ⌘ and dragging to a new location
- Open the folder that contains an item (press ⌘-E)

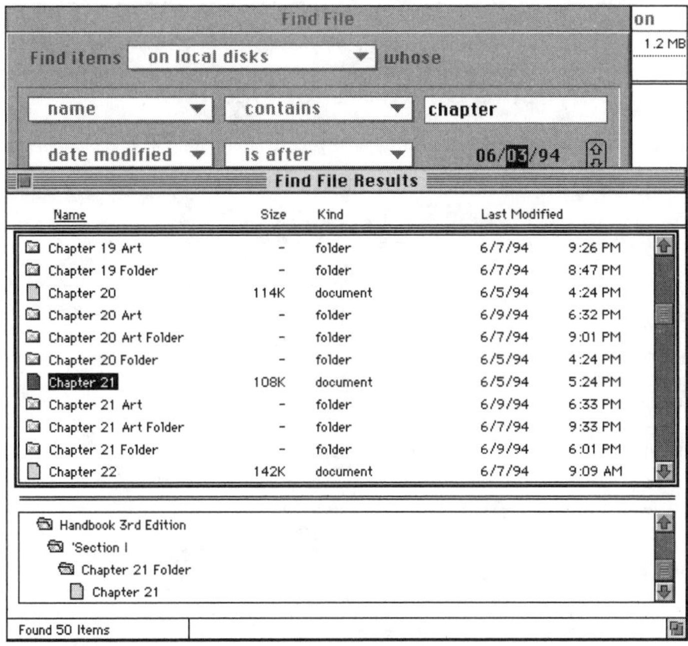

Figure 22-8: The Files I've Found The Find File desk accessory in System 7.5 displays found items in the Results window. You can work with the items in this window — open them, drag them to other disks or folders, throw them away, and more.

Bringing back the old Find dialog box

Apple didn't kill off the old Find dialog box when it included Find File in System 7.5. To display it, press ⌘-Shift-F.

Why would you want to use Find when the Find File does so much more? One reason might be if you *do* want to search for text in Get Info comments. Another, however, is that the Find dialog box opens more quickly than Find File's.

Keyboard Shortcuts for Find File

System 7.5's Find File desk accessory provides an array of keyboard shortcuts. They're listed in the following table.

Find File Shortcuts

To Do This	*Do This*
Select items	Type the first few characters of their name, or use the up- and down-arrow keys
Switch the keyboard focus from the file listing to the folder hierarchy display	Press Tab
Choose More Choices	Press ⌘-M
Choose Fewer Choices	Press ⌘-R
Open an item	Press ⌘-O
Open the folder that encloses the selected item	Press ⌘-E
Print an item	Press ⌘-P
Close the Results or Find File windows	Press ⌘-W

Tips for the Startup Items Folder

As I mentioned earlier, the System Folder contains a folder called Startup Items. Toss an icon in this folder, and the Mac opens it automatically the next time you start up — very handy if you always use a particular program or document. (To keep your file system orderly, don't toss an actual application icon into the folder — use an alias of the icon instead.)

You can use the Startup Items folder to automatically open documents, too. Just put the documents (or, better yet, aliases for them) in the Startup Items folder.

Sounds as startup items

You can use Startup Items to open anything that you can double-click — including sounds. Toss a sound into the Startup Items folder, and you hear a silicon serenade each time you start up.

Copying a sound from the System file to Startup Items

If you'd like to use a sound in your System file, here's how to copy it to the Startup Items folder: Open the System Folder, and then double-click the System file to open it. Locate the sound, and then press Option while dragging the icon to the Startup Items folder. This action puts a copy of the sound in the folder instead of moving the original. (The Option-drag technique for copying an item instead of moving it works throughout System 7.)

Create a things-to-do-tomorrow folder

Want to make sure that certain files get your immediate attention tomorrow morning? Make an alias of the Startup Items folder and put it on your desktop. Before you shut down, stash any documents (or aliases for documents) that you want to work on the next morning in the Startup Items folder alias.

The alternate startup sound

Macs contain an alternate startup sound that normally only plays when there's a hardware problem. On a Power Mac, the alternate sound is of a car crash — appropriate, I suppose, for a noise intended to signify a problem.

You can hear this sound by pressing the interrupt key sequence — ⌘-power key — just after you hear the Mac's normal startup chord. To make your Mac start up normally, press ⌘-Control-power key.

By the way, if you have an older Mac model that accepts the plastic programmer's switch, you can hear *your* alternate startup sound by pressing the switch's interrupt key just after you hear the normal startup chord.

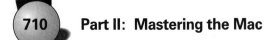

Understanding Enablers

Before System 7.1 came along, Apple often released a new system version with each new Mac model. This scheme was necessary to support the new model's features, but it created headaches as people wondered whether or not to upgrade to the new version or which version was the best for their machines.

Beginning with System 7.1, Apple devised a different scheme for supporting new models: *system enablers.* Like an extension, a system enabler loads during memory at startup time and provides the software that System 7.1 needs to work on a given Mac. This mechanism eliminates the need for Apple to release a machine-specific system software update each time a new Mac model comes out.

The base version of System 7.1 has built-in support for all Mac models that shipped before the release of System 7.1, from the Macintosh Plus through the Macintosh Quadra 950 and PowerBook 145. Macs shipped after System 7.1's release include system enablers specific to that model or family of models. System Enablers are stored in the top level of the System Folder (not in the Extensions folder). They load before any extensions or control panels.

Apple's System 7 Upgrade Kit does not include a full set of system enablers. This can mean trouble if you're on the road and you need to reinstall the system software on a PowerBook that requires a system enabler. If you can't find a dealer who has the enabler you need, you may want to carry along a backup set of the system disks that came with your computer. Or just carry one floppy containing the enabler your PowerBook needs.

With System 7.5, you don't have to worry about having the correct enabler for your machine. The separate enablers for different Mac models have been consolidated into a single universal enabler — the mother of all enablers.

The keys to altering the Mac's startup routine

I've already mentioned that part of the Mac's startup routine involves loading extensions and control panels into memory, opening items in the Startup Items folder, and then restoring the Mac's desktop to its prior state — that is, opening the disk and folder windows that were open when you last shut down.

By pressing the Shift or Option key at various times, you can bypass any or all of these three steps.

- ❖ To bypass the loading of all extensions and control panels, press Shift before the "Welcome to Macintosh" message or Mas OS startup screen appears. The message "Extensions off" appears below the greeting.
- ❖ To bypass the opening of the icons in the Startup Items folder, press Shift as soon as you see the blank menu bar — that is, *before* the Finder's menus appear.
- ❖ To bypass the opening of windows that were previously open, press Option before the disk icons appear on the desktop.
- ❖ To turn off virtual memory, press and hold the ⌘ key during the entire startup process. If you open the Memory control panel after doing this, it will still say

that VM is on, but you can confirm that VM is off by choosing About This Macintosh from the Apple menu — the memory graph will list only the actual amount of RAM your Mac contains.

Bypassing the internal hard drive

If you want to bypass the internal hard drive and force the Mac to start up from an external drive, press ⌘-Option-Shift-Delete until the Mac finds and starts up from an external drive.

System extension loading order

The order in which extensions and control panels load during startup depends on the names and locations of the extensions and control panels.

First, System 7 alphabetically loads the extensions in the Extensions folder, followed by those in the Control Panels folder, and then those in the top level of the System Folder.

You need to keep this loading order in mind when troubleshooting extension conflicts. Also, if you use an extension-management utility (described in Chapter 24), you must put it in the Extensions folder so that it loads before other extensions. (Some extension managers that work as control panels have their own extensions that sit in the Extensions folder.)

For all the details about troubleshooting extension-loading problems — and how you can override System 7's standard loading order — see Chapter 28.

Starting up with System 7.5 extensions only

If you're troubleshooting a problem with system extensions, you can use System 7.5's Extensions Manager to start up with just System 7.5's core set of Apple-supplied extensions. Simply choose System 7.5 Only from the Extensions Manager's Sets pop-up menu.

Tips for the Shutdown Items Folder

The Shutdown Items folder within System 7.5's System Folder holds items that you want the Mac to open just before it shuts down. What in the world would want the Mac to open when you're about to shut down? Here are a few possibilities.

- ❖ A backup program. Instead of relying on your own good sense to back up regularly, force the issue — stash an alias of your backup utility in the Shutdown Items folder.
- ❖ A utility or script that turns off file sharing or performs some other system-related task.

Speak Up with PlainTalk

If your Mac supports Apple's PlainTalk voice-recognition technology, you can access frequently used files quickly by placing them (or their aliases) in the Speakable Items folder within the Apple Menu Items folder. After doing so, you can open the item by saying "open" followed by the item's name. See Chapter 33 for more details about PlainTalk voice recognition.

- Some sounds. Maybe Jackie Gleason saying "Good night, everybody!" or Mystery Science Theatre 3000's mad scientist, Dr. Clayton Forrester, saying, "Push the button, Frank" (that's my shutdown sound).

Using File Sharing

Many Macs are islands, but at least as many are used in places where there are other Macs — offices, classrooms, and user-group meetings. If yours is in the latter category, you'll love System 7's built-in file-sharing features. On the simplest level, System 7 file sharing lets you exchange files between Macs without having to use floppy disks. Connect a cable, click a few times, and one Mac's hard drive icon appears on the other Mac's desktop. You can then shuttle files and folders between the Macs by using standard click-and-drag techniques.

By the way, if you're using file sharing extensively under System 7.5.0 — the original release of System 7.5 — you should strongly consider installing the System 7.5 Update 1.0 package. It boosts file-sharing performance by three to four times. As described in the section "The Various Flavors of System 7 and 7.5," later in this chapter, System 7.5 Update 1.0 upgrades System 7.5 to version 7.5.1. If you have a second-generation Power Mac — a 7200, 7500, 8500, or 9500 — you don't need this update. These Macs run System 7.5.2, which incorporates the update's enhancements.

First steps

Suppose you want to set up a simple file-sharing scheme to exchange files between a PowerBook and a desktop Mac (or any two Mac models). To connect the computers, use a pair of Farallon PhoneNet StarConnectors, which are often discounted to under $20 each. With the cable connected, open the PowerBook's Sharing Setup control panel. Type a name in the Owner Name and Macintosh Name boxes; then click Start in the Sharing area. When the control panel tells you that file sharing is on, close the control panel. (If you don't see the Sharing Setup control panel, use the System 7 Installer disk to install file-sharing software.)

Next, select the PowerBook's hard disk icon (if you just want to share a single folder on the hard disk, select the folder's icon instead) and choose Sharing from the Finder's File menu. In the Sharing window, check the box labeled "Share this item and its contents." Below that item, choose <Any User> from the Owner pop-up menu (see Figure 22-9 "Sharing Strategies"). Close the window, clicking Save when asked to save changes. You've just set up the Mac as a file server.

Now go to the other Mac and open its Chooser desk accessory. Click the AppleShare icon, and the PowerBook name you specified a moment ago appears on the right side of the Chooser. Double-click that name, and a dialog box appears. Click Guest and press Return. In the next dialog box, select the hard drive name and press Return again. In a moment, an icon for the PowerBook's hard drive appears on the desktop. You can now copy files back and forth between the two Macs.

Keep in mind most PowerBooks also offer the SCSI disk mode, which enables you to connect the PowerBook to a desktop Mac and access the PowerBook's hard drive. If you have to transfer a lot of data, you may prefer the faster SCSI disk mode over System 7 file sharing. See the Chapter 25 Quick Tips box "PowerBook Hard Disk Tips" for details on using SCSI disk mode.

File-sharing tips

The sharing scheme I just outlined pairs up well with the Find command's daily backup trick I described earlier. After the two Macs are connected, you can use the Find command to locate the day's files for copying.

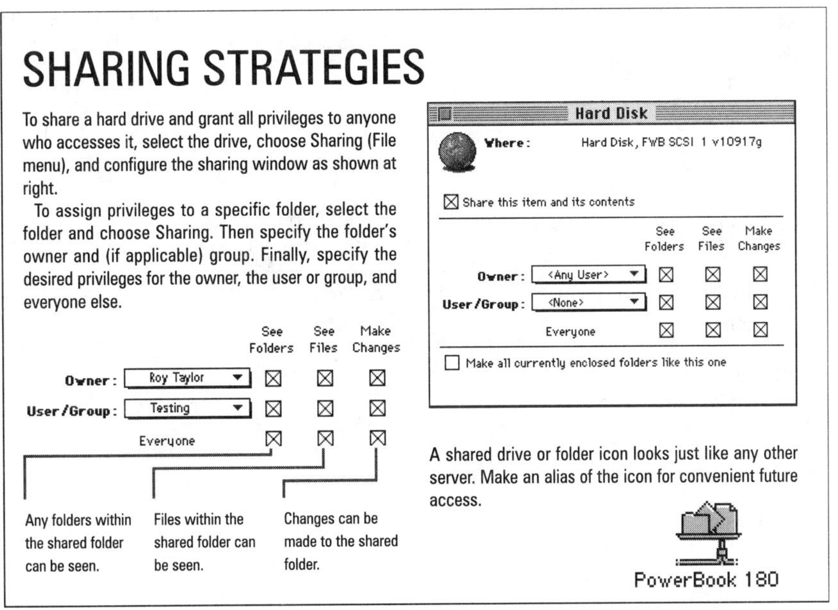

Figure 22-9: Sharing Strategies

Finder 7 Shortcuts

With System 7, it's easier than ever to move around on the desktop. The following list describes Finder 7's capabilities and how to access them quickly. And don't forget about the System 7.5 Find File keyboard shortcuts listed earlier in this chapter.

Finder Shortcuts

To Accomplish This	***Do This***
Eject a disk and remove its icon from the desktop	Drag the icon to the Trash or select the disk and choose Put Away (⌘-Y)
Select an icon from the keyboard	Type the first few characters of the icon's name
Bypass the warning dialog box that appears when you choose Empty Trash	Press Option when choosing Empty Trash
Hide the current application when switching to another application	Press Option while choosing the program you want from the Application menu
Rename an icon	Select it, press Return, and then start typing
Quickly determine whether a file is locked or unlocked	Select the file and press Return; if no border appears around the name, the file is locked
Clean up everything	Choose Select All and then press Option and choose Clean Up All
Clean up selected items only	Press Shift and choose Clean Up Selection
Organize icons by name	Choose By Name from the View menu, choose By Icon or By Small Icon, and then press Option and choose Clean Up by Name
Close all disk and folder windows	Press Option while clicking a close box or choosing Close
Copy a file from one folder to another instead of moving it	Press Option while dragging the file to the destination folder
Copy an item to the desktop instead of moving it	Press Option and drag the item to the desktop
Open an item and close its window	Press Option and double-click the item
Open the folder or disk window that holds the current directory window	Press ⌘ while clicking on the window's title, and then choose the folder or disk name you want

To Accomplish This	*Do This*
Abort a program that seems to have crashed	Press ⌘-Option-Esc and click Force Quit
Open a document with a program that may not have created the document	Drag the document's icon to the program's icon or alias
Skip installing all system extensions during one startup	Hold down Shift during startup
Select the item nearest the upper-right corner of the desktop	Press ⌘-Shift-up arrow
Zoom a directory window to fill the screen	Press Option while clicking the window's zoom box

Selecting Icons from the Keyboard

To Select	*Do This*
The icon to the left or right of the currently selected icon	Press the left-arrow or right-arrow (icon views only) key
The icon above or below the currently selected icon	Press the up-arrow or down-arrow key
The next icon alphabetically	Press Tab
The preceding icon alphabetically	Press Shift-Tab

Keyboard Shortcuts for Outline Views

To Do This	*Press This*
Expand the selected folder's outline	⌘-right arrow
Collapse the selected folder's outline	⌘-left arrow
Expand the entire outline of a selected folder	⌘-Option-right arrow
Collapse the entire outline of the selected folder	⌘-Option-left arrow

To avoid having to thread your way through the Chooser the next time you want to access the PowerBook's hard drive, make an alias of the hard drive icon while you're connected to it. You can automatically connect to the PowerBook by double-clicking the alias. Or stash the alias in the Apple Menu Items folder to access it from that menu.

When you're done with the shared hard drive, drag its icon to the Trash. Then return to the PowerBook and turn file sharing off. You save memory and the Mac runs a bit faster if you turn off file sharing when you aren't using it.

For convenience's sake, I've deliberately avoided discussing the security features in System 7 file sharing. When it's just you, a couple of Macs, and some files to be moved, passwords get in the way. When you're part of a larger network, though, you probably want to set up *access privileges* — settings for who can see and modify shared files and folders.

Access has its privileges

You can use System 7's access privilege settings to lock some people out of certain folders. First, use the Users & Groups control panel to specify a list of *registered users* — people who are allowed access to shared items. You may also want to assemble registered users into *groups* — collections of users who work on related projects or in the same department. After creating users and groups, you can control access privileges for a given folder by selecting the folder and choosing the Sharing command (see Figure 22-10 "Users & Groups" and refer to Figure 22-9 "Sharing Strategies").

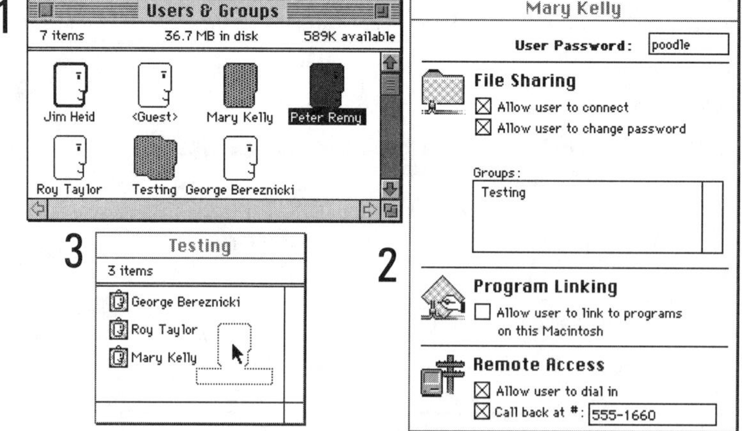

Figure 22-10: Users & Groups With the Users & Groups control panel, you can create a list of people who can access your folders and disks. (1) After opening the control panel, choose New User from the File menu and then rename the new user icon. Double-click a user's icon to change settings. (2) The Remote Access options appear only if you've installed Apple's AppleTalk Remote Access software, which lets you connect to another Mac via a phone modem to exchange files and print documents. You can also assemble users into groups — you can group together the members of a department or the staff for a particular project. To create a group, choose New Group from the File menu. Rename the group icon, and then drag user icons to the group icon. (3) Peter Remy is being added to the Testing group.

In the previous steps, you set up a *peer-to-peer* file-server system. The opposite of peer-to-peer networking is a *dedicated* file server — a Mac and hard disk, running a program such as Apple's AppleShare, that provide centralized storage for a group of Macs. A central file server costs more to set up — the AppleShare software itself retails for over $1,000 — but provides better security and is easier to back up, because shared files are in one place instead of scattered across a network. If you do outgrow peer-to-peer file sharing, you can upgrade to AppleShare and retain your user and group settings. For more details about AppleShare, see Chapter 32.

How to streamline file sharing

There's no question System 7's file-sharing features are priceless for beaming data between two Macs. But you don't want to leave file sharing on all the time — it slows a Mac's performance. I always turn my PowerBook's file sharing on just before I'm about to move some files, and turn it off immediately thereafter.

Toggling file sharing using the Sharing Setup control panel is too much work for me. CE Software's QuicKeys automation utility includes an extension, called System 7 Specials, that lets you turn file sharing on and off with a keystroke. I've set it up so that pressing Control-1 turns on file sharing, and Shift-Control-1 turns it off. Note that no warning dialog box is displayed when you turn off file sharing this way, so you must be certain that your shared volumes aren't actually being accessed — pulling the sharing rug out from under someone is a great way to stir up office animosity. (A similar QuicKeys extension, Choosy, lets you switch between printers without having to use the Chooser desk accessory.)

In the freeware/shareware arena, there's Steve Forgacs' free FileSharingToggle, a simple program that toggles file sharing when run. And no frequent filer should be without Robert Hess' $10 Shaman utility, which can toggle sharing, display icons in the menu bar when sharing is on, and if you have Apple's PlainTalk Speech Manager extension, even speak phrases when someone logs on or off.

System 6 Disks and System 7

Floppy and hard disks that you've used with earlier system versions work with System 7, but when you insert a disk, you see a message saying "Updating disk for new system software." The Finder is creating a desktop database file that enables it to locate the disk's contents. For high-capacity disks, the desktop database file replaces the DeskTop file, which I look at in other chapters. The DeskTop file is still used for disks whose capacity is less than 2MB — in other words, for floppies.

If you use a hard disk or removable high-capacity cartridge with System 7 and then move it to a Mac running System 6, you may notice two new folders: Desktop and Trash. Finder 7 creates these folders to store any icons you moved to the desktop and to store the contents of the Trash. (Yes, under System 7, the Trash is actually a folder — which is why it isn't emptied until you explicitly choose Empty Trash.) You can delete these folders, but Finder 7 creates them again the next time you use that hard disk or cartridge on a Mac running System 7.

Inside the Installer

To install system software — and, for that matter, many application programs — you use a utility that's aptly named Installer. Two basic versions of the Installer utility are in widespread use. Version 4.0 provides an easier interface, better on-line help, and more options than earlier versions.

Using the Installer

When you start Installer, you see one of the two dialog boxes shown in Figure 22-11 "In the Installer." In most cases, you can use the Easy Install option, which automates the installation process.

However, if you want to install only certain portions of your new software — perhaps to save disk space — you can use the custom-install options. In Installer 4.0, choose Custom Install from the pop-up menu in the upper-left corner of the Installer window. In earlier versions, click Customize.

When you specify a custom install, the Installer window changes to reflect the specific options you can choose to install. As Figure 22-12 "Custom Install Options" shows, Installer 4.0 provides more details about the specific installation options you have. Better still, you can resize the window to see more custom install options at once.

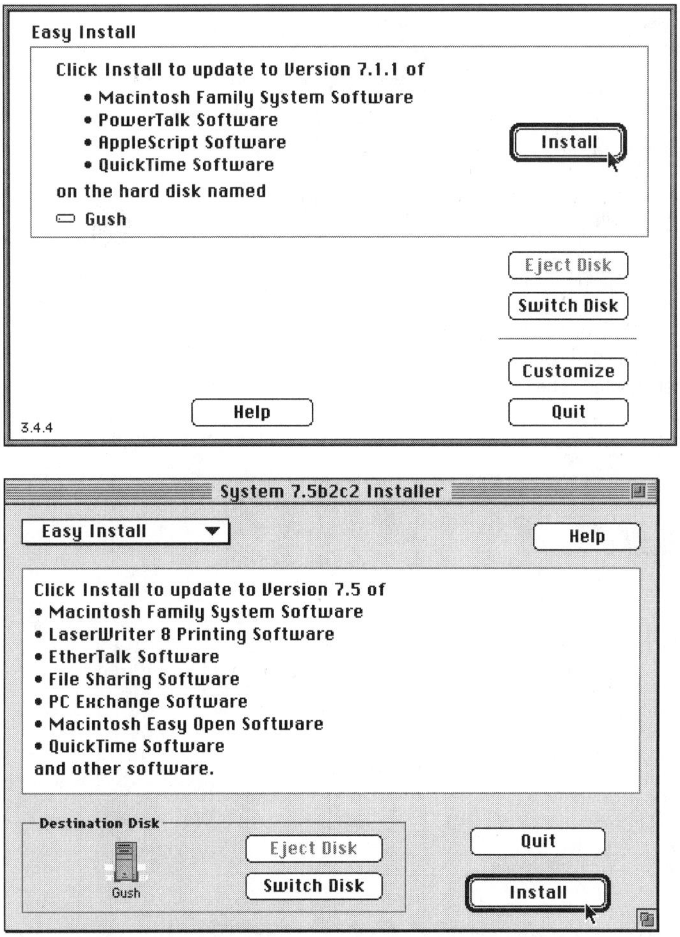

Figure 22-11: In the Installer The Installer utility's main window is your gateway to installation options. Top: Installer versions prior to 4.0 present this simple dialog box. Bottom: Installer 4.0 provides a resizable window and an easier interface.

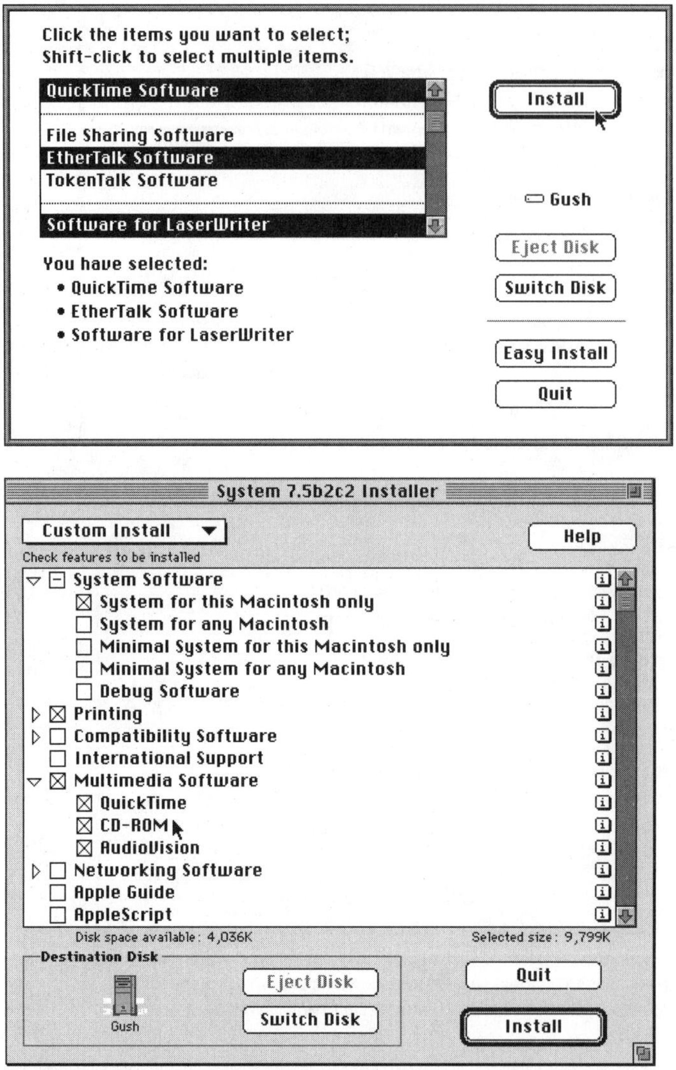

Figure 22-12: Custom Install Options When you choose a custom install, the Installer lists the available options. Top: In Installer versions prior to 4.0, the options are listed like this. Bottom: Installer 4.0 lets you be more specific about what you want to install.

How Installer works

To determine which software to install, Intaller uses a special document called a script. Just a movie script tells the actors what to say and when to say it, an Installer script tells the Installer which software to install and where to install it. When you select an option in the Customize dialog box, for example, the Installer reads its script to determine how to modify your System Folder and then makes the modifications.

The Installer and third-party products

You're likely to encounter the Installer utility throughout your travels in the Macintosh world. Apple makes Installer available to third-party companies, which can create their own scripts to enable you to install their wares.

Several third-party companies have created installer utilities that they license to other companies that, for one reason or another, don't want to use Apple's Installer. One popular third-party installer is Aladdin Systems' InstallerMaker.

These non-Apple installers have their own interfaces and operating styles, but they all provide similar options: an easy-install option that moves everything onto your hard disk and a customize option that lets you selectively install only those items you want.

It's a Setup — from Microsoft

Microsoft has created its own Installer, called Setup, for the latest versions of its Mac applications and for the Microsoft Office suite of programs (Word, Excel, PowerPoint, and Mail). Unfortunately, it's a nightmare. The Setup program tends be extremely finicky — if you move a program it installs to a different folder, for example, the program may not run properly.

Setup is also designed to allow you to do maintenance on your installation — removing a feature you don't need, for instance, or adding one you didn't install originally. This aspect of the program is funky, too, and I often find it easier to just trash the Microsoft programs I've installed and install them again from scratch.

Focus on System 7.5

Most everything in this chapter — and in this book, for that matter — applies to System 7.5 as well to as Systems 7.0 and 7.1. And I've already described System 7.5's fab Find File command. In this section, I focus on the additional differences between System 7.0/7.1 and System 7.5.

The System 7.5 difference

If you've acquired a Mac only recently, you might not be aware of just how System 7.5 differs from its predecessors. Here's an overview.

- *QuickDraw GX and the new GX printing architecture*, described in Chapters 11 and 31, debuted in System 7.5. As I mention in Chapter 11, System 7.5 also includes a GX-savvy version of Adobe Type Manager, called ATM GX.
- *Apple Guide*, the new active-assistance help system described in Chapter 1, also made its maiden voyage.

❖ *Drag and Drop.* Described in Chapters 1 and 27, System 7.5's drag-and-drop technology makes it easier to move information between programs. Items that support drag-and-drop include the Scrapbook, the Movie Player 2.0 application, the Jigsaw Puzzle, the Find File commands, and the Notepad desk accessory, which itself is improved (see the Quick Tips box "Cool Things You Can Do with Drag and Drop").

Cool Things You Can Do with Drag and Drop

With applications that support drag-and-drop (such as WordPerfect 3.1), you can exchange data easily. But you can also do some useful (and fun) things with the accessories that accompany System 7.5.

❖ Easy entry of Find File criteria. As described earlier in this chapter, you can enter information in the Find File window by dragging icons to it.

❖ Custom jigsaw puzzles — and quick PICT file viewing. Store an image as a PICT file, and then drag the PICT file's icon into the Jigsaw Puzzle window. Presto — your own puzzle. This technique is also a handy way to view PICT files without launching a graphics program. (You can also paste an image into the Jigsaw Puzzle window or use its Open command to open a PICT file.) Note: If the image doesn't appear in the Jigsaw Puzzle window, use the Get Info command to increase the memory allocated to the Jigsaw Puzzle.

❖ QuickTime movie editing. If you have Apple's Movie Player 2.0 application, you can edit QuickTime movies by dragging and dropping from one movie window to another. You can even add a text track to a movie by dragging text (from the Notepad, for instance) to a movie window. And you can create movie clipping files by dragging from Movie Player 2.0 out to the desktop.

❖ Quick text file reading. Drag the icon of a text file into the open Notepad window. This is particularly handy for reading "Read Me" files or e-mail that you've downloaded.

❖ Make your own desktop patterns. Just drag a PICT file to the Desktop Patterns control panel, as described in the Quick Tips box "Secrets of the Desktop Patterns Control Panel," later in this chapter.

❖ The secret game of breakout. In System 7.5 (but not 7.5.1 or later), type **secret about box** into the Notepad and then select it and drag out to the desktop. A window appears containing a game of breakout, with the System 7.5 developer's names in each brick. Now *that's* innovation.

❖ *Scriptable Finder.* For the first time, you can create AppleScripts that control the Finder, opening up new possibilities for streamlining repetitive tasks. System 7.5's Apple menu contains a folder, Automated Tasks, that sports some canned scripts with which you can experiment.

Little tweaks and improvements

Many of System 7.5's out-of-the-box enhancements — ones that don't require application program updates or programming — fall into this category.

A better Apple menu

In a direct blow to third-party utilities such as HAM and Menu Extend, System 7.5 provides a hierarchical menu that makes it easier to get to programs and documents buried within folders. Also, the Apple menu sports three folders — Recent Applications, Recent Documents, and Recent Servers — that hold aliases to recently used items in these categories.

You can use the Apple Menu Options control panel to turn the Apple menu hierarchy on and off as well as specify the number of recently used items you want to use.

Finder borders

In the Finder, a border appears within directory windows as you drag items into them to reinforce the notion that you're dragging something into something else. (This interface treatment is part of the drag-and-drop technology.)

The WindowShade feature

The problem with windows is that they can make for a cluttered electronic desktop. To cut down on clutter, use the WindowShade control panel. When it's active, you can hide every part of a window except its title bar by just double-clicking the window.

With the WindowShade control panel, you can customize the WindowShade sequence to require any combination of modifier keys and one to three clicks.

Faster performance

System 7.5 copies files, starts programs, switches between programs, and opens menus faster than System 7.1. And unlike earlier system versions, the System 7.5 disk cache (discussed later in this chapter) actually works well.

A new General Controls control panel

It's bigger and offers new options (see Figure 22-13 "A New General on Duty"). You can prevent items in the Applications folder and System Folder from being renamed or removed — handy for offices or schools. You can specify that the Finder hide itself when you start or switch to a different program, as described in the "Hiding the Desktop and Finder" Quick Tips box later in this chapter. As mentioned earlier in this chapter, you also can specify that the Launcher window appear automatically at startup. And as Chapter 21 described, you can set chime options to have the Mac play sounds at various intervals.

Figure 22-13: A New General on Duty The General Controls control panel in System 7.5 provides options not present in the General control panel used by earlier system versions.

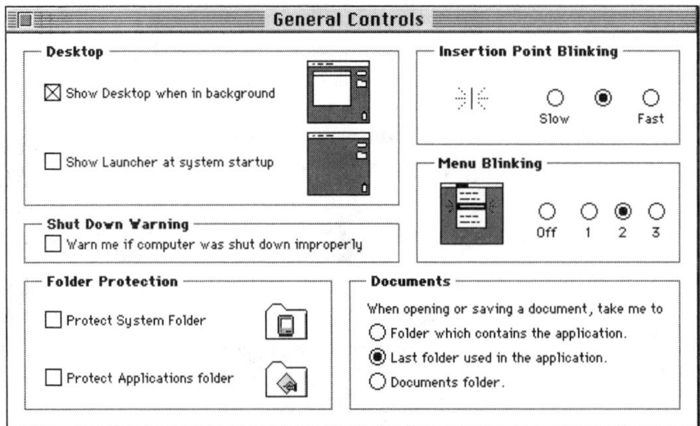

The Desktop Patterns control panel

One item you can no longer adjust with the General Controls control panel is the desktop pattern. In System 7.5, you use the bigger, better Desktop Patterns control panel, which provides some truly cool color patterns (see the Quick Tips box "Secrets of the Desktop Patterns Control Panel")

QUICK TIPS

Secrets of the Desktop Patterns Control Panel

Here are some additional ways to dress up your desktop with the Desktop Patterns control panel.

- ❖ Make your own patterns. Copy a PICT image to the Clipboard, open Desktop Patterns, and choose Paste. You've just created your own pattern. You can also drag a PICT image from the Scrapbook into Desktop Patterns.
- ❖ Add a pattern to System 7.5's utilities. Press Option when Desktop Patterns is open, and its button changes to read Set Utilities Pattern. Click this button, and you apply the current pattern to System 7.5's utilities — Calculator, Jigsaw Puzzle, Find File, Scrapbook, and Key Caps.
- ❖ Tweak an existing pattern. Drag a pattern out to the desktop to create a clippings file. Now open that clippings file using your favorite graphics program (Photoshop, Painter, whatever) and modify it. Save the result, then paste it back into the Desktop Patterns window.

An improved Monitors control panel

You can switch monitor resolutions without having to restart. This feature is especially handy when you're using an AV or Power Mac to videotape a Mac screen image or QuickTime movie. In System 7.5.2, a new control panel, Sound & Displays, takes over these duties (see Chapter 20).

A new CD audio player

The new AppleCD Audio Player provides better audio CD playback features and a flashier interface. See Chapter 25 for more details.

The Auto Power On/Off control panel

This control panel is kind of the ultimate screen saver — it turns your entire Mac off after a specified period of inactivity. You can also specify that the Mac be turned off at recurring intervals — like every day at 5:00. (As if!) This control panel works with all Macs that support soft power (if you can turn your Mac on by pressing the keyboard's power-on key, your Mac supports soft power). You can find more details on this control panel in the section "Environmentally Friendly Computing," in the next chapter.

An improved Scrapbook desk accessory

After ten years, Apple finally added a resizing feature to allow you to change the size of the Scrapbook window (see Figure 22-14, "A Bigger Scrapbook"). The Scrapbook also supports drag-and-drop editing and displays more information about the data in each page.

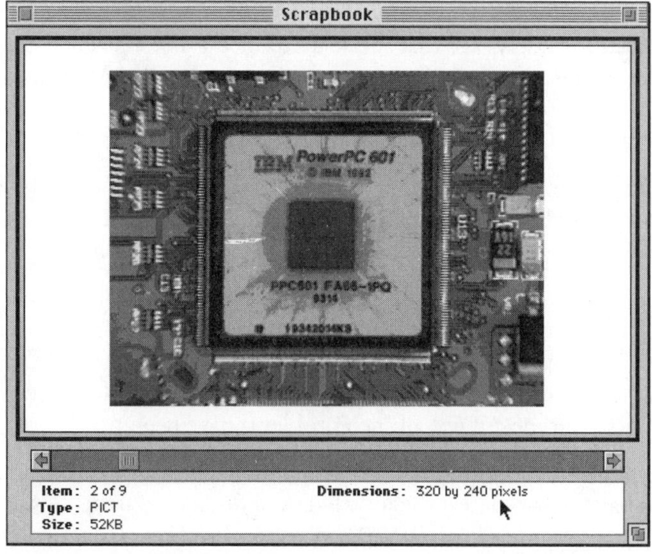

Figure 22-14: A Bigger Scrapbook Tired of that index card-sized Scrapbook? You'll love System 7.5's Scrapbook, which provides a resizable window.

Stickies and a better Notepad

The new Stickies desk accessory lets you put the electronic equivalent of yellow sticky notes on your screen. The new Notepad desk accessory supports drag and drop, much longer notes, and printing.

Extensions Manager goes pro

Many Mac mavens have for years relied on a free extension manager control panel called Extensions Manager to help them selectively activate or deactivate extensions, control panels, and more (see Chapter 24). In System 7.5, Extensions Manager is an official part of the system software. The System 7.5 version, Extensions Manager 3.0, sports a polished interface and even on-line help.

The Various Flavors of System 7 and 7.5

As of August of 1995, Apple has released several updates to System 7 and System 7.5. Let's start with the System 7.5 updates and work our way back.

System 7.5 Update 1.0

This update turns System 7.5 into System 7.5.1. Among its enhancements are the improved Launcher discussed earlier in this chapter, much faster file sharing, faster QuickDraw GX, more native PowerPC code (including a native PowerPC version of Apple Guide) and a whole bunch of little bug fixes. System 7.5.1 also adds keyboard shutdown to all Macs that support soft power (the ability to be turned on by pressing the keyboard's power key).

This update also introduced the Mac OS startup screen, which replaces the "Welcome to Macintosh" message that Apple used since 1984. The change was necessitated by the advent of Mac clones, which aren't called Macintoshes. A welcome addition to the new screen is a progress bar that gives you a rough indication of how far along you are in the startup process.

System 7.5 Update 1.0 also includes version 8.2 of the LaserWriter driver, which provides better support for PostScript fax modems — and lets you press Shift–Tab to tab backwards through the text-entry boxes in Print dialog boxes.

In general, if you're using System 7.5, you should obtain and install this update, particularly if you use file sharing. Some commercial and shareware utilities did have compatibility problems (some examples included Alladin's StuffIt SpaceSaver 3.5, Symantec's Norton Partion 2.0, SpeedyFinder 1.5.9I, and Connectix RAM Doubler 1.5.1), but most if not all such problems have been fixed.

System 7.5 Update 1.0 comes on four disks, but don't be alarmed if its installer utility never asks you to insert the fourth disk. This disk contains PowerTalk- and AppleScript-related items; if you aren't using PowerTalk or AppleScript, the Installer won't ask for this disk.

System 7.5.2

This flavor of System 7.5 is included with the second-generation Power Macs: the 7200, 7500, 8500, and 9500, as well as with the Performa 5200 and 6200 series. It includes all of the enhancements of System 7.5 Update 1.0 and adds some additional ones, including a native PowerPC SCSI Manager, Ethernet network driver, and Resource Manager (an important Mac OS component that application programs use extensively). System 7.5.2 also supports the Sound & Displays control panel and the Energy Saver control panel used by the 7200 and Performa 5200/6200 series.

Gaining Control with the Control Strip

When Apple shipped the PowerBook 500 series in 1994, it introduced a terrific utility called Control Strip, which provides a row of icons that provide quick access to the PowerBooks' power-management features.

Apple gave Control Strip a modular design that lets you add new controls to the strip — and shareware and freeware programmers quickly responded with a slew of them. Several controls are included in the Best of BMUG collection on the *Macworld Power User Clinic* CD.

Unfortunately, original versions of Control Strip worked only on PowerBooks, but the Mac programming community came to the rescue, there, too. A free utility named Control Strip Patcher (available online) modifies Control Strip to work on desktop Macs, too.

For System 7.5.2, Apple officially made Control Strip available to all of us. The second-generation Macs include a desktop version, which includes useful controls for switching monitor settings.

Hide the strip if you aren't using it

Handy as Control Strip is, it does slow down the video-related tasks such as window scrolling. If you aren't using the Strip, it's a good idea to close it.

Control Strip shortcuts

One end of the Control Strip is "attached" to the left or right edge of the display. The Control Strip has a tab on its unattached end. The following table provides a list of Control Strip shortcuts.

To Do This	Do This
Adjust the length of the strip	Drag its tab
Move the strip to a new position on the screen	Hold down the Option key and drag the tab
Hide all but the Control Stip's tab	Click the tab (click the tab again to display the Control Strip)
Make the Control Strip disappear completely	Click the Hide Control Strip button in the Control Strip control panel

The System 7 Tune-Up

If you're using one of the original versions of System 7 — 7.0 or 7.0.1 — you may want to get a copy of Apple's System 7 Tune-Up extension, which modifies the system software to use memory a bit more efficiently and handle low-memory situations better. If there isn't enough memory available to start a program, for example, the Finder asks whether you want to quit a different program in order to make room.

Similarly, if there isn't enough memory to print a document in the background (that is, while you continue to work), the Mac asks whether you want to print it immediately or wait until later. Use the About This Macintosh command to find out which system version you're using. If a bullet character (•) appears after the version number, the tune-up is already installed. If you have System 7.1, you don't need the tune-up — Apple rolled its features into System 7.1.

System Update 3.0

In 1994, Apple released an extension called System Update 3.0. The System Update 3.0 extension is a collection of bug fixes and enhancements to System 7.1, System 7.1.1, and System Software 7.1.2. It also incorporates tweaks and enhancements found in earlier System Update extensions, which include Hardware System Update 1.0, Hardware System Update 2.0, and System Update 2.0.1. If you're running System 7.1, 7.1.1, or 7.1.2, by all means consider installing the System Update 3.0 extension.

What's different in System Update 3.0? For starters, the system enabler files for numerous Macs have been updated. Affected Mac models include the LC III; Quadra 605, 610, 650, 660AV, 800, and 840AV; PowerBook 160, 165, 165c, 180, and 180c; the Color Classic and Color Classic II; and the Power Macs.

System Update 3.0 also modifies the Mac's standard Save and Open dialog boxes so that the boxes show the actual icons for disks, files, and folders. (Previously, the Mac used generic icons for these items.)

System Update 3.0 also includes the SimpleText text editor, a replacement for the venerable TeachText. SimpleText supports multiple document windows, drag-and-drop editing, and multiple fonts, font sizes, and font styles. (SimpleText is also included with System 7.5.)

System Update 3.0 also includes updated versions of the Easy Access control panel, the Apple HD SC Setup disk-formatting utility, the Memory control panel, the PowerBook control panel, the PowerBook Setup control panel, the PowerBook Display control panel, the Battery desk accessory, the TV Setup control panel, the Screen control panel, and the PC Setup control panel.

Understanding Multitasking

Future computer historians will note the late 1980s as the period when *multitasking* began to make its way from mainframes and minicomputers to microcomputers like the Mac. Multitasking — a computer's capability to run numerous programs simultaneously — has been around on big computers for years, but early personal computers lacked the processing speed and the memory capacity needed to load and switch between numerous programs.

Apple took its first steps toward multitasking in 1987 when it released MultiFinder, which provided the most important features of a multitasking operating system — the capability to run several programs at once and to print documents and perform other time-consuming jobs while you continue to work. MultiFinder didn't change much from its initial release to the version that runs under System 6.

The next major step was the development of System 7. System 7 adds enhancements that many people expect of a powerful multitasking operating system, including features that enable programs to communicate with each other to exchange data and commands. As proof of Apple's commitment to Mac multitasking, System 7 doesn't give you the option of running under the "single Finder." In System 7, MultiFinder is always active; indeed, MultiFinder and the Finder are one and the same.

What's in System 7.5 for PowerBooks?

PowerTalk, if you're into that. Also, the improved PowerBook control panel and the new PowerBook control strip, both of which provide better control over, and feedback on, battery life. (The next chapter contains tips for using these items to extend battery life.) You can also display the current battery level in the menu bar.

Other enhancements:

- A sleep key sequence.
- Deferred printing. It's easier to queue up multiple documents when you're on the road and then print them in one fell swoop once you return to the home base.
- File synchronization. System 7.5 includes a utility called File Assistant that synchronizes files between a PowerBook and another Mac — that is, it makes it easier to manage the multiple versions of files that you often get when you use more than one computer. (See Chapter 24 for information about third-party synchronization utilities.)
- The on-the-fly resolution switching feature of the new Monitors control panel is handy if you frequently switch between your PowerBook's display and an external monitor.
- Auto Remounter. This handy control panel, discussed earlier in this chapter, enables a waking PowerBook to automatically remount any file server volumes that you had mounted before putting the computer to sleep.

This section examines some of the technicalities behind the Mac's capability to run several programs at once. You can also find some memory-conservation tips that help you squeeze more out of — and into — your Mac's memory.

Multitasking basics

System 7 lets you have more than one program on-screen simultaneously and switch between them with a mouse click (see Figure 22-15, "Applications on the Menu").

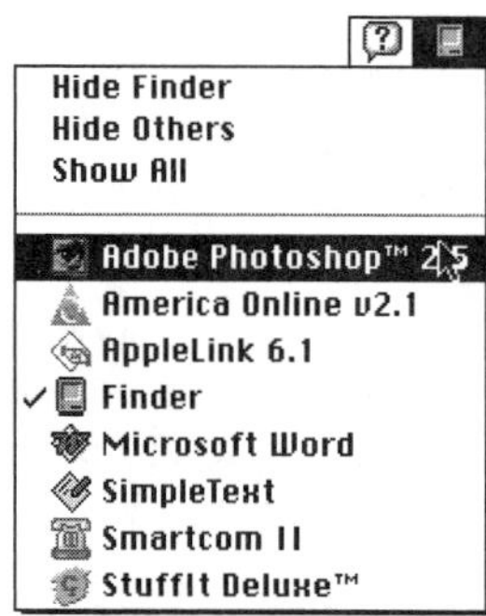

Figure 22-15: Applications on the Menu System 7's Application menu (located at the right edge of the menu bar) lets you quickly switch between programs and avoid screen clutter by hiding windows of applications you aren't using.

When you start an application on a Mac running System 7, the Finder remains visible behind the application's window. If you want to switch back to the Finder — perhaps to start another program or organize some disk files — you need not quit the program you're running. Instead, simply click anywhere within the Finder's desktop or choose Finder from the Application menu. After you return to the Finder, you can start another program. You can continue this process until you run out of memory — which may happen sooner than you expect.

Hiding the Desktop and Finder

Mac Frustration Number 294: You *accidentally* click the gray desktop pattern and find yourself yanked out of the program you were working in and hurled back to the Finder. It's not a bug, it's a feature — by clicking the desktop, you told the Mac, "I wanna work in the Finder."

If you'd rather not have such a hair-trigger Finder, you can configure System 7.5's Finder to hide itself and the desktop when you start or switch to an application program. Just open the General controls panel and uncheck the box labeled "Show Desktop When in Background."

The Performa control panel, included with Performa-model Macs, provides a similar set of features.

Looking under the hood

In the computer world, the process of putting one application on hold and activating a different one is called *context switching*. It's important to understand that context switching isn't multitasking. Programs that are put on hold don't perform any work; they simply hang around on the sidelines, waiting to be called back into action.

System 7's multitasking features surface when you use programs designed for them. When a program is written to recognize and use System 7's multitasking capabilities, it can work *in the background* — that is, when it isn't the active application. A communications program can transfer a file over the phone lines while you type away in a word processor. A database manager can sort a database. A spreadsheet program can crunch through a complex calculation. And almost any program can print, thanks to PrintMonitor, a background printing program included with the Mac (see the Background box "Background on Printing").

Background on Printing

Printing to a laser or ink-jet printer is like standing in line to buy vodka in Russia: the result is great, but you hate the wait. The PrintMonitor application that accompanies System 7 and System 6 MultiFinder lets the Mac print in the background to a PostScript printer and to most Apple printers. PrintMonitor doesn't make your pages appear more quickly: indeed, they probably take longer because PrintMonitor must share processor time with other applications. But PrintMonitor, like any *spooler* (computerese for software that handles background printing), lets you resume work sooner by intercepting data en route to the printer, saving it on disk, and then returning control of the Mac to you while it talks to the printer in the background.

Merriam-Webster hasn't recognized it, but *spool* has joined *radar* and *scuba* in that elite group of acronyms that have lowered their case and evolved into words. The acronym was born when pioneering computer scientists realized that the time they saved by spooling was lost by saying "simultaneous peripheral operations on line" — the catchy phrase that SPOOL once represented.

To activate background printing, use the Chooser desk accessory to select the LaserWriter or other printer driver, and then select the Background Printing On button. (See Chapter 31 for a look at special printing features of System 7.5.) Subsequently, when you issue a Print command, the Mac creates a *spool file* containing the document's contents. System 7 constantly scans for the creation of a spool file.

When System 7 detects a spool file, it starts PrintMonitor, which sends the spool file's contents to the printer in the background. As Chapter 31 describes, PrintMonitor's window lists the documents waiting to be printed and lets you postpone printing, schedule printing for a specific time, and rearrange the order of the waiting documents.

Any program that performs time-consuming tasks that don't require your attention is a candidate for background operation. You aren't likely to see support for background operation in highly interactive applications such as painting programs. The only time-consuming, hands-off task such programs perform is printing, and PrintMonitor takes care of that.

What multitasking isn't

How can the Mac run foreground and background programs simultaneously? It can't. The Mac's system software is a master of deception: it switches its attention from one program to another so quickly that all the programs *appear* to be running at once.

To understand how multitasking operating systems create this illusion, it's important to step back and look at how computers run programs. Nearly all computers, from Macs to mainframes, execute instructions one at a time, in sequence. The exceptions are today's ultra-powerful supercomputers, which use a new computing technique called *parallel processing*, wherein multiple processors execute instructions simultaneously.

In a multitasking operating system, each program you run is called a *task*, or *process*. When a multitasking operating system is running several programs, the computer still executes one instruction at a time, in sequence. However, the operating system switches its attention from one program to the next, executing a certain number of one program's instructions before putting that program on hold and turning to the next one (see Figure 22-16 "Multitasking on the Line"). This *task switching* occurs so quickly that all the programs appear to run simultaneously.

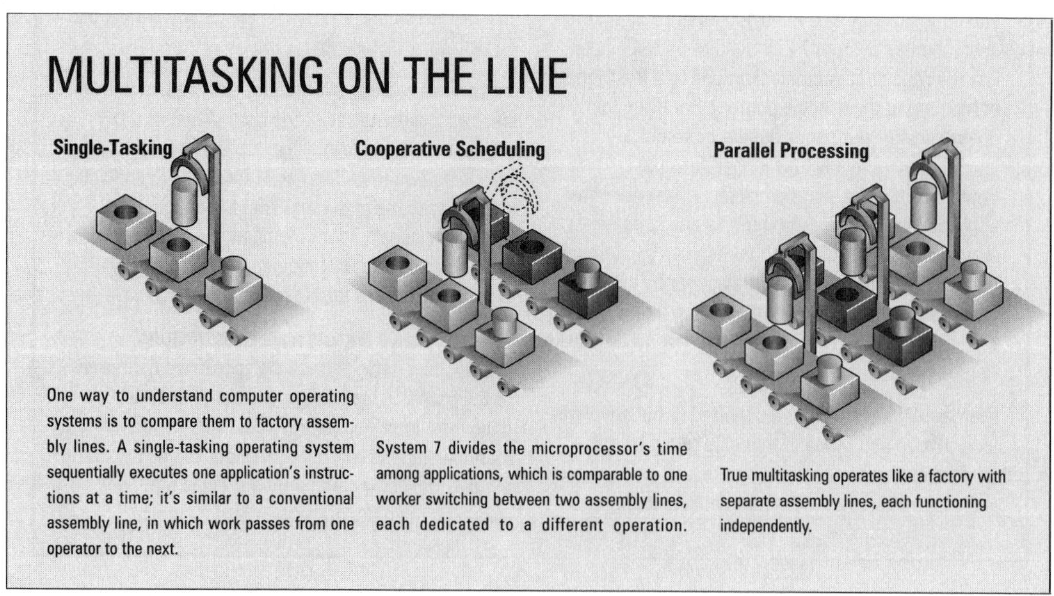

MULTITASKING ON THE LINE
Single-Tasking
Cooperative Scheduling
Parallel Processing
One way to understand computer operating systems is to compare them to factory assembly lines. A single-tasking operating system sequentially executes one application's instructions at a time; it's similar to a conventional assembly line, in which work passes from one operator to the next.
System 7 divides the microprocessor's time among applications, which is comparable to one worker switching between two assembly lines, each dedicated to a different operation.
True multitasking operates like a factory with separate assembly lines, each functioning independently.

Figure 22-16: Multitasking on the Line

How multitasking works

You don't have to understand how the Mac divides its time between programs in order to use it, but a bit of background can help you appreciate the complex juggling that goes on inside a multitasking operating system.

The portion of an operating system responsible for dividing the computer's resources among tasks is called a *task scheduler*. Two basic approaches to scheduling tasks exist — *preemptive* scheduling and *cooperative*, also called *nonpreemptive*, scheduling.

Preemptive versus cooperative

With preemptive scheduling, the task scheduler is tied to the internal heartbeat that all microcomputers use to govern their operation. The task scheduler prioritizes each task, giving each task control of the computer's resources for a specific number of heartbeats. When they've elapsed, the computer's operating system puts the current application on hold, turning its attention to the next one.

With cooperative scheduling, the task scheduler plays a more passive role in allocating processor time. The responsibility for dividing the processor's time is shared among all the applications that are running. An application must be "well behaved" — it must return control of the processor to the operating system at frequent intervals so that other applications get their turn to run. If one program hogs too much of the processor's time, others slow to a crawl. Worse, if a program crashes, the whole system is likely to crash because the haywire application may never return control to the operating system. An operating system that uses cooperative multitasking is a chain that's only as strong as its weakest link.

Traffic lights versus yield signs

The differences between preemptive and cooperative multitasking are like the differences between traffic lights and yield signs. Traffic lights govern the flow of cars in a rigid way: traffic from each side of the street gets a chance to flow only as long as the traffic lights allow it. (Assuming that some yo-yo doesn't run a red light.) Yield signs, however, turn driving into a cooperative effort. Traffic flows smoothly only when all the drivers cooperate and take turns using the intersection.

IBM's OS/2 system software, Microsoft's Windows NT, and Apple's A/UX — a Macintosh version of UNIX (an operating system popular in academic, scientific, and engineering environments) — use preemptive multitasking schedulers. But System 7 (and System 6 MultiFinder) uses the cooperative scheduling approach because it jibes well with the way Mac programs operate.

How Mac programs run

A Mac program spends much of its time waiting for an *event* such as a keystroke or a mouse movement to occur. System 7 senses when a foreground application isn't receiving any events, and says, in essence: "Attention, background task #1! The foreground application isn't receiving any events at the moment, so now's your chance to do some work." It's then up to the background task to say: "Okay, I accomplished something. I'm turning things back over to you, Mac."

Some multitasking gurus criticize cooperative multitasking as not being true multitasking. A true multitasking operating system, they contend, must maintain more control over the allocation of processor time among tasks. Let them whine. The bottom line is that the Mac's cooperative multitasker yields excellent results as long as program developers follow Apple's programming guidelines, which stipulate how applications that perform background tasks should operate.

What's more, the Mac's system software is gradually going the preemptive route anyway. Apple has already shipped a Thread Manager extension that enables programmers to create *multithreaded* programs — programs whose code is divided into parallel paths that can execute independently.

Copland: one step closer to "real" multitasking

In the latter part of 1996, Apple will release a significant new version of the Mac OS. Presently code-named Copland and referred to by some as System 8, this new version will take the Mac OS one step closer to providing full preemptive multitasking. It won't take us all the way there — to avoid causing compatibility nightmares, Apple is wisely taking a slow-and-steady approach to evolving the Mac OS — but it will provide the foundation that future versions of the Mac OS will build on.

Copland will provide several additional benefits, many of which are even more significant, including a greatly enhanced (and fully customizable) user interface and more native PowerPC code. But don't take my word for it — watch the Copland preview segment on the *Macworld Power User Clinic* CD to see for yourself.

The downside of multitasking

As my publisher would be happy to tell you, the more projects you take on, the more time you need to finish each one. The same rule applies to the Mac, whose performance slows when applications run in the background. An application usually runs slower in the background than in the foreground, and a foreground application runs somewhat slower than it would if no background application were running. I say *usually* and *somewhat* because the specific performance penalties depend on what the background and foreground applications are doing. As a general rule, the Mac's overall performance slows with each background task you add.

An example: if you're running PageMaker and also printing a document in the background using PrintMonitor, PageMaker feels less responsive. You may notice a slight delay between the time you press a key and the moment its character appears, or the mouse pointer's movement may seem sluggish and erratic. You also wait longer to see your hard copy because PrintMonitor slows down each time the Mac returns its attention to PageMaker in order to respond to those keyboard and mouse events. Of course, on faster Macs, the slowdown is less noticeable. A Power Mac is better at multitasking than a Quadra, which is better than a Classic or an SE.

On the other hand, when an inactive application isn't performing a background task, it doesn't impose a performance penalty on the currently active application. For example, when Microsoft Word and PageMaker are both running, neither imposes a direct performance penalty on the other because neither is written to perform work in the background.

Other than affecting your stopwatch, another drawback to multitasking is how it hits your bank account. Keeping multiple programs close at hand requires a good-sized hard disk, and keeping them in memory at the same time requires lots of memory. With multitasking and memory, the phrase "the more, the merrier" applies in spades.

Copying Files in the Background

The Finder can copy files in the background while you work in other programs that are already running — great for copying a large number of files to a backup disk.

To indicate that you can switch to another program while something takes place in the background, System 7 introduced a new type of dialog box — the *movable modal* dialog box. As the first part of its name suggests, you can move a movable modal dialog box around on-screen. *Modal* refers to the fact that you can't click outside the dialog box. In the past, virtually all Mac dialog boxes were modal: you couldn't do anything until you confirmed or canceled the dialog box. A movable modal dialog box works a bit differently: it doesn't let you do anything else in the current program, but you can switch to a different program and continue working. The Find command also uses movable modal dialog boxes, as do a few other Finder operations. You can recognize a movable modal dialog box by the stripes that appear in its title bar.

To switch to another program while the Finder is copying a file, you must use the Application menu or the Apple menu — you can't just double-click a program or document icon. (If you try, the Mac simply beeps.) If you use CE Software's QuicKeys or another utility that lets you launch files by pressing a keyboard shortcut, you can also use a shortcut key to start a program.

By the way, Apple's Copland release of the Mac OS will improve on the Finder's multitasking features. Not only will you be able to switch to a different task when files are copying, you'll be able to start *additional* copy operations.

Multitasking Survival Tips

Here are some tips to help you get more out of the Mac's multitasking features.

Save when switching

These days, all major Mac programs are written to coexist with System 7 and other programs. Nonetheless, it's always a good idea to use the active application's Save command before switching back to the Finder or to another open application. If switching programs causes a system crash, at least your latest work is saved. For that matter, it's a good idea to save frequently regardless of what you're doing.

Master System 7 navigation

System 7 makes it easy to create a messy electronic desktop; when several programs are open, switching to a specific window can be difficult. Under System 7, the icon at the right end of the menu bar is actually a menu — the *Application menu.* You can use it to switch between open applications and, better still, to hide the windows of other applications and the Finder. Hiding other windows is a good way to avoid screen clutter (refer to Figure 22-15 "Applications on the Menu"). Alas, it requires a bit more memory because the Mac must save the state of each program's windows before hiding them.

HOW POWER MACS RUN PRE-RISC SOFTWARE

A Power Mac can run software written for a 680X0 (pronounced 68-kay) Mac with the help of an emulator program. The emulator, which is part of the operating system in the Power Mac's ROM, translates 680X0 instructions into equivalent PowerPC instructions. On a Power Mac, System 7 has to decide whether the software it's running—an application, INIT, or System 7 component—is a native program (uses PowerPC code), emulated program (uses 680X0 code), or hybrid program (uses both types of code). Insignia Solutions uses a similar approach to make Windows software run on Power Macs.

To detect what kind of code a program uses, System 7 for PowerPC uses a new component called the Mixed Mode Manager. The manager intercepts every program when launched (A) and decides whether to use the emulator (B) or not (C). For hybrid programs, the Mixed Mode Manager must turn the emulator on and off as the program is running.

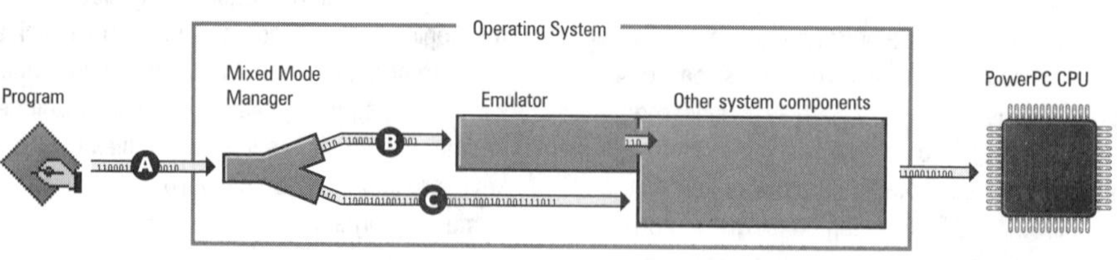

Figure 22-17: How Power Macs Run Pre-RISC Software

Software in the Power Mac Era

If you're a programmer adapting to the Power Mac era, you have many new concepts and programming practices to come to terms with. If you just *use* software rather than creating it, you don't have a lot of learning to do. Power Macs *are* Macs, after all, and their emulation mode runs the vast majority of pre-RISC software (albeit a bit slowly). For background on Power Mac emulation, see Figure 22-17 "How Power Macs Run Pre-RISC Software").

You may want to be aware of a few other concepts relating to software in the Power Mac era. They're detailed in this section.

The Power Mac system software

The Power Macintosh family of RISC-based Macs uses system software that's very similar to that of the rest of the Mac line. In fact, a lot of it is identical. Remember from Chapter 1 that Power Macs run pre-RISC software in emulation mode. Much of the Mac's system software is still pre-RISC software; Apple rewrote only about 10 percent of it in native PowerPC code. But it's that 10 percent that application programs spend most of their time executing.

Enhancements in the second-generation Power Macs

The Power Mac 7200, 7500, 8500, and 9500 as well as the Performa 5200/6200 series incorporate some system software and architectural enhancements that help make them the fastest Macs ever.

- **A new emulator** Called the Dynamic Recompilation Emulator (DRE), this new OS component runs 680X0 programs faster than did the emulator in the first-generation Power Macs. Where the old emulator translated 680X0 code line by line, the new DRE compiles 680X0 programs into native PowerPC code on the fly. Compiled code is stored in a 256K cache; if it's needed again, the emulator retrieves it from the cache instead of recompiling the 680X0 code. Apple claims the new emulator runs 680X0 programs 20 to 30 percent faster than the old one; indeed, Apple says the 9500 series are the fastest "680X0" Macs it has ever made. (By and large, Macworld Lab tests bear this out: the 9500/132 was, on average, 53 percent faster than a Quadra 800, while the 9500/120 averaged 38 percent faster.) The new emulator also provides a small performance boost to native applications, since certain key portions of the Mac OS — such as the Font Manager and the file system — are still in 680X0 code.

  One potential drawback to the new emulator: old programs that use self-modifying code may crash. (Such programs also have compatibility problems when run on 68040 Macs — remember the old 040 Cache Switch control panel?)

❖ **Tweaked system software** As mentioned earlier in this chapter, the latest Power Macs use System 7.5.2, which incorporates the enhancements made in System 7.5 Update 1.0 and adds some additional ones. The Resource Manager, a portion of the Mac OS that programs as well as the OS itself use extensively, was rewritten in native PowerPC code, as was the Ethernet network driver and the SCSI Manager. (Macworld Lab tests show the native SCSI Manager and internal Fast SCSI-2 bus pay off: the 9500/132 was 47 percent faster than an 8100/110 in disk-intensive operations.) Apple also performance-tuned QuickDraw, QuickDraw GX, and the Memory Manager, and honed the Mac OS math library to take better advantage of the 8500's and 9500's 604 chips and yield faster math calculations.

Mac OS 7.5.2 also contains a new mechanism for native-PowerPC device drivers, which among other things, will make possible faster transfers between the Mac and PCI cards. This mechanism, called the Driver Services Library, is one of the first stepping stones to 1996's Copland Mac OS release.

The new system version also does away with the 4GB disk partition limitation of System 7.5 by supporting drive volumes of up to 2 *terabytes* — that's 2048GB. Alas, the Mac's file system still limits file sizes to a maximum of 2GB and allocates disk space rather inefficiently on large volumes. And there's a potential compatibility wrinkle: if you mount a large-capacity drive formatted using the new large-volume driver on a Mac that is running an earlier version of the Mac OS, you'll only be able to access up to 4GB of its contents.

❖ **A foundation for graphics acceleration** Part of the Driver Services Library will make it easier for hardware developers to create accelerated graphics cards. Previously, hardware developers had to devise their own acceleration schemes; now, there's a defined structure for graphics acceleration. And in the little-things-that-count department, the Mac's arrow mouse pointer can now be built into and drawn by a video card, a change that eliminates the flickering pointer you see when a QuickTime movie is playing. (In other Macs, the pointer is drawn by the Mac OS.)

Installation complications

Power Macs complicate the lives of software developers in several ways. Not only do developers have to adapt their programs and programming practices to take advantage of the performance of the PowerPC chips, but they have to do so in a way that doesn't shut out the millions of non-RISC Macs out there.

Separate disks for each

One solution is to include a set of disks for each processor type in the box — a set of 68K disks and a set of Power Mac disks. All those disks take up space and cost money, however, and no Power Mac developer I'm aware of uses this approach.

Smart installation programs

A more sensible approach — and the one most developers use — is to supply software on one set of disks and rely on a *smart installer* to detect the type of machine you have and then install either native Power Mac or 68K code. Aladdin Systems, Apple, and Symantec offer software-installer technologies that support this approach.

Fat binaries

Another popular approach is to install software as a *fat binary*. An application file that's a fat binary contains *both* Power Mac and 68K code and can run on either type of Mac. The downside of a fat binary application is that it is, well, fat — it uses much more disk space than a file containing code for just one type of processor.

But the fat binary approach has a significant advantage: you can move the hard drive containing the software back and forth between a Power Mac and a non-RISC Mac — without having to worry about whether the software can run.

Many programs that include smart installers also provide the option of installing a fat binary. If you anticipate moving a hard drive from one type of Mac to the other, install your software as a fat binary. And consider buying another hard drive.

Understanding the Mac's Memory

If you've been seeing "not enough memory" error messages lately — or if you just bought a memory upgrade and want to put that extra space to work — read on. Few of the Mac's components offer more opportunities for fine-tuning than memory. When you understand how the Mac uses memory, you can make a variety of adjustments to improve overall performance, increase the number of programs you can run simultaneously, or speed up a particular program. And none of these adjustments requires you to open the Mac. You can fine-tune your memory from the comfort of your mouse.

Memory basics

Before looking at memory-maximizing specifics, I'll step back and show you the big picture. Many Macintosh newcomers confuse the Mac's RAM with its hard disk storage, probably because both are described using the same units of measurement: the kilobyte (K), or 1024 bytes; and the megabyte (MB), or one million bytes (technically, 1,048,576 bytes).

RAM is temporary storage space formed by a collection of chips soldered onto the Mac's circuit board or installed in small, plug-in boards. When the Mac is turned off (whether by you or by a power failure), the contents of RAM disappear faster than punch on New Year's Eve. Most Macs come with between 8MB and 16MB of RAM, which you can expand (see Chapter 29).

A hard disk, by contrast, provides permanent storage (or at least it's designed to; drives can fail, making a regular backup routine essential — see Chapter 26).

The many roles of RAM

In the Mac, as in other computers, RAM plays a few roles. It holds a large portion of the Mac OS. When the Mac starts up and displays its "Welcome to Macintosh" message or Mac OS startup screen, it's loading this RAM-based system software from the hard disk.

During startup, the Mac also loads system extensions, enhancements to the system software. You can tell when a Mac is loading system extensions — their icons appear along the bottom of the screen.

The final step in the startup process involves loading the Finder, the program that gives you the desktop and Trash icons. The Finder itself uses roughly 500K of RAM — almost four times the total amount of RAM built into the original Macintosh.

The point is that some of the Mac's RAM is filled right off the bat. You can find out how much RAM your system software and extensions use by choosing the About This Macintosh command from the Finder's Apple menu. A window appears describing how your Mac's RAM is being used (see Figure 22-18 "Window into Memory"). This window can be a memory maximizer's best friend.

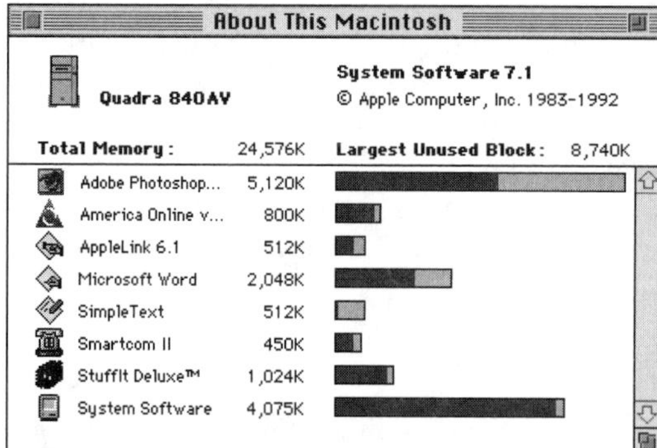

Figure 22-18: Window into Memory The About This Macintosh window displays a bar graph for the system software as well as each open application. Each bar shows how much memory is allocated to that program; the dark-shaded portion of each bar shows you how much of that RAM the program is actually using.

Making room for programs

When you start an application program such as Microsoft Word or ClarisWorks, the Mac sets aside some RAM for the program and then copies the program from the hard drive into that memory. Actually, with most programs, only part of the program is copied into RAM — the part that implements the program's most heavily used features. When you choose a particular command for the first time since starting the program, you may notice a short delay as the Mac retrieves the required software routines from the hard disk. (If your hard disk has an activity light on its front panel, it blinks.) When this happens, the Mac is loading one of the program's *code segments* from disk. (On a Power Mac, it's loading a code fragment — more about this subject shortly.)

Most large programs are divided into numerous code segments. The Mac can load a given segment into memory when it's needed, and it can purge segments from memory to free up space. This scheme enables developers to create programs with smaller minimum memory requirements. On the down side, frequently accessing the hard disk slows performance, especially on a slower Mac. Later, I show you how to minimize segment loading.

How programs store documents

Part of the memory a program receives is reserved for the documents you have open as you work. Some programs store an open document entirely in RAM; common examples include integrated packages such as ClarisWorks and Microsoft Works and drawing programs such as Adobe Illustrator, Macromedia FreeHand, and Claris's MacDraw series. With these programs, the maximum size of a document is limited by the amount of its program's free RAM.

Other programs don't store an open document entirely in RAM, but instead swap portions of the document with the hard disk, keeping in RAM only the portion you're working with at the moment. Most word processors — Microsoft Word, WordPerfect, and Claris's MacWrite Pro — work this way, as do Adobe PageMaker, QuarkXPress, and most database managers, including FileMaker Pro. This approach lets you create much larger documents, but moving around within a document can take longer (it's that relatively slow hard disk again).

Whether a program stashes open documents entirely in RAM or swaps them between RAM and the hard disk may seem like a trivial technical point, but you may need to consider its important ramifications when fine-tuning your short-term memory.

Memory-Maximizing Tips

You can make four basic memory-related adjustments. Notice that each has a potential drawback: weighing each technique's pros and cons is an important part of memory maximizing.

Get Info and memory

If you want to run several programs at the same time but are a little lean on RAM, you can reduce each program's memory requirements to shoehorn both into memory. Each program is likely to run slower because the Mac has to load and discard segments more frequently. And integrated packages and drawing programs are limited to smaller documents.

Conversely, if you want a given program to run faster or you want to create larger documents with an integrated package or drawing program, you can increase its memory allocation. When a program has more RAM to work in, it doesn't have to go out to the hard disk to load code segments as frequently. But less free RAM is available for other programs. For advice about allocating memory, see Figure 22-19, "Allocating Memory" and the section "Virtual Memory on Power Macs," later in this chapter.

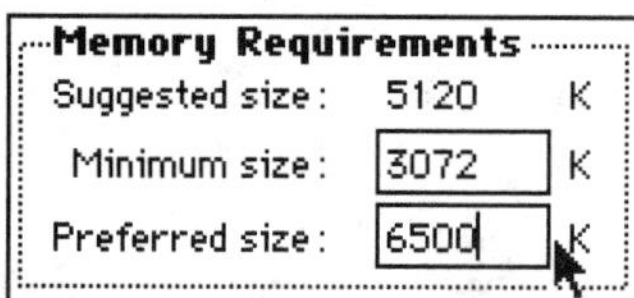

Figure 22-19: Allocating Memory Using the Get Info window, you can adjust a program's current memory size value. If the current memory size is greater than the suggested size, you can safely reduce the current size to match the suggested size. If both memory size values are identical, you can try reducing the current size value, but the program may not run reliably.

Another way to adjust memory sizes is with AppSizer, a shareware control panel from Peirce Software. AppSizer lets you change memory sizes on the fly — that is, at the moment you start a program. This option can be handy if you frequently alternate between various memory-allocation settings depending on the project at hand. AppSizer also lets you temporarily change the memory allocation of a program located on a CD-ROM drive — a feat beyond the Finder's Get Info command.

The disk cache

The *disk cache* — accessed through the Memory control panel — is an area of system software RAM that holds information recently read from the hard disk. If you need this information again, the Mac retrieves it from the cache instead of from the hard disk. A larger disk cache can improve performance if you frequently switch between two programs or perform repetitive tasks. If you work sporadically — if you're never sure which program, command, or document you may use next — a large disk cache is less likely to boost performance. A large disk cache also leaves less free RAM for running programs.

Experiment with various cache sizes (restart the Mac after each adjustment to make your change take effect). If performance doesn't improve, reset the cache to its original size — or even consider reducing its size to free up RAM for other uses.

A better disk cache in System 7.5

In system versions prior to 7.5, the disk cache didn't get — and didn't deserve — a lot of respect. For System 7.5, Apple rewrote the caching software to provide better performance. If you have plenty of RAM (preferably more than 8MB) go ahead and create a large cache—up to a megabyte or so, if you like.

Virtual memory

Virtual memory — accessed through the Memory control panel — blurs the lines between hard disk and RAM storage by tricking the Mac into thinking that part of the hard disk is actually RAM (see Figure 22-20, "Virtually Memory"). This feature lets you run more programs than would otherwise fit into RAM, but switching between programs takes longer than if you had the equivalent amount of real RAM. (Virtual memory doesn't work on the Mac Classic, SE, Plus, LC, or PowerBook 100. To use virtual memory on the original Mac II, you need a Motorola 68851 PMMU chip.)

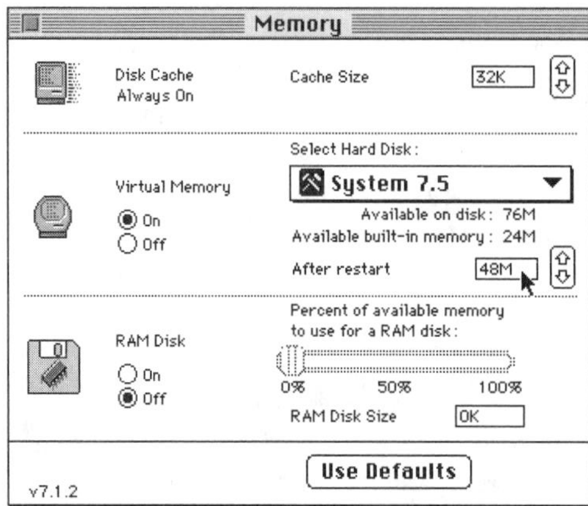

Figure 22-20: Virtually Memory On most Mac models, the Memory control panel lets you set aside some hard disk space as an extension of RAM. The controls at the bottom of the window let you create a RAM disk; if your Mac's Memory control panel doesn't have a RAM Disk section, you need to use a utility such as AppDisk to create a RAM disk.

In theory, you can also use virtual memory to run a program that's too large to fit into RAM. For example, if you want to run a program that requires 4MB of free RAM on a Mac that has only 3MB free, you can use virtual memory to make up the 1MB difference. In practice, however, this feature usually delivers painfully slow performance. You should have enough real RAM to run the largest program in your software library.

As mentioned in Chapter 20, virtual memory and QuickTime don't get along either. VM causes erratic movie playback.

As mentioned earlier in this chapter, you can temporarily turn off VM by pressing the ⌘ key during the Mac's startup sequence. When you do, VM remains off until you restart.

When virtual memory is useful

Virtual memory can be useful if you like to run numerous programs and switch between them. As long as you have enough real RAM to run the largest program comfortably, you don't experience significant slowdowns — only slight delays when you switch between programs.

Virtual memory on Power Macs

For the Power Macs' RISC architecture, Apple rewrote much of the Mac's memory-management software. One side effect of the new world order is that using virtual memory can be *beneficial* when you're using native-mode applications.

This is so because Power Mac software can be divided into chunks called *fragments*. All Power Mac software is loaded into memory as fragments. When virtual memory is active on a Power Mac, native-mode programs can use RAM more efficiently.

Virtual memory itself runs more efficiently on Power Macs. For example, when real RAM needs to be used for something else, the virtual memory software doesn't waste time writing the code that's currently in RAM out to a swap file on the hard drive. When the Mac needs the code again, it simply reads it from the original application file.

The bottom line: using virtual memory on a Power Mac is a good idea if you're using native-mode applications. To get the benefits of VM without its performance penalties, set the amount of VM to be just 1MB larger than the amount of real RAM you have. For instance, if you have 16MB of RAM, set VM to provide a total of 17MB.

Why Does VM Reduce Memory Requirements on Power Macs?

On a Power Mac, the RAM requirements for a program are *lower* when virtual memory is running. When you choose the Finder's Get Info command for an application on a Power Mac, you get an additional message that gives a lower memory requirement when you have VM turned on.

Why? Because of how the Power Mac loads an application into memory. A 68K application stores its code in the CODE resource and uses the Segment Loader to load CODE resources into memory. A Power Macintosh application, on the other hand, stores executable code in the data fork of an application file. This method enables the fat binary approach — a single program that can work on a 68K Macintosh and a Power Mac. (See Chapter 24 for a discussion of resources and data and resource forks.)

With virtual memory turned on, the Virtual Memory Manager on a Power Mac can reuse the data fork of the application as a paging file to help improve performance. As a result, only the needed portions of code get loaded into memory, thus reducing the memory requirements of the application.

Using a RAM disk

Like virtual memory, a *RAM disk* is a software sleight-of-hand. But instead of treating part of the hard disk as RAM, a RAM disk sets aside some memory to act like a disk. Because RAM is faster than a hard disk, anything stored on a RAM disk opens at top speed. Most new Macs let you create a RAM disk by using the Memory control panel. If your Memory control panel doesn't contain a RAM disk option, use a utility program to create a RAM disk. My favorite is AppDisk, a $15 shareware program by Mark Adams, available through on-line services and user groups.

One drawback to a RAM disk is that the RAM it uses isn't available for running programs. Another drawback is that a RAM disk's contents vanish when the power goes. You need to restore the contents of a RAM disk each time you start up your Mac (this rule doesn't apply to the PowerBook 100, 160, 180, 180c, 500-series, or Duo-series models). Connectix Corporation's Maxima and Apple's own PowerBook File Assistant utilities have features that let you save the contents of a RAM disk on PowerBooks other than the 100.

What should you stash in a RAM disk? Ideally, the System Folder as well as the application programs you want to run at top speed. Unfortunately, you need a few megabytes of RAM disk space just to hold System 7's bloated System Folder. (You can pare down the RAM disk's System Folder by removing printer drivers such as the LaserWriter and ImageWriter files, as well the Scrapbook file, file-sharing extensions, and anything else you can live without. You can always restart from your hard drive's System Folder when you need the extra capabilities.)

Extensions, control panels, and memory

I mentioned earlier that system extensions — those programs that load during startup, displaying icons along the bottom of the screen — nibble away at your free RAM. Keep this in mind the next time you're tempted to add an extension that promises to boost your productivity or make you chuckle. Flashy extensions or control panels such as After Dark or Bruce Tomlin's SoundMaster (which plays sounds when you insert and eject disks, throw away files, and perform other activities) are particularly RAM hungry, as are electronic mail extensions such as CE Software's QuickMail and Microsoft Mail.

QuickTime and memory

If you use QuickTime-supporting programs, use QuickTime 1.6 or later — preferably version 2.0, included on the CD that comes with this book. QuickTime 1.5 and earlier versions tend to hog RAM even when you aren't running QuickTime-savvy programs.

PowerBook RAM Disk Tips

If you're using a PowerBook and have a RAM disk large enough to accommodate a System Folder and an application program, use the Startup Disk control panel to specify that your Mac start up from the RAM disk. Then restart. When the desktop reappears, use the PowerBook control panel to put the hard disk to sleep. You can now run from the RAM disk and greatly extend the time between battery charges. You need to wake up the hard disk in order to save documents on it. You can save documents on a RAM disk, but if a system crash corrupts the RAM disk, you lose work.

Running on empty

When you're running low on free RAM, disable any extensions you can do without (extensions you *can't* do without may include ones required by a piece of hardware such as a cartridge drive, scanner, or video card). You can disable extensions or control panels by manually dragging them out of the Extensions or Control Panels folders, both located in the System Folder. An easier way is to use Ricardo Batista's Extension Manager, a free control panel that lets you activate and deactivate extensions and control panels. Several commercial extension managers are also available.

After you disable some extensions or control panels (manually or with an extension manager), choose Restart from the Finder's Special menu. You can also temporarily disable all extensions by restarting and holding down the Shift key until you see the "Welcome to Macintosh" message or Mac OS startup screen with the text "Extensions off" below it.

Using a Less-Memorable PlainTalk Voice

If you use PlainTalk's text-to-speech features, you can use memory more efficiently by choosing voices judiciously. The high-quality male voice uses the most memory — 2.6MB. The compressed female voice, by comparison, uses only 700K. She sounds a bit hoarse, though — you may not want to listen to her all day. You can hear examples of both compressed and uncompressed male and female voices by playing the PlainTalk demonstrations on the *Macworld Complete Mac Interactive CD* included with this book. A QuickTime-based demonstration and a SoundEdit Pro version of the same demonstration are located in the Sounds and Movies folder.

System software and memory

System 7's file-sharing features (discussed earlier in this chapter) require nearly 300K of RAM. If you aren't using file sharing, turn it off with the Sharing Setup control panel. The Mac runs slightly faster, too. Similarly, PowerTalk, QuickDraw GX, AppleScript, and other big-ticket system software enhancements also take their toll on free RAM.

System Update 3.0 also includes updated versions of the Easy Access control panel, the Apple HD SC Setup disk-formatting utility, the Memory control panel, the PowerBook control panel, the PowerBook Setup control panel, the PowerBook Display control panel, the Battery desk accessory, the TV Setup control panel, the Screen control panel, and the PC Setup control panel.

More RAM for your Mac

Of course, the best way to avoid running out of memory is to buy more — RAM prices have never been lower. If you have a Classic, Plus, or SE, upgrade to 4MB. If you have a PowerBook other than the 100, upgrade to at least 6MB (preferably 8MB) to take advantage of a RAM disk. If you have a color Mac, an SE/30, or a Classic II or Performa 200, consider upgrading to 8MB — or beyond, especially if you work with color scanned images, digital sound, or QuickTime movies. (If you add more than 8MB to a Mac II, IIx, or IIcx, use the MODE32 extension to access all the RAM. It's available free through user groups, Apple dealers, or on-line services.) For details on adding memory, see Chapter 29.

But even a hefty RAM upgrade probably keeps the low-memory messages at bay only for a while. They return as you acquire increasingly complex programs and become accustomed to running more of them at once. When that day arrives, remember the techniques I've described here — they can help you cram more into your RAM.

Saving RAM on the IIci and IIsi

If you use the built-in video port on a Mac IIci or IIsi, you can also free up some memory by using the Monitors control panel to switch to the black-and-white (monochrome) display mode. The IIci and IIsi use part of their main RAM to store the bits that represent the screen image. With a standard 14-inch monitor in the 256-color display mode, this area of memory, called the *screen buffer,* requires up to 320K. In monochrome mode, it requires only 38K. This tip doesn't apply to other color Macs: they provide separate video memory, called *VRAM.* (See Chapter 29 for more details about video and VRAM.)

CHAPTER 22 CONCEPTS AND TERMS

- System files fall into several categories: the main players such as the System and Finder files; extensions like Easy Access; control panels (cdevs) such as General, Monitors, and Keyboard; printer drivers like ImageWriter, StyleWriter, and LaserWriter; and miscellaneous files such as PrintMonitor and Finder Help.
- Apple's Installer utility updates the contents of a System Folder. Installer also uses a technique called patching to create a common ground of software features that exist across the Macintosh family.
- The System 7 Finder makes it easy to find and select files (even from the keyboard), view the contents of disks and folders, and customize the Mac's operation to suit your tastes and work habits.
- To add fonts to System 7, you drag them to the System Folder — the Finder stashes them in the appropriate place (in the System file for System 7.0 and in the Fonts folder in System 7.1).
- An alias is a small file that points to a document, an application, a disk, or a folder. When you open an alias, the Mac opens whatever the alias points to. Creating aliases is a great way to have fast access to the items you use most.
- System 7 allows for peer-to-peer file sharing: you can make your disks and folders available to other computers on your network, and theirs can be made available to you.
- Although the Mac's basic operating style is unchanged in System 7, you need to adjust to several changes if you've used earlier versions.
- Multitasking refers to a computer's capability to run multiple programs at once. With preemptive multitasking, the computer gives each task control of the computer's resources for a specific amount of time. With cooperative multitasking — the kind System 7 provides — all the tasks that are running share the responsibility for dividing the processor's time.
- A Mac's performance slows when programs run in the background.
- Two ways to get the most from your Mac's memory are choosing software that uses memory sparingly and adjusting a program's memory requirements by using the Finder's Get Info window.

access privileges
Settings for who can see and modify shared files and folders. Privileges are specified for *users* — people who are allowed access to shared items. You may also assemble users into *groups* — collections of users who work on related projects or in the same department.

alias
A small file (about 1K) that acts as a remote control for another item, usually another file or folder. When you double-click an alias, the Mac opens the item to which the alias points.

background task
An operation, such as printing, that occurs while you work in a different program.

cdev
A technical term for a control panel, short for *control panel device.* A control panel's file type code is the *cdev.*

context switching
The process of putting one application program on hold and activating a different one.

disk cache
An area of system software RAM that holds information recently read from the hard disk. If you need this information again, the Mac retrieves it from the cache instead of from the hard disk. A larger disk cache can improve performance if you frequently switch between two programs or perform repetitive tasks.

fat binary
A program that contains both PowerPC RISC code and 68K-family code. Such a program can run on either type of machine.

file signature
A set of codes that identifies a file's type as well as its creator. The Finder uses the signature to determine which program to start when you open a document icon.

FKEY
Short for *function key, a* small program that is generally available in any application. To run an FKEY, you type a ⌘-Shift-number keyboard sequence.

INIT resource
A snippet of software that's loaded into memory during startup. Extensions and control panels can have INIT resources.

multitasking
A computer's capability to run numerous programs simultaneously.

RAM disk
A software sleight-of-hand that sets aside some memory to act like a disk. Because RAM is faster than a hard disk, anything stored on a RAM disk opens at top speed.

scripting
Creating your own short programs that automate repetitive tasks such as backing up and then deleting older files.

(continued on the next page)

(continued from previous page)

smart installer
In the Power Mac world, an installer utility that detects which type of Mac it's running on and then offers to install native PowerPC code or 68K code or both.

stationery pad
A master for a frequently created document such as a business letter, fax cover sheet, or newsletter. By creating a document and then turning it into a stationery pad (by using the Get Info window), you can reuse its contents without worrying about accidentally saving over them.

system enabler
A special file that loads during memory at startup time (before extensions and control panels load) and provides the software that System 7.1 needs to work on a given Mac. In System 7.5, the separate enablers for different Mac models have been consolidated into a single universal enabler.

virtual memory
Often abbreviated *VM,* a System 7 feature that blurs the lines between hard disk and RAM storage by tricking the Mac into thinking that part of the hard disk is actually RAM. This capability lets you run more programs than would otherwise fit into RAM, but switching between programs takes longer than if you had the equivalent amount of real RAM. VM runs more efficiently on Power Macs than it does on non-RISC Macs.

CHAPTER TWENTY-THREE

Hardware Tips for Every Mac and PowerBook

- Keeping your Mac cool and clean
- Avoiding computer-related aches and pains
- Protecting your computer from power problems
- Squeezing the most juice from your PowerBook
- Saving energy: tips for environmentally friendly computing

In computing's primeval period (30 years ago), computers used vacuum tubes — glowing glass bulbs. One IBM SAGE computer, several dozen of which formed the backbone of the United States' air defense system from 1958 to 1983, used 25,000 tubes. Maintenance was hellish. A staff of technicians worked full-time keeping the four-story behemoth running, and even with a battery of built-in diagnostics, finding a faulty tube often meant turning off the room lights and looking for its weakened glow.

Today, you can service a computer with the lights on. But despite the reliability of solid-state electronics, computers like the Mac still have some mechanical parts that require routine attention. Still, you'd be surprised at how many people ignore the basics of setup and maintenance vital for a healthy Mac. Or maybe you wouldn't. If you're part of the group who believes that preventative maintenance should be prevented, this chapter is for you.

After looking at basic maintenance and setup issues, I present some tips for protecting the Mac against power surges. Then I examine the other critical aspect of Macintosh power: extending battery life in PowerBooks.

Unless otherwise noted, the tips in this chapter apply to the entire Mac family. If you're on the prowl for tips on a specific Mac model, see Chapter 28 for troubleshooting tips and Chapter 29 for upgrade-oriented tips. And don't forget to look up your Mac model in this book's index.

Cleaning Up Your Mac

Although a layer of dust can do damage by acting as a blanket that keeps heat in, electronic chips don't have to sparkle to work. The only items on a Mac that need regular cleaning are the screen and the mechanical parts — the keyboard, mouse, and possibly the floppy disk drive.

Keeping the keyboard clean involves keeping it free of dust and liquids. Each key is a switch with two contacts that close; the key generates a signal when you press it. Dust (or spilled maple syrup) either prevents that signal from being generated or causes a kind of keyboard stuttering: You press *c* and get six of them as the contacts intermittently make and break their connection through the grime.

To dust a keyboard, turn off the Mac and then unplug the keyboard. Take the keyboard into a different room (one without computers), turn it upside down, and blow into the keys with short, powerful breaths. Keep those breaths dry by swallowing a couple times beforehand, and don't think about Grandma's cookies as you work. Better still, rest your lungs and buy a can of compressed air such as Falcon's Dust-Off at a camera store. Read the directions on the can first: with some products, holding the can upside-down or at other odd angles causes icy wet liquid to escape. Don't substitute a bicycle pump, air compressor, or other unfiltered air source. It can make matters worse by blowing dust into the keyboard.

What to do if you spill the Jolt cola

Compared to liquids, though, dust is a minor enemy to keyboards. Crying over spilt milk may serve no purpose, but orange juice or soda spattered on a keyboard is definitely worth a tear or two. When a sugary liquid dries, it leaves behind a sticky residue that can seal or even corrode the key's contacts. If you commit this cardinal sin, take your keyboard to a dealer for a complete cleaning.

If you're in the middle of a big project and can't do without the keyboard, however, you have one small hope. This desperate measure doesn't replace professional service, but it may get you through a crunch. Buy a bottle of spray contact cleaner (not tuner cleaner) at an electronics store. Unplug the keyboard (with the Mac's power off), hold it over a sink, and spray a generous amount of cleaner into the keyboard while repeatedly pressing its keys. Quickly turn the keyboard upside-down to let it drain. Wait half an hour or so, and then reconnect the keyboard and try typing.

If the keyboard works, say a prayer of thanks and vow to take it in for service as soon as possible. If it doesn't, or if one or two keys still act up, try again. If you can't locate contact cleaner, try a bottle of tape-recorder head cleaner. But remember that this technique is a last-ditch effort. If you can live without your keyboard for a while, having it properly cleaned is the best solution.

Cleaning the mouse

Turn the mouse upside-down, remove the retaining plate that surrounds the ball, and then invert the mouse and catch the ball as it falls out. Clean the ball with a lint-free cloth and clean the rollers inside the mouse with a cotton swab moistened with tape head cleaner or alcohol. In any case, cleaning the mouse regularly is a good habit to get into because the mouse picks up dust and lint as you use it.

On the *Macworld Power User Clinic* CD that accompanies this book, you can watch a QuickTime movie showing how to clean the mouse. It's in the Mouse section of the Meet the Mac clinic.

Dusty Drives and Screens

The debate over whether or not to clean floppy disk drives frequently sparks brawls at user-group meetings. Some say that regular cleaning helps prevent disk errors by removing dust and particles that occasionally flake off a disk's surface. Clean-drive advocates swear by disk drive cleaning kits, which contain a disk-like item that houses a circular pad of fiber-based cleaning material. You moisten the pad with cleaning fluid, insert it in the holder, and put the holder in the drive, where it spins like a disk and cleans the heads.

Others say to leave the drives alone unless they're acting up. They claim that cleaning can do more harm than good because of too much or too little fluid, or because dirt and grime in the cleaning pad can act like sandpaper on the drives' heads. I'm from that school. Some of my Macs are approaching their tenth birthdays, and their drives have never been cleaned and have never misbehaved — after near-constant use in houses plagued with woodstove dust in the winter and pollen in the summer. I'm not saying that cleaning is bad for drives, mind you: I'm just presenting both sides of the story. I believe that cleaning is unnecessary if you use high-quality disks and prevent dust from accumulating in your work area.

The screen is another area where improper cleaning can do damage. Most screens have a nonglare coating that common glass cleaners promptly dissolve, turning the screen's finish from matte to glossy. You can keep the screen clean with lint-free tissues (such as Kimwipes) or photographic lens-cleaning tissue.

If you must use a liquid to remove sticky fingerprints, use a cleaning fluid made for computer screens. It won't harm the finish, and some of those products repel dust — at least according to the companies that sell them. Although you can use window cleaner to clean the Mac's case, be sure to spray it on a cloth (not a linty paper towel) rather than directly on the case.

Beating the Heat

Cleaning is important for the Mac's mechanical parts; cooling is vital for its electronic ones. Electronic components have self-destructive lifestyles. Heat is their worst enemy, yet they generate heat as they work. To keep its parts cool, a computer's case must be ventilated so that cool air can replace hot. The designers of the first Macs (ones preceding the SE and II) placed cooling vents at strategic locations in the machine's case to provide convection cooling: the heat created inside the machine rises and exits through the vents in the top of the case, drawing in cooler air through the vents at the bottom. Modern Macs use a similar ventilation technique but supplement it with fans.

You can easily thwart a Mac's ventilation process by blocking a set of vents. If you cram a Mac between books or magazines (or use it on a bearskin rug), you block the lower vents, preventing the intake of cool air. This chokes off the flow of air, allowing heat to build to potentially damaging levels. And damaging doesn't have to mean chip meltdown. Even if it doesn't damage the hardware, too high a temperature can cause a system crash.

To beat the heat, give your Mac room to breathe — an inch or two on the sides and several more on the top. Keep it away from a radiator or other heat source. Also, keep it out of sunlight. Direct sunlight bakes a Mac and causes screen glare to boot. If you're using a Classic, Classic II, SE/30, SE, Plus or, heaven forbid, an earlier model, be especially careful to keep the left side of the machine cool — that's the side where the heat-generating power supply lives.

Keeping Yourself Healthy

Cleaning and cooling keeps your Mac healthy, but what about you? Your equipment should be set up to allow you to use it without having to hire a live-in ophthalmologist and chiropractor. Fortunately, several companies have come to the rescue with gadgets and gizmos that all well-dressed Macs are wearing. Figure 23-1 "A Workstation That Works" illustrates ergonomic issues. The Quick Tips box "Tips for Healthy Computing" describes a few exercises that can help. Also see the Mac References folder on the *Macworld Power User Clinic* CD for more information on computing health issues. An in the *Power User Clinic* itself, check out the Healthy Computing segment.

A WORKSTATION THAT WORKS

Today's ergonomists recognize that there is no perfect position that workers can maintain all day. For most people, a comfortable workstation is one that can accommodate two or more positions, enabling you to adjust your chair, monitor, and keyboard to fit your current task or inclination. Most people find the upright and slightly reclined positions portrayed here best for computer use. If you do a fair amount of traditional desk work, you'll probably want a chair that supports a forward-leaning position as well.

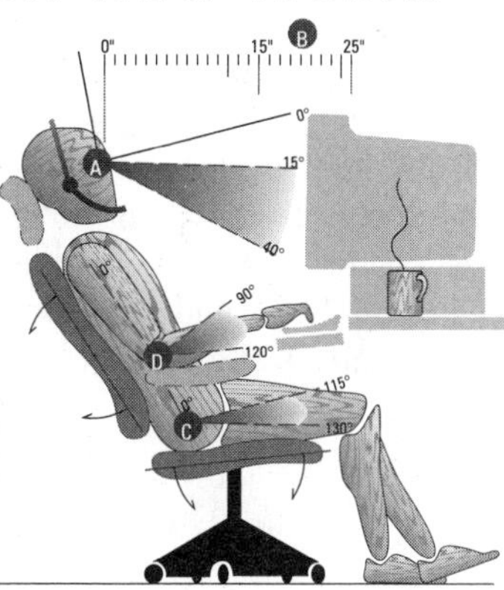

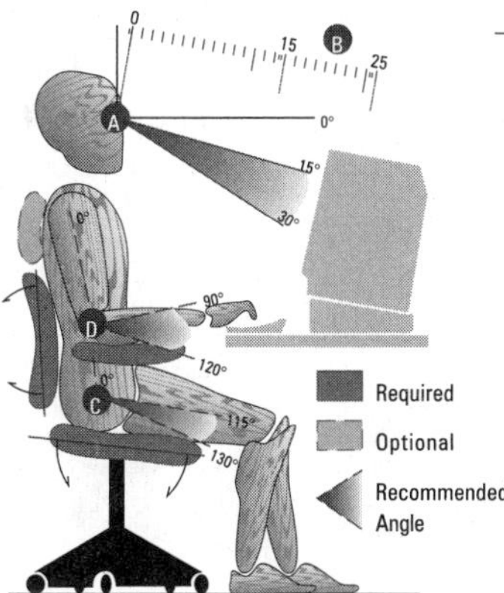

Screen Posture always follows the eyes; screens placed too low or angled improperly are a major source of slouching (A). The distance from the screen to your eyes should be only slightly greater than the distance you normally maintain between reading material and your eyes (B). (Bifocal wearers may require a steeper screen angle than the ones portrayed.)

Chair Seat contours should follow the contours of your back. Adjust chair height so that you don't feel pressure on your tailbone (seat too low) or lower thighs (seat too high). Ergono- mists used to recommend 90 degrees as a good angle between thighs and spine, but recent research shows that more people favor a more open posture (C).

Keyboard Your arms should be relaxed at your side, with elbows a few inches from your body (D). Position your chair and keyboard to minimize reaches. When you change position, from upright to reclined for example, be sure to reposition your keyboard (and screen). An adjustable keyboard stand, which enables you to use the mouse without a stretch, is useful for this purpose, but you can also place the keyboard in your lap.

Desk A comfortable desk height is particularly important if you keep the keyboard on your desk. If you don't have a keyboard stand and you work at a nonadjustable surface that's too high, try raising your chair and putting a platform or box beneath your feet. If your desk is too low, try fastening blocks to the ends of the legs.

Copy Stand If you often look at paper documents when you work, use a copy stand, mounted so that it puts your work in the same plane and at the same height as the screen. If you look at the hard copy more than the screen, orient your chair or screen such that the copy stand, rather than the Macintosh, is directly in front of you.

You Keep moving—motion makes the blood flow. And remember to take a break from computer work every hour.

Prepared with the assistance of Eileen Vollowitz, PT, of Back Designs, in Oakland, California.
—Joe Matazzoni

Figure 23-1: A Workstation That Works

Apple's wrist-friendly keyboard

If you suffer from wrist pain caused by typing, you may want to consider the Apple Adjustable Keyboard, which sports a split keyboard design that supposedly keeps your wrists in a healthier position. You can angle the left- and right-hand sections of the keyboard to up to 30 degrees to find the typing position that feels best. The Apple Adjustable Keyboard also includes detachable palm rests to provide a flat surface to rest your hands when you're not typing; volume control, mute, and record keys (handy — no pun intended — for multimedia work); a separate extended keypad that includes function keys, a numeric keypad, and cursor-control keys; and adjustable feet that let you change the slope of both the main keyboard and the extended keypad.

I commend Apple for going to great lengths to design and build a new and different keyboard, but I'm not sure that the Apple Adjustable Keyboard is the answer to repetitive-stress injuries. For one thing, when you use the keyboard in a split position, you tend to hunch your shoulders forward — a posture that's bad for your back and neck. For another, the separate keypad's keys are tiny, and if you use it extensively, you probably compromise good posture by stretching over to it.

Tips for Healthy Computing

Jane E. Brody writes a syndicated column about health issues for *The New York Times.* What follows are descriptions of exercises she has recommended for keyboard and mouse jockeys. As someone who occasionally suffers from *repetitive-stress injuries* (RSIs), I can vouch for these exercises — they help.

If you feel pain in your arms and wrists, get treatment early. As Brody writes: "Experts caution against trying to work through pain, because that only makes the injury worse and may result in irreversible damage to the nerve that passes through the wrist into the hand."

Limbering-up exercises

1. Clench your fist tightly, and then release, fanning out your fingers. Repeat five times.
2. Grasp the fingers of one hand and gently bend back the wrist. Hold this position for five seconds, and then repeat for the other hand.
3. Grasp the thumb of one hand and gently pull down until you feel the stretch. Hold for five seconds, and then repeat for the other hand.
4. Massage the inside and outside of each hand with the thumb and fingers of the other hand.

Take breaks — and consider talking

In addition to performing these exercises, stand up and take a break every hour or so. Stretch. Move your arms around. When writing or taking notes, don't hold your hands in a tense position over the keyboard as you pause to collect your thoughts.

In the *Macworld Power User Clinic's* Healthy Computing segment, you can watch QuickTime movies showing these exercises.

The Dvorak alternative — and I don't mean John

If you think that your fingers are doing too much walking over the keyboard, a better course of action may be to switch your keyboard layout to the Dvorak layout. A Navy researcher named August Dvorak designed this layout, which puts the most frequently used characters in more accessible positions, in the thirties. (Believe it or not, the conventional typewriter layout was created around the turn of the century in an effort to slow down typists who were causing early typewriter mechanisms to jam.)

Most online services have Dvorak keyboard layouts available that you can use with System 7. Simply drag the layout file to your System Folder icon and click OK when the Finder asks whether it should install the layout in the System file. Next, use the Keyboard control panel to activate the new layout. (For faster access to the layout, use Apple's ResEdit utility to activate System 7's keyboard menu — see the next chapter for details.)

Dvorak International is a nonprofit organization dedicated to helping people convert to the Dvorak keyboard layouts. You can write to Dvorak International at P.O. Box 44, Poultney VT 05764. You can also reach the organization on-line; its America Online address is Dvorak Int.

Tilt-and-swivel stands

For me and many others, a computer monitor is too low to look at for hours on end without developing a pain in the neck. Swivel stands made by firms such as Curtis Manufacturing and Kensington raise the monitor and let you tilt it to a more comfortable viewing angle. You can also try propping up the front of the screen by placing something under it, such as the lid of a disk box or two 1½-inch plastic furniture leg tips (my personal choice).

Many of today's monitors contain built-in tilt-swivel stands. The wonderful Performa 5200 takes this concept to its extreme—the entire computer is built into a tilt-swivel monitor. (You can see this computer in action on the *Macworld Power User Clinic* CD.)

Tilt-and-swivel stands are also available for compact Macs such as the Classic, SE, and Plus. And you'll be glad to know that tilting a Mac does not affect the operation of computer pinball or billiard games.

Taking Care of a PowerBook's Screen

If you're running a PowerBook using the AC adaptor, avoid leaving the computer on for more than 24 hours at a time. Doing so can cause temporary problems with the screen, such as shadows appearing when you move windows. You can fix the problem by putting the computer to sleep for at least several hours.

Clean a PowerBook's screen with soft, lint-free paper or cloth moistened with mild glass cleaner. Don't spray the glass cleaner directly onto the screen.

If you plan to fly with your PowerBook, carry it with you instead of checking it as baggage. If a PowerBook is shipped in an unpressurized airplane cargo hold, its screen may crack.

Don't get in the habit of setting down a pen above the PowerBook's keyboard. One day, you'll close the lid and the pen will crack the screen. Then you'll get to use the pen to write a check for a new one.

Mouse pads

These squares of rubber protect furniture when you use a mouse, and according to their proponents, smooth mouse movement. They're just the thing if you're forced to set up shop on an antique desk. You can also make a mouse pad yourself from wet-suit neoprene or even a piece of clean cardboard, such as the backing of a pad of paper.

Antiglare screens

If you work near a bright window or under a bank of fluorescent lights, screen glare may take its toll on your eyes. Several firms make filters that attach to a monitor's screen. Some filters distort or blur the screen image, however, so be sure to evaluate several before buying one. It may be smarter to rearrange your work area or change its lighting to eliminate the glare. As you shop for screen filters, you encounter some that are advertised as reducing the low-frequency radiation that video tubes give off. There's little evidence that screen filters are effective at blocking monitor radiation.

A safer practice is to sit at arms' length from the front of the Mac's screen, at least four feet away from the sides or back of any other monitor. Keep that latter recommendation in mind if you work in an office: partitions and even walls don't stop low-frequency monitor radiation.

Typing desk

Many desks are too high for comfortable typing. To avoid back and neck strain, a typing desk should be roughly 27 inches high. Get a desk intended for typing, and avoid those so-called computer tables with shelves that place the screen at forehead level. To protect your neck and your ego, you should look down slightly on a computer.

Power Protection

Anyone who has watched an hour's worth of unsaved work vanish into the black hole of a darkened screen knows how traumatic a power failure can be. One minute you're hard at work, and the next you're staring stupefied at a blank piece of glass.

Mac Lesson Number One: The power to be your best exists only when there's power.

But of all the power problems that can occur, power failures constitute a relatively small percentage. A variety of gremlins lurk on the other side of a wall outlet, and some of them can turn a Mac's lights out for good. In the following sections, I look at the kinds of mishaps you may encounter and describe how susceptible your system is to them. Finally, I describe some add-ons that ensure the Mac a healthy flow of juice.

How the Mac uses power

The electricity that powers the Mac's chips, video tube, and other components is quite different from the current you get from a wall outlet. Most of the Mac's electronic components require small amounts of voltage — between 5 and 12 volts — but a wall outlet supplies roughly 120 volts (in the United States and Canada, that is; in Europe, 220 or 240 volts is standard, and elsewhere you may find either 120- or 220-volt systems).

What's more, the Mac's components require *direct current* (DC), while a wall outlet supplies *alternating current* (AC). DC travels continuously, while AC reverses its direction at regular intervals — generally, 60 times per second with 120-volt systems and 50 times per second with 220-volt systems.

All desktop Macs contain a power supply that turns AC voltage from the wall outlet into direct current at the voltage levels needed by the Mac. The power supply also contains filtering circuits that smooth variations in the original current.

A field guide to power problems

Those variations can cause problems. The electricity a power company supplies may seem like pretty consistent stuff, but it isn't. Its voltage fluctuates — sometimes dramatically — and it's prone to various types of *noise*, or interference. Figure 23-2 "Power Problems" illustrates the most common types of power flaws.

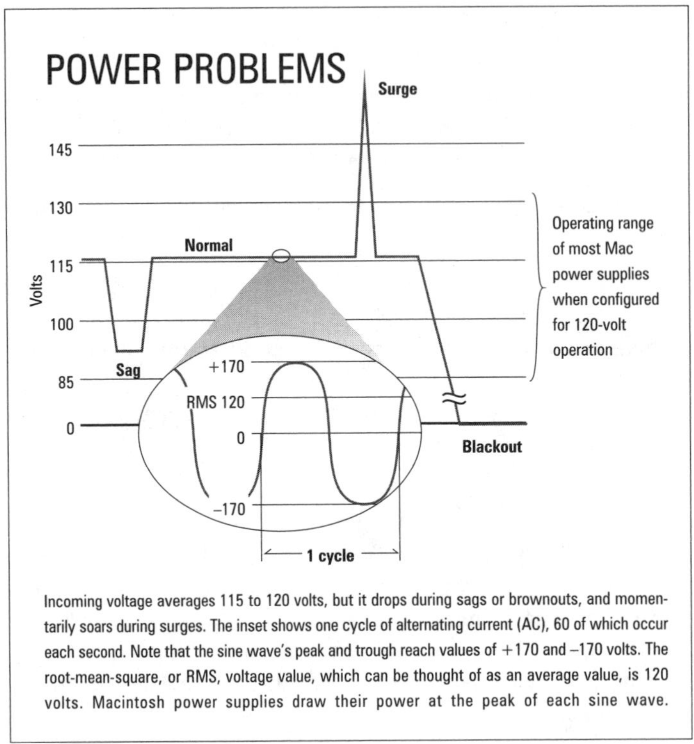

Incoming voltage averages 115 to 120 volts, but it drops during sags or brownouts, and momentarily soars during surges. The inset shows one cycle of alternating current (AC), 60 of which occur each second. Note that the sine wave's peak and trough reach values of +170 and –170 volts. The root-mean-square, or RMS, voltage value, which can be thought of as an average value, is 120 volts. Macintosh power supplies draw their power at the peak of each sine wave.

Figure 23-2: Power Problems

No power at all

Outages, or *blackouts*, occur when the power goes out completely. An overloaded circuit can cause a localized blackout in part of a house or building, while storms and downed power lines usually cause prolonged, area-wide outages. Momentary blackouts can also occur when a utility company switches between various power-distribution circuits while isolating a problem in the lines. Although such blackouts usually last only a fraction of a second, they can go on for several seconds (on the rural northern California coast where I live, longer ones are more common).

Not enough power

Sags occur when the voltage available at the wall outlet drops below roughly 105 volts. Also called *brownouts*, sags can occur when a sudden load is placed on a circuit — such as when an air conditioner or some other power glutton is turned on. Sags can also occur when an electric utility company lowers the voltage in order to reduce demands on its generating equipment during periods of peak usage, such as sweltering summer days and frigid winter nights. Sags generally don't damage the Mac, although a very large one can cause a system error.

Too much power

Surges occur when incoming voltage increases by astronomical amounts for a very brief period (on the order of a few milliseconds, or thousandths of a second). Surges, also called *transients* or *spikes*, can occur when lightning strikes in your vicinity or when the power comes back on after a blackout. Small surges (under 1,000 volts) can be caused by the electric motor in a refrigerator or other appliance turning off and are more common than large surges (1,000 volts or more). A large surge can damage anything that's connected to the circuit; a small one generally doesn't cause permanent damage but can produce a system error and some lost work. Surges as a whole are less common than sags.

Noisy power

Noise covers a range of flaws that affect the quality, not the quantity, of power present. A large electric motor can transmit noise into wiring that can interfere with radio or television equipment on the same circuit. This kind of noise, called *electromagnetic interference* (EMI), generally doesn't affect computer equipment.

The First Line of Defense

How vulnerable is the Mac to blackouts, sags, and surges? Judging from the number of power conditioning products available — and by the alarmist advertising that some manufacturers use — you may think that it's a sitting duck, ready to be humbled by the first surge or sag that comes down the wire.

Not so. The power supplies in the Mac family are designed with sags and surges in mind. Apple's power supplies are designed to work with as little as 85 volts, so the Mac shouldn't blink during brownouts. Mac power supplies can even provide enough juice to keep the machine running during a very brief blackout, the kind caused when utilities switch distribution networks. Apple's power supplies are designed to provide 20 milliseconds of current to a Mac running at what engineers call *full load* — all floppy and hard drive motors on, keyboard and mouse in use, all expansion slots filled, the processor hard at work, and all rear-panel connectors in use at the same time. Because a Mac rarely operates at full load, the power supply can carry you through an outage of a second or two — depending on what's connected to your Mac and how it's being used when the outage occurs.

All Macs are designed to withstand surges of up to 5,000 volts. Indeed, the power supplies in most computer equipment have at least some surge protection built in.

So the Mac's power supply tolerates low-voltage conditions and stands up to surges. Why, then, does an entire industry revolve around power protection? For one thing, no power supply provides enough juice to span an outage lasting more than a couple seconds. Also, surge resistance varies from one piece of equipment to the next; your Mac may withstand a surge, but can your modem, external hard drive, monitor, and scanner?

Many power-protection devices offer convenient features, such as a single switch that turns everything on and off or separate front-panel switches for each item plugged in to the device. Finally, there's the chicken-soup factor: a second stage of power filtering and surge protection can't hurt, and it may well help.

How Surge Suppressors Work

The most popular power-protection device is the *surge suppressor*, which you install between the wall outlet and your computer gear. It reduces incoming surges to innocuous voltage levels. Surge suppressors don't help when the power sags, but they are the least-expensive power protectors.

Surge suppressor considerations

When shopping for a surge suppressor, you face a barrage of jargon and a variety of features, some convenient, some essential. In the jargon department, the two most important specifications are *clamping voltage* and *response time*. The clamping voltage is the point at which the surge suppressor kicks in and starts suppressing; voltages below the clamping voltage are sent along to the equipment. Thus, the lower the clamping voltage, the better; a 340- to 400-volt clamping voltage is best.

Response time is the time required for the surge suppressor to close its electronic gate and prevent the surge from getting through. The faster the response time, the better, because it means that less of the surge sneaks through to the computer. Look for a response time of about 10 nanoseconds or less.

You may also see an *energy dissipation* specification. This term refers to how much juice the surge suppressor's circuitry can absorb before it fails and simply passes the surge on to ground, an event that doesn't harm your equipment but blows out the surge suppressor. Energy dissipation is measured in joules; the higher the value, the more durable the surge suppressor. Inexpensive surge suppressors generally absorb about 50 joules, while heavy-duty suppressors can absorb 300 or more joules.

The easy way to buy a suppressor

The easiest way to choose a good surge suppressor is to make sure that it meets Underwriters Laboratory (UL) specification 1449 (UL 1449 refers to a battery of torture tests, themselves described in another cleverly named document, IEEE 587). A suppressor that complies with IEEE 587 is desirable, but the UL 1449 designation is preferable because it means that an independent laboratory, not the suppressor manufacturer, tested the device. It isn't enough for a suppressor to simply be UL listed; look specifically for the UL 1449 designation.

Beyond technical specifications, you may want to consider other factors (see the Backgrounder box "A Guide to Surge Suppressor Features").

A Guide to Surge Suppressor Features

If you're in the market for a surge suppressor, look beyond the basics and determine whether the suppressor you're considering provides the features listed here.

- *Connections between hot, neutral, and ground* Inexpensive surge suppressors (in the $10 to $20 range) protect only between the hot (current-carrying) and the neutral wires of a wall outlet. For complete protection, you also need protection between the neutral wire and the ground wire (the round hole below the two rectangular ones on a wall outlet) and between hot and ground wires. This scheme is often described as providing three-way protection.
- *Modem protection* A lightning-induced surge can enter the phone lines and fry a modem. Some suppressors provide jacks for a modem or fax machine, a desirable feature for lightning-prone areas. Another UL designation, UL 497A, indicates that a suppressor can successfully protect such communications equipment.
- *Number of outlets* Most surge suppressors provide several outlets and must also provide a master power switch. Some also provide individual switches for each outlet. Some suppressors, such as Curtis Manufacturing Company's Curtis Command Center, are designed to sit beneath a monitor, providing a swivel base for it, and have a power switch for each outlet.
- *Failure alarm* A surge suppressor can fail after absorbing too large a surge; better units provide an alarm that indicates when the suppressor circuit has failed. An alarm may consist of an indicator light (handy if the suppressor is close to your system), an audible buzzer (good if the suppressor is under your desk, out of eyeshot), or both (best).

Complete Power Protectors

For protection against sags and brief blackouts as well as surges, you need a *standby power supply*, which installs between your equipment and the wall outlet and contains batteries that provide 5 to 30 minutes of power. That's more than enough power to span a brief outage or give you time to save and shut down during longer ones.

A standby power supply is often called an *uninterruptible power supply* (UPS), but in fact there's a difference between the two. With a UPS, computer equipment runs continuously from the power supply's batteries, which are constantly being recharged. By contrast, a standby power supply's batteries don't kick in until the power goes off (see Figure 23-3 "How Standby and Uninterruptible Power Supplies Work"). A standby power supply generally costs less than a true UPS and is just as reliable. A standby supply kicks in within milliseconds of an outage or sag, and as I mentioned earlier, the power supplies in your hardware continue to provide power during that period.

Matching the supply to the demand

The amount of power a standby supply can provide depends on what's connected to it. The greater the load on the supply, the faster its batteries discharge. What's more, if you exceed a standby supply's current rating, you eventually blow a fuse in the supply. (Better-quality supplies have overload indicators that light when you're drawing too much current.) Thus, it's important to match the supply to your hardware.

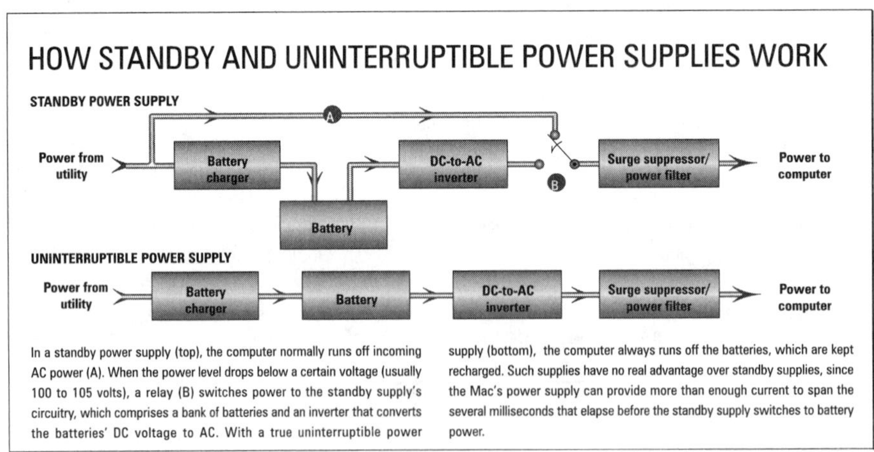

In a standby power supply (top), the computer normally runs off incoming AC power (A). When the power level drops below a certain voltage (usually 100 to 105 volts), a relay (B) switches power to the standby supply's circuitry, which comprises a bank of batteries and an inverter that converts the batteries' DC voltage to AC. With a true uninterruptible power supply (bottom), the computer always runs off the batteries, which are kept recharged. Such supplies have no real advantage over standby supplies, since the Mac's power supply can provide more than enough current to span the several milliseconds that elapse before the standby supply switches to battery power.

Figure 23-3: How Standby and Uninterruptible Power Supplies Work

Standby and uninterruptible power supplies are usually rated in *volt-amps.* A unit rated at approximately 100 volt-amps powers a typical Mac Classic with a hard drive for at least 15 minutes. Such supplies generally cost between $200 and $400. For a modular Mac machine with a color monitor, you need a supply that provides 300 to 400 volt-amps, at a cost of $400 to $500. For a 19-inch monitor, make that at least 400 to 500 volt-amps and $500 to $700. Add another 100 volt-amps to include an external hard drive or tape backup device.

Printers need not apply

Don't bother providing standby power to your laser printer: You need a supply rated at 1,000 volt-amps or more, and they cost between $1,000 and $2,000. And given the fact that you don't lose any work when the laser printer loses power anyway, it makes more sense to simply protect the printer from surges.

Tips for Power Supply Shoppers

Many of the shopping considerations behind surge suppressors apply to standby power supplies, too. Some supplies provide only one rear-panel outlet; others provide several. Some can sit beneath a Mac or a monitor, while others are designed to sit on the floor. The better ones have several indicator lights that warn you when you're overloading the supply, when your electrical wiring is faulty, and when you're running on battery power.

Supplies for servers

More sophisticated supplies provide an interface connector that lets you attach the supply to the Mac's modem or printer port so that the supply can convey status information to the Mac. Such a feature is most useful when you want standby power for a network file server.

If you want standby power for an AppleShare network file server, consider pairing one of American Power Conversion's power supplies with the company's PowerChute software. These well-designed supplies provide interface connectors that can attach to the server Mac's modem port. The PowerChute software monitors the status information; when the power fails and the power supply kicks in, PowerChute sends a warning to all Macs connected to the server telling them how long the server remains available.

If the power doesn't return before the standby power is exhausted, all users are safely logged off the server, which is then shut down normally. Of course, only users who weren't victimized by the outage — or who have their own standby power supplies — see the on-screen warning message, but the warning is only half the value of PowerChute anyway. What's equally important is that the server is safely shut down for you.

Avoid square-wave supplies

Before buying a standby power supply, make sure that it provides either *sine-wave* or *stepped-square wave* output. Inexpensive standby supplies often provide *square-wave* output, which causes considerable electrical stress to monitors and hard drives that can make them wear out faster. Sine-wave output is the most desirable because that's what wall outlets normally supply.

How long will you stand by me?

Finally, be aware that after several years, you need to replace your standby power supply's batteries, which can cost up to 30 percent of the supply's original price. You may want to investigate replacement costs before selecting a unit.

More Power Tips

In this box are some additional tips for avoiding lost work due to power problems.

Check your wiring

Neither a surge suppressor nor a standby power supply can help if your electrical wiring is faulty. Make sure that your wall outlets' third-wire ground holes are connected to a good earth ground. (Check the point where the electrical service enters your house; you should find a copper rod driven into the ground with a heavy wire connecting it to your wiring.)

Also be sure that your hot and neutral lines are wired properly. You can check them yourself by using an inexpensive *line checker* such as Radio Shack's catalog number 22-101. (American Power Conversion's standby supplies contain line-checking features.) To be extra sure, however, double-check with an electrician or your local utility company.

Don't use ground eliminators

Avoid ground eliminators — those little adapters that let you plug a three-pronged power cord into the two-conductor outlets that many older buildings have. Defeating the ground conductor makes the Mac more susceptible to power surges. Have an electrician install a properly grounded, three-conductor outlet.

Unplug during lightning storms

The best way to protect equipment against lightning-induced power surges is to unplug the Mac and everything connected to it during a lightning storm. (Don't forget to unplug the modem from the telephone lines.) A lightning bolt is the ultimate surge; don't count on a surge suppressor to protect you from it.

Save and save often

In the end, one of the best ways to avoid losing work because of power problems is free. Simply follow the advice that Fred Parker, a power-supply veteran at Apple, passed along to me — save often.

Standby power supplies provide more complete protection than surge suppressors but are far less popular. One reason is their cost; another is that they provide only a brief reprieve from darkness. Still, if your power is as unreliable as mine, that reprieve can be priceless. The glow of a Mac screen in an otherwise darkened room is a heartening sight — especially if you haven't saved recently.

Squeezing More Juice from a PowerBook

The new 500-series PowerBooks have the best power features of all PowerBooks to date. Still, battery power is like money: you can't have too much. With this greedy sentiment in mind, here are some tips for extending the life of a PowerBook's battery charge.

Turn down backlighting

Backlighting helps make PowerBook screens as legible as they are, but it's also a major drain on battery power. Consider turning backlighting off and working under a bright light or with your back to a window. You extend battery life significantly.

An easy way to control backlighting is with the PowerBook Display control panel that debuted with System 7.1 (see Figure 23-4 "Controlling Backlighting"). The PowerBook Display control panel turns off backlighting after a specified period of inactivity. The PowerBook control panel that accompanies the 500-series PowerBooks also provides backlight control.

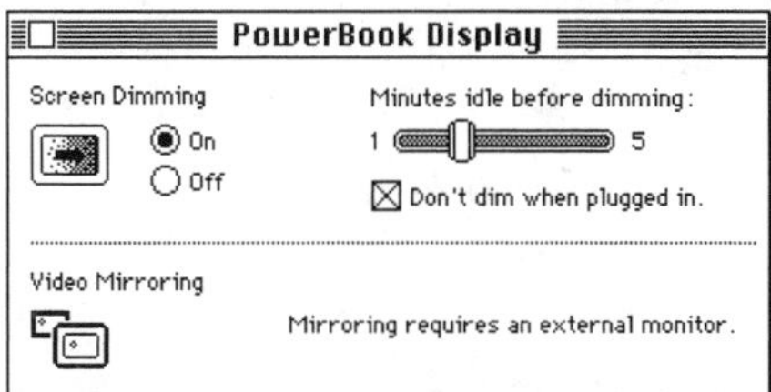

Figure 23-4: Controlling Backlighting The PowerBook Display control panel turns off backlighting after a specified period of inactivity. PowerBook utility packages such as Connectix PowerBook Utilities provide more sophisticated backlight-control options.

When Is It Normal to Not Be Compatible?

The latest PowerBooks have just one serial port, which you can use as a LocalTalk network port or to connect a serial device such as an external modem.

But configuring this dual-personality port isn't always straightforward. If you're using a serial printer such as an Apple StyleWriter and your PowerBook contains the Global Village PowerPort Mercury modem — the modem included in PowerBook 500-series machines sold in the United States — open the PowerBook Setup control panel and select Normal. If your PowerBook contains the Apple Express Modem, open the Express Modem control panel and choose the Use External Modem option; then open the PowerBook Setup control panel and select Normal. (The other option is Compatible — apparently Apple believes it isn't normal to be compatible.)

If you have a PowerBook 200-series machine, you must use the Chooser to turn off AppleTalk. (So much for using LocalTalk to share a StyleWriter connected to a PowerBook.) You don't have to disable AppleTalk on other one-port PowerBooks, nor do you have to disable AppleTalk if you're using the PowerBook's Ethernet connector.

Note that some older Apple printer drivers (such as the StyleWriter II's) show both printer and modem port icons when you select the driver in the Chooser. When faced with this inaccurate list of options, select the modem port icon. Newer drivers display a combined modem/printer port icon.

Tips for the PowerBook control panel

Apple has shipped two basic versions of the PowerBook control panel. The version that debuted with System 7.1 provided a bare-bones interface designed to shield you from the ugly technicalities of power management. The problem was, it didn't help you understand the kinds of activities and work habits that affect battery life.

Apple learned its lesson, and the latest PowerBook control panel lets you choose between easy and custom power-management options (see Figure 23-5 "Comparing PowerBook Control Panels").

For more control over performance and battery usage, click the old PowerBook control panel's Options button to display the Options dialog box. In the new PowerBook control panel, click the Custom switch in the upper-right corner of the control panel's window.

Controlling processor cycling and speed on older PowerBooks

PowerBooks prior to the 500-series models offer two additional power-saving options.

❖ *Processor Cycling* The PowerBook's processor can turn itself off when you aren't using the computer. The moment you move the trackball or touch a key, the processor turns itself back on. When processor cycling is off — when you

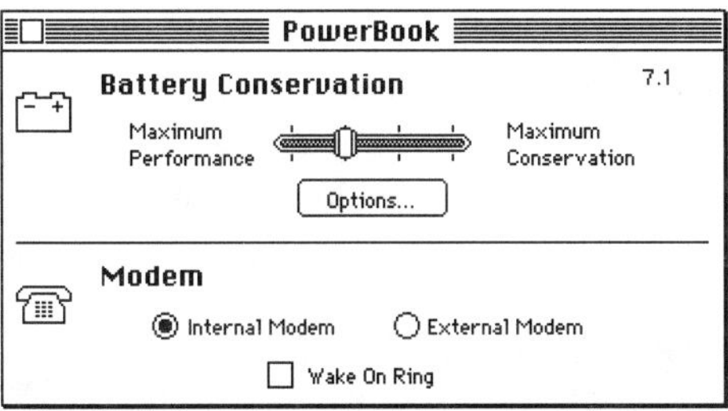

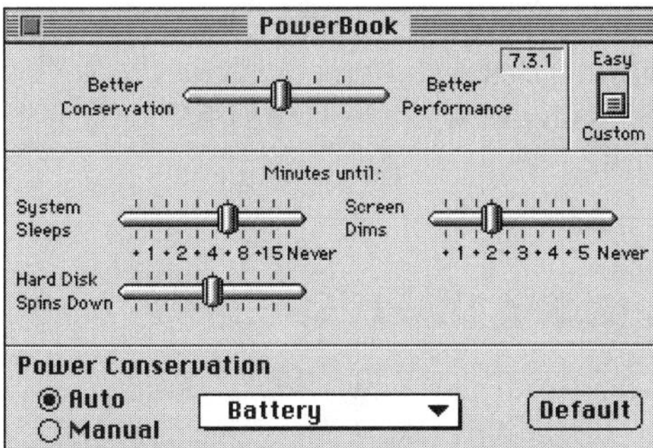

Figure 23-5: Comparing PowerBook Control Panels
Apple has shipped two versions of the PowerBook control panel. The older version is shown at top, the newer version at bottom.

select the Don't Allow Cycling button on the older PowerBook control panel or when you uncheck Allow Processor Cycling on the new PowerBook control panel — the processor remains on all the time. Select the Allow Cycling option for maximum battery life.

- *Processor Speed* Faster PowerBook models such as the 160, 170, and 180 can save battery power by slowing their processors down to 16MHz. With the old PowerBook control panel, select the Reduced Speed button to activate this option. With the new PowerBook control panel, check the Reduced Processor Speed button.

More ways to save power

Here are a few final tips for prolonging battery life.

Don't use System 7 virtual memory

At least not when you're running under battery power. Virtual memory forces the PowerBook to access its hard disk more frequently. Use a RAM disk as your startup disk. As the preceding chapter mentioned, the PowerBook's Memory control panel lets you set up a RAM disk.

Quit your telecom program

And for PowerBooks with modems: when you finish a communications session, quit your communications program. When a communications program is running — even if you aren't actually connected — the PowerBook's modem draws power.

Turn off AppleTalk

Doing so saves power and lets the PowerBook wake up faster. You may want to have AppleTalk turned on when you restart and then turn it off. That way you can turn AppleTalk on and off without restarting. (If AppleTalk is turned off when you start up a computer, certain system software doesn't get loaded, and you must restart to activate AppleTalk. Note that if you have the PowerBook File Assistant extension installed, AppleTalk is always available, thus avoiding the need to restart the system to activate AppleTalk.)

Saving Energy with Desktop Macs

Conserving energy isn't just a good idea for PowerBooks. Businesses and homeowners can cut their electric bills by taking advantage of the power-saving features built into many monitors and Mac models, and provided by several utility software packages. And it isn't bad for the planet, either.

Not watching the monitor? Turn it off!

Most of Apple's monitors provide built-in energy saving features that turn off the monitor after a period of inactivity. Apple monitors that support this feature include the Apple ColorPlus 14-inch Display, newer versions of the Macintosh Color Display (its part number is M1198LL/B), the AudioVision 14 and 17, and the Multiple Scan 15, 17, and 20. (Many third-party monitors have similar features.)

Apple monitors that provide power-down features include a control panel, called Energy Saver, that lets you specify how much time elapses before the light goes out (see Figure 23-6 "The Ultimate Screen Saver"). After the interval elapses, the control panel tells the Mac to stop sending horizontal and vertical sync signals to the monitor. When the aforementioned monitors lose these signals, they shut off. (If you happen to be watching, you might see the image scramble as the monitor dims — that's because it lost those sync signals.)

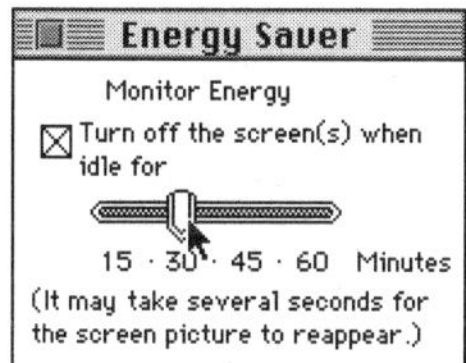

Figure 23-6: The Ultimate Screen Saver The Energy Saver control panel included with Apple monitors will turn off a Mac's monitor after a specified period of inactivity. When you move the mouse or hit a key, the monitor comes back on.

Tips for the Auto Power On/Off control panel

As mentioned in the previous chapter, this control panel lets you specify that the Mac turn itself on and off at intervals you specify. Here are some ways you might put it to work.

- **For the forgetful.** If you sometimes forget to turn your office Mac off before going home for the night, use this control panel to force the issue — specify that the Mac shut itself off during the evening.
- **For unattended backups.** Auto Power On/Off can also be handy for performing unattended backups or other time-consuming tasks. Create a script for a backup session and stash it in your System Folder's Startup Items folder; then use Auto Power On/Off to have the Mac turn itself on in the middle of the night and then off an hour or so later. When it does, the script runs, the backup takes place, and the Mac goes back to sleep.
- **For remote access.** You're going on the road, but you're taking along a PowerBook and plan to access your desktop Mac using Apple Remote Access. Specify that Auto Power On/Off turn your Mac on for several hours each day, and confine your remote-access activities to that window of opportunity (see Figure 23-7 "Work Schedule").

Third-party energy savers

Some third-party screen saver packages include monitor shut-off features. Berkeley Systems' After Dark 3's is called EcoLogic, and has two stages of operation: the first shuts off the monitor after a specified period of inactivity, while the second shuts down the Mac. EcoLogic even estimates how much money you will save in a year—and adjusts its estimate as you adjust sleep intervals.

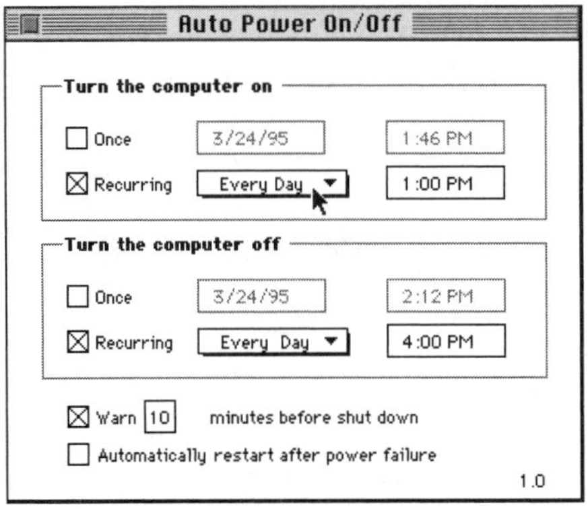

Figure 23-7: Work Schedule With the Auto Power On/Off control panel, your Mac can turn itself on and off at regular intervals or at specific times. Here, the control panel is set to turn the Mac on for a few hours each day.

Then there's Sophisticated Circuits' PowerKey, discussed in Chapter 16, Backgrounder box "More Ways to Put Modems and Telephony to Work." PowerKey includes a control panel that lets you schedule automatic power-up and power-down for not only the Mac but up to three peripherals.

Desktop Macs that go to sleep

The Power Mac 7200, 7500, and 8500 are the first desktop Macs to provide a variety of energy-saving, PowerBook-like sleep modes. These Macs include a greatly enhanced Energy Saver control panel that let you power down the monitor, spin down the hard drive, and put the entire machine to sleep (see Figure 23-8 "The Sleeping Beauty").

In full sleep mode, the 7200 uses less than 30 watts of electricity but springs back to life when you hit a key, move the mouse, or receive an incoming fax call. (The 7500 and 8500 use slightly more.) These features not only help cut energy costs, they make the computer more convenient—it takes less time for the computer to wake up than it does to start up from scratch.

These sleep features also make some of the telephony applications I discussed in Chapter 16 more practical. It's wasteful to leave a desktop computer on all the time just to answer phone calls or receive faxes, but a Mac with energy-saving features can stay asleep until a call actually comes in.

Figure 23-8: The Sleeping Beauty The Energy Saver control panel is the key to the Power Mac 7200, 7500, and 8500 sleep mode. Top: In its simplist mode, Energy Saver lets you specify a sleep interval. To have the Mac shut down instead of sleep, check the Shut Down Instead of Sleeping box. Middle: Click the Show Details button, and you can specify separate intervals for the hard drive and the display. Bottom: To schedule startups and shutdowns, click the Scheduled Startup & Shutdown button.

Tips for the Energy Saver control panel

As Figure 23-8 shows, the Energy Saver control panel's Show Details button reveals separate sleep settings for the monitor and hard drive. Here are some ways you might want to use the two options:

- Monitor. A video display generally uses more juice than the rest of the Mac system, so this might be the device you specify the shortest sleep interval for.
- Hard drive. It doesn't use a lot of juice, but it does make noise. Setting a sleep interval for it will help cut noise pollution in your home, classroom, or office. But it does take several seconds for the drive to spin back up to speed, so you might not want to make the interval too brief.

Alternative Ways to Power a PowerBook

PowerBooks are designed around power conservation, so using one instead of a desktop Mac saves energy right off the bat. Combine a PowerBook with one of the products I'm about to describe to save even more energy.

Running using 12-volt power

Most home alternative-energy products — solar panels, windmills, and the like — generate 12 volts of juice that charges car batteries, which in turn supply power to lights and appliances. You can run a PowerBook from a 12-volt power source using a Lind Electronic Design Automobile Power Adapter, which converts 12-volt DC into the lower-voltage DC required by a PowerBook. (One of these gems enabled me to work through a four-day power outage last January.) A model that powers an Apple StyleWriter printer lists for $49. The PowerBook 100-series and Duo versions costs $69, while the PowerBook 500-series model is $99.

You can also use a DC-to-AC inverter to power equipment from a 12-volt source. Radio Shack sells a variety of inverters, including big honkers that will power a small desktop Mac and monitor. Statpower's Notepower is a compact, 6-ounce inverter that generates enough juice to run a PowerBook using the AC adapter.

Running from the Sun

You can get one step closer to the ultimate power source with Keep It Simple Systems' (800/327-6882) Solar System series — solar panels that, in direct sun, generate enough juice to power a PowerBook. (On cloudy days, they can at least trickle-charge the battery.) The $229 Neptune model I tested was thoughtfully designed: closed, it's an 8- by 14-inch nylon case less than an inch thick. Open it flat, and two amorphous silicon panels begin delivering 8.4 volts to a 10-foot cable that you plug into the PowerBook's adaptor jack. Models are available for all PowerBooks (and other laptops) as well as for Newtons.

Don't Zap Your Mac!

Static electricity can be more disastrous to an integrated circuit than heat. If you've just shuffled across a wool carpet on a dry winter day, touch a metal light switch plate, a radiator, or a cat's nose before touching the Mac. That's especially vital if you're about to install or remove a memory upgrade or an expansion board.

The closer you get to integrated circuit chips, the more important being static-free is. If you live in a static-prone area (one where the humidity is very low), consider using an antistatic wrist strap, available through most computer dealers and mail-order houses, when working with your Mac's innards.

Static electricity can also zap disks, scrambling just enough information to make the disk unreadable. Speaking of floppy disks, they warrant special care, which, as Chapter 26 describes, boils down to no heat, no dust, no bending, and no magnetic fields. And if you have an old Mac and an external floppy disk drive, don't set it to the left of a Mac Plus or SE (near its power supply), near a telephone with a mechanical ringer, or underneath a high-intensity desk lamp (the kind with a transformer in its base). These items generate magnetic fields that can cause disk errors.

CHAPTER 23 CONCEPTS AND TERMS

- A Mac's solid-state electronics are durable and reliable, but you can help their health by keeping your machine clean and cool.
- The mechanical components of the keyboard and mouse are especially prone to damage from dust and liquids. Canned air can keep dust out of the keyboard. Clean the mouse ball and rollers with a cotton swab moistened with tape head cleaner or alcohol.
- Some people believe that regular floppy drive cleaning helps prevent disk errors, while others believe that you should leave drives alone unless they act up. I'm from the latter camp.
- Improper cleaning of your screen can damage its nonglare coating. Use only lint-free tissues and cleaning fluid made for computer screens.
- If you're prone to wrist pain and other keyboard-related injuries, consider a special keyboard such as Apple's Adjustable Keyboard — if your dealer gives you the option to return the keyboard if you aren't happy with it.
- Tilt-and-swivel stands, mouse pads, wrist rests, antiglare screens, and computer furniture are among the accessories you can buy to create a comfortable working environment.
- To avoid repetitive-stress injuries, limber up before working by performing a few simple hand exercises. And stand up and stretch regularly.
- To avoid damaging the Mac's circuitry with a static charge, touch a grounded metal object before working inside the Mac, or consider using an antistatic wrist strap.
- The most common power problems are blackouts (no power), sags (lowered voltage), surges (brief but significant increases in voltage), and noise (poor quality power).
- Apple's power supplies are designed to provide some protection against sags, surges, and noise, but they don't offer protection for other hardware you may have, such as a modem or printer.
- The most popular and least expensive power-protection device is the surge suppressor, which reduces incoming surges to harmless voltage levels.
- The two most important surge suppressor specifications are the clamping voltage and the response time.
- For protection against blackouts and sags, you can use a standby power supply, which contains batteries that provide enough power (usually 5 to 30 minutes' worth) for you to save your work and shut down.

General Terms:

disk drive cleaning kit
A kit usually consisting of a disk-like item containing a circular pad of fiber-based cleaning material. You moisten the pad with cleaning fluid, insert it in the holder, and put the holder in the drive, where it spins like a disk and cleans the heads.

mouse pad
A square of rubber that protects furniture when using a mouse and also supposedly smooths mouse movement.

processor cycling
A PowerBook feature that enables the PowerBook's processor to turn itself off when you aren't using the computer. The moment you move the trackball or touch a key, the processor turns itself back on.

repetitive-stress injury
A term that covers a wide range of health problems caused by performing the same task over and over again. The most common RSI is carpal-tunnel syndrome, an inflammation of the carpal tendon where it passes through the wrist.

surge suppressor
A device designed to protect the Mac from power surges — very brief but potentially damaging increases in the power company's voltage.

tilt-and-swivel stand
An accessory that lets you raise the Mac's monitor and tilt it to a more comfortable viewing angle.

Power-Protection Terms

clamping voltage
In a surge suppressor, the point at which the surge suppressor kicks in and starts suppressing. Voltages below the clamping voltage are sent along to the equipment. Thus, the lower the clamping voltage, the better; a 340- to 400-volt clamping voltage is best.

power supply
A component present in all computers and peripherals that turns alternating current (AC) from the wall outlet into direct current (DC) at the voltage levels needed by the device. The power supply also contains filtering circuits that smooth variations in the original current.

response time
In a surge suppressor, the time required for the surge suppressor to close its electronic gate and prevent the surge from getting through. The faster the response time, the better, because less of the surge sneaks through to the computer.

(continued on the next page)

(continued from previous page)

sag
A power problem that occurs when the voltage available at the wall outlet drops below roughly 105 volts. Also called *brownouts,* sags can occur when a sudden load is placed on a circuit — such as when an air conditioner or some other power glutton is turned on.

standby power supply
A peripheral that installs between your equipment and the wall outlet and contains batteries that provide from 5 to 30 minutes of power.

surge
A power problem that occurs when incoming voltage increases by astronomical amounts for a very brief period (on the order of a few milliseconds, or thousandths of a second). Surges, also called *transients* or *spikes,* can occur when lightning strikes in your vicinity or when the power comes back on after a blackout.

surge suppressor
An add-on that installs between the wall outlet and your computer gear and reduces incoming surges to innocuous voltage levels.

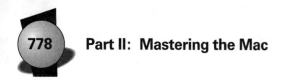

CHAPTER TWENTY-FOUR

The World of Utilities and ResEdit

- Making your computing life easier with utilities
- Putting the Mac on autopilot with macro and scripting utilities
- Extending battery life with PowerBook utilities
- Customizing programs using Apple's ResEdit utility

Utilities are the spice of computing life. I refer not to the local telephone or gas company, but to utility software — programs that make using the Mac easier and more convenient. Utilities form the supporting cast of a computer setup; they work together with the Mac's system software and with your application programs to improve the Mac's performance and enhance its operation.

Try Some of the Mac World's Best Utilities

You'll find a wonderful variety of utilities on the *Macworld Power User Clinic* CD. Among them:

- ❖ Conflict Catcher III. A three-day trial version of Casady & Greene's extension manager. If you have a Power Mac, run this program *now* to see if your computer is being slowed down by extensions.
- ❖ theTypeBook. The full version of Jim Lewis's wonderful font utility.
- ❖ StuffIt Lite. A full working version of Aladdin Systems' famous file-compression utility.
- ❖ Tech Tool. This utility from the Mac repair experts at MicroMat Computer Systems will save, zap, and restore the contents of your Mac's parameter RAM, that special, battery-powered area of memory that stores important information about your system settings — and that can cause system problems if it gets corrupted. See Chapter 28 for details on this great utility.
- ❖ EMMPathy. This utility from the PowerBook pros at VST Technologies can fix the problem that PowerBook 500-series batteries can suffer from if allowed to discharge completely. It, too, is described in Chapter 28.
- ❖ And more. You'll find dozens of great free and shareware utilities in the Best of BMUG collection.

Utilities for Less

Although a large selection of commercial utilities is available, the best place to shop for utilities, extensions, and desk accessories may be a user group or on-line service. While most large software publishers have concentrated on full-blown applications, Mac programming hobbyists and small software firms have churned out more utilities than Dick Clark has TV shows. Here's a small sampling of the most popular free or shareware utilities.

- *Boomerang* by Hiroaki Yamamoto — enhances the Mac's Open and Save dialog boxes with options that let you navigate files and folders quickly. An improved version of Boomerang, SuperBoomerang, is included with Now Software's Now Utilities — along with such goodies as an extension manager, a pop-up menu utility, an Open and Save dialog box enhancer, a menu bar clock, and much more.
- *Compact Pro* by Bill Goodman — a compression utility similar to the StuffIt series.
- *Floppy Fixer* by Frank Beatrous — recovers files from damaged disks.
- *Just Click* by Luis Bardi — lets you switch between programs by clicking on the application menu (as you can with the old System 6 MultiFinder).
- *PwrSwitcher* by David B. Lamkins — lets you switch between programs by pressing the power-on key present on all Apple Desktop Bus keyboards.
- *PowerBar* by Scott Johnson — Similar to the commercial package Square One, it lets you create a palette of icons for convenient program and document opening. Its programmer also happens to live on a street named Macintosh Lane.
- *Sample Editor* by Garrick McFarlane — provides sound-editing features similar to those of Macromedia's SoundEdit series.
- *System 7 Pack* by Adam Stein — provides numerous ways to modify the System 7 Finder.
- *DeskPicture* by Clay Maeckel — replaces the desktop pattern with a PICT image.
- *miniWriter* by David Dunham — a simple text editor desk accessory. Another popular DA word processor is the shareware McSink by John Carpenter. Preferred Publisher's Vantage is a commercial version of McSink with more features.
- *SuperClock* by Steve Christensen — adds a digital clock, calendar, and stopwatch to the Mac's menu bar. It's built into System 7.5.
- *Switch-A-Roo* by Bill Steinberg — lets you switch between any two video modes (such as color and black and white) without having to use the Monitors control panel. (QuicKeys includes an extension, ScreenEase, that provides the same convenience.)
- *AppDisk* by Mark Adams — lets you create a RAM disk and resize it without having to restart the Mac. For details on AppDisk and RAM disks in general, see Chapters 22 and 23.
- *Apollo* by Jeremy Roussak — adds a menu that lets you quickly open often-used applications or documents. Apollo also has teriffic features for changing monitor settings, hiding application windows when you switch programs, and more.
- *ApplWindows* by Hiroaki Yamamoto — modifies the System 7 application menu to not only let you switch programs, but to switch to a specific document window within a given program.
- *Doohickeys* by Jim Luther — a series of small utilities that, among other things, let you eject a cartridge drive without having to shut down System 7 file sharing.
- *ZipIt* by Tommy Brown — a file compression utility that lets you expand and compress ZIP-format archives, the most popular compression format in the DOS/Windows world.

Want to customize your favorite programs' keyboard shortcuts? Need help managing the files on your hard disk? Longing for a way to resurrect that file you accidentally threw away? Want to customize the colors your Mac displays? Need an easy way to move files between programs or between a Mac and a DOS PC? Want to extend the life of your PowerBook's battery charge?

Utilities can perform these feats and many more. In this chapter, I examine the most popular categories of utility software and spotlight several products from each group. Because there's such an abundance of utilities for the Mac, I don't have room to mention each one; so if I leave out a particular program, don't assume it's under par. Computer dealers, user groups, and mail-order software advertisements are good places to learn about the gamut of utilities available in each class. For a look at some first-rate free and shareware utilities, see the Backgrounder box "Utilities for Less."

How Utilities Work

Utilities can provide their Mac-enhancing benefits in several ways. Utilities that work together with your application programs may operate as extensions or as desk accessories (sometimes called DAs, these small programs are usually accessed from the Apple menu).

Utilities may also take the form of *FKEYs*, those small software routines you run by pressing ⌘-Shift along with a number key.

Utilities may also work as *control panels* (cdevs), which show up in the Control Panels folder (see Figure 24-1 "Gaining Control").

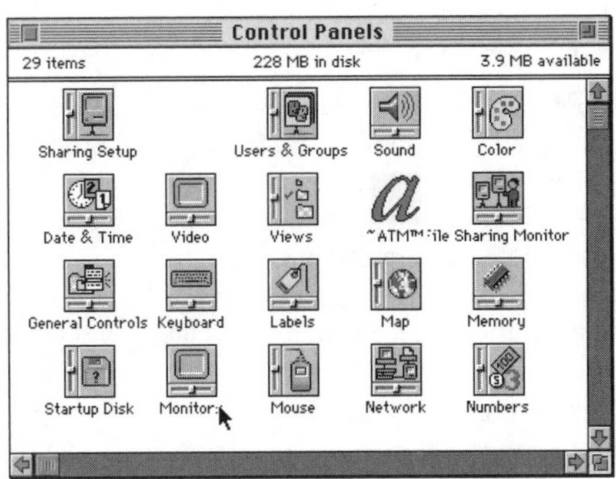

Figure 24-1: Gaining Control Some utilities are control panels, also called cdevs. In System 7, control panels live in the Control Panels folder located in the System Folder.

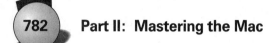

Important Information About Power Macs and Extensions: The Patching Problem

Shortly after the first Power Macs shipped, it became clear there was a problem — a lot of popular utilities, including CE Software's QuicKeys and many screen savers, could slow the machines dramatically.

This problem occurs with utilities that install a large number of patches to tap into the inner workings of the Mac's system software. When these patches are written in the language of the 68000-family processors — and with all pre-Power Mac utilities, they are — they bypass the native-mode system software routines that they're patching, forcing the Power Mac to spend a greater portion of its time running in emulation mode. That can mean slow performance — even when you're running native-mode applications. I've heard of cases where a single startup file caused as much as a forty percent decrease in performance.

How can you tell if a given utility installs these patches? First of all, look for the "Accelerated for Power Macintosh" sticker on the box — if it's there, you know the utility runs in native mode and won't slow down the Power Mac.

Otherwise, just install Casady & Greene's Conflict Catcher III utility. Conflict Catcher III can analyze your startup files and create a report detailing which files install 68K patches over native-mode code — and how many patches they install. It's a great way to performance-tune your Power Mac. (Thanks, Casady & Greene!) Conflict Catcher III, needless to say, runs in native mode.

A full version of Conflict Catcher III is included on the CD that came with this book; it works for three days and then disables itself.

Extensions and DAs

Extensions (which you may also hear referred to as INITs) reside in your hard disk's System Folder and load into memory when the Mac starts up (see Chapter 22). A desk accessory or extension may also add its own menu to the Mac's menu bar.

Utilities that operate as extensions or desk accessories have one common characteristic: Their benefits can surface in any application, from a word processor to a CAD program. One example of an application-spanning extension is Apple's PC Exchange, which lets SuperDrive-equipped Macs access floppies formatted for DOS PCs. An example from the desk accessory camp is Apple's Notepad, which lets you store text notes. And an example from the FKEY camp is the snapshot FKEY, which creates a file containing the Mac's screen image when you press ⌘-Shift-3.

Installation techniques

The way in which you install these application cohorts depends on the type of utility. As Chapter 22 describes, you install an extension by copying it to the System Folder of your startup disk. The Finder stashes it in the Extensions folder (inside the System Folder) after asking you for confirmation.

Utilities that work alone

Instead of working together with your applications, some utilities perform their work alone. Separate applications you start from the Finder are often self-contained job specialists that perform specific tasks, such as backing up hard disks, resurrecting lost files, or transferring files between Macs and other computers.

A well-stocked utility toolkit combines programs from both camps. You're likely to use extensions to enhance your Mac's overall operation, and applications or desk accessories to perform specific tasks.

Navigation Copilots

As you become experienced with the Mac, you start wishing for easier ways to control your programs. You may long for more keyboard shortcuts to eliminate reaching for the mouse. Or you may want to automate frequently performed tasks, such as quitting one program, starting another, choosing a command, and then typing some text. Navigation utilities let you streamline the Mac's operation to suit your work habits and preferences.

Macro utilities

For creating keyboard shortcuts and automating repetitive tasks, use a *macro* or *keyboard enhancement* utility such as Affinity Microsystems' Tempo II Plus or CE Software's QuicKeys. Both let you record and play back keystrokes and mouse movements, and QuicKeys also lets you choose from a roster of built-in shortcuts, such as scrolling to the beginning or the end of a document. I discuss these and other automation utilities in detail later in this chapter.

Iconic launching pads

If you prefer mouse clicking to key stroking, you can create a basic program- or document-launching pad with the Launcher control panel that comes with System 7.5 and Performa models.

A more sophisticated launch pad utility is Binary Software's Square One, which lets you create palettes containing the icons of frequently used documents and programs. Square One also teams up nicely with QuicKeys: you can configure icons so that they execute QuicKeys macros when clicked.

Program and document launchers

If you frequently quit one program and start another, consider Icom Simulations' On Cue II. On Cue II adds a menu to the right edge of the menu bar in which you can add the names of frequently used applications and documents, and then open

them by simply choosing their names. You can even configure On Cue II to display its menu at the mouse pointer's location when you click the mouse while pressing ⌘ and Option — a boon for large-screen users who get tired of making the long trip to the menu bar. (The shareware Apollo provides many of these same features — and then some.)

Lost in Disk Space

Hard disks can be hard work. It's great having megabytes of fast storage on tap, but as a hard disk fills up, managing its contents becomes increasingly difficult.

Fortunately, an entire class of utilities is devoted to simplifying life for hard-disk owners. Take a common problem — the inability to locate a file that you know is sitting somewhere on your hard drive. System 7's Find command is handy and System 7.5's Find File desk accessory is better still. But to complement these tools, consider a disk manager such as PrairieSoft's DiskTop, Aladdin Systems' Desktop Tools, and Working Software's Findswell.

Surrogate Finder

DiskTop mimics many functions of the Finder (see Figure 24-2 "Surrogate Finder"). It lets you copy, rename, and delete files, as well as start programs and open documents. It also lets you copy, rename, and delete files, as well as start programs and open documents and search for files according to a variety of criteria — indeed, a wider variety than the Finder allows.

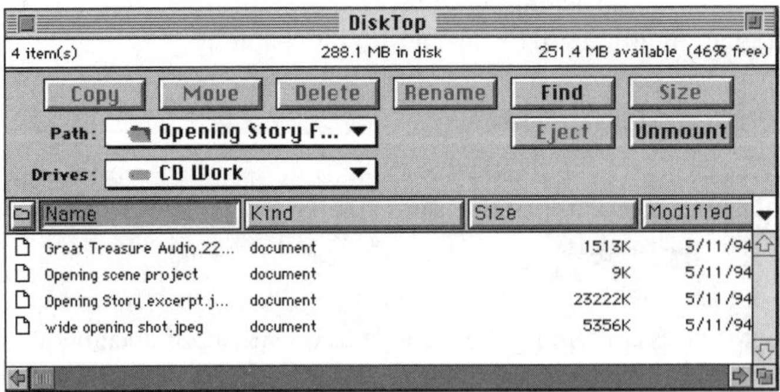

Figure 24-2: Surrogate Finder PrairieSoft's DiskTop enables you to manage disks, start programs, search for files, and open documents without having to return to the Finder.

For example, you can search for all text-only files larger than 10K created by a program other than Microsoft Word between January 1 and January 15. DiskTop program provides some navigation benefits, too, enabling you to quit one program and start another without returning to the Finder. A working version of DiskTop is included on the CD that accompanies this book.

Finding files within dialog boxes

Shortcut (part of Aladdin's Desktop Tools) and Findswell offer an even more convenient way to locate files. Both utilities are extensions that modify the standard Open dialog box all Mac programs use — a logical place to put file-searching features (unless you need to locate a file when using the Finder, whose Open command doesn't display the standard dialog box). Findswell adds a small button; click it, and a dialog box for searching appears. Shortcut turns the disk name that appears above the Eject and Drive buttons into a menu whose commands let you search for files, create new folders, and more.

You can find similar dialog box enhancers in two other utility packages. Symantec's Norton Utilities for the Macintosh includes a dialog box enhancer called Directory Assistance, and Now Software's Now Utilities includes one called Super-Boomerang.

Phrase finders

The aforementioned file ferrets are useful only when you know part or all of the filename you're looking for. When you don't, consider a text-retrieval utility such as Alki Software's Alki Seek, On Technology's On Location, or Virginia Systems' Sonar Professional or Sonar Text Retrieval System. These utilities can search for text contained *within* files. Alki Seek can also search for files based on their names, types, creation dates, and other attributes.

(And don't forget about the System 7.5 Find File trick from Chapter 22: press Option while opening the criteria pop-up menu, and you can search, albeit slowly, for text within files.)

Besides offering another way to locate lost files, a text-retrieval utility can turn the Mac into a powerful research tool. An attorney, for example, may use one to search case-history files for references to a specific case or litigant.

All of these utilities let you perform simple searches for a single word or phrase, or complex Boolean searches, in which you separate multiple words or phrases with OR, AND, or NOT, as in "locate all files containing 'baseball' and 'pitcher' or 'football' and 'quarterback' but not 'hockey' and 'goalie.' " Sonar Professional, in particular, is the program of choice for serious researchers. It can assemble an index of words and phrases, search for synonyms, and even search for words that are within a certain distance of other words such as each occurrence of *trade* that appears within five words of *deficit.*

Disk utilities

Then there's the entire universe of utilities designed to let you partition, back up, recover, optimize, and otherwise tame a hard disk's frontiers. I take a closer look at these utilities and the concepts behind disk backup and disk maintenance in Chapter 26.

Utilities for PowerBooks

The members of the PowerBook family can benefit from every class of utility described in this chapter. (A screen saver can't save a PowerBook's screen any more than it does a desktop Mac's, but you may like the distraction. See the "Screen savers" section later in this chapter for more details.)

But PowerBooks can also benefit from several types of utilities designed for their unique requirements — and quirks. The most popular PowerBook utilities are utility collections such as Connectix's Connectix PowerBook Utilities (CPU) and VST Technologies PBTools.

Better battery-saving options

As I described in the previous chapter, the PowerBook control panel lets you extend a battery charge by specifying that the hard drive spin down and the PowerBook go to sleep after a predetermined amount of time. PowerBook utility packages take this concept to its limit by letting you specify separate sleep settings for *each program* you use.

Basic security

When you're on the road but out to lunch, you don't want someone snooping around on your PowerBook. PowerBook utility packages let you specify a password that must be typed before a sleeping PowerBook wakes up. All packages also offer quick power-on features designed to speed up hand inspections at airports. (It's debatable as to how useful this is, since you can make your PowerBook start up quickly by just pressing the Shift key to disable extension loading.)

Navigation aids

Some people have trouble with PowerBook trackballs and prefer using the keyboard whenever possible. Most PowerBook utility packages provide enhanced keyboard navigation features that let you use the keyboard to choose menu commands and dialog box options. Most packages also have features that enlarge the PowerBook's mouse pointer — ideal for PowerBooks with passive-matrix screens on which the pointer can be hard to see. (Examples of passive-matrix PowerBooks include the 100, 140, 145, 145B, 150, 160, and 520 as well as the PowerBook Duo 210 and 230.)

File synchronization

If you use both a PowerBook and a desktop Mac, you've probably scratched your head now and then wondering which machines' files are the most recent. File-synchronization utilities can save your scalp by automatically updating the contents of the folders you specify. Most PowerBook utility packages include file-sync software. A powerful stand-alone sync package is Leader Technologies' PowerMerge.

The PowerBook 500-series machines include the PowerBook File Assistant utility, which handles file synchronization. This utility is also included with System 7.5.

PowerBook specialists

In addition to the Swiss army knife packages I've described here, there are specialized PowerBook utilities such as Connectix's On The Road, which lets you defer printing and faxing while you're traveling. On The Road lets you set up your PowerBook so that it recognizes various locations — home, office, motel room — when you power on or wake up your PowerBook. On The Road then adjusts key settings accordingly — for example, turning off AppleTalk when you're not connected to the office network.

Miscellaneous Utilities

Before moving on to take a closer look at macro utilities and other advanced customizing tools, here's a quick roundup of some of the other types of utilities that are vying for your memory and hard disk space.

Screen savers

These popular utilities blank the Mac's screen after a specified period of inactivity, supposedly to prevent an image from being burned into the monitor's phosphor coating. The fact is, the phosphor in today's monitors is virtually immune to burn-in. Still, screen savers do provide a fun diversion, especially when they're as entertaining as the popular After Dark, from Berkeley Systems. (If you've seen toasters flying across a friend's screen, you've seen After Dark.) Fans of *Star Trek* will want Berkeley Systems' Star Trek: The Screen Saver, which contains over 15 animated displays — the Enterprise bridge, Klingon battle cruisers, and even tribbles. Screen savers may not save your monitor, but if they give you a few laughs during the day, they may help save your sanity. After Dark versions that showcase characters from Disney and Marvel Comics are also available. There's even a CD-ROM edition of After Dark that includes a "greatest hits" set of screen saver modules.

Connectix's memory utilities

Connectix Corporation offers two noteworthy utilities that enhance, expand, or otherwise work with your Mac's memory.

RAM Doubler is an amazing utility that effectively doubles your Mac's memory. For instance, if you have 8MB of RAM and you install RAM Doubler, you'll suddenly have 16MB of RAM. It's generally reliable and compatible, although it still doesn't provide the performance advantages of the equivalent amount of real RAM.

Maxima is a hot RAM disk utility that uses RAM Doubler technology to provide double-sized RAM disks. It's recommended for Macs with 8MB or more of RAM.

Clipboard enhancers

These utilities add features or conveniences to the Mac's Clipboard data-exchange mechanism. Olduvai's MultiClip Pro provides multiple Clipboards, each of which is editable. The program also provides more features than Apple's Scrapbook desk accessory, including support for multiple scrapbook files and a thumbnail view that shows multiple scrapbook pages in one window. The latest version even supports Adobe Photoshop plug-ins and System 7's publish-and-subscribe features.

Font utilities

These streamline the way the Mac works with fonts. Foremost among them is Adobe's Adobe Type Manager (ATM), which uses PostScript outline font files to provide tack-sharp screen fonts at any size — no jagged-edged type if you choose a size that doesn't exist in your System Folder. ATM also lets you use PostScript printer fonts with non-PostScript printers such as Apple's StyleWriter family.

Adobe's SuperATM uses technology based on that of Adobe's Multiple Master fonts to simulate fonts that aren't present in your system. Adobe's Adobe Type Reunion sorts and organizes fonts by family names, eliminating Font menus that sag to the bottom of the screen.

Jim Lewis's free program, theTypeBook, is one of several utilities that let you quickly create font-specimen books that graphic designers and desktop publishers rely on to help them choose typefaces. (You can find a copy of theTypeBook on the *Macworld Power User Clinic CD* included with this book.)

And don't forget the numerous font-modification utilities covered in Chapter 11.

Screen capture utilities

These replace the Mac's feeble ⌘-Shift-3 FKEY by providing a slew of options for saving a screen image on disk. Programs such as Mainstay's Capture let you copy part or all of the screen — including pulled-down menus — to the Clipboard or save it as a disk file.

MotionWorks' CameraMan and Strata's InstantReplay utilities add the dimension of motion to screen captures. Both let you capture Mac screen activity as a QuickTime movie — great for training applications. InstantReplay is the better of the two; besides being easier to use, it supports QuickTime's MIDI architecture and can convert tracks from an audio CD into QuickTime movies. I used InstantReplay to make the screen recordings in the *Macworld Power User Clinic.*

Workgroup utilities

These let you turn LocalTalk network cabling into a medium for coworker communication and brainstorming. If you're only using LocalTalk cables to connect Macs to laser printers, you're wasting your wires. Farallon Computing's remarkable Timbuktu lets you control one Mac from another Mac on the network (or even from a DOS PC running Microsoft Windows), or simply observe how others are using their Macs. It's also ideal for transferring files between machines. PrairieSoft's Software's In/Out lets you keep track of who's in the office: It's an electronic version of the message boards many offices use. Mainstay's MarkUp enables group editing of documents as they journey through the approval loop: It's an electronic red pencil that works on local networks (see Chapter 3).

Printer utilities

Numerous utilities are available that can enhance your printer's operation, make it easier to manage printers on a network, and even save toner or ink. See Chapter 31 for details.

File transfer and translation utilities

Programs such as DataViz's MacLink Plus/PC Connect bridge the gap between the Mac and the world of DOS PCs and Windows. It includes a cable and software for your Mac and PC that enable you to transfer and translate documents. (I look at these file-translation utilities in greater detail in Chapter 27.) If you work with

3½-inch DOS disks, consider Dayna Communications' DOS Mounter Plus or Apple's own PC Exchange, which is included with System 7.5 as well as with the PowerBook 500-series models. Both are extensions that let you insert 3½-inch PC disks in a SuperDrive and work with them using the Finder. These extensions work with Apple's Macintosh Easy Open software to streamline file translations, too — see Chapter 27.

File-compression utilities

Programs such as Aladdin Systems' StuffIt Deluxe and the shareware StuffIt Classic and Compact Pro let you compress files so they use less disk space. They're priceless for archiving lesser-used files and for sending and receiving files via modem. Symantec's Disk Doubler is another popular file-compression utility. (Aladdin's StuffIt Lite is on the CD included in this book, as is Compact Pro.)

A new generation of file-compression utilities provides its benefits on-the-fly, as you use your Mac. Programs such as Aladdin's StuffIt SpaceSaver (included with StuffIt Deluxe) and Stac Electronics' Stacker for Macintosh automatically compress and decompress files as you work, effectively boosting your hard disk's capacity (see Figure 24-3, "Compression Method Trade-Offs"). On the down side, on-the-fly compression utilities can slow down the Mac and make it difficult to recover damaged files. You might be better off just buying a larger hard disk.

Disk cataloging utilities

A variety of commercial and shareware disk-cataloging utilities is also available to help you keep track of what's on your disks (you'll find one on the CD in the Best of BMUG collection). Several labeling programs are available that read disks you insert and then generate labels that you can print on Avery peel-and-stick label stock.

Security utilities

These software security guards protect your Mac and its data from curious eyes and nefarious spies. To keep wandering hands off your Mac, consider an access-protection utility such as usrEZ's ultraSecure or ultraShield, Casady & Greene's Access Managed Environment (A.M.E.), or Kent-Marsh's NightWatch II, all of which let you electronically lock the keyboard, screen, and mouse.

usrEZ's ultraSecure and ultraShield also provide file-encryption features that scramble documents according to a password you supply. (Compression utilities such as StuffIt Deluxe also enable you to assign passwords to archives, as do high-end backup utilities such as Dantz's Retrospect.)

Disk-security programs such as Kent-Marsh's FolderBolt let you protect files and folders against modification, unauthorized access, and deletion. This utility isn't a kitchen-sink security package; it simply lets you lock folders in any of three ways. You can lock a folder to prevent anyone from opening or modifying its contents

COMPRESSION METHOD TRADE-OFFS

FILE-LEVEL (STUFFIT SPACESAVER, AUTODOUBLER)

Compressing Ⓐ The Mac's operating system, working with a disk driver, saves files to disk (just as it would without a compressor). Ⓑ Operating in the background, the compressor later finds saved files, compresses them, and once the compressed version is successfully saved, deletes the original file. This method is faster than driver-level compression, plus it reduces the chance of losing data if the disk crashes while the driver is compressing a file.

Storing The Mac's disk driver stores all files, decompressed or not, in blocks. The Mac's driver cannot put data from more than one file in a block. If a file, or piece of it, is smaller than the block, that leftover space is wasted. File-level compression does nothing to change this, and many blocks remain only partially filled.

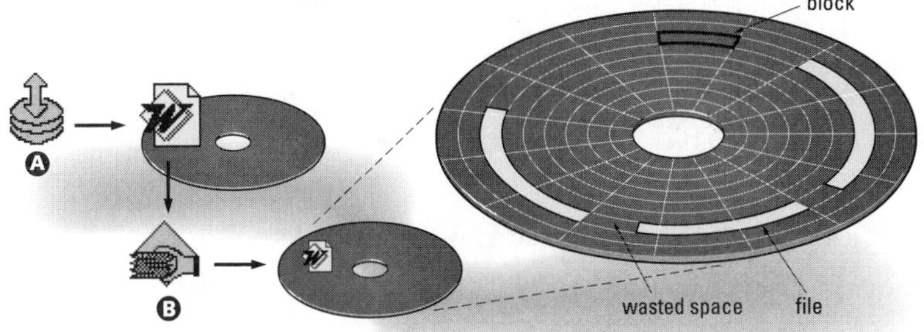

DRIVER-LEVEL (STACKER, TIMES TWO)

Compressing Ⓐ The Mac's operating system works with a disk driver that has been modified by the compression program. The modified driver does all compression as the file is being saved. This method is slower than file-level compression.

Storing A driver-level compressor produces more-compressed files than a file-level compressor, by writing to the disk in a more efficient structure than a standard driver. This modified driver enables blocks to hold data from more than one file, eliminating wasted space. But the nonstandard block structure can interfere with file recovery after a crash.

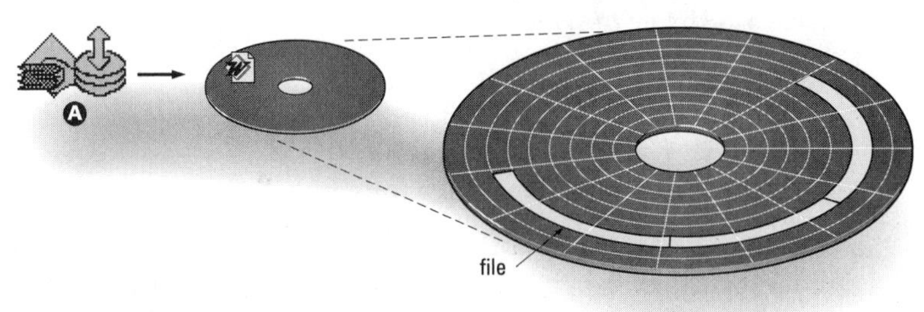

Figure 24-3: Compression Method Trade-Offs

unless he or she has the password you specified when you first locked the folder. You can also designate a folder as read-only: people without the password can access the folder's files but not modify or delete them. And you can designate a folder as a drop box: people can save or copy files to the folder, but they can't open the folder or access its contents.

Diagnostic and virus-detection utilities

Not sure if your Mac is healthy? Utilities such as Apple's Apple Personal Diagnostics may be able to help by testing your system's memory chips and other components. And Apple's Disk First Aid, included with all Macs, is a good first defense against disk-related errors.

Casady & Greene's Conflict Catcher III (included on the CD) is designed to pinpoint conflicts between system extensions — a problem every utility buff has encountered at least once.

Programs such as Symantec's SAM, Datawatch's Virex, and John Norstad's Disinfectant help guard against a virus attack. (Viruses and virus-detection utilities are covered in Chapter 26, and Disinfectant is included on the CD that came with this book.)

Network utilities

An office network is like a freeway: When a problem develops, traffic slows down for everyone. An entire class of utilities is designed to help you troubleshoot network problems and analyze network traffic. Network analysis programs such as Neon Software's TrafficWatch II spy on the data packets that form network traffic, enabling you to determine where problems exist and whether your network wiring scheme can handle the amount of traffic on the network.

Programs such as Dayna Communications' Network Vital Signs and AG Group's Net WatchMan can notify you when a problem, such as a crashed mail server, occurs. Both programs can even contact you over a wireless pager. ("Sorry, fellas — you'll have to play the last few holes without me — the file server just went down.")

For an introduction to networking, see Chapter 32. For a detailed look at network utilities and networking issues, see *Macworld Networking Bible* (IDG Books Worldwide, 1994).

Extension managers

These handy utilities let you selectively disable extensions without having to drag them out of the System Folder. Popular extension managers include Apple's own Extensions Manager (included with System 7.5) and Focus Enhancement's INITPicker. Best of all, however, is Casady & Greene's first-rate Conflict Catcher III, a three-day trial version of which is included on the CD that came with this book.

Utilities that let you manage utilities — now that's the sign of a thriving marketplace. There's no shortage of utilities for the Macintosh, and that's proof of a few things — the gaps still present in the Mac's system software, the vitality of the Mac itself, and most of all, the desire of Mac users to personalize and customize their machines.

Focus on Macros and Scripting

I touched on macro utilities earlier in this chapter. This section provides more details on QuicKeys and Tempo II and also discusses Apple's own AppleScript.

Macro basics

In its simplest form, creating a macro involves choosing a recording command, performing some activities, and then choosing a stop recording command. When you play back the macro, the Mac goes into autopilot while you go do something else.

Programs that let you record and play macros have been available for years: The two veterans are Affinity Microsystems' Tempo II Plus and CE Software's QuicKeys. But these utilities are being joined by a new generation of macro tools that provide finer control over the Mac by enabling you to create scripts — sequences of events that you can not only play back, but edit and embellish. In its most advanced form, creating scripts is a lot like programming. A script can contain *if...then* options that enable it to play back different steps depending on certain conditions: "If I've created any files that haven't been backed up today, run my backup program and then shut down. Otherwise, just shut down."

Macro and scripting features are built into a growing number of application programs, including Microsoft Excel, Word, and Works, ClarisWorks, Lotus 1-2-3, Adobe PageMaker, WordPerfect, and FileMaker Pro. But the latest word in Mac automation is Apple's own AppleScript, an enhancement to System 7 that lets you create scripts that control the Mac's Finder as well as application programs that support AppleScript. In this section, I spotlight AppleScript's benefits and show how it relates to QuicKeys and Tempo II Plus and to the built-in macro and scripting features many programs provide. For some ideas on how to put macros to work, see the Quick Tips box "Ways to Use Macros."

Comparing QuicKeys and Tempo II Plus

With either of these utilities you can accomplish all aspects of Mac automation except creating a customized application, such as a billing program for your company. Although they share similar features, each takes its own approach to macro making.

Ways to Use Macros

Here are just a few of the ways you can put macros to work.

Create custom keyboard shortcuts
A macro doesn't have to perform step-after-step. One of the most common uses for a macro product like QuicKeys is to create keyboard shortcuts that start programs, choose menu commands, and select icons on tool palettes or buttons in dialog boxes. It's a great way to put an extended keyboard's 15 function keys to work.

Streamline system adjustments
If you frequently switch between various monitor settings, network printers and file servers, or other control panel or Chooser-related options, you can set up macros that automate the process. QuicKeys is especially handy for this: It includes an entire category of macro options designed to cut down on trips to the Control Panels folder.

Simulate word-processor style sheets or glossaries
Powerhouse word processors such as Microsoft Word have style-sheet features that automate repetitive formatting, and glossary or AutoText features that let you store and recall often-used text (see Chapter 3). Most other programs lack these features, but you can simulate them by creating macros that choose the desired font and formatting commands, or insert often-used text.

Automate search-and-replace or reformatting operations
Say you're a desktop publisher and one of your first steps in every job is removing the extra space that the folks in the typing pool always put after each sentence. Create a macro that chooses your word processor's Replace command, types two spaces in the Find What box and one space in the Replace With box, and then click Replace All. Similarly, if you frequently retrieve data from the company mainframe computer and then reformat it for importing into a database or spreadsheet, you can set up a macro that does the formatting and importing for you.

Batch-process files
Say you work with Adobe Photoshop and you always apply a certain filter to freshly scanned images. Many Photoshop pros do just that, applying the Unsharp Masking filter to newly scanned images to sharpen them up. You can set up a macro that automatically opens a file in a given folder, applies the filter, saves the file, and then proceeds to the next file.

Create a customized application
With the macro and scripting languages provided by programs such as Microsoft Excel and HyperCard, you can create custom applications that have pull-down menus and dialog boxes that prompt for information and enable users to choose various options. This is macro making at its most ambitious: Indeed, it's actually a form of programming.

Employing the "watch me" (recording your actions as you go) style of macro making I described earlier, Tempo II Plus adds a Command menu to the Mac's menu bar. To begin recording a macro, choose Start Recording from this menu, and then simply perform the steps you want to record: Choose a menu command, type some text, or click a button. When you're done, choose Stop Recording, and Tempo II Plus displays a dialog box for you to save the macro and give it a keyboard shortcut (see Figure 24-4 "In Tempo").

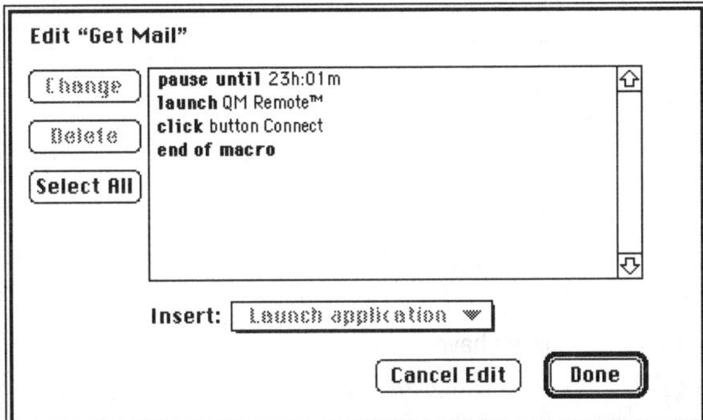

Figure 24-4: In Tempo Affinity's Tempo II Plus adds a Command menu (left) to the menu bar. You use this menu to record, play, and edit macros. This simple macro (right) waits until 11:01 pm, when phone rates drop, and then runs an electronic mail program — in this case, QuickMail Remote — that retrieves any waiting correspondence.

QuicKeys has a record mode that works similarly, but it takes a back seat to the QuicKeys control panel, which is where you'll probably create most of your macros. The QuicKeys control panel's Define menu is packed with predefined shortcuts that insert the time and date, close or scroll through windows, and adjust system settings (see Figure 24-5 "QuicKeys Control"). Other commands in the Define menu let you create shortcuts for clicking buttons, choosing menu commands, typing text, clicking or double-clicking at a specific location within a window, and much more.

Voice Macros: QuicKeys and PlainTalk

If you have an AV or Power Mac, you can create macros that are triggered by spoken commands. In the adjacent figure, the Speech Macro Editor is being used to create a macro that copies some selected text or graphics, opens the Scrapbook, and then pastes the selection into the Scrapbook. The macro runs when you say, "Copy to Scrapbook."

The AV and Power Macs also come with an extension for QuicKeys that lets you trigger QuicKeys macros with spoken commands.

Copy to Scrapbook
Command: Copy to Scrapbook
Context: Anywhere
Script: QuicKeys
Acknowledge
Record
Stop
Run
Menu "Copy" Exactly From "Edit"
Menu "Scrapbook" Apple_Menu
Wait Application "Scrapbook"
Menu "Paste" Exactly From "Edit"
Menu "Close" Exactly From "File"
Wait Window Name_Is "Scrapbook" Not_Exists

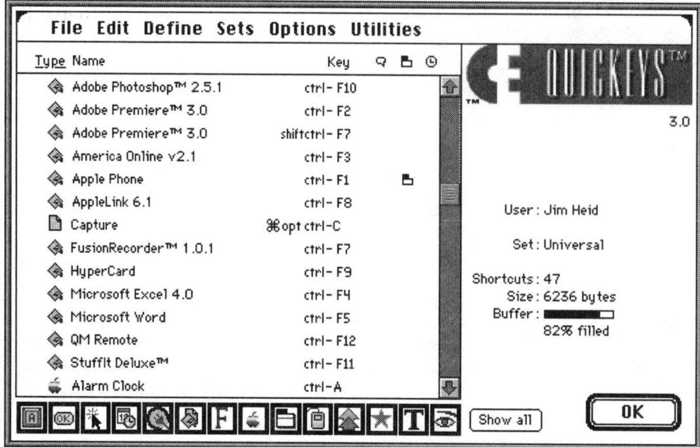

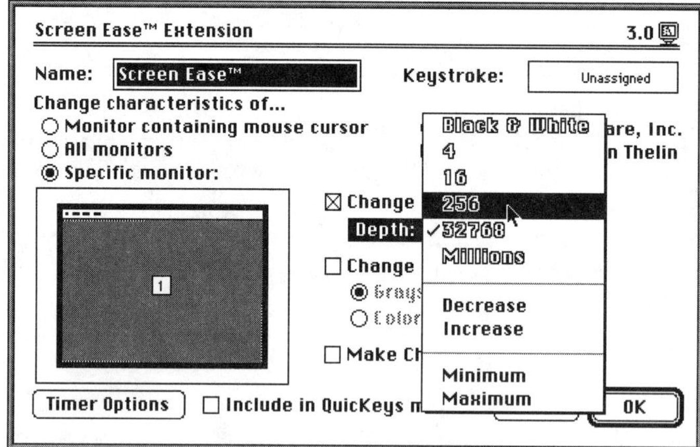

Figure 24-5: QuicKeys Control CE Software's QuicKeys control panel provides menus for creating new macros and lists ones you've already created. The macros shown here allow me to start often-used programs (top) by pressing the Control key along with a function key. QuicKeys' Screen Ease extension (bottom) is just one of many extensions that streamline making system adjustments. Screen Ease lets you switch between frequently used monitor settings without having to open the Monitors control panel. Here, Screen Ease is being set up to switch a monitor from displaying thousands of colors to displaying 256.

Advanced Macro Options

Both QuicKeys and Tempo II Plus let you create universal and application-specific macros. Universal macros, which work in any program, can be used to create keyboard shortcuts for scrolling, resizing windows, starting programs, or typing your name and address — tasks you're likely to perform in more than one program. To create a shortcut that you need in a particular program, use an application-specific macro, which is available only when that program is active.

Most people create keyboard shortcuts for their macros, but both Tempo II Plus and QuicKeys also provide menus that let you start macros using the mouse. Both programs also let you create icons that run macros when double-clicked. They even offer timing options that let you specify that a macro run at certain intervals.

Although macros are relatively simple to create, they may not always be problem free. A number of pitfalls can trip up a novice macro writer, but QuicKeys and Tempo II Plus provide detours around them. (For a guide to solving the most common macro maladies, see the Quick Tips box "Macro Troubleshooting Tips.") You get more reliable macros when you go beyond simply recording a series of events and start taking advantage of the "smart" features that QuicKeys and Tempo II Plus provide.

So which macro utility should you use? I'm partial to QuicKeys. For the simple macros I create — menu command and scrolling shortcuts, file-opening macros — QuicKeys lives up to its name. But Tempo II Plus does have the edge when it comes to creating complex macro sequences whose playback depends on certain conditions being met. QuicKeys' *if...then* capabilities are more limited.

Macro Troubleshooting Tips

Here's how to avoid the macro pitfalls you're most likely to encounter in Tempo II Plus and QuicKeys.

Problem: A file-opening macro you create by invoking your utility's Record command and then double-clicking a file's icon won't work if you subsequently move the icon; when Tempo II Plus or QuicKeys plays the macro, the Mac double-clicks the wrong icon or no icon at all.

Solution: Specify which file or program you want a macro to open. In Tempo II Plus, choose Options from the command menu and click either the Launch Application or Launch File button, and then choose the program or file you want the macro to open. In the QuicKeys control panel, choose File from the Define menu and then select the desired program or document.

Problem: Macros that choose menu commands can fail if a program changes its menu wording as it operates. (For example, most word processors have a Show Ruler command that changes to read Hide Ruler when the ruler is visible.)

Solution: Tell the macro program to choose the command based on its position within a given menu rather than on its wording.

Problem: A macro that clicks a check box within a dialog box can fail if the box is already checked when the macro runs.

Solution: Enable Tempo II Plus's Smart Check Boxes option (in the Preferences dialog box) before recording the macro. In QuicKeys' Button dialog box, select the Only Click If Button Is Off option.

Problem: A macro that clicks a tool in a palette can fail if you move the palette elsewhere on the screen.

Solution: Be sure Tempo II Plus's Enable Smart Features button is selected when recording the macro. In QuicKeys, use the Click Location dialog box to tell QuicKeys to click relative to the document window.

Problem: The macro utility may appear to skip some steps when playing back a multistep macro.

Solution: Add pauses between the steps. Use the Pause command in QuicKeys' Define menu or the Pause for Interval command in Tempo II Plus.

The AppleScript Difference

QuicKeys and Tempo II must provide their smart features because application programs are dumb: They aren't designed to be operated by remote control. But what if an application was designed with automation in mind? What if it provided a vocabulary of explicit commands that a macro utility could use? The vocabulary would incorporate terms specific to the application — cells, ranges, and charts for spreadsheets, for example, fields and records for a database, paragraphs and words for a word processor, or clips and fades in a QuickTime video-editing program. When you performed specific tasks, the application program would "broadcast" messages describing what you did. A macro recorder could record these messages, resulting in a macro that provides explicit instructions instead of simply simulating mouse clicks and keystrokes.

Apple's AppleScript brings this kind of intelligence to the macro world. AppleScript builds on a System 7 mechanism called Apple events, which enables application programs to exchange commands and data. Previous chapters have looked at one aspect of Apple events — the publish-and-subscribe commands that let you create links between documents.

Three flavors of AppleScript support

But just as application programs must be designed to support publish and subscribe, so must they be written to work with AppleScript. A program can support AppleScript on any of a few levels.

Scriptable

This is the most basic form of AppleScript support. It means that the program can be controlled with scripts.

Recordable

A program that is *recordable* can work with a script editor utility to automatically create scripts as you work — much like Tempo II Plus or QuicKeys create macros by recording mouse clicks and keystrokes. You can still create scripts for a program that isn't recordable, but you have to do so by typing the script manually. The System 7.5 Finder is recordable.

Attachable

A program that's *attachable* enables you to assign, or attach, scripts to menu commands or to buttons or other on-screen elements. When you click or otherwise activate an element to which a script is attached, the script runs. You may use this feature to customize the way a certain program's Save command works — say, by adding a logging feature that tracks how much time you spent working with the file.

Forging scripts into applets and droplets

AppleScript also enables you to turn a script into a tiny application program that you can run directly from the Finder. Such a miniprogram is called an *applet*. You can also create a special type of applet, called a *droplet*, that acts like a drop box: You can drag icons for files, folders, or disks to the icon of a droplet, and the droplet runs and then performs some kind of operation on those icons. You may create a droplet that prints the files dragged to it, or creates aliases of them, or copies their names into a database, or duplicates them and then opens the duplicates (see Figure 24-6, "Apple Script").

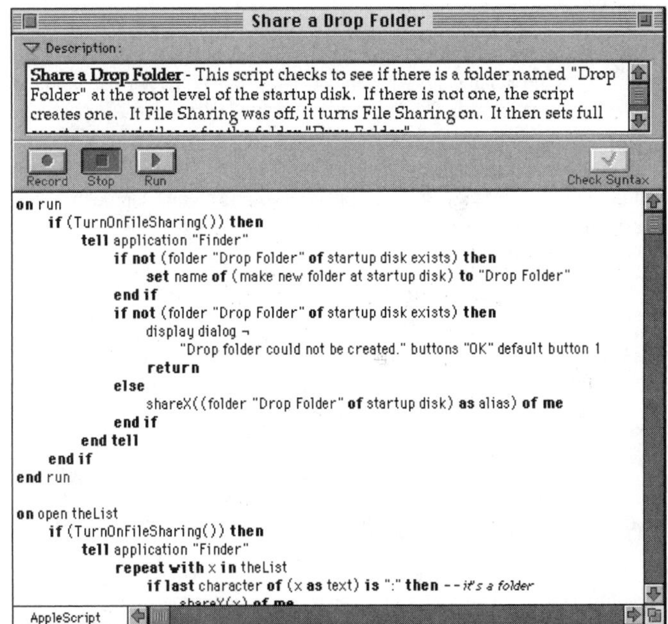

Figure 24-6: Apple Script The script editor included with AppleScript lets you record, play, edit and save scripts. The script shown here is included with System 7.5 (it's in the Automated Tasks folder, accessible via the Apple menu).

AppleScript is included with System 7 Pro and System 7.5. Both include Apple-Script documentation and a utility, called Script Editor, that lets you record, edit, and play back scripts. You can also get an AppleScript developer's toolkit through APDA, Apple's source for developer tools (800-282-2732). The toolkit includes extensive technical documentation.

Scripting in System 7.5

The System 7.5 Finder is not only scriptable, it's recordable — you can create scripts by simply clicking the Record button in the Script Editor utility that accompanies System 7.5 and then performing the actions you want to automate. As you choose commands, the script appears in the Script Editor's window.

Remember Chapter 22's tip about streamlining the Views control panel? By turning on the Script Editor's Record mode and then using the Views control panel, you can create scripts that toggle between detailed and minimalist list views with a double-click. (These and other scripts are available for downloading from the Macworld Online forums on America Online and eWorld.) After creating the scripts, I saved them as applications in the Apple menu, so one click changes my list views to show a lot of information or a little.

One problem is that some System 7.5 components are not yet scriptable. I ran into this roadblock when trying to create a script that would open the Scrapbook and then paste the Clipboard into the Scrapbook. The Scrapbook isn't scriptable, so the Paste command didn't work. Creative scripters can work around limitations like these by combining AppleScript scripts with QuicKeys macros. Still, Apple's slow-and-steady approach to implementing scripting is frustrating.

Recording a script

Recording a script using Script Editor isn't too different from recording a macro with Tempo II Plus or QuicKeys. Click Script Editor's Record button, and then switch to a recordable application program and perform the tasks you want to record. If you position your windows so you can see both the application and Script Editor, you can see script commands appear in the Script Editor's window as you work. When you've finished, you can save the script conventionally or as an applet or a droplet.

With AppleScript, Apple has poured the foundation for heavy-duty scripting, but it's up to the architects and carpenters of the software world to build on it. Expect to see AppleScript support in a growing number of programs, especially now that Apple has added AppleScript support to the System 7.5 Finder.

Also expect to see more sophisticated script editors appearing from third-party utility makers such as UserLand, whose Frontier was the first scripting utility to take advantage of the power of Apple events. When AppleScript hits its stride, there will be no end to the slick ways you can put your Mac to work.

Hard-Core Customizing

If you're a hard-core customizer — the kind of person who putties posters to walls, makes substitutions at restaurants, replaces the buttons on new clothes, and has personalized license plates — you'll want a library of resource-editing utilities. These programs let you customize the way the Mac looks and operates by altering resources, which are small, structured tidbits of information the Mac uses as it runs.

You can perform two basic kinds of customizing tasks with a resource editor. The first involves making cosmetic changes — adding new beep sounds and altering the appearance of windows, scroll bars, dialog box buttons, the mouse pointer, the Trash can, and other icons. The second category involves functional enhancements — changes that actually alter the way the Mac or a certain program runs. You can add or change menu ⌘-key shortcuts, rephrase a dialog box message, add a custom page size to the ImageWriter's Page Setup dialog box, and tailor the way the Finder displays the contents of disks and folders.

This section presents some background on resources and their roles, spotlights some popular resource-editing utilities, and passes along several customizing ideas.

What are resources?

Resources let software developers create and store a program's user interface elements — its menus, dialog boxes, buttons, tool palettes, and so on — separately from the program's software code. This separation makes it easy for software developers to adapt, or *localize*, their programs for different countries. To create a version of a program for use in, say, France, a developer simply alters the program's resources, translating the English menus and dialog box text into French. Besides translating text into other languages, localizing also involves displaying date and currency values in the appropriate format. Without resources, a developer has to substantially change a program's code to adapt the program for another country. With resources, the job can be done in an afternoon by a nonprogrammer.

Resources are grouped by function into *resource types*, which have four-character names such as MENU and LAYO. Each resource is assigned an identification number within its resource type. This scheme makes it possible for resources of different types to have the same ID number — while those within the same group must have unique ID numbers.

When a program needs a given resource (for example, a "Save changes before closing?" dialog box), it requests the resource by its ID number from the Resource Manager, a portion of the Mac's system software whose job is finding and loading the appropriate resource when it's required.

Additional resource advantages

Another advantage of resources is that they can be shared by more than one program, adding consistency to the Mac's operation and saving disk space and memory by putting things all programs can use in a single place (often the System file). A font is a good example of a shared resource. (Incidentally, if you find a resource named WDEF, don't assume your Mac is infected with the virus of the same name. WDEF is a standard definition procedure for creating windows and a general resource located in the System file. See Chapter 26 for more details on viruses and virus-detection measures.)

Resources also enable the Mac to manage its memory more efficiently. A software developer can designate certain resources as *purgeable:* The Mac can clear them from memory when it needs the memory for other uses. When the Mac accesses your disk after you choose a rarely used command, it may be loading a resource that wasn't in memory. And chances are if you choose the same command again a moment later, the Mac won't access the disk because the resource will still be present in memory. Resources enabled the now-ancient 128K and 512K Macs to run programs that otherwise wouldn't have fit in memory. Today's Macs have more memory, but resources still provide their memory-saving advantages. Table 24-1 lists and describes some resources that are ideal candidates for customizing.

Table 24-1
Customizing Candidates

Type	*Description*
ALRT	Template for an alert box's appearance
BNDL	Bundle — the Finder uses BNDL resources to associate files with their icons
CURS	Cursor — defines the appearance of a mouse pointer
DITL	Dialog item list — defines what appears in a dialog or alert box
DLOG	Template for a dialog box's appearance
FKEY	Function key — a ⌘-Shift-number routine
FOND	Font family descriptor
FONT	Font bitmap description
fmnu	Finder menu — contains special menu resources for System 7's Finder; you can edit these resources with ResEdit 2.1.1 or a later version
ICN#	Icon list — a series of icon definitions; generally used by the Finder to show icons in various states (active, inactive, hollow); application icons are ICN# resources
ICON	Icon — a single icon definition, like that of a printer driver you see in the Chooser
icl	Large color icon — System 7 version of cicn, made up of icl8 (8-bit) and icl4 (4-bit) icon resources

Type	*Description*
ics	Small icon — System 7 version of cicn, made up of ics4 and ics8 resources
INTL	International resource — contains data that an application uses to create displays appropriate to a given country (proper date formatting, currency symbols, and so on)
MBAR	Menu bar — defines all the menus in a menu bar
MENU	Defines an individual menu's commands and keyboard shortcuts
NFNT	Font in new-font-numbering-table format
PAT1	Pattern — defines a QuickDraw pattern (the patterns drawing and painting programs show in their palettes)
PAT#	Pattern list — a collection of patterns
PDEF	Contains printing software
PICT	Picture — the pictures that often appear when you choose an About command are usually PICT resources; also appear in Alarm Clock desk accessory and many control panels
ppat	Pixel pattern — used to generate desktop patterns
PREC	Print record — storage area for printer driver data
snd[1]	Sound resource — enables the Mac to play synthesized and digitally recorded sounds
STR[1]	String — a series of characters that may appear in a dialog box or be used by a program; for example, in an error message
STR#	String list — a collection of strings
SIZE	Contains memory-requirements information used by the Finder or System 6 MultiFinder
WDEF	Window definition — describes the appearance of a window
WIND	Window template — used by the Window Manager to create a window

(1) Each of these resources has a space after its name.

Resource Editing Software

Resources enable you to customize a program without having to be a programmer. If you double-click icons and choose menu commands, you can use the latest resource editing tools.

Caution: ResEdit is a power tool. You can irreparably damage the file you're modifying if you're careless. To avoid disaster, always follow the Prime Directive of Resource Editing: Never modify your only copy of a program, system file, or document. Make a duplicate copy of the file and perform your surgery on the copy. And save your work often; most resource editors have a Revert command that lets you fall back on the previously saved version of a file.

Giving your Mac an interface lift

For cosmetic customizing, try a shareware extension called Greg's Buttons, by Greg Landweber. Greg's Buttons replaces the standard black-and-white buttons, check boxes, and radio buttons with attractive, three-dimensional color ones that match System 7's windows and scroll bars. Greg's Buttons adds color to the stop sign, caution, and note alert icons.

For a more complete makeover, there's Dubl-Click Software's ClickChange. ClickChange enables you to change the appearance of the windows, scroll bars, dialog boxes, buttons, pointers, and more (see Figure 24-7 "Mac Makeover"). It also lets you assign colors to virtually every element of the Mac's interface.

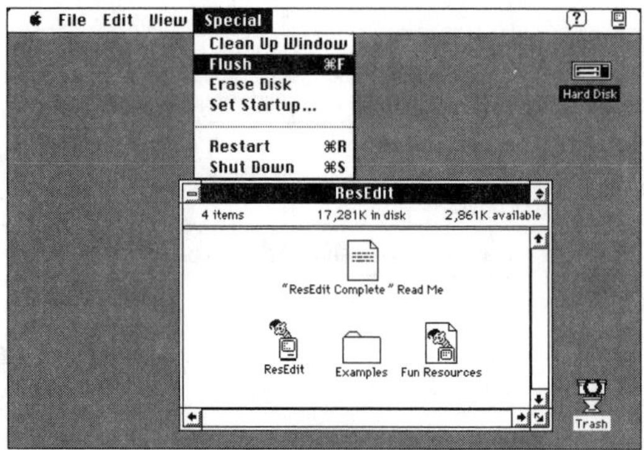

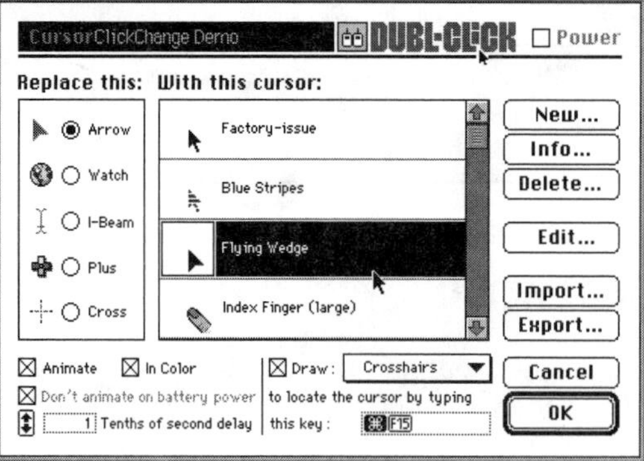

Figure 24-7: Mac Makeover
It may not be tasteful, but it's personal. This Mac (top) is wearing a new window and scroll bar style, thanks to Dubl-Click Software's ClickChange (bottom). ResEdit was used to create the custom Trash icon, the appropriately renamed Empty Trash command, and the Command key shortcuts for the Flush, Restart, and Shut Down commands. The ClickChange screen shows several animated cursor options you may choose as replacements for the wristwatch's moving hands.

ClickChange also works with digitized sounds, which are another type of resource. ClickChange lets you choose from a variety of new system beeps and assign sounds to different events, such as when you insert or eject a disk, drag or resize a window, or even press a key. The utility includes a typewriter sound that goes nicely with the latter option.

But the king of sound customizers is Bruce Tomlin's shareware SoundMaster, which supports the aforementioned aural options as well as several more — including the ability to play a sound when you choose the Finder's Empty Trash command.

Custom ImageWriter paper sizes

A common request of ImageWriter owners is the ability to add custom page sizes to the ImageWriter Page Setup dialog box — perhaps for printing on index cards or special label stock. It's a breeze, thanks to a free utility called PREC Manager by Bill Steinberg. PREC Manager was created back in 1985, but it still works with the System 7.0/7.1 ImageWriter drivers. (It doesn't work with the System 7.5 ImageWriter GX driver, nor is it needed — that driver lets you define your own custom paper sizes.)

The World of ResEdit

To Mac aficionados, customizing resources means using Apple's ResEdit utility, which has been around nearly as long as the Mac itself. ResEdit sports an elegant design that makes many resource editing jobs as easy as clicking and dragging — although you can still wreak havoc by editing resources indiscriminately.

ResEdit is available through user groups and on-line information services such as America Online. You can also buy it from the APDA, Apple's source for developer tools (800-282-2732 in the U.S.). But the best way to get ResEdit is to buy *ResEdit Complete* (Addison-Wesley, 1991). Written by Peter Alley (one of ResEdit's designers) and Carolyn Strange, it's the best guide to understanding and tinkering with ResEdit and resources I've seen. It also includes a disk containing ResEdit 2.1 and a variety of fun resources you can add to your system, including animated mouse pointers and replacement icons for alert boxes and the Trash can. (The toilet icon pairs up well with a SoundMaster-modified Empty Trash command, if you get my drift.)

In addition to *ResEdit Complete*, there's *Apple's ResEdit Reference* (Addison-Wesley, 1990), a somewhat dry overview of ResEdit's capabilities. A better book for the customizer is *Zen and the Art of Resource Editing* (Peachpit Press, 1992). This little volume, written by gurus from the legendary Berkeley Macintosh User Group (BMUG) contains concise overviews of various resource-editing concepts and projects and includes two disks containing ResEdit and a variety of replacement mouse pointer, icon, and keyboard resources. And if you graduate beyond ResEdit (not likely, unless you're a programmer), you'll want MathemÆsthetics' Resourcerer, a resource editor so powerful it makes ResEdit look lame.

A ResEdit primer

When you open a file with ResEdit, its resources appear in a type picker window. To access the resources of a given type, double-click that type's icon. Doing so displays a resource picker window that shows the resources of that type in the file you've opened. Some pickers display their contents graphically, while others use text. Double-clicking a resource in a resource picker window opens that resource for editing.

Some of ResEdit's graphical editors provide fatbits displays for editing icons or fonts (see Figure 24-8 "Editing Icons"). You can customize the icons the Finder uses by editing ICN# resources, but for the Finder to recognize the new icons, you may need to rebuild your disk's Desktop file (restart the Mac while pressing ⌘-Option until you're asked if you want to rebuild the Desktop file, and then click OK). The painting tools, which are also used by ResEdit's font, mouse pointer, and pattern editors, operate like those of HyperCard and most painting programs.

You may prefer to use the icon-customizing features built into the System 7 Finder. See the section "Customizing disk, file, and folder icons" in Chapter 22.

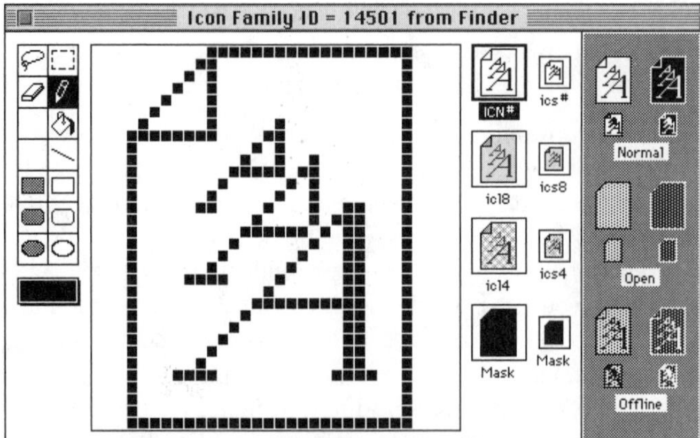

Figure 24-8: Editing Icons ResEdit's icon editor provides a fatbits display. The editor for the Finder's ICN# resources is shown here. Notice that an ICN# resource comprises the same basic icon in several styles: The Finder uses the variants to indicate that an item is selected or not selected, selected and open or not selected and open, and selected but off-line (its disk is ejected but still on the desktop) or not selected but off-line.

A cookbook of ResEdit projects

ResEdit lets you perform all of the customizing jobs that ClickChange and PREC Manager can perform, although those programs are easier to use and, more to the point, are less prone to accidental misuse. But there are customizing tasks that demand ResEdit's power. The following are some customizing examples and tips.

Adding or changing ⌘-key shortcuts

You can use a keyboard enhancement utility such as QuicKeys to change a program's keyboard shortcuts, but the shortcuts don't appear in the program's menus and they won't be copied if you move the program to a different disk. When you alter a program's MENU resources with ResEdit, your custom shortcuts are there for good, or until you change them again (see Figure 24-9 "Modifying Menus").

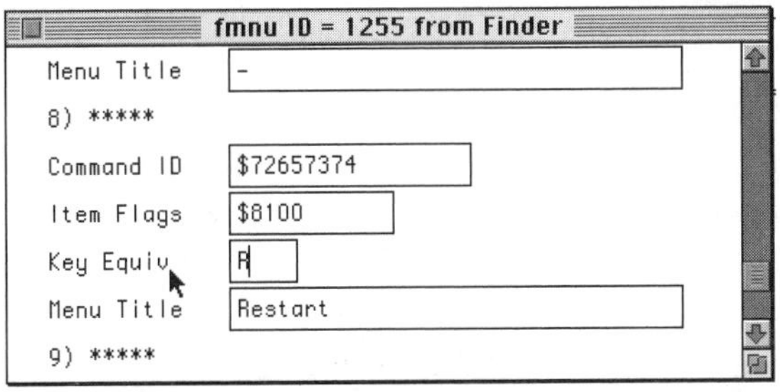

fmnu ID = 1255 from Finder
Menu Title -
8) *****
Command ID $72657374
Item Flags $8100
Key Equiv R
Menu Title Restart
9) *****

Figure 24-9: Modifying Menus With ResEdit, you can add ⌘-key shortcuts to menus. Here, a shortcut is being created for the Finder's Restart commands.

If you want to add keyboard shortcuts to System 7's Finder, you need ResEdit 2.1.1 or later. These versions support the System 7 Finder's special menu resources, which are called fmnu (short for Finder menu).

Rearranging a dialog or alert box

If you're fond of long document names, you may wish that a certain program's Open dialog box showed more of them. By editing a program's DITL resources, you can enlarge the list box to show longer names (see Figure 24-10 "Dialog Enhancements").

You may also want to add descriptive text to a dialog box to remind you of its purpose. If a certain program annoys you by beeping twice when asking if you want to "save changes before closing," edit the appropriate ALRT resource and use ResEdit's Set ALRT Stage Info command to banish the beeps. Using the same command, you can even change an alert box's default button (the one you can choose by pressing Return).

When editing a dialog box, be sure not to remove any items or change them into other items (for example, don't change a check box into a radio button). Also avoid deleting codes that begin with a caret (^) and end with a number, as in ^0 or ^1.

These codes represent placeholders that the Mac replaces with other text. For example, in a dialog message that reads "Save changes to ^0?", the Mac replaces ^0 with a document name.

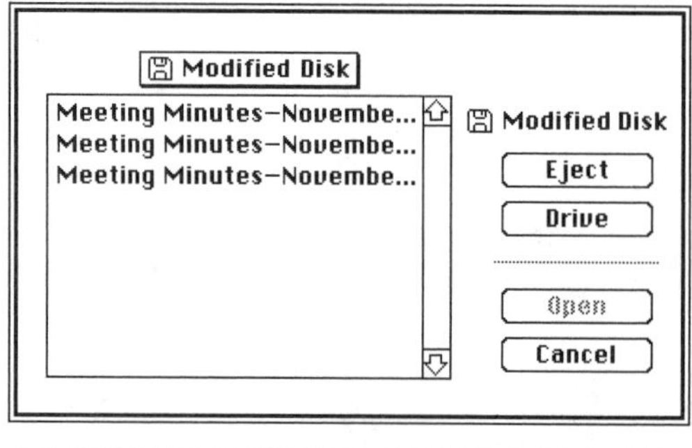

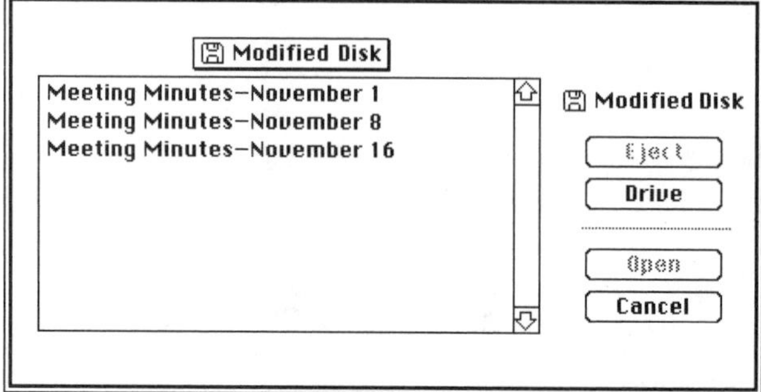

Figure 24-10: Dialog Enhancements Which is which? One pitfall of lengthy document names (top) is that you may be unable to tell one document from another in an Open dialog box. By using ResEdit to enlarge a program's Open dialog box (bottom), you can see those longer document names.

Creating and switching between keyboard layouts

By editing the System file's *keyboard layout* (KCHR) resource, you can rearrange the keyboard layout to suit your tastes. One useful tweak involves changing the Shift-period key sequence to generate a period (not the less-than symbol) and Shift-comma to generate a comma (not the greater-than symbol). With this modification, you can type abbreviations such as "P.O." and "D.C." without having to press and release the Shift key for each period. Other possibilities include moving the typographer's quotes or other often-used Option-key characters to less finger-twisting key positions.

To modify the keyboard layout, start by opening the System file and duplicating an existing layout. (If you bought your Mac in the United States, your layout is named *U.S.*) Then alter the layout as desired, close it, and use ResEdit's Get Info command to rename it, giving it a moniker that reflects your modification (for example, *Easy Quotes*). Finally, save the System file.

The System file can accommodate multiple KCHR resources. When it does, the Keyboard control panel lists each one, as shown in Figure 24-11 "Multiple Keyboards." You can switch between layouts using the Keyboard control panel, but because you're a ResEdit pro by now, you can make switching even easier by activating System 7's Keyboard menu. Using ResEdit, open the System file and open the itlc resource. Locate the radio buttons labeled Always Show Kybd. Icon and check the 1 button. (The Mac consults this bit at startup time: If the bit is set to 1, the Mac displays the keyboard menu.)

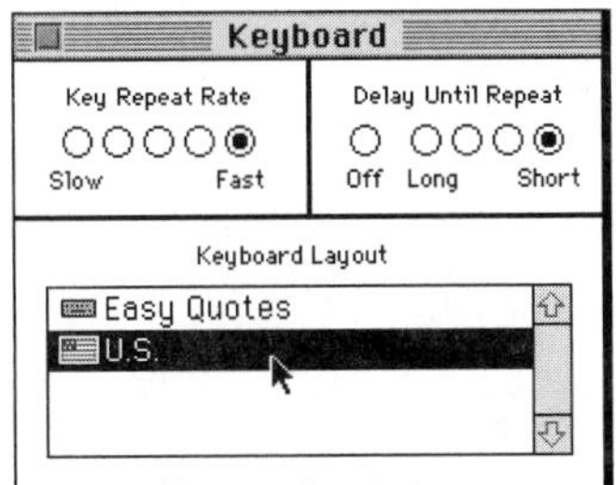

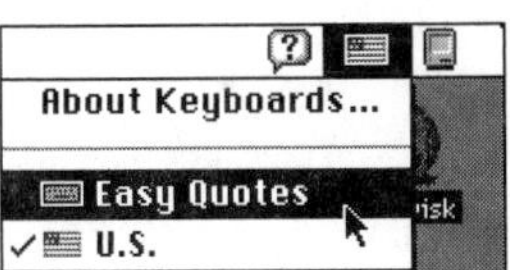

Figure 24-11: Multiple Keyboards By editing and creating KCHR resources (top), you can customize the layout of the Mac's keyboard. You can move a character to a different key sequence by simply dragging it from the upper portion of the display to the desired key location. When your System file contains multiple keyboard layouts (middle), you can switch between them using the Keyboard control panel. If you modify the System file's itlc resource, you can activate System 7's keyboard menu (bottom), which lets you switch layouts without having to use the Keyboard control panel.

The Keyboard menu appears between the Application and Help menus (see Figure 24-11 "Multiple Keyboards"). After you activate the Keyboard menu, you can use it to switch between layouts — no need to use the Keyboard control panel. The Keyboard menu even provides a keyboard shortcut for switching layouts: Press ⌘-Option-spacebar.

Modifying date, time, and number formats

To determine how to display date, time, and numeric values, the Mac uses two System file resources — itl0 (for date values) and itl1 (for time and currency values). By altering the itl0 resource, you can change the date format that the Finder uses in its list views (see Figure 24-12 "Short Dates"). By altering the itl1 resource, you can change the format used for currency and numeric values — handy if you're preparing documents for colleagues in other countries. (In System 7.5, you can change most of these date formats using the Date & Time control panel.)

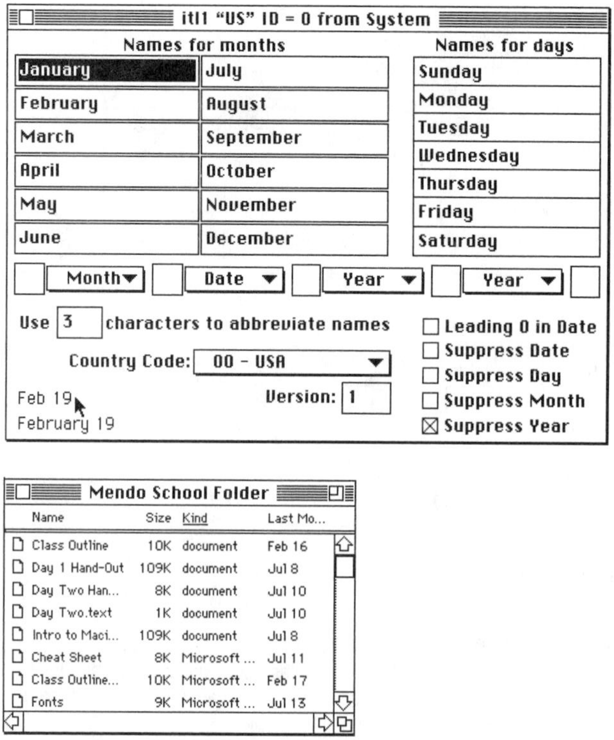

Figure 24-12: Short Dates By editing the System file's itl1 resource, you can customize the names and formats that the Mac uses to display date values. The pop-up menus and check boxes at the bottom of the itl1 editor (top) have been used to change the Mac's date format to display only the month and the date. A Finder window (bottom) uses the new format. To change the format used for time and currency displays, edit the System file's itl0 resource.

Replace the Finder's help screens

The System 7 Finder's Help menu has a command called Finder Shortcuts. When you choose Finder Shortcuts, you can work your way through several windows that list various keyboard shortcuts for the Finder. The text and graphics in those windows comes from numerous PICT resources stored in the Finder file. You can replace those PICT resources with your own images — maybe some of your own quick-reference information or a "this Mac belongs to" message.

Here's how: Open the Finder in ResEdit and double-click the PICT icon. A window appears showing small versions of each PICT resource. Select one and copy it to the Clipboard. Now start a bitmapped graphics program (such as Photoshop or SuperPaint) and paste. Use this image as a sizing template for your own masterpieces.

When you've created your first masterpiece, select it and copy it to the Clipboard. Now switch back to ResEdit, select the PICT resource you want to replace, and paste.

Change the text in font sample windows

When you open a font file's icon, the Finder displays some sample text, using the clever phrase "How razorback jumping frogs can level six piqued gymnasts." Yes, the phrase does manage to use all the letters of the alphabet, but maybe you'd like to change it to the more common "The quick brown fox jumped over the lazy dog's back" — or to something else completely.

With ResEdit, double-click the STR# icon and then locate string number 14516 (in System 7.1 and 7.5, that is; in System 7.0, it's number 14512). Type the message you'd like to appear in the font sample windows.

While you have the STR resource picker open, explore some of the other STR resources. You'll find a lot of familiar messages, and maybe some unfamiliar ones. They're all open for customizing.

Change the suffix for aliases

Normally, the Finder adds the text *alias* to the name of an alias you create. You can change that by editing item 1 of the STR# resource number 20500.

Change the default name for folders

Normally, the Finder names a new folder *untitled folder*. You can change that by editing item three of the STR# resource number 11250.

Customizing Caveats

Before you go crazy with ResEdit or another resource-editing utility, read the following tips for some customizing caveats.

Non-standard applications

ResEdit gives you full access to the resources that the Mac and its programs use, but that doesn't mean you can perform the same modifications on every program. Many programs use resources in nonstandard ways. Microsoft Word, for example, doesn't use MENU resources (fortunately, Word provides its own menu-customizing features). Similarly, Adobe PageMaker's resources aren't stored in the PageMaker application file, but in a System Folder file called PM5 RSRC (PM4 RSRC for PageMaker 4.x). Many Claris drawing programs store MENU resources that list customized views, line, and font settings in their own documents.

Understanding resource overriding

That last example brings up an important point: Resources in a document override those in an application, and resources in an application override those in the System file. For example, the System file contains standard templates for the Open and Save dialog boxes, but many applications override them and provide their own. Thus, modifying the System file's Open and Save dialog boxes may not have any effect on your favorite program.

Replacing your Finder or System files

When you're modifying a Finder or System file, you need a way to replace the original Finder or System file on your startup disk. You can't simply copy the modified version to your startup disk's System Folder because the Mac can't replace a file that's currently in use — that would be like trying to change a car's tires while it's moving.

One way to work around this is to start up with a different system disk and then modify the Finder or System file in your regular System Folder. The system software CD-ROM that accompanies CD-equipped Macs makes a good startup disk for this task; see Chapter 28 for details on starting up with this CD-ROM.

Be tasteful — or at least try

Finally, don't ignore the aesthetic aspects of resource editing, especially if your Mac or programs will be used by someone else. Go ahead: Make your Mac's interface look like a prop from *Pee Wee's Playhouse.* Translate your menu commands into Pig Latin if you like. But don't force your tastes on an unsuspecting colleague. One person's Trash is not necessarily another person's toilet.

CHAPTER 24 CONCEPTS AND TERMS

- Utilities form the supporting cast of your Macintosh setup: They work together with the Mac's system software and with your application programs to improve the Mac's performance and enhance its operation.
- Utilities that work together with application programs may operate as extensions (INITs), desk accessories, function keys (FKEYs), Chooser devices (RDEVs), or control panels (cdevs).
- Some extensions can slow down a Power Mac because they patch native system routines with 68000-family code. Casady & Greene's Conflict Catcher III can spot such offenders.
- Navigation utilities such as CE Software's QuicKeys and Affinity's Tempo II Plus let you create keyboard shortcuts and automate repetitive tasks.
- File-searching utilities such as Claris Clear Choice's RetrieveIt! and Alki Seek give you more file-searching options than the Finder's Find command provides.
- Resource-management utilities such as Suitcase II and MasterJuggler make it easier to work with fonts, FKEYs, sounds, and other system resources.
- Apple's AppleScript takes automation to its limits by enabling you to write scripts that perform tasks when run. An application program must be scriptable in order to be controlled by scripts, and recordable in order to automatically generate scripts as you use it.
- For hard-core customizing, you need a copy of Apple's ResEdit utility. ResEdit lets you tinker with (and damage, if you aren't careful) the resources that programs use as they run.

applet
A tiny application program, created with AppleScript, that you can run directly from the Finder.

attachable
An AppleScript term used to describe a program that enables you to assign, or attach, scripts to menu commands or to buttons or other on-screen elements. When you click or otherwise activate an element to which a script is attached, the script runs.

backup utility
A program that simplifies backing up a hard disk. Examples include Dantz Development's Retrospect or DiskFit series, Inline Design's Redux, or Fifth Generation Systems' Fastback series.

cdev
The technical name for a control panel, which is stored in the Control Panels folder within the System Folder.

disk optimizer
Also called a *defragmentation utility*, a utility that keeps a hard disk running at top efficiency by rearranging its contents so that all files are stored contiguously.

droplet
A tiny application program, created with AppleScript, that you can run directly from the Finder and that acts like a drop box: You can drag icons for files, folders, or disks to the icon of a droplet, and the droplet runs and then performs some kind of operation on those icons.

extension
A program that enhances the Mac's system software by adding features or enabling the Mac to access a device, such as a printer. Examples of extensions include INITs, control panels, and printer drivers.

file-recovery utility
A program that can resurrect files you accidentally delete and repair damaged disks or files. Examples include Symantec's Norton Utilities for the Macintosh, Fifth Generation's Public Utilities, and Central Point Software's MacTools Deluxe or Safe & Sound.

keyboard layout
A resource (with a type of KCHR) that associates the characters in the Mac's character set with keyboard positions. By editing the System file's keyboard layout, or KCHR, resource, you can rearrange the keyboard layout to suit your tastes. The System file can accommodate multiple KCHR resources; you can switch between them using the Keyboard control panel or the Keyboard menu.

macro utility
Also called a *keyboard enhancement utility*, a utility that lets you create keyboard shortcuts, streamline system settings, and automate repetitive tasks.

partitioning utility
A utility that lets you divide a hard disk into multiple partitions, each of which appears on the desktop as a separate disk icon.

RDEV
The technical name for a Chooser device — an icon that appears in the Chooser desk accessory.

recordable
An AppleScript term used to describe a program that can work with a script editor utility to automatically create scripts as you work.

(continued on the next page)

(continued from previous page)

resource-management utility
A utility, such as Fifth Generation Systems' Suitcase II or AlSoft's MasterJuggler (part of the Alsoft Power Utilities package), that simplifies working with fonts, FKEYs, sounds, and other system resources. Also called *font/DA* extender.

resources
Small, structured tidbits of information the Mac uses as it runs. Resources are grouped by function into resource types, which have four-character names such as MENU and LAYO.

script
A series of commands that controls one or more programs when played back.

scriptable
A term used to describe a program that supports AppleScript and therefore can be controlled by scripts.

text-retrieval utility
A program that can search for text contained within files. Examples include Alki Software's Alki Seek, Microlytics' Gofer, On Technology's On Location, Claris Clear Choice RetrieveIt!, and Virginia Systems' Sonar series.

CHAPTER TWENTY-FIVE

Storage: From Floppies to CD-ROMs

- Understanding how floppy disks and hard drives store data
- Maximizing hard disk performance
- Shopping for a hard disk
- Removable media drives: combining hard disk performance with floppy disk security
- Tips for CD-ROM drives

The Mac is a remarkable machine, but how quickly it forgets. The moment the juice is turned off, the Mac becomes a dark and silent box, and your efforts leave its memory chips like air from a bursting balloon.

Because memory forgets, computers have always been paired with mass-storage devices — originally punched cards, and then paper or magnetic tape, and now the current standard, magnetic disks. Storage devices hold the documents you create and the applications you use. In this chapter, you'll tour the mass-storage world, with a focus on hard disks and other high-capacity media. I also provide some tips for organizing a hard disk to maximize its speed and efficiency.

A Magnetic Voyage

In the late seventies, personal computer users wept for joy when floppy disks replaced slow, unreliable cassette tapes as the standard storage device. Floppy disks transformed the microcomputer storage world by allowing *random access* to data. To appreciate that, locate a song in the middle of a compact disc, and then try locating a song in the middle of a cassette tape. You have to access a cassette sequentially — by fast-forwarding and rewinding — but you can jump to any song on a CD. Similarly, a computer can access any spot on a disk almost immediately by moving the drive's heads to that point.

Spinning disks

Inside a floppy disk's plastic case is a disk of flexible (floppy) plastic, coated with iron oxide particles (see Figure 25-1 "Inside a Floppy Disk"). This disk spins at 390 to 600 revolutions per minute as it is being accessed. When the Mac saves a document or copies a file, a read/write head in the disk drive generates a magnetic field that positions the disk's iron particles in patterns corresponding to the zeros and ones that comprise the information being written. When the Mac reads from the disk, the particles re-create the magnetic field in the head.

Making tracks and sectors

A disk is divided into 80 concentric circles called *tracks*, and each track is divided into wedges called *sectors.* The number of sectors in a track depends on the track's location; tracks located near the disk's outer edge have room for more sectors than the smaller tracks closer to the disk's center. The disk's rotation speed varies depending on which tracks the read/write head is accessing.

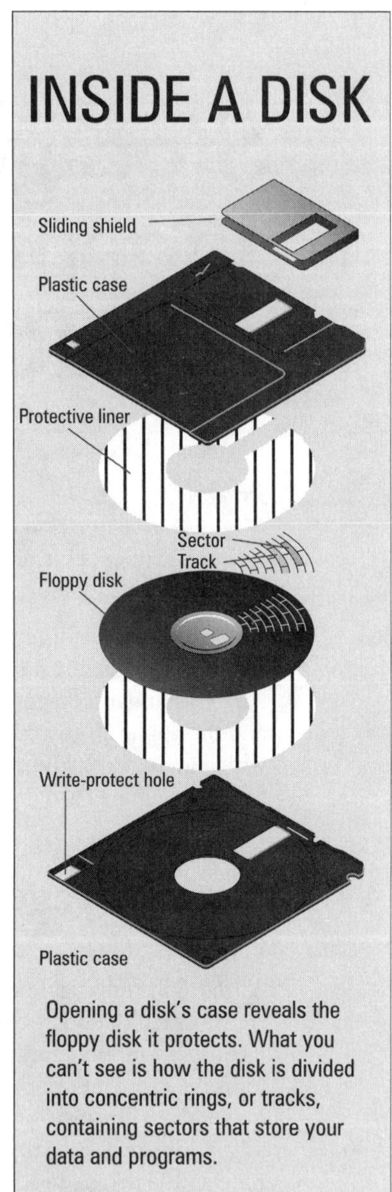
INSIDE A DISK
Sliding shield
Plastic case
Protective liner
Sector
Track
Floppy disk
Write-protect hole
Plastic case
Opening a disk's case reveals the floppy disk it protects. What you can't see is how the disk is divided into concentric rings, or tracks, containing sectors that store your data and programs.

Figure 25-1: Inside a Floppy Disk

You can look at a phonograph album and see grooves, but you can't look at a disk and see tracks and sectors. A disk's divisions aren't physical ones; they're magnetic boundaries recorded on the disk when it's *initialized*, or *formatted.* This software approach to disk formatting enables many other computers to use the same 3½-inch disks that the Mac uses. Fresh out of the box, the disks are identical lumps of storage clay. Each computer's system software sculpts the disk to its own needs by initializing it.

Part of the sculpting process involves creating the tracks and sectors; the other part involves reserving parts of the disk to hold special information. Some tracks hold start-up software — the instructions that either transfer control to the Finder when you start the Mac or eject the disk and display the blinking X icon to indicate that the disk can't start up the Mac. Other tracks hold information about the disk's contents, so the Mac can locate documents and applications and determine where a disk's available space is.

Buying Preformatted Floppies

Many disk manufacturers and computer supply houses now sell preformatted floppies that you can use immediately — no initialization routine required. But isn't buying preformatted floppies a bit like buying presharpened pencils? Have we become so lazy that we can't even format our floppies anymore?

Actually, preformatted floppies are ideal for PowerBooks. If you need a fresh floppy on an airplane at 36,000 feet, you don't want to have to waste precious battery power initializing a disk. A preformatted floppy is ready to use immediately.

Of course, you can save money along with your battery by simply formatting a few floppies yourself before you unplug your PowerBook's AC adaptor. While you're at it, sharpen a few pencils, too.

A Short History of Mac Floppy Drives

The original Mac floppy drive stored 400K. The Mac Plus premiered with 800K disk drives, which doubled storage capacity by using both sides of a floppy disk. 800K drives have two read/write heads, one for each side of the disk. If you have a 128K or 512K Mac or if you choose the Single Sided button in the disk-initialization dialog box, only one side of the disk is used. One reason you may choose the Single Sided option is to create a disk that a Mac with a 400K floppy drive can access.

The drive that ate my data

Some of Apple's original 800K drives had an annoying habit of occasionally refusing to eject a disk completely. They sucked it back in, forcing you to pull out the Universal Disk Disgorger — an unbent paper clip — to rescue the disk, a job that still gets a chuckle out of onlooking DOS/Windows users.

To use the Universal Disk Disgorger — with an old drive or a new one — insert it into the small hole next to the floppy drive and push. Don't pull on the disk — you risk damaging the drive mechanism. You can also use the Disgorger to eject a CD from Apple's CD-ROM drives.

SuperDrive to the rescue

In 1989, Apple introduced the SuperDrive, also called the FDHD (floppy disk high-density) drive. SuperDrives, now standard equipment in all Macs and available as upgrades for older SEs and IIs, store 1.4MB on high-density disks, which have a thinner magnetic coating and smaller magnetic particles.

Dealing with Different Floppy Capacities

A high-density disk's differences can cause problems if you move disks between SuperDrives and 800K drives. If you use an 800K drive to initialize a high-density disk, the drive creates an 800K disk. That disk works properly in 800K drives, but when you insert it in a SuperDrive, you get a message asking if you want to initialize the disk. The message appears because the SuperDrive notices that extra hole in the case and tries to read the disk as a 1.4MB disk. What's more, once the disk has been initialized as an 800K disk, the chances of being able to successfully reformat it as a high-density disk are slim.

The tip? If you'll be swapping files between 800K drives and SuperDrives, don't use high-density floppies as your transfer medium. Instead, format an 800K disk and use it to transfer the files.

A high-density disk has a small hole in its upper-left corner, opposite the write-protect hole. A SuperDrive looks for this hole when you insert a disk. If the hole is present, you can initialize the disk to store its full 1.4MB. If the hole isn't present, the SuperDrive only enables you to create a 400K or 800K disk. And if you're curious, high-density disks spin at 300 rpm (revolutions per minute) regardless of which track the Mac is accessing.

Life in the Hard Drive Era

Fortunately, the hard disk has long-since transformed floppies into a medium for backups and software distribution. A 230MB hard drive can hold the contents of nearly 200 high-density floppies. A 20MB hard drive used to be the power user's choice; today, drives that store hundreds and even thousands of megabytes have become commonplace.

Talk about progress: I remember reviewing external hard drives that stored 10MB, connected to the Mac's serial port, required a floppy to jump-start the Mac — and cost more than a Power Mac. And I have the proud honor of having once reviewed for *Macworld* a 10MB external hard drive that was made by . . . Quark. Yes, *that* Quark. Today's publishing titan used to be a relatively small developer of Apple II and Mac software and hardware.

How a hard drive works

A hard drive may have the capacity of a truck, but it offers the performance of a Porsche. Hard disks transfer data many times faster than floppy disks, and that means less waiting when starting programs and saving files.

A hard disk owes its speed and capacity to several factors. First, its magnetic surface isn't a sheet of flexible plastic, but a polished, precision-machined metal platter whose magnetic particles (and therefore, your data) are packed closer together. Most hard disks contain several platters, stacked like records in a jukebox and sealed in a dust-free enclosure (see Figure 25-2 "Inside a Hard Disk"). The platters spin at least 3600 rpm — six to nine times faster than a floppy disk. And hard disk platters generally spin continuously: A floppy stops when it isn't being accessed and takes about a half-second to get up to speed when the next access begins.

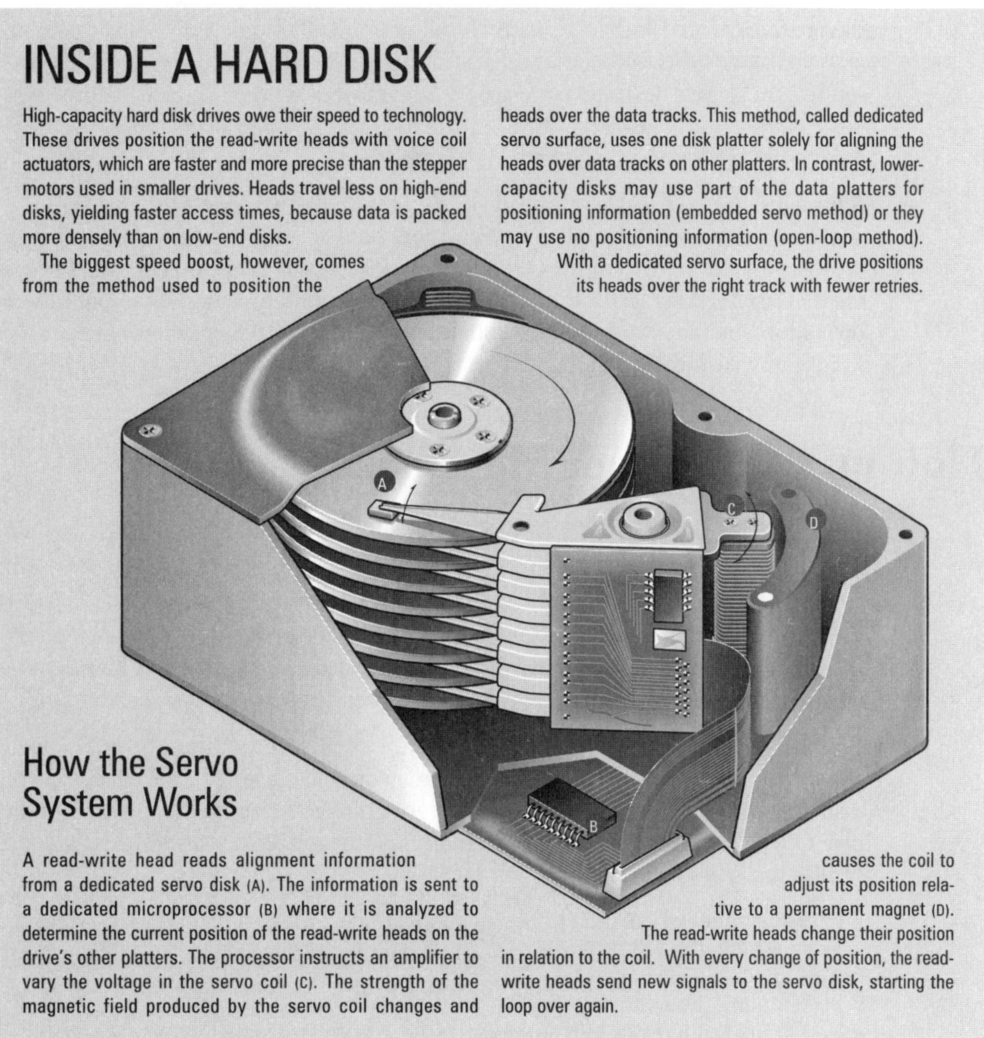

INSIDE A HARD DISK
High-capacity hard disk drives owe their speed to technology. These drives position the read-write heads with voice coil actuators, which are faster and more precise than the stepper motors used in smaller drives. Heads travel less on high-end disks, yielding faster access times, because data is packed more densely than on low-end disks.
The biggest speed boost, however, comes from the method used to position the heads over the data tracks. This method, called dedicated servo surface, uses one disk platter solely for aligning the heads over data tracks on other platters. In contrast, lower-capacity disks may use part of the data platters for positioning information (embedded servo method) or they may use no positioning information (open-loop method).
With a dedicated servo surface, the drive positions its heads over the right track with fewer retries.
A
B
C
D
How the Servo System Works
A read-write head reads alignment information from a dedicated servo disk (A). The information is sent to a dedicated microprocessor (B) where it is analyzed to determine the current position of the read-write heads on the drive's other platters. The processor instructs an amplifier to vary the voltage in the servo coil (C). The strength of the magnetic field produced by the servo coil changes and causes the coil to adjust its position relative to a permanent magnet (D).
The read-write heads change their position in relation to the coil. With every change of position, the read-write heads send new signals to the servo disk, starting the loop over again.

Figure 25-2: Inside a Hard Disk

The specter of the head crash

Unlike the heads in a floppy drive, a hard disk's read-write heads don't touch the disk's surfaces, but ride a hair's width above them. If a hard disk's head does touch the surface, you've got trouble. That's a head crash, and it can occur when the drive is jostled during use, or even when a speck of dust gets between the platter's surface and the head.

A head crash used to damage the platter as the head dug a ditch in the platter's coating. Improved platter surfaces make today's drives more durable (although you still should never move or bump a drive that's in use). *Thin-film coating,* in which the platter is coated with a minutely thin film of metal, is one technology found in many of today's drives. Another safety feature is *automatic head-parking,* which retracts the drive's heads to a safe area when you shut down.

External versus internal drives

A hard disk can live inside or outside a Mac. Internal drives don't use any desk space, and they make moving your Mac more convenient. But if an internal drive breaks, your entire Mac must go to the shop. I'm partial to external drives. They move from one Mac to another in a flash, and with long cables, you can bury them out of earshot under your desk or in a nearby closet. And you don't have to part with your Mac if the worst happens.

How to Manage Your Megabytes

You can make your drive operate faster by following the advice in this section.

Use folders for better performance

A file cabinet lets you create a storage hierarchy; so does the Mac. In this hierarchy, the file cabinet corresponds to the hard disk: It's at the top level of the hierarchy, with folders nested within it.

Beneath the Mac's friendly folder metaphor lie some technicalities that influence performance. When you open a disk's icon by double-clicking it, the Mac scans the disk in order to display its contents. The more files you store at the top level of the disk's hierarchy — that is, not within folders — the longer it takes for the Finder to display the disk's window.

This also applies when you choose an application's Open command: To display a list of available files, the Mac must scan all the files in the current level of the disk's hierarchy. The more files present there, the longer the scanning process takes.

The Mac all but ignores files stored in a folder until you actually open the folder. So, by grouping documents and applications into folders, you'll boost the Mac's performance by reducing the number of files it has to scan at once. And there's the convenience factor: Instead of having to electronically paw through dozens of word processor files, for example, you can go directly to the Proposals folder, the Memos folder, or the Seedy Novel folder, and quickly locate the file you need.

Working with folders

To create a folder, use the Finder's New Folder command (in the File menu). The Finder gives new folders the name *untitled folder*; you'll want to change that to something a bit more appropriate — Documents, Proposals, Graphics Programs, whatever best describes the folder's contents.

At this point, you can open the new folder and follow the same process to create another folder inside it — just as you can nest one manila folder within another. This lets you develop a storage hierarchy that keeps your files orderly. You can nest folders more than a dozen levels deep, but navigating through more than five levels or so becomes cumbersome and time-consuming.

The number of folders you create and the names you give them is up to you. Some people create date-oriented folders — January Work, February Work, March Work, and so on — and then create folders within them for specific types of documents such as memos, publications, and artwork. Some people create 26 folders, one for each letter of the alphabet, and file documents within them.

You'll find a sample filing scheme in Figure 25-3 "Organizing a Hard Disk." It's just a starting point, though: The best filing system is one you've personalized for your work style.

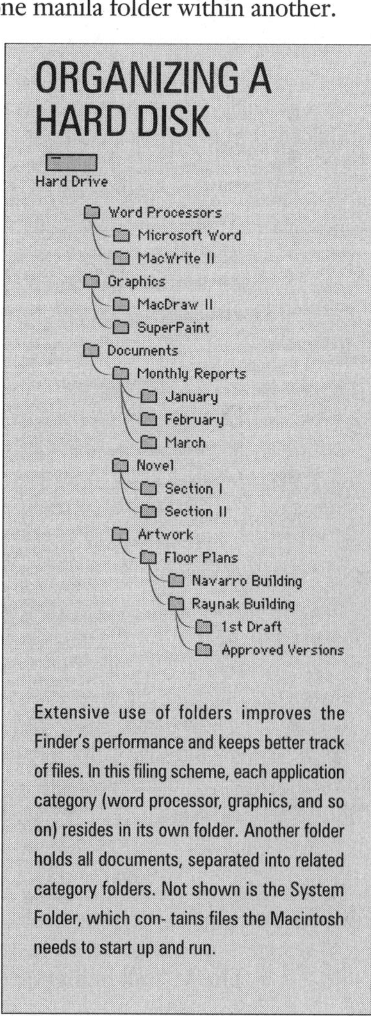

Extensive use of folders improves the Finder's performance and keeps better track of files. In this filing scheme, each application category (word processor, graphics, and so on) resides in its own folder. Another folder holds all documents, separated into related category folders. Not shown is the System Folder, which con- tains files the Macintosh needs to start up and run.

Figure 25-3: Organizing a Hard Disk

Don't forget about Find

Even with an efficient filing system, you may occasionally misplace a file. When you do, use the Find command in the Finder's file menu (or the Find File item in the System 7.5 Apple menu). You can find powerful file- and text-searching features in a variety of third-party utilities, too (see Chapter 24).

PowerBook Hard Drive Tips

Thanks to their rear-panel SCSI connectors, all PowerBooks can tap into the same universe of external storage options as their desk-bound cousins. (To use a SCSI device with a PowerBook Duo model, you need to add an appropriate dock, such as Apple's Duo MiniDock.)

Expanding a PowerBook's hard drive capacity

As for internal hard drives, a PowerBook's tight confines require a 2½-inch hard drive. At this writing, drives of up to 1GB are available in this petite size. (Talk about progress — in the previous edition of this book, the upper limit for PowerBook hard drives was 256MB.) Most hard drive firms sell internal drives for PowerBooks, and some offer trade-in allowances for your existing hard drive. Some firms also offer case kits that let you turn your existing internal drive into an external drive — a nice alternative.

Wake up and go to sleep

A hard disk is one of a PowerBook's major power consumers (the screen backlight is another). Given this, you may think it's best to put the hard drive to sleep whenever possible. Apple reinforces this thinking with the PowerBook control strip, which gives you one-click access to hard drive slumber.

The problem is, it takes four times the amount of power to wake up a sleeping hard disk than it does to keep it spinning. If you frequently alternate between putting the drive to sleep and waking it up, you are using more battery power than if you simply leave the hard disk spinning. You also waste time, because it takes a few seconds for the disk to spin up to operating speed. If you find yourself putting the hard drive to sleep every few minutes, you might be using more power than you're saving.

SCSI Disk Mode

This mode lets you connect the PowerBook to another Mac, which treats the PowerBook's hard drive as an external drive — it's a boon for beaming files between Macs.

SCSI disk mode is supported on the PowerBook 100, 160, 165, 165c, 180, 180c, 500-series models, and Duo-system models equipped with MiniDocks. To set it up, use the PowerBook control panel to specify your PowerBook's SCSI ID (use the Portable control panel for the PowerBook 100). Verify that the PowerBook's hard disk name is different from that of the Mac you're connecting to. Shut down both Macs, then attach a SCSI Disk Adaptor cable to the PowerBook. (Note that cable: it's not the standard SCSI system cable. The Disk Adaptor Cable is dark gray and shorter than the SCSI system cable.) Attach a terminator to the end of the cable.

Make sure all devices in the SCSI chain are off; then connect the other end of the terminator to either a cable leading to the desktop Macintosh or to the end of the SCSI chain (you may need to remove the last device's terminator).

Finally, turn on the PowerBook. If all's well, a diamond shaped symbol (the SCSI symbol — the same icon that's next to the SCSI port on the back of the Mac) begins moving on the screen, bearing a number corresponding to the ID you set. Once you see that, turn on the desktop machine. After it starts, you'll see the PowerBook's hard drive on its desktop.

When you're ready to shut down, first shut down the desktop Macintosh; then power off the PowerBook by pressing and holding the power switch for two seconds, and then releasing. (For the PowerBook 100, press both of the two buttons on the left side of the unit.)

Many of today's PowerBooks can also use PCMCIA (also called PC Card) based hard drives. These removable hard drives combine the capacity of a hard drive with the flexibility of a floppy disk.

Whatever you do, back up

Electrocution aside, the loss of data is the most painful experience a computer peripheral can cause. It's an agony you can avoid by backing up faithfully. I present some guidelines in the next chapter.

Driving to the High End

For color publishers or multimedia producers, a hard drive can't be too fast. Prepress professionals lose money every time they drum their fingers waiting for Adobe Photoshop images to open or save. Fast, high-capacity hard drives are also essential for professional-quality audio and video work. And they're the mainstays of network file servers that supply application programs and documents to an office full of computers. A fast hard drive enables a server to keep up with the data demands of the users connected to it.

Spindle speeding

The latest drives meet these challenges. The availability of Seagate's Elite-2, Elite-3, and Barracuda mechanisms make the latest high-capacity drives faster than their predecessors. One reason these drives are faster is that their internal platters spin faster. A fast spindle speed allows for a faster data transfer rate because more bits pass beneath the drive's heads each second. A fast spindle speed also lowers *latency* — the time it takes for a particular spot on the drive's platters to reach the drive's heads.

Not long ago, the fastest drives had spindle speeds of 4500 and 5400 rpm, compared to the 3600-rpm speed most other drives used. These days, spindles are speeding at 6300 and even 7200 rpm — a dizzying 120 revolutions per second.

Making your Mac keep up

But this extra spindle speed is wasted if the Mac can't keep up. The fastest hard drives can send and receive data faster than any Mac except a Quadra or high-end Centris. On a slower Mac, an ultra-fast drive twiddles its thumbs as it waits for the SCSI bus. In order for a slower Mac to keep up with an ultra-fast drive, you need a SCSI-2 adaptor, which gives your Mac the latest in SCSI interfaces — and one that can better keep up with the hard drive. For details on SCSI-2 adaptors and SCSI in general, see Chapter 26.

More Tech Talk

The speed at which the hard drive's disk spins and the density of the data in its tracks aren't the only factors that contribute to performance. Here's a look at some other technical specifications you can encounter when shopping for a drive.

Average access time

This tells you how long it takes for the drive's heads to locate a given spot on the disk — the mass-storage equivalent to moving a phonograph's tone arm to a given spot on an album. The average access time is measured in milliseconds; the lower the value, the better.

Data transfer rate

This is a measure of how quickly the drive can shuttle bytes to the Mac. The higher the value, the better, but only to a point. Mac Classics, SEs, and Pluses, for example, can't handle as high a transfer rate as a Mac II, which in turn is much slower than a Quadra or Power Mac.

Interleave ratio

This describes the organization of sectors in each track (see Figure 25-4 "Understanding Interleaving"). Generally, the lower the interleave ratio, the better. A 1:1 ratio is best — if your Mac can scarf up sectors at that speed. Back when hard drives were slower, slower Macs such as the SE and Plus needed a 2:1 or even a 3:1 ratio. But the majority of today's drives provide built-in *data caching.* The drive reads an entire track and stores it in a small reserve of memory. When the Mac requests subsequent sectors from that track, the drive sends the data from the cache. Thanks to this caching technique, you can safely use a 1:1 interleave ratio with any Mac.

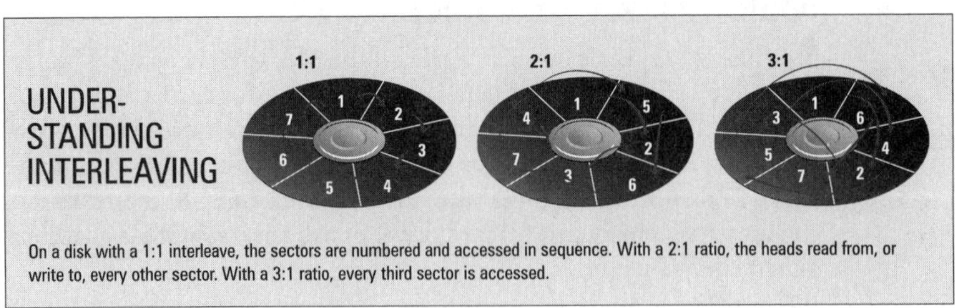

On a disk with a 1:1 interleave, the sectors are numbered and accessed in sequence. With a 2:1 ratio, the heads read from, or write to, every other sector. With a 3:1 ratio, every third sector is accessed.

Figure 25-4: Understanding Interleaving

How important are these specifications?

Performance specifications make for fun party talk, but they really aren't that important for most applications. In day-to-day use, the differences between most drives with similar capacities are minor.

Tips for Faster Driving

Those of you who are always completely satisfied with the speed of your hard drives may skip to a different chapter.

Now that the two of them are gone, the rest of us can concentrate on what is often the weakest link in a Mac's performance chain. Even in the fastest Macs, data slows to a relative crawl when it reaches a hard drive's spinning platters and the head actuator arms that grope across them.

You can employ a variety of tools and techniques to squeeze every drop of speed out of your spindles. You might even have everything you need — you can perform some of the tricks described in this section using the setup software that accompanies most hard drives. For an extra measure of performance or to do advanced drive-tuning, turn to any of several utility packages. Some also streamline working with removable-media SyQuest, Bernoulli, and magneto-optical drives.

Optimizing a drive's performance involves some initial setup and some ongoing maintenance. The setup phases help ensure that the drive and Mac are communicating as fast as they can and that you're using the drive's space efficiently. Ongoing maintenance means using a defragmenting utility to keep the drive's files arranged in a way that allows fastest retrieval.

Formatting: basic setup

All hard drives include a basic formatting utility that prepares the drive for use. Part of the preparation process involves installing the SCSI driver software that the Mac uses to communicate with the drive.

Hard drive vendors often boast that their SCSI drivers are faster than the competition's. Several companies counter with universal driver/formatter packages that work with any hard drive and promise to deliver better performance than the software that came with yours. Well, surprise: for most applications and mainstream drive capacities, there is little significant performance difference between today's drivers.

That's not to say that stand-alone driver/formatter packages such as Casablanca's Drive7, Surf City Software's Lido 7, FWB's Hard Disk Toolkit series, and La Cie's SilverLining don't have something to offer. If you have an older hard drive acquired in the System 6 era, updating its driver could provide a speed kick as well as System 7 compatibility. If you have an AV or Power Mac, installing a driver that supports the SCSI Manager 4.3's asynchronous transfer capabilities can perk up a third-party drive (see the Backgrounder box "Pushing the AV and Power Mac SCSI Envelope").

Some driver/formatter packages also let you specify an interleave ratio, which describes the organization of the wedge-shaped sectors that comprise each track. With the fastest interleave ratio — 1 to 1 — sectors are numbered and read or written consecutively. All of today's Macs and hard drives support a 1:1 ratio. As mentioned earlier in this chapter, older Macs, however, must use a higher ratio because they can't keep up with the speed at which the sectors fly beneath the drive's read/write heads.

By the way, most driver utilities allow you to install a driver without requiring you to reformat the hard disk, but it's much safer to back up first and then reformat the drive with the utility. One driver package — Surf City's Lido 7 — deliberately doesn't support this friendly takeover approach because of the risk of data loss.

Pushing the AV and Power Mac SCSI Envelope

With hard drives and Apple's AV and Power Macs, one area is of special concern: support for SCSI Manager 4.3, the portion of the Mac's system software that communicates with SCSI devices. SCSI Manager 4.3 works together with the fast SCSI circuitry in an AV or Power Mac to allow for particularly speedy data transfers — when a hard drive's SCSI driver supports the new SCSI Manager.

An AV Mac's built-in hard drive does have a SCSI Manager 4.3-compatible driver. If you're connecting a third-party drive to an AV Mac, however, you can boost its performance by 20 to 30 percent by updating its driver to a 4.3-compatible version. Most driver developers have updated their wares to support the new SCSI Manager.

The real performance potential of the new SCSI Manager won't be realized, however, until application software developers rework their programs to take advantage of its capabilities. (Dantz Development has added 4.3 support to its Retrospect series of backup utilities.)

System 7.5.2, the Mac OS version shipped with the second-generation Power Macs, includes a new version of SCSI Manager 4.3 that runs in native mode. This native SCSI Manager is a big contributing factor to the second-generation Power Macs' excellent SCSI performance.

Performance tuning: reckless driving?

Some driver/formatter packages, particularly FWB's Hard Disk Toolkit, let you tweak the low-level controller settings that govern how the drive transfers data. Normally, Hard Disk Toolkit and other driver packages set these options automatically at formatting time: the utility determines what type of mechanism the drive uses and then adjusts its controller options to provide the best overall performance, based on tests done by the driver developer.

If a driver package sets low-level options automatically, can you really improve performance by taking matters into your own hands? You won't find out from these products' manuals, which describe the options but provide little advice for using them.

To be fair, the manuals can't provide specific recommendations for every mechanism. More to the point, different applications tax a drive in different ways — an option that improves the data retrieval in FileMaker Pro might not help saves in Photoshop. Only by testing a drive with your applications and documents can you find the best combination of low-level settings — and there's a good chance those settings are the defaults anyway.

Performance tuning tips

Still, there are two general rules of thumb. To improve performance with large files — opening Photoshop documents, for example — be sure that *prefetching* is enabled. This is a data-access technique that involves reading not only the block of data that the Mac explicitly requested, but also one or more subsequent blocks, which are stored, or cached, in the hard drive's memory buffer. If the Mac needs the cached blocks — and if you're working with a large image file, it probably will — the hard drive supplies them from its cache. Some drive mechanisms allow you to specify the number of blocks that are prefetched. Increasing this number can improve performance, too.

But extensive prefetching can actually slow down small, random-access data transfers — the kind that occur when you're retrieving records from a database, for example. To speed these tasks, try increasing the number of cache segments.

Before adjusting any low-level settings, back up your drive and do some tests, timing the tasks you perform most. Then adjust the settings and check your stopwatch again. You may find a genuine improvement — or you may find that you've spent hours to save a few milliseconds.

In the end, tweaking drive parameters is most worthwhile for people who constantly perform disk-intensive tasks and who own high-capacity (1GB and up) mechanisms, which have a larger number of adjustable parameters. If this describes you, buy Hard Disk Toolkit.

Partitioning: Divide and Conquer

All third-party hard drive formatting utilities support partitioning — the ability to divide the hard drive into a number of smaller-capacity *volumes*, each of which appears on the desktop as a separate drive. (If your older drive's software doesn't support partitioning, this is another good reason to buy a universal formatter.) Most utilities include a control panel or desk accessory that lets you mount and unmount partitions and often perform other tasks such as locking partitions.

One reason to partition a drive is to improve security: most utilities let you encrypt and password-protect partitions as well as lock them to prevent modification. Also, a virus can't infect an unmounted partition.

Good reasons to partition a drive

Partitioning also offers efficiency and performance advantages. When you save a file, the Mac bites off disk space in chunks called *allocation blocks*. The larger the hard drive, the larger the block size. Block sizes start at 500 bytes and increase by 500 bytes for every 32MB of drive capacity: 1K on an 80MB hard drive, 4K on a 230MB, 16K on a 1GB.

Here's the rub: Even if a file contains only one character, the Mac gives it an entire allocation block. The combination of a large hard drive and small files — e-mail messages, memos, small databases — is particularly wasteful: storing 500 tiny files on a 1GB drive wastes 8MB. The solution is to create smaller partitions to hold smaller files.

Partitioning also boosts performance by reducing the amount of searching the Mac must do to locate a particular piece of data. It takes less time to find a file on a 20MB partition than it would if the same file was scattered across a 230MB drive — just as it would take longer to find an article if an encyclopedia was printed as one huge book instead of being partitioned into numerous smaller ones.

There's more. The tracks on the outer edges of a hard drive's platters generally have faster transfer rates than those on the inner edges.

As a result, you can squeeze an extra drop of speed out of a drive by storing your System Folder and other often-used files on a partition that uses the outer tracks.

How can you tell which partition uses the outer tracks? Easy: Partitions are written from the outer edges of the drive platters toward the inner edges, so the first partition you created will be the fastest.

All driver/formatter packages support partitioning, but only Surf City Software's Lido 7, La Cie's SilverLining, and FWB's Hard Disk Toolkit series allow you to change an existing partition's size without erasing its contents.

Optimizing: Squelch Those Seeks

Of all the things that take place within a hard drive, one of the most time consuming is the seek — the drive's read/write heads moving from one track to another. Other things being equal, a drive with a shorter seek time will be faster than a drive with a longer one.

If you've been reading your hard drive utility ads, you probably have nightmares about the specter of file fragmentation. It's what happens as you add and remove files to a hard drive over time. As it recycles disk space freed up by deleted files, the Mac may scatter newly saved files across physically discontiguous tracks. Reading such a file requires more seeks and more time — just as it takes you longer to seek out an article that is scattered throughout a magazine instead of being printed on contiguous pages.

But as hard drives become faster, fragmentation is becoming a bit like ring around the collar — a problem whose seriousness is exaggerated by those who sell remedies for it. With today's hard drives, fragmentation doesn't impair performance to the extent that it used to. Partitioning can reduce its effects, too, since on a partition, files are fragmented over a physically smaller area.

Good reasons to defragment your drives

Still, if you're sensitive to your Mac's performance, fragmentation can cause a drive to feel sluggish over time. I often notice the problem in Open and Save dialog boxes — over time, the drive chatters more and more as I move into and out of nested folders.

Doing away with fragmentation has other benefits.

- ❖ If a drive's directory becomes damaged, a file-recovery utility stands a better chance of being able to rescue a file whose data is contiguous rather than fragmented across the disk.
- ❖ If you use System 7 virtual memory, the amount of available VM is limited to the amount of contiguous free disk space.
- ❖ If you're creating QuickTime movies, you'll get smoother movies if you defragment the hard drive to which you'll be recording.
- ❖ If you're preparing a master hard drive for CD-ROM production, one of the last steps in the production process involves defragmenting the master hard drive so that the CD-ROM's files are contiguous.

Defragmenting tools

One way to defragment a hard drive is to back it up, initialize it, and then restore its contents, beginning with the System Folder and your most-often-used applications and documents. An easier way is to use a defragmenting utility, sometimes called a disk optimizer.

Some universal formatter packages — La Cie's SilverLining and Surf City's Lido 7 — include defragmenting features. Disk optimizers are also included with Symantec's Norton Utilities for Macintosh and Central Point's MacTools Deluxe. The optimizers that accompany these utilities offer smart optimizing features that strategically position certain system files for best performance.

Another excellent optimizer is ALSoft's Disk Express II. Disk Express II can defragment a disk in the background while you work, and it keeps track of the files you use most and optimizes so that those files are physically closest to the drive's directory (see Figure 25-5 "Smart Optimizing"). To speed the Mac's startup, Disk Express II also organizes system extensions so that they're physically stored in the same order in which they load. You can specify that optimization occur at a particular time or let Disk Express II optimize automatically when the percentage of fragmented files reaches a specified value.

Because disk optimizers are included with utility packages, you should evaluate your other needs to determine which package provides the best mix for you. If you don't already have a file-recovery program, consider the Norton Utilities, SuperSet, Public Utilities, or MacTools. If you're already protected, ALSoft's Power Utilities is the best choice. Besides the best all-around optimizer, Power Utilities includes several useful utilities, including Master Juggler, which streamlines working with fonts and sounds (see Chapter 22), and MenuExtend, which puts hierarchical menus in your Apple menu.

If you opt for the Norton Utilities, note that version 3.0 of the SpeedDisk program has a serious bug that can trash data. Be sure to use version 3.1 or later of SpeedDisk.

Fragmentation Display

Anchored
Fragmented
Contiguous
Free

Volume Info:
• Name: 'Documents
• Size: 89,608K
• Last optimized: unknown
• Optimization Index: invalid
• Split Optimize option is On

File Info:
• 1,804 files occupy 78,634K
• 276 files (16%) are fragmented
• Total free space: 10,974K
• Free space fragments: 29
• Largest free space fragment: 7,892K

View
Close

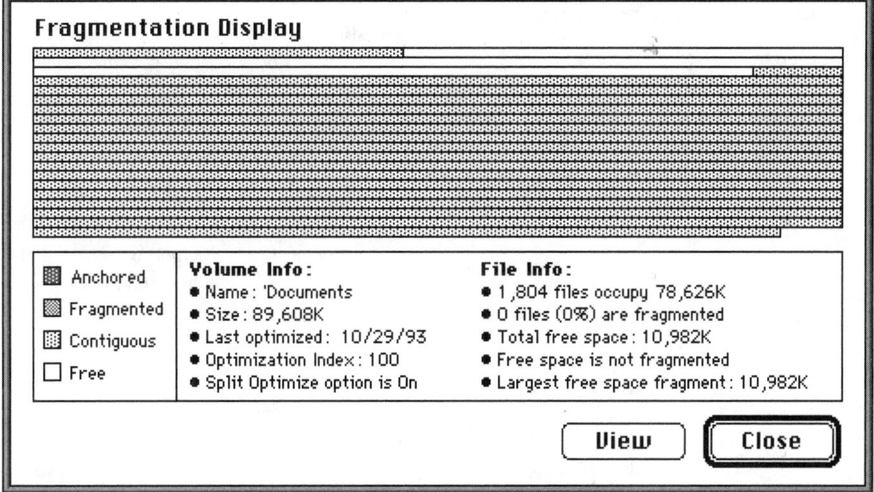

Figure 25-5: Smart Optimizing Most defragmenting utilities provide a graphical display that shows how a disk is fragmented. ALSoft's Disk Express II, shown here, monitors file usage and optimizes so that frequently used files are closest to the disk's directory. Both of these windows show the same drive — before optimizing (top) and after (bottom). In the top window, the tiled square pattern areas indicate fragmented files.

Other Routes to Faster Performance

Here are a few more ways to reduce a hard drive's performance toll.

Rebuild the desktop file now and then
This invisible file stores the information necessary to display the contents of disks and folders. Over time, it can become fragmented and unnecessarily large, saddled with icons for files long since deleted. To rebuild the desktop, hold down the Command and Option keys while restarting the Mac. When the message appears asking if you want to rebuild the desktop, click OK. One catch: You'll lose any comments added to Get Info windows. Public Utilities includes a program that saves and then restores these comments for you; Datawatch's SuperSet includes a rebuilding utility that preserves comments.

Don't use a big memory cache
The cache in the Mac's Memory control panel isn't particularly effective. ("If we didn't get internal information from Apple that they were redoing it, we'd be figuring out how to bypass it," one driver developer once told me.) Keep it small — between 32K and 128K.

Consider a Finder booster
Several products are available that modify the Finder's file-copying routines to provide better performance. Two examples are Fifth Generation Systems' CopyDoubler and Victor Tan's shareware SpeedyFinder (available through user groups and on-line services). If you spend a lot of time copying files to or from file servers or cartridges, one of these products will save you time.

Use folders and aliases extensively
The milliseconds that you might gain with a finely tuned and defragmented drive are lost — with interest — when you spend minutes searching for lost or buried files.

Buy a faster hard drive
If you're slogging along with the 80MB or 230MB drive that accompanied your Mac, supplement it with a 500MB or larger drive. You'll be amazed at how much faster it is.

Of course, as you get accustomed to a fast drive, you'll start wishing it was faster still. When that happens, turn to the tools and techniques I've described in this chapter to give it a mid-life speed kick.

Strength in Numbers — Disk Arrays

Disk arrays operate on the premise that anything one drive can do, multiple drives can do better. More specifically, a disk array ties multiple drive assemblies together in a way that enables them to deliver better performance and, in some cases, better reliability, than a single drive. The array's controller hardware and software tricks the Mac into thinking it's talking to a single drive.

Disk arrays are structured and described according to a framework called *RAID* — redundant array of inexpensive disks — spelled out by researchers at the University of California at Berkeley in 1987. The RAID framework has six levels, numbered 0 through 5 (see Table 25-1). Each RAID level provides a different degree of performance improvement and/or reliability over a *SLED* — a single large expensive disk.

Table 25-1
Levels of RAID

Level	*Title*	*Description*	*Pros*	*Cons*
0	Data Striping without Parity	Data is striped (split) evenly across two drives	Fast performance	Reduced reliability
1	Mirroring	Data is sent to two drives	Increased reliability	Performance suffers; cost per megabyte doubles
3	Parallel Disk Array	Data is transferred in parallel to an array of drives; one drive handles error correction	Reads from the array are fast; data can be restored when a drive fails	Writes can be slow; requires costly controller hardware
5	Independent Disk Array	Reads and writes data and error-checking information across all drives	The fastest and most reliable storage	Costly

Why is RAID fast?

A Level 0 array uses a technique called data striping to split data evenly across two drives, boosting data-transfer rates by enabling disk reads and writes to occur simultaneously. It's this data striping feature that makes disk arrays popular for high-end video production work. On fast Macs such as the Quadra 840AV, it isn't unusual to see transfer rates of 10MB to 20MB per second with high-end arrays and SCSI-2 adapter cards.

The drawback is that the array is only half as reliable as a single mechanism: If one mechanism fails, you lose the contents of both. Despite the acronym's first letter, there's no redundancy in Level 0 RAID.

Why is RAID reliable?

The superior reliability aspects of RAID involve combining two or more drives in a way that ensures that no data is lost, even if one drive breaks. RAID level 1, *mirroring*, involves simply writing the same data to two drives. Several hard drive manufacturers include software with their drives that allows for mirroring.

Hot pluggability

RAID levels 3 and 5 provide superior reliability through more complex data recording methods. These RAID levels even allow for *hot pluggability* — a sloppy buzzword that means you can replace a defective drive within the array without having to shut down the system. RAID levels 2 and 4 aren't used on the Mac.

The Bad News About Disk Arrays and First-Generation Power Macs

Interestingly, many high-performance disk arrays and SCSI-2 adaptors actually transfer data faster on a Quadra 800 and 840AV than on a Power Mac 8100.

There seem to be two reasons behind this. The 68040 processor provides a block-move instruction that's ideally suited to transferring huge amounts of data; many SCSI-2 adapters from firms such as FWB rely on this instruction to blast data to the array. The PowerPC 601 chip provides no equivalent instruction.

Another reason may be that in system versions prior to 7.5.2, SCSI Manager 4.3 is not native, but runs in emulation mode. The second-generation Power Macs use a native-mode SCSI Manager and deliver excellent SCSI performance.

As for more ambitious RAID systems, they're highly specialized and very expensive. And they still can't guarantee that your Mac won't crash or break down or that the power won't go out. It's good that such exotic products are available for the segment of the market that can use and afford them, but the rest of us will have to ride SLEDs — and hope they don't crash.

Installing a disk array

Most disk arrays are external boxes or a combination of boxes connected by cables. The biggest Macs, however — the Quadra 900 and 950 and their same-sized Apple Workgroup Server cousins — can accommodate an internal disk array (see Figure 25-6 "Installing an Internal Array"). An internal array provides better security and a more reliable SCSI chain, since it keeps cable lengths down.

Megabytes to Go: Removable Drives

All hard drives have one similarity — sooner or later, they become full. It happens sooner if you're into megabyte-munching applications such as image scanning or digital video or audio. Or it may happen later, as you acquire more and more software and use it to create more and more documents. Whenever it happens, you'll face the ugly chore of archiving — copying dusty old folders and files to floppy disks to free up space on your hard drive.

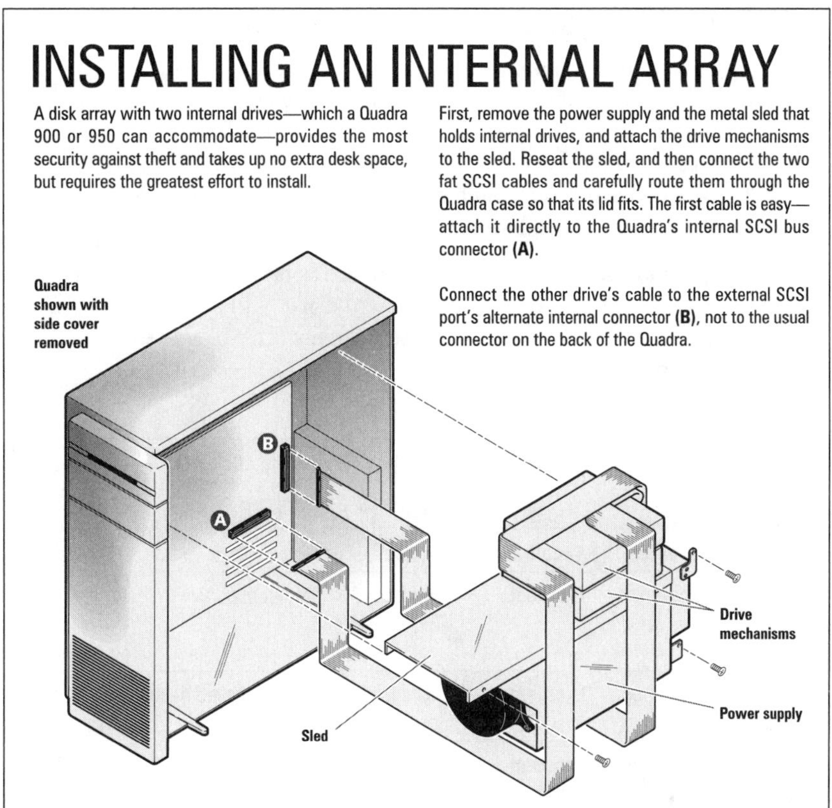

INSTALLING AN INTERNAL ARRAY
A disk array with two internal drives—which a Quadra 900 or 950 can accommodate—provides the most security against theft and takes up no extra desk space, but requires the greatest effort to install.
First, remove the power supply and the metal sled that holds internal drives, and attach the drive mechanisms to the sled. Reseat the sled, and then connect the two fat SCSI cables and carefully route them through the Quadra case so that its lid fits. The first cable is easy—attach it directly to the Quadra's internal SCSI bus connector (A).
Connect the other drive's cable to the external SCSI port's alternate internal connector (B), not to the usual connector on the back of the Quadra.
Quadra shown with side cover removed
B
A
Drive mechanisms
Power supply
Sled

Figure 25-6: Installing an Internal Array

Portability and security

Even if you don't worry about a hard drive's finite capacity, some of its other limitations may concern you. Unless they're installed in a PowerBook, internal hard drives aren't very portable — which makes it harder to move a large number of files to a different Mac. And if you're storing confidential information, you have to resort to security programs, which scramble and unscramble files based on passwords you type. Programs such as Kent-Marsh's FolderBolt do work (and are covered in the next chapter), but they add extra hassles to your work routine — especially if you forget a password.

Although external hard drives are more mobile and can be locked in a safe, you need to wrestle with SCSI cables before you can move them around. What's more, external drives are still delicate instruments that aren't designed for frequent travel. And most can make a big bulge in a briefcase.

Mobility and utility

The ideal storage device would combine the mobility and security of a floppy disk with the speed and space of a hard drive. The good news is that many such devices exist, each with its own merits. Some store as much data as can fit on a half-dozen high-capacity hard drives. But because they're slow, they're useful primarily for backing up hard drives and for secondary storage — holding files you want to have handy but don't need lightning-fast access to.

Others don't store quite as much, but are as fast as many hard drives, making them ideal for backing up or replacing a hard drive. Still other devices can hold the contents of a small library — but those contents can't be erased (see Table 25-2 for the salient points of each technology).

Table 25-2
Storage Options at a Glance

Technology	*Primary*	*Secondary*	*Backup*	*Pros*	*Cons*
Conventional hard drive	Excellent	Excellent	Very Good	Fast; inexpensive	Files must be archived and then deleted when the drive fills
SyQuest removable	Very Good	Excellent	Excellent	Large installed base; inexpensive	Mixed reliability track record
Bernoulli removable	Very Good	Excellent	Excellent	Reliable	Costly, noisy; portable and transportable drives are heavy
Iomega ZIP drives	Fair	Excellent	Excellent	Fairly fast; compact; inexpensive	Relatively low capacity
Erasable optical drives	Poor–Fair	Very Good	Excellent	Large capacity; low cost per megabyte	Costly; too slow for primary storage
WORM drives	Poor	Very Good	Poor	Large capacity; stored data is immune to magnetic fields and erasure	Costly; slow
Tape drives	Poor	Poor	Excellent	Inexpensive; many drives to choose from	Not usable for primary or secondary storage

Media on the Move

The one trait all hard drive alternatives share is that their media — the stuff that holds your data — are removable, like a floppy disk. When you fill one cartridge, eject it and pop in another. Or use cartridges dedicated for certain tasks — word processing, publishing, QuickTime work.

The ubiquitous SyQuest

The most popular removable-media drives in the Mac world are built around mechanisms manufactured by SyQuest and sold by all major (and a lot of minor) hard drive vendors. SyQuest drives are particularly popular among publishers and QuickTime producers, who work with huge files and often need to transport them elsewhere.

The SyQuest mechanism works much like a conventional hard drive, except it uses a single metal platter instead of several, and the platter itself lives in a portable plastic cartridge that you can eject. What about dust, a hard drive's biggest enemy? When you insert a cartridge, the drive spins the platter at high speed for a few seconds in a routine designed to blow foreign intruders away.

The original SyQuest mechanism used 5¼-inch cartridges that held roughly 44MB — the equivalent of over 30 high-density floppy disks. A few years ago, SyQuest unveiled a new mechanism that stores 88MB on similar cartridges. The new drives can read from, but not write to, 44MB cartridges. The 44MB mechanism is still manufactured, and many firms offer both.

Some firms also sell versatile dual-drive models. With such a box, you can use both drives for primary storage or use one to back up the other. Newer generations of SyQuest drives store 105MB or 270MB on 3½-inch cartridges that are about the same size as a floppy disk. Also available are internal drives designed to be installed in Quadra, Centris, Performa, and Power Mac models that have removable drive bays.

The Bernoulli Effect

One of the SyQuest drive's biggest competitors comes from Iomega, whose Bernoulli drives have been around in one form or another for over ten years. Early Mac models stored 20MB on bulky cartridges, but the latest store up to 230MB on cartridges that are slightly smaller than their 5¼-inch SyQuest equivalents. Earlier generations of Bernoulli drives stored 44MB or 90MB.

How a Bernoulli drive works

A Bernoulli drive takes advantage of fluid dynamics principles discovered by eighteenth-century mathematician and physicist Daniel Bernoulli (pronounced burr-NEW-lee). His Bernoulli Theorem states that the pressure of fluid or air decreases when it's moving. In aircraft, the decreased air pressure around moving wings gives them their lift. In bathrooms, the decreased air pressure caused by the shower head's stream pulls the shower curtain in.

In a Bernoulli cartridge, a rush of air causes a flexible disk to be drawn to within a few thousandths of an inch of a rigid metal plate located in the drive (see Figure 25-7 "Inside a Bernoulli Drive"). The disk floats firmly within this air flow, flexing no more than one-thousandth of an inch.

Safe, flexible, and reliable

Because the disk is flexible, a foreign intruder isn't as threatening as it is to a hard disk. When something comes between a Bernoulli disk and its head, the disk flexes and the air flow blows the intruder away. The result is a temporary disk error that the Mac can detect and often correct.

INSIDE A BERNOULLI DRIVE

Bernoulli cartridges closely resemble standard floppy disks. Bernoulli technology uses dual, single-sided platters. The drive heads — which move laterally, read from above and below. The Bernoulli does not filter dust particles, but circulates air to move dust away from the media. Unlike SyQuest and Ricoh removable-media drives, the read-write head do not actually contact the media, so head crashes cannot be caused by dust particles, and disk crashes also are rare. As seen in the detail, the platter flexes toward the head. An air cushion between the two floppy platters allow them to flex inward should a dust particle approach the head. The cartridge also locks in place while in use. This is necessary because unlike other removable-media, the Bernoulli cartridge protrudes from the drive during operation.

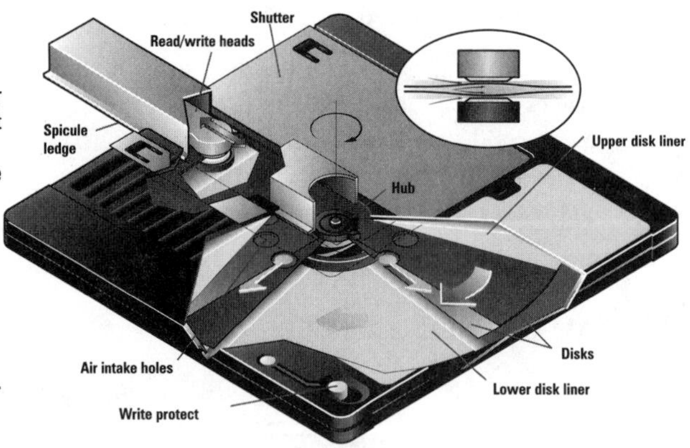

Shutter
Read/write heads
Spicule ledge
Upper disk liner
Hub
Disks
Air intake holes
Lower disk liner
Write protect

Figure 25-7: Inside a Bernoulli Drive

Inside a Bernoulli cartridge, a pair of flexible disks is drawn toward the drive's read/write heads by the air pressure generated by the spinning disks. The same air flow that attracts the media to the heads blows dust away from the media. If a foreign invader withstands the wind and wedges itself between the media and the heads, the disks flex to allow it to pass. It's solid technology that has proven to be very reliable.

Loud for the life of the cartridge

On the down side, the media inside the cartridges does wear out over time, although Iomega warrants cartridges for five years: Most firms selling SyQuest cartridges offer only one- or two-year warranties. Bernoulli drives include a utility that tells you how much cartridge life is left (see Figure 25-8 "How Much Time Do I Have?"). Bernoulli drives are also noisier than SyQuest drives. The heads in older 44MB models required periodic cleaning, but the 90MB and 150MB drives are self-cleaning.

Iomega ZIP Drives

One of today's hottest removable media devices is Iomega's ZIP drive. A ZIP drive uses 3½-inch removable cartridges that store up to 100MB each — not a lot by today's standards, but adequate for backing up and transporting files. The drive itself is small, weighing about a pound and measuring 1½-inches high, 7 inches deep, and 5 inches wide. Removable feet let you position the drive horizontally or vertically.

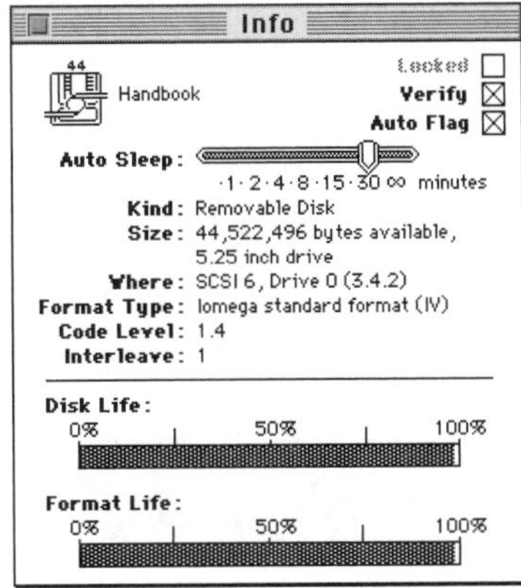

Figure 25-8: How Much Time Do I Have? Iomega's Workshop utility lets you monitor the health of a Bernoulli cartridge. The "sleep" option also lets you specify that a cartridge's disks spin down after a period of inactivity. Designed to conserve battery life on portable Bernoulli drives, this feature also prolongs the cartridge's life — and silences the noisiest part of a Bernoulli drive.

Fast, versatile, and economical

A ZIP drive transfers about 1.25MB per second — comparable to a SyQuest or Bernoulli drive. ZIP drives are available for Macs and Windows machines, making them good tools for cross-platform file swapping. The drives also include a variety of utilities for backup, file-cataloging, and cartridge duplication.

One of the best things about a ZIP drive is its price: less than $200 for the drive itself, and less than $20 each for the cartridges. SyQuest drives, by comparison, sell for $300 and up, while cartridges begin at about $60.

Tape Drives

Finally, there's the lowly but lovely *tape drive,* which uses cartridges containing magnetic tape to store from 115MB to 5GB or more. Numerous tape formats are available; many low-cost to mid-range (115MB to 600MB) tape drives are based on Teac mechanisms. They use special data cassettes that look like exotic, high-precision cassette tapes. They're economical, but pretty slow.

Higher-capacity drives generally use digital audiotape (DAT) mechanisms and special tapes that are similar (though not identical to) DAT cassettes. DAT drives are usually much faster than lower-capacity tape drives. Many drives provide built-in compression hardware that enables them to squeeze more on a tape.

Tape drives are ideal for backing up hard disks and they're economical, with the lowest cost per megabyte of any high-capacity storage medium. But because tapes are a sequential-access medium, they can be slow and they can't be used as primary storage devices. Bernoulli, ZIP, SyQuest, and MO drives are far more versatile.

QUICK TIPS

Tips for Working with Cartridge Drives

Using Bernoulli, SyQuest, or MO cartridge drives is a lot like working with hard or floppy disks, but there are a few differences to keep in mind, especially with SyQuest-based drives.

Ejecting SyQuest cartridges

Ejecting a SyQuest cartridge is a multistep process: Drag the cartridge's icon to the Trash, press a stop button on the drive, and then flip an eject lever on the drive. In a related vein, some SyQuest drives won't recognize a cartridge inserted after you've started up the Mac. Better SyQuest vendors include system extension software that enables the Mac to recognize cartridges inserted after startup. You can use control panels such as Robert Polic's shareware SCSI Probe to mount cartridges inserted after startup. This software is included with Bernoulli drives.

Cartridges and virtual memory don't mix

System 7's virtual memory feature isn't available when your startup drive is a removable cartridge. Virtual memory requires the use of a special file containing the data that System 7 swaps between real memory and the drive. If you were to eject a cartridge containing the swap file, you'd perform the equivalent of removing a car's tires while it was moving, and the results wouldn't be pretty.

As someone who used to use Bernoulli drives for primary storage, I found this particularly frustrating. Then I discovered FWB's Hard Disk Toolkit software, which allows you to enable virtual memory for ejectable cartridges. The software includes a terrific array of features for formatting and fine-tuning drives of all kinds. It includes software that enables the Mac to recognize SyQuest cartridges inserted after startup, as well as formatting software that can overcome the incompatibilities that arise between SyQuest drives from different vendors.

Conquering SyQuest compatibility problems

Although all vendors use the same basic SyQuest mechanism, you can't always move cartridges from one brand of drive to another. Each vendor is responsible for supplying the low-level SCSI driver software that enables the Mac to access the cartridge, and one company's software may not be compatible with another's. If you're buying a SyQuest-based drive to exchange files with someone who already has one, make sure that the two will be able to read each others' cartridges. Similarly, if you're acquiring multiple drives, consider buying from one source.

Another way to avoid SyQuest compatibility woes is to initialize your cartridges using a universal formatter utility such as FWB's Hard Disk Toolkit, Casa Blanca's Drive7, or La Cie's SilverLining.

Letting cartridges adjust to temperature changes

If you're carrying a cartridge around in the winter, allow it to warm up to room temperature before inserting it in a drive. Otherwise, moisture could condense on the platter surface and damage the cartridge as well as the drive. When summer arrives, don't leave cartridges in a sun-baked car, where the heat could cause their cases to warp. And keep cartridges (and all disks, for that matter) away from items that generate magnetic fields, such as speakers, electric motors, and old telephones with mechanical bells.

Swapping cartridges between Macs and PCs

Bernoulli and SyQuest mechanisms are available for Macs and PCs. Some drives include software that lets you create MS-DOS and Mac partitions on the same cartridge. Utilities such as Apple's PC Exchange, Insignia's AccessPC, and Dayna's DOS Mounter also let you work with DOS-format cartridges as though they were Mac disks (see Chapter 27).

CD-ROMs and Compact Discs

Compact discs, those silver platters that have made so many stereos obsolete, have invaded the mass storage world. And I am talking *mass* storage: A 5¼-inch compact disc holds as much as 650MB of data.

Most of today's Macs include or accept optional internal CD-ROM drives. You can also buy external CD-ROM drives, including ones that run on batteries — handy for PowerBooks.

CD-ROM technology

As you saw in previous chapters, a compact disc that stores data is called a CD-ROM. A CD-ROM's data, like that of a ROM chip, is factory-frozen, unable to be erased. For this reason, CD-ROMs are used primarily as a distribution medium for software or data. Many businesses buy commercial CD-ROMs and use AppleShare or System 7's file-sharing features to make the discs' contents available to everyone on a network. Clip art, stock photographs, fonts, encyclopedias, dictionaries, and other research- and education-oriented CD-ROMs are available — not to mention games and interactive multimedia titles.

Multimedia and CD-ROM

As Chapter 20 described, CD-ROMs also play a major part in the multimedia world, where their ability to hold digital audio, QuickTime movies, text, and graphics makes them the best medium currently available for interactive multimedia titles.

Enhanced CDs

A new type of CD format, called *enhanced CD* or *CD Plus*, combines the interactive attributes of CD-ROM with the outstanding audio quality of audio CDs. An enhanced CD can be played not only on an audio CD player, but also in a CD-ROM player. In an audio CD player, the disc plays like any standard audio CD.

In a CD-ROM drive, however, an enhanced CD can also show interactive content: QuickTime movies of music videos or concerts, interactive liner notes, song lyrics, movies of the artist making the album — you name it. Some industry gurus say enhanced CDs will replace conventional audio CDs within a few years; I doubt that will happen — record companies can be rather stodgy when it comes to adopting new technologies — but you can expect to see a growing number of interactive albums appearing.

Playing audio CDs on CD-ROM drives

In addition to providing a SCSI connector for attaching to the Mac, external CD-ROM drives provide standard RCA-type audio-output jacks that you can connect to a stereo. With an internal CD-ROM drive, the audio output is patched directly into the Mac's audio-input circuitry, enabling you to listen to audio CDs through the Mac's speaker — or, better yet, through a pair of speakers connected

to the Mac. (To hear the audio, you must activate the play-through mode using the Sound control panel or the Sound & Displays control panel.)

CD-ROM drives from Apple and many others include a program that lets you play audio CDs and an extension that lets audio-only CDs appear on the Mac's desktop (see Figure 25-9 "Now Taking Requests" and the Quick Tips box "Tips for Playing Audio CDs").

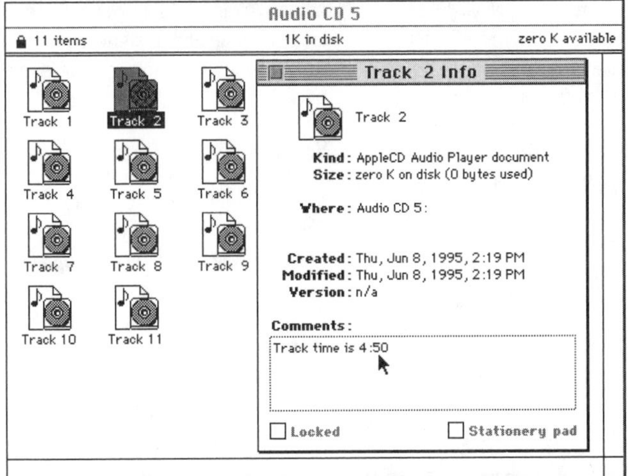

Figure 25-9: Now Taking Requests Top: Apple's CD-ROM drives include the AppleCD Audio Player utility, which lets you not only play audio CDs, but also create playlists that play only those tracks you want to hear, and in the order you want to hear them. Bottom: In System 7.5, you can also play a track from the Finder by double-clicking the track's icon. You can also choose Get Info to see information about a track, including its length.

Tips for Playing Audio CDs

Apple's AppleCD Audio Player utility provides more features than most home stereo CD players. But Apple doesn't tell you much about using them. Here's some background information and some tips.

- *Entering CD and track names.* When you insert an audio CD, the text *Audio CD* appears above the player's play buttons. Click the tiny down arrow below the Normal button, and the player window expands to reveal a list of tracks. Press Tab, and you can type the name of the CD in the box labeled Disc. But don't stop there: press Tab again and the insertion point moves to the track list, where you can type the name of each track on the CD. (Press Tab to move to the next track name and Shift-Tab to move to the previous track name.) When you eject the CD, the player saves your CD and track names, and displays them automatically the next time you insert that CD. (It's able to do this because every audio CD has a unique number of data blocks on it.)
- *Creating playlists.* If you like to hear a CD's tracks in a certain order, program a playlist. Click the Prog button, and the bottom half of the player window changes, displaying a series of boxes labeled Playlist. Drag tracks from the left side of the window to the playlist (refer to Figure 25-9). Within the playlist, drag tracks up or down to change their playback order. Whenever the Prog button is active, the CD's tracks will play back in the order you specified. Notice, too, that the player displays the total playing time of your playlist as you add and remove tracks.
- *Jumping to a specific track.* To skip to and immediately play a specific track, point to the text box above the play buttons and hold down the mouse. Choose the desired track from the pop-up menu that appears. You can also press the left and right arrow keys to move to the next or previous track.
- *Adjusting the playback volume.* You can adjust the playback volume by dragging the volume slider up or down or by pressing the up or down arrow keys.
- *Changing the time display.* Point to the small clock next to the Remaining Time display and hold down the mouse button, and a pop-up menu appears that lets you view the elapsed or remaining time for the currently playing track or the elapsed time for the entire disc or playlist.
- *Customizing the player's colors.* Use the Window Color and Indicator Color menus in the Options menu to change the color of the player's window and pseudo-LED indicators.
- *Back up your player preferences file.* The player stores your track names and playlists in a file named AppleCD Audio Player Preferences, located within the System Folder's Preferences folder. Be sure to back up this file to avoid having to reenter all your track names.
- *Other ways to play audio tracks.* In System 7.5, you can open the player and play a specific track by double-clicking a track's icon in the Finder. You can even make an alias of a favorite track and keep it on the desktop or in your Apple menu. One catch: If you have the wrong CD in the drive when you open the alias, the player isn't smart enough to ask you for the correct CD. If your alias was of track 3, for example, the player simply plays track 3 of whatever CD you've inserted.

How to Convert Audio CD Tracks into QuickTime Movies

QuickTime versions 1.6 and later can convert tracks on an audio CD into audio-only QuickTime movies. One reason you might want to do this is to extract a tune from your favorite CD for use in a noncommercial presentation or multimedia project. (You can't legally use music from a commercial CD in a commercial project without first obtaining permission from the record company or artist.)

Most QuickTime 2.0-compatible movie-playing applications can convert audio tracks. The DesktopMovie shareware utility included on the *Macworld Power User Clinic* CD (in the Movies and Sounds folder) is one of them.

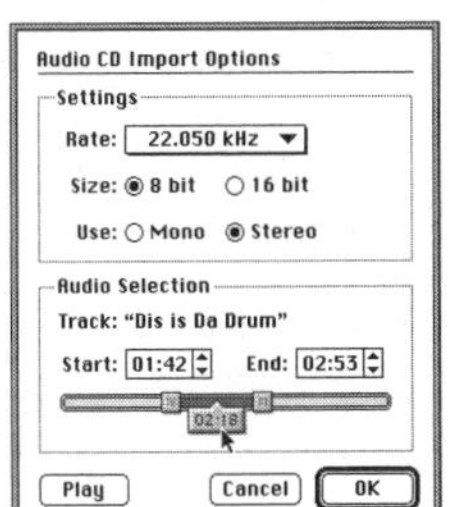

1. **Choose the utility's Open command and locate the desired track in the Open dialog box.**

   When an audio CD track is selected, the Open button changes to Convert.

2. **Click the Convert button or press Return.**

   A Save dialog box appears.

3. **Click the Options button.**

   The Audio CD Import Options dialog box appears (shown at left). You can use this dialog box to choose the audio settings (sampling rate, 8- or 16-bit, and mono or stereo) to be used for the QuickTime movie. You can also specify a selection within the track if you don't want to convert the entire track. Use the Play button to audition your settings.

4. **Choose the desired sound-quality and selection settings, and then click OK or press Return.**

   The Save dialog box reappears.

5. **Specify where you want to store the QuickTime movie, type a name, and click Save or press Return.**

   A progress bar appears during the conversion process (click Stop to cancel).

CDs are not speedy

CD-ROMs have many wonderful attributes, but speed isn't one of them. A typical hard disk can transfer 2MB or more per second, but double-speed CD-ROM drives — the most popular type at this writing — can do no better than 300K per second. The sluggishness is due largely to the fact that a CD-ROM spins slower — at 460 to 1060 rpm in a double-speed drive, versus the 3600 to 7200 rpm of a hard drive.

A new generation of *quadruple-speed* (often called 4X) CD-ROM drives that offer transfer rates in the 600K per second ballpark is now available. Apple's CD600e external drive is one such drive; Apple includes an internal version of this drive in its second-generation Power Macs. (Note that both the AppleCD 600e and AppleCD 600i are not compatible with Apple's DOS Compatibility Card, which lets some Macs run DOS/Windows software. The CD-ROM driver included with the DOS Compatibility Card works only with the AppleCD 150, AppleCD 300, and AppleCD SC Plus CD-ROM drives.)

If you're shopping for a CD-ROM drive, should you spend the extra money for a 4X? It depends. The video on the vast majority of CD-ROM titles is prepared to accommodate the data-transfer rates of double-speed drives, so it won't look any better on a 4X drive. (See Chapter 20's discussion of QuickTime trade-offs for background on movie data rates.) However, all other aspects of the CD's performance — starting up the interactive program, searching for text, moving between screens — will be faster on a 4X drive. A 4X drive will also benefit other types of CDs — such as stock photo collections, PhotoCDs, and text-heavy databases. Indeed, Macworld Lab tests show significant advantages in tests involving searching for text on a CD. If you use these types of CDs extensively, a 4X drive may well be worth the extra cost.

Making your own CDs

Recordable CD-ROM, or *CD-R,* drives that enable you to make your own CD-ROMs — to archive your work, for small-scale CD title distribution, for CD-ROM performance testing, or to send to a mastering house for mass duplication are available.

As with nonrecordable drives, CD-R drives are available in double- or quadruple-speed flavors. 4X drives are considerably faster — in a recent Macworld Lab comparison, a 4X drive took 19 minutes to write a CD, while double-speed models took 37 minutes. Another factor that differentiates drives is the recording software they include; in the same Macworld Lab survey, *Macworld*'s Suzanne Stefanac and Jim Feeley preferred OptImage's CD-It All, a program also sold by Plasmon under the name Toast.

CD-R used to cost $5,000 and up, but today prices have fallen to well under $2,000. If that's still too steep — or if you'd rather wait until the technology matures a bit more (not a bad idea) — remember that many multimedia and publishing service bureaus also offer inexpensive CD archiving services. For a hundred bucks or two, you can have a CD made from the contents of a hard drive or set of cartridges. Given the cost and relative immaturity of recordable CD-ROM drives, that's a bargain.

Optical Storage Meets Magnetic Storage

Relatively slow performance is just one reason that optical-based storage isn't likely to replace magnetic storage any time soon. A more serious hurdle involves developing disks that can be erased and reused: Data is written on a CD-ROM by a laser that burns pits into the disk's surface.

WORMing your way into data

One alternative is offered by *write once, read many times* (WORM) drives. A WORM drive is the storage world's equivalent to indelible ink — once something is written to it, it can't be erased. Storing 400–900MB on a cartridge, WORM drives are specialized beasts most often used for storing data that must not be altered, such as legal and medical records.

Tips for Speeding up a CD-ROM Drive

To many people, the phrase *fast CD-ROM drive* is a contradiction in terms. There's no denying the drives are slow, at least compared to hard drives.

Many firms, including Casablanca Works, FWB, and Charismac Engineering, sell caching utilities that promise to speed up CD-ROM performance. These utilities use a variety of techniques designed to reduce the amount of waiting the Mac has to do for the drive. For example, when the drive is playing back QuickTime movies, the caching utility will tell the drive to read ahead and store additional data in memory, where it can be supplied to the Mac in a flash as soon as it's ready for it.

Many caching utilities have multiple caching schemes, each suited to a particular CD-ROM application. For example, reading zip code data from a CD-ROM database requires different caching techniques than does playing back a QuickTime movie. Casa Blanca Works' DriveCD adjusts its cache size automatically, depending on the type of data it's working with.

Just say MO

But the storage technology that best clears the read/write hurdle uses — you guessed it — magnets embedded in the disk's surface. I'm referring to *magneto-optical* (MO) drives. Also called *erasable optical* (EO) drives, these devices use mechanisms that store 100MB to 125MB on 3½-inch removable cartridges. An older generation of MO drives stores 500 – 600MB on 5¼-inch cartridges.

To write to a cartridge, an MO drive uses a high-powered laser and electromagnet to orient the media's magnetic particles. To read from the cartridge, the drive uses a low-powered laser. Many of today's MO drives can also work as WORM drives. As with CD-ROM drives, however, access time is relatively slow, making MO drives better for long-term storage and retrieval than as substitutes for a conventional hard disk. They're also costly compared to conventional hard drives.

So the lowly magnet continues to serve us well, and it looks like it will even have a place in tomorrow's disk drives. In the next chapter, I show you how to take care of your magnets.

Using PC CD-ROMS on a Power Mac under SoftWindows

With Insignia Solutions' SoftWindows, you can run many Windows applications on a Power Mac. Did you know that you can also work with DOS/Windows CD-ROMs under SoftWindows? Here's how.

First, start SoftWindows. When the C:\> prompt appears (and I never thought I'd write that phrase in this book), type **usecd** and press Return. Then insert the CD.

If this doesn't work, remove the Foreign File Access extension from your Mac's System Folder and restart. Then start SoftWindows and try again. If you're still unsuccessful, put the Foreign File Access file back into your System Folder, restart, and insert the CD. (It should appear on the desktop. If it doesn't, you might have a bad CD.)

Next, from SoftWindows' Setup menu, choose Mac/PC Shared Folders. Locate the CD and then select the drive number to which you want to assign the CD (for example: G:\). Click the Use Macintosh HD button at the bottom of the dialog box. This procedure should let you access the files on the CD from within SoftWindows.

Note that you can only use one CD-ROM drive at a time under SoftWindows.

CHAPTER 25 CONCEPTS AND TERMS

- Floppy and hard disks allow fast, random access to data.
- A floppy disk spins at 390 to 600 revolutions per minute and is accessed by a read/write head in the disk drive. When you initialize a disk, the disk's surface is magnetically divided into 80 concentric circles called tracks, each of which is divided into wedges called sectors.
- The capacity of Mac floppies has steadily increased. The original Mac floppy stored 400K; double-sided floppies doubled that to 800K, while today's high-density floppies store 1.4MB.
- Unlike a floppy disk, a hard disk contains several metal platters, which are stacked like records in a jukebox. Hard disks are faster than floppies in part because their disks spin faster and their magnetic particles are packed closer together.
- Removable-media drives such as SyQuest and Bernoulli drives combine the speed and capacity of a hard drive with the security and convenience of floppies.
- Today's fastest hard drives can transfer data faster than many Macs can accept it. If you don't have a Quadra 800, 840AV, or Power Mac, you may want to add a SCSI-2 adapter to your Mac to get the best performance out of a fast drive. Adaptors are available for these fast Macs that boost their performance even more.

automatic head-parking
A safety feature that retracts a hard drive's heads to a safe area when you shut down.

average access time
The amount of time required for the drive's heads to locate a given spot on a disk.

data caching
A performance-boosting technique in which a drive reads an entire track of data and stores it in a small reserve of memory. When the Mac requests subsequent sectors from that track, the drive sends the data from the cache.

data transfer rate
The speed with which a drive can shuttle bytes to the Mac.

floptical disk
A kind of super floppy that stores roughly 20MB on 3½-inch cartridges that are similar to floppy disks.

fragmentation
A problem in which a hard drive scatters newly saved or copied files across physically discontiguous tracks. The longer you use a disk, the more likely it is that it contains fragmented files. When many files are fragmented, the drive's heads spend too much time in transit, and performance suffers.

head crash
An undesirable event in which a hard drive's read/write head slams into the platter. A head crash can occur when the drive is jostled during use, or even when a speck of dust gets between the platter's surface and the head.

high-density
Floppy disks that have a thinner magnetic coating and smaller magnetic particles than 800K disks. A high-density disk has a small hole in its upper-left corner, opposite the write-protect hole.

initialize
To prepare a disk or other storage medium for use. During initialization, the Mac creates the sectors on the disk as well as special reserved areas that enable the Mac to keep track of files.

interleave ratio
The organization of sectors in each track on a disk.

latency
The time it takes for a particular spot on the drive's platters to reach the drive's heads.

magneto-optical (MO)
A storage technology that combines magnetic and optical storage to offer the high-capacity of the latter with the erase-and-reuse flexibility of the former.

partitioning
Electronically dividing a drive into a number of smaller *logical volumes*. You can mount and unmount these volumes as though you were inserting and ejecting separate disks.

random access
The ability to quickly jump to any location on a storage medium such as a disk.

SCSI-2 adaptor
A plug-in board that gives a Mac a SCSI interface that adheres to the SCSI-2 standard and, therefore, can transfer data more quickly than the Mac's built-in SCSI port.

sector
A wedge-shaped division on a hard or floppy disk.

spindle speed
The number of times per minute that a hard drive's platters revolve.

SuperDrive
The latest Mac floppy disk drives, capable of storing 1.4MB and reading floppies formatted for DOS PCs.

(continued on the next page)

(continued from previous page)

tape drive
A mass-storage device that uses cartridges containing magnetic tape to store between 60MB and 600MB. Tape drives are popular for backing up hard drives.

track
One of many concentric storage paths on a disk.

write once, read many times (WORM)
Abbreviated WORM, a type of optical drive whose media can be written to only once and can't be erased.

CHAPTER TWENTY-SIX

Protecting Your Data and Surviving SCSI

- Developing a backup strategy that protects your work
- Comparing backup programs and devices
- Using file-recovery programs — safety nets for your data
- Safeguarding your Mac against the computer virus threat
- Mastering the SCSI bus — how it works, and when it doesn't

A floppy or hard disk is a friend you can't quite trust. Most of the time, disks are faithful computing caddies that hold your software and documents; it's easy to become smug about this give-and-take relationship. Then one of them develops a case of amnesia, and all of a sudden it's: "Files? What files? I don't have any files." Just like that, you're forced to retype your documents from printouts (if you're lucky enough to have some), or worse, re-create them from scratch. Either way, it's *déjà vu* in its ugliest form.

Disks can betray your trust in a variety of ways. Their microscopic magnetic particles can be led astray by magnetic fields produced by loudspeakers or electric motors. They're susceptible to system errors, computer viruses, SCSI cabling problems, and program bugs, all of which can cause inaccurate information to be written to the disk. They face physical threats from spilled soda to dust to extremes of heat and cold. And hard disks can fall victim to head crashes, in which the read/write heads strike and damage the media surface.

Preparing for a Rainy Day

How do you maintain a relationship with such fair-weather friends? Use an umbrella — a *backup utility*, which stores copies of your files on floppy disks or other storage devices. Backups are to computers what vice presidents are to governments: They don't do much when the sailing is smooth, but when the worst happens, they're indispensable.

Every software library also needs a *file-recovery utility*. One of these rescue squads can save the day if disk problems occur or if you accidentally throw away a file in between backups.

In this chapter, I take a close look at backup and file-recovery utilities, and show how to use both to make your disks more trustworthy companions. I examine the computer virus threat and show how to protect your Mac. I also explore the ins and outs of the SCSI bus — and show what to do when the bus breaks down.

How to Copy a Floppy

Backing up floppy disks is easy — and important. When you buy a new program, your first step should be to make copies of the disks it came on (for backup use only — copying a commercial program for or from someone else is stealing). The instructions in this box show how to copy a floppy disk on a Mac with one or two floppy drives. If your Mac has just one drive — as do all currently manufactured Macs — the floppy copy routine is a bit tricky. To avoid excessive disk swapping, use the following steps.

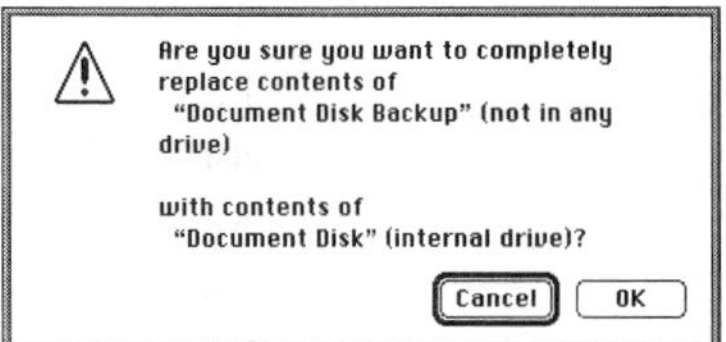

To copy a floppy disk on a Mac with one floppy drive:

1. **Insert the backup disk (not the original) and then choose Eject from the Finder's File menu.**
   The Finder dims the disk's icon to indicate it still "knows" about the disk.
2. **Lock the original disk.**
   To lock the disk, slide its plastic write-protect tab so you can see through the square hole.
3. **Insert the original disk, and then drag its icon to the backup disk's dimmed icon.**
   The Finder asks if you want to replace the backup disk's contents.
4. **Click OK.**
   You will need to swap disks a few times during the copying process.

To copy a floppy disk on a two-drive Mac:

1. **Lock the original disk.**
   To lock the disk, slide its plastic write-protect tab so you can see through the square hole.
2. **Insert the original disk in one drive and the backup in the other.**
   Both disk icons appear on the desktop.
3. **Drag the original disk's icon to the backup's icon.**
   The Finder asks if you want to replace one disk's contents with those of the other; click OK. When the copy is complete, eject both disks; unlock the original if you plan to write to it again.

Backup Basics

A file tucked away on a disk seems safe and sound; after all, the command reads "Save," not "Save until some unforeseen event." But the worst does happen. Disks are damaged or lost. Programs turn kamikaze, crashing and taking files with them. Power surges give hard disks amnesia. Fires start, and sprinkler systems sprinkle. Equipment is stolen. It's enough to make you want police protection, but only a faithfully followed backup strategy can help.

Copying floppies

The techniques described in the Step-by-Step box "How to Copy a Floppy" copy every file from your original floppy disk to the backup disk. As you work with the original (don't forget to unlock it first), you'll probably add to it or modify its files. You have two alternatives for keeping your backups up to date. You can drag only the new or modified files to the backup (clicking OK when asked if you want to replace the existing files), or you can simply recopy the entire disk. The latter takes longer but is easier because you don't have to keep track of which files you modified or added.

Use the Finder's By Date command (it's in the View menu) to look at the original disk's contents sorted according to their creation and modification dates, and then copy only those files with dates past the backup date. You can also determine when a file was created and modified by selecting the file and choosing Get Info from the File menu or pressing ⌘-I. As I mentioned in Chapter 22, you can also use the Finder's Find command to locate all files modified on a given day, and then back up the files by dragging them to a floppy or removable-media cartridge.

How often should you back up a floppy disk that you use to store documents? As often as necessary for your work habits and your peace of mind. If you're using a disk constantly, you may want to back it up every day. The best rule may be to back up anything you aren't willing to re-create.

Hard disks are harder

Backing up a hard disk is, well, harder. A hard disk may streamline your day-to-day computing, but it turns into a ball and chain at backup time. A hard disk can hold thousands of files, making the job of backing up modified files a logistical nightmare. Yet backing up a hard disk couldn't be more important. If you use a computer extensively, a hard disk tends to become a magnetic representation of your life. It's all there — your business plans, personal letters, drawings, programs, and more — and losing it in one fell swoop is about as traumatic an experience as you can have sitting in front of a computer.

To back up a full 230MB drive — a low-capacity drive by today's standards — you need over 160 disks — and a good two hours. Most people can think of better ways to spend their time and disk money. Until their hard disks crash, that is. But thanks to the Mac's ability to keep track of the date and the time that files are created and modified, you need not back up an entire hard disk during each backup session. Backup utilities can read the Mac's digital datebook and back up only those files you've added or changed since the last *full backup.* This task, called an *incremental backup,* takes far less time than a full backup.

Backup Helpers

Several software firms offer backup programs that work with any SCSI hard disk. Examples include Dantz Developments' Retrospect and DiskFit series and Focus Enhancements' Redux Deluxe. Backup programs are also included with Symantec's Norton Utilities for Macintosh and Central Point's MacTools disk utility packages.

The most basic difference between backup programs concerns how the backup program copies files to your backup media. Some programs, including Dantz Development's DiskFit series, copy each file separately and then create on each backup disk a catalog file that the program can use to *restore* the files to the hard disk. On the backup disks you can see each file just as it existed on your hard disk. Need to restore a few files? Simply use the Finder to copy them from the backups to your hard disk. (If a given file won't fit on a single disk at backup time, the utility splits it across multiple disks; you must use the utility to restore such a file.)

Other programs, including Dantz Developments' Retrospect and Focus Enhancements' Redux, copy your files into one large file that spans all your backup disks. Instead of using the Finder, you run the backup utility and tell it to locate and restore the files you need. Norton Fastback, the utility that accompanies Symantec's Norton Utilities, also works this way. Central Point Backup, the utility included with MacTools Pro, offers a choice: you can save backups in a single archive file or as individual, Finder-readable files.

Comparing backup approaches

With the separate-files approach used by DiskFit, you can restore any file that fits on a single backup disk without having to run the backup utility. You'll appreciate that if the utility's master disk becomes damaged, or if you take your backup disks to another machine but forget to take along a copy of the utility.

With the one-file-holds-all approach, if you don't have the backup utility, you don't have any backups — but it does make possible faster backup sessions and some fancy backup gymnastics. Many programs, for example, can compress files as they back them up, reducing the number of backup disks required.

Incremental differences

Another factor to consider is whether a backup program saves or deletes older versions of files you back up. For example, say you begin writing a proposal on Monday morning and then do a full backup on Monday evening. You work on the proposal again on Tuesday and then do an incremental backup. What happens to the backup of Monday's version?

It depends on the program you use. DiskFit and Redux replace older versions of files with their newer versions. That keeps your mountain of backup disks from growing too high, but it also eliminates the option of going back a few days to an earlier version of a file. If you decide Tuesday's version of your proposal stinks — or worse, if your word processing program somehow scrambles the file, and you unknowingly back up the scrambled version — you don't have Monday's version to fall back on. (I'll present a workaround for this potential nightmare shortly.)

In contrast, Retrospect doesn't replace earlier versions of files unless you tell it to. That gives you an extra-strong safety net, but it also means you need more disks to hold your backups. That can be significant if you're backing up large files such as scanned images, digitized sounds, or QuickTime movies.

Choosing Your Backup Weapon

Here are some other points to address before buying a backup utility:

- *Backup selectivity* If you're willing to rely on your original application disks as backups, you can back up documents only and cut your backup time. But some programs give you more flexibility than others in choosing files to back up. Generally, high-end backup programs such as Dantz's Retrospect allow the most control over backup sessions.
- *Specialized media support* If you plan to use a backup medium other than floppy disks, be sure to buy a program that supports your chosen medium. (To find out what other media are available, see the Background box "Media Circus.") Retrospect can back up to virtually anything. DiskFit and Redux Deluxe support tape drives, as long as they display tapes as icons on the Finder's desktop — trouble is, not many tape drives do.
- *Unattended operation* If you use a file server in a busy office, you may want to back it up at night, when it's idle. DiskFit Pro, Norton Fastback, Central Point Backup, and Retrospect are among the utilities that let you specify intervals for unattended backups (see Figure 26-1 "Scheduled Maintenance"). But because no one will be around to shuffle floppy disks, you'll need to use a high-capacity backup medium such as a second hard disk or a tape drive.

Backup Technique #1: Documents Only

Of all the files on a hard drive, none are more valuable than your documents. You can recopy application programs and reinstall system software using your original floppy disks, but documents have no such safety net. So if you're going to back up only one type of file, make it your documents.

For most people, the documents-only backup strategy has another benefit: it dramatically reduces the number of floppy disks required to hold backups. If you work with huge files — digital audio, QuickTime movies, color scanned images — you aren't off the storage hook. Plan to buy a tape drive or other removable-media backup device.

There are several ways to do a documents-only backup, and some of them don't even require a backup program. One technique: Use the Finder to copy the folders for your current projects (you *do* group related documents into folders, don't you?) to a floppy disk or cartridge. To see which folders have been recently modified, choose By Date from the Finder's View menu — your backup candidates appear at the top of the list. Select them, drag their icons to that of a floppy (for small files) or cartridge (for big ones), and sit back.

Another way to find recently created or changed files is to use the Find command in the Finder's File menu: choose Find, click More Choices, and then configure the pop-up menus to locate files created or changed on or after a certain date.

Have a SyQuest, Bernoulli, Iomega ZIP, or magneto-optical cartridge drive? Here's another way to back up without a backup program. Use your hard drive's formatting utility to create one or more partitions, giving each partition the same capacity as a cartridge. (You'll probably need to back up and then reinitialize your hard drive before partitioning it; for details, see the previous chapter.)

Store your documents on these partitions. To back up, simply drag a partition's icon to that of a cartridge. Because their capacities match, you don't have to fret about the partition's contents not fitting on a cartridge. You can even work in other programs while the Finder copies the partition, although your Mac may seem less responsive as it juggles tasks.

The techniques I've described rely on the Finder, but all backup programs also let you specify a documents-only backup, usually by excluding application programs and the System Folder. Most backup programs also let you choose to back up a specific folder, usually by manually selecting it.

- *Programmability* If you have very specific backup needs — perhaps you want to back up all PageMaker and Excel documents at 8 p.m. every Tuesday — consider a program that lets you automate the types of backups you do. Retrospect and Redux Deluxe offer the strongest automation features.

- *Ease of use* Backing up is boring; a program that's difficult to learn won't encourage the practice. Alas, ease of use and power can be at opposite ends of the seesaw. The most powerful backup program — Retrospect — has a fairly steep learning curve. If your backup needs don't demand automation and sophisticated file-selection features, consider a simpler program. Redux and the DiskFit series strike a balance between power and simplicity. The backup utilities that accompany Symantec's Norton Utilities and Central Point's MacTools Pro are also straightforward and easy to use.

Backup Documents Only:Day of Week

Do **Normal Backup** to *Final Handbook CD* Every Mon/Wed/Fri, starting 6/10/94 at 2:00 AM

Cancel OK

Start: 6/10/1994 Fri 2:00 AM

Run on: ☒ Monday ☐ Tuesday ☒ Wednesday ☐ Thursday ☒ Friday ☐ Saturday ☐ Sunday

Action: Normal Backup ▼

Figure 26-1: Scheduled Maintenance Numerous programs can do automatic backups at regular intervals — provided your backup medium can hold all the files that will be copied. Shown here: the scheduling option of Dantz Developments' Retrospect, the Mac world's most powerful backup utility.

Backup Technique #2: Including the System Folder

Your System Folder is a reflection of the way you use your Mac. If a hard drive failure occurs, you need to not only reinstall the basic System Folder from your original disks, but also any fonts and special control panels and extensions you might use.

Then there are the application-preferences settings, which are usually stored in the System Folder's Preferences folder. Most application programs let you tailor their operation by tweaking keyboard shortcuts, icon palettes, and default formatting settings. Programs from Claris and others also store spelling checking dictionaries — including ones to which you've added terms — in the System Folder.

Throw in all the little control panel adjustments you've probably made over time, and it becomes obvious that a well-used System Folder can be almost as arduous to re-create as a folder full of documents. To avoid the manual labor, back it up occasionally. Floppies are a bit impractical — a well-customized System Folder can easily devour a dozen megabytes or more — but a backup program can help. After your first backup session (during which you'll hand-feed a couple of dozen floppies), do an incremental backup to copy only those files that have changed. You'll probably have to handle only a few floppies then.

If you have a removable-media drive of some kind, backing up the System Folder is far easier. You can use the Finder to copy the entire System Folder to a cartridge, or use a backup utility to back up the entire System Folder and then perform incremental backups now and then.

Tips for Using a Backup Program

How will you use your backup program? You'll probably start by doing a full backup, following up with incremental backups at regular intervals. Here are some guidelines and tips.

Make two backups

Your backup disks are prone to the same ailments as your originals. For extra safety, make two backups and alternate them (see Figure 26-2 "Backup Strategies"). And don't store your backups along with your computer. Fire or water won't discriminate between the originals and the backups, and chances are a thief won't either. Practice what the data processing industry calls *off-site storage.*

Large institutions such as banks often rely on secure storage facilities such as those operated by Iron Mountain and other firms. Couriers pick up backup media at the intervals specified by the customer, seal it to show that it hasn't been tampered with, and then take it to a guarded facility containing climate-controlled vaults, motion detectors, and other security systems. (Some sites are carved into caves or mountains and were designed to survive World War III.) If the backups are needed, a courier delivers them within a couple of hours. Iron Mountain says a minimum charge for its services is roughly $75 to $100 per month.

This kind of offsite security is essential for big business, but it's overkill or just too costly for most of us. A safe-deposit box is one economical alternative. A corner of a sock drawer costs even less. Just don't keep all your backups in one place.

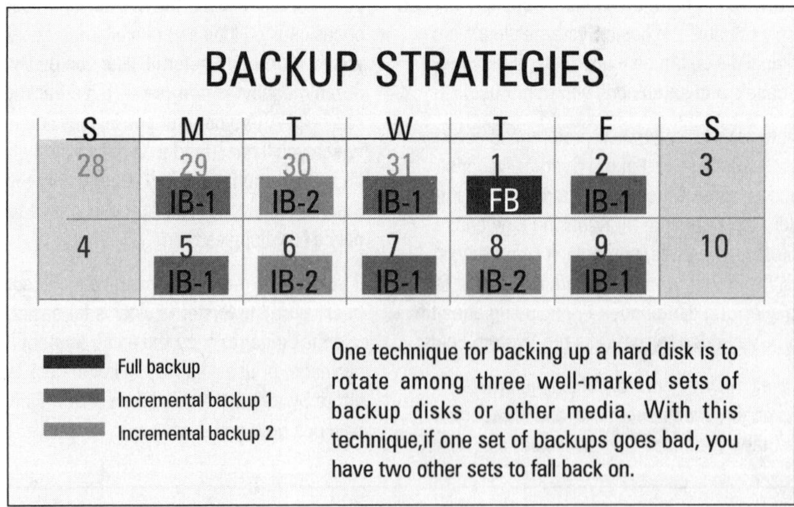

Figure 26-2: Backup Strategies

Test your restore procedures

To make sure everything's working properly, try restoring a folder full of files to a different hard drive. You'll know what to do when the worst happens. You don't want to be trying your program's restore option for the first time when your hard drive crashes.

Have an emergency startup disk or CD

If your hard disk crashes to the point where your Mac won't start up, you'll need a way to get up and running to the point where you can run a backup or disk-repair utility.

Macs that include an internal CD-ROM drive also include a CD that can be used as a startup disk. With some Macs, the CD is named Install Me First; with others, it's named Apple Macintosh CD. Whatever its name, it will get you to the desktop, where you can restore your files. (Depending on how your hard disk crashed, you may first need to reinitialize it using the software that accompanied it.) See Chapter 28 for details on starting up from this CD.

If your Mac didn't include a CD-ROM drive, it probably did include a set of system software disks. (Performa models are the exception; see the Quick Tips box "Backing Up a Performa.") You can use the floppy named Disk Tools as an emergency startup disk.

Symantec's Norton Utilities and Central Point's MacTools Pro include emergency startup floppy disks. One potential problem: These floppy disks may not work on Macs that use system enablers (described in Chapter 22). Both the Norton Utilities and MacTools Pro include an emergency startup disk builder — a utility that will make an emergency startup disk for your particular Mac model. If you're smart, you'll make a couple of emergency startup disks right now and stash them in safe — and separate — places. Go ahead — I'll wait.

Backing Up a Performa

Macintosh Performa models don't include a set of system disks, but they do include a bare-bones backup program, called Apple Backup. So that you can restore your System Folder in the event of a problem, it's a good idea to use Apple Backup to make a backup of the System Folder. It's easy and fun — if you like swapping floppies.

Start Apple Backup and click the Continue button in its welcome screen. In the next screen, specify that you want to back up the System Folder. Apple Backup tells you how many floppies you'll need. Make sure you have the required number, and then insert the first floppy. When it has finished copying to a floppy, the program tells you how to label it. Continue following the instructions on the screen; the program lets you know when you're finished.

Apple Backup can back up to floppy disks only. If you decide to supplement the floppy drive with a *real* backup device — an Iomega ZIP drive, perhaps, or a tape drive — you can graduate to the world of *real* backup programs.

Don't forget customized files

To save time and space on your backup media, you may want to tell your backup program to ignore files in the System Folder. That's generally a safe approach — if you remember to occasionally back up the customized files that live in the System Folder. Such files include word processor spelling-checker dictionaries that contain your own entries, preferences files that store your application preferences, the Scrapbook file, the System 7.1/7.5 Fonts folder, and in system versions 7.0 and earlier, the System file itself.

Verify your backups

Most backup utilities have a *verify* option, which, when active, causes the program to proofread its work as it backs up files. If a disk error causes a file to be written inaccurately, the verification process catches it, and the utility tries again. Verification lengthens the backup process, but that's a small price to pay for more reliable backups.

When to Restore

When do you need to restore the files from the backup disks to the hard disk? The obvious answers: after losing an important file or reformatting the hard disk, which may be necessary after a power failure or kamikaze program crash; after having a hard disk repaired, during which time it was probably replaced or reformatted; or if you're switching to a different hard disk or want a colleague to have a large number of your files.

Another incentive to restore is to improve the hard disk's performance. By backing up and then restoring a drive's contents, you can defragment its contents and make its files contiguous (see Chapter 25 for a discussion of disk fragmentation).

To restore a hard disk so that its files are stored contiguously, first make a full backup (or two, for safety), and then reformat the entire hard disk. Next, restore the system files, the applications, and then the folders and documents in that order. Performing the restoration process in this order ensures that the frequently accessed system and application files will be stored contiguously.

Disk Doctors

What happens if you lose a file in between backups? If you're smart, you'll reach for a file-recovery utility such as Symantec's Norton Utilities for the Macintosh or Central Point's MacTools. These products can often repair and resurrect damaged disks and files. They do so by working intimately with the reserved areas of a disk — areas that don't store documents or applications but instead hold information the Mac uses to keep track of files.

Reserved areas have technical names like volume allocation bitmap and extents b-tree. The Mac takes these magnetic tables of contents at face value; it assumes they're intact and contain valid data. When they don't — when a system crash, program bug, or stray magnetic field scrambles their contents — the Mac may be unable to retrieve part or all of the disk's contents. File-recovery utilities can analyze these areas, often correct inaccurate entries, and thus retrieve files that the Mac thinks are gone (see Figure 26-3 "Recovery Tool").

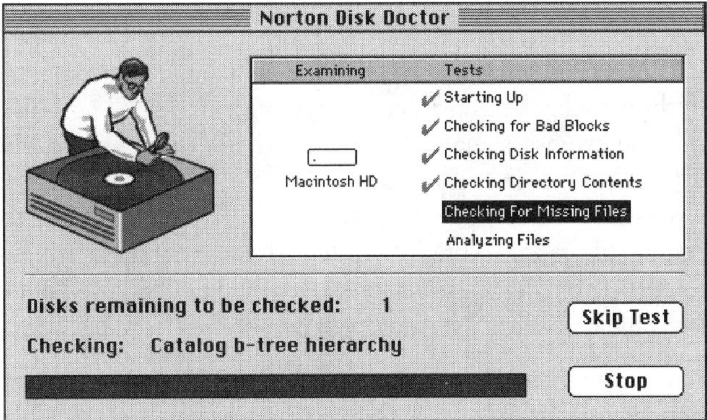

Figure 26-3: Recovery Tool A software rescue squad in action — Symantec's Norton Utilities for Macintosh.

Backing Up a Business

In offices where multiple Macs are connected to one or more file servers, it helps to develop a policy regarding backup. Will users be responsible for backing up their own machines? Will they back up to the file server? And who's responsible for backing up the server?

Making each person responsible for his or her own backups is the easiest approach, but also the most risky — some people just won't do it, and when their drives fail, the entire business suffers.

Backing up to a file server has advantages and disadvantages. On the plus side, you don't need a specialized backup device at each workstation — just buy one tape drive to back up the file server. You can also enforce a stricter backup regimen, either by installing an automatic backup extension on each machine or by using Dantz Development's Retrospect Remote, which lets a network administrator back up users' workstations from the administrator's Mac. The third advantage is that all your backup data is stored in one place.

But this advantage is also a disadvantage. Putting all your digital eggs in one basket makes a regular server backup routine all the more critical. Another drawback is the additional network traffic that backing up generates. To avoid slowing down your office's information highway, back up at night or on weekends.

Another drawback to network backup is that your server probably doesn't have enough storage capacity to back up everyone's entire hard drive. The alternative is to back up only documents to the server, using floppies and master disks to back up System Folders and applications.

And who's responsible for backing up the server? The network administrator, usually, although in many small businesses, it's the office power user — which may be you. Regardless of who the designated backer-upper is, make sure at least two people know how to restore files from the backups. You don't want to be out of business just because the person who backs up is out of the office.

Rescuing trashed files

The aforementioned products can also save the day when you accidentally throw away a file. All three include extensions that spy on you as you use a disk. When you delete a file, the extension makes notations on disk that indicate where that file is physically located on the disk. The file is still there; the Mac has simply removed its entry from the disk's electronic table of contents. Should you need to resurrect the file, you run the file-recovery utility, which reads those notations and re-creates the file's table of contents entry. (Prosecutors for the Iran-Contra trial used similar techniques to resurrect memos Oliver North *thought* he'd deleted from his word processor.)

But there is a catch: If you worked extensively with the disk after deleting the file, some of its contents may have been replaced by newer files. So when you realize you've accidentally deleted a file, stop using that disk until you can run the recovery utility. Even if a recovery utility can't automatically resurrect a file, there's still hope. Most products include *disk editors*, which let you directly view and alter the disk's contents (see Figure 26-4 "Disk Editing").

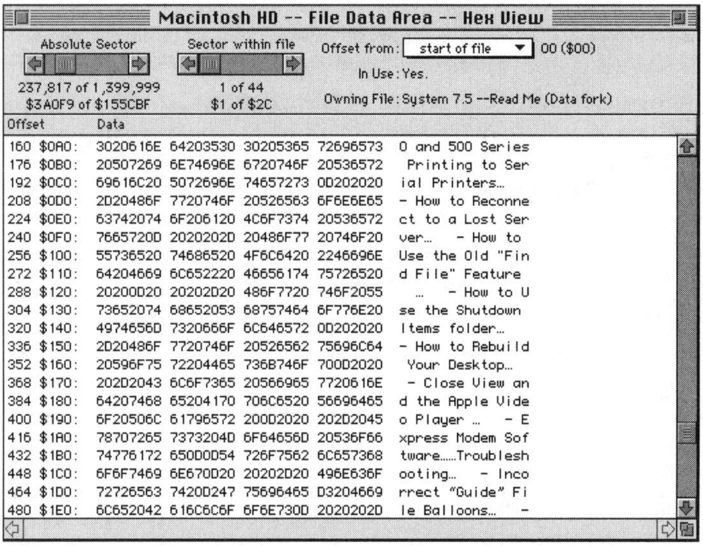

Figure 26-4: Disk Editing When a file-recovery program's automatic recovery features fail you, turn to its disk editor (that of the Norton Utilities is shown here). By searching for text present in the lost file, you may be able to locate some or all of its data and copy it to a new file — or at least retype it. The four-character columns in the left portion of the display show each character's hexadecimal value, while the rightmost column shows the characters themselves.

Good health habits for disks

The previous paragraphs contain several *oftens* and *maybes*. The fact is, file-recovery utilities don't always succeed. A visit to a doctor isn't a substitute for good health habits, nor can a file-recovery utility replace a good backup routine.

And speaking of good health habits, keep disks — floppy or hard — away from excessive moisture, stray magnetic fields, extremes of heat or cold, and dusty environments (see the Quick Tips box "An Ounce of Prevention"). Pack them securely for shipping. (Save your hard disk's original box or your Mac's box, if you have an internal drive.) If you move them from one temperature extreme to another, give the disks time to acclimate before using them. And never move or jostle a hard disk while it's on.

Following these commonsense precautions can lessen the chances that you'll need to restore data from backups or use a recovery program. In short, disks may be fair-weather friends, but you can control the weather.

An Ounce of Prevention

Here are some tips for taking care of floppy disks. I've read some recent Mac books that laugh at this kind of advice; apparently their authors don't store anything important on floppies.

- ❖ Keep disks away from magnetic fields. That includes audio speakers, electric motors, old telephones with mechanical ringers, high-intensity desk lamps, and yes, magnets.
- ❖ Keep disks comfortable. Don't leave them in a sun-baked car or near a radiator or other heat source. If you bring a disk or removable cartridge into a warm building on a winter's day, allow it to warm up to avoid condensation forming on its surface and damaging the drive.
- ❖ Don't place a hard drive or an external floppy disk drive to the left of a Mac Plus or SE. Don't store floppies there, either. The power supply in these Macs generates magnetic fields that can cause disk errors. Apple fixed this problem in the Classic and later compact Mac models.
- ❖ Be gentle. Don't slide a disk's shutter open and touch the inside. Don't trust a disk's plastic case to protect the disk in the mail; cardboard disk mailers are available at office-supply stores.
- ❖ Buy quality disks. You've made a big investment in your Mac and an even bigger investment in the documents you create and the programs you buy — don't skimp on something as relatively inexpensive as a disk. Don't attempt to punch a hole in an 800K disk in order to use it in a high-density SuperDrive. The disk may work for a short time, but it will probably fail. And plastic shavings may damage the floppy drive.
- ❖ Use the write-protect tab to guard against accidental erasure. Slide the tab away from the disk's shutter to lock the disk. You can see straight through the write-protect hole of a locked disk. The Finder indicates a locked disk by displaying a padlock icon in the upper-left corner of the disk's window.

The Virus Threat

Have you had any viruses lately? I refer not to the cold-and-flu variety, but to *computer viruses*, programs that invade the Mac and slow its performance, cause system errors, or — at their most evil — destroy applications and documents.

The term *virus* implies a natural entity that you can't help but pick up now and then, like a cold. The truth is, computer viruses are tools of vandalism — they're bricks heaved through your Mac's windows by people with apparently nothing better to do with their time and programming skill. No cures exist for the viruses that cause colds, but computer viruses could be stopped dead if their creators turned their energies toward being productive, not destructive.

But then, so could war, crime, and pollution. And like them, viruses will be around for some time. What can you do? First, don't lose any sleep over viruses. They exist, but your chances of being victimized by one are small, especially if your Mac isn't on a network and you don't swap software with other users. Second, be prepared — just in case. Arm yourself with knowledge of how viruses spread, of their symptoms and remedies, and of the measures you can take to avoid them.

It came from Ohio

Some of the technical concepts behind viruses have been around for decades, but the first microcomputer viruses appear to have been created in 1983 by Frank Cohen, a University of Cincinnati professor who was researching his doctoral thesis on computer security. Cohen's viruses were created under controlled conditions; none reached the outside world. Interviewed in 1988, when viruses enjoyed a burst of media attention, he admitted to being reluctant to publish his findings, but did so to warn the world of the virus threat. "I had planned to devote my thesis to ways to defend against viruses," he said. "Instead, I used it to prove that you can't defend against them."

Viruses are difficult to fight because they're designed to spread. A virus contains software instructions that enable it to copy itself into legitimate files, called *hosts*. Some viruses infect only application files, while others invade documents or the Mac's system files. Still others begin by infecting a system file and then copy themselves to uninfected applications.

How viruses spread

Most viruses spread when you copy an infected file from one Mac to another, although some spread simply when you insert an infected floppy disk. Now imagine millions of Mac users exchanging files through user groups, office and university networks, and on-line bulletin boards and information services — the propagation possibilities are endless. In 1989, a new virus was discovered in Belgium in early December; by Christmas of that year, it had spread throughout the United States.

A virus doesn't just replicate itself, it also inflicts its own unique symptoms on the machines it infects. Viruses can be malicious or mischievous. A malicious virus may deliberately damage applications, cause system errors, or erase files on a hard disk. A mischievous virus may simply display a message or joke at a predetermined time; its creator is out to soap your windows, not smash them. To date, most Macintosh viruses have fallen into this second category.

But even a mischievous virus can be trouble. It may cause a system error by trying to use memory or resources that a legitimate program is already using. Its programmer may not have tested it thoroughly, or it may conflict with your Mac's combination of hardware and system extensions. The bottom line: There's no such thing as a benign virus.

Names and strains

Most Mac viruses have odd-sounding names — nVIR, Hpat, INIT29 — that reflect the technical makeup of the virus's software. Others are named after their discoverers — Don Ernesto Zucchini was reportedly the first victim of the ZUC virus. Some viruses earn more pronounceable monikers, such as the "Peace" virus, set loose by an attention-hungry editor of a Canadian Mac magazine. It was designed to display a "universal message of peace" on March 2, 1988, and then erase itself. Its victims —including Aldus Corporation, which inadvertently shipped a few thousand infected copies of FreeHand — didn't find the medium appropriate to the message.

Now and then a new strain of an existing virus appears. That's been the case with the nVIR virus, whose original program code was once posted on a computer bulletin board in an attempt to aid creators of antivirus software. It may have helped them, but it also gave budding virus creators a head start in creating new strains.

Table 26-1 "Field Guide to Viruses" lists the names and symptoms of the viruses that have been identified as of mid-1995.

Table 26-1
Field Guide to Viruses

Virus Name	***Nature of Infection***	***Symptoms***	***Comments***
ANTI, ANTI-B, ANTI-ange	Infects applications only (including the Finder), not other system files or documents.	Nondestructive but may cause crashes due to its poor programming.	Disinfected applications aren't identical to original, but generally still run. Best approach is to replace infected application with an uninfected copy from its master disk.
CDEF	Infects DeskTop file only, not system files, programs, or documents.	Slows performance. AppleShare server performance slows significantly.	You can remove this virus from an infected disk by rebuilding its DeskTop file: Press Command and Option while inserting the disk. For hard disks, restart and hold down Command and Option until rebuild dialog box appears. To avoid infecting an AppleShare server, do not grant "make changes" privilege to the server's root directory (desktop level).

Virus Name	*Nature of Infection*	*Symptoms*	*Comments*
CODE 252	Under System 7, generally infects only the System file. Under System 6 without MultiFinder, it can spread to applications. Spreads only between January 1 and June 5 of any year.	If an infected system is started up between June 6 and December 31 of any year, the virus displays the following message: *You have a virus. Ha Ha Ha Ha Ha Ha Ha Now erasing all disks... Ha Ha Ha Ha Ha Ha Ha P.S. Have a nice day.*	No disks are actually erased, but its sloppy programming can cause crashes and damaged files.
Frankie	Infects applications, not documents or system files.	Draws bomb icon, displays the message, *Frankie says: No more piracy*, and then crashes.	Very rare. Doesn't infect genuine Macs. Infects only Atari computers containing certain Mac emulator hardware.
INIT 29 (strains A and B)	Infects any file (document or application) containing resources. Spreads only via applications and System files.	Its poor coding may cause printing problems, INIT conflicts, and MultiFinder crashes. If you insert a locked floppy disk, a dialog box appears saying the disk needs repairs. Normally, this dialog box doesn't appear with locked disks.	INIT 29 can spread very rapidly because it infects unlocked floppies as soon as they are inserted.
MBDF	Infects applications and various system files.	May cause menu-related problems. Lengthens startup process.	This virus originally spread via three Trojan horse games: "10 Tile Puzzle," "Obnoxious Tetris," and "Tetricycle." Its creators, two Cornell University students, were caught and convicted of second-degree computer tampering.
MDEF (strains A, B, C, and D; also called Garfield)	Infects applications, various system files, and documents.	System crashes. On Macs using CE Software's Vaccine, MDEF-A causes menus to work only in infected applications.	Infects system files, applications, and documents. Strains B and C attempt to bypass watchdog INITs. Strain C bugs can cause crashes.
INIT 1984	Infects system extensions only, spreading from one extension to another during startup.	Severely damages files and folders on infected Macs that are started up on any Friday the 13th.	The Disinfectant utility detects and neutralizes this malicious virus.

(continued on the next page)

Table 26-1 *(continued)*			
Virus Name	***Nature of Infection***	***Symptoms***	***Comments***
INIT 17	Infects the System file and then application files. Does not infect documents.	Displays the message, *From the depths of Cyberspace* the first time an infected system is started after 6:06:06 a.m. on October 31, 1993.	Sloppy programming can cause system crashes, especially on 68000-based Macs such as the Classic, SE, and Plus.
INIT-M	Infects all types of files; spreads and attacks under System 7 only.	Severely damages files and folders on infected Macs that are started up on any Friday the 13th. Can cause windows to display improperly. One file or folder on a victimized disk may be renamed to "Virus MindCrime."	Creates a file called FSV Prefs in the System Folder's Preferences folder.
nVIR (strains A and B)	Infects System file first, adding code that subsequently infects each application you run. Finder and DA Handler files usually become infected.	System crashes. Files may disappear. Mac may beep when applications are started. "B" strain causes Mac to say "Don't panic" if System Folder contains the Macintalk file. Otherwise, you may hear random system beeps.	The original program code for nVIR was posted on some bulletin boards and information services. As a result, several clones have appeared: Hpad, nFLU, AIDS, MEV#, and F***, whose actual name can't be printed here. Their symptoms are generally the same.
Peace (also called MacMag, Drew, and Brandow)	Infects System file.	"Message of peace" appeared on March 2, 1988; virus then destroyed itself.	Rare these days, but still could be encountered on old disks.
Scores (also called NASA, Eric, Vult, San Jose Flu)	Infects System file first, lies dormant for two days, then searches for and infects a new application at 3½ minute intervals. Adds invisible files called Scores and Desktop_ (_ character represents a space) to System Folder.	System crashes; printing problems. Miscellaneous problems with MacDraw and Microsoft Excel. May cause insufficient memory messages. Increases size of files it infects by 7K. Notepad and Scrapbook files may have generic document icons (dog-eared page).	System 6.0.4's System file is irreparably damaged and must be replaced with an uninfected copy from its master disk.

Virus Name	*Nature of Infection*	*Symptoms*	*Comments*
T4 (strains A, B, C, and beta)	Infects the Finder and applications. Also attempts to alter the System file.	Mac crashes during startup while loading extensions. Sometimes renames files to *Disinfectant.* May display the message *Application is infected with the T4 virus.*	Originally spread via a game called GoMoku. Disinfected applications are damaged and must be reinstalled. Various strains are similar but are triggered on different dates.
WDEF (strains A and B)	Infects only the invisible DeskTop file contained on all floppy and hard disks. Spreads rapidly through the sharing of floppy disks.	Crashes Mac IIci and Portable. "B" strain causes Mac to beep each time a DeskTop file is infected.	See CDEF comments.
ZUC (strains A and B and C)	Infects applications only, not other System files or documents.	Strange pointer movement when mouse button down —pointer moves and bounces off the screen edges like a billiard ball. Can cause desktop pattern to change.	Applications don't have to be run to become infected. Spreads over networks.
CODE 1	Infects applications and System files, not documents.	Renames the startup drive to "Trent Saburo" when the infected Mac is started on any October 31.	Can cause crashes and other problems.
INIT 9403 (also called SysX)	Infects the Finder and some compression utilities. Believed to infect only Italian versions of the system software.	Destructive! Attempts to completely erase the startup disk as well as any connected drives larger than 16MB.	Found in pirated versions of Connectix RAM Doubler (non-pirated RAM Doubler versions are not infected)

Is your Mac at risk?

Generally, the more Macs your machine comes in contact with, the greater the risk of infection. Consider yourself at risk if any of the following describe you:

- You swap programs, documents, or disks with other Mac users. Even an erased disk can carry the WDEF virus if you erase the disk by dragging its contents to the Trash. If a friend hands you a blank disk to fill with your latest shareware finds, be sure the disk was erased using the Finder's Erase Disk command before you insert it into your Mac.

- You download programs and documents from bulletin boards or information services. Most bulletin boards and information services check incoming files for viruses before making them available to subscribers, but a new virus can slip through undetected if the service's virus-detection software can't recognize it. The Internet is another story — no central authority exists to check posted files for viruses, making the Internet a particularly good place for viruses to propagate. (The fact that it's a worldwide network doesn't hurt, either.)
- You're connected to other Macs on a network. A network is an ideal transmission medium for viruses, especially if several users access applications stored on a file server.
- You use a desktop publishing service bureau or university laser-printer center. Some service bureaus have been criticized for taking a cavalier attitude toward virus checking and prevention. If you use a bureau or central printing station regularly, look into its virus-prevention measures.

Protecting Your Mac from Viruses

If you don't fall into the preceding categories, you aren't immune from viruses, but the threat is minimal. Whether or not you're in the high-risk group, here's how to protect yourself.

Lock floppy disks whenever possible

A virus can't infect a locked disk. *Always* lock the original master disks of an application before inserting them; you'll need virus-free masters in case one of your programs gets infected. To lock a disk, slide its plastic write-protect tab so you can see through the square hole.

Back up religiously

If the worst happens, you'll have something to fall back on — unless the backups are infected, too. To avoid that, keep at least two sets of alternate backups made at different times. Don't neglect to back up the files in your System Folder, too; most viruses attack them first, and by having a backup, you won't have to laboriously reconfigure your System Folder.

Watch out for freeware and shareware

The stuff you download from on-line services is probably safe — on-line forum operators are careful about scanning anything they post for downloading. But, as I mentioned earlier, the Internet is a different story. Small bulletin boards might not be as careful, either. Instead of trustingly copying it to your hard disk, run a

When Infection Strikes

Your Mac is acting up. Should you suspect a virus? Not at first, unless the problem is a dialog box containing a universal message of peace. Most system errors or other problems can be traced to nonviral causes — conflicting system extensions, a damaged disk, loose or damaged printer cables, or application bugs (see Chapter 28 for more troubleshooting advice). I learned this the hard way a while back: I spent two days trying to eradicate a WDEF infection after my system slowed to glacial pace, but the problem turned out to be conflicting system extensions. It goes to show that even the threat of a virus infection can impair your productivity.

After you've eliminated non-viral possibilities, compare your list of symptoms to those in Table 26-1 "Field Guide to Viruses." Run John Norstad's Disinfectant and any other virus detectors you may have. If the detection utility identifies an infection, perform the following steps:

- *Isolate the patient* If you're on a network, disconnect your LocalTalk connector where it attaches to the Mac's printer port. Inform other members of the network before disconnecting your Mac, and be sure they know your machine is infected — theirs probably are, too.
- *Replace the infected files* You did back up yesterday, didn't you? If you don't have healthy backups, use a virus utility to try to repair the damaged files. First, because the disinfecting process itself can damage the files, back up the files the utility says are infected; copy them to floppy disks and be sure to clearly label those disks as infected. If one utility fails to repair the files, try another. If you can't fix a file, delete it. After you successfully repair or delete all infected files, run the detection utility again.
- *Erase the infected disks* Don't use the Finder to erase the disks; you may reintroduce the virus when you insert an infected disk. Instead, use a magnetic bulk eraser such as Radio Shack's catalog number 44-232. A bulk eraser uses a strong magnetic field to scramble the disk's microscopic magnets, so don't use it near your good disks.

freeware or shareware program from a floppy disk first and watch for abnormal behavior, such as system crashes or significantly slowed performance. Use the General Controls control panel (System 7.0 or 7.1) or the Date & Time control panel (System 7.5) or the Alarm Clock desk accessory to change the Mac's date setting, and then run the program again; some viruses lie dormant until a certain amount of time passes. (The Scores virus, for example, waits four days before doing some of its dirty work.) Bypassing your hard disk protects you from *Trojan horse* programs, which appear to be legitimate applications, but which damage or erase files when you run them (see the Background box "Attack of the Trojan Horses").

Protect your networks

Only applications known to be uninfected should be copied to a network file server. If you're in charge of running a server, establish guidelines to prevent anyone else from copying programs to the server. Also consider using the file server for

Attack of the Trojan Horses

A Trojan horse differs from a virus only in that it isn't designed to spread by replicating itself; if a Trojan horse strikes, you can prevent future problems by deleting it (unless the Trojan horse *installs* a virus, as do the Tetricycle and Tetris-Rotating horses). Trojan horses have been relatively rare in the Mac world, but there are several out there.

- ❖ Mosaic and FontFinder surfaced in early 1990 on a bulletin board system in Canada. They appear to be utility programs, but when run, they erase the directory of the Mac's hard disk and display a message: "Gotcha." (Isn't it amazing how uncreative software vandals are?)
- ❖ Steroid appeared later in 1990. It's an extension that promises faster screen displays on Macs with 9-inch, built-in screens. It wipes out disks.
- ❖ Sexy Ladies may have been the first well-known Mac Trojan horse. It's a HyperCard stack that displays cheesy images while erasing data from the disk it's stored on.
- ❖ CPro 1.41 claimed to be an updated version of Bill Goodman's Compact Pro file-compression utility. It wasn't. When run, it erases your startup hard drive and any floppy disk that might be inserted.
- ❖ ChinaT claims to be an extension that provides text-to-speech capabilities (Apple's PlainTalk text-to-speech software was code-named Gala Tea). The only speech ChinaT generates is cursing: It erases hard disks.
- ❖ Tetricycle and Tetris-Rotating claim to be games but merely install the MBDF virus (described in Table 26-1 "Field Guide to Viruses").
- ❖ An unnamed Trojan horse (called Unnamed PostScript Hack in some virus literature) doesn't damage your Mac; it damages your PostScript printer by changing its internal password. Several free utilities are available that protect against this.

document storage only, and running applications from local hard or floppy disks (not a bad approach in any case, given the less-than-blazing speed of LocalTalk cabling).

Consider using more than one

There are programs you can use to scan suspect disks for viruses, remove viruses from infected programs, and guard against future infection. They're often described as the vaccines of the computer world, but the truth is, they're more like chicken soup — not guaranteed cures, but certainly worth trying if you're at risk.

If you suspect a virus infection, see the Quick Tips box "When Infection Strikes" for some tips on what to do.

Mac Medicine

After the Big Mac Viral Epidemic of 1988 (which snared more media attention than victims), programmers on the side of law and order began developing ways to detect, disable, and prevent viruses. Today, you can choose from several commercial virus-detection utilities and nearly a dozen shareware or free ones.

The commercial packages — Datawatch's Virex, Symantec's SAM II, and Central Point's MacTools Anti-Virus (included with MacTools Pro) — include an application program for scanning suspect disks and repairing infected ones, and a *watchdog* extension, which can help prevent infections (see Figure 26-5 "Virus Hunt").

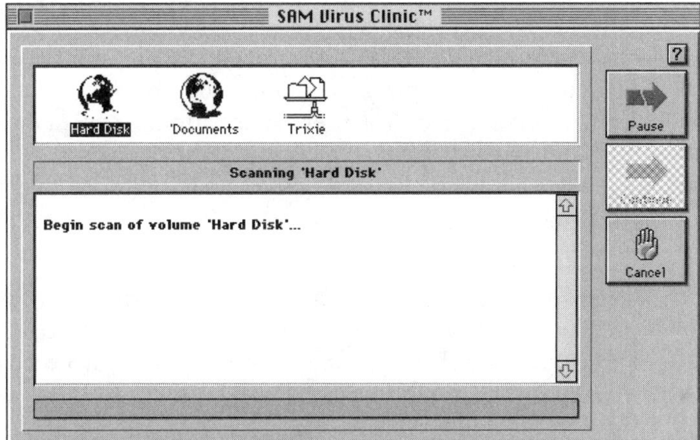

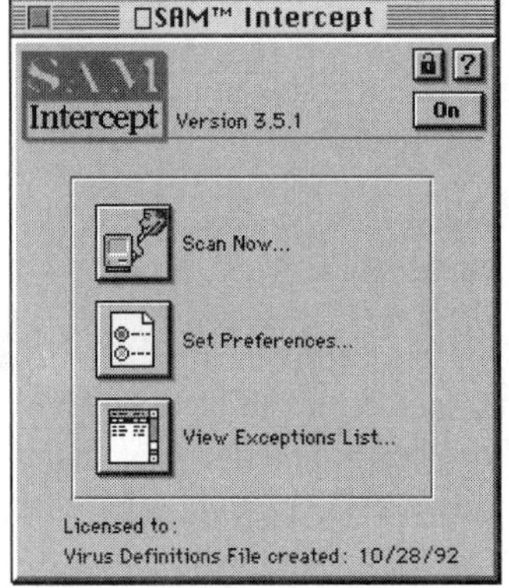

Figure 26-5: Virus Hunt Commercial virus-detection utilities include a scan-and-repair application (top) and a watchdog extension such as Symantec's SAM Intercept (bottom). When a program attempts to modify a file in the way that a virus would, a watchdog extension displays a dialog box that lets you grant or deny access to the file.

Scanning for viruses

It's a good idea to use a virus-detection application's scan mode to check for viruses before backing up. Virex also has a Record/Scan command that saves information about the size and contents of one or more files. If you suspect infection, run the Record/Scan procedure again, comparing the results with the first scan. This is a useful way to spot a new virus that the utility may not otherwise detect.

Watchdog extensions provide several lines of defense against future infections. They automatically scan a newly inserted floppy disk for viruses; if one is found, you can eject the diseased disk and throw it away or you can try to repair it. The extensions also display a warning dialog box if you try to start an infected application. Some watchdogs also keep an eye out for known Trojan horses.

SAM's watchdog extension can also help prevent "unauthorized" modifications to applications and the System Folder. When a program (virus or otherwise) tries to modify an application or system file or attempts to add a new extension to the System Folder, a warning that lets you prohibit or permit the operation appears. Similar warnings can appear when you're installing a new program. (You can also tell SAM to automatically allow a specific type of modification, to eliminate unnecessary warnings.)

As for the free and shareware virus-detection utilities, the most popular are John Norstad's Disinfectant (a detection and repair application with a watchdog extension), Jeffery S. Shulman's VirusDetective (a detection-and-repair DA), VirusBlockade (a watchdog extension), and Chris Johnson's Gatekeeper and Gatekeeper Aid. Disinfectant is included on this book's CD-ROM; See the "On the CD" box at the end of this chapter.

At least one virus-detection utility belongs in every Macintosh user's software library. Start with the programs I just mentioned — they're free, and they may be all you need. For extra protection, consider one of the commercial packages.

Protection for the paranoid

If security is extremely important, you may also consider Casady & Greene's AME. Short for Access Managed Environment, AME provides more security than you'll find at a Secret Service company picnic. You can create a list of people permitted to use your Mac and then define privileges — such as the ability to create or delete files, use printers, or insert floppy disks. For virus protection, you can register your healthy applications as "trusted" and then instruct AME to compare an application to its registration to verify that it hasn't been altered. If it has, AME won't permit it to run.

One Watchdog Is Enough

It's worth noting that watchdog extensions can cause problems if you're not careful. SAM's Intercept INIT, for example, lets you intercept certain activities that some programs perform as part of their normal operation. SAM includes a list of over a dozen software and hardware products that Intercept may not work with properly — one of them is the Virex INIT. With virus utilities, two watchdogs do not necessarily offer twice the protection of one.

No Sure Cures

As I mentioned earlier, a virus-detection utility can't guarantee immunity. It's possible for a new virus to bypass a utility's detection and prevention features. When a new virus appears, a detection utility must be revised to recognize it. Many of today's packages enable you to update the program yourself by typing cryptic character sequences that the utility looks for as it scans for viruses. But the virus has to be discovered before the utility's developer can tell its customers which characters to type.

Your other alternative is to buy individual program updates (often $15 to $25) or subscribe to a series of updates (usually $50 to $75). If a few new viruses appear each year, you'll spend a small sum keeping your medicine cabinet up to date — and you'll be partially unprotected until the latest versions arrive.

Some people believe virus-detection utilities challenge virus writers to create new strains that can bypass their protection measures. They may be right; the WDEF virus contained a stealth mechanism that enabled it to evade most detection utilities when it first appeared.

What Are My Chances, Doc?

How likely are you to get a virus? In a *Macworld* reader survey that ran several years ago, only about eight percent of the readers who responded had been infected. I've never had a virus, and I hang out on a half-dozen information services and run untested shareware with abandon. (As mentioned previously, all commercial online services such as America Online and CompuServe scan uploaded files for viruses before making them available for downloading.) Okay, I'm a hypocrite — a doctor who tells you to watch your diet while his own cheeks bulge with M&Ms.

Or maybe I simply give viruses the attention they deserve. The virus threat is minimal; you'll probably never see one. But they are out there, and new ones can appear at any time.

Coming to Terms with SCSI

For all the talk you hear about viruses, there's a part of your Mac that causes far more problems for far more people: the SCSI bus. Indeed, some types of SCSI problems have symptoms that are similar to those of a virus infection — slow performance, system crashes, and lost files. To be able to differentiate between a virus infection and a SCSI problem, it helps to understand what SCSI is, how it works, and what kinds of problems it can create.

A Brief History of SCSI

Any computer can benefit from the speed and capacity of a hard disk, yet the Macintosh entered the world barely able to communicate with one. The Mac that Steve Jobs unveiled in 1984 lacked a connector for attaching hard drives. Most of the pioneering hard drives that were available attached to the Mac's modem port, which was far too slow to handle the speeds the hard drives were capable of. It wasn't a bottleneck, it was the skinny part of an hourglass.

The Mac languished until early 1986, when Apple introduced the Mac Plus. Besides offering faster performance and more memory, the Plus introduced a new rear-panel connector designed specifically for hard drives and other fast add-ons. This new connector used a high-speed communications scheme called the *Small Computer Systems Interface*, or *SCSI* for short. SCSI saved the Mac by enabling it to communicate with high-speed peripherals at a reasonable speed. Hard drives, image scanners, personal laser printers, CD-ROM drives, tape backup devices, SyQuest and Bernoulli cartridge drives — none of these add-ons would be as popular as they are today without SCSI.

That's the sweet side of SCSI. There's also a bitter side, and it surfaces when you connect several SCSI devices to a Mac — and are suddenly unable to start it. What follows is often a bad dream filled with cable juggling, switch flicking, and head scratching. There's a quirkiness to SCSI, and it's no wonder the acronym is usually pronounced as a word: *scuzzy*.

In this section, I'll explore the bittersweet world of SCSI and pass along some survival tips. I'll also spotlight some recent developments in the SCSI field that promise to deliver fewer headaches and even faster performance.

Public Data Transportation

In computer terms, SCSI is a *bus* — a set of common wires upon which data and instructions flow. A Mac contains several buses. Some enable information to move between the Mac's memory and other internal components; others are designed to enable you to attach additional hardware to the Mac. The SCSI bus falls into the latter category, as do the various internal expansion slots present in most desktop Macs.

But expansion slots are inside the case. The SCSI connector is on the outside so it can attach to external devices. In this regard, SCSI is similar to another bus: the *Apple Desktop Bus* (ADB), which is the connection scheme the Mac's keyboard and mouse use. (Every Mac from the SE on also has an internal SCSI connector that attaches to an internal hard disk.)

SCSI strength 1: speed

The Mac's SCSI port has two basic strengths. First, it's fast. Most Macs' SCSI buses can move a few megabytes per second; the internal SCSI buses on the Power Mac 7500, 8500, and 9500 can shuttle up to ten million characters (10MB) per second. One reason SCSI is speedy is because it transfers the eight bits that comprise a byte in *parallel:* The bits travel alongside each other, each in its own wire, like parade marchers striding eight abreast. By contrast, the Mac's slower modem, printer, and ADB ports transfer data in *serial* fashion: Bits must travel single-file, one after another, like shoppers passing through a check-out line.

But whether data actually travels as quickly as the SCSI bus can carry it depends on the device that you attach to the Mac: A German freeway may have a speed limit of 100 miles per hour, but not every car can sustain that pace. If you connect a hard drive that delivers "only" 2MB per second to a Power Mac 8500, you aren't taking full advantage of the Mac's SCSI capabilities. The lesson: If you're buying a hard drive, look for one that can keep up with your Mac. But don't overbuy: If you attach a 2MB per second hard drive to the SCSI port on a Mac Classic (which transfers only about 650K per second), you won't fully exploit the drive.

SCSI strength 2: expandability

The SCSI port's other strength is that it can accommodate up to seven devices. How can seven devices connect to one port? Through a technique called *daisy chaining:* You connect one device to the Mac, and then connect other devices to each other. Almost every SCSI add-on has two SCSI connectors on its back panel: One connector accepts the cable that attaches to the Mac, and the other accepts the cable that attaches to the next device in the chain. (If you have a device with only one SCSI connector — such as a GCC Technologies PLP laser printer or Apple's PowerCD CD-ROM drive — that device must be the last device on the SCSI chain.)

Tip: Before making any SCSI connections, turn *off* your Mac and any external SCSI devices attached to it. Changing any SCSI connection when a device is on is asking for sizzled circuits.

SCSI's speed and ability to accommodate numerous external devices help explain why Apple adopted the bus back in 1986: It enabled the company to introduce an expandable Mac without having to design a new case and add costly expansion slots. But as you'll see, its versatility is also responsible for the scuzzier aspects of SCSI.

SCSI addressing

If one SCSI port can accommodate several add-ons, how does a device know when information coming from the Mac is intended for it? What keeps a hard drive from responding to commands for a scanner, and vice versa?

SCSI *addresses*, also called *ID numbers*, give every device attached to a SCSI port its own electronic house number. When the Mac transmits information to a device, it sends the device's address along with the information. All the devices on the SCSI chain — including the Mac — constantly monitor the bus for activity, but only the device the information is addressed to responds. The first device to transmit a signal gets control of the SCSI bus — just as the first person in a house who picks up the phone gets control of the line.

And if two devices transmit a signal at the same time? The SCSI ID helps there, too, by assigning priority to each device. On the SCSI totem pole, the higher a device's address, the higher the device's priority. If, say, a hard drive and a scanner both try to access the bus at the same time, the device with the higher address number wins. This is called *bus arbitration.*

SCSI address numbers run from 0 through 6. The Mac itself has an address of 7. If your Mac contains a hard drive, the hard drive's address is always 0. If your Mac has an internal CD-ROM drive, the CD-ROM drive's address is always 3. External

SCSI and PowerBooks

PowerBooks have the same basic SCSI advantages and potential problems as desk-bound Macs. This box describes some PowerBook particulars that relate to SCSI.

The SCSI disk mode

As described in the previous chapter, the PowerBook 100, 160, and 180, as well as the Duo and 500-series models, offer a *SCSI disk mode* that enables you to attach the PowerBook to another Mac's SCSI port as though it were an external hard drive. Once connected, the PowerBook hard drive appears on the other Mac's desktop. It's an ideal way to transfer files created on the road.

To connect a PowerBook to another Mac via SCSI, you need an HDI-30 SCSI Disk Adaptor Cable (Apple part number M2539LL/A). Connect the Disk Adaptor Cable to a SCSI System Cable. Depending on the Mac you're connecting to, you may also need one or more SCSI terminators; check your PowerBook's manual for details.

Cable considerations

All PowerBook models (as well as the Duo Dock) do not use the 25-pin SCSI connector other Macs provide, but instead use a smaller connector called an HDI-30. To connect a PowerBook to a SCSI device, use Apple's Apple HDI-30 SCSI System Cable (part number M2538LL/A). You'll probably need to also use a Peripheral Interface Cable because the HDI-30 SCSI System Cable is only 18 inches long.

SCSI devices such as hard drives and scanners have rear-panel switches that let you change their IDs (see Figure 26-6 "A Guide to SCSI Components"). Two houses can't have the same address, nor can two SCSI devices. If you connect a device whose ID matches that of a divice already on the drain, disk errors may occur, or the Mac may not start up at all. When that happens, shut everything off and follow the advice in the Quick Tips box "Surviving with SCSI."

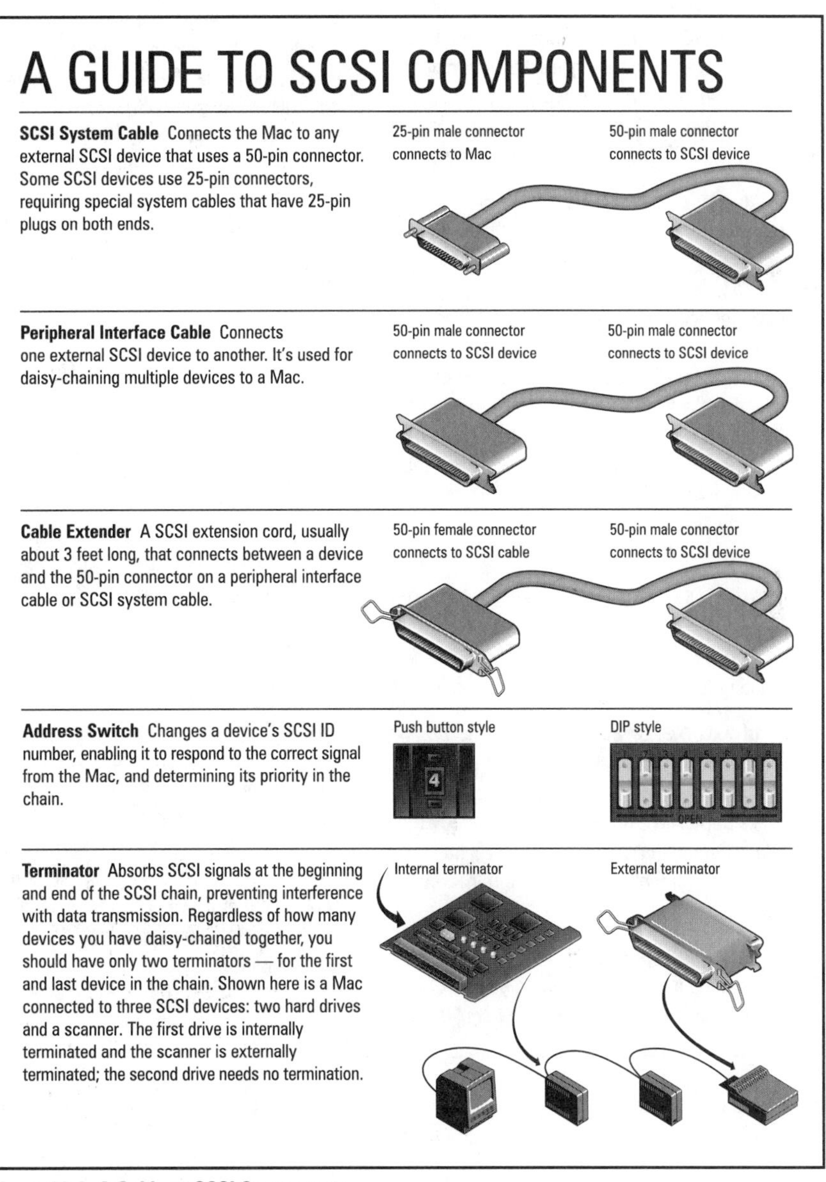

A GUIDE TO SCSI COMPONENTS
SCSI System Cable Connects the Mac to any external SCSI device that uses a 50-pin connector. Some SCSI devices use 25-pin connectors, requiring special system cables that have 25-pin plugs on both ends.
25-pin male connector connects to Mac
50-pin male connector connects to SCSI device
Peripheral Interface Cable Connects one external SCSI device to another. It's used for daisy-chaining multiple devices to a Mac.
50-pin male connector connects to SCSI device
50-pin male connector connects to SCSI device
Cable Extender A SCSI extension cord, usually about 3 feet long, that connects between a device and the 50-pin connector on a peripheral interface cable or SCSI system cable.
50-pin female connector connects to SCSI cable
50-pin male connector connects to SCSI device
Address Switch Changes a device's SCSI ID number, enabling it to respond to the correct signal from the Mac, and determining its priority in the chain.
Push button style
4
DIP style
Terminator Absorbs SCSI signals at the beginning and end of the SCSI chain, preventing interference with data transmission. Regardless of how many devices you have daisy-chained together, you should have only two terminators — for the first and last device in the chain. Shown here is a Mac connected to three SCSI devices: two hard drives and a scanner. The first drive is internally terminated and the scanner is externally terminated; the second drive needs no termination.
Internal terminator
External terminator

Figure 26-6: A Guide to SCSI Components

Surviving with SCSI

Here are some tips to help you avoid SCSI problems.

Buy quality cables

The best SCSI cables are *double-shielded:* The wires that carry the SCSI signals are wrapped with two layers of metal shielding to trap electrical interference that can cause data errors, especially in long SCSI chains or on fast Macs such as Quadras and Power Macs. Apple's SCSI cables are first-rate but costly.

Keep the cable length down

In theory, the total length of all the SCSI cables in a chain can be up to seven meters (about 23 feet). If you have a loud hard drive, you can attach one or two three-foot peripheral interface cables together to move the drive further away from your desk. But don't go overboard. Long cable runs can cause data errors, especially if you use cheap SCSI cables or if a cable's shielding is damaged. Avoid cable runs of more than six feet between devices, and keep the total length of the SCSI cabling below 15 feet. With SCSI cabling, less is better.

Clip those cables

The little wire clips on SCSI connectors help ensure a tight connection. But when you're in a hurry to connect a device or reorganize the order of devices, it's tempting to not use the clips. Use them.

Demand external or active termination

Try to avoid buying internally terminated devices if you can. If you're torn between two otherwise identical external hard drives, for example, buy the one that is not internally terminated. You'll have one less device to worry about in future termination travails.

Check those addresses

Before installing a new device, examine its SCSI address switch and make sure it won't conflict with a device already on the chain. Consider writing a device's address on a label and then attaching it to the front panel. When SCSI problems occur, you won't have to bend over each device to determine its address. When changing a device's address, keep in mind that the address also determines the device's priority. If you're working with two external hard drives and you want the Mac to start up from a specific one, be sure to give that drive the higher address. (You can also use the Startup Disk control panel to override this startup order.) You can assign addresses in any order: For example, you can use ID numbers 3 and 5, skipping over ID number 4.

Power up properly

In general, you should always turn on external SCSI devices first and then switch on the Mac. Also, Apple recommends that all SCSI devices be switched on while the Mac is on, even if you aren't using some of them. Neither rule seems carved in stone, however. Many people (myself included) turn all their devices on and off from a single power switch without problems. I usually have no trouble leaving one or more devices off, too, although now and then, I encounter a device that must be on in order for the Mac to start up.

Keep some SCSI tools on hand

A free control panel called SCSI Probe (by Robert Polic) lets you examine the devices on a bus and if you've turned on a drive after starting up the Mac, you can use SCSI Probe to make the drive's icon appear on the desktop. (In computer lingo, this is called *mounting* the drive.) FWB's terrific Hard Disk Toolkit contains a similar control panel. Hard Disk Toolkit also lets you test a hard drive and fine-tune it for best performance.

SCSI meets the terminator

For the Mac to know where the SCSI bus begins and ends, the bus needs small electronic components called *terminators*. Terminators are the bumpers on the front and back of the SCSI bus: They absorb colliding SCSI signals, preventing them from electrically reflecting within the cabling and interfering with reliable data transmission. If you attach more than one SCSI device to a Mac, you'll also need to grapple with terminators. Improper termination is another common source of SCSI woes.

Internal and external termination

As Figure 26-6 shows, terminators can be internal or external. Internal terminators are usually installed directly on a device's circuit board; external terminators attach to a device's rear-panel SCSI connector. Some devices also provide convenient termination switches that let you activate or deactivate internal termination.

In theory, termination is simple: Two's company, and three's a crowd. Specifically, the first and last device in the SCSI chain must each have a terminator connected to it. If your Mac contains an internal hard drive, the drive has an internal terminator. If you have one external SCSI device attached, it needs a terminator, too. If you have two or more external SCSI devices, those in between the first and last device must *not* be terminated. Having more than two terminators on the SCSI bus can cause startup problems, data errors, and even hardware damage.

Tip: The Mac IIfx uses special SCSI circuitry that requires nonstandard terminators, which usually have black plastic cases instead of the common gray ones. Be sure to use only the black, IIfx-style terminators with this Mac.

Determining termination

How do you know whether your new SCSI gizmo is internally terminated? It isn't always easy to tell, which is why Apple recommends that hardware manufacturers not use internal terminators in external devices. (An external terminator is easy to spot: It's dangling off the back of the box.) Still, some companies use internal termination, perhaps because including an external terminator would add expense. Generally, a device's manual should state whether it's internally terminated, although hard drive vendors have been known to contradict their own manuals.

IDE Drives: Storage for the Low End

The Quadra 630 and Performa 630 series, the Power Mac 5200, the LC 580, and the PowerBook 150 don't use the SCSI bus for their internal hard drives. Instead, these Macs use a hard drive interface called Integrated Drive Electronics, or IDE. In an IDE drive, the controller chips that enable the computer to communicate with the drive mechanism are built into the drive itself. IDE drives tend to cost less than their SCSI counterparts — which makes them ideal for low-cost Macs.

Generally, the only time you have to concern yourself with the fact that you have a non-SCSI internal hard drive is if you need to format the drive. Older versions of many third-party formatter utilities — the programs I discussed in the previous chapter — do not support IDE drives. You should use the formatter utility that came with your Mac or be sure you buy an IDE-compatible third-party driver.

Ontrack Computer Systems' Disk Manager Mac and Casa Blanca Works' Drive7 are two such packages. Both support both IDE and SCSI drives and can actually boost your IDE drive's performance by tweaking the handshaking methods used by the drive as well as enabling its internal cache memory. The degree of performance improvement depends on the IDE drive you have. And unlike Apple's IDE software, both packages let you create multiple partitions and assign passwords to them.

All This and SCSI-2

A Power Mac 8500's 10MB-per-second transfer rate sounds (and is) fast, but SCSI isn't stopping there. A new version of the SCSI specification, *SCSI-2,* promises data transfer rates of 10MB to 40MB per second — essential speeds for video and high-end color applications, where 100MB files aren't uncommon. The key performance-enhancing aspects of SCSI-2 are *Fast SCSI* and *Wide SCSI.* Fast SCSI doubles the bus's transfer rate to 10MB. Wide SCSI adds lanes to the bus's freeway, expanding SCSI's parallel data path from eight bits wide to 16 and eventually 32 bits.

Numerous high-end hard drives that support fast and wide SCSI are available. And the Power Mac 7500, 8500, and 9500 contain an internal Fast SCSI-2 bus that can exploit them. For other Macs, you need a SCSI-2 adaptor card such as FWB's SCSI JackHammer or PCI JackHammer or Atto's SiliconExpress. These plug into a NuBus or PCI slot and provide a Fast SCSI-2 port. They're ideal for use with disk arrays (discussed in the previous chapter) and are popular among high-end digital video producers.

Keep in mind only a few costly high-capacity hard drives can approach the transfer rates these boards are capable of. As a rule, the lower your hard drive's capacity, the less likely it is to benefit from a SCSI accelerator.

Special SCSI-2 cabling considerations

But the advent of SCSI-2 may create the potential for even more SCSI headaches. SCSI-2's fast transfer rates make high-quality cables and correct termination more essential than ever. Moving up to SCSI-2 also means becoming familiar with new cabling and termination schemes. There isn't room on the back of a SCSI-2 adaptor card for the conventional 50-pin Centronics-style connectors you're probably used to working with. Instead, fast SCSI-2 cards use a high-density 50-pin connector, called an HD-50, whose smaller pins are packed together like rush-hour bus riders.

Take care when attaching the cable's connector to the card; the weight of the cable and the force required to mate the connectors can loosen the card — a scenario for disaster. You may want to connect the cable while the Mac's case lid is still removed, using one hand to steady the card as you make the connection. (And speaking of cables, buy only double-shielded, twisted-pair SCSI cables for any fast hard drive: Bargain-basement cables are likely to cause data errors and reduced performance.)

Wide SCSI-2 adaptors and drives use yet another type of connector, which has 68 pins. Wide SCSI-2 devices also provide *active termination* features, in which circuitry within the drive automatically terminates the SCSI bus — no futzing with terminators. A growing number of vendors are providing active termination in standard SCSI devices.

Dual SCSI buses on high-end Macs

SCSI is also evolving within the Mac family. The Quadra 900 and 950 contain two electrically separate SCSI buses. As discussed in the previous chapter, some disk arrays take advantage of the two buses; one of the drives in the array connects to the Quadra's external bus, while the other attaches to the internal bus. Specialized driver software separates the two buses and allows data striping across the two mechanisms.

The Power Mac 8100 also has a dual channel SCSI bus, with two physical connectors on the logic board. The first SCSI channel supports only the internal hard drive and is capable of transfer rates of up to 4.5MB per second. The 8100's second channel supports any additional internal or external SCSI devices. The two SCSI buses are independent of each other — each has its own SCSI controller chip.

Many of the second-generation Power Macs provide even better SCSI performance. As mentioned earlier, the Power Mac 7500, 8500, and 9500 provide internal Fast SCSI-2 buses that can handle transfer rates of up to 10MB per second.

Special termination issues for the 8100

As with other Macs, the 8100's SCSI buses must be terminated at both ends. The first SCSI channel is terminated by the internal hard drive and the logic board.

Termination for the second channel is a bit more complicated. For CD-ROM equipped 8100s, the cable for the CD-ROM has an additional SCSI connector and a terminator on it similar to that of the Quadra 900 and 950. If your Power Mac 8100 does not have an internal CD-ROM drive, termination is provided by the logic board. Any external device must also be terminated.

The faster processing rates and tighter tolerances of the Power Macintosh family make it even more important to use high-quality cables and terminators. Refer back to the Quick Tips box "Surviving with SCSI," earlier in this chapter, for advice.

Looking Ahead: SCSI-3, Fiber Channel, and FireWire

There are several new implementations of SCSI on the horizon, but they all fall under one umbrella: *SCSI-3*. This latest version of the venerable SCSI standard supports the existing SCSI protocols as well as several different interface designs and data-transfer schemes. These new SCSI interfaces will be available as cards that plug into the PCI expansion slots of second-generation Power Macs — NuBus slots are just too slow to accommodate the new flavors of SCSI.

Three of the four SCSI-3 implementations will simplify your life by eliminating the aggravation of setting address switches and adjusting terminators — the devices will configure themselves when you plug them in. SCSI-3 shatters the seven-device limit, in some cases supporting up to 127 devices on a single bus. And the devices themselves will be hot-pluggable: you won't have to shut down the Mac to install them.

Shifting into Serial

As I mentioned earlier in this chapter, SCSI has always been a parallel bus — the bits that make up each byte of data travel alongside each other, each in its own wire. In the past, parallel buses have always been faster than their serial ones, just as a multilane freeway can carry more cars than a one-lane road.

But bits aren't cars and cables aren't freeways, and at a certain point, a parallel interface becomes a liability. To speed up a parallel interface you can add more wires to its cables, and you can speed up the clock that regulates the bus. Both changes increase the risk of interference between wires, which limits cable lengths and requires more electrical shielding; more shielding means more wires, and the bigger connectors that more wires demand all increase the cost.

Serial buses, with fewer wires packed in side by side, are resistant to interference, even at very high clock speeds and over very long cables. It's for these reasons that three of the four SCSI-3 protocols rely on serial data transmission techniques. Through sophisticated signaling schemes, serial SCSI protocols can blast more data through less-expensive cables than their parallel predecessors.

But First, Ultra SCSI

Making the transition to serial SCSI commits hard drive and interface manufacturers to a major engineering effort. While waiting for the technical and political dust to settle, some storage vendors are turning to a SCSI-3 spec that is an enhanced version of the parallel SCSI architecture, called *Ultra SCSI*.

By doubling the SCSI clock rate from 10 MHz to 20 MHz, Ultra SCSI promises a doubling of the maximum sustained transfer rate: while Fast and Wide SCSI-2 maxes out at 20MB per second, Ultra SCSI supports rates of up to 40MB per second.

Ultra SCSI's downside is that, as a parallel bus, it doesn't address SCSI's finicky cabling requirements. If anything, Ultra SCSI's fast transfer rates make issues such as cable length and cable quality more critical.

Tuned in to Fiber

The SCSI-3 protocol that's generating the most excitement in the high-end Mac storage world is *Fiber Channel*. While Ultra SCSI provides a solid performance boost using tried-and-true, but potentially finicky, methods, Fiber Channel promises a quantum leap in transfer rates — taking advantage of the high clock-speeds that parallel buses can use reliably.

Fiber Channel's name implies the use of fiber optic cables, and indeed, the Fiber Channel standard supports them. But Fiber Channel also supports good old copper wires, including twisted-pair (telephone-like) and coaxial cabling.

Fiber Channel's promises are enticing: copper cable lengths up to 100 meters long, and fiber cables up to 10 kilometers long. No address switches or terminators to configure. Hot-pluggable devices — up to 127 of them per bus. And transfer rates of up to 100MB per second.

Fiber Channel supports several topologies — methods of connecting devices to each other — but the one most likely to surface in the personal computer world is called Fiber Channel-Arbitrated Loop, or FC-AL. In the FC-AL topology, the devices on the bus are connected in a circle and talk to each other to determine which one can transmit data on the bus at a given time — hence the phrase arbitrated loop.

Apple's Fire in the Wire

Then there's *FireWire*, also known by the less-catchy name P1394, the preliminary standard on which it's based. The initial FireWire specification allows for transfer rates of up to 20MB per second over inexpensive 9-pin cables. The cables use heavy-duty connectors, similar to those used on home video games, designed to withstand repeated plugging and unplugging. FireWire supports up to 63 hot-pluggable devices on a bus; cables between devices can be up to 4.5 meters long.

Originally touted as a SCSI replacement for hard drives and other storage devices, FireWire is evolving into an interface for multimedia devices such as video cameras, digital still cameras, and video cassette recorders. Indeed, Apple's implementation of FireWire places special emphasis on *isochronous* — real-time — data, such as video feeds and audio. (Sony plans to build FireWire connectors into digital video cameras.)

FireWire doesn't allow for the sizzling transfer rates or kilometer-class cable lengths of Fiber Channel, but with its relatively inexpensive controllers and widespread use in consumer electronics, FireWire is likely to be simpler and less expensive than other flavors of SCSI-3. If Apple or another vendor ships a FireWire interface card for PCI Macs and Windows machines, and if enough FireWire-equipped devices become available to make the card worth buying, then drive manufacturers might be enticed into building FireWire-based mechanisms. If not, don't expect to see FireWire affecting the storage world.

SCSI Manager 4.3: what's the difference?

In mid-1993 Apple released version 4.3 of the SCSI Manager — the portion of the Mac's system software that deals with SCSI devices. The new SCSI Manager supports the SCSI-2 command set as well as more sophisticated data-transfer and SCSI communications techniques. For example, the new manager supports *disconnect/reconnect,* which enables a device to electronically disconnect and release control of the SCSI bus while processing a command from the Mac and then reconnect when it's again ready to communicate with the Mac. This enables the Mac to submit data requests to multiple devices so that those requests are executed in parallel — ideal for disk arrays.

The new manager also supports *asynchronous* SCSI communications. This enables the Mac's central processor to initiate a SCSI data transfer operation and then go on to other tasks while the transfer takes place.

The improved SCSI Manager also takes advantage of the *direct-memory access* (DMA) chips present in some Mac models, including the IIfx, the AV Macs, and the Power Macs. DMA support enables these Macs to perform other jobs while data is transferred to or from a SCSI device. SCSI Manager 4.3 also takes full advantage of the two SCSI buses present in many Quadra models and in the Power Mac 8100 to enable you to connect up to 14 devices.

As mentioned in Chapter 22, the second-generation Power Macs ship with System 7.5.2, which includes a version of SCSI Manager 4.3 that runs in native mode.

In short, SCSI remains as useful to the Mac family today as it was in 1986. It's the bus that saved the Mac, helped lower the cost of hard drives, and still enables even low-end Macs to tap into a variety of powerful add-ons. Some occasional scuzziness is a small price to pay for all that.

ON THE CD

Try These Essential Virus-Protection and SCSI Tools

The *Macworld Power User Clinic* CD contains several of the virus-protection and disk/SCSI-related items that I discussed in this chapter.

- Disinfectant. The full version of John Norstad's essential virus-protection utility; it's in the Virus Checkers folder of the Best of BMUG collection.
- Virus References. Full details on the viruses that have been identified to date. You can access this information through the Best of BMUG's Virus Checkers folder or through the Mac References folder.
- SCSI Probe. Robert Polic's must-have control panel for checking SCSI addresses and mounting SCSI devices.
- DiskDup+. Roger Bates' terrific shareware utility, which you'll find in the Best of BMUG's File/Disk Utilities makes backing up floppies a breeze. It even makes disk labels.
- The Best of BMUG collection also contains a variety of disk-related utilities.

CHAPTER 26 CONCEPTS AND TERMS

- Because they can store thousands of files, hard disks are more difficult to back up than floppy disks.
- A full backup is a backup of all the files on a hard drive; an incremental backup copies only those files you've added or changed since the last full backup.
- Points to consider when shopping for a backup utility include network support (if you use AppleShare or System 7 file sharing); backup selectivity (the ability to exclude certain files, such as applications and system files, from a backup routine); and the method used to store backup files (Finder-readable backups versus backups that must be restored using the utility itself).
- Viruses are tools of vandalism created by twisted programmers. Malicious viruses can damage your system software, applications, and documents. Mischievous viruses may simply display a message on the screen but can still be dangerous due to sloppy programming.
- Although the virus threat is real, your chances of being victimized by one are small, especially if your Mac isn't on a network and you don't swap software or disks with other users.
- Generally, the more Macs your machine comes into contact with, the greater the risk of infection.
- To help guard against infection, lock floppy disks whenever possible (viruses can't infect locked disks) back up regularly; run a new free or shareware program from a floppy disk; and use one or more virus-detection utilities to scan for and guard against infections (don't combine utilities indiscriminately, however).
- The Mac's SCSI bus is a versatile connection scheme for hard drives and other performance-oriented add-ons, but it can also be the source of headaches.
- Common SCSI problems include incorrect termination, duplicated SCSI ID addresses, and data-transfer errors caused by cheap or faulty cabling.
- SCSI-2 is an enhanced version of the SCSI standard that allows for faster data transfers.

active termination
A SCSI termination scheme, provided by Wide SCSI-2 devices and some conventional SCSI devices, in which circuitry within the drive automatically terminates the SCSI bus — no futzing with terminators.

address
Also called an *ID number,* a unique electronic house number that every device attached to a SCSI port must have. When the Mac transmits information to a device, it sends the device's address along with the information.

asynchronous transfers
An advanced SCSI-2 data-transfer technique that enables the Mac to initiate a SCSI data-transfer operation and then go on to other tasks while the transfer takes place.

backup utility
A program that stores copies of your files on floppy disks or other storage devices.

daisy chaining
A device connection technique, used by SCSI, in which you attach one device to the Mac and then connect other devices to each other.

disconnect/reconnect
An advanced SCSI-2 data-transfer technique that enables a device to electronically disconnect and release control of the SCSI bus while processing a command from the Mac and then reconnect when it's again ready to communicate with the Mac.

disk editors
Utility programs that let you directly view and alter a disk's contents, including disk areas that are normally inaccessible.

Fiber Channel
A particularly promising SCSI-3 protocol that can use fiber-optic cables as well as copper wires. Fiber Channel supports up to 127 hot-pluggable devices per bus and transfer rates of up to 100MB per second.

file-recovery utility
A program that can resurrect damaged files as well as files that you threw away by mistake.

FireWire
Also called P1394, a SCSI-3 protocol that allows for transfer rates of up to 20MB per second over inexpensive 9-pin cables. The cables use heavy-duty connectors, similar to those used on home video games, designed to withstand repeated plugging and unplugging. FireWire supports up to 63 hot-pluggable devices on a bus; it's designed primarily for multimedia devices such as digital still and video cameras.

full backup
A backup session that copies all files located on a given drive.

incremental backup
A backup session that copies only those files you've added or changed since the last full backup.

(continued on the next page)

(continued from previous page)

parallel
A data-transmission technique in which bits travel alongside each other, each in its own wire, like parade marchers striding eight abreast. The Mac's SCSI bus transfers data in parallel. Compare with *serial.*

restore
The process of copying files from backup media such as floppy disks to the hard drive.

SCSI-3
A new version of the SCSI standard that supports multiple cabling and transmission schemes, many of which use exotic serial data-transmission techniques to provide extremely fast performance, better reliability, and more flexibility. See *FireWire, Fiber Channel, UltraSCSI.*

SCSI disk mode
A SCSI feature offered by some PowerBook models that enables you to attach the PowerBook to another Mac's SCSI port as though it were an external hard drive. Once connected, the PowerBook hard drive appears on the other Mac's desktop.

serial
A data-transmission technique in which bits travel single-file, one after another, like shoppers passing through a check-out line. The Mac's modem, printer, and ADB ports transfer data in serial fashion. Compare with *parallel.*

terminator
An electronic component that tells the Mac where a SCSI bus begins and ends. Terminators are the bumpers on the front and back of the SCSI bus: They absorb colliding SCSI signals, preventing them from electrically reflecting within the cabling and interfering with reliable data transmission.

Trojan horse
A program that appears to be legitimate, but which damages or erases files or installs a virus when you run it.

UltraSCSI
A high-speed SCSI-3 protocol. By doubling the SCSI clock rate from 10 MHz to 20 MHz, Ultra SCSI promises a doubling of the maximum sustained transfer rate: up to 40MB per second.

verify option
A backup utility option that, when active, causes a program to proofread its work as it backs up files. If a disk error causes a file to be written inaccurately, the verification process catches it, and the utility tries again.

viruses
Programs that invade the Mac and slow its performance, cause system errors, or destroy applications and documents. A virus contains software instructions that enable it to copy itself into legitimate files, called *hosts.*

watchdog extension
A system extension that can help prevent virus infections by prohibiting certain types of activities that a virus is likely to perform — such as modifying the System file.

CHAPTER TWENTY-SEVEN

Exchanging Data

- Exchanging files between programs and computers
- Understanding Clipboard formats
- Creating hot links with System 7 publish and subscribe and Microsoft OLE
- Converting files between Macs and DOS PCs
- Creating portable documents

Remember the videotape format wars of the eighties — Beta versus VHS? You couldn't play one type of tape in the other type of machine, and until Beta died its slow death, video stores stocked both formats.

Before that, the standards battle was between the 8-track tape and the cassette. Before that, it was long-playing records versus fast-spinning 78s. And in the last century, railroads had a hard time agreeing on how much distance there should be between the tracks. As the industry joke goes, the great thing about standards is that there are so many to choose from.

In the Mac world, this lack of standards hits home as you start using more and more application programs and find that you need to move information between them. Maybe you want to include a scanned image in a document you've created with a publishing program. Or you want to move a database file created with Microsoft Works on a PowerBook to your desktop Mac, which is running FileMaker Pro. Or perhaps a client gave you a WordPerfect file, but you use Microsoft Word.

In each of these cases, you need to contend with *file formats* — the way a particular program stores information when you use the Save command. In this chapter, I examine some of the technical issues behind exchanging data with disk files, with the Clipboard, with System 7's publish-and-subscribe features, and with the drag-and-drop data exchange features of System 7.5. I also show how to use the file-conversion features many popular programs provide, and I spotlight some programs that can convert files from one format to another.

The Format of Things

Ideally, you should be able to use one program to open another program's documents without thinking about file formats — just as you can play a compact disc using any brand of CD player.

The complex nature of application programs makes this ideal world impossible, at least for now. Each category of program works with information in a different way, and each has its own information-storage requirements. A word processor needs to store long strings of text characters as well as formatting information — fonts and type sizes, headers and footers, page numbers, and margins. A spreadsheet program needs to store the numbers and formulas you enter as well as column-width and text-formatting information. A publishing program must store formatted text and graphics as well as layout-related details such as the location of ruler guides. A database manager needs to store the data you enter and also the data-entry screens and reports you design.

You can see the common thread here: Programs must store not only what you type with the keyboard and draw with the mouse, but also the formatting codes necessary to re-create a document's appearance on the screen and on the printed page.

Import/export restrictions

A program's own file format is often called its *native* format. For example, Microsoft Word's native files are Word documents, and QuarkXPress's native files are QuarkXPress publications. A non-native file is often called a *foreign* file. To Microsoft Word, for example, a WordPerfect document is a foreign file. The process of saving a file in a non-native format is called *exporting*. And as you may guess, bringing data in from a different program is called *importing*.

Many programs are capable of opening and saving files in competing programs' native formats. Among word processors, for example, Microsoft Word can open and save WordPerfect documents, and vice versa. Among spreadsheet programs, Microsoft Excel can open and save Lotus 1-2-3 documents, and vice versa.

But there can be flies in the ointment. A document's formatting can change when being imported or exported because one program may not support all the features of the other. Even worse things can happen: For example, if you try to use WordPerfect to open a Microsoft Word document saved using Word's fast-save option, WordPerfect crashes. The solution: Disable Word's fast-save option using Word's Options dialog box.

Figure 27-1 "File Conversion Roadmap" maps out the basic steps you must take to determine how to get foreign files into a format you and your Mac can understand.

Filters for files

The file-conversion features in most of today's programs can be expanded through the use of conversion filters, also called converters or translators. A filter is a small file that tells a program how to convert a particular type of foreign file. Filters usually reside within a specific folder on your hard drive; when you start a program, it determines which filters are present and then adjusts its Open and Save dialog boxes to reflect those conversion options.

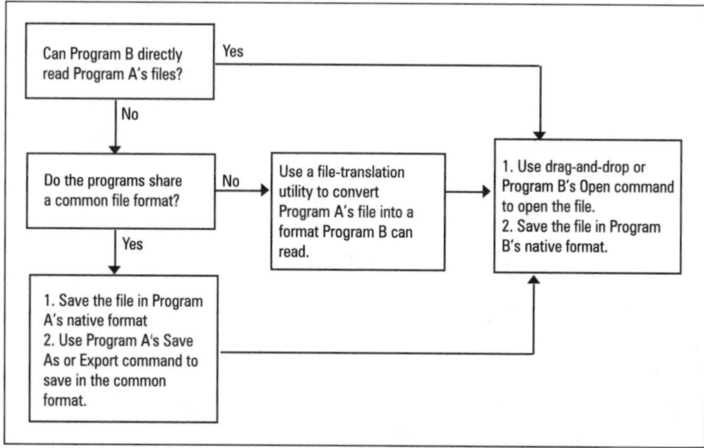

Figure 27-1: File Conversion Roadmap Taking a data-exchange trip? Use this roadmap as a guide to choosing the best approach.

The filter approach has its advantages. You can save disk space by deleting unneeded filters or by not installing them to begin with. Better still, you can add additional filters as they become available; many developers make new filters available for downloading through on-line services such as America Online, eWorld, and CompuServe. (For details on downloading software from on-line services, see Chapter 17.)

The XTND conversion technology

Many programs support a file-translation technology called *XTND*. Originally developed by Claris and now under Apple's wing, XTND establishes a standard design for filters, so any filter designed for XTND can be used with any program that supports XTND. This standardization also makes it possible for companies to sell libraries of file translators that work with any XTND-compatible program. DataViz's MacLink Plus/Translators is one such package, offering over 150 translators.

Converting Foreign Files

So how do you determine whether Program A can import Program B's documents? You may start by checking Program A's documentation: Most manuals contain a chapter or appendix on exchanging files with other programs. If you don't have the manual or you can't bring yourself to read it, there are two techniques you can try.

Drag-and-drop

This technique works with System 7 only. Simply drag the icon of the document you want to import to the icon of the application program. If the program can open the document, the program's icon becomes highlighted (see Figure 27-2 "Opening Foreign Files"). Release the mouse button while the program's icon is highlighted, and the Mac starts or switches to the program, which then opens the document.

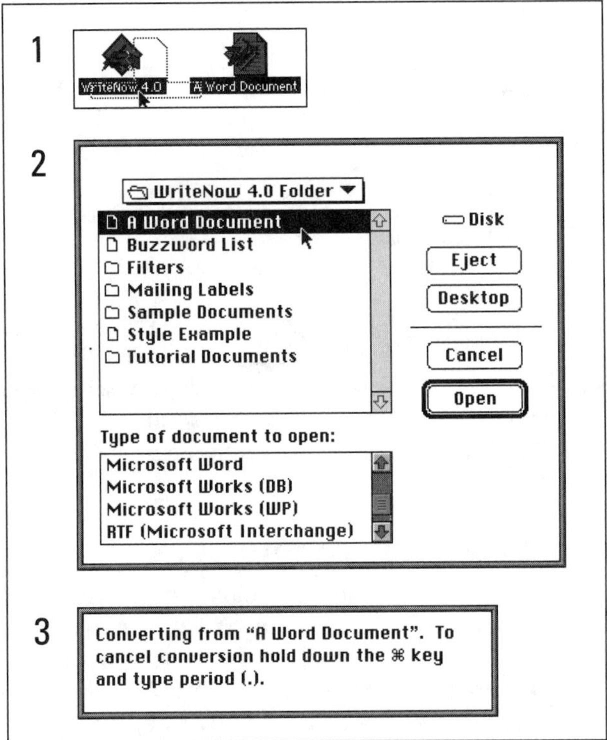

Figure 27-2: Opening Foreign Files With System 7, one way to open a foreign file is to drag its icon to that of the program. When the program's icon becomes highlighted (1), release the mouse button. Here, a Word document is being dragged to the icon of SoftKey's WriteNow. A more-reliable technique is to start the program and then choose its Open command (2). When you open a foreign file, most programs display a conversion box similar to this one (3).

Use the program's Open command

Because the Finder doesn't know which import filters you may have installed, this technique is more reliable than the previous one. Start the program you want to use to open the document, choose Open from the File menu, and then navigate your way to the folder containing the document. If the program is able to open the document, its name appears in the Open dialog box. (In many programs, you can narrow down the list of files displayed by choosing the type of file you're looking for from a pop-up menu in the Open dialog box.) When you double-click the document, you'll probably see a message saying the program is converting a foreign file.

After the import

When a program imports a file, that file's contents usually appear in a new, untitled window. When you choose the Save command, you will need to supply a name for the document. Don't type the same name as the original foreign file unless you really want to replace it. It's better to use a different name, one that reflects the fact that you've converted the file. For example, if you used Word to open a foreign file named Business Plan, you might name the new file Business Plan/Word.

Importing and exporting in publishing programs

Desktop publishing programs put a different spin on the import-export routine. In Adobe PageMaker, instead of using the Open command to import a document, you use the Place command. In QuarkXPress, you use the Get Text or Get Picture command. With both programs, an imported file doesn't appear in a new, untitled window, but in the currently active publication window. Both PageMaker and QuarkXPress include filters for a large variety of file formats — any publishing program must, because one of its chief roles is to enable you to combine text and graphics created in other programs.

Interchange Formats

If one program can't directly read another program's documents, you need to find a file format that both programs do support. This parcel of common ground is often an *interchange* file format — a file format designed for moving data between programs.

Table 27-1 summarizes the most common interchange file formats in the Macintosh world.

Table 27-1
Common Ground

Format	*Application*	*Pros*	*Cons*
Document Content Architecture (DCA)	Word processing	Supported by many PC programs and IBM word processors, and by MacLink Plus/PC and Apple File Exchange	Font, style, and size information are lost
Data Interchange Format (DIF)	Spreadsheets and database management	Supported by many programs and by MacLink Plus/PC	Cell formatting and widths are lost
Encapsulated PostScript (EPS)	PostScript graphics and special effects	Supported by many DOS PC programs	Applies to PostScript devices only
PICT	Object-oriented graphics	Supported by the DOS PC version of PageMaker; translators available for converting to Microsoft Windows graphics	Minimal DOS PC support
Symbolic Link (SYLK)	Spreadsheets and database management	Retains some formatting information, including commas, column widths, and cell alignment	Font, style, and size information is lost
Tagged-Image File Format (TIFF)	Bitmapped graphics	Supported by many PC and Macintosh scanners; not tied to specific computer or graphics resolution	Files can be large and time-consuming to load
Rich-Text Format (RTF)	Word processing	Retains most formatting information, including font, styles, and sizes; supported by Mac and Windows versions of PageMaker and QuarkXPress	Not supported by some Mac word processors

Word processor formats

For word processor documents, the best interchange file format is the *rich-text format*, or *RTF*. This format, developed by Microsoft, is supported by Microsoft Word as well as WriteNow, WordPerfect, Adobe PageMaker, and others. RTF files retain all text formatting and even graphics. The least desirable interchange format is the *text-only* file, which discards nearly all formatting information.

Nothing but the text

Standards are rare in computing, but there is one that enables you to exchange data between any two programs — and for that matter, any two computers. It's the American Standard Code for Information Interchange — ASCII, for short — and it's the least common denominator in the world of data exchange.

ASCII (pronounced *ask-ee*) is a set of 256 codes, each representing a letter, number, special character, or a control code (a rudimentary formatting function such as a tab or carriage return). All computers use the ASCII character set, and thus, can exchange text and rudimentary formatting (tabs and carriage returns). Among the wonders that ASCII makes possible are text-oriented on-line services such as CompuServe, which can be accessed using any computer equipped with a modem.

Most programs that deal with text can save and open files containing only ASCII codes. In the Mac world, such ASCII files are called *text-only* files. By saving a document as a text-only file, you lose its formatting information, but at least you can transfer its text to another program.

Making a text-only file

To save a document as a text-only file, first be sure you've saved the document in its native file format. Next, choose the application's Save As command and select the text-only option (see Figure 27-3 "How to Make Text Only"). Give the text-only file a different filename to avoid replacing the original. Avoid editing at this point, because any changes you make won't be saved in the original, formatted document. For this reason, it's best to create a text-only file only when you're ready to open the file with the importing application.

Some word processors make you perform an extra step when saving text-only files. After you confirm the Save As dialog box, they ask if a carriage return should be put at the end of each line or only between paragraphs. If you plan to open the document with a word processor or publishing program, choose Paragraphs. Choosing Line Breaks tells the program to place a carriage return at each line ending. All those extra returns defeat the importing program's word wrap feature, making reformatting difficult.

Opening a text-only file

The steps required to open a text-only file in the importing application depend on the program. With most word processors and spreadsheets, simply use the Open command. If you haven't yet started the program, you can use the drag-and-drop technique described earlier in this chapter.

With publishing programs, you usually import text-only files using a Place or Get Text command. Most programs assign preset font, style, and size values to unformatted ASCII text, so you may want to adjust those presets before opening the file. Check the formatting and file-importing sections of your program's manual for details on such features.

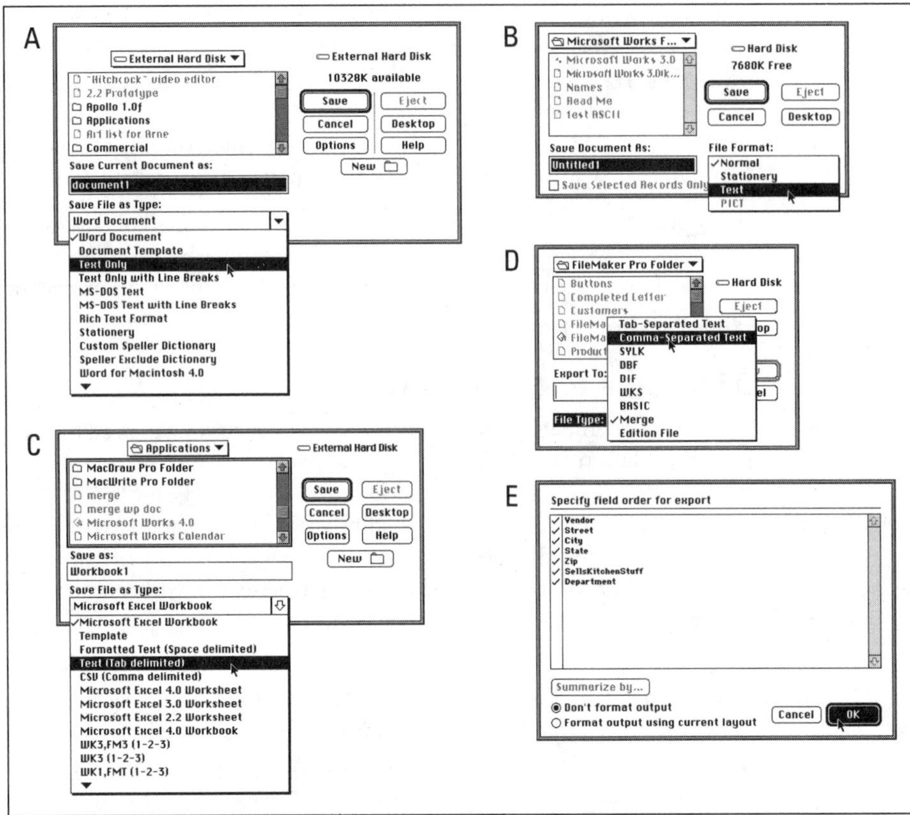

Figure 27-3: How to Make Text Only Most Mac applications let you save documents in ASCII, or text-only, form. With Microsoft Word (A), choose Save As, and then choose the desired format from the pop-up menu. With Microsoft Works (B), choose Save As and choose the Text format. With Excel (C), choose Save As, and then click the Options button and choose Text. With FileMaker Pro (D), choose Export Records from the Import/Export submenu (in the File menu), and then choose the desired format from the pop-up menu. Next, select the fields to be exported (E) and then click OK.

Spreadsheet and database exchange formats

For swapping spreadsheets and databases, a common interchange format is the *symbolic link*, or *SYLK*, file. If you save a spreadsheet as a SYLK file, you will lose font, style, and size information, but you will save rudimentary formatting such as column widths and cell alignment. All popular spreadsheet and database programs can open and save SYLK files. You can also exchange databases through text-only files, although you'll lose all formatting.

If you need to exchange a spreadsheet or a database file, use the exporting program's Save As or Export command to create a file in a format the importing program can interpret. If both programs support an exchange format such as SYLK, use it. Advanced data managers such as ACI's 4th Dimension and Microsoft's

Avoiding Font Foibles with SuperATM and FontChameleon

When you're moving files between two computers — whether Macs or PCs — you may encounter formatting problems if both machines don't have the same fonts. If you open a document that uses fonts you don't have on your system, you're likely to see a lot of oddly spaced text in the Courier font.

One solution to this problem is to make sure the destination computer contains all the fonts used in the original document — not always a practical option. Another solution is to use Adobe's SuperATM, an enhanced version of the legendary Adobe Type Manager utility, which uses PostScript Multiple Master fonts to let the Mac display smooth-looking text at any point size. SuperATM does this, too, but it also automatically generates substitute fonts whose widths match those of missing ones. The resulting document won't look exactly like the original, but at least its line endings and overall formatting will be the same.

Ares Software's FontChameleon technology, described in Chapter 11, provides similar font-matching features.

FoxBASE+/Mac offer many ways to exchange data. You can, for example, often import data from and export it to ASCII files directly, or you can use a *print-to-disk* option to create an ASCII file containing those records that appear in a given report.

Delimiters — boundaries for bytes

If you must resort to the lowly ASCII file, you'll encounter an additional data-exchange wrinkle. In order to separate the rows and columns of a spreadsheet or the fields and records of a database, the program must insert codes called delimiters. As I described in Chapter 8, delimiters are boundaries that tell the importing program where one field or cell ends and the next begins.

The most common field or cell delimiter is a tab character (ASCII code 9); the most common row or record delimiter is a carriage return (ASCII code 13). A *tab-delimited text file* is an ASCII file whose data items (cells or fields) are delimited by tabs. Some programs and programming languages create text files that use commas as delimiters. Commas cause problems, however, because they can appear within values themselves ("10,000", "Raynak, Margaret"). Programs that delimit with commas do what I did in the previous sentence — enclose each data item within quotes and then separate each quoted item with a comma.

Graphics exchange formats

There are interchange formats aplenty for graphics. For bitmapped graphics such as scanned images, you'll probably want to use the *tagged-image file format,* or *TIFF.* For object-oriented graphics such as illustrations created with MacDraw, the *PICT* format is a good choice (for color images, use the PICT2 format). For PostScript

Using Search-and-Replace to Massage Delimiters

If you're working with two programs that don't support the same delimited format, don't give up. Massage the exported file using a word processor, changing the exported file's delimiters into ones the importing application understands. For example, if you want to import a comma-delimited text file into a database program that can import only tab-delimited text files, open the text file in your word processor and use its search-and-replace feature to replace the quotes and comma delimiters with tab characters.

illustrations created by programs such as Macromedia FreeHand and Adobe Illustrator, use the *Encapsulated PostScript*, or *EPS*, format. Each of these formats is supported by major graphics programs as well as desktop publishing software and even many word processors, including Microsoft Word, WordPerfect, and MacWrite Pro.

Using a native format as an interchange format

Several programs' native file formats have become so widely supported that they can serve as interchange formats. For example, every Mac word processor I know of can open and save MacWrite documents. If you need to transfer files between two programs that can't read each other's files but do support the MacWrite format, you can use this format as an intermediary step.

Always save before exporting

Before exporting a document from a given program, first save the document in the program's native format — in case you have to edit the original later. To save the document in a foreign format in most programs, you use the Save As command and then choose the desired format from a pop-up menu or button list (see Figure 27-4 "Pick a Format"). Some programs, including Claris FileMaker Pro, provide an Export command instead. Adobe PageMaker and QuarkXPress provide Export commands that let you export text from a publication. You might use their Export commands if you want to create a word-processor file containing some or all of a publication's text.

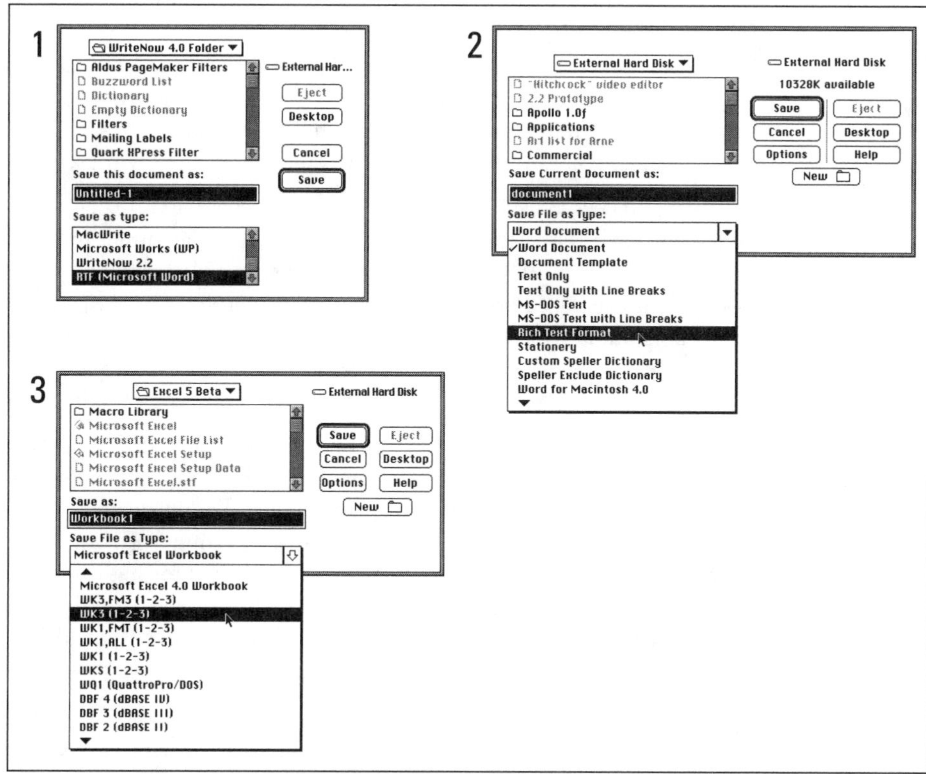

Figure 27-4: Pick a Format The key to saving documents in foreign formats is usually the Save As command. Typically, a program — such as WriteNow (1) or Microsoft Word (2) or Microsoft Excel (3) — lists supported file formats in its Save As dialog box.

The Clipboard and Beyond

The Mac provides other ways to exchange data between programs, techniques that are either faster and easier or more sophisticated than exporting and importing disk files.

All mainstream Mac programs provide Cut, Copy, and Paste commands that let you move small amounts of information between documents and between programs. These commands are the keys to the Mac's Clipboard, the Mac's basic data-exchange system for moving text and graphics between documents and programs (see Chapter 1 if you need a Clipboard refresher course).

Many programs also support an advanced data-exchange system that is built into System 7. Unlike the Clipboard, System 7's publish-and-subscribe feature makes it easy to update information that you transfer between programs: When the bar graph changes in the original program, the version you included in the word-processed document changes, too.

How the Clipboard works

Most of the time, the Clipboard's operation is straightforward. But there can be times when things don't quite paste the way you wanted them to. After pasting some text from one program to another, you may find that the text appears in a different font or size, or that you can no longer edit it. To understand why these formatting problems can occur, it helps to step back and examine how the Clipboard works.

When you cut or copy something to the Clipboard, your application program stores it in one or more Clipboard formats. Just as a file format describes how information is organized on disk, a Clipboard format describes how information is stored in memory by the Clipboard.

Flavors of formats

The Mac provides four standard Clipboard formats. The *PICT* format stores information (whether text or graphics) as a picture. The *TEXT* format stores only text, with no font or type-size formatting information. The *styl* format stores text as well as font and size information. The *snd* format stores sounds. (If you have the QuickTime system extension installed, a fifth standard format is available: the *moov* format, which stores the frames from a QuickTime movie. And if you have Apple's QuickDraw 3D installed, a sixth format is available: *3DMF*, QuickDraw 3D's standard 3-D metafile format.)

Besides these standard Clipboard formats, the Clipboard also supports private data formats — formats defined by a specific program. Private formats are designed to reflect the type of information a particular program creates, and retain more formatting information than is retained by the standard Clipboard formats.

Application programs usually place data on the Clipboard in one or more standard formats as well as one or more private formats. Why so many formats? To increase the odds of being able to retain as much formatting as possible when you paste the information into another program.

Clipboard formats in action

When you choose Paste, the receiving program peruses the Clipboard in search of a private format it can understand. If it finds one, it pastes the data using the private format, thereby retaining all formatting information. If the program doesn't find a private format it understands, it uses whichever standard format — TEXT, PICT, or styl — it prefers. For example, word processors work with text, so they generally choose the styl or TEXT format. Graphics programs work with images, so they may prefer the PICT format. Figure 27-5 "Understanding Clipboard Formats" summarizes these formatting follies.

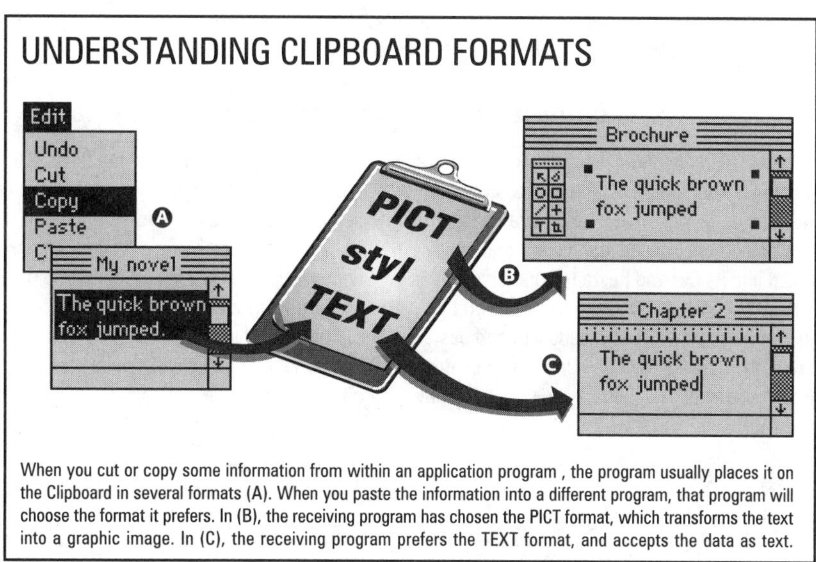

When you cut or copy some information from within an application program , the program usually places it on the Clipboard in several formats (A). When you paste the information into a different program, that program will choose the format it prefers. In (B), the receiving program has chosen the PICT format, which transforms the text into a graphic image. In (C), the receiving program prefers the TEXT format, and accepts the data as text.

Figure 27-5: Understanding Clipboard Formats

An example may help clarify how programs treat Clipboard formats. Say you've just copied several cells from a Microsoft Excel spreadsheet because you want to paste them into a Word document. One of the many Clipboard formats Excel uses is called RTF — short for rich-text format, a format that retains formatting information. (The RTF Clipboard format is very similar to the RTF file format I described earlier in this chapter.) Microsoft Word can read this format, so when you paste the cells into a Word document, all the cell formatting is retained.

But what if you paste the cells into WordPerfect, which can't read the RTF Clipboard format? In this case, WordPerfect uses a Clipboard format it does understand — TEXT — and accepts the contents of the cells, but without any formatting.

So, when some text you paste loses its formatting, it's probably because the only Clipboard format both programs support is the TEXT format, which discards formatting information. To retain formatting when using the Clipboard to transfer text between programs, use programs that support each other's private Clipboard formats or the styl format. If you can't, disk files may be a better medium for transferring text between two programs because both programs probably support at least one file format that retains formatting information.

Data Exchange Recommendations for Beginners

Publish and subscribe and System 7's other cutting-edge data-exchange features are impressive, but in the real world, they're often overkill. I've encountered many Mac owners who haven't yet mastered the Clipboard and its Cut and Paste features. If you're in this group, spend some time exploring the Edit menu. Copy a chart from a spreadsheet and paste it into a word processor. Stash your name and address in the Scrapbook desk accessory so you won't have to retype it.

After coming to terms with the Clipboard, you'll probably start thinking of ways to use publish and subscribe to streamline your data-exchange endeavors. You'll start combining programs to create documents you couldn't create with any single program. The way in which the Mac lets you sling text and graphics between programs has always been one of the machine's unique strengths. Take advantage of it.

Determining formats

How can you tell which Clipboard formats a program uses? I have yet to find a manual that tells you, so you need to do some experimenting. Select some information, choose Copy, and then open the Scrapbook and choose Paste. The Scrapbook window lists the Clipboard formats in which the data is stored (see Figure 27-6 "Finding Formats").

Exchanging Data with Drag-and-Drop

As I mentioned in earlier chapters, a growing number of programs — among them, Microsoft Word and Excel, Adobe PageMaker, QuarkXPress — support drag-and-drop editing: you can move information within a document and even between document windows by simply dragging it with the mouse.

What these programs don't allow you to do is drag and drop information between *programs*. You can't, for instance, drag a paragraph from Microsoft Word to PageMaker. At least not yet. (You *can* drag and drop between Microsoft's latest programs, dragging and dropping a table from Excel 5 into Word 6, for example.)

Drag-and-drop in System 7.5

With System 7.5, Apple has included new drag-and-drop system software that makes it possible to drag and drop information between programs. Developers must adapt their products to take advantage of the new Drag Manager, as it's called, but once they do, it will be easier than ever to shuttle information between programs. (One developer that *has* adopted drag-and-drop is Novell — its WordPerfect 3.1 word processor supports the Drag Manager.)

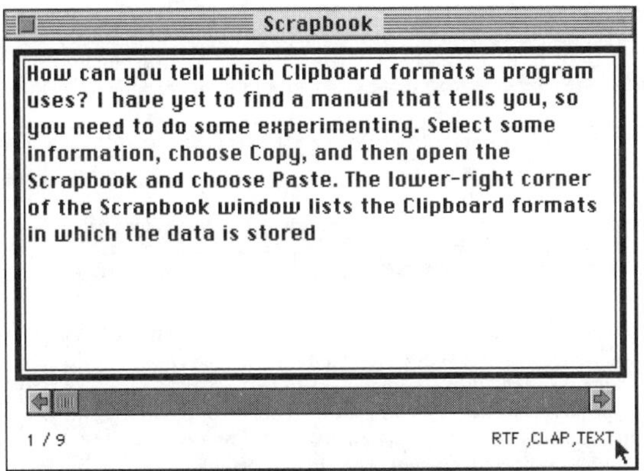

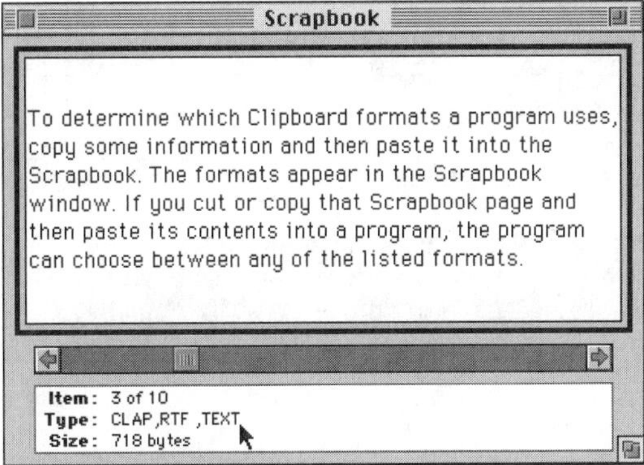

Figure 27-6: Finding Formats To determine which Clipboard formats a program uses, copy some information and then paste it into the Scrapbook. In system versions prior to 7.5, the formats appear in the lower-right corner of the Scrapbook window (top). In System 7.5, they appear in the lower left — and they're even labeled with the word *Type* (bottom). If you cut or copy that Scrapbook page and then paste its contents into a program, the program can choose between any of the listed formats.

How drag-and-drop works

As described in Chapter 22, many parts of System 7.5 support drag-and-drop right out of the box: the Scrapbook, the Notepad, and the Find File window, for example, not to mention the Jigsaw Puzzle and, in System 7.5.1 and later, the Launcher. (QuickTime 2.0's Movie Player 2.0 application also supports drag-and-drop.) Figure 27-7 "Drag-and-Drop in Action" illustrates the process of dragging some text from the Scrapbook to the Notepad.

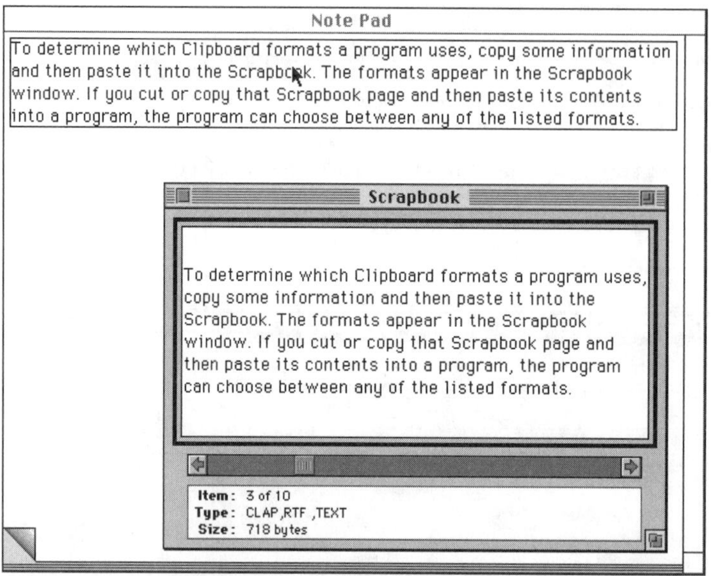

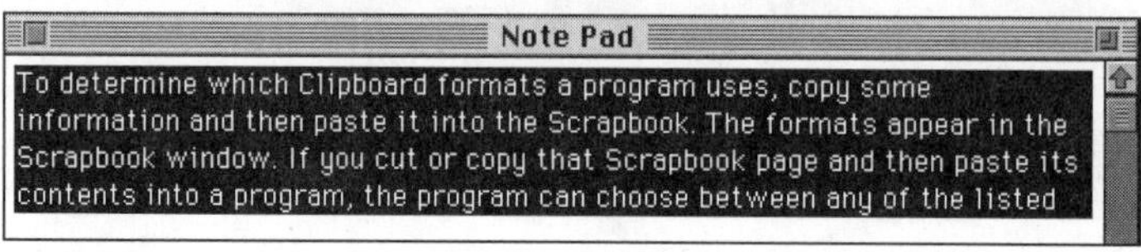

Figure 27-7: Drag-and-Drop in Action Apple's drag-and-drop technology lets you move information between programs without cutting and pasting. Top: Some text being dragged from the Scrapbook to the Notepad. Note the border that appears within a document window when the mouse pointer is within it. Middle: The text after being dropped into Notepad. Bottom: To create a clippings file, drag the selected information to the Mac's desktop.

Drag-and-drop eliminates the multistep process of opening an application, copying the selected data, switching to an open document, and pasting the data—instead, you simply drag the data where you want it.

Here's a scenario that illustrates how drag-and-drop might work with applications that support it: Wendy is using a drawing program and creates a graphic that she wants to add to a word-processor document. She simply selects the graphic and drags it into position in the document. The graphic now appears in both the drawing program and the word-processing document—without copying and pasting.

Creating a clippings file

Wendy could also drag the graphic onto her desktop, where it becomes a *clippings* file that she can drag into other files later. For example, she might save her mailing address or company logo as a clippings file so that she could drag it into any document when she needed it.

If you have System 7.5, you can experiment with drag-and-drop by playing with the Scrapbook and Notepad. Try making a clippings file — drag an item out of the Scrapbook and onto the desktop. Then drag that clippings file into the Notepad window. A few minutes with this great technology will make the Clipboard seem archaic by comparison.

Using Publish and Subscribe

When you copy and then paste something from one document to another, there's no connection between the receiving document and the original document. If the information in the original document changes, you need to repeat the copy-and-paste routine in order to update the information in documents containing it.

System 7's publish-and-subscribe data-exchange system enables you to link documents so that when information changes in one document, copies of it in other documents are updated automatically. The publish-and-subscribe system also lets you exchange data between Macs connected over a network — another feat the Clipboard can't match. Most popular programs support publish and subscribe; check out your favorite program's Edit menu: If you see a submenu named Publishing or Editions or commands such as Create Publisher and Subscribe To, the program supports publish and subscribe.

To use publish and subscribe, you must first select the information you want to exchange and choose Create Publisher from the Edit menu. When you perform this step, the Mac creates a file called an *edition*, which contains a copy of the information you published. As with the Clipboard, the information may be stored in a variety of formats (indeed, editions support the same standard formats — PICT, TEXT, and styl — as the Clipboard).

To put the published information into a document, choose Subscribe To from the Edit menu. The Mac automatically selects the last edition you created.

An optional third step involves telling the Mac when you want new versions of the publisher to be updated. You can specify that information be updated automatically whenever the original document is saved, or only when you explicitly request it (see Figure 27-8 "Updating Options").

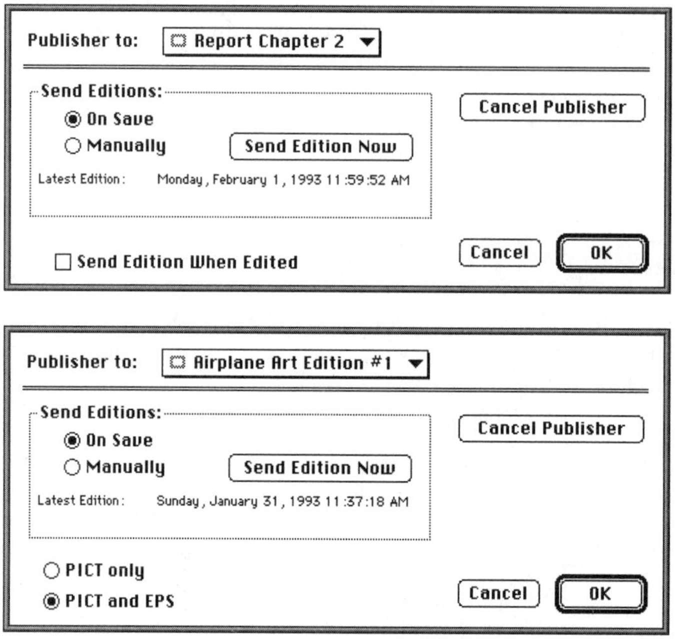

Figure 27-8: Updating Options A program's Publisher Options dialog box lets you specify when updated information should be sent to subscribers — automatically when you save the document or only when you specify. Most programs add additional options to their Publisher Options dialog box. Microsoft Word (top) lets you specify that editions be updated as soon as you make changes (choosing this option can slow Word's performance). Adobe Illustrator (bottom) lets you specify whether the edition should contain a PICT version of the image or both PICT and Encapsulated PostScript (EPS) versions.

Publish and Subscribe in Business

In this scenario, you work in an office whose responsibilities include assembling a monthly status report for the executive staff. The report is written by several managers, and each manager's contribution undergoes several revisions before the final version is complete. (This is a common scenario not only for status reports, but for technical manuals and proposals, too.)

By using publish and subscribe along with System 7's file-sharing features, you can streamline the process of assembling and updating each report. Each time a contributor alters and then saves his or her section, the master version of the report is changed to reflect the latest version. There's no copying and pasting needed, and no fretting about whether someone's latest draft has been incorporated.

I use Microsoft Word for the word processor, but you can substitute any word processor that supports publish and subscribe, including WordPerfect or Claris MacWrite Pro.

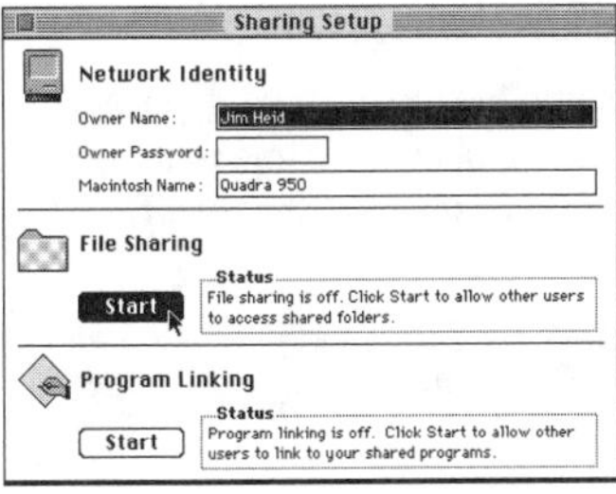

To set up your Mac for file sharing:

1. **Open System 7's Sharing Setup control panel and in the File Sharing section, click Start.**
2. **Select your hard disk icon or the icon of a folder on your hard disk and then choose Sharing from the Finder's File menu.**
3. **In the Sharing window, check the box labeled *Share this item and its contents*.**
   Specify access privileges for the drive or folder if you like. See Chapter 22 for details.
4. **Close the Sharing window and click Save or press Return when asked to save changes.**
   After performing the above steps, use the AppleShare option in each Mac's Chooser desk accessory to connect to the shared hard disk or folder. The process of connecting to a shared hard disk is described in more detail in Chapter 22.

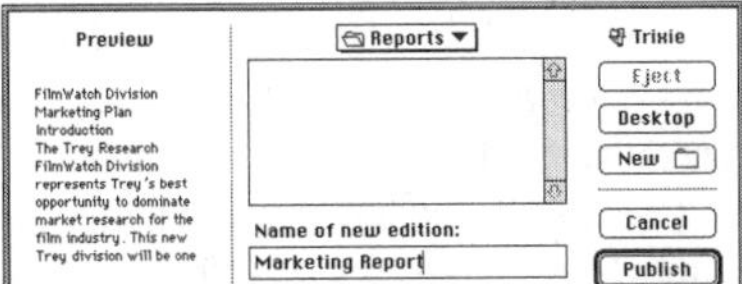

To publish a contribution to the report:

1. **Write your section, formatting it as you normally do, and then save it on your own — not the shared — hard drive.**
2. **Choose Word's Select All command (Edit menu).**
   Word selects the entire document.
3. **Choose Create Publisher from the Edit menu's Publishing submenu.**
   The Create Publisher dialog box appears.

(continued on the next page)

(continued from previous page)

4. **Click the Desktop button and then locate and double-click the name of the shared hard drive.**
   This tells Word to save the edition file on the shared drive.
5. **Type a name for the edition file and then click Publish.**

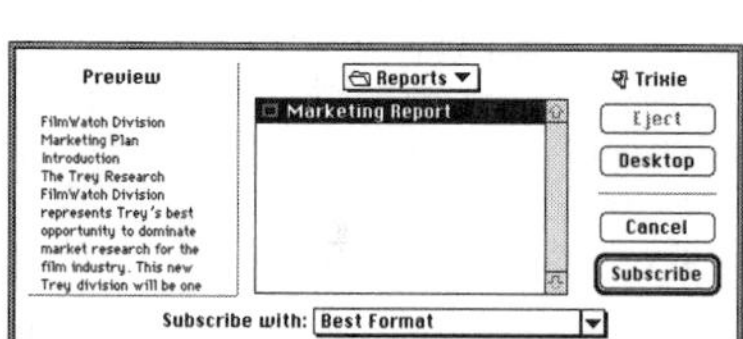

To assemble the report from each component:

1. **Choose New from Word's File menu.**
   A new, untitled document window appears.
2. **Create any special title page you may want.**
3. **Choose Subscribe To from the Edit menu's Publishing submenu.**
   The Subscribe dialog box appears.
4. **Navigate your way to the shared hard drive, and then locate and double-click the name of the edition file containing the first section of the report.**
   Word inserts its text.
5. **If you want the next section to begin a new page, insert a page break after the text by pressing Shift-Enter.**
6. **Repeat Steps 1–5 until you've inserted all sections.**

You can't perform major editing on published information that you've subscribed to. You can reformat all of the text in a publisher — change its font, size, and style as well as margins and line spacing — but you can't, say, correct a misspelled word or change the font for an individual heading. This is why each contributor performs formatting at his or her machine. (Remember that style sheets, which are covered in Chapter 4, can help automate formatting.)

Keep in mind that each contributor can use publish and subscribe *within* his or her own section. Wendy may use it to link a graph created in Lotus 1-2-3 to the original spreadsheet that generated it, and Roy may use it to incorporate inventory figures from an accounting program. As the underlying documents change, a game of digital dominos occurs: Each contributor's section is updated, causing the master report to be updated, too. (You can even take the game one domino further: If you publish the final report and then subscribe to it within Adobe PageMaker, the publication will be updated with each version.

Publish and Subscribe in Graphic Design

Say you're a designer using Adobe PageMaker to create a brochure for some new clients who keep changing their minds about the logo design, which you created in Adobe Illustrator. Rather than go through the work of exporting and importing the logo each time it's revised, you can use publish and subscribe.

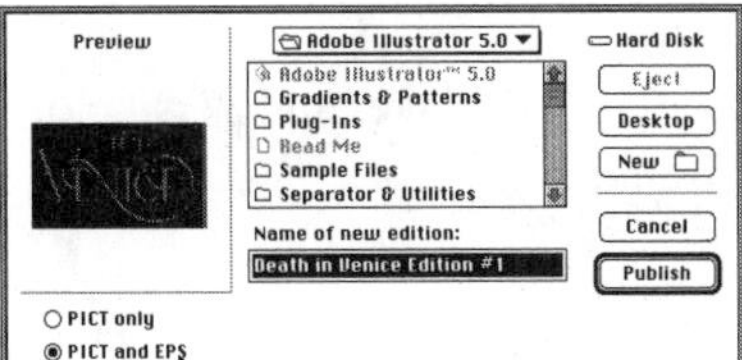

To publish the logo in Illustrator:

1. **Select the logo by clicking it once.**
2. **Open the Publishing submenu (in the Edit menu) and choose Create Publisher.**
   The Create Publisher dialog box appears.
3. **Be sure the button labeled PICT and EPS is checked.**
4. **Type a name for the edition file and click Publish.**
   At this point, you can quit Illustrator if you like. If you have enough memory to keep both Illustrator and PageMaker open, you may want to do so in order to see publish and subscribe in action.

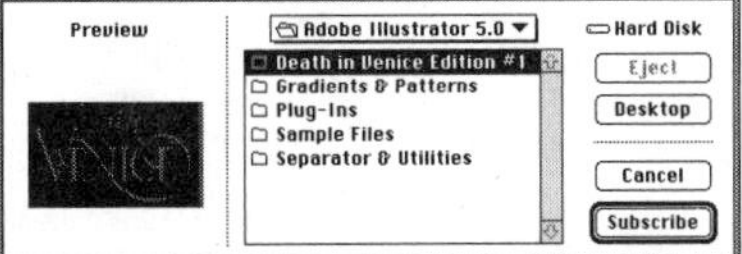

To subscribe to the logo in PageMaker:

1. **Open the Editions submenu (in the Edit menu) and choose Subscribe To.**
2. **Be sure the correct edition file is selected and then click Subscribe.**
   In a moment, the PageMaker mouse pointer changes shape to indicate that it's "loaded" with a PostScript illustration.
3. **Click on the layout to place the illustration.**
   Now when you change the original logo and then save it, the version in PageMaker will be updated to match it.

OLE — Data Exchange, Microsoft Style

Some Microsoft programs, including Word and Excel, support an additional data-exchange system called *object linking and embedding*, or *OLE*. (Adobe PageMaker and Persuasion also support OLE.) OLE was developed by Microsoft and is a key data-exchange mechanism in the Microsoft Windows operating environment.

OLE is popular in the Windows world but is less so in the Mac world, where Apple, not Microsoft, sets the standards. (Didja hear that, Bill Gates?!) Nonetheless, OLE is supported by several of the Mac's most popular programs — Microsoft Excel, Word, and Works as well as Adobe PageMaker and Persuasion — so it deserves a look.

Exchanging data by linking

Linking is similar to using publish and subscribe, in that the data you exchange can be updated when the original information changes. But linking also differs: It doesn't use edition files and it doesn't work across computers on a network. Also, to establish links between two files created in different programs — such as a Word document and an Excel spreadsheet — you must have enough memory to have both programs open simultaneously. And, obviously, you need to have both programs. This isn't the case with publish and subscribe, where one program can access editions created with any program.

A Look Ahead at OpenDoc

OLE is also worth examining because future versions of the Mac's system software will support similar data-exchange techniques. Apple is working on a data-exchange system, called OpenDoc, that will enable what's often called *in-place editing:* the ability to edit imported data without having to return to the application program that created it. For example, in the world of Open Doc, if you double-click a spreadsheet table that you imported into a word processor document, your menu bar changes to reflect the spreadsheet program's menus. If you double-click a graphic after you've finished your editing, your word processor's menus and tools are replaced by those of your graphics program.

Besides making data exchange more efficient, OpenDoc should enable developers to create smaller application programs that can work together, rather than the current trend toward huge, bloated programs that try to do everything themselves. Like System 7's publish-and-subscribe mechanism (and unlike Microsoft's OLE), OpenDoc will also let you exchange data across networks.

You establish a link by first cutting or copying some information in a program that supports links, and then using a Paste Special or Paste Link command. After you establish a link, you can control how and when it's updated, usually by using an Edit menu's command called Link Options.

Exchanging data by embedding objects

Embedding is the other half of OLE: It's similar to pasting, except that the program in which you embed information keeps track of the name of the program that created the information. Information that you embed is called an *object.* If you need to modify an embedded object, you double-click on it, and an *object window* opens that contains the information. If the object came from a different program, the Mac starts or switches to that program, which opens the object window.

After you modify the object and close the object window, the information is updated in the document in which you embedded it. If you embed an object from a different program and you want to edit the object, your Mac must have enough memory to run both programs simultaneously.

Comparing OLE and publish and subscribe

OLE is often faster and more convenient than publish and subscribe. On the down side, OLE doesn't let you link documents across a network (unlike publish and subscribe) and it's supported by only a few Microsoft programs as well as Adobe PageMaker. Also, OLE can get confused if you rename files or move them to other folders or disks. System 7's publish-and-subscribe feature doesn't get lost as easily.

The Quick Tips box "Data-Exchange Techniques Compared" compares the three data-exchange techniques in more detail.

In the end, if you work primarily by yourself and you use Microsoft programs or PageMaker or Persuasion, you lean toward linking and embedding. On the other hand, if you work on a network and you use a wide variety of applications, publish and subscribe is probably the better exchange medium.

Exchanging Files with PCs

So far, I've covered exchanging files between Mac programs. Swapping files between Macs and DOS/Windows PCs involves traversing similar minefields, but to get to them you first have to move the files from one machine to the other. There are four basic ways to move documents between Macs and PCs.

Transferring with a disk drive

Using utilities such as Apple's PC Exchange (included with System 7.5), the 1.4MB SuperDrives built into today's Macs can directly access 3½-inch MS-DOS floppy disks (see Figure 27-9 "DOS on the Desktop"). The disk drive approach is easy and

Data-Exchange Techniques Compared

Included in this box is a comparison of the three data-exchange techniques.

Technique	*Pros*	*Cons*
Publish and Subscribe	Supported by a large number of programs. Doesn't require programs to be open simultaneously. Works across networks, and many users can subscribe to a single edition. You can subscribe to an edition created by a different program without having to have that program on your Macintosh.	Requires three files; it can be cumbersome to move files to a different machine via floppy disks.
Linking	Requires a maximum of two files (the source and destination), making transporting linked files more practical. Faster and more convenient than publish and subscribe for linking data within a document.	Currently supported by relatively few programs. If you're linking between two programs, you must have the second program and your Mac must have enough memory to open both simultaneously. Other users can't access a linked file simultaneously.
Embedding	Requires only one file, making it easy to transport files. Changes in an object are automatically reflected in your document.	Supported by relatively few programs. If you're linking between two programs, you must have the second program and your Mac must have enough memory to open both simultaneously. Other users can't access an embedded object.

convenient, but it can be slow. Also, a floppy disk's limited capacity makes this option unsuitable for moving large numbers of files or large documents such as scanned images.

PC Exchange and third-party disk-access utilities I examine shortly do more than just enable DOS media to appear on the Mac's desktop. They also help the Mac's Finder determine which program to open when you double-click a PC file's icon. For a look at how they accomplish this, see the Background box "From Extensions to Signatures" later in this chapter.

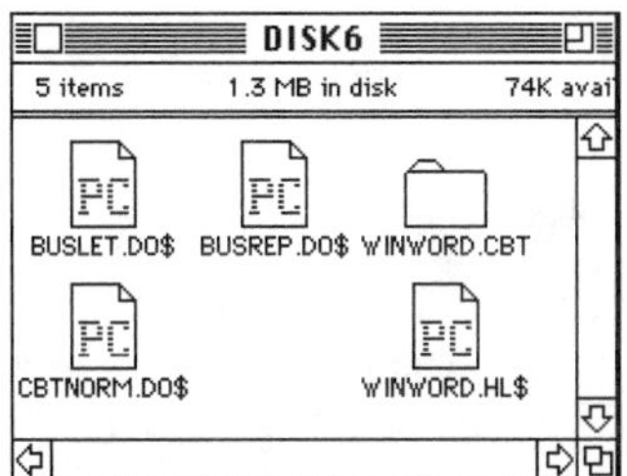

Figure 27-9: DOS on the Desktop
With utilities such as Dayna Communications' DOS Mounter Plus and Apple's PC Exchange (included with System 7.5 and the PowerBook 500 series), you can work with MS-DOS floppies using the Finder. MS-DOS subdirectories even appear as folders.

Swapping files on high-capacity media

The file-access products and concepts I've discussed so far also apply to high-capacity media: Bernoulli and SyQuest cartridges, magneto-optical drives, and to some extent, even CD-ROMs. Both PC Exchange and Insignia Solutions' AccessPC can mount DOS-format cartridges, as can Dayna Communications' DOS Mounter.

To mount DOS cartridges with PC Exchange, you need version 2.0.2 or later. (Version 2.0.3 is the most current at this writing.) There's no need to install any additional software, but you do need to perform a couple of special steps. First, open the PC Exchange control panel, and then click Options; a list of your Mac's SCSI devices appears. Click the entry for your cartridge drive, and a check mark appears next to it; this tells the Mac to load driver software for the drive when you restart, which is your final step. (For more PC Exchange insights, see the Quick Tips box "Tips for PC Exchange.")

Insignia's AccessPC includes a driver file for DOS-format removable cartridges. AccessPC even lets you format DOS cartridges using the Mac's Erase Disk command; PC Exchange requires that you use the formatting software that came with the DOS version of the drive. AccessPC also has the unique ability to access the hard drive files created by Insignia's SoftWindows program. When you install SoftWindows, it creates a huge file that it treats as though it were a separate, DOS-format hard drive. In the Mac's Finder, this file appears as a single icon — you can't open it to access the DOS/Windows files it contains. But AccessPC lets you mount the file as though it were a DOS-format hard drive, giving you one more way to move files between SoftWindows and the Mac OS.

Tips for PC Exchange

Swapping files with PC Exchange? Here are some survival tips, most of which apply to third-party products such as Dayna's DOS Mounter and Insignia's AccessPC.

Leave at least 5K free on a DOS disk. The Mac needs this space to store information about the appearance and position of the file and folder icons on the disk.

Don't delete any directories named RESOURCE.FRK. If you work with a DOS disk on the Mac and then mount the disk on a DOS machine, you might see this directory. It contains resource information that Mac-format documents contain.

Standardize on a PC Exchange Preferences file. This file, located in the System Folder's Preferences folder, stores your extension-mapping settings. If you want everyone in the office to have the same settings, copy this file to each user's machine. Don't rename the file.

Drag to the Trash to eject DOS-format cartridges. The Finder's Eject Disk command isn't available for DOS-format removable-media cartridges.

Eject DOS-format cartridges before turning on file sharing. You can't turn on System 7 file sharing when a removable-media DOS cartridge is mounted.

Eject a DOS-format cartridge before restarting or shutting down. Otherwise, you're likely to see a "sad Mac" icon when you restart.

As for CD-ROMs, Apple's CD-ROM drives include an extension, named Foreign File Access, that, together with additional files, enables DOS-format CDs to appear on the desktop. You can access files on these CDs using the same translation tools and techniques I've described so far. You can also use Windows CDs within SoftWindows, although the current version doesn't support multimedia CDs very well. A better way to run DOS multimedia titles is using Apple's Power Macintosh DOS Compatibility Card, which emulates the SoundBlaster sound-output circuitry most such titles require.

Transferring with a file-transfer package

Products such as DataViz's MacLink Plus/PC include a cable that connects to each machine as well as specialized communications software for each machine (see Figure 27-10 "Transfer Tools"). With this technique, you can swap files that won't fit on a floppy disk. Most packages can also use modems to transfer files over phone lines — handy when the machines aren't close enough for a direct cable connection. You'll often find niceties, too, such as a logging feature that records who's accessed your machine, and password protection for guarding against unauthorized access. The cons: You need to learn the transfer software and juggle cables if you normally have different devices connected to your serial ports.

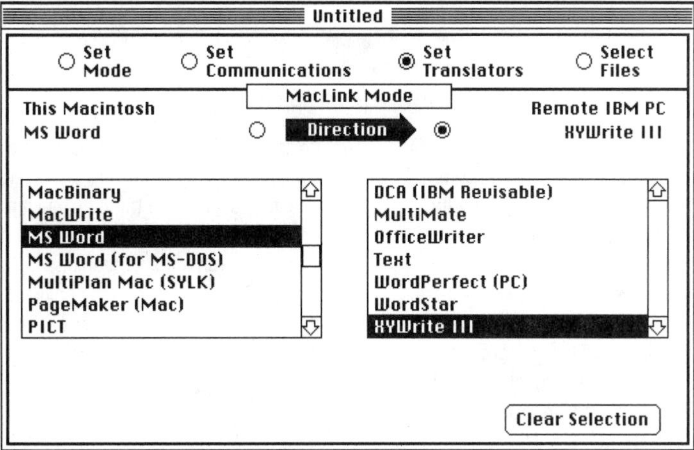

Figure 27-10: Transfer Tools With Dataviz's MacLink Plus/PC, the first step in transferring files is to specify how (or whether) to translate them. When you click on a file format in one scroll box, the other scroll box changes to list only those formats MacLink Plus/PC can translate to. Here, MacLink Plus/PC is set up to translate a Microsoft Word document into XyWrite III format. After choosing translators, you click the Select Files button to select the files to be moved.

Easier opening with Macintosh Easy Open

The smoothest road to file transfers involves combining DataViz's MacLinkPlus Easy Open Translators, a library of file-translation modules that work with Macintosh Easy Open (MEO), an Apple extension that's included with System 7.5. Insignia Solutions' AccessPC (a DOS-mounting utility) includes Macintosh Easy Open as well as a version of MasterSoft's Word for Word translators, which can convert between all popular DOS/Windows and Macintosh word processors.

When you double-click a document that normally can't be opened because its creator is missing, Easy Open steps in and searches for programs and translation utilities that are capable of opening the document and then lists them for you (see Figure 27-11 "Opening Made Easier"). After you select an alternate program, Easy Open manages the conversion of the document by using that program's built-in translation capabilities or by using a translation utility you'd previously installed.

Transferring with a network

Put your Mac and PC on a network — either by adding a LocalTalk expansion board to the PC or by using Ethernet — and the two computers can swap files using System 7 file sharing, AppleShare, or third-party network products such as Novell NetWare.The pros: It's relatively fast and very convenient, especially if you transfer files frequently. You can access the other camp's hard disks as if they were connected to your machine, opening files directly or transferring them using the

From Extensions to Signatures

As you may recall from Chapter 24, a Macintosh file is identified in the disk directory by special codes — collectively called a *signature* — that identify the application in which the document was created. The signature enables you to open a document by double-clicking it. When you do, the Mac consults the document's signature to determine which program to start. If you don't have that program, a message appears saying the document "could not be opened, because the application program that created it could not be found."

Application programs also use signatures to narrow down the list of files in their Open dialog boxes. When you choose a program's Open command, its Open dialog box shows only those documents the program knows how to open. That's because the program checks the signature of every file and displays only those files whose signatures — and therefore, whose formats — it recognizes. This often confuses newcomers, who wonder why a document they can see when using the Finder doesn't show up when they switch to a program and choose the Open command.

The parts of a signature

A document's signature has two components — a creator code and a type code. The creator code identifies the program that created the document; this is the part of the signature the Mac uses when you double-click a document to open it. The type code identifies a document's file format — a Word document, a PageMaker document, and so on. A program uses the type code to determine which files to display in its Open dialog box.

Both the type and creator signatures are four-character codes; for example, a Microsoft Word document has a type code of WDBN and a creator code of MSWD. Both codes are stored within a document; you can't see them by looking at the document's icon or by opening the document. However, you can examine and even change a document's type or creator code using utilities such as Apple's ResEdit or PrairieSoft's DiskTop, included on the CD-ROM that accompanied this book.

Changing signatures

Changing a signature doesn't change a file's internal format, but it can still be useful. For example, if a colleague gives you a TIFF image on a DOS disk, you can change the file's type code to TIFF in order for it to show up in a Mac graphics program's Open dialog box. (Normally, a PC file has a type code of TEXT: Most Mac graphics programs will think such a file is a text-only file and will, therefore, not display it in their Open dialog boxes.)

Utilities such as Dataviz's MacLink Plus, Apple's PC Exchange, and Dayna's DOS Mounter Plus automatically give PC files signatures that enable you to open the files by double-clicking. They do this by associating a specific Mac signature with a specific PC *file extension* — a three-character suffix that appears after a PC file's name. For example, when you double-click a PC document whose name ends with DOC — the extension used by the PC version of Microsoft Word — PC Exchange tells the Mac to start Microsoft Word.

These utilities also let you modify their extension maps to better suit your software library. For example, if you use Claris Resolve, you may want to modify the extension map so that transferred Lotus 1-2-3 files acquire Resolve's signature instead of Excel's.

Finder. And a networked PC can share a PostScript laser printer with Macs. The cons: It's relatively expensive; PC LocalTalk boards cost a few hundred dollars, plus $50 to $75 for each network connector kit. Networks require setup and maintenance time, and their software reduces the memory available for programs. (See Chapter 32 for more details on networks.)

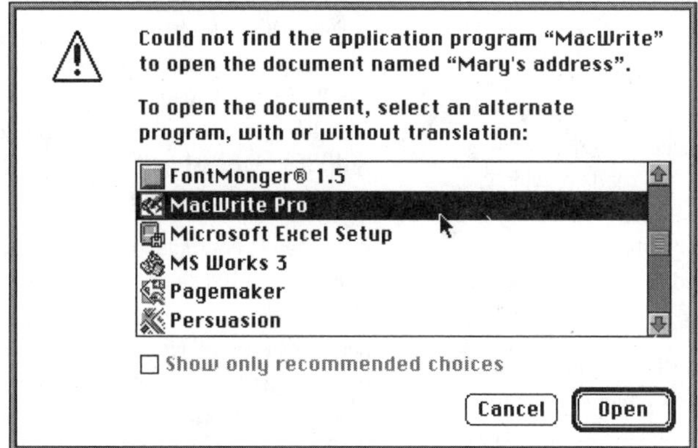

Figure 27-11: Opening Made Easier Apple's Macintosh Easy Open software, included with many third-party translation tools as well as System 7.5, puts an end to annoying "application not found" dialog boxes by giving you a choice of programs that can open the document.

Transferring with communications software

If you already have communications programs for your Mac and PC, you can swap files using modems or a null modem cable (the ImageWriter I cable works well). If you use modems, you can upload files to a communications service and then download them to the other platform. Or you can call the other computer directly (see the Quick Tips box "Computer to Computer").

The pros: It's generally inexpensive because you may not need to buy any additional software. And communications services make convenient "drop boxes" that eliminate the need for two people to be at their machines at the same time to exchange files. The cons: It's slow and filled with technical hurdles. Communications services can be costly for large transfers because you're charged for the time you spend on-line.

Computer to Computer

Using a communications program to transfer files between computers can be a trying experience. Here are some tips that will help you make a successful transfer.

- *Get the right cable* For direct cable connections, be sure your cable is wired properly. Standard RS-232C cables don't work; your cable must be wired as a null modem, which tricks each machine into thinking it's talking to a modem. A competent computer dealer can supply the cable you need.
- *Check your settings* Both the receiving and transmitting programs must speak the same language at the same speed. Typical settings for cable connections are 9600 bps, 8 data bits, 1 stop bit, and no parity. For 1200-bps modems, use 1200 bps instead of 9600. And to see what you're typing, turn both programs' local echo options on.
- *Use transfer protocols* File-transfer protocols eliminate garbled data by "proofreading" data as it's sent. The most popular transfer protocol is called XMODEM, although it's being supplanted by a faster, more convenient protocol called ZMODEM. If you're using XMODEM for Mac-to-Mac transfers, be sure to use MacBinary XMODEM; it transfers the special information in Mac files, such as their signatures and icons.
- *Plan ahead* For modem transfers, talk to the other person and settle on communications settings and transfer protocols, and on who should call whom. Next, the person at the receiving end puts his or her program in answer mode and the sender invokes his or her program's dial command. When a connection is made, type a few characters to verify settings and then invoke the transfer commands.

Life in the Portable Document Age

For people who routinely need to shuttle documents from one computer — or computing platform — to another, one of the most exciting developments in data exchange involves programs such as Adobe Acrobat, No Hands Software's Common Ground, Novell's WordPerfect Envoy, and Farallon Computing's Replica.

These packages are designed to overcome the classic problems of file exchange — Computer B not having the same application programs and/or fonts as Computer A. All four programs also let you electronically send documents created on your machine to other machines, regardless of the operating system, hardware configuration, and font configuration they use. This makes them suitable not only for corporate document distribution and archiving, but also for electronic publishing — on CD-ROMs, on-line services, and the Internet.

This section examines these portable document tools and also looks at the portable-document features provided by QuickDraw GX, which is included with System 7.5.

How Acrobat works

Adobe Acrobat cleverly combines several of Adobe's best technologies — the PostScript language, with its device independence; Multiple Master fonts, with their stretch-and-squeeze versatility; and Adobe Type Manager, with its ability to whip up a tack-sharp font in any font size.

An electronic document created using Acrobat is called a *Portable Document Format* (PDF) file. A PDF file is a PostScript-based file format that preserves the text, graphics, and formatting of the original document. To create a PDF file, you use the Acrobat PDF Writer. The PDF Writer works like a printer driver: Select it using the Mac's Chooser desk accessory, choose your application program's Print command, and the PDF Writer displays a special Print dialog box (see Figure 27-12 "Creating a PDF File").

The PDF Writer translates the Mac's QuickDraw graphics commands into Acrobat's PDF format. PDF files carry information about the fonts used in your document — their widths, names, and styles — as well as the text and graphics of the document. Built-in compression features reduce file sizes dramatically. (For example, color and gray-scale images can be compressed by a factor of 10 to 1.)

Reading PDF files

After you create a PDF file, you can beam it to a colleague, who can use the Adobe Acrobat Exchange or Reader applications to read the file. These programs decompress PDF files and use Adobe Multiple Master fonts to mimic the typefaces used in the document. (If the actual typefaces are available on your colleague's system, the program uses them.)

To make it easy to scan a document, the Acrobat Exchange displays thumbnails of each page. When you find a page you want to read, you can use a zoom command to enlarge it to normal size (see Figure 27-13 "Reading a PDF File").

Acrobat Exchange also provides annotation features that let you attach electronic Post-it notes to documents. Acrobat Exchange even treads into the hypertext world, offering a linking feature that lets you create cross-references within or across PDF documents.

Searching for information

One of the advantages of electronic documents is that they can be searched easily — a big plus for, say, a 500-page manual. Acrobat has a simple Find command that lets you locate text. It also provides a sophisticated search function that lets you perform "sounds like" searches and complex logical searches (for example, find *Mac or Windows or Apple*).

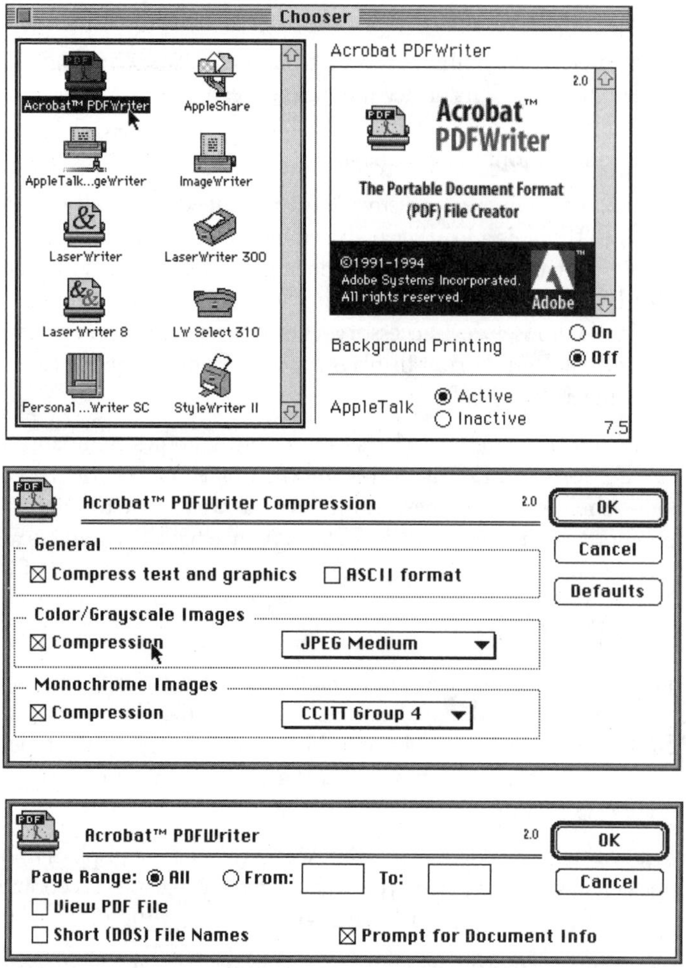

Figure 27-12: Creating a PDF File Creating a PDF file with Adobe Acrobat is a lot like printing a document, except that the document's contents go to disk instead of to a printer. First, select the Acrobat PDF Writer using the Chooser desk accessory (top). Next, you might fine-tune page setup options, such as the type of compression the PDF Writer uses when saving graphics present in the original document (middle). Finally, choose the Print command and specify the pages you want to save in PDF form (bottom).

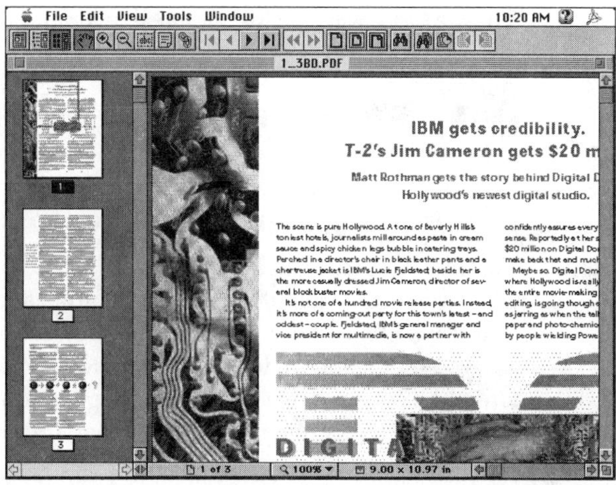

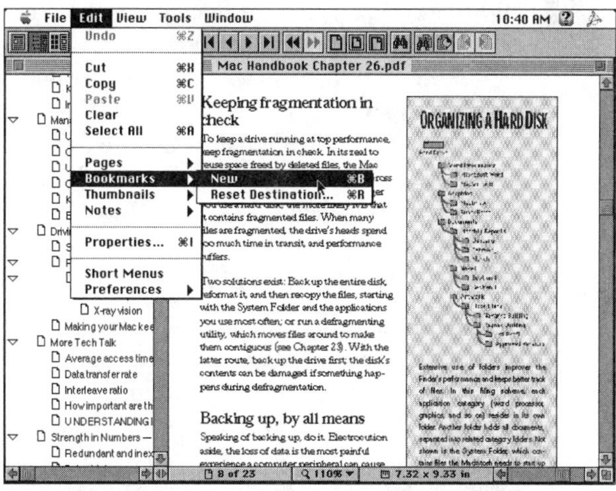

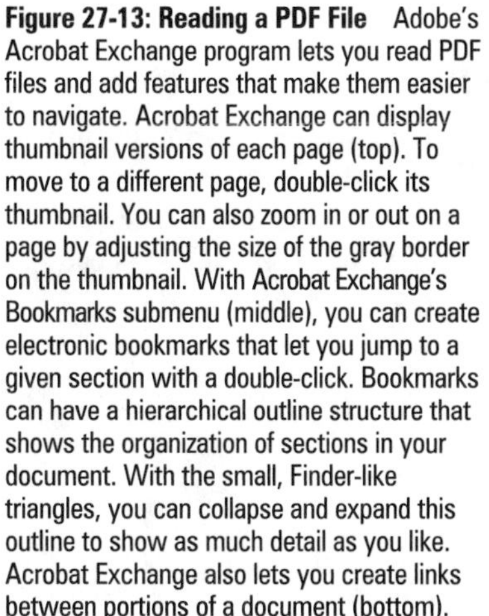

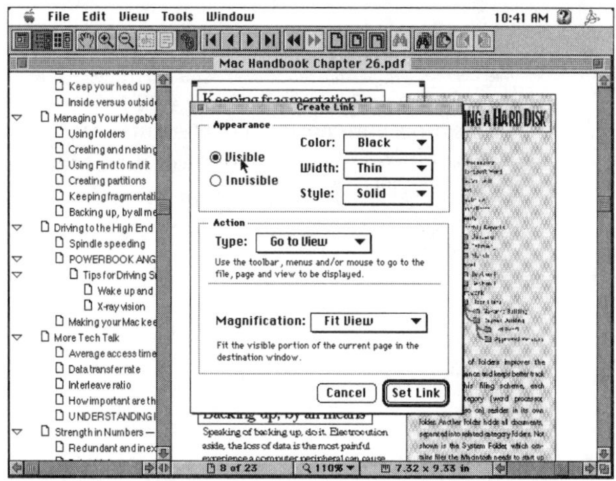

Figure 27-13: Reading a PDF File Adobe's Acrobat Exchange program lets you read PDF files and add features that make them easier to navigate. Acrobat Exchange can display thumbnail versions of each page (top). To move to a different page, double-click its thumbnail. You can also zoom in or out on a page by adjusting the size of the gray border on the thumbnail. With Acrobat Exchange's Bookmarks submenu (middle), you can create electronic bookmarks that let you jump to a given section with a double-click. Bookmarks can have a hierarchical outline structure that shows the organization of sections in your document. With the small, Finder-like triangles, you can collapse and expand this outline to show as much detail as you like. Acrobat Exchange also lets you create links between portions of a document (bottom).

To make text available for advanced searching, however, you must first process it with the Acrobat Catalog program, which builds *indexes* for PDF documents. (An index is a list of all the words used in the documents as well as the page numbers where each word appears.) The big catch: Acrobat Catalog is available for Windows machines only.

Common Ground, Envoy, and Replica

Common Ground, Envoy, and Replica are Acrobat's biggest competitors. All three differ from Acrobat in that they aren't intimately tied to PostScript. They're also generally faster and more straightforward. Common Ground is particularly easy to use: you simply drag a document icon over Common Ground's AutoMaker application. Both Common Ground and Replica also provide printer drivers that let you create portable documents using your applications' Print commands.

For distributing portable documents, Common Ground and Replica enable you to embed a viewer within the documents themselves, so readers can simply double-click the documents and begin reading — they don't have to install a separate viewer utility, as they do with Acrobat. Common Ground even lets you choose whether you want to embed a Mac or Windows reader, enabling you to do your authoring on the Mac and distribute self-contained portable documents to both platforms. You can also distribute the reader applications separately from the portable documents themselves.

Choosing a portable document package

So how do Acrobat, Common Ground, Envoy, and Replica compare? In a recent Macworld Lab survey, Common Ground finished first. It and Adobe Acrobat did a much better job of retaining font fidelity than did Envoy and Replica. Common Ground 2.0 promises even better fidelity, thanks to its use of Bitstream's TrueDoc font technology, which is designed to retain character shapes more faithfully than technologies such as Adobe's SuperATM.

Frame Technology's FrameViewer

If you use Frame Technology's FrameMaker (discussed in Chapter 9), you can turn publications into portable documents with Frame's FrameViewer software. One unique capability of FrameViewer is that its documents can contain links to graphics files instead of containing the graphics themselves. With this approach, you can update graphics without having to update the portable document file that they appear in.

Data Exchange and Portable Document Tools

The *Macworld Power User Clinic* CD contains several items useful to data swappers and portable document readers.

- The Best of BMUG collection contains a variety of file-conversion utilities for text and graphics files.
- The Mac References folder contains Adobe's Acrobat Reader application, which lets you read and navigate Acrobat PDF files. And there's a PDF file for you to play with: a chapter from this book (actually, a chapter from the second edition of this book — some of its content is a bit dated by now, but you can still experiment with the navigation and searching techniques used with portable documents).

QuickDraw GX and portable documents

QuickDraw GX supports a new type of document file format, called a portable digital document (PDD) or print and view document. With QuickDraw GX, you can use any program to create a portable document that can be opened, viewed, and printed on any other Macintosh that's running QuickDraw GX. The file retains all of the graphics and typographic information of the original document, even if the other Mac doesn't have the same application or fonts used to create the document.

QuickDraw GX's portable document features aren't nearly as flexible as those of Acrobat, Common Ground, Replica, or Envoy. You can't, for example, search for text in a GX portable document — all text is turned into a bitmap image. GX also lacks document-annotation and hypertext-linking features, and it isn't available on Windows machines, so you can't distribute portable documents across platforms.

Creating a portable digital document

You can create a portable digital document by using an application program's Print dialog box or by dragging an existing document icon to a PPD Maker desktop printer icon (desktop printer icons are discussed in Chapter 31).

Before using a program's Print command to create a portable digital document, be sure to select the PDD Maker GX icon in the Chooser desk accessory (see Figure 27-14 "Making PDD Files").

Next, open the document for which you want to create a PDD and then choose your application program's Print command. If the program supports QuickDraw GX's enhanced Print dialog box and you click the dialog box's More Choices button, you can use the Include pop-up menu to specify the level of font embedding you want to use for the document.

Make your choices, click Save, and a dialog box appears for you to name the PDD file.

If your program doesn't support QuickDraw GX's Print dialog box, you won't see the Include pop-up menu until you click the Print dialog box's Save button. The Include pop-up menu is in the Save dialog box that appears when you click Save.

Once you create a PDD, you can open, read, and print it using the Simple Text utility or any program that can read PDD files.

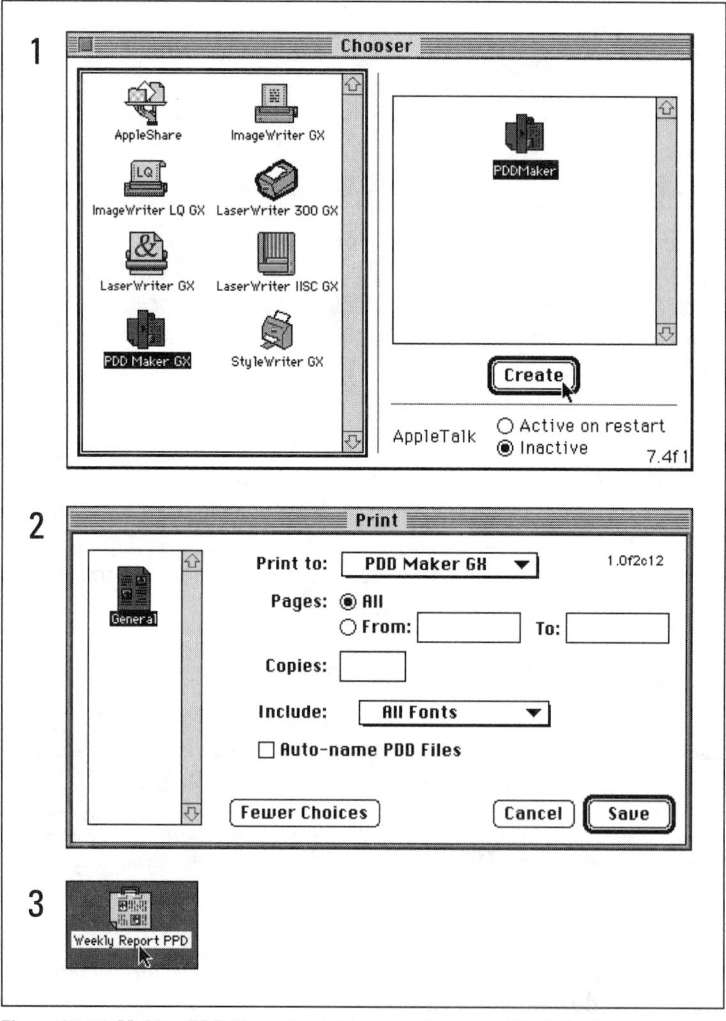

Figure 27-14: Making PDD Files Here's how to make a portable digital document with QuickDraw GX. (1) First, be sure the PDD Maker GX icon is selected in the Chooser desk accessory (you might want to click Create to make a desktop printer icon for the PDD Maker). (2) Open your document, choose Print, and specify font-embedding options. (3) The portable document appears with this icon.

CHAPTER  CONCEPTS AND TERMS

- Every type of program has its own document-storage requirements. The organization of data in a file — the characters, their formatting codes, and the file signature — is called a file format.
- The key to exchanging files between programs is to find a file format that both programs understand. Oftentimes, this means using an interchange format — a file format designed for exporting and importing data — such as TIFF, EPS, RTF, or SYLK.
- ASCII (the American Standard Code for Information Interchange) is a set of 256 codes, each representing a letter, number, special character, or control code such as a tab. Most programs that deal with text can save and open text-only files — files containing only ASCII codes.
- There are four basic ways to move documents between Macs and PCs — with a disk drive, with a file-transfer package, over a network, or using communications software.
- The Mac's Clipboard stores information in a variety of formats. If information you paste loses its formatting, it's probably because the receiving program does not understand the original program's Clipboard formats.
- System 7's publish-and-subscribe feature and Microsoft's OLE technology let you create links between documents so that you don't have to repeat the cut-and-paste routine when the information in an original document changes.
- Several products enable you to exchange formatted documents between computers, even if the machines don't share the same application programs and fonts.

ASCII
Pronounced *ask-ee*, is a set of 256 codes, each representing a letter, number, special character, or a control code. ASCII stands for American Standard Code for Information Interchange.

Clipboard format
The structure of information is stored in memory by the Clipboard. When you cut or copy something to the Clipboard, a program stores it in one or more Clipboard formats.

delimiters
Characters, such as commas or tabs, that serve as boundaries that tell an importing program where one field or cell ends and the next begins. The most common field or cell delimiter is a tab character (ASCII code 9). The most common row or record delimiter is a carriage return (ASCII code 13).

edition
A small file that contains a copy of the information you publish using a program's Create Publisher command.

exporting
The process of saving a file in a non-native format.

file extension
A three-character suffix that appears after a DOS file's name and often indicates which program created the document. Extensions are similar to (but more primitive than) Macintosh file signatures.

file format
The way a particular program stores information when you use the Save command.

filters
Also called *converters* or *translators,* a small file that tells a program how to convert a particular type of foreign file.

foreign file
A non-native file format, either an interchange format or a format created by a different program. To Microsoft Word, for example, a WordPerfect document is a foreign file.

importing
The process of bringing data into a program from a different program.

interchange file format
A file format designed for moving data between programs. Examples include RTF, PICT, TIFF, and EPS.

native file format
A program's own file format — the type of file the program creates unless you specify otherwise. Compare with *foreign file.*

object linking and embedding
Abbreviated OLE, a Microsoft-developed data-exchange mechanism similar to System 7's publish-and-subscribe system.

(continued on the next page)

(continued from previous page)

Portable Document Format
Abbreviated PDF, a file format designed by Adobe Systems for its Acrobat product.

print-to-disk option
An option, provided by some database programs, that lets you create a text-only file containing those records that appear in a given report.

rich-text format
Abbreviated RTF, a Microsoft-developed format, designed primarily for swapping documents between word processors, that retains all text formatting and even graphics.

signature
Special codes that identify the application in which a Mac document was created. A document's signature has two components — a *creator* code and a *type* code. The creator code identifies the program that created the document; this is the part of the signature the Mac uses when you double-click a document to open it. The type code identifies a document's file format — a Word document, a PageMaker document, and so on.

symbolic-link format
Abbreviated SYLK, a common interchange format for swapping spreadsheets and databases.

tab-delimited text file
An ASCII file whose data items (cells or fields) are delimited by tabs.

tagged-image file format
Abbreviated TIFF, a file format, originally developed by Aldus, commonly used to store bitmapped graphics such as scanned images.

XTND
A file-translation technology that establishes a standard design for filters so that any filter designed for XTND can be used with any program that supports XTND.

CHAPTER TWENTY-EIGHT

28 Troubleshooting

- Setting up your system
- Troubleshooting common Macintosh problems
- Tracking down printer and network problems
- Solving GeoPort and Express Modem problems
- Working out Power Mac problems
- Clearing up AV and speech recognition problems

The Mac is reliable, but not infallible. And when problems do occur, the Mac's friendly facade can even work against you by hiding technical difficulties behind error messages that provide few clues to the problem. At times like these, the Mac almost seems to say, "Sorry, something is wrong, but I won't bore you with the details."

This chapter is a guide to troubleshooting common hardware and software problems. I've organized symptoms into general categories — startup and system problems, disk and Finder problems, and printing and network problems, Power Mac problems, and so on. I've provided at least one suggestion for each.

Before you look at troubleshooting specifics, here are some tips on setting up a system.

Setting Up Your System

When the first Macs came out, setting up a Mac meant plugging it in, pouring some Perrier, and listening to the New Age music on the guided tour cassette. These days, you have to wrestle with SCSI cables, expansion boards, and a slew of system files. When you're done, you may feel like sipping something a little stronger.

This section is a roadmap to follow when setting up a system. These tips aren't intended to replace the setup instructions in your hardware and software manuals. Always consult your manuals first for information specific to your hardware and software.

Step 1: Install expansion boards

If you bought any expansion boards for your Mac, install them first. The components on expansion boards and on the Mac's main logic board are extremely sensitive to static electricity, so be sure you're static-free before removing the Mac's case. (Don't shuffle across any carpets, and touch a metal light switch plate or other grounded object before starting. Consider using a wrist grounding strap if you're working in a very dry environment.)

Don't remove an expansion board from its static-free bag until you're ready to install it. You can install most NuBus boards in any slot, but check your boards' manuals to see if they have any special restrictions. And be sure your Mac is unplugged before installing or removing any board.

Step 2: Tame the SCSI bus

The next step in setting up a Mac is to properly connect it to its peripherals — the keyboard, mouse, printer, external hard disk, and any other add-ons. The most difficult aspect of Mac cabling involves interconnecting peripherals such as hard disks, scanners, and tape-backup drives. These devices connect to the Mac's SCSI bus, which is covered in Chapter 26.

Keep two rules in mind when setting up SCSI peripherals:

- *Be sure each device has a unique ID number* Use the highest number (6) for an external hard disk. Use lower numbers for lower-priority hardware such as a scanner or tape-backup drive. You don't have to number devices sequentially; you can use ID number 6 for a hard disk and ID number 3 for another device, skipping over numbers 4 and 5.
- *Be sure to terminate the SCSI chain properly* Determine whether your hardware contains internal terminators, and never place more than two terminators on the bus (see Figure 28-1 "SCSI Wiring").

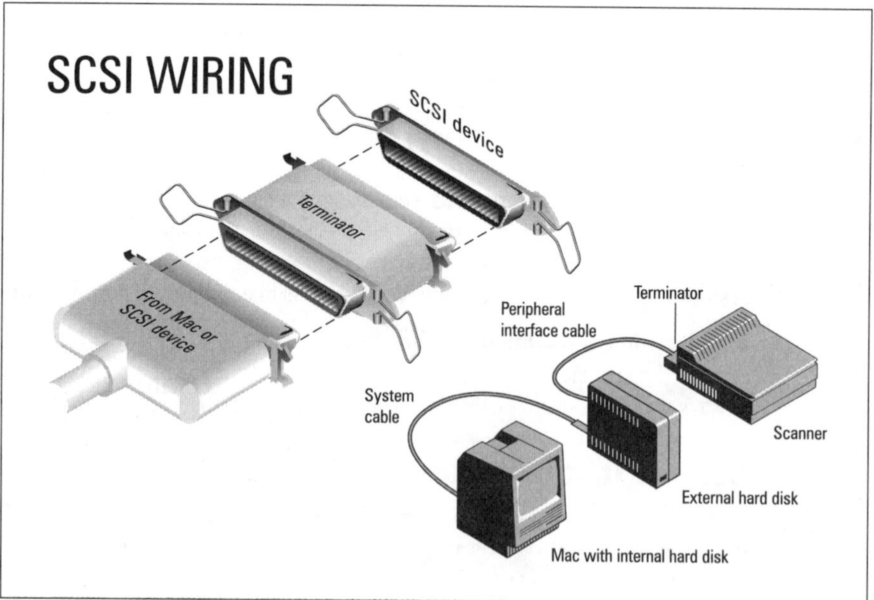

Figure 28-1: SCSI Wiring

Step 3: Finish wiring

After you've tamed SCSI, your remaining wiring chores are child's play. They involve attaching the mouse and keyboard, and perhaps also connecting to an ImageWriter, StyleWriter, or LaserWriter printer.

On every Mac from the SE on, the mouse and keyboard use the Apple Desktop Bus (ADB). Like SCSI, the ADB lets you daisy-chain numerous peripherals to a single connector. But unlike SCSI, ADB devices automatically configure themselves when you switch on the Mac; you don't have to fret with ID numbers and termination.

Where to connect the keyboard and mouse

Back when Macs provided two ADB ports, you had to wrestle with whether to attach the mouse to the keyboard's free ADB port or directly to the Mac's second ADB port. Today's Macs provide just one ADB port, sparing you of this decision. But if your monitor has ADB ports — current Apple monitors do — you must decide whether to connect your input devices to the monitor's ADB port (and then connect the monitor's ADB port to the Mac's) or to the Mac itself.

Connecting the input devices to the monitor's ADB port gives you a bit more flexibility in where you put the Mac itself. It also lets you move the keyboard further away from the monitor — handy if you like to type with your feet up and the keyboard on your lap (not the best position for your posture and wrists, but people do it anyway).

Connecting a printer

As for printers, connecting to an ImageWriter, StyleWriter, Personal LaserWriter, or LaserWriter Select is straightforward: Each of these printers connects via a serial cable to the Mac's modem or printer port.

But PostScript-based LaserWriters and other PostScript printers can be tricky. These printers use Apple's LocalTalk networking system to enable you to share their printing prowess with an office full of Macs and PCs.

The tricky part of LocalTalk wiring involves structuring the network properly. In a LocalTalk network, the network signals must run in a line, not a circle (see Figure 28-2 "A Network Diagram"). And be sure to position cables and connectors so that people won't trip over them or inadvertently disconnect them by moving their Macs.

(Many laser printers provide Ethernet ports, which are faster than their LocalTalk counterparts. See Chapter 32 for details on connecting an Ethernet network.)

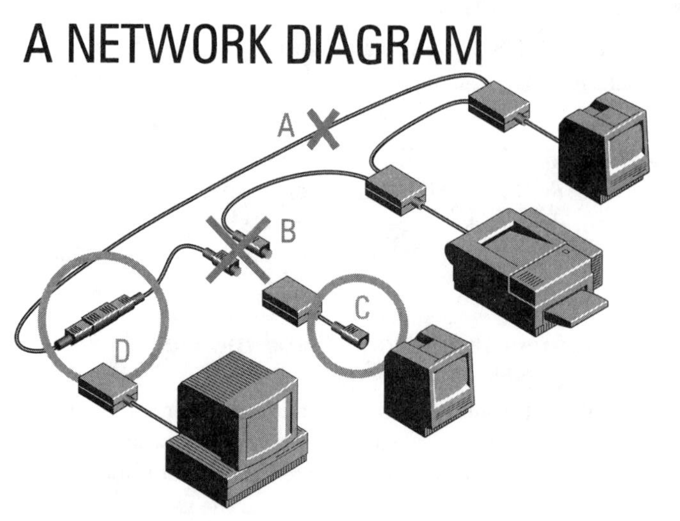

LocalTalk connectors attach cables to all the networked devices—Macs, printers, or DOS/Windows PCs equipped with LocalTalk expansion boards. Avoid a common wiring trap: never connect the first and last device on a network to create a closed loop (A). Other problems include loose connections and dangling unconnected cables (B). If you need to remove a device, either unplug its connector box (C) or insert a cable extender between the two dangling cables (D).

Figure 28-2: A Network Diagram

Step 4: Install system software

After setting up your hardware, turn your attention to software. Time spent planning your software installation will be rewarded with faster, more efficient operation later on.

All current Macs include internal hard drives with preinstalled system software, so you don't have to worry about installing the Mac OS itself. However, if you buy an external hard drive or removable media drive and you want to use it as your startup drive, you need to install the system software on it, or at least copy the System Folder from your internal hard drive to the external drive and then use the Startup Device control panel to designate it as the startup drive.

To install the System Folder and its contents on an external hard disk or cartridge, use Apple's Installer program, located on the system software disk labeled Install. If your Mac came with an internal Apple CD-ROM drive, you can install the system software from the CD that accompanied the Mac. Details on the Installer appear in Chapter 22.

If you connected a new printer in the previous step, you may need to install its driver software. (I say "may" because Apple preinstalls the drivers for its printers. To find out whether your System Folder already contains a driver for your new printer, just open up the Chooser from the Apple menu. If you see an icon corresponding to your printer, you're all set.) For more details on printer drivers, see Chapters 30 and 31.

If you have any hardware that included extensions, control panels, or other driver software, install the software now. Usually that means simply copying one or more system extensions to the System Folder, although some hardware products include their own installer program or use the Apple Installer.

After installing your system software, you're ready to install your application programs. Generally, that means running an Installer utility located on the application's master disk. It's a good idea to restart the Mac with extensions off (hold down the Shift key until you see the message *Extensions off*) before installing applications — some extensions can interfere with the installation process. Be sure to follow the instructions in your program manuals.

See Chapter 25 for tips on creating a filing scheme that helps you find what you've stored.

How to Do a "Clean Install" of the Mac OS: And Why It's a Good Idea

One of the best ways to cure serious system problems such as frequent crashes is to reinstall the Mac's system software. You can do so by using the system disks or system software CD-ROM that came with your Mac.

You *could* just run the Installer utility to reinstall the system software over your existing folder, but it's better to do what's called a *clean install* — that is, not to fix up the old System Folder, but to create a shiny new one.

There are two ways to do a clean install:

- ❖ Open your existing System Folder and move the System file into any other folder, such as the Extensions folder or the Preferences folder. Then run the Installer. (By "hiding" the System file, you trick the Mac into thinking the disk doesn't have a System Folder.)
- ❖ Run the Installer and press ⌘-Shift-K at the main Installer screen. A message appears asking whether you want to update your existing System Folder or to install a new one. Select Install New System Folder.

After you've done a clean install, you will need to restore your favorite fonts, Apple menu items, and the like. That's the bad news. But the good news is that you will have a spanking-fresh Mac OS installation, and that will almost certainly cure your crashes.

Startup Problems and System Crashes

You connected a hard disk, scanner, or some other SCSI device, but the Mac doesn't recognize it.

- ❖ Check all the SCSI devices to make sure they are connected properly, with the right number of terminators in the right positions. (See Chapter 26 for details on SCSI.) Then, with the power off, disconnect and firmly reconnect all SCSI cables. Use the metal cable snaps to lock them into place.
- ❖ Make sure each device has a unique SCSI ID number. If two or more SCSI devices have the same number, one or more of them may not work.
- ❖ Be sure you've installed any system extension software that accompanies the device. Some scanners, for example, won't work unless their system extensions are in the System Folder.
- ❖ Be sure the total length of the cabling in your SCSI chain is less than 30 feet (the shorter the better: some users say no longer than 20 feet) and that no single link between peripherals is more than six feet long (again, the shorter the better).

The Mac doesn't start from a hard disk that was previously working.

- ❖ If you've added any new SCSI devices since the last successful startup, double-check your SCSI cabling, termination, and address switches. SCSI is a common source of startup problems.
- ❖ The disk's startup information — its *boot blocks* — may be damaged. If the Mac's screen flashes the "where's the disk?" icon, or if the Mac crashes during startup, displaying the frowning Mac icon, bad boot blocks may be to blame (but also see the next section on misbehaving extensions). You can make repairs using a utility such as Symantec's Norton Utilities for the Macintosh or Central Point Software's MacTools, both of which are discussed in Chapter 26.
- ❖ One or more files in the System Folder may have been damaged. Try reinstalling the system software from an emergency startup floppy. (See Chapter 26 for details on creating such a floppy.)
- ❖ The hard disk's *driver software*, which enables the Mac to recognize and access the hard disk, may be damaged. If your hard disk came with a diagnostic program, run it. Many hard disks enable you to reinstall the driver software without reinitializing (which would erase the contents of the disk).

Understanding the "Rescued Items" Folder

When the Mac crashes and takes unsaved documents with it, don't despair. Well, okay, you can despair, but don't give up hope. After restarting the Mac, open the Trash and look for a folder called *Rescued items from [your hard disk name].* If you find such a folder, drag it out of the Trash window and onto the desktop. Now open the folder. You may see documents with bizarre names such as *Word Temp-3.* If you do, start the program you were using and try opening the file — it may contain part or all of the document you were working on when the crash occurred. If it does, thank your lucky stars and then save the document.

How's this work? Many programs create temporary files — the software equivalent of scratch paper — as they work. So even if you haven't saved a document recently (or at all), some or all of your precious keystrokes may still have been squirreled away on disk. When System 7 starts up after a crash, it looks for these temporary files and stashes them in the rescued items folder.

A disclaimer: A temporary file is rarely a mirror image of a document. When you open a temporary file, don't expect to find an entire document with all its formatting intact. More often, you'll find a mish-mash of formatting codes and oddball characters, with some real text sprinkled throughout the file. But if that real text includes work you'd otherwise have to re-do, you can consider your rescue mission a success.

Oh, and why does System 7 put the rescued items folder in the Trash, where it's one command away from oblivion? Don't ask me. Just be grateful for the feature — and remember to save often.

- The crash may have corrupted the contents of the Mac's *parameter RAM*, the battery-powered memory that holds Control Panel settings, such as the time, date, and current startup disk. (On a PowerBook, the parameter RAM also holds your system sleep settings.) Try resetting the parameter RAM. To reset the parameter RAM under System 7, start up or restart the Mac while holding down the ⌘, Option, P, and R keys. To reset the parameter RAM under System 6.x, start the Mac with a different disk, and then hold down the ⌘, Shift, and Option keys while opening the Control Panel. A dialog box asks if you want to "zap" the parameter RAM. Click Yes; then restart.
- To zap the parameter RAM on a Mac Plus or earlier machine, you must remove the computer's battery — regardless of which system you're running. Leave the battery out for 20 to 30 minutes before reinstalling it.

ON THE CD

TechTool: A Power Tool for Resetting and Restoring PRAM — And For Learning Your Mac's Birthday!

Resetting the Mac's parameter RAM (PRAM) is a common and useful troubleshooting technique: sometimes the Mac just needs you to clear its head.

But the standard PRAM-reset key sequence — pressing ⌘-Option-P-R as the Mac is starting up — isn't a perfect solution. For one thing, it's a finger-twisting sequence that you must issue at just the right time. But more significant, this sequence doesn't clear *all* of the Mac's PRAM. It clears only 64 bytes of it; there's another 192-byte area that isn't touched — and it could be that *these* bytes contain corrupted information that's causing whatever problem you're experiencing.

One way to clear all of the Mac's PRAM is to remove the lithium battery on the Mac's logic board. Given that this battery is actually soldered in place on some Macs, this isn't exactly a convenient solution. A better way is to use a utility that zaps all of the PRAM for you. I've included just such a utility on the *Macworld Power User Clinic* CD: TechTool, from Micromat Computer Systems, makers of MacEKG and DriveTech, two outstanding diagnostic utilities.

When you start TechTool, you get an astonishingly detailed report on your system configuration (see the adjacent figure). Two of the most interesting tidbits

of info are the date of your Mac's manufacture and the number of hours that it has been in use — yes, your Mac knows its birthday and has a built-in odometer! This information, by the way, comes from that secret 192 bytes of PRAM.

TechTool can save the contents of your Mac's PRAM on disk. It's a good idea to save the PRAM when your Mac *isn't* acting up. That way, when you have to reset the PRAM, you can quickly restore its contents without having to manually work through half the control panel settings in your System Folder. And you'll be glad to know that TechTool will not reset your Mac's birthday or odometer count.

Before using TechTool, be sure to read its on-line help for important information about rebuilding the desktop or resetting PRAM.

When you started up your Mac II-family machine, the speaker produced an unusual startup sound and the machine did not start up.

- ❖ A faulty Mac II-class machine can produce any of three "I'm not feeling well" sounds. One is a single, high-pitched tone, which generally indicates a memory problem. Try replacing memory boards (SIMMs) one at a time to isolate the faulty one.
- ❖ Another abnormal startup sound consists of two high-pitched tones, with the second higher than the first. This, too, usually indicates a memory problem.

- The third and most common abnormal startup sound consists of four notes, one after the other, each higher than the previous one. (Musicians: It's a broken A-major chord.) This can refer to SCSI problems, a loose or damaged memory SIMM, or loose cable connections. When you hear this one, think back on the last hardware add-on you installed and double-check that it's installed correctly. Double-check all cables, turn the Macintosh off, and then try again. If the problem persists, consider taking the computer to a service technician.

When you start up your CD-ROM-equipped Mac with a CD in the drive, the Mac freezes. Upon restarting, you hear the "chord of death" discussed in the previous section.

This problem can occur if the CD you've inserted contains invalid information in its boot blocks. (Chances are the CD was mastered improperly — a CD that isn't intended to be used as a startup disk should not have any boot blocks at all.) Eject the CD, shut the Mac off for at least 10 seconds to clear its digital head, and then restart.

You try to start your Mac using a CD-ROM inserted in the built-in CD-ROM drive, but the Mac starts up from the hard disk instead.

In order to force the Mac to start up from the CD, you must press ⌘-Option-Shift-Delete — a real finger-twister — before the smiling Mac icon appears. The best approach is to shut the Mac off, insert the CD in the drive, and then press the ⌘-Option-Shift-Delete sequence while turning the power on. Another technique is to open the Startup Disk control panel and select the CD-ROM drive as the startup disk.

For some information on the startup CD-ROM that accompanies CD-equipped Macs, see the Backgrounder box "Starting Up from a CD-ROM."

You added a new system extension, control panel, desk accessory, or font, and now the Mac crashes during startup when you try to use the system extension, or when you try to start a program that was previously working properly.

- System extensions that load during startup can conflict with each other or with applications. First, remove the suspect extension from the appropriate folder within the System Folder (start the Mac with a different system disk if necessary), and then restart. If the Mac doesn't crash, blame the extension. You can often cure system extension conflicts by renaming the offending extension so that it loads in a different order (the Mac loads system extensions in alphabetical order). If that fails, contact the extension's developer. The Quick Tips box "Extension Troubleshooting Strategies" provides more guidelines for solving extension woes.

Extension Troubleshooting Strategies

When your System Folder is laden with extensions, finding the one that's causing a crash can be time-consuming and frustrating. In this box, I describe some techniques that may help.

Step 1: Try starting up without them

With System 7, you can bypass all extensions by pressing the Shift key while the Mac is starting up. Hold the Shift key down until the message *Extensions off* appears below the *Welcome to Macintosh* message. If the desktop appears, chances are the problem is with your extensions — proceed to the next step. If the Mac still doesn't start up, the hard drive's System Folder or boot blocks may be damaged as described earlier in this chapter.

Step 2: Find the troublemaker

One strategy for troubleshooting extension conflicts is to drag all extensions out of the System Folder and then put them back one-by-one, restarting after each, until the big bomb appears. To save time, you may try dragging only half the extensions out and then adding one or two at a time.

Step 3: Downsize your extension collection

While you're contemplating all the time that troubleshooting wastes, think about your collection of extensions and consider getting rid of ones that aren't absolutely essential to your work. The more extensions you use, the greater the chance that two of them won't get along. Other pluses to downsizing your extension collection: Your Mac will start up faster and will have more free memory for your programs.

Medicine for curing extension woes

The Extension Manager control panel that accompanies System 7.5 is a good tool for solving extension-conflict problems. You can also use it to create and switch between sets of extensions.

But the ultimate weapon for fighting extension problems is Casady & Greene's Conflict Catcher III. Besides letting you manage (disable and enable) extensions and letting you know how much memory each uses, Conflict Catcher III can help you track down extension conflicts. As mentioned in Chapter 22, Conflict Catcher III can also ferret out extensions that may be slowing down a Power Mac by patching over native-mode system software routines. Also as mentioned there, you'll find a fully functional (but three-day trial) version of Conflict Catcher III on the CD that came with this book.

- ❖ If the Mac crashes only when you try to use the new desk accessory, the desk accessory itself may be damaged or improperly installed. Remove the desk accessory, and then reinstall it. If the problem persists, it may be that the desk accessory's disk is defective, or the desk accessory may not be compatible with your system configuration; contact the desk accessory's developer.
- ❖ System 6 only: If the Mac acts up after you add a desk accessory or a font, the System file (which holds both) may be damaged. Restart using a different system disk, and copy its System file to the disk that's giving you trouble. Make sure you're using the latest version of Font/DA Mover. If the problem persists, the desk accessory or font may be damaged. It's also possible that the desk accessory is incompatible with your version of the system software; check with the desk accessory's developer.

Starting Up from a CD-ROM

Macs with built-in CD-ROM drives can start up from a CD inserted in the drive. One reason you may want to start up from the CD is to reinstall the system software on the hard drive.

The CD that accompanies a Mac with a built-in CD-ROM drive contains System 7.5 as well as a folder full of utilities (including Disk First Aid and HD Setup), an interactive tutorial on Macintosh basics, the HyperCard Player (which lets you open HyperCard stacks), and other goodies, such as PowerTalk and QuickDraw GX, stashed in a folder named Extras. The CDs that come with Power Mac also include a folder full of demonstration applications that you can play with.

You can install the system software directly from the CD, or you can use the DiskCopy utility (also included on the CD) to make a set of backup floppy disks.

Because the CD-ROM is so much slower than a hard drive, the CD is not meant to be a permanent startup disk, but used as a backup and archive of system software.

- When you run MultiFinder under System 6.x, newly installed fonts and desk accessories don't always appear in the Font or the Apple menu (if this happens, try restarting the Mac). It's best to install fonts and desk accessories from the Finder.

You added a new extension, but it isn't loading during startup.

- Make sure that the new extension is stored in the System Folder, and then restart. If you're using System 7, be sure the extension is in the Extensions folder, located within the System Folder.
- Don't press any keys during startup, and be sure the Caps Lock key isn't depressed; often you can bypass loading a particular extension by pressing certain keys.

The Mac crashes when you start a program or open a desk accessory, and the ID number in the bomb dialog box is 12, 15, 25, 26, or 28.

- An ID=15, ID=25, or ID=28 system crash often indicates insufficient memory. Restart, and then try one or more of the following: Remove system extensions; use the Memory control panel to disable or reduce the size of the RAM cache. (System 6.x only: Use the Finder's Set Startup command to specify that the Mac not use MultiFinder.) Restart again to make the changes take effect.
- An ID=26 crash indicates that the Mac's attempt to start the program was unsuccessful, perhaps due to corrupted data in memory or a damaged application file. Restart and try again. If the Mac still crashes, reinstall the application from its master disk.

❖ An ID=12 crash indicates that the software you're attempting to run is trying to access a system software feature that isn't supported by your current hardware and/or system software combination. For example, you may be trying to run a color program on a Mac Classic, or you may be trying to run a program that requires System 7 under System 6.x. Check the program's system requirements and verify that your Mac meets them.

❖ Other system error ID numbers, such as 1, often indicate an extension conflict of some kind. See the Quick Tips box "Extension Troubleshooting Strategies" for advice on dealing with conflicting extensions.

The Mac appears to have frozen — it doesn't respond to mouse clicks or keystrokes.

❖ Press ⌘-Option-Esc. If a dialog box appears asking if you want to "force-quit" the application, click Force Quit. (You can't click anything if the mouse pointer is frozen, too. If that's the case, you need to press the reset switch if your Mac has one, or just power-down, wait 10 seconds, and then restart.) If the Mac responds to the Force Quit button, thank your lucky stars and immediately save any unsaved documents. Then restart the Mac to clear its head and get back to a healthy state.

❖ If the Mac doesn't respond, try ⌘-Option-Esc again. If this doesn't work, you need to reset the machine. To do so, hold down ⌘ and Control while pressing the keyboard's power key. This sequence works on most current Mac models. Some models also have a reset switch; the Power Mac 7100, for example, has one on the left-front corner of the case.

Troubleshooting PowerBooks

This box contains some advice for solving common PowerBook problems.

The speaker pops occasionally

As the old computer industry joke says, "this isn't a bug — it's a feature." Ten to 20 seconds after producing a sound (such as an error beep), the PowerBook cuts power to its sound chip in order to save battery power. When the power goes, pop goes the speaker. To eliminate the pop, insert a miniplug (Radio Shack catalog number 274-368) in the PowerBook's speaker jack. You won't hear a peep (or a pop).

When the PowerBook is connected to a network, it never goes to sleep.

If the PowerBook has the recharger cord plugged in, open the Chooser and check to see if AppleTalk is on. If it is, you've found the reason: Apple designed the PowerBook's EverWatch power-management features with the assumption that if the recharger is plugged in and AppleTalk is on, you're at your office and you want the PowerBook to be as fast and responsive as possible. (Note that the PowerBook only detects whether the recharger cord is plugged in, not whether there's current flowing through the recharger.)

The other possibility for the PowerBook not going to sleep is that AppleTalk is on and you're connected to a shared hard disk or network electronic mail service. In this case, the PowerBook is detecting periodic network activity and thus stays awake. (Simply having AppleTalk active and being plugged into a LocalTalk network does not keep the PowerBook awake when the power cable is not connected.)

A program slows dramatically while performing a time-consuming task. Moving the trackball wakes up the system, and processing continues.

The power consumption of the PowerBook's microprocessor is reduced automatically when it detects that no activity requiring its attention has taken place for a period of time. This is called *processor cycling.* The processor comes back up to speed instantaneously when you resume using the computer. The problem is, some programs don't work properly with processor cycling on. Try turning off processor cycling while using the program. Use the PowerBook control panel to turn off processor cycling.

The PowerBook doesn't run on the battery but operates normally when plugged into AC power.

PowerBook 100: Check that the storage switch on the back of the computer (next to the power connector) is in the up position. This switch disables battery power but enables you to use the unit with AC power. Another possibility: A fuse on the logic board can blow if the computer's lithium batteries aren't removed before the unit is taken apart. It's also important that the unit be completely reassembled before the batteries are reinstalled. Have the fuse replaced by a technician. And think at least twice before venturing into the PowerBook's tight confines.

Other PowerBook models: A fuse on the logic board may have blown. The black insulating "O" ring on the tip of the AC adaptor may be damaged and shorting out against the logic board. Have the adaptor repaired and the fuse replaced by a technician.

Your single-serial-port PowerBook (for example, a 520c) displays an error message when you try to use an Apple StyleWriter or other printer connected to the modem port.

As I mentioned in Chapter 23, PowerBooks with a combined printer/modem port can have problems with serial printers or external modems. For some background and advice, see the Chapter 23 PowerBook Angle box "When Is It Normal to Not Be Compatible?"

Also note that a single-serial-port PowerBook containing a Global Village TelePort II modem can't use a StyleWriter printer unless you first disable the modem software and then restart.

Your 500-series PowerBook is not recognizing or charging a battery.

The 500-series PowerBooks use so-called Intelligent Batteries that can become dumb and refuse to charge. Batteries that exhibit this problem typically have an extremely low charge — because, perhaps, you waited too long to charge the battery, or you stashed it in a drawer for three months. Since the power-management features of the 500-series batteries depend on having a certain amount of juice available, the PowerBook can have trouble recognizing the battery and charging it.

Look for these symptoms of a dumbed-down battery: the battery gets extremely hot during charging; the battery doesn't show up in the Control Strip's battery monitor module (a grayed-out battery appears instead); the battery becomes completely discharged after only a day or two of sleep. If you find one or more of these symptoms, you can fix the battery using an Apple utility called Intelligent Battery Recondition; it's available on-line or from Apple dealers. VST Systems' EMMPathy is a freeware utility that also restores the smarts to a dumb battery. It's included on this books' CD.

Disk and Finder Problems

When you copy files using the Finder, an error message says that some files couldn't be written or read and asks if you want to continue.

- If the Mac couldn't write some files, the destination disk could be at fault. If you're copying multiple files, try copying one at a time. If that doesn't work, the destination disk may be magnetically or physically damaged. A temporary fix that usually works for me is to use the Finder's Duplicate command to duplicate a small file on the destination disk. This causes subsequently copied files to be stored on a different area of the disk. Make sure you back up the disk as soon as possible and then erase it. If problems surface after erasing, the disk may be physically damaged. Throw out a damaged floppy; a damaged hard disk can be repaired.
- If the Mac couldn't read some files, the source disk may be the culprit. If it's a floppy or removable hard disk, try ejecting and reinserting the disk; it may not have been seated properly. If you have two floppy drives, insert the source disk in the other drive. If these techniques fail, the source disk may be damaged. Use a disk-repair utility to scan the disk for errors, a process called *verifying*. See Chapter 26 for more details on disk-repair and file-recovery utilities.

When you double-click a document, the Finder says it can't be opened because "the application is busy or missing" or "cannot be found."

- If you don't have the application that created the document, you can't open the file from the Finder, but you may be able to open it from within another application. For example, you can open MacWrite documents from within most word processors by using the word processor's Open command. Macintosh Easy Open, included with System 7.5 (and discussed in Chapter 27), look for other programs that *can* open the document. If you see the message above, you don't have MEO installed.
- The document may not be intended to be opened from the Finder (for example, a document that stores your working preferences or a spelling checker dictionary). If the document has a generic document icon, it probably can't be opened from the Finder (see Figure 28-3 "Generic Errors"). But again, you may be able to open it from within an application.
- The document, its application, or the disk's desktop database files (which contain information about the disk's contents) may be damaged. This is less likely than the previous situations, but it's possible. Every document file has a signature that identifies the application that created it. If this signature is damaged, either in the document or in the desktop database file, the Finder won't know which application to open. Try rebuilding the desktop (see Figure 28-4 "Rebuilding the Desktop") or using a disk utility to examine the document's file signature.

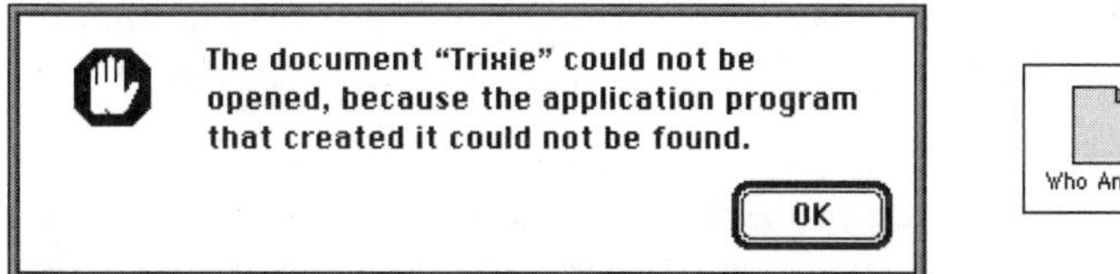

Figure 28-3: Generic Errors When you see this error message (left), it means the Finder was unable to locate the application that created the document. Oftentimes, this occurs when you try to open or print a document that isn't intended to be opened from the Finder. Examples of such a document include an application's temporary work file or settings file, which stores your working preferences. Such documents often have generic document icons (right).

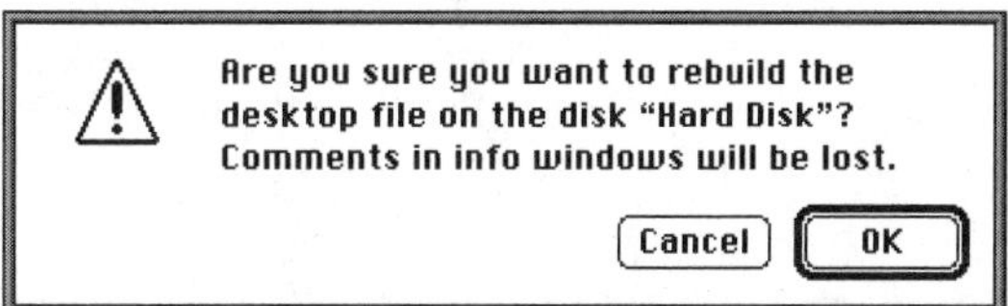

Figure 28-4: Rebuilding the Desktop One solution to certain disk ailments involves rebuilding the desktop file by restarting the Mac and then holding down the ⌘ and Option keys before the Finder's menu bar appears. Doing so causes the Finder to display the message shown here. Note that rebuilding the desktop file causes the Finder to lose any Get Info comments you may have added to that disk.

- A special file attribute, called the *bundle bit*, may be set (that is, turned on) for a file other than the application itself (such as a spelling checker dictionary). As a result, the desktop database has become confused. Most disk utilities can repair this problem.

Multiple icons for a single hard disk appear on the desktop.

- This is a potentially nasty problem that indicates a SCSI problem — two or more devices with the same ID, improper termination, or faulty cabling. This problem can result in damage to the data on the hard drive. Shut down immediately, turn the Mac off, and double-check all SCSI connections, address switches, and terminators.

When you insert a disk, the Mac tells you that it needs minor repairs and asks if it should perform them.

- This usually indicates a damaged Desktop file, which, like the desktop database files mentioned earlier, helps the Mac keep track of the files on a disk. (In System 7, the Desktop file is used on floppy disks only. In System 6, it's used for high-capacity media, too.) If you click OK, the Finder rebuilds the Desktop file.

When you insert an older disk or removable cartridge or you connect an older hard drive, the Mac tells you that it's "updating disk for new system software."

- This doesn't indicate a problem. The Finder is simply scanning your old disk (which was formatted under System 6 or an earlier version) and creating a System 7 desktop database file that enables it to keep track of the disk's contents.

When you insert a disk, the Mac tells you that it's damaged or unreadable and asks if you want to initialize it.

- Just say no — unless you want to erase the disk. If the disk has important data on it, click Cancel to eject it. Then try inserting the disk again and/or restarting the Mac; if the same message appears, the disk is sick. Use a disk utility to diagnose its ailments and, if possible, recover its contents. (Use the utility to copy those contents to another disk and then try making repairs on the copy, in case the recovery process backfires.)
- If you elect to initialize the disk and the Mac displays a message saying "Initialization Failed!" you'll know the disk is defective. Throw it out. Even if the initialization succeeds, think twice about using the disk for important work. It could be about to fail permanently.

When you choose Empty Trash, the Finder says that the Trash couldn't be emptied because one or more items were locked.

- Open the Trash and verify that the file isn't really locked: Using the Finder, select it and choose Get Info. If the Locked box is checked, click it to unlock the file. Then try throwing it away. You can also delete locked items by pressing Option while choosing Empty Trash.

When Trouble Hits, Retrace Your Steps

When the Mac suddenly starts acting up, think about what you've done recently. Did you just install a new program, control panel, or system extension, connect a new device, or reorganize your SCSI chain? Retrace your most recent steps: The answer to your problem may be in one of them.

If all you find are footprints, check your SCSI bus, system software, and extensions as described throughout this chapter.

- These problems can also occur when you throw away a file that the Mac is currently using — or thinks it's using. When you open a file, the Mac alters the disk's directory to indicate that the file is in use. These notations may remain unchanged until you quit the application — even if you use the application's Close command. Try quitting the application, and then throwing the document away. If that fails, hold down the Option key while dragging the document into the Trash. Then hold down Option again while choosing Empty Trash. If this fails, restart and then throw the file away. The restarting process should close the file properly. If you frequently encounter this problem with a specific disk, try rebuilding the disk's desktop.

You selected a disk (or a removable-media cartridge or a CD) and chose Put Away or dragged its icon to the Trash, but the Finder tells you that the operation can't be completed because it contains items that are in use or because the disk is being shared.

- Have you started a program or opened a document on that disk? If so, you won't be able to eject the disk until you quit the program and/or close the document.
- Have you made a removable cartridge available to other users with System 7's file-sharing feature? If so, you won't be able to eject the disk until you turn file sharing off. (A free utility, UnmountIt by Jim Luther, lets you unmount and eject sharable volumes when file sharing is on.) Also, System 7.5.1 and later versions do not have this problem; they will allow you to eject a cartridge when sharing is on.

The Mac asks you to insert a disk that you ejected long ago.

- When you use the Eject command (or the Eject button in an Open or Save dialog box), the Mac remembers that the disk still exists and may ask to see it again. Dragging an icon to the Trash or selecting the icon and choosing Put Away (⌘-Y) causes the Mac to forget the disk, guaranteeing you won't be asked for it again.

The Finder frequently displays the messages saying that there isn't enough memory to keep certain windows open, to open a desk accessory, or complete another operation.

- The Finder has run out of memory. Close some windows, eject disks, unmount file server volumes, and then try again.

When you eject a disk, a Finder error message appears saying that "the disk is so full that the folder changes couldn't be recorded."

- If a disk is full or nearly full, there may not be enough free space for the Finder to record the changes you've made to the disk's icon arrangement, Get Info comments, or folders. Click OK to close the error dialog box, reinsert the disk, delete at least one file, and then try again.

The Finder isn't saving custom settings you make in the Views control panel. Or you get a message saying "The system extension PowerPC Finder Update cannot be used."

- These problems generally indicate a damaged Finder Preferences file, which stores Finder settings. Open the System Folder's Preferences folder, locate Finder Preferences, and then drag it to the Trash and choose Restart from the Special menu. After the desktop reappears, empty the Trash.

Printing and Network Problems

The Mac reports that it can't locate or access the printer.

- Verify that the startup disk you're using contains at least 100K of free space — preferably more, particularly if you're printing graphics. Many applications create temporary files during printing and can't print if the startup disk is locked or nearly full.
- Check to make sure that the printer is connected and on-line (for ImageWriters and StyleWriters, press the Select button; most laser printers have a button labeled Online that makes the printer available or not available).
- Verify that the printer's paper supply hasn't run out.
- Use the Chooser to make sure that the printer driver and the proper connection port are selected. Then choose the Page Setup command, verify your print settings, click OK, and try again.
- For laser printers: Be sure the printer is on and that its paper tray contains paper and is properly seated. Use the Chooser to select the printer's driver. If you're using a PostScript printer and the printer's name doesn't appear in the Chooser window, the printer may not be warmed up, or you may have a LocalTalk wiring problem (refer to Figure 28-2). After the printer's name appears in the Chooser, select it, and then use Page Setup to verify print settings, and try again.

When you print to a laser printer, an error message appears saying that the printer was initialized with an earlier version and needs to be reinitialized.

- This problem is far less common today than in the past. It occurs when you use different LaserWriter driver versions on different machines in your network instead of standardizing on one version. Today's LaserWriter drivers — versions 7.x and 8.x — don't cause this problem. Still, in a network setting, it's a good idea to standardize on one driver version.

When you try to print a document on a PostScript printer, PrintMonitor or your application program reports that a PostScript error occurred.

PostScript errors represent a broad category of printing problems. They can be caused by complex PostScript illustrations, such as the informational graphics in this book. Simplify the illustration if possible — cut complex paths into smaller paths, raise flattening so that fewer line segments are required, or simplify clipping paths in masks by reducing the number of anchor points.

Memory errors can occur if a document contains more downloadable fonts than will fit in the printer's memory. Check the Unlimited Downloadable Fonts box in the Page Setup dialog box's Options dialog box and try again.

Another cause of memory errors can be an illustration that contains nested Encapsulated PostScript (EPS) files. Say you import a custom logo into an illustration to create a piece of clip art. Then you import that illustration into another illustration, which you then import into a page layout program. Each step in this scenario increases the amount of nesting of dependent EPS files. Consider breaking nested elements into separate files.

Memory-related PostScript errors are less common with Level 2 PostScript devices, which can allocate additional memory when necessary.

An excellent source of information on PostScript related printing problems is Systems of Merritt (Mobile, AL). The company sells a variety of PostScript books and utilities.

GeoPort and Express Modem Problems

You're experiencing frequent crashes or slow performance when transferring files or sending faxes using a GeoPort-equipped Power Mac.

- If you're using version 1.0 or 1.1 of the GeoPort software, upgrade to version 2.0 or later (see Chapter 16). Versions 1.x of the GeoPort software have problems with Power Macs. (If you're desperate, try disabling virtual memory and making sure there are no faxes in the Waiting to Be Sent folder.)

The modem appears to be dialing properly (you hear the Touch-Tone beeps coming from the Mac's speaker), but a recording says your call can't be completed.

❖ Try again to make sure you're not having phone line problems. If the problem persists, try restarting the Mac. I've encountered situations where a Quadra 840AV Mac's Express Modem software gets weird if you've been using a program, such as Adobe Photoshop, that makes extensive use of the DSP chip (which produces the Touch-Tone beeps). Restarting always clears up the problem.

You're having trouble connecting to another computer using a GeoPort and the Express Modem software. The computers seem to establish a connection, but then the connection is dropped right away.

❖ Be sure you've selected the Express Modem software in your telecom program's setup dialog box. And try turning off error correction. You can do this with the modem command **&Q0** in the modem setup string (see Chapter 16).

You want the GeoPort adaptor to answer an incoming call when the modem is in originate (rather than auto-answer) mode. (You can trick an external modem into doing this by issuing an ATDT command when the phone is ringing.) With the GeoPort, however, you get an error message saying the port is in use.

❖ With the GeoPort and Express Modem software, there's a delay of six seconds between the time that a ring is detected and when you can issue an **ATDT** command. To eliminate this delay, type **ATH1DT** instead of **ATDT**. The **H1** forces the modem to go off-hook. Once the modem is off-hook, the **DT** command tricks the modem into thinking it is the originator of the call.

When you begin an outgoing modem or fax call, you get an error message saying that you "cannot use the Express Modem now because the sound output rate is incorrect."

❖ For the GeoPort to work, the sound sampling output rate must be 24 kHz. You can specify this using the Sound control panel. Open Sound, choose Sound Out from the control panel's pop-up menu, and choose 24 kHz from the Rate pop-up menu. Close the Sound control panel and try again. (On the Power Mac 7500 and 8500, use the Sound & Displays control panel to set the sampling rate.)

You're trying to print some faxes from the Fax Viewer application and you get a cryptic error message with the number 108 in it.

❖ This happened to me — the problem turned out to be that my startup disk was full. Trash some unneeded files and try again.

Power Mac Problems

Your computer seems to be running slowly, even when you're using native applications.

- ❖ You may be using one or more system extensions that patch native-mode system software with 68000-family code. Run Casady & Greene's Conflict Catcher III (included on this book's CD-ROM) and see the sections in Chapter 22 for details on this problem.

You just installed the Power Macintosh Upgrade Card, but you can't get the Mac to restart in Power Macintosh mode.

- ❖ After using the upgrade card's control panel to specify that the Mac start up in Power Mac mode, you must shut down the computer and then turn it back on. Simply restarting isn't enough because the computer's chips don't get reset unless they are powered off. (A hard reset — the Control-⌘-power key keyboard sequence — will shut power off but can corrupt the System file.)
- ❖ Did you recently reset the parameter RAM? If so, the computer will boot up in 68K mode. Use the upgrade card's control panel to specify that the Mac start up with the upgrade card.

You've installed some video RAM upgrade SIMMs in a Power Mac 7100 or 8100, and now you're having weird video problems.

- ❖ You may have installed the wrong kind of SIMMs. The VRAM expansion card SIMMs for the 7100 and 8100 have the same pin configuration and size, but they're electrically different and they aren't interchangeable. How can you tell them apart? The SIMMs for the Power Macintosh 7100 have two chips per SIMM, while SIMMs for the Power Macintosh 8100 have four chips per SIMM.

You've installed a VRAM Expansion Card and when you open the Monitors control panel, the lowest setting that's available is 256 colors/grays.

- ❖ Apple decided that the Power Macs are fast enough with the VRAM Expansion Card to be able to support 256 colors/grays at similar speeds as lower settings. Thus, the VRAM Expansion Card provides only the 256, Thousands, and Millions settings. The AV card provides the standard array of settings — from two colors to millions.

You're having problems using a DOS/Windows CD-ROM under SoftWindows.

❖ As befitting the DOS/Windows world, you have to go through several gyrations to get DOS/Windows CDs to show up in SoftWindows. You'll find all the ugly details in Chapter 25's Quick Tips box "Using PC CD-ROMs on a Power Mac under SoftWindows."

When you insert an audio CD, a message appears saying that the disk isn't readable and asking if you want to initialize it.

❖ Make sure you have the Foreign File Access and Audio CD Access files in your Extensions folder. The Mac needs these files to recognize audio CDs.

❖ Do you have both PC Exchange and Dayna Communications' DOS Mounter installed? If so, remove one of them from your System Folder — when both utilities are installed, the Mac can have problems with audio CDs. (You don't need both anyway — they perform the same function; see Chapter 27.)

AV and Speech Recognition Problems

You've added items to the Speakable Items folder, but the Mac isn't recognizing them when you issue spoken commands.

❖ When you add an item to the Speakable Items folder, you must restart the Mac in order for the PlainTalk speech recognition technology to recognize them. Restart and try again.

You're trying to capture video on the Quadra 840AV or 660AV, and you're only able to capture gray-scale, not color, information. You have a monitor larger than 16 inches.

❖ This isn't a bug; it's a shortcoming of the machine. These Macs' on-board video memory isn't fast enough to digitize video data on 19- or 21-inch monitors. Your only choice when using a large screen monitor is to work with the 8-bit gray-scale display. Connect the Mac to a smaller monitor to do color QuickTime captures.

When you connect your AV Mac to a television monitor, the image is clear but if you select a solid desktop pattern, the color is off. For example, a red desktop starts out blue at the top of the screen but fades to red and to purple. The problem happens at all Monitor control panel color settings.

❖ This discoloration can occur because TV sets have marginal color purity specifications compared to computers. You can get some improvement by adjusting the gamma setting: Open the Monitors control panel and, while holding down the keyboard's Option key, click the control panel's Options button. Gamma-adjustment settings appear in the left side of the Options dialog box. Select the gamma one for television, and the color should improve. (In the monitor world, gamma correction matches the computer's color tables to the monitor or television set the computer is connected to. This is necessary because no two monitors or televisions reproduce color identically.)

The QuickTime movies that you digitize have jerky motions and the sound breaks up.

❖ You may have specified too large a movie window size or an inappropriate compressor. Or background operations (such as printing) may have caused an interruption when you were digitizing the movie. See Chapter 20 for tips on making smooth QuickTime movies.

You've forgotten the passwords that you assigned to TV stations on a Mac equipped with a TV tuner card.

❖ Sorry — you'll have to call a locksmith. Just kidding. This one's easy: just open the Preferences folder (within the System Folder) and locate the TV Preferences file. Trash it, restart, and your passwords will be gone.

For More Help

I've presented the most common Mac ailments here, but I haven't explored problems specific to a given program or third-party product. Your best sources for that kind of help are user groups, manuals, and firms' technical support hotlines.

But before you call the latter, be sure to compile the information the support technician will need to diagnose the problem. Take time before trouble strikes to write down your system configuration — the amount of memory, the system version (choose About this Macintosh from the Finder's File menu), the names of the extensions, control panels, and desk accessories you've installed, and a list of your peripherals. When a problem occurs, note the steps that caused it.

And before you call, take a few deep breaths. A support technician can't help you if you're panicked and panting. When you're at that level of despair, you need a different kind of hotline.

CHAPTER 28 CONCEPTS AND TERMS

- If the Mac doesn't recognize a hard disk, scanner, or other SCSI device, check all SCSI devices to make sure each has a unique address. Also verify that you have the correct number of terminators in the correct positions and that your SCSI cabling is secure and undamaged.
- If the Mac doesn't start up from a hard disk that was previously working, the disk's startup information (its boot blocks) may be damaged. Other possibilities include SCSI problems or a damaged System Folder.
- If the Mac crashes during startup, conflicting extensions may be to blame.
- When you copy files using the Finder and an error message says that some files couldn't be written, the destination disk could be damaged.
- Common causes of printing problems include loose or damaged cables, insufficient free space on your startup disk, or the printer being offline.
- When setting up your system, use this sequence: First, install your expansion boards, connect any SCSI peripherals, connect your mouse, keyboard, and (for modular Macs) your monitor, install the system software, and then install your application programs.

boot blocks
The portion of a disk that the Mac reads in order to begin its startup process.

driver
Software that enables the Mac to recognize and access a device such as a hard disk or printer.

parameter RAM
The battery-powered memory that holds Control Panel settings, such as the time, date, and current startup disk. On a PowerBook, the parameter RAM also holds your system sleep settings.

PART III

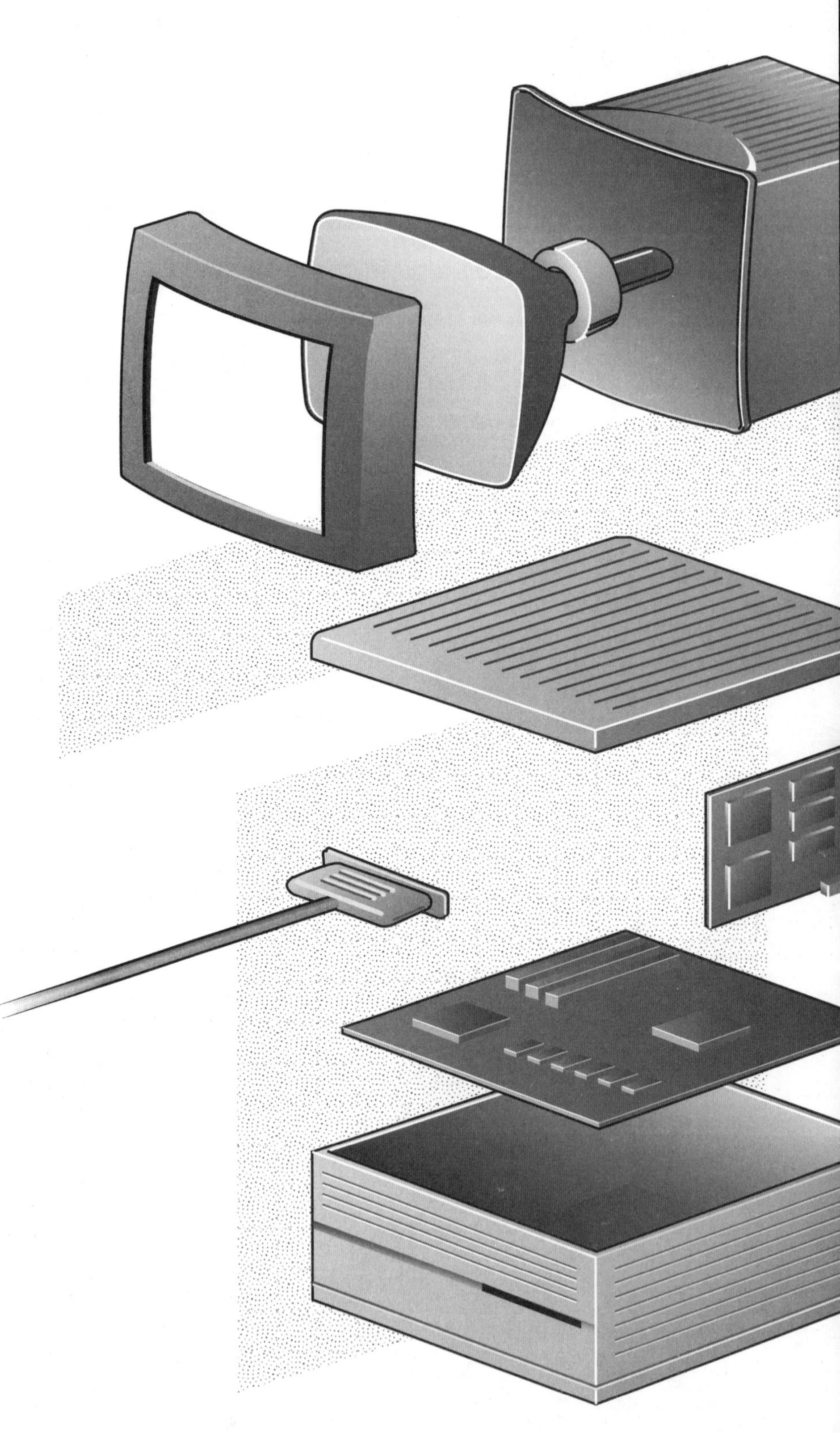

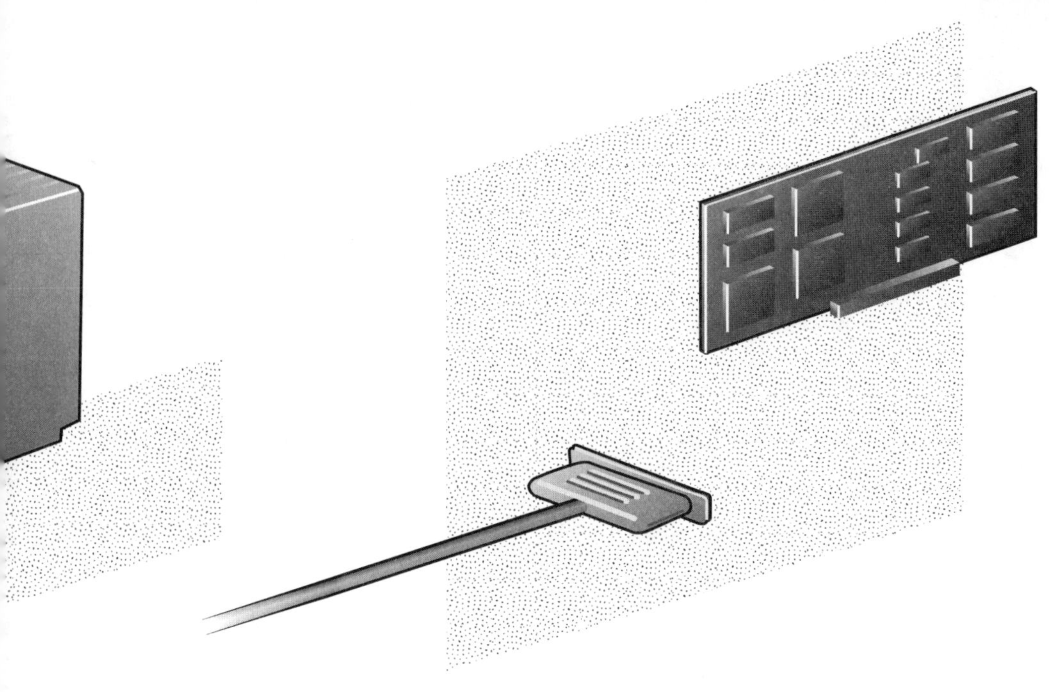

Expanding the Mac

CHAPTER TWENTY-NINE

Upgrading Strategies

- Assessing the hardware upgrade options for each Mac
- Surveying PowerBook upgrades
- Improving your Mac's video features
- Understanding and installing memory upgrades
- Deciding between an upgrade or a new Mac

Buying into the Mac world is like boarding a moving train. You stand alongside the tracks, waiting until the right model comes along, and then you time your leap and hold on as money flutters from your pockets. Whew — you made it.

But where are you heading? Toward a dead-end spur? Is a new model going to pass as you settle into your seat? And if this train can't take you to your destination, will you be able to transfer to one that can?

Every Mac owner has faced worries like these at one time or another — especially now that the second-generation Power Macs have arrived. Should you sell your old Mac and buy a new one? Will a third-party accelerator board or other upgrade suffice? Will your upgraded machine be compatible with new Macs?

These aren't easy questions to answer, but one thing is certain: An old Mac may not be the newest or fastest train on the tracks, but it can still take many people where they want to go. (And it sure beats walking.) But more to the point, you can upgrade an old Mac to give it most of the features in Apple's current offerings. And if you do have one of the newest Macs, hardware upgrades can make a good thing even better.

In this chapter, I outline the most common upgrade options available for old and new Macs; my goal is to help you map out an upgrade path that makes the most of your Mac and your money. I also provide some background into how the Mac's memory works and how the Mac creates its knock-out screen displays.

Check Out These Roadmaps for the Upgrade Path

The *Macworld Power User Clinic* CD contains several items of interest for anyone about to tread the upgrade path.

The Installing Upgrades segment of the *Macworld Power User Clinic* is an introduction to installing expansion cards and memory upgrades, and is one way to get to Newer Technology's Guru utility, which describes the memory and video-memory upgrade options available for all Macs.

In the Second-Generation Power Macs interview, Power Mac product line manager Dave Limp demonstrates how easy it is to add memory to the Power Mac 7200 and 7500, both of which contain an innovative hinged tray that provides fuss-free access to the main logic board. In this interview, you can also learn more about the PCI expansion bus and the processor-upgrade cards that the Power Mac 7500, 8500, and 9500 use.

In the Performa Update interview, Performa product manager Eric Gee demonstrates the ease of upgrading the all-in-one Performa 5200 and describes some of the Apple upgrades available for it.

Assessing Your Hardware Options

Before you can devise an upgrade strategy, it helps to know what your options are. Hardware upgrades fall into two broad categories — ones that make your Mac faster and ones that add new features, such as color or additional storage. The most common upgrades within these categories (which often overlap) are detailed in the following sections.

Memory

More memory helps programs run faster and enables you to run more of them at once. More memory also lets you create larger documents with programs that keep entire documents in memory instead of swapping between memory and disk. (Examples include drawing programs such as Deneba's Canvas and the Claris MacDraw series, spreadsheet programs such as Microsoft Excel, and integrated packages such as ClarisWorks.) Most significantly, more memory lets you run today's increasingly complex — and increasingly bloated — application programs. I discuss memory upgrade issues in more detail later in this chapter.

Hard disks

All current (and many discontinued) Macs include an internal hard drive, but it tends to fill faster than a hall closet. The Mac's SCSI bus can accommodate multiple drives, however, and dozens of companies are eager to sell you one. See Chapter 25 for the scoop on storage.

Accelerator boards

These silicon brain transplants replace your Mac's *central processing unit* (CPU) with a faster, flashier one.

- Accelerators for the old Plus, SE, Classic, and Performa 200 usually replace those machines' 68000 CPU with a 68030. You'll have a hard time finding such products these days; the Mac family has evolved and prices have fallen so much that it generally doesn't make much sense to install an accelerator in a 68000-based Mac.
- Accelerators for the Mac II family usually replace the 68020 or 68030 with a 68040 — the brain behind the Centris and Quadra families.
- Accelerators for the Quadra line provide either a faster 68040 or a PowerPC chip.
- Microprocessor upgrade boards for the Power Mac 7500, 8500, and 9500 enable you to replace your computer's PowerPC processor with an even faster one.

Logic board

This upgrade involves an Apple dealer replacing your machine's main circuit board — its *logic board* — with a different one. Logic board upgrades are restricted to models that have cousins in the same basic case. You can upgrade a Quadra 800, 840AV, or Power Mac 8100 to a Power Mac 8500, for example.

Logic board upgrades Apple has offered in the recent past include Classic to Classic II; LC or LC II to LC III; LC II or LC III to LC 475; Centris/Quadra 610 to Quadra 660AV or Power Mac 6100; Quadra 650 to Power Mac 7100; Quadra 800 to Quadra 840AV or Power Mac 8100; Quadra 900 to Quadra 950; and Mac II and IIx to Mac IIfx. You may find dealers or mail-order houses that still have these elderly upgrades available, but unless the price is low, you're probably better off with a new Mac.

Logic board upgrades generally cost more than accelerator upgrades, but they have a significant advantage: they provide new features, such as GeoPort connectors or audio/video digitizing ports. On the downside, a logic board upgrade may require you to buy new memory — the memory installed in your existing Mac may not be fast enough or the right kind for the logic board you're buying.

Video

All currently manufactured Macs (as well as most discontinued ones) include video circuitry on their logic boards. With many models, you can increase the number of colors displayed on certain monitors by adding additional video memory, called *VRAM*. Most Macs also accept plug-in video boards that control color or large-screen monitors or add other display talents, including the ability to attach the Mac to videocassette recorders (see Chapter 20).

Multiple monitors

You can connect more than one monitor to most Macs by adding additional video cards or slower SCSI video adaptors. In a Mac connected to multiple monitors, each monitor is driven by its own video circuitry and has its own VRAM.

What's slick about this approach is that it lets you mix and match different types of video hardware and displays — a color monitor and a two-page color display, an AudioVision monitor and a full-page monochrome display, a PowerBook's LCD screen and a color video projector. And you can drag windows from one display to another, or even position a window to span displays. Because the Mac keeps track of each monitor's capabilities, it can adjust the way it displays the window on each monitor.

Ethernet interfaces

Ethernet is a networking system that transfers data much more quickly than does the Mac's built-in LocalTalk port. Ethernet is built into many mid-range and high-end Macs, including the Centris, Quadra, and Power Mac families as well as the PowerBook 500-series. A variety of Ethernet adaptors is available for other Macs, including PowerBooks. And high-speed Ethernet cards — ones that can shuttle 100MB per second across a network — are available for PCI Power Macs.

Tips for Working with Multiple Monitors

A large-screen monitor is a great way to enhance your Mac — you can see more of a document on the screen at once, you do less scrolling, and tasks such as page layout, graphics, and movie editing are more efficient.

But if one monitor is great, two monitors are even better. By connecting a second monitor to your Mac, you can

- Stash toolbars and auxiliary windows on the second monitor. For example, I keep Microsoft Word's Find dialog box and toolbars on my second monitor, freeing up space on the other monitor for text. Most programs save the position of their windows when you quit and restore them to those positions when you use them again.
- Expand your electronic desktop. If you're working with multiple documents or application programs, it's far easier to spread them out across two monitors than it is to keep switching between them.
- Mix and match monitor settings. If there's one monitor you use primarily for text editing, set it to a minimum number of colors — for example, 2 or 4. Your word processing documents will scroll much faster.

Aliases (discussed in Chapter 22) are terrific tools for multi-monitor setups. For example, make an alias of the Trash icon and then position the alias on your second monitor. That way, when you need to throw away a file, you won't have to drag the icon all the way across two monitors.

Coprocessors

These specialized microprocessors work along with the Mac's CPU, lightening its load. *Math coprocessors* speed up calculations in spreadsheets and other number-crunching programs. Math chips are often built into or offered for accelerator boards and are available on plug-in expansion cards for the Mac LC and IIsi. (Other Mac IIs and the SE/30 include math chips; the LC can accept one via its expansion slot.)

Graphics coprocessors, also called *graphics accelerators*, are generally used with or included on 24-bit video cards, which enable Macs to display images with photographic realism — though they must move megabytes of data to do so. Without a graphics accelerator, true color can require true patience.

Digital signal processor (DSP) upgrades can provide the kinds of sophisticated features built into the AV and Power Mac models — sophisticated audio, faster Photoshop filtering operations, and telecommunications features such as fax modems and voice telephones. These days, most DSP cards are Photoshop accelerators; see Chapter 13 for details.

Sound-recording hardware

Most Macs contain sound-recording circuitry that, with appropriate software, lets you "attach" recorded comments to documents and send voice mail messages to other Macs on a network. AV and Power Macs have sophisticated audio circuitry that can record stereo sound with near CD-quality. And as I describe in Chapter 21, you can add professional-level sound-recording features to many Macs by adding third-party cards, such as Digidesign's Audiomedia II.

Cache memory boards

These special-purpose memory boards provide a speed kick to Power Macs by storing the most recently used instructions and data in a small amount of high-speed memory that the processor can access faster than main memory. Many Power Mac models include a cache card; you can get a bigger speed boost by replacing it with a larger one. More on cache cards later in this chapter.

Assessing Your Slot Options

Some Macs are less receptive to upgrades than others. The Classic, Plus, and earlier machines are particularly resistant to improvement. They're sealed boxes, with no expansion slots for accepting plug-in boards, such as video boards, accelerators, and high-speed networking boards. To work around this, pioneering upgrade developers generally used the *Killy Clip*, a clip that straddled the machine's processor and thus tapped into the signals that would otherwise be provided by an expansion slot.

Upgrading most other Macs is generally straightforward, because all other models provide at least one slot (see Table 29-1). With the single-slot Macs — models that include the SE, SE/30, LC series, Centris 610, Quadra 660AV, Power Mac 6100, and Mac IIsi — there isn't much room to grow, so you'll need to choose upgrade options carefully. More to the point, you'll need to decide whether it makes more sense to just buy a new Power Mac.

Table 29-1
Counting Slots

Macintosh Model	***NuBus Slots***	***PDS Slots***
Plus and earlier; Classic, Classic II	0	0
SE	0	1
SE/30	0	1
Color Classic, Color Classic II	0	1
LC family, Performa 400 series, Quadra 630	0	1
Performa 5200, 6200	0	1
II, IIx, IIfx	6	0 (IIfx, 1)
IIcx	3	0
IIci	3	1
IIsi, Centris 610, Centris/ Quadra 660AV, Power Mac 6100*	1	1
IIvx, Performa 600	3	1
Centris/Quadra 650, Power Mac 7100	3	1
Quadra 700	2	1
Quadra 900, 950	5	1
Quadra 800, 840AV, Power Mac 8100	3	1
Duo Dock	2*	0*
Macintosh Model	***PCI Slots***	
Power Mac 7200, 7500, 8500	3	
Power Mac 9500	6	

*These models provide one slot that can accommodate either a PDS board or a NuBus board (a NuBus board requires an adaptor card).

How to get more NuBus slots

You've run out of NuBus slots? Consider a NuBus expansion chassis from Second Wave. The Expanse NB8 and Expanse NB4 are desktop boxes that provide eight and four NuBus slots, respectively, as well as a power supply and fan. There's even room in the chassis case for an internal SCSI hard drive.

How the NuBus Works

NuBus is named for a standard that was developed at the Massachusetts Institute of Technology and refined in 1985 by a standards committee comprising representatives from MIT, AT&T, Texas Instruments, Apple, and others. The NuBus standard specifies everything from how expansion boards access the internal bus to such physical details as the distance between the slot's pins.

NuBus slots overcome two of the classic drawbacks of slots — forcing users to fuss with small switches inside the case that tell the computer what hardware you've installed, and making it harder for software developers to write software that runs on different system configurations.

Every NuBus board contains a *configuration ROM* — a read-only memory chip that identifies the board and describes its capabilities. When you switch on a NuBus Mac, its Slot Manager consults each board's configuration ROM and then sets up your system accordingly. Thus, installation is usually a plug-and-play proposition.

Apple tackled the software compatibility problem by designing the Mac's system software to act as an intermediary between programs and your hardware. Properly written Mac programs avoid accessing hardware directly; instead, they use Macintosh Toolbox routines, which access the hardware. So as long as software developers follow Apple's guidelines, their programs will run on any Mac, regardless of the boards it contains.

In recent years, Apple has extended Slot Manager support to the PDS slots that many machines provide. Thus, a PDS expansion board can also have a configuration ROM and set itself up automatically at startup time.

Variations on the NuBus Theme

The NuBus slots in the Centris/Quadra 660AV, Quadra 840AV, and Power Macs support a newer version of the NuBus standard, called *NuBus-90.* Among other things, the NuBus-90 specification allows for faster data transfers across the bus — an important advantage for audio and video applications, which involve transferring megabytes of data.

Compact Mac models such as the Quadra 610 and 660AV and the Power Mac 6100 can accept NuBus cards that are up to 7 inches long and use a maximum of 10 watts of power. Other NuBus-capable Macs can accept cards up to 12 inches long. A bigger selection of large cards is available.

To use a NuBus board with the Mac IIsi, Centris 610, Quadra 660AV, or Power Mac 6100, you need an adaptor such as Apple's NuBus Adaptor Card. This card contains the chips that enable the IIsi to communicate with a NuBus card. (The IIsi adaptor card also includes a math coprocessor.) The adaptor card also contains the 96-pin NuBus connector into which you plug your NuBus board, which runs from front to back within the computer's case, parallel to the logic board.

The Power Mac 7100/66 has some design limitations that hamper the performance of its NuBus slots, making this Mac less suitable than others for applications such as digital video. Apple fixed the problem in the Power Mac 7100/80.

How the PCI Bus Works

The second-generation Power Macs use a new expansion bus design called PCI, short for *peripheral component interconnect.* PCI slots are also currently found in many high-performance DOS/Windows machines; indeed, PCI's popularity in the DOS/Windows world is one reason Apple has adopted it for the Mac. Another reason is that PCI offers faster performance than NuBus, which isn't all that Nu anymore.

PCI was originally developed by Intel and is now under the control of an independent standards committee of which Apple is a member. A PCI card's connectors differ from those of NuBus cards, but otherwise PCI cards look pretty much like any other expansion card.

The real difference between PCI and NuBus shows up on a stopwatch. The PCI slots on the second-generation Power Macs support sustained transfer rates of about 90MB per second — many times faster than NuBus (see the adjacent figure, "Why PCI is Faster than NuBus"). That makes possible accelerated video expansion boards that provide real-time scrolling on large monitors, ultra-fast Ethernet network interfaces, and warp-speed SCSI accelerators.

WHY PCI IS FASTER THAN NUBUS

PCI runs both faster and more efficiently than NuBus. PCI's 33 MHz speed yields a theoretical maximum throughput of 132MB per second. NuBus's limit is 40 MBps. But the Mac's operating system and the nature of the buses themselves limit the data-transfer rate to less than the maximum. Likely top data-transfer rates are 32 MBps for the PCI Power Macs and 16 MBps for NuBus Macs.

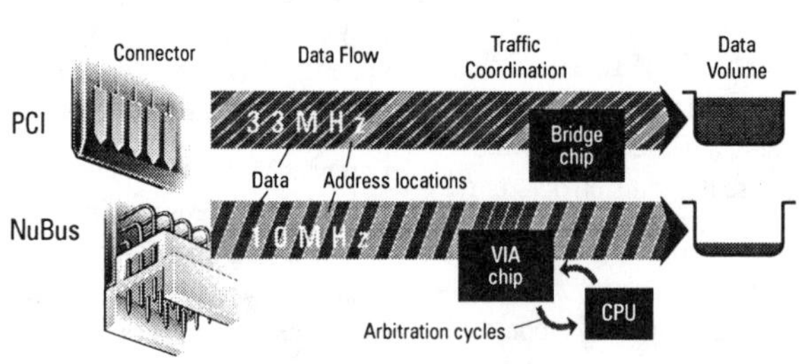

Every PCI transfer is a burst transfer, where one address is followed by many data blocks. Sustained NuBus transfers need a separate address for each data block. This added overhead slows the effective transfer rate. Between data transfers, NuBus and the Mac's CPU must stop the flow of data to arbitrate the next transfer. PCI doesn't interrupt data flow because it sets up the next data transfer while the current transfer is still running.

Cross-Platform Pluses

PCI not only provides dramatically faster performance than NuBus, it also makes it far easier for hardware developers to create cards that work in PCs as well as Macs. Apple says that if a developer adheres to the PCI 2.0 specification when designing a card, it will only have to write some software to make the card work with PCI Power Macs. That sounds too good to be true, but several major PCI developers I talked to confirmed this was their experience.

PCI makes it easier for businesses to mix PCs and Power Macs by letting them buy expansion cards that work in both. And because PCI cards sell in such greater volumes, they cost less. For example, an accelerated 24-bit graphics card for NuBus can cost $1000 to $2000. ATI Technologies' Xclaim GA, the accelerated 24-bit video card that Apple includes with some Power Mac 9500 configurations also sells separately for less than $700. (The card includes 2MB of video RAM, upgradable to 4MB, and supports 24-bit color on resolutions as high as 1152 by 840 pixels.)

This isn't to say there won't be hurdles on the path to cross-platform expansion — PC hardware developers will need to pay careful attention to the plug-and-play and ease-of-use requirements that Mac owners take for granted — but there's no denying that the move to PCI has major benefits.

Easing the Transition from NuBus to PCI

To ease the transition from NuBus, Second Wave has introduced PCI versions of its NuBus expansion chassis. The $595 Xpanse PN200 contains two NuBus slots and draws its power from the Mac's SCSI connector — clever. The $995 Xpanse PN400 contains four slots and the $1895 Xpanse PN800 contains eight. These larger chassis contain their own power supplies and also accept optional SCSI drive bays.

Upgrade Strategies: Compact Macs

Here's my upgrade recommendation for the compact Mac models: don't do it. Sell your compact Mac or pass it along to someone and buy a newer Mac instead. If your budget, your desk space, or your loyalty prohibit this, here are some options.

- *Plus or earlier:* Sell it or supplement it with a new machine.
- *SE:* Accelerators and large-screen monochrome monitor adaptors (sorry, no color) may still be available, but you'd get better performance and a better hedge against obsolescence with a newer Mac, such as a Performa 5200 or 6200.
- *SE/30:* Install an upgrade board for acceleration, Ethernet networking, or color video.
- *Classic and Classic II (Peforma 200):* Some dealers may still be able to locate the Classic II logic board upgrade for the Classic, but a new Mac is a better move.
- *Color Classic:* Add a VRAM upgrade for 16-bit (32,000 colors) video. Install an upgrade board for acceleration, Ethernet networking, or 24-bit color video.

Upgrade Strategies: LC and Performa Families

In this section, I spotlight some upgrade options for the LC and Performa lines.

- *LC and LC II (Performa 400, 405, 430):* An upgrade from the LC III to the Performa 475 is available. You may still be able to find the LC III logic board upgrade for the LC and LC II, but a new Mac makes more sense.

- *LC III (Performa 450):* A video RAM upgrade gives you more colors. A math coprocessor speeds complex math calculations and 3-D graphics rendering. Accelerator boards are also available.
- *LC 475, 575, and LC 630 (Performa 470, 570, 630 series):* DayStar's PowerCard lets these reasonably fast 68LC040 Macs join the PowerPC party.
- *LC 5200 (Performa 5200), Performa 6200:* These PowerPC-based Performas accept TV tuner, video digitizing, and fax/modem or Ethernet networking cards — and, of course, memory upgrades.

Upgrade Strategies: Mac II Family

- *II, IIx:* Apple used to offer a logic board upgrade that turned a II or IIx into a IIfx but has long-since discontinued it. You may be able to find one at a dealer, but think twice before buying it. For one thing, you'll also need to buy memory: the IIfx can't use your Mac II or IIx's existing SIMMs. For another, if you have a Mac II, you'll probably want the SuperDrive upgrade, too. When you're finished, you'll have a machine that's still slower than today's *low-end* Macs. An accelerator board is a better bet — a new Mac is better still.

Tips for Mapping Out an Upgrade Strategy

Upgrade options fall into one of two categories: minor and major. A minor upgrade might involve simply adding additional video memory in order to be able to display more colors. A major upgrade, on the other hand, usually involves adding an accelerator or buying a logic board upgrade.

Part of mapping out an upgrading strategy involves deciding just how content you are with your current system. If you're pleased with its performance but you simply want better video features, for instance, a video RAM upgrade or new video card will probably do the job. On the other hand, if your machine is showing its age in several areas, a logic board upgrade or all-new Mac may be in order.

Finally, now that the Power Macs make up the majority of the Mac product line, keep in mind that a Power Mac logic board or processor upgrade will provide better performance than a 68030- or 68040-based accelerator — provided, of course, that the programs you rely on are available in native-mode form.

Comparing PowerPC Upgrade Options

So you've decided you want to upgrade to a PowerPC-based Mac. You have another decision to make: whether to buy a logic board upgrade — assuming one is available for your Mac — or a third-party PowerPC upgrade card. (In the past, this decision was a bit more complicated, as Apple sold its own upgrade card. In June of 1995, however, Apple turned over its PowerPC upgrade card business to DayStar Digital.)

Here's some advice to help you decide.

Comparing PowerPC Upgrade Cards

Unlike logic board upgrades, PowerPC processor upgrade cards let you switch back and forth between PowerPC and 68K operation. If one of your favorite programs isn't available in native-mode form, you can start up under the Mac's 68K processor. This feature makes an upgrade card a great way to ease your transition into the Power Mac world.

Upgrade cards also have the edge on price. DayStar's PowerCard 601 sells for less than $700. Its 601 chip runs at twice your Mac's original clock rate; for instance, in a Quadra 700, which has a 25 MHz 68040, the upgrade card's 601 chip runs at 50 MHz, while in a Quadra 630, which has a 33 MHz 68040, the card runs at 66 MHz.

DayStar's higher-performance upgrade cards are the PowerPro family. Several PowerPro models are available. If you have a Quadra/Centris 650 or a Quadra 610, 700, 800, 900, or 950, you can choose from 80 MHz or 100 MHz models. These also provide their own SIMM slots that can accept up to 128 MB of 64-bit memory.

Less-expensive PowerPro 601 cards are available for the Centrs/Quadra 610 and the Centris/Quadra 650, 800, and 950. These cards run at speeds of between 40 MHz and 66 MHz, depending on the Mac they're installed in. They lack the on-board SIMM slots provided by the costlier PowerPro models, but they do provide 1MB of cache memory.

The Argument for Logic Board Upgrades

Logic board upgrades cost more, but they provide more. Besides being faster, they give you two GeoPort connectors (on a Power Mac, both the modem and printer ports are GeoPort connectors), support for PlainTalk speech recognition, and 16-bit, CD-quality audio.

The bad news is that logic board upgrades are available for only a few Macs. You can upgrade a Quadra 800 or 840AV or a Power Mac 8100 to a Power Mac 8500. And you might still be able to find logic board upgrades that turn a 68K Mac into a Power Mac 6100, 7100, or 8100. I don't recommend these, however; the second-generation machines are so superior to their predecessors — and so reasonably priced — that it makes more sense to buy one of them instead of upgrading to a now-discontinued Power Mac model.

Why doesn't Apple offer second-generation logic board upgrades for other desktop Macs, such as the Quadra 650 or even the Power Mac 7100, which was more recently discontinued? Blame it on the case. The Power Mac 7200 and 7500 use a new case design and logic board layout, so Apple can't offer a logic board upgrade for older Macs.

Why the new case? One reason is for easier upgrading; more on this later in this chapter. But the other reason is that the 7100-style case — which originally housed 1992's Mac IIvx and IIvi — was not able to adequately absorb the radio interference generated by the kind of fast processors that the second-generation Power Mac models can use.

- *IIcx:* Almost all IIcx machines contain soldered rather than socketed CPU chips, and that means problems for accelerator boards. (DayStar Digital offers a chip-pulling service for customers of its accelerator boards.) Note that after adding an accelerator, some weak spots remain, including a relatively slow SCSI port and no Ethernet networking. A new Mac is probably a better bet.
- *IIci:* This is one of the few Mac II-family machines for which a PowerPC upgrade card is available. The DayStar Turbo 601 provides a 66 MHz PowerPC 601 chip and 256K of Level 2 cache memory. A 100 MHz version is also available. Best of all, you can restart using the IIci's 68030 for those times when you need 680X0 compatibility.
- *IIsi:* The DayStar Turbo 601 turns this featherweight Mac II into a PowerPC-based machine. Given this machine's single expansion slot, however, a new Mac may make more sense.
- *IIvx (Performa 600):* The DayStar Turbo 601 is also available for this machine, as is the Power Mac 7100/66 logic board upgrade. (Think twice about the latter if you're interested in digital video work; as described earlier, the 7100/66 has relatively slow NuBus slots.) For thousands of colors on most monitors instead of 256, add a VRAM SIMM to bring video memory up to 1MB. If you're interested in multimedia, CD-ROMs, or Kodak's PhotoCD system, consider adding Apple's CD-600i internal, quadruple-speed CD-ROM drive.

Upgrade Strategies: Centris/Quadra Families

The Macs in the Centris and Quadra clans are beginning to show some gray around the temples, but they still have plenty of life in them.

- *Quadra 605:* Add a VRAM upgrade to display thousands of colors on larger monitors. DayStar offers a PowerPC upgrade card for this value-packed Mac.
- *Centris/Quadra 610:* Add a VRAM upgrade to display thousands of colors on larger monitors. A PowerPC upgrade card is available from DayStar. Some dealers may still have the Power Mac 6100 logic board upgrade, but I don't recommend it.
- *Quadra 630:* If you didn't get them when you bought your 630, you can add the Apple Video System boards discussed in Chapter 20 to provide TV-in-a-window as well as video digitizing capabilities. PowerPC upgrade cards are also available from DayStar Digital.

- *Centris/Quadra 650:* Add a VRAM upgrade to display thousands of colors on larger monitors. DayStar's PowerPro or PowerCard PowerPC cards are available. Some dealers may still have the Power Mac 7100/66 logic board upgrade, but I don't recommend it.
- *Centris/Quadra 660AV:* Add a VRAM upgrade to display thousands of colors on larger monitors. Some dealers may still have the Power Mac 6100 logic board upgrade, but I don't recommend it; DayStar does not offer a PowerPC upgrade card for the 660AV.
- *Quadra 700:* Add a VRAM upgrade to display millions of colors on larger monitors. DayStar Digital's PowerPro 601 accelerator provides PowerPC performance.
- *Quadra 800 and 840AV:* Add a VRAM upgrade to display millions of colors on larger monitors. Each of these fast Quadras can also be upgraded to a second-generation Power Mac 8500.
- *Quadra 950:* DayStar Digital's PowerPro 601 accelerator provides PowerPC performance.

Upgrade Strategies: First-Generation Power Macs

This section spotlights some upgrade options for the first-generation Power Mac models: the 6100, 7100, and 8100. Before sinking a lot of money into one of these machines, however, you should strongly consider whether a second-generation Power Mac might make more sense — it could be cheaper, and it would definitely be better.

The two factors that could swing the decision in favor of souping up your first-generation Power Mac are memory and expansion cards. If you have a large amount of memory in your first-generation Power Mac, there's a good chance you won't be able to use it in a second-generation machine. (I have more to say about this later in this chapter.) If you have a significant investment in NuBus cards, you'd need to buy a Second Wave NuBus/PCI expansion box. Replacing a large amount of memory and accommodating your NuBus cards can boost the cost of a second-generation Power Mac sky-high.

The AV Technologies card

All three Power Macs accept a card called the AV Technologies card, which adds video-in and video-out features. (The AV configurations include this card. Non-AV configurations include a basic video card.)

The AV Technologies card installs in the Power Mac's processor-direct slot and provides three ports: a 15-pin connector for a monitor, an S-video input, and an S-video output. (An adaptor that lets you attach composite video cables is included.)

The AV card provides a 40-pin DAV connector identical to that of the Quadra 660AV and 840AV. The DAV connector taps into the AV card's raw video input signal; it also connects to the digital audio signal input for the Power Mac's 16-bit sound chip. (NuBus cards can also access these video and audio signals directly: third-party developers designing NuBus cards for the 7100AV and 8100AV have designed their cards to use a flat ribbon cable that plugs into the DAV connector on the AV card.)

Power Mac AV models include two adaptor cables that let you connect your AV card to standard television sets, camcorders, videodisc players, and VCRs. The input cable connects pin 3 (the luminance signal) of the AV card's video output connector to the signal pin of the RCA plug.

The video and graphics system on the AV Technologies card is built around two banks of 80ns VRAM, with a total capacity of 2MB. As with the 660AV and 840AV, application programs can use the VRAM as a single frame buffer (video input is disabled) or as two frame buffers, one for video and one for graphics.

A Level 2 cache

All first-generation Power Macs include or accept an optional Level 2 cache memory SIMM that can boost performance by holding recently used data and instructions in an area of fast memory. When the PowerPC processor is executing a program, it first checks its 32K internal cache, then the Level 2 cache, and then main memory (DRAM) for instructions. Because cache memory is faster than DRAM, the processor can access it more quickly.

All Power Mac models accept a SIMM-based Level 2 cache whose size can range from 128K to 1MB. Many models include a 256K cache card. For a 10 to 20 percent performance boost, get a 512K or 1MB cache card. You can install a Level 2 cache yourself; simply plug its SIMM into the 160-pin connector on the main logic board.

Something interesting to note: Tests done by Macworld Lab indicate that a large cache provides a bigger performance benefit when you're running 68K applications in emulation mode than when you're running native-mode programs.

Video memory upgrades

The first Power Macs came with great video features right out of the chute — the 6100, 7100, and 8100 were the first Macs to come equipped to drive two monitors. Even the second-generation Power Macs don't have this feature; on them — and on other desktop Macs — driving multiple monitors means adding video cards. (There's one exception, sort of: If you upgrade a Power Mac 8500's video memory to 4MB, you can connect a TV monitor and a computer monitor simultaneously. But the TV monitor's relative fuzziness makes it unsuitable for anything except playing QuickTime movies and monitoring an incoming video signal.)

The Power Mac 7100 and 8100 each provide a single VRAM memory upgrade slot; plug a VRAM SIMM into the slot and you get more colors on large monitors. You can expand a 7100's VRAM to a total of 2MB (allowing for millions of colors on a 14-inch monitor and thousands on a 21-inch monitor). You can expand an 8100's VRAM to a total of 4MB, for millions of colors on monitors as large as 21 inches — dreamy.

The Power Mac 8100-to-8500 Upgrade

As I've mentioned elsewhere in this chapter, the Power Mac 8100 is the only first-generation Power Mac that you can upgrade to a second-generation model — specifically, the amazing 8500. Should you consider this upgrade? Again, the answer depends on the amount of RAM and the number and type of NuBus boards your 8100 contains. If you have scads of RAM, you'll spend a fair amount replacing it with the DIMM-based memory that the 8500 uses. (You may be able to install some of it in the 8500 using SIMM-to-DIMM adaptor cards, which I describe later in this chapter.)

Similarly, if you have a few NuBus cards, you'll either need to replace them with their PCI equivalents or buy a NuBus expansion chassis from Second Wave. And note that the Second Wave chassis do not support cards, such as Radius' SpigotPower AV, that use the 8100's digital audio-video (DAV) connector. Yet another factor to consider: if you've connected two monitors to your 8100, you'll need to buy a video card for the 8500, which comes equipped to drive just one monitor. If you have a fully laden Power Mac 8100, you might find that these hidden costs behind the 8100-to-8500 upgrade are just too high.

Upgrade Strategies: Second-Generation Power Macs

Apple's second-generation Power Macs — the 7200, 7500, 8500, and 9500 — have more features than a movie theater complex. Here's how to make them even better.

Processor upgrades

One of the best things about the Power Mac 7500, 8500, and 9500 is the processor-upgrade slot, which lets you upgrade the computer's processor with a faster one. For details on the processor-upgrade slot, see the Chapter 1 Backgrounder box "Inside Apple's Processor-Upgrade Technology" and the Second-Generation Power Macs interview on the *Macworld Power User Clinic* (see the "On the CD" box earlier in this chapter).

Cache memory

The Power Mac 7200, 7500, and 8500 provide a slot for a Level 2 cache card. (In the Power Mac 9500, 512K of cache memory is soldered to the main board.) The Power Mac 8500 includes 256K of cache memory; replace its 256K cache SIMM with a larger one for better performance. The 7200 and 7500 do not include a cache SIMM, but they have a slot for one — adding one is a good way to provide a modest speed kick.

Video memory upgrades

The Power Mac 8500 and 7500 include 2MB of video memory, expandable to 4MB. Upgrading to a full 4MB of VRAM provides 24-bit color on monitors as large as 21 inches and, on the 8500, eliminates having to shut down the Mac's monitor when printing to video.

Both 7200 models share similar on-board video features, although the 7200/90 goes a bit further than the 7200/75. Both include 1MB of video memory; the 7200/75 can be upgraded to 2MB (allowing for 24-bit color on 16-inch monitors), while the 7200/90 supports up to 4MB. In their stock configurations, the machines use a 32-bit-wide graphics bus; when upgraded, the VRAM DIMMs interleave to 64 bits wide.

Upgrade Strategies: PowerBooks

This section presents some upgrade strategies for PowerBook-family machines.

PowerBook 500 expansion

The PowerBook 500 series sports a modular design that makes hardware expansion far easier than in the 100-series models (see Figure 29-1, "The Pull-Apart Power-Book"). This design lets the 500-series machines offer a larger array of expansion options, many of which you can install yourself.

PowerPC chips

The PowerBook 500-series models' processors are mounted on small daughtercards that plug into the main board. Apple will offer a PowerPC 603e processor upgrade card for the 500-series machines, probably by late 1995. (See Chapter 1 for a comparison of the PowerPC-family chips.)

Screens

The PowerBook 520, 520c, and 540 screens can be upgraded to active-matrix LCD screens, which provide faster display performance and a brighter image.

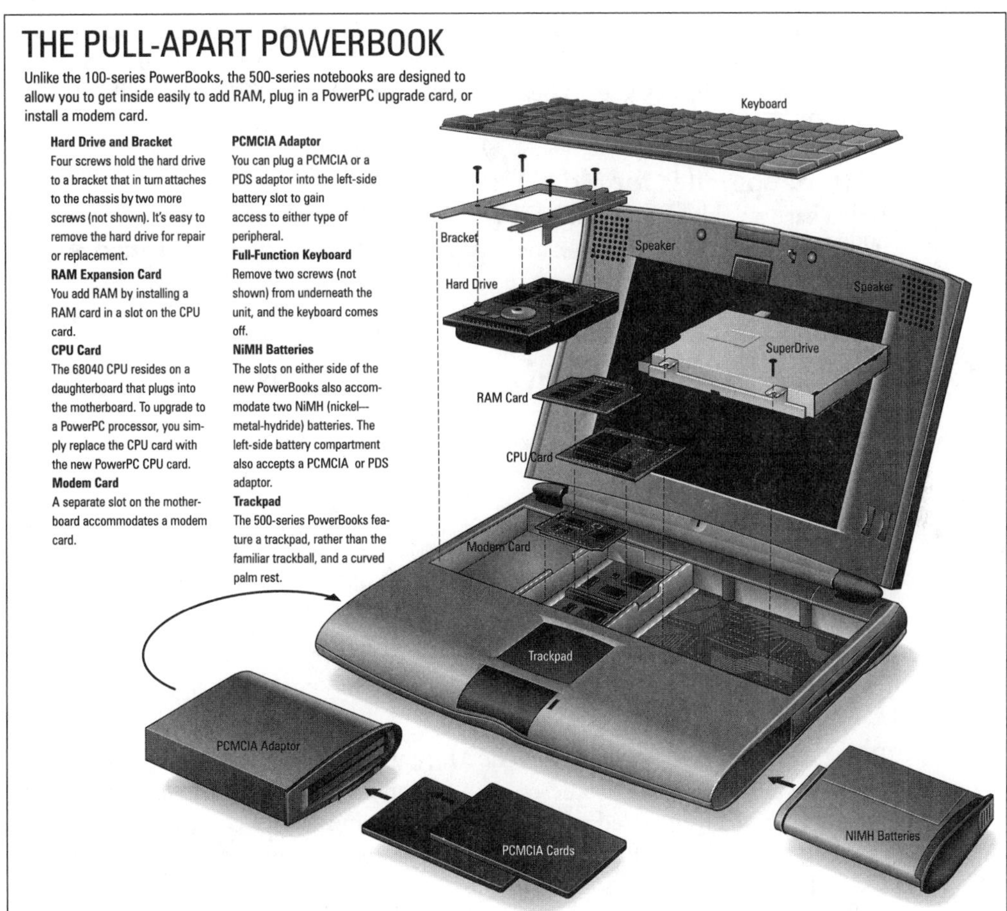

THE PULL-APART POWERBOOK
Unlike the 100-series PowerBooks, the 500-series notebooks are designed to allow you to get inside easily to add RAM, plug in a PowerPC upgrade card, or install a modem card.
Hard Drive and Bracket
Four screws hold the hard drive to a bracket that in turn attaches to the chassis by two more screws (not shown). It's easy to remove the hard drive for repair or replacement.
RAM Expansion Card
You add RAM by installing a RAM card in a slot on the CPU card.
CPU Card
The 68040 CPU resides on a daughterboard that plugs into the motherboard. To upgrade to a PowerPC processor, you simply replace the CPU card with the new PowerPC CPU card.
Modem Card
A separate slot on the motherboard accommodates a modem card.
PCMCIA Adaptor
You can plug a PCMCIA or a PDS adaptor into the left-side battery slot to gain access to either type of peripheral.
Full-Function Keyboard
Remove two screws (not shown) from underneath the unit, and the keyboard comes off.
NiMH Batteries
The slots on either side of the new PowerBooks also accommodate two NiMH (nickel—metal-hydride) batteries. The left-side battery compartment also accepts a PCMCIA or PDS adaptor.
Trackpad
The 500-series PowerBooks feature a trackpad, rather than the familiar trackball, and a curved palm rest.
Keyboard
Bracket
Speaker
Hard Drive
Speaker
SuperDrive
RAM Card
CPU Card
Modem Card
Trackpad
PCMCIA Adaptor
PCMCIA Cards
NiMH Batteries

Figure 29-1: The Pull-Apart PowerBook

Memory

The PowerBook 500-series models can accept up to 36MB of RAM. You can add the RAM by plugging a RAM card into the slot on the CPU card.

PCMCIA cards (PC Cards)

The optional PowerBook PCMCIA Expansion Module slides into the left-hand battery chamber on the PowerBook and lets you install two Type II or one Type III PCMCIA cards (which, these days, are more commonly known as PC Cards).

Type II cards are 5mm thick and often provide features such as memory and network interfaces; Type III cards are larger but can accommodate a wider array of hardware, including tiny hard disk drives.

Apple has done a fine job of applying its hardware/software integration expertise to the PC Card module. When you insert a Type III hard drive module, the drive icon appears on the desktop. When you want to remove a PC Card, simply drag it to the Trash, and a tiny spring within the module ejects the card.

Battery upgrades for older Duo models

If you have an older PowerBook Duo, such as a 230, consider buying one of the new Type III NiMH batteries used by the newer Duos, such as the 280 and 280c. The Type III batteries provide more operating time between charges.

Memory Upgrade Details

In this section, I provide some background into how memory chips work and outline the memory-upgrade options available to each Mac model.

Memory background

There are many types of memory, but most fall into either of two broad categories: *ROM* and *RAM*. You can't venture into the Mac world without encountering these two acronyms, so it helps to understand the concepts behind them.

Prerecorded memory

ROM stands for *read-only memory*. The Mac can read the contents of a ROM chip, but it can't change them. As I describe in Chapter 1, a ROM chip's software is in there for good, prerecorded at the factory like the music on a compact disc. The only real threat to ROM is an electrical mishap, such as a power surge or a spark of static electricity.

RAM — memory that forgets

As Chapter 1 describes, RAM performs the vital job of storing the documents you create and the software you use to create them. RAM is the Mac's temporary workspace: When you start a program, one of the Mac's first jobs is to copy the program from disk into RAM. Similarly, the Finder loads into RAM when you start up the Mac.

RAM chips are often referred to as *DRAM* (pronounced *dee-RAM*) chips. *D* is for *dynamic* and reflects the chip's need for a periodic electronic nudging, or *refresh signal,* that enables it to retain its contents. The other major type of RAM chip, *static RAM,* doesn't require a refresh signal and therefore uses less power. But static RAM chips are more expensive than their dynamic counterparts; as a result, most deskbound computers use DRAM chips. All-in-one PowerBooks such as the 170, 180, and 180c use *pseudo-static RAM* chips, which contain their own refresh circuitry.

The scoop on SIMMs

The DRAM chips used in deskbound Macs are connected in groups of eight on small plug-in circuit boards called *Single Inline Memory Modules*, or *SIMMs*. (The Mac Portable and PowerBook models use their own specialized memory boards.)

Understanding RAM chip capacities

The amount of information a DRAM chip can hold is determined by the chip's *density*, which is measured in kilobits. One kilobit, or *Kbit* for short, equals 1,024 bits. The most common DRAM sizes are 256-Kbit, 1-megabit, and 4-megabit. A 1MB SIMM ties eight 1-megabit DRAM chips together on a plug-in circuit board. A 4MB SIMM uses eight 4-megabit DRAMs.

The dreaded composite SIMM

A composite SIMM uses lower-density RAM chips to construct a single bank of memory. A composite SIMM uses many smaller DRAM chips along with additional circuitry to trick the Mac's memory controller circuitry. An example of a composite SIMM is a 16MB SIMM that uses 32 4-megabit DRAM chips. A noncomposite 16MB SIMM uses eight 16MB chips.

Composite SIMMs are less expensive than noncomposite SIMMS because they are made with less expensive components. But they pose timing and electrical problems in some Macs, particularly ones optimized for maximum DRAM performance, such as the Quadra 800 and 900 series.

Composite SIMMs often cause AV Macs to have trouble reading floppy disks, especially 800K disks. What's more, the additional circuitry in the composite SIMMs can cause random memory failures due to higher electrical currents and increased system noise. In short, avoid composite SIMMs.

Memory speeds

When shopping for SIMMs, you'll see specifications that describe their speed — 100ns chips, 80ns chips, and so on. The time required for the Mac to successfully read from or write to a DRAM chip is called its *access time*. For example, the Mac Classic requires DRAMs with an access time of 120 nanoseconds (*ns*, or one billionth of a second). The faster Mac LC III and LC 520 require 80ns DRAMs, while the Quadra 840AV needs 60ns DRAMs. The Power Macs can use 80ns DRAMs, thanks to special caching circuitry. Table 29-2 lists Mac family DRAM speed requirements.

When shopping for Mac memory upgrades, look for chips whose access time equals or is faster than that required for your Mac. You can use DRAMs with a faster access time than your Mac requires. For example, 80ns DRAMs work fine in a Mac IIsi, but they won't improve performance because the Mac IIsi's circuitry is designed for the timing of 100ns DRAMs.

There is one good reason to buy faster DRAMs than your Mac requires: if you upgrade to a faster model, you can use your old SIMMs.

Table 29-2
Memory Speed Limits

Mac Model	*DRAM Speed Requirement*
Plus, SE	150ns
Classic, SE/30, II, IIx, IIcx	120ns
IIsi, LC, LC II, Classic II; Performa 200, 400, 405, 430	100ns
Quadra 800, Centris/Quadra 660AV, Power Mac 7200, 7500, 8500, 9500	70ns
Quadra 840AV	60ns
All others	80ns

Bank deregulation: 72-pin versus 36-pin SIMMs

Beginning with the Mac LC III, Centris series, and Quadra 800, Apple switched from SIMMs containing 36 pins to ones with 72 pins. (The Mac IIfx requires special, 64-pin SIMMs.) The newer SIMM design has several advantages — some practical, others technical. On the practical side, the 72-pin SIMMs are common in the DOS PC world. This means businesses that mix Macs and PCs can also mix SIMMs — a real convenience.

On the technical side, the 72-pin SIMMs eliminated one of the common hassles of Mac RAM expansion — dealing with banks of SIMM slots. Older Macs that used 36-pin SIMMs provided sets of SIMM slots; each set of four was called a *bank*. When expanding memory in such a Mac, you had to take care to fill each bank in a specific way. For example, in a Mac IIci, which had two banks of four slots each, you had to fill all four slots in a bank with SIMMs of the same capacity. And if you mixed SIMM capacities in the two banks, you had to put the higher-capacity SIMMs in Bank B if you used the IIci's built-in video. These arcane rules didn't exactly reinforce the Mac's ease-of-use reputation.

68000-family Macs that use 72-pin SIMMs spare you from this agony. In a Quadra 840AV, for example, there's no difference between a slot and a bank — a slot *is* a bank. So in these Macs, the overly technical "banking regulations" are things of the past. Simply fill as many of the slots as you like, and the Mac will use whatever RAM it finds.

First-generation Power Mac memory upgrades

Memory upgrades for first-generation Power Macs are pretty straightforward. All first-generation Power Mac models use 80ns, 72-pin SIMMs that are identical to the 80ns, 72-pin SIMMs used by 68000-family Macs.

One difference: Because the first-generation Power Macs provide 64-bit memory addressing, you must add two SIMMs at a time. The two SIMMs must be located in physically contiguous slots and their capacities and speeds must be the same — shades of the old "banking regulations" that old Macs impose. First-generation Power Macs can use 4MB, 8MB, 16MB, and 32MB SIMMs.

Second-generation Power Mac memory upgrades

As Chapter 1 stated, second-generation Power Macs introduce a new memory-expansion board: the 168-pin *dual* in-line memory module, or *DIMM*. Also used in some workstations and newer, high-end PCs, DIMMs provide a 64-bit-wide data bus that eliminates the hassle of having to buy SIMMs in pairs and install them in physically contiguous slots. Not that there isn't a benefit to doing so: if you install two identically sized DIMMs, the Power Mac's memory architecture ties them into a 128-bit memory bank, interleaving access to them and providing, Apple says, a 10- to 15-percent performance boost.

DIMMs cost roughly 5 to 10 percent more than equivalent SIMMs, and for a couple of reasons. First, DIMMs require buffer circuitry that SIMMs do not. Second, because DIMM sockets grasp the modules differently than do SIMM sockets, DIMMs must use gold-plated contacts — SIMMs generally use less-expensive tin-lead contacts. Over time, however, as DIMMs begin to sell in greater volumes than SIMMs, the price scales may tip.

Using your existing SIMMs

Newer Technology and SimmSaver Technology, both of Wichita, Kansas, have created DIMM expansion units that allow you to use existing 72-pin SIMMs in a second-generation Power Mac. That's great news for anyone with a healthy investment in SIMMs — at least in theory. At this writing, the second-generation Power Macs are brand new, and it's too early to say whether these devices will be reliable — the high-speed memory subsystems in the second-generation Power Macs could be sensitive to the additional circuitry that a SIMM-to-DIMM adaptor uses.

Installing an upgrade in a second-generation Power Mac

Adding memory upgrades to a Power Mac 7200 or 7500 is a cinch. Flick two plastic latches to remove the top of the case — no screws. Inside, the storage devices and power supply are mounted on a hinged chassis that swings up to allow complete access to the motherboard beneath. (The case also has an additional bay that can accommodate a 3½-inch device, such as a second internal hard drive.)

As for the Power Mac 8500 and 9500, they aren't so easy. In both machines, you must remove the logic board to access the DIMM or VRAM SIMM slots. Unless you're experienced at working with circuit boards and have a steady hand, I recommend having a dealer install upgrades in these machines.

Accessing More Than 8MB on an Older Mac

System 7 enables the Mac to access more than 8MB of memory, but the ROM chips in some Macs — the II, IIx, IIcx, and SE/30 — are not what Apple calls *32-bit clean;* that is, they don't follow all the rules necessary to operate under 32-bit addressing. As a result, these Macs can't access more than 8MB of RAM.

Fortunately, this problem is easy to fix: Simply use the MODE32 control panel. MODE32 was developed by Connectix Corporation, and it has since been licensed by Apple. MODE32 is included with many memory upgrades and is also available free through user groups and on-line services. If you use System 7.1 or a later version, you can also use Apple's 32-Bit System Enabler, also available through on-line services and user groups.

Special considerations for the II and IIx

Also note that the original Mac II and IIx can't use standard 4MB SIMMs. Instead, you need special nine-chip SIMMs that contain a *programmable-array logic* (PAL) chip. If you want to use 4MB SIMMs on an original II or IIx, be sure to specify that you're buying them for this machine.

There's more. In the original Mac II, Bank A can't use SIMMs larger than 2MB. To use 4MB, 8MB, or 16MB SIMMs, you must put them in Bank B. Also, if you're using Bank B, Bank A must be filled with 2MB or smaller SIMMs. (Bank A is the right-hand set of four SIMM slots as you face the front of the Mac.) This is a problem unique to the Mac II; it's caused by problems in the Macintosh II ROMs (MODE32 doesn't fix the problems, either). You can fix this problem by installing the FDHD Apple SuperDrive Upgrade kit, which includes a set of Mac IIx ROMs.

Without this upgrade, the largest memory configuration on a Mac II is 20MB: four 1MB SIMMs in Bank A and four 4MB SIMMs in Bank B. With Mac IIx ROMs, the maximum memory the computer will support is 128MB (eight 16MB SIMMs).

Installing a Memory Upgrade

Installing memory isn't hard, but it is delicate. The memory slots in many Macs use plastic retaining clips that are easily broken. (Most newer Macs provide memory slots with metal clips that are easier to work with and more durable.) A slot with a broken clip won't hold the upgrade tightly enough for reliable operation; you'll probably have to replace the Mac's entire logic board.

Most companies that sell RAM upgrades include informative booklets and even videos that show how to tackle the job. The *Macworld Power User Clinic*'s Installing Upgrades segment will also introduce you to the steps involved. Before you start, heed the static electricity precautions I've outlined previously: If you live in a static-prone area (one where the humidity is very low), consider using an anti-static wrist strap, available through most computer dealers and mail-order houses.

If you're feeling clumsy, have a technician install the memory upgrade for you. It won't cost much, especially compared to replacing a damaged logic board.

A Closer Look at Video Upgrades

Given the Mac's graphical personality, it isn't surprising that some of the most popular upgrades involve video. This section describes Mac video upgrade issues.

Reviewing video basics

I'll start by examining how color Macs display their images. You may recall from previous chapters that the Mac uses a bitmapped display. On a monochrome Mac such as a Classic II, each screen dot, or pixel, corresponds to one bit in the Mac's memory. When a given bit has a value of one, its corresponding pixel is on, or black. When a bit has a value of zero, its pixel is off, or white.

Because a bit can have only one of two values (1 or 0), a bitmapped display that uses one bit per pixel can display only two colors — black or white. Shades of gray can be simulated by *dithering*, in which groups of pixels are combined into patterns. The Mac's gray desktop is an example of a dithered pattern formed by evenly spaced, alternating black and white pixels.

The color and gray-scale difference

The secret to displaying color or true shades of gray is to assign additional bits to each pixel — what many people refer to as increasing the *pixel depth*. Each additional bit lets a color Mac store more information about the pixel. Two bits per pixel can represent four colors. Four bits can represent 16 colors, and eight can represent 256 colors. You can tell a color Mac how many bits to assign each pixel by using the Monitors control panel or, on the Power Mac 7500 and 8500, the Sound & Displays control panel (see Figure 29-2, "Bits and Pixels").

How many bits do you need?

Most older color Macs have color video circuitry that can assign a maximum of eight bits to each pixel, so they can display a maximum of 256 colors or gray shades simultaneously. This is excellent for gray-scale image processing and adequate for creating business presentations and graphs.

The video circuitry in most of today's desktop Macs can assign up to 16 bits to each pixel, allowing for 32,768 colors — ideal for viewing QuickTime movies and adequate for basic image processing.

Most Quadras and all Power Macs can work with up to 24 bits per pixel, allowing for 16.7 million colors — just the ticket for professional-level video, 3-D rendering, electronic photography, and image processing.

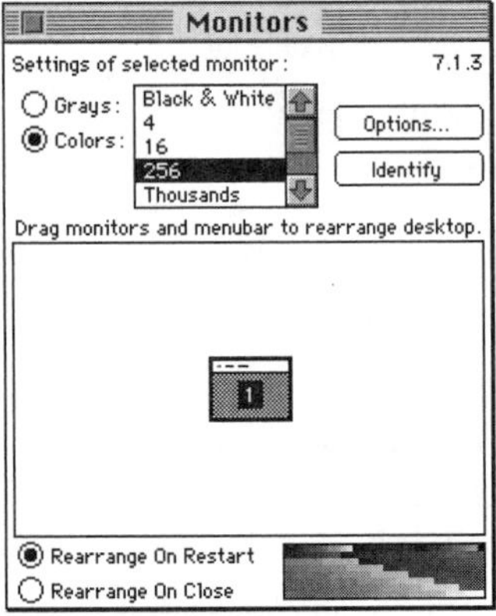

Figure 29-2: Bits and Pixels The Monitors control panel lets you specify how many bits the Mac should assign to each pixel, and whether it should display colors or shades of gray. If you have more than one video board installed (as is the case here), you can also specify where the menu bar should appear.

Expanding Video RAM

Most of today's Macs with built-in color video can accept VRAM expansion boards that allow for the display of more colors on certain monitors. If you have such a Mac, expanding its video RAM is a great (read *cheap*) way to enhance its display capabilities.

To expand video RAM, install SIMMs in the slots provided on the Mac's logic board. Table 29-3 shows what you need for each relevant model.

In previous editions of this book, this would be the time I'd refer you to a gigantic table listing the video-expansion capabilities of each Mac model. Well, these are the mid-1990s, and times have changed. Now, I'll refer you to the *Macworld Power User Clinic* CD and the GURU utility it contains. GURU, created by the gurus at Newer Technology, lists the video-expansion features of every Mac model. It's

Understanding Video Bit Depth

How can only two bits represent four colors; or eight, 256 colors; or 16, thousands of colors? In a color Mac's VRAM, the bits that represent each pixel can be on (assigned a value of 1) or off (assigned a value of 0) in different combinations.

For example, when two bits are assigned to each pixel, four on-off combinations exist — both bits on; both bits off; one bit on, second bit off; and second bit on, first bit off.

When four bits are assigned to each pixel, you get 16 on-off combinations. With eight bits per pixel, you get 256 combinations. Internally, the Mac uses 32 bits to describe colors, giving it the ability to create more than 16 million different hues (see Figure 29-3, "Looking Behind a Color Monitor"). But remember, the number of colors that can actually be *displayed* at once depends on the Mac and monitor size you use.

easier to use than a gigantic table — and better still, when Newer Technology updates it to reflect new Mac models, I'll post it for downloading from the Macworld Online forums on eWorld and America Online. (See Appendix A for details on downloading the free *Macworld Power User Clinic* electronic updates.)

LOOKING BEHIND A COLOR MONITOR

The digital information that represents an image goes through several transformations before appearing on the Mac's screen. Each screen pixel starts life out as a chunk of 32 bits (A)—8 bits define red, 8 define green, and 8 define blue. The remaining 8 bits (the alpha channel) are reserved for special effects that vendors may opt to support. Lines of 32-bit information are queued up in a buffer on the video display board; the lines are separated into 8-bit chunks, and each chunk is sent to a converter that transforms it from digital to analog information (B). The board electrically intensifies each analog signal so that it can drive its corresponding electron gun (C). The higher the intensity, the more saturated the color. The red, green, and blue guns fire their color signal at the corresponding color phosphors on a monitor's screen (D).

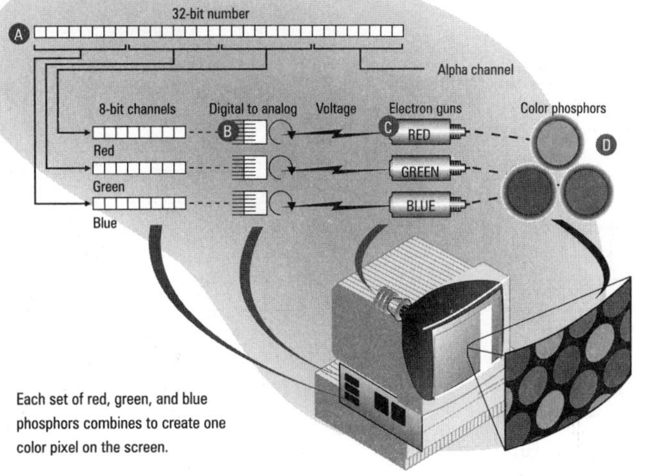

Each set of red, green, and blue phosphors combines to create one color pixel on the screen.

Figure 29-3: Looking Behind a Color Monitor

Video and the IIci and IIsi

For IIci and IIsi owners, there's a price to pay for on-board video. In its 16- and 256-color modes, the on-board video in the IIci and IIsi provides slower performance than does a plug-in video board, which provides its own video memory. That's because the Mac's CPU often has to wait to access memory because the video circuitry accesses the same bank of memory in the course of creating screen images. Two office workers can use the same filing drawer to store different things, but they cannot access the drawer at the same time.

What kind of performance penalty can you expect? In tests performed by Macworld Lab, a Mac IIsi using built-in video was almost twice as slow in 256-color mode as a IIsi using a NuBus video board. This performance penalty doesn't apply to other Macs with built-in video — they provide dedicated video RAM. And because the video circuitry uses part of the Mac's main memory to hold the screen image, less memory is available to run programs — up to 320K less in the 256-color mode.

So what's the tip? To speed up a IIci or IIsi and free up some memory, install a video board.

Table 29-3
VRAM Upgrade Options

Mac Model	*VRAM SIMMs Needed*
LC III (Performa 450), Performa 460 series	One 256K SIMM
Centris 610, 650, Quadra 605, Performa 470 series, LC 475	Two 256K SIMMs
Quadra 700, 800	Two 256K SIMMs or six 256K SIMMs
Quadra 840AV, 900, 950	Four 256K SIMMs
Mac IIvx, Performa 600, Quadra 605, LC 475, Performa 470, LC, LCII (Performa 400, 405, 430), PowerBook Duo Bock	One 512K SIMM
Power Mac 7200/75	One 1MB SIMM
Power Mac 7200/90	Three 1MB SIMMs
Power Mac 7500, 8500	Two 1MB SIMMs

Upgrade or New Machine?

Buying the right upgrade requires pinpointing your present Mac's weaknesses: Do programs take too long to start or documents too long to open? You may need a faster hard disk. After a program starts, does it run sluggishly? What aspects of its operation are sluggish? Do calculations take too long? A math coprocessor or an accelerator or logic board upgrade may be in order. Do color graphics ooze onto the screen? You may need a graphics accelerator. If you answer "all of the above," think about getting a new, faster machine.

Last, but far from least, it's important to assess your financial options to determine which will cost less — upgrading an existing Mac or selling it and buying a new one. In the Mac's early days, upgrading an existing machine usually made better financial sense because the only alternative was a considerably more expensive new machine. As Apple continues to lower prices, the decision isn't as easy. Given the cost of hardware upgrades — and the compatibility and reliability risks that sometimes accompany them — a new machine may be the smarter buy, especially now that the second-generation Power Macs are here. And even if a new machine costs slightly more, the extra features it provides may be worth the cost.

There's another plus to buying a new machine: You get a blank slate that's ready to accept all the upgrade options that will be developed for it. That knowledge will be comforting when the next convoy of new trains rolls out of Apple Station.

CHAPTER 29 CONCEPTS AND TERMS

- You can upgrade an older Mac to give it most, if not all, of the features present in current machines. You can also upgrade a new Mac to make a good thing even better.
- Hardware upgrades fall into two broad categories — ones that make your Mac faster and ones that add new features, such as additional storage or the ability to display more colors.
- The most common upgrades are memory, hard drives, accelerator boards, logic boards, video memory, Ethernet networking boards, sound-recording hardware, and cache memory boards.
- The two basic categories of memory are ROM (*read-only memory,* which permanently holds portions of the Mac's system software) and RAM (*random-access memory,* which holds the programs you're running, open documents, and RAM-based portions of the Mac's system software).
- Some Macs are less receptive to upgrades than others. The Classic, Classic II, Plus, and earlier machines do not contain expansion slots for plug-in boards.
- When you're considering whether to upgrade an older Mac or buy a new one, it's important to pinpoint your Mac's weaknesses and then assess your financial options to determine which will cost less.

32-bit clean
A phrase that refers to software that follows Apple's guidelines for operating in a 32-bit environment. Software that is not 32-bit clean may crash under System 7 if 32-bit addressing is enabled (in the Memory control panel). Also, the ROM chips in older Macs are not 32-bit clean, and thus, limit those models to a maximum of 8MB of RAM. You can work around this limitation by using Connectix's MODE32 extension or, with System 7.1 and later versions, Apple's 32-Bit System Enabler.

access time
The time required, in nanoseconds (billionths of a second abbreviated *ns*), to successfully read to or write from a RAM chip. Some Macs require faster RAM chips than others; the IIci needs 80ns RAM chips, while the Plus and SE can use slower chips. You can use chips with a faster access time than your Mac needs, but they won't speed up processing; the computer's circuitry is designed for chips with a specific access time.

bank
In older Macs (ones that use 36-pin SIMMs), a set of four SIMM slots. In newer Macs (ones that use 72-pin SIMMs), a bank is a single SIMM slot.

bit
Short for *binary digit,* the smallest unit of computer storage. A bit can represent one of two states — 1 (on) or 0 (off).

bus
An internal freeway that carries data between the Mac's memory, its microprocessor, and a variety of support chips. All Macs contain two primary buses — the *address bus*, which carries signals from the microprocessor that specify where in memory data is to be stored or retrieved, and the *data bus*, which carries the data itself. Expansion slots provide electronic on-ramps and off-ramps to this digital freeway.

byte
The workhorse of information storage, equal to 8 bits. One byte can represent any of 256 values, since its 8 bits can be on or off in 256 different combinations. A byte can represent a single character. Storing the alphabet requires 26 bytes.

configuration ROM
A read-only memory chip, present on a NuBus or PDS expansion card, that identifies the card and describes its capabilities.

density
The capacity, in bits (not bytes), of an individual RAM or ROM chip. The most common densities are 256 kilobits and 1 megabit. By tying 25 6-Kbit, 1-Mbit, or 4-Mbit RAM chips together in groups of eight, a SIMM board can store 256K, 1MB, or 4MB, respectively.

DIMM
Short for *dual inline memory module,* the type of memory-expansion cards used by second-generation Power Macs.

DRAM
Pronounced *dee-ram,* an acronym for *dynamic random-access memory,* the most common type of RAM chip in the computer world. The amount of information a DRAM chip can hold is determined by the chip's *density,* which is measured in kilobits.

gigabyte
1,024 megabytes, abbreviated as *GB.*

Killy Clip
A clip, used in some accelerator boards for compact Macs, that straddles the machine's processor and thus taps into the signals that would otherwise be provided by an expansion slot.

kilobit
1,024 bits, abbreviated as *Kbit.* The capacities of individual RAM chips are measured in Kbits.

kilobyte
1,024 bytes, abbreviated as *K.*

megabit
1,048,576 bits, abbreviated as *Mbit.*

megabyte
1024 kilobytes, abbreviated as *MB.*

(continued on the next page)

(continued from previous page)

NuBus slot
An expansion connector named for a standard developed at the Massachusetts Institute of Technology and refined in 1985 by a standards committee comprising representatives from MIT, AT&T, Texas Instruments, Apple, and others. The NuBus standard specifies everything from how expansion boards access the internal bus to such physical details as the distance between the slot's pins.

PCI
Short for *peripheral component interconnect,* the expansion slot scheme used by second-generation Power Macs. PCI slots are faster than their NuBus predecessors.

pixel depth
A phrase often used to describe how many bits are assigned to each screen pixel. For example, a Mac that can display millions of colors can be described as having a 24-bit pixel depth.

processor-direct slot
An expansion connector that allows access to all of the control, address, and data signals of the Mac's micro-processor.

RAM
An acronym for *random-access memory,* the memory that stores the programs you run and the documents you create.

ROM
An acronym for *read-only memory.* The Mac can read the contents of a ROM chip, but it can't change them. A ROM chip's software is in there for good, prerecorded at the factory like the music on a compact disc.

SIMM
An acronym for *Single Inline Memory Module,* the small circuit board that holds individual RAM chips (usually eight). You expand a Mac's memory by adding SIMMs. *Low-profile* SIMMs are the thinnest. *Composite SIMMs* are fatter and may not fit in some Macs.

VRAM
An acronym for *video RAM* — the memory that stores the bits that form a Macintosh screen image.

CHAPTER THIRTY

Picking a Printer

- Surveying the types of printers available for the Macintosh
- Comparing ink-jet and laser printers
- Understanding the difference between PostScript and QuickDraw printers
- Determining what kinds of features your printer needs
- Shopping for a color printer — is one in your future?

No matter how you use the Mac, chances are you need to commit your work to paper. In this chapter, I look at the types of printers available for the Mac, focusing on the most popular category — the laser printer.

What Kind of Printer?

Macintosh printers fall into four general categories. In this section, I give an overview of each category — an introduction that sets the stage for the rest of the chapter.

Dot-matrix printers

Printers such as Apple's ImageWriter II are successors to the typewriter — they create text and graphics by striking an inked ribbon. But where a typewriter uses preformed characters, a dot-matrix printer uses a grid, or matrix, of fine wires located in a *print head* that moves from left to right across the page. By firing these wires in specific patterns, the printer can produce graphics and text in any typestyle. Where print quality is concerned, dot-matrix printers are on the bottom of the totem pole. However, because they're impact printers, they can print on carbon or carbonless multipage business forms, such as invoices — a feat the other printers discussed here can't match. Dot-matrix printers are also ideal for printing mailing labels because they can accept continuous-feed paper stock (paper whose sheets are attached to each other, accordion-style).

Ink-jet printers

Apple's StyleWriter series and Hewlett-Packard's DeskWriter are higher-class cousins of dot-matrix printers. Instead of using an inked ribbon and print wires to produce images, an ink-jet printer uses several dozen microscopic nozzles that spray extremely fine streams of ink at the paper. Besides making the printer much quieter than its dot-matrix counterparts, this scheme allows for much finer print quality, or *resolution*. For example, the ImageWriter II has a maximum resolution of 144 dots per inch (dpi), while the current members of the StyleWriter family can print at 720 by 360 dpi. (The original StyleWriter and StyleWriter II printed 360 dpi.)

Laser printers

Laser printers use photocopier-like mechanisms to produce text and graphics with resolutions of 300 dpi and up. Laser printers are much faster than dot-matrix or ink-jet units — even the least expensive models can print up to several pages per minute. Laser printers are also the preferred units for desktop publishing and proofing because their resolution is high enough to accurately render the subtleties of typographic fonts and to print newspaper-quality halftones of scanned images.

Color printers

These specialized scribes use a variety of complex techniques to apply colored ink, dye, or wax to paper — usually to special paper, at that, although plain-paper color printers are now available. Low-end color printers are used for printing attention-getting overhead transparencies and business graphics. High-end units are often used for proofing color publications, scanned images, and illustrations that will be printed on four-color printing presses.

For critical color publishing applications, however, most publishing pros still rely on photographic *Matchprints* produced by color-separation service bureaus. But because such prints often cost $50 to $100 each, many publishers use color printers first to look for obvious errors in color balance or placement.

Ink-jet Details

As mentioned earlier, ink-jet printers are capable of much higher output resolution than dot-matrix units. But ink-jet output still isn't in the laser league (see Figure 30-1 "Print Output Comparisons"). Up close, even the naked eye can discern sloppy character edges created by ink seeping into the paper's fibers as it dries. Scanned images and large black areas have a mottled look. You can minimize these flaws by photocopying printed pages, but handle them gently: ink-jet output can smear in its first few seconds of life.

The

The

The

Figure 30-1: Print Output Comparisons Output samples from three types of printers, enlarged 200 percent. Top: Ink-jet output; middle: 300-dpi output; bottom: 600-dpi laser output. The high resolution of ink-jet and laser printers enables them to more accurately render the subtleties of true typographic fonts. But note the fuzzy-edged quality of ink-jet output caused by the ink spreading into the paper's fibers as it dries.

Today's ink-jet printers no longer require special paper, as did some pioneering models of the mid-80s, but they're still more finicky than lasers. They can't handle heavy card stocks, for instance, and they don't always print envelopes well. And output quality varies dramatically depending on the quality of paper you use. You also wait longer to see it; most personal laser printers can churn out several pages in the time it takes an ink-jet to produce one.

Comparing StyleWriters and DeskWriters

Apple's StyleWriter family and Hewlett-Packard's DeskWriter are popular Mac-specific desktop ink-jet printers that produce 300-dpi or sharper output.

DeskWriters are equipped with a LocalTalk connector, enabling them to be shared on a network. (DeskWriters manufacturered prior to May 1990 lack a LocalTalk connector.) By comparison, the StyleWriter models connect via a serial cable to the Mac's modem or printer port. They can still be shared on a network, however, thanks to drivers that incorporate what Apple calls GrayShare — or, for color-capable StyleWriters, ColorShare.

If you're connecting to a LocalTalk network, connect the StyleWriter to your Mac's modem port, since the printer port is used for LocalTalk connections. (If you have a modem, you might want a port splitter box, which lets you connect multiple serial devices to the modem port and switch between them.) If you're using Ethernet, you can connect the StyleWriter to the modem or printer port. You then use the Chooser's Setup button to turn printer sharing on (see Figure 30-2 "Share that StyleWriter").

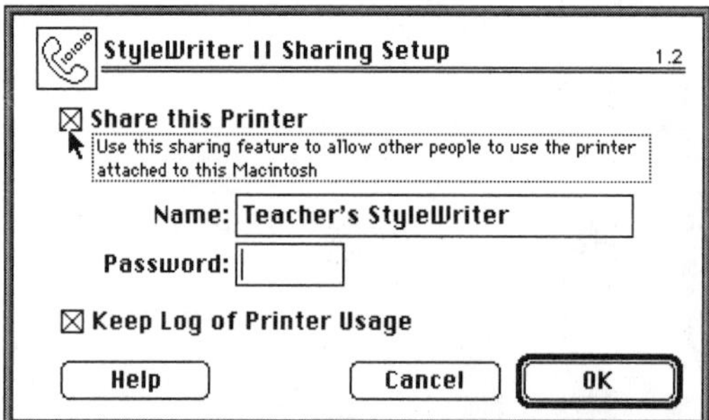

Figure 30-2: Share that StyleWriter To share an Apple StyleWriter printer on a network, click the Setup button in the Chooser (not shown here) to display the Sharing Setup dialog box. Then check the Share this Printer box. If you like, you can give the printer a name that will appear in the Chooser windows of other Macs on the network, and a password that must be typed before other users can print.

GrayShare and ColorShare work much like System 7's file sharing; just as activating file sharing turns your Mac into a file server, activating printer sharing turns it into a print server. And you know how your Mac slows down when its hard drive is being accessed over the network? It happens with printer sharing, too — in spades. When someone prints to the StyleWriter connected to your Mac, it's *your* Mac that has to crunch through the document and control the printer. During the print job, you'll notice distracting delays between keystrokes and jerky mouse movement and your Mac divides its time between you and someone else's print job. That's the price you pay for sharing.

The Hewlett-Packard DeskWriter 540 can be shared on a network without slowing down the Mac it's attached to. The DeskWriter 540's resolution is 600 by 300 dots — it prints 600 dots horizontally and 300 vertically.

Their slow, light-duty mechanisms don't exactly make the StyleWriter and DeskWriter ideal workgroup printers. But sharing can be useful in home offices containing more than one Mac (maybe a desktop machine and a PowerBook) and in classrooms.

The latest StyleWriters

In the middle of 1995, Apple revamped its StyleWriter line, adding some new models and updating the StyleWriter's driver software. The latest drivers provide the desktop printer icons and print-queue windows that debuted in System 7.5's QuickDraw GX, but don't require you to install GX, which has stiff memory requirements and minimal application support. For details on the new drivers, see the Chapter 31 section "The wonders of the desktop printer icon."

Here's what the StyleWriter family tree looks like:

- The StyleWriter 1200 is the least expensive model; it prints in black and white only. It's the successor to the StyleWriter and StyleWriter II but provides 720 by 360 resolution.
- The StyleWriter 2200 is a compact, color-capable StyleWriter that can run on batteries. It's discussed in the PowerBook Angle box, "Printers for PowerBooks," later in this chapter.
- The Color StyleWriter 2400 is a color ink-jet that prints 720 by 380 dpi. The 2400 provides one black cartridge and one tricolor cartridge containing cyan, yellow, and magenta inks. If you don't need color, you can yank both cartridges and replace them with Apple's High-Performance Ink Cartridge. This black-only cartridge sports more ink nozzles than the smaller cartridges, a characteristic that allows the print head to spew more ink during each pass across the page, improving speed dramatically.
- Color StyleWriter Pro is Apple's top-of-the-line ink-jet printer. It provides four separate ink cartridges — one each for cyan, yellow, magenta, and black. As a result, it can print more pages between ink refills — roughly 300 pages, compared to 100 pages for the Color StyleWriter 2400.

Which StyleWriter is for you? For black-and-white work on a budget, you can't beat the StyleWriter 1200. If you can spend a bit more, however, consider the Color StyleWriter 2400 — it's every bit as good a printer for black-and-white work, and it has the added benefit of being a first-rate color printer, too.

Laser Printer Details

The marriage of Mac and laser printer is a happy one — even if it does require a hefty dowry. Lasers cost less than ever, but finding the perfect partner still isn't easy. Today's laser printer shopper faces a raft of specifications and technical issues. In this section, I examine the technical processes behind laser printers and present the issues you'll want to consider when shopping for one.

Mechanics and electronics

A laser printer's output results from a collaboration between an engine and a controller. The engine is the mechanical half of the duo; it works much like a photocopier. The engine helps determine print quality and speed, and it defines how well the printer can handle different kinds of paper, such as envelopes. The controller determines the printer's typographical features — the range and quality of the fonts, styles, and sizes — as well as its compatibility with Mac applications and with other computers.

The controller also guides the engine's imaging mechanism, telling it where to apply the *toner* powder that forms the image. And because describing the appearance of a page requires complex calculations, the controller also helps determine printer speed. In nearly all of today's Mac-compatible printers, the controller is housed within the printer's case and contains its own microprocessor and memory chips. As I'll explain shortly, however, some low-end printers use the Mac's processor and memory as their controller.

Because the controller defines the printer's overall capabilities, your quest for the perfect printer should begin with a look at its brains.

Watch your language — PostScript versus QuickDraw

The primary difference between printer controllers lies in the type of commands they respond to. *PostScript* controllers use commands written in PostScript, a programming language created by Adobe Systems for describing the appearance of pages. A PostScript controller is a powerful computer in itself. It typically has 2MB of memory or more, a microprocessor, and ROM chips containing the PostScript language *interpreter* as well as a selection of *font outlines*, mathematical formulas the controller can use to create text in virtually any size and orientation.

Examples of Apple PostScript printers include Apple's original LaserWriter and LaserWriter Plus, the LaserWriter IINT and IINTX, the LaserWriter Select 310 and 360, the Personal LaserWriter 320, the LaserWriter 4/600PS and 16/600PS, and the LaserWriter Pro series. Texas Instruments, HP, and QMS are among the third-party firms that offer PostScript machines for the Mac world.

Printers for PowerBooks

I've worked with several portable printers and found that portability and capability are at opposite ends of the see-saw. The better the printer, the larger and heavier it is — and the less likely you are to want to lug it around. The smaller the printer, the slower and more limited it is — and the less likely you are to want to use it. It's an adventure in compromise, and it's difficult to find a winner.

The WriteMove II

For portability, you can't beat the GCC Technologies WriteMove II. Cut a box of aluminum foil in half vertically for a rough idea of how small this 2.5-pound puppy is. A sock would make a nice carrying case.

The WriteMove II runs on a rechargeable battery and also includes a cleverly designed AC adaptor, whose prongs fold down so as not to puncture your briefcase. Technically, the printer isn't an ink-jet — it uses a 360-dpi thermal-wax transfer mechanism built by Citizen. The thermal-wax output doesn't smear when wet, and large black areas don't mottle the paper the way liquid ink does. The WriteMove II's ink ribbon is only a bit larger than a microcassette tape. The printer supports a multistrike ribbon that you can use until it's threadbare, or a single-strike film ribbon that produces dark, crisp output. (Do stock up, though: the printer goes through ribbons like a gift wrap department.)

The WriteMove II lacks a sheet feeder: you have to hand-feed each page, and properly aligning the top of the page can be cumbersome. Also, this printer is s-l-o-w. But there's nothing smaller — and its film-ribbon output is superb.

Hewlett-Packard DeskWriter 310 and 320

The DeskWriter 300 series machines are interesting birds. In their most portable configurations, they measure 2.5 inches high by 12 inches wide by 5.75 inches deep. They also hold just one sheet of paper at a time; you must hand-feed the printer for multipage documents. An optional sheet feeder accepts up to 60 sheets. The DeskWriter 310 accepts an optional color kit. The 310's resolution is 300 dpi; the 320's is 600 by 300 dpi.

The Apple Portable StyleWriter

The now-discontinued Apple Portable StyleWriter is a slightly repackaged version of a battery-powered Canon ink-jet, the BJC-10sx. At an almost portly 4.5 pounds, the Portable StyleWriter is nearly twice as heavy as the WriteMove II. A sheet feeder, handy for multipage jobs, is an extra-cost option. The Portable StyleWriter can't print in color — in fact, it can't even print in gray-scale. Think of it as a text-only printer.

The Apple StyleWriter 2200

This machine replaced the Portable StyleWriter, and it's not bad. It prints 720 by 360 dpi in black and white, and 360 by 360 dpi in color. It weighs 3.1 pounds — more than a pound less than the Portable StyleWriter it replaced — includes a built-in 30-sheet paper feeder, and accepts an optional rechargeable battery that prints roughly 200 pages on a charge.

Table 30-1
PostScript versus Non-PostScript

PostScript	***Non-PostScript***
Processing occurs in printer, requiring complex controller, but freeing Mac for other tasks	Processing occurs in Macintosh, allowing simpler, less-expensive controllers, but requiring Mac memory and hard disk space
Many font outlines stored in printer's ROM	All fonts stored on Macintosh hard disk
Background printing built into the Mac's system software	Not all QuickDraw printers support spoolers or work with the Mac's background printing feature
Printer can be shared by Macs and DOS PCs	Limited Mac sharing capabilities; no PC support
Large selection of fonts	Currently a smaller selection of fonts unless you use Adobe Type Manager
Controller can shadow text, and print along an irregular path	Some effects are not available or are application-dependent
PostScript printers are ideal proofing devices for imagesetter output	Spacing of some fonts may not match PostScript counterparts, making proofs less accurate
Can use applications that generate PostScript effects	PostScript-specific applications often produce inferior output
Most PostScript printers can also emulate other printers, such as the HP LaserJet	QuickDraw printers generally have no emulation features
Printer can be used with other PostScript-supporting computers	Printer must be used with Macintosh computers

QuickDraw-based printers use the Mac as the controller, so they don't contain the complex controllers that PostScript printers require. And because QuickDraw printers make the Mac do more of the work, they generally cost less. But they often do less, too (see Table 30-1 for ten points of comparison). Now that GCC Technologies has yanked its venerable Personal LaserPrinter series off the market, Apple is the only company selling a QuickDraw-based laser printer: the Personal LaserWriter 300, a fine little laser that can be had for about $600. (Incidentally, many of the technical details behind QuickDraw laser printers apply to other types of QuickDraw-based printers, such as ImageWriters, StyleWriters, and Hewlett-Packard DeskWriters.)

Comparing font-handling capabilities

Another important differentiating factor between printers concerns the techniques they use to produce text. Outline fonts combined with PostScript's wide array of graphics-manipulation commands give PostScript printers tremendous typographic versatility. Need a 10-foot-high *W* filled with a checkerboard pattern? Want to produce a record label with the musician's name set in a circle, with a shadow behind it? Chores like these are a cinch for PostScript.

As I describe in the next chapter, you can also supplement a PostScript printer's built-in, or *resident*, fonts with downloadable fonts, whose outlines are stored in separate files within your System Folder and downloaded to the printer's memory before printing.

QuickDraw printers can use TrueType fonts or, when paired with the Adobe Type Manager utility, Type 1 PostScript fonts. Although these printers use outline fonts, they still aren't as typographically talented as their PostScript cousins. The problem isn't the fonts, but the underlying language that positions them on the page: QuickDraw lacks PostScript's wide array of graphics operators, and because of that, QuickDraw printers still can't produce all the special text effects of their PostScript competitors.

Apple's QuickDraw GX, an improved version of the basic text-and-graphics routines responsible for everything you see on the Mac's screen, gives QuickDraw printers dramatically enhanced typographic capabilities. But in order for many of these capabilities to become realities, application developers must adapt their programs to take advantage of QuickDraw GX.

Although these developments give QuickDraw printers a shot in the typographic arm, QuickDraw printers still deliver inferior results with PostScript-oriented drawing programs such as Macromedia FreeHand and Adobe Illustrator — unless you use PostScript emulation software such as TeleTypesetting Company's T-Script (see the Background box "How to Print PostScript on a QuickDraw Printer").

They don't share alike

The differences between printer-driving languages are also important if you plan to share a printer with other computers. Since QuickDraw is confined to Macs, you can't use a QuickDraw printer with a DOS/Windows machine.

Sharing a QuickDraw printer on a network generally isn't as easy or convenient. By contrast, every PostScript printer contains a LocalTalk connector and built-in print server software, which enables it to be used with up to 32 Macs (and PCs equipped with LocalTalk boards). A growing number of printers include or accept optional Ethernet interfaces — ideal for printing scanned images, which tend to bog down a LocalTalk network.

How to Print PostScript on a QuickDraw Printer

PostScript emulation software lets you overcome the language barrier between QuickDraw and PostScript. A PostScript emulator resides on your Mac's hard disk and acts as an intermediary between your application programs and a non-PostScript printer. After installing the emulator, you use the Chooser desk accessory to select its driver. Thereafter, when you issue a Print command, the emulator intercepts and saves on disk the PostScript instructions that would otherwise be sent to a PostScript printer. The emulator's PostScript interpreter then takes over, using the Mac's processor and memory to translate the PostScript into instructions your printer can understand.

Several PostScript emulation packages used to be available for the Mac, but only one has endured: TeleTypesetting's T-Script. It supports dozens of output devices, from dot-matrix printers to ink-jets to lasers. One of the most interesting features it provides is the ability to act as a print server for other Macs on a network. You can use another Mac's Chooser to select the emulator's driver and then print as though you were printing to a LaserWriter. The emulator receives the PostScript instructions over the network and then processes the job.

To get PostScript output from a Color StyleWriter Pro or Color StyleWriter 2400, use GDT Softworks' StyleScript. StyleScript is an actual Adobe PostScript interpreter that GDT has tweaked to work specifically with the Color StyleWriters. Note you'll need 8MB minimum free memory and up to 12MB for large PostScript images.

A PostScript emulator can be a remarkably inexpensive way to get PostScript output, but there are other prices to pay. The emulator's performance is dependent on your Mac's. A Quadra-class machine with a math coprocessor chip or a Power Mac delivers acceptable performance, but lesser Macs will tax your patience. And there's always the chance that a complex PostScript document won't print: emulators have historically had more compatibility problems than PostScript printers, including PostScript clones.

Another PostScript plus is its industrywide support. PostScript is available on output devices ranging from laser printers to typesetters, and it's supported by a wide range of computers. PostScript's popularity lets you move files between printers or computers while retaining file formatting. For example, you can print proofs of a document on a 300 dots per inch (dpi) PostScript laser printer, and then take your file to a service bureau for output on a 2540-dpi PostScript imagesetter. Similarly, you can transfer a document created using the Mac version of PageMaker to a DOS PC running PageMaker or QuarkXPress, and its line breaks and character spacing will remain intact.

Tip: Microsoft Windows supports and includes TrueType outline fonts. Now that TrueType is firmly entrenched in both the Mac and Windows worlds, exchanging documents and retaining their formatting is easier. If you're creating a document that you know will end up on the other platform, use only TrueType fonts. You're likely to have less reformatting to do.

How Printers Use Their Internal Memory

Every page that you're printing must ultimately be described as a *bitmap* — an array of bits, each corresponding to one dot on a page. A full-page bitmap for a 300-dots-per-inch printer is roughly 1MB in size. All that data has to be stored somewhere. In PostScript printers, it's stored in the controller's *page buffer*, an area of printer memory. In QuickDraw printers, it's generally stored on the Mac's hard disk and transferred to the printer during the print job.

Printers that use outline fonts must translate those outlines into bitmaps in the type sizes needed for the page you're currently printing. Because some character bitmaps will probably be needed again later, PostScript printers store them in an area of memory called the *font cache*. Retrieving a character bitmap from the font cache is much faster than creating a new one from the outline.

On a PostScript printer, a fixed amount of printer memory is reserved for the font cache. The Mac's TrueType outline font technology creates a font cache in the Mac's memory.

Other PostScript Issues

All PostScript printers are compatible with the Mac, but there can be significant differences among printers. Some questions worth asking include the following.

Does it use an Adobe interpreter?

To avoid the cost of licensing PostScript interpreters from Adobe Systems, some manufacturers have developed their own. Some of these so-called PostScript *clones* provide faster performance, but PostScript is a complex language and incompatibilities can arise, especially if you print complex illustrations created with programs such as FreeHand or Illustrator. If you print typographically simple documents, such as memos, manuscripts, and legal contracts, you may never encounter problems. (Of course, if you print simple documents, you may not need a PostScript printer to begin with.)

I used to have serious reservations about PostScript clones, but today's machines have fewer problems than their predecessors. In the past, PostScript clones had major problems handling Type 1 downloadable fonts, the downloadable font format used by Adobe and many other font developers. Type 1 fonts contain instructions that the printer's controller uses to optimize the appearance of each character at a given size. These instructions, called *hints*, are encrypted, and clone developers were loath to crack the code, fearing lawsuits from Adobe. Adobe has since published the Type 1 specifications, however, so today's PostScript clone interpreters can, well, take the hints. The latest high-resolution engines help sharpen their text output, too.

Is it a Level 1 or Level 2 interpreter?

Unless you're considering an older used printer, this isn't an issue anymore — all printer manufacturers I'm aware of have adopted Level 2 PostScript. Level 2 PostScript offers several advantages over Level 1. Among other things, it uses a printer's memory more efficiently; it provides image decompression features that reduce printing times; and it allows for faster print jobs by storing, or *caching*, elements that repeat on each page. Level 2 also provides significant features for color printing, including support for multiple *color rendering dictionaries* — sets of data that tell a printer how to produce various colors.

For a couple of years, most of Level 2's advantages were only theoretical — the Mac's printer driver didn't take advantage of them. Now that Apple and Adobe have shipped the LaserWriter 8 driver (also known as PSPrinter), the Mac can take better advantage of Level 2 machines. I have a lot more to say about LaserWriter 8 in the next chapter.

How much memory is provided?

Most PostScript laser printers provide at least 2MB to 5MB of memory, divided into three areas: the page buffer, the font cache, and *virtual memory*, or *VM* — general work space that also holds downloadable fonts. (By the way, virtual memory as it applies to PostScript printers is unrelated to System 7's virtual memory feature.) The font cache holds the bitmaps for characters that have already been printed on a page. When the font cache fills — which can happen when you print a document with a large mix of type styles and sizes — the controller must purge some of the character bitmaps it has laboriously created and then create the new ones it needs.

If the purged characters are needed again, the controller must re-create their bit maps from the font's outlines. The more memory a printer provides, the larger its font cache and VM. A larger font cache means faster performance, and more VM means more room for downloadable fonts. Many printers also accept memory-expansion options. In many cases, adding memory improves the printer's capabilities — it may let you print using higher resolution setting, for example, or may enable a resolution-enhancement feature.

Does it have a RISC chip?

Original PostScript controllers used 68000-family processors, but today's machines use high-speed *RISC* (reduced instruction-set computer) processors whose internal architecture is streamlined for top performance. If you print complex documents containing illustrations, scanned images, and scads of type sizes and styles — elements that make a controller sweat — avoid buying an older, 68000-family based machine such as an Apple LaserWriter IINT or IINTX.

TrueType and Multiple Master Fonts Need More Memory

No matter which PostScript printer you choose, if you plan to print TrueType or Adobe Multiple Master fonts, consider a model that provides (or can be upgraded to) at least 3MB of memory. Just as today's larger programs demand more memory from a Mac, the latest font technologies require more memory in a printer. And to think that the February 1985 issue of *Macworld* magazine called the original LaserWriter's 1.5MB "an enormous amount."

How does it handle TrueType fonts?

Before an outline font can be printed (or displayed, for that matter), the outline must be translated into a bitmap of the point size required. This job is performed by a piece of software called a *rasterizer*, also called a *scaler*. Adobe's Adobe Type Manager utility is the best-known rasterizer; Apple's TrueType also contains its own scaler. A PostScript printer performs its own rasterizing; with QuickDraw printers, the Mac does the rasterizing.

Although PostScript and TrueType both rely on outline fonts, each uses a different format of outline and thus requires its own rasterizer. Because of these dueling font formats, the Mac must perform some extra effort to print a TrueType font on a PostScript printer (see Figure 30-3, "Printing TrueType Fonts," and the Backgrounder box "TrueType Fonts in a PostScript World"). Don't feel like you have to memorize every step described in this box — there isn't a quiz at the end of this chapter. What's important to remember is this: If you plan to frequently print TrueType fonts on a PostScript printer, look for a printer containing the TrueType rasterizer.

Can it accept a hard disk?

Some printers can accept an optional SCSI hard disk. A hard disk attached to a printer stores downloadable fonts, making them available to all machines on a network and eliminating downloading time (20–30 seconds per font). A hard disk also acts as an extension to the font cache, which further improves printer performance.

Can it imitate other printers?

Older software for DOS machines and other computers may not support PostScript, but it generally does support letter-quality printers or Hewlett-Packard LaserJets. Most PostScript printers provide emulation modes that enable them to respond to commands for such printers. If emulation modes are important to you, look for a printer that provides *automatic emulation sensing*. Emulation sensing enables a

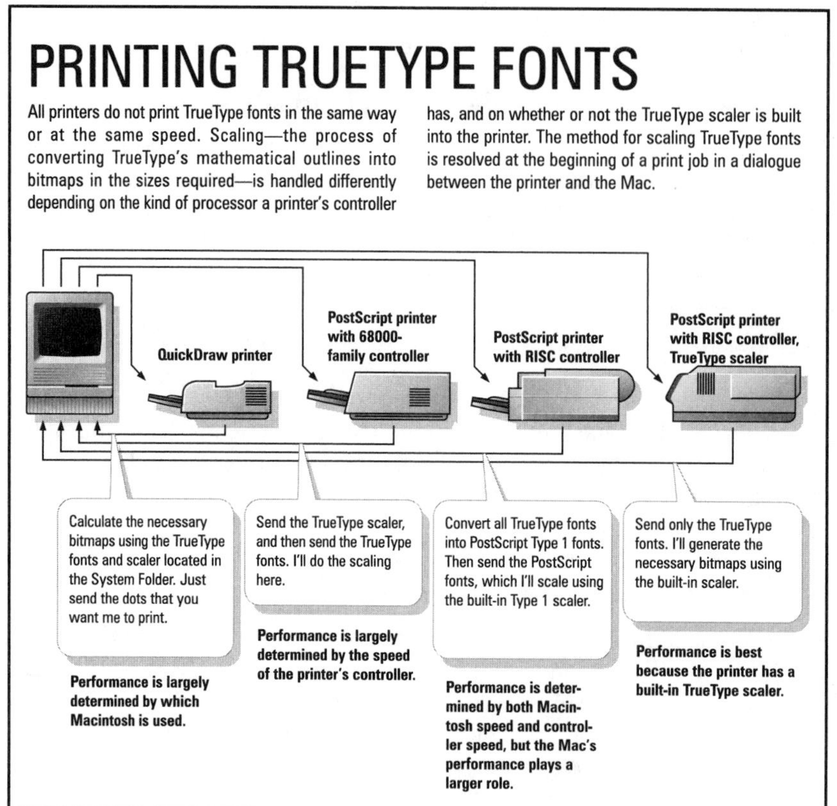

PRINTING TRUETYPE FONTS
All printers do not print TrueType fonts in the same way or at the same speed. Scaling—the process of converting TrueType's mathematical outlines into bitmaps in the sizes required—is handled differently depending on the kind of processor a printer's controller has, and on whether or not the TrueType scaler is built into the printer. The method for scaling TrueType fonts is resolved at the beginning of a print job in a dialogue between the printer and the Mac.
QuickDraw printer
PostScript printer with 68000-family controller
PostScript printer with RISC controller
PostScript printer with RISC controller, TrueType scaler
Calculate the necessary bitmaps using the TrueType fonts and scaler located in the System Folder. Just send the dots that you want me to print.
Performance is largely determined by which Macintosh is used.
Send the TrueType scaler, and then send the TrueType fonts. I'll do the scaling here.
Performance is largely determined by the speed of the printer's controller.
Convert all TrueType fonts into PostScript Type 1 fonts. Then send the PostScript fonts, which I'll scale using the built-in Type 1 scaler.
Performance is determined by both Macintosh speed and controller speed, but the Mac's performance plays a larger role.
Send only the TrueType fonts. I'll generate the necessary bitmaps using the built-in scaler.
Performance is best because the printer has a built-in TrueType scaler.

Figure 30-3: Printing TrueType Fonts

printer to switch into an emulation mode when it determines that incoming data isn't PostScript code. Without emulation sensing, you need to flick a switch or use a printer's front-panel buttons to switch between PostScript and emulation modes.

What ports does it provide?

All PostScript printers provide a LocalTalk port for connecting to Macs and LocalTalk-equipped IBM PCs (and compatibles). Most PostScript printers also provide RS-232C serial ports; some also have Centronics parallel ports — the dominant printer port in the IBM world. To use the printer with computers lacking LocalTalk, you need one of the latter two ports. A growing number of PostScript printers also include or accept optional Ethernet connectors for tapping into high-speed networks. Ethernet's extra performance is particularly helpful if you're printing large scanned images, a job that involves shuttling lots of data over the network.

TrueType Fonts in a PostScript World

To print a TrueType font, the LaserWriter driver (or the PSPrinter driver) and a PostScript printer must perform a multistep process (see Figure 30-3).

First, the LaserWriter driver looks in the printer to see if the required fonts are located in its RAM or ROM or on a hard disk attached to the printer. If the fonts are found, the job proceeds. If the fonts aren't present in any of those places, the LaserWriter driver looks in the System Folder for downloadable PostScript fonts. If they're found, they're downloaded and the job continues.

If the downloadable PostScript fonts aren't in the System Folder, the LaserWriter driver looks in the System Folder for TrueType outline fonts. Then the LaserWriter printer driver queries the printer to determine whether it contains the TrueType scaler. If the printer contains the TrueType scaler, the Mac simply downloads the TrueType outline to the printer, whose scaler handles the rasterizing. This is the most efficient method of printing a TrueType font on a PostScript printer; alas, not all printers contain the TrueType rasterizer. (Apple's latest PostScript printers do, as do a growing number of third-party printers.)

If the printer lacks the TrueType scaler and its controller uses a 68000-family processor, the Mac downloads the TrueType scaler to the printer's memory, essentially teaching the printer how to handle TrueType fonts. The font outlines themselves are downloaded next.

If the printer lacks the TrueType scaler and has a RISC-based controller, the Mac has even more work to do. The TrueType scaler won't run on a RISC-based printer, so the Mac must convert the TrueType font to a Type 1 PostScript font and then download the converted font. This is often the most time-consuming method of printing a TrueType font on a PostScript printer.

Does it accept a fax modem board?

Several printers can accept an optional PostScript fax modem board. With a fax board, you can send documents to any standard fax machine; if you send them to another printer equipped with a PostScript fax board, the documents are printed at full resolution, using fonts present in the destination printer — no fax jaggies. The received fax looks as if you printed it from a Mac on your own network. It's remote printing without the snail-like performance provided by modems and software such as Apple Remote Access. Note that the board doesn't give the printer scanning capabilities, so you can't send faxes of hard copy documents.

Print Engine Considerations

A print engine forms images by using a series of evenly spaced parallel lines that are painted on a photosensitive drum or belt by a laser beam or some other light source (see Figure 30-4, "Inside an Engine").

With the bitmapped image of the page as a guide, the engine uses a light source (usually a laser) to expose its photosensitive drum or belt (A). In a write-black engine (shown here), the areas to be printed have an electrical charge that attracts toner as the drum rotates past the toner compartment (B). In a write-white engine, the areas not to be printed have a charge that repels toner. Because written-to areas are not completely solid, write-white engines produce more solid blacks (C). When the drum meets the developing cylinder (D), charged toner particles are attracted to areas of the drum that have an opposite charge (E). An electrically charged wire attracts toner from the drum onto the paper (F). After a discharge brush removes all electrical charges from the paper (G), heat rollers fuse toner to the paper (H). A cleaning blade removes any remaining toner from the drum (I), and a second wire neutralizes the drum's electrical charge (J) so that it may be written to again.

Figure 30-4: Inside an Engine

Resolution

All laser printers used to produce 300-dpi output. Thanks to improvements in print engines and the plastic toner that they apply, 600 dpi is the new baseline. Dataproducts offers 800-dpi machines, and Lexmark's Optra line and Xante's Accel-a-Writer line hold the current record with their 1200 dpi. (Note that some printers may require you to add to their base memory configurations in order to reach their resolution potential.) These higher resolutions make for a more

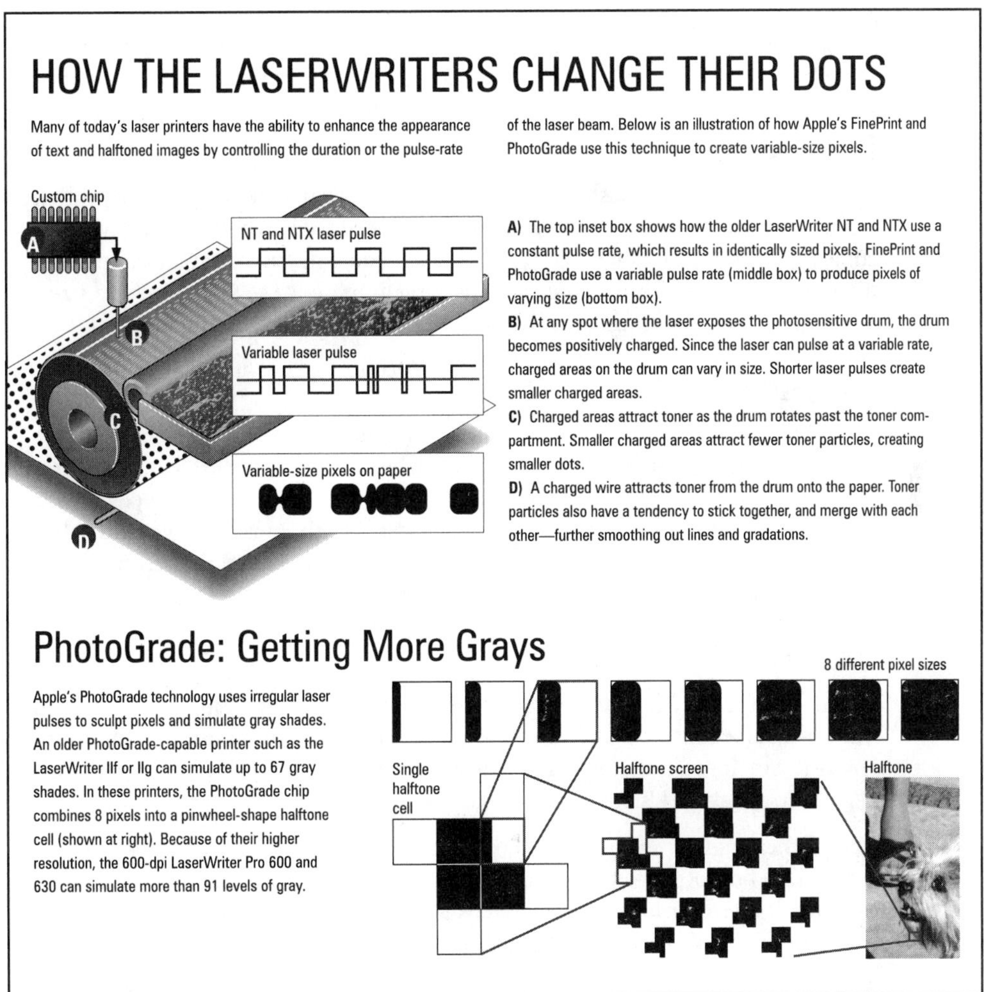

HOW THE LASERWRITERS CHANGE THEIR DOTS
Many of today's laser printers have the ability to enhance the appearance of text and halftoned images by controlling the duration or the pulse-rate of the laser beam. Below is an illustration of how Apple's FinePrint and PhotoGrade use this technique to create variable-size pixels.
Custom chip
A
B
C
D
NT and NTX laser pulse
Variable laser pulse
Variable-size pixels on paper
A) The top inset box shows how the older LaserWriter NT and NTX use a constant pulse rate, which results in identically sized pixels. FinePrint and PhotoGrade use a variable pulse rate (middle box) to produce pixels of varying size (bottom box).
B) At any spot where the laser exposes the photosensitive drum, the drum becomes positively charged. Since the laser can pulse at a variable rate, charged areas on the drum can vary in size. Shorter laser pulses create smaller charged areas.
C) Charged areas attract toner as the drum rotates past the toner compartment. Smaller charged areas attract fewer toner particles, creating smaller dots.
D) A charged wire attracts toner from the drum onto the paper. Toner particles also have a tendency to stick together, and merge with each other—further smoothing out lines and gradations.
PhotoGrade: Getting More Grays
Apple's PhotoGrade technology uses irregular laser pulses to sculpt pixels and simulate gray shades. An older PhotoGrade-capable printer such as the LaserWriter IIf or IIg can simulate up to 67 gray shades. In these printers, the PhotoGrade chip combines 8 pixels into a pinwheel-shape halftone cell (shown at right). Because of their higher resolution, the 600-dpi LaserWriter Pro 600 and 630 can simulate more than 91 levels of gray.
8 different pixel sizes
Single halftone cell
Halftone screen
Halftone

Figure 30-5: How the LaserWriters Change Their Dots

versatile printer — besides being able to crank out spreadsheets and memos, a high-resolution printer can also produce camera-ready output for in-house newsletters and low-budget catalogs and directories.

But resolution specs don't tell the entire story. Many manufacturers supplement sharper engines with resolution-enhancement schemes: examples include Apple's PhotoGrade and FinePrint, Lexmark's PictureGrade, and Hewlett-Packard's Resolution Enhancement Technology, which started the trend. These technologies vary in implementation and effectiveness, but conceptually, they're identical: each plays games with the printer's laser beam to finely control the size and position of each dot of toner, thereby improving sharpness (see Figure 30-5 "How the LaserWriters

Change Their Dots"). Technologies such as PhotoGrade and PictureGrade enhance the look of scanned images and gray shades, while Apple's FinePrint and HP's RET sharpen text and object-oriented graphics.

Engine speed

Most laser engines can push paper at a pace of between 4 and 20 pages per minute (ppm). In many cases, however, you see these speeds only when printing multiple copies of the same document or very simple documents, such as manuscripts in the Courier font. With documents containing graphics or several fonts and sizes, performance is often limited by the printer's controller, not its engine.

Engine life

If you churn out hundreds of copies of documents or share a printer in a busy office, you need an engine designed to take a beating and keep on feeding. Two specifications refer to an engine's durability — *engine life*, measured in pages; and *duty cycle*, the number of pages you can print per month. Heavy-duty printers have duty cycles in the 40,000-page-per-month range. If you exceed the recommended duty cycle rating, you're asking for mechanical trouble.

Ease of feeding

You need to replenish your printer's toner supply every few thousand pages or so. For no-fuss feeding, you can't beat the single-cartridge system used in Canon-built engines, which you'll find in printers from Apple, Canon, QMS, Hewlett-Packard, and others. (Lexmark's engines are also easy to set up.)

Many other engines use multipart consumables kits, which may comprise a toner cartridge, a photoconductor belt or drum, and a small bottle that holds used toner. You install these components separately, a job that isn't difficult, but that can lead to messy spills if you aren't careful.

Alas, the disposable cartridges used in Canon engines are an environmentalist's nightmare, each contributing several pounds of plastic to the local landfill. Happily, you can recycle cartridges — and save money in the process — by sending them to one of the growing number of cartridge remanufacturing services (see the Backgrounder box "Saving Green").

Pushing Paper

Paper trays aren't as glamorous as laser beams, but they're at least as important. If a printer runs out of paper too often, if its trays are awkward to load, or if it folds and mutilates envelopes, it will boost your blood pressure instead of your productivity.

Large or prolific offices will want a printer that provides at least two paper trays. You can configure a multi-tray printer to link its trays so that when one runs out, the other kicks in. Or you can put letterhead in one tray and second sheets in the

Saving Green

A used toner cartridge isn't used up — many of its internal parts are good for tens of thousands of pages. By reusing or recycling toner cartridges, you can at least postpone all that plastic's journey into forever.

Toner cartridge remanufacturers disassemble cartridges, clean and replace parts as needed, and then replenish their toner supply — for about half of what new cartridges cost. Many remanufacturers are starting to handle non-Canon toner cartridges, too. Using a recycled cartridge won't void your printer's warranty, degrade print quality, or hurt your printer. If you choose a reputable recycler, that is. Some fly-by-night operations simply drill a hole in the cartridge and fill it with toner — an approach that invites poor output quality at best, and printer damage at worst. Ask for recommendations at a user group or desktop publishing service bureau, or ask a remanufacturer for references.

If you still prefer to buy brand-new cartridges, at least consider recycling your spent ones. Hewlett-Packard, Apple, Lexmark, Compaq, and other firms have cartridge recycling programs that usually involve returning the spent cartridge to the manufacturer using a postage-paid label included with the cartridge.

other, or high-quality paper in one tray and el-cheapo bond in the other. (See Chapter 31 for more details on using multiple paper trays.) The paper-handling champion is HP's LaserJet 4Si MX, which includes two 500-sheet trays and accepts an optional duplexer than enables the printer to print on both sides of a sheet. Lexmark's Optra series includes one 500-sheet tray and accepts a second tray as well as a duplexer. HP's LaserJet 4M Plus also accepts a duplexer. Texas Instruments' microLaser series are the low-cost paper handling leaders, each providing two 250-sheet trays as standard equipment. The trays themselves are well designed and easy to load, too.

Paper capacity is one thing; paper size is another. Most laser printers can handle paper up to 8½ by 14 inches — legal size. But several workgroup-oriented machines can print on sheets up to 11 by 17 inches — ideal for publishing or proofing tabloid-size newsletters or two-page spreads.

Then there's the lowly manual-feed slot — and the dreaded envelope. Many printers crease and mutilate envelopes so that it looks like the Postal Service has already gotten to them. Of the dozens of laser printers I've tested for *Macworld* over the last ten years, only one — Lexmark's Optra LX — was consistently able to print envelopes without creasing them. The Optra LX boasts an envelope conditioning feature that eliminates creasing by briefly opening and closing the printer's fusing rollers (which use heat and pressure to affix the plastic toner onto the paper) as the envelope travels through them. The mechanism makes a kerchunking noise that's just loud enough to be annoying to anyone sitting next to the printer. Perhaps that's why you can disable the feature with the printer's front panel.

How to Talk to PC Printers

Laser (and ink-jet) printers designed for the IBM PC world often cost less than their Mac-specific cousins. If you're willing to stray from the pack, you can use one of these PC printers with a Mac. All you need is the proper cable and driver software that the PC printer can understand.

Several PC printer packages were available in recent years, but only one has endured: GDT Softwork's PowerPrint. (As for the competition, which included products such as Orange Micro's Grappler LX and Insight Development's MacPrint, "We either beat 'em or bought 'em," a GDT representative once told me. Indeed, GDT offers PowerPrint upgrades to Grappler and MacPrint owners.)

PowerPrint includes a serial-to-parallel cable as well as a couple of disks containing printer drivers. One end of PowerPrint cable connects to your Mac's modem or printer port; the other end sports a soap-bar-sized plastic box that plugs into a PC printer's parallel connector and contains the serial-to-parallel convertor circuitry. GDT thoughtfully includes little plastic caps that protect the connector's pins when the cable is crammed into a briefcase along with a PowerBook.

The PowerPrint drivers are straightforward and packed with slick features. All drivers provide a draft mode that spews text (but no graphics) onto the page in no time flat. The drivers for laser and ink-jet printers provide a unique *photocopy reduction* mode that shrinks a page image without changing margins. (The reduction option in Apple's printer drivers will make text smaller but cause line endings to change.)

Other goodies include great on-line help (including balloon help) and a Preview button that shows how a document will appear before you commit it to paper. There's also support for multiple paper bins, so you can print, for example, page one from one bin and the rest of a document from another. There's even a Paper Size button that lets you define custom paper sizes for offbeat stocks such as index cards. The PowerPrint drivers generally support the highest resolution a printer provides — 360 dots per inch for Canon ink-jet machines and up to 600 dpi for laser printers.

Other Flavors of PowerPrint

Of course, connecting PowerPrint's cable to the printer port means disabling AppleTalk and forgoing access to LocalTalk printers and file servers. If you can't bear the isolation, consider GDT's PowerPrint/LT, a version of PowerPrint that uses LocalTalk instead of a serial connection. (Technically, LocalTalk is a serial connection, too, but you know what I mean.) PowerPrint/LT's pint-sized LocalTalk adaptor box plugs into a PC printer's serial port; you can then plug any standard LocalTalk connector into the adaptor box.

PowerPrint/LT not only lets you retain your connection to printers and file servers on a LocalTalk network, it also lets everyone on the network share the PC printer. You simply install the appropriate PowerPrint/LT drivers on each Mac in the network, select the printer in the Chooser, and print.

It's worth noting that you can share a PC printer using the standard PowerPrint package, but through a somewhat awkward scheme that involves using System 7 file sharing to set up one Mac as a print server for the other Macs on the network. Conceptually, this is similar to the way sharing works with Apple's StyleWriters, and it has the same drawbacks: your Mac's performance is slightly slower when file sharing is on, and it can be considerably slower when other users are printing documents to the shared printer. There's also a legal angle: the PowerPrint license agreement stipulates that software be used on only one computer at a time. Thus, if two people want to print to a shared printer simultaneously, you'll need two copies of PowerPrint. Avoid all the pitfalls and expense by just buying PowerPrint/LT.

Many PC-centric offices use networks built around Novell NetWare servers. If yours is among them, consider GDT's PowerPrint/NW, which combines the standard PowerPrint drivers with software that taps into NetWare print servers. And if you're among the 37 people who actually use System 7.5's QuickDraw GX technology, you might investigate PowerPrint/GX. PowerPrint/GX, which provides support for QuickDraw/GX's desktop printer icons as well as its enhanced Print and Page Setup dialog boxes.

PowerPrint Power Tips

Here are some tips for getting the best results out of PowerPrint.

- *Experiment with different drivers if your printer supports more than one language.* The results from color printers, in particular, can vary dramatically depending on the driver you choose. For all printers, make the Epson LQ driver your last choice — its language doesn't allow for as much precision in spacing than others.
- *Use Courier or Monaco for draft output.* PowerPrint's draft mode uses a printer's default resident font, which is usually a monospaced font. By formatting a document in a monospaced font, you'll avoid odd character spacing when using draft mode.
- *Convert EPS images to TIFF format before printing.* Because PowerPrint isn't a PostScript driver, it can't do full justice to EPS images. You can improve results, however, by opening an EPS image in a program such as Photoshop and then saving it as a TIFF file, which doesn't require PostScript for best results.
- *Use a lower resolution for low-memory lasers.* To print a full page at 300 dpi, PowerPrint requires that a laser printer contain at least 1.5MB of memory. Problem is, in their base configurations, many HP and compatible laser printers come with less. To print a full page on such machines, use the Print dialog box's Resolution pop-up menu to specify a lower resolution, such as 75 or 150 dpi.
- *For best results from dot-matrix machines, use unidirectional printing.* (In the Print dialog box, click Options and then click the Unidirectional button.) In this mode, PowerPrint controls the print head so that it's printing only when traveling from left to right. This mode is slower than bidirectional printing, but it often gives better results.

Focus on Color Printers

Most people rely on monochrome printers for their day-to-day work, but more and more are buying color machines — to proof publications, create package mock-ups, print scanned or video-captured images, produce overhead transparencies, and just punch up their documents.

The increasing interest in color isn't surprising. Color printer prices have never been lower and print quality has never been better. The complex hardware and software required to accurately mix and apply pigments continue to mature: today's color consumers need not feel like pioneers chasing rainbows. In this section, I describe the technologies and issues behind color printing.

Color printer basics

There are many ways to put color on paper, but all involve applying pigments in three colors — cyan, yellow, and magenta. These *primary colors* can be mixed to produce other colors. Equal amounts of cyan and yellow, for example, produce green, and equal amounts of magenta and cyan make blue. Equal amounts of all three primaries produce black, although many printers apply a separate black pigment to obtain richer blacks. This technique of mixing cyan, yellow, and magenta to produce colors and also applying black where needed is called *CMYK* or *process* color (the *K* stands for black). Color printing presses also produce their output by using the same four ink colors — which is why they're often described as four-color presses.

A color printer's pigments can take several forms, from liquid ink that is sprayed through microscopic nozzles to solid wax that is melted onto the page by heated rollers. Because of this variety of technologies, color printers are categorized according to the makeup of their pigments — ink-jet and *phase change* ink-jet printers, *thermal wax transfer* printers, and *dye sublimation* printers. There are even a few color laser printers with powdered toner in four colors — guess which four. (For a look at how various color printing technologies work, see Figure 30-6, "Color Printing Technologies Illustrated.")

Pigments and dots

You may think that a color printer mixes pigments in the quantities needed for a given color and then applies that color to the page. Not so. Instead, most printers overlay dots of whichever primary colors are needed: To print a red dot, the printer overlays one yellow and one magenta dot. With this scheme, red, green, and blue dots are easy to create: The printer just applies equal amounts of two primaries. So, a color printer can easily produce eight colors — cyan, yellow, magenta, black, red, green, blue, and white. (To produce white, the printer applies no pigments at all — thus, its white is only as white as the paper you use.)

What about the rest of the spectrum? Ideally, a color printer could create other colors by applying pigments in unequal amounts — for example, a lot of magenta and just a tad of cyan. Some high-end color printers can do just that, but the majority have just one dot size. To produce colors other than the eight just listed, they must resort to dithering — that patterning process I describe in Chapter 14.

How color dithering works

Dithering involves applying cyan, yellow, magenta, and black dots in complex patterns that trick the eye into seeing other hues. But the eye isn't that easily fooled. Dithering results in impure colors, and it can give color output a speckled look as if you tried to tone down a bright paint by sprinkling pepper on it. What's more, the quality of the dither patterns — the arrangements of colored dots — can vary from one printer vendor to the next.

If you're printing pie charts, text, and line drawings such as architectural diagrams, you can avoid dithering by using only the basic eight colors listed in the preceding section. Otherwise, there's no escaping it — except to buy a high-end color printer that can produce continuous-tone images.

The challenge of photographs

Nothing pushes the envelope of color printing like a scanned color photograph. A scan not only requires extensive dithering, it also requires halftoning: Its continuous tones must be converted into a series of dots that a printer (or printing press) can produce.

As you may recall from Chapter 14, in a halftone of a black-and-white photo, gray shades are simulated by dots of varying size — larger dots for darker grays, smaller dots for lighter ones. To create these dots, a printer combines the smallest dots it can create into clusters called cells and then turns on varying numbers of dots within each cell.

Color halftoning

Halftoning a color image is a similar, but trickier, process. First, the image must be separated into cyan, yellow, magenta, and black components; each resulting separation uses dots of varying size to represent the amount of each primary color required to simulate the image's hues. Then each screen is rotated to a different angle, causing all the screens' dots to overlap and form sets of small circles called rosettes.

At the high resolutions used in professional printing, these rosettes are small enough to be invisible at normal reading distances. (You can see them if you try; look closely at the cover of this book.) But at the 300-dpi resolution provided by some color printers, the rosettes are bigger than the blooms on Jack's beanstalk. You may not mind this chunky look if you're using a color printer to produce rough mockups. But if you're printing color output to check an image's color balance, the fat rosettes, plump halftone dots, and dither patterns will complicate your job by obscuring image details.

These drawbacks aren't present in the film recorder world or in the upper stratum of color printing, where dye-sublimation printers live. Costly dye-sublimation color printers can do jaw-dropping justice to color scans, thanks to their translucent pigments. The five-figure Iris SmartJet color ink-jet printer also handles photos beautifully, thanks to its ability to print variable-size dots.

COLOR PRINTER TECHNOLOGIES ILLUSTRATED

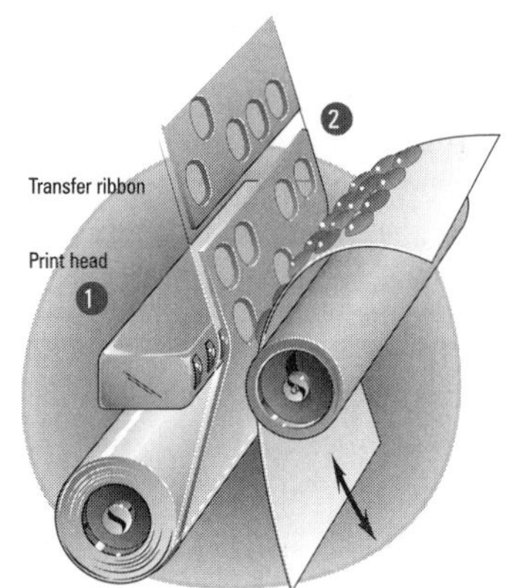

Thermal-Wax Transfer Printer

A thermal-wax transfer printer contains a roll of transfer ribbon on which wax-based pigments in each process color (cyan, magenta, yellow, and black) are positioned one after another. The transfer ribbon is sandwiched between the print head, which contains thousands of heating elements, and the paper (1). The print head's heating elements are turned on and off to melt the wax as needed, causing individual dots to adhere to the paper (2). The paper passes by the ribbon and the print head four times, once for each process color.

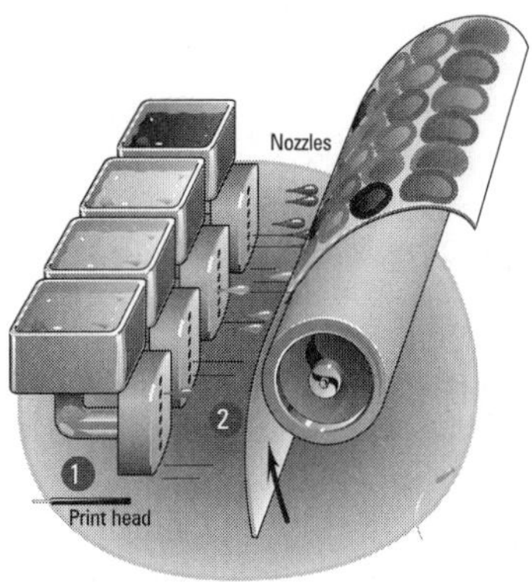

Ink-Jet Printer

A color ink-jet printer sprays drops of ink onto the page through microscopic nozzles in the printer's print head. To spray a drop of ink, some ink-jet printers send an electronic signal to a piezoelectric diaphragm within the head (1), forcing a drop of ink from the nozzles (2). Others, such as Hewlett-Packard's HP DeskWriter and the Apple Color StyleWriter Pro, use a heating element to create bubbles that expand, forcing drops of ink from the print head. Because an ink-jet printer lays down all four colors in one pass, it poses fewer registration problems than do multipass printers.

Film Recorder

Unlike a printer, a film recorder uses red, green, and blue light to produce images on 35mm slide film. A controller board translates commands from the Mac into video signals and sends them to a high-resolution monochrome cathode-ray tube (1). A filter wheel (2) rotates to produce the required amount of each primary color, which travels through a lens and into a camera adapter that attaches to the front of the film recorder. With the proper adapter, a film recorder can also accept 4-by-5-inch Polaroid print or transparency film.

Figure 30-6: Color Printing Technologies Illustrated

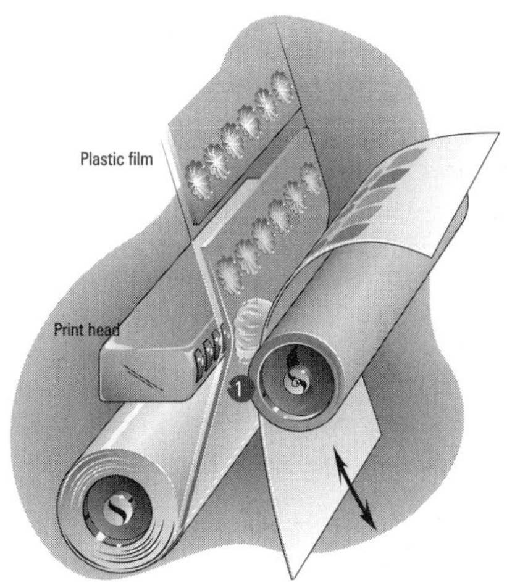

Dye Sublimation

Dye-sublimation printers pass plastic film coated with cyan, magenta, yellow, and black (C, M, Y, and K) dye across a print head containing about 2400 heating elements. This dye goes from solid to gaseous form when heated (1). Coated paper, designed to absorb the gaseous dye on contact, passes across the film four times (once per color) as it contacts the print head. Each heating element can produce 255 different temperatures—the hotter, the more dye is transferred. This variable dye density produces continuous-tone images.

Phase Change Ink Jet

Phase-change printers melt blocks of C-, M-, Y-, and K-color wax in ink reservoirs. The melted ink is sprayed onto the page through tiny perforations in print-head nozzles (1), in a single pass, as with typical ink-jet printers. Unlike the water-based inks used in typical ink jets, the wax-based inks in solid-ink printers solidify on the page very quickly, inhibiting absorption that can reduce image sharpness. This allows phase-change ink jet printers to use relatively absorbent plain paper. High-pressure rollers then flatten the dots and fuse them to the page (2).

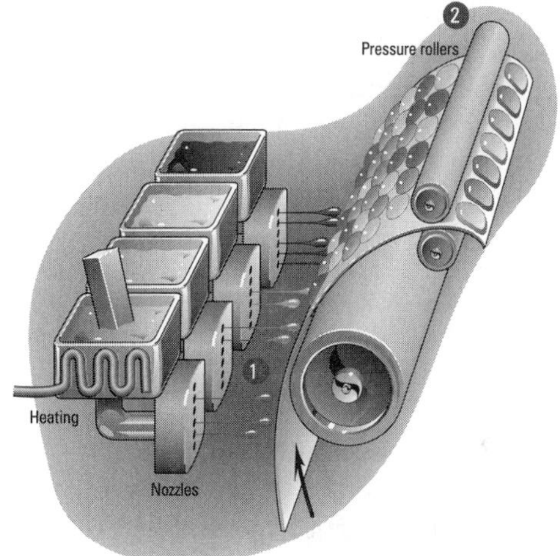

Color Laser

Color laser printers use a four-chamber developing unit that holds colored (C, M, Y, and K) plastic toner powder. After a light source exposes an image on a photosensitive drum (1), exposed portions of the drum take on an electrical charge that attracts toner as the drum rotates past the developing unit (2). This process is repeated four times, once for each color. After each exposure, the paper passes across the toner-coated drum. When the four passes are completed, heated rollers fuse the toner to the page (3).

Figure 30-6: Color Printing Technologies Illustrated *(continued)*

From Screen to Paper — Matching Woes

If you think the muddy waters of rosettes and screen angles are sloppy, put on your hip boots. One of the most complicated aspects of color output involves matching the colors you see on the screen with the colors your printer produces. This isn't critical for presentations and simple color-coding applications: Who cares if a printed bar chart's hues differ from what you saw on the screen?

But color matching is essential for color publishing. When publishers specify certain colors for a design or spend hours tweaking the color in scanned photographs, they want the final printed output to match what they saw on their screens. Publishers also need printers that can accurately reproduce colors in printing industry color-specification systems, such as Pantone and Trumatch.

One problem behind screen-to-printer matching is that monitors and printers use different ingredients to mix their colors. Printers use cyan, yellow, magenta, and black pigments, and monitors use red, green, and blue light. Printing inks create colors by absorbing, or subtracting, light reflected from paper; monitors create colors by adding light to a screen. In color jargon, printers use a *subtractive color model* (the CMYK model), and monitors use an *additive color model* (the *RGB* model).

Converting between color models

Because of this fundamental difference, documents you print must often go through a transformation process in which their RGB colors are translated into CMYK counterparts. But the phrase "something got lost in the translation" can apply to color transformations as readily as it does to language. Printers can't produce the same range of colors you see on the screen — technically speaking, they have different *color gamuts*. As a result, when you print an image, its RGB colors must be converted, or mapped, to their closest available CMYK colors. The result: The color that prints isn't what you saw on-screen.

The paper used for printing is another variable in color matching. Paper isn't always completely white, and any tint is going to alter colors by changing the way light is reflected. But this isn't a serious issue for most color printers because most require that you use the manufacturer's paper. (Where plain-paper output is concerned, color printer vendors are being pulled from two sides. Business people want to be able to print charts and graphs on company stationery, but publishers need a pure white stock that provides consistent output.)

Other color-matching snags

Other problems in color matching arise even before your output meets the printed page. Monitors themselves vary. An image displayed on your monitor is likely to look different on your coworkers' monitors — for that matter, it may look different on *your* monitor a month from now.

Over the years, numerous firms, including Kodak and Electronics for Imaging (EFI), have developed color-management systems — software, and in some cases, calibration hardware — that promise greater fidelity between the screen and the printed page.

For screen-to-printer matching, Apple may be the final arbiter. Its ColorSync extension to the Mac's System software enables developers of printers, scanners, and monitors to create *device profiles* that describe their hardware's color characteristics. ColorSync then works with application programs to adjust colors as they journey from one device to another.

Color-management systems such as ColorSync are often paired with color calibration hardware such as Kodak's ColorSense. A calibrator uses an optical sensor that attaches to the front of a display. The sensor enables the Mac to compare the color a monitor is producing to the color the Mac's video signals are telling it to produce. If there are variations — and there probably will be — the calibrator's software can adjust the video signals to compensate, enabling the display to produce the colors it's supposed to.

Color Printer Shopping Considerations

Grouping color printers into the general categories — ink-jet, thermal wax, laser, and dye-sublimation — is convenient for price and basic comparisons, but your shopping list needs to address other things, too. For starters, you need to choose between a PostScript and a QuickDraw printer; all the information in this chapter's section "Watch your language — PostScript versus QuickDraw" also applies to color printers.

Here's an overview of other key issues to examine.

Media flexibility

Want to print on plain paper? Forget dye-sublimation printers: they require special, expensive paper designed to absorb the printer's dyes. Liquid ink-jets such as Apple's StyleWriters do a respectible job on plain paper, although cheap paper can produce mottled-looking output.

Color laser printers as well as the Tektronix Phaser 340 solid ink-jet (also called phase-change ink-jet) deliver excellent results on typical copier bond and letterhead stock. However, the Phaser 340's unique ink formulation prevents double-sided printing.

Thermal-wax printers remain the finicky bunch where paper is concerned. Thermal-wax technology benefits from extremely smooth paper; a sheet of copier bond or textured letterhead has pits and valleys that prevent the wax from adhering. All thermal-wax vendors sell special, ultra-smooth paper that provides excellent results.

The Sharp-built print engine used in several thermal-wax machines from General Parametrics, Tektronix, and Digital Equipment Corporation accepts a special ink ribbon that sacrifices its black panel in favor of a primer medium that is applied to areas of the page that will contain ink. The primer attempts to smooth the paper's rough surface, but it's only effective on high-quality plain paper that's relatively smooth to begin with, such as Hammermill Laserprint. With typical photocopier bond, output is mottled. Thermal wax machines remain best suited to printing transparencies as well as on their own special paper.

The finish and durability of output varies from one technology to another. Liquid ink-jet output smears when wet. Solid ink-jet output has a textured matte finish that can crack after repeated folding. Thermal wax gives printed areas of the page an appealing gloss. Pages from a dye-sublimation printer are glossy all over.

As for color laser printers, the finish depends on the engine. The QMS and Xerox machines I've tested produce a semi-glossy finish, but the edges of characters and of shapes (such as the bars in a chart) have a slightly fuzzy, out-of-focus appearance. The Apple Color LaserWriter is less glossy and doesn't suffer from this fuzziness. And the HP Color LaserJet produces a matte finish identical to that of a monochrome laser printer. Indeed, with a document containing only black text and line art, it's impossible to tell the Color LaserJet's output from that of a monochrome laser printer.

ON THE CD

See the Apple Color LaserWriter in Action

Of the latest crop of color laser printers, Apple's Color LaserWriter is the easiest to set up; its Canon-built print engine uses the fewest number of components. The Color LaserWriter relies on slide-in toner cartridges that will look and feel familiar to anyone who's fed a monochrome laser or photocopier.

In the Imaging Products segment of the *Macworld Power User Clinic*, you can see exactly what's involved in setting up the Color LaserWriter and learn what else sets it apart from other color lasers.

And while you're using the CD, check out the Stupid Printer Tricks clinic to learn about some interesting ways to use your printer; see the next chapter's "On the CD" box for more details.

The Trend Toward Combination Dye-Sub/Thermal-Wax Printers

Seiko's Professional ColorPoint PSF and Fargo's Primera Pro and Pictura 310 are hybrid thermal-wax/dye-sublimation machines. Remove the thermal-wax ribbon and paper and replace them with their dye-sub equivalents, and these printers can produce photorealistic, continuous-tone prints. Businesses can benefit by being able to print gorgeous transparencies that are free of the dither (dot) patterns that thermal-wax and laser printers must use to simulate fine color gradations. Publishers can benefit by using the less-expensive thermal-wax paper for rough proofs, and then switching to the dye-sub stock for final proofs.

Of the three, the Seiko machine does the best job of straddling the thermal-wax and dye-sub camps: besides delivering superior output quality, it automatically senses which type of ribbon you've installed. The Fargo machines require you to check a dialog box option; if you forget, the paper jams. Also, Macworld Labs testing has found that the Fargo machines' color balance is significantly different in each mode. You wouldn't want to use their thermal-wax prints to tweak color balance if you planned to print the final proof in dye-sub mode.

The Fargo machines have additional drawbacks. They're slow and they lack built-in PostScript, relying instead on a nicely designed QuickDraw-based driver. Fargo sells PostScript interpreter software — a version of Adobe's Configurable PostScript Interpreter, or CPSI. CPSI runs on the Mac to which the printer is connected, so its performance depends on the Mac's.

Still, the Primera Pro and Pictura 310 have their appeal. The $1,895 Primera Pro is by far the least expensive dye-sub machine around, and the $4,995 Pictura 310 is the only tabloid-size dye-sub printer you'll find for under $5,000 (or, for that matter, for under $10,000). Fargo's machines may not be the fastest or most sophisticated thermal and dye-sub color printers available, but they are the only ones that won't traumatize your accountant.

Resolution

In past years, most color printers had a relatively coarse resolution of 300 or 360 dots per inch. A growing number of machines provide 600-dpi or 600 by 300-dpi modes. Color lasers, in particular, provide excellent resolution. Apple's Color LaserWriter provides true 600-dpi resolution, and the the Xerox 4900 Color Laser Printer provides a 1200 by 300-dpi mode. In this mode, the printer's laser beam pulses four times faster than in 300-dpi mode, enabling the printer to apply four times the number of dots in the horizontal direction.

Many machines also employ resolution-enhancement techniques — fine-tuning dot sizes, for example — to further improve the quality of text and scanned images. The HP Color LaserJet provides HP's Resolution Enhancement technology, for example, while the Apple Color LaserWriter employs Color PhotoGrade.

Teaching a Color QuickDraw Printer to Speak PostScript

As mentioned elsewhere in this chapter, QuickDraw printers such as the Color StyleWriter Pro and the Hewlett-Packard DeskWriter 560C give mediocre results when used with PostScript-oriented programs such as Adobe Illustrator and Aldus FreeHand. In the past, the answer has been PostScript clone interpreters that run on the Mac, such as TeleTypesetting Company's T-Script.

DeskWriter 560C, Color StyleWriter Pro, and Color StyleWriter 2400 users have another choice: true Adobe PostScript Level 2 interpreters that run on the Mac. HP offers a PostScript Level 2 software driver kit for the DeskWriter 560C.

GDT Softworks offers similar software, the $149 StyleScript, for the Apple Color StyleWriter Pro and Color StyleWriter 2400. StyleScript is based on Adobe's Configurable PostScript Interpreter (CPSI), which up to now, has been used only on high-end printers, such as 3M's $20,000 Rainbow dye-sublimation printer. CPSI has stiff memory requirements, though — 8MB minimum, and up to 12MB for large PostScript images, according GDT Softworks. Even on a fast Mac, you won't get sizzling performance, and your Mac will slow as it processes print jobs. But you will get the least-expensive color PostScript output available.

Cost per page

Another factor that may influence your choice is the cost per page. Laser and ink-jet printers are very economical with pages that are mostly blank — most manufacturers base their consumables' replacement intervals on pages where only five percent of the area contains pigment. Thermal wax output is costlier with such documents because the printer uses an entire set of ink panels for each page regardless of its contents. For transparancies, however, which typically use colored backgrounds and thus have much higher coverage percentages, thermal wax machines are often more economical.

Speed

Color printer performance is often measured in minutes per page, not pages per minute. Producing color output requires additional processing time, as the controller — whether built-in or Mac-based — figures out how much cyan, yellow, magenta, and black ink to apply in order to create various hues. For QuickDraw printers, this means that the faster your Mac, the faster the printer.

The actual printing takes longer, too. In ink-jet printers, a print head skitters from left to right, painting the page in narrow passes. Thermal-wax and dye-sublimation printers — which heat dye-impregnated film to transfer color to paper — are much faster, but are still slower than monochrome lasers.

Color lasers provide better performance; indeed, if you're printing a black-and-white document, a color laser's performance can approach that of a monochrome machine. In the most recent survey of business color printers that I wrote for *Macworld*, the color lasers we tested were, as a group, the fastest machines around.

Another excellent performer, however, was Tektronix's Phaser 340 solid-ink printer; its controller delivered exceptional performance with PostScript illustrations and typographically complex jobs. The Phaser 340 accepts an optional attachment that turns the printer into a color photocopier. The Phaser CopyStation is essentially a scanner that connects to the Phaser 340's SCSI port. It's a nice way to make a good printer even better.

Time to Buy a Color Printer?

Between falling prices, rising quality, and improving performance, desktop color printers are closer than ever to entering the mainstream of personal-computer peripherals. At the low end, they *have* arrived: machines such as the Color StyleWriter 2400 are versatile printers for small businesses, home offices, and schools.

In the business world, color printers will play second fiddle to monochrome machines for the foreseeable future. One reason is cost: today's color printers are slower and more expensive to buy and operate than monochrome printers.

Another reason is practical: many of the documents produced in businesses are photocopied for distribution, and the vast majority of copiers are color blind. Adding color charts or diagrams to a multipage report means printing the color pages separately and then collating them into the final product — a labor-intensive job.

That doesn't mean there hasn't been solid progress in business color. Today's printers are better than ever, and the best of them come closer than ever to meeting not only specialized color printing needs, but ordinary ones, too. If you've got the checkbook and the room for one, take the plunge. Just don't plan to put your monochrome workhorse out to pasture.

CHAPTER  CONCEPTS AND TERMS

- Ink-jet printers cost less than laser printers, but their output quality is inferior.
- A laser printer generally has two basic components — an engine, the photocopier-like mechanism that transfers toner to paper, and a controller, the circuitry that accepts commands from the Mac and governs the engine.
- In a QuickDraw printer, the Mac serves as the controller. This reduces the printer's cost but means the Mac must act as the controller.
- A QuickDraw printer can't be used with a DOS PC. Also, most QuickDraw printers aren't as easy to share on a network as PostScript machines.
- The three predominant color printer technologies are ink-jet (good), thermal-wax transfer (better), and dye-sublimation (best).
- Dye-sublimation printers are best for printing scanned photographs because they can produce continuous-tone images. Other color printers must resort to dithering.
- Color management software such as Apple's ColorSync is designed to enable printed colors to match those displayed on the screen.

additive color
The process of creating colors by projecting colored light. With additive color, the three primary colors are red, green, and blue.

all ports active
A printer feature in which all the connection ports are always listening for data when a print job arrives at one port, other ports are temporarily disabled.

CMYK
An abbreviation for *cyan, magenta, yellow,* and *black,* the four process colors used in the color printer world.

color gamut
The range of hues a color printer can produce.

controller
The printer circuitry that governs the engine according to commands received by the Mac. In QuickDraw printers, the Mac acts as the controller.

device profile
A description of the color-rendering capabilities of a given device, such as a monitor or printer. Color-management systems such as Apple's ColorSync use device profiles.

downloadable font
A PostScript font whose outline is stored in your System folder and downloaded to the printer's memory before printing.

duty cycle
A print engine specification that describes the maximum number of pages you can print per month without risking mechanical problems.

emulation modes
Special operating modes provided by some PostScript printers that enable a printer to imitate a non-PostScript printer.

emulation sensing
A feature provided by some PostScript printers that enables a printer to switch into an emulation mode when it determines that incoming data isn't PostScript code. Without emulation sensing, you need to flick a switch or use a printer's front-panel buttons to switch between PostScript and emulation modes.

engine
The printer mechanism that transfers toner, ink, wax, or dye to paper.

font cache
In a PostScript printer, an area of controller memory that stores already rasterized fonts in the likely event they will be needed again in that document. TrueType creates a font cache in the Mac's memory.

font outlines
Mathematical formulas the Mac or a printer can use to create text in virtually any size and orientation.

GrayShare
An Apple printer driver technology that provides enhanced resolution for grayscale images and lets you share a printer on a LocalTalk network.

hints
Instructions built into a font that TrueType or a PostScript controller uses to optimize the appearance of each character at a given size and resolution.

interpreter
The portion of a PostScript printer's controller that deciphers the PostScript code being sent from the Mac.

PostScript
A programming language created by Adobe Systems for describing the appearance of pages. When you print a document to a PostScript printer, the Mac's LaserWriter driver creates a PostScript program that describes the document's appearance.

PostScript clone
A printer whose interpreter understands PostScript but was created by a firm other than Adobe.

primary colors
The three basic colors from which all colors can be created. With subtractive color (mixed pigments such as paint or ink), the three primary colors are cyan, yellow, and magenta. With additive color (mixed light), the primaries are red, green, and blue.

print head
The component in an ink-jet or dot-matrix printer that moves from left to right across the page, applying ink as it goes.

rasterizer
Also called a *scaler,* the software responsible for translating a font outline into a bitmap of the point size and resolution required.

resident font
A font built into a printer. Compare with *downloadable font.*

resolution
The number of dots per inch a printer (or other output device) can render. Laser and ink-jet printers generally have resolutions of 300 to 600 dots per inch.

resolution enhancement
Techniques that involve finessing a print engine's laser beam in a way that smooths character edges and, in some printers, improves gray-scale output.

rosettes
Small patterns of C, M, Y, and K dots that form a color halftone.

self-centering manual-feed slot
A print engine convenience feature that makes it easy to manually feed envelopes. Such a slot uses two adjustable guides — move one, and the other moves accordingly.

subtractive color
The process of creating colors by absorbing, or subtracting, light reflected from paper. With subtractive color, the three primary colors are cyan, yellow, and magenta.

toner
A fine plastic powder that laser printer engines melt onto paper to produce output.

toner scatter
An undesirable artifact produced by some laser printers that causes small type to appear heavy and overexposed, with hollow portions of characters such as *e* and *b* partially filled in. Toner scatter occurs because of stray electrical charges generated by a relatively imprecise corona wire, the component that attracts toner from the photoconductive drum to the paper.

virtual memory
Abbreviated *VM,* general work space in a PostScript printer that also holds downloadable fonts. Not to be confused with System 7's virtual memory feature.

CHAPTER THIRTY-ONE

Printer Power Tips

- Printing on paper, film, mimeos, and mailers
- Printing labels and T-shirt transfers
- Improving the performance of PostScript printers and the LaserWriter 8 driver
- Using the enhanced printing features in QuickDraw GX

This chapter begins with a look at the universe of paper, film, mimeo masters, and mailers that you can run through a printer. Next, there's a collection of tips for PostScript printers and the LaserWriter 8 driver. I wrap up with background and tips on the enhanced printing features in QuickDraw GX and in LaserWriter 8.3 and the latest StyleWriter drivers.

Today's Paper

A printer without paper is like a camera without film. And there are almost as many types of paper as there are types of film. Whether you use a dot-matrix printer such as Apple's ImageWriter II, an ink-jet printer such as an Apple StyleWriter or Hewlett-Packard DeskWriter, or a laser printer such as one of Apple's LaserWriters, you'll find a wonderful variety of vehicles for your documents.

Paper for dot-matrix printers

Although the selection of alternative print media is growing, paper remains the preeminent output medium. Here are some tips for choosing the best stock for your printer and your print jobs.

For dot-matrix printers, ImageWriters and their ilk accept single sheets that you load as though loading a typewriter. The ImageWriter II accepts an optional sheet feeder that eliminates having to hand-feed page after page. A less-expensive alternative to hand-feeding is to use *fanfold,* also called *pin-fed,* paper. Fanfold paper is a single, long sheet of paper that's perforated and folded to lie in a stack. The left and right edges of the sheets have perforated strips containing holes that are grasped by sprockets in the printer.

After printing a document, you separate the sheets and tear off the perforated strips. This chore is sometimes called *bursting*, but "boring" is more accurate. To cleanly remove the perforated strips, fold them back and forth a few times before tearing; even then, many papers leave little nubs behind, each a dead giveaway that the document was printed on fanfold paper. To get cleaner edges, use a high-quality fanfold paper with finer perforations. Paper and computer supply houses often use terms such as *invisible perf* or *satin edge* to describe such stock.

Besides white and off-white colors such as ivory and gray, fanfold paper comes printed with horizontal green or blue bars — that classic computer paper look. The alternating bars of color and white supposedly help lead the eyes across lines of numbers.

You'll also find fanfold paper whose sheets are prepunched to fit in standard three-ring binders. And Lyben Computer Systems of Troy, Michigan, is one source for Banner Band, 45-foot long rolls of paper with perforated sprocket edges, but no cross perforations. Available in several colors, it teams up well with Broderbund Software's BannerMania program.

Printing with impact

One advantage dot-matrix printers have over ink jet printers and laser printers is that they're *impact* printers, and can print on the carbonless multipart paper that businesses depend on for invoices and other forms. Most supply houses sell blank multipart forms; you can also buy forms printed with your company name and logo from mail-order business form houses such as New England Business Services (800-225-6380).

Because dot-matrix printers are impact printers, you can also use them to create stencils for mimeograph machines. AB Dick's 2060 stencil masters are designed specifically for dot-matrix printers. You can also use AB Dick's less-expensive F-1960 masters if you remove their plastic backing before printing. (Use an old ribbon when printing the masters to avoid gumming up the ImageWriter's print head with stencil wax.) You'll get better mimeos if you avoid printing solid black or dark patterns on the masters.

Paper for laser printers

Laser printers use photocopier like mechanisms, so any paper designed to run through copiers gives satisfactory results. Like fanfold paper, photocopier bond is available prepunched for three-ring binders.

When you want more than just satisfactory results, use a paper such as Hammermill's Laser Plus, CG Graphic Arts Supply's Laseredge series, or Georgia Pacific's Nekoosa Laser 1000. Available through most large office supply outlets, these papers' smooth, bright-white finish makes them ideal for printing camera-ready documents you'll supply to a print shop. If you use wax or spray adhesive to mount the output, use Hammermill's Laser Plus, which contains a coating, called a *wax holdout*, that enables the wax to adhere without soaking into the paper.

Feeding Without Fuss

Buying exotic paper is one thing; getting it to run through a printer without jamming is another. Most laser printers can automatically feed paper weights ranging from 16 to 28 pounds. (Most photocopier bond is 20-pound stock; the measurement refers to the weight of 500 sheets, or a ream, of 17 × 22-inch paper.) To print on heavier stocks, use the manual feed slot, which provides a straighter and therefore, less jam-prone, paper path. Check your printer's manual to determine its paper-handling limits.

Unless you've bought an optional envelope cassette, you'll also want to use the manual feed slot to print envelopes. Check your printer's manual for details on the margin settings you need to use, or just experiment. After you find the settings that work for you, save them in a template or stationery document that you can reuse. Information management and electronic address book programs such as Adobe TouchBase Pro also have features that simplify envelope printing. Most word processors also include a selection of envelope stationery documents.

Specialty laser papers

Premium typewriter bond such as Eaton's 28-pound Impressions series delivers fine results in most laser printers. If you're feeling green, you'll be glad to know recycled paper is available for dot-matrix and laser printers. Many office supply stores and mail-order houses sell recycled fanfold paper in white or with green bars. And Paper Direct (800-272-7377) sells a large selection of white, colored, and special-finish recycled stocks.

A staggering selection of specialty papers is available for laser printers, and the best source I've found for it is Paper Direct. Its mail-order catalog lists speckled granite, parchment, linen, and marble finishes along with pinstripes and borders. The Electrix and Firebrites series come in vibrant fluorescent and Day-Glo colors. The Perfs and Scores collection comprises several types of perforated or scored stocks. One is scored so that it folds three times, and has a perforated area that makes an ideal tear-off reply card. Another is similarly scored but contains a perforated Rolodex card. Still another has a slot for a business card. They're an economical way for a small business to produce expensive-looking brochures. Lyben Computer Systems stocks colored and textured specialty paper manufactured by The Legacy Company. Letraset's Copy FX collection also sports several specialty stocks.

Paper for the ink-jet set

The factor that most affects ink-jet output quality is the paper you use. Cheap photocopier bond works well in a laser printer, but in an ink-jet printer, its coarse fibers soak up the wet ink before it has a chance to dry, causing mottled-looking output.

Which End Is Up?

Regardless of the paper you choose, you'll get better results if you print on the correct side. Because of the way paper is made, each side of a sheet has different characteristics. The correct side to use for printing is the *felt* side, which is smoother than the *wire* side. Most paper manufacturers indicate the felt side on the label attached to the paper's wrapper. If you've removed the paper from its wrapper (a bad idea because it exposes the paper to humidity), you'll need to print some tests. The side that gives the sharpest results is the felt side. If you're using watermarked bond, hold a sheet up to the light: If the watermark's text or design is reversed, you're looking at the wire side. (This felt-versus-wire side issue applies to laser printing, too, but print quality doesn't degrade as dramatically if you laser-print on the wire side.)

You can get better results by using paper designed for ink-jet printing, such as Ink-Jet Ultra and Ink-Jet Cotton, both of which are sold by Paper Direct. Most computer- and office-supply houses sell similar stocks.

Because of its textured surface and high cotton content, high-quality watermarked bond — the kind of paper often used for corporate letterheads — can deliver disappointing results with StyleWriters. One workaround is to print a business letter on plain stock and then photocopy that page onto your letterhead.

To keep the address on an envelope from smearing if it gets wet, cover it with a piece of transparent tape.

Beyond Paper: Alternative Media

Printers aren't just for paper anymore. Peel-and-stick labels, Rolodex cards, mimeograph stencils, clear and colored plastic film, preprinted checks, and stiff card stock are among the paper alternatives most printers accept. You'll even find laser printer toner cartridges that enable you to create iron-on transfers for T-shirts, and products that add color to laser-printed documents.

Transparency and overhead stock

Businesses and schools rely on overhead transparencies for presentations and instruction. Transparency film also makes attractive, see-through covers for reports. And, as I'll describe shortly, it teams up well with peel-and-stick labels.

The only transparency film designed for dot-matrix printers I've found is 3M's Type 186 Impact Dot-matrix Transparency Film (order number 78-6969-6505-8).

For HP DeskWriters, use Avery's 5277 transparency film. For StyleWriters, Apple recommends 3M CG3480 film. And for laser printers, there's 3M's Type 154 Laser Printer Transparency Film (order number 78-6969-6085-1) and Avery's ColorFrames film, which has colored borders in a variety of hues. James River's ProTech line also has transparency film in several colors.

If you plan to reuse transparencies, consider mounting them in cardboard frames such as 3M's Type 9070 Transparency Mounting Frames. Frames eliminate distracting light leaks around the transparency's edges, they make transparencies easier to handle and sort, and they provide an area where you can write notes. The Image Frame also protects the transparency with a layer of clear plastic that you can write on and erase, and it's prepunched for storage in three-ring binders.

Labels: output with a peel

Peel-and-stick labels have a thousand-and-one uses, and nearly as many varieties are available for all types of printers. Avery's selection is the largest, with everything from mailing labels to audio- and videotape labels. Most labels are white paper, but several clear plastic sizes are available for laser printers. Their matte finish, similar to that of Scotch Magic Transparent Tape, makes the label stock nearly invisible when applied.

Formatting for labels

Formatting documents so that the text printed in the right place on each label used to be a chore — page after wasted page, a ruler and margin tweak between each one. Fortunately, Avery labels have become so popular that many programs — including Adobe PageMaker, Claris FileMaker Pro and ClarisWorks, and Microsoft Word and Works — include template documents designed for the most common sizes. Simply open one of these templates and substitute its placeholder text with your own, and then load up the printer and go.

Label-printing software

Then there are dedicated label-printing programs such as Avery's MacLabelPro and Williams & Macias' StickyBusiness series and MySoftware's MyLabelDesigner series. Label-printing programs combine basic page-layout features with built-in templates for label stocks. StickyBusiness and StickyBusiness Plus are identical except that the latter includes a variety of barcode fonts and can print a variety of barcodes. MyLabelDesigner and MyAdvancedLabelDesigner are also similar, but the latter provides built-in database management features.

All labeling programs work similarly. You generally begin by selecting the type of label you want to create from a menu. Labeling programs make this particularly easy by not only describing each supported label stock, but also including its brand name and part number. For instance, in StickyBusiness, choosing the menu item named AV 5196 Diskette summons the template for Avery's disk label stock. In MySoftware's MyLabelDesigner programs, the menus normally don't list Avery part numbers; to display them, choose the awkwardly named Show Avery Part #s command from the Labels menu.

It's at this first stage of label making that one of the differences between packages surfaces — some programs support a wider range of label stocks than others. For understandable reasons, Avery's MacLabelPro supports only Avery label stocks. (MacLabelPro actually shares a common heritage with the Williams & Macias programs — back in 1990, Avery licensed a version of StickyBusiness to distribute as MacLabelPro.) MySoftware's MyLabelDesigner programs include just over 100 templates.

The StickyBusiness programs are the reigning template champs; each ships with over 500 templates that support not only Avery labels, but also stocks from other suppliers, including New England Business Services (a large mail-order supplier of preprinted labels, invoices, and other business forms); Inmac (a mail-order office- and computer-supply house); and even United Parcel Service. Both StickyBusiness programs also support dedicated label printers such as CoStar's LabelWriter machines.

Laying out labels

After you specify the label size, a label program sets up an untitled window that contains a rectangle corresponding to that size (see Figure 31-1 "Creating Labels"). All label programs provide tools for creating text, lines, and boxes. The MyLabelDesigner and StickyBusiness programs can import PICT or EPS graphics files; you can also paste graphics from the Mac's Clipboard. You might use these features to add a company logo or a scanned image to labels. The StickyBusiness packages have a unique Grab Icon command that can import icons stored in application programs. This feature can be handy when you're creating labels for disks or removable-media cartridges; more on this aspect of label making shortly.

The layout features in a label program are crude compared to those of a publishing program. Forget about having fine control over letter spacing, for example; if you want kerning and other spacing controls, you'll have to use a publishing or illustration program. In many ways, the label programs even fall short of the layout features you find in an integrated package such as ClarisWorks. For example, none of the programs tested has a Group command, which lets you combine numerous objects into a single object that you can move and resize. MyLabelDesigner and MyAdvancedLabelDesigner have additional limitations; for instance, they don't let you draw diagonal lines (only horizontal and vertical ones), and they provide just three line widths. But at least the MyLabelDesigner programs let you zoom in on a design to do detailed work; StickyBusiness doesn't.

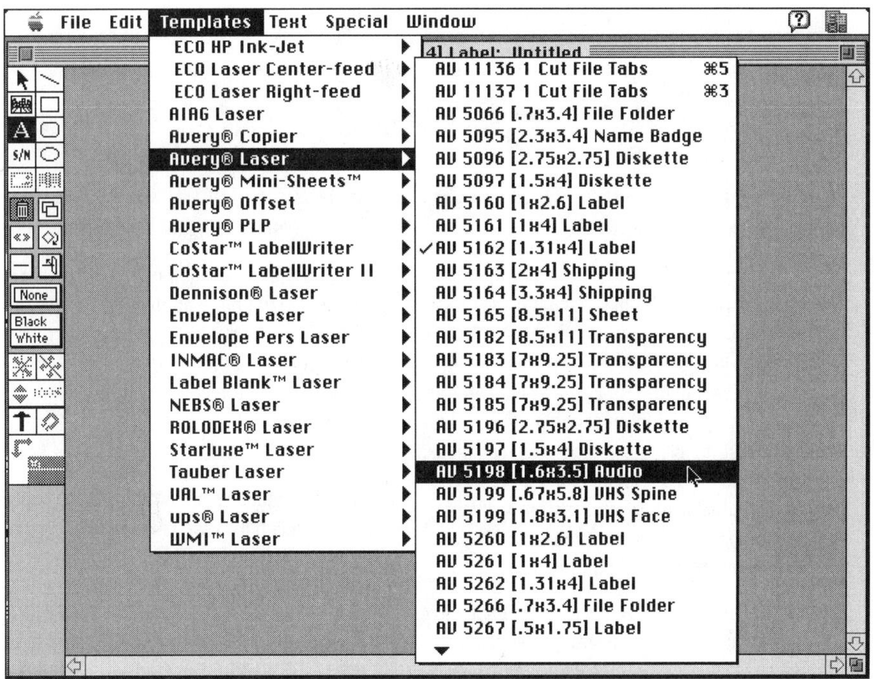

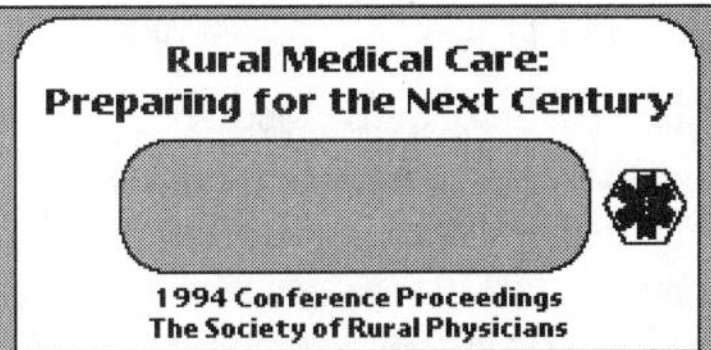

Rural Medical Care:
Preparing for the Next Century
1994 Conference Proceedings
The Society of Rural Physicians

Figure 31-1: Creating Labels Creating a label begins with selecting the desired stock (top). Williams & Macias' StickyBusiness, shown here, provides the largest array of label templates: over 500. After choosing the stock, you use the program's layout tools to create the label (middle). When printing the label, you can specify that the program begin printing at a specific point on the label sheet (bottom).

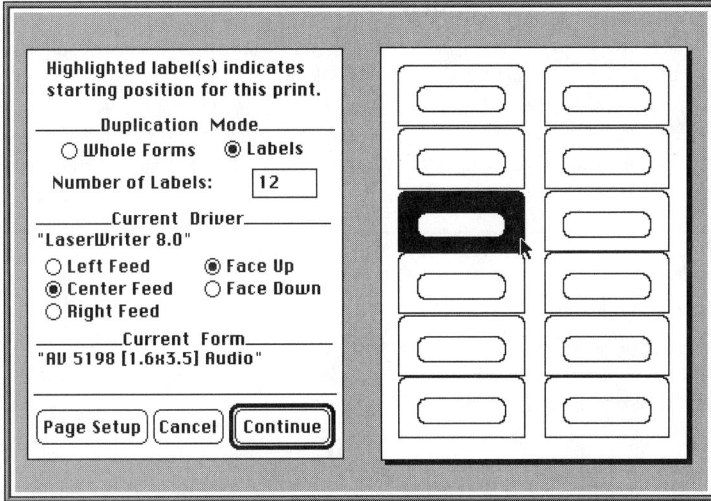

Tips for Printing Labels

Formatting is only half the challenge of label printing; the other half is getting label stock to run through a printer. Here are some tips for specific types of printers.

- ❖ **ImageWriter II.** When using fanfold label stock, never use the ImageWriter's paper-feed knob to wind the labels backward. Doing so is likely to cause a label to peel off inside the printer, where it can get stuck to internal components. Also, with most fanfold label stocks, it isn't necessary to start printing at the top of the page — the amount of space between each row of labels is usually identical, even when one row is separated from the next by perforations.
- ❖ **StyleWriter series.** Apple's ink-jet printers can feed label stocks directly from their paper trays. Because label stock is thicker than paper, however, slide both of the printer's paper-thickness adjustment levers to the envelope position. One lever is next to the sheet feeder, and the other is inside the printer, just above the ink cartridge. When manually feeding labels into an original StyleWriter, use the rear manual-feed slot instead of the front one.
- ❖ **Laser printers.** Some laser printers, including Apple's LaserWriter II line, can feed label stock directly from their paper trays — convenient for lengthy label-printing sessions. Other laser printers don't provide a straight-enough paper path to feed label stocks automatically; the stock goes through too many twists and turns in the print engine, and that increases the chance of a label peeling off inside the machine — a five-star headache. With such machines, use only the manual-feed slot to feed labels.

Regardless of which printer you use, it's always a good idea to print a page of labels on plain paper first. Combine this test page together with a sheet of label stock and then hold the sandwich up to a bright light to check the positioning and alignment of each label.

Dedicated Label Printers

Finally, if you'd rather not tie up your main printer with labeling jobs, consider a dedicated label printer such as Seiko's Smart Label Printer Pro or CoStar's LabelWriter XL or LabelWriter XL Plus. The Seiko machine is not much bigger than a desktop tape dispenser and prints on roll-fed labels that measure $1^1/_8 \times 3^1/_2$ inches. The CoStar machines are slightly bigger, but they support larger labels — up to $2^1/_4 \times 4$ inches. CoStar sells a variety of label sizes.

I tested a Seiko Smart Label Printer Pro and a CoStar LabelWriter XL. Despite their manufacturers' marketing claims, neither produces laser-quality output; both use 203-dot per inch thermal printing mechanisms. Still, the print quality is more than adequate for mailing labels and the like. The CoStar printer is the better of the two; besides supporting larger labels, it includes vastly superior software that provides basic mailing list management features, support for bar codes, and a label serial number feature. And with the addition of an interface box, the CoStar machines can be shared on a network.

Specialized labeling features

If all labeling programs did was combine bare-bones layout features with templates for common label sizes, there wouldn't be much incentive for using them. Fortunately, most programs do more.

As mentioned earlier, MyAdvancedLabelDesigner has a built-in database manager that's suitable for keeping track of mailing lists. Both MySoftware programs can also import text-only files created with a database manager, so you can use data from a program such as FileMaker Pro. StickyBusiness lacks a built-in data manager but provides a print-merge feature that lets you combine data from a text-only file with repeating text, such as your return address, that you've added to a template.

As you might expect, a label program's real prowess is printing. Label programs have a variety of features designed to cut down on label waste and make label printing an easier process. For example, if your labeling life involves printing just a few labels now and then, you probably have a lot of label sheets that are only partially used. You can tell a label program to skip those blank spots when it begins printing, and thus not have to begin each printing session with a full sheet. Label programs also let you print multiple copies of the same label. All of the programs tested also have a serializing feature that prints a unique serial number on each label — a great feature if you're a software developer using the program to print labels for disks.

And speaking of disks, it's worth noting that Williams & Macias also sells a program called MyDiskLabeler III, whose sole specialty is printing disk labels. MyDiskLabeler III's layout features are similar to those of StickyBusiness, but the program includes only templates for floppy disks, SyQuest cartridges, and other storage media. More to the point, MyDiskLabeler III can read the directories of disks or cartridges and print their contents on the labels. You can also create and print reports that list the contents of a disk or cartridge. If you rely on SyQuest cartridges for backing up or transporting files, these features can be valuable tools for documenting the contents of the cartridges. Williams & Macias sells its own line of SyQuest labels for laser printers; the firm also sells a variety of other label stocks, as does MySoftware Company.

Choosing a labeling program

If you print only a few labels now and then and you already have a program that includes label templates, you might not want to bother with stand-alone label software. If you can benefit from the additional features a label program provides, then get one of the StickyBusiness packages from Williams & Macias: StickyBusiness if you don't need bar-coding features, or StickyBusiness Plus if you do. They support the widest array of label stocks, they provide the best layout features, and the programs themselves are easier to use and better designed than MySoftware's packages. Both StickyBusiness packages also include a desk accessory, QuickStick, that lets you dash off a quick label.

How to Make Laminated Cards

By combining transparency film with full-sheet label stock such as Avery's 5353, you can create rugged laminated plastic cards. After laying out the card, choose the Page Setup command and click the Options button. In the Options dialog box, check the Flip Horizontal box, and then click OK. (With the QuickDraw GX print dialog boxes, choose Page Setup, click More Choices, select the LaserWriter Options item, and check the Flip Horizontal box.)

Next, print the document on the transparency film. Attach the label stock to the film, with the toner side (the side whose contents appear backwards) facing the stock, and then trim. Because the toner is sandwiched between the label and film, it won't scratch off.

Printers for labels

If you print loads of labels, consider Costar's LabelWriter II, a tiny printer that prints just labels. (The LabelWriter Plus prints larger labels.) Costar also makes the AddressWriter and the larger AddressExpress, both of which print envelopes, postcards, and pinfeed labels.

Card Games

Database programs such as FileMaker Pro haven't completely replaced index cards and Rolodex files. In fact, by printing a database on card stock, you can have the best of both worlds — electronic sorting and revision along with the reliability of hard copy.

ImageWriter card options

ImageWriters can print on standard index cards; continuous-feeding fanfold cards are also available in several sizes and colors. Avery also makes Rolodex cards in fanfold form. For easier formatting and feeding, consider modifying the ImageWriter print driver so that its Page Setup dialog box offers an index card option. You can use Apple's ResEdit utility or, better still, a free program called PREC Manager, available from user groups and on-line services. For details on modifying resources, see Chapter 22.

Laser printer card options

For laser printers, Paper Direct's Perfs and Scores collection includes several noteworthy card stocks. There's an 8½ × 11-inch sheet perforated into eight business card-size rectangles, another perforated into four postcards, and a third divided into eight Rolodex cards. If you're doing a small mailing, consider the Postal Service's prestamped postcards. They roll through an ImageWriter well, and can be used with most laser printers' manual feed slots.

Table tents and door hangers

Paper Direct also sells a variety of offbeat card stock. The Table Tent stock lets you create your own table tents — you know, those little placards you see on restaurant tables: "Save room for our irresistible desserts!" Several styles are available; each has a different pattern or background.

The Door Hangers series is fold-out cards containing a large hole that enables you to hang them from doorknobs. If your company is having an off-site sales meeting or convention, you might use Door Hangers to print daily agendas or reminders to hang on each employee's hotel room door. A bed and breakfast might use it to print daily menus for guests. A smart-aleck teenager might use them to print pithy messages for parents and siblings.

Fruit of the Laser

I've saved my favorite alternative output medium for last. I had to: It was in the dryer. You can buy toner cartridges for many laser printers that let you create iron-on transfers for fabrics, baseball caps, mugs, plaques, and a lot more. Easy Transfer Cartridges, from a company of the same name (800-336-1599), are filled with sublimation dye, the same pigment used in high-end color printers.

Printing a transfer

An Easy Transfer Cartridge lives up to its name. Simply replace the printer's standard cartridge with an ETC, choose the LaserWriter driver's Flip Horizontal option as described earlier, and then print to a high-quality stock (Hammermill's Laser Plus worked beautifully for me).

Applying the transfer

To transfer the resulting output to fabric, a household iron on its cotton or linen setting works well, although you can blur large transfers if you move the iron too quickly. The company recommends using a dry mounting press (most school graphic arts and photography departments have them). The first ETC cartridges required you to use fabric composed of at least 50 percent polyester, lest the transfer come out in the wash. Fortunately for cotton lovers, the latest ETC cartridges work with all-cotton fabrics, too.

Creating color transfers

If you're adventuresome — and you have a graphics program that does color separations (Macromedia FreeHand and Adobe Illustrator do, as does Fractal Design Painter) — you can print full-color images by printing them in four passes, once each for a cyan, magenta, yellow, and black cartridge. Obtaining accurate registration (ensuring that each color prints in the correct place) for each pass is difficult, however.

ETC cartridges are available in a rainbow of colors and for numerous popular printer models. A sample transfer, and literature that lists compatible surfaces, is free.

Finishing Touches

The cliché notwithstanding, books *are* often judged by their covers. This section describes ways to polish a final product.

Letraset's Color Tag foil

To add appeal to laser-printed or photocopied documents, you can add color using Letraset's Color Tag system, a wallet-sized electric iron and heat-sensitive colored foil. Place the foil over the part of a document to be colorized, and burnish it with the iron. When you peel off the foil, the color adheres to the toner that the printer or copier applied. The foil comes in 72 colors and in metallic and matte finishes. The results are stunning.

Stupid Printer Tricks, Apple's Color LaserWriter, and theTypeBook

In the *Macworld Power User Clinic*'s Stupid Printer Tricks segment (sorry, Mr. Letterman), you can watch yours truly demonstrate some of the printer tips described in this chapter. Will I burn myself creating an iron-on T-shirt transfer with a laser printer? Will the Letraset ColorTag foil go on smoothly? Will I drench myself in ink when refilling a StyleWriter cartridge? Tune in to find out.

When you're done, check out the Imaging Products segment to see the Apple Color LaserWriter in action.

And when you're ready to start taming your font collection, start up Jim Lewis's fabulous font-specimen utility, theTypeBook. With this utility, creating font catalogs is as easy as choosing a few commands. theTypeBook can print font samples in six different formats, including charts showing which key sequences summon special characters.

Paper Direct LaserColor foil

Paper Direct's LaserColor foil provides the same stunning gloss as Letraset's Color Tag system but uses your laser printer or photocopier to do it. After printing the item you want to colorize, attach the foil to the output and then run the page through your laser printer or copier (by printing or copying a blank page). The heated fuser rollers in the printer or copier affix the foil to the page — just as the Color Tag's iron does.

Binding options

The best way to enhance and present a large document is to bind it. VeloBind Corporation manufactures binding equipment of all sizes, from the Personal VeloBinder, which binds up to 45 pages, to the Model 750, which joins up to 750. The firm also sells attractive cover stocks and tab dividers. Bind-it Corporation's Covermate 600 is a thermal binding machine that produces *perfect-bound* books of up to 2¼ inches wide. (This book, like most, is perfect bound.) Bind-it's Covermate 25 uses less-expensive plastic-comb binding.

Utilities for Power Printing

Numerous utilities are available that can enhance your printer's operation, make it easier to manage printers on a network, or just cut down on toner use. Here are some examples. Note that all but the last utility, Peirce Print Tools, are designed for non-QuickDraw GX printing (indeed, GX's enhanced printing features eliminate the need for many of these utilities).

- *Print Central* This network utility from Adobe lets you set up a centralized print server on a dedicated Macintosh. Print Central sports numerous options that streamline printing in a busy office, such as the ability to route print jobs to whichever printer is least busy. You can also specify security options to keep some printers (such as your color machine) off limits to certain users (like the guy who keeps printing scanned images of his kids).
- *Blue Parrot* This control panel from Casa Blanca Works lets you monitor the status of the printers on your network. By knowing which printers are in use before choosing the Print command, you can route your job to an idle machine — or at least to one with a smaller number of pending jobs.
- *Toner Tuner* This clever utility from Working Software adds a slider to the Print dialog box that lets you save laser printer toner by adjusting the darkness of output.
- *Peirce Print Tools* This amazing set of print extensions for QuickDraw GX lets you do everything from log print jobs to save paper and toner to create customized special effects. It's covered in more detail later in this chapter.

I've covered the most popular kinds of print media here, but there isn't room to describe every kind of specialty paper and output accessory. Paper Direct sells a sampler kit containing hundreds of paper and envelope samples, and the price is credited to your first order. And most office supply stores stock a large selection of labels, paper, and binding equipment. Try them out. Classy papers and alternative output media are more tools you can use to convey your messages — and they're a fun way to give your printer a break from the same old stock.

Tips for StyleWriters

I've already provided some recommendations for ink-jet paper. This section contains some additional tips for the ink-jet set.

Thinking about ink

A StyleWriter's disposable print head contains about an ounce of ink. The ink itself is 70 to 90 percent water. Because the ink's pigments are water soluble, ink-jet output can smear easily before it dries — or after if it gets wet. Your pages may not be exposed to raindrops very often, although your envelopes might be. As I mentioned earlier, to protect the address on an envelope, cover it with a piece of transparent tape.

If you are printing something that will be exposed to moisture, you can improve durability by spraying a page with Krylon Crystal Clear or other artist's fixative. And don't forget about the photocopier. Besides getting more durable output, you'll improve the quality of the output itself. A photocopier's plastic toner creates "blacker blacks" than liquid ink's. The photocopies also won't have that wavy, mottled look that often plagues ink-heavy pages.

Refilling ink cartridges

Apple says a StyleWriter II or 1200 ink cartridge is good for about 500 double-spaced text pages. When the ink is spent, you throw away the cartridge and buy a new one. Or do you? The cartridge's components are good for more than just a few hundred pages, and if you can get more ink into the cartridge, you can get more pages out of it.

In the early days of ink-jet printing, some people used syringes to inject spent cartridges with fountain-pen ink. Things are a bit more civilized now; several companies sell refilling kits that replenish a cartridge. Refilling is easy but can be messy. (I trashed a favorite T-shirt in my first try.)

The first few pages I printed with a refilled cartridge were streaked and disappointing, but things improved after a few cartridge cleanings (click the Print dialog box's Options button and then check the Clean Ink Cartridge Before Printing box). Indeed, I couldn't discern between output created with a fresh cartridge and a refilled one.

The question is, is it worth the trouble? It does cost less, and if you're on a tight budget, the answer is probably yes. But don't think you're doing the environment any favors; refilling kits contain about as much disposable cardboard and plastic as does a new print cartridge. (By comparison, refilling a larger, more complex laser cartridge can be environmentally correct.)

Cleaning the ink cartridge

I mentioned the StyleWriter driver's Clean Ink Cartridge Before Printing check box. This box can be your best friend when streaks appear on your output. Streaking can occur when paper dust and fibers clog the ink nozzles. During the cleaning, the StyleWriter wipes the surface of the ink nozzles to remove paper fibers, caps the ink cartridge with a rubber cover, and then pumps a small amount of fresh ink into the nozzles. The entire job takes about 13 seconds. The StyleWriter performs the cleaning process automatically when you first switch it on after plugging it in, when you replace the ink cartridge, and when more than 72 hours have elapsed since the last cleaning.

One final ink tip: Always remove the ink cartridge before transporting an ink-jet printer; otherwise, you may find any inky mess when you reach your destination. This is especially true if the printer will be shipped by air; the lower pressure in some airliner cargo holds is likely to cause ink to pump from the cartridge. Ship a partially used cartridge in a zip-top plastic bag.

HP Offers Free DeskWriter Repair Kit

If you have a Hewlett-Packard DeskWriter 510 or 520 (or DeskJet 550C or 560C) that was manufacturered between June 1993 and March 1994, you should know about a free repair kit that Hewlett-Packard has released. These printers can develop paper feed problems, such as reporting that they're out of paper when they really aren't. The problems are caused by the rubber that HP used in the printer's paper-feed rollers — after a few years, the rubber hardens somewhat and becomes slick and less able to grab sheets of paper. The repair kit lets you fix the problem.

To find out if your printer has the defective rollers, check its serial number — if its number begins with US3 through US43, call HP at 800-656-2324 for a roller-repair kit.

Tips for PostScript Printers

If you use a laser printer in an office, chances are it's a PostScript printer. Some non-PostScript laser printers are available for the Mac — examples include GCC's PLP series and Apple's Personal LaserWriter LS and LaserWriter Select 300 — but PostScript printers' superiority for graphics and publishing work and their ability to be easily shared on a network have made them the preferred printers in the Macintosh business world.

Since Apple's original LaserWriter appeared in 1985, I've worked with well over 100 PostScript printers in the course of writing *Macworld*'s printer roundups. In this section, I present a collection of PostScript printer tips and techniques for improving performance, managing fonts, and upgrading your printer. The following tips also apply to color PostScript printers.

No startup page

I'll start with an easy one. When you switch on a PostScript printer, it ruminates for a minute or two and then prints a *startup page* listing information about the printer: the number of pages it has printed, the fonts it contains, and the settings of its various ports. Occasionally, these statistics are useful, but most of the time, the startup page just wastes time, toner, and paper.

You can disable the startup page in a few ways. The low-tech solution involves simply pulling the printer's paper tray out an inch or two when you first switch it on. When the printer's on-line indicator illuminates, indicating the machine is warmed up and ready for print jobs, slide the tray back into place.

A better method is to explicitly tell the printer to stop printing its startup page. Most of today's PostScript printers sport calculatorlike keypads you can use to adjust various settings — including whether a startup page is printed.

If your printer doesn't have a keypad (none of Apple's do), you need to run a utility program on your Mac to disable the startup page. Apple's PostScript printers include a utility called Apple Printer Utility; if you have a non-Apple PostScript printer, you may be able to obtain a copy from an Apple dealer. You can use Apple Printer Utility to disable the startup page and adjust a variety of other printer settings.

Two older, less-capable programs called LaserWriter Utility and LaserWriter Font Utility were included with Apple printers before the Apple Printer Utility shipped in 1994. The LaserWriter Font Utility is also widely available through on-line services and user groups. Both programs have a Utilities menu containing a command called Start Page that lets you enable or disable the startup page.

Name that printer

When you use the Chooser desk accessory to select a PostScript printer, the printer's name appears in the Chooser's device list. Usually, the name corresponds to the printer's model number — *LaserWriter Pro 630*, for example. With the aforementioned utilities, you can change the name to something more descriptive — *Art Department Printer* or *5th Floor LaserWriter* or *Trixie's Printer* or *Lil' Gutenberg* (see Figure 31-2 "What's in a Printer Name?"). Naming a printer is especially valuable if your network contains two or more printers of the same model, a situation that can make it impossible to tell which printer in the Chooser is which.

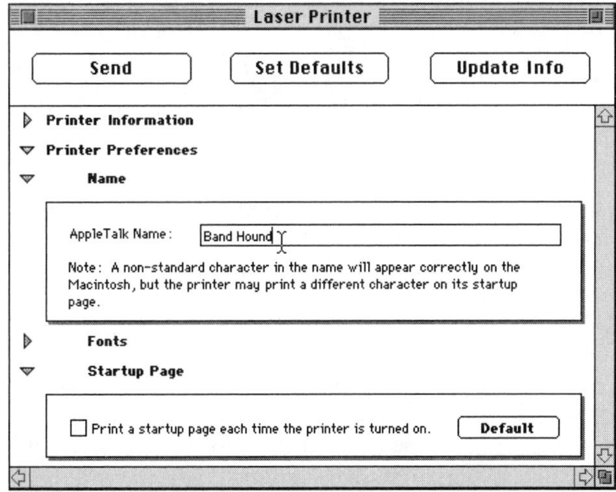

Figure 31-2: What's in a Printer Name? With the Apple Printer Utility, you can change a PostScript printer's name. This window also shows the option for disabling the printer's startup page.

If you can't round up LaserWriter Utility, check the disks that came with your printer. An older Apple utility called The Namer also lets you change a printer's name.

Font Downloading Strategies

You probably already know that you can supplement the fonts built into a PostScript printer with *downloadable* fonts — ones that reside on your Mac's hard disk and are transferred to the printer's memory. When you print a document, the Mac's PostScript printer driver — the system file named LaserWriter — queries the printer to determine if it contains the required fonts. If it doesn't, the driver automatically downloads the fonts and then clears them from the printer's memory at the end of the job.

Automatic downloading is convenient, but there's a catch: One downloadable font takes up to 20 seconds to transfer over the LocalTalk cabling you probably use. If you use a few downloadable fonts — say, New Baskerville with italic and bold — you add a minute to the time required to print a document. And if you print a document a few times in the course of fine-tuning its formatting, the wasted time piles up even more.

Manual downloading

One answer is manual downloading. By taking the time to download "by hand" the fonts you plan to use, you remove the need for automatic downloading during print jobs. Fonts downloaded manually remain in the printer's memory until you nix the power or reset the printer.

You can download fonts using the Apple Printer Utility or its older siblings (see Figure 31-3 "Downloading Fonts Manually"). A more-convenient option is a $20 shareware control panel called Startup Downloader, by Manuel Veloso. With Startup Downloader, you specify sets of fonts that you want to manually download. Startup Downloader then creates a tiny (20K) application program that, when run, downloads the fonts. If you put these mini-programs in your hard disk's Startup Items folder, the fonts are downloaded when you start up the Mac. It's manual downloading made automatic. (Or maybe I should call it Manuel downloading.)

Where downloadable fonts live

Regardless of the downloading tool you use, it helps to know where your downloadable font files are located. In System 7.0, downloadable PostScript fonts are stored in the Extensions folder; in System 7.1 and 7.5, they live in the Fonts folder. Both folders are located within the System Folder. In system versions prior to 7.0, PostScript fonts reside within the top level of the System Folder.

(If you use MasterJuggler or Suitcase, you *can* store your printer font files elsewhere; see Chapter 22 for details.)

The downside to manual downloading

There are some drawbacks to manual downloading. Each font you manually download leaves less room in the printer's memory for fonts that may be automatically downloaded during print jobs. At worst, you may receive an error message during a print job stating that the document couldn't be printed. In this case, you need to reset the printer to clear its memory: You can't selectively remove fonts that you've manually downloaded.

One possible solution to this printer-memory problem is buried within the Page Setup dialog box: Click the Options button and then check the box named Unlimited Downloadable Fonts in a Document. When this box is checked, the LaserWriter driver purges automatically downloaded fonts as soon as they're used.

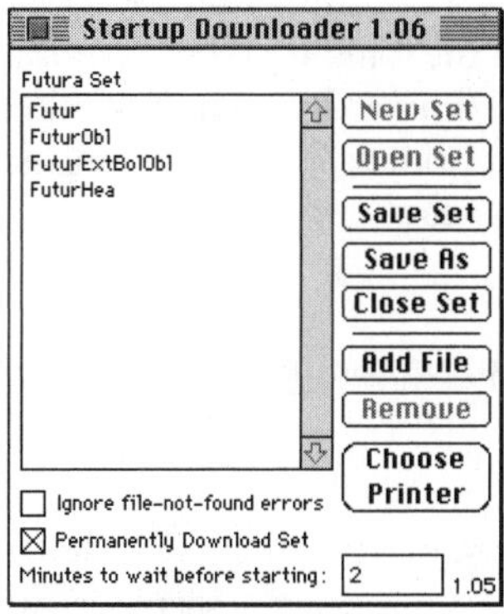

Figure 31-3: Downloading Fonts Manually
You can download fonts manually with a utility such as Apple's Apple Printer Utility (top), which here shows a list of fonts selected for downloading. Manuel Veloso's shareware Startup Downloader control panel (middle) creates tiny application programs that download sets of fonts when run (bottom) .

However, if a given font is needed again, it must be downloaded again, lengthening print times. For this reason, a better solution is to strike a balance between manual and automatic downloading: Manually download only those fonts you use most and let the LaserWriter driver download the bit players for you.

A hard drive for your printer

The best alternative to the downloading dilemma is to attach a hard disk to your printer's SCSI port — if it has one. Some SCSI-equipped printers include Apple's LaserWriter IINTX, IIf and IIg, and LaserWriter Pro 630 and 810; GCC's BLP II and BLP IIs; Texas Instruments' microLaser Turbo series; and NEC's SilentWriter2 990. Most color PostScript printers also have SCSI ports.

Apple's LaserWriter Pro 630 has two SCSI interfaces: one external and one internal. Many third-party hard drive vendors sell 2½-inch hard drives with appropriate brackets for the 630. APS Technologies even sells a kit that lets you install a spare PowerBook internal drive — maybe the one you have left over when you upgraded your PowerBook's hard drive — in a LaserWriter Pro 630.

How to use a printer hard drive

When you attach a hard drive to a printer, you can use a font-downloading utility to download fonts to the drive. Then, when the fonts are required during a print job, the printer transfers them from its hard drive to its memory — almost instantly. A hard drive also makes a PostScript printer faster at printing documents containing a large variety of fonts, sizes, or styles.

Don't trash your printer font files

In the ideal world, you could reclaim some precious storage space from your Mac's hard drive by deleting the printer font files after downloading them to the printer's hard drive.

The problem is, if you use the Adobe Type Manager utility (and who doesn't?), deleting the printer font files prevents ATM from generating sharp screen characters at any size. If you work primarily with small text sizes, this drawback won't be significant. Just be sure you've installed bitmaps for the sizes you need. If you create a lot of display type, though, you may want to leave the printer fonts on your hard disk.

Check compatibility before buying a drive

Note that some hard drives can't be formatted as font drives. The printer must be able to tell how much space is available on the disk; some third-party drives don't support the required SCSI commands. If you're buying a drive to attach to a PostScript printer, verify with its manufacturer that it can work with one.

If your printer lacks a SCSI port, you can still boost its capacity for downloadable fonts by adding a memory upgrade or font card to the printer (see the Background box "Printer Upgrade Options").

Printer Upgrade Options

Hardware upgrade options vary from printer to printer — some machines accept second paper trays or envelope feeders, for example. But some upgrade categories apply to most or all PostScript printers.

Memory

Most PostScript printers accept memory upgrades. Adding more memory increases the printer's downloadable-font capacity and boosts its overall performance, particularly with graphically complex documents. With some printers, adding memory also increases the printer's *image area,* and thus lets you print closer to the edges of the page. With low-end printers such as Texas Instruments' now-discontinued microLaser PS17, you must add memory in order to print legal-size (8½ × 14-inch) pages. (Another way to increase the image area is to click the Page Setup dialog box's Options button and then check the Larger Print Area box. This slows printing and leaves less room for downloadable fonts, however.) Some printers even provide better output quality when equipped with more RAM. Boost an Apple LaserWriter IIf's memory to at least 5MB, and you can take advantage of its PhotoGrade technology to print better-looking scanned images. Boost an IBM/Lexmark LaserPrinter 4019 to 5MB, and its resolution jumps from 300 dots per inch to 600 dpi.

Font cartridges

Apple's now-discontinued LaserWriter IINTX contains an internal slot that accepts a circuit board containing additional fonts. Other printers — including numerous models from QMS, Texas Instruments, Okidata, and IBM/Lexmark — provide front-panel slots that hold font cartridges. Fonts in a font cartridge don't have to be downloaded; besides boosting the printer's performance, this frees more of its RAM for lesser-used downloadable fonts, and it reduces data traffic on your network.

The best source for font cartridges is Sonnet Technologies, whose FontCards sell for between $199 and $249 and contain between 10 and 18 Adobe typefaces. Sonnet will also create customized cartridges containing the fonts you use most, including any custom fonts you may have created using programs such as Macromedia Fontographer.

Controller upgrades

Xante Corporation sells numerous hardware upgrades for Apple's original LaserWriter, for the LaserWriter II series, and for other popular printers from Hewlett-Packard, Canon, QMS, and others. Xante's AccelaWriter series boosts resolution to 600 dpi and provides faster performance as well as SCSI ports for hard disks. Xante's upgrades (along with the firm's laser printers) also sport an innovative feature called Virtual Disk Technology that enables you to permanently download fonts to the printer. The ImageUp! board from NewGen Systems provides similar benefits (sans the Virtual Disk Technology) for HP LaserJet series II printers.

Tips for the LaserWriter 8 Driver

I've mentioned the LaserWriter driver file a few times: It's the link between your Mac and a PostScript printer. Over the years, Apple has released numerous updates to the LaserWriter driver.

The latest version in the non-QuickDraw GX world is LaserWriter 8. Some of LaserWriter 8's enhancements are aimed at color printers and imagesetters, but many are also useful for the Mac in the gray flannel suit. For example, the driver provides dialog box options that let you access the extra amenities many printers

More Quick Printer Tips

Here are a few more quick tips for PostScript printers.

Manually download frequently used fonts
I've spent a good part of this chapter on this tip, but it's worth repeating. There isn't a better way to inexpensively improve performance with downloadable fonts.

Don't use city name fonts like New York or Geneva with PostScript printers
Besides looking inferior to true PostScript fonts, these fonts may require the printer to perform additional calculations that slow performance.

Print in black and white when proofing
If you're proofing a page with color or gray-scale images, you'll see it sooner by choosing the Black & White option. In the LaserWriter 8 driver, click the Print dialog box's Options button and then choose Black and White from the Print pop-up menu. If you're using QuickDraw GX, you can't specify black and white printing.

Uncheck Larger Print Area or Unlimited Downloadable Fonts
They slow the printer by commandeering printer memory that would otherwise be used to handle the calculations required to print a page.

Avoid mixing a slew of fonts, sizes, and styles
This is the best way to boost a PostScript printer's performance. And not only will you see your pages faster, but the pages you see will look better.

have: enhanced resolution, multiple paper bins, fax modem cards, and even duplex mechanisms for printing on both sides of a page.

This section is a collection of LaserWriter 8 tips and tricks. If you're using QuickDraw GX or are thinking of doing so, you'll find details on QuickDraw GX printing later in this chapter. You'll find QuickDraw GX provides many of the same printing options — and then some.

One more thing before we start: In the middle of 1995, Apple shipped LaserWriter version 8.3, which provides QuickDraw GX's user interface and printing-management enhancements without actually requiring you to install QuickDraw GX. LaserWriter 8.3 is included with Apple's Color LaserWriter and LaserWriter 4/600 PS and is also available for downloading from on-line services. It requires System 7.1.1 or later. Unless otherwise noted, everything in this section applies to LaserWriter 8.3. Later in this chapter, I'll describe the enhanced features that LaserWriter 8.3 (and QuickDraw GX) provide.

How LaserWriter 8 works

The key to LaserWriter 8's ability to support unique printer features is a special file called a *printer description file* (PDF). PDF files reside in a folder named Printer Descriptions, which is within your System Folder's Extensions folder. True to its name, a PDF lists a specific printer's capabilities: its resolution, paper-handling features, and more.

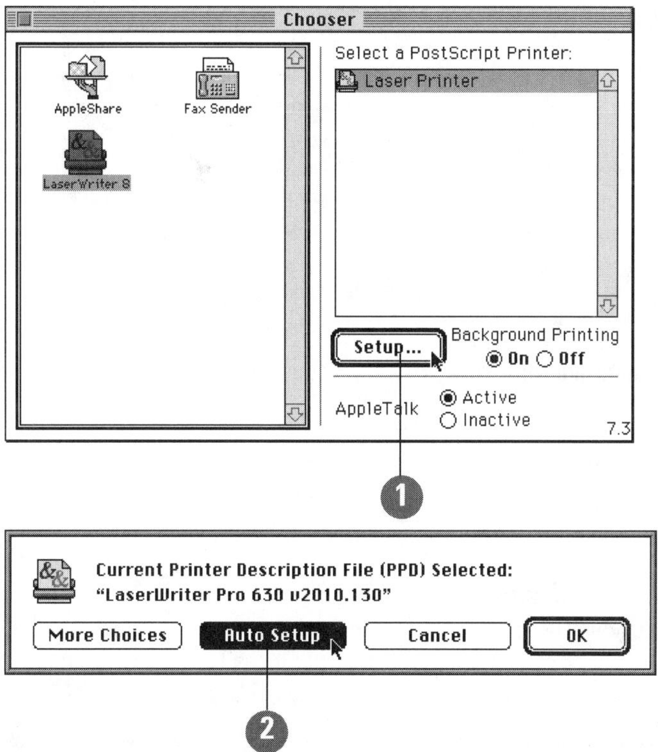

Figure 31-4: Setting Up LaserWriter 8 After installing LaserWriter 8, open the Chooser (top), select your printer, and click the Setup button (1). This displays another dialog box (bottom) that lets you manually or automatically configure the driver for your printer. When you click the Auto Setup button (2), the driver queries the printer to learn its brand and model, and then it selects the matching PDF file. You can also manually select a different PDF by clicking the More Choices button and then clicking the Select PPD button. You might do this when preparing a print-to-disk file for an imagesetter or color printer that you don't actually have.

A PDF is a text-only file that you can open with any word processor. Not that you ever have to: PDFs are accessed automatically by the Chooser desk accessory as part of an easy configuration process that you perform after installing LaserWriter 8 (see Figure 31-4, "Setting Up LaserWriter 8").

After the driver knows what your printer is capable of, it can adjust its Page Setup and Print dialog boxes accordingly — a trick earlier versions of the driver couldn't perform.

Pick your paper

A growing number of PostScript printers include or accept optional multiple paper bins. Thanks to PDFs, LaserWriter 8 lets you tap these trays in several ways. Two or more trays make it easy to mix and match stocks without having to walk over to

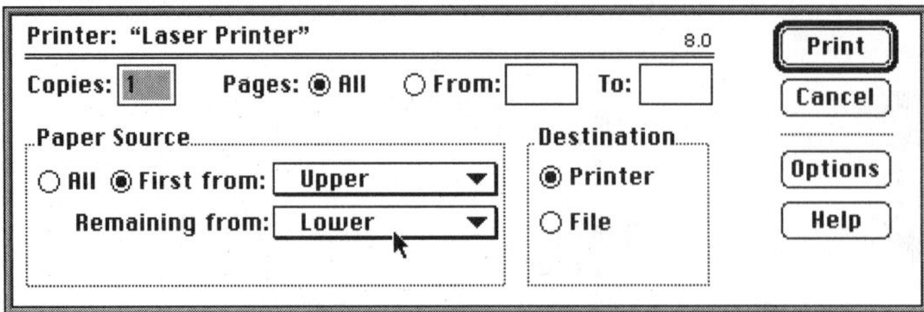

Figure 31-5: Paper Feeding Options The Paper Source pop-ups in LaserWriter 8's Print dialog box let you mix and match paper within a print job. Here, the first page of a document will be printed using the paper in the printer's upper tray, while the remaining pages will use the paper in the lower tray.

the printer and slide trays in and out. In an office, multiple bins can help you avoid the fist fights that often occur when, say, one person installs transparency stock just as another person begins a 48-page print job.

Here are a few ways you might put two trays to work.

Multipage business letters

Put letterhead in the upper tray and second sheets in the lower one. Then, in the Paper Source area of the Print dialog box, choose Upper for the first page, and Lower for the remaining pages (see Figure 31-5 "Paper Feeding Options").

Here's a variation of this technique for a printer that has one paper cassette and one multipurpose tray, such as Apple's LaserWriter Pro series: put second sheets in the cassette and letterhead in the multipurpose tray. Then select First From Multipurpose Tray and Remaining From Cassette. If you write more one-page letters than multipage ones, reverse this scheme.

Printing rough proofs

Put el-cheapo copier bond in the upper tray and high-quality laser paper in the lower one. When you're proofing a document for typos and layout errors, use the upper tray. When you're ready for final output, use the lower one.

Mixing paper and transparencies

Put laser stock in one tray and transparency stock in the other. (Check your transparency stock's box to verify that it can be fed automatically — some transparency stocks must be manually fed.)

If your printer has just one paper bin, you can still use the Paper Source options to streamline stock switching. For multipage business letters, put second sheets in the paper tray. When it's time to print, choose Manual for the letterhead page and Auto Select for the remaining pages.

Printing thumbnail pages

LaserWriter 8's Page Setup dialog box contains a pop-up menu, called Layout, that lets you print multiple pages reduced to fit on a single sheet of paper. Choose the 2 Up option, and your printer will print two pages on each sheet of paper. Choose 4 Up, and the printer shoehorns four pages onto a sheet. On the printed output, each scaled-down page is framed by a black border.

You can use this feature to save paper and toner when you're printing simple documents such as text manuscripts or electronic mail messages. You'll be surprised at how readable the text remains when it's reduced, especially with two-up printing. Text printed in four-up mode is a bit small — if the bottom rows of an eye chart give you trouble, don't go smaller than two-up.

Using the 2 Up or 4 Up option is also a handy way to print thumbnail versions of a large document for convenient filing. It's great for printing storyboards of presentations or video productions. And for you desktop publishers, using two-up printing is a good way to gauge how a two-page spread will appear when printed.

Making greeting cards

I doubt Adobe and Apple had the following application in mind when they created the 4 Up option, but you can use it as a quick-and-dirty method of creating a small greeting card or invitation. Start by creating a four-page document. Put the card's front on page one and its back on page two, and format these pages so they appear upside-down on the Mac's screen. (You'll probably want to use a graphics or publishing program for the job, although you can also use a word processor that provides drawing features, such as Microsoft Word or WordPerfect.) Next, create the card's inside pages (right-side up) on pages three and four. Finally, choose Page Setup, select the 4 Up option, and then print. Folding the output puts each page in the right order and orientation. Trim the sheet to remove the page borders if you like. (Later I'll describe a free utility that prevents the borders from being printed.)

Here's another slick Page Setup feature previous LaserWriter drivers lacked: If you click the graphic representation of the page — the picture of the dogcow — the graphic is replaced by a text listing of your printer's exact imageable area (the portion of the page upon which the printer can apply toner). This can be a handy way of finding out just how close to the edges of a page you can get. (This information, by the way, comes from the PDF.)

Before leaving the Page Setup dialog box, you might want to explore some of the features in the Options dialog box, which appears when you click the Options button. These features are largely unchanged from LaserWriter 7.x, but if you're new to driver exploration, you may have never encountered them. An easy way to familiarize yourself with them is to turn on System 7's balloon help feature and point to each option.

The power of the Print dialog box

I've already touched on the best new feature of the LaserWriter 8 Print dialog box: the Paper Source options that let you bounce between bins. Clicking the Print dialog box's Options button reveals more options that you can use to fine-tune print jobs and save time in the process (see Figure 31-6 "Exploring Print Options").

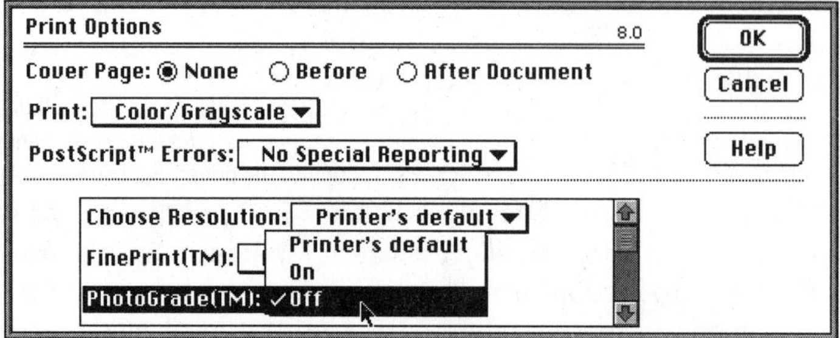

Figure 31-6: Exploring Print Options Clicking the Print dialog box's Options button reveals another dialog box that lets you control unique printer features. Here, the PhotoGrade feature provided by many Apple LaserWriters is being disabled for faster printing.

If you're proofing a document containing scanned images or illustrations containing color or gray shades, you can cut printing times — often dramatically — by choosing the Black and White option instead of Color/Grayscale. In a similar vein, if your printer has a halftone-enhancement feature such as Apple's PhotoGrade, you can probably reduce printing times by disabling it: click Options, locate the PhotoGrade pop-up menu, and choose Off. (Generally, disabling a text-enhancement feature — for example, Apple's FinePrint or Hewlett-Packard's Resolution Enhancement Technology — will not decrease printing times.)

Options you select in the bottom portion of the Print dialog box revert to their original, printer-resident settings after a document is printed. For instance, if you disable PhotoGrade to get faster output of a given document, PhotoGrade will be reenabled after the document is printed.

Creating print-to-disk and EPS files

LaserWriter 8's Print dialog box contains an area labeled Destination, whose buttons let you aim the document at the printer (the normal setting) or at a disk file. The latter option is most often used by desktop publishers who are going to be using a service bureau to get high-resolution imagesetter output. Printing a document to disk and then supplying the disk file eliminates the need for the service bureau to have the application that created the document: to print the document, the bureau downloads the print-to-disk file to its imagesetter. (It can be more involved than this; always consult with a service bureau before providing it with a print-to-disk file.)

The Hacker's Guide to LaserWriter 8

Leave it to the Mac community to find a way to make a good thing better. While exploring America Online, I found a utility that can perform several modifications to the LaserWriter 8 driver.

Printer Defaults 1.1.1, a free utility created by John Rawnsley, can modify the driver not to print page borders in the two- and four-up modes; to limit the maximum number of copies you can print; to add a two- or four-up pop-up menu to the Print dialog box; to not require AppleTalk to be active (useful for generating print-to-disk files when you aren't connected to a network); and much more.

If you're comfortable working with Apple's ResEdit utility (described in Chapter 24), you can perform several additional modifications, including adding additional n-up options to the Page Setup dialog box. (This can be handy if you have a tabloid-size printer, whose 11 × 17-inch sheets can easily accommodate six or even eight reduced-size pages.) You'll find instructions in a file named LaserWriter 8.x Hacks, created by Don Markuson.

Whether you use Printer Defaults or ResEdit as your modification weapon, don't make any changes to your sole copy of the driver. For safety's sake, make a duplicate and then modify the copy. To make a dupe using the Finder, select the driver — it's in the Extensions folder, within the System Folder — and choose Duplicate from the File menu. Also, if you're in charge of managing drivers on a network, you might want to copy the same modified driver to each user's System Folder so that everyone will have the same printing options.

LaserWriter versions 8.1.1 and later build on the print-to-disk feature with an option that lets you create an encapsulated PostScript (EPS) version of a single page within a document. One use for this feature is to create a page-within-a-page effect: that is, to print a small, reduced version of a page in another document. (For example, you might include a page from a report or manual on a slide that's part of a presentation.) Another use is to export an EPS image from a program that doesn't provide an EPS export command.

In the Destination area of the Print dialog box, click the File button (notice the Print button changes to read Save). In the Pages area of the dialog box, specify the single page for which you want to create an EPS file (for instance, to create an EPS file of page 2, type *2* in the From and To text boxes). Click the Save button, and a Save dialog box appears. From its Format menu, choose either of the two EPS Mac options. (The EPS Mac Enhanced Option yields better results but uses more disk space.) Type a name for the file and click Save. You can now import the resulting file into any application program that can read EPS files.

LaserWriter 8 and PostScript fax

If your printer contains a PostScript fax board, the Destination area of the Print dialog box contains a third button, Fax, that you choose when you want to fax a document instead of print it. LaserWriter 8.1.1 and later versions provide a fax log feature that keeps track of outgoing faxes.

LaserWriter 8.2f, included with Apple's fax-capable lasers (for example, the LaserWriter 16/600 PS) can use a printer's SCSI hard drive to store incoming and outgoing faxes. Because a hard drive provides more storage than the printer's RAM, you can receive and transmit faxes that you'd otherwise have to spread out over multiple transmissions. To configure the printer to store fax data on the hard disk, you must download a PostScript file named UseDiskForFax to the printer. This file — and the Apple Printer Utility you use to download it — is included on the disks that came with the printer.

For more information on PostScript faxing, see the previous chapter and Chapter 16.

Printing with QuickDraw GX

QuickDraw GX is the biggest thing to happen to Macintosh printing since PrintMonitor made it possible to work and print at the same time. From reading Chapter 11, you already know about the font- and type-related enhancements QuickDraw GX brings to the table. This section summarizes QuickDraw GX's improved printing features and provides tips for using them.

As I've mentioned before, in mid-1995 Apple endowed several of its non-GX printer drivers with some of GX's best printing features. Specifically, LaserWriter 8.3 and the drivers for the StyleWriter 1200, 2200, and 2400 support the desktop printer icons and print-management features that previously required QuickDraw GX.

But there are still some things that these drivers can't do that GX can. In the following sections, when I say "GX," I'm referring to a feature that *requires* QuickDraw GX. When I say "GX or Apple's latest non-GX drivers," I'm referring to a feature that is available with GX as well as with LaserWriter 8.3 and the StyleWriter 1200, 2200, and 2400 drivers.

What's new?

Here's a summary of the new printing features in QuickDraw GX.

A new way to work with and switch between printers

Although you still use the Chooser desk accessory from some printer-related tasks, QuickDraw GX and Apple's latest non-GX drivers provide a special type of icon called the *desktop printer*, an icon that represents a specific printer and a specific print queue (a list of jobs waiting to be printed). Desktop printer icons provide another way to print documents — just drag their icons to the desktop printer icon. And they make possible a flock of fun little printer tricks I'll describe shortly.

More ways to manage pending print jobs

The old PrintMonitor application, which handles background printing in non-GX systems, doesn't provide much control over jobs that are waiting to be printed. With the desktop printer windows in QuickDraw GX and Apple's latest non-GX drivers, you can become a control freak, pausing print jobs, redirecting them to different printers, scheduling them to print at a certain time, and much more.

- *More versatile document-printing options* With QuickDraw GX, you can specify custom paper sizes, give names to paper trays, and more.
- *An expandable design that makes it easy to add printing features* QuickDraw GX provides an expandable architecture that lets Apple and third-party developers add printing features through the use of *printing extensions.* Just as system extensions enhance the Mac — adding a screen saver, for instance, or a keyboard-shortcut utility — printing extensions add printing features. Examples include extensions that print watermarks (such as the word *Confidential*) on pages or automatically print pages in the correct order for binding.

A note about application compatibility

Chapter 11 stated that application programs must be adapted to take advantage of many of QuickDraw GX's features. This applies to QuickDraw GX printing, too — to an extent. Some printing-related features in QuickDraw GX will require GX-aware application programs, but many of the enhancements work with GX-unaware programs, too.

QuickDraw GX's new Print dialog boxes

Programs that support QuickDraw GX printing use a new style of Print and Page Setup dialog box (see Figure 31-7 "New Ways to Set Up and Print"). Each dialog box contains a More Choices button that, when clicked, expands the dialog box to reveal more printing options; more about this later.

The wonders of the desktop printer icon

Your first job before printing with QuickDraw GX or Apple's latest non-GX drivers is to make a desktop printer icon for your printer. When you use the Chooser to select the icon for a printer, a button called Create appears. Click it or press Return, and a desktop printer icon appears on the desktop a moment later (see Figure 31-8, "Making a Desktop Printer Icon").

So your desktop has this cool icon that looks like a printer. What can you do with it?

Page Setup
Paper Type: US Letter
1.0f2c12
Orientation:
Scale: 100 %
More Choices
Cancel
Format

Print
Print to: Laser Printer
1.0f2c12
Pages: All
From: To:
Copies: 1
More Choices
Cancel
Print

Figure 31-7: New Ways to Set Up and Print QuickDraw GX-aware application programs use new Page Setup (top) and Print (bottom) dialog boxes.

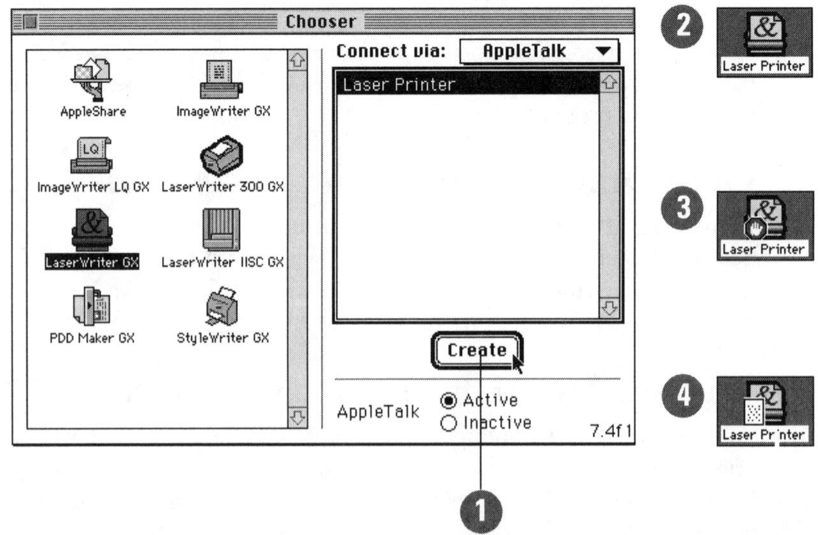

Figure 31-8: Making a Desktop Printer Icon To make a desktop printer icon, select the printer in the Chooser and then click Create (1). The desktop printer icon appears on the desktop (2). The bold border around the icon indicates that this is the default printer — the one that jobs will go to unless you specify otherwise. When a printer's queue has been paused, a small stop sign appears in the printer's icon (3). When a job is printing, a small page icon appears (4).

Drag documents to it to print them

This is the drag-and-drop equivalent to the Print command that the Finder has always had. Drag a document icon to a desktop printer icon, and the Finder starts or switches to the program that created the document and presents its Print dialog box.

Share it with other Macs on your network

Select a desktop printer and choose Sharing from the Finder's File menu, and you can make the desktop printer icon available to other Macs on your network. (This doesn't work with LaserWriter 8.3.) You can even assign a password to a desktop printer to keep certain people from using it — another way to keep that guy in the office from printing out family photos on the color printer.

Make an alias of it

To access a desktop printer icon from the Apple menu, make an alias of it and then put the alias in the Apple Menus Items folder.

Rename it

You can change a desktop printer icon's name using the Finder's standard icon-naming techniques. You might use a descriptive name that reflects a certain setting — such as Print After Midnight for an icon whose print queue is set to start after midnight.

The Printing menu

When a desktop printer is selected, the Finder adds a menu named Printing to the menu bar. This menu is one of the gateways to the industrial-strength printing features in QuickDraw GX and Apple's latest non-GX drivers.

Bossing your print jobs around

The real power of a desktop printer icon surfaces when you open it. Double-click a desktop printer icon, and a window appears listing jobs that are waiting to print (see Figure 31-9 "Waiting to Print"). It's this window that lets you boss your print jobs around.

Pausing the queue: lining up jobs for later

Say you want to gang up a bunch of print jobs that you'll send to the printer during a long lunch break. Select a desktop printer icon and choose Stop Print Queue from the Printing menu. This erects a temporary road block between the print queue and the printer itself.

Now use your application programs' Print commands as you normally would. (Be sure the printer whose queue you've paused is selected as the current printer — with the printer's icon selected, choose Set Default Printer from the Printing menu.) As you "print" documents, their *print files* line up one behind another in the printer's queue. You can spot a paused queue by the stop sign icon that appears in the desktop printer's queue window.

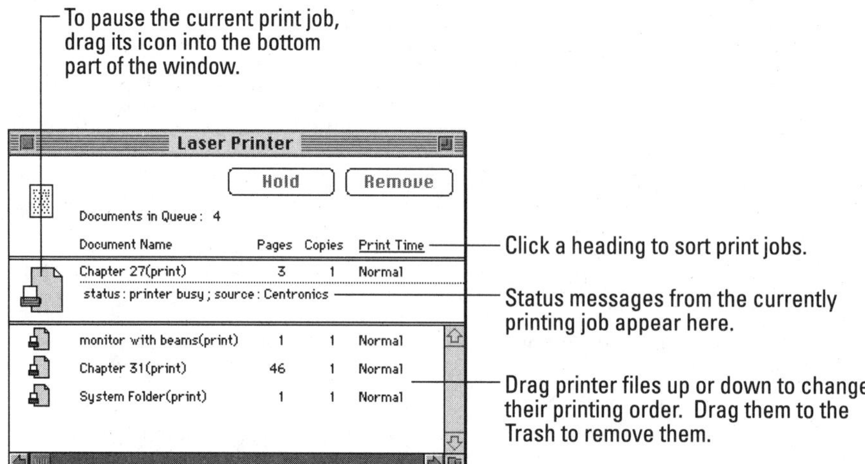
To pause the current print job, drag its icon into the bottom part of the window.
Laser Printer
Hold
Remove
Documents in Queue: 4
Document Name
Pages
Copies
Print Time
Chapter 27(print) 3 1 Normal
status: printer busy; source: Centronics
monitor with beams(print) 1 1 Normal
Chapter 31(print) 46 1 Normal
System Folder(print) 1 1 Normal
Click a heading to sort print jobs.
Status messages from the currently printing job appear here.
Drag printer files up or down to change their printing order. Drag them to the Trash to remove them.

Figure 31-9: Waiting to Print The desktop printer window lists jobs that are in the queue and lets you organize and redirect them.

You can reorganize the order of these pending print jobs so that one comes out before another or you can redirect one or more jobs to a different printer if you like (see the next two tips).

To take down the roadblock and begin printing the jobs you've queued up, choose Start Print Queue from the Printing menu. To schedule the jobs to print at a certain time, select them (with the queue window open, choose Select All from the Finder's Edit menu), and then choose Set Print Time from the Printing menu. Specify the time in the dialog box that appears. Finally, choose Start Print Queue from the Printing menu.

Reorganizing the print queue

Seconds after sending a 50-page report off to print, you realize you need to print out an urgent memo. In the predesktop printing world, you'd have to cancel the big job, print the small one, and then reprint the big one starting where you left off.

In the world of desktop printing, you can postpone the big job and sneak in the small one. In the queue window, select the job and choose Hold Print Request from the Printing menu — or simply drag the job down into the bottom half of the window. Now, print your memo.

When you've finished, you can resume the big print job by dragging it back into the status area of the desktop printer window or by selecting it and choosing one of the two Resume commands in the Printing menu. (Choose Resume on Page One to restart the entire job, or Resume On Page to start printing from a certain page.)

Scheduling Printing in the Print Dialog Box

Using the desktop printer window to specify a print time is just one way to schedule print jobs under QuickDraw GX. Another way is to use the Print Time option in the Print dialog box.

Click More Choices and scroll through the list of options on the left side of the dialog box until you see the Print Time option. Select it, and a series of scheduling options appears in the dialog box, as shown in the adjacent figure.

Tip: You can use the keyboard to type the time and date. Just press Tab to move from one set of numbers to the next; press *A* for AM and *P* for PM.

As the figure shows, you can also designate a job as urgent to push it ahead of other documents that might be waiting to print. You can also choose to display an alert message when the job begins and/or ends.

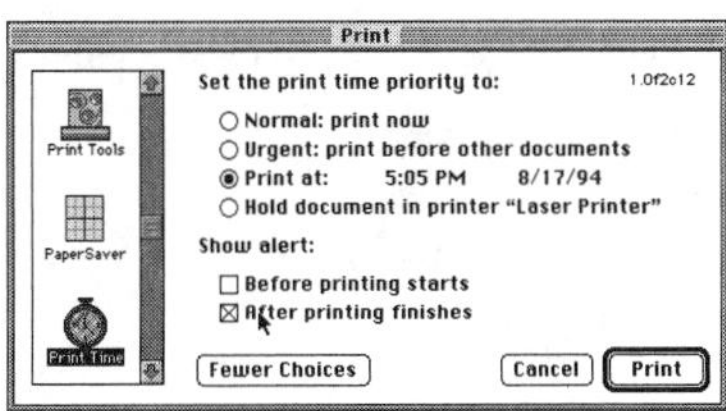

Redirecting a print job

Say that instead of pausing that 50-page print job, you decide to print it on a different machine in your network — one that isn't busy at the moment. In the old days, that meant going to the Chooser, selecting the new target printer, returning to your application program, and choosing its Print command. With GX and Apple's latest non-GX drivers, you can simply drag the print file to the desktop printer icon for the desired printer.

Viewing a print job

You can look at a pending print job by simply double-clicking it. The Finder opens the Simple Text application, which opens the print file and displays it.

You can't edit the print file or even copy part of it to the Clipboard, although you can print it again by choosing Simple Text's Print command.

Redirecting print jobs within the Print dialog box

Being able to redirect a print job by dragging a print file to a different desktop printer is exciting enough, but QuickDraw GX's printing flexibility doesn't stop there. If you're using a GX-aware application program, you can redirect a job to a different printer *before* you okay the Print dialog box — just choose the desired printer's name from the Print To pop-up menu in the Print dialog box.

Adding print features with printing extensions

If you think the GX printing features I've described so far are neat, fasten your seatbelt. The real power of the GX printing architecture is that it's extensible — by adding printing extensions, you can add printing features to *all* of your application programs.

Printing extensions show up in the Page Setup or Print dialog box when you click the More Choices button (see Figure 31-10 "Expanded Printing Options").

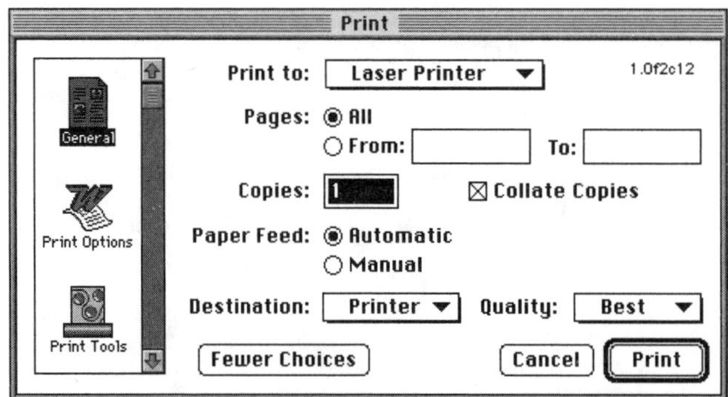

Figure 31-10: Expanded Printing Options When you click the More Choices button in the GX Print dialog box, additional options appear. Printing extensions are listed along the left edge of the dialog box. Tip: You can use the keyboard's arrow keys to select printing extensions.

The awesome Peirce Print Tools

There's one single product that illustrates the power of printing extensions so well that Apple often used it when demonstrating QuickDraw GX before its release. I'm referring to Peirce Software's Peirce Print Tools, a collection of printing extensions that adds the following printing features to any application program (see Figure 31-11 "Peirce Printing").

Back-to-front printing

Many laser printers deliver their output in reverse order, forcing a shuffling job to get pages back in the right order. Peirce Print Tools' BackToFront option eliminates this hassle.

Border printing

This cute option lets you print a border on each page. A variety of border designs is included, from simple rectangles to diamonds.

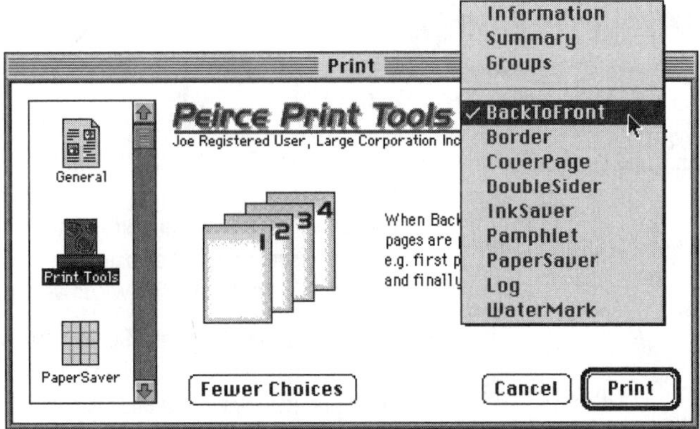

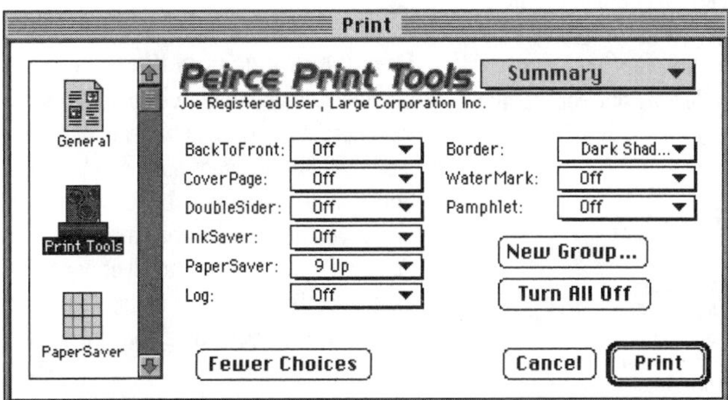

Figure 31-11: Peirce Printing Peirce Print Tools adds numerous printing features. When you choose a specific feature, the Print dialog box changes to reflect its options (top). To control all options from one place, choose the Summary option (bottom).

Cover pages

The old LaserWriter driver provided a cover page option since the very beginning. Peirce Print Tools' CoverPage option provides a variety of cover page designs and includes a utility that lets you create your own cover pages.

Double-sided printing

No, Peirce Print Tools can't turn a single-sided printer into a duplex printer. But it does the next-best thing. The DoubleSider option makes it easier to print on both sides of a page by letting you first print the odd-numbered pages and then even-numbered ones. Print the odd pages by selecting the Fronts Only option, then flip the sheets over, put them back in your printer, and print the even pages by selecting the Backs Only option.

Save ink and toner

The InkSaver option saves ink or toner by reducing the darkness of the entire document — similar to Working Software's Toner Tuner. It's handy when you're proofing pages.

Power Tips for Peirce Print Tools

Here are a few tips for getting more out of Peirce Print Tools.

Using PPT with GX-unaware applications

If Peirce Print Tools' options show up in the GX Print dialog box, does that mean you can only use them with GX-aware programs?

Fortunately, no. Peirce Print Tools include an extension that adds a menu to the menu bar whenever a GX-unaware program displays its Print dialog box. (Yes, you can still access the menu when the Print dialog box is displayed). As the adjacent figure shows, you can access all Peirce Print Tools options from this menu.

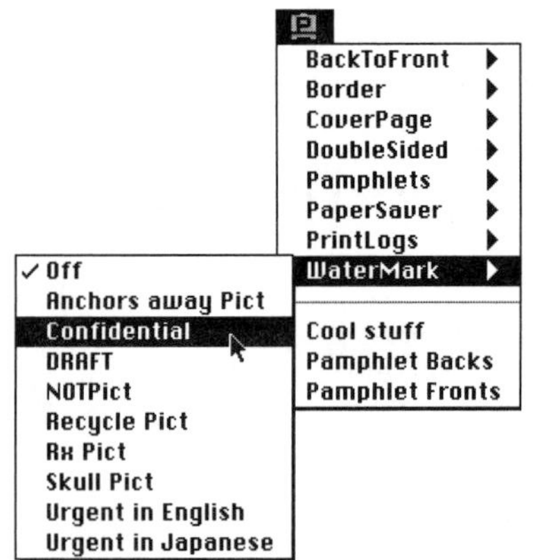

Using the Summary window to control settings

If you want to make adjustments in several Peirce Print Tools options, choose Summary from PPT's pop-up menu. This changes the Print dialog box to display pop-up menus for all of PPT's options. You can jump from one to the next in a flash. The only things missing from this display are the cool-looking previews that each of PPT's windows displays.

Another great feature of the Summary window is the Turn All Off button. Click it when you want to disable all PPT printing options in one fell swoop — it's a lot faster than working your way through each pop-up menu.

Creating groups of settings

Chances are you might use different sets of settings for different types of documents. When you print drafts of your business plan, maybe you use the Confidential watermark and double-sided printing. When you print your e-mail messages, maybe you use the PaperSaver and a cover page. PPT lets you save each set of printing options as a *group.* Once you save a set, you can activate it instantly by choosing its name.

Creating a desktop printer for each group

Another fast way to switch between sets of PPT options is to create a different desktop printer icon for each set. For that watermark-and-double-sided scenario I just outlined, create a desktop printer and name it Proposal Printing. For the e-mail printing scenario, create a desktop printer and name it Print E-mail. Then simply select the desired desktop printer from the Print To pop-up menu in the Print dialog box, or drag documents to the desktop printer's icon.

Pamphlet printing

This amazing option makes it easy to create bound booklets or pamphlets. It changes the order in which pages print so that the pages are in the proper order when they're folded and bound. (In the publishing world, this is called *imposition.* Think of the Pamphlet option as imposition for the rest of us.)

Paper saving

This option is similar to the LaserWriter 8 driver's n-up option, described earlier. PaperSaver lets you print between 2 and 16 pages reduced to fit on a single sheet of paper.

Print logging

The Log option keeps a log of the jobs that have been printed on a particular desktop printer — ideal for billing purposes or for just monitoring how a given printer is being used.

You can view the print log using a utility that comes with Peirce Print Tools. You can also export some or all of the log in a variety of formats for importing into a spreadsheet or database manager.

Watermarking

Chapter 3 described watermarks, which are text or graphics superimposed over the contents of each page. Peirce Print Tools' WaterMark option lets you create your own watermarks and print them in a variety of darkness settings. You can also specify that watermarks print on all pages, on only the first page, or on all pages except the first. Several canned watermarks are included; you can also create your own using the Peirce Print Tools Utility's watermark editor, which lets you add graphics, specify the rotation angle for the watermark, and much more.

Just you watch: You'll be able to tell when a person has Peirce Print Tools because all of his or her documents will have borders and watermarks on them. Use these features sparingly.

The Future of QuickDraw GX

When QuickDraw GX shipped, most people seemed impressed with its user interface enhancements but unimpressed with its high memory requirements and application-compatibility problems. As I mentioned in Chapter 11, very few application developers have created programs that take full advantage of GX's features.

Is QuickDraw GX doomed? Not on your life. For one thing, Apple is making steady improvements. System 7.5.1 and later versions of the Mac OS include QuickDraw GX 1.1.1, which uses less memory and is faster. But more to the point, the next version of the Mac OS — the version currently called Copland — will reportedly use QuickDraw GX exclusively; you won't have any choice. So even if you haven't installed QuickDraw GX yet, it might be worth your while to familiarize yourself with its capabilities and new Print dialog boxes. GX may be taking a while to get off the ground, but Apple seems determined to make it fly.

CHAPTER 31 CONCEPTS AND TERMS

- Office-supply stores and specialty mail-order houses such as Paper Direct are great sources for special paper stocks, transparency film, peel-and-stick labels, and other print media.
- ImageWriters and other dot-matrix printers are impact printers unlike ink-jet and laser printers; dot-matrix printers can print on carbon and carbonless multipart business forms.
- For ink-jet printers, you get the sharpest output by using smooth paper and printing on the proper side.
- When you want top quality from a laser printer, use an ultra-smooth laser paper such as Hammermill's Laser Print or Laser Plus.
- You can print iron-on transfers for T-shirts and other fabrics using Easy Transfer Cartridges.
- Techniques for improving a PostScript printer's performance include disabling the startup page, manually downloading often-used fonts, attaching a hard disk to the printer if it supports one, and expanding the printer's memory.
- QuickDraw GX adds significant new printing capabilities to the Mac's system software. Applications must be GX-aware in order to display the GX print dialog boxes.

desktop printer
In QuickDraw GX and Apple's latest non-GX drivers, an icon that represents a specific printer and its corresponding settings. You can print documents by dragging them to a desktop printer icon and manage a printer's queue by opening the desktop printer icon.

downloadable font
A font that resides on your Mac's hard disk and is transferred to the printer's memory.

fanfold paper
Also called *pin-fed* paper, a single, long sheet of paper that's perforated and folded to lie in a stack. The left and right edges of the sheets have perforated strips containing holes that are grasped by sprockets in the printer. After printing a document, you separate the sheets and tear off the perforated strips.

felt side
Also called the *top side,* the smoother side of a sheet of paper — and the side you should print on, particularly if you have an ink-jet printer. Compare with *wire side.*

image area
The area of a page that a printer can actually produce output on. Most laser printers, for example, can print to within roughly a quarter of an inch of the edges of the page. In non-QuickDraw GX systems, you can increase the image area by checking the Larger Print Area option in the Page Setup dialog box's Options dialog box.

impact printer
A printer that produces output in the manner of a typewriter — by striking a ribbon that transfers ink to the paper. Nonimpact printers include ink-jet and laser printers.

print file
In QuickDraw GX and Apple's latest non-GX drivers, a file that's waiting to print. You can drag a print file's icon to redirect it to another printer or change its order in the print queue. Another name for a print file is a *spool file.*

printing extension
In QuickDraw GX, a software add-on that provides additional printing features, such as the ability to print watermarks on each page or print multiple pages on a single sheet of paper. Peirce Software's Peirce Print Tools is an example of a printing extension.

ream
Five hundred sheets of paper.

sheet feeder
An add-on, available for ImageWriters and some ink-jet printers, that holds a stack of paper, eliminating having to hand-feed page after page.

startup page
A page printed by a PostScript printer shortly after it's switched on, listing information about the printer — the number of pages it has printed, the fonts it contains, and the settings of its various ports.

wire side
The rougher side of a sheet of paper, the wire side is the side that is in contact with the paper manufacturing equipment's wire brushes. If you print on the wire side using an ink-jet printer, your output is likely to look somewhat splotchy. Compare with *felt side.*

CHAPTER THIRTY-TWO

Networking Basics

- Following the roadmap to a fully networked office
- Assessing the options and benefits of networking
- Comparing System 7 file sharing and AppleShare
- Phoning home with Apple Remote Access

If you use two or more Macs, chances are you can benefit from connecting them to each other to form a network. Wait! Don't turn the page! It's true that networking has its technicalities — bandwidths and bridges, twisted pairs and topologies — but even if you're new to the Mac, you can set up a small network without immersing yourself in the technicalities. Small-scale Mac networking can be surprisingly easy and economical.

What's to gain? For one thing, your Macs can share an expensive add-on such as a laser printer or hard drive. It's easier to buy a big-ticket item when you know that all your Macs will be able to share it.

Beyond sharing hardware, you can share information and ideas. Using *file server* software, you can store in one place files everyone needs to access — client databases, product fact sheets, downloadable laser printer fonts, or boilerplate templates for frequently produced documents. Using *electronic mail* software, you can send messages and files to coworkers. And with *multiuser* database software, everyone can access the same database file at once, eliminating the need to store a separate copy on each person's machine — and fretting over whose version is the latest.

Many people are intimidated by networking not only because of the jargon that surrounds it, but also because it provides so many sharing options. The best way to conquer both fears is to start small and add new capabilities as you need them — and as you master those you already have.

This chapter presents a roadmap you may want to follow in your journey to a networked office. Along the way, I examine networking's benefits and look at some products. For a detailed look at the wide world of Macintosh networking, see *Macworld Networking Bible, 2nd Edition* (IDG Books, 1994).

Hardware You Can Share

Sharing hardware doesn't mean just hard drives and laser printers. Here's a sampling of the other types of hardware you can share on a network.

- *ImageWriters* Using Apple's ImageWriter II/LQ LocalTalk Option board, you can share an ImageWriter II.
- *Telephone modems* Modems such as Shiva's NetModem series can be shared on a network. A network modem can't serve an office full of communications junkies, but it is ideal for several people who just check their e-mail now and then.
- *Fax modems* Cypress Research Corporation's FaxPro II system lets you set aside a modem-equipped Macintosh for your network's faxing needs. With a fax server, the Macs on your network are free from the grunt work of receiving faxes and converting documents for faxing. FaxPro II also lets you create a database of documents that you fax frequently — brochures, price lists, technical notes, and so on. A document in a fax database has already been converted into faxable form; when you need to fax it, the server simply dials and faxes the converted document. See Chapter 16 for more details.
- *Serial devices* With Shiva's NetSerial, you can put virtually any serial device — modem, pen plotter, daisy-wheel printer — on a network.
- *Alternate storage devices* You can share tape backup drives, erasable optical drives, and removable-media drives such as Bernoulli and SyQuest drives. You can even share CD-ROMs with System 7 file sharing or an AppleShare server, provided the server's hard disk has enough free space to keep track of the CD-ROM's vast number of files.

Phase 1 — Sharing a Printer

At its simplest level, Macintosh networking means sharing a PostScript-based printer such as Apple's LaserWriter 16/600 PS or any of the other numerous Mac-compatible PostScript printers that are available. Like a co-op vacation home, a PostScript printer is a less painful purchase when a large group can enjoy it. As Chapter 30 describes, many non-PostScript laser and ink-jet printers, including Apple's StyleWriter series, can also be shared on a network.

Sharing a PostScript printer is particularly easy because all you need are cables that interconnect the Macs and the printer. You don't need any special networking software; Apple's LaserWriter printer driver, included with the Mac's system software, contains all the smarts needed to communicate with any Mac-compatible PostScript printer.

Similarly, all PostScript printers contain built-in software that enables them to listen for numerous machines and handle print jobs on a first-come-first-served basis. In short, the Macintosh and the printer already know how to talk with each other: Your job is to add the lines of communication.

Apple's lines of communication

Those lines can take a few forms. If you want the Apple brand name, endow each Mac and printer with a LocalTalk Connector Kit, which includes a 6-foot length of LocalTalk cable and a small connector box that plugs into a Mac's rear-panel printer connector or into the printer itself. The connector box's nine parts electrically isolate the network's components, helping to prevent wholesale equipment carnage should one item short out.

The cable itself isn't too different from what you'd find in a stereo system. It contains a pair of wires twisted around each other, surrounded by a braided wire shield that keeps electrical interference out and helps prevent the signals in the cable from interfering with nearby radios or TVs. Included with the connector kit is a small connector called a *cable extender*, used for attaching two cables to each other. If you need longer cable lengths — perhaps to reach a Mac in another room — Apple offers 30- and 75-foot LocalTalk cables.

The PhoneNet alternative

Apple's cabling is usually discounted below its retail prices, but you can save even more by using one of the LocalTalk cabling alternatives, such as Farallon Computing's popular PhoneNet cabling system. PhoneNet connector boxes often sell for half the price of Apple's.

Another plus is that PhoneNet uses ordinary telephone wiring rather than the special cabling LocalTalk requires. PhoneNet can often use the telephone wiring already present in a building (see Figure 32-1 "A Quick Network over Phone Wiring"). That can save you a fortune in cable costs, especially if your Macs are far apart. Adaptors are also available that let you mix LocalTalk and telephone cabling on the same network — helpful if you're already using one kind of cabling and decide to add more machines to your network.

LocalTalk wiring tips

Whether you use LocalTalk or a LocalTalk-compatible cabling scheme, you'll hook up your Macs and printers as shown in Chapter 28 (Figure 28-2 "A Network Diagram"). Be sure each cable is snugly attached to its connector, and tuck the cables safely behind desks so people won't trip over them or jerk them loose with desk chairs.

Also avoid the common pitfall of leaving a cable dangling, without going into a connector. The end points of a LocalTalk network are connectors to which only one cable is attached. In this case, the network isn't properly terminated — its end point isn't defined, and it won't work properly.

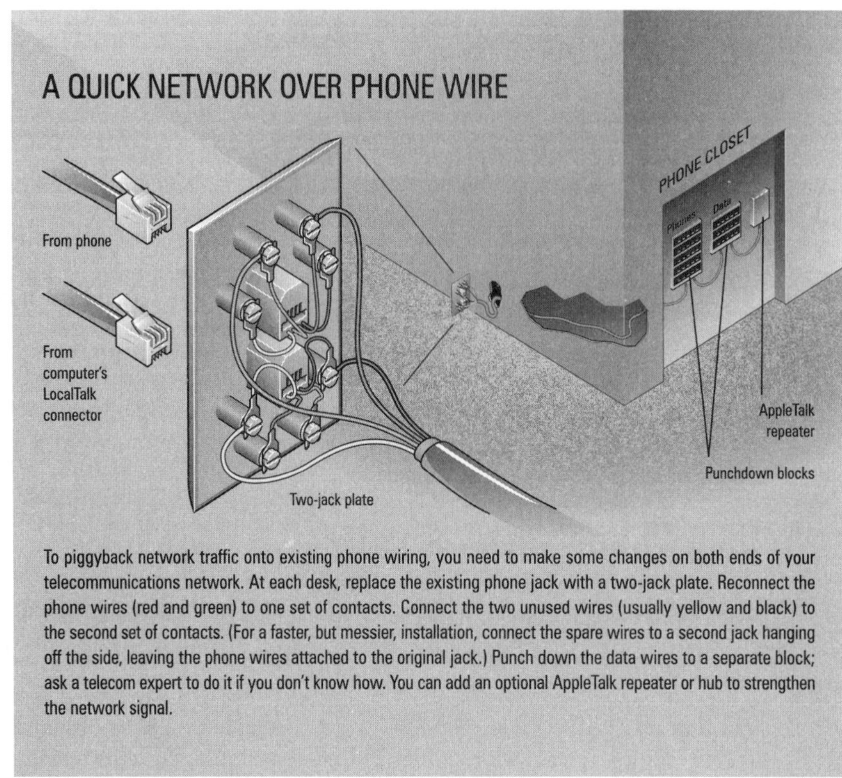

A QUICK NETWORK OVER PHONE WIRE
PHONE CLOSET
From phone
From computer's LocalTalk connector
AppleTalk repeater
Punchdown blocks
Two-jack plate
To piggyback network traffic onto existing phone wiring, you need to make some changes on both ends of your telecommunications network. At each desk, replace the existing phone jack with a two-jack plate. Reconnect the phone wires (red and green) to one set of contacts. Connect the two unused wires (usually yellow and black) to the second set of contacts. (For a faster, but messier, installation, connect the spare wires to a second jack hanging off the side, leaving the phone wires attached to the original jack.) Punch down the data wires to a separate block; ask a telecom expert to do it if you don't know how. You can add an optional AppleTalk repeater or hub to strengthen the network signal.

Figure 32-1: A Quick Network over Phone Wiring

Ethernet: networking in the fast lane

LocalTalk is adequate for small networks that transfer or print primarily text-oriented documents rather than huge graphics files. If this doesn't describe you — if you have a huge office, if you deal with huge files, or both — you'll want to build your network around Ethernet instead.

LocalTalk transfers data at the relatively slow pace of 230,000 bits per second (230Kbps). Ethernet, by comparison, runs at 10 *million* bits per second (10Mbps). Not all Macs can handle data rates that fast, of course, but even on slower machines, Ethernet is several times faster than LocalTalk. The bottom line: If you frequently transfer large files over your network — scanned images, sounds, QuickTime movies — Ethernet will deliver far more satisfying performance.

Best of all, you can mix and match LocalTalk and Ethernet on the same network. You may set up some Ethernet highways for your publishing or scanning workstations, and use LocalTalk for the rest of the machines.

Ethernet cabling exposed

Ethernet networks can use any of several types of wires: *thin-wire* and *thick-wire* Ethernet each use a different type of coaxial cable — stuff similar to what cable TV companies use. As you might guess, thick-wire Ethernet, which is also called *10Base5*, uses thicker cabling than thin-wire, which also goes by the catchy name *10Base2*. Thick-wire Ethernet cabling costs more and is more cumbersome to work with, but it has the distance advantage: you can have up to 500 meters of cable between each network device, as opposed to the 200-meter limit of thin-wire.

These days, more and more Ethernet networks are built on a different kind of cabling, called *10BaseT* or *twisted-pair*. 10BaseT cabling is similar to telephone wiring. Because it doesn't contain the costly metal shielding that coaxial cable does, 10BaseT cabling is a lot cheaper.

Making Ethernet connections

So much for cables — what about connectors? Ethernet ports are built into most current desktop Mac models as well as the PowerBook 500 series and many laser and color printers. These ports are called *AAUI* connectors, short for *Apple Attachment Unit Interface*.

How do you connect them to each other? In Ethernet's earlier days, setting up even a tiny Ethernet network required buying a piece of hardware called a *hub*, which as its name implies, forms the central connection point for the network.

With a hub, you connect a small box, called a *transceiver*, to the Mac, and then run a cable from the transceiver to the hub. The transceiver is responsible for converting the signals on the Ethernet cable into the digital data required by your Mac's Ethernet port.

Catching the EtherWave

Hubs are still essential for larger Ethernet networks, but for small-scale Ethernet — several Macs and a printer or two — there's an easier, less-expensive alternative: Farallon Computing's EtherWave adaptors. Smaller than a paperback book, an EtherWave adaptor has a cable that plugs into the Mac's Ethernet connector.

The EtherWave adaptor also has two jacks, into which you plug 10BaseT cabling. The real beauty of the EtherWave system is that you can connect up to eight devices to each other without having to buy a hub. EtherWave combines the ease and convenience of LocalTalk with the data-transfer speeds of Ethernet. (And if you do have a hub, EtherWave makes it easier to add devices to it.)

EtherWave adaptors are available in several flavors. The EtherWave PowerBook Adaptor connects to a PowerBook's SCSI port, providing the performance of SCSI disk mode without the aggravations. The EtherWave Printer Adaptor lets you put a LocalTalk printer on an Ethernet network.

Ethernet and second-generation Power Macs

As I mentioned in Chapter 1, second-generation Power Macs — the 7200, 7500, 8500, and 9500 — contain not only AAUI Ethernet connectors, but also 10BaseT connectors. If you're using an Ethernet hub and 10BaseT cabling, you can connect a second-generation Power Mac to your network without having to buy a transceiver.

The fast PCI slots present in second-generation Power Macs also make possible high-speed Ethernet cards that can transfer data at many times the speed of the Mac's built-in Ethernet ports. These cards use a new standard called *Fast Ethernet*, which is rated at up to 100Mbps. Farallon and Asanté Technologies are among the first companies to offer Fast Ethernet cards for second-generation Power Macs.

Installing printing software

After you unite the machines, you need to configure each Macintosh for network printing.

If you're sharing a PostScript laser printer, be sure it's warmed up (wait until it prints its startup page or until its Online indicator is on). Next, use each Mac's Chooser (in the Apple menu) to activate AppleTalk. If, after you click the Activate button, the bottom of the Chooser window reads Active After Restart, you'll need to restart the Mac in order to load the AppleTalk software. Finally, use the Chooser to select the LaserWriter printer driver icon. (If you don't see this icon, you need to install the printer driver from the Mac's system disks or from the disks that accompany the printer.)

Next, specify a user name for your machine using the Sharing Setup control panel. Use the name of the person who uses that Mac, or a name that describes the Mac's purpose, such as Publishing Station. This name enables the LaserWriter driver to provide useful feedback when you're printing — more about that shortly.

If you're sharing a non-PostScript printer such as an Apple StyleWriter, activate its sharing software. For details on sharing a StyleWriter, see the section "Comparing StyleWriters and DeskWriters" in Chapter 30.

Make a desktop printer icon

If you're using QuickDraw GX or Apple's latest non-GX printer drivers, you'll want to create a desktop printer icon for your printer in order to access all the neat print job-management features that desktop printing provides. For instructions and details on other network-related printing features, see the Chapter 31 section "Printing with QuickDraw GX."

Testing your setup

After you perform these steps, close the Chooser and try printing a short document. If your test document doesn't print, retrace your steps and double-check the cables. If it does print, perform these steps on each Mac in the network.

If you always use the same printer, you need to perform the previous chores only once; the Chooser remembers that you've chosen the LaserWriter driver as well as the user name you typed and the name of the printer you selected. However, if you switch between two or more LaserWriters or other printers, you need to use the Chooser each time you change printers. This does not apply if you're running QuickDraw GX, which lets you aim a print job at whatever printer you like, at any time.

Phase 2 — Electronic Mail

After you string the lines between machines, you can add additional capabilities to a network by adding appropriate software. The next step may be to add software that lets you transfer files between Macs, enabling you to say good-bye to the so-called "sneaker net" — copying files to floppy disks and carrying them to other machines in your office.

Several categories of network software let you move files between machines. One is *electronic mail*, or *e-mail*, software such as CE Software's QuickMail or Casady & Greene's SnapMail. With e-mail software, you send files as *enclosures* that accompany messages you type (see Figure 32-2 "Files Enclosed"). When messages arrive at their electronic mailbox destination, the recipients can save the enclosed files on their own disks. You can even request a return receipt message, which notifies you when a message is read. In large offices, e-mail not only makes it easy to transfer files, it also helps eliminate distracting phone calls and annoying games of phone tag.

E-mail details

Each brand of e-mail software has its own operating style, but all require similar setup steps. First, you designate one Mac as the *e-mail server*, the electronic post office that stores messages and forwards them to their addressees. You can still use the server Mac to run other programs, but you'll notice it slows down when people are sending and retrieving mail as it divides its time between postal duties and running other programs.

For this reason, it's important to carefully consider which Mac in a network is best suited to being a server. You should use a machine with several megabytes of free hard disk space. If you anticipate heavy mail volume, consider using a faster Mac for the server. And if you plan to run other programs on the server Mac, make sure you use a machine that's reliable: If someone in your office likes to run prerelease versions of software (which may contain bugs) or games (which often monopolize the Mac's hardware), that person's Mac is not an ideal server.

Setting up the e-mail server

After you choose a server, you set up the e-mail server software, which usually comprises a system extension that loads the server software into the Mac's memory during startup and an *administrator* program that you use to create a mailbox for each person in the network. Finally, install on each Mac the e-mail *client* software, which generally includes a desk accessory that lets the user read and send mail and a startup document that lets the Mac notify the user when a message arrives.

After the initial setup, the administrator's job becomes custodial. Using the administrator program, he or she adds and removes users as needed, helps users who have forgotten their passwords, and works to keep the mail moving. Each user can — and should — change his or her password when signing on to the system for the first time.

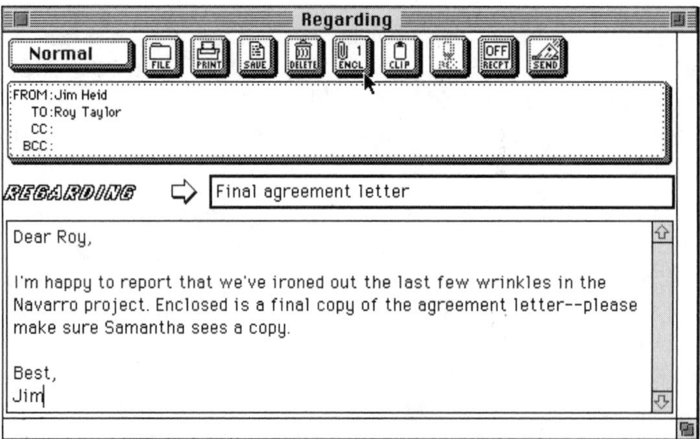

Figure 32-2: Files Enclosed With electronic-mail software such as CE Software's QuickMail, shown here, you can enclose disk files with messages. The recipient clicks on the ENCL button to retrieve the file from the mail server.

Choosing e-mail software

QuickMail can each easily meet the needs of any network. But a better choice for small-scale e-mail systems is Casady & Greene's SnapMail. Or, if you have System 7.5 or System 7 Pro, you can use the built-in e-mail software that PowerTalk provides. More about this option shortly.

Transferring files from Timbuktu

For a variation on the file-transfer theme, you may want to investigate Farallon Computing's Timbuktu Pro (see Figure 32-3 "I'm in Control"). Timbuktu Pro can

Standardize on Version Numbers

If you're setting up a network to share a PostScript printer, be sure all Macs use the same version of the LaserWriter driver. If you mix System 6 and System 7 LaserWriter drivers on the same network, you're likely to become a casualty of what's often described as "LaserPrep wars" — a conflict between the two drivers. The result of the conflict is an error message saying that you need to restart the printer — and a lot of waiting.

To avoid LaserPrep wars, be sure to use the same version of the LaserWriter driver on each Mac in your network. In fact, it's a good idea to standardize on the same system and application software versions, too. Networks are more reliable and easier to troubleshoot when everyone is using the same software versions.

transfer files, but it isn't an e-mail package; instead it lets you control one Macintosh from another — for example, to help someone who's struggling to master a difficult program.

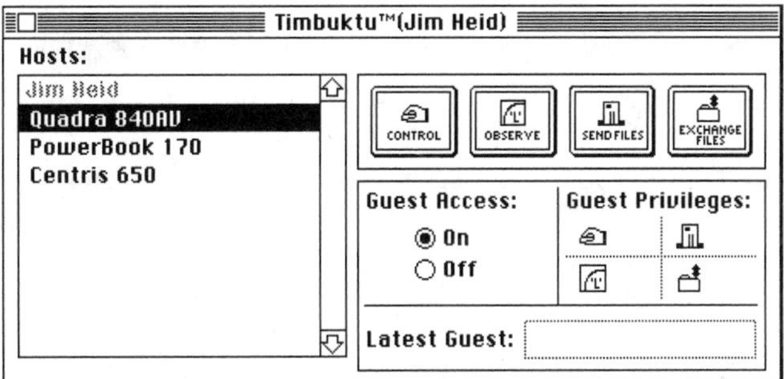

Figure 32-3: I'm in Control Farallon Computing's Timbuktu software lets you transfer files between Macs and control one Mac from another. Timbuktu's desk accessory, shown here, also lets you specify passwords to protect against unauthorized access to your files or your Mac.

You can also take over all the screens in the office — great for group training sessions. And you can use one Mac's modem or ImageWriter printer from another Mac. With Farallon's Timbuktu/Remote, you can even control a Mac over the telephone lines, although you need a 9600-bps or faster modem for tolerable performance. More about Timbuktu/Remote and other remote-access tools later in this chapter.

Timbuktu is also available for DOS PCs running Microsoft Windows. With the Windows and Mac versions of Timbuktu, you can not only transfer files between the two platforms, but control one from the other.

Focus on PowerTalk

Just as System 7 file sharing gives Macs built-in peer-to-peer file sharing, Apple's PowerTalk, included with System 7 Pro and System 7.5, gives Macs built-in peer-to-peer electronic mail.

PowerTalk is a set of workgroup-oriented services built around what Apple calls the Apple Open Collaboration Environment, or AOCE. Just as programs can reach out and tap into QuickTime to get movie features, or QuickDraw GX to get nifty graphics and printing features, they can tap into PowerTalk to get communication-related features.

AppleMail: basic e-mail

PowerTalk's AppleMail program lets you create and send messages as well as read incoming ones (see Figure 32-4 "Checking AppleMail"). As with other e-mail systems, you can enclose files with messages. Because PowerTalk works in a peer-to-peer fashion, you don't need to set aside a Mac to act as a mail server.

When you want the increased performance and reliability that a central server provides, you can use Apple's PowerShare Collaboration Server, which can also run along with the AppleShare file-serving software discussed later in this chapter.

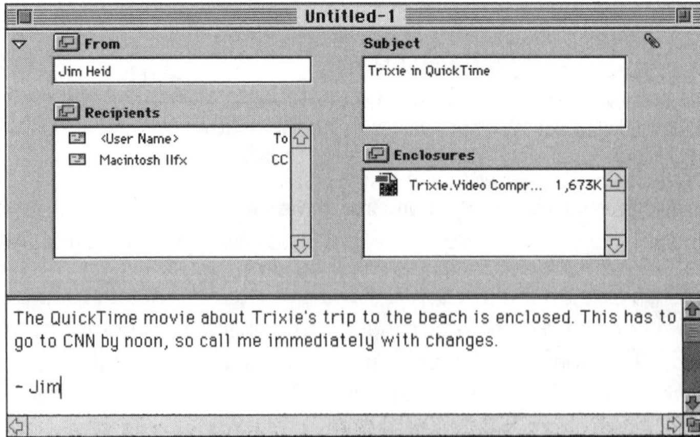

Figure 32-4: Checking AppleMail PowerTalk's AppleMail application lets you send messages and files to other users on your network.

The real power of PowerTalk

PowerTalk and AOCE represent more than just built-in e-mail. AOCE provides a library of standard features and software routines that developers can use to add electronic mail and other network collaboration features to their programs. When a program supports PowerTalk, it can provide direct access to all the communications services you use. (For example, when PowerTalk is installed, Microsoft Word 6 and Excel 5 each provide a Mail command and a Mail toolbar, both of which enable you to send and receive mail from within those programs.) From local e-mail to on-line service e-mail to faxes and even voice-mail messages, PowerTalk brings communication to the Mac's desktop.

PowerTalk also adds several new icons to the Mac's desktop (see Figure 32-5 "PowerTalk's Desktop Additions").

Figure 32-5: PowerTalk's Desktop Additions PowerTalk adds these new icons to the Mac's desktop.

The Mailbox

The Mailbox holds your incoming and outgoing correspondence. (After you set up PowerTalk for the first time, the icon's name changes to your name.) The Mailbox's *In Tray* window holds incoming mail messages (see Figure 32-6 "Picking Up the Mail"). In PowerTalk's world, the In Tray is the central repository for incoming mail — regardless of that mail's place of origin. Your Internet e-mail can appear in the same place as incoming faxes and network e-mail — no need to manually check a variety of services to keep in touch.

If you use Cypress Research's MegaPhone software (discussed in Chapter 16), you can even specify that incoming voice-mail messages appear in your PowerTalk In Tray. To do so, choose Preferences from MegaPhone's File menu and then choose the Voice Messaging option from the Topic pop-up. Finally, check the box labeled Direct Messages to PowerTalk In Tray. (If you don't have PowerTalk installed, this box is disabled.)

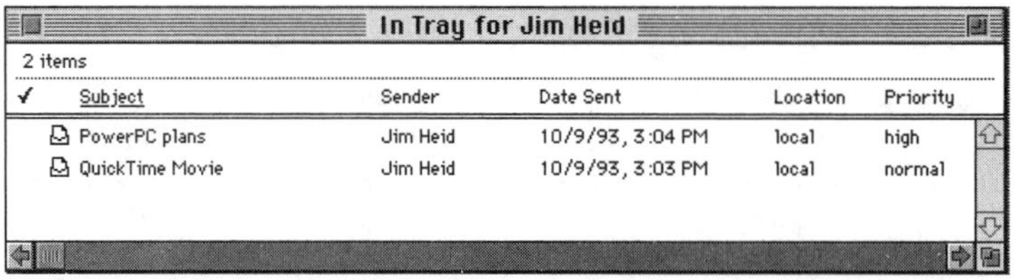

In Tray for Jim Heid

2 items

✓	Subject	Sender	Date Sent	Location	Priority
	PowerPC plans	Jim Heid	10/9/93, 3:04 PM	local	high
	QuickTime Movie	Jim Heid	10/9/93, 3:03 PM	local	normal

Figure 32-6: Picking Up the Mail The In Tray shows the mail you've received. With the Mailbox menu's Preferences command, you can specify that your Mac notify you when new mail arrives by displaying a dialog box, playing a sound, flashing the Apple menu — or by doing all three.

Catalogs

These hold icons that represent the network services (printers, file servers, and so on) you use as well as the people you keep in touch with — their names, their addresses (both physical and electronic), even their hobbies and favorite foods, if you like. Catalogs can contain contact information for individual users or for groups of users — much as a file server can store access privileges for individual users and for groups.

The Key Chain

The Key Chain provides a single log-on procedure for the communication and network services you use, whether they're on your office network or on an on-line service. True to its name, the Key Chain puts all your keys in one place. Once you unlock your key chain, you can access all the services it knows about without having to constantly type passwords. You can lock the Key Chain when you're going to be away from the computer for a while, and you can use the PowerTalk Setup control panel to lock the Key Chain automatically after a period of inactivity.

Information cards

To help you keep track of contact information and send documents, PowerTalk provides a special type of document called an *information card.* An information card can reside in a catalog, on your desktop, on a file server, or within a certain folder on a disk.

An information card contains four electronic pages, each of which stores a different type of information (see Figure 32-7 "Give Me Information"). Once you've created an information card for a person on your network, you can send a file to that person by dragging the file's icon to the person's information card.

The drag-and-drop angle

If you always send a daily memo to a certain group of people, create a *group icon*, and then drag each user's icon to it. Thereafter, you can transmit the memo by dragging its icon to the group icon.

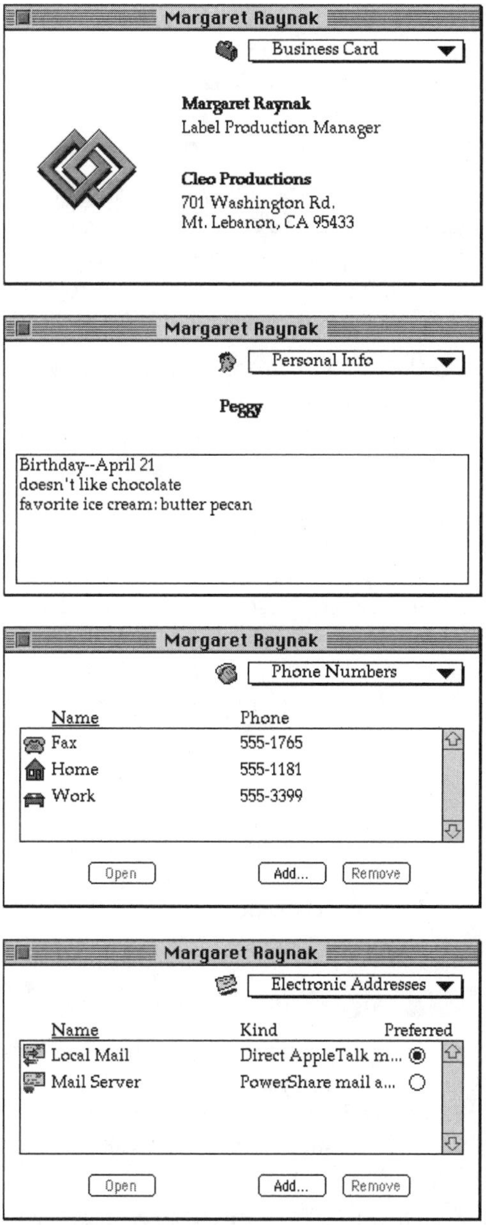

Margaret Raynak

Business Card

Margaret Raynak
Label Production Manager

Cleo Productions
701 Washington Rd.
Mt. Lebanon, CA 95433

Margaret Raynak

Personal Info

Peggy

Birthday--April 21
doesn't like chocolate
favorite ice cream: butter pecan

Margaret Raynak

Phone Numbers

Name	Phone
Fax	555-1765
Home	555-1181
Work	555-3399

Open Add... Remove

Margaret Raynak

Electronic Addresses

Name	Kind	Preferred
Local Mail	Direct AppleTalk m...	◉
Mail Server	PowerShare mail a...	○

Open Add... Remove

Figure 32-7: Give Me Information Information cards hold contact details about users or groups. Shown here are the four electronic pages a card contains (from top to bottom): a business card page for basic contact information; a personal info page for listing birthdays, shoe sizes, and other essential data; a phone numbers page for listing telephone numbers; and an electronic addresses page for listing e-mail and fax contact information.

The real power of PowerTalk becomes apparent when you consider that some of the members of the group might be on your office network, while others are across the country, at the other end of modem lines or fax machines.

Streamlining collaboration with personal catalogs

PowerTalk lets you create any number of *personal catalogs*, each of which can hold frequently used information cards. If a certain project requires you to work with certain network resources and people, you can create a personal catalog for that project. Just as folders let you group related documents together, personal catalogs let you group related information cards together.

Programs that support PowerTalk can access the catalogs you create. With a PowerTalk-compatible word processor, you could, for example, fax a document to someone whose fax number was stored in a catalog. You can use the Get Info command to designate a certain catalog as the *preferred catalog* — the one PowerTalk-compatible programs use unless you specify otherwise.

PowerTalk automatically places one personal catalog, named *Personal Catalog*, in the Apple menu for you. When a catalog window is open, a Catalogs menu appears whose commands let you create new user or group information cards as well as create new personal catalogs. When a catalog window is open, the Finder's View menu lets you narrow down the display of catalog items to view only certain types, such as file servers. A Find In Catalog command in the Apple menu also makes it easier to find items in catalogs.

Sign in, please

A common office chore involves signing off on pieces of paper, such as purchase orders. PowerTalk provides a digital signature feature that lets you electronically sign a document. A document's recipient can then be certain that the document wasn't altered.

Is PowerTalk for you?

If you work alone, you probably won't want to bother with PowerTalk. If you work on a small network and you haven't yet taken the e-mail plunge, PowerTalk's built-in e-mail is a good place to start. If you're on a large network that already uses an e-mail system, chances are the e-mail software's developer has enhanced its product to take advantage of PowerTalk.

In the long run, the real power of PowerTalk won't surface until popular application and communications programs are updated to take advantage of it. When that happens, PowerTalk should make it easier to keep in touch.

Phase 3 — Creating a File Server

E-mail products can eliminate sneaker wear but not worries over whose version of a certain document is the most current. If anything, swapping files between different machines only fuels those fears. And having important files scattered across the hard drives and floppy disks in an office makes backing up difficult.

The solution? Use file-server software to make one or more hard drives available to the entire network. A file server is an electronic version of the office filing cabinet, providing shared storage for files that everyone needs (or that only certain people need: You can create private folders that can't be used without a password). Backing up is simplified because all the important documents are stored in one place. And the entire office can take advantage of that high-capacity hard drive you just bought.

Or so go the claims. In reality, a network's hard drive isn't nearly as fast as a *local* one (attached directly to your Mac) because LocalTalk and even Ethernet transfer data more slowly than the Mac's SCSI port does. For example, Microsoft Excel takes about 10 seconds to start from my local hard drive but over 30 seconds to start from my file server. What's more, putting all that extra data on a network's cabling slows down everything else that takes place on the network, such as printing and exchanging e-mail. Thus, it's best to use a file server to store only documents, not programs.

Distributed and dedicated servers

File servers come in two flavors: *distributed* and *dedicated* (see Figure 32-8 "Server Approaches Compared"). With distributed serving, anyone in the network can turn his or her machine into a file server by making one or more folders — or the entire contents of a hard drive — available to others. Once that's done, anyone on the network can *mount* it and use it as though it were a local drive.

Apple's System 7 provides distributed file-serving features; for details on using them, see Chapter 22. The distributed approach is often called *peer-to-peer* file serving because each machine on the network is considered an equal as far as file serving is concerned.

With the dedicated approach, you set aside, or *dedicate*, one Mac and its hard drive to act as a server for everyone. A dedicated file server generally isn't used to run applications, although you might also use one to act as an e-mail server.

Apple's AppleShare software supports between 120 and 200 users depending on the version you buy. AppleShare 3.0 runs on 680X0-family Macs and supports up to 120 users. AppleShare 4.0 runs on 68040 Macs and Power Macs and supports up to 150. AppleShare Pro runs on Apple's Workgroup Server 95 and supports up to 200 users, 5000 open files, and up to 20 server hard drives.

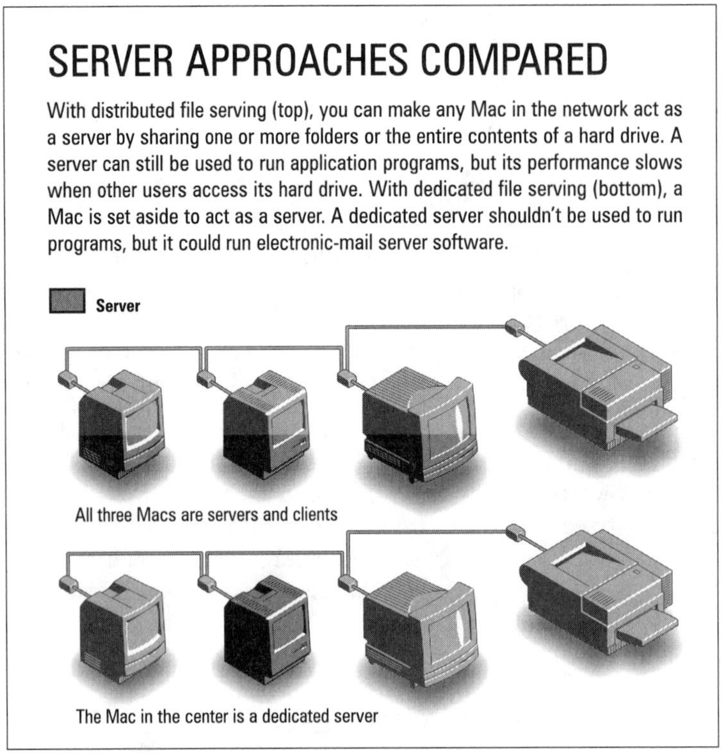

SERVER APPROACHES COMPARED

With distributed file serving (top), you can make any Mac in the network act as a server by sharing one or more folders or the entire contents of a hard drive. A server can still be used to run application programs, but its performance slows when other users access its hard drive. With dedicated file serving (bottom), a Mac is set aside to act as a server. A dedicated server shouldn't be used to run programs, but it could run electronic-mail server software.

Server

All three Macs are servers and clients

The Mac in the center is a dedicated server

Figure 32-8: Server Approaches Compared

Clearly, distributed file serving is the more economical approach. System 7 requires no extra hardware beyond cabling. But one downside to distributed file serving is that someone can turn off the file sharing drive at any time, with disastrous results for anyone using it. System 7 provides some safeguards for this, but it still can happen. And of course, a Mac acting as a file server slows down when others are accessing its hard drive.

Combining AppleShare and System 7 file sharing

Can AppleShare and System 7 file sharing coexist on the same network? Yes, but only to a degree. The server Mac can access shared folders or drives that other Macs have made available through System 7's Sharing command.

However, you can't start System 7 file sharing on the server Mac — the File Sharing area of its Sharing Setup control panel is missing. The only way to share folders on the server Mac is through AppleShare.

Save Money: Create a Headless Server

If you use a Mac without a built-in monitor as a dedicated server, you can cut the cost of your server by several hundred dollars or more by not buying a monitor or keyboard for that Mac. Such a server is often called a *headless* server.

To set up a headless server, use the monitor and keyboard from a different Mac in your office. Place the AppleShare File Server icon (or an alias of it) in the Startup Items Folder. Then shut down the server Mac, disconnect the monitor and keyboard, and then start the server up again.

AppleShare 3.0 and later versions let you run the AppleShare Admin program from another Mac on your network, so if you need to perform minor maintenance on the server, you don't have to reinstall the video hardware and keyboard. You will need to reinstall the video hardware and keyboard, however, if you want to run the Admin program on the server itself or if you want to run applications on the server.

Focus on AppleShare

This section describes how to set aside a Mac to be a file server and how you may use AppleShare's additional security options to control access to the server's contents.

Three steps to server setup

Installing AppleShare requires three basic steps:

1. Install the server software on one Macintosh.
2. Install the workstation software on each of the other Macs in your network.
3. Configure the server by supplying user and group names, specifying access privileges, and performing other administrative tasks.

In the world of AppleShare, the person in charge of setting up and maintaining the server is the *administrator*. The administrator uses a program called AppleShare Admin to perform the previous steps.

Installing AppleShare

To install the AppleShare server or workstation software, you use Apple's Installer utility. The server disk's installer script copies to the Mac's hard disk the AppleShare Admin program, the AppleShare File Server program (which actually starts the server), and an extension named File Server Extension. After installing this software, restart the server Mac to load the extension.

After you've installed the server software and restarted the server Mac, you're ready to create users and groups. With AppleShare, you do this using the AppleShare Admin program. If you had previously set up users and groups on the server Mac using System 7's file-sharing features, AppleShare Admin offers to convert the users and groups into its own format.

This convenience feature means you can start out with System 7's file-sharing features and then progress to AppleShare without losing users and groups and their access privilege settings.

If you're unfamiliar with the concepts and steps behind creating users and groups, you may want to review the section "Access has its privileges" in Chapter 22.

Consider defragmenting your drive

If you've used the server Mac's hard drive extensively, your server will provide better performance if you defragment its hard drive. See Chapter 25 for details on defragmenting utilities and techniques.

Specifying security options

AppleShare provides password and other security features that help ensure the privacy of each user's data on the server. During the setup phase, you may want to use the File Server Preferences dialog box to take advantage of the security options AppleShare provides. With the File Server Preferences dialog box in AppleShare's Admin program, you can specify that passwords expire after a certain amount of time, and more.

While you're putting things under lock and key, you may want to also specify access information for individual programs and documents. You can use the Access Information command to specify that documents and programs be copy-protected so that users can't copy them from the server to their machines. You can specify that only certain folders — not the entire hard disk — be available to others on the network. You can also specify the maximum number of users that can access a given program or document.

Table 32-1 lists some typical access privilege settings. Table 32-2 shows which privileges you need in order to perform various tasks.

Table 32-1
Access Privilege Reference

If You Want to...		*Set Privileges Like This...* *See Folders*	*See Files*	*Make Changes*
Give everyone on the network all access privileges	Owner	•	•	•
	User/Group	•	•	•
	Everyone	•	•	•
Share a folder with one person or group	Owner	•	•	•
	User/Group	•	•	•
	Everyone			
Keep a folder private so that only you can access it from other machines	Owner	•	•	•
	User/Group			
	Everyone			
Keep a folder private but allow others to drop files or folders into it	Owner	•	•	•
	User/Group			•
	Everyone			•

Table 32-2
Access Privilege Sampler

If You Want to...	*Set Privileges Like This...* *See Folders*	*See Files*	*Make Changes*
Copy a file to a folder			•
Copy a file from a folder	•	•	
Copy a folder to a folder	•		•
Copy a folder from a folder	•		
Create a file	•	•	•
Create a folder	•		•
Delete a file	•	•	
Move a folder to a folder	•		•
Move a folder from a folder	•		•
Open a file		•	
Save changes to a file		•	•

Back Up Your Users & Groups Data File

AppleShare's Admin utility creates a file called Users & Groups Data File that stores the user and group names you've created. When you alter your user and group settings, make a backup copy of the Users & Groups Data File. If you switch hard drives or if something happens to your old file server, you can copy the backup file to your new server and not have to re-create all your user and group names.

To back up the Users & Groups Data File, open the server's System Folder and then open the Preferences folder. Drag the Users & Groups Data File to a floppy disk. Keep your backup in a safe place — preferably in the same safe place you use to store your server backups.

Preparing to serve

After you've set up your server and created or updated your user and group lists, you're ready to put the server into action. To do so, run the AppleShare File Server program. After a few moments, the AppleShare server windows appear, indicating that the server is up and running.

Application Software Considerations

Because file server software turns a hard disk into a shared storage area, it's possible that more than one person could try to modify the same document at the same time. One part of a file server's job involves keeping track of who's opened what.

It does so through *file-access protocols* — rules built into the file-serving software that specify how users can access files. A *file-locking* protocol locks a file against alteration after one person has opened it.

The multiuser difference

But some tasks, especially database management and accounting, benefit from users being able to simultaneously modify a file. Your file server can accommodate such tasks if you use *multiuser* software — programs that allow multiple users to access and modify the same documents. With a multiuser database manager such as Claris FileMaker Pro, for example, a secretary can enter new client records, a sales representative can print a sales report, and a shipping clerk can update inventory figures — at the same time, from the same database.

A multiuser program handles these simultaneous requests without file clobbering through a *record-locking* protocol, which enables multiple users to access a file, but only one person to modify a given record. Apple's AppleTalk Filing Protocol (AFP) is a set of file-sharing rules that developers of network-compatible applications follow.

Some real-world examples

How do some of the leading software packages handle file and record locking? Here are some examples.

- Microsoft Works lets numerous users open the same file, but only the one who opened it first can modify it. Anyone else must use the Save As command to give it a new name. Microsoft Excel works similarly.
- Adobe PageMaker lets numerous users open a template or a copy of a publication, but only one person at a time can open an original publication.
- Microsoft Word lets you open a document that is in use by someone else, but you can't save any changes unless you save the document under a different name, on a different drive, or in a different folder. If you open a document that someone else has gotten to first, Word displays a message letting you know that the file is in use.
- Claris MacDraw II and MacDraw Pro both let multiple users open a file, but only the person who opens it first can save changes normally (that is, by using the Save command). If others try to save changes they've made, a message asks if they want to save the changed document under a new name, replace the original, or not save the changes after all.
- Claris FileMaker Pro, ACI's 4th Dimension, and Microsoft's FoxPro+/Mac are multiuser database managers that let numerous users work simultaneously with a database file. However, only one person at a time can modify a given record (one entry in the database, such as someone's name and address). Multiuser data managers also provide security features that let you make certain information available to only certain people. In a personnel database, for example, you might want to give everyone access to employee names and phone extensions but only certain managers access to salary information.

As you can see, not all programs behave in the same way on a network. After setting up a network for file serving, test your applications to see how they behave when more than one person tries to open a document.

Remote Control with Apple Remote Access

If you have employees who travel frequently or work at home, you may want to give your network *remote access* features to allow those users to dial in and access the file server, e-mail system, and even laser printer.

Apple's Apple Remote Access is a software package that lets a remote Macintosh connect to another Macintosh that's also running Apple Remote Access. To use Apple Remote Access, you need two modems — one connected to the office-based Macintosh and one connected to the remote Macintosh.

Required equipment

Apple Remote Access works with 2400-baud modems, but 9600-bps or faster modems provide much better performance. With a 2400-bps modem, remote network access can seem slower than the Pony Express. With a 9600-bps or faster modem, however, performance is acceptable — not as fast as a local network node, but fast enough for electronic mail to still seem electronic.

You can use one copy of the Apple Remote Access software on up to three Macs. If you need remote access on more than three Macs, you must buy additional copies of Apple Remote Access.

Setting up for incoming calls

After installing the Apple Remote Access software on one of your office-based Macs, use the Remote Access Setup control panel to configure it to accept calls (see Figure 32-9 "Now Taking Calls").

With Apple Remote Access, you can use the standard System 7 Users & Groups control panel to create lists of users and groups who are eligible to access the network from a remote location. For added security, you can specify a *call-back number* for each user (see Figure 32-10 "I'll Get Right Back to You").

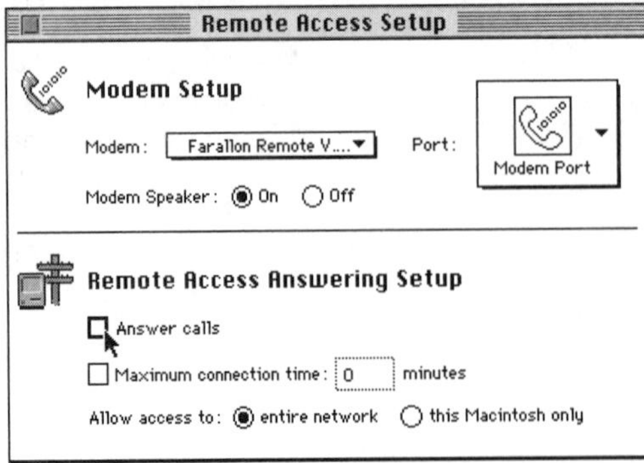

Figure 32-9: Now Taking Calls To set up Apple Remote Access, open the Remote Access Setup control panel and check its Answer Calls box. You can also specify whether you want to grant remote access to only the Mac that's running Apple Remote Access, or to the entire network that Mac is attached to. The second option provides more security by preventing access to other machines on your network.

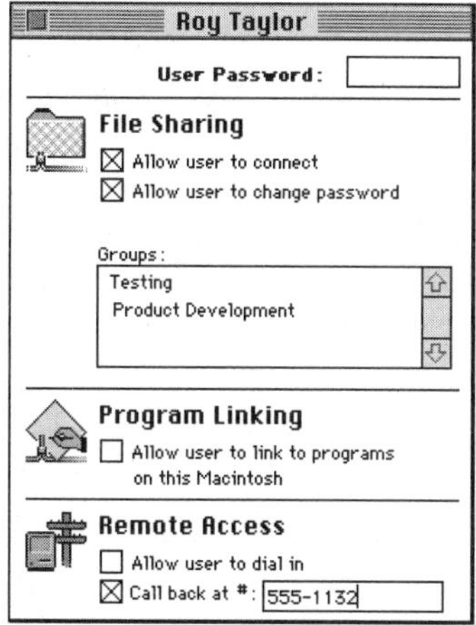

Figure 32-10: I'll Get Right Back to You With Apple Remote Access, when a user for whom you've specified a call-back number dials in, your modem temporarily disconnects the user and then immediately dials the call-back number to reestablish the connection.

Special Steps for Sharing Removable Media

Both AppleShare and System 7's file-sharing software enable you to make removable media such as SyQuest and Bernoulli cartridges and CD-ROMs available to the Macs on your network. If you use AppleShare, use the AppleShare Admin program to mount and unmount cartridges or CD-ROMs and to make them available to the network.

With System 7's file-sharing software, sharing removable media isn't as straightforward. You need to insert the cartridge or CD-ROM *before* using the Sharing Setup control panel to turn file sharing on. If you turn file sharing on, insert a cartridge or CD-ROM, and then choose Sharing, a dialog box appears stating that "not all volumes are available for file sharing." If you see this somewhat arcane message, turn off file sharing, insert the cartridge, and *then* turn file sharing on.

A similar problem can surface if you try to eject a cartridge after sharing it. If you drag the cartridge's icon to the Trash or select the icon and choose Put Away, an error message appears saying that the disk "could not be put away because it is being shared." This message appears even if you never used the Sharing command to make that cartridge available. The solution: Turn off file sharing. (This hassle doesn't occur in System 7.5.1 or later versions, which do allow you to eject a cartridge when sharing is on — provided, of course, that no other Macs on your network have mounted the cartridge.)

To avoid both of these hassles, remember this rule: If you want to share a cartridge, insert the cartridge before turning file sharing on. To eject that cartridge, first turn file sharing off. Or use a free utility called UnMount It, by Jim Luther — it lets you eject removable media without having to turn off file sharing.

Mac, phone home

To connect from a remote Macintosh, use the Remote Access control panel on the remote Mac to select the modem you're using. Then start the Remote Access program that came with Apple Remote Access. A new, untitled *connection document* appears (see Figure 32-11 "A New Remote Connection"). To make the connection, click Connect.

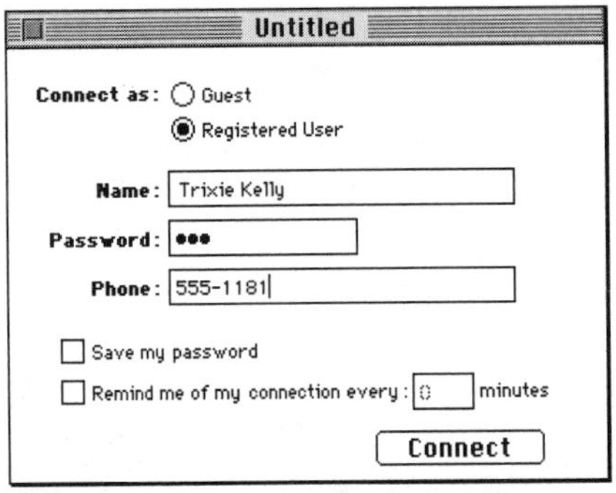

Untitled
Connect as: Guest
Registered User
Name: Trixie Kelly
Password: •••
Phone: 555-1181
Save my password
Remind me of my connection every : 0 minutes
Connect

Figure 32-11: A New Remote Connection
Creating a new connection document in Apple Remote Access. Select the Guest or Registered User option as appropriate. If you're connecting as a registered user, type your user name and password in the appropriate text boxes and then type the phone number for the home base's modem. When the two modems are on speaking terms, a status window appears.

With a connection established, you can use the Mac's Chooser desk accessory to select remote printers, file servers, and electronic mail systems. Everything works as though you're connected to a local network, except that the remote network appears to respond in slow motion. (For some remote access survival tips, see the Quick Tips box "Timesaving Tips for Apple Remote Access").

Electronic mail and remote access

CE Software's QuickMail takes an especially versatile approach to remote access by being able to talk to any computer with a modem. If you dial into a QuickMail server using a computer other than a Mac, QuickMail discards the Mac interface and presents special text menus for accessing the system. Combine that capability with a low-end laptop computer, and you have an inexpensive way to keep in touch.

Timesaving Tips for Apple Remote Access

A remote access session can seem like a dream in which you're trying to run with legs made of lead. You can prevent the dream from turning into a nightmare by following the tips in this box.

- ❖ If you're accessing a remote file server, don't leave its directory windows open on your screen. The Finder updates directory windows now and then, and the updates take more time when you're connected via modem. Close a remote volume's directory window as soon as you're done with it. As soon as you're done with a remote volume, drag its icon to the Trash. Note that this does not disconnect you from the remote Macintosh.
- ❖ Don't run an application program stored on a remote file server. If you try, Apple Remote Access displays a warning saying that the program will "take a long time to be opened." Believe it — and then click Cancel.
- ❖ Think twice about printing a document containing downloadable fonts or bitmapped graphics such as scanned images. You'll get the fastest remote printing times if you stick with fonts that are built into the remote network's printer.
- ❖ Use the connection-reminder option in the remote access connection document window (it's labeled *Remind me of my connection*). When you choose this option, a notice appears at specified intervals reminding you that you're connected to a remote machine — and paying phone charges all the while.
- ❖ You can use the call-back option to reverse the phone charges on lengthy remote access sessions. You'll need to make a brief call to establish initial contact, but then the remote system will call you back, and thus become responsible for phone charges.
- ❖ If you plan to transmit electronic mail to the remote system, prepare your outgoing messages before connecting. If you'll be copying files to a remote server, compress them first using a utility such as Aladdin Systems' StuffIt. Compressed files take less time to transfer over the phone lines.

Don't quit your on-line service yet

Remote-node setups allow network e-mail systems to span the miles, but commercial e-mail and on-line services such as CompuServe, eWorld, and America Online still have their place. For starters, their multiline phone networks can accommodate thousands of callers at once. With remote-node access, only one person at a time can call in to check his or her mail. If you exchange e-mail via the Internet or on-line services such as CompuServe, you'll be glad to know that QuickMail and SnapMail provide gateway features that unite a network and a service by automatically dialing the service at specified intervals and sending or retrieving mail to or from the service.

Other remote access products

Another way to establish remote access connections is by equipping one of your office-based Macs with a Shiva NetModem. The NetModem includes software that lets you dial into the network from a remote Macintosh. Shiva also sells a DOS program called DOS Dial-In that lets DOS machines dial in to a LocalTalk network. DOS Dial-In could be of special interest to people who use DOS portable computers and want to exchange documents and e-mail with remote networks.

For a variation on the remote-access theme, combine ARA with Farallon Computing's Timbuktu Pro, which lets you actually control a remote Mac or even a Windows PC. You can run programs, choose their commands, print documents — but of course, in slow motion. Note the subtle but important difference between Apple Remote Access and Timbuktu/Remote: ARA allows you to dial in to a remote network to access its services, while Timbuktu Pro allows you to see what's on a remote Mac's screen and control the Mac as if you were sitting at it. You can't control or view the screen of a remote Mac using ARA alone. (If you're on a budget, you can buy Timbuktu/Remote, which doesn't require ARA but also has fewer features.)

Other Networking Options

After you master printer sharing, electronic mail, and file serving, you may want to investigate more advanced networking options. If you use Windows PCs, you can tie them into the network using Apexx Technology's PCTalk adaptor, which plugs into a PC's parallel printer port and adds a LocalTalk connector. Apexx's EtherChain plugs into the parallel port and adds a 10BaseT Ethernet connector. You can also turn a PC into a server for Macs using software such as Novell's NetWare. And QuickMail is available for PCs, so you can create a central e-mail post office for a network that uses both platforms.

Then there's *groupware*, a genre of network-oriented software designed around the fact that people usually collaborate on projects. Mainstay's MarkUp lets multiple users electronically annotate a document and keeps track of when comments were made. PrairieSoft's In/Out lets you track the whereabouts of the employees in your office. Lotus also sells Mac client software for its popular Notes product.

At the high end you'll find products that enable the Mac to tap into minicomputer- and mainframe-based networks such as those from IBM and Digital Equipment Corporation (DEC). Macs are especially popular among users of DEC's VAX minicomputers: It's been estimated that over half of all VAX installations also use Macs.

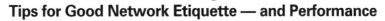

QUICK TIPS

Tips for Good Network Etiquette — and Performance

Following these basic rules can help make communal computing work smoothly.

- ❖ *Run applications locally:* Avoid running large applications from a server. They'll perform slowly and bog down the network. Small, fast-loading applications work well from a remote server, but a complex program like PageMaker can make a network snail slow. Run large applications locally; use the server primarily for sharing and storing documents.
- ❖ *Don't run unreliable software:* Never run prerelease software or untested shareware on a network, especially on a machine that's being used as a server. A crash for one can mean a crash for all.
- ❖ *Don't delete indiscriminately:* Don't throw away a file with a cryptic name; it may be a work file that another user's application has created. Check with others before deleting files you don't recognize.
- ❖ *Release volumes you don't need:* When you're done with a server volume, release it by dragging the volume's icon to the Trash at the Finder or by selecting the icon and choosing Put Away from the Finder's File menu.
- ❖ *Don't break connections:* If you must unplug a LocalTalk connector, make sure all users have saved their work. Reliable network software can usually reestablish a connection, but don't count on that. If you must detach from the network, disconnect your machine by unplugging its network box from your Macintosh, not by unplugging the cables that go into the network box.
- ❖ *Share applications carefully:* Many programs weren't written with network use in mind, and can crash when used by more than one person at the same time. Be sure a program is designed for network use before storing it on a shared hard disk. And don't ignore the legal ramifications of networking. You may be required to buy a special license or purchase multiple copies of a program to use it on a network.
- ❖ *Back up religiously:* The crash of one person's hard disk leads to depression; the crash of a shared hard disk can lead to a riot.

Conquer the Basics First

But before venturing into these waters, master the basics. Add one capability at a time to your network, and be sure everyone understands it before expanding further. And don't ignore your network-administration duties: Develop a filing system for your server. (For some additional tips on managing your network, see the Quick Tips box "Tips for Good Network Etiquette — and Performance.") Be on the alert for viruses — as I explain in Chapter 26, networks enable them to spread easily.

Follow these basic guidelines, and you'll have fewer technical problems and questions to answer. In short, you'll increase your net's worth.

CHAPTER 32 CONCEPTS AND TERMS

- Networking enables Macs and LocalTalk-equipped DOS PCs to share expensive hardware such as laser printers. You can also use electronic mail and file-server software to share ideas and information with coworkers.
- Sharing a PostScript printer is relatively easy: Apple's LaserWriter driver (and Adobe's PSPrinter driver) can communicate with any Mac-compatible PostScript printer. All you add are cables.
- Electronic mail software lets you transfer files between Macs as enclosures that accompany messages you type.
- File server software lets you turn one or more hard disks into a central storage area that can hold documents or applications. Security features enable you to assign passwords to folders containing sensitive data.
- File server software provides file-locking protocols that prevent multiple users from trying to modify the same file. Record-locking protocols enable multiuser database managers to allow many users to access a file, but only one user at a time to modify a given record.
- Dial-in access features enable you to tap into your network using a telephone modem. For acceptable performance, however, you need a 9600-bps or faster modem.
- To get reliable results from your network, start small and add new services one at a time, testing often.

10BaseT
Also called *twisted pair,* the most economical type of cabling for Ethernet networks. 10BaseT cabling is similar to telephone wiring.

AAUI
Short for *Apple Attachment Unit Interface,* the type of Ethernet connector provided by most Macs and current Apple PostScript printers. To connect a Mac to an Ethernet network, you attach a transceiver box to the AAUI port. Second-generation Power Macs also provide a 10BaseT connector that eliminates the need for a transceiver box when connecting to 10BaseT networks.

administrator
The person in charge of setting up and maintaining a network. Often seen pulling his or her hair out or weeping quietly.

AppleTalk Filing Protocol
Abbreviated *AFP,* a set of file-sharing rules that developers of network-compatible applications follow.

cable extender
A small adaptor, included with a LocalTalk connector kit, used for attaching two cables to each other.

call-back number
In Apple Remote Access, a number you specify that helps ensure security by disconnecting and then calling back anyone who dials in.

client
Anyone who is on the receiving end of network services such as a file server. Also the person who often makes life miserable for the administrator.

dedicated file serving
A disk-sharing approach in which one Mac and its hard drive is set aside to act as a server for everyone. A dedicated file server generally isn't used to run applications, although you may also use one to act as an e-mail server.

distributed file serving
A disk-sharing technique in which anyone on the network turns his or her machine into a file server by making one or more folders — or the entire contents of a hard drive — available to others. Apple's System 7 provides distributed file-serving features. The distributed approach is often called *peer-to-peer* file serving because each machine on the network is considered an equal as far as file serving is concerned.

electronic mail software
Programs that let you send messages and files to coworkers on a network. Examples include CE Software's QuickMail and Microsoft Mail.

enclosure
In electronic mail, a file that usually accompanies a message you send. When a message arrives at its destination, the recipient can save the enclosed file on his or her own disks.

Ethernet
A high-speed networking system that's built into a growing number of Mac models and laser printers. Ethernet adaptors are also available for existing Macs, including PowerBooks.

file server
A computer whose hard drive (or a portion thereof) has been made available to other users on a network.

file-access protocols
Rules built into the file-serving software that specify how users can access files. A *file-locking* protocol locks a file against alteration after one person has opened it. A *record-locking* protocol enables multiple users to access a file but only one person to modify a given record.

headless server
A file server that lacks a monitor or keyboard.

hub
In an Ethernet network, the central connection point for each device. With a hub, you connect a small box, called a *transceiver,* to the Mac and then run a cable from the transceiver to the hub.

local hard drive
A hard drive attached directly to your Mac — as opposed to a drive that you access over a network.

mount
To connect to a server so that its folders and icons appear on your Mac's desktop.

multiuser database
A database program that enables multiple network users to access the same database file at once, eliminating the need to store a separate copy on each person's machine.

thin-wire
Also called 10Base2, a type of coaxial cabling used in Ethernet networks. Thin-wire networks can have between 200 meters between network devices. Also see *10BaseT* and *thick-wire.*

thick-wire
Also called 10Base5, a type of coaxial cabling used in Ethernet networks. Thick-wire networks can have between 500 meters between network devices. Also see *10BaseT* and *thin-wire.*

CHAPTER THIRTY-THREE

Input Devices

- Understanding how input devices work
- Shopping for alternatives to Apple's keyboard and mouse
- Talking to the Mac with PlainTalk speech recognition
- Surveying input devices for PowerBooks
- Getting artistic with graphics tablets

The Mac's *input devices* — its keyboard and mouse — are your links to the Mac, letting you move around the screen in the direction of your choice. And like most people, you're probably content using Apple's stock input devices. After all, one mouse or keyboard is the same as another, right?

Actually, you can choose from a large and varied selection of alternative input devices. Some are keyboards and mice that may appeal to people who find Apple's input devices uncomfortable or too expensive. Others fall into the different-strokes-for-different-folks category: *Trackballs* don't require as much desktop space as mice, while *graphics tablets* offer pen-like control for drawing and drafting applications. And then there's the *trackpad* that many PowerBooks provide (and that's also available for desktop Macs), and the *voice-recognition* capabilities of Apple's AV and Power Macs.

This chapter describes the most popular input devices available for the Mac family, spotlights some products from each class, and provides some tips for using them.

Keyboard Considerations

In the Mac world, most alternative input devices are alternatives to the mouse. True, a pointing device is the cornerstone of the Mac's graphical interface, but the keyboard is essential too, especially for typing-intensive applications such as word processors, data managers, and spreadsheets.

A guide to Apple keyboards

Apple offers several keyboards for the Mac — the Apple Keyboard II; the Apple Extended Keyboard II; the newest one, the AppleDesign keyboard; and the Apple Adjustable Keyboard, which is covered in Chapter 23.

- The Apple Keyboard II has a layout similar (but not identical) to the old Mac Plus keyboard. The standard typewriter layout is supplemented by four arrow keys for moving the Mac's blinking insertion point, and a calculator-like numeric keypad for fast number entry. Many word processors also use the numeric keypad for scrolling.
- The Apple Extended Keyboard II supplements the standard keyboard's typewriter, arrow, and numeric keypad keys with additional scrolling keys and a row of 15 *function keys.* Many programs use the function keys as keyboard shortcuts for often-used menu commands. You can also create your own function-key shortcuts using a macro utility such as CE Software's QuicKeys or Affinity Microsystems' Tempo II (see Chapter 24).
- The AppleDesign keyboard also provides a 105-key extended layout. This keyboard also provides adjustable height controls. The primary difference between the AppleDesign keyboard and the Extended Keyboard II is that the AppleDesign keyboard has a permanently attached ADB cable and one ADB port, while the Extended Keyboard II has two ADB ports.
- The Mac Plus and portly Portable included their own keyboards; the Apple Keyboard II is included with the Classic II, LC III, and most Performa models.
- The Apple Keyboard II, Extended Keyboard II, and the Apple Adjustable Keyboard are also sold separately; when you buy a Centris, Quadra, Power Mac, or PowerBook Duo Dock, you need to choose a keyboard.

The Inbound Bus

Most alternative input devices connect to the Mac's *Apple Desktop Bus* (ADB), an expansion system designed for input devices. ADB, used on all Macs except the Plus and its predecessors, is a simple expansion system designed for input devices. The Mac provides two ADB connectors, as do many ADB input devices. You can attach multiple input devices to a single connector by *daisy-chaining* them — attaching one device to another. Although the ADB can accommodate up to 16 devices, Apple warns against attaching more than three to each connector because ADB signals deteriorate as the cable length increases.

The Mac's ADB connectors also provide a source of power, so you don't need a separate power supply or power outlet for each device. The battery-powered Mac Portable and PowerBooks, however, require low-power ADB devices designed to draw less juice — more about this later.

Before connecting or disconnecting an ADB device, first shut off the Mac, or it may fail to recognize one or more of the devices. Another incentive to turn off the Mac is that ADB connectors may short-circuit momentarily when installed or removed, damaging the input device or the Mac itself. Some people who travel with a Mac have also reported problems with the connectors wearing out after repeated use, so it's wise not to attach and detach ADB devices too frequently.

Make mine extended

I recommend an extended keyboard for anyone with enough desk space to accommodate it. Even if you never create any macros, you'll find its additional scrolling keys useful for navigating through documents. The keyboard's layout almost matches that of the latest IBM keyboards — useful if you switch between Macs and PCs or use Insignia Solutions' SoftWindows software, which lets PowerMacs run Windows programs.

The key to power

Apple's ADB keyboards also offer a *power-on key* that turns on Mac II, Centris, and most Quadra and Power Mac models. If you're running System 7.5.1 or a later version, the power key also lets you turn power off as well as on. With older Macs, the power-on key has no effect. You can, however, put it to work by using Sophisticated Circuits' PowerKey — which provides three outlets that supply juice when you press the power-on key. PowerKey Remote lets you activate power over the phone — handy for fax modems or for use with Apple Remote Access (described in Chapter 32).

Competing keyboards

If you haven't bought a keyboard yet, or if you're thinking of upgrading from a standard to an extended version, consider a non-Apple keyboard. Not only do these products cost less than Apple's Extended Keyboard II, many offer useful features — missing from Apple's models — providing even more value for the money. For example, most alternative keyboards provide a useful comma- and period-lock feature that prevents you from getting angle-bracket symbols (< or >) when you press the comma or period key while holding down the Shift key. (You can use the ResEdit utility to modify your Mac's keyboard layout to prevent this, too — see Chapter 24.)

Comparing keyboard alternatives

Two alternative extended keyboards include Interex's Mac-105 Enhanced keyboard, which provides two ADB ports; and Microspeed's Keyboard Deluxe, which provides three ADB ports.

Key Tronic Corporation's MacPro Plus provides a layout similar to that of the Extended Keyboard II, but with a larger Return key that supposedly reduces data-entry errors. The MacPro Plus also provides interchangeable Caps Lock and Ctrl keys and period- and comma-lock features. Key Tronic's Trak Pro is a keyboard with a built-in trackball.

Don’t buy until you try

But there’s another, more subjective, reason to consider a non-Apple keyboard — how it feels. The pressure required to generate a keystroke, how well the keys respond to fast typing, the sound they make when pressed and released: These characteristics combine to give every keyboard its own personality. If you find Apple’s keyboards uncomfortable or unresponsive, give the competition a try. But remember, you will stroke those keys millions of times, so don’t buy a keyboard until you’ve test-driven it.

Pointing Alternatives

Since its invention in 1963, the mouse has become the world’s premier pointing device. Apple builds a first-rate rodent that meets most users’ needs — and, unlike a keyboard, it’s conveniently included with each machine (see the Background box “A Field Guide to Apple Mice”). But tastes in input devices do vary, and certain tasks benefit from a different approach to pointing.

Although Apple’s mice are among the best, they’re mechanical beasts prone to wear and breakdown. The mouse mechanism uses a rubber ball that requires a smooth surface on which to roll, lest the pointer jerk across the screen. The ball and the rollers it touches accumulate dirt and require periodic cleaning. An extremely dusty environment — a factory, a wood-heated house, or my office — can choke an Apple mouse to death.

Alternative mice

A mouse that doesn’t share these shortcomings is Mouse Systems Corporation’s aptly named Little Mouse. Designed for ADB-equipped Macs, the Little Mouse is an *optical* mouse: Rather than measuring the movement of a rubber ball, it measures the light reflected from a 7 by 8-inch pad covered with a grid of minute dots (see Figure 33-1 “How Pointing Devices Work”).

Aside from its button, the Little Mouse has no moving parts to wear out or get cheesy. It’s also smaller and lighter than an Apple mouse. The required mouse pad does add to desktop clutter, but many people prefer to use a mouse pad even with a conventional mouse because the mouse glides nicely on a pad’s smooth surface. I used a Little Mouse for a few weeks and found it a worthy alternative to an Apple mouse. (I also switched back to my Apple mouse, so I suppose that says something, too.)

Other contenders include Mouse Systems’ A3 mouse and Logitech’s MouseMan, both of which provide not one button but three, and let you program them to issue ⌘-key sequences or execute macros. People who use Apple’s AU/X version of the UNIX operating system may like these mice because UNIX windowing systems often use a three-button mouse. Kensington’s Thinking Mouse provides four programmable buttons.

HOW POINTING DEVICES WORK

Mechanical Mouse

In an Apple mouse, a rubber ball touches two capstans, which are connected to slotted wheels sandwiched between two light-source- and-photosensor pairs (A and B). When the ball rolls, the capstans turn the wheels, whose slots interrupt the light. Each interruption is interpreted by the Mac as one increment of movement. The sensors are offset slightly so that, as the wheels turn, they produce a pair of signals with a pause between. The direction a wheel turns is indicated by which sensor, A or B, produces the first signal in each pair. Trackballs work similarly, except only the ball (not the entire housing) moves.

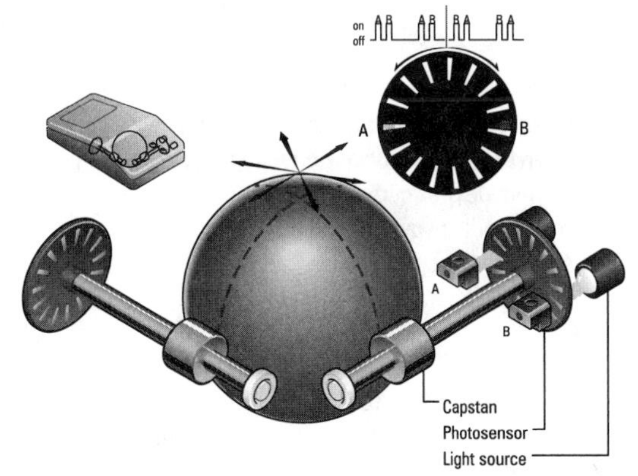

Optical Mouse

In an optical mouse, light from two light sources (A and B) reflects off a pad covered with a fine grid of dots. The image of the grid is projected onto two separate photosensors. One senses vertical movement (C) and the other horizontal movement (D). As the reflection of the grid passes over the sensors, circuitry within the mouse counts the dots to determine the distance the mouse has moved in either direction.

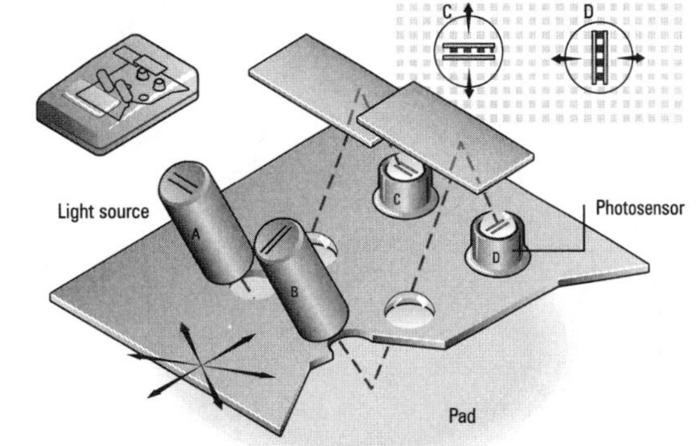

Graphics Tablet

In a graphics tablet, a drawing stylus or cursor exchanges minute radio signals with the tablet through a grid of wires that crisscross the drawing area. The tablet determines the location of the stylus and transmits the location information to the Macintosh. The stylus doesn't need to touch the tablet surface itself; this means you can trace a drawing, even through several pages of a book.

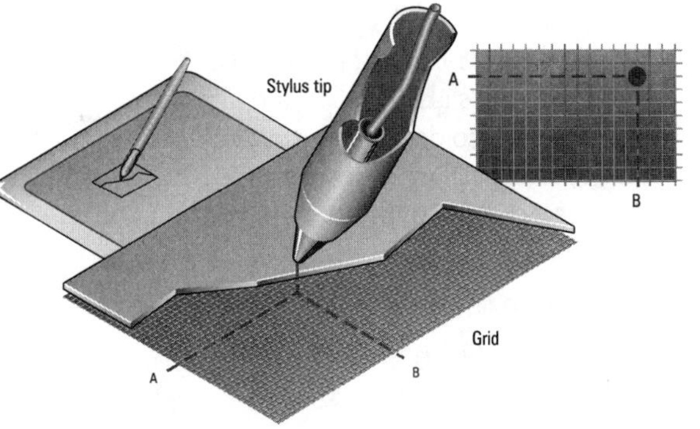

Figure 33-1: How Pointing Devices Work

A Field Guide to Apple Mice

Apple has shipped several mice over the Mac's lifetime. One species is electro-mechanical, using the ball to drive two wheels whose edges are ringed with metallic encoders. A current is made and broken as the encoders spin past electrical contacts. The other mice use the opto-mechanical design described in this chapter.

Here's how to tell the rodents apart:

- ❖ The electro-mechanical ADB mouse has a heavy gray ball with a sliding retainer ring and is made in the United States.
- ❖ The first opto-mechanical ADB mouse has a lighter black ball with a rotating retainer and is made in Taiwan. Some people complain that this mouse's lightweight ball prevents smooth pointer movement.
- ❖ The second ADB opto-mechanical mouse has a heavy gray ball with a rotating retainer and hails from Malaysia.
- ❖ The newer Apple Desktop Bus Mouse II has a comfortable, rounded shape. Its ball is located closer to the front of the mouse, a location that Apple says allows for more precision with less hand effort.

Incidentally, the original Apple mouse — the non-ADB mouse — was born in 1983 along with Apple's Lisa and the Apple IIe. The Macintosh 128K, 512K, 512K Enhanced, and Plus used this mouse, as did the Apple IIe and IIc.

Cordless mice

If you use the Mac to give presentations using programs such as Adobe Persuasion and Microsoft PowerPoint, you probably don't like being tethered to the Mac by the mouse's tail. The answer: A cordless mouse. Numerous cordless mice are available; some examples include Spark International's Spark Cordless Mouse, DynaPoint's Cordless DynaMouse, and Proxima's Cyclops. All use an infrared link instead of a wire. They run on rechargeable batteries and provide a sleep mode that conserves juice when they aren't moving.

Pointing without rolling

But even a tailless mouse requires some desk space in which to roam. If you just can't spare that kind of real estate, consider a trackball — a plastic ball that sits on rollers housed within a small case that, like a keyboard, occupies a fixed location on your desk. To move the Mac's pointer, you roll the trackball with your fingers. A trackball's ability to fit and work in a small space is what makes it the pointing device on PowerBook 100- and 200-series models.

Most trackballs provide two buttons. One works just like a standard mouse button, while the other works like a mouse button that sticks. This second button lets you drag icons, windows, or other items without holding down a button: Click the button once to start dragging, and then click it again to stop. By giving your hand one less chore to perform, a locking-click button can help you make more precise pointer movements, and it eliminates the finger fatigue that hours of delicate dragging can cause.

Comparing trackballs

Some trackballs — such as Kensington Microware's Turbo Mouse, Logitech's TrackMan, and Mouse Systems' A3 Trackball — let you combine their buttons to perform special tasks. For example, you can configure it to issue an often-used keyboard command, such as ⌘-S for Save. This technique of pressing two or more buttons simultaneously is called *chording*.

(Note that Kensington Turbo Mouse models prior to version 4.0 can crash a Power Mac. If you have an older Turbo Mouse and you've just upgraded to a Power Mac, contact Kensington for upgrade details.)

Other ADB-compatible trackballs include MicroSpeed's three-button MacTrac and HyperTrac, which includes slick software that senses which program you're using and switches to the appropriate set of button shortcuts. And there's Curtis Manufacturing's MVP Mouse, which can accept an optional foot pedal for clicking.

Something to consider when trackball shopping is the size of the ball itself. Some people find that a smaller sphere gives more control, while others (myself included) prefer a bigger ball. See how comfortable you are with the size and position of the trackball's buttons; they vary from one trackball to the next. And if you're left-handed, opt for a trackball that lets you reverse the functions of the single-click and locking-click buttons.

Tips for Avoiding a PowerBook Trackball

A PowerBook's trackball is harder for many people to operate than a mouse. The trackball on the Power-Book Duo models can be especially frustrating because of its small size.

The best way to avoid problems with the trackball is to avoid using it. Every large PowerBook model has an Apple Desktop Bus (ADB) port into which you can plug a conventional mouse. The PowerBook Duo models can connect to a mouse when docked to a Duo MiniDock or Duo Floppy Adaptor. Be sure to use a low-power mouse: It has a symbol on the bottom of it that looks a bit like a *C.*

You can often avoid using the trackball by relying on the keyboard for scrolling, issuing commands, and even selecting icons. This is a good excuse to memorize your programs' ⌘-key shortcuts — and to seek out programs that offer a wide selection of them.

It's also a good reason to buy a keyboard-enhancement utility such as CE Software's QuicKeys to create your own keyboard shortcuts. As I describe in Chapter 24, you can create keyboard shortcuts that open desk accessories and control panels as well as frequently used files.

The PowerBook's system software contains a large selection of keyboard-navigation options. You can use the keyboard to select icons, choose devices in the Chooser, and start programs. For details on the Finder's keyboard-navigation options, see the section "System 7 Keyboard Shortcuts" in Chapter 22.

The Apple Trackpad

The Apple trackpad is a different kind of input device. As mentioned in Chapter 1, the trackpad relies on a principle called *coupling capacitance* to sense the presence of your finger (see Figure 33-2 "How the Trackpad Works"). Some elevator buttons — those kind that don't actually depress when you press them — also use coupling capacitance. If it's good enough for an elevator, Apple figures, it's good enough for a PowerBook.

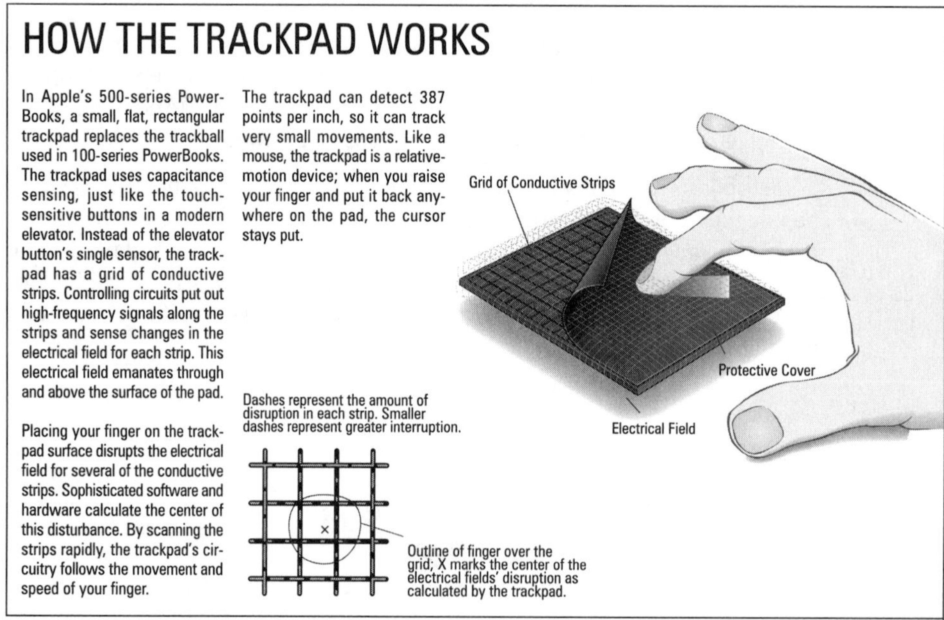

HOW THE TRACKPAD WORKS
In Apple's 500-series PowerBooks, a small, flat, rectangular trackpad replaces the trackball used in 100-series PowerBooks. The trackpad uses capacitance sensing, just like the touch-sensitive buttons in a modern elevator. Instead of the elevator button's single sensor, the trackpad has a grid of conductive strips. Controlling circuits put out high-frequency signals along the strips and sense changes in the electrical field for each strip. This electrical field emanates through and above the surface of the pad.
Placing your finger on the trackpad surface disrupts the electrical field for several of the conductive strips. Sophisticated software and hardware calculate the center of this disturbance. By scanning the strips rapidly, the trackpad's circuitry follows the movement and speed of your finger.
The trackpad can detect 387 points per inch, so it can track very small movements. Like a mouse, the trackpad is a relative-motion device; when you raise your finger and put it back anywhere on the pad, the cursor stays put.
Grid of Conductive Strips
Protective Cover
Electrical Field
Dashes represent the amount of disruption in each strip. Smaller dashes represent greater interruption.
Outline of finger over the grid; X marks the center of the electrical fields' disruption as calculated by the trackpad.

Figure 33-2: How the Trackpad Works

Actually, the trackpad has some significant advantages over the trackball other PowerBooks use:

- No moving parts. There's nothing to break or get dirty.
- Low power consumption. The trackpad uses less power than a trackball, and that's significant in a battery-operated device.
- It's smaller and lighter. This allowed Apple to devote more space to other internal components.
- Its proportions match the screen's. There's a more-direct correlation between the trackpad and the screen than there is with a trackball.

Alternative Input Devices for the PowerBook Line

A PowerBook's input devices are built in, but that doesn't mean there isn't room for improvement. This box lists some alternatives you may consider.

Numeric keypads

If you work with numbers extensively, you can add an external numeric keypad to the PowerBook. Keypads such as Sophisticated Circuits' PowerPad and Kensington's NoteBook KeyPad allow for calculator-like number entry and also provide Page Up, Page Down, Home, End, and other convenient scrolling keys.

Alternative trackballs

Given that a PowerBook provides a built-in pointing device, I'm not sure why you'd want to connect an external one — unless you didn't like the built-in one, that is. If that's the case, consider MicroSpeed's MicroTrac trackball, which provides three programmable buttons.

Alternative balls for the trackball

These aren't so much input devices as a fashion accessories. APS Technologies, CoStar, and other firms sell replacement balls for the trackball — little billiard balls, multicolored balls, you name it.

Keyboards

On PowerBook 100- and 200-series models, the keyboard is about 2 percent narrower and 5 percent shorter than Apple's standard desktop keyboards. As a result, the keyboard may feel cramped, especially if you have large hands or you're used to conventional Mac keyboards. And take it from me, working on a cramped keyboard for long periods can cause big problems. So, if you frequently use a PowerBook in the office, attach an external keyboard to its ADB port. Use an extended keyboard and you'll get the added benefit of function keys, a numeric keypad, and navigation keys.

A trackpad for your desktop Mac

The trackpad is now available as an ADB device for desktop Macs (or for trackball-equipped PowerBooks). It's called the Alps GlidePoint; it sells for well under $100, weighs less than two ounces, and isn't much bigger than a business card. It even fits on the wrist rest of a classic PowerBook.

The GlidePoint provides three buttons and includes software that lets you program them to issue commands. As an alternative to using the buttons, you can also click and drag using only the trackpad — something the PowerBook 500-series trackpad doesn't allow. To click or double-click, just tap once or twice. To drag, tap twice and hold your finger down on the second tap. To complete the drag, just lift your finger.

I tested a GlidePoint and found it took some getting used to, particularly for fine pointer movement and drag-and-drop operations. But as I've said elsewhere in this chapter, tastes in pointing devices vary — if you're unhappy with mice and trackballs, give the GlidePoint a try.

Tips for the trackpad

Here are a few tips for the trackpad.

You have to use your finger

You can't use a stylus, a pen, or even a long fingernail to work the trackpad. These devices, unlike your body, do not conduct electricity, and the trackpad relies on that in order to operate.

Rock your finger for precise positioning

The trackpad is very sensitive, able to measure 387 dots per inch in the horizontal and vertical directions. For extra-precise positioning, just rock your finger on the pad — you'll be able to move the mouse pointer in single-pixel increments.

Use the trackpad control panel to fine-tune sensitivity

Like the mouse, the trackpad uses acceleration curves: The faster your finger moves across the pad, the faster and further the pointer moves across the display. If your finger darts across the pad, the pointer will traverse the display completely. If the finger moves slowly, the pointer does, too. If you find the pointer moves too quickly, use the Trackpad control panel to specify a slower setting. In Apple's user testing, most people preferred the fourth setting up from the slowest setting.

Pens and Tablets

As effective as mice and trackballs are, they still lack the familiar feel of a pen or pencil, making them second-best tools for drawing and drafting. For these tasks it's hard to beat a *graphics tablet,* also called a *digitizing tablet.* Tablets provide a flat drawing area upon which you scrawl using a pen-like *stylus* whose tip contains a switch that mimics a mouse button.

Most tablets have a drawing area that's covered with a clear plastic sheet, or *overlay,* under which you can tuck artwork to be traced. A newspaper artist may use a graphics tablet and a drawing program such as Macromedia FreeHand or Adobe Illustrator to trace a map or diagram to accompany a story. Many tablet pens accept ink-filled cartridges, enabling you to place a sheet of paper on the tablet's surface to see on paper what you're drawing on-screen.

Tablet work areas vary widely in size, and as the size increases, so does the price. One inexpensive tablet, Wacom's ArtPad, provides a tiny work area that measures 4 by 5 inches. Wacom sells other sizes ranging from 6 by 8 inches to 18 by 25 inches. CalComp's DrawingSlate II line comprises pads as small as 6 by 9 inches and as large as 12 by 18 inches. And then there's SummaGraphics's SummaFlex, an 18 by 24-inch flexible pad that you can roll up like a beach towel.

Absolute versus relative motion devices

Their pen-on-paper operating style isn't all that makes tablets superior drawing tools. Equally important, tablets are *absolute-motion* pointing devices, while mice, trackballs, and trackpads are *relative-motion* pointing devices. Your blind mouse can't report its physical location: It doesn't know whether it's at the edge of the desk or in the middle. When you pick up the mouse and set it down elsewhere, the pointer doesn't suddenly jump to a different spot on the screen. Mice and trackballs simply report that they're moving a certain distance in a certain direction.

In contrast, each point on a graphics tablet corresponds to a point on the Mac's screen. Pick up a tablet's stylus and then touch it to a different part of the drawing area, and the Mac's pointer *does* suddenly jump to a different part of the screen. It's this operating style that makes tablets ideal for tracing and drawing. Most tablets also provide a relative-motion mode that you can use when you want mouse-like operation.

Graphics tablets are also better able to discern small degrees of movement. Mice and trackballs can generally discern 200 to 300 units of movement per inch, but graphics tablets typically detect 1,000 units or more per inch. The higher a pointing device's resolution, the better suited it is to precise drawing because it's able to register even minute movements.

Pressure-sensitive tablets

Most of today's graphics tablets are pressure sensitive: pressing harder with the stylus gives you a darker or wider line. Fractal Design's Painter, Adobe Photoshop, Adobe Illustrator, and Aldus FreeHand are among the graphics programs that support pressure-sensitive tablets.

Cordless pens

The pens on early graphics tablets had connecting wires that attached to the tablets, but all of today's tablets use cordless pens. By eliminating the pen-to-tablet umbilical, tablets take one more step toward providing a natural-feeling drawing surface. Most tablets, including Wacom's and Kurta's, also accept a mouse-like *cursor* containing a lens with cross-hairs that aid in precise positioning. (By the way, this is the only place in this book where you'll find the word *cursor*. The arrow you move around on the Mac's screen is called a *pointer*.)

Wacom offers a particularly large array of cordless pens, including several that write with real ink. Put a piece of paper on your Wacom tablet and pick up an UltraPen with Ink, and you can draw on paper as well as on-screen. Besides allowing artists to work in a more familiar manner, this is useful for applications that require a paper signature as well as an electronic one — driver's license applications, for example, or credit card receipts.

Specialized Input Devices

Keyboards, mice, trackballs, and graphics tablets represent the mainstream of input devices. In the backwaters are some specialized devices, which are described in this box.

Joysticks

Anyone who's seen a video game has seen a joystick; it's a moving appendage similar to a car stick-shift with a button on top. Advanced Gravis' MouseStick II and Kraft Systems' KM-30 also provide buttons alongside the stick. The MouseStick II provides several goodies, including adjustable stick tension and programmable buttons that transmit commands when pressed. Joysticks remain best suited to game playing, but they can also be used as mouse replacements.

A distant cousin to the joystick is Altra's Felix, for ADB-equipped Macs. Felix uses a short, stubby stick that moves within a one-inch area. Altra says the stick's tight area of travel makes it feel more precise and natural than a mouse or conventional joystick. Try it before you buy it.

Devices for handicapped users

Several input devices have been created for handicapped users who are unable to operate a keyboard or mouse. Prentke Romich Company's (Wooster, OH) HeadMaster headset enables users to direct the mouse pointer by moving their heads. A control unit measures the change in the headset's position and reproduces the electrical output of a desktop mouse. A puff switch on the headset replaces the mouse button — blowing into the switch is the same as pressing the mouse button.

The Standard HeadMaster has a wire running from the headset to the computer. The Remote HeadMaster replaces this wire with an infrared link that enables a user to leave the workstation without assistance. Prentke Romich Company sells programs that put an image of a keyboard on the screen and enable text to be entered by pointing to the desired letter and activating the puff switch. The software provides word-prediction features that finish words for you and other functions that increase writing speed.

Touch screens

For a while, it was thought that touch-sensitive computer screens would be ideal alternatives to desktop pointing devices. In the early eighties, Hewlett-Packard even released a computer with a built-in touch screen. It flopped, partly because no popular software supported it, but also because users' arms got tired.

Touch-sensitive screens do have their place, however. They're often used for computerized directories or information kiosks in stores, museums, trade shows, and the like. They're also useful in factory environments where there aren't any desktops.

Microtouch Systems' Mac 'n' Touch SA-14 is a 14-inch touch-sensitive color monitor that includes a driver for translating touch to pointer movement.

Templates and macros

Finally, to help earn their keep, many tablets accept *command templates* that give you one-click access to frequently used commands. A template package includes a disk and a printed sheet that slips beneath the tablet's plastic overlay and contains labeled boxes in which you click to issue commands. Of course, locating the right box and then clicking in it can take as long as choosing the command with the mouse. But it never hurts to have another option for choosing commands, and some people do find templates ideal alternatives.

Talk To Me: Speech Recognition

Apple's AV Macs and PlainTalk voice-recognition technology enable you to use some hardware of your own — your mouth — as an input device. PlainTalk can aid users who have disabilities, and it enables you to rest your wrists now and then by choosing menu commands and activating palette tools with spoken commands.

Macs capable of speech recognition include utilities for creating voice-activated macros that open files, scroll windows, adjust system settings, and select palette tools. You can also open often-used files by placing them (or aliases of them) in the Speakable Items folder, within the Apple Menu Items folder. PlainTalk also lets you choose menu commands in any application program that uses standard MENU resources. (Most programs do, although Microsoft Word does not.)

Activating voice recognition

You activate PlainTalk's voice-recognition features by using the Speech Setup control panel, shown in Figure 33-3 "Listen Here, Mac." Speech recognition requires roughly 2MB of system memory. (Given this and the memory required by PlainTalk's text-to-speech features, and it's easy to see why the AV and Power Macs ship with at least 8MB of memory. To reduce the amount of memory used for speech, select a compressed voice for feedback to spoken commands, or set feedback to None rather than having voice feedback.)

If you're using an AudioVision 14 monitor, be sure to connect the sound-in plug to the external sound input port on the back of the computer, and that the AudioVision's built-in microphone is turned on.

Normally, PlainTalk is set up to require you to speak a name before reciting a command — just as a dog trainer gets a pup's attention by saying its name before giving a command. PlainTalk's preset name is *computer*. As Figure 33-4 "Name That Mac" shows, you can use the Speech Setup control panel to change that, but it's worth noting that Apple fine-tuned PlainTalk to be particularly sensitive to the word *computer*. If you find your Mac isn't listening as well as you'd like, it may be because you gave it a name that it has trouble understanding.

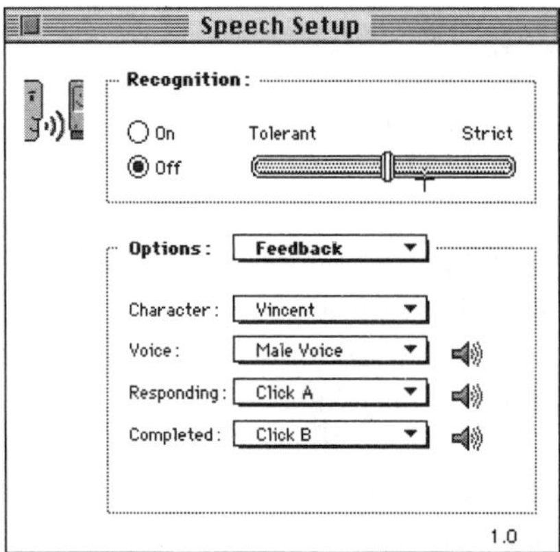

Figure 33-3: Listen Here, Mac You activate PlainTalk speech recognition using the Speech Setup control panel. The Tolerance slider lets you adjust recognition: Moving it closer to Strict results in more accurate recognition, although the system may ask you to repeat commands more often. Moving the slider closer to Tolerant reduces the need to repeat commands, but increases the chances of the machine picking up background speech or noise and interpreting it as a command.

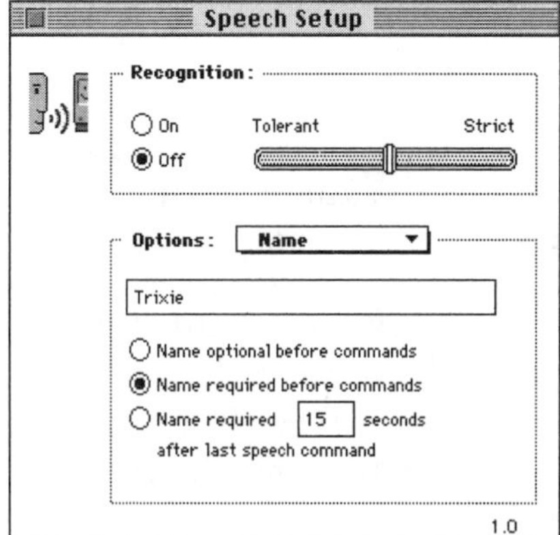

Figure 33-4: Name That Mac With an AV Mac's Speech Setup control panel, you can specify a name for the Mac. When issuing spoken commands, you precede the commands with the name. You can also specify whether the name is required or optional.

You can also disable the name requirement, but this has a risk: The Mac could overhear you and perform a command you did not intend it to. Imagine telling a coworker, "The branch office has shut down," and then turning to your Mac to find it's turned itself off.

When voice recognition is on, PlainTalk displays a feedback window that shows the commands you've given (see Figure 33-5 "Monitor Your Speech"). If PlainTalk doesn't recognize a command, the window displays the message, *Pardon me?*

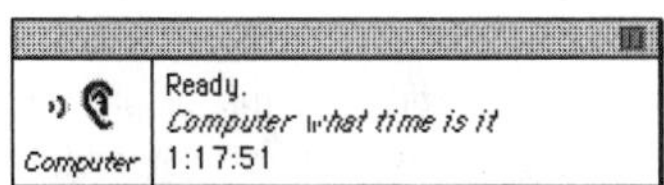

Figure 33-5: Monitor Your Speech
PlainTalk's speech recognition feedback window displays commands and responses. The small sound waves adjacent to the ear (which is named Vincent), indicate that the computer's microphone is picking up sound. Although the AV and Power Macs can serve as telephones (see Chapter 16), PlainTalk doesn't support speech recognition over the telephone. Phone lines and phone mouthpieces don't provide the required fidelity.

DSP limitations on the 660AV and 840AV

Also, the amount of digital signal processing required for voice recognition means you can't use voice commands while also using the AV Mac's GeoPort connector to conduct a 9600-bps data communications session. The Power Macs don't have this limitation.

Is speech recognition ready for prime time?

PlainTalk speech recognition makes for a fun demonstration for friends, but I've found it only marginally useful in my day-to-day routine. It just isn't fast and accurate enough.

So until the next big breakthrough occurs, keyboards and mice will probably remain the preeminent input devices. And when you think about it, do you really want to work in an office full of people who are barking at their computers?

How PlainTalk Recognizes You

Third-party voice-recognition products such as Articulate Systems' Voice Navigator require extensive training: You sit in front of a microphone and repeatedly speak the words you want the system to recognize. Thereafter, the system compares what you said to what it knows, looking for matches.

PlainTalk doesn't require advance training. Apple digitized hundreds of voices and developed methods of isolating and identifying the sound characteristics that transcend individual voices and even dialects. A sibilant *s,* a percussive *k,* a long *o:* The frequency patterns produced by these and other spoken sounds are generally consistent regardless of dialect or inflection. PlainTalk can recognize 51 distinct building blocks of speech, which are called *phonemes.*

When you issue a spoken command, the Mac's analog-to-digital converter generates a stream of digital data from the analog signal produced by the microphone. The PlainTalk recognition software analyzes this data to determine the volume of various frequencies. The Mac then compares the results to its database of phonemes, making tens of thousands of comparisons and decisions within a few milliseconds. (If that sounds impressive, remember that a puppy can do the same thing — and detect emotion, too.) When PlainTalk determines that it has recognized a word, it generates an Apple event message that is sent to the active application program. The program then responds to the event accordingly.

In order to be fully voice operated, an application program must support Apple's AppleScript (discussed in Chapter 24). If your favorite programs don't yet support AppleScript, you can still create simple voice activated macros using QuicKeys and the Speech Macro Editor included with an AV Mac. And you can issue menu commands if the program uses standard MENU resources.

CHAPTER 33 CONCEPTS AND TERMS

- The mouse is the cornerstone of the Mac's graphical environment, but the keyboard is an essential component for typing-intensive tasks such as word processing, data management, and spreadsheet analysis.
- Mice come in several forms. Besides the standard Apple mouse, there are optical mice that measure the light reflected from a pad covered with a grid of tiny dots; multiple-button mice whose extra buttons let you issue ⌘-key sequences; and cordless mice that use infrared links instead of wires.
- A trackball is a mouse alternative comprising a plastic ball that sits on rollers housed within a small case. You move the pointer by rolling the trackball with your fingertips.
- For drafting and drawing applications, a graphics tablet is often preferred to the mouse.
- Other alternative input devices include joysticks, touch-sensitive screens, and head-mounted pointing devices designed for handicapped users.
- Apple's PlainTalk voice-recognition technology, available in AV and Power Macs, enables you to issue spoken commands.

absolute-motion pointing device
A pointing device, such as a graphics tablet, that can report its position to the Mac. Compare with *relative-motion pointing device*

chording
The technique of pressing two or more mouse or trackball buttons simultaneously.

cursor
A mouse-like device, used with a graphics tablet, that contains a lens with cross-hairs that aid in precise positioning.

function keys
Special keys, present on some keyboards, that often correspond to often-used menu commands. You can also create your own function-key shortcuts using a macro utility such as CE Software's QuicKeys.

graphics tablet
Also called a *digitizing tablet,* an input device that provides a flat drawing area upon which you scrawl using a pen-like *stylus* whose tip contains a switch that mimics a mouse button. Some tablets are pressure sensitive. Most tablets have a drawing area that's covered with a clear plastic sheet, or *overlay,* under which you can tuck artwork to be traced.

numeric keypad
A small keyboard (or portion of a keyboard) that provides a set of number keys arranged in a calculator-like layout for convenient number entry. Many word processors also use the numeric keypad for scrolling.

optical mouse
A mouse that detects movement by measuring not the rolling of a rubber ball, but the light reflected from a pad covered with a grid of minute dots.

pointing device
A hardware peripheral that lets you control the position of the Mac's on-screen pointer. The most common pointing device is a mouse.

power-on key
On a Mac keyboard, the key with a hollow, left-pointing triangle. On Mac II, Centris, most Quadra family machines, and Power Macs, pressing the power-on key switches the Macintosh on. On other Macs, the power-on key has no effect.

relative-motion pointing device
A pointing device, such as a standard mouse, that simply reports that it's moving a certain distance in a certain direction. A relative-motion pointing device can't report its physical location: For example, it doesn't know whether it's at the edge of the desk or in the middle. When you pick up the mouse and set it down elsewhere, the pointer doesn't suddenly jump to a different spot on the screen.

trackball
A mouse alternative comprising a plastic ball that sits on rollers housed within a small case that, like a keyboard, occupies a fixed location on your desk. To move the Mac's pointer, you roll your fingers across the trackball.

trackpad
The pointing device on the PowerBook 500-series machines. The trackpad relies on a principle called coupling capacitance to sense your finger's location.

APPENDIX A

Using the Macworld Power User Clinic CD

This appendix describes the contents of the *Macworld Power User Clinic* CD and provides some tips for using it.

What's On the CD-ROM?

There are two main parts to the CD: the *Macworld Power User Clinic*, a multimedia production that complements the book; and the software libraries, which contain over 100MB of free software, shareware, sounds, fonts, QuickTime movies, and reference materials.

Navigating the CD

When you insert the *Macworld Power User Clinic* CD, a standard Finder window appears. Table A-1 describes the CD's main icons.

What is the Macworld Power User Clinic?

The *Macworld Power User Clinic* is an interactive companion to the book. It uses QuickTime movies, animations, and color graphics to supplement the information in the book. The *Clinic* also contains numerous excerpts from the book and has a Find command that lets you locate text.

Using the Macworld Power User Clinic

Before starting the *Macworld Power User Clinic*, be sure to do the following:

- If you haven't already, install QuickTime 2.0 and the Star Ratings files as described in the Step-by-Step box, "How to Install QuickTime 2.0 and the Star Ratings Files."
- Use the Monitors control panel or the Sound & Displays control panel to set your monitor for Thousands of colors. If your video hardware doesn't support the Thousands setting, use the 256 colors setting. (Note that the movies look better with the Thousands setting.)

- If you have a Power Mac, use the Memory control panel to specify a 512K RAM cache. This helps the movies on the *Macworld Power User Clinic* play back smoothly — it also helps your Power Mac's overall performance. After changing the RAM cache size, restart the Power Mac to put your changes into effect.

- Connect your Mac to a set of speakers or at least headphones. This isn't a requirement, but you'll get far more out of the CD's movies if you listen to them through something other than a Mac's built-in speaker. See Chapter 21 for details on connecting the Mac to audio systems.

To start the *Clinic*, double-click its icon. After a few moments, the main contents screen appears.

As the main screen shows, the *Macworld Power User Clinic* is divided into three primary sections: Clinics, Interviews, and Reviews. To work with a section, click its entry.

At Least Read This!

Even if you don't read this entire appendix, at least read this section — it contains important information about setting up a Power Mac to run the *Macworld Power User Clinic*, about working with the programs on the CD's "The Best of BMUG" collection and about installing the Macworld Star Ratings files in your System Folder.

Many of the programs are ready to run directly from the CD-ROM. (Of course, the programs will run much faster if you copy them to a hard disk.) However, some programs may create items in your System Folder that refer to the CD.

The right way to install DarkSide

Specifically, the installer for the screen saver DarkSide of the Mac creates an alias in your System Folder's Startup Items folder. (Aliases are discussed in Chapter 22.) If you run the DarkSide installer from the CD, your Mac will ask you to insert the CD every time you start up or restart. Unless you're really nuts about this CD, you probably won't want this. Therefore, if you want to install DarkSide, copy the Dark Side folder to your hard drive and *then* run the installer from the hard drive. In general, this is a good approach to follow when installing a program.

If you find your Mac is asking for the CD when you start up or that you can't eject the CD (the Mac says some "items are in use"), chances are you ran an installation program that creates an alias in your System Folder that refers to the CD. Check in your System Folder's Startup Items, Control Panels, and Extensions folders for these aliases. (Of course, if the Mac doesn't let you eject the CD, also make sure that no programs or documents on the CD are open. Also be sure that System 7 file sharing is turned off.)

Check the "read me" files

As a general rule, it's a good idea to read the "read me" file for a given program to learn about any special installation procedures it may require.

Power Mac users: Set up a 512K RAM cache

if you're using a Power Mac, open the Memory Control and set your RAM cache to 512K. This helps the movies on the *Macworld Power User Clinic* play back smoothly — it also helps your Power Mac's overall performance. After changing the RAM cache size, restart the Power Mac to put your changes into effect.

Install the Star Ratings Files folder

In order for the *Macworld Power User Clinic*'s Find command to work, you *must* copy the Star Ratings Files folder from the CD to your System Folder. For details, see the Step-by-Step box, "How to Install QuickTime 2.0 and the Star Ratings Files," later in this appendix.

Table A-1:
Macworld Power User Clinic CD at a Glance

Folder	***Contents and Comments***
Put in System Folder	The QuickTime 2.0, QuickTime Musical Instruments extensions, the QuickTime PowerPlug, and the Apple Multimedia Tuner. To install QuickTime 2.0, drag these items to the System Folder of your startup disk and then restart your Mac. (See the detailed installation instructions later in this appendix.) This folder also contains your first set of Macworld Star Ratings files, which are used by the *Power User Clinic*. If you want the *Power User Clinic's* search feature to operate, you must install these files as described later in this appendix.
Macworld Power User Clinic	To start the *Power User Clinic*, open this icon. (Be sure to install QuickTime 2.0 and the Star Ratings Files folder first.)
More Software	This folder contains many of the utilities and programs that I mention in the book. The TechTool and EMMpathy utilities are here, as are Alias Director, File Buddy, SoundTrecker, and more. This folder also contains the Adobe Acrobat Reader and sample chapter discussed in Chapter 27.
The Best of BMUG	Roughly 100MB of shareware and freeware, organized into the following categories: AfterDark, Business, Education, Entertainment, Fonts, PowerBooks, Power Mac, Telecom, Utilities, Sound, and Graphics.
Movies and Sounds	A small collection of fun digitized sounds and QuickTime movies. You can use the Peter's Player or Desktop Movie applications in this folder to play these and other QuickTime movies.
Mac References	A library of useful electronic reference materials for the Mac. When you're looking for details on memory upgrade options, viruses, computing health hazards, or Mac bulletin board systems, look here.

How to Install QuickTime 2.0 and the Star Ratings Files

The instructions in this box describe how to install QuickTime 2.0 and the Star Ratings Files on your system.

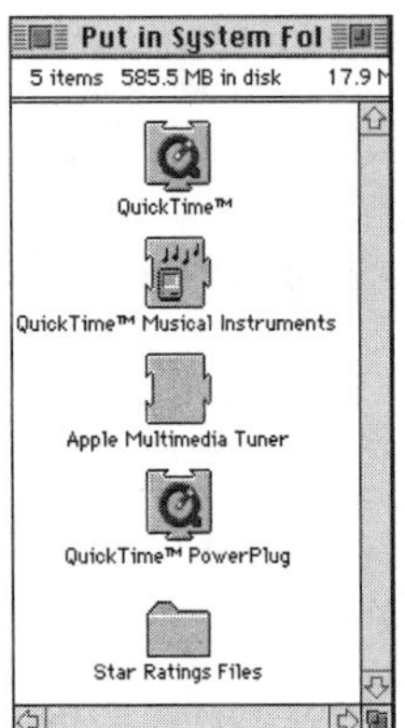

To install QuickTime 2.0 and the Star Ratings files:

1. **If you're already using an older version of QuickTime, remove it from your System Folder.** (It's located within the Extensions folder.)

   You might just want to drag the icon out to your desktop. After installing QuickTime 2.0 and then restarting, you can delete the earlier version of QuickTime.

2. **On the CD, open the folder named Put in System Folder.**

   You see a window containing the icons, shown at left.

3. **If you have a Power Mac, select everything in this folder. If you do not have a Power Mac, select everything *except for* the QuickTime PowerPlug file.**

   The QuickTime PowerPlug extension works only with Power Macs. It won't hurt anything if you install it on a non-Power Mac, but you will waste a bit of disk space.

4. **Drag the items you've selected to the icon of your System Folder.** (Be sure to drag them to the *icon* of the System Folder — if you drag them into the open System Folder window, they won't be installed properly.)

   The Mac informs you that some of the items have to be installed in the Extensions folder. Click OK. After the Finder has copied the files, it notifies you that some items were put in the Extensions folder and one item was put in the (System Folder. Click OK.)

5. **Restart your Mac by choosing Restart from the Special menu.**

Clinics

The Clinics provide information relating to this book, and use QuickTime movies, digital sounds, color graphics, and text to do so. Here's a quick description of all eight clinics:

- **Meet the Mac.** This segment provides overviews of how the components in a Mac system operate. The centerpiece of this segment is an illustration of a Mac system. When you point to a component without clicking, that component's name flashes to identify it. When you point to a component and click, you go to that component's screen, where you watch a movie about the component and read relevant text from the *Handbook*. You can also jump to a component's screen by clicking the buttons along the right side of the Meet the Mac screen. Finally, you can take a quick tour of the Mac's ports and connectors by clicking the Back Panel button. Doing so displays the Back of the Mac screen; point to a port, and a window pops up describing it and referring you to relevant chapters in the *Handbook*.
- **Multimedia Theater.** In this segment, you can hear the Mac's sound features and compare the effects of various sampling rates. Every book tells you that higher sampling rates yield higher quality sound, but use more disk space. With this Clinic, you can actually click the bars in a graph to *hear* examples of various sampling rates. This Clinic also contains some cool QuickTime movies, including one created with a 3-D rendering program, a demonstration of Apple's QuickTime VR, and a time-lapse movie that I created using Adobe Premiere.
- **Mastering the Mac OS.** The opening screen of this Clinic shows a typical Finder desktop. Point to the items on the desktop, and windows appear describing them, providing tips for them, and referring you to relevant chapters in the book. In some cases you can also click on the items to display text tips from the book.
- **Stupid Printer Tricks.** Chapter 31 describes how you can add color to laser printer output and create iron-on T-shirt transfers. This Clinic contains QuickTime movies that illustrate both tricks. You can also read some of the printer tips from Chapter 31 here.
- **PowerBook Power Tips.** This Clinic contains a QuickTime movie that demonstrates some alternative power sources for PowerBooks, including a solar panel. You can also read power-management tips here.
- **Healthy Computing.** Chapter 23 discusses ergonomics issues and provides some tips for healthy computing. In this Clinic, you can read some of these tips and also watch QuickTime movies illustrating four useful exercises that can help you limber up before work sessions.
- Installing Upgrades. This Clinic is an introduction to installing memory upgrades. You can watch QuickTime movies illustrating how to install a SIMM and read some of the upgrade-related tips from Chapter 29.

How to Get and Install Your Free Online Updates

Each month, Macworld posts a new set of Star Ratings to the Macworld Online forum on America Online. You can read these Star Rating directly on Macworld Online, or you can save them to your hard drive and use them along with Macworld Power User Clinic. I'll also post regular updates to the book's text, including details on new Mac models, developments in the world of Mac clones, new software details, and — heaven forbid — corrections to the book.

To get your free online updates to the *Macworld Power User Clinic*, you must have an account on America Online. (If you don't, call 800–249-9300.)

After signing on to AOL, make your way to the Macworld Online forum. The fastest way to do so is to use the keyword feature: press Command-K, type *macworld,* and press Return.

Once in the Macworld Online forum, click the Product Forum icon. In the window that opens, double-click the Books icon. You'll find the my updates here.

To download an update, double-click its name and then click the Download Now button in its window. What you'll be downloading is a self-extracting archive containing the Star Ratings files and update files. (The file's name is Mac Handbook Update.sea.) Now and then, I may include additional goodies, such as a hot new freeware or shareware utility.

After the download is complete

1. Double-click the file Mac Handbook Update.sea. In a moment, an information dialog box appears. Read it, and then click Continue. A Save Dialog box appears next, with the name *What's New* supplied in the Save As area.
2. Specify that the What's New file be stored in your Star Rating folder, within your System Folder. If you like, you can navigate your way to the Star Ratings Files folder and then click Save — when the installation program asks if you want to replace the existing What's New file, click Replace. Or, you can save the What's New file on your desktop and then drag it into the Star Rating Files folder. Your end goal is to put the What's New file in the Star Ratings Files folder. (Don't change the name of this file' if you do, the *Macworld Power User Clinic* won't be able to locate it.)
3. A message appears saying that one of the files already exists. Click the Replace All Duplicates button. (What you're doing here is telling the archive extractor utility to replace the old files with the new ones that you just downloaded.)

   When the installation process is complete, the archive extractor quits. You can throw away the file named Mac Handbook Update.sea.

   To read the update, start up the Macworld Power User Clinic and choose the What's New command from the References menu. You can also print the update from this screen. (The What's New file is a standard text only file, so you can also open and print it with a word processor.

Updating Your Star Ratings

To get the latest Macworld Start Ratings, click the Star Ratings icon in the main Macworld Online screen A window appears listing each category. To read the latest ratings for a given category, double-click its name.

If you like, you can update your Star Rating collection so that you can read and print the latest rating within the *Macworld Power User Clinic*. The steps for updating a category are straightforward: Open the category, choose Save, edit the file name to remove the issue date, and then save the file in your Star ratings File folder. Here's a step-by-step look at the process:

1. Open the category you want to update and then choose Save from the File menu. A Save dialog box appears.
2. Make your way to the Star Rating Files folder within your hard drive's System Folder. (The pop-up menu at the top of the Save dialog box should read Star Rating Files.) *Don't click Save yet.*
3. In the test entry portion of the Save As dialog box, delete the issue date numbers and the space that precedes the category name. For example, if the text entry box says **12/95 Input Devices**, delete the 12/95 as well as the space after it. The text that remains should be the category name only, with no numbers or spaces in front of it.
4. Click Save or press Return. A dialog box asks if you want to replace the exiting category file. Click Replace. (If you don't see the Replace? dialog box, you didn't edit the file name properly or save it in the correct location.
5. Repeat steps 1-4 for each category that you want to update.

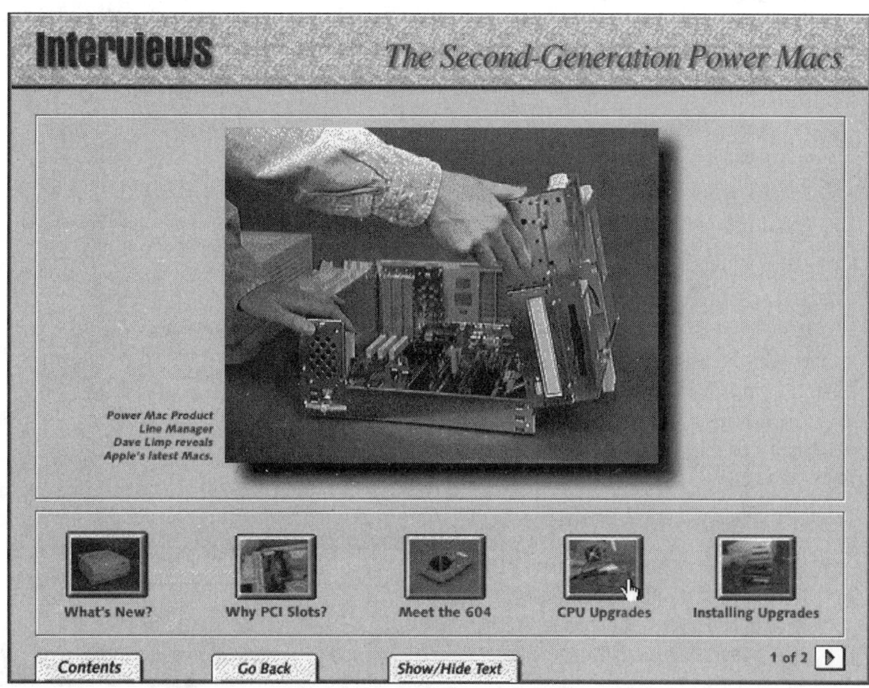

Figure A-1: Navigating a Segment. Click a movie's button to play or hide it.

Interviews

In this section, you can watch interviews I conducted with the product managers of the second-generation Power Macs, the Performa 5200 and 6200, the QuickTake 150 and Color LaserWriter, and the forthcoming Copland Mac OS. You'll hear a bit of Apple propaganda now and then, but you'll also get some solid information on some of Apple's latest products. Many of these segments also include Mac screen recordings that illustrate the concepts or features being discussed.

The Interviews section also contains an interview with Grammy- and Oscar-winning music legend Herbie Hancock, who is an avid Macintosh user — indeed, he used the Mac in the production of his latest album, *Dis is Da Drum* (Mercury Records). This interview contains some concert footage that I shot at the Los Angeles Macintosh Group's 1995 MacFair convention.

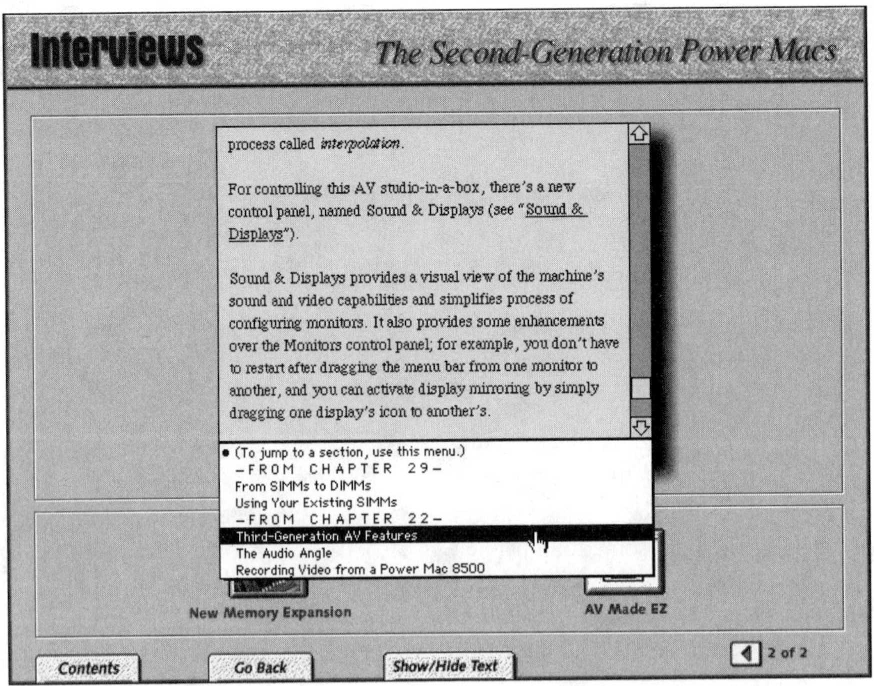

Figure A-2: Working with Text. By clicking the Show/Hide Text button that appears on most *Macworld Power User Clinic* screens, you can read and navigate through text from this book.

Reviews

This section contains Macworld's Star Ratings reviews, capsule reviews of hundreds of Mac hardware and software products. Using the Find command, you can search for products or companies. Be sure to visit the Macworld Online forum on America Online to download the latest updates — and also to visit with *Macworld* contributors and fellow readers, download software, and read articles and reviews from *Macworld*, the Macintosh authority.

A closer look at the segments

Most of the segments in the *Macworld Power User Clinic* work similarly. When you make your way to a specific section, you see a screen containing buttons for movies, as shown in Figure A-1: "Navigating a Segment".

To play a movie, click its button. To close the movie before it has finished, click the button again or press the Return key.

If you want to skip to a different movie while a movie is playing, just click the button for the movie you want. The *Macworld Power User Clinic* automatically closes the current movie and then opens the new one.

To move around *within* a movie — for example, to go back to watch a portion of it again — you must display the movie's controller bar. To do so, click once within the movie, and then click the little movie badge icon that appears in the movie's lower-left corner. This displays the standard QuickTime controller.

Working with and searching for text

When a given screen contains text from this book, you can read it by clicking the Show/Hide Text button. When you do, a scrolling text box appears, as shown in Figure A-2: "Working with Text."

Notice that the text box has a pop-up menu adjacent to it. You can jump to a specific section within the text box by choosing its name from this pop-up menu.

When you see underlined text within a text box, you can click the underlined text to make something happen. In most cases, a graphic will appear. In other cases, you'll jump to a different section of the *Macworld Power User Clinic.*

You can also search for text located anywhere on the CD by using the Find command. To do so, choose Find from the Search menu. (I'll describe how to access the menu bar in a moment.) You can also bring up the Find dialog box by pressing Command-F.

When your search text is found, it flashes and a dialog box appears asking if you'd like to continue searching. To continue the search, click Find or just press Return. To stop the search, click Stop Search or press Command-period.

Navigating with the menu bar

One thing that often annoys me about CD-ROMs is that you can't access the Apple or Application menus without quitting the CD's interactive program. This means you can't switch to a different program, adjust your control panel settings, check your alarm clock, or perform any other tasks while the CD is running.

Not so with the *Macworld Power User Clinic.* I gave it a menu bar that not only provides access to the Apple and Application menus, but also lets you quickly jump around within the *Clinic* itself.

To display the menu bar, just move the mouse pointer to the top of the screen. As it approaches the top, the menu bar appears. When you move the pointer away from the top of the screen, the menu bar disappears. You can also show or hide the menu bar by pressing Command-spacebar.

Exploring the Best of BMUG Collection

As mentioned earlier, the "Best of BMUG" folder contains nearly 100MB of free software and shareware, all of it compatible with Power Macs and System 7.5.

The best way to explore the "Best of BMUG" library is to dive into each folder and read the "Read Me" files that accompany each program. Most of these files are in SaintEdit format. SaintEdit is a great shareware text editor utility that's also included on the CD. (Choose its About command to learn how it got its name.)

By the way, if you have Apple's PlainTalk text-to-speech software installed, you can have SaintEdit read files aloud. Just choose Speak to Me from its Bedtime Stories menu. SaintEdit can even read aloud in the background — as I'm writing this in Microsoft Word, SaintEdit is reading a file to me.

If you make any of the shareware programs or fonts a part of your regular computing routine, please take the time to pay the author's requested shareware fee. Help keep the shareware system alive!

Enjoy the CD!

I hope you enjoy the *Macworld Power User Clinic* CD as much as I enjoyed putting it together. My sincere thanks and appreciation go to every individual and company that contributed, with special thanks to Maryellen Kelly; to everyone at BMUG and LAMG; to Herbie Hancock, Melinda Murphy, and Darrell Smith; to Trixie; and to Roy and Wendy.

Please send your comments and suggestions to JIMHEID (AppleLink and America Online), or to 76174,556 (CompuServe).

Index

— Symbols —

— A —

— B —

— C —

— D —

(continued)

— E —

— F —

(continued)

(continued)

—H—

(continued)

(continued)

— M —

(continued)

— N —

— O —

— P —

— Q —

(continued)

— T —

— U —

—V—

(continued)

—X—

—Y—

—Z—